PROSE WRITERS OF GERMANY

Frederic Henry Hedge

Introduction by
James A. Good

THOEMMES PRESS

This edition published by Thoemmes Press, 2002

Thoemmes Press
11 Great George Street
Bristol BS1 5RR, England

http://www.thoemmes.com

The Early American Reception of German Idealism
5 Volumes : ISBN 1 85506 992 X

Reprinted from the 1849 edition

Introductions and editorial selection
© James A. Good, 2002

British Library Cataloguing-in-Publication Data
A CIP record of this title is available from the British Library

Publisher's Note

The Publisher has gone to great lengths to ensure the quality of this reprint but points out that some imperfections in the original book may be apparent.

This book is printed on acid-free paper, sewn, and cased in a durable buckram cloth.

INTRODUCTION

Frederic Henry Hedge (1805–90) is one of the most important American intellectuals of the nineteenth century. He possessed a wealth of intellectual resources and was exceptionally well versed in the main currents of Western thought of his time. Thomas Carlyle, who was an important influence on Hedge, once remarked to Ralph Waldo Emerson, "Wherever new thought is marching onto the field, there we find Mr. Hedge in the front rank."[1] With William Ellery Channing, Hedge was one of the two most important leaders of American Unitarianism, uniting the movement with a consistent theology and defending it from external attack. But Hedge is most remembered for his relationship to the American transcendentalists. With his intellectual qualities, Hedge naturally emerged as a "teacher of teachers," leading the transcendentalists in their earliest studies of German philosophy and theology.[2] In the following, I shall discuss Hedge's life and intellectual development and briefly discuss his philosophical relationship to the Boston transcendentalists.

Hedge's preparation for the intellectual prominence he attained began at home where, during his childhood, his father and a series of Harvard graduate students privately tutored him. Hedge's father, Levi Hedge, was descended from a distinguished, well-educated New England family of ministers and academics. Levi was Harvard's first professor of philosophy, teaching there from 1792 to 1832. An important defender of Scottish common sense philosophy in America, Levi used his own *Elements of Logick, or a Summary of the General Principles and Different Modes of Reason* (1816), which emphasized post-Lockean

---

[1] "To Ralph Waldo Emerson," 31 August 1847, *Correspondence of Thomas Carlyle and Ralph Waldo Emerson, 1834-1872*, ed. C.E. Norton (Boston: Houghton, Mifflin Company, 1883), 2: 140.

[2] William H. Lyon, *Frederic Henry Hedge: Seventh Minister of the First Parish in Brookline* (Brookline, Mass.: First Parish in Brookline, 1906), 13.

Scottish thought and remained a standard logic text at Harvard for many years. Under his father's tutelage, Hedge was always rather shy and bookish, fond of both prose and poetry. He demonstrated a talent for languages at an early age, reading Greek and Latin by age ten. When he reflected on his childhood, Hedge noted, "he had no companions in study," nor any "class rivalry to cramp or cheer."[3] George Bancroft, who later emerged as a famous historian, was Hedge's most important tutor. At the age of twelve, Hedge passed Harvard's entrance exam, but his father decided to send him, with Bancroft, to Germany to gain a more complete education before he entered Harvard. Hedge's education in Germany was a crucial component of his intellectual development.

When Hedge and Bancroft arrived in Germany, Bancroft sought out the assistance of Edward Everett, a colleague of Hedge's father who was also in Germany at the time. Everett helped Bancroft place the young Hedge in Göttingen where he attended the gymnasium, Gotha. Although Bancroft successfully pursued his own plan to study at the Universities of Berlin and Heidelberg, he was frequently troubled by his responsibility for Hedge who, in isolation from his family, had to learn how to interact with other students.[4] Unable to meet the expense of Hedge's boarding in Göttingen on the allowance he received from the boy's father, after six months Bancroft moved Hedge to the gymnasium at Ilfeld in Hanover. Hedge never fit in well at Ilfeld and, after some disciplinary problems, Bancroft moved him once more, this time to the gymnasium at Schulpforte in Saxony. Hedge finally found his element at Schulpforte, where he began to develop a mastery of the German language and literature, including Goethe and the

---

[3] Quoted in Joseph Henry Allen, *Sequel to "Our Liberal Movement,"* (Boston: Roberts Brothers, 1897), 64.

[4] Interestingly, Bancroft attended Hegel's lectures at the University of Berlin for part of a term. In his journal and a letter of 1820 he described Hegel as "sluggish" and stated that he stopped attending the lectures because Hegel's vocabulary was unintelligible. Quoted in Alvin S. Haag, "Some German Influences in American Philosophical Thought from 1800 to 1850" (Ph.D. diss., Boston University, 1939), 194. Nevertheless, like Hedge, Bancroft remained interested in German philosophy, and in 1825 he published "Writings of Herder" in the *North American Review*. Richard Arthur Firda, "German Philosophy of History and Literature in the *North American Review*: 1815-1860," *Journal of the History of Ideas* 32 (1971): 138.

THE EARLY AMERICAN RECEPTION
OF GERMAN IDEALISM

Volume 3

Selected and Introduced by
James A. Good
Rice University, Texas

History of American Thought

The Early American Reception of German Idealism
Selected and Introduced by **James A. Good**,
Rice University, Texas

Volume 1
Introduction
Psychology; or a View of the Human Soul (1841)
Frederick Augustus Rauch

Volume 2
Introduction
The Remains of the Rev. James Marsh, D.D. (1843)

Volume 3
Introduction
Prose Writers of Germany (1849)
Frederic Henry Hedge

Volume 4
Introduction
Rational Psychology (1849)
Laurens Perseus Hickok

Volume 5
Introduction
The Science of Thought (1869)
Charles Caroll Everett

German idealists. Fifty years later Hedge reminisced about his German education, claiming, "I am a German by intellectual descent…. Germany is the fatherland of my mind. It was there I first drew the breath of intellectual life and imbibed my first ideas of poetry and philosophy."[5] Hedge and Bancroft spent four years in Germany, returning to the United States in 1822. The following year Hedge entered Harvard as a junior.

Though Hedge's first inclination was to study science at Harvard, under his father's influence he chose theology instead. At Harvard a modest talent for poetry writing fully bloomed and only his dislike of mathematics prevented him from graduating with highest honors. During his two years at Harvard, Hedge befriended several who would become transcendentalists, perhaps most importantly Margaret Fuller. Fuller and Hedge shared an interest in German literature and became lifelong friends. When Hedge graduated from Harvard in 1825 he was considered for a position as a German instructor, but he decided to enter the Divinity School instead. His most influential Divinity School professors included Henry Ware, Sr., George Ticknor, and Andrews Norton. Although Norton later became one of the transcendentalists' most adamant critics, Hedge developed a respect for him at this time despite the fact that he was "conscious of his limitations and sometimes galled by his intolerance."[6] With Ticknor he was able to study the German higher criticism of the Bible. As Hedge immersed himself in his studies, he developed a friendship with Emerson that was immensely important to both men for the rest of their lives. Hedge's encouragement led Emerson to publish many of his early poems, but he was unable at this time to interest Emerson in German literature. Because of the historical importance of Hedge's influence on Emerson, it is worth quoting from his reminiscence of their friendship at this time at some length. Hedge recalled, "I tried to interest him in German literature, but he laughingly said that as he was not entirely ignorant of the subject, he should assume that it was not worth knowing. Later he studied German, mainly for

---

[5] Hedge, "Address to Germans of Boston, Faneuil Hall, July, 1876," *The Index* 27 August 1870, 2–3.

[6] Quoted in Octavius Brooks Frothingham, *Recollections and Impressions* (New York: G.P. Putnam's Sons, 1891), 29–31.

the purpose of acquainting himself with Goethe, to whom his attention had been directed by Carlyle."[7] A few years later Hedge became Emerson's closest advisor on German thought and, among the transcendentalists, his knowledge of the German language, literature, and philosophy earned him the nickname "Germanicus Hedge." George Ripley confirmed this depiction of Hedge when he described him as the "fountain...of the very atmosphere of German thought."[8]

Hedge graduated from the Divinity School in 1829 first in his class of nine. In the same year he was ordained at the Congregational Church and Society in West Cambridge, Massachusetts, and he married Lucy L. Pierce, daughter of the Rev. John Pierce of Brookline, Massachusetts. In West Cambridge, Hedge often met at a local bookstore with Fuller, Emerson, George Ripley, and Convers Francis where they discussed the latest trends in European thought.

Hedge's publishing career began in 1833 with "Coleridge's Literary Character," which appeared in the *Christian Examiner*. In that article Hedge reviewed Coleridge's ideas and displayed his knowledge of German thought by elucidating Colderidge's debt to German idealism. As Henry A. Pochmann notes, Hedge's "essay on Coleridge was the first clear and specific exposition of Kant, Fichte, and Schelling published in the United States by a native-born American."[9] The twenty-one-page essay was a review of the American editions of Colderidge's *Biographia Literaria* (1817), James Marsh's edition of the *Aids to Reflection* (1829), and *The Friend* (1831), as well as the three-volume London edition of Coleridge's *Poetical Works* (1829). After a brief discussion of Coleridge's speculative powers, Hedge complained about Coleridge's lack of clarity on German idealism, and used that opportunity to engage in "a few explanatory remarks respecting German metaphysics." In the discussion that followed, Hedge demonstrated a thorough understanding of Kant's

---

[7] Quoted in James Elliot Cabot, *A Memoir of Ralph Waldo Emerson* (New York: Houghton Mifflin, 1888), 139.

[8] George Ripley and George Bradford, "Philosophical Thought in Boston," in Justin Winsor, *Memorial History of Boston, including Suffolk County, Massachusetts* (Boston: J. R. Osgood and Company, 1881–83), 4: 307.

[9] Henry A. Pochmann, *German Culture in America: Philosophical and Literary Influences: 1600-1900* (Madison: The University of Wisconsin Press, 1957), 144.

Critiques, Fichte's *Wissenschaftslehre*, and Schelling's *System des transcendentalen Idealismus*. Although Kant revolutionized philosophy, explained Hedge, his successors rightly moved beyond his analytic method and his narrow focus on epistemological problems to "the whole world of intelligences, with the whole system of their representations."[10] Hedge then criticized Fichte's subjectivism and tendency toward skepticism, favoring Schelling's system of objective idealism. Yet Hedge never identified himself, in this essay or any other publication, with any particular school of thought. First and foremost, he was always a preacher primarily interested in ethics rather than philosophy or theology, but his principle debt to German idealism was its opposition to Lockean sensationalism and its alternative vision of man and his relationship to the world. The impact Hedge's article made on American transcendentalism cannot be overestimated. Moreover, the article's importance was not limited to the United States; Emerson was so impressed by it that he immediately recommended it to Thomas Carlyle.[11]

During the next two years, Hedge published highly regarded articles on Emmanuel Swedenborg and on the pretensions of phrenology.[12] Hedge later claimed that these articles, in addition to the previous one on Coleridge, reacted "against the orthodoxy expounded at the Harvard Divinity School" and "looked in the transcendental direction."[13] Indeed, these articles were the first American statement of transcendentalism. Thus Hedge has been accurately described as "one of the earliest and most influential of transcendentalists."[14] To his contemporary transcendentalists,

---

[10] Hedge, "Coleridge's Literary Character," *Christian Examiner* 14 (March 1833): 121.

[11] "Emerson to Thomas Carlyle," 20 November 1834, *The Correspondence of Emerson and Carlyle*, ed. John Slater (New York: Columbia University Press, 1964), 110. Cf. Harold Clarke Goddard, *Studies in New England Transcendentalism* (New York: Columbia University Press, 1908), 33.

[12] Hedge, "Emmanuel Swendenborg," *Christian Examiner* 15 (1833): 193–218; Hedge, "Pretensions of Phrenology Examined," *Christian Examiner* 17 (1834): 249–269.

[13] Quoted in Caroline H. Dall, *Transcendentalism in New England: A Lecture Before the Society for Philosophical Enquiry, Washington, D.C., May 7, 1895* (Boston: Roberts Brothers, 1897), 16.

[14] Goddard, *Studies in New England Transcendentalism*, 33.

the articles were "seminal" to their movement; according to Perry Miller, they brought the movement into being.[15]

In 1833 Hedge received an offer to become minister of the Independent Congregational Church in Bangor, Maine. Initially he was reluctant to accept the offer, but when Emerson preached there and reported to him about the liberal thinkers in the congregation, Hedge reconsidered and moved to Bangor in 1835. The congregation included Congregationalists, Unitarians, and Methodists, many of whom were among the wealthiest and most educated people in the lumber boomtown of Bangor. Hedge's tenure in Bangor began inauspiciously enough. Just as they were about to move, his wife Lucy grew ill and she and their two young children were unable to join him for several months. Hedge was also engaged in a protracted salary dispute with the congregation. Once those issues were resolved, however, Hedge settled into the position and was well received.

In 1836, Hedge, Emerson, Francis, James Freeman Clarke, and Amos Bronson Alcott attended the first meeting of the informal group that came to be known as the "Transcendental Club" at the home of George Ripley in Boston. Theodore Parker, Margaret Fuller, Orestes A. Brownson, Henry David Thoreau, Nathaniel Hawthorne, William Ellery Channing, and others, attended subsequent meetings. To the initiated, the group was known as the "Symposium," in honor of Plato, or as "Hedge's Club" because meetings were generally called when Hedge was in town. How frequently the group met over the course of the next three or four years we do not know because of its informality and lack of records, but members agreed that, within the group, Hedge's mind was the most philosophically trained. Many of the men were ministers who were trained at the Harvard Divinity School and subsequently left the church when they adopted the "New Views" on religion. Significantly, Hedge was among the few ministers who were sympathetic to the New Views but continued their careers within the church.

---

[15] Joel Porte, *Representative Man: Ralph Waldo Emerson in His Time* (New York: Oxford University Press, 1979), 55; Nelson R. Burr, *A Critical Bibliography of Religion in America* (Princeton, NJ: Princeton University Press, 1961), 242; Perry Miller, *The Transcendentalists: An Anthology* (Cambridge, Mass.: Harvard University Press, 67.

In 1835, Hedge first proposed that the group publish a literary journal devoted to "spiritual philosophy."[16] The project was postponed when Hedge moved to Bangor and thus could not serve as editor of the journal. Hedge raised the idea again in 1839; this time the group founded its literary organ, *The Dial*, with Fuller as editor and Ripley as assistant editor. Hedge contributed an article, two translations, and one poem to *The Dial* during its brief four-year existence, yet his interest and involvement in the journal soon languished, possibly because of a growing disenchantment with some of the more radical tendencies of the transcendentalist movement. It is clear that Hedge's involvement with the transcendentalists complicated his relationship to the Bangor congregation, as some deacons began to express doubts about his orthodoxy in 1841 and 1842.[17]

Despite this adversity, Hedge published his first major volume in 1847, *Prose Writers of Germany*. Although the transcendentalists advocated the development of original American thought, they also sought to bring foreign masterpieces to the attention of the American people because they believed such works would stimulate original expression by native artists and intellectuals. Much like Margaret Fuller's writings on Goethe in *The Dial* and George Ripley's published translations of German and French writers in *Specimens of Foreign Standard Literature*, Hedge's *Prose Writers of Germany* is part of this latter effort. The book is an anthology of excerpts from the writings of German writers presented, most for the first time, in English translation. Hedge sought to select "the Classics" of German prose in the sense of "writers of the first class."[18] Altogether the book included twenty-eight selections and involved eight translators besides Hedge. The first effort of such a scale in the United States, the book went through five editions.

Soon after *Prose Writers of Germany* was published, Hedge took a leave of absence from his Bangor pulpit for a tour of

---

[16] Quoted in Orie W. Long, *Frederic Henry Hedge: A Cosmopolitan Scholar* (Portland, Maine: The Southworth-Anthoensen Press, 1940), 23.

[17] See Bryan F. Le Beau, *Frederic Henry Hedge Nineteenth Century American Transcendentalist: Intellectually Radical, Ecclesiastically Conservative* (Allison Park, Penn.: Pickwick Publications, 1985), 26.

[18] Frederic Henry Hedge, *Prose Writers of Germany* (Philadelphia: Carey and Hart, 1847), iii.

England, Belgium, Germany, and Italy. In England, he met Carlyle who was duly impressed with his intellect and character. Although his trip to Germany only confirmed his love for that country, Italy was his greatest delight. He spent the winter in Rome with Margaret Fuller, who was playing a supporting role in the 1848 revolution as the wife of Marchese Ossoli. Hedge returned to Bangor in December of 1849, and submitted his letter of resignation to his congregation there with the hope of moving closer to Boston.

When a professorship at Harvard was not forthcoming, he accepted an offer for the pulpit of the Westminster Congregational Society in Providence, Rhode Island. Hedge and his family spent less than seven years in Providence, but they developed close, lifelong ties with several members of the congregation. During these years, Hedge received an honorary Doctor of Divinity degree from Harvard and published *Christian Liturgy, for the Use of the Church* and, with the assistance of Frederick D. Huntington, *Hymns for the Church of Christ*; both books appeared in 1853. He left Providence in 1857 to accept the more prestigious pulpit of the First Parish of Brookline, Massachusetts.

Within a year after his move to Brookline, Hedge was appointed Lecturer on Ecclesiastical History at the Harvard Divinity School and editor of the *Christian Examiner*.[19] Under his leadership, the *Christian Examiner* became one of the leading journals of the day. In 1859 he was elected president of the American Unitarian Association. Serving four successive terms as its president, Hedge was widely regarded as one of the most effective presidents of the American Unitarian Association during a period in which it faced serious internal discord and factionalization. Hedge displayed an impressive ability to remain bold and daring in his liberal religious writings while rising above party squabbles within the association, garnering respect from all.

In all of this, Hedge's literary production did not abate. In 1860 he published *Recent Inquiries in Theology*, a collection of essays

---

[19] Charles Carroll Everett, one of the other authors in the Early American Reception of German Idealism series, studied at the Harvard Divinity School from 1858 to 1859. Everett was named the first Bussey Professor of Theology at the Divinity School in 1869, where he remained until his death in 1900. Thus Hedge and Carroll were colleagues from 1869 to 1881. Crawford Howell Toy, "Charles Carroll Everett," *The New World: A Quarterly Review of Religion, Ethics, and Theology* 9 (1900): 715.

and reviews by English religious thinkers on contemporary theological issues. All of the essays were consistent with Hedge's liberal religion; all were opposed to the agnostic implications of Lockean epistemology. In 1865, Hedge published *Reason in Religion*, perhaps his most important book. Many of his contemporaries regarded the book as the most important expression of liberal religion of the time, establishing Hedge as the intellectual leader of liberal Unitarianism. Hedge followed the publication of this book with *The Primeval World of Hebrew Tradition* (1870) and *Ways of the Spirit and Other Essays* (1877). Throughout these years, Hedge also managed to published journal articles too numerous to list and maintained an increasingly busy speaking schedule. He resigned his position in Brookline in 1872, devoting himself full-time to his academic career at Harvard where he was appointed professor of German, a position he held until his retirement in 1881.

Hedge remained active after his retirement, regularly lecturing at Alcott's Concord School of Philosophy until 1887, speaking on many important occasions, including a notable eulogy on the death of Emerson in 1882, and receiving an honorary LL.D. from Harvard in 1876. Also in 1876, he published *Hours with German Classics: Masterpieces of German Literature Translated into English*. This book was followed by *Atheism in Philosophy* in 1884, in which he argued that excessive philosophical speculation dangerously undermined belief in the existence of God, and in 1888 he published *Martin Luther and Other Essays* and *Metrical Translations and Poems*. In the last few years of his life, Hedge suffered from eczema and was unable to sustain literary efforts; he died on 21 August 1890 at his home in Cambridge. The following year Hedge's *Sermons* was published.

From the time of his death to the present day, Hedge's philosophical relationship to the transcendentalists has been a recurring theme in the secondary scholarship on his thought. Although he acknowledges the originality of Hedge's thought, Bryan Le Beau has argued that Hedge should be viewed as a transcendentalist. According to Le Beau, Hedge "fully accepted the most basic tenet [of transcendentalism], which held that man had the innate capacity to arrive intuitively at truths not open to the understanding." Le Beau's argument that Hedge was a transcendentalist is persuasive, but it is perhaps more interesting to note points on which Hedge's thought was most original. As

Le Beau notes, "no one party within Unitarianism or one school of philosophy could claim Frederic Hedge."[20]

All of Hedge's mature thought displayed a profound debt to German idealism. Moreover, unlike many of the transcendentalists, Hedge went beyond the exposition of German idealism found in the writings of Coleridge and Carlyle, preferring the German of the original authors. From the idealists, Hedge took a critical stance toward the philosophy of Locke and the Scottish philosophy Hedge's father had so eloquently espoused. Much like Diogenes Teufelsdröckh ("devil oppressed"), the primary character of Thomas Carlyle's *Sartor Resartus* ("The Tailor Retailored"), Hedge also rejected the deterministic and mechanical Newtonian philosophy as a product of mere understanding. Through pure reason, Hedge believed, man could discover his moral autonomy in a deeply spiritual, organic and purposive universe. The understanding was limited to the realm of natural science, while reason operated in the realm of moral faith. This allowed Hedge to be a vigorous champion of science without concern that it would undermine faith. Hedge agreed with Schelling that nature and spirit are not opposed to one another, but are aspects of the one true and divine reality. Hence, for Hedge, God is immanent in nature, and reality, which continually progresses, testifies to God's loving nature revealed to reason through divine revelation. Thus like the other transcendentalists, Hedge believed social progress was inexorable.[21] Natural and spiritual man, for Hedge, were not static ontological realities, but were labels for stages of growth. By developing our natural capacities, with the assistance of divine grace, we can receive the truths of divine revelation and enter into conscious communion with God.

In his social thought, Hedge embraced the idealists' rejection of the atomistic individualism of the British political tradition. According to the post-Kantian idealists, we do not form societies in spite of our differences; we come together in social units because of our differences. For Hedge, each individual needs all others, and by devoting ourselves to the common good we contribute to society and simultaneously advance our own

---

[20] Le Beau, *Frederic Henry Hedge*, 167.

[21] Paul F. Boller, Jr., *American Transcendentalism, 1830-1860: An Intellectual Inquiry* (New York: G.P. Putnam's Sons, 1974), 144.

spiritual growth. Our social interdependence culminates in political unity and the creation of states. As the state becomes subject to the machinations of political parties, however, it is dissociated from society and focuses its energy on its own perpetuation rather than the common good. For Hedge, this process was inevitable until social cooperation was perfected. Nevertheless, according to Hedge, the tendency toward good in the world is greater than the tendency toward evil. Because he placed greater emphasis on man's social context than other transcendentalists, his political thought was what he described as an "enlightened conservatism." He rejected social and political revolution because, he claimed, "There is no standpoint out of society from which society can be reformed. 'Give me where to stand' was the ancient postulate. 'Find where to stand' says modern Dissent. 'Stand where you are' said Goethe, 'and move the world.'"[22] According to Hedge's view, there is no place for quick and radical change; rather, the truly spiritual person is content to await the fullness of time.

Hedge's thought was also more conservative than that of most of the other transcendentalists in that it was a self-consciously Christian transcendentalism.[23] Hedge sought to counter the natural religion of the Enlightenment, according to which God was reduced to a dispassionate, uninvolved first mover. At the same time, he could not return to the Calvinism of his father's generation. Thus he sought to promote a liberal Christianity that emphasized God's immanence and love. This sort of religion, for Hedge, went beyond the understanding, and thus the Enlightenment, to a direct communion with the absolute being that dwells in nature and in us all at a level deeper than self-consciousness. Reason and reflection, for Hedge, can provide us with living truth, as opposed to the merely logical truth of the understanding. The starting point for philosophy and true religion is the divine root in man. In some ways this divine root was similar to the Scottish doctrine of the moral sense that was ingrained in Hedge as a child. But Hedge resolutely rejected the

---

[22] Hedge, *Martin Luther and Other Essays* (Boston: Roberts Brothers, 1888), 144.

[23] This is a primary theme of Ronald Vale Wells, *Three Christian Transcendentalists: James Marsh, Caleb Sprague Henry, Frederic Henry Hedge* (New York: Columbia University Press, 1943).

traditional notion of original sin, although he did not deny that we have the ability to sin. Sinfulness can be overcome by our divine nature, however, through self-culture and discipline. Moreover, Hedge's emphasis upon man's social context led him to emphasize the social aspects of the Gospel more than most of the other transcendentalists. His religious thought most differed from Emerson and other more radical transcendentalists in his emphasis on Scripture as the primary source of divine revelation. Where Emerson found revelations all around him, Hedge emphasized more traditional Christian sources.[24]

Hedge's contribution to three congregations of the Unitarian Association, as well as the Association itself, and to the Transcendental Club, firmly establishes his importance in American intellectual and religious history. In his writings he offered a liberal reconstruction of New England Protestantism that probably paved the way for the Social Gospel that followed soon after his death. Unlike Emerson and other, more radical transcendentalists, Hedge hoped to further the effectiveness of the Christian church during a time of philosophical evolution. He tried to rethink the fundamental tenets of Christianity in terms of a new philosophy that was inspired by German and English Romanticism. In all of his work, including the present volume, Hedge promoted the latest European thought in America with an aim toward facilitating the genesis of an American version of Christianity that was philosophically respectable but that avoided the more radical transcendentalism of Emerson. In this regard, Hedge is accurately classified as one of the Christian transcendentalists.[25]

James A. Good
Rice University, Texas, 2002

---

[24] Peter Carafiol, *Transcendent Reason: James Marsh and the Forms of Romantic Thought* (Tallahassee, Florida: University Presses of Florida, 1982), 101.

[25] I believe Wells makes a strong case for grouping Hedge with James Marsh, the author of Volume Two in the Early American Reception of German Idealism series, and Caleb Sprague Henry, minister and professor of mental and moral philosophy at New York University. Wells, *Three Christian Transcendentalists*.

PAINTED BY C.A. SCHWERDGEBURTH ENGRAVED BY J. SARTAIN.

GOETHE.

PROSE WRITERS

OF

GERMANY

BY

FREDERIC H. HEDGE

ILLUSTRATED WITH PORTRAITS

Die deutsche Nation ist nicht die ausgebildetste, nicht die reichste an Geistes- und Kunstprodukten, aber sie ist die aufgeklaerteste, weil sie die gruendlichste ist, sie ist eine philosophische Nation.—Fr. H. Jacobi.

SECOND EDITION

PHILADELPHIA
PUBLISHED BY CAREY AND HART
1849

PREFACE

THE volume of translations which is now offered to the Public, though bearing the title, "Prose Writers of Germany," in conformity with the series of publications to which it belongs, is far from pretending to be a complete exhibition of the prose literature of that nation.

The impossibility of representing in adequate specimens, the vast body of writers who might claim to be represented under this title, together with the unsatisfactoriness of brief extracts, has induced the editor to adopt a different course,—to give few writers and large samples, and instead of a "collection," as Mr. Longfellow has characterized his "Poets and Poetry of Europe," to make a selection.

Every selection is liable to the charge of partiality; and those who are much conversant with German literature will doubtless miss some favorites who shall seem to them entitled to a place in these pages. It is believed however that the Classics, in the stricter sense, (writers of the first class) are mostly here. With regard to the rest, access or want of access to their writings has had some share, as well as personal preference, in determining the admissions and the omissions.

Some difficulty has been found in reconciling a just apportionment of space in our pages to different writers with the prescribed limits of the work. The difficulty, the editor is aware, has not been entirely overcome. While want of room has compelled him to omit altogether some writers whom he would gladly have introduced into the present selection, he regrets that the same necessity has required him in several instances to limit his extracts.

The editor avails himself of this opportunity to thank those who have assisted him in the work of translation. Besides his indebtedness to existing publications, especially to Carlyle's German Romance, he has to acknowledge the contributions of J. Elliot Cabot, Esq.,* Rev. J. Weiss,† Rev. C. T. Brooks,‡ Mr. Geo. Bradford,§ and Mr. Geo. Ripley.‖ The extracts from Möser, with the exception of the first, and that from Hamann, are by the same, anonymous, contributor. Likewise the translations from Hegel are by an anonymous friend possessing peculiar qualifications for that difficult task. Above all, his thanks are due to the Rev. Mr. Furness of Philadelphia, who has kindly taken upon himself the general superintendence of the work while passing through the press.

BANGOR, MAY, 1847.

---

* In the translations from Kant with the exception of the last, and in the translation from Schelling.

† In the translation from Schiller.

‡ In the extracts from the Titan of Jean Paul.

§ In the translation from Goethe's Wahlverwandtschaften.

‖ In the translation from Schleiermacher.

CONTENTS.

MARTIN LUTHER .... Page 9
    On Education 11
    Concerning God the Father 15
    Concerning Angels 16
    Simple Method how to Pray 18
    Prayer at the Diet of Worms 20
    Selections from Letters—Letter to the Elector Frederic 20
    To the Elector John 23
    To Caspar Guttel 23
    To his Wife 25
    To his Wife 25
    To his Wife 26

JACOB BOEHME 35
    To the Reader 37
    Of God and the Divine Nature 37
    Of God's First Manifestation of Himself in the Trinity 38
    Of Eternal Nature after the fall of Lucifer, &c. 38
    Of the Creation of Angels, &c. 41
    Describing what Lucifer was, &c. 41
    Of the Third Principle, or Creation of the Natural World 42
    Of Paradise 42
    Concerning the Supersensual Life 43
    Concerning the Blessing of God in the Goods of this World 44
    On True Resignation 45

ABRAHAM A SANCTA CLARA 46
    On Envy 46

JUSTUS MÖSER 50
    Letter from an Old Married Woman, &c. 52
    How to Attain to an Adequate Expression of Our Ideas 54
    Moral Advantages of Public Calamities 55

IMMANUEL KANT 57
    From the Critique of the Judgment 63

CONTENTS.

The Notion of Adaptation in Nature	65
Judgment by Means of Taste, Aesthetic	66
The Pleasure that Determines the Aesthetic Judgment	67
The Pleasure Derived from the Agreeable	67
The Pleasingness of Good, Connected with Interest	67
Comparisons of the Three Kinds of Pleasure	68
The Beautiful What	68
Comparison of the Beautiful with the Agreeable	68
An Aesthetic Judgment, when not pure	69
Of the Ideal of Beaûty	70
Plan of an Everlasting Peace	71
Of the Guaranty of an Everlasting Peace	73
Supposed Beginning of the History of Man	74
Remark	77
Conclusion of the History	78
Concluding Remark	79
JOHANN GOTTHOLD EPHRAIM LESSING	**81**
From Laocoon	85
From the Educator of the Human Race	91
Fables	95
Extract	98
MOSES MENDELSSOHN	**99**
Letter to J. C. Lavater	102
Supplementary Remarks	106
On the Sublime and the Naive	107
JOHANN GEORG HAMANN	**119**
The Merchant	121
CHRISTOPH MARTIN WIELAND	**128**
Philosophy Considered as the Art of Life	130
Letter to a Young Poet	132
On the Relation of the Agreeable and the Useful	138
From the Dialogues of the Gods	141
JOHANN AUGUST MUSÄUS	**154**
Dumb Love	158
MATTHIAS CLAUDIUS	**182**
Dedication to Friend Hans	182
Advertisement to Subscribers	182
Speculations on New Years' Day	183
The Sorrows of Young Werther	183
On Prayer	183
A Correspondence	184
On Klopstock's Odes	185

CONTENTS.

JOHANN CASPAR LAVATER	187
On the Nature of Man	191
Of the Truth of Physiognomy	193
Of the Universality of Physiognomical Sensations	195
On Freedom and Necessity	196
Of the Excellence of the Form of Man	197
Of the Congeniality of the Human Form	198
Resemblance between Parents and Children	200
Observations on the Dying and the Dead	202
Of the Influence of Countenance on Countenance	202
Of the Influence of the Imagination	203
Male and Female	204
FRIEDRICH HEINRICH JACOBI	206
From the Flying Leaves	209
Learned Societies	220
JOHANN GOTTFRIED VON HERDER	231
Love and Self	236
Tithon and Aurora	242
Metempsychoris	248
JOHANN WOLFGANG VON GŒTHE	263
The Vicar of Wakefield	270
From the Elective Affinities	278
Confessions of a Fair Saint	282
Indenture	304
The Exequies of Mignon	305
Extracts	306
Novelle	345
The Tale	353
JOHANN CHRISTOPH FRIEDRICH VON SCHILLER	365
Upon Naive and Sentimental Poetry	372
JOHANN GOTTLIEB FICHTE	383
The Destination of Man	384
JOHANN PAUL FRIEDRICH RICHTER	405
Rome	407
Leibgeber to Siebenkäs	411
Second Extract from "Flower, Fruit and Thorn pieces"	413
Dream	415
Letter to my Friends	417
The Marriage	418
Thoughts	420
AUGUST WILHELM VON SCHLEGEL	423
Lectures on Dramatic Literature	424

CONTENTS.

FRIEDRICH DANIEL ERNST SCHLEIERMACHER 441
    Discourse IV. Church and Priesthood 441

GEORG WILHELM FRIEDRICH HEGEL 446
    Introduction to the Philosophy of History 447
    Who thinks abstractly? 456

JOHANN HEINRICH DANIEL ZSCHOKKE 459
    The Poor Vicar 459

FRIEDRICH VON SCHLEGEL 472
    Lectures on the Philosophy of History 473

NOVALIS (FRIEDRICH VON HARDENBERG) 489
    From Heinrich von Oefterdinger 491
    From the Fragments 496

LUDWIG TIECK 498
    The Elves 501

FREDERIC WILLIAM JOSEPH VON SCHELLING 509
    On the Relation of the Plastic Arts of Nature 510

ERNST THEODOR AMADEUS HOFFMANN 521
    The Golden Pot 522

ADALBERT VON CHAMISSO 544
    The Wonderful History of Peter Schlemihl 547

PAINTED BY HOLBEIN ENGRAVED BY J. SARTAIN

LUTHER.

MARTIN LUTHER.

Born 1483. Died 1546.

"*Japeti de stirpe satum Doctore Luthero
Majorem nobis nulla propago dabit.*"

To MARTIN LUTHER belongs, with strict propriety, the foremost place in this collection intended to represent the German mind. Luther is regarded by his countrymen as the original of that mind,—the prototype of all that is most distinctive in German modes of thought and speech. Other writers of German had attained to eminence before him. Tauler, in particular, the celebrated mystic of Strasburg, is still an honored name. Nevertheless, the national-intellectual life of Germany dates from Luther as its parent source, and is emphatically referred to him by a grateful posterity. There is scarcely another instance in history, in which an individual, without secular authority or military achievement, has so stamped himself upon a people and made himself, to so great an extent, the leader, the representative, the voice of the nation. He has been to Germany, in this respect, what Homer was to Greece.

While devoting himself to the regeneration of the national religion, he unconsciously conferred upon the national literature a service as signal in its kind, as any which the church derived from his labors. He first gave to that literature an adequate organ. He created the language* which is now written and spoken by educated Germans. For though a constant approximation to the modern High German is undoubtedly visible in the writings of his immediate predecessors,—as e. g. in Albrecht Dürer, the painter, and the translator of the *Gesta Romanorum*,—there is still a great stride between their language and the Lutheran, in point of movement and well-defined inflection. On the whole, the modern High German must be considered as having first attained its full development and perfect finish in Luther's version of the Bible. By means of that book, it obtained a currency which nothing else could have given it. It became fixed. It became universal. It became the organ of a literature which, more than any other since the Greek, has been a literature of ideas. It became the vehicle of modern philosophy,—the cradle of those thoughts which, at this moment, act most intensely on the human mind.

Martin Luther was born at Eisleben, in Saxony, during a visit of his parents to that city, November 10, 1483. His father, Hans Luther, a poor miner, who had previously resided in the village of Mohra, removed to Mansfeld the following year; and here it was that Martin received the first rudiments of education. At the age of twenty, he obtained the degree of Master at the University of Erfurth. His father had destined him to the study of the Law, but Theology drew him with irresistible attraction. He became a monk of the Augustine order, at Erfurth, and, in process of time, Doctor of Divinity, at Wittenberg.

He began his labors, as a reformer, in the year 1517, with an attack on the sale of Indulgences, in ninety-five propositions, which he sent forth into the world, as it were a cartel aimed at Tetzel and Rome. Three years later we find him at the Diet of Worms, defending himself and his doctrine before the emperor Charles V. and the German princes. That was the most remarkable assembly ever convened on earth,—an empire against a man! Lucas Cranach's picture represents Luther as he stood there, so lone and strong, with his great fire-heart,—a new Prometheus, confronting the Jove of the sixteenth century and the German Olympus. "Here I stand, I cannot otherwise. God help me! Amen." Immediately upon this followed his translation of the Bible, which was his best defence; and

---

* "Er schuf die Deutsche Sprache." Heine. This may seem too strongly put, when we consider the necessary laws of language. The Lutheran was not a creation out of nothing, certainly; but it was the evolution of a perfect and harmonious form out of a rude and undigested mass.

from this time, until his death, which occurred on the 18th February, 1546, such a succession of labors in behalf of the Reformed religion, as to justify the epitaph,

"*Pestis eram vivens, moriens, tua mors ero Papa!*"

Luther is represented as a man of low stature* but handsome person, with a "clear brave countenance," lively complexion, and falcon eyes. Antonio Varillas† says; "Nature gave him an Italian head upon a German body; such was his vivacity and diligence, his cheerfulness and health." His voice was clear and penetrating, his eloquence overpowering. Melanchthon, on beholding his picture, exclaimed, "*Fulmina erant singula verba tua.*" Another contemporary said of him, that he was a man "to stop the wrath of God." Another calls him the third Elias. He was a husband and a father, fond of society, of a free and jovial nature, much given to music, himself a composer and an able performer on the flute. A man of singular temperance and great industry. He throve best on hard work and spare diet. An easy life made him sick. As to his character, a man without guile, open, sincere, generous, obliging, patient, brave, devout. "He was not only the greatest," says Henry Heine,‡ "but the most German man of our history. In his character all the faults and all the virtues of the Germans are combined on the largest scale. Then he had qualities which are very seldom found united, which we are accustomed to regard as irreconcileable antagonisms. He was, at the same time, a dreamy mystic and a practical man of action. His thoughts had not only wings but hands. He spoke and he acted. He was not only the tongue but the sword of his time. Moreover, he was, at the same time, a scholastic word-thresher and an inspired, God-intoxicated prophet. When he had plagued himself all day long with his dogmatic distinctions, in the evening he took his flute and gazed at the stars, dissolved in melody and devotion. He could scold like a fishwife, and he could be soft, too, as a tender maiden. Sometimes he was wild as the storm that uproots the oak, and then again, he was gentle as the zephyr that dallies with the violet. He was full of the most awful reverence and of self-sacrifice in honor of the Holy Spirit. He could merge himself entirely in pure spirituality. And yet he was well acquainted with the glories of this world, and knew how to prize them; and out of his mouth blossomed the famous saying,

"*Wer nicht liebt Wein, Weiber und Gesang,
Der bleibt ein Narr sein Lebenlang.*"

He was a complete man, I would say, an absolute man, one in whom matter and spirit were not divided. To call him a spiritualist, therefore, would be as great an error as to call him a sensualist. How shall I express it? He had something original, incomprehensible, miraculous, such as we find in all providential men,—something awfully *naive*, blunderingly wise, sublimely narrow;—something invincible, demoniacal."

The position which Luther holds in the estimation of his countrymen, as father of the German language and literature, together with the intrinsic worth of his writings, has seemed to me to justify more copious extracts, than one who knows him only as the great Reformer or the dogmatic theologian, might expect to find in a work like this. I have endeavored to preserve in the translation the slight taste of antiquity which marks the writer of the sixteenth century; although the language of Luther is less antiquated than that of contemporary English writers. In fact the antiquity resides in the thought rather than the idiom. The idiom is substantially that of the present day.

The following specimens, with the exception of the letters, are taken from the edition of Luther's works by Walch, in twenty-four vols. 4to. The letters are from the complete collection published by Martin Leberecht de Wette, in five vols. 8vo. Berlin. 1826.

---

* "Untergesetzter Statur." See *Des seligen Zeugen Gottes. D. Martin Luther's Lebens umstände in 4. Th. von Friedrich Siegmund Keil. Leipzig.* 1764.
† *Liber hist. de haeres,* quoted by Keil.
‡ Zur Geschichte der Religion und Philosophie in Deutschland. Salon, vol. 2d. Hamburg. 1835.

ON EDUCATION.

FROM A DISCOURSE ON THE SPIRITUAL ADVANTAGES ARISING FROM THE FURTHERANCE OF SCHOOLS, AND THE INJURY CONSEQUENT ON THE NEGLECT OF THEM.

Now if thou hast a child that is fit to receive instruction, and art able to hold him to it and dost not, but goest thy way and carest not what shall become of the secular government, its laws, its peace, &c., thou warrest against the secular government, as much as in thee lies, like the Turk, yea, like the Devil himself. For thou withholdest from the kingdom, principality, country, city, a redeemer, comfort, cornerstone, helper and saviour. And on thy account the emperor loses both sword and crown; the country loses safe-guard and freedom, and thou art the man through whose fault (as much as in thee lies) no man shall hold his body, wife, child, house, home and goods in safety. Rather thou sacrificest all these without ruth in the shambles, and givest cause that men shall become mere beasts, and at last devour one another. This all thou wilt assuredly do, if thou withdraw thy child from so wholesome a condition, for the belly's sake. Now art thou not a pretty man and a useful in the world? who makest daily use of the kingdom and its peace, and by way of thanks, in return, robbest the same of thy son, and deliverest him up to avarice, and labourest with all diligence to this end, that there may be no man who shall help maintain the kingdom, law and peace; but that all may go to wreck, notwithstanding thou thyself possessest and holdest body and life, goods and honour by means of said kingdom.

I will say nothing here of how fine a pleasure it is for a man to be learned, albeit he have never an office; so that he can read all manner of things by himself at home, talk and converse with learned people, travel and act in foreign lands. For peradventure there be few who will be moved by such delights. But seeing thou art so bent upon mammon and victual, look here and see how many and how great goods God has founded upon schools and scholars, so that thou shalt no more despise learning and art by reason of poverty. Behold! emperors and kings must have chancellors and scribes, counsellors, jurists and scholars. There is no prince but he must have chancellors, jurists, counsellors, scholars and scribes: so likewise, all counts, lords, cities, castles must have syndics, city clerks, and other learned men; nay, there is not a nobleman but must have a scribe. Reckon up, now, how many kings, princes, counts, lords, cities and towns, &c. Where will they find learned men three years hence? seeing that here and there already a want is felt. Truly I think kings will have to become jurists and princes chancellors, counts and lords will have to become scribes, and burgomasters sacristans.

Therefore I hold that never was there a better time to study than now; not only for the reason that the art is now so abundant and so cheap, but also because great wealth and honour must needs ensue, and they that study now will be men of price; insomuch that two princes and three cities shall tear one another for a single scholar. For look above or around thee and thou wilt find that innumerable offices wait for learned men, before ten years shall have sped; and that few are being educated for the same.

Besides honest gain, they have, also, honour. For chancellors, city clerks, jurists, and people in office, must sit with those who are placed on high, and help counsel and govern, And they, in fact, are the lords of this world, although they are not so in respect of person, birth and rank.

Solomon himself mentions that a poor man once saved a city, by his wisdom, against a mighty king. Not that I would have, herewith, warriors, troopers, and what belongs to strife done away, or despised and rejected. They also, where they are obedient, help to preserve peace and all things with their fist. Each has his honour before God as well as his place and work.

On the other hand, there are found certain scratchers* who conceit that the title of writer is scarce worthy to be named or heard. Well then, regard not that, but think on this wise: these good people must have their amusement and their jest. Leave them their jest, but remain thou, nevertheless, a writer before God and the world. If they scratch long, thou shalt see that they honour, notwithstanding, the pen above all things; that they place it† upon hat and helmet, as if they would confess, by their action, that the pen is the top of the world, without which they can neither be equipped for battle nor go about in peace; much less scratch so securely. For they also have need of the peace which the emperors, preachers and teachers (the lawyers) teach and maintain. Wherefore thou seest that they place our implement, the dear pen, uppermost. And with reason, since they gird their own implement, the sword, about the thighs; there it hangs fitly and well for their work; but it would not beseem the head; there must hover the plume. If, then, they have sinned against thee, they herewith expiate the offence, and thou must forgive them.

There be some that deem the office of a writer to be an easy and trivial office; but to ride in armour, to endure heat, cold, dust, thirst and other inconvenience, they think to be laborious. Yea! that is the old, vulgar, daily tune; that no one sees where the shoe pinches another. Every one feels only his own troubles,

---

* *Scharrhansen*, men who scratch for money, and think of nothing else. Tr.
† The word *Feder*, feather, is used indifferently in German to denote pen or plume. Tr.

and stares at the ease of others. True it is, it would be difficult for me to ride in armour; but then, on the other hand, I would like to see the rider who should sit me still the whole day long and look into a book, though he were not compelled to care for aught, to invent or think or read. Ask a chancery-clerk, a preacher or an orator, what kind of work writing and haranguing is? Ask a schoolmaster what kind of work is teaching and bringing up of boys? The pen is light, it is true, and among all trades no tool so easily furnished as that of the writing-trade, for it needeth only a goose's wing, of which one shall everywhere find a sufficiency, *gratis*. Nevertheless, in this employment, the best piece in the human body, (as the head) and the noblest member, (as the tongue) and the highest work (as speech) must take part and labour most; while, in others, either the fist or the feet or the back, or members of that class alone work; and they that pursue them may sing merrily the while, and jest freely, which a writer cannot do. Three fingers do the work (so they say of writers), but the whole body and soul must coöperate.

I have heard of the worthy and beloved emperor Maximilian, how, when the great boobies complained that he employed so many writers for missions and other purposes, he is reported to have said; "what shall I do? They will not suffer themselves to be used in this way, therefore I must employ writers." And further: "Knights I can create, but doctors I cannot create." So have I likewise heard of a fine nobleman, that he said, "I will let my son study. It is no great art to hang two legs over a steed and be a rider; he shall soon learn me that; and he shall be fine and well-spoken."

They say, and it is true, the pope was once a pupil too. Therefore despise me not the fellows who say "*panem propter Deum*" before the doors and sing the bread-song.* Thou hearest, as this psalm says, great princes and lords sing. I too have been one of these fellows, and have received bread at the houses, especially at Eisenach, my native city. Although, afterward, my dear father maintained me, with all love and faith, in the high school at Erfurt, and, by his sore sweat and labour, has helped me to what I have become,—still I have been a beggar at the doors of the rich, and, according to this psalm, have attained so far by means of the pen, that, now, I would not compound with the Turkish emperor, to have his wealth and forego my art. Yea I would not take for it the wealth of the world many times multiplied; and yet, without doubt, I had never attained to it, had I not chanced upon a school and the writers' trade.

Therefore let thy son study, nothing doubting, and though he should beg his bread the while,

---

* A song or psalm which the poor students of Luther's time sang, when they went about imploring charity at the doors of the rich.

yet shalt thou give to our Lord God a fine piece of wood out of which he can whittle thee a lord. And be not disturbed that vulgar niggards contemn the art so disdainfully, and say: Aha! if my son can write German and read and cipher, he knows enough; I will have him a merchant. They shall soon become so tame that they will be fain to dig with their fingers, ten yards deep in the earth, for a scholar. For my merchant will not be a merchant long, when law and preaching fail. That know I for certain; we theologians and lawyers must remain, or all must go down with us together. It cannot be otherwise. When theologians go, then goes the word of God, and remains nothing but the heathen, yea! mere devils. When jurists go, then goes justice together with peace, and remains only murder, robbery, outrage, force, yea! mere wild beasts. But what the merchant shall earn and win, when peace is gone, I will leave it to his books to inform him. And how much profit all his wealth shall be to him when preaching fails, his conscience, I trow, shall declare to him.

I will say briefly of a diligent pious school-teacher or magister, or of whomsoever it is, that faithfully brings up boys and instructs them, that such an one can never be sufficiently recompensed or paid with money; as also the heathen Aristotle says. Yet is this calling so shamefully despised among us, as though it were altogether nought. And we call ourselves Christians!

And if I must or could relinquish the office of preacher and other matters, there is no office I would more willingly have than that of schoolmaster or teacher of boys. For I know that this work, next to the office of preacher, is the most profitable, the greatest and the best. Besides, I know not even, which is the best of the two. For it is hard to make old dogs tame and old rogues upright; at which task, nevertheless, the preacher's office labours, and often labours in vain. But young trees be more easily bent and trained, howbeit some should break in the effort. *Beloved! count it one of the highest virtues upon earth, to educate faithfully the children of others, which so few, and scarcely any, do by their own.*

ON THE SAME SUBJECT.

FROM AN EXHORTATION OF M. LUTHER TO THE COUNCILMEN OF ALL THE CITIES OF GERMANY TO ESTABLISH AND MAINTAIN CHRISTIAN SCHOOLS.

LET us consider our former misery and the darkness wherein we have been. I deem that Germany has never before heard so much of God's word as now. One finds no trace of it in history. If, then, we let it pass thus, without thanks or honour, it is to be feared we shall suffer yet more horrible darkness and plagues. Dear Germans! buy while the market is at the door. Gather while the sun shines and the weather is good. Use God's grace and word while it is there. For you shall know that God's grace and word is a travelling shower which does not appear again where it has once been. It dwelled once with the Jews, but gone is gone;—now they have nothing. Paul brought it into Greece, but gone is gone;—now they have got the Turk. Rome and Italy have had it once; gone is gone;—now they have got the Pope. And ye Germans must not think that you will have it forever; for ingratitude and neglect will not suffer it to remain. Therefore seize and hold fast whoever can. Idle hands have slender years.

Yea! sayest thou, though it be fitting and necessary to have schools, of what use is it to teach the Latin, Greek and Hebrew tongues, and other fine arts? Could we not teach, in German, the Bible and God's word, which are sufficient for salvation? Answer: Yes, I know alas! too well, that we Germans must always be and continue beasts and wild animals. So the surrounding nations call us, and we deserve it well. But I wonder we never say: of what use are silks, wine, spices and outlandish wares of foreign nations? seeing we have wine, corn, wool, flax, wood and stones in German lands—not only a sufficiency for support, but also a choice and selection for honour and adornment? We are willing to contemn the arts and languages which, without any injury, are a great ornament, use, honour and advantage, both for the understanding of the Sacred Scriptures, and for the conduct of worldly government; and are not willing to dispense with outlandish wares which are neither necessary nor useful, and moreover distress and ruin us. Have we not good reason to be called German fools and beasts?

Indeed, if there were no other use to be derived from the languages, it ought to rejoice and animate us that we have so noble and fine a gift of God; wherewith he has visited and favoured us Germans above all other lands. It doth not appear that the Devil would suffer these same languages to come forward by means of the High-schools and Cloisters; on the contrary they have always raved most vehemently and still rave against them. For the Devil smelled the roast,* that if the languages revived, his kingdom would get a hole which he could not easily stop up again.† Now, since he hath not been able to prevent their revival, he thinks

---

* "To smell the roast" is a proverbial expression with the Germans, equivalent to our "smell the rat," i. e. to suspect mischief. Tr.

† The study of the Greek and the Hebrew is said to have been discouraged by the clergy prior to the Reformation, in order to prevent a nearer acquaintance with the Scriptures. "They have discovered," says a monk of that period, "a new language which they call the Greek; beware of it, for it is the mother of all heresies. I see in the hands of some a book written in that language, called the New Testament. It is a book full of thorns and poison. And as to Hebrew, my beloved brethren, you may be sure that whoever meddles with that will immediately become a Jew." Tr.

still to keep them so poorly, that they shall decline and fall away again of themselves. It is no welcome guest that hath come into his house with them; therefore he means to entertain him in such a way that he shall not long remain. There be few of us that perceive this wicked trick of the Devil, my dear masters! Therefore, beloved Germans! let us here open our eyes, thank God for the noble treasure and take fast hold of it, that it may not again be wrested from us, and the Devil wreak his spite. For we cannot deny this, that howbeit the gospel came and comes daily through the Holy Spirit alone, yet it came through the instrumentality of the languages, and, by means of them, has advanced, and by means of them must be preserved. For straightway, when God was minded to let his gospel go forth into all the world through the apostles, he gave tongues for that end. And he had before diffused the Latin and Greek tongues so widely in all lands, by means of the Roman Government, to the end that his gospel might bring forth fruit speedily far and near. Thus also hath he done now. No one knew why God caused the languages to revive, until now, when it is evident that it was done for the gospel's sake, the which he was minded afterward to reveal, and thereby to discover and destroy the kingdom of Antichrist. For this cause also he gave Greece to the Turks, that the Greeks who were driven out and scattered abroad might carry forth the Greek tongue and become an introduction to the study of other languages also.

And let us understand this, that we shall not be able to preserve the gospel without the languages. The languages are the sheath in which this sword of the Spirit is hid. They are the casket in which this jewel is borne. They are the vessel in which this drink is contained. They are the cupboard in which this food is laid. And, as the evangile itself showeth, they are the baskets which hold these loaves and fishes and fragments. Yea! if we should so err as to let the languages go, (which God forbid!) we shall not only lose the gospel, but it shall come to pass, at length, that we shall not know to speak or write, neither Latin nor German aright. Of this let the miserable and dreadful example of the High-schools and Convents be a proof and a warning; where they have not only lost all knowledge of the gospel, but have so corrupted the Latin and the German language that the wretched people have beome mere beasts, cannot write or speak correctly, either Latin or German, and have also well nigh lost their natural reason.

Yea! sayest thou, many of the Fathers have attained to blessedness, and have also taught, without languages. That is true. But to what dost thou impute it, that they have so often failed in the Scriptures? How often does St. Augustin fail in the psalms, and in other expositions? So also Hilary, yea all who have taken upon themselves to expound Scripture without the languages. Was not St. Jerome compelled to translate the Psalter anew from the Hebrew, because, when men argued with the Jews out of our Psalter, they mocked and said it was not so written in the Hebrew, as our people quoted it?

Thence comes it that since the time of the apostles the Scripture has remained so obscure and that no certain and permanent exposition of it hath been written. For even the holy Fathers (as I have said) have often failed, and because they were ignorant of the languages, they are seldom agreed, but one goes this way, another that. St. Bernard was a man of a large spirit, insomuch that I might almost place him above all other teachers who have become celebrated, both ancient and modern. But see, how he so often sports with the Scriptures, (howbeit spiritually) and quotes them aside of their true meaning! For this cause the sophists have said that the Scriptures were dark, and have thought that in its own nature the word of God was so obscure and spoke so strangely. But they see not that the whole difficulty lies in the languages. Nothing more simple than the word of God has ever been spoken; so we understood the tongues. A Turk must needs speak obscurely to me—because I know not his language—whom, nevertheless, a Turkish child of seven years can well understand.

Neither let us be deceived for that some boast themselves of the Spirit and think meanly of the Scripture. Some also like the Brethren, the Waldenses, deem the languages not to be useful. But, dear friend, Spirit here, Spirit there,—I have also been in the Spirit and have also seen Spirits, (if ever it be lawful to boast of one's own flesh) perhaps more than these same people shall see in a year, howsoever they boast themselves. Also, *my* spirit has proved itself somewhat, while theirs is quite silent in a corner and does little else than protrude its praise. I might have led a pious life and have preached well enough in quiet. But the Pope and the Sophists and the whole Government of Antichrist I should have been forced to leave as they are. The Devil cares not for my spirit so much as for my language, and my pen in the Scriptures. For my spirit takes nothing from him save myself alone. But the holy Scriptures and the languages make the world too narrow for him and injure him in his kingdom. So then, I cannot praise the Brethren, the Waldenses, in that they despise the tongues. For though they should teach aright, they must often fail of the right text, and remain unarmed and unfurnished to battle for the faith against error.

Now, although, as I have said before, there were no soul and no need of schools and languages for God's sake and the Scriptures,—yet were this alone a sufficient reason for establishing everywhere the very best schools both for boys and girls,—that the world has need of skilful men and women in order to maintain outwardly its secular condition. The men should be fit to govern Land and People; the women should be well able to guide and preserve house, children and servants. Now must such men be made out of boys and such women must be made out of little girls. Therefore it is important to train and educate little boys and girls aright for such work. I have said above that the common man does nothing toward this end, neither can he, neither will he, neither knows he. Princes and lords ought to do it, but they are occupied with sleigh-riding, with drinking and with mummery; they are laden with grave and important affairs of the kitchen, the cellar and the chamber. And though some would do it willingly, the others must needs scare them with the fear of being called fools or heretics. Therefore, my beloved Council-men, it remains in your hands alone. You have space and vocation for it more than princes and lords.

Thou sayest let each one teach and train his own. Answer: Yes! we know very well what kind of teaching and training that is. Even when it is carried farthest and succeeds well, it amounts to nothing more than a little discipline of forced and decent manners. For the rest, they are mere blocks of wood, and know nothing either of this or of that, and can neither counsel nor help. But if they were taught and trained in schools or elsewhere, where there are learned and able masters and mistresses, who teach languages and other arts and histories, they would hear the history and the sayings of all the world;—how it fell out with this or that city or kingdom or prince, man or woman; and they would be able, in a short time, to bring before them, as it were in a mirror, the being, life, counsels and designs, the successes and failures of the whole world, from the beginning; whence they might learn to order their thoughts and adjust themselves to the course of the world, in the fear of God. And they should be made witty and wise by these histories, knowing what to seek and what to avoid in this outward life; and should be able moreover to advise and govern others. But the education which is given at home, without such schools, attempts to make us wise by our own experience. Ere that comes to pass we shall be dead a hundred times over, and shall have acted inconsiderately all our life long. For experience requires much time.

How much time and trouble are bestowed in teaching children to play at cards, to sing and to dance. Why will we not spend as much time in teaching them to read and other accomplishments, while they are young and have leisure and capacity and disposition for them? I speak for myself: if I had children and were able, they should not only hear me languages and histories, but they should also sing and learn music and the whole of the mathematics. For what is all this but mere child's play, in which the Greeks aforetime instructed their children, and by means of which they afterward became wonderfully skilful people and capable of many things? Yea! what grief it is to me now, that I did not read more poets and histories, and that no one instructed me in these matters. Instead thereof, I have been made to read the Devil's filth, philosophers and schoolmen, with great cost and labour and injury, so that I have enough to do to get rid of it all.

Thou sayest, who can give up his children and train them all, for squires? They must attend to the work at home. Answer: My opinion is not that we should establish such schools as there have been heretofore, where a youth would pore for twenty or thirty years over Donatus and Alexander and learn nothing after all. We have a different world now, and things are otherwise managed. My counsel is that the boys should be suffered to go to school an hour or two each day and none the less work at home the rest of the time,—learn a handycraft and do whatever is wanted of them. Let both go together, seeing they are young and can wait. Besides, do they not spend ordinarily tenfold as much time at marbles and ball and in running and wrestling?

So likewise a girl may find time enough to go to school an hour a day, and still wait upon her work at home. They sleep away and dance away and play away more time than that. The only difficulty is this, that there is no hearty desire to train the young and to help and instruct the world with fine people. The Devil loves, rather, coarse blocks and good-for-nothing people, that man may not fare too well upon the earth.

Therefore, dear masters, take to heart the work which God so imperatively demands of you, to which your office binds you, which is so necessary to the young, and which neither the world nor the Spirit can do without. Alas! we have long enough been rotting and corrupting in darkness. All too long have we been "German beasts." Let us, for once, make use of our reason, that God may mark our gratitude for his gifts, and that other lands may take note that we too are men, and such as can either learn something useful of them or teach them something;—so that by us also the world may be made better. I have done my part. It was my desire to counsel and help the German land. And albeit some may contemn me in this thing and give to the winds my faithful advice and pretend to better knowledge, I must even endure it. I well know that others might have done better; but seeing they are silent, I have done as well as I could. It is better to speak right forth, however unskilfully, than always to be silent on this head. And I am in hope that God will arouse some among you, to the end that my true counsel may not wholly fall in the dust, and that you will consider not him that speaketh but ponder the thing itself and let it go forward. * * * * *

Herewith I commend you to the grace of God. May he soften and kindle your hearts so that they shall earnestly take the part of these poor, suffering, forsaken youth, and, by Divine aid, counsel and help them to a happy and Christian government of the German land, in body and soul, with all fulness and redundancy, to the praise and honour of God the Father, through Jesus Christ our Saviour! Amen.

Given at Wittenberg, Anno, 1524.

CONCERNING GOD THE FATHER.

FROM AN EXPOSITION OF THE CHRISTIAN CREED, DELIVERED AT SMALCALD IN THE YEAR 1537.

ART. I. "*I believe in God the Father, the Almighty, Creator of Heaven and Earth.*"

Here, it is first of all held up to us, that we know and learn whence we are derived, what we are and where we belong. All wise men have ever been concerned to know whence the world and ourselves have proceeded, but have not been able to discover. They have supposed that man is born by chance, without a master by whom his birth is ordained and brought to pass, and that he lives and dies by chance, like other beasts. Some have advanced farther and have pondered this subject until they were forced to conclude that the world and man must have proceeded from an eternal God, because they are such mighty and glorious creations. Nevertheless, they have not been able to attain to any true knowledge thereof. But we know it well, howbeit not of and from ourselves but from the word of God which is here brought before us, in the creed. Therefore wouldst thou know whence thou and I and all men are derived, listen and I will tell thee. It is God the Father, the almighty creator of heaven and earth, an only God, who has created and preserves all things. Now thou knowest it. It is indeed a simple doctrine to look at, and a plain sermon. And yet no man, be he as wise as he could be, was able to find it, save he who came down from heaven and revealed the same to us.

The wise man, Aristotle, concludes that the world existed from eternity. To that one must say, that he knew nothing at all of this art. But when it is said that heaven and earth are a creation or work made by him who is called an only God and made out of nothing; that is an art above all arts. And thus it is with me and thee and the world. Sixty years ago I was nothing as yet. And so, innumerable children will be born after us who as yet are nothing. So the world six thousand years ago was nothing, and, in time, will be nothing again. And so, all was brought out of nothing into being, and shall be brought out of being into nothing again, until all is created anew, more glorious and fair. This, I say, we know, and the Holy Scripture teacheth it us, and little children have it presented to them thus, in the words of the creed —"I believe in God the Father, &c."

Therefore, learn first of all, from this, whence thou comest; namely from him who is called

Creator of heaven and earth. That may be counted a great and sublime honour, which I ought reasonably to accept with great joy, that I am called and am a creature and work of the only and most high God. The world seeketh after honour with money, force and the like. But it hath not the piety rightly to consider and reflect upon this honour, concerning which we pray, through the mouth of young children, here in the creed, that God is our master, who has given us body and soul, and preserves them still from day to day. If we rightly believed this, and deemed it true, there would spring from it great praise and boasting; for that I can say, the Master who has created the sun, he has also created me. As now the sun boasts its beauty and its glory, so will I boast and say: I am the work and creature of my God.

With this honour should every man be satisfied, and say with joy, I believe in God, Creator of heaven and earth, who has hung his name about my neck, that I should be his creature, and that he should be called my God and Maker. It is a children's sermon and a common saying, nevertheless, one sees well who they be that understand it. We deem it no particular honour that we are God's creatures, but that any one should be a prince or great lord, we open eyes and mouth. Yet are these but human creatures, as Peter calls them, and an afterwork. For, if God did not come first with his creature, and make a man, there could be no prince. Yet do all men clamour about such an one, as if it were some great and precious thing, whereas it is much greater and more glorious to be a creature of God. Therefore should servants and maidservants and all men accept this high honour, and say, I am a man. That is a higher title than to be a prince. Not God, but men make the prince, but God alone can make me a man.

It is said of the Jews, that they have a prayer wherein they praise God for three things. First, that they are created men and not irrational animals. Secondly, that they are created male and not female. Thirdly, that they are created Jews and not heathen. But that is praising God as fools are wont, by flouting and vilifying other creatures of God, at the same time. So doth not the Psalmist praise him. He includes all that God has made, and says, Praise the Lord on the earth! ye whales and all the deeps! &c.

Furthermore, this article teacheth us not only who hath created us and whence we are, but also where we belong. This is shown us by the word *Father*. He is at the same time Father and Almighty Creator. The beasts cannot call him Father, but we are to call him thus and to be called his children. With this word he showeth what destination he hath appointed us, having first taught us whence we are and what praise and honour have been bestowed upon us. What is the end and purpose of the whole? This,—that ye shall be children and that I will be your Father. That I have not only created you and will preserve you here, but that I will have you to children, and suffer you to be my heirs, who shall not be thrust out of the house like other creatures, oxen, cows, sheep, &c., that either perish all, or else are eaten, but, besides that ye are my creatures, ye shall also be forevermore my children and live alway.

Thus do we pray and confess, when we say in the creed, *I believe in God the Father*, that, in like manner as he is Father and liveth forever, we also, as his children, shall live forever and shall not perish. Therefore are we by so much a higher and fairer creation than other creatures, that we are not only creatures of God and his work, but are destined also to live forever with our Father.

This is an article with which we should day by day converse, that, the longer we taste thereof, the more we may prove it; for it is impossible, with words or with thoughts, to comprehend what is meant by God the Father. A sated and weary heart may hear but doth not consider it. But the heart which rightly received such words would often think thereon with joy, and when it looked upon the sun, moon, and other creatures, would recognise herein a special favour, that it is called a child of God, and that God is willing to be and remain our Father, and that we shall evermore live and remain with God.

This then is the first article, whence we briefly learn that a Christian is a fair and glorious creation that cometh from God, and that the end which he craves and for which he is destined, is eternal life.

CONCERNING ANGELS.

FROM A DISCOURSE ON GOOD AND EVIL ANGELS, PREACHED AT WITTEMBERG, AT THE FEAST OF MICHAELMAS, 1533; FROM THE WORDS: "TAKE HEED THAT YE DESPISE NOT ONE OF THESE LITTLE ONES! FOR I SAY UNTO YOU, THAT IN HEAVEN, THEIR ANGELS DO ALWAYS BEHOLD THE FACE OF MY FATHER WHICH IS IN HEAVEN." MATT. XVIII. 10.

* * * Seeing then, that the Feast of St. Michael, and of all the angels, exists, we will retain the same in our churches. Not for secular reasons alone, and the income which is derived from it; but much rather for spiritual reasons. Because it is useful and necessary that Christians should continue in the right understanding of angels,—so that the young people may not grow up, neither learning nor knowing what dear angels purpose and do; and have no joy therein, and never thank God the Lord for this gift and benefit.

* * * * * * *

Now beginneth the Lord a sermon for children, and saith, "Take heed that ye despise not one of these little ones," &c. There thou hast a clear text, which thou oughtest, with certainty, to believe. For this man, Christ, knows, of a surety, that children have angels, which do not make the children, but help to preserve them whom God hath created. So then, we preachers and parents ought to begin where Christ began, and impress upon children that they have angels. * * * After this manner would I train a child from early youth, and say to him, Dear child, thou hast an own angel. If thou prayest morning and evening, this angel shall be near thee and shall sit by thy little bed. He has a little white coat, and he shall nurse thee and rock thee and take care of thee, that the bad man, the Devil, may not come nigh thee. Also, when thou lovest to say thy *Benedicite* and thy *Gratias* before meat, thy little angel will be near thy table, and will wait upon thee and guard thee and watch, that no evil may befal thee, and that thy food may do thee good. If this were impressed upon children, they would learn and accustom themselves from youth up to the thought that the angels are with them. And this would not only serve to make them rely on the protection of the dear angels, but also cause that they should be well-behaved, and learn to stand in awe, and to think: Though our parents are not with us, yet the angels are here; they are looking after us, that the evil Spirit may do us no mischief.

This, peradventure, is a childish sermon, but, nevertheless, it is good and needful; and so needful and so simple that it may profit us old folks also. For the angels are not only present with children, but also with us who are old. So says St. Paul, in the first epistle to the Corinthians, xi. 10, "For this cause ought the woman to have a power on her head, because of the angels." Women should not be adorned in the church and in the congregation as if they were going to a dance, but be covered with a veil for the sake of the angels. St. Paul here fetcheth in the angels, and saith that they are present at the sermon, and at sacred offices and divine service. This service of the angels doth not seem to be precious, but herein we see what are genuine good works. The dear angels are not proud as we men; but they walk in divine obedience, and in the service of men, and wait upon young children. How could they perform a meaner work than to wait day and night upon children? What doth a child? It eats, weeps, sleeps, &c. Truly, an admirable thing, that the holy ministering Spirits should wait upon children who eat, drink, sleep, and wake! To look at it, it doth indeed seem a lowly office. But the dear angels perform it with joy, for it is well pleasing to God, who hath enjoined it upon them. A monk, on the contrary, saith, shall I wait upon children? That will I not do. I will go about higher and greater works. I will put on a cowl and will mortify myself in the cloister, &c. But if thou wilt consider it aright, these are the highest and best offices, which are rendered to children and to pious Christians. What do parents? What are their works? They are the menials and the servants of young children. All that they do—they themselves confess—they do for the sake of their children, that they may be educated. So do also the dear angels. Why, then, should we be ashamed to wait upon children? And if the dear angels did not take charge of children, what would become of them? For parents, with the help of prince and magistrate, are far too feeble to bring them up. Were it not for the protection of the dear angels, no child would grow to full age, though the parents should bestow all possible diligence upon them. Therefore hath God ordained, and set for the care and defence of children, not only parents, but also emperors, kings, princes, and lastly, his high and great Spirits, the holy angels, that no harm may befall them. It were well that the children were impressed with these things.

On the other hand, one should also tell children of the wiles of the Devil and of evil spirits.ABC child, one should say to them, if thou wilt not be pious, thy little angel will run away from thee, and the evil Spirit, the black *Popelmann*, will come to thee. Therefore, be pious and pray, and thy little angel will come to thee, and the *Popelmann* will leave thee. And this is even the pure truth. The Devil sits in a corner, and if he could throttle both parent and child, he would do it not otherwise than gladly. * * * * *

Thus are the dear angels watchmen also, and keep watch over us and protect us. And were it not for their guardianship, the black Nick would soon find us, seeing he is an angry and untiring Spirit; but the dear angels are our true guardians against him. When we sleep, and parents at home and the magistrate in the city and the prince of the country sleep likewise, and can neither govern nor protect us, then watch the holy angels and guard and govern us for the best. When the Devil can do nothing else, he affrighteth me in my sleep, or maketh me sick that I cannot sleep. Then no man can defend me; all they that are in the house are asleep; but the dear angels sit at my bed-side, and they say to the Devil: Let this man sleep, &c. This is the office which the angels perform for me, unless I have deserved that God should withdraw his hand from me, and not permit his angels to guard and defend me, but suffer me to be scourged a little, to the end that I may be humbled, and acknowledge the blessing of God which he conferreth upon me by the ministry of the dear angels.

Further, it is the office of the dear angels to protect and accompany me when I journey,— to be with me by the way. When I arise in the morning and perform my prayer, and pronounce the blessing of the morning and go forth into the field, I am to know that God's angels are with me,—that he keeps good watch over me against the devils that are around me, behind and before.

* * * This doctrine comforteth and rejoiceth us, and causeth that we take courage in our necessities, and think within ourselves: Thou art alone, it may be, and yet thou art not alone;

the dear angels given thee by God are present with thee. Thus we read in the second book of Kings, c. vi. When the prophet Elisha was about to go forth from the city of Dothan with his servants, he saw a great army of the king of Syria, which had come to take him. Nevertheless the prophet went forth. This was an excellent boldness that the prophet should go forth with his servant against so large a host and a nation of warriors. The servant was affrighted, and said, "Alas, my master! what shall we do?" But the prophet was undismayed, and said, Fear not: for they that be with us are more than they that be with them. Such was his defiance and courage. The servant could not see it, but the prophet prayed that the Lord would open the eyes of his servant. Then he saw that the mountain was full of horses and chariots of fire round about Elisha.

So, likewise, we read of the patriarch Abraham, that he sent out his servant to bring home a wife for his son Isaac. And when the servant knew not the way, Abraham said, "The Lord God of heaven shall send his angel before thee, and thou shalt take unto my son a wife from thence." Abraham sends his servant out as one would throw a feather into the air. It doth not trouble him that his son Isaac is not acquainted with the bride, and doth not know where she is to be found; but he saith: The Lord will let his angel go with thee, who shall show thee the way; and thou shalt find the bride. Is it not a fine thing that the angel of the Lord must be present and woo a wife for Isaac? It sounds foolish in the ear of Reason, that an angel should trouble himself as to how we wed. * * * And David also, in the thirty-fourth Psalm, saith: "The angel of the Lord encampeth round about them that fear him and delivereth them." *Castra metatur angelus Domini*, the angel of the Lord erects a bulwark, he saith. An angel can soon do that. In a trice he can make a rampart and a bulwark about a city, and it shall be an excellent wall.

In like manner, we read that the bad and the good angels contend and war with each other. We know not how this is, neither do we behold it; but the Holy Scripture declareth it.

How many devils were there, thinkest thou, last year, at the diet at Augsburg? Every bishop brought as many devils there as a dog hath fleas at St. John's time. But God sent thither also more numerous and more powerful angels, so that their evil purpose was defeated. And howbeit the devils stood in our way, and we were forced to separate ere peace was made, yet were our enemies unable to accomplish aught that they meditated and desired.

In the Revelation of St. John, cap. xii., it is written that the old dragon, the Devil, and Michael contended one against the other. The Devil had his angels and came up against Michael: and Michael had his angels also. That must have been a grand and mighty warfare in which the holy angels and the devils strove thus with each other. The Devil is strong in understanding, power and wisdom; but Michael with his angels was too strong and powerful for him, and thrust him out of heaven. That is a warfare which is carried on every day in the Christian world. For heaven is Christendom on the earth. There good and evil angels contend. The Devil hinders men from receiving the gospel, creates enthusiasts and factious spirits. Even among us, he maketh many to be sluggish and cold. That is the Devil's army in which he placeth himself and fighteth against us. But Michael with his angels is with us. He awakeneth other pious preachers, who continue in the pure doctrine and in the truth, that all may not perish. For one preacher can save twelve cities, if God will.

I myself do often feel the raging of the Devil within me. At times I believe; at times I believe not. At times I am merry; at times I am sad. Yet do I see that it happeneth not as the evil multitude wish, who would not give so much as a penny for preaching, baptism and sacrament. Now although the Devil is beyond measure wicked and hath no good thing in purpose, yet do all orders proceed and remain according to wont. * * * *

If we keep these instructions of which I have spoken, then shall we continue in the true understanding and faith, and the dear angels will continue in their office and honours. They will do what is commanded them by God, and we shall do whatsoever is commanded us. That thus we and they may know and praise God for our Creator and Lord, Amen.

DR. MARTIN LUTHER'S
SIMPLE METHOD HOW TO PRAY.

WRITTEN FOR MASTER PETER BALBIERER. (BARBER.)

DEAR MASTER PETER.

I give you as good as I have, and will show you how I myself manage with prayer. Our Lord God grant unto you and every one to manage better. Amen!

First, when I feel that I am become cold and indisposed to prayer, by reason of other business and thoughts, I take my psalter and run into my chamber, or, if day and season serve, into the church to the multitude, and begin to repeat to myself—just as children use—the ten commandments, the creed, and, according as I have time, some sayings of Christ or of Paul, or some psalms. Therefore it is well to let prayer be the first employment in the early morning, and the last in the evening. Avoid diligently those false and deceptive thoughts which say: Wait a little, I will pray an hour hence; I must first perform this or that. For, with such thoughts, a man quits prayer for business which lays hold of and entangles him, so that he comes not to pray, the whole day long.

Howbeit works may sometimes occur which are as good, or better than prayer, especially if necessity require them. There is a saying to this effect, which goes under the name of St. Jerome: "All the works of the faithful are prayer." And there is a proverb: "Whoso labours faithfully, he prays twice." The meaning of which saying must be, that a believer fears and honours God in his labour, and thinks of his commandment—to do wrong to no man,— not to steal nor take advantage, nor to betray. And, doubtless, such thoughts and such faith make his work a prayer and an offering of praise. On the other hand, it must be equally true that the works of the unbelieving are mere curses, and that he who labours unfaithfully curses twice. For the thoughts of his heart in his employment must lead him to despise God and to transgress his law, to do wrong to his neighbour, to steal and to betray. What are such thoughts but mere curses against God and man? * * * Of constant prayer, Christ indeed says, men ought always to pray. For men ought always to guard against sin and wrong, which no man can do except he fear God and set his commandment before his eyes. Nevertheless, we must take heed that we do not disuse ourselves to actual prayer, and interpret works to be necessary which are not necessary, and by that means become at last negligent and indolent, and cold and reluctant to pray. For the Devil is not indolent nor negligent around us. And our flesh is alive and fresh toward sin and averse from the spirit of prayer.

Now when the heart is warmed by this oral communion and has come to itself, then kneel down or stand with folded hands and eyes toward heaven, and say or think, in as few words as possible, &c. &c.*

Finally, observe that thou must ever make the "Amen" strong, and not doubt but that God assuredly heareth thee with all his grace, and saith "yea" to thy prayer. And think that thou kneelest or standest not alone, but the whole Christendom, or all pious Christians, with thee, and thou among them, in consenting unanimous supplication which God cannot despise. And quit not thy prayer until thou hast said or thought,—"Go to now, this prayer hath been heard with God; that know I surely and of a truth." That is the meaning of Amen.

Also, thou must know that I would not have thee to repeat all these words in thy prayer, for that would make it, at last, a babble and a vain empty gossip—a reading from the book and after the letter, such as the rosaries of the laity and the prayers of priests and monks have been. My purpose is to awaken the heart and instruct it what kind of thoughts to connect with the Lord's prayer. If the heart be rightly warmed and eager for prayer, it can express these thoughts with very different words, perhaps with fewer,

perhaps with more. For I, myself, do not bind myself to precisely these words and syllables, but say the words to-day after this fashion, to-morrow otherwise, according as I feel warm and free. I keep as nearly as I can to the same thoughts and meaning. But it will sometimes happen that, while engaged with some single article or petition, I walk into such rich thoughts that I leave the other six.* And when these rich and good thoughts come, one ought to give place to them and let other prayers go, and listen in silence, and on no account offer any hindrance; for then the Holy Ghost himself preaches, and one word of his preaching is better than a thousand of our prayers. And so I have often learned more in one prayer than I could have got from much reading and composing.

Wherefore, it is of the greatest importance that the heart be disengaged and disposed to prayer; as saith the Preacher, (cap. iv. 17,) "Prepare thy heart before prayer, that thou mayest not tempt God."† What else is it, but tempting God, when the mouth babbles while the heart is distracted with other things? Like that priest who prayed after this fashion: "*Deus in auditorium meum intende;* Fellow, hast thou unharnessed the horses? *Domine ad adjuvandum me festina;* Maid, go and milk the cows! *Gloria Patri et Filio et Spiritui Sancto;* Run, boy, as if the Devil were after thee!" &c. Of such prayers I have heard and experienced much in Popedom, in my day. * * * But now, God be praised, I see well that that is not prayer, in which one forgets what one has said. For a true prayer is conscious of all its words and thoughts, from the beginning to the end of the prayer.

Even so a good and diligent barber‡ must fix his thoughts, his purpose and his eyes, with great exactness upon the razor and the hair, and not forget where he is, in the stroke or the cut. But if he chooses to chat much at the same time, or hath his thoughts or his eyes elsewhere, he is like to cut one's mouth and nose, and throat into the bargain. Thus each thing—if it is to be done well—requires the entire man, with all his senses and members. As the saying goes: *Pluribus intentus, minor est ad singula sensus:* he who thinks of many things thinks of nothing, and does nothing aright. How much more must prayer—if it is to be a good prayer—possess the heart entirely and alone.

This is briefly said of the "Our Father," or of prayer, as I myself am wont to pray. For, to this day, I suck still at the *Paternoster*, like a child. I eat and drink thereof like a full-grown man; and can never have enough. It is to me, even more than the psalter, (which notwithstanding, I dearly love,) the best of all prayers. Assuredly, it will be found that the

---

* Here follows, in the original, after a brief invocation, a paraphrase of the Lord's Prayer.

* Luther divides the Lord's Prayer into seven petitions.
† The text here quoted is probably the first verse of the fifth chapter of Eccl.; but it differs widely from the common English version.
‡ Luther was probably writing to a barber by profession.

right Master hath ordained and taught it. And it is a pity upon pities that such a prayer of such a Master, should be babbled and rattled over by all the world, so entirely without devotion. Many pray, it may be, some thousand *Paternosters* a year; and if they should pray a thousand years, after that fashion, they would not have tasted or prayed one letter or tittle thereof. In fine, the *Paternoster* (as well as the name and word of God) is the greatest martyr upon earth, for every one tortures and abuses it; few comfort and make it glad by a true use of it.

LUTHER'S PRAYER
AT THE DIET OF WORMS.

ALMIGHTY, eternal God! What a strange thing is this world! How doth it open wide the mouths of the people! How small and poor is the confidence of men toward God! How is the flesh so tender and weak, and the Devil so mighty and so busy through his apostles and the wise of this world! How soon do they withdraw the hand, and whirl away and run the common path and the broad way to hell, where the godless belong. They look only upon that which is splendid and powerful, great and mighty, and which hath consideration. If I turn my eyes thither also, it is all over with me; the bell is cast and the judgment is pronounced. Ah God! Ah God! O, Thou my God! Thou my God, stand Thou by me against the reason and wisdom of all the world. Do Thou so! Thou must do it, Thou alone. Behold, it is not my cause but thine. For my own person I have nothing to do here with these great lords of the world. Gladly would I too have good quiet days and be unperplexed. But Thine is the cause, Lord; it is just and eternal. Stand Thou by me, Thou true, eternal God! I confide in no man. It is to no purpose and in vain. Everything halteth that is fleshly, or that savoureth of flesh. O God! O God! Hearest Thou not, my God? Art Thou dead? No! Thou canst not die. Thou only hidest Thyself. Hast Thou chosen me for this end? I ask Thee. But I know for a surety that Thou hast chosen me. Ha! then may God direct it. For never did I think, in all my life, to be opposed to such great lords; neither have I intended it. Ha! God, then stand by me in the name of Jesus Christ, who shall be my shelter and my shield, yea! my firm tower, through the might and strengthening of thy Holy Spirit. Lord! where stayest Thou? Thou my God! where art Thou? Come, come! I am ready, even to lay down my life for this cause, patient as a little lamb. For just is the cause and Thine. So will I not separate myself from Thee forever. Be it determined in Thy name. The world shall not be able to force me against my conscience, though it were full of devils. And though my body, originally the work and creature of Thy hands, go to destruction in this cause—yea, though it be shattered in pieces—Thy word and Thy Spirit, they are good to me still! It concerneth only the body. The soul is Thine and belongeth to Thee, and shall also remain with Thee, forever. Amen. God help me! Amen.

SELECTIONS FROM LUTHER'S LETTERS.

FROM A COLLECTION IN FIVE VOLS. 8vo., PUBLISHED BY DR. W. M. L. DE WETTE, PROFESSOR OF THEOLOGY AT BASLE. BERLIN. 1826.

Extract from a Letter to the Elector Frederic and Duke John of Saxony, containing an admonition to those princes to suppress, according to the authority entrusted to them by God, the rebellious spirit which at that time possessed the peasantry in various parts of Germany, and which manifested itself in the destruction of churches and in other riotous acts.

To the most Serene, the High-born Princes and Lords, Duke Frederic, Elector of the Roman Empire, and John, Duke of Saxony, Landgrave of Thüringen and Margrave of Meissen —my most gracious Masters:

Grace and peace in Christ Jesus our Saviour. —This fortune hath ever the Holy Word of God, that wherever it appeareth, Satan opposeth it with all his power; first, with the fist and insolent force; and where that will not avail, he assaileth it with false tongues, with erring spirits and teachers. Where he cannot quell it with his might, he would suppress it by means of cunning and lies. Thus did he in the beginning, when the gospel first came into the world. He assaulted it mightily with the Jews and the Gentiles, shed much blood, and made Christendom full of martyrs. When that availed not, he brought on false prophets and erring spirits, and made the world full of heretics and sects. * * * So must it be now, that it may be seen that it is the genuine Word of God, because it happeneth unto it as it hath happened in all time. Pope and emperor, kings and princes assail it with the fist, and would fain quell it with force. They damn it, blaspheme it, and persecute it unheard and unknown, like men devoid of sense. But judgment hath been pronounced, and their defiance condemned long ago. (Ps. 2.) "Why do the heathen rage and the people imagine a vain thing? The kings of the earth rise up and the rulers take counsel together against the Lord and against his Anointed. But he that sitteth in the heavens shall mock at them; the Lord shall have them in derision. Then shall he speak unto them in his wrath and vex them in his sore displeasure." Thus, of a certainty, shall it happen to our raging princes. And they will have it so, for they will neither see nor hear. God hath blinded and hardened them, that they shall run upon destruction and be shattered in pieces. They have been sufficiently warned.

All this Satan seeth well, and perceiveth that such raging will come to nought. Yea! he noteth and feeleth that the more it is oppressed (as is the wont of God's word) the more doth it spread and increase. Therefore he will now attack it with false spirits and sects. And we must consider this, and not suffer ourselves to be deceived by it. For it must be so, as Paul saith to the Corinthians: " For there must be also heresies among you, that they which are approved may be made manifest among you." So then, Satan being cast out, after that he hath wandered about one year or three, through dry places, seeking rest and finding none, he hath settled down in your Electoral and Princely Graces' dominions, and hath made him a nest at *Alstädt*, and thinks to fight against us under cover of our own peace and shelter and protection. For Duke George's kingdom, howbeit it is near, is far too kind and gentle toward this undaunted and unconquerable spirit, (for so it boasteth itself,) to prevent the manifestation of its bold daring and defiance. It shrieks and wails horribly, and complains of its sufferings, whereas no one hath yet touched it, neither with the fist, nor with the mouth, nor with the pen. They dream to themselves some great cross which they suffer. So wantonly and without all reason must the Devil lie. O! he cannot by any possibility hide himself.

Now it is a special joy to me that our own proceed not after this fashion. And they themselves boast that they are not of our party, and that they have learned nothing and received nothing from us. No! they come from heaven, and hear God himself speaking with them as with the angels; and it is a poor thing that Faith and Love and the cross of Christ are preached at Wittenberg. God's voice, say they, thou must hear thyself, and must suffer and feel God's work within, that thou mayest know how heavy thy pound is. Scripture is naught—" *Bah! Bible, bubble, babble!*" &c. &c. If we should speak such words of them, their cross and suffering I ween would be dearer than the cross of Christ, and they would esteem it more highly. So willing is that miserable spirit to bear the credit of cross and suffering, and yet they cannot bear that one should entertain the least doubt or question that their voice is from heaven and their work of God; but they will have it straightway believed by force, without consideration. So that I have never read or heard of a more high-minded or prouder "*Holy Spirit*," (if such it be.) But here is neither time nor room to judge their doctrine. I have examined and judged it twice, I think, ere this, and, if need be, can judge it again, and will, by the grace of God.

I have written this letter to your Princely Graces chiefly for this cause, that I have heard and have also gathered from their writing, how this selfsame spirit will not rest its cause upon the Word alone, but is minded to carry it on with the fist, and would fain rise with force against the magistracy, and straightway set on foot a veritable rebellion. Here Satan suffereth the rogue to peep forth. It is too palpable! * * * Therefore, your Princely Graces, here is no time to sleep or loiter, for God demands and will have an answer touching the negligent use of the sword which he hath committed to you in earnest. Neither is it excusable, before the people and the world, that your Princely Graces should tolerate rebellious and insolent fists.

* * * First, it must needs be a bad spirit which cannot manifest its fruit in any other way than by destroying churches and cloisters, and burning saints, which the most abandoned villains in the world can do as well, especially when they are safe and unresisted. I would think more of this Alstädt Spirit if it would go up against Dresden, or Berlin, or Ingolstadt, and there storm and break down cloisters and burn saints.

Secondly, that they boast themselves of the Spirit availeth nothing, for we have the word of St. John for it, to prove first the Spirits whether they be of God. Now is this Spirit not yet proved, but dashes on with impetuous vehemence, and rages wantonly, according to its own pleasure. If it were a good Spirit, it would first suffer itself to be proved and judged in humility, as the Spirit of Christ doth. * * * What manner of Spirit is that which fears in the presence of two or three and cannot bide a dangerous assembly? I will tell thee. He smelleth the roast.* He hath had his nose hit once or twice by me in my cloister at Wittenberg. Hence he fears the soup, and will not stand, save where his own people are, who say yea, to his precious words. If I (who have no Spirit at all and have no voice from heaven) had suffered such a word to be heard of me by my papists, how would they have cried victory, and have stopped my mouth!

I cannot boast myself and bid defiance with such lofty words. I am a poor miserable man. I did not open my cause with excellency of speech, but, as Paul confesses of himself, with weakness and fear, and much trembling. And *he* might, notwithstanding, have boasted of a voice from heaven, had he chosen. How humbly I attacked the Pope, how I besought and entreated, let my first writings prove. Nevertheless, with this poor spirit of mine, I have done that which this world-eating spirit of theirs hath not yet attempted, but, on the contrary, hath thus far shunned and fled, after a very knightly and manly fashion; and hath even most nobly boasted of such evasion, as of a knightly and sublime act of the Spirit. For I stood up to dispute at Leipsic before the most dangerous of all assemblies. I appeared at Augsburgh before my greatest enemy, without escort. I stood up at Worms before the emperor and the whole empire, albeit I knew beforehand that my escort were betrayed, and that wild, strange malice and treachery were levelled against me.

Weak and poor as I then was, yet such was

---

* Smells a rat.

the state of my heart,—had I known that as many devils were aiming at me as there were tiles on the roofs at Worms, I would none the less have ridden in; and yet I had never heard aught, as yet, of the voice from heaven and of God's pounds and works, and of the Alstädt Spirit. Item: I have been made to answer for myself, in corners,—to one, to two, and to three, to whomsoever, and where and howsoever they listed to question me. My timid and poor spirit hath been forced to stand forth, free as a flower of the field, and could not appoint either time, or person, or place, or mode, or measure, but must be ready and willing to give an answer to every man, as St. Peter teacheth.

And this Spirit, which is as high above us as the sun is above the earth, which scarce considers us as worms, appoints for himself only unperilous, friendly, and safe judges and hearers, and will not stand and answer to two or to three in sundry places. He feels somewhat that he does not love to feel, and thinks to scare us with swelling words. Well! we can do nothing but what Christ gives us. If *He* shall leave us, then shall a rustling leaf perchance affright us; but if He will keep us, that spirit shall yet be made sensible of its lofty boasting.*

But I would fain know whether,—seeing the Spirit is not without fruit, and that theirs is so much loftier than ours,—whether it bears nobler fruit than ours? Truly, it ought to bear other and better fruit than ours, seeing it is better and nobler. So we teach and profess, that the Spirit which we preach bears the fruits spoken of by Paul to the Galatians—"love, joy, peace, longsuffering, gentleness, goodness, faith, meekness, temperance." In fine, the fruit of our Spirit is the fulfilling of the ten commandments of God. Now then, the Alstädt Spirit, that will not leave ours in peace, must, of a surety, yield something higher than love and faith, long-suffering and peace; notwithstanding St. Paul reckons love to be the highest fruit. It must do much better than God hath commanded. I would fain know what that is, since we are assured that the Spirit imparted by Christ is given for this end only, that we fulfil the commandment of God. * *

I perceive as yet no particular fruit of the Alstädt Spirit, except that it is minded to strike with the fist, and to destroy wood and stone. Love, peace, long-suffering, goodness, gentleness,—they have thus far been very sparing in their exhibition of. Doubtless, they would not have the fruits of the Spirit become too common. But I can show, by the grace of God, much fruit of the Spirit among our people. And, if it comes to boasting, I might set up my single person—the meanest and most sinful of all—against all the fruits of the whole Alstädt Spirit, much as they blame my life. But, to accuse the doctrine of any man because of the infirmities of his life —that is not the Holy Spirit. For the Holy Spirit reproveth false doctrine, and beareth them that are weak in faith and in life, as Paul teacheth, Rom. xiv. and in all places. Neither am I troubled that the Alstädt Spirit is so unfruitful, but because it is a lying Spirit, and setteth itself up to judge the doctrine of others.

* * * Be this then the conclusion of the whole matter, my gracious Masters. Your Graces shall not hinder the function of the Word. Let them preach away as much as they please, and against whom they please, for, as I have said, there must be sects, and the Word of God must take the field and fight. * * * If their Spirit be the true one, it will not be afraid of us, but maintain its ground. If our Spirit be the true one, it will not be afraid of them, nor of any man. Let the Spirits tilt and charge against each other. If, meanwhile, some are led astray, so be it! It is according to the course of war. Where there is fighting and strife, some must fall and some must be wounded. But he that striveth honourably shall receive a crown.

But if they attempt to do more than to fight with the word; if they go about to destroy and to smite with the fist;—then your Graces shall take hold, whether it be we or whether it be they, and straightway forbid them the land, and say to them: "We will willingly bear with you, and see you contend with the Word for the maintenance of the true doctrine; but keep the fist still, for that is our business; or else take yourselves out of the land." For we who bear the Word of God must not fight with our fists. * * * Our work is to preach and to suffer, not to defend ourselves and to strike. Christ and his apostles destroyed no churches and broke in pieces no images, but won hearts with God's word, and then churches and images fell of themselves. So should we do likewise. * *

What need we care for wood and stone, if we have men's hearts? See how I do. I have never laid hands on a single stone. I have destroyed and burned nothing in the cloisters. And yet, through my word, the cloisters are now empty in many places, — even under those Princes who are opposed to the gospel. Had I attacked them with storm, like these prophets, the hearts of men in all the world would have remained captive, and I should only have destroyed here and there a little wood and stone. Who would have been the better for that? Honour and fame may be sought that way, but, assuredly, the good of souls is not sought by such means. There be some who think that I, without carnal weapons, have done the Pope more injury than a mighty king could have done. But these prophets, willing to do something special and better, and not being able, leave the saving of souls and take to assailing wood and stone. That is the new and wonderful work of this high Spirit.

If they argue that the Jews were commanded in the law of Moses to destroy all idols, and to abolish the altars of the false gods, the answer is, they themselves know that God, from the beginning, has wrought with one word and

---

* i. e. be made sensible of the vanity of it.

faith, but with diverse kinds of saints and works. * * * * * *

Nay, if it were right that we Christians should storm and break down churches like the Jews, it would follow further that we ought to put to death all who are not Christians, as well as destroy images,—as the Jews were commanded to slay the Canaanites and the Amorites. Then the Alstädt Spirit would have nothing more to do but to shed blood; and all who did not hear their "voice from heaven" must be slain by them, that there might remain no occasion of offence among the people of God. Which offence is much greater from living unchristian men, than from images of wood and stone. * *

The removing of offences must be accomplished by the Word of God. For though all outward offence were destroyed and done away, it would avail nothing, unless the hearts of men were brought from unbelief to the true faith. For an unbelieving heart will always find new cause of offence; as it came to pass among the Jews, who erected ten idols where they destroyed one. Wherefore, we must employ the true method, according to the New Testament, of banishing the Devil and offences; that is, the Word of God. With that we must turn away the hearts of men from evil; and then, peradventure, the Devil with all his splendour and his power shall fall of himself.

Here will I rest the matter for the present, humbly beseeching your Princely Graces earnestly to discountenance such storming and swarming, that these matters may be managed by the word of God alone, as befitteth Christians; and that all occasion of tumult, for which Master *Omnes** is ever more than too much inclined, may be averted. For they be no Christians who, not content with the Word of God, are fain to lay hold with their fists also, and are not rather ready to suffer all things,—yea, though they boast themselves filled with ten Holy Spirits and filled again.

May God's mercy strengthen and keep your Princely Graces evermore! Amen! Given the 21st August, Anno 1524.

Your Princely Graces'
Obedient MART. LUTHER, Doctor.

TO THE ELECTOR JOHN.

A LETTER OF ACKNOWLEDGMENT IN RETURN FOR A PRESENT OF SOME ARTICLES OF CLOTHING.

GRACE and peace in Christ! Most Serene, High-born Prince, and Gracious Lord! I have long delayed to thank your Electoral Princely Grace for the clothes and garment sent and presented to me. But I will humbly entreat your Electoral Princely Grace not to believe them that speak of me as one that hath need. Alas!

* The mob.

I possess more, especially from your Electoral Princely Grace, than my conscience will bear. It befitteth me not, as a preacher, to have superfluity, neither do I desire it.

Hence I receive your Electoral Princely Grace's all too generous and gracious favour in such wise, that I straightway fear. For by no means would I willingly, here in this life, be found with those to whom Christ saith: "Wo unto you that are rich, for ye have had your reward." Moreover, to speak after the manner of this world, I would not be burthensome to your Electoral Princely Grace, since I know that your Electoral Princely Grace hath so much of giving to do that it may not have more than enough for its need. For too much bursts the bag.

Wherefore, although the liver-coloured cloth had been too much, yet, that I may be grateful to your Electoral Princely Grace, I will also wear the black coat in honour of your Electoral Princely Grace, howbeit it is far too costly for me, and were it not your Electoral Princely Grace's gift, I could nevermore wear such a coat.

For this cause, I entreat that your Electoral Princely Grace will wait until I complain and beg, myself, to the end that your Electoral Princely Grace's anticipation of my wants may not make me shy of begging for others who are much more worthy of such grace. For without this, your Electoral Princely Grace does too much for me. Which Christ shall graciously and richly recompense. That he may do so, I pray from my heart. Amen.

Your Electoral Princely Grace's
Obedient MARTINUS LUTHER.
The 17th Aug. 1529.

EXTRACT

FROM A LETTER TO CASPAR GUTTEL, PREACHER AT EISLEBEN. WRITTEN AGAINST THE ANTINOMIANS. JANUARY, 1539.

* * * I MARVEL much how the rejection of the Law and the Ten Commandments can be imputed to me, seeing there are so many and such various expositions of the Ten Commandments by me, which are daily preached and made the subject of exercises in our churches; to say nothing of the Confession and the Apology and our other books. Moreover they are sung in two different ways, and painted and printed, and done in woodcuts, and repeated by the children, morning, noon, and evening, so that I know of no way in which they are not practised, save (alas!) that we do not paint and practise them in our conduct and life as we ought to do. And I myself, old and instructed as I am, repeat them daily, word for word, like a child. So, if any one had received a different doctrine from my writings and yet saw how diligently I handled the Ten Commandments, he ought to have accosted me in this wise: "Dear

Doctor Luther, how is it that thou insistest so strongly on the ten commandments, seeing it is thy doctrine that they ought to be rejected?" So ought they to have done, and not to have mined in secret behind me, to wait for my death, to make of me what they listed, after that. * * * * * * *

I have taught indeed, and still teach, that sinners should be moved to repentance by preaching, or by the contemplation of the sufferings of Christ, that they may see how great is the wrath of God against sin, for which no other remedy could be found than that the Son of God should die for it. Which doctrine is not mine but St. Bernard's. What do I say? St. Bernard's? It is the doctrine of all Christendom. It is the preaching of all the prophets and the apostles. But how doth it follow therefrom, that the Law should be done away? I find no such consequence in my dialectic, and I would like to see and hear the master who could demonstrate the same. * * * For the devil knoweth that Christ may soon and easily be withdrawn, but the Law is written in the core of the heart and cannot by any possibility be done away. * * * But he goeth about to make people secure, and teacheth them to regard neither the Law nor sin, that when, hereafter, they are suddenly overtaken by death or an evil conscience, who before had been accustomed only to sweet security, they may sink, without help, into hell, because they have learned nothing but sweet security in Christ. * * * It is only sorrowful and suffering hearts that feel their sin, and they are to be comforted, for the dear Jesus can never be made sweet enough to such. * * * But these spirits are not such Christians, because they are so secure and of good courage. Neither are their hearers such, for they also are secure and well to do. A fine and beautiful maiden singeth in a certain place—an excellent singer—" He hath fed the hungry with good things, and the rich he hath sent empty away, He hath put down the mighty from their seats and exalted them of low degree. And his mercy is on them that fear him." (Luke i. 50, 52, 53,) If this *magnificat* be correct, God must be an enemy of spirits that are secure and that fear him not. And such spirits must they be, who put away Law and sin. * * * For this I will and may boast with truth, that no papist of this time is, with such conscience and earnest, a papist as I have been. For what is now a papist is not so, from the fear of God, as I, poor wight, was forced to be. But they seek other things, as any one may see, and they themselves know it. I have had to experience that saying of St. Peter: "*Crescite in cognitione Domini.*" I see no Doctor, no Council, no Fathers—though I should even distil their books, as it were, and make a *quinta essentia* out of them—who have accomplished the "*crescite*" at once, at the beginning, in such sort, as to make the *crescite* a *perfectum esse*. By token, St. Peter himself was forced to learn his own *crescite* from St. Paul, Gal. ii. 11, and St. Paul from Christ himself, who must say to him: "Sufficit tibi mea gratia," &c. 2 Cor. xii. 9.

Dear God! can they not bear that the holy Church should confess herself a sinner and believe in forgiveness of sins, and pray for the same, in the Lord's prayer?

Ah! I ought, in reason, to have peace with mine own. To have to do with the papists were enough. One might well nigh come to say with Job and with Jeremiah: "Would that I had never been born!" So likewise might I almost say: Would that I had never come with my books! I care nothing for them. I could bear that they had already perished, all of them, and that the writings of these high spirits were offered for sale in all the bookstalls as they desire,—that they might have their fill of fair fame. Then again, I must not esteem myself better than our dear Goodman of the house,—Jesus Christ,—who, also, here and there complaineth: "In vain have I laboured, and my trouble is lost."* But the Devil is lord of this world. And I could never believe, myself, that the Devil should be lord and god of this world, until now that I have pretty much experienced that this also is an article of faith: *Princeps mundi, deus hujus sæculi*. But God be praised! it will remain unbelieved, peradventure, by the children of men; and I, myself, believe it but feebly. For every man is well pleased with his own way, and all hope that the Devil is beyond the sea, and God in our pockets.

But, for the sake of the pious who wish to be saved, we must live, preach, write, do all and suffer all. Otherwise, when we behold so many devils and false brethren, it were better to preach nothing, to write nothing, to do nothing, but only to die quickly and be buried. They pervert and blaspheme all things, and make of them nothing but mischief and a cause of offence, even as the Devil rideth and guideth them. There will and must be fighting and suffering. We cannot have it better than the dear prophets and apostles, to whom it happened also after the same fashion. * * *

It was a special presumption and arrogance in them that they also must needs bring forth something new and peculiar, that people might say, "I opine truly, this is a man! He is another Paul! Must they of Wittenberg alone know all things? I have a head too!" Yea! a head indeed, that seeketh its own honour and befooleth itself with its own wisdom! * *

From all which we see, and might, if we would, understand the history of the churches from the beginning. It hath happened so in all time. Wherever God's word hath arisen and his flock been gathered together, the Devil hath become aware of the light, and hath blown against it, out of every corner;—puffed and

---

* These words are given as a quotation from Isaiah, xlix. 4.

stormed with great and strong winds to put out the divine light. And if one or two winds were checked and fended off, he hath evermore blown through some new hole, and stormed against the light. And there has been no end nor cessation, neither will be until the last day.

I hold that I alone (not to speak of the elders) have suffered more than twenty storm-winds and factions which the Devil hath blown. First, there was Popedom. Yea! I think all the world should know with how many storm-winds, Bulls and books the Devil hath raged against me from that quarter; how miserably they tore, devoured and destroyed me; and how I only breathed upon them a little now and then, with no effect, save that they became the more wrathful and mad to blow and to spit, without ceasing, to this day. And when I had now well nigh ceased to fear this manner of the Devil's spitting, he bursts me another hole by means of Münzer and that uproar, wherewith he had near blown out my light. And when Christ had almost stopped that hole, he tears me sundry panes out of my window with Karlstadt, and breezes and fumes, so that I thought he would carry away the light, wax and wick together. But here too, God helped his poor torch and preserved it, that it went not out. Then came the Sacramentists and the Baptists, pushed open door and window, and thought to quench the light. Perilous they made it, but their will they accomplished not.

And though I were to live yet a hundred years, and could lay all future storms and factions, as, by the grace of God, I have laid past and present ones, I see well that no rest would be secured by such means to our posterity, seeing the Devil lives and reigns. Wherefore I also pray for an hour of grace,* and desire no more of this stuff. Ye, our posterity! do ye continue to pray and diligently to follow after the word of God! Preserve God's poor taper! Be warned and armed! as those who must expect every hour that the Devil will break you a pane or a window, or tear open door or roof, to put out the light. For he will not die before the last day. I and thou must die, and when we are dead he shall remain the same that he hath ever been, and cannot cease from storming.

I see yonder, from afar, how he puffeth out his cheeks, till he becometh red in the face, and intendeth to blow and to storm. But as our Lord Christ, in the beginning, (even in his own person,) smote those puffed cheeks with his fist, and caused them * * * so will he do now and ever forth. For he cannot lie who saith, "I am with you always unto the end of the world:" * * * Jesus Christ, "*heri et hodie et in sæcula,*"—who was, and is, and shall be. Yea! so the man is called, and so no other man is called, and so no other shall be called.

For thou and I were nothing a thousand years ago; nevertheless, the Church was preserved without us. It must have been his doing whose name is "*qui erat*" and "*heri.*" So, now, too, we exist not by our own life, and the Church is not preserved by our means, —— and we and it must go to destruction together, as we daily experience, were there not another man who evidently sustains both the Church and us —— whose name is "*qui est*" and "*hodie.*" Even so shall we contribute nothing to the preservation of the Church when we are dead; but it will be his doing whose name is "*qui venturus est*" and "*in sæcula.*" And what we now say of ourselves, as touching these things, that have our forefathers also been constrained to say, as the Psalms and the Scripture witness; and our posterity shall also experience the same, and they shall sing with us and the whole Church, Ps. 124, "Had it not been the Lord who was on our side, now may Isràel say." * * * For this time enough of such complaining! Our dear Lord Christ be and remain our dear Lord Christ, praised in eternity! Amen.

TO HIS WIFE.

To my Gracious Lady,* Catherine Luther, of Bora and Zulsdorf, near Wittenberg, — my Sweetheart.

Grace and peace, my dear maid and wife! Your Grace shall know that we are here, God be praised!—fresh and sound; eat like Bohemians,—yet not to excess—guzzle like Germans, —yet not much;—but are joyful. For our gracious Lord of Magdeburg, Bishop Amsdorf, is our messmate. We know nothing new but that Doct. Caspar Mecum and Menius have journeyed from Hagenau to Strasburg, in the service and in honour of Hans von Jehnen. M. Philipps† is nice again, God be praised! Tell my dear Doct. Schiefer, that his King Ferdinand will have a cry, as if he would ask the Turk to be godfather, over the Evangelical Princes. Hope it is not true, it would be too bad. Write me whether you got all that I sent you, as lately, 90 Fl. by Wolf Paerman, &c. Herewith I commend you to God. Amen. And let the children pray. There is here such a heat and drought that it is unspeakable and insupportable, day and night. Come dear Last Day! Amen. Friday after Margarethæ, 1540. The Bishop of Magdeburg sends thee friendly greeting.

TO HIS WIFE.

To the rich Lady at Zulsdorf, Lady *Katherin Lutherin*,—bodily resident at Wittenberg, and mentally wandering at Zulsdorf, — my beloved,—for her own hands. In her absence to be broken and read by Doct. Pomeran, Preacher.

---

* i. e. for the final hour.

* *Jungfer,* literally, virgin. Luther's letters to his wife are generally marked by a dash of irony, particularly in the superscriptions. † Melanchthon.

—————* grant that we may find a good drink of beer with you! For, God willing, to-morrow, as Tuesday, we will set out for Wittenberg. It is all dung with the Diet at Hagenau,—pains and labour lost, and expenses in vain. Howbeit, if we have done nothing else we have brought M. Philipps out of hell, and will fetch him home again, from the grave, with much joy, if God will, and by his grace, Amen. The Devil out here is, himself, possessed with nine bad devils; he is burning and doing mischief, after a frightful fashion. More than a thousand acres of wood in the Thuringian forest belonging to my most Gracious Master have been burned and are yet burning. Moreover, there is tidings to-day that the forest of Werda is also on fire, and many others beside. No attempts to quench the flames are of any avail. That will make wood dear. Pray and cause prayers to be said against the wicked Satan, who seeketh, vehemently seeketh to ruin us not only in body and soul but also in name and estate. May Christ our Lord come from heaven and kindle a bit of a fire too, for the Devil and his angels, that he shall not be able to quench! Amen! I am not certain whether this letter will find you at Wittenberg or at Zulsdorf, else I would have written more. Herewith I commend thee to God, Amen! Greet our children, our boarders and all. Monday after Jacobi 1540.

TO HIS WIFE.

To the deeply learned Lady *Katharin Lutherin*,—my Gracious Housewife at Wittenberg.

Grace and Peace! Dear Kate, we sit here and let ourselves be martyred, and would fain be off; but methinks that cannot be, under a week. Thou mayest tell M. Philipps to correct his postil. He never understood why our Lord, in the gospel, calls riches thorns. Here is the school to learn that. But I shudder to think that thorns, in the Scripture, are always threatened with fire. Wherefore I have the greater patience, if haply, by the help of God, I may be able to bring some good to pass. Thy sons are still at Mansfeld. For the rest, we have enough to eat and to drink, and should have good days, were it not for this vexatious affair. I think the Devil is mocking us. May God mock him again! Pray for us! The messenger is in great haste. St. Dorothy's day, 1546.

TO HIS WIFE.

To my dear Housewife, *Katharin Lutherin*, Doctoress, Self-martyress, my Gracious Lady,—for her hands and feet.

Grace and Peace in the Lord! Dear Kate,

* A line is wanting here.

do thou read John and the little catechism, concerning which thou once saidst, that all contained in that book is by me. For thou must needs care, before thy God, just as if he were not Almighty, and could not create ten Doctor Martins if the single old one were to drown in the Saale, or the Oven-hole, or Wolf's Vogelheerd. Leave me in peace with thy anxiety. I have a better guardian than thou and all the angels are. He lies in the crib, and hangs upon the Virgin's teats, but sitteth, nevertheless, at the right hand of God, the Almighty Father. Therefore be in peace. Amen!

I think that hell and the whole world must now be emptied of all their devils, who,—peradventure all on my account,—have come together, here in Eisleben. So firm and hard the matter stands. * * * Pray! pray! pray and help us that we may do well! For I was minded to grease the wagon to-day, *in ira mea*, but pity for my fatherland withheld me. I too am become a jurist. But it will not go. It were better they let me remain a theologian. * * * They demean themselves as they were God; which they were best cease from betimes, ere their God-head becomes a devil-head, as it happened unto Lucifer, who could not remain in heaven by reason of his arrogance. Well, God's will be done! * * * The domestic wine. here is good, and the Naumburg beer is very good, except that I think it makes my breast full of phlegm with its pitch. The Devil has spoiled us the beer, in all the world, with his pitch, and, with you, the wine, with sulphur. * * * And know that all the letters which thou hast written have arrived here; and to-day came that which thou wrotest *next* Friday, together with the letter of *M. Philipps*,—that thou mayest not be impatient. The Sunday after Dorothy's day, 1546.

Thy dear Lord,
M. LUTHER.

TO HIS WIFE.

To my friendly, dear Kate Luther, at Wittenberg. For her own hands, &c.

Grace and Peace in the Lord! Dear Kate, we arrived to-day, at 8 o'clock, in Halle; but could not proceed to Eisleben, for there met us a great Anabaptist with billows of water and cakes of ice, covering the country, and threatening us with baptism. For the same cause we could not return again, on account of the Mulda; but were forced to lie still at Halle, between the waters. Not that we thirsted to drink of them. We took, instead, good Torgau beer and good Rhenish wine, and comforted and refreshed ourselves with the same, while we waited till the Saale should have spent her wrath. For, since the people and the coachmen and we ourselves, were fearful, we did not wish to venture into the water and tempt God. For the Devil is our enemy and dwelleth in the water, and prevention is better than complaining, and there is no need to give the Pope and his officers occasion for a foolish joy. * * * For the present, nothing more, except to bid thee pray for us and be good. I think if thou hadst been with us, thou wouldst also have counselled us to do as we have done. Then, for once, we had followed thy counsel. Herewith be commended to God. Amen. Halle, on the day of Paul's conversion, anno 1546.

MARTINUS LUTHER, Doct.

TO HIS FATHER.

A LETTER OF CONSOLATION IN SICKNESS.

To my dear Father, Hans Luther, citizen at Mansfeld in the valley.—Grace and Peace in Jesus Christ our Lord and Saviour! Amen.

Dear Father, Jacob, my brother, has written me that you are dangerously sick. Seeing then that the air is now bad, and that otherwise there is danger from all quarters,—also in regard of the times, I am moved with anxiety on your account. For although God has hitherto given and preserved to you a firm and hardy body, yet doth your age, at this time, cause me anxious thoughts. Albeit, without that, we are none of us secure of our life a single hour, neither ought we to be. Wherefore, I had been beyond measure delighted to come to you bodily, but my good friends have dissuaded me therefrom, and I myself must think that I ought not to tempt God by venturing upon danger, for you know with what favour lords and peasants regard me.

But great joy would it be to me,—so it were possible—that you, together with the mother, would suffer yourselves to be brought hither to us; which my Kate also with tears desireth, and we all. I hope it; we would wait upon you after the best manner. To this end have I despatched Cyriac to you, to see if your weakness might allow of it. For whether, according to the will of God, you are destined for longer life here, or for life hereafter, I would, from my heart, as is fitting, be bodily near you, and, according to the fourth* commandment, with childlike faith and service, prove myself grateful toward God and you.

Meanwhile, I pray the Father,—who hath created and given you for a father to me,—from my heart's ground, that he would strengthen you according to his groundless love, and enlighten and preserve you by his Spirit, that you may know, with joy and thanksgiving, the blessed doctrine of his Son, our Lord Jesus Christ, to which you have now, by his grace, been called, and have come out of the horrible former darkness and errors. And I hope that

---

* According to the Lutheran Catechism, which adopts the Roman Catholic arrangement of the Decalogue.

his Grace which hath given you this knowledge, and therewith hath begun his work in you, will preserve and continue it to the end, into yonder life and the joyful future of our Lord Jesus Christ. Amen!

For he hath already sealed this doctrine and faith in you, and confirmed it with tokens, to wit: that you have suffered, for my name's sake, much reviling, contumely, scorn, mockery, contempt, hatred, enmity, and danger, together with us all. But these are the true signs wherein we must be like unto our Lord Christ, as St. Paul saith, Rom. viii. 17, that we may be glorified together with him.

Wherefore let your heart be refreshed and comforted now in your weakness, for we have, in yonder life with God, a sure and faithful helper, Jesus Christ, who, for us, hath destroyed death together with sin, and now sitteth there for us, and, together with all the angels, looketh down upon us and tendeth us, when we go out, that we need not care, nor fear to sink, nor fall into ruin. For he hath said it and promised, he will and cannot lie nor deceive us. Thereof there can be no doubt. Ask! saith he, and ye shall receive, seek and ye shall find! Knock and it shall be opened unto you! And the whole psalter is full of such comfortable assurances, especially the 91st psalm, which is particularly good to be read by all that are sick. * * * But, if it be his will that you be still withheld from that better life, and continue to suffer with us in this troubled and unblest vale of sorrows, and to see and hear our misery, and, together with all Christians, help to bear and overcome it, he will also give you grace to accept all this with willing obedience. For this cursed life is nothing else but a right vale of sorrows. The longer one remaineth in it, the more sin, wickedness, plague and misery one sees and experiences, and there is no cessation nor diminution of the same until we are beaten upon with the spade. Then, at last, it must cease and suffer us to sleep contentedly, in the peace of Christ, until he shall come and wake us again with gladness. Amen!

Herewith I commend you to Him who loveth you better than you love yourself, and hath proved his love in that he hath taken your sins upon himself, and paid with his blood, and hath given you to know the same by his gospel and to believe it by his Spirit. * * * The same, our dear Lord and Saviour be with you and by you, until—God grant it may come to pass here or yonder—we see each other again in joy. For our faith is sure, and we doubt not that we shall shortly see each other again with Christ; seeing the departure from this life to God is much less than if I should come hither from you at Mansfeld, or you should go hence from me at Wittenberg. That is true, of a certainty. It is but an hour of sleep, and then all shall be changed.

Howbeit, I hope that your pastor and preacher will show you richly a true service in these things, so that you scarce shall need my gossip, —yet could I not omit to excuse my bodily absence, which, God knows, grieveth me from the heart.

My Kate, Hänschen, Lenichen, Aunt Lehne and the whole house greet you and pray for you faithfully. Greet my dear mother and all our friends! God's Grace and Power be and remain with you forever! Amen.

Your dear son,
MARTINUS LUTHER.

Wittenberg, 15th February, anno 1530.

TO HIS SON JOHN.

GRACE and peace in Christ, my dear little son. I see with pleasure that thou learnest well and prayest diligently. Do so, my son, and continue. When I come home I will bring thee a pretty fairing.

I know a pretty, merry garden wherein there are many children. They have little golden coats, and they gather beautiful apples under the trees, and pears, cherries, plums and wheatplums;—they sing and jump and are merry. They have beautiful little horses, too, with gold bits and silver saddles. And I asked the man to whom the garden belongs, whose children they were? And he said, They are the children that love to pray and to learn, and are good. Then I said, Dear man, I have a son too, his name is Johnny Luther. May he not also come into this garden and eat these beautiful apples and pears, and ride these fine horses? Then the man said, If he loves to pray and to learn, and is good, he shall come into this garden, and Lippus and Jost too, and when they all come together they shall have fifes and trumpets, lutes, and all sorts of music, and they shall dance, and shoot with little cross-bows.

And he showed me a fine meadow there in the garden, made for dancing. There hung nothing but golden fifes, trumpets, and fine silver cross-bows. But it was early, and the children had not yet eaten; therefore I could not wait the dance, and I said to the man: Ah! dear sir! I will immediately go and write all this to my little son Johnny, and tell him to pray diligently, and to learn well, and to be good, so that he may also come to this garden. But he has an aunt Lehne, he must bring her with him. Then the man said, It shall be so; go and write him so.

Therefore, my dear little son Johnny, learn and pray away! and tell Lippus and Jost too, that they must learn and pray. And then you shall come to the garden together. Herewith I commend thee to Almighty God. And greet aunt Lehne, and give her a kiss for my sake.

Thy dear Father,
MARTINUS LUTHER.

Anno 1530.

TO JONAS VON STOCKHAUSEN.

A LETTER OF ADVICE INSTRUCTING HIM HOW TO CONTEND WITH HIS WEARINESS OF LIFE. WRITTEN THE 27th NOV., 1532.

To the severe and firm Jonas von Stockhausen, Captain at Nordhausen, my Gracious Master and good friend.

Grace and peace in Christ! Severe, firm, dear Master and friend. It hath been made known to me by good friends how hardly the foul Fiend assaileth you with weariness of life and desire of death. O! my dear friend, here is high time not to trust, by any means, nor to follow your own thoughts, but to hear other people who are free from such buffetings. Yea! bind your ear firmly to our mouth, and let our word enter your heart; so shall God through our word comfort and strengthen you.

In the first place, you know that man shall and must obey God, and diligently guard him, self against disobedience to his will. Since then you are sure and must comprehend that God gives you life, and will not yet have you dead, your thoughts should yield to his Divine will, and you should obey him cheerfully, and have no doubt that such thoughts, as disobedient to the will of God, are, of a certainty, shot and thrust with force into your heart by the Devil. Wherefore you behove to resist them firmly, and forcibly bear, or tear them out again.

To our Lord Christ, also, life was sore and bitter, yet would he not die without his Father's will, and he fled death, and preserved life while he could, and said, My hour is not yet come. And Elias and Jonas, and other prophets, called and cried for death, by reason of great sorrow and impatience of life, and, moreover, cursed their birth, their day and life. Yet were they constrained to live and to bear their weariness with all their might, until their hour came.

Truly, you behove to follow these words and examples, as the words and admonitions of the Holy Spirit, and to spue out and throw from you the thoughts which drive you the contrary way. And, though it may be sore and difficult to do, let it seem to you as if you were bound and fettered with chains, out of which you must twist and work yourself loose, till the sweat breaks from you. For the Devil's darts, when they stick so deep, may not be drawn forth with laughter, nor without labour; but with force must they be torn out.

Wherefore it is needful that you take heart and comfort against yourself, and speak with indignation against yourself: "Nay, fellow! be thou never so unwilling to live, yet shalt thou and must thou live; for my God will have it so, and I will have it so. Get you gone! ye devil's thoughts of dying and death, into the abyss of hell. Ye have nothing to do here," &c. And grind your teeth together against such thoughts, and set up such a hard head for God's will, and make yourself more obstinate and stiff-necked than any curst boor or shrew, yea, harder than any anvil of iron.

If you shall so attack yourself and contend against yourself, God will surely help you. But if you do not struggle nor defend yourself, but leave such thoughts free to plague you at their leisure, you will soon be lost.

But the best of all advice is, not to fight with them always, but, if you can, to despise them,— to act as though you felt them not, to think of something else, and to speak in this wise: Come! Devil, do not teaze me! I cannot now attend to thy thoughts; I must ride, drive, eat, drink, do this or that;—also, I must be merry now. Come again to-morrow! &c. And take in hand whatever else you can, play and the like, that you may be able, freely and easily, to despise such thoughts, and send them from you, even with coarse, uncivil words, as: Dear Devil, if thou canst come no nearer to me, then ———— ————, &c., I cannot wait for thee now.

Let them read you, as touching such matters, the example of the "Louse-cracker," of the "Goose-fife," and the like, in *Gerson, de cogitationibus blasphemiæ*. This is the best counsel; and our prayer, and the prayers of all good Christians, shall help you. Herewith I commend you to our dear Lord, the only Saviour, and true conqueror, Jesus Christ. May he maintain his victory and triumph against the Devil in your heart, and rejoice us all by his aid and his wonders in you; which we comfortably hope and pray, according as he hath bidden and assured us. Amen!

DOCTOR MARTINUS LUTHER.
Wittenberg, Wednesday after Catharinæ.

TO THE LADY VON STOCKHAUSEN.

LUTHER COUNSELS HER IN RELATION TO THE MELANCHOLY OF HER HUSBAND.

To the honourable and virtuous Lady N. von Stockhausen, Captain's lady at Nordhausen, —my gracious and kind friend.

Grace and peace in Christ! Honourable and virtuous Lady! I have written, in haste, a brief letter of consolation to your dear Lord. Well! the Devil is hostile to you both, for that you love his enemy, Christ. You must pay the price of that, as he himself saith: "Because I have chosen you, therefore the world hateth you and the prince thereof; but be of good cheer." Precious, in the sight of God, are the sufferings of his saints. But now, in haste, I can write but little. Take heed, before all things, that you leave not your husband one moment alone; and let him have nothing wherewith he might do injury to himself. Solitude, to him, is pure poison, and therefore the Devil himself driveth him to it. But it were well to tell or to have read in his presence, many stories, new tidings, and strange matters. It will not be amiss, if, at times, they are idle and false tidings, and tales of Turks, Tartars, and the like;—if haply he may be incited thereby, to laugh and to jest. And then, down upon him with comfortable words of Scripture. Whatsoever you do, let it not be lonesome or still about him; that he may not sink into thought. It shall do no harm, if he should be made angry on account thereof. Pretend as if you were sorry for it, and scold, &c. But still do it the more. Take this in haste, for want of better. Christ, who is the cause of such sorrow, will help him, as he hath lately conferred help on yourself. Only hold fast! you are the apple of his eye. Whoever toucheth that, toucheth him. Amen!

DOCTOR MARTINUS LUTHER.
Wittenberg, Wednesday after Catharinæ, 1532.

TO CHANCELLOR BRÜCK.

A LETTER OF ENCOURAGEMENT IN RELATION TO THE CAUSE OF THE REFORMERS.

To the estimable right learned Master Gregory Brück, Doctor of Laws, the Elector of Saxony his Chancellor and Counsellor, my gracious Master and friendly, dear Gossip.

Grace and peace in Christ! Estimable, right learned, dear Master and dear Gossip. I have written now several times to my most gracious Lord and to our friends, so that I think I have overdone the matter,—especially, as concerneth my most gracious Lord;—as if I doubted that the aid and grace of God were more abundant and more powerful with his Electoral Princely Grace than with me. I have done it at the instigation of our people, of whom some are so careful and cast down, as if God had forgotten us,—who cannot forget us except he first forget himself. Then were our cause not his cause, nor our doctrine his Word. Otherwise, if we be assured and doubt not that it is his cause and Word, then is our prayer certainly heard, and aid is already decreed and prepared, and we shall be helped. It cannot fail. For he saith: "Can a woman forget her child, that she should not have compassion on the fruit of her womb? And though she should forget, yet will not I forget thee," &c.

I saw lately two miracles. First, as I looked out at the window, I saw the stars in the heavens and the whole fair dome of God; yet did I see no pillars on which the Master had placed this dome. Nevertheless, the heavens fell not, and the dome stands yet fast. Now there are some that seek for such pillars. They would fain lay hold of and feel them. And because they cannot do this, they struggle and tremble as though the heaven must certainly fall, for no other reason than because they cannot seize or see the pillars. Could they but lay hold of these, the heaven would stand firm.

Next, I saw also great thick clouds hover over us with such weight that they might be likened to a great sea. Yet saw I no floor upon which they rested or found footing, nor any vessels in which they were contained. Still they fell not down upon us, but greeted us with a sour face and flew away. When they were gone, then shone forth both the floor and our roof which had held them,—the rainbow. That was a weak, thin, small floor and roof; and it vanished in the clouds; and, in appearance, was more like an image, such as is seen through a painted glass, than a strong floor. So that one might despair on account of the floor, as well as on account of the great weight of water. Nevertheless, it was found in truth, that this almighty image (such it seemed) bore the burden of the waters and protected us. Yet there be some who consider, regard and fear the water and the thickness of the clouds and the heavy burden of them, more than this thin, narrow and light image. For they would fain feel the strength of the image, and because they cannot do this, they fear that the clouds will occasion an everlasting sin-flood.

Thus, in friendly wise, must I jest with your Honour, and yet write without jesting; for I have had special joy, in that I learned that your Honour hath had, before all others, good courage and a cheerful heart in this, our buffeting. I had hoped that, at the least, a *pax politica* might have been obtained, but God's thoughts are far above our thoughts. And it is even right, for He, as St. Paul saith, heareth and doth *supra quam intelligimus aut petimus.* "For we know not how to pray as we ought." (Rom. viii. 26.) If he should hear us now, after the same manner in which we pray,—that the emperor may give us peace,— it might be *infra*, not *supra quam intelligimus*, and the emperor, not God, should have the glory. * * * * But this work which God hath vouchsafed to us by his Grace, he will also bless and further by his Spirit. He will find way, time and place to help us, and will neither forget nor delay. They have not yet accomplished the half of what they undertake, the *viri sanguinis.* Nor have they yet all returned to their homes, or whither they would go. Our rainbow is weak, their clouds are mighty, but *in fine videbitur cujus toni.* Your Honour will pardon my gossip, and comfort Magister Philip and all the rest. Christ shall also comfort and preserve me our most gracious Lord. To Him be praise and thanks in eternity! Amen! To His Grace I also faithfully commend your Honour.

MARTINUS LUTHER, Doct.

Ex Eremo, 5 Aug. anno MDXXX.

TO JOSEPH LEVIN METZSCH AT MILA.

ANSWER TO THE QUESTION WHETHER INHERITED DEBTS ARE TO BE CONSIDERED AS A PART OF THE CROSS LAID UPON US BY GOD.

To the severe and firm Joseph Levin Metzsch, at Mila, my kind, good Master and friend. Grace and peace in Christ! Severe, firm, dear master and friend. Whereas you are moved to know if pecuniary debt, inherited from parents, be also a cross imposed by God,— you may suppose that every scourge wherewith God scourgeth his children is a portion of the holy cross. Seeing then that debts, or need, or poverty are no light scourge, for him who knows not how to bear them, they are also, without doubt, a perceptible particle of the holy cross, with the children of God who know how to bear and to use it. But, like every other chastisement of the dear Father, it ought not to terrify the conscience, as a serious disfavour, but to comfort and strengthen it, as a fatherly rod or fox-tail.* For whether one fall into debt wantonly or carelessly, or whether one innocently inherit it, it is nevertheless appointed by God, and the rod is laid upon us through our own carelessness and wantonness. Herewith be commended to God! Amen.

MARTINUS LUTHER.

12th March, 1520.

TO THE POPE, LEO X.

EXTRACTS.

Luther, in this letter, defends himself from the charge of having attacked the person of the Pope; expresses his willingness to do all that is required of him, except to recant or renounce the right of private interpretation, and admonishes the Pope not to listen to flatterers, but to those who speak the truth.— This letter was originally written in Latin, and afterwards translated by Luther himself into German.

To the most Holy Father in God, Leo the tenth, Pope at Rome, all blessedness in Christ Jesus our Lord! Amen.

Most holy Father in God, the troubles and the controversy in which I have been entangled now, these three years, with certain wild men, compel me, from time to time, to look toward thee, and to think of thee. Yea! seeing it is believed that thou art the only principal cause of this controversy, I cannot avoid to think of thee without cessation. For though I am compelled by some of thy unchristian flatterers, who, without all reason, are incensed against me,— to appeal from thy chair and judgment to a free Christian council in my cause; yet have I never so estranged my mind from thee, as not, with all my powers, to wish the best at all times to thee and thy Romish Chair, and, with diligent, hearty prayer, as much as I was able, to implore the same from God. True it is, that I have taken upon myself greatly to despise and to overcome them that hitherto have been at pains to threaten me with the loftiness and greatness of thy name and power. But there is now one thing which I may not despise, which also is the reason that I write to thee again; and that is, that I perceive that I am maligned and misinterpreted, and am said not even to have spared thy person.

* A kind of whip.

But I will freely and openly confess that, so far as I am conscious, as oft as I have made mention of thy person, I have ever said the best and most honourable things concerning thee. And if, at any time, I have not done so, I can, myself, in no wise commend it, and must confirm the judgment of my accusers with full confession, and wish for nothing more dearly, than to sing the counterpart of this my insolence and wickedness, and to retract my faulty word. I have called thee a Daniel in Babylon; and how diligently I have defended thy innocence against the slanderer Sylvester, every one who reads it may superabundantly understand. * * *

* * * But this is true, I have freely attacked the Romish Chair, which they name the Roman Court, concerning which thou thyself must confess,—and no one upon earth can confess otherwise,—that it is viler and more shameful than ever was Sodom or Gomorrah or Babylon. And, as far as I perceive, its wickedness henceforth is neither to be counselled nor helped. Everything there has become altogether desperate and bottomless. Wherefore it hath vexed me, that under thy name and the semblance of the Romish Church, the poor people, in all the world, have been cheated and injured. Against which I have contended and will yet contend, while my Christian spirit liveth within me. * *

* * * Meanwhile thou sittest, holy Father Leo, like a sheep among the wolves, and like Daniel among the lions, and like Ezekiel among the scorpions. What canst thou alone do among so many wild monsters? And though three or four learned and pious Cardinals should fall to thy lot, what were they among such a multitude? Ye should sooner perish with poison ere ye could undertake to help the matter. It is over with the Romish Chair. God's wrath, without cessation, hath overtaken it. It is opposed to the general Councils. It will not suffer itself to be instructed nor reformed. Yet shall not its raging and unchristian manners hinder it from fulfilling that which is said of its mother, the ancient Babylon, "We would have healed Babylon and she is not healed,—we will let her go." Jer. li. 9.

Haply, it were thy task and that of the Cardinals to prevent this misery; but the sickness mocks medicine;—horse and carriage obey not the coachman. This is the cause why I have ever so grieved, thou good Leo, that thou hast been made a pope at this time, who wert well worthy to have been pope in better times. The Roman Chair is not worthy of thee and the like of thee; rather the evil Spirit ought to be pope, who also surely doth reign in Babylon, more than thou.

O! would to God thou wert rid of the honour, as they call it,—thy most mischievous friends,—and mightest maintain thyself with some prebend, or with thy paternal inheritance! Truly, none but Judas Iscariot and his like, whom God hath rejected, should be honoured with such honour. For tell me, whereunto art thou yet of use in Popedom? Save, that the worse and more desperate it grows, the more vehemently it abuseth thy power and title to injure the people in body and soul, to increase sin and shame, and to quench faith and truth. O! thou most unhappy Leo! thou sittest in the most dangerous of all chairs. Verily! I tell thee the truth, for I bear thee good-will. * * *

* * * I will speak yet farther. It had never entered my heart to storm against the Roman Court nor to dispute concerning it. For since I saw that there was no help,—that cost and pains were lost, I treated it with contempt, gave it a letter of dismission, and said; Adieu dear Rome! That which stinketh, let it stink on! and that which is filthy, let it be filthy still! (Revel. xx. 11.) And so I betook myself to the silent, quiet study of the Holy Scriptures, that I might become profitable to them among whom I dwelt. And, when now I laboured not unfruitfully in this matter, the evil Spirit opened his eyes and became aware of the same. Straightway he stirred up, with a mad ambition, his servant John Eck,—a special enemy of Christ and the truth,—and bade him drag me, unawares, into a disputation;—seizing upon a word touching the popedom that had escaped me by chance. * * * * *

* * * So now I come, holy Father Leo, and laying myself at thy feet, entreat thee, if it be possible, to put forth thine hand, and to place a bridle upon those flatterers who are enemies of peace, and yet pretend peace. But, as to retracting my doctrine, of that nothing will come. And let no one take it upon himself, except he wish to entangle the matter in still greater confusion. Moreover, I may not suffer rule or measure in the interpretation of the Scripture, seeing that the word of God, which teacheth all freedom, must not and shall not be bound. If these two articles be allowed me, nothing else shall be laid upon me, that I will not do and suffer with all willingness. I am an enemy to strife and will incense or provoke no one, but neither will I be provoked. And if I be provoked I will not be without a word, spoken or written, God willing. Thy Holiness may with short and easy words take it upon thyself, and extinguish all this controversy, and thereupon be silent and command peace, which I have, alway, been altogether eager to hear.

Wherefore, my Holy Father, do not listen to thy sweet ear-singers, who say that thou art not mere man, but united with God, and hast all things to command and to require. It may not be, and thou wilt not effect it. Thou art the servant of all the servants of God, and art in a more dangerous and miserable condition than any man upon the earth. Let them not deceive thee, who lie to thee and pretend that thou art lord of the world; and who will not suffer any one to be a Christian except he be subject to thee;—who babble that thou hast power in heaven, in hell, and in purgatory. They are thy enemies, and seek to destroy thy soul.

* * * They err all, who say thou art above the Council and universal Christendom. They err who give to thee alone the power to interpret Scripture. They, all of them, seek nothing else than how they may sanction their unchristian doings in Christendom by means of thy name; as the evil Spirit, alas! hath done through many of thy predecessors. In brief, believe none who exalt thee, but only them who humble thee. That is God's judgment, as it is written: "He hath put down the mighty from their seats, and exalted them of low degree." Luke i. 52.

See how unlike are Christ and his vicegerents! For they would all fain be his vicegerents, and, verily, I fear, they are too truly his *vicegerents*. For a vicegerent is so in the absence of his lord. If then a pope reigneth in the absence of Christ, who dwelleth not in his heart, is he not too truly the vicegerent of Christ? * * * But what may such a pope be except an antichrist and an idol? How much better did the apostles, who called themselves, and suffered themselves to be called, only servants of Christ, who dwelt in them, and not vicegerents of an absent Christ.

Peradventure I am impudent, in that I seem to instruct so great a height, from which every one should receive instruction,—and as some of thy poisonous flatterers represent thee,—from which all kings and judgment-seats receive judgment. But I follow in this St. Bernard, in his book addressed to pope Eugene, which all popes ought to know by heart. I do it, not with the design to instruct thee, but from a pure fidelity of care and duty which, of right, constraineth every man to take thought for his neighbour even in those things which are secure, and suffereth us to regard neither honour nor dishonour, so diligently doth it consider a neighbour's danger and mishap. Wherefore, since I know that thy Holiness floateth and hovereth at Rome,—that is, upon the highest seas,—with countless dangers raging on all sides, and liveth and worketh in such misery that, haply, thou hast need of the help, even of the meanest Christian, I have thought it not unmeet that I should forget thy majesty until I had fulfilled the duty of brotherly love. I may not flatter in so serious and dangerous a matter, in which,—if there be some who will not understand that I am thy friend and more than subject,—there shall yet be found one who understandeth it.

In conclusion, that I may not appear empty before thy Holiness, I bring with me a little book,* which has gone forth under thy name; for a good wish and a beginning of peace and good hope; from which thy Holiness may taste with what kind of business I would fain occupy myself, and not unprofitably, if thy unchristian flatterers would let me. It is a little book, if thou regardest the paper; but yet the whole sum of a Christian life is comprehended in it, if the sense be understood. I am poor and have nothing else wherewith I may make proof of my service; neither canst thou be benefited more than with spiritual benefits. Herewith I commend myself to thy Holiness, whom may Jesus Christ preserve forevermore! Amen.

Wittenberg, 6th September, 1520.

TO BARBARA LISCHNERIN.

EXTRACT.

LUTHER SEEKS TO PACIFY HER IN REGARD TO HER DOUBTS OF FUTURE BLESSEDNESS.

Grace and peace in Christ! Virtuous, dear Lady! Your dear brother, Jerome Weller, hath made known to me that you are greatly troubled with doubts respecting the eternal Providence. For which I am heartily sorry. May Christ, our Lord, deliver you therefrom! Amen.

For I know the sickness well, and have lain in the hospital with it, even unto eternal death. Now would I fain, over and above my prayers, counsel and comfort you. But writing in such matters is a feeble thing; yet, as much as in me lies, will I not refrain therefrom, if God will give me grace for the work. And I will make known to you how God hath helped me to escape such buffetings, and with what art I yet preserve myself from them day by day.

First, you must fix it firmly in your heart, that such thoughts are assuredly the inflation and the fiery darts of the Devil. So saith the Scripture, Prov. xxv. 27, "He that searcheth the height of majesty shall be cast down."* Now are such thoughts nothing but a searching of the Divine Majesty; they would fain search his high Providence. And Jesus Sirach saith: "*Altiora ne quæsieris*," "Thou shalt not inquire after that which is too high for thee;" but what God hath commanded thee, that look after. For it profiteth thee nothing to gaze after that which is not commanded thee. And David also complaineth that he had brought evil upon himself, when he would inquire after things that were too high for him.

Wherefore it is certain, that this cometh not from God but from the Devil. He plagues the heart therewith; that men may become enemies of God and despair; which, notwithstanding, God hath strictly forbidden in the first commandment; and he willeth that men shall trust and love and praise Him by whom we live.

Secondly, when such thoughts occur, you shall learn to ask yourself: "Friend, in what commandment is it written that I should think of these things or handle them?" And if no such commandment is found, then learn to say: "So get thee gone, thou ugly Devil! Thou wouldst fain drive me to care for myself; whereas God everywhere speaketh: "I care for thee; look

---

* Liber de Libertate Christiana.

* English version: For men to search their own glory is not glory.

unto me and wait that which I shall appoint, and let me care," — as St. Peter teacheth, —1 Pet. v. 7: "Cast all your care upon him for he careth for you;" and David, Ps. lv. 22: "Cast thy burden upon the Lord and he shall sustain thee."

Thirdly, albeit, such thoughts do not immediately cease, (for the Devil doth not willingly desist,) you likewise, on your part, must not cease, but must still turn your heart away from them, and say: "Hearest thou not, Devil, that I will not have such thoughts? And God hath forbidden them. Get thee gone, I must now be thinking of his commandments, and let him care for me himself the while. If thou art so exceeding wise in such matters, then get thee to heaven, and dispute with God himself. He can sufficiently answer thee." And, in this way, you must still send him from you, and turn your heart toward the commandments of God.

FROM A LETTER

TO THE CHRISTIANS AT ANTWERP, IN WHICH LUTHER CAUTIONS THEM AGAINST FALSE TEACHERS.

Grace and peace from God our Father and the Lord Jesus Christ! My very dear masters and friends in Christ! I am moved by Christian love and carefulness to send this writing unto you. For I have learned how that Spirits of error are bestirring themselves among you, which have the boldness to hinder and defile the Christian doctrine, as happeneth in various places. * * * * *
* * * This one will have no baptism, that one denies the sacrament, another supposes a world between this and the last day. Some teach that Christ is not God; some say this and some say that; and there are almost as many sects and creeds as there are heads. There is no simpleton now so rude, but if he dream or imagine somewhat, the Holy Spirit must have inspired it, and he claims to be a prophet. *
* * * So then, dear friends, there hath come among you also a Spirit of disorder, in bodily shape, who would fain cause you to err, and lead you astray from the right understanding, into his conceits. Therefore take heed and be warned! But that you may the better avoid his tricks, I will here relate some of them.

One article is: he holds that every man hath the Holy Spirit.

The second: The Holy Spirit is nothing else than our own reason and understanding.

The third: Every man believes.

The fourth: There is no hell or damnation, but only the flesh is damned.

The fifth: Every soul will have eternal life.

The sixth: Nature teaches that I should do unto my neighbour as I would that he should do to me; and to will this is faith.

The seventh: The Law is not violated by evil lust, so I do not gratify the lust.

The eighth: He who hath not the Holy Spirit, hath also no sin, for he hath no reason.

All these are mere wanton articles of folly, and excepting the seventh, not worth answering. And your love shall do right to despise this Spirit. For he is as many others are now, here and there, who care not much what they teach, and only desire that men may speak of them, and have to do with them. And the Devil also seeketh this uneasiness, that he may wrestle with us, and the while hinder us, so that we forget the true doctrine, or converse not with it. Even so he useth to deceive the people with other hobgoblins, that they may miss their way, &c. And he setteth their mouth agape, that they cannot attend to their business the while. Just so this Spirit does with you, in these articles.

Wherefore, be warned, for God's sake, and take heed that ye despise and let go all that presenteth itself as new and strange, and which it is not necessary to the salvation of the soul to know. For, with such goblins, he seeketh to catch the idle. * * * * *

We have all enough to do, our whole life long, to learn the commandments of God and his Son Christ. When we are well instructed in these, we will further inquire into these secret articles, which this Spirit stirreth up without cause, only that he may obtain honour and fame. So then continue in the way, and learn what Paul teacheth the Romans, and look at my preface there, that you may know which is the right method of learning in the Scriptures; and withdraw yourselves from useless prattlers. Herewith I commend you to God. And pray for me! Amen.

TO HIS MESSMATES.

HE COMPARES THE ACTIONS OF THE BIRDS ABOUT HIM TO A DIET.

Grace and peace in Christ, dear Masters and friends! I have received the letters written by you all, and have learned how it fareth on every hand. That you, on your part, may learn how it fareth here, I give you to know that we, namely I, Master Veit and Cyriac, go not to the Diet at Augsburg, but we have come to a diet of a different sort, elsewhere.

There is a *rookery* just beneath our window like to a little forest. There the jackdaws and the crows have established a diet. There is such a riding to and fro,—such a screaming day and night without cessation, as if they were all drunk, full and mad. Young and old chatter together, so that I wonder how voice and breath can hold out so long. And I would like to know if any of this nobility and military gentry are left with you; for methinks they have assembled together here, from all the world. I have not yet seen their emperor, but the nobility and the great fellows hover and wriggle constantly before our eyes. They are not very splendidly clad, but simply, in uniform colour, all alike black, all alike gray-eyed, and all alike sing one song; yet with a pleasant difference of young and old, great and small. They care not for great palaces and halls; for their hall is arched with the fair wide heaven; their floor is the field, wainscotted with beautiful green bows; and the walls are as wide as the ends of the world. Neither do they care for steed or harness. They have feathered wheels with which they can fly from the firelocks and escape from wrath. They are grand, mighty lords; but what they will decree, I know not yet.

But so far as I have learned from their interpreter, they intend a mighty expedition and warfare against wheat, rye, oats, malt, and all kinds of grain; and there will be many a knight made in this cause, and great deeds will be done.

Thus do we sit here at the diet, and hear and see with great joy and love how the princes and lords, together with the other estates of the empire, sing and luxuriate so joyfully together. But a special joy have we when we see in what a knightly fashion they wriggle, wipe their bills, and overthrow the defence, that they may conquer and acquire glory against corn and malt. We wish them joy and weal, and especially that they may be spitted upon a hedge-stake. But I hold that they are nothing else but sophists and papists, with their preaching and writing; whom I must needs have before me in a heap, that I may hear their lovely voice and discourse, and see how useful a gentry it is, to devour all that is on the earth, and, in return, to chatter for pastime.

To-day we have heard the first nightingale, for they have not been willing to trust April. Hitherto we have had only splendid weather. It hath not rained once, except yesterday, a little. With you peradventure it may be otherwise. Herewith be commended to God, and keep house well!

Martinus Luther, Doct.
From the Diet of the Malt-Turks, 28th April, anno 1530.

JACOB BOEHME.*

Born 1575. Died 1624.

This celebrated mystic, whose speculations procured for him, in his own age, the significant title of "*Philosophus Teutonicus*," appears in strong contrast with the great Reformer by whose side he is placed in these pages.† He may be regarded as the antipodes of Luther in all the leading tendencies of his mind. Luther's fame rests on his character, — that of Boehme is derived from his thought. The one was a man of action, with an eye to practical effect in all that he wrote and did; the other was a quietist, whose spirit reposed with intense inwardness on itself, and who knew no world but that of his own dreams. Luther sought to ground a popular theology, Boehme strove to penetrate the deepest mysteries of Being. Luther aimed at what was needful or profitable for the daily use and conduct of life, Boehme aspired to the highest truth. The one laboured to instruct the masses, the other to instruct himself. The former had his sphere in the actual, the other in the absolute. They relate to each other as Paul and John.

Boehme, like Luther, was a son of the people. His birthplace was Alt Seidenberg, in Lower Lusatia, near Görlitz, where he afterward practised his craft. His parents were peasants of the poorest sort; his calling that of shoemaker. Born to narrow fortunes and humble hopes, the shoemaker of Görlitz, like his English fellow-craftsman, the shoemaker of Leicester, was "one of those to whom under ruder or purer form, the Divine Idea of the Universe is pleased to manifest itself, and across all the hulls of ignorance and earthly degradation, shine through, in unspeakable awfulness, in unspeakable beauty, on their souls."‡ He received no instruction from books until his eleventh year, and then, from no other but the bible, the ability to read which, was the extent of his schooling. But, before this, he had received instruction of a different sort, while tending cattle in the fields.

"His daily teachers had been woods and rills,
The silence that is in the starry sky,
The sleep that is among the lonely hills."

And there the God who delights to pour out his Spirit in vessels of this quality,—"*Der stets den Schäfern gnädig sich bewies*," — drew near to his soul in the eternal melodies of Nature. Established in his calling at Görlitz, "sitting in his stall, working on tanned hides, amid pincers, paste-horns, rosin, swine-bristles, and a nameless heap of rubbish," he continued to see visions and to dream dreams, and believed himself the recipient and medium of Divine revelations. At three different times, according to his own account, he was environed with supernatural light, which attended him, in one instance, for seven successive days. "Replenished with heavenly knowledge," he went out into the fields, and "viewing the herbs and the grass, he saw into their essences and properties, which were discovered to him by their lineaments, figures, and signatures."* The first reflection of this illumination was the "Aurora," or "The Morning-redness in the East," which he wrote with no view to publication, but merely by way of record and memorandum,—"that the mysteries revealed to him might not pass through him as a stream." It became public without his consent, and was seized and condemned as heretical by the Senate of Görlitz, at the instigation of a clerical persecutor. The author was admonished to write no more books, but to confine himself to his proper calling. As if the proverb, "*Ne sutor*," &c., had been made expressly for him, Boehme meekly promised obedience, not doubting, in his simplicity, that he had committed

---

* Called by English writers, *Behmen*. This corruption seems past recovery.

† Although placed by his side, in accordance with the plan of this work, Boehme is more than half a century removed from Luther in chronological order. The interval between them is far from being a blank in the literary history of Germany. It contains many names of note;—among which those of Zwingli, Ulrich von Hutten, Sebastian Frank, and Johann Fischart, would claim a distinguished place in a complete survey of German literature,—but none which properly come within the scope of this Collection.

‡ Carlyle.

* See "Jacob Behmen's Theosophick Philosophy, unfolded in divers Considerations and Demonstrations, by Edward Taylor. With a short account of the life of Jacob Behmen." London, 1691.

an error. A silence of seven years ensued. At the expiration of this term, having meanwhile removed from Görlitz to Dresden, and experiencing new motions of the Spirit, he no longer hesitated to write and to publish. He composed, in rapid succession, a large number of works, in which he endeavors to communicate his revelations; struggling painfully with want of culture and of language, in his attempts to express ideas so far beyond the range of that experience which had furnished the only dialect he knew. Latin words and scientific terms, picked up in conversation with scholars, without any clear understanding of their import, are brought in to eke out his slender vocabulary; and serve only to enhance the obscurity, by the unusual and illegitimate sense in which they are employed. "Art," he says, "hath not written here, neither was there any time to consider how to set it punctually down, according to the right understanding of the letters, but all was ordered according to the direction of the Spirit, which often went in haste. And though I could have written in a more accurate, fair, and plain manner, yet the reason was this, that the burning fire did often force forward with speed, and the hand and pen must hasten directly after it, for it cometh and goeth as a sudden shower."—"I can write nothing of myself, but as a child which neither knoweth nor understandeth, but only that which the Lord vouchsafeth to know in me."

Never, since the days of the Apostles, has such defective scholarship been united with such intellectual fecundity and such important results. Jacob Boehme has been a guide and a prophet to men of the profoundest intellect, of the most exalted station, and the most distinguished piety. Religious sects have been founded on his doctrine, and called by his name. William Law, the most devout of English mystics, was his disciple, and published an English edition of his works. Schelling, the most cultivated of German Transcendentalists, author of the "Philosophy of Identity," bears witness to the depth and wealth of his intuitive wisdom, and reflects it in his Ontology. Goethe, in his youthful speculations, seems to have borrowed from him the leading idea of his cosmogony.* King Charles I. of England is said to have sent a special messenger to Görlitz to learn of Boehme, and, after reading, in the English, the "Answers to the forty questions of the soul," to have declared, that "if, as he had been informed, the author was no scholar, it was evident that the Holy Ghost yet dwelled in men."

It is not easy to collect the true form of Boehme's philosophy out of the thick obscurity of his writings. And it is more difficult still, to separate the pure idea from the form, in a system so complicated with Christian mythology and Christian dogmatics. One knows not how much or how little may be intended by the theological phraseology in which the author has clothed his speculations, where biblical terms are often so warped from their literal import. But if we divide the various systems of philosophy, according to their ontological characteristics, into three classes; viz: the Magian or Dualistic,—the Unitarian, with its numberless varieties, theistic, atheistic, and pantheistic, from Anaximander to Spinoza,—and, thirdly, the Platonic or Trinitarian;—the speculations of Boehme will be found in the last of these divisions. He belongs to the Platonic family of philosophers, by virtue of the triune nature which he ascribes to Being. His system* supposes three Principles, in which all Being is comprised. The first Principle, or the Father,—" the eternal Darkness," like the το εν of the Platonic Trinity, is destitute of intelligence in itself (αλογος), although the Father of intelligence. It is not so much God as the source of God. "*Fons deitatis.*" From this first Principle proceeds, by eternal generation, the second Principle, the Son, "the eternal Light." And from these two proceeds, by eternal generation, the third, "the Outbirth," which is the immediate cause of the material creation. These three Principles are undivided in God; but, through the fall of Lucifer and his angels, they have become separated in Nature and in man. Man, in his natural state, partakes of the first Principle, and of the life which proceeds from the third. He becomes possessed of the second only by regeneration in Christ. Furthermore, these three Principles are manifested in seven elements or "Fountain Spirits," as they are denominated by Boehme. The first is called

---

* The idea that the material universe was created out of the ruins of a fallen, spiritual world. See "Aus meinem Leben," Book VIII.

* For an account of this system, see "A Compendious View of the Grounds of the Teutonic Philosophy, published by a gentleman retired from business." London, 1770.

Astringency; the second, Attraction; the third, Anguish; the fourth, Heat. These four constitute the first Principle. The fifth is Light; the sixth, Sound. These two constitute the second Principle. The seventh is the Body generated by the other six, in which they live and work, and which represents the third Principle.

A full account of this system would far exceed the limits and design of this sketch. The points which have been mentioned are those which seemed to be most characteristic and fundamental, as well as most necessary for the right understanding of the extracts given below. As to the practical part of Boehme's doctrine, it may be summed up in his own words,—said to have been written in an album—which contain, in fact, the substance of all practical philosophy.

"Wem Zeit ist wie die Ewigkeit
Und Ewigkeit is wie die Zeit
Der ist befreit von allem Streit,"*

When he felt himself seized with what he supposed to be his last sickness, he caused himself to be removed to his old residence, Görlitz, and having, as it is said, predicted the hour of his death, departed, saying, "Now I go hence into Paradise."

TO THE
READER OF THESE WRITINGS.*

It is written, "The natural man understandeth not the things of the Spirit, nor the mysteries of the kingdom of God, they are foolishness unto him, neither can he know them:" therefore I admonish and exhort the Christian lover of mysteries, if he will study these high writings, and read, search, and understand them, that he do not read them outwardly only, with sharp speculation and reasoning; for in so doing, he shall remain in the outward, imaginary ground only, and obtain no more than a counterfeited colour or feigned shadow of them.

For a man's own reason, without the light of God, cannot come into the ground of them, it is impossible; for let his wit be never so subtil, it apprehends spiritual things but, as it were, the shadow in a glass.   *   *   *   *   *

Now if any would search the divine ground, that is, the divine Revelation, or manifestation, that God has been pleased to make of himself, he must first consider with himself, for what end he desires to know such things, whether he desires to practise that which he might obtain, and bestow it to the glory of God, and the welfare of his neighbour; also whether he desires to die to earthliness, and to his own will, and to live in that which he seeks and desires, and to be one spirit with it.

If he have not a purpose, that, if God should reveal himself and his mysteries to him, he would be one spirit and have one will with God, and wholly resign and yield himself up to him, that God's Spirit may do what he pleases with him, and by him, and that God may be his knowledge, will and working; he is not yet fit for such knowledge and understanding.

For there are many that seek mysteries and hidden knowledge, merely that they may be respected and highly esteemed by the world, and for their own gain and profit; but they attain not this ground, "where the Spirit searches all things, even the deep things of God."

It must be a totally resigned and yielded will, in which God himself searches and works, and which continually pierces into God, in yielding and resigned humility, seeking nothing but his eternal native country, and to do his neighbour service; and then it may be attained. He must begin with effectual repentance and amendment, and with prayer that his understanding may be opened from within; for then the inward spirit will bring itself into the outward understanding.

But when he reads such writings and yet cannot understand them, he must not presently throw them away, and think it is impossible to understand them; no, but he must turn his mind to God, beseeching him for grace and understanding, and read again, and then he shall see more and more in them, till at length he be drawn, by the power of God, into the very depth itself, and so come into the supernatural and supersensual ground, namely, into the eternal unity of God, where he shall hear unspeakable and effectual words of God, which will bring him back and outward again (by the divine effluence) to the very grossest and meanest matter of the earth, and afterward back and inwards to God again; then it is that the Spirit of God searches all things with him, and by him, and so he is rightly taught and driven by God.

*   *   *   *   *   *   *   *

Of God and the Divine Nature.

*   *   *   *   *   *   *   *

The soul, which has its original out of God's first principle in creation, and was breathed from God into man in the third principle, (that is, into the sidereal and elementary birth,) is

---

* From the "Compendious View of the grounds of the Teutonic Philosophy."

* To whom time is as eternity,
And eternity as time,
He is freed from all strife.

capable of seeing further than any other creature into the first principle of God, out of and in and from the essence of which it proceeded. And this is not marvellous, for it does but behold itself in the rising of its birth, out of which it came originally, and, by the power of its light, can see the whole depth of the Father in the first principle, by which he manifested himself in creation.

This the devils also see in a degree; for they also are out of the same first principle, they also wish that they might not see nor feel it; but it is their own fault that they separated themselves from the second principle, which is called, and is God, one in essence and threefold in personal distinction, which is shut up to them.

* * * * * * * *

When I consider *what God is*, then I say, *He is the One!* in reference to the creature, as an eternal nothing. *He has neither foundation, beginning nor abode;* he needs not either space or place; he begetteth himself in himself, *from eternity to eternity; and the outgoing out of the will in itself is God.*

He is neither like or resembleth any thing, and has no peculiar place where he dwells; *the true heaven where God dwells is all over and in all places, for wheresoever he was before the creation, there he is still, namely, in himself,* the Essence of all essences; *all is generated from him, and is originally from him.*

* * * * * * *

God, without nature and creature, has no name, but is called only the eternal Good, that is, the eternal One! the Profundity of all beings! There is no place found for him, therefore can no creature rightly name him: for all names stand in the formed word of power, but *God is*, himself, *the root of all power, without beginning and name;* therefore said he to Jacob, " Wherefore askest thou what is my name?"

* * * * * * *

OF GOD'S FIRST MANIFESTATION OF HIMSELF IN THE TRINITY.

God is the will of the wisdom; the wisdom is his manifestation.

In this eternal generation we are to understand three things; namely, 1. An eternal will. 2. An eternal mind of the will. 3. The egress, efflux, or effluence from the will and mind, which is a spirit of the will and mind.

The will is the Father: the mind is the conceived comprehension, or receptacle of the will, or the centre to something; and it is the will's heart, that is the Son of God; and the egress of the will and mind is the power and spirit.

* * * * * * *

And as we perceive that in this world there is fire, air, water, and earth, also the sun and the stars, and therein consist all the things of this world; so you may conceive, by way of similitude, that the Father is the fire of the whole, holy, constellations, and that the Son, namely, his heart, is the sun which sets all the constellations in a light, pleasant habitation; and that the Holy Ghost is the air of the life, without which neither sun nor constellation would subsist.

* * * * * * *

OF ETERNAL NATURE AFTER THE FALL OF LUCIFER, AND OF THE CREATION OF THIS WORLD, AND OF MAN.

Reader, understand and consider my writings aright. We have no power or ability to speak of the birth of the Deity, for it never had any beginning from all eternity; but we have power to speak of God our Father, what he is, and how the eternal geniture is, and of the nativity, birth, and working of nature.

And though it is not very good for us to know the austere, earnest, strong, fierce, severe, and original birth of nature, as it came to be separated, and first manifested by the apostasy of Lucifer, and into the knowledge, feeling, and comprehensibility of which our first parents brought upon themselves, and upon us their posterity, through the poisoning venom and infection they received, by the instigation and deceit of the devil; yet we have very great need of this knowledge, that we thereby may learn to know the devil, who dwells in the most strong, severe, and cruel birth of all, and to know our own enemy, SELF, which our first parents awakened and roused up, and we carry within us, and which we ourselves now are.

* * * * * * *

I know very well, and my spirit and mind shows me, that many will be offended at the simplicity and meanness of the author, for offering to write of such high things, and will think he has no authority to do it, and that he sins, and runs contrary to God and His will, in presuming, being but a man, to go about to speak and say what God is. For it is lamentable, that, since the fall of Adam, we should be so continually cheated by the devil, as to think that we are not the children of God, nor of his essence, or offspring.

Your monstrous, outward, bestial form or shape indeed is not God, nor of his essence; but the hidden man, which is the soul, is the proper essence of God, forasmuch as the love in the light of God, is sprung up in your centre, out of which the Holy Ghost proceeds, and wherein the second principle of God consists. How then should you not have power and authority to speak of God, who is your Father, of whose essence you (the regenerated) are, as a child is the Father's own substance? The Father is the eternal power, or virtue; the Son is the heart and light continuing eternally in the Father; and all regenerated souls continue in the Father and the Son; and now seeing the Holy Ghost proceeds from the Father and the Son, the eternal power of the Father is in you, and the eternal light of the Son shines in you.

* * * * * * * *

If you lift up your thoughts and minds, and ride upon the chariot of the soul, (as is beforementioned,) and look upon yourself, and all creatures, and consider how the birth of life in you takes its original, and what the light of your life is, whereby you can behold the sun, and also look with your imagination beyond the sun into a vast space to which the eyes of your body cannot reach, and then consider what the cause might be that you are more rational than the other creatures, seeing you can, by the operations of your mind, search into every thing; you will, if you be born of God, attain to what God and the eternal birth is; for you will see, feel, and find, that all creation must yet have a higher root, from whence it proceeded, which is not visible, but hidden. Now if you farther consider what preserveth all thus, and whence it is, then you will find the Eternal that has no beginning, the Original of the eternal principle, namely, the eternal, indissoluble band of Father, Son and Holy Spirit. And then, secondly, you will see the separation; in that the material world, with the stars and elements, are out of the first principle of creation, which contains the outward and third principle of this world. For you will find in the elementary kingdom or dominion, a cause in every thing wherefore it generates and moves as it does; but you will not find the first cause whence it is so; and that therefore there must be two several principles, for you find in the visible things a corruptibility, and perceive that they must have a beginning, because they have an end, and these two principles are the first and third.

You find in all things a glorious power and virtue, which is the life growing and springing of every thing, and that therein lies its beauty and pleasant welfare. Now look upon an herb or plant, and consider what is its life which makes it grow, and you shall find in the original, harshness, bitterness, fire, and water, whence proceeds the pleasant smell and colours, for if it be severed from its own mother that generated it at the beginning, then it remains dead.

Thus you see that there is an eternal root which affords this, and must be a principle, which the stock itself is not, and that principle has its original from the light of nature. * *
* * * * * * *

But what do you think was before the times of the creating of this world? For out of that proceeded the root of this earth and stones, as also the stars and elements. But of what consists the root? You will find therein nothing else but bitterness, harshness, astringent sourness and fire, and these are but one thing, namely, the pure, eternal element, and from which all outward, natural things were generated after the fall of Lucifer; for, before his fall, there was but one pure element. Now in these forms you cannot find God; the pure Deity being incomprehensible, unperceivable, almighty, and all powerful. Where is it then men may find God?

Here open your noble mind, and search further. For seeing God is only good, whence comes the evil? And seeing also that he alone is the life, and the light, and the holy power, as is undeniably true, whence comes the anger of God? Whence comes the devil, and his evil will? And whence has hell-fire its original? Seeing there was nothing before God manifested himself in creation, but only God, who was, and is a Spirit, and continues so in eternity. Whence then is the first matter of evil? Here blind reason gives this judgment, that there must needs have been in the spirit of God, a will to generate the source and fountain of anger and evil.

But the Scripture says, the devil was created a holy angel; and it further says, "Thou art not a God that wills evil;" and, by Ezekiel, God declares, "that as sure as he lives, he wills not the death of a sinner;" and this is testified by God's earnest and severe punishing of the devil, and of all sinners, that he is not pleased with death.

What then is the first matter of evil in the devil? And what moved him to anger, seeing he was created out of the original, eternal Spirit of God? Or whence is the original of evil, and of hell, wherein the devils shall remain forever, when this world, with the stars, elements, earth, and stones, shall perish in the end of time?

Beloved Reader, open the eyes of your mind here, and know, that no other anguish or source of punishment will spring up in Lucifer than his own quality, or working property; for that is his hell which he himself formed; and because the light of God is his eternal shame, therefore is he God's enemy, because he is no more in the light of God.

Now, nothing can be here produced by reason, that God should ever have used any matter out of which to create the devil, for then the devil might justify himself, that he was made evil, and created of evil matter. But God created him out of nothing but merely and entirely out of his own divine essence, as well as the other angels; as it is written, "Through him and in him are all things." And his only is the kingdom, the power and the glory; and all is in him, as the Holy Scriptures witness. And if it were not thus, no sin could be imputed to the devil, nor to men, if they were not eternal, and had their being out of God himself.
* * * * * * *

If, therefore, you will speak or think of God, you must consider that he is All. * *
* * * * * * *

And seeing that he himself witnesses, that his is the kingdom and the power, from eternity to eternity; and that he calls himself Father, (and the Son, the Second Person in the Trinity, begotten of his Father,) therefore we must seek for him in the original of his manifesting himself in the tri-une One; namely, Father, Son, and Spirit; from whom all creation proceeded;

and we can say no otherwise, but that the first principle in creation is God the Father himself, as the source, or fountain of life.

Yet there is found in the original of life the most fierce and strong birth, namely, harshness, bitterness, anguish, and fire; of which we cannot say that it is God; and yet is the most inward first source of all light, and that *is* in God the Father; according to which he calls himself an angry, zealous, or jealous God, and a consuming fire. And this source is the first principle, and that is God the Father in the originality, or first manifestation of himself, at the beginning in creation.

* * * * * * *

And in this first principle, prince Lucifer, at the extinguishing in himself the light of the second principle, continued; and is ever the same abyss of hell; wherein the soul also continues which extinguishes that light which shines from the heart of God, (into every man that cometh into the world,) being then separated from the second principle. For which cause also, at the end of time, there will be a separation or parting asunder of the saints of light from the damned, whose source of life will be without the light of God, and the working fountain of their condition as a boiling, springing torment.

* * * * * * *

I will now write of the second principle, of the clear, pure Deity; namely, of the heart of God, that is, the power, glory, or lustre of God the Father, in the Son. In the first principle, I have mentioned harshness, bitterness, anguish, and fire, yet they are not separate but one only thing, and they generate one another in the first source of all creation. And if now the second principle did not break forth, and spring up in the birth of the Son, then the Father would be a dark valley; and the Son, who is the heart, the love, the brightness, and the sweet rejoicing of the Father (in whom the Father is well pleased) opens another principle.

This is now what the evangelist John says, chap. 1, "In the beginning was the word; and the word was with God; and the word was God. The same was in the beginning with God. All things were made by him, and without him was not anything made. In him was life." And he is another person than the Father, for in his centre there is nothing else but mere joy, love and pleasure. * * *

The evangelist says further, "And the life was the light of men." Here, O man, take now this light of life, which was in the word and is eternal; and behold the Being of all beings, and especially thyself; seeing thou art an image, life, and derive thy being of the unsearchable God; and a likeness as to him. Here consider time and eternity; heaven and hell; this world; light and darkness; pain, and the source; life and death. Here examine thyself, whether thou hast the light and life of the Word in thee; so shalt thou be able to see and understand all things: for thy life was in the word, and was made manifest in the image which God created; it was breathed into it from the Spirit of the Word. Now lift up thy understanding in the light of thy life; and behold the formed Word! Consider its generation, for all is manifest in the light of life.

Although here the tongue of man cannot utter, declare, express nor fathom this great depth, where there is neither number nor end; yet we have power to speak thereof, as children talk of their father.

Now being to speak of the holy Trinity, we must, first, say that there is one God, and he is called God the Father and Creator of all things, who is almighty, and all in all; whose are all things, and in whom and from whom all things proceed, and in whom they remain eternally. And then we say, that he is three in persons, and has, from eternity, generated his Son out of himself, who is his heart, light and love: and yet they are not two, but one eternal essence. And further we say, the Scripture tells us that there is a Holy Ghost, which proceeds from the Father and the Son, and there is but one essence in the Father, Son, and Holy Ghost.

* * * * * * * *

But the Holy Ghost is not known or manifested in the original of the Father before the light, or son [break forth] but when the soft fountain springs up in the light, then he goes forth as a strong almighty spirit in great joy from the pleasant source of water and of the light; and he makes the forming [shaping, figuring] and images [or species], and he is the centre in all created essences; in which centre the light of life, in the light of the son or heart of the father, takes its original. And the Holy Ghost is a several person, because he proceeds [as a living power and virtue] from the Father and the Son; and confirms the birth, generating or working of the holy Trinity.

* * * * * * * *

Thus God is one only undivided essence, and yet threefold in personal distinction, one God, one Will, one heart, one desire, one pleasure, one beauty, one almightiness, one fulness of all things, neither beginning nor ending: for if I should go about to seek for the beginning or ending of a small dot, or punctum, or of a perfect circle, I should be confounded.

And although I have written here of the springing of the second principle, and the birth of the divine essence in the Trinity, as if it took a beginning, yet you must not understand it as having any beginning, for the eternal manifestation of the pure Deity is thus, without beginning or end; and that in the originalness in creation: for I am permitted to write as far as of the originalness, to the end that man might learn to know himself, what he is, and what God in the Triune One, heaven, angels, devils, and hell are. And also what the wrath of God and hell fire is, by the extinguishment of the divine light.

OF THE CREATION OF ANGELS, AND OF LUCIFER; DESCRIBING HOW HE WAS IN THE ANGELICAL FORM, AND HOW HE IS NOW IN HIS OWN PROPER FORM, BY HIS REJECTING, AND THEREBY EXTINGUISHING, THE DIVINE LIGHT OF THE SECOND PRINCIPLE IN HIMSELF.

Behold, O child of man, all the angels were created in the first principle, and by the flowing forth of the Holy Spirit were formed, and bodied in a true angelical and spiritual manner, and enlightened from the light of God, that they might increase the paradisical joy, and abide therein eternally; 'but being they were to abide eternally, they must be formed out of the first principle which is an indissoluble band;' and they were to look upon the heart or Son of God, to receive his light, and to feed upon the word, which food was to be their holy preservation, and to keep their image clear and light; even as the heart or Son of God in the second principle, manifests and enlightens the Father, namely, the first principle; and in those two principles the divine power, the pure elements, paradise, and kingdom of heaven spring up.

Thus it is with those angels that continued in the kingdom of heaven in the first paradise; they stand in the first principle in the indissoluble band, enlightened by the Son in the second principle; their food is the divine word; and their thoughts and mind is in the will of the Trinity in the Deity. The confirming and establishing of their life, will, and doings, is the power of the Holy Ghost: whatever the Holy Spirit does in the regenerating of paradise, and the holy wonders, the angels rejoice at, and sing the joyful Hallelujahs of Paradise concerning the pleasant saving and eternal birth. All they do is an increase of their heavenly joy, delight, and pleasure in the heart or Son of God; and they sport in holy obedience in the will of the eternal Father; and to this end their God created them: that he might be manifested, and rejoice in his creatures, and his creatures in him; so that there might be an eternal sport of love, in the centre of the multiplying of the pure eternal nature in the indissoluble eternal band.

But this sport of love was spoiled by Lucifer himself, who is so called, because of the extinguishment of the light of the Son of God in him, and his being cast out of his throne.

DESCRIBING WHAT HE THEN WAS, AND ALSO WHAT HE NOW IS.

He was the most glorious prince in heaven, and king over many legions of angels, and had he introduced his will into the divine meekness, and the light of the Son of God, and continued in the harmony wherein God had created him, then he would have stood, and nothing could have cast him out of the light. For he, as well as the other angels, was created of the pure eternal nature, out of the indissoluble band, and stood in the first Paradise. He felt and saw the generation of the holy Deity in the birth of the second principle, namely, of the heart or Son of God, and the outflowing of the Holy Ghost; his food was of the word of the Lord, and therein he should have continued an angel of light.

But he saw his own great beauty and glory, and that he was a prince standing in the first principle, and in his own desire went into the centre, and would himself be God. He despised the birth of the Son and heart of God, and the soft and very lovely influence, working, and qualification thereof. He entered with his will into SELF, and meant to be a very potent and terrible Lord in the first principle, and would work in the strength of the fire, in the centre of nature; he therefore could no longer be fed from the word of the Lord, and so his light went out by the heart or Son of God departing from him; for thereby the second principle was shut up to him; and presently he became loathsome in Paradise, and was cast out with all his legions that stuck to and depended upon him.

And so he lost God, the kingdom of heaven, and all paradisical knowledge, pleasure and joy; he also presently lost the image of God, and the confirmation of the Holy Ghost; for because he despised the second principle, wherein he was an angel and image of God, all heavenly things departed from him, and he fell into the dark vale, or valley of darkness, and could no more raise his imagination up into God, but remained in the anguishes of the first four forms of the original of nature.

For he is always shut up in the first principle, (as in the eternal death,) and yet he raises himself up continually, thinking to reach the heart of God, and to domineer over it; for his bitter sting climbs up eternally in the source or root of the fire, and affords him a proud will to have all at his pleasure, but he attains nothing. His food is the source or fountain of poison, namely, the brimstone spirit: his refreshing is the eternal cold fire: he has an eternal hunger in the bitterness; an eternal thirst in the source of the fire. His climbing up is his fall, and the more he climbs up in his will the greater is his fall: as one standing upon a high clift would cast himself down into a bottomless pit, he looks still further, and he falls in further and further, and yet can find no ground.

Thus he is an eternal enemy to the heart or Son of God, and to all the holy angels, and he cannot now frame any other will in himself.

His angels or devils are of very many several sorts; for, at the time of Lucifer's creation, he stood in the kingdom of heaven in the point, locus, or place, where the Holy Ghost in the birth of the heart of God in Paradise, did open infinite and innumerable centres in the eternal birth of pure eternal nature; and therefore their quality was also manifold, and all should have been and continued angels of God, if Lucifer had not corrupted and thereby destroyed them: and so now every one in his fall continues in his own essences, excluded from the light of the second principle, which they extinguished in themselves: and so it is with the soul of man, when it rejects the light of God, and it goes out of that soul.

OF THE THIRD PRINCIPLE, OR CREATION OF THE MATERIAL WORLD, WITH THE STARS AND ELEMENTS; WHEREIN THE FIRST AND SECOND PRINCIPLE IS MORE CLEARLY UNDERSTOOD.

The eternal and indissoluble band, which is the first principle wherein the essence of all essences stands, is not easily nor in haste to be understood; therefore it is necessary that the desirous reader should the more earnestly consider himself what he is, and whence his reason, his inward senses, and thoughts do proceed, for therein he finds the similitude of God, especially if he considers and meditates what his soul is, which is an eternal, incorruptible spirit.

For if the reader be born of God in true resignation, there is no nearer way for him to come to the knowledge of the third principle, than by considering the new birth, how the soul is new born by the love of God in the light, and how it is translated out of darkness into the light by a second birth. And now every one finds by experience, that falls into the wrath of God, and whereof there are terrible examples, that the soul must endure uneasiness and torment in itself, in the birth of its own life, so long as it is in the wrath of God; and then if it be born again, there is great exulting joy arises in it; and thus there is found very clearly and plainly two principles; also God, Paradise and the kingdom of heaven.

For you find in the root of the original of the spirit of the soul, the most inimicitious, irksome source, torment, or working property, wherein the soul without the light of God is like all devils, being an enmity in itself, striving against God and goodness, and climbing up with pride in the strength of the fire, in a bitter, fierce, malicious wrathfulness against God, against heaven, against all creatures in the light of the second principle, and also against all creatures in the third principle of this world, setting up themselves alone.

Now the Scripture witnesses throughout, and the new-born man finds it so, that when the soul is new born in the light of God, then it is quite otherwise, and contrary to what it was before. It finds itself very humble, meek, courteous, and pleasant; it readily bears all manner of crosses and persecution; it turns the outward body from out of the way of the wicked; it regards no reproach, disgrace or scorn, put upon it from the devil or man; it places its confidence, refuge and love in the heart or Son of God; it is fed by the word of God, and cannot be hurt or so much as touched by the devil; for although it is in its own substance, and stands in the first principle in the indissoluble band, it is enlightened with the light of God in the Son or second principle, and the Holy Ghost (who goes forth out of the eternal birth or generation of the Father, in the light of the heart or Son of God) goes in it, and establishes it the child of God; therefore all that it does, living in the light of God, is done in the love of God; and the devil cannot see that soul, for the second principle, in which it then lives, and in which God, and the kingdom of heaven is, as also the angels and Paradise, is shut up from him, and he cannot get to it.   *   *   *   *   *
*   *   *   *   *   *   *   *

Therefore, O man, consider with thyself, where thou art; namely, on one part, [that is, thy body and outward carcass of clay, thou art a guest for awhile in this outward world, travelling in the vanity of time] under the influence of the stars, and four elements; one other part, [namely, thy soul in its own self and creaturely being, that is, in its fallen state, without the divine light or regeneration] in the dark world among the devils; and as to the third part, [namely, thy divine image and spirit of love, in the eternal light] in the divine power in heaven: that property which is master in thee, its servant thou art; prank and vapour as stately and gloriously as thou wilt in the sun's light, yet thy fountain shall be made manifest to thee.

OF PARADISE.

Moses says, that, when God had made man, he planted a garden in Eden, and there he put man, to till and keep the same; and caused all manner of fruits to grow, pleasant for the sight and good for food; and planted the tree of life also, and the tree of knowledge of good and evil in the midst.

Here lies the veil before the face of Moses, in that he had a bright shining countenance, that sinful Israel cannot look him in the face; for the man of vanity is not worthy to know what Paradise is; and albeit it be given us to know it according to the inward, hidden man, yet by this description we shall remain as dumb to the beast, but yet be sufficiently understood by our fellow scholars in the school of the great master.

Poor reason, which is gone forth with Adam out of Paradise, asks where is Paradise to be had or found? Is it far off or near? Or, when the souls go into Paradise, whither do they go? Is it in the place of this world, or without the place of this world above the stars? where is it that God dwells with the angels? and where is that desirable native country where there is no death? Being there is no sun nor stars in it, therefore it cannot be in this world, or else it would have been found long ago.

Beloved reason; one cannot lend a key to another to unlock this withal; and if any have a key, he cannot open it to another, as antichrist boasts that he has the keys of heaven and hell; it is true, a man may have the keys of both in this life time, but he cannot open with them for any body else; every one must unlock it with his own key, or else he cannot enter therein; for the Holy Ghost is the key, and when any one has that key, then he may go both in and out.

Paradise was the heavenly essentiality of the second principle. It budded in the beginning of the world through the earthly essentiality, as the eternity is in the time, and the divine power is through all things; and yet is neither comprehended or understood of any earthly thing in self-hood.

In Paradise the essence of the divine world penetrated the essence of time, as the sun penetrates the fruit upon a tree, and effectually works in it into a pleasantness, that it is lovely to look upon and good to eat; the like we are to understand of the garden of Eden.

The garden Eden was a place upon the earth where man was tempted; and the Paradise was in heaven, and yet was in the garden Eden; for as Adam before his sleep, and before his Eve was made out of him, was, as to his inward man, in heaven, and, as to the outward, upon the earth; and as the inward, holy man penetrated the outward, as a fire through heats an iron, so also the heavenly power out of the pure, eternal element penetrated the four elements, and sprang through the earth, and bare fruits, which were heavenly and earthly, and were qualified, sweetly tempered of the divine power, and the vanity in the fruit was held as it were swallowed up, as the day hides the night, and holds it captive in itself, that it is not known and manifest.

The whole world would have been a mere Paradise if Lucifer had not corrupted it, who was in the beginning of his creation an hierarch in the place of this world; but seeing God knew that Adam would fall, therefore Paradise sprang forth and budded only in one certain place, to introduce and confirm man in his obedience therein. God nevertheless saw he would depart thence, whom he would again introduce thereinto by Christ, and establish him anew in Christ to eternity in Paradise, therefore God promised to regenerate it anew in Christ, in the Spirit of Christ in the human property.

There is nothing *that is nearer you, than heaven, Paradise, and hell;* unto which of them you are inclined, and to which of them you tend or walk, to that in this life-time you are most near. *You are between both; and there is a birth between each of them. You stand* in this world *between both the gates,* and you have both the births in you. *God beckons to you in one gate,* and calls you; *the devil beckons you in the other gate* and calls you; *with whom you go, with him you enter in.* The devil has in his hand, power, honour, pleasure, and worldly joy; and the root of these is death and hell-fire; On the contrary, God has in his hand, crosses, persecution, misery, poverty, ignominy, and sorrow; and the root of these is a fire also, but in the fire there is a light, and in the light the virtue, and in the virtue the Paradise; and in the Paradise are the angels, and among the angels, joy. The gross fleshly eyes cannot behold it, because they are from the third principle, and see only by the splendour of the sun; but when the Holy Ghost comes into the soul, then he regenerates it anew in God, and then it becomes a paradisical child, who gets the key of Paradise, and that soul sees into the midst thereof.

But the gross body cannot see into it, because it belongs not to Paradise; it belongs to the earth, and must putrefy and rot, and rise in a new virtue and power in Christ, at the end of days; and then it may also be in Paradise, and not before; it must lay off the third principle, namely, this skin or covering which father Adam and mother Eve got into, and in which they supposed they should be wise by wearing all the three principles manifested on them. Oh! that they had preferred the wearing two of the principles hidden in them, and had continued in the principle of light, it had been good for us. But of this I purpose to speak hereafter when I treat about the fall.

Thus now in the essence of all essences, there are three several distinct properties, with one source or property far from one another, yet not parted asunder, but are in one another as one only essence; nevertheless the one does not comprehend the other, as in the three elements, fire, air, water; all three are in one another, but neither of them comprehend the other. And as one element generates another and yet is not of the essence, source, or property thereof; so the three principles are in one another, and one generates the other; and yet none of them all comprehends the other, nor is any of them the essence or substance of the other.

The third principle, namely, this material world, shall pass away and go into its ether, and then the shadow of all creatures remain, also of all growing things [vegetables and fruits] and of all that ever came to light; as also the shadow and figure of all words and works; and that incomprehensibly, like a nothing or shadow in respect of the light, and after the end of time there will be nothing but light and darkness; where the source or property remain in each of them as it has been from eternity, and the one shall not comprehend the other.

Yet whether God will create more after this world's time, that my spirit doth not know; for it apprehends no farther than what is in its centre wherein it lives, and in which the Paradise and the kingdom of heaven stands.

CONCERNING THE SUPERSENSUAL LIFE.*

A DIALOGUE BETWEEN MASTER AND DISCIPLE. FROM THE SIXTH BOOK OF THE WORK ENTITLED "THE WAY TO CHRIST."

1. The Disciple said to the Master: How

* Translated from the Extract in Künzel's "Drei Bücher Deutscher Prosa."

may I attain to the supersensual life, that I may see God and hear him speak?

The Master said: If thou canst raise thyself for a moment thither, where no creature dwelleth, thou shalt hear what God saith.

2. The Disciple said: Is that near or far?

The Master said: It is in thee, and if thou canst be silent and cease, for an hour, from all thy willing and brooding, thou shalt hear unspeakable words of God.

3. The Disciple said: How may I hear, if I cease from all willing and brooding?

The Master said: If thou wilt cease from all brooding and willing of thine own, then the eternal Hearing and Seeing and Speaking shall be revealed in thee, and shall discern God through thee. Thine own hearing and willing and seeing hinders thee, that thou canst not see nor hear God.

4. The Disciple said: Wherewith shall I hear and see God, seeing he is above nature and creature?

The Master said: If thou keepest silence, thou art what God was before nature and the creature, and out of which he made thy nature and creature. Then shalt thou hear and see with that wherewith God, in thee, saw and heard, before thine own willing and seeing and hearing did begin.

5. The Disciple said: What doth hinder me that I cannot attain thereunto?

The Master said: Thine own willing and hearing and seeing, and because thou dost strive against that whence thou hast proceeded. With thine own will thou separatest thyself from God's willing, and with thine own seeing thou seest only in thy willing. And thy willing stoppeth thine hearing with the obstinate concupiscence of earthly, natural things, and leadeth thee into a pit, and overshadoweth thee with that which thou desirest, so that thou canst not attain to the supernatural, supersensual.

6. The Disciple said: Seeing I am in nature, how can I pass through nature into the supersensual deep, without destroying nature?

The Master said: To that end three things are requisite. The first is, that thou shouldst surrender thy will unto God and let thyself down into the deeps of his mercy. The second is, that thou shouldst hate thine own will, and not do that whereunto thy will impelleth thee. The third is, that thou shouldst bring thyself into subjection to the Cross, that thou mayest be able to bear the assaults of nature and creature. If thou doest this, God will in-speak into thee, and will lead thy passive will into himself,— into the supernatural deep, and thou shalt hear what the Lord speaketh in thee.

7. The Disciple said: It were necessary that I should quit the world and my life, in order to do this.

The Master said: If thou leave the world, thou wilt come into that whereof the world is made. And if thou losest thy life, and comest into impotence of thine own faculty, then shall thy life be in that, for the sake of which thou didst leave thy life,—that is in God, whence it came into the body.

8. The Disciple said: God has created man in the life of nature, that he may have dominion over all creatures upon the earth, and be lord of everything in this world. Therefore, surely, he ought to possess it for his own.

The Master said: If, in the outward alone, thou governest all animals, then thou art with thy will and thy government according to the manner of beasts, and exercisest only a symbolical and perishable dominion, and bringest thy desire into the beastly *Essence* wherewith thou wilt become infected and entangled, and acquire the nature of a beast. But if thou hast left the symbolical way, thou shalt stand in the super-symbolical and shalt reign over all creatures, in the ground out of which they were created. And then nothing upon earth shall harm thee, for thou wilt have relations with all things, and nothing will be foreign from thee.

CONCERNING THE BLESSING OF GOD IN THE GOODS OF THIS WORLD.*

FROM THE WORK ENTITLED "THE THREEFOLD LIFE OF MAN."

MAN has free permission to disport himself, on the earth, in whatsoever employment he will. Do what he will, everything stands in the miraculous power of God. A swineherd is as dear to him as a Doctor, so he be pious and confide purely in God's will. The simple is as useful to him as the wise. For with the wise man he rules, and with the simple he builds. Both are equally instruments of his wondrous deeds. Each has his calling wherein he passeth his time; and all are equal before him. * * *
* * * As the flowers of the earth do not envy one another, although one is more beautiful and more powerful than another, but all, in a friendly manner, stand side by side, and each rejoices in the other's virtue;—and, as a physician mingles together various kinds of herbs of which each gives forth its power and its virtue and all minister unto the sick;—so, likewise, do we all please God, as many of us as enter into his will. We all stand together in his field. And as thorns and thistles spring forth from the ground and choke and devour many a good herb and flower; so, likewise, is the godless who trusteth not in God, but buildeth upon himself, and thinketh: "I have my God in my box, I will board and leave great treasures to my children, that they also may sit in the place of mine honour; that is the true way;"—and therewith rendeth many a heart that it also waxeth careless and thinketh that is the right way to happiness; that a man possess riches, and power and honour, he hath happiness. Yet, if we

---

* From the above-mentioned work of Künzel.

consider it, it happeneth to one as to another; and the poor soul is none the less lost. For the rich man's dainties taste no better to him than the hungry man's morsel of bread. Everywhere there is care, grief, fear, sickness, and, at last, death. It is all a fighting with shadows, in this world. The mighty sitteth in the dominion of the spirit of this world, and he that feareth God sitteth in the dominion of divine power and wisdom. The dominion of this world endeth with the body, but the dominion in the Spirit of God endureth forever.

OF TRUE RESIGNATION.*

If we would inherit the filiation, we must also put on the new man, which can inherit the filiation, which is like the Deity. God will have no sinner in heaven, but such as are born anew, and become children, who have put on heaven.

A man must wrestle so long, until the dark centre that is shut up so close, break open, and the spark in the centre kindle, and from thence immediately the noble lily, twig and branch, sprouts, as from the divine grain of mustard-seed, as Christ says. A man must pray earnestly, with great humility, and for a while become a fool in his own reason, and see himself as void of understanding thereon, until Christ be formed in this new incarnation.

And then when Christ is born, *Herod* is ready to kill the child; which he seeks to do outwardly by persecutions, and inwardly by temptations, to try whether this lily branch will be strong enough to destroy the kingdom of the Devil, which is made manifest in the flesh.

Then the destroyer of the serpent is brought into the wilderness, after he is baptized with the Holy Spirit, and tempted and tried whether he will continue in resignation in the will of God: he must stand so fast, that if need require, he would leave all earthly things, and even the outward life, to be a child of God.

No temporal honor must be preferred before the filiation, but he must with his will leave and forsake it all, and not account it his own, but esteem himself as a servant in it only, in obedience to his master; he must leave all worldly property. We do not mean that he may not have, or possess anything; but his heart must forsake it, and not bring his will into it, nor count it his own; if he sets his heart upon it, he has no power to serve them that stand in need, with it.

Self serves only that which is temporary; but resignation has rule over all that is under

---

* From " the Way to Christ.'

it. Self must do what the Devil will have it to do in fleshly voluptuousness and pride of life; but resignation treads it under the feet of the mind. Self despises that which is lowly and simple; but resignation sits down with the lowly in the dust: it says, I will be simple in myself, and understand nothing, lest my understanding should exalt itself, and sin. I will lie down in the courts of my God, at his feet, that I may serve the Lord in that which he commands me. I will know nothing of myself that the commandment of the Lord may lead and guide me, and that I may only do what God doth through me, and will have done by me: I will sleep until the Lord awaken me with his spirit; and if he will not, then will I cry out eternally in him in silence, and wait his commands.

Beloved Brethren, men boast much now-a-days of Faith, but where is that faith? The modern faith is but the history. Where is that child that believes that Jesus is born? If that child were in being, and did believe that Jesus is born, it would also draw near to the sweet child Jesus, and receive him, and nurse him.

Alas! the faith now-a-days is but historical, and a mere knowledge of the story that the Jews killed him, that he left this world, that he is not king on earth in the animal man, but that men may do as they list, and need not die from sin, and their evil lusts; all this the wicked child self-rejoices in, that it may fatten the Devil by living deliciously.

This shows that true faith was never weaker since Christ's time than it now is; when, nevertheless, the world cries aloud, and says, we have found the true faith, and contend about a child, so that there was never worse contention since men were on earth.

If thou have that new-born child which was lost and is found again, then let it be seen in power and virtue, and let us openly see the sweet child Jesus brought forth by thee, and that thou art his nurse; if not, then the children in Christ will say, thou hast found nothing but the history, namely, the cradle of the child.

Beloved Brethren, this is a time of seeking and of finding: it is a time of earnestness; whom it touches, it touches home: he that watches shall hear and see it; but he that sleeps in sin, and says in the fat days of his voluptuousness, all is peace and quiet, we hear no sound from the Lord; he shall be blind. But the voice of the Lord has sounded in all the ends of the earth, and in the trouble that is upon the face of the earth a smoke arises, and in the midst of the smoke there is a great brightness in the divine light that is in the children of God. Hallelujah. Amen. Shout unto the Lord in Sion, for all mountains and hills are full of his glory: he flourishes like a green branch, and who shall hinder it?

ABRAHAM A SANCTA CLARA.

Born 1642. Died 1709.

This celebrated ecclesiastic—the most popular preacher of his day, was descended from noble ancestors, and bore the family name of *Ulrich Megerle*. His parents, Jacob and Verona Megerle, resided at *Krähenhennstetten*, a village near the city of Möskirch, in Suabia. He distinguished himself in early youth by his industry and talents, and an ardent thirst for knowledge. He received a classical education at the Latin schools at Möskirch, Ingolstadt and Salzburg. In his eighteenth year he entered the order of the barefooted Augustine monks, at Mariabrunn, and studied philosophy and theology in a convent of that order at Vienna. Two years later, having been consecrated priest and made doctor of theology, he went as holiday-preacher to the convent of Taxa, near Dachau, in Bavaria. From there he returned to Vienna, where he soon acquired an extended fame by his popular eloquence. In 1669 he was made imperial court-preacher by Leopold I., an office which he filled with general acceptance for twenty years. During this time he rose from grade to grade in his order, and became successively provincial procurator, lector, pater spiritualis, prior and definitor of his province. As prior, he attended the meeting of the general chapter of his order, in Rome, 1689, preached there several times with great applause, and was presented by pope Innocent XI. with a consecrated cross.

As definitor, he contributed greatly to the improvement of several of the convents of his order. He died at Vienna, December 1st, 1709, in the sixty-eighth year of his age.

As a pulpit-orator, Pater Abraham a Sancta Clara was distinguished by a broad humor, in which he resembles some of his contemporaries in the English and Scottish churches. By Protestants he was, for a long time, considered as a mere clerical zany, or spiritual buffoon. But he glowed with a genuine enthusiasm for virtue and religion, was deeply convinced of the truth of what he taught, and possessed a profound knowledge of man and the world, sound practical morality, a complete mastery of his native language, great affluence of imagination, a brilliant wit, an animated delivery, and an excoriating satire. On the other hand, his characteristic faults were utter want of taste, a perpetual striving after effect, delight in puns and antitheses, a fondness for the *bizarre*, and a style which, though suited to his peculiar manner, is altogether beneath the dignity of his subject. He was an orator for the people in the full sense of the word, and although beyond his age in many respects, conformed himself to the tastes and habits of the times. He was devoted to his order, which he served with great fidelity and beneficent effect during the whole of his active life.

ON ENVY.

FROM A WORK ENTITLED "JUDAS THE ARCH VILLAIN."

* * * * *

I have always heard indeed that:
As the bell is, so it dingeth,
As the singer, so he singeth,
As the spawn is, so the fish,
As the cook, so is the dish.
As the cobbler, the shoe will look,
As the writer, so the book.
As the leech is, so the salve,
As the cow, so is the calf.
As the teacher, so the rede,
As the pasture, so the feed.
As the soil is, so the crop,
As the dancer, so the hop.
As the tree is, so the pear,
As the ma'am, the maidens are.
As the soldier, so the battle,
As the herdsman, so the cattle.
As the lord, the servants be,
As the parent, the progeny.

I have always heard, have always read, have always written, have always said that these things are so; but now I perceive that not always as the parents are, so is the progeny. Adam a good father; Cain, his son, an arch villain; Noah, the father, a saint; Ham, the son, a scamp; Abraham, the father, God-blessed;

Ishmael, the son, God-cursed; Isaac, the father, an angel; Esau, his son, a devil; Jacob, the father, a lamb; Reuben, the son, a ram; David, the father, a friend of God; Absalom, the son, a foe of God, &c. Yea, I know and I can show a lady before whose beauty Helena of Greece must hide herself, a lady before whose white face lilies must blush with shame, a lady before whose grace of form Spring comes too late with its decorations, a lady whose countenance is more sun-bright than the sun, before whose loveliness the morning-red pales with wonder; and yet this beautiful and elect lady has a daughter who is to view, like a heap of impurity; for she is savage as a dung-heap, black as a coal-heap, inopportune as a funeral-heap, stiff-necked as a stone-heap, unclean as an ant-heap, ugly as a dirt-heap, yea as the Devil himself. This most beautiful lady is Virtue, Honour, Science—everything good; but the daughter which she produces is cursed Envy. In the island of Malta there are no serpents, in Sardinia there are no wolves, in Germany there are no crocodiles, in Tuscany there are no ravens, in Hellespontus there are no dogs, in Iceland there is nothing poisonous, but in the whole world there is not a place where there is no envy.

Daniel lived at court, and was quite a distinguished lord at court; nay he rose so high that he was all-potent with King Darius, and that prince never saw better than when Daniel was the apple of his eye; and well shall it be with every monarch who has such a right hand as was the faithful Daniel. Nevertheless, this pious minister experienced, at last, a change in his king, from the best wine into the sharpest vinegar. For he commanded by an inhuman decree that Daniel should be cast into the den of lions, that those voracious animals might be gorged with so stately a crumb. But the meat was too good for such guests. Now I read it in thy forehead, how thou art tickled with curiosity to know the crime and misdeed of Daniel. Perhaps he was untrue to his king? though truth, at court, is generally quite genuine and almost brand-new, because it is so seldom used. Perhaps he suffered himself to be bribed with *denarii*, and afterwards used spadilles against his own *king*,* whereby he lost his game? Perhaps he betrayed the designs and ripe resolves of the king to the opposite party, and so blabbed blameably out of school? Perhaps he divided the king's rents and moneys, as the wolf divided the sheep? The wolf, namely, divided six sheep with the shepherd, in this way: The first is mine, the second ought to be yours; but he took it likewise to himself; the third is mine again, the fourth, in strict justice, should be yours; but he took that also, &c.; so that at last nothing was left to the shepherd. Perhaps Daniel had been sleepy in his service at court, and made his appearance only on occasions when some offices had become vacant? Perhaps Daniel had shown a friendly rudeness or a rude friendliness to one or the other of the court-dames? Nothing of the kind! Not at all! Daniel was a right, upright, well-disposed, just, intelligent, conscientious minister at court; not a guilty but a guiltless, not a blameable but a blameless servant, and a prophet besides, and an interpreter of dreams into the bargain, and a chronicler on the top of that. If so, what was it then that plunged him into the tyrannous lions-den? Ask not long! A court-dog bit him, a court-cat scratched him, a court-arrow pierced him. He burned his mouth with a court-soup, he knocked his head against a court-door. Understand me right; it was envy among the ministers and courtiers at court that caused him to fall. So it happened to Henry, Count of Holstein, at the court of Edward III., king of England. So it happened to Belisarius, the great war-chief, at the court of the emperor Justinian. So it happened to Aristides, to Scipio, to Themistocles, to Tully, to Epaminondas, to Socrates, to Pompey, to Iphicrates, to Conon, to Chabrias. But those are all foreign names. So it happened to many Ferdinands, Henrys, Rudolphs, Casimirs, Philips, Conrads, Wolfgangs, &c., whom cursed envy plunged into misery. O, envy! O, envy! * * * * * * *

Goodly brothers had Joseph. Gen. 37. If these be brothers, then sloe-bushes may be called grape-vines. If these be brothers, then the wolf may be called the burgomaster of the sheep Not brothers were they, but brooders of all evil. When the honest youth, Joseph, out of brotherly love and sincerity, told them his dream,—of which it might be easily surmised that it was no empty vision but a prophecy of his future good fortune,—they straightway grew pale at the relation. What! said they, thou young pigeon-bill! wilt thou be a king, and shall thy fortune mount so high that we shall bow the knee to thee and serve thee? Nay, the Devil bend thy neck, arrogant booby! &c. They were so embittered against him that they could not look upon him. Yea they were driven so far by damned envy, that they resolved to throttle this their brother. But let us reason together a little, ye shepherds! (although you ought more properly to have been swine-herds.) Hear me. Either it is true that your brother is to be king, or it is not true. If it be not true, then laugh at the empty dream, and rather banter this young A. B. C.-smith with brotherly jests. Put a shepherd's staff in his hand instead of a sceptre, and say laughingly, God save your majesty! &c. But if it is true that he is to be king, then you ought not to be angry with him on that account, but rather to rejoice, and to say: So then Joseph is to be a king! That is the greatest honour for us, and everlasting renown for our whole family. Well, we shall no longer wear our dirty shepherds' knapsacks, but every one of us will be a gentleman, and how good it will seem when we are called, my lord! Then, of

---

* An allusion to the game of quadrille, or ombre. Tr.

a surety, brother Reuben will be made chief master of ceremonies; then, certainly, brother Zebulon will have the situation of president of the chamber; brother Issachar cannot fail to become chief of the kitchen department; he loves a good bit, anyhow. Brother Simeon, without doubt, will be lord chamberlain, for he knows how to sport the compliments. Think on me! brother Ashur will be master of the chase. How he will hunt! Then we will have a different state of things. Now we must stuff our hungry stomachs with sour turnips; then they will serve up to us other bits. O, God grant that our brother may be a king! That is the kind of talk that Joseph's brothers should have held. But cursed envy perverted their understanding, disordered their reason, and they would rather suffer evil days and laborious days than to see Joseph exalted to royal dignity. O, hellish envy! The envious man is contented with his own poverty if he only sees that his neighbour is not rich. The envious man finds satisfaction in his own misery if he only notes that it is not well with his neighbour. The envious man complains not of his want of understanding and his ignorance if he only perceives that his neighbour also hath not much faculty. The envious man is willing to remain abject if he only finds that his neighbour does not rise. The envious man laments not his mis-shape and his scarecrow face if he only knows that his neighbour is not fair. O, cursed envy! thou sippest and suckest out of gall, honey, and out of honey, gall; for thy neighbour's good is to thee an evil, and thy neighbour's evil is to thee a good. O! O! O! * * * *
* * * *

The envious are, how are they? They are like muck-chafers, which from the fairest roses suck only poison, not honey; so the envious seek in their object only what is defective, the good they pass over in silence. The envious are, how are they? They are like files or rasps, which devour, gnaw, bite and tear other things, but destroy themselves also thereby. So the envious seek to injure their neighbour and waste the health of their own body and soul. The envious are, how are they? They are like wells, which are generally cool when the weather is warm, and generally warm when the weather, especially in winter, is cold; so is it well with the envious when it is ill with others, and ill with them when it is well with others. The envious are, how are they? They are like the thunderbolt which, for the most part, strikes only lofty edifices, not those which are low; so the envious hate those whom God has exalted. The envious are, how are they? They are like the quails. Those evil birds sigh when the sun rises; so the envious sigh and are pained when they see their neighbours rise, and grow in riches and honour. The envious are, how are they? They are like a tree beneath which young trees are growing, but the great tree oppresses them with its branches, for it cannot bear that other trees shall grow to equal it. So the envious labour diligently to prevent that any one should rise from low to high estate. The envious are, how are they? They are like men sick of a fever, to whom sweet food tastes bitter. Even so nothing more embitters the envious than when they perceive that their neighbour enjoys good and sweet fortune. The envious are, how are they? They are like flies, which usually plague men there where they are sore or wounded. So the envious seek only that in their neighbour which is blameworthy; what is virtuous and commendable they freely pass over in silence. The envious are, how are they? They are like buckets in a well; when one goes down the other mounts, when one goes up the other descends. So it is well with the envious, and he prospers greatly when he sees his neighbour fall, and when his neighbour mounts, the envious is cast down thereby.

O, thou cursed vice! Thou art a maggot of the soul; further yet, thou art an imposthume of the heart; further yet, thou art a pest of the five senses; further yet, thou art a poison of the limbs; further yet, thou art a dangerous fever of the blood; further yet, thou art a giddiness of the brain; further yet, thou art a darkness of the understanding; further yet, thou art a hangman and torturer and tyrant of the human body. Other vices have a little pleasure and imaginary delight. The wooing of Bathsheba sugared the heart of David somewhat. When Herod shared the board and bed of his brother's wife, he enjoyed a momentary satisfaction. When Nebuchadnezzar set up for a god, and, in his arrogance and pride, suffered himself to be worshipped; the reputation of the thing tickled him a little. When the rich man gorged himself every day, his daily gormandizing, no doubt, gave him pleasure. When Achan made too long fingers and stumbled over the seventh[*] commandment, he enjoyed becoming rich without labour. * * In short, all other vices have on them and in them and with them a honey, although in small weight, but the envious finds nothing but sorrows. * * * * *

An envious man may eat what he will and how he will and when he will and as much as he will and whence he will, he will nevertheless remain dog-meagre, because everything, with him, is changed into poison. * * * Therefore God the Lord himself asked Cain, after he had washed his hands in his brother's blood : "*Quare concidit facies tua?*" "Cain, why hath thy countenance fallen?" The fellow was as lean as a ramrod; but there was no other cause for it than damned envy, which is a poison to human health.

* * * * * *

Of what country the prodigal son was, is not precisely known; but I believe he was an Irish-

---

[*] The eighth, according to the division of most Protestant sects. Tr.

ABRAHAM A SANCTA CLARA.

man.* What his name was, is not generally understood; but I believe it was *Malefacius.* From what place he took his title (seeing he was a nobleman), has not yet been discovered; but I believe it was *Maidsberg* or *Womenham.* What was the device in his coat of arms, no one has described; but I believe it was a sow's stomach in a field *verd.*

This chap travelled with well-larded purse through various countries and provinces, and returned no better but rather worse. So it often happens still, that many a noble youth has his travels changed to travails. Not seldom also, he goes forth a good German and returns a bad *Herman.*† What honour or credit is it to the noble river Danube that it travels through different lands, through Suabia, Bavaria, Austria, Hungary, and at last unites with a sow?‡ The pious Jacob saw, in his journey, a ladder to heaven; but alas! many of our Quality find, in their journeys, a ladder into hell. If, nowadays, a man travel not, he is called a Jack-in-the-corner and one who has set up his rest behind the stove. But tell me, dear half-Germans! (for whole Germans ye have long ceased to be.) Is it not true? Ye send your sons out that they may learn strange vices at great cost in stranger-lands, when, with far less expense, they might be acquiring virtues at home. They return with no more point to them than they went out, except that they bring home some new fashion of *point*-lace. They return no more gallant, unless it be that gallant comes from the French *galant.* They return more splendidly clad, but good habits were better than to be finely habited. New-fashioned hats, new-fashioned periwigs, new-fashioned collars, new-fashioned coats, new-fashioned breeches, new-fashioned hose, new-fashioned shoes, new-fashioned ribbons, new-fashioned buttons, — also new-fashioned consciences creep into our beloved Germany through your travels. Your fool's-frocks change too with every moon; and soon the tailors will have to establish a university and take Doctors' degrees, and afterwards bear the title of Right-reverend Doctors of fashion.

If I had all the new fashions of coats for four and twenty years, I would almost make a curtain before the sun with them, so that men should go about with lanterns in the day-time. At least, I would undertake to hide all Turkey with them, so that the Constantinopolitans should think their Mahomed was playing blind-the-cat with them. An old witch, at the request of king Saul, called the prophet Samuel from the dead, that he might know the result of his arms.

It will soon come to pass, that people will want to call from the dead the identical tailor and master who made the beautiful Esther's garment, when she was so well-pleasing in the eyes of Ahasuerus. * * * * *
* * * So the prodigal son learned but little good in foreign lands. His doing was wooing; his thinking was drinking; his Latin was "*Proficiat,*"* his Italian, *Brindisi,* his Bohemian, *Sasdravi,* his German, *Gesegnet's Gott.** In one word, he was a goodly fellow always mellow, a vagrant, a *bacchant,* an *amant,* a *turbant,* a *distillant,* &c. Now he had wasted his substance in foreign provinces and torn his conscience to tatters as well as his clothes. He might, with truth, have said to his father what the brothers of Joseph said, without truth, to Jacob when they showed him the bloody coat, "*fera pessima,*" &c., "an evil beast hath devoured him." An evil beast devoured the prodigal son; an evil beast, the golden eagle, an evil beast, the golden griffin, an evil beast, the golden buck, an evil beast, the golden bear. These tavern-beasts reduced the youngster to that condition that his breeches were as transparent as a fisherman's net, his stomach shrunk together like an empty bladder, and the mirror of his misery was to be seen on the sleeve of his dirty doublet, &c. And now when the scamp had got sick of the swine-diet, more wholesome thoughts came into his mind and he would go straight home to his old father and seek a favourable hearing at his feet; in which he succeeded according to his wish. And his own father fell quite lovingly on the neck of the bad *vocativo,* for which a rope would have been fitter. Yea, he was introduced with special joy and jubilee into the paternal dwelling, sudden preparations were made for a feast, kitchen and cellar were put in requisition, and the best and fattest calf must be killed in a hurry and cooked and roasted. Away with the rags and tatters! and hurrah! for the velvet coat and the prinked up hat and a gold ring! Bring on your fiddlers! *allegro!*

Meanwhile, the other brother comes home and hears from afar a fiddling, and a fifing, and a scraping, and a dancing, and a hopping, and a shouting, &c. Holloa! he says, what's that? The devil and his grand-mother! What's to pay now? Surely my sister is not having a wedding! I heard nothing about any bride when I went out this morning. While he hovers in these thoughts, some one reaches him a glass of wine out of the window and the house-servant runs toward him with the tidings that his brother, who fared so ill in foreign parts, was come home, and he must come in immediately and sit down to a roast of veal. At this he became entirely pale with sheer envy, and, while they waited on his brother in that style, he sat down before the door of the house and bit his nails,

---

* An untranslateable pun. *Irrländer,* literally, err-lander, one who wanders from country to country, a vagabond. Tr.

† The translator is in doubt as to the meaning of this quip. Perhaps Herman stands for the Spanish *Hermano;* and the meaning is—a bad brother, a loose companion.

‡ The river Save, called in German *Sau,* which is the German for sow. This river joins the Danube between Semlin and Belgrade. Tr.

* *Proficiat* or *prosit,* a salutation at drinking, equivalent to "Your health." Tr.

and gnashed his teeth, and scratched his head, and turned up his nose, and sighed from his heart, and fasted and tormented himself so with his envy, that he had well nigh been struck with apoplexy. O fool! How much better would it have been, had the *gispus* gone in and welcomed his brother home! And if he had given him an old felt, it would have done no harm, seeing he had brought no hat with him. And if he had sat down to table with him and helped to make way with the roasted calf, and pledged him heartily in a few healths, and hopped about to the voice of the clear-sounding horns, and worn through a pair of shoe-soles and half another with dancing, it would have been much better and God would not have been so much offended thereat. But with his fasting and his envy, which tormented him more than the fiery serpents did the people of Israel, he deserved hell. In other cases affliction is a road to heavenly courts, and suffering a way to eternal joys; and pains are the outriders of eternal merriment; but the torments of the envious fool are the earnest-money of eternal damnation. * * * * * *
* * * * * * * *

JUSTUS MÖSER.

Born 1720. Died 1794.

THE following account of this genial writer and true-hearted man, as well as the first specimen from his writings, is from Mrs. Austin's German Prose Writers. The other translations are furnished by a friend.

The writings of Möser are little known in this country, yet they are distinguished by a vigorous, homely good sense, a freedom from all affectation, a knowledge of the condition of the laboring classes, and a zeal for their improvement and happiness, which obtained for him, not unjustly, the name of the Franklin of Germany. He was born in 1720, at Osnabrück, where his father filled high offices under the government. He early gave proofs of great talents, which were judiciously cultivated by his mother. He studied law at Jena and Göttingen; but the open book of human life was his favorite and most important study. As a man of business, he was the able and zealous defender of oppressed innocence, and resisted alone the arbitrary will of the then ruler of Osnabrück. The confidence of his countrymen raised him, in 1747, to the honorable post of "Advocatus Patriæ," and the Landstande appointed him Secretary and Syndic of the Order of Knights. His noble character was put to the test during the troubles of the Seven years' War, and secured him the respect of Duke Ferdinand of Brunswick. He was employed for eight months in London in transacting the affairs of the troops subsidized by England, and his residence in that country added much to his practical experience. He was for twenty years (during the minority of the English prince, who, in 1761, was acknowledged protestant bishop and sovereign of Osnabrück), virtually, though not nominally, chief counsellor of the regent. Nothing but Möser's great talents, knowledge of business, and industry, united to his unswerving integrity, fairness and disinterestedness, would have enabled him to steer his course, free from all suspicion or reproach, between the conflicting interests of the sovereign and the states, both of whom he served. For six years he was justiciary of the criminal court of Osnabrück; and on his resignation, was appointed privy referendary of the government, which post he held till his death, January 8th, 1794.

Möser's objects in writing were far higher than the gratification of the vanity, or the acquisition of the fame, of an author; yet there is no writer whose works have a more enduring reputation. They may serve as a model for all who are inspired with the noble desire of rendering intelligible to the people their own true interests;—the highest office in which genius, wit, learning, or eloquence, can ever be employed.

Gifted in an eminent degree with a sound mind in a sound body, he devoted both to the service of his country and of mankind, and he closed a happy, useful, and honorable life at the age of 74, "having had much to rejoice, little to sadden, and nothing to offend him," as he himself thankfully acknowledged. There is a beautiful passage in Goethe's life,* of which I subjoin an abridged translation.

"The little essays or papers of this admirable man, relating to matters of social and political interest, had been printed some years before in the Osnabrück newspaper, and had been pointed out to me by Herder, who suffered nothing of merit to pass unobserved. Möser's daughter was now occupied in collecting them.

"They were all conceived in one spirit, and are all distinguished for their intimate knowledge of the condition of the middle and lower classes, and indeed of the whole fabric of society. The author, with a perfect freedom from prejudice, analyzes the relations of the several classes to each other, and also those existing between the several towns and villages of the country. The public revenues and expenditure, the advantages and disadvantages of the various branches of industry, are brought distinctly before us, and old times compared and contrasted with new.

---

* Dichtung und Wahrheit, book XIII.

"The internal condition of Osnabrück, and its relation to other countries, particularly England, are clearly stated, and practical consequences deduced. Though he calls them 'Patriotic Fantasies,' their contents are in fact true and practicable.

"And as the whole structure of society rests on the basis of family, he devotes his especial attention to that. He treats, seriously or sportively, of the changes in manners and habits, dress, diet, domestic life, and education. It would be necessary to make an inventory of every incident of social life, if we would exhaust the subjects which he handles. And how inimitable is the handling! It is a thorough man of business speaking to the people in a weekly paper, in order to render intelligible to all the intentions and projects of a wise and benevolent government; by no means in a merely didactic style, but in a variety of forms, which we might almost call poetical, and which certainly deserve to be called rhetorical, in the best sense of the word. He is always master of his subject, and has the art of giving a lively color to the most serious; sometimes assuming one mask, sometimes another, sometimes speaking in his own person, with a gay and tempered irony; vigorous and true, sometimes even rough and almost coarse, but in every case so appropriate, that it is impossible not to admire the talents, the good sense, the facility, lightness, taste and originality of the writer. In the choice of his subjects, his profound knowledge of them, enlarged views, skilful and appropriate handling, deep and yet gay humor, I can compare him to none but Franklin."

Nothing can be added to this just and beautiful description of Möser's "Patriotische Fantasien." It remains only to say, that his "History of Osnabrück," is equally remarkable for the accurate antiquarian knowledge it exhibits. He left some other works, among which is a defence of the German language and literature, in answer to Frederic the Great.

LETTER

FROM AN OLD MARRIED WOMAN TO A SENSITIVE YOUNG LADY.

You do your husband injustice, dear child, if you think he loves you less than formerly. He is a man of an ardent, active temper, who loves labour and exertion, and finds his pleasure in them; and as long as his love for you furnished him with labour and exertion he was completely absorbed in it. But this has, of course, ceased; your reciprocal position, — but by no means his love, as you imagine,—has changed.

A love which seeks to conquer, and a love which has conquered, are two totally different passions. The one puts on the stretch all the virtues of the hero; it excites in him fear, hope, desire; it leads him from triumph to triumph, and makes him think every foot of ground that he gains, a kingdom. Hence it keeps alive and fosters all the active powers of the man who abandons himself to it. The happy husband cannot appear like the lover; he has not like him to fear, to hope, and to desire; he has no longer that charming toil, with all its triumphs, which he had before, nor can that which he has already won be a conquest.

You have only, my dear child, to attend to this most natural and inevitable difference, and you will see in the whole conduct of your husband, who now finds more pleasure in business than in your smiles, nothing to offend you. You wish—do you not?—that he would still sit with you alone on the mossy bank in front of the grotto, as he used to do, look in your blue eyes, and kneel to kiss your pretty hand. You wish that he would paint to you, in livelier colours than ever, those delights of love which lovers know how to describe with so much art and passion; that he would lead your imagination from one rapture to another. My wishes, at least for the first year after I married my husband, went to nothing short of this. But it will not do;—the best husband is also the most useful and active member of society; and when love no longer demands toil and trouble,—when every triumph is a mere repetition of the last,— when success has lost something of its value along with its novelty,—the taste for activity no longer finds its appropriate food, and turns to fresh objects of pursuit. The necessity for occupation and for progress is of the very essence of our souls; and if our husbands are guided by reason in the choice of occupation, we ought not to pout because they do not sit with us so often as formerly by the silver brook or under the beech tree. At first I too found it hard to endure the change. But my husband talked to me about it with perfect frankness and sincerity. "The joy with which you receive me," said he, "does not conceal your vexation, and your saddened eye tries in vain to assume a cheerful look; I see what you want,—that I would sit as I used to do on the mossy bank, hang on all your steps, and live on your breath; but this is impossible. I would bring you down from the top of the church steeple on a rope ladder, at the peril of my life, if I could obtain you in no other way; but now, as I have you fast in my arms, as all dangers are passed and all obstacles overcome, my passion can no longer find satisfaction in that way. What has once been sacrificed to my self-love, ceases to be a sacrifice. The spirit of invention, discovery, and conquest, inherent in man, demands a new career. Before I obtained you I used all the virtues I possessed as steps by which to reach you; but now, as I have you, I place you at the top of them, and you are the highest step from which I now hope to ascend higher."

Little as I relished the notion of the church tower, or the honour of serving as the highest step under my husband's feet, time and reflection on the course of human affairs convinced me that the thing could not be otherwise. I therefore turned my active mind, which would perhaps in time have been tired of the mossy bank, to the domestic business which came within my department; and when we had both been busy and bustling in our several ways, and could tell each other in the evening what we had been doing, he in the fields, and I in the house or the garden, we were often more happy and contented than the most loving couple in the world.

And, what is best of all, this pleasure has not left us after thirty years of marriage. We talk with as much animation as ever of our domestic affairs; I have learned to know all my husband's tastes, and I relate to him whatever I think likely to please him out of journals, whether political or literary; I recommend books to him, and lay them before him; I carry on the correspondence with our married children, and often delight him with good news of them and our little grandchildren. As to his accounts, I understand them as well as he, and make them easier to him by having mine of all the yearly outlay which passes through my hands, ready and in order; if necessary, I can send in a statement to the treasury chamber, and my hand makes as good a figure in our cash-book as his; we are accustomed to the same order, we know the spirit of all our affairs and duties, and we have one aim and one rule in all our undertakings.

This would never have been the case if we had played the part of tender lovers after marriage as well as before, and had exhausted our energies in asseverations of mutual love. We should perhaps have regarded each other with ennui, and have soon found the grotto too damp, the evening air too cool, the noontide too hot, the morning fatiguing. We should have longed for visitors, who when they came would not have been amused, and would have impatiently awaited the hour of departure, or, if we went to them, would have wished us away. Spoiled by effeminate trifling, we should have wanted to continue to trifle, and to share in pleasures we could not enjoy; or have been compelled to find refuge at the card-table,—the last place at which the old can figure with the young.

Do you wish not to fall into this state, my dear child? Follow my example, and do not torment yourself and your excellent husband with unreasonable exactions. Don't think, however, that I have entirely renounced the pleasure of seeing mine at my feet. Opportunities for this present themselves far more frequently to those who do not seek, but seem to avoid them, than to those who allow themselves to be found on the mossy bank at all times, and as often as it pleases their lord and master.

I still sometimes sing to my little grandchildren, when they come to see me, a song which, in the days when his love had still to contend with all sorts of obstacles, used to throw him into raptures; and when the little ones cry, "Ancora! ancora! grandmamma," his eyes fill with tears of joy. I asked him once whether he would not now think it too dangerous to bring me down a rope-ladder from the top of the church steeple, upon which he called out as vehemently as the children, "O, ancora! grandmamma, ancora!"

P. S.—One thing, my dear child, I forgot. It seems to me that you trust too entirely to your good cause and your good heart, (perhaps, too, a little to your blue eyes,) and do not deign to try to attract your husband anew. I fancy you are, at home, just as you were a week ago, in society, at our excellent G——'s, where I found you as stiff and silent as if you had met only to tire each other to death. Did you not observe how soon I set the whole company in motion? This was merely by a few words addressed to each, on the subject I thought most agreeable or most flattering to him. After a time the others began to feel more happy and at their ease, and we parted in high spirits and good humour.

What I did there, I do daily at home. I try to make myself and all around me agreeable. It will not do to leave a man to himself till he comes to you, to take no pains to attract him, or to appear before him with a long face. But it is not so difficult as you think, dear child, to behave to a husband so that he shall remain forever in some measure a lover. I am an old woman, but you can still do what you like; a word from you at the right time will not fail of its effect. What need have you to play the suffering virtue? The tear of a loving girl, says an old book, is like a dew-drop on the rose; but that on the cheek of a wife is a drop of poison to her husband. Try to appear cheerful and contented, and your husband will be so; and when you have made him happy, you will become so, not in appearance, but in reality.

The skill required is not so great. Nothing flatters a man so much as the happiness of his wife; he is always proud of himself as the source of it. As soon as you are cheerful, you will be lively and alert, and every moment will afford you an opportunity of letting fall an agreeable word. Your education, which gives you an immense advantage, will greatly assist you; and your sensibility will become the noblest gift that nature has bestowed on you, when it shows itself in affectionate assiduity, and stamps on every action a soft, kind, and tender character, instead of wasting itself in secret repinings.

HOW TO ATTAIN TO AN ADEQUATE EXPRESSION OF OUR IDEAS.

Your complaint, dearest friend, that you can seldom satisfy yourself perfectly, in expression and execution, when you attempt to impart weighty and interesting truth, may, likely enough, be well founded; but I am not yet convinced, that this arises from any deficiency of language. All words, especially dead words on paper, to which indeed the physiognomy is wanting, to assist expression, are but very imperfect signs of our thoughts and feelings, and we are often more affected by another's silence, than by the finest written discourse. But these signs, too, have their accompaniments, to the feeling and thinking reader; and as he who understands music, does not employ the notes slavishly,* so the reader, who has the necessary capacity, can, by the help of written words, accompany the writer in his elevation, and draw out of his soul, all that remained behind.

I should rather say, that your thoughts and feelings were not sufficiently developed, when you made an attempt to express them. Most writers content themselves with thinking over their subject calmly, then forming what they call a plan, and handling their theme accordingly; or they avail themselves of the heat of the first impulse; and their glowing imagination presents us a fresh painting, often glaring and powerful enough, and yet the result disappoints their expectations. But indispensable as it is, that he, who would express forcibly a great truth, should revolve it beforehand, order his expressions, and handle his theme, according to its nature, with all energy; this is not yet the precise method by which we can attain to a powerful expression of our sentiments.

However evident to me a truth may be, after I have gained instruction on the subject from books and my own reflections, and however well acquainted with it I may seem to myself, I do not venture to form my plan immediately and to treat it accordingly. I rather reflect, that it has innumerable windings and aspects not directly obvious, and I must first strive to master as many of these as possible, before I communicate myself, or consider the plan and expression. Accordingly, as soon as I feel inspired by my subject and prepared for utterance, I first throw all that comes into my mind upon paper. Another day, if the subject attracts me anew, I proceed in the same way, and this I repeat so long as the fire and the impulse last, penetrating ever deeper into the subject. So soon as I have put something on paper and relieved the mind of its first burden, it gradually extends its grasp and gains new views, which nearer images at first concealed. The farther it penetrates, and the more it discovers, the more fiery and passionate it becomes in behalf of its beloved object. It is continually discovering more beautiful relations, feels itself lighter and freer in comparison, gets acquainted and familiar with all parts, dwells upon and delights in their contemplation, and does not desist, till the last grace is bestowed.

And now when I have got so far, and have commonly spent many days and nights,—morning and evening hours,—while I lay down the pen at the least appearance of languor, I begin, in the hours of business, to read over what I have written and to reflect how I shall arrange my plan. Generally, during this employment, the best method of arrangement discloses itself, or if I cannot decide upon it, I lay my paper aside and wait for a happier hour, which must come wholly of itself, and does come readily, after one has once become familiar with a truth. But the best way of presenting the subject, is always that, and that only, which grows out of the subject itself during the process. Thus I begin to arrange gradually all I have gained in this way out of my own mind, to strike out what is not appropriate, and bring every thing into its place.

Commonly, all that I first set down, comes to nothing; but there are scattered particulars which I now find necessary to note, with the general result. I retain more of the subsequent efforts in which there is a tendency to greater precision; and the final improvements conduce, for the most part, only to the perspicuity and ease of my essay. The order or arrangement of the argument follows of itself, the main design, and the colouring I leave to the hand which, without the necessity of special guidance, paints with power and warmth what the heated imagination feels with increasing force.

Yet I will not say, that, in this respect, you can immediately trust yourself. Every principle has its own place, and it does not operate with one as with another. Suppose I would prove to you the doubtful value of previous preparation, and should begin by saying, "Garrick admired Clairon, as the greatest actress of France, but thought it rather small in her, that she could decide in her own room, in cold blood, upon the degree of rage to which she would rise, as Medea." You might easily discern the justness of the comparison, but not feel all I wish you to feel in reading it. Garrick never disposed his parts beforehand; he merely wrought himself up into the situation of the person he had to represent, and then left it to his mighty soul, to exercise all its art, according to the feeling of the moment. And so must every one do, who would conceive forcibly great sentiments.

The colouring is easier when separated from the general tone, but, in connexion with it, more difficult. On this subject, it is not easy to furnish rules. It is mastered only by attentive observation of nature, and much experience of what should be adopted or rejected, expressed strongly or slightly. Subordination in the grouping is the principal thing, and if you are happy and accurate in this, the various stand-points, from

---

* i. e. with a slavish confinement to the written signs. Tr.

which your readers will survey your delineation, deserve only a general consideration.

Among a million of men, there is perhaps not more than one, who knows how to put his soul on the stretch so far, that it produces all it is capable of producing. Great numbers possess a multitude of impressions, whether from art or nature, concealed within, without being themselves conscious of it. The soul must be placed in circumstances of emotion, it must be warmed in order to unfold itself fully, and excited to enthusiasm in order that it may yield up all that is in it. Horace recommends wine as a gentle torture of the soul. Others regard fondness for the subject in hand, as mightier, than the thirst for discoveries. Every one must make the experiment for himself. Rousseau never gave the first movements of his soul. He who offers these only and nothing more, presents such truths alone as are common, and known to all men. He, on the other hand, practised often ten times over the system, which I have proposed to you, and did not desist, so long as there was any thing to be drawn forth. When a great man pursues this course, we may be pretty certain, he will press farther, than any have done before him. Whenever you are conscious of being stronger in feeling, than in expression, be assured that your soul is sluggish, and refuses to bring forth all that is in her. Assail her, when you feel the time has come, and compel her to exert herself. All the ideas, with which she has been at any time impressed, and those, which she herself has produced unconsciously from these impressions, must be put into motion and glow. She must compare, resolve, and feel what she could never do without this stimulus; she must be enamoured and warmed with her great subject. But where there is this love for the subject, there needs no arrangement. Scarcely can one tell when it is done, how he passed from one point to another.

THE MORAL ADVANTAGES OF PUBLIC CALAMITIES.

"O, if it were only Easter, if only the long winter-evenings were over!" said to me last autumn a tenant, who had not reaped for himself, his wife and seven children, so much as would keep them till Martinmas. The flax he had sown had not come up, and the last year's scarcity had already disabled him from paying his rent.

"Now," said I to him yesterday, "Easter is come and the long winter is over, and I see you are still alive, with your wife and all your children. I suppose you have earned your bread with difficulty, but it could never have tasted so good, as it has this winter, when it was the rarest thing you had."

"It was indeed very difficult," he replied, "you see my house is altogether miserable, my wife and children naked, and myself enfeebled. It has been so hard for us. The flax we still had, was soon spent. A pound of bread cost a skein, and there were only three who could spin, and nine who must eat. There was no work to be had out of the house, and when Christmas came, our flax was spun and gone. Ah, thou melancholy Christmas!—My wife had already pawned her petticoats and caps; we could not go to God's church. There was nothing besides in the house, on which we could raise any money, but the cow. I wished to drive her away to sell, but my wife and children held her fast embraced, and we all cried out, and stood so a long sad time. I walked out at last, for I could no longer endure my misery. I staid away two hours, that I might not see my own dying with hunger. But it was always as if six horses drew me back; I must return home. I passed by an oven filled with bread; and want, the sweet savour and opportunity made me a thief; so miserable had I become. With this stolen bread we solemnized our Christmas. But I rose the next morning before day, took my cow, and carried her to the man from whom I had stolen the bread. With a thousand tears I acknowledged to him the deed; and the man, whom I had known as hard and avaricious, gave her to me again and a bushel of rye also. Since then, my landlord, to whom I am yet in debt for the past year, and whom I could not have spoken to before, because he had nothing left himself, has given me aid. Ah, Sir! there is still pity in the world, there are still secret virtues, which we do not find out till the time of need!"

The last remark of the good man pleased me. "But what will you do now?" I asked. "I must now to Holland," said he, "to earn something to pay my debts. But I have no money for the journey, and since I have received so much from all I know, I can apply to nobody, and so my cow must still——" Here he could say no more for sobbing, and tears rolled down his sorrowful face.—"And who knows whether I shall ever return from Holland, since I find myself so weak after such a wretched winter, and must make great exertions now, to earn only so much as I owe for corn and rent."

I provided him for his journey, his maintenance, his children; and now I made haste to think over the secret virtues, which want discloses in so many hearts. How great, how noble, thought I, has many a heart shown itself in the present scarcity! What concealed fountains of virtue have been opened by want, and how many thanks do we owe to Providence for these trials.

Prosperous and easy times, long continued, finally lull men to sleep. The poor man is ungrateful, because help comes promptly, and prompt help renders him negligent in his business. The philosopher amuses himself with an ideal world, and the statesman with idle projects. Mere voluptuous passions arise from repose, and find an easy gratification. The virtues hold their even way with the civilities. Nothing compels feeling and decision. Interest in the public good slackens, and all goes on so indifferently well, that even the greatest genius is only half developed. But if want breaks in, if peril demands heroes, and a universal call summons the soul; if the State is striving against its downfall; if its dangers are increasing with every neglected moment; if the most frightful crisis can only be diverted by the greatest sacrifice; then all is action and greatness; the orator waxes mighty, the genius surpasses his own hopes, courage and constancy inspire the friend; heart and hand open with equal promptitude; performance follows resolve, and the soul is astonished at its own powers. It finds in itself unknown virtues, mounts ever higher, and discerns from new elevations an ever widening field of duty. Great things, and things adored in a state of tranquillity, vanish with its flight; and man shows himself once more a creature worthy of the Godhead.

How many seeds of virtue would never germinate, and how few would ripen, if there were no want, no adversity! To how many have not their own hearts been revealed by the sight of a poor man wasting away! And how many a poor man has not been inspired by hunger, with feeling, gratitude and inclination for labour, which before he had neglected! Will not also many of our country-people discern, better than before, the worth of moderation and frugality? and many have learnt to do without a multitude of things, which they formerly thought absolutely necessary? I do not now refer to the political uses of public calamities; that would lead to other considerations. How salutary, how instructive, as well for the heart as for the understanding, is thus the present scarcity! The good Providence seems to have ordained that this should occur, at least once, in every generation. Without this awakening, many would lead a very stupid life. The more refined part of mankind certainly take sufficient pains to deserve abundant chastisement, and — when they do not receive enough in this way — to torment themselves. But their sensibility needs but a slight occasion to call it into action; and Heaven needs not punish any land in order to chastise some few fools. Too great, or too unfeeling, to suffer by a public calamity, they are left to the martyrdom of their own imagination.

IMMANUEL KANT.

Born 1724. Died 1804.

A SLIGHT acquaintance with the German literature of the last half-century, discovers the vast influence, on all its productions, of the critical and transcendental philosophies. These terms, which are sometimes confounded, designate two distinct branches of speculation. The critical philosophy begins and ends with Kant. The transcendental, to which it gave birth, developed itself with various phases in the systems of those philosophers, who, after him, attained successively the highest eminence, as metaphysicians; particularly, Fichte, Schelling, Hegel. The transcendental philosophy, although, in one sense, the offspring of the critical, differs from it in its positive, systematic and constructive character; whereas, in the critical, the negative and destructive tendency predominates. Kant has, properly speaking, no system; he is analytic, not synthetic. Both these philosophies, however, are parts of one movement, and may properly enough be comprised under one denomination. The term transcendental, according to the current use, has this comprehension at present, and is likely to retain it.

The history of European philosophy exhibits perhaps no other instance of a movement so succinct, so defined and complete;—so epic as that represented by the four names which have been mentioned. Kant, the critic, prepares the way by analyzing our cognitions, and disencumbering the ground of traditional errors. Fichte, the idealist, pursues to its last results the subjective path of philosophical inquiry. Schelling, the pantheistic realist, takes the objective direction. Finally, Hegel, the encyclopedist, describes the outermost circle and lays the ground-plan which embraces and classifies all branches and topics of philosophy in one comprehensive system.

To the influence of this philosophy on the national mind, German literature owes some of its most distinctive features; in particular, that thoughtful tone and that profound spirit which so strongly characterize it. If it be inferior to others in some particulars; if it has less of creative genius and affluence than the English, less of grace and plausibility than the French, of artistic perfection than the Italian, of romantic and popular interest than the Spanish; it is superior to all these in intensity and depth. It presents a greater amount of ideas in proportion to its extent, acts more powerfully on the mind in proportion to the genius embarked in it; has more of that quality which is called suggestive than any literature of modern Europe. And for these properties it is principally indebted to the efforts and speculations of those great men who have labored so assiduously to found a science of absolute truth.*

Immanuel Kant was born at Königsberg, in old Prussia, April 22d, 1724. His father pursued the business of a saddler in one of the suburbs of that city. In his ninth year, he was put to school at the *Collegium Fredericianum*, where he distinguished himself by his application, and laid the foundation of that vast erudition by which he was afterwards distinguished. In 1740, he entered the university of his native city, where he first studied theology, and afterwards applied himself to philosophy and the exact sciences. After leaving the university, he held the office of private tutor in several families, and resided for nine years with Count Hüllesen of Arnsdorf. In 1755, he returned to Königsberg, and took the degree of Master of Arts. For fifteen years he lectured, in connection with the university, on logic, metaphysics, physics, and mathematics. In 1770, he was made Professor *ordinarius* of logic and metaphysics; which office he retained till 1794; refusing several more lucrative offers from other universities. He died, February 12th, 1804, in his eightieth year; having never travelled above seven miles from

---

* "German literature is inextricably interwoven with German philosophy. There is not a fairy-tale of Tieck, not a song of Goethe, not a play of Schiller, not a criticism of Schlegel, not a description of Humboldt, in which this undercurrent is not perceptible. Nay, however paradoxical it may appear, I will venture to affirm that German music has received much of its peculiar character from the same source, that the compositions of Beethoven, Weber, Spohr, Mendelssohn, are deeply tinctured with the same spirit."—*Mrs. Austin.*

his native city, but leaving a name which had traversed the civilized world. Kant remained unmarried, but was social in his habits, and a welcome visitor in the first families of Königsberg, who knew how to prize the greatest intellect of the age. He was an agreeable companion, and entertained his company with amusing anecdotes, of which he possessed an inexhaustible store, and which he related in a very dry manner, with unmoved countenance, exciting great merriment in others. He dressed with elegance, and was fond of cards; seldom passing an evening without a game of l'hombre, which he considered as the only certain means of withdrawing his mind from strenuous thought, and composing himself to rest.

Reichardt, in the "Urania" for 1812, has given a spirited sketch of his person and habits. "He was utterly dry in body and mind. More meagre, nay withered, than his little body, perhaps none ever existed; colder and more purely secluded within himself, no sage ever lived. A high, cheerful brow, a fine nose and bright clear eyes, distinguished advantageously the upper part of his countenance. But the lower part, on the other hand, was the most perfect expression of coarse sensuality, which showed itself to excess, especially in eating and drinking. He loved a good table in cheerful company." "So boundless a memory as Kant possessed one shall seldom find. His lectures were rendered exceedingly interesting thereby. His lectures on physics and physical geography, in particular, were very instructive and pleasing to young people, by reason of his measureless acquaintance with history, travels, biography, novels, and all departments which could furnish materials for enriching and illustrating those sciences. Although he had his notes before him, he seldom looked at them, and often repeated whole columns of names and dates from memory."

"The life-history of Immanuel Kant," says Heine, "is difficult to describe. For he had neither life nor history. He lived a mechanically regular, almost abstract bachelor-existence, in a still, retired street of Königsberg, an ancient city on the north-eastern boundary of Germany. I do not think that the great clock of the cathedral in that place accomplished its daily task in a more passionless and regular manner than its countryman, Immanuel Kant. Rising, coffee-drinking, writing, reading lectures, dining, walking,—everything had its set time; and the neighbours knew with perfect accuracy that it was half-past three o'clock, when Immanuel Kant, in his grey body-coat, with his rattan in his hand, came out of his house-door, and bent his steps toward the little linden-alley which, for his sake, is still called the philosopher's walk. Eight times he walked up and down that alley, at all seasons of the year; and when the weather was dull, and the grey clouds portended rain, his servant, old Lampe, was seen walking behind him with anxious concern, carrying a long umbrella under his arm, like a picture of providence.

Strange contrast between the outward life of the man and his destructive, world-to-pieces-crushing thought! Truly, if the citizens of Königsberg had suspected the entire import of that thought, they would have felt a far more shuddering horror for that man than for the executioner,—an executioner who beheads only men. But the good people saw in him nothing more than a professor of philosophy, and when, at the set time, he passed along, they gave him friendly greeting, and perhaps set their watches by him."

His fame, at present, rests chiefly on his labors as a metaphysician. But, in his own day, he was scarcely less distinguished by his contributions to the exact sciences than by his investigation of the intellectual powers and the ideal world. He published important treatises on various subjects connected with physical science, of which the most celebrated is the "Universal Natural History and Theory of the Heavens." In this work he seems to have anticipated some of the subsequent discoveries in astronomy. In particular, he conjectured the existence of another planet beyond Saturn, more than twenty years before Sir W. Herschel had discovered the Georgium Sidus. The following is an extract from the passage in which this conjecture is propounded. "Should there not be between Saturn, the outermost of the planets which we know, and the least eccentric comet, which descends to us from a distance, perhaps ten times greater, another planet whose motion approaches more nearly to the cometary than that of Saturn?" * * * "The law which determines the relation between the eccentricity of the planetary orbits and their distance from the sun supports this conjecture."*

* *Allgemeine Naturgeschichte und Theorie des Himmels. Erster Theil.*

Kant's moral character, distinguished for probity and a high sense of honor, was held in the highest estimation by his fellow-citizens.

There is an entertaining biography of him by Borrowsky, a personal friend.

For the following "Remarks" on Kant's philosophy, the editor is indebted to the translator of the extracts which are given from the "Critique on the Faculty of judging," and the "Plan for an everlasting peace."*

INTRODUCTORY REMARKS.

[IN reading Kant's writings, the observation often forces itself upon us, that the words will very well bear a construction quite opposite to that he himself seems to put upon them; and we discover that they are equally intelligible and harmonious from two entirely distinct points of view. It is true, indeed, of all honest and thorough discussion of principles, that its application is infinitely wider than the particular intent of the writer. Thus a profound remark in Morals is equally applicable to Physics, Art, and Politics. But in Kant, born to represent an important step in the progress of Modern Philosophy, this double meaning, passing easily into open contradiction, accompanied too by the most entire earnestness and strictness of inquiry, is particularly remarkable, and has given occasion to much difference of opinion as to the whole scope and fundamental character of his philosophy.

Thus he is commonly cited as the founder of modern Transcendentalism, which in the popular estimate is equivalent to Mysticism; yet where the aim is rather to find fault than to understand, it is easy too to make him out a materialist and a skeptic. This peculiarity, allied to and resulting from the very nature of his system, as we shall hereafter see, must be understood and kept in view in the study of his writings, and particularly in the Critique of the Judgment, (from which the longest of our extracts is taken); which it renders one of the most interesting, but most difficult of his writings.

Kant's starting-point is altogether with the Materialists, or as they call themselves of late, the Common-sense, or Inductive Philosophers. In common with all the world of his time, and with most persons of the present day, he assumes that our knowledge is limited, both in extent and in degree; that we know in part, and parts only.

Nevertheless, the fact that we have Experience, of some kind, whatever be its value, remains unshaken; and with this he commences his examination of our Cognitive Faculty; having for his aim to discover, and after the rigidest scrutiny, set down, as Knowledge, only what we certainly know; leaving all that belongs to Opinion, Faith or Feeling, to stand on its own basis.

As his Test of Certainty, he appeals directly to the private intuition, or consciousness, not relying on Experience, however often repeated; for, as he says, this, though it may be amply sufficient for the uses of everyday life, is yet easily distinguishable from absolute and original certainty. This latter he calls Knowledge *à priori*, by which is to be understood, not a knowledge preceding Experience, but deriving its support from something prior to and independent of Experience. For example, our conception of a triangle, though suggested by the actual figure, cannot be derived from it; for there is no perfect triangle; none perfectly adequate to the conception.

It is obvious that on the strict application of this test, most of our so-called Knowledge must take another name; and the inquiry occurs: whether there be anything in Experience deserving to be called Knowledge.

Kant answers that there is: viz. That in all our perceptions of outward things, they must appear as existing in Space and Time. This is not the result of Experience; for all Experience must presuppose it; and whatever validity we may allow our knowledge of phenomena, of this at least we are certain, that they can appear to us only in Space and Time.

These, then, are the *forms* of our perceptions; not indicating anything in the nature of the objects perceived, but mere subjective forms.

Accordingly, he divides Knowledge into two kinds; Knowledge of Forms, (subjective Knowledge); and Knowledge of subject-matter, (objective Knowledge); and he says that of the latter we not only have nothing, but cannot even conceive of the possibility of our ever having any knowledge of things *as they are in themselves.*

It would not be possible for us in the brief space devoted to this sketch of Kant's philosophy, to give even a general account of his development of his theory of Perception, nor of his critique of the Understanding. Suffice it to say that on this principle of the subjectiveness of all Knowledge, he proceeds to construct a system of subjective Knowledge, (Understanding); embracing, according to him, all our proper cognitive faculty.

It is evident, however, from what has already been said, that as Knowledge relates only to the forms and conditions of Experience, it must depend entirely upon the possibility of Experience; and where this is impossible, Knowledge must also be impossible. Now, Kant

---

* J. Elliot Cabot, Esq.

finds certain conceptions in the mind, not only unconnected with, but, by their very nature, transcending all possibility of Experience. For example, our conceptions of God, Freedom, and Immortality, to which no possible sensuous experience can be adequate. Such conceptions Kant calls *Transcendental Ideas;* and the faculty conceiving them, *Reason.* The Transcendental Ideas lay claim to absolute certainty and objectivity, without reference to Experience. This is evidently in contradiction to the theory of Knowledge according to the Understanding. Finite perception is deceptive, and must appeal to Experience as the test of its correctness. The claims of the Transcendental Ideas to theoretic Knowledge, therefore, must be considered as an overweening pretence, and they should rather be called transcendent, than transcendental. They cannot give us any information as to the nature of any object; but, at most, like empirical conceptions, declare some law of the subject. And in support of this he shows that every Transcendental Idea contains a contradiction; that is, when we endeavour to give it a theoretic application, to declare what it asserts concerning its object, two opposite propositions of equal apparent truth are the result. Thus our idea as to the extent of the Universe,—it is equally easy to maintain that it is infinite, or that it is finite; eternal, or having originated in Time, and so on. And these *Antinomies of Pure Reason*, as he calls them, he shows are inherent in all Ideas.

To the Transcendental Ideas he accordingly assigns a merely subjective application.

Wherever the Subject and the Object coincide, there, according to him, is the true province of the Transcendental Ideas, for then they have objective validity. Thus in the *practical* Ideas, as Kant styles them; for instance the Idea of Duty; here the conception (Subject) and the Object, (the course of life to be pursued,) coincide. So of the idea of God. Considered theoretically, that is, if we attempt to discover his nature, we are baffled and fall into contradictions, from the weakness of human powers;—such conceptions are transcendent, not transcendental. But considering God as the foundation of the moral order of the Universe, of the idea of Duty, we are in no danger of error, for here both ends of the problem are within our reach.

Kant's skepticism is therefore wholly theoretical; and he consoles himself for the unwelcome results of his inquiries by the reflection that all the practical and solid interests of humanity remain untouched; and that only our vain assumption of knowledge, unsuited to our nature and position, is affected. It is of no importance whether our notions of God are correct, theoretically, or not; it is sufficient that we have a subjective (practical) knowledge of him, in the Idea of Duty.

Kant's method, as already explained, is empirical, or so to say, *narrative.* He begins with certain universally-admitted facts, and proceeds to examine their consequences and relations, as they fall under his hand, but without searching out their foundation or ultimate significance.

Thus he gives us the *forms*, Space and Time, as if for aught he knows there may be others that he has not yet discovered. And he does not inquire why it is that these and no others should exist. They stand there without our knowing whence or how. But if we examine into their nature we discover them to be essentially connected with the nature of sensuous Perception; and they conduct us to new points of view in relation to Kant's system.

All Knowledge must presuppose some connection between the Subject and the Object; the mind and the thing; and whichever it may be that acts on the other, there is at all events a communication between them. And moreover this empirical communication must depend upon an original and essential connection. If we could imagine two essentially and primarily distinct kinds of Matter, they could not act upon each other, nor could there be any communication between them. For Matter can act or be acted upon only according to its laws. But the laws of Matter are its essence, and if they act according to the same laws they must be identical. It is necessary, therefore, and an antecedent condition of the perception of things, that both they and we should be parts of one identical nature. So too in proceeding beyond mere sensuous perception,— the abstract rules formed by the Understanding, e. g. the common hypotheses in Physics, presuppose a like identity, for they are formed by generalization, and this is impossible without at least a dim idea of a common centre of all things. The reason why animals, or men reduced to a mere animal existence, do not generalize nor form rules, except to a very limited extent, is that this Idea is not present in their consciousness, (or only very dimly,) but exists *outside* of them, as Instinct.

So that the simplest Experience presupposes an entire continuity throughout the Universe as its fundamental condition. This series or continuity, considered abstractly, is Space. Space is not the *idea*, but the *abstraction* of the material Universe; for it belongs to subjective perception and Understanding, which have nothing to do with Ideas; but it is a sufficient recognition, by the sensuous faculty, of what the Reason afterwards comes to know as concrete Truth. Thus we cannot imagine a limitation of Space, nor of a place where it is not. The edge, or boundary of Space, or a vacuum where there is Extension without Space, is an absurdity. And it is equally impossible to imagine an object not in Space.

Space is in fact the abstraction of the Infinite displayed in the Finite. For Matter, though necessarily connected with and supported by Spirit, is yet its direct opposite. Every one of the qualities of Matter is antagonistic to the corresponding spiritual quality. Thus Spirit is infinite and eternal; Matter finite and transitory. Or rather, Matter, if it could be considered by itself, would be a mere negation, and is incapable of being expressed without its opposite. For transience, for example, implies a certain duration. The material Universe, therefore, is an embodied contradiction, and Space of course a mere suspension or abstraction of this. Thus Space is both the affirmative condition and the negation of Extension; for there is no unlimited Extension, and limitation is equivalent to negation.

So of Time. It differs from Space only as quality from quantity; Intension from Extension; the inward from the outward sense, so called. As Matter is limited in extent, so also it is transient in substance; and as Space contains both extension and limitation, so Time is embodied Change, i. e. persistence and transience: we cannot arrest any particle of it, as the Present, for as we pause, it is already Past. Every-day experience shows us that our notion of Time depends upon the number of events that have successively impressed us and then given place to others. Amid a rapid succession of interesting events, a week, when past, seems a month, and a month a year, for we date from each succeeding event. On the other hand, to measure Time for economic purpose, we employ astronomic changes, since here the succession is unvarying.

It is the profound remark of an ancient Hindoo book, that Time is the connection of Matter and Spirit. And the same is true of Space.

The interesting point here, and that to which the preceding inquiries tend, is this: That not the Transcendental Ideas alone, but the commonest and simplest experience must necessarily contain a contradiction, to the Understanding. Time is the contradiction of Eternity, yet also of the moment, or point in Time; Space is the opposition of Unity, yet also of the point in Space. And it is also very remarkable that Kant in the table which he gives of the different classes of possible judgments, and also in his table of Categories, or classes under which all pure conceptions of the Understanding may be reduced, has in each instance distributed them under various heads, *by threes*, of which two are contraries and the third their result; without giving any deduction, or reason for so doing. Thus under the head of Quantity, in judgment, he gives: Universal, Particular, and Special; and under the same head in the Categories, he gives: Unity, Multiplicity, and Totality; and so on through the whole. The truth is that each of these classes contains, not only three kinds of judgment, or of conceptions, but also the three elements necessary to every judgment and every conception; viz. the contradiction and its result. Thus if I say: This paper is white, here we have the general attribute, *white*, the limitation, to this piece of paper, (negation of other paper); and the result, this special piece of paper. So of all conceptions, and so of all knowledge; there is no possible act of cognition that does not embrace this element of contradiction. It is the combination of outside and inside, light and darkness, extent and limitation, requisite to every sensuous impression; and it is the puzzle in the highest problems that employ the mind of man. Thus in Civil Government, the cöexistence of personal freedom, (which supposes each individual supreme and unlimited), with Society, in which he is only a part. So in Religion, the fierce disputes that have agitated the world now for eighteen centuries, arise solely from the impossibility, and at the same time the ever-recurring necessity, of conceiving Man to be at once human and divine, finite and infinite; and the difficulty of reconciling the doctrine of Immortality and possible perfection, with the common views of humanity, on any other ground. A finite immortal is the most tremendous of contradictions. This is the cause of the horror with which the doctrine of the mere humanity of Jesus Christ is looked upon by most persons.

But these contradictions and these impossibilities are such only to the Understanding; that is, the mind employed only with particulars. The contradiction truly exists in the Universe, and to him who does not transcend it, does not see it and its contrary united in an harmonious synthesis, it is final. But in reality it is superficial, and Reason, or the mind contemplating things as a Whole, readily resolves it. Then it is no longer contradiction, but the necessary organism of the Idea.

Kant, from his point of view, was quite right in making knowledge subjective only, for he confines his inquiries as to the Cognitive faculty entirely to the Understanding, or subjective Reason, to the very nature of which, this antagonism of the subjective and objective, and their absolute separation, is altogether essential.

There is another branch of Kant's enquiry, touched upon in the beginning of these remarks, but which our limits forbid our discussing at much length; leading, however, to the same point. This is the distinction he makes between the *phenomenon*, or *appearance of a thing*, and *the thing itself*, and his doctrine that we can know nothing of the latter, but that all our perception and knowledge is confined to the former. This evidently follows from his premises.

For if all our intercourse with things is that of one thing with another, it must evidently be merely outward, like all relations of things to each other.

If we bring two bodies together, they touch only their outer surfaces; an inward union is impossible. Modern Chemistry has shown experimentally that the transformations of Matter are merely apparent, and consist solely of various combinations of the same particles. Bodies apparently the most distinct, for example, starch, gum, sugar, fat, and the woody fibre of plants are the same or nearly so, in composition. For Matter, as has been well said, has no inside, but only outside, and is capable only of outward relations.

This Kant shows, psychologically, in our sensuous perceptions. For what do we after all mean, when we say we perceive a thing, for instance a tree? Plainly nothing more than that we see certain colours and outlines apparently connected and belonging to some thing.

But whether there is anything really existing in that place, or whether it be only something within myself, or the effect of another thing, I cannot (with absolute certainty) tell. For our senses are our only evidence, and they pretend to nothing more than a perception of appearances. To another intelligence, or to differently constructed senses, the object may appear quite different. At first sight, indeed, it might seem that we do entirely rely upon the report of our senses; but let any one compare his knowledge of any outward fact with his perception of a mathematical truth, and he will find the former much the weaker. We may admit the possibility of our being persuaded to change our notions as to the colour, shape, and other qualities of any object; but we cannot for an instant admit the possibility of being convinced that two and two do not make four. Now evidently there are no degrees of certainty; we either know, or we do not know.

Kant accordingly comes to the conclusion that we cannot, properly speaking, *know* anything of the real nature or substance of objects: and that all we can hope to know about them is their effect upon ourselves; or at the most, the forms and rules of this subjective effect.

Nevertheless our claim of objective knowledge continues: in spite of the contradiction of the Understanding, there is an instinctive feeling that it is not absolute, but only the different sides of one truth. And in truth the contradiction here too belongs only to the Understanding, transcending its province. It is true, that of anything absolutely objective, really foreign to our nature, we can know nothing objectively; and more than this, as we have seen above, we could not have even subjective knowledge of an absolute object; it would be for us a mere non-entity.

But this antithesis of Subject and Object is entirely subordinate and belongs wholly to the Understanding Reflection and consciousness indeed by nature require it, and depend upon it; but it is the prerogative of Reason to see through and reconcile all distinctions and oppositions, not indeed annihilating them, but appointing to them their proper sphere.

So that this contradiction to the Understanding is so far from interfering with the validity of the Transcendental Ideas (conceptions of the Reason) that it is essential to their nature. Knowledge is not rendered impossible by it, but all knowledge, down to the merest sensuous perception, is shown by Kant himself (properly understood), to contain and require it.

Kant is not the only philosopher who has arrived at these contradictions. They are necessarily present in the Understanding; and in all empirical philosophy, logically carried out, this is made evident. The only escape is either in the feebleness that cannot understand its own results; or in wilfully ignoring them, which is the course pursued by Cousin, and more avowedly by the "Scotch School."

But the interesting feature in Kant's inquiry, and that which gives it its place in the History of Philosophy, arises from the faithfulness with which it is made. His rigid and faithful examination of facts of consciousness brought him to principles, which his adherence to the common point of view made him reject or overlook, but which in fact involved a revolution in Philosophy. His close analysis revealed the contradiction contained in those propositions which seem most solid and certain to the Understanding, and this showed the true province and the limitations of this faculty (or rather this direction of the mind), by pushing to their necessary consequences the common principles. It is not sufficient to contradict or refute Error; it is requisite moreover to show that it is an embodied self-contradiction and self-refutation, and to see this the repugnant elements must be displayed. It is this dialectic that makes the value of Kant's Critique, and it is not the less interesting for being unconscious.

Among the extracts we have given from Kant's writings, that from the Critique of the Judgment is intended as a specimen of his method and style in his strictly scientific works. This book is remarkable as displaying in the most striking manner the contradiction above alluded to. Thus in his principle that Beauty is a *subjective fitness;*—when it is evident, and indeed he himself has explained, that fitness necessarily implies an object, something for which the thing is fit; and when he speaks of a *"normal regularity without law,"* etc.,—here and throughout we have the material standpoint, and also the idealistic, to which the former necessarily leads. This extract may also serve as a specimen of Kant's scientific style, which is perfectly uniform throughout his more important works. Its crabbed, harsh character, and the frequent use of unusual words, or at least of words used in unusual senses, will no doubt excuse us in the eyes of our readers from giving extracts of sufficient length, to afford any adequate means of judging of Kant's general merits as a philosopher. But what is given may be enough at least to correct or prevent some false impressions; being as we have said, as far as it goes, a fair specimen of the whole.

The other extracts exhibit Kant rather as a philanthropist and a well-read scholar than as a philosopher, and both in matter and in style are much less abstruse and peculiar.

FROM THE
CRITIQUE OF THE JUDGMENT.

THE domain of our general cognitive faculty comprehends two provinces, one embracing our conceptions of Nature, and the other the idea of Freedom; for in each of these it has *a priori* authority. Philosophy is divided accordingly into *theoretical* and *practical.* * * * The system of laws, relating to our conceptions of Nature, is derived from the Understanding, and is theoretical. That arising from the idea of Freedom, is derived from the Reason, and is exclusively practical. * * * The subject-matter to which the laws of the cognitive faculty apply, is nothing else than the aggregate of all objects of possible experience, considered merely as phenomena. * * * The provinces of Understanding and of Reason therefore are different, though their subject-matter is the same, and they do not interfere with each other 'for this reason,'* that conceptions relating to Nature give us objects as present to Perception (*Anschauung*),† though not as the things themselves, but only as phenomena; the idea of Freedom on the other hand has to do with the thing itself, but not as an object of sensation. Thus neither can give a theoretical knowledge of its Object (nor even of the subject thinking), in its essential nature, for this would be the Supersensuous; the idea of which must indeed be presupposed as the foundation of the possibility of Experience, but can never be raised and enlarged into a cognition. * * * Now, although an impassable chasm is established between the province of the conception of Nature (as the Sensuous), and that of the idea of Freedom (the Supersensuous), so that no passage is possible from the former to the latter, as if they were two different worlds, one of which could have no influence upon the other; yet there exists an *obligation* that the latter should exert an influence over the former: that is, that the idea of Freedom should actualize in the sensible world, the end sought by its laws. It must be conceivable therefore, that Nature should admit at least the possibility of a coincidence with the ends to be accomplished in the sensible world in accordance with the laws of Freedom. There must therefore be a ground of unity between the supersensuous foundation of Nature, with the principle of Freedom; and this, though we can have no 'complete' cognition of it, either theoretical or practical, yet makes the transition possible from the one system of views to the other. * * * * * *

But among the higher cognitive faculties there is one that forms a connecting link between the Understanding and the Reason. This is the Judgment, concerning which we have reason (from analogy) to conjecture that it also has, if not a peculiar province, yet a principle peculiar to itself, and *a priori*, though certainly subjective. * * * For all the faculties or capabilities of the mind may be reduced to three, which are not farther reducible to any common principle; viz: the Cognitive faculty the sentiment of Pleasure or Pain and Desire. The laws of the cognitive faculty are given by the Understanding alone, * * * and those of Desire, (as subject to the idea of Freedom), by the Reason. Between these lies the sentiment of Pleasure; as the Judgment between Understanding and Reason. It is therefore at least to be conjectured, that the Judgment also must contain an *a priori* principle of its own; and as Pleasure or Pain is necessarily connected with Desire, a transition must thus be formed between the pure cognitive faculty, i. e. from the province of Nature, to that of Freedom; just as in its logical employment it renders possible a connection of Understanding with Reason. * * * A reference to this analogy is familiar even to the common understanding, and we often call beautiful objects in Nature or Art by names which seem to presuppose a moral judgment. We call trees majestic and splendid; or fields smiling and happy; —even colours are said to be innocent, modest, tender, &c. * * * Taste makes possible as it were the passage from the pleasures of sense to habitual moral interest, without too abrupt a transition. * * * * *

Judgment is the faculty of conceiving the Particular as contained in the Universal. Where the Universal, (the rule, the principle, the law,) is given, Judgment, which subordinates the Particular to it, is *determinative*. But where the Particular is given, for which the Universal is to be sought, it is merely *reflective*.

The determinative Judgment has only to subordinate particulars to the general transcendental laws furnished by the Understanding; the law is given *a priori*. But so manifold are the forms in Nature, the modifications as it were of the general transcendental principles of Nature, left undetermined by the laws furnished *a priori* by the pure Understanding (since these apply only to the possibility of Nature in general, as perceptible by the senses), that there must exist for them laws, which indeed as empirical, may be *accidental* to the view of our understanding, but which, if they are to have the name of laws, (as the idea of nature demands), must be considered as necessary, and as proceeding from a principle of unity among the manifold particulars.

The reflective Judgment, whose province it is to ascend from the Particular in Nature to the Universal, is therefore in need of a principle, and this it cannot derive from Experience, since its very aim is to establish the unity of all empirical principles under principles higher though likewise empirical, and thus to establish the possibility of a systematic subordination

---

* The words between commas ' ' here and elsewhere are inserted to render the sense more clear. Tr.

† I am obliged (reluctantly) to translate *Anschauung* by *Perception*, instead of *Intuition*, since by the latter word we mean an *intellectual beholding*, which is never Kant's sense. Tr.

among them. Such a transcendental principle, the reflective Judgment therefore must give to itself, and cannot take it from anything else, (since it would then be determinative); nor yet impose it upon Nature, since all study of the laws of Nature must conform to Nature, as something independent of the conditions of reflection.

Now as the general laws of Nature* have their foundation in the Understanding, the principle in question can be no other than this, that the particular, empirical laws (as far as they are left indeterminate by the general laws,) are to be considered as so connected together as if Nature had been subjected to these also, by an Understanding (though not by ours), so as to render possible a system of Experience according to particular natural laws. Not as if such an Understanding must actually be postulated, (for it is only the *reflective* and not the *determinative* Judgment that requires this idea as its principle)—but the reflective faculty prescribes it as a law for itself, and not for Nature.

Now since the conception of an object, as containing at the same time the reason of the actual existence of the object, is called the *end*, and since the harmony of a particular thing with that in the nature of things which is possible only from their adaptation to *ends*, is called the *fitness* of its form, it follows that the principle of Judgment, as respects the Form of things, under the laws of Experience, is *the fitness of Nature in her manifold variety*. That is, by this view, Nature is so conceived as if there were an Understanding that contained a principle of union among her various empirical laws.

The *fitness* of Nature, therefore, is a special conception *a priori*, having its origin solely in the reflective Judgment. For we cannot ascribe to natural objects anything like an aiming of Nature in them at ends, but only use this conception in aid of our study of Nature in relation to the connection of Phenomena which is given by empirical laws. * * * *

This transcendental conception of a *fitness* in Nature belongs neither to our conceptions of Nature nor to the idea of Freedom, since it attributes nothing to the object (Nature), but only gives the way in which we must proceed in the study of the objects in Nature, with a view to a complete coherent system of Experience. It is thus a subjective principle (maxim) of the Judgment; and hence we are rejoiced, as if at a happy accident, favourable to our endeavours, (and in fact relieved from a necessity), when we meet such a systematic unity among merely empirical laws; although we must necessarily presuppose that such a unity exists, without being able to comprehend or prove it. * *

The Understanding is indeed in possession of general laws of Nature *a priori*, without which Nature could not be an object of Experience. It is requisite, however, that there should also exist a certain order in the rules of Nature that relate to particulars, which are known to the Understanding only by Experience, and as far as it is concerned, accidental.*

These rules, without which there could be no passing from the general possibility of Experience to an actual experience,† the Understanding must conceive as laws, (i. e. as necessary); since otherwise they would form no order of Nature :—though it does not perceive, and may never comprehend them. So that although the Understanding can declare nothing *a priori* as to the nature of objects, yet in compliance with these laws of 'particular' Experience, as we call them, it is necessary to presuppose an *a priori* principle :—viz. that a cognizable order of Nature under these laws, is possible ; and to lay this at the foundation of all study of Nature. As for instance is expressed in the following propositions: That there is in Nature a system of genera and species comprehensible by us;— that these approach a common type, so that a transition from one to the other, and thus to a higher order, is possible: That though at first it seems to us unavoidable to suppose, for the specific variety of effects in Nature, an equal variety of causes, yet they may perhaps be embraced under a few principles, with the discovery of which we are to employ ourselves, &c.

This harmony of Nature with our cognitive faculty is presupposed *a priori* by the Judgment as the foundation of its examination of Nature in her 'particular or' empirical laws. For the Understanding the objective *existence* of this harmony, is accidental;—the Judgment alone ascribes it to Nature, as 'an adaptation or' fitness to our cognitive faculty, transcending Experience. For without presupposing this, we should have no order of Nature under particular laws, and hence no clue for experience and inquiry into these laws in their manifold variety. For it is easily conceivable, notwithstanding all the uniformity of Nature in her general laws, without which 'even' the *form* of an empirical cognition would not be possible, that nevertheless, the variety of particular laws and their effects might be so great that it would be impossible for our Understanding to discover in Nature any comprehensible system of subdivision into genera and species, by which one should throw light upon the other, and render it possible for us to combine so confused (or,

---

* Space and Time, the (subjective) conditions of the existence of Phenomena. Tr.

* That is, the Understanding knows only their existence, and not *why* they exist, (their principle) : — so that it cannot pronounce them necessary. Tr.

† The general possibility of Experience is given *a priori*, in Space and Time; but in order to have any experience of an actual thing, there must pre-exist a synthesis or union of various particulars in a more general whole. We cannot perceive an isolated quality ; e. g. colour without extension, or vice-versa. This union Kant calls the Unity of Apperception, and declares it to be a necessary antecedent of Experience. Tr.

properly speaking, so infinitely complex) a mass into a coherent experience. * * *

This harmony of Nature, amid the complexity of her particular laws, with our need of finding in her, general principles, must, as far as our faculties reach, be considered accidental, but yet as a necessary postulate of our Understanding, and hence as a fitness in Nature to the aim of our Understanding in its striving after Knowledge. The general laws of the Understanding, which are at the same time laws of Nature, are as necessary to Nature (though 'subjective, or' arising from spontaneity) as the laws of motion. * * * But that the order of Nature under particular laws in all their possible variety and dissimilarity, transcending our powers of comprehension, is yet in reality fitted to our cognitive faculties, is, so far as we can see, accidental; and the discovery of this order is the business of the Understanding, which is thus directed to its true function, the introduction of unity of principle among these various particular laws. This design the Judgment is forced to ascribe to Nature; since the Understanding can furnish no such law. * * *

The Judgment is thus in possession of an *a priori* principle of the possibility of Nature, but it is only a subjective one, whereby a law is prescribed, not to Nature, but to itself in its study of Nature. This law we may call *the law of Specification in Nature*, as to her empirical laws.

This is not seen *a priori* in Nature, but postulated, as the principle according to which we must conceive the subdivision of her general laws, and the subordination under them of her particular laws. So that when it is said that Nature subdivides her general laws according to a principle of fitness to our cognitive faculty, * * * we neither give a law to Nature, nor learn one from her by Experience, though this may confirm it. For this only is intended; that however Nature may be constituted as to her general principles, we must at all events pursue our study of her empirical laws according to this principle and the maxims founded on it; since it is only so far as this is done, that we can proceed in the employment of our Understanding in Experience, and the acquisition of Knowledge.

The attaining of any end is connected with a feeling of Pleasure, and where the condition of attaining the end is an *a priori* notion; (as in the present case, a principle of the reflective Judgment), the feeling of Pleasure is placed on a foundation *a priori*, and of universal validity.

Now although we do not and cannot trace the slightest feeling of Pleasure from the coincidence of our perceptions with the laws and universal ideas of Nature, (the Categories); since the Understanding proceeds without 'conscious' aim, by the necessity of its nature; yet on the other hand the discovery that two or more apparently heterogeneous laws are embraced under one common principle, is the occasion of very marked satisfaction, often indeed of an admiration, which does not cease even when we are familiar with the object.

It is true 'that in many cases' we no longer feel any pleasure to arise from the comprehensibility of Nature, and her unity amid the divisions of genera and species (whereby alone Experience and knowledge of her particular laws is possible); but it must certainly have been felt at one time; and it is only because the commonest experience would not be possible without this harmony, that it has gradually lost itself in the mere cognition, and is no longer distinguished. * * * On the other hand, a view of Nature which should declare at the outset, that at the slightest advance beyond the commonest experience we should come upon a heterogeneousness of her laws, making the combination of particular laws under general principles of Experience, impossible for our Understanding, would be altogether repulsive to us: *for* this is opposed to the principle of the (subjective) harmony of Nature in her divisions, with the reflective Judgment.

This postulate of the Judgment however is so undefined as to the extent to which this principle of the ideal fitness of Nature to our cognitive faculty is to be allowed, that if we should be told that a deeper or wider knowledge of Nature from observation must at last reveal to us a complexity in her laws, not reducible to a single principle by any human understanding; we should have nothing to object: though it is more agreeable to us when hopes are afforded, that the more we penetrate into Nature, or become acquainted with outward, as yet unknown laws, the more simple and consonant we shall find her principles, amid all the apparent heterogeneousness of her empirical laws. * * *

THE NOTION OF ADAPTATION IN NATURE, APPLIED TO ÆSTHETICS.

The merely subjective in the notion of an object; i. e. its relation to the Subject, and not to the thing, forms the *æsthetic** character of the notion; but that which aids, or may be employed in determining the nature of the thing as an object of knowledge, is its *logical validity*.

In the cognition of a sensible object, both these relations occur. * * * Sensation expresses both the merely subjective in our notions of outward things, and also their material (real) principle, whereby their actual existence is declared. * * * But that subjective element in a notion, which can in no case form part of a cognition, is the *pleasure* or *displeasure* connected with it. For by pleasure or the contrary, I know nothing of the object, though the sentiment may result from a cog-

---

* Æsthetic with Kant means *sensuous;* dependent on, or belonging to the senses. Tr.

nition. Now the *adaptedness* of a thing, as given in perception, is no quality of the object, for that could not be perceived, though it may be inferred from a knowledge of the thing. So that this adaptedness, preceding the cognition, and not even aiming at knowledge of the object, yet still immediately connected with its notion, is that subjective element in the notion, which cannot form any part of cognition.

The object therefore is said to be *adapted*, only because its image 'or notion' is immediately connected with the feeling of pleasure; and the notion 'itself is an æsthetic notion' as to the fitness of the object. The only question is whether such a notion of fitness exists.

When the mere apprehension of the form of a sensible object, unconnected with any conception or definite knowledge, is attended with pleasure, the notion is thereby referred, not to the object, but merely to the subject; * and the pleasure can express only the harmony of the object with the cognitive faculties exercised in the reflective Judgment; thus a mere subjective, formal adaptedness of the object. For such apprehension of forms by the Imagination can never take place without some comparison (even though unconscious) on the part of the reflective Judgment, of the apprehensions with its faculty of connecting sensations with ideas. When therefore in this comparison the Imagination (the faculty of *a priori* perceptions) is unexpectedly brought into harmony with the Understanding (the faculty of conceptions), by means of the notion of an object, and thereby a feeling of pleasure awakened; in such case there must appear to us to exist a *fitness* of the object to the reflective Judgment. This is an *æsthetic judgment* as to the fitness of the object; neither founding itself upon, nor giving any conception of the thing itself.

Whenever the form of an object (abstracted from its material influence upon us, as Sensation), in merely considering it, without reference to any conception of its nature, is found by the Judgment to cause pleasure by its mere image, this pleasure the Judgment decides to be necessarily connected with the notion; not merely for the particular person, but for all. The object in such case is said to be *beautiful;* and the ability to judge by means of this pleasure (and thus to form judgments of universal validity), is called Taste.   *   *   *

JUDGMENT BY MEANS OF TASTE, IS ÆSTHETIC.

In order to determine whether a thing is beautiful or not, we do not refer the notion to its object, through the Understanding (as in cognition); but to the Subject, and the feeling of pleasure or displeasure, through the Imagination.   *   *   *   *

All notions may refer to objects, except those relating to the sentiment of pleasure or displeasure, for this denotes nothing in the Object, but only an affection of the Subject.   *   *   *

An *objective* fitness can be known only from the reference of particulars to a certain end, thus only from a conception 'of the nature of the object.'   *   *   *   It is either outward adaptedness, i. e. *usefulness;* or inward adaptedness, i. e. the *perfection* of the thing.—That the satisfaction derived from an object, whence we call it beautiful, cannot depend on any notion of its usefulness, is sufficiently evident from what has been said. For then it would not be a pleasure derived immediately from the object, which is the essential condition of a judgment concerning Beauty. But an objective, *inward* fitness, i. e. Perfection, comes nearer to the predicate of Beauty, and it has hence been held by distinguished philosophers, that Perfection, indistinctly conceived, is synonymous with Beauty.— It is of the greatest importance in a Critique of Taste, to determine whether Beauty can be resolved into the idea of Perfection.

In order to judge of objective fitness, we must always have the conception of an *end*, and where the fitness is not outward, (Usefulness), but inward; the conception of an inward end which shall contain the ground of the inward possibility of the object. Now as *end* is something the idea of which may be considered as the ground of the possibility of the object itself, in order to conceive of an objective fitness in a thing, the conception of *what it ought to be* must precede it.   *   *   *   The merely *formal* element in the notion of a thing: i. e. the combination of the Manifold into one, (leaving its nature undetermined), gives of itself no knowledge of objective fitness; since as we abstract from the particular thing, as an end, (that which it ought to be), nothing is left but the subjective fitness of the notions in the mind of the beholder;   *   *   *   but nothing as to the perfection of any object.   *   *   *   Thus, for example, if I come upon a grassy spot in the woods, around which the trees stand in a circle, and do not image to myself any purpose; (as for instance, that it might be used for a rustic dance); the mere *form* will not give me the least idea of perfection. But to conceive of formal, objective fitness, without any end proposed; that is the mere *form* of a perfection;   *   *   *   is a complete contradiction.

Now Taste is æsthetic Judgment: i. e. it rests upon subjective grounds, and cannot have any conception, (and thus not that of a particular end), as its motive. Therefore the idea of Beauty, as a formal, subjective fitness, by no means involves any perfection of the thing; and the distinction between the ideas of the Beautiful and of the Good, (as if they differed only in logical form, the former merely a confused, the latter a distinct idea of Perfection), is without foundation. For then there would be no *specific* difference between them, and an æsthetic judgment would be at the same time cognitive.   *   *

But I have already shown that the æsthetic Judgment is peculiar in this, that it gives no knowledge whatever, (not even confused), of its Object, * * * but refers the image, wherein an Object is presented 'to the mind,' merely to the subject. * * * * *

THE PLEASURE THAT DETERMINES THE ÆSTHETIC JUDGMENT, IS ENTIRELY UNCONNECTED WITH INTEREST.

Interest is the pleasure that we connect with the notion that a certain thing exists. It is therefore constantly connected with Desire; which is either its motive, or necessarily connected therewith. Now when it is asked whether a thing is beautiful or not, we do not seek to know whether the existence of the thing can be of any importance to us, or to any one: but only what is our judgment respecting it, apart from the question of its existence? If any one ask me whether the palace I see before me, is beautiful, I may indeed say that I am not fond of things made only to be stared at; or I may answer after the manner of the Iroquois Sachem, who liked nothing in Paris better than the *restaurans;* or I may scold in Rousseau's style, about the vanity of the great, who waste the sweat of the people on such superfluities; or finally, I can easily persuade myself that if I were upon an uninhabited island, without hope of ever seeing men again, and by my mere wish could conjure up such a palace, I should never give myself even this trouble, if I already had a hut that suited me. All this may be granted; but this is not now the question. The point is only whether the mere image of the thing in my mind is accompanied by pleasure; however indifferent I may be as to its existence. It is easy to see that it is what I make out of the notion within me, and not that wherein I am dependent on the existence of the object, that enables me to say that it is *beautiful,* and to prove that I have Taste.

Every one must confess that a judgment concerning Beauty, with which the slightest *interest* is mingled, is quite partial, and no pure æsthetic judgment. We must be altogether disinterested, and indifferent as to the existence of the thing, in order to judge in matters of Taste.

We cannot better illustrate this point, (which is of special importance), than by contrasting with the pure, disinterested* pleasure of the æsthetic judgment, pleasure that is connected with interest. * * * * *

THE PLEASURE DERIVED FROM THE AGREEABLE, IS CONNECTED WITH INTEREST.

The Agreeable is that which is pleasing to the senses, in Sensation. * * * By Sensation we understand an image received through the senses, referring to an object; and, to prevent the continual danger of misunderstanding, we shall call that which constantly and necessarily remains subjective, and can in no case constitute a notion of an object, by the customary name of *Feeling.*

The green colour of the meadows belongs to objective sensation, as the perception of a Sensible object; but the *agreeableness* of the colour belongs to subjective Sensation, whereby no object is given; *i. e.* to Feeling. * * *

Now, that my judgment of a thing, declaring it to be *agreeable,* expresses an *interest* in it, is clear from this, that it excites by means of Sensation, a *desire* for such things; hence the pleasure presupposes, not a mere judgment concerning it, but a reference of its existence to my condition, so far as affected by such an object. * * * It is not mere approbation I bestow on it, but inclination is excited by it; and those sensations which are the most vividly and intensely agreeable, are so far from being connected with Judgment as to the object of the sensation, that those who are constantly bent on enjoyment willingly disclaim all Judgment.

THE PLEASINGNESS OF GOOD IS CONNECTED WITH INTEREST.

Good is that which is pleasing to us, through the Reason, by its bare idea. We say that a thing is good *for something,* (useful), when it pleases us as means only; but we call that good *in itself* which pleases by itself. But in each is contained the idea of purpose, and thus the relation of the Reason to a volition, (at least in possibility); consequently, a pleasure at the *existence* of an object or an action; *i. e.* Interest.

In order to pronounce a thing good, I must know what sort of a thing it is; that is, I must have a conception of its nature. Flowers, fanciful pictures, interwoven figures, such as are called Arabesques, convey no particular idea, and yet are pleasing. 'On the other hand,' the pleasure derived from Beauty is necessarily dependent on the notion of an object, and thus contains the *indication* of some conception, though it does not determine its precise character. Herein it is distinguished from the Agreeable, which rests entirely upon Sensation. * *

The Agreeable and the Good are distinguished from each other, it is true, in the commonest experience. We say unhesitatingly of a highly-seasoned dish, prepared with every provocative of appetite, that it is *agreeable,* and at the same time that it is not *good;* since it is pleasing immediately to the senses, but mediately, *i. e.* through a consideration of its consequences, it is disagreeable. * * * But notwithstanding this difference, they agree in this, that they are always connected with an interest in the object; not only the agreeable, and that which is good as means, (the Useful), but also absolute and universal Good, viz: moral Good, which carries with it the highest interest, since it is the object of the Will, (that is, of Desire, determined by Reason). But to will anything, and to take

---

* A judgment as to an object giving Pleasure, may be entirely *disinterested,* but yet very *interesting:* i. e. it does not found itself upon any interest, but produces it. Such are all purely moral judgments. * * * *

pleasure in its existence—that is, to take an interest in it, are identical.

COMPARISON OF THE THREE KINDS OF PLEASURE.

The Agreeable and the Good have each a reference to Desire, and carry with them, the one a pathological, the other a pure practical satisfaction, produced not by the mere notion of the thing, but by its existence.   *   *   *
'On the contrary,' the æsthetic Judgment is purely contemplative; that is, indifferent to the existence of the object, and regards only the relation which the nature of the thing bears to the feeling of pleasure or displeasure.   *   *
It results, therefore, that Taste is the faculty of judging of an object or a sentiment, by means of the pleasure or displeasure arising from it, unconnected with any interest. The object of such pleasure is called *beautiful*.

THE BEAUTIFUL IS THAT WHICH, APART FROM ANY CONCEPTION, IS CONSIDERED AS AFFORDING PLEASURE TO ALL.

This definition of the Beautiful follows from the foregoing definition of it as the object of disinterested pleasure. For, when any one perceives that the pleasure afforded by a thing is unconnected with interest, that thing he cannot consider otherwise than as pleasing to all. For as the pleasure is founded upon no private inclination, or consideration of interest, but, on the contrary, as the mind feels itself entirely unbiassed in the satisfaction attributed to the object, the pleasure cannot depend upon any private circumstances or conditions; it must therefore be considered as founded in an attribute common to all, and a like pleasure must be presumed to be felt by every one.   *   *
So that Taste must necessarily be considered as the power of judging of that by which even Feeling may be communicated, and thus as aiding in the accomplishment of what is sought by every one's natural inclination.

A man left on a desert island would ornament neither his hut nor his person, for himself. He would not seek for flowers, much less plant them, for ornament. It is only in society that it occurs to him to be not only a man, but a man of Taste, (the commencement of civilization); for as such is one considered who is desirous of communicating his pleasure to others, and expert in doing so, and who is not satisfied with an object unless he can share with others the pleasure it affords. Hence we expect and require of every one this regard to universal communication, as it were from an original contract dictated by Humanity itself.   *   *   *

Here is a pleasure which, like all pleasure or displeasure not resulting from the idea of Freedom, (that is, from the previous determination of the higher faculty of Desire, by pure Reason), cannot be understood from conceptions, as if necessarily connected with the notion of an object, but only through reflective Perception; and thus like all empirical judgments, can claim no objective necessity, nor *a priori* validity. But the æsthetic judgment, like all empirical judgments, claims only acquiescence from every one, which notwithstanding its essentially accidental nature, it well may. The only astonishing and remarkable point is, that it is no empirical conception, but a feeling of Pleasure, (and thus no conception whatever), which is to be attributed to every one, and connected with the notion of the thing, as if it were a predicate belonging to its cognition. A single empirical judgment, for example, when we find a movable drop of water in a rock-crystal, rightly demands that every one should find it so, since it is formed according to the universal conditions of the determinative Judgment, and the laws of all possible Experience. So he who feels pleasure in the mere contemplation of the form of an object, without reference to a conception, properly claims the agreement of all, although it is a private and empirical judgment, since the ground of this pleasure is to be sought in the universal though subjective condition of reflective judgments.   *   *   *   So that the pleasure in an æsthetic judgment is dependent indeed on an empirical notion, and cannot be connected *a priori* with any conception; (we cannot determine *a priori* what will be agreeable to Taste, or the contrary; we must make the experiment); but it is the foundation of the judgment, since it depends merely upon reflection and the universal though subjective conditions of the harmony on which all cognition of objects is founded.   *   *   *   *

We therefore speak of the Beautiful as if Beauty were something in the nature of the thing, and as if our Judgment were *logical*, (giving a knowledge of the object through conceptions ' of its nature'); whereas it is only *æsthetic*, and contains only a relation of the object to the subject. And this because the æsthetic judgment herein resembles the logical judgment, that it may claim universal validity.

This universality, however, cannot be derived from conceptions, for there is no transition from conceptions to the feeling of pleasure or displeasure, except in the purely practical ('moral') laws; and these are accompanied by interest, and thus distinguished from the pure æsthetic Judgment.

Accordingly the æsthetic judgment must contain, together with the consciousness of being divested of all Interest, a claim to universal validity, independent of objective universality; that is, a subjective universality.

COMPARISON OF THE BEAUTIFUL WITH THE AGREEABLE BY MEANS OF THE ABOVE CRITERION.

As to the Agreeable, it is felt by every one, that a judgment founded upon his private feeling, and asserting only that the object is pleasing to him, is confined to himself. Then when a man says: This Canary wine is pleasant: he will not object if any one correct his expression, and tell him he should rather say: It is pleasant *to me.* * * * To one person the colour of violet is soft and pleasing, to another dead and flat. One man is fond of wind-instruments, another of stringed instruments. To contend about such things, and to pronounce the judgment of others, differing from our own, incorrect, as if there were a logical opposition between them, would be folly. As to the Agreeable the maxim holds, therefore, *that every one has a taste of his own,* in matters of Sense.

As to the Beautiful, however, the case is quite different. Here it would be absurd for any one pretending to Taste to think to justify himself by saying that the object, (the building we see, the garment that person wears, the concert we listen to, the poem that is to be criticised), is beautiful *to him.* For he should not call it *beautiful,* if it pleases him alone. There may be many things pleasing and attractive to him, but this is nothing to any one else: if he declare anything to be beautiful, he attributes the same pleasure to others; he judges not for himself alone, but for all; and speaks of Beauty as a quality of the thing.

We say, therefore, the thing *is beautiful;* not *expecting* the assent of others, from having often found them to agree with us in opinion, but *requiring* it. We find fault with men if they judge otherwise, as wanting in that Taste which should be an universal attribute.

As to the Beautiful, therefore, we cannot say that every one has a taste of his own. For this would be to declare that there is no such thing as Taste; that is, no æsthetic judgment that can properly claim the assent of all.

In respect to the Agreeable, there is indeed a degree of unanimity in men's judgments, in reference to which some are said to have Taste and others not; and this not as signifying a perfection of the organs of Sense, but of the faculty of judging as to the Agreeable. Thus one who knows how to regale his guests with various luxuries, (agreeable to the different senses,) so as to please all, is said to have Taste. But the universality is here only comparative, and thus this kind of Taste is capable only of *general rules,* as being derived from Experience, and not of universal laws, such as the æsthetic judgment claims to establish for the Beautiful. * *

It is to be remarked, however, in this place, that the æsthetic Judgment presupposes nothing more than a general assent, * * * thus the *possibility* of an æsthetic judgment possessing universal validity. It does not *postulate* the assent of every person, (for this belongs only to a *logically* universal judgment, which can be supported by demonstration), but only *demands* this assent, as an example of the rule, the confirmation of which is sought, not from conceptions, but from the agreement 'in feeling' of other persons. * * * Whether any particular person who thinks to pronounce an æsthetic judgment do really judge in accordance with this principle, may be uncertain; but that he does refer to it, and therefore that his judgment is æsthetic, is declared by the use of the word Beauty. * * * * *

AN ÆSTHETIC JUDGMENT, WHEREIN AN OBJECT IS PRONOUNCED BEAUTIFUL AS CONNECTED WITH A PARTICULAR IDEA, IS NOT PURE.

There are two kinds of Beauty; Beauty *detached (pulchritudo vaga),* and Beauty adherent *(pulchritudo adhærens).* The former presupposes no idea of the object; the latter presupposes an idea, and an adequate perfection of the thing. Under the first class are embraced the 'independent and' self-subsisting beauties of any object; the other includes (as dependent and attached to the idea of some particular thing) objects conceived to exist for a special end. The beauty of flowers is free, detached Beauty. What the flower actually is, only the botanist knows; and even he, though he sees in it the reproductive organ of the plant, yet in judging of it as an object of Taste, pays no regard to this natural end. This Judgment, therefore, is founded upon no perfection of any sort; no inward fitness regulating the management of the parts. Many birds, such as parrots, humming-birds, the birds of Paradise, and various sea-shells, are beautiful in themselves; not as connected with an object with reference to its design, but independently and of themselves. So drawings *a la grecque,* arabesque borders, &c., signify nothing, represent no particular object, and express no particular idea, but are free, detached Beauty. So what are called *fantasies,* in Music (without theme); indeed all Music without text may be considered as of this kind.

In judging of detached Beauty, in its form, the æsthetic Judgment is pure. It presupposes no idea of a design to be accomplished, which should be represented by the object; for by this the freedom of the Imagination, sporting as it were in contemplation of the object, would only be restrained. But human Beauty (whether of a man, a woman, or a child); the beauty of a horse; of a building (church, palace, arsenal, or summer-house), presupposes the idea of design, which determines what the thing should be; the idea of perfection. It is therefore merely *adherent* Beauty. Thus also the connection of the Agreeable (in Sensation), with Beauty, which properly concerns only Form, disturbs the purity of the Judgment; so also connection with the Good (that is, something for which the thing, from its design, is good), is likewise destructive of the purity of the æsthetic Judgment.

'For example' we might add much that is pleasing when seen by itself, to a building, were it not that it is intended for a church: it might ornament a figure to cover it with tracery-work, and delicate, yet regular lines, as in the tatooing of the New Zealanders; were it not that it is a human being: this countenance might have much more delicate features, and a softer and more pleasing outline, were it not intended to represent a man, or indeed a warrior. So the pleasure derived from the inward design of a thing, which determines its precise character, is founded upon an idea; but that derived from Beauty is by nature such that it presupposes no conception, but is connected immediately with the image of the thing.

Now if the æsthetic judgment is made dependent on design, and thus a judgment of the Reason, it is no longer a pure æsthetic judgment.

It is true that this advantage is gained by the connection of æsthetic with intellectual pleasure, that 'the principle of' Taste becomes *fixed*, and though not universal, yet it is capable of being subjected, as to certain things, to fixed rules. These rules, however, are then no longer rules of Taste, but of a union of Taste with Reason; i. e. the Beautiful with the Good. * *

OF THE IDEAL OF BEAUTY.

As to Taste, 'therefore,' there are no objective rules * * to determine what is beautiful. For all Judgment from this source is æsthetic, that is, subjective Feeling and not a conception of any object, that determines it. To seek a principle of Taste which should give indefinite conceptions a universal criterion of the Beautiful, is a fruitless endeavour, since what is sought is impossible and self-contradictory.

That this feeling (of pleasure or displeasure) shall be capable of being generally communicated, and this without any conception 'of the nature of the object;' and the general approximate agreement of all ages and all nations, in relation to this feeling, as to certain objects is the empirical though obscure criterion of Taste, scarcely reaching to conjecture, which, as so many examples show us, has a deep-hidden foundation in the common nature of Man; in the common principles of Judgment as to the Forms under which objects are presented to us.

Hence some products of Taste are considered as models; not as if Taste could be acquired, by imitation; for Taste must be a faculty of the individual; but he who copies a model, shows himself expert, as far as he copies correctly; but Taste involves the power of judging of the model itself.

From this it follows that the highest model, the prototype of Taste can be only an Idea, which every one must awaken in himself. * *

An *Idea* is properly a conception of Reason; an *Ideal* is the image of some thing adequate to the Idea. Each such prototype of Taste rests indeed upon the vague idea of a *maximum* 'of Beauty,' but can be reached only by representation, and not by conceptions. It is therefore more properly called an Ideal 'than an Idea' of Beauty; and this, though we may not possess it, yet we strive to produce within ourselves. But since it depends upon representation, and not upon conception, it is an Ideal of the Imagination only; the Imagination being the faculty of Representation. Now how do we arrive at this Ideal of Beauty? *A priori*, or by Experience? And also, what kind of Beauty is capable of an Ideal?

It is to be observed in the first place, that the Beauty for which we are to expect an Ideal, is not *vague*, but *fixed* Beauty, 'controlled by' a conception of objective fitness. An Ideal therefore is not the object of a perfectly pure æsthetic judgment, but of one partaking in a measure of the nature of an idea. That is, the principles by which we judge concerning an Ideal, have for their foundation some idea of Reason, according to definite conceptions, and this idea determines *a priori*, the design upon which rests the possibility of the object. An Ideal of beautiful flowers; of fine furniture; of a beautiful view, is inconceivable. Even indeed as to Beauty dependent on adaptation to particular ends, an Ideal is often inconceivable; for example, an Ideal of a beautiful dwelling-house, of a beautiful tree, garden, &c.; probably because the purpose is not sufficiently definite and fixed by the notion of the thing, and thus the fitness is almost as 'floating and' unattached to a 'particular' object, as in the case of *vague* or detached Beauty.

Man, as 'a being,' having the end of his existence within himself, and able to determine its aims by means of Reason, or, where he is obliged to take them from the outward world, yet able to compare them with fundamental and universal aims, and to form an æsthetic judgment from the comparison, Man alone can present an Ideal of Beauty, in like manner as Humanity alone, among all earthly things, can afford an Ideal of perfection in him, as Intelligence. * * * *

The Ideal of the human form consists in the expression of the moral nature, without which it cannot afford a universal and *positive* pleasure, (as distinguished from the merely negative satisfaction of an academically correct representation). * * * * * *

The correctness of such an Ideal of Beauty is tested in this; that it permits no intermixture of sensuous satisfaction with the pleasure derived from the object, and yet excites a strong interest in it.

* * * * *

Taking the result of the above investigations, we find that all depends on the conception of Taste; and that this is the faculty of judging of an object according to the free, yet normal action of the Imagination. * * * But that the Imagination should be free, and yet essentially subject to law, that is, that it should contain an *autonomy*, is a contradiction.

The Understanding alone gives the law. But if the Imagination is compelled to proceed according to a definite law, the product will be determined as to its Form, according to certain conceptions of the perfection of the thing, and in this case the pleasure will not be owing to Beauty, but to Goodness, (to Perfection, though mere formal Perfection), and the judgment will be no æsthetic judgment.

It is thus a normal regularity, without law; a subjective harmony of the Imagination and the Understanding, without any objective harmony, (wherein the notion is referred to a precise conception of the object); and it is thus alone that the freedom and regularity of the Understanding can co-exist with the peculiar nature of an æsthetic judgment.

We find regular, geometrical figures, a circle, a square, a cube, &c., commonly given by critics of Taste as the simplest and most undoubted examples of Beauty; and yet they are called *regular*, because they can only be conceived of as mere representatives of a particular idea, which prescribes to the figure the law by which alone it exists. Thus one of the two must be wrong; either this judgment of the critics, in ascribing Beauty to these figures, or ours, which declares fitness, without conception, essential to Beauty.

Now it is not necessary to select a man of taste, in order to discover that greater pleasure is afforded by the figure of a circle than by a scrawl, and more in an equilateral and equiangular triangle than in one of uneven shape and as it were deformed. For this requires only common sense, and not Taste. Where we find a purpose, for example, to determine the size of a place, or to make accessible the relations of the parts to each other and to the whole; —here regular figures, and those of the simplest kind are required; and the pleasure depends not immediately upon the image of the figure, but on its applicability to various purposes. A room whose walls form unequal angles, a garden of such a shape, in short all disturbance of symmetry, as well in the forms of animals, (e. g. to be one-eyed), as of buildings or flower-beds, is unpleasant, because inappropriate; not only practically, as relates to a particular use of these things, but also in judging of them generally, as adapted to various purposes. This is not the case with the æsthetic judgment, which if pure, unites pleasure or displeasure with the mere view of the object, immediately, without reference to any employment or end. * * * All stiff regularity, approaching the mathematical, is unpleasant, from its affording no continued exercise of the perceptive powers; and where neither knowledge nor a special end is sought, it is tedious. On the other hand whatever affords a ready and agreeable exercise to the Imagination, is always new, and we do not tire of beholding it.

Marsden, in his description of Sumatra, makes the remark that in this island the wild beauties of Nature everywhere surround the beholder, and thus have little attraction for him; whereas a pepper-garden, where the poles upon which this plant climbs, form parallel lines of alleys, had a great charm for him when he came upon it in the midst of the forest; and he concludes from this that the apparently lawless beauty of the wilderness is pleasing only as variety, to one who has become tired of regularity.

But he would have only to make the experiment of spending a day in his pepper-garden, to see that when the Understanding has satisfied the craving for order which everywhere accompanies it, the object is no longer interesting, but on the contrary imposes an irksome restraint upon the Imagination; whereas the profusion of Nature, lavish even to extravagance in that country, where it is subjected to no rules of art, would afford constant nourishment to his taste.

Thus the song of birds, irreducible to any musical rules, seems to have more freedom, and thus to offer more to the Taste, than even the human voice, though exercised according to all the rules of Music. For we sooner tire of the latter, if often and long repeated. * * *

A distinction is also to be made between beautiful objects, and beautiful views of objects, (which may be indistinct, from distance). In the latter case pleasure seems to arise not so much from what is seen, as from what we are led to imagine in the field of view; that is, from the fancies with which the mind pleases itself, being constantly excited by the variety upon which the eys falls; thus for example in the varying shapes in a wood-fire, or a murmuring brook; neither of which are beautiful, but which have a charm for the imagination, by the excitement they afford. * * * For the Imagination (as a productive faculty of Cognition), has great power in creating as it were another Nature, from the material furnished by actual Nature. With this we occupy ourselves when 'the world of' experience seems too common-place; we re-model it, still indeed according to the laws of analogy, but also on principles that lie higher up in the Reason, and which are as truly natural to us as those in accordance with which the Understanding apprehends empirical Nature.

Herein we feel our freedom from the law of association that attaches to the empirical use of this faculty, and according to which indeed Nature furnishes us with material; but this is wrought by us into something quite different and superior to nature. * * *

FROM THE
"PLAN FOR AN EVERLASTING PEACE."*

NATIONS, 'considered collectively' as States, may be judged by the same rules as individuals, who, in the state of nature (i. e. of independence of outward laws), are obnoxious to each other by their mere contiguity, and each of whom

---

* *Zum ewigen Frieden.* Königsberg. 1795.

may and ought, for the sake of his own safety, to demand of the other to enter into a compact with him, of the nature of a civil government, whereby each may be secured in his right. * * * The attachment of savages to their lawless freedom, 'and their preference of' unceasing conflict to submission to the restraint of laws to be established by themselves—and thus of insane freedom to that in accordance with Reason—is looked upon by us with profound contempt, and considered as rudeness, want of civilization, and bestial degradation of humanity. It would seem, therefore, as if cultivated nations, united into separate States, must hasten to escape as soon as possible from so degraded a condition. Instead of this, however, the majesty of every *State* (for the majesty of a *people* is an absurd expression) is thought to consist precisely in this, that it is subject to no restraint from outward laws, and the glory of its chief magistrate to be, that without exposing himself to danger, he has many thousands at his command, ready to be sacrificed for a matter that does not concern them at all;[*] and the difference between the savages of Europe and those of America consists principally in this, that whereas many tribes of the latter have been entirely eaten up by their enemies, the former know how to make a better use of the conquered than to feed upon them, and prefer increasing by them the number of their subjects, and thus of the implements for yet more extensive wars.

When we consider the depravity of human nature, which shows itself openly in the uncontrolled relations of nations (whilst in the condition of civil government it is in a great measure veiled),—it is much to be wondered at that the word *Right* has not as yet been dispensed with, as pedantic, in military politics, and that no State has yet dared openly to declare itself for this opinion. For Hugo Grotius, Puffendorf, Vattel, &c. (no very comforting counsellors), are still faithfully cited in justification of warlike attacks, though their code, whether philosophical or diplomatic, has not and cannot have the least *legal* force, since States as such are subject to no common outward authority; and though there is no instance where a State has ever been induced by any arguments armed with the voices of such mighty men, to desist from its intention.

This reverence which every State pays (at least in words) to the idea of Right, proves that there exists in Man (though as yet undeveloped) the germ of a more complete mastery over the evil principle within, and a hope of similar victory in others. For otherwise States intending to make war upon each other would never make use of the word *Right*, unless it were in mockery, as the Gallic prince, who declared : "That it was the preference that Nature has given to the stronger over the weaker, that the latter should obey."

The mode by which States maintain their rights is never legal process, as where an outward tribunal exists, but only War, and this and its favourable event, Victory, do not decide the right; a treaty of peace terminates only the existing war, and not the *state of War*, a new pretext being easily found. * * * Reason, 'therefore,' from the throne of the supreme moral authority, entirely condemns War, as a means of obtaining justice, and on the other hand makes Peace an immediate duty. But Peace cannot be made or secured without a compact among nations. So that a league of a peculiar nature is demanded, which we may call *a league of Peace (fœdus pacificum)*, and which would be distinguished from a *compact of peace (pactum pacis)*, in this, that the object of the latter is to put an end only to *one war*, but that of the former to abolish War forever. * * *

The practicability (objective reality) of this idea of a *Federation*, to extend by degrees over all States, and thus lead to an everlasting Peace, may be easily shown. For if by good fortune a mighty and enlightened nation should be able to form itself into a republic (which from its nature must be inclined to lasting peace), this would give a centre for the federative union of other states, to collect around it, and thus secure the freedom of each, according to the idea of international Law, and to spread itself out by degrees farther and farther by repeated unions of this kind.

* * * * * * * *

The idea of international Law, as *a right to make War*, that is, a right to determine what is just, not by universal laws limiting the freedom of each, but by one-sided maxims, through force, —it is utterly without meaning, unless we understand by it, that it is quite right that men with such views should perish by mutual annihilation, and thus find everlasting Peace in the wide grave, that covers all the horror of violence, together with its authors.

There is no other way in accordance with Reason, for States to escape from the condition of lawlessness in their relations to each other, than by giving up, like private individuals, their wild (lawless) freedom, and submitting to public laws.

* * * * * * *

Since the communion (more or less close) between the nations of the earth, has extended so far that an act of injustice done in one part of the earth is felt in all, the idea of cosmopolitan Law is no fantastic nor exaggerated notion, but the necessary complement of the unwritten code, as well of civil as international Law; necessary to the public Law of the human race in general, and thus to eternal Peace, with the approach of which we can flatter ourselves only on this condition. * * * *

If it is our duty 'to strive for' this state of

---

[*] Thus a Bulgarian prince answered the Grecian emperor, who good-naturedly wished to decide their dispute by a duel :—" A smith who has tongs will not pull red-hot iron out of the fire with his fingers."

public Law, and if at the same time there is a well-grounded hope that it may be actualized, though only in an infinitely extended approximation, then an everlasting Peace, to succeed the hitherto falsely so called *treaties of Peace*, (properly *truces*), is no empty idea, but a problem to be solved progressively, and continually approaching the goal, since the periods of equal progress are, we hope, constantly becoming shorter. *   *   *   *   *

ON THE GUARANTY OF AN EVERLASTING PEACE.

This guaranty is given by nothing less than the great Artist, Nature, (*natura dædala rerum*), from whose mechanical course the design shines visibly forth, to produce through the very dissensions of men an involuntary concord. We give therefore to Nature, considered as the overpowering influence of a Cause unknown to us in the laws of its action, the name of Fate; but viewing it as adaptation to a design running through the Universe; as the recondite wisdom of a higher Cause whose energy is directed towards the objective destination* of the human race, we name it Providence; not, indeed, that we, properly speaking, *know*, or can even *infer* it, from these contrivances of Nature; but we are obliged to *suppose* it, to form any conception of their possibility, according to the analogy of human contrivances. The relation, however, and the harmony 'of this Cause' with the end immediately prescribed to us by Reason (in Morals) is an idea in theory transcending our powers, but practically, (for instance,. as to the idea of the duty of Peace, and the employment of the mechanism of Nature to this end), established, and its reality well-founded. *   *   *   *   *

Before examining farther into the nature of this guaranty, it will be necessary first to consider the situation in which Nature has placed the actors in her great theatre, and which makes the secure establishment of Peace finally necessary; and afterwards the manner in which she brings this about.

The arrangement provided by Nature for this end consists in this: 1. That she has taken care that in all parts of the earth, men shall be able to live; 2. That she has scattered them, by means of War, in all directions, even to the most inhospitable regions, in order that these may be peopled; 3. That, by the same means, she has compelled them to enter into relations more or less founded upon Law.

It is admirable that even the cold deserts on the Arctic Sea produce moss, which the reindeer digs from under the snow, to be itself the food or the steed of the Ostiacs or Samoides; or that the salt sand wastes provide the camel, created as it were for crossing them; in order not to leave these regions unoccupied. *   *   *

---

* That is, the destiny of the race, in History, as distinguished from Virtue, the destination of the individual. Tr.

K

But 'the inhabitants of these countries' were driven thither probably by War alone. *   *   * Nature, in providing that it should be possible for man to inhabit every part of the earth, at the same time despotically willed that they *should* inhabit every part, even against their inclination, and without connecting with this necessity the moral constraint of an idea of Duty, but choosing War as the means of accomplishing this purpose. Thus we see nations, the identity of whose language testifies to their common origin, as the Samoides on the Frozen Ocean and a nation of similar language a thousand miles distant, on the other side of the Altai mountains; between whom a different (Mongolian) nation, an equestrian and warlike people, has thrust itself, and thus driven one portion of the tribe to such a distance, into the most inhospitable regions, whither they would certainly never have spread from their own inclination. So the Fins in the northernmost parts of Europe, called Laplanders, and the Hungarians, with whom they are related in language, are now widely separated by the Gothic and Sarmatian races that have penetrated between them. And what can have driven the Esquimaux, (a race quite different from any of the American, and perhaps consisting of ancient European adventurers), into the North; and the Pescheras in South America into Terra del Fuego, except War; of which Nature avails herself as means of peopling all parts of the earth? *   *   *   *   *

Thus much concerning what Nature does *for her own purposes*, with the human race, considered as a race of animals.

Now comes the question, which touches the most important point in the design of an everlasting Peace. 'What does Nature to this' intent, as to the aim which Man's reason makes his duty; that is, what does she in furtherance of his *moral endeavour ;* and how does she guaranty that what Man *ought* to do, but does not, according to his nature as a free being, he shall nevertheless do, without prejudice to his freedom, by a natural necessity. *   *   *

When I say of Nature that *she wills* this or that to take place, I mean by this, not that she makes it our duty, (for this belongs solely to the free practical Reason), but that *she does it herself*, whether we wish it or not: (*fata volentem ducunt, nolentem trahunt*).

1. Even if a nation were not driven by internal discord to submit to the restraint of public laws, yet War would accomplish this from without; for, according to the beforementioned provision of Nature, every nation finds in its neighbourhood another nation pressing upon it, against which it must inwardly organize itself into a State, in order to be prepared for resistance. Now the republican form of government is the only one perfectly adapted to the rights of Man, but also the hardest to establish, and yet more difficult to preserve. So that many maintain that it would have to be a commonwealth of

angels, since men, with their selfish inclinations, are not capable of so sublime a form of government. But here Nature comes to the assistance of this universal Will, so honoured, but practically so powerless; and this by means of these same selfish inclinations. So that it requires only a good organization of the State, (which surely is within the power of men), so to array these forces against each other, that the one shall prevent or neutralize the evil effect of the other; so that the result for the Reason will be the same as if neither existed. Thus a man, though not morally good, may be compelled to be a good citizen. Paradoxical as it may sound, the problem of civil organization may be solved by a nation of devils, provided they have understanding. It runs thus:— "So to order and organize a multitude of rational beings, all requiring universal laws for their protection, but each secretly inclined to make himself an exception to their operation, that though they conflict in their private feeling, yet these feelings shall so counteract each other that in civil relations the result will be the same as if they had no such evil feelings."

Such a problem must be capable of a solution. For it is not the moral improvement of mankind, but only the mechanism of Nature, as to which we inquire how it is to be employed in the affairs of men, so to direct the conflict of hostile sentiments among a people, that they shall oblige each other to submit to compulsory laws, and thus bring about a condition of tranquillity in which laws are effective. This may be seen even in actually existing States, though very imperfectly organized; they approach in outward condition very near to what the idea of Right commands, though inward morality is certainly not the cause; for good government is not the product of Morality, but, vice-versa, a good moral development of a nation is to be expected only from good government.

So that the mechanism of Nature, through selfish inclinations, which are naturally opposed to each other in their outward effects also, serves as an instrument to prepare the way for what Reason aims at, the law of Right; and thus, as far as depends on the State, to further and secure inward as well as outward Peace.

We may say, therefore, that Nature imperatively *demands* that the right shall finally prevail. What is neglected at first brings itself about at last, though with much discomfort. * *

2. The idea of international Law presupposes a separation of many independent, neighbouring States, and though this in itself is a state of War (unless a federative union repress the outbreak of hostilities), yet even this is more in accordance with Reason than an amalgamation, by a power overgrowing the others and passing into a universal monarchy. For laws are always weakened in proportion to the increase of the area of government; and a soulless despotism, after having rooted out the germs of good, falls at last into anarchy. Nevertheless it is the desire of every State (or of its rulers) thus to bring about a state of enduring Peace, by monopolising, if possible, the government of the whole world. But Nature will have it otherwise.

She makes use of two means to prevent nations from intermingling, and to separate them: the difference of *Language*, and the difference of *Creed*, which indeed carries with it an inclination to mutual hatred, and an excuse for War; but yet, in the advance of culture, and the gradually increasing friendly intercourse of mankind, leads to greater harmony of principles, and to a peaceful understanding, brought about and secured, not like the despotism above spoken of (on the grave of Freedom), by the exhaustion of all forces, but by their equilibrium amid the liveliest contention.

3. As Nature wisely separates nations, though the will of each State, supported too by principles of international law, would seek for union, by cunning or violence;—so on the other hand she unites nations whom the idea of cosmopolitan Right would not have protected against violence and war, by mutual interest.

This is the spirit of Commerce, which cannot coëxist with War, and which, sooner or later, takes possession of every nation. For as among all means of influence under the command of the governing authority of the State, the power of money is most to be relied on, States are compelled (not precisely by moral motives) to encourage Peace; and in whatever quarter of the world War threatens to break out, to prevent it by negotiations, as if in constant league to this end. * * * * * * *

Thus does Nature guaranty everlasting Peace, by the very mechanism of human passions; not indeed so securely that future Peace can be (theoretically) *prophesied;* but practically she is successful, and renders it our duty to labour to bring about this end, as no mere chimera.

SUPPOSED BEGINNING OF THE HISTORY OF MAN.

To strew conjectures in the *course* of a history, in order to fill up a gap in the narrative, may be regarded as allowable; since that which went before, as remote cause, and that which came after, as effect, may furnish a tolerably safe guide to the discovery of the intermediate causes, and thus make the transition intelligible. But to *create* a history entirely out of conjecture, seems to be little better than laying the plan of a novel. Such a history ought not to be called a *conjectural history*, but a mere fiction. Nevertheless, that which ought not to be hazarded in relation to the progressive history of human affairs, may yet be attempted in relation to the first beginning of the same, so far as that beginning is the work of Nature. For here, it is not necessary to invent. Experience will suffice, if we assume, that experience, in the first beginning of things, was neither better nor worse than now,—an assumption which agrees with the analogy of nature, and has nothing presumptuous in it. A history of the *first unfolding* of freedom from an original capacity in the nature of man, is something very different from the history of freedom in its *progress*, which can have no other basis than received accounts.

Conjecture, however, must urge no extravagant claims to assent. It must announce itself not as serious occupation, but only as an exercise permitted to the imagination, under the guidance of reason, by way of recreation and mental hygiene. Accordingly, it must not measure itself with a narrative on the same subject, which has been proposed and believed as actual history, and whose evidence depends on far other grounds than those of natural philosophy. For this reason, and because I am attempting here a mere pleasure-excursion, I may count on the privilege of being allowed to avail myself of a certain ancient, sacred document, and of fancying that my excursion made on the wings of imagination, though not without a guiding thread deduced by reason from experience, has hit the exact line which that document historically describes. The reader will turn over the leaves of the document (first book of Moses, from the second to the fourth chapter), and, following step by step, see whether the course pursued by philosophy according to ideas, coincides with the one which is there indicated.

Not to lose ourselves in merely fantastic conjectures, we must begin with that which cannot be deduced by human reason from antecedent natural causes, viz. the *existence of man*. We must suppose him existing in fully developed stature, in order that he may be independent of maternal aid. We must suppose a *pair*, in order that he may propagate his species; and yet but a *single* pair, in order that war may not spring up at once, between those who are near together and yet estranged from each other; and that Nature may not be charged, on the score of various parentage, with having made no sufficient provision for union, as the chief end of human destination. For the unity of the family from which all men were to derive their origin, was undoubtedly the best means to bring about this end. I place this pair in a region secured against the attack of beasts of prey, and richly furnished by nature with the means of support; that is, in a kind of *garden*, and in a climate forever genial. Farther still, I contemplate them at that period only, at which they have already made important progress in the ability to use their powers. I begin therefore not with the utter rudeness of nature, lest there should be too many conjectures for the reader, and too few probabilities, if I were to attempt to fill up this gap, which probably comprises a long period of time.

The first man, then, could stand and walk; he could speak (Gen. ii. 20.) and even talk, that is, speak according to connected ideas (v. 23.), consequently, think. All these faculties he was forced to acquire for himself, for if they had been inborn, they would be hereditary, which is contrary to experience. But I here assume that he is already possessed of these faculties, and direct my attention exclusively to the development of the *moral* in his doing and abstaining, which necessarily presupposes the faculties in question.

At first, the novice is guided solely by instinct, that *voice of God* which all animals obey. This allowed him certain articles of food and forbade others. (Gen. iii. 2. 3.) It is not necessary however, to suppose, for this purpose, a special instinct which has since been lost. It might have been simply the sense of smell, its relation to the organ of taste, and the known sympathy of the latter with the instruments of digestion. Hence a capacity, the like of which may still be observed, to predict the suitableness or unsuitableness of any particular species of food. It is not even necessary to suppose this sense stronger in the first pair than it is now; for it is well known what difference exists in the powers of perception, between those who are occupied with their senses alone and those who are occupied, at the same time, with their thoughts, and thereby diverted from their sensations.

So long as inexperienced man obeyed this call of Nature, he found his account in so doing. Soon, however, Reason began to stir and he sought to extend his knowledge of the means of subsistence beyond the bounds of instinct, by a comparison of that which he had eaten with that which resembled it, in the judgment of another sense than the one to which the instinct attached,—the sense of sight. (Gen. iii. 6.) This experiment might have had a happy issue, although instinct did not advise, provided it did not forbid. But it is a property of reason to be able, with the help of imagination, to elaborate artificial desires not only without a natural impulse, but even against the impulses of nature. These desires which, in their first manifestation, we call wantonness, gradually produce a whole swarm of unnecessary and even of unnatural propensities, to which we give the name of luxury. The occasion of the first defection from natural instinct, may have been a trifle, but the consequence of this first experiment was, that man became conscious of his reason, as a faculty capable of extension beyond the limits within which other animals are held; and this consequence was of great importance and had a decisive influence on his way of life. Although, therefore, it may have been merely a fruit, the sight of which tempted him to partake of it by its resemblance to other pleasant fruits, of which he had already partaken; yet if we add the example of an animal to whose nature such fruit was adapted, whereas it was not adapted to the nature of man, and, consequently, forbidden to him by an opposing natural instinct;—this circumstance would give to reason the first occasion to practise chicanery with Nature (Gen. iii. 1.) and, in spite of her prohibition, to make the first experiment of a free choice; which experiment, being the first, probably did not result according to expectation. No matter how insignificant the injury which ensued, man's eyes were opened by it. (Gen. iii. 7.) He discovered in himself the capacity to select his own life-path, instead of being confined to a given one, like other animals. The momentary pleasure which the perception of this advantage might awake in him, must have been followed immediately by fear and anxiety. How was he, who, as yet, knew nothing according to its hidden qualities and remote effects,—how was he to proceed with his newly discovered power? He stood, as it were, on the brink of an abyss. From the single objects of his desire, as they had hitherto been indicated to him by instinct, he learned their infinity, an infinity in which he was as yet unprepared to choose. It was not possible for him however to return from this state of freedom once tasted, to that of servitude, or subjection to the law of instinct.

Next to the instinct of nourishment, by which Nature preserves the individual, the instinct of sex, by which she provides for the preservation of the species, is the most important. Reason, once called into action, began without much delay to manifest its influence here likewise. Man soon found that what, with other animals, is transient and for the most part dependent on periodical impulse, was capable of being prolonged and even increased, in his case, by means of the imagination, which acts with greater moderation indeed, but also with greater permanence and uniformity, the more the object is withdrawn from the senses; and that, by this means, the satiety which the satisfaction of a merely animal desire brings with it, might be prevented. Accordingly, the fig-leaf (v. 7.) was the product of a far greater exercise of reason, than that which appeared in the first stage of its development. For to render a propensity more intense and more permanent by withdrawing the object of it from the senses, shows a consciousness of some degree of power of reason over impulses, and not merely, like that first step, a capacity to serve them to a greater or less extent. *Denial* was the artifice which led from the joys of mere sensation to ideal ones, from mere animal desire to love, and, with love, from the feeling of the merely agreeable, to the taste for the beautiful, first in man, and then in nature. Propriety,—the disposition to inspire respect in others by the decent concealment of whatsoever might produce contempt,—as the true foundation of all genuine social union, gave moreover the first hint to the cultivation of man, as a moral being.—A small beginning, but one which makes an epoch, by giving a new direction to thought, is more important than the whole immeasurable series of extensions given to culture, in consequence of it.

The third step in the progress of reason, after it had connected itself with the first felt and immediate necessities, was the deliberate expectation of the future. This faculty, by means of which not only the present life-moment is enjoyed, but the coming and often far distant time made present, is the most decisive mark of the advantage possessed by man in being able to prepare himself, according to his destination, for distant ends; but it is also, at the same time, the most inexhaustible fountain of cares and troubles, occasioned by the uncertain future, from which all other animals are freed. (vs. 13—19.) The man, who had himself and a wife, together with future children, to support, anticipated the ever-growing difficulty of his labour. The woman anticipated the evils to which Nature had subjected her sex, and the added ones which the stronger man would lay upon her. Both saw with fear, in the back ground of the picture, after a toilsome life, that which indeed befalls inevitably all creatures, but without occasioning them any anxiety, namely, death. And they seemed to reproach themselves for the use of reason which had brought all these evils upon them, and to count it a crime. To live in their posterity, who might experience a happier lot, and, as members of a family, lighten the common burden, was, perhaps, the only consoling prospect which still sustained them. (Gen. iii. 16—20.)

The fourth and last step in the progress of reason, and that which raised man entirely above the fellowship of the beasts, was this, that he comprehended, however, obscurely, that he is truly the *aim of Nature*, and that nothing which lives upon the earth can rival him in this. The first time that he said to the sheep: "that skin which thou wearest, Nature gave thee not for thine own sake but for mine," and so saying, took it from the animal and put it upon himself; (v. 21.) he became conscious of a prerogative which, by virtue of his nature, he possessed above all other animals. He no longer regarded these as his associates in creation, but as means and instruments committed to his will, for the accomplishment of whatsoever ends he pleased. This conception includes, though dimly, the converse; viz. that he could not say the same of his fellowman, but must regard him as an equal partaker with himself of the gifts of Nature. We have here a remote preparative for those limitations which reason was hereafter to impose upon the will of man in regard to his fellow, and which are even more necessary than inclination and love, to the constitution of society.

And thus had man,—in consideration of his title to be an end unto himself, to be regarded as such by every other and by none to be used merely as a means to other ends,—entered into an *equality with all rational beings* of whatsoever rank. (Gen. iii. 22.) It is here, and not in the possession of reason, considered merely as an instrument for the satisfaction of various propensities, that we are to look for the ground of that unlimited equality of man even with higher beings, who may be incomparably superior to him in natural endowments, but no one of whom has therefore a right to manage and dispose of him at pleasure. This step in the progress of reason is therefore simultaneous with the dismissal of man from the mother-lap of Nature;—a change which was honourable indeed, but at the same time dangerous, inasmuch as it drove him forth from the unmolested and safe condition in which his childhood was nursed, as it were from a garden which had maintained him without any care on his part, (v. 23.) and thrust him into the wide world, where so many cares and troubles and unknown evils awaited him. Hereafter, the burdens of life will often elicit the wish for a paradise — the creature of his imagination—where he may dream or trifle away his existence in quiet inactivity and uninterrupted peace. But reason, restless and irresistibly impelling him to unfold the capacities implanted in him, stations itself between him and that region of imaginary joys, and will not permit him to return into that condition of rude simplicity out of which it has drawn him forth. (v. 24.) It impels him to undergo with patience the labour which he hates, to chase the gauds which he despises, and to forget even death so terrible to him, in the pursuit of those trifles whose loss is more terrible still.

REMARK.

From this sketch of the first history of man it appears, that his departure from the Paradise which reason represents as the first residence of his species, was nothing else than the transition from the rudeness of a merely animal nature, to humanity, from the leading strings of instinct to the guidance of reason, — in a word, from the guardianship of Nature, to a state of freedom. Whether man has gained or lost by this change, can no longer be a question, if we regard the destination of the *species*, which consists solely in progress toward perfection; however defective may have been the first attempts, and even a long series of successive attempts to penetrate to this end. Nevertheless, this course which, for the species, is a progress from worse to better, is not exactly such for the individual. Before reason was awakened, there was neither command nor prohibition, and consequently no transgression. But when reason began its work, and, weak as it was, came into collision with animalism in all its strength, it was unavoidable that evils, and what was worse, with the growing cultivation of reason, vices should arise, which were entirely foreign from the state of ignorance, and consequently of innocence. The first step out of this state, therefore, on the moral side, was a *Fall;* on the physical, a number of life-ills, hitherto unknown, were the effect; consequently, the *punishment* of that Fall. So the history of *Nature* begins with good, for it is the *work of God;* but the history of *Freedom* begins with evil, for it is the *work of man.*

For the individual who, in the use of his freedom, has reference only to himself, the change was a loss. For Nature, whose aim in relation to man, is directed to the species, it was a gain. The former, therefore, has reason to ascribe all the evils that he suffers, and all the evils that he does, to his own fault; at the same time, however, as a member of the whole, (the species) he must admire and commend the wisdom and propriety of the arrangement.

In this way, we may reconcile, with each other, and with reason, the oft misinterpreted, and, in appearance, successively conflicting assertions of the celebrated J. J. Rousseau. In his work on The Influence of the Sciences, and in that on The Inequality of Men, he very correctly exhibits the unavoidable contradiction which exists between culture and the nature of man, as a physical race of beings, in which each individual is to fulfil entirely his destination. But in his 'Emil' and his 'Social Contract' and other writings, he endeavours to solve the difficult problem, and to show how culture must proceed in order to unfold, according to their destination, the faculties of Humanity as a moral species, so that there may no longer be any conflict between the natural and the moral destination. From this conflict,[*] since culture has not

---

[*] To mention but a few instances of this conflict between the effort of Humanity to fulfil its moral destination on the one hand, and the unchangeable observance of the laws implanted in man's nature, adapted to a rude and animal condition on the other hand, I adduce the following. The epoch of man's majority, *i. e.* the impulse as well as the capacity to propagate his species, is set by Nature at the age of sixteen or seventeen years; an age at which the youth, in a rude state of Nature, becomes literally a man; for he possesses then the power to maintain himself, to beget children, and to maintain them, together with his wife. The simplicity of his wants makes this easy. In a state of cultivation, on the other hand, many means, acquired skill, as well as favourable external circumstances, are necessary for this purpose; so that, civilly, this epoch is deferred, on an average, by at least ten years. Nature, meanwhile, has not changed her period of maturity to suit the progress of social refinement, but obstinately insists on her own law, which she has calculated for the preservation of the human race, as an animal species. Hence arises an unavoidable conflict between the purposes of Nature and the customs of Society. The natural man has already attained to manhood at an age when the civil man is still a youth, or even a child. For we may call him a child who, on account of his years, (in a state of civilization) cannot even maintain *himself*, much less his kind; although he has the impulse and the capacity, and, consequently, the call of Nature to beget his kind. Assuredly, Nature has not implanted instincts and capacities in living beings, merely that they may war against and suppress them. The tendencies of Nature, therefore, are not designed for a state of civilization, but solely for the preservation of the human species as a race of animals. There is an unavoidable collision between nature and civilization, in this particular, which only a perfect civil polity — the highest aim of culture — can do away. At present, the interval in question (between natural and civil majority) is usually beset with vices and their consequences, the manifold evils of humanity.

Another example which proves the truth of the propo-

yet rightly commenced, much less completed its course, according to true principles, educating alike the man and the citizen, arise all the real evils which oppress human life, and all the vices which dishonour it. The propensities which lead to those vices, and on which the blame is laid in such cases, are good in themselves, and have their end as natural endowments. But these natural endowments, being calculated for a state of Nature alone, are trenched upon by progressive culture, and, in turn, re-act upon culture, until perfected Art returns to Nature again; which is the final goal in the moral destination of the human species.

CONCLUSION OF THE HISTORY.

The beginning of the next period was the transition of man from an era of peace and ease to one of labour and discord, as a prelude to social union. And here again we must make a great leap, and suppose him at once in possession of tame animals, and of fruits which he could multiply by sowing and planting: (Gen. iv. 2.) although it must have been a long process, by which he arrived from the rude life of

---

sition, that Nature has implanted in us two tendencies to two different ends, viz., of man as an animal and of man as a moral species, is the *Ars longa vita brevis* of Hippocrates. Science and art might be carried much farther by a single mind which is made for them, after it has once attained the requisite maturity of judgment by long discipline and acquired knowledge, than by successive generations of learned men; provided that single head could live through the whole period, occupied by those successive generations, with the same youthful power of intellect. Now Nature has evidently taken her determination respecting the duration of human life, from a very different point of view than the promotion of science. For when a man of the happiest intellect stands on the brink of the greatest discoveries, which he is authorized to expect from his skill and experience, old age comes in; he grows dull, and must leave it to another generation, beginning with the A. B. C., and going over the whole ground again which he has been over, to add another span to the progress of culture. Accordingly, the progress of the human race toward the fulfilment of its entire destination appears to be continually interrupted, and in continual danger of falling back again into primitive rudeness. And the Grecian philosopher did not complain entirely without cause, when he said " it is a pity that man must die then when he has just begun to understand how he ought to live."

We may take, for a third example, the inequality of the human condition. Not the inequality of natural endowments nor of the gifts of Fortune, but that inequality in universal human rights, concerning which Rousseau complains with much truth, but which is inseparable from culture as long as it proceeds without a plan, as it must for a long time, and to which Nature certainly did not destine man, seeing she gave him freedom, and reason to restrain that freedom solely by its own universal and external legality, which we call civil right. Man was intended to work his way gradually out of the rudeness of his natural tendencies, and while he lifts himself above them, nevertheless to take heed that he does not sin against them; a faculty which he does not acquire till late, and after many unsuccessful attempts. In the meanwhile, Humanity sighs under various evils which, from inexperience, it inflicts upon itself.

---

a hunter to the first of these possessions, or from the irregular digging of roots and gathering of fruits to the second. At this point, the division between men who had hitherto lived peaceably side by side, behoved to begin; the consequence of which was the separation of those addicted to different modes of life, and their dispersion over the earth. The life of the shepherd is not only easy, but affords also the most certain support, since there can be no want of feed in a soil which is uninhabited far and wide. On the other hand, agriculture or planting is very toilsome, dependent on the uncertainty of the weather; consequently insecure, and requiring, moreover, permanent buildings, ownership of the soil, and sufficient power to defend it. But the herdsman hates this property in the soil, which limits the freedom of his pasturage. With regard to the first point, the agriculturalist might seem to envy the herdsman as more favoured by Heaven than himself (v. 4.); in fact, however, he was much troubled by him as long as he remained in his neighbourhood; for the browsing cattle did not spare his plantations. Since now it was easy for the herdsman, after the damage which he had caused, to withdraw himself to a distance and thus escape reprisals, seeing he left nothing which he could not as well find everywhere else, it was probably the husbandman who first used violence against these trespasses which the herdsman thought lawful, and who, since the occasion for these trespasses could never entirely cease, was compelled, unless he would lose the fruits of his long diligence, to remove as far as possible from those who led a nomadic life. (v. 16.) This separation makes the third epoch.

A soil, on the working and planting of which (especially with trees), the support of life depends, requires fixed habitations; and, for the defence of these against all assaults, a multitude of men who shall assist each other. Consequently, men addicted to this mode of life, could no longer disperse by families, but must keep together and establish villages, (improperly called cities), in order to protect their property against hunters or hordes of vagrant herdsmen. The first necessities of life, the production of which involved various pursuits (v. 20.), might now be exchanged, the one for the other. The necessary consequence of this was culture, and the beginning of the arts, as well of amusement as of industry. (vs. 21, 22.) But what is most important, there was also some arrangement toward a civil constitution and public justice; at first, indeed, with respect only to gross acts of violence, the avenging of which was now no longer left to individuals, as in the savage state, but committed to a legalized power which kept the whole together; that is a kind of Government, beyond which there was no executive force (vs. 23, 24.) From this first rude institution, all human arts, among which that of society and civil security is the most profitable, could gradually unfold themselves, the human race multiply, and like swarms of bees diffuse itself from a common centre, by sending forth cultivated colonists. With this period, also, the *inequality* among men,—that rich fountain of so much evil, but also of all good—began and continued to increase.

So long, indeed, as the nomadic, herd-tending nations which acknowledge God alone for their ruler, hovered around the inhabitants of cities, and the husbandmen, who had a man (magistrate) for their master* (vi. 4.), and, being sworn foes of property in land, assumed a hostile attitude toward them, and were hated by them in turn, there was continual war between the two, or, at least, continual danger of war; and therefore both nations could enjoy, internally at least, the inestimable blessing of freedom. For the danger of war is even now the only thing that qualifies Despotism. Wealth is required in order that a State may become a Power; but without liberty there can be no wealth-producing industry. To supply the place of this, in a poor nation, there must be a general participation in the maintenance of the common weal. And this again cannot exist without a feeling of liberty.

In time, however, the growing luxury of the city-dwellers, particularly the art of pleasing, by which the city women eclipsed the dirty nymphs of the wilderness, could not but prove a powerful temptation to those herdsmen to form connexions with them, and thus to suffer themselves to be drawn into the splendid misery of the cities. Then, with the amalgamation of two once hostile nations,—putting an end to all danger of war, but, at the same time also, to all liberty,—it came to pass that the despotism of powerful tyrants on the one hand, together with a culture scarcely yet commenced, — soulless luxury in abject slavery, combined with all the vices of the savage state — on the other hand irresistibly diverted the human race from that progressive cultivation of their capacity for good, prescribed to them by Nature, and thereby rendered them unworthy of their very existence, as a species intended to rule over the earth, and not merely *to enjoy as brutes or to serve as slaves.* (v. 17.)

CONCLUDING REMARK.

The thinking man feels a sorrow that may even lead to moral corruption, of which the thoughtless knows nothing. He feels, namely, a discontent with that Providence which guides the course of the world at large, when he reflects on the evils which oppress the human race to so great an extent, and seemingly without the hope of anything better. It is of the greatest importance, however, *to be satisfied with Providence,* notwithstanding it has prescribed to us a path so full of toil in our earthly world; partly that we may still take courage amid our difficulties; partly, lest, in ascribing these evils to Fate, we forget our own guilt, which perhaps is the sole cause of them, and so neglect to seek a remedy for them in self-reformation.

It must be confessed that the greatest evils which afflict civilized nations arise from *war:* not so much indeed from that which actually is, or has been, as from the never-ending, ever-increasing *preparation* for that which is to be. To this end are applied all the forces of the State and all the fruits of its culture, which might be used for still further culture. Freedom is, in many points, materially invaded, and the motherly care of the State for individual members, changed to requisitions of inexorable severity; which, nevertheless, are justified by the fear of external danger. But, would this culture, would the intimate union of the various classes of the Commonwealth for the mutual furthering of their prosperity, would the same population, nay, would that degree of freedom, which, under very restrictive laws, still exists,— would they be found, were it not for that *respect for Humanity* which the constant dread of war enforces in the Heads of States? Look at China, which, though she may suffer a sudden invasion, yet, in consequence of her situation, has no powerful enemy to fear; and where, consequently, every trace of freedom is obliterated! In that stage of culture, therefore, at which the human race at present stands, war is an indispensable means for the promotion of further culture; and not till the progress of culture is completed (God knows when), would a perpetual peace be salutary for us; and not till then would it be possible. Accordingly, so far as this point is concerned, we ourselves are to blame for the evils of which we so bitterly complain; and the sacred record is quite right in representing the amalgamation of nations into one Community, and their perfect deliverance from external danger, while their culture has scarcely yet commenced, as a hindrance to all further culture, and a lapse into irremediable corruption.

The second cause of discontent among men is the order of Nature with respect to the shortness of life. It is true, one must have estimated very erroneously the value of life, to wish it longer than it actually is; for that would be only prolonging a struggle with perpetual difficulties. On the other hand, however, one can hardly blame a childish judgment for fearing death without loving life, or for thinking,— difficult as it may be to spend a single day in tolerable contentment, — that there are never days enough in which to repeat the torment. But when we consider, with how many cares the means of maintaining so short a life afflict us, and how much injustice is perpetrated

---

* The Arabian Bedouins still call themselves children of a former *Sheik,* the founder of their tribe (as *Beni Aled,* &c.). This personage, however, is by no means a ruler, and can exercise, of his own will, no authority over them. For in a nation of herdsmen, as no one possesses real estate which he would have to leave behind, any family that is discontented may easily separate itself from the tribe, and go to strengthen another.

in the hope of some future, though equally transient good, it is reasonable to conclude, that, if men could look forward to a life of eight hundred years or more, the father would no longer be secure of his life from the son, the brother from the brother, friend from friend; and that the vices of so long-lived a race would reach such a height as to render man worthy of no better fate, than to be swept from the earth in a general flood. (vs. 12, 13.)

The third wish, or rather empty longing, (for one is conscious that the object can never be attained) is the shadow-image of that *golden age* so much praised by the poets :—a state in which men are to be freed from all imaginary necessities imposed by luxury, and contented with the simple wants of Nature; where there is to be a perfect equality of condition, everduring peace; in a word, the pure enjoyment of a careless life spent in idle dreaming or in childish sports. This longing, which makes the Robinson Crusoes and the voyages to the South Sea Islands so attractive, illustrates the satiety which the thinking man experiences in a state of civilization, if he seeks its value in enjoyment alone, and balances the counterweight of indolence, when admonished by reason to give value to life, by means of action. The vanity of this desire of a return to the period of simplicity and innocence, is abundantly evident, when, from the above representation of his original condition, we learn that man could not maintain himself in it, precisely, because it does not satisfy him; and that he is still less disposed to return to it again. So that, after all, the present laborious condition is to be regarded as his own choice:

Such a representation of his history is therefore profitable to man, and conducive to his instruction and improvement, as showing him that he must not charge Providence with the evils which afflict him; also, that he is not justified in imputing his own crimes to the transgression of his first Parents, creating an hereditary tendency to similar transgressions in their descendants, (for voluntary actions have nothing hereditary in them), but that, on the contrary, he may, with perfect justice, regard their actions as his own, and, accordingly, take to himself the whole blame of the evils arising from the misuse of his reason; since he cannot but be conscious that he would have done precisely as they did, in similar circumstances, and that the first use which he made of his reason would have been,—in spite of the admonitions of Nature,— to abuse it. This point of *moral* evil being adjusted, those which are strictly *physical* will hardly be found to yield a balance in our favour, if tried by a debt and credit account of guilt and desert.

And so the result of an attempt to construct a history of primitive man by the aid of philosophy, is contentment with Providence and the course of human things on the whole, as proceeding not from good to bad but from worse to better. To this process every one, for his part, is called upon by Nature herself, to contribute according to his power.

PAINTED BY TISCHBEIN.   ENGRAVED BY J. SARTAIN.

LESSING.

JOHANN GOTTHOLD EPHRAIM LESSING.

Born 1729. Died 1781.

LESSING was the son of a Lutheran Clergyman; his birthplace, Kamentz in Upper Lusatia.

Biography, fond to trace the promise of future greatness in childish caprices, pleases itself with the circumstance, that at the age of five, he was unwilling to have his picture taken otherwise, than with a great pile of books by his side. So great, it is intimated, was the child's passion for Letters!

At the age of twelve he was sent to the High-school at Meissen in Saxony, where he labored with great diligence and laid the foundation of his extensive erudition. At seventeen he entered the university of Leipzig, where his parents wished him to study theology. But following the bent of his own genius, he studied everything else instead; and though a constant hearer of the celebrated Ernesti, he otherwise gave no heed to prepare himself for the sacred office. He felt the secret '*Drang*,' which indicated another calling, and in fact before he left Leipzig had already begun his literary career, as a writer for the stage. The Drama was his first love; but he did not confine himself to that, nor to any one province of literature. Indeed there is scarcely one which his learning and his genius have not illustrated.

In 1750 he went to Wittenberg to prosecute his theological studies in compliance with the earnest solicitation of his parents. His younger brother, Johann Gottlieb, was already a student at this university; and the two, in conjunction, published several essays in theology and polite literature, which procured them much honor from the Public, and some odium from the orthodox.

Lessing however did not remain long in Wittenberg, nor did he ever become a preacher. He went to Berlin, and lived as author by profession, in intimate communion with Mendelssohn, Nicolai, Rammler, and others, supporting himself by his pen. Some of his principal works, particularly Emilia Galotti and the Laocoon, were published during this period, and while holding the office of secretary to General Tauenzien, at Breslau. In 1760 he was made member of the Royal academy of sciences at Berlin. In 1766 he accepted a situation connected with the theatre at Hamburg, as theatrical critic, and there wrote his *Dramaturgie*. In 1770 he was made librarian to the library at Wolfenbüttel, in the Duchy of Brunswick-Wolfenbüttel, where, with the exception of a tour to Italy, made in the company of the hereditary Prince of Brunswick, he remained until his death. Here he published his Nathan the Wise, and several theological treatises. The latter involved him in vexatious controversies, and subjected him to persecutions which embittered the remainder of his days, and, as it is thought, abridged their term. He died in the beginning of his fifty-third year; too soon for the interests of literature, too late for his own peace.

The life comprehended in this brief outline was singularly unblessed. Lessing was not made of the stuff which thrives in the world of men. He was one of those illstarred geniuses, who, owing to some fatality or some defect, or, quite as often perhaps, to some unwonted and unaccommodating virtue, fail to find an equal and congenial sphere for the exercise of their faculties, and are never at one with their destiny. His erratic course, not wholly free from folly,* was crossed with frequent vexations and bitter disappointments. He had the misfortune, among others, to lose, soon after marriage, a beloved wife to whom he had been betrothed for six years.—"Six years," says Hegel†—"what a long time for a betrothed pair! and, in this interim, almost nothing but vexation and suffering through sickness. And then the duration of the marriage,—only three years! Who can help thinking, in such a case, of the vanity of man and his dearest cares? Should we not think that, if a man could know this

---

* He is accused of having been addicted to games of hazard.

† " Ueber Lessing's Briefwechsel mit seiner Frau." Hegel's Vermischte Schriften.

(81)

beforehand, he would prefer an earlier death than Nature had intended, to such a life?"

"That a man like Lessing," says Heine,* "could never be happy you will easily comprehend. Even if he had not loved the truth, and if he had not everywhere fought for it, of his own free will, he must nevertheless have been unhappy, for he was a Genius. They will pardon thee everything, said lately a sighing poet; they will pardon thy riches, they will pardon thy high birth, they will pardon thy handsome figure, they will even pardon thy talent, but to genius men are inexorable. Therefore is the history of great men always a martyr-legend. If they suffered not for great Humanity, they suffered for their own greatness, for their great manner of being, for their unphilistine ways, their dissatisfaction with ostentatious common-place, with the smirking meanness of their environment;—a dissatisfaction which naturally drives them into extravagances, e. g. into the play-house, or even into the gambling-house, as happened to poor Lessing. * * * * *

It is heart-rending to read in his biography, how Destiny denied this man every joy, and how it was not even permitted him to recreate himself from his daily conflicts, in the peaceful bosom of a family. Once only, Fortune seemed disposed to favor him. She gave him a beloved wife, a child. But this happiness was like the sunbeam which gilds the wing of a passing bird. It passed as soon. The wife died in giving birth to her first child; the child immediately after birth. Concerning the latter, he wrote to a friend these horribly witty words: "My joy was but brief. And I was unwilling to lose him,—this son. For he had so much sense! So much sense! Do not think that the few hours of paternity have made me such an ape of a father. I know what I say. Was it not a proof of sense, that he came so unwillingly into the world?—that he suspected mischief so soon? Was it not a proof of sense, that he seized the first opportunity to be off again?—I had hoped, for once, to have some comfort like other people. But it proved a bad business for me."

"There was one sorrow of which Lessing never spoke with his friends; that was, his awful loneliness, his spiritual isolation. Some of his cotemporaries loved him, no one understood him. Mendelssohn, his best friend, defended him with zeal when he was accused of Spinozism. The zeal and the defence were as laughable as they were superfluous. Be quiet in thy grave, old Moses! thy Lessing, to be sure, was on the way to this dreadful error, this pitiable calamity — Spinozism. But the All-highest, the Father in heaven rescued him, at the right moment, by death. Be quiet, thy Lessing was not a Spinozist, as slander would have it. He died a good deist, like thee and Nicolai, and Teller, and the Universal German Library!"

This life, so unsuccessful, so tragic, in its personal aspects, was eminently successful in its fruits. German literature is indebted to Lessing as scarcely to any other name in its annals. He has been to it what Luther was to the language,—the father of a new era and order of things. That era of the German intellect which has just transpired, that era which gave to Germany her present intellectual position among the nations, and which, through her influence, has become an era in the progress of the universal mind, dates from Lessing, its earliest representative in general literature; as Kant was its earliest representative in philosophy. He first delivered his countrymen from the tyranny of French forms, and, placing before them the true models of all time, particularly Shakspeare and the Greeks, led them back to Nature, and, through Nature, to new creations. Great as a poet,—although his sublime ideal of the poet's function led him to disclaim that title,—* he was still greater as a critic, and, therein, a true son of his country, a

---

* Salon, vol. ii.

* He thus speaks of himself at the close of the *Dramaturgie:* "I am neither actor nor poet. It is true men have sometimes done me the honour to rank me in the latter class. But it is only because they misunderstood me. They should not infer so liberally from some dramatic attempts which I have hazarded. Not every one who takes the brush in his hand is a painter. The oldest of those attempts were made at that age when we are so willing to mistake pleasure and facility for genius. Whatever is tolerable in the later ones, I am very conscious that I owe it wholly and only to criticism. I feel not in me the living fountain which struggles forth, of its own force, and, by its own force, shoots up in such rich, fresh and pure rays. I have to squeeze everything out of me by pressure and pipes. * * * I have therefore always been shamed or vexed, when I have heard or read anything in dispraise of criticism. It has been said to stifle genius; and I had flattered myself that I derived from it something which approaches very near to Genius. I am a cripple, and cannot possibly be edified by a philippic against crutches. But, to be sure, as the crutch may help the lame man to move from place to place, but can never make him a runner, so it is with criticism."

genuine representative of the national mind. Germany has produced no greater critic than Lessing. And when we say this, we place him at the head of that "group" in the "Phalanx" of Letters. Herder testifies of him, that "no modern writer has exercised a greater influence on Germany, in matters of taste and of refined and profound judgment on literary subjects." "Lessing's judgments have, for the most part, been confirmed by time. What then seemed sharp, is now thought just; what was then hard, is now sober truth." I know scarce any one who could speak of himself, as a writer, with greater modesty and dignity than Lessing. And generally, he is, without question, in extent of reading, in critical acumen, and in many-sided, manly understanding, the *first* critic of Germany."* His dissertation on the Fable is affirmed by the same author, to be the "most concise and philosophic theory concerning any species of composition, that has been written since Aristotle."

But Lessing wrought even more powerfully, by his character and example, as the fearless advocate of truth, and the uncompromising enemy of all narrowness, and false enlightenment, and pretence,—of all half-culture and half-truth,—than by his critical theories. This is Heine's view of him. "Since Luther, Germany has produced no greater and better man than Gotthold Ephraim Lessing. These two are our pride and our delight. Like Luther, Lessing acted not only by means of certain specific performances, but by stirring the German nation to its depths, and producing a wholesome mental commotion with his criticism and his polemics. He was the living criticism of his time, and his whole life was polemic. That criticism made itself felt in the widest domain of thought and feeling; in religion, in science, in art. That polemic overcame every adversary, and grew stronger with every victory. Lessing, according to his own confession, required such controversy, for the development of his own mind. He resembled that fabulous Norman who inherited the talents, knowledge, and faculties of the men whom he slew in battle, and, in this way, at last, was endued with all possible advantages and excellences. It may be supposed that such a battle-loving champion must occasion no small noise in Germany, quiet Germany, which, at that time, was more sabbath-still than now-a-days. People were confounded at his literary boldness. But this very quality was of great service to him. For "*oser*" is the secret of success in literature as well as in revolutions—and in love. At Lessing's sword trembled all. No head was secure from him. * * * Whom his sword could not reach, he slew with the arrows of his wit. * * * Lessing's wit is not like that *Enjouement*, that *Gaîté*, those springing *saillies* which are known in this country. His wit was not the little French grey-hound, that runs after its own shadow; it was more like a great German cat, that plays with the mouse before devouring it. * * * Thus, by his controversies, he has rescued many a name from well-deserved oblivion. Several tiny authors he has, as it were, spun round with the most genial ridicule, with the most costly humor; and now they are preserved to endless ages in his works, like insects caught in a piece of amber. While killing his adversaries, he made them immortal. Who of us would ever have heard of that Klotz on whom Lessing has expended so much ridicule and acuteness? The rocks which he hurled upon that poor antiquary, and with which he crushed him, are now his indestructible monument.

It is worthy of note that the wittiest man in Germany was also, at the same time, the most honest. Nothing can equal his love of truth. Lessing made not the slightest concession to falsehood, even when, after the usual fashion of the worldly wise, he could promote the cause of Truth by it. He could do everything for the truth except to lie for it. Whoso thinks, said he once, to recommend Truth by all sorts of masks and paints, would fain be her pimp; but her lover he never was.

To no one is the beautiful saying of Buffon—"the style is the man"—more applicable than to Lessing. His manner of writing is entirely like his character, true, firm, unadorned, beautiful and imposing by its inherent strength. His style is the style of Roman architecture; the greatest solidity with the greatest simplicity."

His influence in Theology has been as great, perhaps, as in Criticism and Art, although less generally acknowledged, and although most vehemently resisted at the time. In Theology, as in every other department, he was a reformer, at war with the prevailing opinions of his time; and was persecuted, as only theological

---

* Herder's Zerstreute Blätter. II. Th. "Gotthold Ephraim Lessing."

reformers are. He published some fragments of an anonymous skeptic, found in the library at Wolfenbüttel, containing doubts which Lessing wished to have solved, but which he was accused of circulating with impious designs against the essential truths of Christianity. In the storm of abuse occasioned by these publications he appeals from Lutheran Divines to Luther himself. "O! that he could judge me;—he whom I would prefer of all others for my judge! Luther, thou! Great misunderstood! And by none more misunderstood than by those short-sighted, headstrong men who, with thy slippers in their hands, saunter screaming or indifferent along the path prepared by thee. Thou hast delivered us from the yoke of Tradition: who shall deliver us from the more intolerable yoke of the Letter! Who shall bring us at last a Christianity such as thou wouldst now teach, such as Christ himself would teach!"*

That judgment, in the spirit of Luther, which he so vainly craved during his life, was liberally accorded to him, by all the best minds of Germany, after his death; and by none more liberally than by Herder, than whom he could not have wished for himself—among the living —a fitter judge. "Lessing's last days," says this writer,† "were destined to be embittered by a theological controversy from which, if the Public has not yet derived all the benefit which he certainly expected and intended, it can hardly be considered his fault.‡ He published the 'Fragments, by an anonymous Author,' relating to the Resurrection and other points of biblical history. I, who knew Lessing personally, who knew him at the time when the above-mentioned pieces had probably come into his hands, and, as I now infer from many expressions of his, were then exercising his mind intensely; I, who also heard him converse on subjects of this kind, and believe myself to be sufficiently acquainted with his character in what relates to manly love of truth;—I am convinced, for my own part, (for others, I neither pretend nor care to be,) that he procured the publication of these pieces solely and purely for the interests of Truth, for the sake of freer and manly inquiry, examination and confirmation on all sides. He has affirmed this himself so often, so strongly, so plainly;—the whole manner in which he published these Fragments, and, as a layman, gave here and there his thoughts upon them, sometimes in the way of refutation;—Lessing's general character, as it must have impressed every one who knew him (and those who did not should be cautious in their judgment of it);—all this is to me a pledge of his pure philosophical conviction, that hereby also he should occasion and effect something useful, to wit,—I repeat it again,—free investigation of the truth,—of truth so important, as this history must be to every one who believes it, or who believes on it. If, of all truths and histories, this truth and this history alone may not be investigated,—may not be investigated in relation to every doubt and every doubter,—that is not Lessing's fault. But, in our day, no theologian and no religionist will maintain this. If we grant this one proposition,—that Truth must and can be investigated;—that Truth gains with every free and earnest examination, precisely in that degree and proportion in which it is cognizable by us, and consequently, only in such measure binding upon us;—if we grant this proposition, which the history of all times, and religions, and peoples, especially the history and truth of the Christian religion, wherever it has been questioned and assailed, incontrovertibly proves: then Lessing has won. And then, instead of talking of crooked, malicious, wicked designs, we should thank him that he has given us occasion for the investigation and confirmation of the most important truths; in short, for triumph.

* * * * * * * *

I thanked him, always, for making me acquainted with doubts which occupy me and bring me farther; which develope thoughts in me, although not in the smoothest way.

* * * * * * * *

And where art thou now, noble truth-seeker, truth-perceiver, truth-defender? What seest, what discernest thou now? Thy first glance beyond the bounds of this darkness, of this earth-mist; in what a different, higher light did it reveal to thee all which thou sawest and soughtest on earth! To seek the truth, not to have discovered it; to strive for the good, not to have already embraced all goodness;—this was here thy contemplation, thy serious em-

---

* "Durch die Fragmente des Wolfenbüttelischen Ungenannten veranlasste Schriften."
† Zerstreute Blätter. II. "Gotthold Ephraim Lessing."
‡ The strictest theologian will scarcely deny at present that the publication of the fragments has been of service. The surest proof of which is that if they were to appear now they would scarcely attract the attention which men then involuntarily bestowed upon them. A sign that we have advanced.

ployment, thy study, thy life. Eye and heart thou soughtest ever to keep awake and sound; and to no vice wast thou so opposed, as to vague, creeping hypocrisy, to our customary, daily half-lie and half-truth, to the false politeness which is never helpful, to dissembling philanthropy which never desires to be, or can be beneficent;—but most of all (agreeably to thy office and vocation) to that wearisome, drowsy, half-truth which, in all our knowing and learning, like rust and cancer, gnaws, from early childhood, in human souls. This monster, with all its frightful brood, thou assailedst like a hero, and bravely hast thou fought thy fight. Many passages in thy books, full of pure truth, full of manly, firm sentiments, full of golden, eternal goodness and beauty, will encourage, instruct, confirm, awaken men who, also, like thee, shall serve the truth entirely; so long as truth is truth and the human mind is what it was created to be; who shall serve every truth; even though, at first, it may seem dreadful and hateful;—persuaded that, in the end, it will prove, nevertheless, to be wholesome, refreshing, beautiful. Wherever thou hast erred, where thy acuteness and thine ever active, lively mind lured thee aside into by-ways;—in short, where thou wast a man, thou erredst, assuredly not willingly, and strovest ever to become a *whole* man; a progressive, growing spirit."

Vitis ut arboribus decori est, ut vitibus uvæ,
Tu decus omne tuis : postquam te fata tulere
Ipsa Pales agros, atque ipse reliquit Apollo.
Spargite humum foliis inducite fontibus umbras,
Et tumulum facite et tumulo superaddite carmen.
" Candidus ignotum miratur lumen Olympi
Sub pedibusque videt nubes et sidera Daphnis."

"FROM LAOCOON."*

LAOCOON, OR THE LIMITS OF PAINTING AND POETRY.

PREFACE.

The first one who compared Painting with Poetry, was a man of refined feeling, who had experienced in himself a similar effect from these two arts. Both, he perceived, represent absent things as present, appearances as reality. Both deceive, and the deceptions of both give pleasure.

A second sought to penetrate into the interior of this pleasure, and discovered that, in both cases, it flows from the same source. Beauty, the first notion of which we derive from corporeal objects, has general rules which will bear application to various objects,—to actions, to thoughts, as well as to forms.

A third, who reflected on the value and distribution of these general rules, observed that some of them obtain most in Painting, others in Poetry, and that in regard to one class therefore Painting may assist Poetry, in regard to the other, Poetry Painting — with illustrations and examples.

The first was the *Amateur,* the second the Philosopher, the third the Critic.

---

* The Laocoon of Lessing is the masterpiece of German criticism, as his Emilia Galotti is the masterpiece of German Tragedy. It unites, with extensive erudition and rare penetration, a poet's feeling for beauty and art. The general subject is announced in the preface, the greater part of which is given above. But, in addition to the arguments which bear directly on that subject, it contains many general reflections on art and poetry, of great value. The brief extract which is here offered, contains Lessing's answer to the question, why Laocoon does not 'cry,' in the representation of the sculptor, as well as in that of the poet?

The two first were not likely to make a false use, either of their feelings or their conclusions. In the observations of the critic, on the other hand, the principal point is the correctness of the application to specific cases; and since there are fifty witty critics to one of penetration, it would be a wonder if this application were always made with that caution which is necessary to maintain a just balance between the two arts.

If Apelles and Protogenes, in their lost works on painting, confirmed and illustrated the rules of that art by the already established rules of poetry, we may rest assured that they did it with that moderation and accuracy with which we still see Aristotle, Cicero, Horace, Quintilian, in their works, apply the principles and experiences of Painting to Eloquence and Poetry. It is the prerogative of the ancients, in nothing, to have done, either too much or too little.

But we moderns have thought to surpass them in many things, by converting their little pleasure-paths into highways, although the shorter and safer highways have dwindled, by that means, into bypaths that lead through wildernesses.

The dazzling antithesis of the Greek Voltaire, that painting is silent poetry, and poetry a speaking picture, would scarcely be found in any text-book. It was one of those conceits in which Simonides abounded, in which that portion which is true is so obvious, that men think they must overlook what is indefinite and false in them.

The ancients, however, did not overlook it. On the contrary, while they limited the saying of Simonides to the effects produced by the two arts, they did not forget to insist that, notwithstanding the perfect similarity of these effects, they differed, nevertheless, as well in the objects as in the manner of their imitation. (Τλη και τροποις μιμησεως).

But just as if no such difference existed, many of the latest critics have drawn from that coincidence between painting and poetry, the most crude conclusions. At one time, they force poetry into the narrow bounds of painting; at another, they give to painting the entire dimensions of the wide sphere of poetry. All that is lawful in the one they concede to the other; all that pleases or displeases in the one must needs be pleasing or displeasing in the other also. Full of this idea, they pronounce the most shallow judgments with the most confident tone. They treat the differences observed between the works of a poet and a painter handling the same theme, as faults which they charge upon the one or the other, according as their taste inclines more to the one or the other art.

And this false criticism has, to some extent, misled the *virtuosi* themselves. It has engendered a fondness for sketching in poetry, and introduced allegory into painting. Men have attempted to make the former "a speaking picture," without properly understanding what Poetry can or ought to *paint*; and to make the latter "a silent poem," not considering in what degree Painting is capable of expressing universal conceptions, without departing too far from her destination and becoming a kind of arbitrary *writing*.

To counteract this false taste and these unfounded judgments is the principal design of the following essays. Their origin is accidental, and their growth has followed rather the order of my reading than the methodical development of general principles. They are, therefore, not so much a book, as irregular *collectanea* for a book.

As I make the "Laocoon" my point of departure, and often recur to it, I have determined to give it a share in the title.

I.

The universal and principal characteristic of the Greek master-pieces in painting and in sculpture, according to Herr Winkelmann, is a noble simplicity and a quiet grandeur, as well in the attitude as in the expression. "As the depth of the sea," he says, "remains for ever quiet, however the surface may rage, so the expression, in the figures of the Greeks, discovers, in the midst of passion, a great and calm soul.

"This soul paints itself in the face of the Laocoon, and not in the face alone, under the most vehement suffering. The pain apparent in all the muscles and sinews of the body, and which, without considering the face and other parts, we seem almost to feel ourselves, in the painful drawing in of the abdomen alone,—this pain, I say, manifests itself nevertheless with no degree of violence in the face, or in the whole attitude.

He raises no such fearful cry as Virgil sings of his Laocoon; the opening of the mouth does not permit it; it is rather an anxious and oppressed sigh, as described by Sadolet. The pain of the body and the greatness of the soul are expressed with equal force in the narrow structure of the figure, and, as it were, weighed, the one against the other. Laocoon suffers, but he suffers like the Philoctetes of Sophocles; his misery touches our soul, but we wish, at the same time, to resemble this great man in his capacity of endurance.

"The expression of so great a soul far transcends the imitation of mere natural beauty. The artist must have felt in himself the strength of mind which he has impressed upon his marble. Greece possessed artists and philosophers in the same person, and had more than one Metrodorus. Wisdom joined hands with Art, and breathed into her figures a more than common soul, &c."

The observation on which this criticism is based, that the pain of Laocoon does not show itself in his countenance with that degree of vehemence which might be expected from its intensity, is perfectly correct. Further, it is indisputable that, in this very circumstance, in which a half-critic might judge the artist to have fallen below Nature and not to have reached the true pathos of pain, his wisdom is most conspicuously manifest.

But, in regard to the reason which Herr Winkelmann assigns for this wisdom, and in regard to the universality of the rule which he deduces from this reason, I venture to be of a different opinion.

I confess, the depreciating side-glance which he throws at Virgil, first caused me to doubt; and then the comparison with Philoctetes.

"Laocoon suffers like the Philoctetes of Sophocles." How does this character suffer? It is singular that his suffering should have left such a different impression upon our minds. The complaints, the screams, the wild execrations with which his pain filled the camp, interrupting the sacrifices and all solemn acts, sounded not less terribly through the desert island. They were the cause of his being banished thither. What tones of impatience, of misery, of despair! The poet made the theatre resound with his imitation of them.

A cry is the natural expression of bodily pain. Homer's wounded warriors fall, not seldom, with a cry to the ground. Venus, when injured, shrieks aloud,* not that she may be characterized by this cry as the luxurious Goddess of pleasure, but that Nature may have her due. For even the iron Mars, when he feels the lance of Diomed, cries so horribly, "as if ten thousand mad warriors were shrieking at once," that both armies are terrified.† Notwithstanding Homer elevates his heroes so far above human nature in some things, they always remain true to it, when it comes to the feeling of pain or affront, and to the expression

* Iliad, E. v. 343. † Iliad, ib. 859.

of that feeling by cries or tears or by railing. In their deeds they are beings of a higher order; but, in their sensations, they are veritable men.

I know, we more refined Europeans, of a wiser posterity, understand better how to govern our mouth and our eyes. Courtesy and grace forbid cries and tears. The active courage of the first, rude age of the world has transformed itself, with us, into a suffering one. Yet even our ancestors were greater in the latter, than in the former kind. But our ancestors were barbarians. To suppress all pain, to look with unflinching eye on the stroke of death, to die laughing under the bites of adders, to mourn neither one's own sin nor the loss of one's dearest friend,—these are traits of the old Northern heroism. Palnatoko gave the citizens of Joms command, to fear nothing, nor so much as to name the word fear.

Not so the Greek! He felt and he feared. He gave utterance to his pains and his grief. He was not ashamed of any human weakness; but he allowed none to withhold him from the path of honour, or to hinder him in the fulfilment of his duty. What was savageness and callousness with the barbarians, was, with him, the result of principle. Heroism, with him, was like the hidden sparks in the flint, which sleep peacefully so long as they are not awakened by external force; and neither take from the stone its smoothness nor its coldness. With the barbarian, heroism was a bright, devouring flame which raged without ceasing, destroying or blackening, at least, every other good quality in his nature. When Homer leads the Trojans to battle, with wild shouts, and the Greeks, on the other hand, in resolute silence,— the commentators remark well, that the poet intended hereby to describe the former as barbarians, and the latter as civilized nations. I wonder they have not noticed a similar characteristic contrast in another passage. The hostile armies have concluded an armistice. They are occupied with the burning of their dead,— an employment which does not pass without hot tears on both sides; δαxρυα θερμα χεοντες. But Priam forbids his Trojans to weep; ιδ' εια xλαιειν Πριαμος μεγας. He forbids them to weep, says Madame Dacier, because he fears that they will make themselves too tender, and enter the conflict with less courage, on the morrow. Good! but I ask why must Priam alone fear this? Why does not Agamemnon also give the same command to his Greeks? The meaning of the poet lies deeper. He designs to teach us, that only the civilized Greek can weep and be brave at the same time; whereas the Trojans, in order to be so, must first extinguish every feeling of humanity. Νεμεσσωμαι γε μεν ιδεν xλαιειν, he makes the intelligent son of the wise Nestor say, in another place.

It is worthy of note, that among the few tragedies that have come down to us from antiquity, there are two in which bodily pain constitutes not the least part of the misery, with which the hero suffers. The Philoctetes and the Dying Hercules. The latter, also, like the former, is represented by Sophocles as wailing, moaning, weeping, and crying. Thanks to our decent neighbours, those masters of propriety, a howling Philoctetes, a crying Hercules, would now be most ridiculous and intolerable characters on the stage. True, one of their newest poets* has ventured upon Philoctetes. But did he dare to show them the true Philoctetes?

Even a Laocoon is numbered among the lost pieces of Sophocles. Would that Fate had spared us this Laocoon! From the very slight notices of it, which the ancient grammarians have given, it is impossible to determine how the poet handled this subject. But of this I am sure, that he did not represent Laocoon as more stoical than Philoctetes and Hercules. Everything stoical is untheatrical, and our compassion is always commensurate with the suffering expressed by the object that interests us. It is true, if we see that object bear his misery with a great soul, that greatness of soul will provoke our admiration. But admiration is a cold feeling which precludes every warmer sentiment and every clear representation, with its vacant stare.

And now I come to my inference. If it is true that cries, under the infliction of bodily pain,— more especially, according to the old Greek view of the subject,—are perfectly consistent with greatness of soul; then the desire of representing such a soul, cannot be the reason why the artist was nevertheless unwilling to imitate those cries in his marble. On the contrary, there must be some other reason why, in this particular, he departs from his rival, the poet, who expresses these cries with the most deliberate intention.

II.

Whether it be fable or history, that the first essay in the plastic arts was made by Love,— this much is certain, that she was never weary of guiding the hand of the great, old masters. For, whereas, at the present day, painting is pursued, in its whole extent, as that art which imitates bodies in general, upon surfaces, the wise Greek confined it within much narrower limits. He restricted it to the imitation of those bodies which are beautiful. Their artists painted nothing but the beautiful. Even vulgar beauty, the beauty of inferior orders, was, with them, only an incidental theme,—their exercise, their recreation. Their works aimed to please by the perfection of the object itself. They were too great to demand of the spectator, that he should content himself with the mere cold enjoyment arising from a successful likeness,— from the contemplation of their own skill. Nothing in their art was dearer to them, no-

---

* Chateaubrun.

thing seemed to them more noble, than the aim of the art.

"Who would wish to paint thee, since no one likes to look upon thee?" said the ancient epigrammatist,* of a very deformed person. Many a modern artist would say: "Be thou as deformed as it is possible to be; I will paint thee notwithstanding. Though no one loves to look upon thee, yet shall men look with pleasure on my painting, not because it represents thee, but as a proof of my art which knows how to copy such a scarecrow so accurately."

True, the propensity to glory in mere skill, undignified by the worth of its object, is too natural not to have produced, among the Greeks also, a Pausonius and a Pyreicus. They had such painters, but they rendered them strict justice. Pausonius, whose department was below the beauties of ordinary nature,— whose depraved taste loved best to represent the unsightly and defective in the human form,—lived in the most contemptible poverty. And Pyreicus who painted barber's-rooms, dirty workshops, asses and kitchen-herbs, with all the diligence of a Dutch artist,—as if things of that sort were so charming and so rare in nature, acquired the name of Rhyparographer, or painter of filth; although the luxurious rich purchased his pictures for their weight in gold, as if to help their nothingness by this imaginary value.†

The magistrates, themselves, did not think it unworthy their attention, to detain the artist forcibly within his proper sphere. The law of the Thebans, which required the imitation of the beautiful and forbade the imitation of the deformed, is well known. It was not a law against bunglers, as it is generally, and even by Junius himself,‡ considered to be. It condemned the Greek *Ghezzi*,— the unworthy artifice of obtaining a resemblance by exaggerating the deformities of the originals; in a word,— caricature.

We laugh when we are told that even the arts were subject to civil laws, with the ancients. But we are not always right when we laugh. Unquestionably, the laws must not arrogate to themselves any power over the sciences, for the object of the sciences is truth. Truth is necessary to the soul, and it is tyranny to place the slightest restriction on the gratification of this essential want. But the object of the arts, being pleasure, is not indispensable. Therefore it may well depend on the legislator, what kind of pleasure he will allow, and in what degree he will allow it.

The plastic arts especially, besides the inevitable influence which they exert on the character of a nation, are capable of an effect which demands the close inspection of the Law. If beautiful men produced beautiful statues,

---

* Antiochus. (Antholog. Lib. ii. Cap. iv.)
† Hence Aristotle advises that his pictures should not be shown to young people, that their imagination might be kept pure from ugly images. Aristot. Polit. L. 8. C. 5.
‡ De Pictura. vet. lib. ii. cap. iv.

these again reacted upon those; and the state was indebted to beautiful statues, among other causes, for its beautiful men. With us, the sensitiveness of maternal imagination appears to express itself only in monsters.

From this point of view, I think, I see a truth in certain ancient traditions which have been rejected, without qualification, as lies. The mothers of Aristomenes, of Aristodamas, of Alexander the Great, of Scipio, of Augustus, of Galerius,—all dreamed, during their pregnancy, of serpents. The serpent was a symbol of godhead, and the beautiful statues and paintings of Bacchus, of Apollo, of Mercury, of Hercules, were seldom without a serpent. The honest women had feasted their eyes on the god, during the day; and the confounding dream awakened the image of the beast. Thus I rescue the dream, and surrender the explanation which the pride of their sons, and the impudence of flatterers have made of it. There must have been some reason why the adulterous fancy was always a serpent.

But I wander out of my way. I only wished to establish this point, that with the ancients beauty was the highest law of the plastic arts.

And, this point established, it follows necessarily, that everything else, to which the plastic arts might likewise extend, must yield, altogether, where it was found incompatible with beauty; and where it was compatible with beauty, must, at least, be subordinated to that.

I will go no farther than the expression. There are passions and degrees of passion which manifest themselves in the countenance, by the ugliest distortions, and throw the whole body into such violent attitudes, that all the beautiful lines which define it in a state of rest, are lost. Accordingly, the ancient artists either abstained altogether from the representation of these passions; or they reduced them to a lower degree,—one in which they are susceptible of some measure of beauty.

Rage and despair disfigured none of their works. I venture to affirm that they have never represented a Fury.*

They reduced anger to earnestness. With the poet, it was the angry Jupiter who hurled the lightning; with the artist, it was only the earnest.

Lamentation was softened into concern. And where this could not be done,—where lamentation would have been as belittling as it was disfiguring,—what did Timanthes in that case? His picture of the sacrifice of Iphigenia,— wherein he apportions to each of the spectators the degree of sorrow, proper to each, but covers the face of the father, which should have exhibited the most intense of all;—is well known, and many handsome things have been said concerning it. One says: "the painter had so exhausted himself in sad countenances, that he

---

* Except on coins, whose figures belong not to Art, but to the language of symbols.

despaired of his ability to give the father a sadder one."* "He confessed by this," says another, "that the grief of a father, in such a case, is beyond all expression."† For my part, I see here neither the incompetence of the artist, nor the incompetence of the art. With the increase of the passion, the traits of countenance corresponding to that passion are proportionally marked. The highest degree of it has the most decided expression; and nothing in art is easier than to represent what is decided. But Timanthes knew the limits which the Graces have assigned to his art. He knew that the degree of lamentation which became Agamemnon, as father, manifests itself in distortions, which are always ugly. He carried the expression of grief only so far as beauty and dignity could be combined with it. What was ugly he would fain have passed over, or would fain have softened; but since his composition did not allow of both, what else remained but to conceal it?—What he might not paint, he left to be conjectured. This concealment is a sacrifice which the artist made to beauty. It is an example showing, not how expression may be carried beyond the bounds of art, but how it must be made subject to the first law of art, the law of beauty.

Now, applying this to the Laocoon, we see clearly the reason which I am seeking. The master laboured for the highest beauty possible, under the given conditions of bodily pain. Bodily pain, in all its deforming vehemence, was incompatible with that beauty. It was necessary therefore, that he should reduce it,—that he should soften cries into sighs. Not because crying betrays an ignoble soul, but because it disfigures the countenance, in a manner which is disgusting. Do but tear open the mouth of Laocoon, in imagination, and judge! Let him scream and see! Before, it was a creation which inspired compassion, because it united pain with beauty. Now, it has become an unsightly, an abominable creation, from which we are fain to turn away our faces, because the sight of pain awakens displeasure; and that displeasure is not converted into the sweet sentiment of pity by the beauty of the suffering object.

The mere wide opening of the mouth, setting aside the violent and disgusting derangement and distortion of the other parts of the countenance, produced by it,—causes, in painting, a spot and in sculpture, a cavity, which produces the most disagreeable effect in the world. Montfaucon discovered little taste when he declared an old, bearded head, with wide, gaping mouth, to be a Jupiter delivering an oracle.‡ Must a god scream when he discloses the future? Would an agreeable outline of the mouth render his speech suspicious? Neither do I believe Valerius, when he says that Ajax, in the abovementioned picture of Timanthes, is represented as screaming.* Far inferior masters, and that too, in times when art had already degenerated, do not let even the wildest barbarians, when suffering the terrors of death beneath the sword of the conqueror, open the mouth so wide as to scream.

It is certain that this reduction of extreme bodily pain to a lesser degree of feeling was observable in various ancient works of art. The suffering Hercules in the poisoned garment, by an unknown master, was not the Sophoclean Hercules, who shrieked so dreadfully, that the Locrian rocks and the Eubœan Cape resounded with his cries. He was more gloomy than wild. The Philoctetes of Pythagoras Leontinus seemed to communicate his sufferings to the beholder, an effect which the slightest touch of the horrible would have prevented.

III.

But, as has been hinted, art, in modern times, has had its limits greatly enlarged. It is contended that the sphere of its imitations embraces the whole extent of visible nature, of which the beautiful is only a small part. Truth and expression are said to be its first law; and as Nature herself always sacrifices beauty to higher ends, so the artist also is required to subordinate the beautiful to his general calling, and to pursue it no further than truth and expression permit. Enough that by truth and expression, deformities of Nature are changed into beauties of Art.

Suppose we leave uncontested, for the present, the worth or unworthiness of these views, may there not be other considerations, independent of these, which should induce the artist to set bounds to expression, and not to take it from the extreme point of the action represented?

I think that the single moment of time, to which the material limits of art confine all its imitations, will lead to such considerations.

Since the artist can use but one moment of everchanging nature, and the painter, more especially, can use that moment only from a single point of view; and since their works are made, not to be seen merely, but to be contemplated, and to be contemplated repeatedly and long, it is evident that in the selection of that single moment and that single point of view, too much care cannot be had to choose the most fruitful. But only that is fruitful which gives the imagination free play. The more we see, the more we must be able to imagine; and the more we imagine, the more we must think we see. Now, in the whole course of a passion,

---

* Pliny, lib. xxxv. sect. 35.
† Valerius Maximus, lib. viii. cap. 2.
‡ Antiq. expl. T. I. p. 50.

* He enumerates the degrees of grief expressed by Timanthes as follows:—Calchantem tristem, moestum Ulyssem, clamantem Ajacem, lamentantem Menelaum.— A screaming Ajax would have been an ugly figure; and since Cicero and Quintilian do not mention it in their descriptions of this work, I am the rather justified in regarding it as an addition, with which Valerius has enriched it, out of his own head.

there is no one moment which possesses this advantage in so slight a degree, as the climax of that passion. There is nothing beyond it; and to exhibit to the eye the uttermost, is to bind the wings of Imagination, and to compel her, since she is unable to exceed the sensible impression, to occupy herself with feebler images, below that impression, shunning, as limitation, the visible fulness expressed. When, therefore, Laocoon sighs, Imagination can hear him cry; but when he cries, she can neither rise one step above that representation, nor sink one step below it, without beholding him in a more tolerable, and, consequently, less interesting condition. She hears him merely groan, or she sees him already dead.

Further, since this single moment receives from art an unchangeable duration, it should express nothing that can be conceived only as transient. All phenomena to whose essence, according to our notion, it belongs, to break forth suddenly, and suddenly to vanish,—to be what they are for one moment only,—all such phenomena, whether pleasing or terrible, acquire, through the prolongation given to them in works of art, so unnatural an aspect, that the impression is weakened each time we look upon it, until, at last, the whole subject produces only shuddering or disgust. La Metrie, who caused himself to be painted and engraved as a second Democritus, laughs but the first time he is seen. If we look at him often, the philosopher becomes a buffoon, and the laugh changes to a grin. So of cries. The violent pain which extorts the cry is either soon relieved, or else it destroys the sufferer. Although, therefore, a man of the greatest patience and fortitude may cry, he does not cry unceasingly. And it is only this appearance of perpetuity in the material imitations of art, that makes his crying seem like feminine impotence or like childish petulance. This, at least, the author of the Laocoon was bound to avoid, even though the act of crying were not incompatible with beauty, or though his art would allow him to express suffering without beauty.

Among ancient painters, Timomachus seems to have delighted most in scenes of vehement passion. His raving Ajax and his infanticide Medea were celebrated paintings. But, from the descriptions we have of them, it appears that he well understood and knew how to seize that point, where the beholder does not so much see as imagine the uttermost,—that appearance with which we do not so necessarily connect the idea of transitoriness, that we are displeased with the prolongation of it. The Medea he did not represent at the moment when she is actually slaying her children, but at the moment previous to that, when maternal love is yet contending with jealousy. We foresee the result of this conflict. We tremble in anticipation of beholding soon the *cruel* Medea only, and our imagination far surpasses all that the painter could exhibit to us of that dread moment. But for that very reason, the continued irresolution of Medea is so far from displeasing, in a work of art, that we even wish it had been so in reality,—that the conflict had never been decided, or had been protracted, until time and reflection should have assuaged the fury of passion, and secured to the maternal sentiment the victory. Timomachus earned great and frequent praises by this proof of wisdom, which gave him a decided superiority over another unknown painter, who was foolish enough to exhibit Medea at the very height of her madness, and thus to give that fleeting and transient fit of extreme rage, a permanence which is an outrage against Nature. A poet who reproaches him with this want of judgment, says wittily,—addressing the picture itself,—"Dost thou then forever thirst after the blood of thy children? Is there ever a new Jason, ever a new Creusa incessantly irritating thee? To the Devil with thee, then, even in the picture," he adds, full of disgust.

Of the Raving Ajax of Timomachus, some judgment may be formed from the account of Philostratus.* Ajax was not represented in it, as he storms among the herds, chaining and slaying oxen and rams instead of men. But the master exhibits him, on the contrary, as he sits exhausted there, after these mad exploits, and revolves the intention of destroying himself. And that is truly the "raving Ajax," not because he raves at this moment, but because it is evident that he has been raving, and because the extent of his madness is seen most vividly in the shame and despair which overwhelm him at the recollection. The storm is inferred from the wrecks and the corpses which it has cast upon the strand.

IV.

I review the reasons assigned, why the author of the Laocoon was obliged to observe a certain measure in the representation of bodily pain; and I find that they are all derived from the peculiar nature of his art, and its necessary limits and requirements. They will hardly be found applicable to poetry.

Without inquiring at present, how far the poet can succeed in depicting corporeal beauty, it is indisputable that, as the whole immeasurable domain of perfection is open to him, so the visible form, by means of which perfection becomes beauty, is only one of the least of those aids by which he contrives to interest us in his characters. Oftentimes he neglects this aid altogether, assured that when his hero has once obtained our good-will, we shall be so much occupied with his nobler qualities, that we shall not think of his personal appearance; or so won by them, that, if we do think of the person, we shall give it, of our own accord, a beautiful, or at least an indifferent look. At all events, he will not find it necessary to consult

---

* Vita Apoll. lib. ii. cap. 22.

the eye in each particular trait, which is not expressly designed for the eye. When Virgil's Laocoon cries, who considers that a large mouth is necessary for this purpose, and that a large mouth is not becoming. Enough that "Clamores horrendos ad sidera tollit" is sublime to the ear, whatever it may be to the eye. If any one requires here a beautiful image, he has entirely missed the impression which the poet intended.

Again, the poet is not required to concentrate his sketch into a single moment. He can, if he pleases, take each action at its origin and carry it through to its termination. Each of those variations, which would cost the painter a separate picture, costs him but a single stroke. And though this one stroke, in itself considered, might offend the imagination of the hearer, it is so well prepared by what preceded, or so qualified and compensated by what follows, that it loses its individuality, and, taken in connection with the rest, produces the most charming effect. Although, therefore, it were really unbecoming for a man to cry out in the extremity of pain; how can this trifling, transient impropriety injure, in our estimation, one whom we have already learned to know and to love, as the most careful of patriots, and the most devoted of fathers? We refer his cries, not to his character, but solely to his intolerable pain. This is all that we hear in his cries; and it was only by means of them, that the poet could make that pain apparent to his readers.

Who then will reproach him? Who will not rather confess that, if the artist did well not to represent Laocoon as crying, the poet did equally well to let him cry.

FROM "THE EDUCATION OF THE HUMAN RACE."*

What education is to the individual, revelation is to the whole human race.

Education is a revelation which is made to the individual; and revelation is an education which has taken place and is still taking place with the whole human race.

Whether any advantage may accrue to the science of education, by considering education from this point of view, I shall not here inquire. But unquestionably, it may be of great use in theology, and may help to resolve many difficulties, to regard revelation as an education of the human race.

Education gives man nothing which he might not have had from himself; it only gives him that, which he might have had from himself, more rapidly and more easily. So too, revelation gives mankind nothing which the human reason, left to itself, might not also have attained to; but it gave them and gives them what is most important, sooner.

And as, in education, it is not a matter of indifference, in what order the faculties of man are unfolded, as education cannot communicate all things at once,—even so God, in his revelation, has found it necessary to observe a certain order, a certain measure.

Although the first man had been furnished, at the outset, with the notion of an only God, yet this notion, being not an acquired, but an imparted one, could not possibly continue, in its purity, for any length of time. As soon as human reason, left to itself, began to work upon it, it separated the one Immeasurable into several Immeasurables, and gave to each of these parts its own peculiar characteristic.

Thus arose, in a natural way, polytheism and idolatry. And who knows how many million years human reason might have wandered about in these aberrations, notwithstanding everywhere and at all times, individual men perceived that they were aberrations; had it not pleased God, by a new impulse, to give it a better direction?

But since he could not and would not reveal himself again to each individual, he selected a single nation for his special training: and that the most rude and savage of all, in order to begin with them from the foundation.

This was the Israelitish nation, concerning which, it is not even known, what kind of worship they had in Egypt. For slaves so degraded, as they were, were not allowed to take part in the worship of the Egyptians; and the God of their fathers had become wholly unknown to them.

Perhaps the Egyptians had expressly forbidden them any god or gods, had taught them to believe that they had no god or gods, that to have a god or gods was a prerogative of the superior Egyptians. Perhaps they had taught them this in order to tyrannize over them with the greater show of justice. Do not Christians at the present day pursue very much the same course with their slaves?

To this rude people, therefore, God caused himself at first to be proclaimed as the God of their fathers, in order first to familiarize them with the idea, that they too had a God of their own.

By means of the miracles with which he brought them out of Egypt, he proved himself, in the next place, a God who was mightier than all other gods. And while he continued to manifest himself as the mightiest of all, a distinction which only one can possess, he accus-

---

* This Essay is considered as one of great importance in speculative theology. It contains the germ of all that is most valuable in subsequent speculations on these subjects. The greater part of it is given above. The little that has been omitted seemed not to be essential to the fair presentation of the author's idea. The original is divided into formal propositions, numbering one hundred. It was thought best to omit the formality of the numbers in the translation.

tomed them gradually to the notion of an only God.

But how far was this conception, of an only God, below the true transcendental idea of unity, which reason, so long afterward, learned to deduce, with certainty, from the idea of infinity.

The nation was very far from being able to raise itself to the true conception of the One, although the more enlightened among the people had already approximated more or less nearly to this idea. And this was the true and only cause why they so often forsook their own, and thought to find the only, that is, the most powerful God, in some other divinity, of another nation.

But what kind of moral training was possible for a nation so rude, so unskilled in abstract thought, so completely in its childhood? Only such a one as corresponds with the period of childhood; an education by means of immediate, sensual rewards and punishments.

So here again, education and revelation coincide. As yet, God could give his people no other religion and no other law than one, by the keeping or transgressing of which, they might hope to be happy or fear to be wretched, here on earth. For, as yet, their thoughts extended no further than the present life. They knew of no immortality of the soul; they longed for no future state of being. To have revealed to them those things to which their reason as yet was so little adequate, what else would this have been, on the part of God, but to commit the fault of the vain pedagogue, who would rather urge his pupil forward and make a display of his proficiency, than instruct him thoroughly?

But wherefore, it may be asked, wherefore this education of so rude a people, with whom it was necessary to begin thus at the very beginning? I answer, to the end that individuals among them might, in process of time, be used, with so much the greater safety, as educators of other nations. God educated in them the future teachers of mankind. This the Jews became; and only they could become this,—only men of a nation so trained.

For, further. When the child had grown up, under blows and caresses, and was now arrived to years of discretion, all at once, the Father sent it abroad. And there, at once, it acknowledged the advantages it had enjoyed without acknowledging them in its Father's house.

During the time that God had led his chosen people through all the stages of a childish discipline, the other nations of the earth had advanced, in their own way, by the light of reason. Most of them had remained far behind the chosen people, but some of them had outstripped it. And thus it happens with children who are suffered to grow up by themselves. Many remain quite rude, but some cultivate themselves to an astonishing degree.

But these favoured few prove nothing against the use and the necessity of education. And so the few heathen nations which, up to this period, seemed to have got the start of the chosen people, even in the knowledge of God, prove nothing against revelation. The child of education begins with slow but certain steps; it is late in overtaking many a more happily organized child of Nature, but it does overtake it at last, and, thenceforward, can nevermore be overtaken by it.

As yet the Jewish nation had worshipped, in their Jehovah, rather the mightiest than the wisest of all the gods; as yet they had feared him, as a jealous God, rather than loved him. And this too may serve as a proof, that the conceptions they had formed of their highest and only God, are not exactly the true conceptions, those which we ought to have of God. But now the time had arrived when these conceptions of theirs were to be enlarged, ennobled, rectified. For this purpose, God made use of a quite natural method;—a better and more correct standard, by which they had now the opportunity of estimating him.

Hitherto, they had measured him only with the miserable idols of the small and rude nations, their neighbours, with whom they had lived in a state of perpetual jealousy: but now, in their captivity, under the wise Persians, they began to measure him with the Being of all beings, whom a more disciplined reason had learned to acknowledge and to adore.

Revelation had guided their reason, and now, all at once, reason threw light upon their revelation.

This was the first mutual service which both rendered to each other; and so far is this reciprocal influence from being derogatory to the author of both, that, without it, one of the two would be superfluous.

The child, sent into foreign lands, saw other children, who knew more and behaved better than himself. Mortified, he asked himself, why do not I know that too? Why do not I also live thus? Might not this have been taught to me also in my Father's house? Might not I also have been held to this? Then he looks up his elementary books once more, with which he had long been disgusted, for the sake of casting the blame upon them. But behold! he recognizes that it is not the fault of the books, but purely his own fault, that he did not long ago possess the same knowledge and live in the same manner.

Thus enlightened respecting their own national treasures, the Jews returned and became an entirely different people, whose first care was to make this light permanent among themselves. Soon there was no more thought of defection or idolatry. For one may become faithless to a national *god*, but never to God, when once a true knowledge of him has been attained.

Theologians have sought to explain this entire change of the Jewish people, in different ways. And one who has well exposed the insufficiency of these different explanations, assigns, as the true reason of this change, the visible fulfilment of the prophecies uttered and written respecting the Babylonish captivity and the restoration from the same. But this reason, too, can be true only as it supposes more elevated conceptions of God, now first attained to. Now, for the first time, the Jews must have perceived, that working miracles and foretelling the future belonged to God alone. Hitherto, they had ascribed both to the false idols; and this was the reason that miracle and prophecy had hitherto made so feeble and transient an impression on their minds.

Without doubt, too, the Jews became more familiar with the doctrine of immortality, under the Chaldeans and Persians. They obtained a still more intimate acquaintance with it, in the schools of the Greek philosophers in Egypt.

But it was not with this doctrine, in their sacred writings, as it was with that of the unity and the attributes of God. And therefore the belief in the immortality of the soul, could never be the belief of the whole people. It was and continued the belief only of a particular sect.

A *preparation* for the doctrine of the immortality of the soul may be found in the divine threat to visit the sins of the fathers upon the children, to the third and fourth generation. This accustomed the fathers to live, in imagination, with their latest posterity, and to feel, in anticipation, the misery they might bring upon their innocent heads. An *allusion* to this doctrine is found in whatever would excite curiosity and give occasion for questions; as, for example, the often recurring phrase, "gathered to his fathers," as synonymous with dying. An *indication* of it is found in whatever contained a germ from which the unrevealed truth could be developed. Of this character, was the inference which Christ drew from the expression, "the God of Abraham, of Isaac and of Jacob." This indication, indeed, seems to me capable of being developed into a strict demonstration.

In these preparations, allusions, and indications, consists the positive perfection of an elementary book. Its negative perfection consists in this, that the way to those truths which are still kept back, is not closed or obstructed.

But every elementary book is suited only to a particular age. For the child, that has outgrown it, to linger over it longer than was intended, is injurious. For, in order to connect any kind of use with this detention, it is necessary to suppose more in the book than it actually contains, to import into it more than it will bear. It is necessary to seek and to make too many allusions and hints, to shake out* the allegories too assiduously, to interpret the examples too minutely, to press the words too far. In this way, the child acquires a narrow, perverted, hairsplitting mind, becomes fond of mystery, superstitious, and impatient of everything that is

---

* *i. e.* As one shakes a vessel or cloth, to empty it completely of its contents. Tr.

easy and intelligible. This is the way in which the Rabbins treated their sacred books. This was the kind of character which they, thereby, impressed on the mind of their people.

A better teacher must come and snatch the elementary book, which he has exhausted, out of the pupil's hands.—Christ came.

God designed to embrace, in one plan of education, only that portion of the human race, which was already united in itself, by language, by action, by government, and by other natural and political relations. And this portion was now ripe for the second great step in the progress of their education. That is, this portion of mankind had advanced so far in the exercise of their reason, as to be capable of and to require nobler and worthier motives for their moral conduct, than the temporal rewards and punishments which had guided them hitherto. The infant becomes a boy. Sweetmeats and toys give place to the growing desire to be as free, as honoured and as happy as he sees his older brothers and sisters.

The better sort among that portion of mankind had long been accustomed to be governed by a shadow of these nobler motives. The Greek and the Roman did everything, that they might continue to live in the memory of their fellow-citizens, after death. It was time that another, actual life, to be expected after this, should influence their actions. And thus Christ became the first reliable, practical teacher of the immortality of the soul.

The first reliable teacher — reliable, on account of the prophecies which seemed to be fulfilled in him, on account of the miracles which he performed, on account of his own resurrection from the dead, with which he sealed his doctrine. Whether we are able, at this day, to demonstrate this resurrection and these miracles, I shall leave out of view. I shall also leave out of view the question, what was the person of Christ? All this may have been important to secure the reception of his doctrine then, but it is no longer so necessary to the understanding of his doctrine now. The first practical teacher. For to suppose, to wish, to believe the immortality of the soul, as a philosophical speculation, is one thing; to conform one's inward and outward life to it, is another thing. And this, at least, was first taught by Christ. For, though it was the belief of many nations, before him, that evil actions would be punished in the life to come, it was only those actions which were injurious to society, and which therefore had a penalty attached to them already by society. It was reserved for him alone to recommend inward purity of heart with a view to another life.

His disciples faithfully disseminated this doctrine. And if they had rendered no other service than to procure the more general diffusion, among various nations, of a truth which Christ seemed to have designed for the Jews alone, they ought, even on this account, to be reckoned among the educators and benefactors of the human race. True, they mingled this one great doctrine with other doctrines, the truth of which was less apparent, and the use of which was less edifying. How could it be otherwise? Let us not, therefore, reproach them. Rather let us seriously inquire whether even these associated doctrines did not give a new impulse and direction to human reason.

This much, at least, is matter of experience, that the books of the New Testament, in which these doctrines, after some time, found a repository, have furnished and still furnish the second better elementary book for the human race. For seventeen hundred years they have occupied the human understanding more than all other books. More than all other books, they have enlightened it, even though it were by means of that light which the human understanding itself has carried into it. No other book could possibly have become so generally known among different nations. And, unquestionably, the converse of such entirely dissimilar modes of thought, with the same book, has aided the human understanding more than if each nation had had an elementary book of its own, peculiar to itself.

Moreover, it was highly essential that each nation should, for a time, regard this book as the *Non plus ultra* of its knowledge. For the boy, too, must look upon his elementary book, in this light, at first, that his eagerness to finish may not hurry him on to things for which he has laid as yet no sufficient foundation. And, what is still of the highest importance, beware, you of superior ability, who stamp and glow with impatience at the last page of this elementary book; beware of betraying to your schoolmates what you suspect, or begin already to discern. Until they have come up with you, these weaker brethren, rather look back yourself once more into this elementary book, and examine if that which you regard as a peculiarity in the method, or as intended to fill up a gap in the didactic portions, be not something more than that.

You have seen, in the infancy of mankind, in the doctrine of the unity of God, that mere truths of reason are taught, at first, as truths directly revealed, in order to diffuse them more rapidly, and to ground them more firmly. You experience the same thing in the boyhood of mankind, in the doctrine of the immortality of the soul. This doctrine is *preached*, in the second, more perfect elementary book, as revelation; not *taught* as the result of human reasoning. As it no longer needs the Old Testament to teach the unity of God, and as we gradually begin to be able to dispense with the aid of the New, in regard to the doctrine of the immortality of the soul, may there not be mirrored there still other doctrines which it is designed that we shall wonder at as revelations, until reason has learned to deduce them from and to connect them with other established truths?

For example, the doctrine of the Trinity. What if this doctrine were designed to guide the human understanding at last, after numberless aberrations to the right and to the left, to the recognition of the truth that God cannot be *one* in the same sense in which finite things are one,—that even his unity must be a transcendental unity, not excluding a kind of plurality? Must not God at least have the most perfect conception of himself? *i. e.* a conception in which everything is contained, that is contained in himself. But could everything be contained in that conception which is contained in himself, if, of his necessary actuality,* as of his other qualities, there were merely a conception, a bare possibility? This possibility exhausts the essence of his other qualities, but does it also of his necessary actuality? I think not. Consequently, either God can have no perfect conception of himself, or this perfect conception is just as necessarily actual, as he is himself. My reflection in the mirror is an empty image of me, and nothing more; because it has only that of me, from which rays of light are thrown upon the surface of the mirror. But if this image contained everything, without exception, that is contained in me, it would no longer be a mere image, but an actual duplicate of myself. If I think I see the same duplication of the being of God, it is not so much an error of mine, perhaps, as it is the inability of language to express my conception. This much is indisputable, that those who wished to make this idea popular, could hardly have chosen a more appropriate and intelligible expression than that of a *Son* whom God generates from all eternity.

And the doctrine of hereditary sin. How, if everything should convince us, at last, that man, in the first and lowest stage of his humanity, is not sufficiently master of his actions, to be capable of obeying a moral law?

And the doctrine of the satisfaction made by the Son. How, if everything should force us, at last, to assume that God, notwithstanding that original incapacity of man, chose rather to give him moral laws and to pardon all transgressions of the same, in consideration of his Son, that is, in consideration of the self-subsistent extent of all his perfections, before which and in which, every imperfection of the individual vanishes; that he chose rather to do this, I say, than not to give him moral laws, and thereby to exclude him from that moral felicity which cannot be conceived as possible, without those laws?

Let it not be objected, that this kind of reasoning concerning the mysteries of religion is forbidden. The word mystery signified, in the first ages of Christianity, something very different from that which we understand by it now; and the development of revealed truths into truths of reason is absolutely necessary, if

---

* The copy before me has *Wirksamkeit* (activity) which I take to be a misprint for *Wirklichkeit*. Tr.

ever men are to be helped by them. At the time when they were revealed, they were not yet truths of reason; but they were revealed in order to become so. They were the *Facit*, as it were, which the arithmetical teacher tells his scholars beforehand, in order that they may have some regard to it, in their reckoning. If the scholars were to content themselves with the *Facit* announced to them beforehand, they would never learn to reckon, and so fail to fulfil the purpose for which the good master gave them a clue in their labours.

And why may we not be guided by a religion, with whose historical truth, if you please, there are so many difficulties, to nearer and better conceptions of the Divine Being, of our own nature and our relations to God, conceptions to which human reason would never have attained of itself?

It is not true, that speculations concerning these things have ever done mischief, or proved injurious to society. Not the speculations themselves, but the folly, the tyranny, of attempting to suppress them, of not allowing their own to those who had their own, is liable to this reproach. On the contrary, these speculations, whatever may be their result in individual cases, are unquestionably the most fitting exercise of the human understanding, generally, as long as the human heart, generally, is only capable, at the utmost, of loving virtue for the sake of its eternally happy consequences. For, with this self-interestedness of the human heart, to exercise the human understanding, also, on those things only, which concern our bodily necessities, would tend rather to blunt than to sharpen it. It needs, positively, to be exercised with spiritual objects, if ever it is to attain its perfect illumination, and produce that purity of heart which shall make us capable of loving virtue for its own sake.

Or is the human race destined never to reach this highest grade of culture and purity? Never! Let me not imagine this blasphemy, thou All-good! Education has its aim, with the race, not less than with the individual. That which is educated is educated for some end. The flattering prospects which are opened to the youth, the honour and affluence which are held up before him,—what are these, but means by which he is educated to become a man, a man who, though these prospects of affluence and honour should fail, shall still be capable of doing his duty? Is this the aim of human education? And does the Divine education fall short of this? What Art can accomplish with the *individual*, shall not Nature accomplish with the *whole?* Blasphemy! Blasphemy!

No! it will come! it will surely come, the period of perfection, when, the more convinced his understanding is of an ever better Future, the less man will need to borrow from that Future the motives of his actions; when he will choose the good because it is good, and not because arbitrary rewards are annexed to it which are only to fix and strengthen his wandering gaze, at first, until he is able to appreciate the interior and nobler reward of well-doing. It will surely come, the period of a new, eternal gospel, which is promised us, even in the elementary books of the New Covenant. Proceed in thine imperceptible course, Eternal Providence! Only let me not despair of thee, because imperceptible. Let me not despair of thee, even though thy steps, to me, should seem to retrograde. It is not true, that the shortest way is always a straight one. Thou hast, in thine eternal course, so much to take along with thee! So many sidelong steps to make! And what if it be now, as good as proved, that the great, slow wheel which brings the race nearer to its perfection, is put in motion, only by smaller, quicker wheels, of which each contributes its part to the same end?

Not otherwise! The path, by which the race attains to its perfection, each individual man— some earlier, and some later — must first have gone over. "Must have gone over in one and the same life? Can he have been a sensual Jew and a spiritual Christian in the same life? Can he, in the same life, have overtaken both these?" Perhaps not! But why may not each individual man have existed more than once in this world? Is this hypothesis, therefore, so ridiculous, because it is the oldest? because it is the one which the human understanding immediately hit upon, before it was distracted and weakened by the sophistry of the schools? Why may not I, at one time, have accomplished, already here on earth, all those steps toward my perfection, which mere temporal rewards and punishments will enable man to accomplish; and, at another time, all those, in which we are so powerfully assisted by the prospect of eternal compensations? Why should I not return as often as I am able to acquire new knowledges, new talents? Is it because I carry away so much, at one time, as to make it not worth the while to return? Or, because I forget that I have been here before? It is well for me that I forget it. The remembrance of my former states would allow me to make but a poor use of the present. Besides, what I am *necessitated* to forget now, have I forgotten it forever? Or because, on this supposition, too much time would be lost to me? Lost? What have I then to delay? Is not the whole eternity mine?

FABLES.

ZEUS* AND THE SHEEP.

The sheep was doomed to suffer much from all the animals. She came to Zeus and prayed

---

* The Father of the Gods is, by German writers, more often designated by his Greek than by his Latin name. The translator has thought best to retain this appellation where it occurs in the original.

him to lighten her misery. Zeus appeared willing, and said to the sheep: I see indeed, my good creature, I have made thee too defenceless. Now choose in what way I may best remedy this defect. Shall I furnish thy mouth with terrible teeth and thy feet with claws?

Ah! no, said the sheep, I do not wish to have anything in common with the beasts of prey.

Or, continued Zeus, shall I infuse poison into thy spittle?

Alas! replied the sheep; the poisonous serpents are so hated.

What then shall I do? I will plant horns in thy forehead, and give strength to thy neck.

Not so, kind Father! I might be disposed to butt like the he-goat.

And yet, said Zeus, thou must, thyself, be able to injure others, if others are to beware of injuring thee.

Must I? sighed the sheep. O! then, Kind Father, let me be as I am. For the ability to injure will excite, I fear, the desire. And it is better to suffer wrong than to do wrong.

Zeus blessed the good sheep, and from that time forth, she forgot to complain.

THE BLIND HEN.

A hen which had become blind continued to scratch for food as she had been used. What availed it the industrious fool? Another hen, that could see, but wished to spare her tender feet, never forsook the side of the former, and without scratching enjoyed the fruit of scratching. For as often as the blind hen turned up a corn, the seeing one devoured it.

The laborious German compiles the *collectanea* which the witty Frenchman uses.

THE WOLF ON HIS DEATHBED.

A wolf lay at the last gasp, and was reviewing his past life. It is true, said he, I am a sinner, but yet, I hope, not one of the greatest. I have done evil, but I have also done much good. Once, I remember, a bleating lamb that had strayed from the flock, came so near to me, that I might easily have throttled it; but I did it no harm. At the same time, I listened with the most astonishing indifference to the gibes and scoffs of a sheep, although I had nothing to fear from protecting dogs.

I can testify to all that, said his friend the fox, who was helping him prepare for death. I remember perfectly all the circumstances. It was just at the time when you were so dreadfully choked with that bone, which the good-natured crane afterwards drew out of your throat.

ÆSOP AND THE ASS.

Said the ass to Æsop: The next time you tell a story about me, let me say something that is right rational and ingenious.

You something ingenious! said Æsop; what propriety would there be in that? Would not the people say you were the moralist and I the ass?

HERCULES.

When Hercules was received into heaven he paid his respects to Juno before all the other divinities. The whole Heaven and Juno were astonished. Dost thou show such preference to thine enemy? Yes, replied Hercules, even to her. It was her persecution alone, that furnished the occasion of those exploits, with which I have earned Heaven.

Olympus approved the answer of the new God, and Juno was reconciled.

THE BOY AND THE SERPENT.

A boy played with a tame serpent. My dear little animal, said the boy; I would not be so familiar with thee had not thy poison been taken from thee. You serpents are the most malicious and ungrateful of all animals. I have read how it fared with a poor countryman who, in his compassion, took up a serpent,—perhaps it was one of thy ancestors,—which he found half-frozen under a hedge, and put it into his bosom to warm it. Scarcely had the wicked creature begun to revive, when it bit its benefactor; and the poor, kind countryman was doomed to die.

I am amazed, said the serpent. How partial your historians must be! Ours relate the affair very differently. Thy kind man thought the serpent was actually frozen, and, because it was one of the variegated sort, he put it into his bosom, in order, when he reached home, to strip off its beautiful skin. Was that right?

Ah! be still! replied the boy. When was there ever an ingrate who did not know how to justify himself?

True, my son, said his father, who had listened to the conversation. Nevertheless, when you hear of an extraordinary instance of ingratitude, be sure to examine carefully all the circumstances, before you brand a human being with so detestable a fault. Real benefactors have seldom had ungrateful debtors;—no! I will hope, for the honour of humanity,—never. But benefactors with petty, interested motives,—they, my son, deserve to reap ingratitude instead of acknowledgments.

THE YOUNG SWALLOW.

What are you doing there? demanded a swallow of the busy ants. We are collecting stores for the winter, was the ready answer.

That is wise, said the swallow; I will do so too. And immediately she began to carry a number of dead spiders and flies into her nest.

But to what purpose is that? asked her mother at last. To what purpose? Stores for the ugly winter, dear mother. Do thou gather likewise. The ants have taught me this providence.

O! leave to earthly ants this small wisdom; replied the old one. That which befits them, befits not the nobler swallows. Kind Nature has destined us for a happier fate. When the rich Summer is ended, we go hence; we gradually fall asleep on our journey, and then warm marshes receive us, where we rest without wants, until a new Spring awakens us to a new life.

THE APE AND THE FOX.

Name to me an animal, though never so skilful, that I cannot imitate! So bragged the ape to the fox. But the fox replied: And do thou name to me an animal so humble as to think of imitating thee!

Writers of my country! Need I explain myself more fully!

ZEUS AND THE HORSE.

Father of beasts and of men!—so spake the horse, approaching the throne of Zeus,—I am said to be one of the most beautiful animals with which thou hast adorned the world; and my self-love leads me to believe it. Nevertheless, might not some things in me still be improved?

And what in thee, thinkest thou, admits of improvement? Speak! I am open to instruction, said the indulgent god with a smile.

Perhaps, returned the horse, I should be fleeter if my legs were taller and thinner. A long swan-neck would not disfigure me. A broader breast would add to my strength. And, since thou hast once for all destined me to bear thy favourite, man,—the saddle which the well-meaning rider puts upon me might be created a part of me.

Good! replied Zeus, wait a moment. Zeus, with earnest countenance, pronounced the creative word. Then flowed life into the dust; then organized matter combined; and suddenly stood before the throne, the ugly *camel*.

The horse saw, shuddered and trembled with fear and abhorrence.

Here, said Zeus, are taller and thinner legs; here is a long swan-neck; here is a broader breast; here is the created saddle! Wilt thou, horse! that I should transform thee after this fashion?

The horse still trembled.

Go! continued Zeus. Be instructed, for this once, without being punished. But to remind thee, with occasional compunction, of thy presumption,—do thou, new creation, continue!— Zeus cast a preserving glance on the camel;—and never shall the horse behold thee without shuddering.

THE RAVEN.

The fox saw how the raven robbed the altars of the gods, and lived, like them, upon their sacrifices. And he thought within himself: I would like to know, whether the raven partakes of the sacrifices because he is a prophetic bird; or whether he is considered a prophetic bird, because he is so bold as to partake of the sacrifices.

THE EAGLE AND THE FOX.

Be not so proud of thy flight! said the fox to the eagle. Thou mountest so high into the air for no other purpose but to look farther about thee for carrion.

So have I known men who became deep-thinking philosophers, not from love of truth, but for the sake of lucrative offices of instruction.

THE SWALLOW.

Believe me, friends! the great world is not for the philosopher,—is not for the poet. Their real value is not appreciated there; and often, alas! they are weak enough to exchange it for a far inferior one.

In the earliest times, the swallow was as tuneful and melodious a bird as the nightingale. But she soon grew tired of living in the solitary bushes, heard and admired by no one but the industrious countryman, and the innocent shepherdess. She forsook her humbler friend and moved into the city. What followed? Because the people of the city had no time to listen to her divine song, she gradually forgot it, and learned, instead thereof, to—build!

THE RAVEN.

The raven remarked that the eagle sat thirty days upon her eggs. "And that, undoubtedly," said she, "is the reason why the young of the eagle are so all-seeing and strong. Good! I will do the same."

And since then, the raven actually sits thirty days upon her eggs; but, as yet, she has hatched nothing but miserable ravens.

THE SPIRIT OF SOLOMON.

An honest old man still bore the burden and heat of the day. With his own hands he ploughed his field; with his own hand he cast the pure seed into the loosened bosom of the willing earth.

Suddenly under the broad shadow of a Linden-tree, there stood before him a godlike apparition. The old man was astounded. I am Solomon, said the phantom, with a voice which inspired confidence. What dost thou here, old man?

If thou art Solomon, replied the old man, how canst thou ask? In my youth, thou sentest me to the ant: I considered her ways, I learned from her to be diligent and to hoard. What I then learned, I still practise.

Thou hast learned thy lesson but half, returned the Spirit. Go to the ant again! And now learn from her, also, to rest in the winter of thy days, and to enjoy what thou hast gathered!

THE SHEEP.

When Jupiter celebrated his nuptials, and all the animals brought him gifts, Juno missed the sheep.

Where is the sheep? asked the goddess. Why does the good sheep delay to bring us her well-meant offering?

The dog took upon himself to reply, and said:

Be not angry, Goddess! It is but to-day that I saw the sheep. She was very sad, and lamented aloud.

And why grieved the sheep? asked the Goddess, beginning to be moved.

Ah wretched me! she said; I have, at present, neither wool nor milk. What shall I bring to Jupiter? Shall I, I alone, appear empty before him? Rather will I go and beg the shepherd to make an offering of me.

At this moment,—together with the prayer of the shepherd,—the smoke of the offered sheep ascended to Jupiter through the clouds,—a sweet-smelling savour. And now had Juno wept the first tear, if ever tears bedewed immortal eyes.

THE POSSESSOR OF THE BOW.

A man had an excellent bow of ebony, with which he shot very far and very sure, and which he valued at a great price. But once, after considering it attentively, he said: "A little too rude still! Your only ornament is your polish. It is a pity! However, that can be remedied," thought he. "I will go and let a first-rate artist carve something on the bow." He went, and the artist carved an entire hunting-scene upon the bow. And what more fitting for a bow than a hunting-scene?

The man was delighted. "You deserve this embellishment, my beloved bow." So saying he wished to try it. He drew the string. The bow broke!

THE AGED WOLF.*

The mischievous wolf had begun to decline in years, and conceived the conciliating resolution of living on a good footing with the shepherds. Accordingly, he took up his march and came to the shepherd whose folds were nearest to his den. Shepherds! said he, you call me a blood-thirsty robber, which I really am not. To be sure, I must hold by your sheep, when I am hungry; for hunger hurts. Protect me from hunger; only give me enough to eat, and you shall be very well satisfied with me; for really, I am the tamest and most gentle of creatures, when I have had enough to eat.

When you have had enough? Very likely; replied the shepherd. But when will that be? You and avarice never have enough. Go your ways!

---

* From "The History of the aged Wolf," in seven fables.—The first fable.

MEROPS.

I want to ask you something, said a young eagle to a contemplative and profoundly learned owl. They say there is a bird called Merops, who, when he ascends into the air, flies with the tail first, and with the head turned toward the earth. Is that true?

No, indeed! answered the owl; it is a silly invention of man. He may be a Merops himself; for he is, all the time, wishing to fly to heaven, but is not willing, for one moment, to lose sight of the earth.

THE WASPS.

Foulness and corruption were destroying the proud fabric of a war-horse which had been shot beneath its brave rider. Ever-active Nature always employs the ruins of one creation for the life of another. And so there flew forth a swarm of young wasps from the fly-blown carrion. Ah! cried the wasps, what a divine origin is ours! The most superb horse, the favourite of Neptune, is our progenitor.

The attentive fabulist heard the strange boast, and thought of the modern Italians, who conceive themselves to be nothing less than the descendants of the ancient, immortal Romans, because they were born among their graves.

THE PEACOCKS AND THE CROW.

A vain crow adorned herself with the feathers of the richly-tinted peacocks, which they had shed, and when she thought herself sufficiently tricked out, mixed boldly with these splendid birds of Juno. She was recognized, and quickly the peacocks fell upon her with sharp bills, to pluck from her the lying bravery.

Cease now! she cried at length, you have your own again! But the peacocks, who had observed some of the crow's own shining wing-feathers, replied: Be still, miserable fool! these too cannot be yours! And they continued to peck.

EXTRACT
FROM LESSING'S THEOLOGICAL WRITINGS.

IF God should hold all truth inclosed in his right hand, and in his left only the ever-active impulse to the pursuit of truth, although with the condition that I should always and forever err; and should say to me: Choose! I should fall with submission upon his left hand, and say: Father, give! Pure Truth is for Thee alone!

ENGRAVED BY J. SARTAIN.

M. MENDELSSOHN.

MOSES MENDELSSOHN.

Born 1729. Died 1786.

A JEW by birth and conviction, this able writer and excellent man is celebrated, not less for the services rendered to his own people, his "kinsmen according to the flesh," by his labors as a Hebraist and expositor of Jewish affairs, than for those which literary Germany associates with his honored name. No man has done more to soften the rigor of that hostility which embittered the lot of the German Israelite, a century ago. Since Maimonides, no Jewish writer, not excepting the famous Manasseh Ben Israel, has exerted a greater influence on the Jewish mind.* Since Nathaniel, no one has better deserved the commendation bestowed on that disciple: "An Israelite, indeed, in whom there is no guile!" He was one of those who have wrought even more by what they were than by what they did. His writings are a valuable contribution to the literature of his country; but his character, as an upright, magnanimous and religious man, is a legacy to his brethren, more valuable than his writings, and "richer than all his tribe."

Mendelssohn† was a native of Dessau. His father Mendel who taught the Jews' school in that city was wretchedly poor and could give him nothing but the *Mishna* and the *Gemarra;* himself more familiar with Hebrew roots than with any more substantial nourishment. He speaks of being roused at three o'clock, A. M., in the winter, wrapped in a cloak and carried to the "seminary," when only seven years old.

At an early age he fell in with the *More Nebochim,* or *Guide of the Perplexed,* a work of Maimonides, the intense study of which made an era in his life; and that in two ways. It laid the foundation of his mental culture, and also of his bodily disease and suffering.

"Maimonides," he said, "is the cause of my deformity,* he spoiled my figure, and ruined my constitution; but still I doat on him for many hours of dejection, which he has converted into hours of rapture. And if he has unwittingly weakened my body, has he not made ample atonement by invigorating my soul with his sublime instructions?"

At fourteen, we find him an adventurer at Berlin, without the means of procuring a single meal. In his distress, he applied to Rabbi *Frankel,* who had been his teacher at Dessau; "and there he happened to meet with *Mr. Hyam Bamberg,* a benevolent man, and an encourager of aspiring young Jews, who allowed him, on the Rabbi's intercession, an attic to sleep in, and two days' board weekly." His first object was not to get a living but to get an education. He had come to Berlin for this purpose, and to this he devoted several successive years of intense application, under all the difficulties and discouragements which may be supposed to hamper a youth so circumstanced; without teachers, without books, with seldom enough to satisfy his hunger, and to whom a belly-full was, as Lamb says, 'a special Providence.' The manner in which he studied Latin illustrates his indomitable energy in the pursuit of knowledge. Having mastered the nouns and the verbs and procured an old second-hand dictionary, he set himself to translate into Latin Locke's "Essay on the Human Understanding," a task which he actually accomplished, at that early stage of his progress; fighting his way through difficulties, metaphysical and philological, with a painful laboriousness unknown, out of Germany, in modern times.

His only means of support during this period, in addition to the charity of *Herr Bamberg,* was an occasional *groschen* obtained by copying Hebrew for his old master. He subsisted principally on dry brown bread, and when purchasing a loaf, "he would notch it,

---

* I speak only of those whom Israel has acknowledged and retained. Spinoza, unquestionably the greatest intellect that has sprung from the seed of Abraham since the dispersion, can hardly be ranked as a Jewish writer.

† The following sketch is taken chiefly from the "Memoirs of Moses Mendelssohn, &c.," by M. Samuels. Second Edition. London, 1827.

* Mendelssohn was hump-backed and extremely small and feeble in person.

according to the standard of his means, into so many meals; never eating according to his appetite, but according to his finances."

In this way he spent several years of hardship and suffering, during which, however, he had by dint of incredible exertions, made himself thoroughly acquainted with the principal languages and the mathematics. But now a kind Providence brought him acquainted with a wealthy manufacturer of the Jewish faith, who received him into his house, as the tutor of his children, then into his counting-room, as clerk, and finally into his silk-manufactory, first as manager, and soon after as partner. A new tide in his affairs set in with this connection. An immediate support, not ample at first, but sufficient for his wants, was secured to him, and he now commenced his career as an author, devoting his days to business, and his nights to Letters. About this time, he became acquainted with Abbt, Nicolai and Lessing. With the latter, he formed an intimate friendship, from which he derived incalculable benefit in the way of literary and philosophic culture, and which he always regarded as among the most fortunate circumstances of his life. "Lessing loved Mendelssohn," says his biographer, "for his excellent heart and highly cultivated understanding, and Mendelssohn was no less attached to Lessing for his inflexible consistency and his transcendent abilities. A union founded on esteem and friendship was cemented between them, which neither time nor long separation, nothing indeed but death could dissolve. The noble monument of their mutual affection, preserved to posterity in the latter pages of the *Morgenstunden*, will endure as long as virtue and science are cherished and cultivated among mankind." In Lessing, than whom no man was ever more free from the prejudices of creed and nation, Mendelssohn found a hearty sympathy and an effective fellow-laborer in his various projects for bettering the condition of the German Jews; an object, which, then and at all times, lay nearest his heart. Indeed the known friendship of so eminent a man for one of that tribe, in defiance of all the prejudices of his age, was scarcely less important to the Jews in general than it was to Mendelssohn in particular.

One of the first, perhaps the very first literary effort by which he became distinguished beyond the pale of his own communion, was his "Philosophical Dialogues," a work which owed its origin to the following circumstance. "Lessing once brought to Mendelssohn a work written by a celebrated character, to hear his opinion upon it. Having given it a reading, he told his friend that he deemed himself a match for the author, and would refute him. Nothing could be more welcome to Lessing, and he strongly encouraged the idea. Accordingly, Mendelssohn sat down and wrote his "Philosophical Dialogues," in which he strictly redeemed his pledge of confuting the author; and carried the manuscript to Lessing for examination. 'When I am at leisure,' said Lessing, 'I will peruse it.' After a convenient interval, he repeated his visit, when Lessing kept up a miscellaneous conversation, without once mentioning the manuscript in question; and the other, being too bashful to put him in mind of it, was obliged to depart. The same thing happened at several subsequent meetings. At last, he mustered sufficient resolution to inquire after it. Want of leisure was pleaded as before, but now "he would certainly read it. Mr. Mendelssohn might, in the mean while, take yonder small volume home with him, and let him know his opinion of it." On opening it, Mendelssohn was not a little surprised to see his own Dialogues in print. "Put it into your pocket," said Lessing, good-naturedly, "and this Mammon along with it. It is what I got for the copyright; it will be of service to you." He afterward, at the instigation of Nicolai and Lessing, collected all his philosophical lucubrations, and published them under the title "*Philosophische Schriften.*" Three editions of this work which appeared, anonymously at first, but afterward with the author's name, were exhausted in a short time.

Through his connection with Herr Bernard, Mendelssohn soon became rich, as a Jew should be, and, being rich, he married, as a rich Jew should do. His wife was a daughter of *Abraham Gaugenheim* of Hamburg. By her he had several children, among them a son who gave rise to one of his most celebrated works — the "*Morgenstunden,*" (Morning-hours.) This book consists of lectures on the existence of God, — the result of many years' inquiry on that subject — the original design of which was to instruct his oldest son, Joseph, his son-in-law and other Jewish youths in the rudiments of religion. The lessons were given before the hours of business, whence the title *Morgenstunden.* The work is a fragment, the death of the author arresting its progress soon after the publication of the first volume.

The most popular of his works and that which contributed most to his celebrity abroad, was his Phaedon, a work on the immortality of the soul, based on Plato's dialogue of that name —in fact a translation of Plato, with much additional matter of his own. In less than two years it went through three large German editions and was translated into the English, French, Dutch, Italian, Danish, and Hebrew.

Mendelssohn's fame was at its height, and zealous Christians were wondering that so enlightened and exemplary a man should retain the faith of his Fathers, when his peace and religious liberty were somewhat rudely assailed—though with no unkind intentions—by a challenge from Lavater, who, with an obtuse zeal which knew no scruple on the score of delicacy, sought to drag him into theological controversy. The good Lavater, with all his humanity, was a little intolerant in matters of religion. A religious man and not a Christian by profession, was an idea for which he could find no room in his philosophy. It was not enough that Mendelssohn was all that a Christian should be; he insisted on a formal and public renunciation of Judaism in favor of Christianity. In order to bring about this result, he dedicated to him his translation of Bonnet's "Inquiry into the evidences of Christianity," with the request that he would refute it, in case he should find the argument untenable; and that, if it should seem to him conclusive, he would "do what policy, love of truth and probity demanded, what Socrates doubtless would have done, had he read the work and found it unanswerable;" thus offering him the alternative, either to incur the odium of his own people by formally abjuring the faith of his Fathers, or to draw down upon himself the wrath of the Christian clergy by a public assault on their religion.

To a timid and sensitive nature like Mendelssohn's, constitutionally averse from all controversy and especially from controversy in religion, such a challenge was perfectly overwhelming. Prostrate with ill health at the time, he suffered intensely from this attempt to drag him forth from the strict reserve which he had always maintained on these subjects. But rallying himself to reply, he adroitly put by both horns of the threatened dilemma, in a letter which satisfied all parties and which drew from Lavater a public apology and retracttation of his peremptory challenge.

The agitation caused by this transaction aggravated Mendelssohn's constitutional complaints and brought on a severe sickness which threatened his life and, for a long time, incapacitated him for intellectual labor. After his recovery, he published his commentary on Ecclesiasticus ; soon after, his translation of the Pentateuch, "a work," says his biographer, "which forms an epoch in the history of modern Judaism, and which, for its vast utility and the immense good it has wrought, entitles the author to the eternal gratitude of his nation." To this was added a metrical translation of the psalms. Then followed a work which excited a good deal of attention in Germany, at the time, entitled "*Jerusalem, oder über religiöse Macht und Judenthum.*"* It contained a plea for toleration founded on the principles of the social compact, together with an able defence of Judaism. It is still the best treatise on these subjects.

Mendelssohn was doomed to experience another severe trial of his sensibility, in an attack on his friend Lessing, by Friedrich Heinrich Jacobi. This eminent author published a volume of "Letters to Mr. Mendelssohn on the Doctrine of Spinoza," in which he charged Lessing with being an "implicit Spinozist." Mendelssohn endeavored to refute the charge in a work entitled "Moses Mendelssohn to the friends of Lessing." The answer was considered triumphant and drew from Kant† the remark, " It is Mendelssohn's fault that Jacobi thinks himself a philosopher."

But the excitement of a controversy so repugnant to his gentle nature, acted fatally on his long enfeebled constitution and reduced him to that degree that a trifle sufficed to snap the slender thread which bound him to this world. Returning from the synagogue one frosty morning, he took a cold of which he died within four days; on the 4th January 1786, in his fifty-eighth year.

"Mendelssohn died as he had lived, calm and placid, and took an earthly smile with him

---

* Jerusalem, or on religious power and Judaism.

† Speaking of Kant, it is worthy of note that Mendelssohn, in the earlier part of his career, was the successful competitor of this distinguished philosopher in a contest for the prize awarded by the Royal Academy of Berlin, to the best essay on the question: "Are metaphysics susceptible of mathematical demonstration?"

into eternity. When his death became known, the whole city of Berlin was a scene of unfeigned sorrow. The citizens of all denominations looked on his death as a national calamity."

"Mendelssohn was of a short stature, very thin, and deformed in the back. His complexion was very dark and sallow; hair black and curly; nose rather large and aquiline. A gentle smile played around his mouth which was always a little open. Nothing could exceed the fire of his eyes, and there was so much kindness, modesty, and benevolence portrayed on his countenance that he won every heart at first sight. His vaulted brow and the general cast of his features bespoke a vast intellect and a noble heart."

"From sensual gratification he abstained firmly to the end. It was inconceivable that the quantity of food to which he restricted himself could nourish a human body. Yet Providence had blessed him with affluence; his fortune enabled him to live genteelly and keep a hospitable table; and it was affecting to see him press his guests to partake of viands and liquors which he himself, though never so desirous, durst not venture to taste."

His disinterestedness was without limits and his beneficence corresponded with his means.

Professor Rammler erected to him a monument with this inscription:

MOSES MENDELSSOHN,
BORN AT DESSAU OF HEBREW PARENTS,
A SAGE LIKE SOCRATES,
FAITHFUL TO THE ANCIENT CREED,
TEACHING IMMORTALITY,
HIMSELF IMMORTAL.

Besides the works which have been mentioned, he published several others in German and some in Hebrew.

LETTER TO J. C. LAVATER,*

IN ANSWER TO A CHALLENGE EITHER TO REFUTE BONNET'S EVIDENCES OF CHRISTIANITY, OR ELSE TO ADOPT THE CHRISTIAN RELIGION.

Honoured Philanthropist,

You were pleased to dedicate to me your translation from the French of Bonnet's Inquiry into the Evidences of the Christian Religion, and most publicly and solemnly to conjure me "to refute that work, in case I should find the main arguments in support of the facts of Christianity untenable, or should I find them conclusive, to do what policy, love of truth, and probity bid me, what Socrates would have done had he read the work, and found it unanswerable;" which, I suppose, means, to renounce the religion of my fathers, and embrace that which Mr. Bonnet vindicates. Now, were I ever mean-spirited enough to balance love of truth and probity against policy, I assure you I should, in this instance, throw them all three into the same scale.

I should deem myself beneath a worthy man's notice, did I not acknowledge, with a grateful heart, the friendship and kindness you manifest for me in that dedication, which I am fully persuaded flowed from a pure source, and cannot be ascribed to any but benevolent and philanthropic motives. Yet I must own that it appeared to me exceedingly strange, and I should have expected anything rather than a public challenge from a man like Lavater.

It seems you still recollect the confidential conversation I had the pleasure of holding with yourself and your worthy friends in my apartment. Can you then possibly have forgotten how frequently I sought to divert the discourse from religious to more neutral topics, and how much yourself and your friends had to urge me before I would venture to deliver my opinion on a subject of such vital importance? If I am not mistaken, preliminary assurances were even given that no *public use* should *ever* be made of any remarkable expression that might drop on the occasion. Be that as it may, I will rather suppose myself in error than tax you with a breach of promise. But as I so sedulously sought to avoid an explanation in my own apartment amidst a small number of worthy men, of whose good intentions I had every reason to be persuaded, it might have been reasonably inferred that a *public one* would be extremely repugnant to my disposition; and that I must have inevitably become the *more* embarrassed when the voice demanding it happened to be entitled to an answer at any rate. What then, sir, could induce you to single *me* thus, against my well-known disinclination, out of the many, and force me into a public arena which I so much wished never to have occasion to enter? If even you placed my reserve to the score of mere timidity and bashfulness, these very foibles would have deserved the moderation and forbearance of a charitable heart.

But my scruples of engaging in religious controversy never proceeded from timidity or bashfulness. Let me assure you that it was not only from the other day that I began searching into my religion. No, I became very early sensible of the duty of putting my actions and opinions

---

* From the "Memoirs of Moses Mendelssohn," by M. Samuels. For an account of this correspondence, see the biographical sketch given above.

to a test. That I have from my early youth devoted my hours of repose and relaxation to philosophy and the arts and sciences, was done for the sole purpose of qualifying myself for this important investigation. What other motives could I have had? In the situation I was then in, not the least temporal benefit was to be expected from the sciences. I knew very well that I had no chance of getting forward in the world through them. And as to the gratification they might afford me — alas! much esteemed philanthropist!— the station allotted to my brethren in the faith, in civil society, is so incompatible with the expansion of the mind, that we certainly do not increase our happiness by learning to view the rights of humanity under their true aspect. On this point, too, I must decline saying any more. He that is acquainted with our condition, and has a human heart, will here feel more than I dare to express.

If, after so many years of investigation, the decision of my mind had not been completely in favour of my religion, it would infallibly have become known through my public conduct. I do not conceive what should rivet me to a religion to appearance so excessively severe, and so commonly exploded, if I were not convinced in my heart of its truth. Let the result of my investigation have been what it may, so soon as I discovered the religion of my fathers *not* to be the *true* one, I must of course have discarded it. Indeed, were I convinced in my heart of *another* religion being true, there could not, in my opinion, be a more flagitious depravity than to refuse homage to truth, in defiance of internal evidence. What should entice me to such depravity? Have I not already declared, that in this instance, policy, love of truth, and probity, would lead me to steer the same course?

Were I indifferent to *both* religions, or derided and scorned, in my mind, revelation in general, I should know well enough what policy suggests, when conscience remains neutral. What is there to deter me? Fear of my brethren in the faith? Their temporal power is too much curtailed to daunt me. What then? Obstinacy? Indolence? A predilection for habitual notions? Having devoted the greatest portion of my life to the investigation, I may be supposed to possess sufficient good sense not to sacrifice the fruit of my labours to such frivolities.

Thus you see, sir, that, but for a sincere conviction of my religion, the result of my theological investigations would have been sealed by a public act of mine. Whereas, on the contrary, they have *strengthened* me in the faith of my fathers; still I could wish to move on quietly without rendering the public an account of the state of my mind. I do not mean to deny that I have detected in my religion human additions and base alloy, which, alas! but too much tarnish its pristine lustre. But where is the friend of truth that can boast of having found *his* religion free from similar corruptions? We all, who go in search of truth, are annoyed by the pestilential vapour of hypocrisy and superstition, and wish we could wipe it off without defacing what is really good and true. Yet of the essentials of my religion I am as firmly, as irrefragably convinced, as you, sir, or Mr. Bonnet, ever can be of those of yours. And I herewith declare, in the presence of the God of truth, your and my creator and supporter, by whom you have conjured me in your dedication, that I will adhere to my principles so long as my entire soul does not assume another nature. My contrariety to your creed, which I expressed to yourself and to your friends, has since, in no respect, changed. And as to my veneration for the moral character of its founder! had you not omitted the reservations which I so distinctly annexed to it, I should concede as much now. We must finish certain inquiries once in our life, if we wish to proceed further. This, I may say, I had done, with regard to religion, several years ago. I read, compared, reflected, and—made up my mind.

Yet, for what I cared, Judaism might have been hurled down in every polemical compendium, and triumphantly sneered at in every academic exercise, and I would not have entered into a dispute about it. Rabbinical scholars, and rabbinical smatterers, might have grubbed in obsolete scribblings, which no sensible Jew reads or knows of, and amused the public with the most fantastic ideas of Judaism, without so much as a contradiction on my part. It is by virtue that I wish to shame the opprobrious opinion commonly entertained of a Jew, and not by controversial writings. My religious tenets, philosophy, station in civil society, all furnish me with the most cogent reason for abstaining from theological disputes, and for treating in my publications of those truths only which are equally important to all persuasions.

Pursuant to the principles of my religion, I am not to seek to convert any one who is not born according to our laws. This proneness to conversion, the origin of which some would fain tack on the Jewish religion, is, nevertheless, diametrically opposed to it. Our rabbins unanimously teach, that the written and oral laws, which form conjointly our revealed religion, are obligatory on our nation only. "Moses commanded us a law, even the inheritance of the congregation of Jacob." We believe that all other nations of the earth have been directed by God to adhere to the laws of nature, and to the religion of the patriarchs. Those who regulate their lives according to the precepts of this religion of nature and of reason, are called virtuous men of other nations, and are the children of eternal salvation.

Our rabbins are so remote from *Proselytomania*, that they enjoin us to dissuade, by forcible remonstrances, every one who comes forward to be converted. We are to lead him to reflect that, by such a step, he is subjecting himself needlessly, to a most onerous burthen; that, in his present condition, he has only to observe the precepts of a *Noachide*, to be saved; but the moment he embraces the religion of the Israelites, he subscribes gratuitously to all the rigid rites of that faith, to which he must then strictly conform, or await the punishment which the legislator has denounced on their infraction. Finally, we are to hold up to him a faithful picture of the misery, tribulation, and obloquy, in which the nation is now living, in order to guard him from a rash act, which he might ultimately repent.

Thus, you see, the religion of my fathers *does not wish* to be extended. We are *not* to send missions to both the Indies, or to Greenland, to preach our doctrine to those remote people. The latter, in particular, who, by all accounts, observe the laws of nature stricter than, alas! we do, are, in our religious estimation, an enviable race. Whoever is not born conformable to our laws, has no occasion to live according to them. We alone consider ourselves bound to acknowledge their authority; and this can give no offence to our neighbours. Let our notions be held ever so absurd, still there is no need to cavil about them, and others are certainly at liberty to question the validity of laws, to which they are, by our own admission, not amenable; but whether they are acting manly, socially, and charitably, in ridiculing these laws, must be left to their consciences. So long as we do not tamper with *their* opinions, wrangling serves no purpose whatsoever.

Suppose there were amongst my contemporaries, a Confucius or a Solon, I could, consistently with my religious principles, love and admire the great man, but I should never hit on the extravagant idea of converting a Confucius or a Solon. What should I convert him for? As he does not belong to the congregation of Jacob, my religious laws were not legislated for him; and on doctrines we should soon come to an understanding. Do I think there is a chance of his being saved? I certainly believe, that he who leads mankind on to virtue in this world, cannot be damned in the next. And I need not *now* stand in awe of any reverend college, that would call me to account for this opinion, as the *Sorbonne* did honest Marmontel.

I am so fortunate, as to count amongst my friends, many a worthy man, who is not of my faith. We love each other sincerely, notwithstanding we presume, or take for granted, that, in matters of belief, we differ widely in opinion. I enjoy the delight of their society, which both improves and solaces me. Never yet has my heart whispered, "Alas! for this excellent man's soul!"—He who believes that no salvation is to be found out of the pale of his own church, must often feel such sighs rise in his bosom.

It is true, every man is naturally bound to diffuse knowledge and virtue among his fellow-creatures, and to eradicate error and prejudice as much as lies in his power. It might therefore be concluded, that it is a duty, publicly to fling the gauntlet at every religious opinion, which one deems erroneous. But all prejudices are not equally noxious. Certainly, there are some which strike directly at the happiness of the human race; their effect on morality is obviously deleterious, and we cannot expect even a casual benefit from them. These must be unhesitatingly assailed by the philanthropist. To grapple with them, at once, is indisputably the best mode, and all delay, from circuitous measures, unwarrantable. Of this kind are those errors and prejudices which disturb man's own, and his fellow-creatures' peace and happiness, and canker, in youth, the germ of benevolence and virtue, before it can shoot forth. Fanaticism, ill-will, and a spirit of persecution, on the one side, levity, Epicurism, and boasting infidelity, on the other.

Yet the opinions of my fellow-creatures, erroneous as they may appear to *my* conviction, do sometimes belong to the higher order of theoretical principles, and are too remote from practice, to become immediately pernicious; they constitute, however, from their generality, the basis, on which the people who entertain them have raised their system of morality and social order; and so they have casually become of great importance to that portion of mankind. To attack such dogmas openly, because they appear prejudices, would be like sapping the foundation of an edifice, for the purpose of examining its soundness and stability, without first securing the superstructure against a total downfall. He who values the welfare of mankind more than his own fame, will bridle his tongue on prejudices of this description, and beware of seeking to reform them prematurely and precipitately, lest he should overset what *he* thinks a defective theory of morality, before his fellow-creatures are firm in the perfect one, which he means to substitute.

Therefore, there is nothing inconsistent in my thinking myself bound to remain neutral, under the impression of having detected national prejudices and religious errors amongst my fellow-citizens,—provided these errors and prejudices do not subvert, directly, either their religion or the laws of nature, and that they have a tendency to promote, *casually*, that which is good and desirable. The morality of our actions, when founded in error, it is true, scarcely deserves that name; and the advancement of virtue will be always more efficaciously and permanently effected through the medium of truth, where truth is known, than through that of prejudice or error. But where truth is not known, where it has not become national, so as to operate as powerfully on the bulk of the people as deep-rooted prejudice—there *prejudice* will be held almost sacred by every votary of virtue.

How much more imperative, then, does this discretion become, when the nation, which, in our opinion, fosters such prejudices, has rendered itself otherwise estimable through wisdom and virtue, when it contains numbers of eminent men, who rank with the benefactors of mankind! The human errors of such a noble portion of our species, ought to be deferentially overlooked by one, who is liable to the same; he should dwell on its excellences only, and not insidiously prowl to pounce upon it, where he conceives it to be vulnerable.

These are the reasons which my religion and my philosophy suggest to me, for scrupulously avoiding polemical controversy. Add to them, my local relations to my fellow-citizens, and you cannot but justify me. I am one of an oppressed people, who have to supplicate shelter and protection of the ascendant nations; and these boons they do not obtain everywhere, indeed nowhere, without more or less of restriction.* Rights granted to every other human being, my brethren in the faith willingly forego, contented with being tolerated and protected; and they account it no trifling favour, on the part of the nation, who takes them in on bearable terms, since, in some places, even a *temporary domicile is denied them*. Do the laws of Zurich allow your circumcised friend to pay you a visit there? No.— What gratitude then do not my brethren owe to the nation, which includes them in its general philanthropy, suffering them, without molestation, to worship the Supreme Being after the rites of their ancestors? The government under which I live, leaves nothing to wish for in this respect; and the Hebrews should therefore be scrupulous in abstaining from reflections on the predominant religion, or, which is the same thing, in touching their protectors, where men of virtue are most tender.

By those principles, I have resolved invariably to regulate my conduct; unless extraordinary inducements should compel me to deviate from them. Private appeals, from men of worth, I have taken the liberty tacitly to decline. The importunities of pedants, who arrogated to themselves the right of worrying me publicly, on account of my religious principles, I conceived myself justified in treating with contempt. But the solemn conjuration of a Lavater, demands at any rate this public avowal of my sentiments: lest too pertinacious a silence should be construed into disregard, or — into acquiescence.

I have read, with attention, your translation of Bonnet's work. After what I have already stated, conviction becomes, of course, foreign to the question: but, even considered abstractedly, as an apology of the Christian religion, I must own, it does not appear to me to possess the merit which you attach to it. I know Mr. Bonnet from other works, as an excellent author; but I have read many vindications of the same religion, I will not only say by English writers, but by our own German countrymen, which I thought much more recondite and philosophical than that by Bonnet, which you are recommending for my conversion. If I am not mistaken, most of your friend's hypotheses are even of German growth; for the author of the *Essai de Psychologie*, to whom Mr. Bonnet cleaves so firmly, owes almost every thing to German philosophers. In the matter of philosophical principles, a German has seldom occasion to borrow of his neighbours.

Nor are the general reflections premised by the author, in my judgment, the most profound part of the work; at least the application and use which he makes of them, for the vindication of his religion, appear to me so unstable and arbitrary, that I scarcely can trace Bonnet in them. It is unpleasant, that my opinion happens to be so much at variance with yours; but I am inclined to think, that Bonnet's internal conviction, and laudable zeal for his religion, have given to himself a cogency in his arguments, which, for my own part, I cannot discover in them. The major part of his consequents flow so vaguely from the antecedents, that I am confident I could vindicate any religion by the same ratiocination. After all, this may not be the author's fault; he could have written for those only who are convinced like himself, and who read merely to fortify themselves in their belief. When an author once agrees with his readers about the result, they will not fall out about the argument. But at you, sir, I may well be astonished; that *you* should deem that work adequate to convince a man, who, from his principles, cannot but be prepossessed in favour of its reverse. It was probably impossible for you to identify the thoughts of a person, like me, who is not furnished with conviction, but has to seek it. But if you have done so, and believe, notwithstanding, what you have intimated, that Socrates himself would have found Mr. Bonnet's arguments unanswerable, one of us is, certainly, a remarkable instance of the dominion of prejudice and education, even over those who go, with an upright heart, in search of truth.

I have now stated to you the reasons why I so earnestly wish to have no more to do with religious controversy; but I have given you, at the same time, to understand that I could, very easily, bring forward something in refutation of Mr. Bonnet's work. If you should prove peremptory, I *must* lay aside my scruples, and come to a resolution of publishing, in a counter-inquiry, my thoughts, both on Mr. Bonnet's work, and on the cause which he vindicates. But, I hope you will exonerate me from this irksome task, and rather give me leave to withdraw to that state of quietude, which is more congenial to my disposition. Place yourself in my situation; take my view of circumstances, not yours, and you will no longer strive against my reluctance. I should be sorry to be led into the temptation

---

* Justice and gratitude require me to observe, that this was written in the middle of the last century. *Enlightened* Europe presents in our days, but one state to verify it.

of breaking through those boundaries, which I have, after such mature deliberation, marked out to myself.

I am, with most perfect respect,
yours sincerely,
MOSES MENDELSSOHN.
Berlin, the 12th of December, 1769.

To this Lavater replied in a second Letter, which gave rise to another publication on the part of Mendelssohn, entitled,

SUPPLEMENTARY REMARKS.

* * * * * * * *
* * * As to what regards Bonnet's work, I confess, that my judgment on it referred entirely to the purpose for which it was recommended to me by Mr. Lavater. I might, it is true, have taken for granted, that it was not at all Mr. Bonnet's aim to oppugn, by his Inquiry, any religious persuasion whatsoever, least of all Judaism; but that he had only the benevolent intention of leading, by means of a more wholesome philosophy, back into the paths of truth, the sceptics and weak in faith of his own church, who have been deluded by a false philosophy, to laugh at religion, Providence, the immortality of the soul, the resurrection, and retribution, as absurd superstitions. In this light I should have considered Mr. Bonnet's work, in order to form a more correct estimate of its merits.

But the unlucky dedication had at once deranged the proper aspect of things. And as that was the point from which I started, and not knowing that the author had disapproved of the translator's proceeding, I read the whole performance under the impression, that it was levelled against myself, and those of my persuasion. In this view, then, the use and application which Mr. Bonnet makes of philosophical principles, could not but appear to me loose and arbitrary; and I *could* say, with propriety, that I was confident I could vindicate, in the same manner, any religion one pleases. * * * * * I will mention a single point by way of illustration.

Mr. Bonnet constitutes miracles the infallible criterions of truth; and maintains that if there be but credible testimony that a prophet has wrought miracles, his divine mission is no longer to be called in question. He then actually demonstrates, by very sound logic, that there is nothing impossible in miracles, and that testimony concerning them may be deserving of credit.

Now, according to *my* religious theory, miracles are not, indiscriminately, a *distinctive* mark of truth; nor do they yield a moral evidence of a prophet's divine legation. The public giving of the law, only, could, according to our creed, impart satisfactory authenticity; because the ambassador had, in this case, no need of credentials, the divine commission being given in the hearing of the whole nation. Here no truths were to be confirmed by actual proceedings, no doctrine by preternatural occurrences, but it was intended it should be believed, that the divine manifestation had chosen this very prophet for its legate, as every individual had himself heard the nomination. Accordingly, we read (Exod. xix. 9.), "And the Lord said unto Moses, Lo, I come unto thee in a thick cloud, that the people may hear when I speak unto thee, and believe thee forever:" (Exod. iii. 12.) "And this shall be a token unto thee, When thou hast brought forth the people out of Egypt, ye shall serve God upon this mountain." Our belief in a revealed religion is, therefore, not founded in miracles, but on a public legislation. The precept to hearken to a wonder-working prophet (Deut. xviii. 15.) is, as our rabbins teach, a mere implicit law, as given by the legislator, and quite independent of the intrinsic evidence of such wonders. So does a similar law (Deut. xvii. 6.) direct us to abide, in juridical cases, by the evidence of two witnesses, though we are not bound to consider their evidence as infallible. Further information on this Jewish elemental law will be found in Maimonides' Elements of the Law, chap. 8, 9, 10. And there is an ample illustration of this passage of Maimonides, in Rabbi Joseph Albo, Sepher Ikkarim, sect. i., cap. 18.

I also meet with decisive texts in the Old Testament, and even in the New, showing that there is nothing extraordinary in enticers and false prophets performing miracles;* whether by magic, occult sciences, or by the misapplication of a gift truly conferred on them for proper purposes, I will not pretend to determine. So much, however, appears to me incontrovertible, that, according to the naked text of Scripture, miracles cannot be taken as *absolute criterions* of a divine mission.

I could, therefore, perfectly well maintain that an argument, founded on the infallibility of miracles, does not decide any thing against the believers in my religion, since we do not acknowledge that infallibility. My Jewish principles will fully bear me out in the assertion, that I would undertake to vindicate, by similar reasoning, any religion one pleases; because I do not know any religion which has not signs and miracles to produce; and surely every one has a right to place confidence in his forefathers. All revelation is propagated by tradition and by monuments. There, I suppose, we agree. But, according to the fundamentals of my religion, not miracles only, but

---

* How are we, for instance, to account for the Egyptian magicians? In the Old Testament (Deut. xiii. 2.), a case is laid down, when we are not to hearken to a prophet or a dreamer of dreams, even if he give a sign or a wonder, but put him to death. In the New Testament, it is distinctly said (Matt. xxiv. 24.), "For there shall arise false Christs and false prophets, and shall show great signs and wonders," &c. Not to mention other texts.

a public giving of the law, must be the *origin* of tradition.

It will now be seen that the assertion of mine, which Mr. Lavater calls singular, is not only compatible with the belief in a revelation, but that it even emanates from the very elements of my religion. As an Israelite, I have argued on Israelitish principles. How could I have done otherwise, under the impression that Mr. Bonnet meant to controvert those principles? But now that I am aware that this excellent author's design was to oppugn the unbelievers of his own church only, and to show *them* that the doctrines which they revile, are, by far, more reconcilable with sound reason than their own fantastic deliration, many difficulties which I have met with on reading the German translation, of course vanish of themselves; and I must own, that, so far as its scope goes, the work is more important, and more worthy of Mr. Bonnet's pen, than I had, at first, an idea of.

ON THE SUBLIME AND THE NAIVE IN POLITE LITERATURE.*

In reading Longinus his treatise on the sublime, one cannot but regret that the work of Cæcilius, treating of the same matter, has been lost. Longinus, it is true, says of him, that "he merely laboured to give us an idea of the sublime, by an infinite number of examples, as if no one knew what it was, but wholly omitted what is most essential, that is, the method by which we may accustom our minds to a true elevation." But as Longinus occupied himself exclusively with the latter,—taking the former for granted, either as something which every one, as he thought, must be acquainted with, or as known to his Terentian, at least, out of Cæcilius; we are in want of a very necessary part of the knowledge of the sublime, to wit, a lucid explanation of it; and those translators and commentators of Longinus who have endeavoured to supply this defect, do not appear to have been very successful in their attempts.

Perhaps the idea of the sublime, which, as Longinus says, constitutes the highest perfection in writing, may be rendered somewhat clearer by the principles which have been established in the foregoing essays† on the nature of the sentiments and on the sources of the fine arts in general.

We have seen that the strictly beautiful has its own determinate limits which it may not pass. When the whole extent of the object is not taken in by the senses at once, it ceases to be *sensuously beautiful* and becomes *monstrous* or *disproportionately great in extension*. The sensation which is then awakened is one of a mixed character indeed, but one which has something repulsive for well-educated minds accustomed to order and symmetry. The senses discover the boundaries at last, but cannot, without difficulty, embrace and combine them in one idea.

When the limits of this extension are still farther removed, they may vanish entirely, at last, to the senses, and then arises the sensuous immeasurable. The senses, perceiving something connected, wander about to discover its limits and lose themselves in the illimitable. Thence, as was shown in the first treatise,* arises, at first, a shuddering which comes over us, and then something like giddiness which often obliges us to take our eyes from the object. The vast ocean, a far extended plain, the innumerable host of the stars, every height or depth whose limits are not discoverable, and other like objects of Nature, which seem immeasurable to the senses, awaken this kind of sensation, which, as is there set forth more minutely, is, in some cases, exceedingly pleasant, but, in others, may occasion discomfort.

The artist also avails himself of these sensations on account of their agreeableness, and endeavours to produce them by imitation. The imitation of the sensuous immeasurable is denominated, in general terms, the *grand*. By this term is understood not a limited magnitude, but one which seems to be limitless, and is adapted to produce an agreeable awe. There is, in art, a particular method of producing this sensation, where the immeasurable itself cannot be represented. It is to repeat, at equal intervals of time or space, a single impression, unaltered, uniform, and very often. The senses, in that case, detect no symmetrical process, no rule of arrangement from which the end of this repetition might be inferred; they are thrown into a state of restlessness which resembles the awe produced by the immeasurable. An instance, in architecture, is a straight colonnade in which the columns are like and separated from each other by equal distances. A colonnade of this kind has something grand which immediately disappears when the uniformity of the repetition is interrupted and a prominent contrast introduced at certain intervals. The monotonous iteration of a single sound after equal pauses has the same effect in music, and is used to express veneration, the terrible, the awful. In literary composition there are arts of speech which produce the same effect. Sometimes it is done by the multiplication of conjunctions,— of the connecting *and*:

Und das Geschrei und der tödtenden Wuth und der donnernde Himmel.

---

* *Belles lettres, Schöne Wissenschaften,* literally Beautiful sciences. I prefer the above as being more English and customary, while it answers more exactly to the subject matter of this treatise. Tr.

† See "Mendelssohn's philosophische Schriften," in two vols., Berlin, 1777, from which this essay is taken. Tr.

* *Zusätze zu den Briefen über die Empfindungen,* p. 36. Tr.

So too,

——— *und* ist noch *und* denkt noch *und* fluchet.

Sometimes too by the multiplication of verbs or nouns without the connecting *and*. Longinus gives an example from Xenophon: They dashed their shields against each other, they crowded, they struggled, they slew, they fell. * * *
* * * * * * * *

The climax which increases in regular gradations has a similar effect; but this pleases also for other reasons, which it would be out of place to enlarge upon here.

As there is an illimitable in extended magnitude, whose effects we have just described, so there is an illimitable in intensity, or unextended magnitude, which produces similar effects. Power, genius, virtue, have their unextended immeasurable, whose effects also awakens a sensation of awe, and which has at the same time this advantage, that it does not, by tedious uniformity, terminate at last in satiety and disgust, as is apt to be the case with the immeasurable in extension. They are various as they are great, and, as it was remarked in the passage already referred to, the sensation which they excite is unmixed on the part of the object; and therefore it is that the soul affects these with so much eagerness. We commonly call the intensively great, powerful; and the powerful, in its perfection, we designate with the special appellation of sublime. We may say then, generally, that everything which is, or appears immeasurable in the degree of its perfection, is called sublime. We call God the most sublime of beings. We call a truth sublime, which concerns a very perfect nature, as God, the universe, the human soul; which is of immeasurable value to human kind, or for the discovery of which a great genius was required. In the fine arts and in letters, the sensuously perfect representation of the immeasurable will be grand, powerful or sublime, according as the magnitude relates to extension or number, to a degree of strength, or particularly to a degree of perfection.

The sensation produced by the sublime is a compound one. The greatness arrests our attention; and since it is the greatness of perfection, the soul clings with pleasure to that object, and all collateral ideas are thrown into obscurity. The illimitableness awakens an agreeable awe which pervades us wholly, while the variety prevents us from being satiated, and gives the imagination wings to penetrate farther and ever farther. All these sensations blend together in the soul; they flow into each other, and grow to a single sentiment which we call admiration. If, therefore, we wished to describe the sublime according to its effects, we might say it is the sensuously perfect in art which is capable of exciting admiration.

Every perfection which, by its greatness, surpasses our ordinary conceptions, which exceeds the expectation we had of a certain object, or which outdoes all that we had imagined of perfection, is an object of admiration. The determination of Regulus to return to Carthage, although well advised of the tortures which awaited him there, is sublime, and excites admiration, because we had not supposed that the duty of keeping one's promise, even with an enemy, could exert such power over the human heart. The unexpected reconciliation of Augustus with Cinna, in the celebrated tragedy of Corneille, produces the same effect, because the character of this prince had prepared us for a very different course of conduct. In Canute, the mercy shown to Ulfo does not create so sudden a sensation, because it was not so unexpected in view of the character of the ever merciful Canute.

Finally, the attributes of the Supreme Being, as recognized in his works, awaken the most extatic admiration, because they surpass all that we can imagine of greatness, perfection, sublimity.

Since the great and the sublime are so nearly related, we see why artists so often maintain the sublime by means of the great, and, as it were, by sensible impressions of the great, prepare us for the intellectual conception of the sublime. They magnify the measure or the proportions of those things which they desire to represent as sublime. They make use of a bright lustre which dazzles by its intensity, or of an obscurity which causes the boundaries of objects to disappear, but never of a moderate light. The image of the sublime is never fully drawn; single traits are hyperbolically exaggerated, and the rest left indefinite, in order that the imagination may lose itself in their vastness.

——— "I stretch my head into the clouds,
My arm into eternity."

We accompany the sublime in poetry with the great in music, with the artificially immeasurable in iteration, &c.; not because all that is great is also sublime, as is generally supposed, but because similar sensations mutually support each other, and because the great is precisely the same in respect to the external senses, that the sublime is in relation to the inner sense. Therefore, the impression on the inner sense must needs be strengthened when the external senses are, by means of similar impressions, attuned in harmony with it.

Admiration in regard to the productions of the fine arts, as well as the perfection which is expressed by it, may be of two different kinds. Either the object to be represented possesses in and of itself qualities which are admirable; in which case the admiration of the object becomes the dominant idea in the soul; or the object is not particularly remarkable in and of itself, but the artist possesses the skill to bring out its qualities and to place them in an uncommon light; and then the admiration is directed rather to the imitation than to the archetype, rather to the excellences of art than to the excellences of the object. And as every work is an embodying of the perfections of the master, so the admiration, in the latter case, regards more especially the artist and his characteristic excellences. We admire his great wit, his genius, his imagination, and other faculties of the soul which harmonize together for so worthy an end; and whose invisible nature he has found means to manifest in his work. That which especially pleases us in art, considered as art, refers to the intellectual endowments of the artist, which are brought to view in his works. When these exhibit the marks of genius or of extraordinary talent, they excite our admiration.

This classification will furnish opportunities of deciding how far the sublime is compatible with ornate expression, and in what cases it rejects such expression. We will begin with that species in which the admiration arises immediately from the object itself.

Perfections of the external condition are of too little worth to excite the admiration of a man of understanding. Hence riches, splendour, authority and power without merit are justly excluded from the province of the sublime.

"Those things," says Longinus very strikingly, "the contempt of which is considered as something great, can never possess real sublimity in themselves." In fact we admire not so much those who possess great wealth or hold distinguished posts of honour, as those who might have these things, but who, from a noble magnanimity, reject them. Therefore the representation of these things in architecture and the arts of embellishment, where advantages of external condition come into consideration, may be showy, proud, splendid;—but true sublimity is attained only by means of a noble simplicity, i. e. by the avoidance of all which would seem to place much value on those advantages. Not the lavish use of wealth and splendour, but a wise indifference toward them exalts the soul and teaches us to know its real dignity. They must be objects of importance with the spendthrift, if he wishes to shine with them.

Physical perfections, as, for example, uncommon strength or bravery, a beautiful form in an insignificant posture, a beautiful countenance whose features indicate neither intellect nor sentiment, an extraordinary nimbleness in the motions of the limbs without grace or attraction, &c., may indeed excite a slight degree of admiration, but we are never so charmed as we are in contemplating great mental perfections. A great intellect, great and noble sentiments, a happy imagination combined with penetrating sagacity, generous and vehement emotions which rise above the conceptions of ordinary minds, whether they have a true or only an apparent good for their object, and, in general, all great qualities of mind which surprise us unexpectedly, ravish our soul and lift it, as it were, above itself. The immeasurably great which is there implied, and which seems new, because unsuspected, fixes the attention of the mind and enfeebles all collateral ideas, uncongenial with it, to such an extent that the soul finds no transition to other objects, but, for awhile, is lost in wonder. When this inability to quit the object continues for a time, that state of mind is called astonishment.

This admiration, however, may be likened almost to a flash of lightning, which dazzles us for a moment and disappears, unless its flame is maintained and nourished by the fire of a gentle sentiment. When we love the object which we admire, or when, by undeserved suffering, it merits our compassion, then admiration alternates with a more affectionate sentiment, in our minds; we wish, we hope, we fear for the object of our love or of our compassion; and we admire his great soul which is raised above hope and fear. When the artist, by his magic power, can transport us into this frame of mind, he has reached the summit of his art, and satisfied art's worthiest aims. It is a spectacle pleasing to the gods, says an ancient philosopher, when they behold a good man struggling with fate, sacrificing everything but his virtue. Ecce spectaculum dignum, ad quod respiciat intentus operi suo Deus: ecce par Deo dignum, *vir fortis cum mala fortuna compositus!**

These then are the principal kinds of admiration which flow directly from the object itself without reference to the perfections of the artist. We will examine how far external embellishment of expression is compatible with them.

The truly sublime, as has been stated in the foregoing remarks, occupies the faculties of the soul to such an extent, that all collateral ideas connected with it must needs disappear. It is a sun which shines alone and eclipses all feebler lights with its splendour. Moreover in the moment when we perceive the sublime, neither wit nor imagination can perform their functions, to turn our thoughts in any other direction; for no other similar idea was ever connected in our mind with the object of admiration, so as to follow naturally in its own train according to the laws of the imagination. Whoever doubts this, let him consider that, according to our explanation, the unexpected, the new is an essential condition of the sublime. It is this, precisely, that causes the strong impression which admiration makes on our minds, and which is not unfrequently succeeded by astonishment, or even by a kind of stupor—a loss of consciousness.

Hence it is evident that excessive ornament is incompatible with the sublime of the first class. Any amplification, by means of collateral ideas, is unnatural; for all such ideas are necessarily thrown, as it were, into the darkest shade. The analysis of the main idea would weaken admiration by its slowness; it would allow us to feel the sublime only by little and little. On the other hand, comparisons and other ornaments of speech are still more out of place, since wit and imagination, from which

---

* Seneca, de Providentia, C. II.

they spring, suspend their functions during the contemplation of the sublime, and allow the soul the repose which is necessary to dwell on that idea and to think it over in all its grandeur. The main idea of the sublime is properly that,

"Judicis argutum quod non formidat acumen."

We may say of it, *volet hoc sub luce videri;* whereas of collateral ideas it may be said, *hoc amat obscurum.* Therefore the artist, in the representation of this species of the sublime, should cultivate a naive, inartificial expression, which leaves the reader or spectator to imagine more than is said. Nevertheless, the expression must be derived from actual vision (*anschauend*), and if possible refer to particular instances, in order that the mind of the reader may be roused and inspired to meditation.

We will illustrate these thoughts by some examples. This proposition, what God willed, that came to pass, contains the same lofty idea which we admire in the well-known "God said, Let there be light, and there was light." But the former expression is abstract and therefore not sufficiently inspired. This sensuous act, "said,"—this individual object, light, make the idea an intuition, and give it life.

Reges in ipsos imperium est Jovis
Cuncta supercilio moventis,

is an unusually sublime conception; but substitute *mente* or *voluntate* instead of *supercilio,* or *regnantis* instead of *moventis,* and a portion of the sublimity vanishes, because the concrete ideas are changed to abstract ones. The omnipotent wink, *supercilio,* the sensuous action, *moventis,* produce in our imagination the sublime image of the Jupiter of Phidias. We see the omnipotent, if I may use the expression, face to face, *Qui totum nutu tremefacit Olympum.*

In the following passage of Horace,

Si fractus illabatur orbis
Impavidum ferient ruinæ,

the danger which threatens the wise man is perfectly painted, while the state of his soul by which it is more particularly designed to excite our admiration, is indicated by only one word, *impavidum.* Substitute

Si fractus illabatur orbis,
Justum et tenacem propositi virum
Impavidum ferient ruinæ;

and where then is the admired sublimity? The misplaced circumlocution has detained the impatient mind of the spectator, eager for the issue, too long, and suffered the fire of expectation to become extinct. The same remark will apply to the sacred psalmist, in reference to that passage in which he carried out a similar idea more worthily perhaps than Horace. "Therefore will we not fear though the earth be removed and though the mountains should be carried into the midst of the sea." The danger, in this case, is described as minutely, but with far greater truth than in Horace. But how could the influence of trust in God be expressed more simply and artlessly,—"we will not fear"—for which the Hebrew needs but three syllables.

Observe, by the way, the careful selection of phrases in both these great poets, if it may be allowed us to compare them together. Horace describes the quality of mind of a Stoic philosopher, whom the thought, that destiny is necessary and immutable, has rendered insensible to all untoward accidents. He may anticipate every evil; the ruins of the world actually smite him, *feriunt ruinæ,*—but he is not dismayed. No calamity can overtake him unprepared. He has armed himself against every stroke of Fate. The sacred poet, on the other hand, is speaking of the state of mind of a good man, who reposes entirely on God and places his trust in him. He may be alarmed when sudden danger threatens, but his thoughts recur to God. Therefore he is not afraid.

Some objects are, in their nature, so perfect, so sublime, that they cannot be reached by any finite thought, nor correctly indicated by any sign, nor represented as they are by any pictures; such are God, the universe, eternity, &c. Here the artist must strain all the powers of his mind to find the worthiest figures by which these infinitely sublime ideas may be brought sensuously before the mind. He may do so the more safely that the thing signified must always remain greater than the sign he employs; and consequently his expression, however full he may make it, will always be naive in comparison with the thing. The sacred poet sings:

Lord, thy mercy reaches above the heavens,
And thy truth above the clouds,
Thy justice is like the mountains of God,
And thy right an unfathomable deep!

* * * * *

The sublime in sentiment, or the heroic, which, as we remarked above, is an inferior variety of the sublime of the first class, consists in those perfections of the affective powers which excite admiration. When the hero himself is introduced and made to utter such sentiments in person, he should express himself as briefly and as inartificially as possible. A great soul utters its sentiments gracefully and emphatically, but without parade of diction. It argues greater perfection when our noble sentiments have become, as it were, a second nature; when we think greatly and act greatly without knowing it or without making any particular merit of it. Hence we are pleased with the emphatic brevity of the old Horatius, "Qu'il mourut;"—of Brutus in Voltaire, "Brutus l'eut immolé"—and the artless offer of friendship in Corneille, "soyons amis, Cinna!"

To this class belongs the answer of that Spartan who, when a Persian soldier boasted that the arrows and javelins of the Persian army would cover the sun, replied, Then we shall fight in the shade. The epitaph of Simonides on the Lacedæmonians, who fell in battle at Thermopylæ, is of the same kind;

Dic hospes Spartæ nos te hic vidisse jacentes
Dum sanctis patriæ legibus obsequimur.*

* Cicero. Tuscul. Quæst. L. I.

These patriotic men considered their death as sufficiently compensated, if Sparta learned that they had fallen, while obeying the sacred laws of their country.

But though the heroic soul is thus immovable in its sentiments and thus brief and emphatic in the expression of them, when the determination has once been formed; it must show itself rich and inexhaustible in thought, when deliberating on its actions, and while yet uncertain which the path is that virtue prescribes. It must be neither obstinate nor rash, and, in doubtful cases, must weigh the reasons for and against its purposed course with great caution, before it inclines to one or the other side. Then, the sublime in sentiment admits of the richest ornament in expression. All the fire of rhetoric is brought into requisition, in order to exhibit the motives, on both sides, in the strongest light. The undetermined soul wavers as if driven by waves from one side to the other, and carries the hearer with it in every direction, until it recognizes the voice of virtue which puts an end to its irresolution.

Immediately, all doubts are removed, all obstacles overcome, the resolve stands firm and nothing can cause it to vacillate again.

From the sublime of this last description have arisen the monologues in tragedies, which, in modern times, since the Chorus is done away, have come very much into vogue. The monologue of Augustus in the tragedy of Cinna, (Act VI. sc. III.) that of Rodogune in the tragedy of that name, (Act III. sc. 3.) of Agamemnon in the tragedy of Iphigenia, (Act IV. sc. 3.) of Cato in Addison, (Act. V. sc. 1.) of Æneas in the Dido of Metastasio, (Act. I. sc. 19.) are masterpieces in their kind. But they are all outdone by the celebrated soliloquy of Shakspeare's Hamlet, Act. III. sc. 2.

* * * * * * *

Among all the varieties of the sublime, the sublime of passion,—when the soul is suddenly stunned with terror, remorse, anger, and despair,—requires the most artless expression. A mind in commotion is occupied singly and alone with its own passion, and every idea which would withdraw it from that, is torture to it. The soul labours under the multitude of conceptions which overwhelm it. In the moment of vehement emotion they all press forward for utterance, and since the mouth cannot utter them all at once, it hesitates and is scarce able to pronounce the single words which first offer themselves.

What, for example, could Œdipus say, in that terrible moment when, by the confession of the ancient servant, the whole mystery was explained to him, and he felt that the terrible imprecation which he had pronounced against the murderer of Laius must fall upon himself?

Wo! wo! now all is plain!

Sophocles makes him exclaim. Œdipus, to whom so many oracles, testimonies and circumstances were known in relation to this matter, which seemed now to contradict each other, and now to contradict his own consciousness, perceives at length, with horror, that they perfectly agree, and that he is the most miserable of men. Wo! wo! is the expression of Nature in the first stupor, the sigh which the wretch heaves forth when he can find no words. And the first idea which could arise again in the soul of Œdipus must needs have reference to the agreement of the circumstances. "Now all is clear."

Seneca, on the contrary, who seems to have thought this much too quiet, makes his Œdipus, on the same occasion, rave after a very different fashion:

Dehisce tellus tuque tenebrarum potens
In Tartara ima rector umbrarum rape.

One sees that the more foaming the words, the colder the heart; for we feel that it is the stilted poet, not the wretched Œdipus whom we hear.

In Shakspeare's Macbeth, Macduff learns that Macbeth has seized on his castle and murdered his wife and children. He falls into a profound melancholy; his friend endeavours to comfort him, but he hears nothing; he is meditating the means of revenge, and breaks forth at last into those terrible words:

He hath no children!

These few words breathe more vengeance than could have been expressed in a whole oration.

When Joseph could no longer contain himself for grief, and had removed all the bystanders, in order to discover himself to his brethren, what words should he find to express the condition of his soul? How make known to his brethren, in one word, that he was the individual whom they had abused, but their brother still? "*I am Joseph*," he says; "*doth my Father yet live?*" "And they could not answer him, for they were troubled at his presence."

Longinus has remarked, that the true sublime may sometimes be attained by mere silence. "The sublime," he says, "in the ninth division of his treatise, "is nothing but the echo of a great mind. And therefore we sometimes admire the mere musing of a man, even when he utters no word, like the silence of Ajax in Hell,* which has in it more sublimity than all which he could have said." This eloquent silence is imitated by Virgil,† who says of Dido, when addressed by Æneas in the Elysian fields:

Illa solo fixos oculos aversa tenebat,
Nec magis incepto vultum sermone movetur
Quam si dura silex aut stet Marpesia cautes.
Tandem proripuit sese, atque inimica refugit
In nemus umbriferum.

Among the moderns, Klopstock has likewise attempted to make use of this sublime silence, in that passage where Abdiel is addressed by the repentant Abaddon, who was his friend before they fell, with what success I will not undertake to say.

Where this dumb rhetoric, if it may be called

* Odyssee, B. XI. v. 563.   † Æneid, B. VI. v. 469.

so, is connected with the sublime in passion, at the right point, it is capable of producing the most happy effect on the mind of the attentive spectator. In the Œdipus of Sophocles, (Act IV. sc. 3.) the Corinthian shepherd says to Œdipus in the presence of Jocaste that he may return without fear to Corinth; that Merope is not his mother, nor Polybius his father; that he himself, the shepherd, had discovered him on the mountain Cithæron, and brought him from thence to Corinth. This declaration must needs strike the mind of Jocaste like a thunderbolt. She is now fully informed with regard to her terrible fate. She had caused her son to be exposed on that very mountain, for fear that he might some time murder his father Laius according to the oracle. Œdipus was found on that mountain, and is now her husband. The dark sayings of Tiresias and the whole of the terrible mystery are suddenly made clear to her soul. But she is dumb. Grief has so stupified her that she stands there like a pillar. Her husband and son continues to inquire of the shepherd. What despair must have shown itself in her looks during this conversation! Œdipus, tormented by the most dreadful doubts, is impelled by his rashness to put a question to her also. Now she suddenly wakes from her death-slumber.

Joc. How, what did he say? For the sake of heaven, if thou lovest thyself, cease to inquire farther. I am sufficiently miserable thus.
Œdip. Be calm! And though I were descended from three-fold slaves, it cannot dishonour thee.
Joc. Nevertheless, obey me! Be entreated! O do it not!
Œdip. Nay! I must bring the truth to light.
Joc. Ah! Knowest thou what weighty reasons I have for preventing thee!
Œdip. It is even these secret reasons which double my uneasiness.
Joc. (aside). Miserable! O that thou mightest never learn who thou art!
Œdip. Bring hither the other shepherd speedily. Let the queen be ashamed of my condition if she will, and be proud of her own.
Joc. Alas! alas! Thou most miserable of all mortals! This is all that I have to say to thee. I can endure it no longer. (*Exit.*)

So speaks the true sublime in passion. The dumbness of Jocaste, so long as the discourse was not addressed to her, the wild, despairing looks, the oppression, the convulsive trembling in every joint, with which a good actress would accompany this dreadful silence, produce the utmost terror in the spectators, who are kept in a state of constant expectation by the impatience of Œdipus, and the near development of the great mystery. They are not yet indeed fully informed as to the fate of Jocaste; but so much the more terrible are the anticipations to which her conduct, the responses of the oracles, and the sayings of Tiresias, give rise.

At length, she speaks; but what words! what perplexity! "How? What said he?" &c. In departing, she gives us plainly enough to understand what purpose she nourishes in her breast, and hastens to execute without witnesses. "This is all that I have to say to thee; I can endure no longer!" Who does not now tremble for her life? Who does not follow her with the eyes, and wish that she might not be left to herself, in her despair? Œdipus, only, is too much occupied with himself, and apprehends no danger on her part. She departs, and we learn, in the beginning of the fifth act, that our fear was but too well founded.

So much for the sublime of the first class, in which the ground of admiration is to be found in the object itself, which is brought before us. Perhaps I have dwelt on it too long; but the sublime in sentiment required a more detailed exposition from the circumstance that, among all the examples of the sublime which Longinus adduces, there is to be found scarcely one which can be ranked in this class. I except the case of the silence of Ajax, which really belongs here, as also the well-known exclamation of that hero: "O! Father Zeus! deliver the Greeks from darkness! Let it be light, that our eyes may see once more. In the light of day destroy us, if thou hast so determined!"—which Longinus quotes in his ninth section.

The second class of the sublime is that in which the admiration is directed rather to the art of representing than to the representation itself; and, therefore, as was shown above, recurs, for the most part, to the genius and the wonderful abilities of the author. The object in itself may contain nothing lofty, nothing extraordinary; but we admire the great talents of the poet, his happy imagination, his power of invention, his deep insight into the nature of things, into characters and passions, and the noble manner in which he has known how to express his excellent thoughts. A man rolling in the agonies of death, on the field of battle, is not, in itself, a remarkable object. But who does not admire the genius of a Klopstock in describing this circumstance. It was a happy conception, in the outset, — and one which opened a field for great thoughts,—to place an atheist instead of an ordinary man in this situation.

——— And the victor approaching,
And the rearing steed, and the din of the sounding armour,
And the cries and the rage of the slaying and the thundering
  heaven
Storms over him. He lies and sinks with cloven head,
Stupid and unconscious among the dead, and thinks he is passing
  away.
Again he lifts himself up and still is, and thinks still, and curses,
Because he still is, and spurts with his pale dying fingers
Blood toward heaven; curses God and would fain yet deny him.

That which the painters call *fracas*, — the wild tumult on a field of battle,—which is here described with admirable traits, throws the mind of the reader into the utmost commotion. The raving despair of the atheist, who now feels that there is a God, in the midst of this terrible uproar, attracts our whole attention and fills us with disgust and amazement. The horrible, the dreadful assails us on every side. On all hands we have the sensibly immeasurable, which causes a shuddering sensation, one after another, and, agreeably to the explanation given above, maintains the feeling of the sublime. What a thought,

> Curses God and would fain yet deny him!

* * * * *

But there are also some objects entirely devoid of interest in themselves, which give the artist not the least advantage and leave it entirely to the power of his genius, how far they shall appear sublime to us, *i. e.*, how far they shall excite our admiration. An example of this kind is the passage quoted by Longinus from Demosthenes. "Will ye then—confess to me—will ye then run back and forth continually and ask among yourselves what is there new? What can be more new than that one man from Macedonia makes war upon all Greece? Is Philip dead? No, by the Gods! he is only indisposed. But O! ye Athenians, what is that to you? Suppose, that which is human should happen to him; assuredly you would make to yourselves another Philip." What is there great in this passage? What else awakens the idea of the immeasurable here, but the wonderful mind of the orator who knows how to avail himself so felicitously of the most insignificant circumstances, in order to give life, emphasis, and inspiration to his discourse?

No one is more happy in taking advantage of the commonest circumstances and making them sublime, by a fortunate turn, than Shakspeare. The effect of this species of the sublime must necessarily be stronger, the more unexpectedly it surprises us and the less prepared we were to anticipate such weighty and tragic consequences from such trivial causes. I will give one or two examples of this, out of Hamlet. The king institutes public entertainments in order to dissipate the melancholy of the prince. Plays are performed. Hamlet has seen the tragedy of Hecuba. He appears to be in good humour. The company leaves him; and now mark with astonishment the tragic consequence which Shakspeare knows how to draw from these trivial common circumstances. The prince soliloquizes,

> O! what a rogue and peasant slave am I!
> Is it not monstrous that this player here,
> But in a fiction, in a dream of passion,
> Could force his soul so to his own conceit,
> That from her working all his visage wanned;
> Tears in his eyes, distraction in 's aspect,
> A broken voice and his whole function suiting
> With forms to his conceit! And all for nothing!
> For Hecuba!
> What 's Hecuba to him or he to Hecuba,
> That he should weep for her? What would he do
> Had he the motive and the cue for passion
> That I have?

What a master-trait! Experience teaches that persons afflicted with melancholy find unexpectedly in every occasion, even in entertainments, a transition to the prevailing idea of their grief; and the more it is attempted to divert them from it, the more suddenly they fall back. This experience guided the genius of Shakspeare wherever he had to depict melancholy. His Hamlet and his Lear are full of these unexpected transitions causing terror to the spectator.

In the third act, Guildenstern, a former confidant of Hamlet, at the instigation of the king endeavours to sound him and to ascertain the secret cause of his melancholy. The prince detects his purpose and resents it.

> *Guild.* O, my lord! if my duty be too bold, my love is too unmannerly.
> *Ham.* I do not well understand that. Will you play upon this pipe?
> *Guild.* My lord, I cannot.
> *Ham.* I pray you.
> *Guil.* Believe me I cannot.
> *Ham.* I do beseech you.
> *Guil.* I know no touch of it, my lord.
> *Ham.* 'Tis as easy as lying. Govern these ventages with your finger and thumb, give it breath with your mouth, and it will discourse most eloquent music. Look you, these are the stops.
> *Guil.* But these cannot I command to any utterance of harmony; I have not the skill.
> *Ham.* Why, look you now, how unworthy a thing do you make of me! You would play upon me; you would seem to know my stops; you would sound me from my lowest note to the top of my compass: and there is much music, excellent voice in this little organ; yet cannot you make it speak. 'S blood! do you think I am easier to be played on than a pipe! Call me what instrument you will, though you can fret me you cannot play upon me.

None but Shakspeare must venture to introduce such common matters upon the stage, for no one but he possesses the art to use them. Must not the spectator, in this case, be as much amazed as Guildenstern, who feels the superior address of the prince, and withdraws, covered with shame?

If the artist wishes to give us, in his work, a clear and sensible proof of those perfections which he possesses in the highest degree, he must direct his attention to the highest beauties which can animate his description. The little touches of the pencil, it is true, attest the finishing hand of the master, his diligence and his care to please. But it is not in them, certainly, that we are to look for the sublime which deserves our admiration. Admiration is a tribute which we owe to extraordinary gifts of mind. These are what we call genius in the strictest sense. Accordingly, wherever, in a work of art, there are found sensible marks of genius, there we are ready to accord to the artist the admiration which is his due. But the unimportant adjuncts, the last finish—that which belongs indeed to the picture, but does not constitute an essential part of the picture—exhibits too plainly the diligence and the care which it has cost the artist; and we are accustomed to deduct so much from genius as we ascribe to diligence.

It appears then that, in this class of the sublime, the artist is free to use the whole wealth of his art in order to place in their true light the beauties which he has introduced by a happy thought. And herein this kind distinguishes itself from the former in which the naive and inartificial mode of treatment is preferable. Nevertheless, even here, the artist must not honour with too much care and labour those little beauties which perhaps would occupy minds of a lower order for a long time; and he may only then not reject them, when they offer themselves, as it were, unbidden.

I shall content myself with adducing a single example. The sacred Psalmist says of the Sun, (Ps. xix. 6.)

"He cometh forth like a bridegroom out of his chamber,
And rejoiceth like a hero to run a race."

Both images are uncommonly sublime and in the last, especially, Hogarth finds a similarity of thought to the celebrated antique—the Apollo—whom the artist has happily characterized, as the God of day, by the swiftness with which he seems to step forth and to shoot his arrows; —if the arrow can be regarded as intended to signify the rays of the sun. But these great beauties, even in the hands of so great a master as Rousseau, if not entirely dissipated, are at least very much degraded from their sublimity by too diligent elaboration.

Cet astre ouvre sa carriére
Comme un Epoux glorieux,
Qui dés l'Aube matinale
De sa couche nuptiale
Sort brillant et radieux.
L' universe à sa presence
Semble sortir du neant.
Il prend sa course, il s'avance,
Comme un superb geant.

Here we find eight words of the original text spread out into nine verses; but how have they suffered by this extension! *   *   *
*   *   *   *   *   *   *

For the rest, it is evident from our explanation, that this second class of the sublime may consist in the thoughts as well as the expression; and—as it respects the thoughts—in the understanding as well as the imagination, in the creative power, in the comparisons, in striking sentences, sentiments, descriptions of characters, passions, the manners of men and objects in Nature;—and, as it respects the expression—in the use of ornate diction, in the choice of epithets designating the most sensuous qualities, in the arrangement and connection of words, and finally, in the euphony and harmony of the periods. For the artist may display his extraordinary talents by all these beauties.

It will not be necessary to remind the reader that both kinds of the sublime are often found united in works of art. In the essay on the first principles of art it has been already observed, with respect to imitation, that our pleasure in a successful likeness of imitative art is far greater than our pleasure in a form produced by Nature herself, because in the former case, the idea of the artist comes in and heightens the enjoyment. Now this is true not only of imitation, but of all beauty, as it was also there remarked. They please far more when they are viewed, at the same time, as expressions of the perfections of the artist who produced them. Although he must not seek, of himself, to appear and to shine, yet there will always remain some footprints of genius which occasionally betray him and indicate the giant who stamped them there. Therefore, in many cases, subjective sublimity may be united with objective. But the expression will admit of more or less ornament, according as our admiration is directed rather to the object itself, or to the skill of the artist. This must depend, in particular cases, on the nature of the subject to be handled and on the design of the artist.

It would be superfluous, moreover, to illustrate all these remarks with examples, since the treatise of Longinus, who seems to occupy himself singly and exclusively with the second species of the sublime, is in every one's hands. My design was merely to make the idea of the sublime, which is often talked about in connection with works of the fine arts, a little clearer; and I am satisfied if I have not been wholly unsuccessful in this attempt. I shall content myself with adding one or two remarks.

Longinus says, in the seventh division of his work, "You may be assured, in general, that that is really beautiful and sublime which pleases always and all men." Perrault is not satisfied with this proposition of Longinus, and says of it, in his answer to the eleventh observation of Boileau on Longinus, that, according to this precept, the sublime would be extremely rare, since men of different age, different education and mode of life conceive the same thing in very different ways. It seems to me that Perrault is right, so far as the sublime of the second class is concerned. It requires oftentimes a very deep insight into the mysteries of art, to be able to admire the talents of the artist. And how small is the number of the noble ones who possess this insight! But the sublime in the object, and, especially, the sublime in sentiment, surely move men of all classes, as soon as they understand the words by which it is expressed.

Nay, men of ordinary minds, whose feeling is not entirely perverted, must admire the sublime in sentiment the more, the more it exceeds their way of thinking and the less they had supposed the human soul to possess such perfections. It is objected that the most refined critics have disputed with regard to certain passages, whether they are to be classed with the sublime. For example, the passage from the holy scriptures, "God said, Let there be light, and there was light," belongs unquestionably to the sublime of the first class, and yet its sublimity has been doubted by many discerning minds. Where then, in this case, is the agreement which we are to regard as a criterion of the sublime of the first class? But let it be considered that the opponents of Longinus have never doubted that the fact in itself—"God said, Let there be light, and there was light"— is sublime. Only they have refused to concede that it was the intention of the Lawgiver to say something sublime with these words; that is, they allowed to this passage a sublimity of the first class, and only doubted whether that of the second class could be ascribed to it. One sees too, with wonder, in the controversies respecting this passage, how little the critics have been willing to understand one another. The one party appeals continually to the sublimity of the act and the simplicity of the language, the other party is silent on this point and speaks only of the purpose of the Lawgiver, who, to speak after the manner of men, did not assuredly mean in this passage, to tax his mental faculties to say something sublime. Had they explained themselves, the controversy would have been at an end.

Longinus, therefore, is not only right in saying that what pleases always and all men is really beautiful and sublime, but, so far as the sublime of the first class is concerned, we may invert the proposition and say that the sublime must always please and please all men. The words of the Greek critic, which immediately follow, prove moreover that he is actually speaking of the sublime of the first class, when he says that it pleases always and all men, although he has never expressly pointed out this essential distinction. He says: "When people of various tastes, of dissimilar habits, differing in knowledge and in years, have been moved by the same thing, the consent of so many diversities affords us so much the greater certainty, that what is so admired must infallibly possess sublimity."

For the rest, since the sublime is found only in connection with great and extraordinary powers of mind, ordinary wit or the faculty of seeing, in things that differ, unimportant resemblances, is justly excluded, as well from the sublime of the first, as of the second class. Pointed antitheses, epigrammatic conceits, farfetched and artificial wit, may amuse and entertain us pleasantly enough for a time, but they can never excite admiration. They may even hinder it, inasmuch as they are marks of a little mind which makes an insignificant relation, discovered by it, a matter of importance. The smallest soul has something more important to do, in a moment of strong emotion, than to notice insignificant allusions and relations and to dwell upon them. Only an indifferent mind can be so oppressed with ennui as to find entertainment in trifles.

All this, however, applies only to common, hair-splitting wit. There is a great and noble kind founded not in empty likenesses and idle allusions and relations, but in fruitful truths and often in worthy sentiments. This higher wit is a fruitful source of the sublime and the admirable in the fine arts. Even the most vehement passion does not exclude antitheses which rest on some important truth or sentiment. The good writers of antiquity knew only this genuine species of wit, which entertains, moves and instructs at the same time. In the place of this, some of their followers introduced an empty shimmer, which rather dazzles than illumines.

The following are examples of sublime thoughts clothed in wit.

The answer of Alexander when Parmenio said to him; "I would accept the offer of Darius if I were Alexander;" "So would I," replied the prince, "if I were Parmenio."

"He who would fear nothing," says an ancient philosopher, "let him learn to fear God." From this probably arose the sublime verse of Racine:

Je crains Dieu, cher Abner, et n'ai point d'autre crainte.
Athalie, Act I. Sc. 1.

Omnia terrarum subacta
Præter atrocem animum Catonis.—*Horat.*

Neque Cato post libertatem vixit neque libertas post Catonem.
Senec.

Tout etait Dieu excepté Dieu même; et le monde que Dieu avait fait pour manifester sa puissance, semblait être devenu un temple d'idoles.—*Bossuet. Hist. Univ.*

Fern unter ihnen hat das menschliche Geschlecht,
Im Himmel und im Nichts, ein doppelt Bürgerrecht.
Aus ungleich festem Stoff hat Gott es auserlesen,
Halb zu der Ewigkeit, halb aber zum Verwesen.
Zweideutig Mitteldng von Engeln und von Vieh,
Es überlebt sich selbst und stirbt und stirbet nie.
Haller.

* * * * * * *

Examples of pathetic or passion-moving antitheses:—

How doth the city sit solitary that was full of people! The greatest among the nations, the princess of the provinces is become tributary!—*Jerem. Lam.* c. i, v. 1.

Anibalem pater filio meo potui placare. Filium Anibali non possum.——Vultum ipsius Anibalis quem armati exercitus sustinere nequeunt, quem horret populus Romanus,—tu sustinebis? ——Deterreri hic sine te potius, quam illic vinci. Valeant apud te meæ preces, sicut pro te hodie valuerunt.—*Tit. Liv.* I. 23.

Leve toi triste objet d'horreur et de tendresse;
Leve toi cher appui qu'esperait ma vieillesse:
Viens embrasser ton pere! Il t'a du condamner,
Mais s'il n'etait Brutus il t'allait pardonner.
Va, ne t'attendris point; sois plus Romain que moi;
Et que Rome t'admire en se vengeant de toi.
Brutus, Act V. Sc. 7.

The sublime, in general, and especially that of the first class, stands in such close connection with the naive in expression, as has been already suggested above, that it may not be unsuitable to inquire here wherein the naive consists, and how far it may be used in the works of the fine arts.

We have no German word to denote this property. 'Natural,' 'artless,' expresses too little. Men often, in common life, express themselves naturally and artlessly without being naive. 'Noble simplicity,' on the other hand, expresses too much and denotes only a certain species of the naive. We often say of certain comical expressions, that they are naive, although they are anything but noble. We must, therefore, make use of this outlandish word; but we will endeavour to ascertain the idea which is usually connected with it.

Simplicity is unquestionably a necessary ingredient of naiveté. As soon as an expression becomes profound, vivid, highly ornate, naiveté must be altogether denied it; and, so far, the sublime in expression is opposed to the naive. But mere simplicity is not enough. Beneath this simple exterior there must lie a beautiful thought, an important truth, a noble sentiment or passion, which utters itself in an inartificial manner. A merely simple expression leaves us unaffected, but when a beautiful thought dwells, like a lofty soul, in this unadorned body, our heart is touched with a soft emotion, and we exclaim with pleasure, How naive! The country-manners prevalent in our times are extremely simple; but are they naive like the manners of the Arcadian shepherds and other citizens of the golden age, which probably never existed except in the imagination of the poet? And what other reason is there for this difference, but the noble sentiments imputed to the latter, in addition to their external simplicity? Perhaps then, we may establish the following definition: When an object is noble, beautiful, or is associated with important consequences, and is indicated by a simple sign, we call the designation naive.

This definition would be perfectly applicable to all those cases in which the person, into whose mouth the naive saying is put, has really beautiful, noble or significant thoughts, and only makes use of simple expressions. For example, Virgil says in his third eclogue,

> Malo me Galatea petit, lasciva puella,
> Et fugit ad salices, et se cupit ante videri.

This is uncommonly naive. The hiding of Galatea appears to be mere innocent sport; but there is a tender affection at the bottom of it. She provokes the shepherd by this agreeable play to pursue her behind the willows. She could not more happily signify to him her secret passion.

* * * * * * *

The epigrammatic inscription on the brazen cow of Myron,

> Herdsman, wherefore hurriest thou
> Back so far for me?
> Why thy goad upliftest now
> And urgest me to flee?
> I am the artist Myron's cow
> And cannot go with thee,

is naive for the same reason; because, at first sight, it seems to be a mere narrative, but, in reality, contains a very flattering compliment to the artist.

Derision also sometimes assumes the air of innocent narrative in order to conceal its design, and thereby to make the satire more biting. Praise and blame are both the more emphatic, the less designed and the more accidental they appear.

* * * * * *

> On dit que l'Abbe Roquette
> Preche les sermons d'autrui:
> Moi qui sçais qu'il les achete,
> Je soutiens qu'ils sont a lui.
> *Boileau.*

> Huissiers, qu'on fasse silence!
> Dit en tenant audience
> Un President de Baugé;
> C'est un bruit a tête féndre,
> Nous avons deja juge
> Dix causes sans les entendre.
> *J. B. Rousseau.*

Praise sometimes wears the mask of reproach, and is all the more flattering:

> Helas qu'est devenu ce tems, cet heureux temps
> Ou les Rois s'honoraient du nom de fainéans!

And so, inversely, blame sometimes takes the guise of eulogy, whereby the irony is rendered more severe.

* * * * * * *

La Fontaine loses his benefactress, Madame de Lasabliere, and meets his friend, M. d'Hervart. "My dear La Fontaine," said his honest friend, "I have heard of the misfortune which has befallen you. You resided with Madame de Lasabliere; she is dead. I wished to propose to you to come and live with me." "I was just going there," answered La Fontaine.

Generally, the naive in moral character consists in an external simplicity, which unintentionally discovers internal worth; in ignorance of the world's ways; in unconcern about false interpretation, in that confiding manner which is not founded in stupidity and want of ideas, but in magnanimity, innocence, goodness of heart, and an amiable persuasion that others are not worse disposed toward us, than we are toward them. If, therefore, we regard the external conduct of men as the sign of their internal character and worth, the naive, here too, will require simplicity of expression, together with dignity and significance in the thing expressed.

It is the same with the naive in the human countenance, which is so essential to the painter and sculptor. It is always the unstudied, the artless in exterior, undesignedly evincing internal excellence. Since the features, the airs and gestures of men are signs of their propensities and sentiments; since every feature in the countenance expresses a propensity, and every mien an emotion corresponding to it, a naive character is ascribed to the *tout ensemble* of all the features and gestures, when, as it were, without design, without pretence, without self-consciousness, they discover a happy and harmonious combination of tendencies and sentiments. Hence the naive in the character of a child, when, amidst the otherwise monotonous features of a childish face, tender germs of meekness, love, innocence and graciousness appear.

Grace, or elevated beauty in movement, is also connected with the naive, inasmuch as the movements which charm us are natural, have an easy flow, and slide gently one into another, and unintentionally and unconsciously indicate that the motive forces in the soul, from which these voluntary motions flow, sport and unfold themselves in the same unstudied, harmonious, and artless manner. Hence, the idea of innocence and of moral simplicity is always associated with a lofty grace. The more this beauty of motion is combined with consciousness and appears to be the work of design, the more it departs from the naive and acquires a studied character; and, when the accompanying internal emotions do not agree with it, an affected character. Nothing is so disgusting as insipid naiveté, or an outward simplicity which appears to have designs and makes pretensions.

On the other hand, when simplicity in motion betrays, at the same time, want of thought and want of feeling, it is called stupidity; and when inactivity is added, we have the *niais*. In general, then, according to these considerations, it requires, in all cases, an artless external simplicity, together with internal worth or significance, to constitute the naive.

There are cases, however, where he who speaks naively has really nothing more in his mind than the words he makes use of express, and consequently discovers, on his part, no more of internal worth than appears outwardly, but where the hearers, by means of other circumstances, are enabled to connect a good deal more with those words which seem so indifferent, or to draw important consequences from them.

* * * * * * *

The well-known passage in Gellert:*—

"What did you say, Papa? You made a mistake;
You said I was only fourteen years old."
"No! fourteen years and seven weeks,"

is uncommonly naive, because the speaker, (Fiekchen), without perceiving it, betrays the secret wishes of her heart. She means to set her father right, to show him that he has miscalculated by seven weeks, and, in doing so, shows how carefully she must have calculated herself. Contrary to her purpose, therefore, she says more than she meant to say; and yet we call her answer naive.

Thus we sometimes, from haste, let fall a naive word, whereby we betray an important secret.

* * * * * * *

When this takes place in the heat of passion, a naive betrayal of the most secret thoughts may have a very tragic effect. There is a trait of this kind in the Romeo and Juliet of Herr Weisse. The Countess Capulet, who is far from suspecting that her Juliet is in love with Romeo, but, on the contrary, has reason to suppose that she hates this Montague, as all her family hate and prosecute him, because he has killed her cousin Tybalt, (on account of whose death Juliet pretends to be inconsolable, while the absence of Romeo is the real cause of her grief) — this Countess Capulet comes to cheer her daughter, and to inform her that the Count of Lodrona has applied for her hand.

Mad. Capulet. I bring you joyful news, Juliet; joyful for us all, especially joyful for you.
Juliet (*quickly*). Has Romeo been pardoned? — (*Frightened*). Alas! how weak my head is. Is Romeo punished?

A French writer (Dict. Encycl. Art. Naiveté) makes a distinction, which seems to be warranted by the use of language, between naiveté and *a* naiveté. A naiveté, he says, is the name we give to a thought, a trait of the imagination,

* Fabeln und Erzählungen, 2 B. s. 115.

a sentiment which escapes us against our will and may sometimes injure us; an expression originating in vivacity, carelessness, inexperience of the ways of the world. Of this description is the answer of a wife to her dying husband, who was designating the person whom he wished her to marry after his death: "Take him," said he, "you will be happy with him!" "Ah, yes," replied she, "I have often thought of it."

Naiveté, on the other hand, is the language of fine genius and of discerning simplicity. It is the most simple picture of a refined and ingenious idea; a masterpiece of art in him in whom it is not natural.

But, since both kinds of the naive have certain marks in common, it will be necessary, in order not to exclude any of them, to extend our definition of the naive somewhat. When, by a simple expression, something is understood to be designated, which is important in itself or may have important consequences, whether it be the design of the speaker to imply more than he says, or whether without purpose, and, sometimes, against his purpose, he betrays more than he says, the expression is called, in each of these cases, naive.

* * * * *

The effects of the naive are, first, an agreeable astonishment, a slight degree of wonder at the unexpected significance which lay concealed beneath an outward simplicity. We love to fix our attention on an object which reveals to us more and more, the longer we dwell upon it, which performs, as it were, more than it seemed to promise. If now, this interior significance arises from a high degree of perfection, there ensues the feeling of awe which accompanies the sublime; but combined with a joyous sensation which approaches very nearly to laughter. For the simplicity of the expression forms a kind of contrast with the importance of the thing signified, or with the consequences flowing from it, which tempts to laughter, and the sense of this contrast, if not suppressed by stronger sentiments, manifests itself in actual laughter. When overpowered by the sublime, it is no longer laughter, which the contrast produces, but the trace of a gracious smile which plays about the lips and loses itself in lofty admiration. This is always the feeling which we have when surprised by the naive in moral character. The man devoid of sentiment, who judges according to appearance, will not witness the morally naive without laughing; for he sees nothing more than the contrast with the customs of the world which he knows better, and the strangeness of that too certain confidence in the goodness of others, which provokes him to loud laughter. The man of sensitive heart, on the contrary, sees through to the inner worth, recognises the magnanimity from which that indecision and seeming strangeness spring; and while his lips move themselves to laugh, a feeling of awe comes over his heart and resolves the laugh into wondering meditation. The naive in the features of the countenance produces a similar effect, only that the inclination to laugh, in this case, will manifest itself with much weaker indications, because the contrast here is not so obvious. The man devoid of sentiment will contemplate it with indifferent eyes because the air and the features seem to him unmeaning; and, with the more discerning, the contrast produces no other effect than a gentle opening of the lips and an almost imperceptible lengthening of the mouth, which is rather an approval than a smile.

If the essence of the naive is an evil,—not a dangerous one,— a weakness, an error, a folly which is not followed by any perceptible misfortune, the naive is merely ludicrous. In this case, the effect will differ according as the individual, from whom it comes, intends that more should be understood than he says, or, unintentionally, betrays more than he says. In the former case, he makes us laugh; in the latter, he makes himself ridiculous. Of this examples enough have been given above, and the application is so easy that we may reasonably leave it to the reader.

But when the essence of the naive consists in actual danger, a misfortune which befalls some one in whose fate we are interested, the naive is tragic, and when the danger is a dreaded consequence of the naive, the effect is terrible and prostrates every feeling of the ludicrous. An example of this is the above-mentioned passage from Romeo and Juliet. Another, equally striking, is the too ingenuous confession of Monime in the Mithridates of Racine; when this princess suffers herself to be betrayed into confidential communications by the wily Mithridates and confesses to him her love-affairs, but perceives with terror, during the relation, that Mithridates loses colour and begins to grow pale with rage.

But when the dreaded evil is not a consequence of the naiveté, but is connected with it in some other way,— as sign with the thing signified,— the smile which the perception of the contrast provokes may consist with the saddest emotions. Andromache smiles at the simple fears of the little Astyanax, and, at the same time, scalding tears roll down her cheeks. The whole pit laughs at the innocence of the little Arabella,* without detriment to the tragic sensation. Nay, our compassion for these children is the more lively, the more they show by their naive conduct, that they are unconscious of the misfortune in which they are most nearly concerned. Whence it is evident, how unfounded is the opinion of some critics, who would have all sentiments which contain any touch of the ludicrous, banished from the tragic stage.

This matter deserves further discussion, but it does not belong to the object which I had proposed to myself.

---

* An allusion to Lessing's "Miss Sarah Sampson." Tr.

JOHANN GEORG HAMANN.

Born 1730. Died 1788.

The "Magus of the North," as he was pleased to style himself in his contributions to the periodical literature of his time, is a name little celebrated beyond the select circle of his admirers, but greatly honored within that circle. Hamann was one of those who waken an intense interest in a few, and none at all in the mass.

A native of Königsberg, in compliance with the wishes of his father, he studied theology at the university in that city. But an impediment in his speech and a preference for criticism, philology and poetry, induced him to devote himself principally to those pursuits and to make the Law his nominal profession. In 1752 he entered the family of the Baroness of Budberg, in Kurland, as a private tutor; afterward that of General von Witten in the same capacity, and in 1755 became domesticated with a merchant in Riga where he grew so familiar with the business of commerce, that he undertook a mercantile expedition to Holland and England. The ill success of this enterprise occasioned him deep chagrin, and, while in London, he resolved on a change of life. He turned his attention to religion, but without resuming theology as a profession. He returned to Riga where he resided a few years, and afterward to his native city; devoting himself to literary pursuits and particularly to ancient literature and the Oriental languages. In 1764 he made the tour of Germany and Switzerland, and went to Warsaw in the capacity of travelling tutor to a nobleman from Kurland. In 1777 he received an appointment under the Prussian Government to an office connected with the Customs-department, in Königsberg. In 1784 a pension bestowed by a kind patron gave him a pecuniary independence and the means of devoting himself entirely to letters. But, before he could reap the full benefit of this provision, he was overtaken by death, on a journey for the benefit of his health, June 21st, 1788.

Hamann is indebted for his reputation to the testimony of a few names of the highest mark, such as Herder, Jacobi, Goethe, and Jean Paul, rather than to any great popularity which his works have had with the German Public. He belonged to that class of writers who love the shade and lose more by obscurity than they gain by originality; — who repel, by the uncouth shapes, in which their thoughts are disguised, more readers than they attract by the rarity and pickedness of the thoughts themselves. He is a humorist, but of a sombre complexion, with a strong dash of cynicism. At the same time, a deep religious sentiment pervades his writings which show him to be an orthodox believer, according to the letter, like his contemporary—in all else, his antipodes—Matthias Claudius. "The *Kernel* of his works," says Herder, "contains many seed-corns of great truths, new observations and the results of a wonderfully extensive reading; the *shell* is a laborious texture of strong expressions, allusions and word-flowers. He read much and with taste (*multum et multa*), but the balsam-odors from the ethereal table of the ancients, mixed with occasional vapors of Gaul and the steam of British humor, formed a perfect cloud around him. His observations often combine a whole view in a single view-point; but let the reader stand at that view-point, otherwise he will see everything askew, and common mould instead of microscopic forests. Every thought of his is an unstrung pearl; every thought is wrapped in the very word without which it could neither have been thought nor spoken."

"The great Hamann," says Jean Paul, "is a deep sky full of telescopic stars, with many a nebula which no eye can resolve." And again, "Hamann's style is a river which the storm drives back toward its source, making it innavigable for Dutch market-boats."

But the best account of Hamann is that given by Goethe in his autobiography.*

"Since I was tempted to the Sibylline character which I gave to these leaves, as well as

---

* " Aus meinem Leben." Zwölftes Buch.

to the publication of them, by Hamann, this seems to me a proper place to speak of that worthy and influential man, who was to us then as great a mystery, as he has been to his country ever since. His "Socratic Memorabilia" excited attention and were especially dear to those who could not adjust themselves to the dazzling spirit of the times. They seemed to reveal a deep-thinking, thorough man, who, while he was well acquainted with the public world and literature, still held to something secret and inscrutable, and expressed himself in a very peculiar way concerning it. He was regarded indeed, by those who ruled the literature of the day, as an abstruse enthusiast; but the upstriving youth of the country yielded itself without resistance to his attraction. Even "the silent in the land," as—half in jest and half in earnest—they were called; those pious souls, who without confessing to any particular communion, formed an invisible church, turned their attention toward him, and to my Klettenberg, as well as to her friend Moser, the 'Magus of the North,' was a welcome phenomenon. One inclined the rather to come into relations with him, since it was understood that, though distressed with the narrowness of domestic circumstances, he could still maintain this beautiful and lofty way of thinking. With President von Moser's great influence, it would have been easy to provide a tolerable and comfortable existence for a man of such simple habits. In fact an opening was made and the mutual understanding and approximation between them had gone so far, that Hamann undertook the long journey from Königsberg to Darmstadt. But the president being accidentally absent, that strange individual — for what reason, no one knew — immediately returned. Notwithstanding, a friendly correspondence was still maintained. I possess to this day two letters of the Königsberger to his patron, which bear witness to the wonderful greatness and intensity of their author.

"But so good an understanding was not long to remain. These pious persons had imagined him pious too, after their fashion. They had regarded him with reverence as the 'Magus of the North,' and supposed that he would always continue to present a venerable aspect. But already in his 'Clouds,' an afterpiece to the 'Socratic Memorabilia,' he had given some offence; and when, after that, he published the 'Crusades of a Philologian,' which not only exhibits on its title-page the goats-profile of a horned Pan, but on one of the first leaves of which, also, a large cock, in wood-engraving, beating time to young cockerels who stand before him with notes in their claws, shows himself, in the highest degree, ludicrous;—whereby certain pieces of church-music, not approved by the author, were intended to be ridiculed;—then arose, among the well-meaning and persons of delicate feeling, an aversion which the author was soon made to perceive, while he, on his part, not edified thereby, withdrew himself from a nearer connection with them. * * * * * *
* * * * * * *

"The principle to which the various declarations of Hamann may be reduced, is this: 'All that man undertakes, whether with word or deed, or however performed, should be the result of the union of all his powers; every partial effort is to be condemned.' A glorious maxim! but difficult to observe. With respect to life and art it may do very well. But in every communication by word which is not poetical, there is great difficulty in carrying it out. For the word, in order to express anything, in order to mean anything, must detach itself, must individuate itself. Man, when he speaks, must, for the moment, become one-sided; there can be no communication, no doctrine, without separation. But as Hamann, once for all, resisted this separation and undertook to speak as he felt, imagined, thought, with perfect unity, and demanded the same of others, he came into collision with his own style and with all that others might produce. In order to perform the impossible, he grasps at all the elements. The deepest, mysterious intuitions, where Nature and Spirit meet in secret, the illuminating flashes of the understanding which burst forth from such meeting, the significant images that hover in those regions, the sayings of sacred and profane writers crowding upon him, and whatever else may adjoin itself, humoristically, hereto,—all this forms the wondrous whole of his style, of his communications. Unable to associate with him in the deeps, to wander with him on the heights, to make ourselves masters of the forms which float before him, to discover the sense of a passage, which is merely indicated, in an infinitely extended literature; — it grows ever thicker and darker around us, the more we study him. And this darkness will increase with coming years, because his allusions are directed principally to certain peculiarities dominant, at the time, in literature and life. In my collection there are some of his printed sheets in which he has cited, with his own hand, in the margin, the passages to which he alludes. On turning to those passages, one is met again by an equivocal double-light which is in the highest degree agreeable; only one must renounce entirely what is usually called understanding. Such leaves, therefore, deserve to be called Sibylline, because one cannot contemplate them in and for themselves, but must wait for an opportunity to recur to their oracles. Every time we consult them, we think to find something new, because the indwelling sense of each passage touches and moves us in manifold ways.

"Personally, I have never seen him, nor come into any immediate relation to him through letters. He seems to me, in the connections of life and friendship, to have been, in the highest degree, clear, and to have felt very correctly the relations of men to each other and to himself. All the letters that I have seen of him were admirable and much more intelligible than his other writings, because here, the reference to time and circumstances, as well as to personal relations, was much more evident. And yet I thought to perceive in them, that, feeling with the greatest naiveté the superiority of his mental gifts, he always thought himself a little wiser and more knowing than his correspondents, whom he treated ironically rather than heartily. If this was true of particular cases only, yet those cases constituted, for me, the majority, and a reason for not wishing to come any nearer to him."

The principal works of Hamann are the "Memorabilia of Socrates," "Golgotha and Scheblimini," and "Sibylline Leaves by the Magus of the North." The specimen given below does not verify the peculiarities mentioned in these quotations. It was a youthful essay which the author was hardly willing to publish with the rest of his works. It is given not as a characteristic, but, simply, as the most intelligible specimen of an author whom, on account of his peculiar position in German Literature, it was thought best to represent in this Collection. The translation is by an anonymous friend of the editor.

THE MERCHANT.

FROM HAMANN'S SCHRIFTEN, HERAUSGEGEBEN VON FRIEDRICH ROTH. BERLIN. BEY G. REIMER. 1821. VOL. I.

Supplement to a translation of Dangeuil's Remarques sur les Avantages et les Desavantages de la France et de la Gr. Bretagne, par Rapport au Commerce et aux autres Sources de la Puissance, &c.

THERE are virtues, which originate like colonies, as others seem to be the growth of the age. Our sensitiveness to what we now name the world, or honour, would be as incomprehensible to the ancients, as it is difficult to the moderns to imagine a passionate love of country, or to feel it themselves.

History furnishes most indubitable proofs of special care taken by the most ancient nations for the regulation of civil society. Their policy extended from divine service to the theatre, dancing and music. Everything was employed by them as an implement of the government. One spirit united families, whose activity and exercise were promoted even by domestic dissensions. This spirit made them fruitful in projects, and the performance corresponded.

The common weal seems to have been extinguished since the period when, instead of citizens, there were vassals who assumed to be masters of their own actions and their property, when they had paid homage to their chief. To this chief it was, in part, no longer possible, in part no longer necessary, to be a father to his country. In these times, the prince was perhaps an armed Hobbes, or a prototype of Machiavel, or a Vespasian, ruling by tax-gatherers and vampires; or the slave of priests. His inclinations, his court, and certain classes, took the place of the public welfare. He imitated those philosophers who took the earth for the centre of the universe.

The style of our offices has likewise served to divert the mind from the common weal. To seem worthy of a place which can seldom be the object of the wishes of a rational man, we bring ourselves betimes into, I know not what, entanglements. How many submit for the sake of daily bread, and from the fear of man, to slavish cringing, and to perjury!

* * * * * *

Aiming at a yearly income and a comfortable livelihood, zeal to imitate or excel others in a pageantry of trifles, hence arises the monopoly which every one pursues in his class. The accumulations of prosperity and avarice dissipate the minds of our youth too much to leave space enough for great passions and power for great undertakings. How many, besides, find their fortune already complete, having thought as little of building it up, as of building up themselves. One may say, in truth, of places of honour and estates, that to despise both, we need only look at their possessors.

Witty minds have not failed to remark, on the derision expressed by nature, in that she appoints, on this earth, the cattle in the field to be more learned than we, and the bird in the heavens more wise. But has it not been her intention that man should owe his prerogatives to the social affections; should early accustom himself to reciprocal dependence; seeing betimes the impossibility of dispensing with others? Wherefore has she sought to compensate death, not by a cold mechanism, but by the soft and ardent inclination of love? Wherefore has her Author provided by laws, that marriage should spread, and that families, by ingrafting with families, should form new bonds of friendship? Wherefore are his goods so differently appointed to the earth and its dwellers, but to render them social? The fellowship and inequality of men are also nowise among the projects of our wit. They are no inventions of policy, but designs of Providence, which, like all other laws of nature, man has partly misunderstood, and partly abused.

Nothing reminds us more impressively of the advantages of union than the benefits which flow from commerce in human society. Through this it is, that that is everywhere, which is anywhere. It satisfies our wants, it prevents satiety by new desires, and these it allays too. It maintains peace among nations, and is their horn of plenty. It furnishes them with arms, and decides their doubtful fortune. Men labour for it, and it rewards their diligence with treasures. It enlarges their intercourse, develops their powers, makes itself not only their weapon, but employs their genius, their courage, their virtues, their vices. Every harbour, every canal, every bridge, every floating palace and army, are its works. Through its influence, the arts are awakened and extended. Our sideboards and the toilets of the ladies are adorned with its gifts. The poisons of our kitchens, and the antidotes of our physicians pass through its hands. It atones for frugality by profusion. Its exercise consists in exact integrity, and from its gains the patriot distributes prizes, and performs his vows.

What happy changes may not the world promise itself from the commercial spirit, now beginning to prevail, if it should be purified by insight and noble impulses? Perhaps we may not vainly flatter ourselves with the hope that, through its influence, the love of the public good will be re-established, and the virtues of the citizen raised from their ashes to their original splendour.

The demand of commerce for liberty promises to hasten the happy return of that blessing to man. The unrestrained energy, the unimpeded skill of each individual, and all that each undertakes not at variance with the common good, will gradually banish that unbridled audacity with which every one in our times allows himself in everything, and aims to make possible whatever he considers useful to himself alone.

Inestimable good! without which men can neither think nor act, whose loss robs him of every privilege! By thee, trade blooms, and extends through all ranks! Each resumes his ancient and natural rights, which we had renounced from servile passions and prejudices!

Holland has, to the advantage of her trade, abolished tyrannical persecution for conscience' sake, and adopted among her fundamental laws that freedom of opinion which is as reasonable as it is beneficial. Why should it not tend to the renown of the Roman tax-gatherers, that they were the first who concerned themselves to relieve their countrymen from the blindness of superstition?*

The spirit of trade may perhaps abolish in time the inequality of ranks, and level those heights, those hills, which vanity and avarice have thrown up, in order not only to receive sacrifices thereon, but to control with more advantage the course of nature. The incapacity of the idle ceases to be a mark of distinction gratifying to his pride, where the effort, and labour, and sweat of contemporaries make their life costly, and alone claim consideration and favour. The laurels wither with the decay of the fathers. Their rest on the bed of honour has become to us more indifferent than to their useless posterity, who enjoy the same repose on the cushions of prosperity and tedium. These dead are here, to bury completely the glory of their dead. Trade is, at the same time, the shovel which stirs the heaped-up gold, like the corn, and preserves it either for the bosom of the earth, or for the enjoyment of her children. Through it, gold is not only increased and made fruitful, but also useful, and a medium of life for man. But where it stands highest, the citizen must be most moderate in his gains, since, were all the world to have enough, none would have too much or too little.

Men knew formerly very little of the principles of trade. It was pursued rudely, and was so much contemned, as to be left almost entirely to the Jews. Now, on the other hand, men have with much sagacity aimed to make a science of commerce. Although its objects and ideas are in part arbitrary, and depend on the imagination; yet men have attempted to unite the theory of trade, and its exercise with as much exactness as the astronomers to found their reckonings on imaginary lines and hypotheses. How much weighty insight, have not the prince and the people gained besides, by a thorough examination of the sources of trade?

---

* Cicero says, De Nat. Deor. III. 19, that they were the first who considered it absurd to believe those gods who had been men. Self-interest led them to this rational conclusion, because the lands consecrated to the Immortals were exempt from taxes. Whether we have profited more from distempered and false, or suffered more from great and noble views, may be a problem.

That instructive satire on monarchs, which the inventor of chess, according to the fancy of a distinguished poet* had in mind, is no longer a picture of our kings. They have better learned to appreciate the worth of their subjects. They now know that the state becomes great, only when they promote population by abundant sustenance, regard idleness as an injury to their violated majesty, punish it with contempt and hunger, consider it the masterpiece of their wisdom, to multiply the hands of diligence, as well as to lighten its labour, and watch over the education of orphans and foundlings.

The subject has learnt better to understand and to employ the fruits of the soil and his own sweat. Philosophy is no longer sculpture. The scholar is called back from the Spanish castles of the intellectual world, and from the shades of the library, to the great theatre of nature and her doings, to living art, and her implements, to social employments, and their moving springs. He is an attentive spectator, a scholar, an intimate of the peasant, the artisan, the merchant, and through universal observation and research, becomes the helper and teacher of all.†

When even the common man becomes an object of importance to the state, because its strength flows from his preservation, industry, and increase, then the interest, which the commonwealth takes in the industry of every day-labourer, is sure to instil into him, in time, nobler sentiments. "If those artisans had known," says Plutarch, "that through their labour, Amphion would surround a city with walls, or Thales still a tumult of the people, with what ambition, what delight, had they carved the lyres of these men!"‡

Trade has served for a demonstration of all these truths, and the pursuit of it has confirmed their force. When, therefore, the deceitful, lying, avaricious disposition of an ancient nation* is ascribed to their calling, when reference is made to a modern country, rendered habitable by skilful industry, and powerful by trade, where the moral virtues, and the smallest offices of human love are regarded as wares; when it is said that with the art of calculation that resoluteness cannot exist, by which the renunciation of selfishness, and magnanimous sentiments are attained, that attention to trifles limits the circle of mental vision, and reduces elevation of thought, it is certainly the duty of the merchant to refute these charges.

Was it the fault of religion, that in those dark times of superstition, the spiritual order adopted a sort of *assiento*-contract,† that the priest carried on a most lucrative stock-jobbing, derived premiums from the fear of hell, sold the church-soil to the dead, taxed the early days of marriage, and made a profit on sins, which he for the most part invented himself?

We laugh at the wise Montaigne, who was anxious, lest the introduction of powder and shot should annihilate bravery. Let us feel a more earnest anxiety for the moral results of trade. Much pains have been taken certainly to perfect the science, but perhaps too little thought has been given to forming the merchant. The spirit of trade should be the spirit of traders, and their morals, the groundwork of its reputation. Both should be better encouraged by rewards, supported by laws, and upheld by examples.

"The occupation most useful to society," says an ancient writer,‡ "should assuredly be followed with emulation, I mean agriculture, which would prosper greatly, if rewards were offered, giving it the preference. The commonwealth would hereby gain infinite advantage, the public revenues be increased, and sobriety be associated with improved industry. The more assiduous the citizens became in their occupations, the less would extravagance prevail. Is a republic favourably situated for commerce, honours shown to trade would multiply merchants and commodities. If on any one who discovered a new source of gain, without detriment to the commonwealth, a mark of honour should be conferred, public spirit would never be extinguished. In short, were every one convinced, that rewards would accompany whatever was done to promote the public good, this would be a great impulse to discover something valuable. But the more men have at heart the general welfare, the more will be

---

* No prince this game invented, that will I dare to say,
Too plainly, his own image before him, it doth lay,
For idly while he sitteth, the monarch little knows,
The peasant, whom he vexeth, defendeth his repose.
The sovereign is the queen, to raise and to depress,
And the inglorious king, to all men valueless,
To the high place, he dozing fills, doth owe
The crown, that decks in state his empty brow.

Regnier lends the last touch to this picture, in his fourteenth satire.

" Les fous sont aux échecs les plus proches des Rois."

† I appeal merely to that great monument, that has been raised by two philosophers in France to the glory of their native land. One cannot refuse admiration to the Encyclopædia, to which I here refer, on the score of the mechanic arts. This gigantic work, which appears to need a Briareus (I know not whether my memory furnishes me with the right name of the heaven-stormer with the hundred hands), could fall to no more capable and enterprising undertaker, than M. Diderot. Besides his articles, which do honour to him and the work, I am delighted to refer to the essay of Boulanger on the compulsory labourers, on the dams and bridges, under the title *Corvée*. (Ponto et Chaussées.)

‡ In his Essay on the Duty of Philosophers to associate with Public Men.

---

* The Carthaginians, Cicero's second oration against Rullus.

† A contract between the King of Spain and other powers for introducing negro-slaves into the Spanish colonies.

‡ Xenophon, in the Conversation between Hiero and Simonides.

devised and undertaken for its sake." This rich passage exhausts almost all I could say, or could wish to say. My readers will therefore be content with the gleaning only of a few remarks.

Our merchants should above all be stimulated by these considerations, to make their calling, not merely a gainful trade, but a respected rank. I remember to have read, that in Guinea, the merchant is the nobleman, and that he pursues trade by virtue of his dignity, and royal privileges. On his elevation to that rank, the king forbids the waves to injure the new nobleman, or merchant. This monarch doubtless prizes his merchants highly, because from them comes his greatness, and wonders perhaps that our kings grant nobility only to soldiers and courtiers, or even drive a trade with it, and sell it for ready money.

The nobility of the merchant must not be confounded with military nobility. The prerogatives of the latter are founded on the circumstances of the times when it arose. Nations plundered one another, remained nowhere at home, lived like robbers, or had to defend themselves against robbers. Kings believed they could immortalize themselves only by conquests. These required blood and noble blood. The military order had consequently the highest rank, and whoever distinguished himself in this, was ennobled. The pretensions of these heroes were allowed to descend to their children, that, inflamed by the deeds of their ancestors, they might make it their glory, like them, to die. This was an artifice, to transmit a certain spirit to the children, and to elevate the military class, which at that time was the only privileged one. This being the origin and the purpose of their nobility, those are the genuine knights, who, born in the counting-rooms of acquisitiveness instead of the tent, are trained to be voluptuaries and cowardly prodigals. They might make use of their weapons, like the discarded patron of Venice.*

Our times are no longer warlike and the deeds of the most renowned heroes,

"From Macedonia's madman to the Swede,"

will appear to us soon like the adventures of Don Quixote. The nation, which distinguished itself by the sword to the last, has become much more honourable and mighty through the plough. Men no longer desolate other lands by conquests, but conquer their own by trade. If war is still carried on, it is as a defence against jealous rivals, or to establish the balance of power. We prepare, not now for triumphs, but to enjoy peace; and the time is perhaps near, when the peasant and citizen will ennoble their class.

The merchant has thus, as it were, taken the place of the soldier. Does not his rank, consequently, deserve to be elevated by like respect, and like means? The profession of arms has become great through the nobility. Commerce must become great through merchants, that is, such merchants, as do not think it necessary to gain honour by purchased privileges merely, but place their dignity in the prosperity of trade, and hold those gains unworthy, which would poison its sources. To devastate, to destroy, to become rich, this is the only thing, in which the military spirit of the nobility shows itself in the mercantile profession.

The rewards, marks of honour, and privileges of the merchant must give him in the eyes of his countrymen a visible distinction, that continually admonishes him to uphold the flourishing prosperity of the country, which the soldier must devastate against his own will, with the same courage, ambition, and elevation of mind.

Thanks be to the age in which we live! our merchants need as little to be cheats, as our nobility ignoramuses. If there are yet among Christians, persons, whose whole soul is made up of avarice, who aim to enrich themselves by usury and deceit, they must not be ennobled. Besides, what avail them those certificates of liberality, for which ancestors are assigned them, but to make them exhibit a ridiculous resemblance to that species of mouse whose wings render his rank among animals ambiguous?

I come to the morals of the mercantile class, on which depends the pursuit, as well as the prosperity of trade. Good faith, honesty, love of the commonwealth, must be here the moving springs, like diligence in manufactures, workshops, and agriculture;—double objects of equal elevation, which claim all the care and thought of the government, because from their union springs the good of the whole nation.

If the merchants were regarded as mediators between the different members of the State,* with how much right would their avocations become more public and solemn! The common weal, as it were, compensates them. On its preservation depend their rank and occupation. It must therefore take more interest in their condition; but on the other hand, the merchant should be more mindful of the obligations they are under to the public, and the consideration they owe it on this account.

Public credit is the soul of trade; it rests on the confidence, which individual citizens acquire through honourable dealing. This sum of the private credit of numerous citizens of the same place, taken together, is a deposit, which should be sacred to all the members of the community, because it involves in itself the immediate interest of each member, to support ac-

---

* St. Theodore, whose statue is in St. Mark's place, holding a shield in the right hand, and a lance in the left. The Venitians, instead of this martial saint, have taken St. Mark for their patron since his bones were brought to the city, by their merchants.—*Amelot de la Houssage.*

* Hume's Essays.

cording to his means, the credit of the rest, and to protect it from all adulteration and diminution. Whoever brings the public faith under suspicion, deserves severer punishment than the man who robs the public coffer entrusted to him.

Readiness to pay is a result of the moral character of the debtor, which speaks well to the creditor for his wisdom and honesty. This readiness furnishes not only the best security for the gold committed to strange hands, but serves as a pledge against possible misfortunes. The virtue of a merchant should thus bear the same relation to his good name, as the ware to the coin.

But chiefly the merchant presupposes the upright citizen, because the welfare of trade must be often in opposition to his own private advantage. To maintain the former, demands therefore sacrifices from the disinterestedness and self-denial of the latter. Mere rapacity renders the merchant sharp-sighted to the greatness of the advantage, without his picturing to himself the consequences to his fellow-citizens, and to commerce. He swallows down each bit, and considers neither the wants of the future nor the bones with which he will be choked. The present and the certain prevent his discerning a greater good, which might compel an expenditure of time, or which he must share with others. Thus he disregards for the sake of his own advantage, not only the public revenue, but even the interests of his own posterity. The stream may fail, the harbour be destroyed—nothing but his own loss is of importance in his eyes, and the profits of a year will be preferred, without a scruple of conscience, to the gain of a century.

Plato* describes both the riches and the poverty of the artisan as the ruin of his profession. " Is he rich," says he, " think you he will be anxious about his work? No, he and his art will be ruined by indolence and neglect. Is he needy, how can he procure suitable implements? He is clumsy, and leaves behind him, in his children and apprentices only bunglers." Let us be assured, that the merchant's love of gain is far more detrimental to the improvement of trade. And does not experience teach us that the very vices, whereby property has been or can be acquired, at the same time destroy its value? The counting-room is a school of deceit and avarice; what wonder? when the household is a temple of disorder and waste! The exchange is ashamed of these freebooters, and the city of their memory. Trade execrates their oppressions, and the public their profession.

The merchant, on the other hand, who loves his country, its present and future welfare, plants trees that may give shade to his posterity. He abhors as a theft all gain which is contrary to the general good of commerce. He seeks by wise undertakings, to attract to the country new branches of trade. He supports and upholds the old, which, if they do not immediately bring him fruit a hundred fold, yet employ the hands of his fellow-citizens, and with the ruin of which, numerous other lateral branches would be destroyed. This merchant is no phantom. I myself know merchants who have greatness of soul enough to make the expansion of trade, and not private gain, their ultimate object, who think not only of its arithmetic, but also of its morals and its utility. Holland should bore through her dams, if she had not merchants, who out of love to her soil, can employ their millions in a trade which now yields little, or is indeed the occasion of loss, like the whalefishery. The merchant is therefore capable of great sentiments. To encourage them is worth the pains.

The green cap, the broken bench formerly terrified the cheat. Wherein does he now find his security, but in the defence, which he durst not stoop to himself, but which is offered him, and in the ruin of better citizens. Hope and compassion, which are left him, inspire boldness, while the final disgrace renders fear and repentance inactive.

An ancient nation is spoken of,* where the taste for beauty cost lovers dear. From their contributions a bridal treasure was collected for those daughters of the land whom nature had refused to furnish with recommendations. How near does not this come to the use, made at present, of the virtue of an honourable man?

If a city contains not more than one upright citizen, it is on his account the laws were made, and on his account the magistracy instituted. Not to accommodate those offenders, who are studious only to infringe and corrupt justice, are the laws entrusted to you, fathers of the city! but to support this honest man, that he may not be wearied out, terrified, or impeded, that unhindered, he may do all the good his patriotic soul devises and his magnanimous heart suggests for the benefit of the commonwealth. Then will his zeal, in gratitude for your support, find fresh nutriment, and his example become the pattern and inheritance of his house.

Let us argue from single individuals to whole families. They are the elements of civil society; consequently, their social influence is indisputably greater than men seem to recognise. The welfare of the community is bound up with the virtues and vices, the flourishing and decay of certain families. A single family has often been sufficient to corrupt the morals of a whole State, to impress its own form on the mass, or to fix it there; to bring certain principles and customs, on which business depends, into favour or contempt. Mahomet was first the prophet of his own family, and afterwards of a great people. Ought not the cares of the magistracy to extend to the fostering of some families, and the depression of others?

If it is justifiable policy, in opening the view of a building, that adorns a certain part of the

---

* Republic. B. IV.   * Herodotus, I. 96.

city, to remove a few miserable hovels, if it is a duty to transfer to the mouth of the stream such trades as taint the purity of its waters, and to remove them from the place where it enters their walls, there is a far more urgent call on the magistracy, to protect families whose integrity is exposed to the vexations of envy, and the rage of wickedness, to uphold them as the keystone of the laws, and on the other hand, to watch those whose views spread secret poison among their fellow-citizens.

The family mania, whose mere name excites suspicions of an infectious disease, is in our days greater than ever. The selfishness, which unites whole families in extorting from the community the same assistance that relations are obliged to lend each other, has extended a detrimental indulgence to the children of great families, to whom men, in spite of stupidity and worthlessness, hardly venture to refuse preferences and offices any longer, and who, through the baseness of their intercessors and patrons, are sometimes placed in a position to justify themselves again, by the choice of others. Hence those conspiracies to put down merit, the rewards of which they seek to marry with their like, in case of need to disarm the laws, or give their expounders cunning. Hence those nurseries of old customs, to whose service certain houses are more devoted, than the corporations at Ephesus to their Diana. To this prevailing evil there could not be a more forcible check, than through the family spirit itself, whose application as much to the public good generally, as to commerce in particular, I would here recommend.

The family spirit, of which I speak, deserves at least more attention, than the author of the Fable of the Bees claims for a certain portion of ignorance, which he holds must be maintained, in every well-constituted community. This spirit consists in a remarkable strength of certain natural gifts or propensities, which through the impression of domestic example, and the consequent training, becomes hereditary and is transmitted. I premise here particularly a certain amount of social tendencies, and the seeds of citizen-like virtues, (for why should not these be capable of imitation and degeneracy, like other tendencies and dispositions?) an amount which would enable us to forget our private good in the public approbation and welfare, to prefer the honour of the order, to which we devote ourselves, and its social advantages, above self-preservation and individual advantage.

It is this family spirit which has built cities, and through which they subsist. It was doubtless most active when their foundations were laid and the walks first marked out. None of those small communities thought of anything else but the city; even when his own house began to occupy him, the thoughts of the individual were far from being directed from the public works to his own building, but this latter was always subordinate to the former. The city was completed, yet was still a subject of discourse; each was still occupied in the work undertaken; one still inquired of another, what was to be supplied and added? Children and children's children carried out and improved the plan which the first founder had devised. The more distant the times, the more obscure was the tradition of the value, the nature and the circumstances of an inheritance, which had cost many generations, and for the rent of which the care and management should be undertaken by us. The peril of capital in hands, which have not earned it, is great. The zeal, the blessings, the wishes, wherewith the first founders of our dwelling-places bequeath them to their latest possessors in spite of their ingratitude, kindles yet perhaps some sparks in the souls of a few families, who make known and reveal to us the spirit of the first benefactors. It is these patriots to whose families every city should offer the right and honour of representing those by whom it was built and founded.

If there are besides, families which have inherited from their ancestors the true principles of trade, and a genuine love of it, these are the lifeguardsmen, from whose services commerce receives warmth and splendour. They are to be regarded as the dam, which gives security to its course, as the lighthouse, by which the wandering mariner directs his path, and at whose sight the stranger rejoices. Such families should not be allowed to go to decay, but rather be encouraged, distinguished, preferred, so that the spirit which animates them may be immortal; for with them trade rises and falls, and under its ruins they must be buried.

These thoughts have not entered into my mind by mere accident. They are founded in some degree on a stray paper, which I had partly in view, and of which in part this seems to be written in continuation. The author would not be injured by a publicity to which every thing that is found, is exposed. For the rest, I am as little inclined to gratify the curiosity of readers by an account of the accident, which threw this paper into my hands, as to trouble myself about their conjectures. My view in the communication of this fragment will be in part justified by its perusal.

* * * * * * *

"This family from the grandfather downward, has closely interwoven its own consequence with the good of the community. The grandfather died and left behind, by will, to his numerous heirs, some hundred thousands, which for the extension of commerce, and to draw the Polish merchandise to Miza, he had lent to the Poles, according to the wishes of their kings. The war ruined this scheme. The son received nothing but the debts of his father, and carried on likewise an extensive trade. This man did every thing, although the result was unfortunate. How much would he not have undertaken in better circumstances! In his civil offices he concerned himself, merely, for the improvement of general commerce, and his views were far from being limited to his own especial benefit. The former, and not the latter, he regarded as the inheritance of his family. Careless in his domestic economy, he was the more zealous to frame for the good of the city new plans and institutions, which are yet in existence. He always appealed to the old laws, and was urgent to be judged thereby. The word public he uttered with reverence. He loved the Pole, in spite of all his folly and levity, because he furnished commodities for trade, and hated the Englishman, so respectable as he is otherwise, because he employed his countrymen as beasts of burden, as carriers to his customers. He sighed over the existing decay; and zeal for the public good at last destroyed him. He lived like a Roman with his great deeds, eating roots, and he was proud to be a citizen. He was called obstinate, but none presumed to perpetrate any baseness before his eyes. Whoever knows men, understands their language. An obstinate man means a man, who can be brought to no conclusion without reflection, who does not lay aside and alter the plan, by which he wishes to proceed, according to the fancy of every one, but continues true to the precepts of sound reason and conscience, and is far above the judgments of complaisant, frivolous people. The children of this citizen inherited the spirit and the principles of their father, which perhaps are no longer suitable to our times. Love for the public good is their passion; it gives them penetration and courage, whereby they are an offence to those, who ride in gilt coaches, and adorn themselves with the spoils of trade. They resist the seductions of strangers, who come to us as to savages, to carry on our commerce. If this family wish to assert the principles of their father, against their competitors, they are compelled to resolve on their own ruin. Their plans were well laid, and aimed likewise at the extension of the commerce of Poland and Curland, to Holland and France, for which a good friend sacrificed himself. Nevertheless, they failed through rivals, with whom all methods are good, whereby they can cut rushes for their own roofs, through the dishonesty of agents, corrupted by the impunity, —as things go now,—of acting against the laws, and the shallow ambition of making a fortune without a good name. Men admire Marius, sitting on the ruins of Carthage, the greatest of commercial cities, and amidst its fallen heaps raising himself above the vicissitudes of his own destiny. I have not yet forgotten the words of a dying son of this house, with which he consoled his brother, by whom he was honoured as a second father. They merit to be preserved, "Who knows, my brother, whether the ruin of a house like ours may not conduce to general progress? Men will thereby come to the knowledge, how much is due to honourable citizens, and be warned, not to be so hard with others." This man felt himself stronger perhaps in cold blood, than Glover in the midst of his inspiration, when he conceived the noble sentiment, with which his hero devoted himself and his handful, exclaiming, "Freedom and my country!"

CHRISTOPH MARTIN WIELAND.

Born 1733. Died 1813.

WIELAND was a native of Suabia. His father, a Lutheran divine, who, at the birth of this son, resided in Oberholzheim, removed soon after to Biberach, where Wieland spent his childish years.

His early education was superintended by his father in person. At the age of seven he read Latin. At twelve he gave indications of his poetic genius in German and Latin verse. At fourteen he was put to school at Klosterbergen, near Magdeburg, where he remained two years, and then continued his studies under private instruction at Erfurt. In 1750, he entered the University of Tübingen as a student of law, but devoted himself chiefly to literary pursuits. Thence he sent the first cantos of an epic poem to Bodmer at Zurich, who was so much struck with this juvenile performance, that he invited the young poet to reside with him. He remained in Switzerland eight years, writing and publishing several minor works. At the end of this period he returned to Biberach, where he was made a member of the Council, and appointed Director of Chancery, and where he married, in 1765. In 1769, he was elected Professor of Philosophy at Erfurt, an office which he retained but three years, and then accepted an invitation from the Duchess Amalia, of Weimar, to superintend the education of her sons. Wieland had already become distinguished as an author. His *Agathon*, his *Musarion*, his *Don Silvio de Rosalva*, had placed him at the head of the national literature of that day. His translation of Shakspeare, the first in the German language, had also been published some time before. With the leisure of his new office and the security of a pension for life, he now devoted himself with increased zeal to literary pursuits. Amidst his numerous engagements and a constant series of publications, original and translated, prose and verse, he undertook the German Mercury, a monthly periodical, which he edited during the rest of his life. In 1798, he purchased with the proceeds of his literary labors an estate at Osmansstädt, near Weimar, where he intended to pass the remainder of his days; but, after the death of his wife, at the solicitation of the Duchess, he returned to Weimar, and there resided until his death, which occurred January 20th, 1813.

In Wieland we notice first his singular fertility. The industry of the man is amazing, and enlarges our idea of the capabilities of a human life. His translations from Shakspeare, Horace, Lucian, Cicero, would alone be sufficient to establish his reputation for literary diligence. When we add to these some fifty volumes of original productions, and consider, moreover, how much of his time was spent in editorial labors and official duties, we have an example of productiveness which has few parallels in the history of letters, and which places Wieland on a level, in this particular, with Lope de Vega, Voltaire, and Sir Walter Scott.

As to quality, it must be confessed that Wieland's excellence lies rather in the manner than in the matter. He is more graceful than energetic, more agreeable than impressive, more sportive than profound. 'Words that burn' are not found on his page, nor thoughts that make one close the book and ponder, and rise up intellectually new-born from the reading. But then he has charms of manner that lure the reader on and hold him fast. And when we speak of him as not profound, we speak in relation to German standards. Unlike the generality of his countrymen, he occupied himself with the show of things rather than their substance; with phenomena rather than laws. He loved to discourse pleasantly, rather than to investigate conscientiously, or to settle accurately. What Goethe says of him is very characteristic; that "in all he did he cared less for a firm footing than for a clever debate."

As a poet, he has been accused of licentiousness. Voluptuousness would be a more proper designation. His poetry is certainly liable to objection on that score. At the same time, it is free from coarseness and from all that — in his own phrase — 'offends against the Graces.' It should be observed too, that Wieland's life was pure and exemplary in all respects. Whether prose or poetry, his writings are distinguished by elegance of style and perfect finish. He elaborated all that he wrote with great care, and declared that he spent one-sixth part of his time in copying.

His intellectual life is divided into two periods distinctly marked in his works. He began his literary career a zealous enthusiast. His first productions are strongly tinctured with religion, and treat, in part, of religious subjects. He afterward became an Epicurean (theoretically) in morals; a materialist, or common-sense man, in philosophy; placed experience above faith; believed in no ideas but those which are derived through the senses; and good-humoredly satirized all lofty aspiration, and everything which leaned, as he thought, to spiritual excess. It would be difficult to find another author whose earlier and later productions exhibit such a contrast as those of Wieland.

Bouterwek, in his "History of German Poetry and Eloquence," thus characterizes him: "The names of Klopstock and Wieland denote opposite extremes. While Klopstock carried the poetry of the supersensual, in its most solemn earnestness, to excess, Wieland laughingly turned his back on supersensual things, and declared war against all extravagance. His poetry was not meant to be trifling, any more than his character was trifling; but he would have it subordinate to a philosophy which he had learned, in the French school, to regard as the only sound one. In this way, Wieland became a philosophical poet of sensualism, such as Germany had never seen before. But far from advocating a sensualism which degrades man to a beast, he wished to establish that form of virtue which, according to the doctrine of Shaftesbury, he held to be of the same origin with the love of the beautiful, as the only true one, in opposition to all which seemed to him extravagant and fantastic. Conscious of the strictest purity in his own morals, he never doubted that a poet, especially in the capacity of satirist, might, without scruple, paint the most voluptuous charms of sense as seductively as was consistent with the laws of beauty. Only what offended the Graces — according to his principles — was to be strictly excluded from the domain of poetry. This æsthetic morality which Wieland introduced into German literature, operated beneficially as a counterpoise to the false rigorism by which criticism in Germany was oppressed." "Satire has never contended with such polished weapons, as in Wieland's writings, against that enthusiasm to which no modern nation is so much inclined as the German." "With all his faults and defects, and whatever a one-sided criticism may bring forward to his disparagement, he is still one of the great poets who are the pride of German literature." "He had imbibed so much of the taste of the French, along with their philosophy, that he bore the name of the '*German Voltaire*' in Germany and out of Germany. But in all that Voltaire has written there is not a trace to be found of Wieland's ideal of moral loveliness. Among Italian poets, Ariosto is the one whose humor agrees best with Wieland's manner." "His Muse rather smiled than laughed." "This inextinguishable cheerfulness, united with such knowledge of mankind, such refinement of wit and taste, such fulness of imagination, with so soft, so luxurious, so apparently careless, and yet so cultivated a style, is found in no other poet."

The following extract from Goethe's Eulogy of Wieland is taken from Mrs. Austin's "Characteristics of Goethe."

"The effect of Wieland's writings on the public was uninterrupted and lasting. He educated his age, and gave a decided impulse to the taste and to the judgment of his contemporaries. And whence proceeded this great influence which he exercised over the Germans? It was the consequence of the vigor and frankness of his character. Man and author were, in him, completely blended; his poetry was life, his life poetry. Whether in verse or in prose, he never concealed what was his predominant feeling at the moment, nor what was his general frame of mind. From the fertility of his mind flowed the fertility of his pen. I use the word *pen* not as a rhetorical phrase; it has here a peculiar appropriateness; and if pious reverence ever hallowed the quill with which an author wrote his works, assuredly that which Wieland used was worthy of this distinction. He wrote everything with his own hand, and very beautifully; at once freely and carefully. He kept what he had written ever before his eyes, examined, altered, improved it; unweariedly cast and recast; nay, had the patience, repeatedly, to transcribe whole works of considerable extent. And this gave his productions the delicacy, the elegance, clearness, the natural grace which cannot be attained by mere drudgery, but by cheerful, genial attention to a work already completed.

"Our friend was capable of the highest enthusiasm, and, in youth, gave himself completely up to it. Those glad bright regions of the golden time, that paradise of innocence, he dwelt in longer than others. His natal roof, hallowed by the presence of his father, a learned pastor; the ancient cloister of Bergen beneath its shade of antique times on the shores of the Elbe, where his pious teacher lived in patriarchal simplicity; the still monastic Tübingen; the simple dwellings of Switzerland, surrounded by gushing brooks, washed by clear lakes hemmed in by rocks; in all he found his Delphi; in all, the groves and thickets in which, even when arrived at manhood, he still revelled. Amid such scenes he felt the mighty attraction of the movements which the manly innocence of the Greeks has bequeathed to us. He lived in the lofty presence of Cyrus, Araspes and Panthea. He felt the Platonic spirit move within him. * * * * * But precisely because he had the good fortune to linger so long in these higher regions, because he was permitted so long to regard all that he thought, felt, imagined and dreamed, as the most absolute reality, was the fruit, which he was at last compelled to pluck from the tree of knowledge, the more bitter to him. Who may escape the conflict with the outer world? Our friend, like the rest, was drawn into the strife; reluctantly he submitted to be contradicted by life and experience. And as, after long struggling, he could not succeed in combining these noble images with the ordinary world, these high intents with the necessities of the day, he determined to accept the actual, as necessary; and declared what had hitherto appeared to him truth, to be fantastic visions. * * * *
He declared war on all that cannot be shown to exist in reality; first on Platonic love; then on all dogmatizing philosophy, especially the two extremes—the Stoic and the Pythagorean. * * * * * *

"It has been acutely remarked by some foreigners that German authors take less heed of the public than those of other nations; and that, therefore, it is easy to discern, in their writings, the man educating himself, the man who wants to owe something to himself; and consequently, to read his character. This was peculiarly true of Wieland, and it would be the more interesting to follow his writings and his life with this view, since suspicions have been cast upon his character, drawn from these very writings. Many men still misunderstand him, because they imagine the many-sided must be indifferent, the mobile must be infirm and inconsistent. They do not reflect that character regards the practical alone. Only in what a man does, in what he continues to do and persists in doing, can he show character; and in this sense, there never was a firmer, more consistent man than Wieland. When he gave himself up to the variety of his sensations, to the mobility of his thoughts, and permitted no single impression to obtain dominion over him, he showed, by that very process, the firmness and certainty of his mind. He loved to play with his conceptions, but never—I take all his contemporaries to witness—never with his opinions. And thus he won and retained numerous friends."

PHILOSOPHY CONSIDERED AS THE ART OF LIFE AND HEALING ART OF THE SOUL.

MEN had lived, and perhaps lived many thousand years, before one of them hit upon the thought that life could be an *art;* and, in all probability, every other art, from the arts of Tubalcain to the art of catching flies,—which *Shah Baham*, a *peritus in arte*, assures us, is not so easy a matter as some people imagine,—had long been invented, when, at last, the sagacious Greeks, along with other fine arts and sciences, invented also this famous *art of life*, called *Philosophy:* or, if they did not altogether invent it, first reduced it to the form of art, and carried it to a high degree of refinement.

By far the greater part of the children of men never dreamed that there was such an art. People lived without knowing how they did it, very much as Mons. Jourdain in Moliere's "Citizen Gentleman," had talked prose all his life, or as we all draw breath, digest, perform various motions, grow and thrive, without one in a thousand knowing or desiring to know by what mechanical laws or by what combination of causes all these things are done. And in this thick fog of ignorance innumerable nations in Asia, Africa, America, and the Islands of the South Sea, white and olive, yellow-black and pitch-black, bearded and unbearded, circumcised and uncircumcised, tattooed and untattooed, with and without rings through the nose, from the giants in Patagonia to the dwarfs on Hudson's Bay, &c. &c., live to this hour. And not only so, but even of the greatest portion of the inhabitants of our enlightened Europe, it may be maintained with truth, that they know as little about said art of life and that they care as little about it as the careless people of Otaheite or the half-frozen inhabitants of *Terra del Fuego*, who are scarcely more than sea-calves.

The strangest part of this business is, that all these people, who, according to a very moderate calculation, constitute nearly the whole human race,—like their ancestors as far back as Adam and Eve, who also knew nothing of the aforesaid fine art,—notwithstanding their ignorance, live away as courageously as if they were finished masters of it. Nay more, the greater part of these bunglers get on so well, as it respects all the most essential and important functions of human life, that scarcely one of the hired masters and professors of the art can hold a candle to them.

Cicero says somewhere, "Nature is the best guide of life," which probably means, that Nature shows us best how we may help ourselves through this earthly state. Further, he says, "No one can fail who suffers himself to be guided by her." On this guidance, therefore, it would seem that men must always have relied. This same Nature, they thought, which teaches us to breathe, eat, drink, to move hands and feet, &c., teaches us also how to use our senses, our memory, our understanding, and all our other powers; teaches us what is fitting and what is not fitting. It requires only so much attention as every object enforces of itself, to see and feel whether it is friendly or hostile. Our nose and our tongue teach us, without any other instruction, what fruits, herbs and roots, &c., are good to eat. At a pinch, hunger teaches the same, without much circumstance. Nature has provided for all pressing necessities. Either the thing which we require exists already;—and then we have whatever is needed to seize and enjoy it;—or, at least, the materials of it exist; and then we have just so much understanding, power, and natural dexterity in our members, as is necessary to form those materials to our use and purpose. What does not succeed the first time, will succeed the tenth or the twentieth. If two arms are not sufficient, four, six, eight will accomplish it. Every new trial adds something to our knowledge of the thing, and to our faculty. We learn by errors and failures, and become masters by practice, without perceiving how it has come about. And this same Nature which carries us so far, always conceals from us what lies too far to be reached from the place assigned us; makes us happy by ignorance, and has given us this beneficent sluggishness, of which the world-reformers make so much complaint, for no other purpose but that the everlasting desire to improve our condition may not cause us to fall from the frying-pan into the fire, and that we may not fare like that man who, in order to feel better, physicked himself to death, and had for his epitaph: *Per star meglio sto qui.*

So Nature teaches all men how to live, who have not run away from the instruction and discipline of the good Mother. And, in all this, as you perceive, there is no art. It is Nature herself, bodily. The celebrated *Quam multis non ego!* of the ancient philosopher is the native philosophy of all Samoyedes, Laplanders, Esquimaux, &c.—a philosophy in which the New Hollanders or the New Walesmen, as the honest people must suffer themselves to be called, according to the arbitrary pleasure of the gentlemen with the firelocks, who have the command, appear to have made the greatest progress. Let no man come and say that such a life is an oyster-life. Call it, if you please, a continual childhood; but honour Nature who conducts these her children, by the shortest route, to the *beate vivere* at which we enlightened people seldom or never arrive, merely on account of the great multitude of roads which lead to it.

The wise Theophrastus (not Paracelsus, but the scholar and successor of the divine Aristotle) lived ninety years, and when he came to die, he complained against Nature because "she has given man so little time to live, and because an honest fellow must die at the very moment when he has begun to comprehend a little the art of life." When did ever a New Hollander make so unreasonable a complaint? When *he* has come to be an hundred years old (which is nothing rare with them), he has lived just one hundred years, and rises satisfied from the banquet of Nature;—and truly, a banquet that, in which Nature furnishes such poor entertainment, that the strictest candidate for canonization need not scruple to share it.

But—let me remark in passing—I am very far from believing that Theophrastus made the foolish speech which is imputed to him. The people around his bed did not exactly understand what he said, and then some schoolmaster came along, a good while after, and tried to make sense of it, and made nonsense. I would bet that Theophrastus meant neither more nor less than this; that he regretted he had not been wise enough, sixty or seventy years before, to see that he might have saved himself the trouble of studying, as art and science, what Nature would have taught him far better and more surely, without study, if he had had the simplicity of mind to heed her instruction. It was not innocent Nature but his own folly that he blamed, as most men are wont to do in his case; although they might as well let it alone; for what is the use of repentance when one has no time left for amendment?

Notwithstanding all that has been said, it is by no means my intention to dispute the value, whatever it may be, of the above-mentioned art of life.

It has somewhere been said, that art is, at bottom, nothing else than Nature herself, who, by means of man, as her most perfect instrument, unfolds and brings to perfection under a different name, what before she had merely sketched, as it were, or hastily begun. If art is that, and so far as it is that, it is worthy of all honour.

Yes, even then, when it merely comes in aid of enfeebled or corrupted Nature, it is, like the art of medicine, sometimes beneficial, although often just as uncertain and just as ineffectual as that. When Nature no longer suffices for the support of life, then, to be sure, art must patch and prop, and plaster and doctor as well as it can. Or, to speak more correctly, even in this case, the good, universal Mother has provided for her darling child. She has remedies in her store-chamber for every wound or disease of the outward or the inward man, so that art has nothing to do but to observe and to exhibit. The simpler then the remedies are, the less they have been tampered with, the better for the sufferer. And still, the successful issue must be expected from Nature alone. If she has strength enough left to raise herself up by the hand of art, well and good; — if not, then, for art too, nothing remains, but to let the sick man die and to embalm the dead. Art cannot supply the power of life where it is wanting.

It was long ago that philosophy, on account of this resemblance to the healing art, received the name of "medicine for the soul." And truly, this qualification seems better adapted to secure its acceptance, than when it claims to teach us to live according to the rules of art. For who that has the free use of his natural powers does not feel that he can live without it? On the other hand, when it presents itself only as physician, then the well know that they have nothing to do with it.

The Indians in the islands of the South sea, it seems, are unacquainted with medicines. With them slight wounds or illnesses heal themselves; and of great ones they die — as we do. And as they are so fortunate as to have no idea of a soul in and of itself, as a man in their apprehension is always a man, made out of one piece, so they know nothing of particular diseases of the soul; or if ever they experience an attack of this kind, the hunger-cure, for which they have but too frequent opportunity, is generally the most effectual remedy.

On the other hand, when the progress of refinement in a nation has gone so far, that body and soul, instead of being as they should be one person, are treated as two powers with different interests, each having its separate establishment, like naughty husbands and wives; what is more natural than, that bad consequences should result from such an ill-starred union? Man is then no longer that noble being in whom all is sense and power and soul, in whom, so to speak, everything corporeal is spiritual, and everything spiritual, corporeal. He is an unnatural, Centaur-like compound of animal and spirit, in which the one lives at the other's expense, in which the animal creates for itself necessities, the spirit passions, projects and aims of which the natural man knows nothing. Each oppresses, drags, worries and exhausts the other as much as it can, and a vast number of bodily and mental diseases are the ultimate fruit of this putting asunder what God had joined together. In such cases, when the evil has reached its height, that "medical art for the soul" may offer its aid with some degree of success; and either relieve the patient by purging, bleeding and clysters; or, at least, by means of agreeable opiates, procure for him a delusive rest.

But this art has never yet been found able to effect a radical cure; and we may boldly maintain, that when a nation has once fallen into the hands of the two Goddesses of Healing, it is irrecoverably lost; not because one must needs burst with their medicines, but because whenever they are resorted to, the evil has already proceeded too far to admit of entire restoration.

I said Philosophy might the rather maintain its place, as healing art for the soul, because then, the well would know that they had nothing to do with it. But as all arts love to make themselves more important than they are, so this art too has found means to impose itself upon all the world as indispensable. Like its sister art, which ministers to the body, it will not allow any one to be entirely well. According to its doctrine and its ideal of health, the whole earth is one great lazar-house of bodily and mental diseases, and there is no man well enough to dispense with its prescriptions. Happily, this assumption is not conceded to either of these arts. Nature knows nothing of ideals. As long as a man feels himself sound, he has a right to think himself sound; and, without troubling himself whether others object to that view or not, he lives straight forward as a healthy man; and (like Voltaire's Zadig) reads not a letter of all the learned dissertations, in which gentlemen undertake to prove it impossible that he should be well. There are cases, it is true, in which a sick man is only the more dangerously sick, because unconscious of his malady. But these cases are rare, and cannot deprive the great mass of those who feel well, of their traditional right to that feeling.

LETTER TO A YOUNG POET.

WELL then, my young friend! No man can escape his destiny; and if you too are destined to the laurel-wreath and the dark cell of the divine Tasso, or to the spital and the postumous fame of the Portuguese Camoens, can I, weak mortal, prevent it?

I have heard your confession and have pondered well the whole case. Your inward vocation seems indeed to admit of no doubt.

Such tension of the inner and the outer senses! All so sharply tuned that the softest breath of Nature causes the entire organ of the soul to vibrate harmoniously like an Æolian harp; and every sensation gives back, with heightened beauty and the purest accord, like a perfect echo, the melody of the object, and grows ever sweeter as it gradually dies away.

A memory in which nothing is lost, but everything imperceptibly coalesces into that fine, plastic, half spiritual substance from which Fancy breathes forth its own new and magical creations.

An imagination which, by an involuntary, inward impulse, idealizes each individual object, clothes everything abstract in determinate forms, to the simple sign supplies imperceptibly ever the thing itself or an image resembling it, in short, which embodies all that is spiritual and purifies and ennobles into spirituality all that is material.

A warm and tender soul which kindles with every breath, all nerve, sensation and sympathy; which can imagine nothing dead, nothing unfeeling in Nature, but is ever ready to impart its own excess of life, feeling, passion to all things about it, ever with the greatest ease and rapidity to metamorphose others into itself and itself into others.

A passionate love for the wonderful, the beautiful and the sublime in the material and the moral world, a love avowed from earliest youth and never false to itself.

A heart which beats high at every noble deed and revolts with horror from every bad, cowardly and unfeeling one.

Add to all this, together with the most cheerful temperament and quick circulation, an inborn propensity to reflect, to search within, to pursue your own thoughts, to rove in a world of ideas, and, together with the most social disposition and the most delicate vivacity of sympathetic inclinations, an ever predominant love for solitude, for the silence of the forest, for all that promotes the quiet of the senses, all that disengages the soul from the burdens by which it is hampered in its free and peculiar flight, or that rescues it from the distractions which interrupt its inward occupations.

To be sure, if all this does not constitute native endowment for a poet to be, if it is not sufficient to assure a youth that—to speak with the philosopher among the poets—it is the Muses themselves that have sent him this beautiful phrenzy, which he can no more shake off than Virgil's Cumæan Sibyl can shake off the prophetic god—*

Be easy, my friend! I recognise and reverence the indelible character by which Nature has consecrated you to the priesthood of the Muses, and since, according to the divine Plato, it is only necessary that the Muses' fury, in order to produce the finest effects, should seize a tender and uncoloured soul, I must be greatly deceived or you will do honour to the theory of our philosopher.

I do not consider it exactly an infallible diagnostic of a genuine inward vocation,—nevertheless it is generally at least the case,—that an almost irresistible impulse to the art in which they are destined to excel manifests itself in future *virtuosi*, in poets, painters, &c., from their earliest youth. And this sign of election, my young friend, is also found in you.

You say, "As far as I can look back into the first years of my life, I cannot remember the time when I did not make verses. The inborn sensibility of my ear to the music of fine verse, the rapture which dissolved me, when, even in my boyhood, I declaimed certain passages in which the versification was particularly good from ancient or modern poets, especially from the Æneid and Horace's Odes, the often repetition and dwelling on those lines, on which, even when I read them to myself, I know not what internal, spiritual ear feasted, as on the dying echo of the song of the Muses, —all this, with me, preceded instruction. And so it came to pass, that I made all kinds of verses and observed a number of rules before I had the least idea — in the way of learned knowledge — of prosody, rhythm, poetic numbers, imitative harmony, and the like. Nothing could equal my love for the poets, except the ease with which I understood them, the interest they inspired in me, and the almost ecstatic rapture in which I continued for hours in the enjoyment of some particularly beautiful passage, and the visions which it conjured up in my soul. With Virgil, Haller, Milton, and the five first cantos of Klopstock, I forgot eating and drinking, play, sleep, myself and the world. I experienced, indeed, from my early youth, the same opposition from those who had charge of my education,—whether as a natural or a hired duty,—which Ovid, Ariosto, Tasso, and so many other celebrated poets had to contend with. But strong nature prevailed, and the Genius, or the evil Spirit, as you would rather call it, that possessed me, was not to be expelled, neither by fair means nor foul. Even when I made no verses, my guardians, the enemies of the Muse, gained nothing. All the ideas and knowledges with which they endeavoured to stuff my mind, either fell through or were transmuted into poetic matter. Whatever I studied, physics, metaphysics, ethics, history, politics,—everything, with me, was converted into epopee and drama. And while the teacher, with the air of a mystagogue, was explaining the monadology of Leibnitz, my imagination was developing the plan of a poem on the origin of Venus from the foam of

---

* Wieland, of all writers, indulges most frequently in that very convenient figure called *aposiopesis* by the rhetoricians, of which the above is a specimen. Tr.

the sea; or I was making the statue of Pygmalion start into life before my eyes, or I was explaining to myself how the great principle of the Orphic cosmogony, Love, like the lyre of Amphion, could unite the elements into a world by its attractive energy."

What can I answer, my dear friend, to facts of such potency? I seem to hear my own history. All this, word by word, was my own case, five and thirty years ago: and if, notwithstanding these plain indications of Nature, I would still keep you on this side of the dangerous Rubicon, I have at least quite other reasons for so doing than distrust of your talent and ability.

The very first flowers of the fertile soil which has fallen to your lot, notwithstanding you think so modestly of them yourself, would be sufficient to inspire me with the fairest hopes respecting you, and the rather, precisely because, with so decided a natural vocation and so much preparatory discipline and years of study, you are still so little satisfied with your own productions, and are almost as much offended by praise which you cannot persuade yourself that you have merited, as others would be by the most merited censure. I know no more decided criterion of true talent, than this difficulty of satisfying one's self, this unwearied striving after something higher, this unaffected contempt of present attainments, compared with what one trusts hereafter to be, and this delicate feeling of the beauties in the works of other men, and of the deficiencies in one's own; qualities which I have so often had occasion to notice in you, and which are so seldom found in poets, young or old.

Wonder at me as much as you please, my dear friend! But it is precisely my well-grounded conviction that Mother Nature really designed to make a poet of you, and that, if you should give yourself up to your inclination, you would become wholly a poet and therefore lost for all other modes of life,—it is even this that makes me tremble for you. Unhappily, the good mother has thought of everything else except the one important point, that she ought to have brought over Plutus to her plan. How could she forget that poets, no more than birds of Paradise, can live on flower-odours; and that the very man who has all the elementary Spirits at his command, and whom it costs but a stroke of the pen to summon the most splendid magic banquet-table out of the ground, is, of all men in the world, the nearest to starvation, unless by chance some compassionate Genius (who, however, is not to be counted on) has provided better for him than Nature, the Muses, or he himself.

It would be a very different affair, indeed, if you intended to follow the wise counsel which *Herr Klinggut* gives his friend, to pursue poetry, which he deems to be in every point of view a very uncertain business, only as a collateral employment by the side of some lucrative office or other honest subsistence in the learned or civil line.   *   *

  *   *   *   *   *

But the verses, which in that case, are sent "to Dessau to the press," are of a quality conforming; and it must be confessed that the poets of narrower income, have, generally, very different views in regard to this matter. He who makes verses only then when he knows of nothing else in God's world to do, will be just such a kind of poet as one, who attends to painting only in lost hours, will be a Raffael.

What I now say is between ourselves. The Graces forbid that I should deprive the gentlemen, who know how to spend their waste hours to so good advantage, of their pastime! Suffice it that you, my young friend, happily or unhappily for yourself, are not of this category. Your love for the Muse is a serious passion which must decide the fate of your life.

You will be everywhere—in all the events, relations, employments, business, sorrows and joys of your earthly pilgrimage—a poet. You will always think, feel, speak, act as only a poet thinks, feels, speaks, acts; and though, for ten years in succession, you should not have made a single verse, yet all that you had seen, heard, tried, done, and suffered in those ten years, would either have been poetry or have been turned to poetry; and at the end of this— to the Muses, apparently, lost—period of your life, there would lie more germs and embryos of poems of all kinds in your soul, than you would have time to unfold, though you should reach the age of Bodmer or of Nestor.

But alas! this is not all. You will also commit follies which only a poet can be guilty of. With the most fortunate head and the best of hearts, you will stand, every moment, in a false light before the world; you will always hear complaints and reproaches, and still you will always injure only yourself; and whatever pains you may take to persuade men that you are a harmless, innocent, well-meaning being, men will stare at you as a strange animal, will not know what to make of your way of thinking and being, and will entertain, every minute, serious doubts of your understanding and your heart.

All this, my beloved, diffuses very unpleasant consequences over the life of the individual who is endowed with this admired and despised, envied and hated, flattered and almost always badly rewarded talent, which gives him such singular advantages over ordinary men,— so much power over *their* imagination, and such inexhaustible means of helping himself,—in his *own.*

The golden λαϑε βιωσας, the unnoticed, narrow path through life—the eternal wish of all souls which are made for the quiet enjoyment of Nature and for living with their own ideas—will become for you a tree of Tantalus. A hateful celebrity, which you will find it impossible to escape, will poison your rest and inundate you with an inexhaustible flood of thousand-fold, worthless, but all the more troublesome, petty annoyances, which will not even leave you the poor illusion of being at least rewarded with love for the pleasure you have conferred upon the world.

A love for the Muses, like yours, generally terminates like the passion of an inexperienced pair of turtle-dove souls, who, in the place of all other dower, bring to each other an unbounded treasure of fondness, and have forgotten all provision for the necessities of life in the sweet delusion that love will always be meat and drink to them. The enchanted lover by the side of his beloved, is perfectly assured that a straw-built shed, is a fairy palace; that, with her beaming eyes, he needs no light; in her warm bosom, no firing; in short, that, in the ocean of bliss in which his intoxicated soul is rioting, like the gods in heaven, he needs nothing except—that the sweet illusion should last forever. But this is the very point in which he has reckoned without his host.

It has not been considered that hours, days, months, perhaps whole years will come, in which fancy, deprived of its magic power, will deliver us up to the disagreeable feeling of the present; and that, with its deceitful nature, it magnifies the evils which oppress us as much, as, in happy hours, it enhances what is pleasant in our condition. It has not been taken into the account, that even if it were according to nature, never to wake of ourselves from the beautiful Endymion-dream in which we have been lapped, yet the sober people about us would certainly not fail, either from good will or ill will to shake and shove us until they had played us the evil trick which the Corinthian experienced at the hands of his relatives, who drugged him with hellebore until all the splendid tragedies disappeared, which he thought he saw on the empty boards.

This circumstance alone would be sufficient to justify all my solicitude regarding the way of life on which you are about to enter. The true poet, however rare—according to the aforesaid Herr Klinggut—the louis d'or and the sugarplums may be with him, yet finds himself in about the same situation in which a possessor of the philosopher's stone might be. Both perhaps—the one with his talisman in his head and heart, the other with his powder in his pocket—might be happy, if it were only possible to conceal their secret from all the world. But since this is out of the question, they may both be sure that means enow will be found to make them pay dearly for the advantage which they possess over other honest people.

When, my friend, I indulge these fears for your future happiness, the louis d'or and the sugarplums are the least that I am thinking of. The latter, with all things thereto pertaining, confectionary and wines,—all, except the order-insignia, you will come to taste, it may be, but too often; and so much money as a poet needs who lays no claims to a villa like Boileau's and Pope's, or even to a Ferney, may also be found. Horace dined as often as he pleased, at the tables of the great at Rome, resided as often and as long as he pleased, in the splendid house of Mæcenas or in his elegant villa at Tibur, had his own little Sabinum,—knew scarcely any other plague than those which he had to endure from authors, from the Public, from his own celebrity, through the misfortune of being the first lyric poet of Rome; and yet he was often so hard pressed with all this, that, notwithstanding his love for the Muses, he swore he would be hanged if he had not rather sleep away his time than to make verses.

Read what this amiable poet—a refined man of the world, as well as a man of genius and distinguished acquirements—says in many parts of his letters, especially in the nineteenth, to Mæcenas, and in the second of the second book, to Julius Florus, of the discomforts and plagues of the poet's calling. And read also, if you please, the notes of his newest commentator,* who appears to have understood the author more clearly and intimately than many others, for the simple reason, that he had had very much the same experience himself. Since we must once for all fulfil our destiny, it is well at least to know what we have to expect, and how much or how little we can build on those receipts which are considered the surest.

Among all the beautiful visions which cheer and animate a young poet, when he enters on the long and painful career whose goal so few of the thousands that run in it ever reach, the most delightful perhaps is this: 'the hope that something more than applause,—the empty *digito monstrari et dicier hic est*—that the love of the nation for which he labours, will be the prize of his unwearied efforts.' Do not, my friend, flatter yourself with so vain a hope. The highest on which you can count are moments of favour, brief effervescences occasioned by the pleasure which you have conferred upon us in these moments, and for which it is thought that you are abundantly recompensed by the condescension which permits itself to be entertained by you. From the moment that we perceive or imagine that you are striving for our approbation, we look upon you with the same eyes with which we regard all other pretenders to the character of *virtuosi* in the entertaining arts, and you stand, whether you like it or not, on the same level with jugglers, rope-dancers, and histrionic performers. All your exertions to attain a high degree of perfection we regard as simply your duty, and wo unto you, if you do not always surpass yourself, or ever hold yourself at liberty to sleep upon your laurels!

You will not find this thought very encouraging; but I have not yet told you the worst.

---

* Wieland here refers to himself. Tr.

Your relation to the Public, as poet, is much less advantageous than if you had the honour to be a great *Kadenzen-macher* or the Parisian Grand-Diable. For these arts, every man possesses a standard of perfection, and can judge, with more or less correctness, how much is required to perform this or that miracle. But with the poetic art the contrary is the case. Among a thousand readers, scarcely one has a clear and definite idea of the difficulties and of the highest in art. The readers or hearers know whether the poet interests them or makes them gape. But that is all. And, since a very indifferent and a very careless work may have something interesting as well as a masterpiece, you may expect that when your work has ceased to be the curiosity of the fair,* the first novel which is new, which has a little wit, here and there an astonishment, a pathetic passage, or a slippery picture, will seize the attention of the reading world and displace your work though all the nine Muses had helped you produce it. Do not hope, by any strain of your faculties, by any ideal perfection for which you have striven with all the powers of your mind, to obtain what, according to your ideas of art, and with a full consciousness of what you have accomplished, seems to you but simple justice. That you will never obtain; not because men intend to deny you justice, but because they have no conception of all that which it is necessary to know, in order to render it.

When a poetical work, in addition to all other essential qualities of a good poem, is what Horace calls *totum teres atque rotundum*, when, together with the finest polish, it possesses the greatest ease, when the language is uniformly pure, the expression always adequate, the rhythm always music, when the rhyme always comes of itself in its proper place without being foreseen, when the whole stands forth as if cast at one casting or blown with one breath, and nowhere shows a trace of labour or effort, it may be set down as certain that such a production has cost the poet, whatever his talent, infinite pains. That lies in the nature of the case; and since perhaps there is no European language in which it is more difficult to compose beautiful verses than in ours, the labour and the effort required to arrive at any degree of perfection in such a language must be proportionally greater.

But do not fancy, if ever you should succeed in producing such a work, that the reader will give you the least credit for that which you have performed over and above what was required. He would have been quite satisfied, as daily experience shows, with less. Nay, what is worst of all, this very ease, this smoothness, this roundness which has cost you so much, and which the occasional but rare connoisseur acknowledges with becoming coolness,

---

* New publications in Germany are generally brought out at the semi-annual fair of Leipsic. Tr.

will only injure your work with the great mass. " I suppose it does not cost you the least trouble to write such verses," is the compliment which will greet you on every side. And as men are accustomed to estimate a work in proportion to the apparent difficulty of producing it, so yours will incur a kind of contempt on account of that very thing on which you have most congratulated yourself. It will be read perhaps with more pleasure than many other works of the same season. But because men think that no thing is easier than for you to manufacture such things, you will scarcely have finished one before people will expect you another like it, as if you had done nothing as yet. And if you are so disobliging or lazy or unfruitful, as not to fulfil the expectation of your patrons with all speed, some new fabrication which contains something to laugh at or to weep at, will take the attention of the leisure world and the work on which your whole soul has impressed itself, the work of your love, of your night watches, the work for which you have summoned all your powers, on which you have expended all your talent, all your knowledge of the mysteries of art, will be confounded with the mushrooms which spring up in a single night, will be thrown into a corner, and, in a short time, be as clean forgotten as if it had never been.

All this, my friend, is something so natural, such an everyday affair, it has been from the same causes so universal in all nations, at least in certain periods, that it would be ridiculous to complain of it. True, it is not very pleasant to be surprised with experiences of this kind; and, at the moment when this shall happen to you, you will be more than once tempted to envy the happiness of every honest Bœotian who, with just that portion of human sense which he brought with him, eats his bread in the sweat of his face, and, for want of the doubtful advantage of having ten thousand people whom he never saw mentioning his name and undertaking to pass judgment on him and his merits or demerits, is richly indemnified by the enjoyment of a life which glides unknown but peacefully down the stream of time.

I should never have done if I were to reckon up to you all the varieties of vexation and discomfort which await you on the other side of the *Aganippe*, which is the perilous Rubicon for you. I doubt not that, as to many of them, I should tell you nothing but what you knew before. But do not forget to take into the account the delicate sensibility and irritability of a poetic organization. A thousand things which will embitter your life are trifles in themselves considered; but for the nervous system, for the imagination, for the heart of a poet, they will be heavy sorrows. A single perverse or malicious criticism, one stupid look of a hearer at a passage which ought to have given him an electric shock, or the question: "What was your meaning in that passage?" at some delicate stroke of irony, will render you insensible to the approbation of thousands; and for the sake of one such citation as you have seen of some quite virginal stanza of a favourite poem in a book where you certainly did not expect it, a citation or rather adulteration by some harmless academic philosopher, who wished to honour the poet, you will wish that you could annihilate your best work.

I say nothing of the treatment you have to expect from others, brothers in art, connoisseurs, critics, reviewers, &c. You will, if I am not greatly deceived in you, adopt Horace's method in regard to all gentlemen of this description. Expect then also Horace's fate; that is, to be read with pleasure in secret, to be deluged with praise to your face, and publicly to be honoured on every occasion with critical shrugging of the shoulders, or at best with silence. A common soldier who by mere dint of talent and merit should rise to the office of field-marshal, would be a great rarity. But an author who, without belonging to a clique, without having made disciples, without having let his reputation to the potentates of the Republic of Letters for the time being, without having adopted young authors in clientele, and so created for himself a sturdy band of followers who shall be always ready to attack with foot and fist all who may have incurred the disfavour of their patron: an author, I say, who, without all these aids, and, what must not be forgotten, without being protected by the ægis of golden mediocrity, should arrive merely by his own merits at the quiet possession of an undisputed property in fame and authority with his contemporaries, would be a still greater rarity. Strange things sometimes happen in this world, and some one may win the golden prize; but who can calculate that he shall be that one?

On the whole, if an extended and decided fame, and the advantages connected therewith are the goal for which you run, you may prepare yourself betimes to find every conceivable hindrance in your way, and at last perhaps to see people arrive there before you, who, instead of running in the prescribed path, jump the barriers, cut across the field, and by a happy impudence appropriate the prize which they never could have won in the ordinary course. "The race is not to the swift," says Solomon, "nor the battle to the strong, but time and chance happeneth to all."

You know, my dear friend, how many reasons I have for feeling the liveliest interest in your affairs. I see you entering on a path which probably will not lead you to the temple of Fortune; and yet I have not the heart to keep you back. I myself love the art, to which you are about to devote yourself with such decided capacity, too well not to experience a kind of inward rebuke when seeking to deter you from it. And how can I help foreseeing the answer with which you will beat to the ground at once all that I can oppose to your resolution? Nor is it my design to deter you; I would only compel you, before you choose your part for ever, to consider the dangers and discomforts of the path which seems to you so charming.

In Horace's day, poetry chanced to be the way in which a kind of fortune could be made. He says it was necessity, which dares everything, that impelled him to make verses.

Ibit eo quo vis, qui zonam perdidit.

With us, I fear, it is just the reverse. The narrow path across the Helicon is generally the direct road into the arms of the beggarly goddess whom Horace wished to escape. Perhaps you may live to witness a happier day for the German Muses. Perhaps some other prince is destined to realize the glory which was despised by the great king,* who, after forty years laden with every other kind of fame, in which he had done nothing for our literature, and was entirely unacquainted with it, finally contented himself with the merit of publicly upbraiding us with its barrenness and defects. Perhaps— but no!—these hopeful perhapses are after all very uncertain, and in fact far more improbable than many now dream. Rather therefore picture to yourself the worst; and since, in any case, you have no great talent for the philosophy of Aristippus, and are not strongly disposed, whatever the advantages to be gained by it, to expend much incense on the gods of this world, or on those who dispense their favours, examine yourself carefully, whether in the lap of your beloved Muse you can be happy with a meal of potatoes and cold water?

And if then, my friend, all things considered, you are resolved to venture, promise me with hand and mouth (since I have told you beforehand the worst that can happen) never in your life, however it may fare with you, to complain of the envy of your rivals and guild-brethren, of the indifference of the great, and the ingratitude of the Public.

Nothing is at once more unjust and more foolish than to whine because things are as they have always been, and because the world, instead of revolving around our own dear little self, in its eternal on-rush takes us along with it, like imperceptible atoms, without being aware of it.

Mankind around us, from the greatest to the least, have so much to do with themselves and their own necessities, so much with their own plans, wants, passions and the momentary suggestions of the good or evil Demon, which every one, will he or nill he, must bear on his shoulders, that it is not to be wondered at, if they do not trouble themselves much about our affairs. And yet, if you help a man in his need or confer a pleasure upon him when, where, and as he desires, he will thank you for it sincerely at the moment. But how can we demand of him that he should thank us also for unasked and unavailing services, or that he shall feel obliged

---

* Frederic II. Tr.

to us when we have sung his ears full at the wrong time? How can we demand that other men, amid the pressure of their business, cares, dissipations, entertainments, shall attach the same importance that we do to the art which we pursue, the objects with which our soul is filled, the work with which we are occupied and with which they perhaps do not know what in God's world to do. How can we reasonably demand that they should have as practised an ear for the music of our verses, that they should notice the finer beauties of a poetic picture as accurately or estimate them as highly as if they had made such matters a special study for many years?

It lies in the nature of things that much in works of wit, of taste, of art, must be lost to the mere amateur. But the Public are not therefore unjust toward writers of distinguished merit nor without a feeling of the value of the masterpieces of the poetic art. See how well every day manufactures, *sine pondere et arte*, are received, where there is anything in them that can please. The reading world wishes to be entertained and amused in a great variety of ways, and it loves variety so much, that an author must be altogether insipid who does not succeed in attracting notice, and in being for a time at least distinguished among the daily increasing crowd of competitors. Even in the easiest and most artless kind,—that which has scarcely anything of poetry, except vividness of expression and rhyme — wit or humour or the felicitous ejaculation of a momentary feeling is enough to make an author beloved and esteemed by a nation. Let not the fault therefore be in yourself, my young friend. Deserve public approbation, and it will not be denied you. Spread all your sails, and, not content with ordinary prizes, enrich our literature with works which, instead of entertaining for the moment only, shall possess themselves of the entire soul of the reader, bring all his organs of sensation into play, warm and enchant his imagination with an unbroken illusion, afford nourishment to his mind, and to his heart the sweet enjoyment of its best feelings,—its moral sense, its interest in others' joys and sorrows, its admiration of all that is beautiful and great in Humanity. And, depend upon it, the Public will feel all the gratitude for such a work, which you can reasonably desire.

I add this clause, because it would be madness to expect more of men than they can give. And by what right do authors alone demand from their nation more justice, more gratitude, more equality and constancy than any other man of merit—in whatever category he may be —can expect from it?

I have thought this little digression necessary, that you may not consider that, which I have now stated merely as fact respecting the disagreeable circumstances in the life of a poet, as a lamentation wrung from me by the feeling or the memory of my own experiences. In every conceivable mode of life and in all conceivable circumstances, the life of man is compassed about with manifold actual, imaginary, natural and self-made plagues; and in the surprise of the moment, a very small pain may sometimes extort from us a loud cry. But who would be in despair at unavoidable, universal and therefore very endurable ills? *Quisque suos patimur manes.* It needed no reference to my own case, in order to speak to you of universal experiences, common to all times and to all nations where literature has flourished.

You, my friend, know me well enough to know that I am satisfied with my lot in every point of view. From my youth up, I have loved art more than what is called fame and success; and always the unadulterated feeling of a few noble souls, the unexpected kind-hearted thanks of some brave, upright man, who could have no private purposes in praising me, have been more to me than the calm approbation of the connoisseur or the loud applause of the multitude; although, in a career of more than thirty years, these too have not been wanting. But I should arrogate to myself a merit to which I have no claim, were I to deny that, after spending the greater part of my life in the service of the Muses, I have done more for myself than for others. It was the pure truth— and will probably remain true to the end of my days—that I said to my Muse, from the fulness of my heart, more than fifteen years ago, when living at the farthest extreme of South Germany, entirely secluded from our Parnassus and without any literary connexions,

> If thou pleasest not, if world and connoisseur agree
> To disparage thy merit,
> Let thy consolation be, in this calamity,
> That with sweet pains thou hast conferred much joy on me.
> Thou art still, O Muse! the happiness of my life,
> And if no one listens to thee, thou singest to me alone.

I am greatly mistaken if, in the course of your life, this sentiment does not become your sentiment also. And so, whichever way your fate may lead you, I have still this consolation always, that a fountain of happiness is springing up within you, which can sweeten every care of life and double the enjoyment of its highest pleasures, and which, even when it begins to fail, will still have a few nectar-drops left for your solace, in the days in which we have no pleasure.

ON THE RELATION OF THE AGREEABLE AND THE BEAUTIFUL TO THE USEFUL.

BALZAC, whose "Letters," once so admired, would furnish an inexhaustible fund of antitheses, *concetti* and other witticisms for epigrammatists by profession, was often in the predicament of saying something very flat when he imagined that he had said something very ingenious. Nevertheless, he sometimes made a good hit, as one who spends his whole life in chasing after thoughts necessarily must.

In the following passage I am pleased with the concluding thought, notwithstanding its epigrammatic turn, on account of the simplicity and luminous truth of the image in which it is clothed. "We must have books," he says, "for recreation and entertainment, as well as books for instruction and for business. The former are agreeable, the latter useful; and the human mind requires both. The Canon-law and the codes of Justinian shall have due honour, and reign at the universities, but Homer and Virgil need not therefore be banished. We will cultivate the olive and the vine, but without eradicating the myrtle and the rose."

I have two remarks to make, however, respecting this passage. In the first place, Balzac concedes too much to those pedants, who turn up their noses at the favourites of the Muses and their works, when he reckons the Homers and the Virgils among the merely agreeable writers. Antiquity, more wise in this respect, thought differently; and Horace maintains with good reason, that there is more practical philosophy to be learned from Homer than from Crantor and Chrysippus.

In the next place, it seems to me on the whole to indicate rather a mercantile than a philosophical way of thinking, when people place the agreeable and the useful in opposition to each other, and look upon the former with a kind of contempt in comparison with the latter. Presuming that what we understand by the agreeable is something that violates neither law nor duty nor sound moral sentiment, I say that the useful, as opposed to the agreeable and the beautiful, is common to us with the lowest brute; and that when we love and honour that which is useful in this sense, we do only what the ox and the ass do likewise. The value of such utility depends on the greater or less degree of indispensableness which attaches to it. So far therefore as a thing is necessary to the preservation of the human species and of civil society, so far it is good indeed, but not on that account excellent. Accordingly, we desire the useful, not on its own account, but only on account of certain advantages which we derive from it. The beautiful on the other hand we love by virtue of an intrinsic superiority of our nature over the merely animal. For man alone of all animals is endowed with a delicate feeling for order and beauty and grace. Hence, he is so much the more perfect, so much the more a man, the more extended and intense his love for the beautiful, and the greater the refinement and accuracy with which, by mere sensation, he can distinguish different degrees and kinds of beauty. And therefore, moreover, it is only the beautiful in art as well as in the mode of life and in morals, that distinguishes social, developed, refined man from savages and barbarians. Nay, all the arts without exception, and the sciences too, owe their growth almost exclusively to this love for the beautiful and the perfect, inherent in man, and would still be infinitely removed from that degree of perfection to which they have risen in Europe, if men had attempted to confine them within the narrow limits of the necessary and the useful, in the common acceptation of those words.

Socrates did so, and if ever he was mistaken in anything, it was in this. Keppler and Newton would never have discovered the laws of the mundane system,— the noblest product of human thought,— if, in conformity with his precepts, they had confined geometry to mere mensuration, and astronomy to the mere necessities of travel by land and sea, and to the making of almanacs.

Socrates exhorted painters and sculptors to combine the agreeable and the beautiful with the useful; just as he urged mimic dancers to ennoble the pleasure which their art was capable of yielding, and to entertain the heart together with the senses. According to the same principle, he behoved to admonish those labourers who occupy themselves with things essential, to combine the useful as far as possible with the beautiful. But to deny the name of beautiful to everything that is not useful is to confound ideas.

It is true, Nature herself has established a relation between the useful, and the beautiful and graceful. But these are not desirable because they are useful, but because it is the nature of man to enjoy a pure satisfaction in the contemplation of them, a satisfaction altogether similar to that which we derive from the contemplation of moral excellence, and as much a want of rational beings as food, clothing, shelter, are wants of the animal man.

I say of the animal man because they are common to him with all other, or at least, with most other animals. But neither these animal necessities, nor the power and the effort to satisfy them, constitute him a man. In providing food, in building his nest, in choosing a mate, in training his young, in battling with others who would deprive him of his food, or take possession of his dwelling,—in all this he acts, materially considered, as an animal. It is the way and manner in which man—unless reduced to the condition of a brute, and kept therein by cogent, external circumstances—performs these animal functions, that distinguishes him from and raises him above all other orders of animals, and characterizes his humanity. For this animal that calls itself man, and this only, possesses an inborn feeling for beauty and order, possesses a heart disposed to communication of itself, to sympathy with sorrow and with joy, and to an infinite diversity of agreeable and beautiful sentiments. Only this animal possesses a strong propensity to imitate and to create, and labours unceasingly to improve what he has invented and made.

All these qualities together distinguish him essentially from other animals, make him their lord and master, subject land and sea to his dominion, and lead him from step to step so far, that, by the almost unlimited extension of his artistic powers, he is enabled to transform Nature herself, and, from the materials which she furnishes, to create for himself a new world, more perfectly adapted to his particular ends.

The first thing, in which man displays this his superiority, is the refinement and ennobling of all those wants, impulses and functions which he has in common with other animals. The time which he requires for this purpose is not to be considered. Enough that he finally arrives at that point where he is no longer necessitated to beg his sustenance from mere chance, and where the greater certainty of a richer and better support allows him leisure to think also of perfecting the other necessities of life. He invents one art after another, and each increases the security or the pleasure of his existence. And so he ascends continually from the indispensable to the convenient, from the convenient to the beautiful.

The *natural* society into which he is born, combined with the necessity of securing himself against the injurious consequences of a too great extension of the human species, leads him at last to *civil* society and civilized modes of life.

But here too, no sooner has he provided for the necessary, for the means of internal and external security, than we find him occupied, in thousand-fold ways, with beautifying this his new condition. Imperceptibly small villages are transformed into large cities, the abodes of the arts and of commerce, and points of union for the different nations of the earth. Man spreads himself ever farther in all senses and in all directions. Navigation and traffic multiply relations and pursuits by multiplying the wants and the goods of life. Wealth and luxury refine every art whose mother was want and necessity; leisure, ambition, and public encouragement promote the growth of the sciences, which, by the light they diffuse over all the objects of human life, become rich sources of new advantages and enjoyments.

But in the same proportion in which man adorns and improves his external condition, his feeling for the morally beautiful is also unfolded. He renounces the rude and inhuman uses of the savage state, he learns to abhor all violent conduct toward his kind, and accustoms himself to laws of justice and propriety. The manifold relations of the social condition unfold and determine the ideas of politeness and etiquette, and the desire of pleasing others and of gaining their esteem teaches him to restrain his passions, to conceal his faults, to turn his best side out, and to perform whatsoever he does, in a decent manner. In a word, his manners improve with the rest of his condition.

Through all these gradations he raises himself at last to the highest perfection of mind, possible in this present life, to the great idea of the whole of which he is a part, to the ideal of the fair and good, to wisdom and virtue, and to the worship of the inscrutable, original Power of Nature, the universal Father of Spirits, to know whose laws and to do them is his greatest privilege, his first duty and his purest pleasure.

All this we denominate, with one word, the progress of Humanity. And now let every one answer for himself the question, whether man would have made this progress if that inborn feeling of the beautiful and the graceful had remained inactive in him? Take from him this, and all the results of his dormant power, all the monuments of his greatness, all the riches of Nature and Art of which he has possessed himself, disappear; he relapses into the brutal condition of the inhabitants of New Holland; and, with him, Nature herself relapses into savage and formless chaos.

What are all these steps by which man gradually approaches perfection but successive embellishments, embellishments of his necessities, his mode of living, his habitation, his apparel, his implements, embellishments of his mind and heart, his sentiments and passions, his language, manners, customs, pleasures?

What a distance from the earliest hovel to a building of Palladio! From the canoe of a Carib to a ship of the line! From the three blocks by which, in the remotest ages, the Bœotians represented the three Graces, to the Graces of Praxiteles! From a village of Hottentots or wild Indians to a city like London! From the ornaments of a woman of New Zealand to the state-dress of a sultana! From the dialect of the natives of Otaheite to the languages of Homer, of Virgil, Tasso, Milton and Voltaire!

What innumerable gradations of embellishment must men and human things have passed through before they could overcome this almost measureless interval!

The desire to beautify and refine, and the dissatisfaction with the lower grade as soon as a higher was known, are the true, the only, and the very simple forces by which man has been urged onward to the point at which we find him. All nations which have perfected themselves are a proof of this proposition. And if there are any to be found which, without any special impediment, physical or moral, have always remained stationary in the same degree of imperfection, or which betray an entire want of those motives to progress, which have been mentioned, we should have reason to regard them rather as a particular species of man-like animals than as actual men of our own race and kind.

If now, as no one will deny, everything which tends to perfect man and his condition deserves the name of useful, where is there any ground for this hateful antithesis which certain

Ostrogoths still make between the useful and the beautiful? Probably these people have never thought what the consequences would be, if a nation, which has reached a high degree of refinement, should banish or let starve its musicians, its actors, its poets, its painters, and other artists; in a word, all who minister in the kingdom of the Muses and the Graces;—or, what would be quite as bad, if it should lose its taste in all these arts.

The loss of things which are incomparably less important would make a great gap in its prosperity. If one should reckon up to you what the consequences would be to the French, if only the two little articles, fans and snuff-boxes, were stricken out from the number of European necessities, and if you were to consider that these are but two little twigs of the countless branches of that industry elicited by the love for playthings and trinkets, wherewith all the large children in trowsers and long coats around us are affected, and if you were to calculate how useful to the world even these useless things are, and were to reflect that the departments of the beautiful and the useful are not exclusive departments, but are so manifoldly intertwined with each other that it is impossible ever to define with certainty and precision their respective boundaries, in short, that there exists such an intimate relation between them that almost all that is useful is or may be made beautiful, and all that is beautiful useful;—if you were to consider all this, you would—

But there are some people who, like the Abderites, grow no wiser by considering. He whose head has, once for all, a crook in it, will never, in his life, be brought to see things as they are seen by all the rest of the world who look straight before them.

And then there is still another class of incorrigible people who have always been avowed contemners of the beautiful, not because their head is placed awry, but because they call nothing useful that does not fill their purse. Thus, the trade of a sycophant, a quack, a dealer in charms, a clipper of ducats, a pimp, a *Tartuffe*, is certainly not beautiful; it is therefore perfectly natural that this gentry should manifest on every occasion a profound contempt for that kind of beauty which yields them nothing. Besides, to how many a blockhead is stupidity useful! How many would lose their whole authority, if those among whom they had won or stolen it, had taste enough to distinguish the genuine from the false, the beautiful from the ugly! Such persons, to be sure, have weighty, personal reasons to be enemies of wit and taste. They are in the condition of the honest fellow who had married his homely daughter to a blind man, and was unwilling that his son-in-law should be couched.

But the rest of us, who can only gain by being made wiser,—what Abderites we should be if we suffered ourselves to be persuaded by these gentlemen who are interested in the matter, to become blind or to remain blind, in order that the ugliness of their daughters may not come to light!

FROM THE DIALOGUES OF THE GODS.*

DIALOGUE VI.

Mercury brings to the banqueting Gods the information that they have been formally deposed in the Roman Senate — under the government of the Emperor Theodosius the great — Jupiter discusses this event with great moderation, and reveals to the Gods consoling glimpses of the Future.

SPEAKERS.

JUPITER, JUNO, APOLLO, MINERVA, VENUS, BACCHUS, VESTA, CERES, VICTORIA, QUIRINUS, SERAPIS, MOMUS AND MERCURY.

Jupiter and Juno, with the other inhabitants of Olympus, are sitting in an open hall of the Olympian palace, at sundry large tables. Ganymede and Antinous are pouring out nectar for the gods, Hebe, for the goddesses. The Muses perform table music, the Graces and the Hours dance pantomimic dances; and Jocus, from time to time, provokes the blessed gods to loud laughter, by his caricatures and his lazzi. In the moment of the greatest merriment, Mercury comes flying in, in great haste.

Jupiter. You are late, my son; how you look! What news do you bring us from below there?

Venus, to Bacchus. He seems to have a heavy load of it; how troubled he looks!

Mercury. The newest that I bring with me is not very well calculated to enhance the mirth which, I see, reigns here at this moment.

Jupiter. At least your looks are not, Mercury. What can have happened so bad as to disturb even the gods in their enjoyment?

Quirinus. Has an earthquake destroyed the Capitol?

Mercury. That would be a trifling affair.

Ceres. Has a violent eruption of Ætna devastated my beautiful Sicily?

Bacchus. Or has an untimely frost blighted the Campanian vines?

Mercury. Trifles! Trifles!

Jupiter. Well! Come! Out with your tale of wo!

Mercury. It is nothing more than— (*He hesitates.*)

Jupiter. Do not make me impatient, Hermes! What is 'nothing more than?'

Mercury. Nothing, Jupiter, but that at Rome on a motion made in the Senate by the Imperator in his own person, and carried by an overwhelming majority, you have been FORMALLY DEPOSED.

---

* These dialogues were suggested to Wieland by his translations of Lucian. Some of them are mere *jeux d'esprit* in imitation of that author on whom he had expended three years' labour. Some have a deeper meaning. The author says of them, "I do not wish for readers who need to be informed that they have a very serious purpose." Tr.

(*The gods all rise from the table in great commotion. Jupiter, who alone remains seated, laughing.*) Is that all? That is what I have been expecting this long while.

All the gods at once. Jupiter deposed! Is it possible? Jupiter!

Juno. You talk like a crazy man, Mercury.—Æsculapius, do feel of his pulse!

The gods. Jupiter deposed!

Mercury. As I said, formally and solemnly, by a great majority of voices, declared to be a man of straw — what do I say? a man of straw is something; — less than a man of straw, a nothing: robbed of his temples, his priests, his dignity as supreme protector of the Roman empire!

Hercules. That is mad news, Mercury!—But, as true as I am Hercules, (*flourishing his club*) they shall not have done me that for nothing!

Jupiter. Be quiet, Hercules!—So then, Jupiter Optimus Maximus, Capitolinus, Feretrius, Stator, Lapis, &c. &c., has finished his part?

Mercury. Your statue is thrown down, and they are now busily employed in demolishing your temple. The same tragedy is going on in all the provinces and corners of the Roman empire. Everywhere legions of goat-bearded, semi-human beings, with torches and crowbars, hammers, mattocks and axes are falling to work and destroying with fanatic rage the venerable objects of the arch-old popular faith.

Serapis. Wo is me! What will be the fate of my splendid temple at Alexandria and my superb colossal image! If the desert of Thebais spews out but one half of its sacred Satyrs against them, it is a gone case.

Momus. O! you have nothing to fear, Serapis. Who would dare to touch your image, when it is an understood thing at Alexandria, that, on the least outrage committed against it by any sacrilegious hand, heaven and earth will tumble into ruins and Nature sink back into ancient chaos?

Quirinus. Only, one cannot always depend on that sort of tradition, my good Serapis! It might happen to you as it did to the massive-gold statue of the goddess Anaitis at Zela, with regard to which, it was also believed, that the first one who offered any violence to it, would be struck dead on the spot.

Serapis. And what happened to that statue?

Quirinus. When the Triumvir, Antony, had routed Pharnaces at Zela, the city, together with the temple of Anaitis, was plundered; and no one could tell what had become of the massive-gold goddess. Some years after, it happened that Augustus was spending the night at Bononia with one of Antony's veterans. The Imperator was splendidly entertained, and, at table, the conversation happening to turn on the battle of Zela and the plunder of the temple of Anaitis, he asked his host, as an eyewitness, whether it was true that the first one who laid hand on her fell suddenly dead to the ground?—You behold that rash man before you, said the veteran, and you are actually supping from a leg of the goddess. I had the good fortune to seize upon her first. Anaitis is a very good person, and I gratefully confess, that I am indebted to her for all my wealth.

Serapis. That is poor consolation which you give me, Quirinus! If such things are going on in the world as Mercury reports, I can promise myself no better fate for my colossus at Alexandria. It is really dreadful that Jupiter can look so composedly on such enormities!

Jupiter. You would do well, Serapis, if you would follow my example. For a Divinity of Pontus, you have enjoyed the honour of being worshipped from East to West long enough, and you can hardly expect that your temples should fare better than mine, or that your colossus should last longer than the god-like masterpiece of Phidias. Surely you do not look to be the only one that stands upright, when all the rest of us are fallen.

Momus. Fy! Fy! Jupiter, what have you done with your famous thunderbolts, that you submit so quietly to your fall?

Jupiter. If I were not what I am, I should answer that foolish question with one of them, witling!

Quirinus to Mercury. You must tell it to me again, Mercury, before I can believe you. Do you mean to say then, that my Flamen is abolished? my temple closed? that my festival is no longer celebrated? Have the enervated, slavish, unfeeling Quirites degenerated to this degree of ingratitude toward their founder?

Mercury. I should deceive you, if I were to give any other account.

Victoria. Then I need not ask what has become of my altar and my statue in the Julian Curia. The Romans have so long forgotten the art of conquering, that I find nothing more natural than that they should not even be able to bear the presence of my image any longer. With every look which they cast upon it, it would seem to reproach them with their shameful degeneracy. Victoria has nothing more to do with Romans whose very name has become an insult among Barbarians, which only blood can wash out.

Vesta. Under such circumstances they will be sure not to let the sacred fire burn any longer in my temple. Heaven! What will be the fate of my poor virgins?

Mercury. O, they will not touch a hair of their heads, venerable Vesta! They will let them very quietly die of hunger.

Quirinus. How times change! Formerly, it was a dreadful misfortune for the whole Roman Empire, if the sacred fire, on the altar of Vesta, went out.

Mercury. And now, there would be a deal more fuss made, if the fire should go out in some Roman cook's-shop than, if the Vestals should let theirs expire twice every week.

Quirinus. But who then, in future, is to be the patron and protector of Rome, in my stead?

Mercury. St. Peter with the double key has bespoken this little office for himself.

Quirinus. St. Peter with the double key! Who is he?

Mercury. I do not exactly know, myself. Ask Apollo; perhaps he can give you more information on the subject.

Apollo. That is a man, Quirinus, who, in his successors, will govern half the world for eight hundred years; although he himself was only a poor fisherman.

Quirinus. What! Will the world let itself be governed by fishers?

Apollo. At least by a certain kind of fishers, by fishers of men, who with a very ingenious kind of bow-net, called *decretals*, will gradually catch all the nations and princes of Europe. Their commands will be regarded as divine oracles and a piece of sheep-skin or of paper sealed with St. Peter's fisher's-ring will have power to create and depose kings.

Quirinus. This St. Peter, with his double key, must be a mighty conjuror!

Apollo. Not at all! The strangest and most miraculous things in the world come about, as you ought to know by this time, in a very natural way. The avalanche, which overwhelms a whole village, was at first a little snow-ball; and a stream which bears large vessels is a gurgling rock-fountain in its origin. Why may not the successors of a Galilean fisherman, in a few centuries, become masters of Rome, and, by means of a new religion, whose chief priests they have constituted themselves, and with the aid of an entirely new morality and system of politics which they know how to rear upon that religion, become at last, masters for a time of half the world? Did you not yourself tend the herds of the King of Alba, who was a very small potentate, before you placed yourself at the head of all the banditti in Latium, and patched together the little robbers-nest, which, in process of time, became the capital and queen of the world? St. Peter, it is true, made no great figure in his life-time, but he will see the time when emperors shall hold the stirrups for his successors, and queens with all humility kiss their feet.

Quirinus. What things one lives to see, when one is immortal!

Apollo. To be sure, it requires a good deal of time and no little art to make that progress in man-fishing. But the fishes must be stupid enough, who will let themselves be caught by them.

Quirinus. Meanwhile, we are and remain all of us deposed, eh?

Mercury. It seems likely to stop at that, for the present.

Several gods. Better not be immortal, than experience such things.

Jupiter. My dear sons, uncles, nephews, and cousins, all and severally! I see that you treat this little revolution, which I have very quietly seen approaching this long while, more tragically than the thing is worth. May I ask you to sit down again in your places, and let us discuss these matters calmly and candidly over a glass of nectar. Everything in nature has its time, everything is liable to change, and so too are human opinions. They ever change with circumstances, and if we consider what a difference only fifty years makes between the grandsire and the grandson, it really will not seem strange that the world should appear to take an entirely new shape in the course of one thousand or two thousand years. For at bottom it is only in appearance after all. It remains forever the same comedy though with different masks and names. The foolish people there below have practised superstition with us long enough, and if there are some among you who thought themselves benefited by it, I must tell them that they were mistaken. One would not grudge that mankind should grow wiser at last, if they can. By heaven! it were none too soon. But that is not to be thought of, at present. True, they always flatter themselves that the last folly of which they have become conscious, is the last they shall commit. The hope of better times is their everlasting chimera, by which they are forever deluded, in order to be forever deluded again; because they will never come to understand that not the time, but their own inborn, incurable folly, is the cause why their condition never improves. For it is, once for all, their lot not to be able to enjoy anything good with a pure enjoyment, and to exchange one folly, of which they have grown weary at last, like children of a worn-out doll, for a new one, with which, for the most part, they fare worse than before. This time, it actually looked as if they would gain by the exchange, but I knew them too well not to foresee that they were not to be helped in this way. For though Wisdom herself should descend to them, in person, and dwell visibly among them, they would not cease to hang ribbons and feathers and rags and bells about her, until they had made a fool of her. Believe me, Gods, the song of triumph, which they are raising, at this moment, on account of the glorious victory they have obtained over our defenceless statues, is a raven-cry prophetic of wo to posterity. They think to improve, and will fall from the frying-pan into the fire. They are weary of us, they wish to have nothing more to do with us. So much the worse for them! We need them not. If their priests pronounce us unclean and evil spirits and assure the foolish people that an ever-burning gulph of brimstone is our dwelling, why need that trouble us? Of what importance is it to us, what conceptions half-reasoning creatures of earth may form of us? or in what relation they place themselves to us, and whether they smoke us with a sickening compound of the stink of sacrifices and incense, or with hellish brimstone? Neither the one nor the other reaches to us. You say, they do not know us, when they wish to withdraw themselves from our government. Did they know us better while they served us? What the poor people call their religion is their concern not ours. It is they alone who gain or lose by ordering their life rationally or irrationally. And their descendants, when hereafter they shall feel the consequences of the unwise decrees of their Valentinians, their Gratiani, and their Theodosii, will find cause enough to regret the unwise provisions which will accumulate on their giddy heads a flood of new and insupportable evils, of which the world had no conception as long as it adhered to the old faith or the old superstition. It would be a very different affair, if they really improved their condition under the new arrangement! Who of us would or could blame them for that? But it is just the opposite! They resemble a man, who, for the sake of driving away some trifling evil with which he might live to the age of Tithonus, suffers ten others, which are ten times worse, to be fastened upon him. Thus, for example, they raise a great outcry against our priests, because they entertained the people, who are everywhere superstitious and will always remain so, with delusions, which however benefited the State as well as themselves. Will their priests do better? At this moment they are laying the foundation of a superstition, which will benefit no one but themselves, and which, instead of strengthening the political constitution, will confound and undermine all human and civil relations,—a superstition which will lie like lead on their brains, exclude every sound conception of things, natural and moral, and, under pretence of a chimerical perfection, will poison humanity in every man in the very germ. When the worst has been said that can be said with truth of the superstition which has hitherto fooled the world, men will be forced, hereafter, to confess, that it was far more human, more innocent, and more beneficial, than the new one which is substituted in its place. Our priests were infinitely more harmless than those to whom they must now yield. They enjoyed their authority and their income in peace, were in harmony with every one and assailed no man's faith. These are greedy of dominion and intolerant, they persecute one another with the uttermost rage on account of the most insignificant verbal subtleties, decide by a majority of voices what must be thought concerning unthinkable things and what must be said concerning unspeakable things, and treat all, who think or speak otherwise, as enemies of God and man. It was a thing scarce heard of for a thousand years, that the priests of the gods came into collision with the civil authority, until encroached upon by these raving iconoclasts. The new priesthood on the contrary, since their party has been in power, have not ceased to confound the world. As yet, their pontiffs work under ground, but soon they will grasp at the sceptres of kings and assume to be vicegerents of their God, and under this title arrogate to themselves an hitherto unheard of dominion over heaven and earth. Our priests indeed, as was proper, were not very zealous promoters—or at least they were not avowed enemies—of philosophy, from which they had nothing to fear under the protection of the laws. Least of all, did they dream of subjecting the thoughts and opinions of men to their jurisdiction, and of hindering their free circulation in society. Theirs, on the other hand, who, as long as they were the weaker party, made so much boast of having Reason on their side and always placed her in the van, whenever attacked by ours,— now that she would only be an hindrance to them, in their farther operations,—will dismiss her from their service and will not rest until they have made all dark around them, until they have withdrawn from the people all means of enlightenment and stamped the free use of the natural judgment as the greatest of all crimes. Formerly, while they lived on alms themselves, the wealth and decent living of our priests was an abomination to them; now that they are driving with full sails, the moderate revenues of our temples are much too small to satisfy the necessities of their pride and vanity. Already their pontiffs at Rome, through the liberality of superstitious and wealthy matrons, whose enthusiastic sentimentality they know how to avail themselves of in so masterly a manner, by the most shameless legacy-hunting, and a thousand other arts of the same sort, have placed themselves in a condition to surpass the first persons in the State, in splendor, luxury, and expense. But all these fountains, although grown to rivers by ever new accessions, will not satisfy these insatiable men. They will invent a thousand unheard of means to tax the simplicity of rude and deluded men; even the sins of the world they will convert to golden fountains by their magic art, and, to render these fountains more productive, they will invent a monstrous number of new sins, of which the Theophrasts and the Epictetusses had no conception.

But why do I speak of all this? What is it to us what these people do or leave undone, or how well or ill they avail themselves of their new dominion over the sickly souls of men who are enervated and crippled by lust and bondage? They who deceive the rest are themselves deluded. They too know not what they do. But it becomes us to treat them with indulgence as diseased and insane, and, without regard to their gratitude or ingratitude, in future also, still to confer upon them as much good as their own folly may yet leave us the opportunity of doing. The unhappy! Whom but themselves do they injure, when of their own accord they deprive themselves of the beneficent influence by which Athens became the school of wisdom and of art, and Rome the lawgiver and mistress of the earth, by which both attained a degree of culture to which even the better descendants of the barbarians, who are now about to divide among themselves the lands and wealth of these degenerate Greeks and Romans, will never be able to rise. For what is to become of men from whom the Muses and the Graces, Philosophy and all the beautifying arts of life and the finer enjoyment of life have withdrawn themselves, together with the gods, their inventors and protectors? I foresee with one glance all the evil that will thrust itself in, in the place of the good, all the unformed, the perverted, the monstrous and misshapen that these fanatical destroyers of the beautiful will rear on the ashes and the ruins of works of genius, of wisdom and art, and I am disgusted with the loathsome spectacle. Away with it! For, so truly as I am Jupiter Olympius, it shall not always remain so, although centuries will elapse before Humanity reaches the lowest abyss of its fall, and centuries more before, with our aid, it works its way once more above the slime. The time will come when they will seek us again, invoke our aid once more, and confess that they are powerless without us. The time will come when with unwearying diligence they will drag forth from the dust once more, or excavate from rubbish and corruption every ruined or defaced relic of those works which, by our influence, have once sprung from the mind and hands of our favourites, and exhaust themselves in vain, with affected enthusiasm, to imitate those miracles of genuine inspiration and the actual afflatus of divine powers.

Apollo. Most surely it will come, Jupiter, that time! I see it as if it stood already before me, in the full glory of the present. They will again erect our images, will gaze upon them with a feeling of awe and wonder, will use them as models for their idols, which had become frights in barbarous hands; and—O! what a triumph! their pontiffs themselves will take pride in erecting the most magnificent temple to us, under a different name!

Jupiter. (*with a large goblet of nectar in his hand*) Here's to the Future! (*to Minerva.*) My daughter, we'll drink to the time when you shall see all Europe converted into a new Athens, filled with academical lyceums, and perhaps shall hear the voice of philosophy from the midst of the forests of Germany, more clear and free than formerly from the halls of Athens and Alexandria.

Minerva. (*slightly shaking her head*) I am glad, Father Jupiter, to see you of such good cheer in view of the present aspects; but you will pardon me if I believe as little in a new Athens as in a new Olympus.

Quirinus. (*to Mercury*) I can't get that Peter with the double key, who is to be my successor, out of my head, Mercury! How is it with that key? Is it an actual or emblematic, a natural or a magic key? Where did he get it, and what will he unlock with it?

Mercury. All that I can tell you about it, Quirinus, is, that with this key he can unlock Heaven or Tartarus to whom he pleases.

Quirinus. He may unlock Tartarus to whom he will for all me; but as to Heaven!—that is a very different matter.

Mercury. Indeed, they are preparing to people Heaven with such an enormous quantity of new gods of their sort, that there will hardly be any room left for us old ones.

Jupiter. Leave that to me, Hermes! They could easily deprive us of our temples and territories on the earth; but, in Olympus, we have been established too long to be crowded out. For the rest, as a proof of our perfect impartiality, we will concede to the new Romans the right of apotheosis, notwithstanding their insolence, under the same conditions as to the old. As I understand, most of their candidates who lay claim to this promotion are not persons of the best society. Therefore, before we admit any one, with St. Peter's permission we will examine him a little. If it shall appear that, in virtue of his other qualities and merits, he can maintain his place among us, no objection shall be made on account of the golden circle round his head; and Momus himself shall not twit him with the miracles which are wrought with his bones or his wardrobe.

Juno. You may do as you please with regard to the men, Jupiter; but I protest against the introduction of the ladies.

Venus. There are said to be some very pretty ones among the number.

Jupiter. We will talk about that when the case occurs. And now—not a word more *de odiosis!* A fresh cup, Antinous!

DIALOGUE VIII.

JUPITER, NUMA, *afterward* AN UNKNOWN.*

Jupiter. How happens it, Numa, that we have not seen you now, for several days, at the table of the Gods?

Numa. The accounts which Mercury lately brought us from Rome left me no rest until I had seen with my own eyes how matters stood.

Jupiter. And how did you find them?

Numa. I say it with heavy heart, Jupiter, but probably I tell you nothing new, when I say that your authority with mortals appears to be irrecoverably lost.

Jupiter. Did you not hear what Apollo said at table the other day?

Numa. He gave you very distant consolation, Jupiter; and even this consolation turns at last on a verbal quibble. It is just as if a Chaldean soothsayer had comforted Alexander the Great, when about to die of a miserable fever at Babylon in the midst of the enjoyment of his conquests, with the assurance that two thousand

---

* He is so still to most persons at the present day, and he appears here to give some important information respecting his true character and aim.

years after his death a noble descendant of the great Wittekind would wear his picture in a ring. Such a thought may be very agreeable as long as one is in good condition; but it is a poor indemnification for the loss of the first throne in the world.

Jupiter. I should have thought, friend Numa, that your residence in Olympus would have corrected your notions of such things!

Numa. I know very well that a decree of the senate at Rome cannot deprive you of the influence which you have on the affairs of the world below; but—

Jupiter. (*smiling*) Speak out plainly what you think! My ear has grown patient of late — 'But' what?

Numa. Your influence, after all, cannot be very considerable; or else I cannot conceive how you could suffer yourself to be deprived of the divine authority and the high privileges which you have enjoyed for so many centuries throughout the Roman world, without so much as stirring a finger.

Jupiter. I can pardon my Flamen for not comprehending a thing of this sort; but you, Numa!—

Numa. To speak candidly, Jupiter, although I may be considered in some sort the founder of the old Roman religion, it was never my intention to give more nourishment to the superstition of the rude Romans than was absolutely necessary to polish them. I did not indeed make any essential change in the service of those gods which a primeval, popular belief had long established in the possession of the public veneration. Nevertheless, it was my aim to keep the way open, so to speak, to a purer knowledge of the Supreme Being, and at least to prevent the coarsest kind of idolatry by not allowing the Godhead to be represented in the temples, neither in the likeness of beasts nor even of men. I regarded even then the different persons and names, which the faith of the forefathers had exalted into gods, either as symbols of the invisible and unfathomable arch-Power of Nature, or as men whom the gratitude of posterity for great services conferred on social and civil life, had raised to the rank of publicly worshipped, guardian spirits.

Jupiter. And ocular evidence has taught you that you did not err greatly, in this latter notion at least; although I am not of your opinion as it regards the images of the gods.

Numa. Had there been Phidiasses and Alkameneses in Latium in my day, it is probable that these artists might have led me too to a different way of thinking.

Jupiter. If, then, you have never held us for anything else than we are, whence your surprise that we are quite willing to let it pass, when the inhabitants of the earth have also advanced so far as to regard us in the same light?

Numa. It may be owing to the habit of living among you, and of seeing you so long in possession of the worship of mankind. Both these circumstances have placed you in a strange kind of *chiaroscuro* to my eye, and have given me imperceptibly, perhaps, too high an opinion of your nature and dignity. In short, I confess that it will be difficult for me, Jupiter, to accustom myself to a different way of thinking.

Jupiter. I am half inclined to come forth from the *chiaroscuro*, and to draw away the veil from the secrets of my family, concerning which so many excellent people on the earth have cudgelled their brains to no purpose.

Numa. I am sure you will lose nothing by it.

Jupiter. One always gains by the truth, friend Numa!— You know that no one of us, Olympians, long as we have existed and far as our sight extends, can refer to a time when this immeasurable whole began to be, whose existence, on the contrary, is the most convincing proof that it had no beginning. On the other hand it may be affirmed with the same certainty, that, of all its visible parts, no one has always existed precisely as it is. Thus, for example, the earth which we once inhabited has undergone several great revolutions, of which, in part, some traces have been preserved by oral tradition among the oldest nations. Of this kind is the tradition current among the Northlanders, the Indians and the Egyptians, that there was a time when the earth was inhabited by gods. In fact, the inhabitants of the earth in this first period, if they can be called men, were a kind of men who would compare with the present race, as the Olympian Jupiter of Phidias, with the Priapus-images of fig-tree wood which the country people stick up to protect their gardens; so far did they surpass in size and beauty, bodily strength and mental powers, the men of after times. With them and by means of them, the earth enjoyed a state of perfection which was worthy of its then inhabitants. But, in the course of thousands of years, it has undergone great changes. A part of the posterity of the first inhabitants degenerated in the different regions of the earth, over which their increase compelled them to spread themselves. Extraordinary events, earthquakes, volcanoes, floods, changed the shape of the planet. While whole countries were swallowed up in the ocean, others gradually emerged from the waves; but the greater part of the old inhabitants of the earth perished in this fearful revolution of things. The few who remained, wandered singly, amazed and dispirited, among the ruins of Nature. Here and there, indeed, accident brought a Deucalion and a Pyrrha together, but their descendants soon degenerated, through want and misery, into beastly savages. Meanwhile, the earth gradually recovered from the chaotic state which naturally resulted from those terrible convulsions, and became evermore fitted for the habitation and subsistence of its new inhabitants. The new races with which it was peopled supported themselves scantily with hunting and fishing, and where these failed, with acorns and other wild fruits. They dwelt, for the most part, in forests and caves; and the most of them were so rude, that they did not even know the use of fire. Happily, a family of that first and more perfect race had preserved itself on the summit of Imaus, with all their original excellences, and in the enjoyment of all the advantages derived from the arts and sciences invented by their ancestors. Necessitated by similar catastrophes to relinquish the seats of their inheritance, they scattered themselves to the east and to the west, and wherever they came, their arrival was like the appearance of beneficent gods. For, besides a cultivated language and gentle manners, they brought all the arts, of which no trace was to be found among those wild-animal-men, and the want of which was the very cause which had degraded them to that inhuman animality. You will comprehend, friend Numa, that they were received as gods by these wretched creatures, and that, by all the good which they communicated, by the arts of agriculture, by the breeding of domestic animals, the planting of fruit trees, whereby they became creators of a new world, by the civil societies whose founders, by the cities whose builders and lawgivers they became, by the pleasant arts of the Muses, whereby they diffused milder manners, more refined pleasures, and a sweeter enjoyment of life,—you will comprehend, I say, that by all these benefits they had deserved so well of mankind, that, after their death, (of which their ascension into this purer element was the natural consequence) they came to be honoured as *guardian gods* by a grateful posterity. You will further comprehend, that they who once conferred so many and such great benefits on mortals, after their transition to a higher mode of life, should still find pleasure in caring for men who had received from them all that made them men, and in general to watch over the preservation of all that of which they had been, in some sense, the creators.

Numa. Now, suddenly, everything which, before, I had seen only as in a mist, is made clear to me.

Jupiter. And now too, it will be clear to you, I hope, why I said I was very willing that men should become sufficiently enlightened to regard us as nothing more than we actually are. Superstition and priestcraft, powerfully supported by poets, artists and mythologians, had gradually converted the service which was paid us, and which we accepted, only on account of its beneficial influence on Humanity, into a mad idolatry, which neither could nor ought to continue, which was necessarily undermined by an ever-growing culture, and like all human things, must finally fall back into itself. How could I desire that that should not ensue, which, according to the eternal laws of necessity, must needs ensue?

Numa. But these fanatical innovators are not contented with merely purifying a service so ancient, and founded on such important benefits; they destroy, they annihilate it! They rob you of that which they actually owe to you; and far from reducing the ideas of the nations respecting the gods of their fathers to the standard of truth, they carry the madness of their impious insolence so far as to pronounce you evil demons and hellish spirits, and to treat you as such.

Jupiter. Do not be angry, good Numa! Was I not also forced, while my altars yet smoked, to endure every coarse and indecent tale with which the poets entertained their gaping hearers at my expense? What does it signify to me what is thought or said of me there below, since the period has once for all arrived, when the service of Jupiter has ceased to be beneficial to men? Shall I force them with thunderbolts to have more respect for me? Of what importance can it be to me, whether they assign Olympus or Tartarus to me for a dwelling? Am I not secure against all the consequences of their opinion? Or will Ganymede pour out for me one cup the less of nectar on their account?

Numa. But it is of importance to them, Jupiter, not to deprive themselves of all the benefits which the world has hitherto enjoyed under your government, by the abandonment of all communion between themselves and you, into which they are now suffering themselves to be betrayed.

Jupiter. I thank you for your good opinion of my government, friend Pompilius! There are certain wise people below there, who do not think quite so highly of my influence in human things, and—strictly considered—they may not be so far out of the way. One cannot do more for people than they are receptive of. I have never liked to employ myself with working miracles, and so every thing goes its natural course,—mad enough, as you see, and yet, on the whole, not so bad but that one may get on with it. And so it will remain for the future, I think. Whatever I can contribute to the common good, without sacrificing my repose, I shall always be pleased to do. But as to playing the enthusiast and letting myself be crucified for ingrates and fools—that is not in Jupiter's line, my good Numa!

The Unknown appears.

Numa. Who may that stranger be, who is coming towards us yonder? Or are you already acquainted with him, Jupiter?

Jupiter. Not that I remember. He has something in his appearance, which indicates no common character.

The Unknown. Is it permitted me to take part in your conversation? I confess, it hath drawn me hither from a considerable distance.

Jupiter. (*aside*) A new kind of magnetism! (*To the unknown.*) You know then, already, whereof we were speaking?

The Unknown. I possess the faculty of being where I wish to be; and where two are inquiring after truth, I seldom fail, visibly or invisibly, to make the third.

Numa. (*shaking his head, softly to Jupiter*) A queer customer!

Jupiter. (*without minding Numa, to the Unknown*) In that case, you are an excellent companion! I rejoice to make your acquaintance.

Numa. (*to the Unknown*) May I ask your name? and whence you come?

The Unknown. Neither the one nor the other has anything to do with the subject matter which you were discussing.

Jupiter. We were speaking merely of facts. And these, as you know, appear differently to each observer, according to his stand-point and the quality of his eyes.

The Unknown. And yet each thing can be seen correctly only from one point of view.

Numa. And that is—?

The Unknown. The centre of the Whole.

Jupiter. (*aside, to Numa*) In that man there is either a great deal, or nothing.—(*To the Unknown.*) You know the Whole then?

The Unknown. Yes.

Numa. And what do you call its centre?

The Unknown. Perfection; from which everything is equally remote and to which everything approximates.

Numa. And how does each thing appear to you from this centre?

The Unknown. Not fragmentary, not as it is in particular places and periods of time, not as it relates to these or those things, not as it loses or gains by its immersion in the atmosphere of human opinions and passions, not as it is falsified by folly or poisoned by corruption of heart; but as it relates to the whole, in its beginning, progress and issue, in all its forms, movements, operations and consequences;—that is, in the measure in which it contributes to the eternal growth of the perfection of the whole.

Jupiter. That is not bad!

Numa. And seen from this point of view, how do you find the subject of which we were speaking when you came,—the great catastrophe which, in these days, without respect or mercy, has overthrown everything that, for so many centuries, was most venerable and sacred to the human race?

The Unknown. It followed necessarily, for it had been a long while preparing; and it needs at last, as you know, but a single blast to overthrow an old, ill-joined, thoroughly ruinous fabric, and one, moreover, which was founded on the sand.

Numa. But it was such a magnificent structure, so venerable in its antiquity, possessing, with all its variety, so much simplicity, so beneficent in the protection which Humanity, the laws, the security of the States enjoyed so long under its lofty arches! Would it not have been better to repair than to destroy it? Our philosophers at Alexandria had formed such beautiful projects not merely to restore its former authority but even to give it a far greater splendour and especially a symmetry, a beauty, a convenience which it never had before! It was a Pantheon of such great extent and such ingenious construction that all the religions in the world — even this new one if it would only be peaceable — might have found space enough within its walls.

The Unknown. It is a pity that, with all these apparent advantages, it was nevertheless built only on the movable sand! And as to peaceableness!—how can you expect that, in a matter of such great importance, truth and delusion should agree together?

Numa. That is a very easy matter, if only mankind will agree among themselves. They are never more grossly deluded than when they imagine themselves in exclusive possession of the truth.

The Unknown. If it is not their destination to be deceived — and that, surely, you will not maintain — then it cannot and will not be their lot to wander forever in error and delusion, like sheep without a shepherd. Between darkness and light, twilight and half-light is certainly better than complete night! but only as a transition from that to pure all-irradiating daylight. The day has now dawned, and would you lament that night and twilight are past?

Jupiter. You love allegory, as I hear, young man! I, for my part, love to speak roundly and plainly. I suppose you mean to say that men will be made happier by this new order of things? I hope they may, but as yet I see very poor preparations for it.

The Unknown. Without fail the condition of these poor mortals will be better and infinitely better. Truth will put them in possession of that freedom which is the most indispensable condition of happiness: for truth alone makes free.

Jupiter. Bravo! I heard that five hundred years ago in the *Stoa* at Athens, until I was sick of it. Propositions of this kind are just as indisputable and contribute just as much to the welfare of the world as the great truth, that once one is one. As soon as you will bring me intelligence that the foolish people below there have become better men than their fathers, since that a great part of them believe differently from their fathers, I will call you the messenger of very good tidings.

The Unknown. The corruption of mankind was so great that even the most extraordinary provisions could not remedy the evil at once. But, assuredly, they will grow better when truth shall have made them free.

Jupiter. I believe so too, but, it seems to me, that is saying no more than if you should say, that as soon as all men are wise and good they will cease to be foolish and perverse; or that, when the golden age arrives in which every man shall have abundance, no one will suffer hunger any more.

The Unknown. I see the time actually coming when all who do not purposely close their hearts to the truth, will, by means of it, attain to a perfection of which your philosophers never dreamed.

Jupiter. Have you been initiated in the mysteries of Eleusis?

The Unknown. I know them as well as if I had been.

Jupiter. Then you know what is the ultimate aim of those mysteries.

The Unknown. To live happily, and to die with the hope of a better life.

Jupiter. You seem to be a great philanthropist; do you know anything more salutary for mortals than this?

The Unknown. Yes.

Jupiter. Let me hear it, if I may ask.

The Unknown. To give them in reality what those mystagogues at Eleusis promised.

Jupiter. I fear that is more than you or I will be able to perform.

The Unknown. You have never tried, Jupiter.

Jupiter. Who likes to speak of his services? But you may easily suppose that I could not have attained to the honour which has been paid me by so many great and powerful nations for several thousand years, without having served them to some extent.

The Unknown. That may have been a long while ago! He who is unwilling to do more for man than he can do '*without sacrificing his repose,*' will not accomplish much in their behalf. I confess, I have laboured sore.

Jupiter. I like you, young man. In your years this amiable enthusiasm, which sacrifices itself for others, is a real merit. Who can offer himself up for mankind without loving them? And who can love them without thinking better of them than they deserve?

The Unknown. I think neither too well nor too ill of them. I pity their misery. I see that they may be helped; and they shall be helped.

Jupiter. It is even as I said. You are full of courage and good-will, but you are still young: the folly of earth's people has not yet made you tender. When you are as old as I am, you will sing a different song!

The Unknown. You speak as might be expected of you.

Jupiter. It seems scandalous to you to hear me talk thus, does it? You have formed a great and benevolent plan for the good of mankind. You burn with the desire to execute it. You live and have your being in it; your farseeing glance shows you all its advantages; your courage swallows up all difficulties; you have set your existence upon it; how can you help believing that it will be accomplished? But you have to do with *men*, my good friend! Do not be offended, if I speak exactly as I think: it is the privilege of age and experience. You seem to me like a tragic poet who undertakes to perform an excellent piece with nothing but crippled, dwarfed, halt and hunchbacked actors. Once more, my friend, you are not the first who has undertaken to accomplish something great with men; but I tell you that, as long as they are what they are, all such attempts will come to nothing.

The Unknown. For that very reason, they must be made new men.

Jupiter. New men! (*laughing*) That, indeed! If you could only do that! But I think I understand you. You mean to remodel them, to give them a new and better form. The model is there; you have only to form them after yourself. But that is not all that is required. Nature must furnish the clay for your creation; and you will have to take that as it is. Think of me, my friend! You will take all possible pains with your pottery, and when it comes out of the furnace, you will see yourself disgraced by it.

The Unknown. The clay — to continue your figure — is not so bad in itself, as you think. It can be purified and made as plastic as I require it, in order to make new and better men out of it.

Jupiter. I rejoice to hear it. Have you made the experiment?

The Unknown. I have.

Jupiter. I mean, on the large scale. For success in one piece out of a thousand, does not decide the matter.

The Unknown. (*after some hesitation*) If the experiment on the large scale has not yet succeeded according to my mind, I know, at least, why it could not be otherwise. It will be better in time.

Jupiter. In time? Yes, to be sure! we always hope the best from time. And who would undertake anything great without that hope? We shall see how time will fulfil your expectations. I can promise you little good for the next thousand years.

The Unknown. You have, I see, a small scale, old King of Crete! What are a thousand years, compared with the period required for the completion of the great work of making a single family of good and happy beings out of the whole human race?

Jupiter. Ah! you are right. How many thousand years have the Hermetic philosophers been labouring on their *stone*, without completing it? And what is the undertaking of those wise masters compared with yours?

The Unknown. Your jest is unseasonable. The work which I have undertaken, is just as possible as that the seed of a cedar should grow to a great tree; only that the cedar does not, it is true, attain its perfection as rapidly as a poplar.

Jupiter. And you should have as much time for the accomplishment of your work as you desire, if it depended only on that. But the certain and enormous evils, with which mankind for so many centuries are to purchase the hope of an uncertain good, give the thing a different shape. What shall we think of a plan intended to benefit the human race, which

13*

so fails in the execution, that a large portion of the human race, for a period whose duration is incalculable, are rendered beyond all comparison more miserable and (what is worse still) more depraved in head and heart than they ever were before? I appeal to ocular evidence, and yet all that we have witnessed since the murder of the brave enthusiast, Julian, was but a small prelude to the immeasurable calamities which the new hierarchy will bring down on poor foolish mortals who suffer themselves to be lured into the unsuspected snare, by every new song which is piped to them.

The Unknown. All these evils about which you complain, in the name of Humanity,—you who formerly took their misery so little to heart,—are neither the conditions nor the consequences of the great plan of which we speak. They are the obstacles which oppose it from without, and with which the light will have to contend but too long, until it has finally overcome the darkness. Is it the fault of the wine when it is spoiled in mouldy vessels? Since it is the nature of the case, that mankind can advance in wisdom and goodness, only by imperceptible degrees; since from within and without such an infinite number of enemies are labouring against their amendment; since the difficulties increase with every victory and even the most effective measures, from the mere circumstance that they have to pass through human heads and to be confided to human hands, become new obstacles; how can you be surprised that it is not in my power to procure for my brethren the happiness which I have designed for them at a less cost? How gladly would I have relieved them of all their misery at once! But even I can effect nothing in opposition to the eternal laws of necessity. Suffice it that the time will come at last.—

Jupiter. (*somewhat vexed*) Well then! we will let it come; and the poor fools to whom you are so kindly disposed, must see, meanwhile, how they can help themselves! As I said, my sight does not extend far enough to judge of so far-looking and complicated a plan as yours. The best of it is, that we are immortal and therefore may hope to see the result at last, however many Platonic ages we have to wait for it.

The Unknown. My plan, great as it is, is at bottom the simplest in the world. The way in which I am sure of effecting the general happiness is the same by which I conduct each individual to happiness; and the pledge of its safety is, that there is no other. For the rest, I end as I began: it is impossible not to be deceived, so long as one regards things fragmentarily and as they appear in the particular. They are, in reality, nothing but what they are in the whole; and the perfection which unites all in one, toward which everything tends and in which everything will finally rest, is the only view-point from which everything is seen aright. And herewith, fare ye well! (*He vanishes.*)

Numa. (*to Jupiter*) What say you to this apparition, Jupiter?

Jupiter. Ask me again fifteen hundred years hence.

DIALOGUE IX.
JUPITER AND JUNO.

Jupiter, *half-sitting, half-reclining on a couch strown with roses.* Juno, *sitting at his feet.*

Jupiter. And is this all, dear Juno, that you have to ask of me? You might have requested an impossibility; and to oblige you I would have attempted to make it possible.

Juno. You are very gallant, Jupiter. I shall never expect anything unreasonable of you.

Jupiter. The kings and the nobility have always belonged to your department, and the least you can expect of my affection is, that I should leave you unmolested in your own sphere.

Juno. Nor do my wishes extend any farther than that. For since I know your present principles, it would be asking too much to require that you, for your own part, should take a livelier interest in kings.

Jupiter. I perceive you think I incline too strongly to the side of the people. There may be some foundation for that opinion; but in fact it is only because it has been one of my first principles of government to take the side of those who are likely to retain the right at last. The present time is not favourable to the 'Shepherds of the people.' It is now the people's turn; and I am afraid, my love, that I am doing very little for you and your clients, when I swear to you that I will place no hindrances in the way of the measures which you shall adopt for their advantage.

Juno. I trust things have not yet come to that pass, that the inhabitants of the earth have only to imagine that we have no more power over them, in order to be independent of us.

Jupiter. As I said, you can try. I leave you perfect freedom; only I foresee that, as matters stand, you will have but little pleasure in the result.

Juno. I would rather you did not foresee that. If I were suspicious—

Jupiter. That you have always been a little, lady of my heart! But this time you would do me injustice. It is my serious intention to keep my promise to you, and to leave the governing gentlemen below there to your powerful protection and—to their fate.

Juno. I confess, Jupiter, I do not exactly understand how the king of gods and of men can be so indifferent in the affairs of kings, and, without moving a finger, can look quietly on and see his sub-delegates gradually changed into theatre-princes and card-kings.

Jupiter. It will not come to that so easily, my dearest.

Juno. It *has* come to that already in some places, and it will come to that everywhere at last, if we fold our hands in our laps any longer.

Jupiter. We shall not assuredly make a man like Henry IV. of France, or Frederick the only, out of a king of cards; and he who lets a king of cards be made of himself deserves nothing better.

Juno. That is a mere evasion, sir husband. You know very well that such kings as you have named are extremely rare products of Nature and circumstances; and so much the better. The kings at bottom are our vicegerents after all, and for that purpose the ordinary ones are good enough, provided we do not let them fall.

Jupiter. The compliment which you are pleased to pay me in those words is not very flattering; but, *basta!* We will not enter into any explanation on this subject. I shall not let my vicegerents, as you call them, fall, as long as they can stand on their own legs. My office is to let no one be oppressed if I can help it. Only, dear wife, do not let us forget the great truth, that kings exist for the sake of the people, and not the people for the sake of the kings.

Juno. With your permission, sir husband, that is an old saw, which, like most wise sayings of the kind, seems to say a great deal, and in fact says very little. Kings exist to govern the people, and the people must let themselves be governed by them. That is the thing; and so old Homer, even in his day, understood it, when he makes the wise Ulysses say to the stupid populace of the Grecian army: "The government of many is not good! Let one only be ruler, one only be king."* And, that no one may imagine the sceptre to depend on arbitrary will, he wisely adds, that it is Jupiter himself from whose hand kings receive this sign of supreme power. This is truth, and I know no higher.

Jupiter. I am very much obliged to you and to old Homer! But to speak candidly, what might pass for true in a certain sense, in those rude times of the world's first youth, is no longer so when applied to a people who through experience and cultivation have reached that point at last where they are masters of their own reason, and have grown strong enough to shake off the yoke of ancient prejudices and errors. Nations, indeed, have their childhood as well as individuals; and, as long as they are ignorant and weak and foolish like children, they must be treated like children, and governed by blind obedience to an authority which is not responsible to them. But nations do not, any more than individuals, remain children for ever. It is a crime against Nature to wish to keep them in perpetual childhood by force or fraud; or, as is generally the case, by both. And it is both folly and crime to treat them as children still, when they have already ripened into men.

Juno. I willingly concede, Jupiter, that a high degree of culture requires a different kind of government from that which is most fitting for a people that is yet entirely rude, or that is still in the first stages of its culture. But all the philosophers of the earth will never cause that ten millions of men, who together constitute a nation, shall have two millions of Epaminondasses and Epictetusses at their head; and so the saying of Ulysses will always remain true:

"Truly we cannot all reign, not all be kings, we Achaians,
Nor is polycracy good; let one and one only be ruler,
One only king!"

Jupiter. Granted! Only let every people, when it has arrived at that point where it can understand its own rights and calculate its own powers, for which in fact nothing more is required than an ordinary share of common sense, —let every such people have the privilege of managing its own political institutions. (*Juno shakes her head.*) I mean, they should be allowed to empower those of their number in whose judgment and integrity they have most confidence, to adopt such measures as shall hinder the arbitrary power of the individual and of the few who know how to possess themselves of his favour and confidence from doing mischief, from wasting the powers of the state, corrupting its morals, and making a crime of wisdom, virtue, and the candour which says aloud what it believes to be true; in short—

Juno. O! you are perfectly right there, Jupiter! Kings must not be suffered to do that. They must be restrained by religion and laws, of course! They must know that they receive their sceptre from the hands of Jupiter alone.

Jupiter. Dear wife, do not harp upon this string any more, if I may make the request. I know best how the matter stands. But suppose it were as you say, the people would be little benefited if kings had no one over them beside me. I should have to remind them of it with thunder and lightning every moment, or they would govern exactly as if there were no Jupiter over them, although they should sacrifice whole hecatombs to me every morning with the greatest ceremony.

Juno. I do not mean that religion shall be the only thing which they respect—

Jupiter. (*somewhat passionately*) The worst kings will always respect us most,—they who have made the great Ulyssean principle: that kings have their sceptre from me, one of the first articles of faith, and thereon grounded a blind subjection which is made the most sacred duty of the people.

Juno. But I say that they must govern according to laws whose end is the common good.

Jupiter. The common good!—A beautiful saying! And who shall give them these laws?

Juno. O! Themis has published them long ago all over the world! Where is there a nation so barbarous as not to know the universal laws of justice and right?

Jupiter. So innocent as you affect to be, child! Suppose now kings and their tools, or rather imperious courtiers and servants and their obe

---

* See Iliad, B. II. vs. 204, 205. Tr.

dient instruments the kings, in spite of old Themis and her antiquated laws, should govern only according to their own will and pleasure, and because they have the power and are answerable to no one should do as much evil or—what is the same thing to the people—should suffer as much evil to be done as they please; How then?

Juno. That is the very thing that we must prevent, Jupiter! Else why are we in the world?

Jupiter. We! Well, to be sure, my darling, you are right there!—only that the more reasonable class of men view the thing from another side. We mortals, they think, are after all the only ones who have suffered under the former government. We can help ourselves; and we will help ourselves. He who trusts that others will do for him that which he can do for himself, and in the doing of which no one is so much interested as himself, will always be poorly served.

Juno. How you talk! If mortals below there should hear you talk in this way—

Jupiter. We are speaking between ourselves, child! If *we* do not see clearly!—I do not object however that all men should know that I, for my part, always hold with him who does his duty. I am very willing that people should grow wiser. There was a time when they showed me unmerited honour. All the mischief that was done by lightning among them was placed to my account; and dear Heaven knows what foolish things I often had to hear, when the lightning struck my own temple or passed by many rogues to fall on some innocent person. Now that the brave North American, Franklin, has invented the lightning-rod, and since the people know that metals, high trees, the pinnacles of towers, and things of that sort are natural conductors of lightning, my thunderbolts are ever less feared. But I never think of being jealous about it.

Juno. We have imperceptibly fallen into a moralising vein, dear Jupiter!

Jupiter. And morals, you think, have nothing to do with politics?

Juno. Not that exactly. But I think that politics have a morals of their own, and that what is the rule of right for the subjects is not always so for the monarchs.

Jupiter. I remember the time when I thought so too. It is a very convenient and pleasant way of thinking for kings; but times change, my love!

Juno. If *we* only remain firm, there is nothing to fear.

Jupiter. Hear me, Juno! You know that I possess the privilege of seeing somewhat farther into the Future than the rest of you. Your confident tone sometimes tempts me to discover to you more than I had originally intended.

Juno. And what mystery may that be which makes you look so serious?

Jupiter. Everything, dear Juno, is subject to the eternal law of change. The time has now arrived for monarchies to cease; and (*in a lower tone*) our own tends to its decline as well as the rest. It is not much to be regretted, for it was only patchwork after all.

Juno. You speak as in a dream, Jupiter.

Jupiter. First reigned Uranus and Gaia; then came the kingdom of Saturn; this gave place to mine; and now—

Juno. And now? You do not mean to abdicate your kingdom in favour of the National Assembly at Paris, do you?

Jupiter. And now the kingdom of Nemesis has come!

Juno. The kingdom of Nemesis?

Jupiter. The kingdom of Nemesis! So I am assured by a primeval oracle long forgotten by gods and men, which Themis uttered while still in possession of the Delphian soil, and which I recall again in these days.

"When after long revolving centuries," says the oracle, "there shall be a kingdom on the earth in which the tyranny of kings, the insolence of the great, and the oppression of the people keep equal pace with the cultivation of all the faculties of Humanity, and both at last are so near their acme, that in a moment the eyes of all the oppressed are opened and all arms raised for revenge, then inexorable but ever just Nemesis, with her diamond bridle in one hand and her scale which measures with a hair's breadth exactness in the other, will descend upon the throne of Olympus to humble the proud, to exalt the depressed, and to exercise a strict retribution upon every sinner who has trampled the rights of Humanity under foot, and who in the intoxication of his insolence would acknowledge no other laws than the extravagant demands of his passions and his humours. Content to reign under her, Jupiter himself will then be nothing more than the executor of the laws which she will enact for the nations of the earth. An age more golden than the Saturnian will then be diffused among innumerable generations of better men. Universal harmony will make one family of them, and mortality will be the only difference between the happiness of the inhabitants of earth and of Olympus."

Juno. (*laughing*) That sounds splendidly, Jupiter!—And you believe in this fine poetic dream, and are resolved, as it would seem, with your hands in your lap, to await its fulfilment?

Jupiter. (*gravely*) I am resolved to submit myself to the only Power which is above me, and if you would take good advice, you would follow my example, and quietly let come what must come at last, though we should all so forget ourselves as to attempt to hinder it.

Juno. O! certainly I shall let come what I can't hinder! But why therefore remain inactive? Why divest ourselves, before the time, of the power which we actually possess, to oblige an old oracle? and not rather summon all our powers to restrain the Demon of rebellion and the rage for governing which has taken possession of the people? I insist on my old Homeric Oracle: " The government of many is bad!" Nations must enjoy the privileges of liberty under a paternal government; nothing is more reasonable. But they must not attempt to govern themselves, they must not attempt to throw off the indispensable yoke of relations and duties, and to introduce an equality which is not in the nature of men or of things, and which makes the deluded happy in a moment of intoxication, only to make them more fearfully sensible of their actual misery, on awaking.

Jupiter. Be unconcerned, my best of wives! Nemesis and Themis will know how to reduce to the right measure what is now too much or too little, too rash or too one-sided.

Juno. I am not yet disposed to abdicate my share in the government of the world to another I still feel courage in me to preside over my office myself; and if you always hold with those who do their duty, I promise myself your approbation. At least I have your word that you will not labour against me.

Jupiter. And I swear to you by the diamond bridle of Nemesis, that I will keep it as long as you are wise enough to bridle yourself. Do as you think best, but do not compel me to do my duty, my dear!

Juno. (*embracing him*) Let the beautiful Antinous fill you your great cup with nectar, Jupiter; and take your ease. You shall be satisfied with me.

JOHANN AUGUST MUSÄUS.*

Born 1735.   Died 1787.

JOHANN AUGUST MUSÄUS was born in the year 1735, at Jena, where his father then held the office of Judge. The quick talents, and kind lively temper of the boy, recommended him to the affection of his uncle, Herr Weissenborn, Superintendent at Allstadt, who took him to his house, and treated him in all respects like a son. Johann was then in his ninth year: a few months afterwards, his uncle was promoted to the post of General Superintendent at Eisenach; a change which did not alter the domestic condition of the nephew, though it replaced him in the neighbourhood of his parents; for his father had also been transferred to Eisenach, in the capacity of Councillor and Police Magistrate. With this hospitable relative he continued till his nineteenth year.

Old Weissenborn had no children of his own, and he determined that his foster-child should have a liberal education. In due time he placed him at the University of Jena, as a student of theology. It is not likely that the inclinations of the youth himself had been particularly consulted in this arrangement; nevertheless he appears to have studied with sufficient diligence; for in the usual period of three years and a half, he obtained his degree of Master, and what was then a proof of more than ordinary merit, was elected a member of the *German Society*. With these titles, and the groundwork of a solid culture, he returned to Eisenach, to wait for an appointment in the Church, of which he was now licentiate.

For several years, though he preached with ability, and not without approval, no appointment presented itself; and when at last a country living in the neighbourhood of Eisenach was offered him, the people stoutly resisted the admission of their new pastor, on the ground, says his Biographer, that "he had once been seen dancing." It may be, however, that the sentence of the peasants was not altogether so infirm as this its alleged very narrow basis would betoken: judging from external circumstances, it by no means appears that devotion was at any time the chief distinction of the new candidate; and to a simple rustic flock, his shining talents, unsupported by zeal, would be empty and unprofitable, as sounding brass or a tinkling cymbal. At all events, this hindrance closed his theological career: it came in good season to withdraw him from a calling, in which, whether willingly or unwillingly adopted, his history must have been dishonest and contemptible, and his gifts could never have availed him.

Musäus had now lost his profession; but his resources were not limited to one department of activity, and he was still young enough to choose another. His temper was gay and kindly; his faculties of mind were brilliant, and had now been improved by years of steady industry. His residence at Eisenach had not been spent in scrutinizing the phases of church preferment, or dancing attendance on patrons and dignitaries: he had stored his mind with useful and ornamental knowledge; and from his remote watch-tower, his keen eye had discerned the movements of the world, and firm judgments of its wisdom and its folly were gathering form in his thoughts. In his twenty-fifth year he became an author; a satirist, and what is rarer, a just one. Germany, by the report of its enemies and lukewarm friends, is seldom long without some Idol; some author of superhuman endowments, some system that promises to renovate the earth, some science destined to conduct, by a north-west passage, to universal knowledge. At this period, the Brazen Image of the day was our English Richardson: his novels had been translated into German with unbounded acceptance;* and *Grandison* was figuring in many weak heads as the sole model of a true Christian gentleman. Musäus published his *German Grandison* in 1760; a work of good omen as a first attempt, and received with greater favor than the popularity of its victim seemed to promise. It co-operated with Time in removing this spi-

---

* From Carlyle's German Romance.

* See the Letters of Meta, Klopstock's lady, in *Richardson's Life and Correspondence*.

(154)

ritual epidemic; and appears to have survived its object, for it was reprinted in 1781.

The success of his anonymous parody, however gratifying to the youthful author, did not tempt him to disclose his name, and still less to think of literature as a profession. With his cool sceptical temper, he was little liable to over-estimate his talents, or the prizes set up for them; and he longed much less for a literary existence than for a civic one. In 1763, his wish, to a certain extent, was granted: he became Tutor of the Pages in the court of Weimar; which office, after seven punctual and laborious years, he exchanged for a professorship in the *Gymnasium*, or public school of the same town. He had now married; and amid the cares and pleasures of providing for a family, and keeping house like an honest burgher, the dreams of fame had faded still farther from his mind. The emoluments of his post were small; but his heart was light, and his mind humble: to increase his income he gave private lessons in history and the like, "to young ladies and gentlemen of quality;" and for several years took charge of a few boarders. The names of Wieland and Goethe had now risen on the world, while his own was still under the horizon: but this obscurity, enjoying as he did the kind esteem of all his many personal acquaintances, he felt to be a very light evil; and participated without envy in whatever entertainment or instruction his famed contemporaries could afford him. With literature he still occupied his leisure; he had read and reflected much; but for any public display of his acquirements he was making no preparation, and feeling no anxiety.

After an interval of nineteen years, the appearance of a new idol again called forth his iconoclastic faculty. Lavater had left his parsonage among the Alps, and set out on a cruize over Europe, in search of proselytes and striking physiognomies. His theories, supported by his personal influence, and the honest rude ardor of his character, became the rage in Germany; and men, women, and children were immersed in promoting philanthropy, and studying the human mind. Whereupon Musäus grasped his satirical hammer; and with lusty strokes, defaced and unshrined the false divinity. His *Physiognomical Travels*, which appeared in 1779, is still ranked by the German critics among the happiest productions of its kind in their literature; and still read for its wit and acuteness, and genial overflowing humour, though the object it attacked has long ago become a reminiscence. At the time of its publication, when everything conspired to give its qualities their full effect, the applause it gained was instant and general. The author had, as in the former case, concealed his name: but the public curiosity soon penetrated the secret, which he had now no interest in keeping; and Musäus was forthwith enrolled among the lights of his day and generation; and courteous readers crowded to him from far and near, to see his face, and pay him the tribute of their admiration. This unlooked-for celebrity he valued at its just price; continuing to live as if it were not; gratified chiefly in his character of father, at having found an honest way of improving his domestic circumstances, and enlarging the comforts of his family. The ground was now broken, and he was not long in digging deeper.

The popular traditions of Germany, so numerous and often so impressive, had attracted his attention; and their rugged Gothic vigor, saddened into sternness or venerable grace by the flight of ages, became dearer to his taste, as he looked abroad upon the mawkish deluge of Sentimentality, with which *The Sorrows of Werter* had been the innocent signal for a legion of imitators to drown the land. The spirit of German imagination seemed but ill represented by these tearful persons, who, if their hearts were full, minded little though their heads were empty: their spasmodic tenderness made no imposing figure beside the gloomy strength, which might still in fragments be discerned in their distant predecessors. Of what has been preserved from age to age by living memory alone, the chance is that it possesses some intrinsic merit: its very existence declares it to be adapted to some form of our common nature, and therefore calculated more or less to interest all its forms. It struck Musäus that these rude traditionary fragments might be worked anew into shape and polish, and transferred from the hearths of the common people, to the parlors of the intellectual and refined. He determined on forming a series of *Volksmährchen*, or Popular Traditionary Tales; a task of more originality and smaller promise in those days than it would be now. In the collection of materials, he spared no pains; and despised no source of intelligence, however mean. He would call children from the street; become a child along with them, listen to their nursery tales, and reward his tiny narrators with a *dreyer* apiece. Sometimes he assembled a knot of old women, with their spinning-wheels, about him; and amid the hum of their industrious implements, gathered stories of the ancient time from the lips of the garrulous sisterhood. Once his wife had been out paying visits: on opening the parlor door at her return, she was met by a villanous cloud of tobacco-smoke; and venturing forward through the haze, she found her husband seated by the stove, in company with an old soldier, who was smoking vehemently on his black stump of pipe, and charming his landlord, between whiffs, with legendary lore.

The *Volksmährchen*, in five little volumes, appeared in 1782. They soon rose into favor with a large class of readers; and while many generations of novels have since that time been ushered into being, and conducted out of it, they still survive, increasing in popularity rather than declining. This pre-eminence is owing less to the ancient materials, than to the author's way of treating them. The primitive tradition often serves him only as a vehicle for interesting description, shrewd sarcastic speculation, and gay fanciful pleasantry, extending its allusions over all things past and present, now rising into comic humor, now sinking into drollery, often tasteless, strained, or tawdry, but never dull. The traces of poetry and earnest imagination, here and there discernible in the original fiction, he treats with levity and kind sceptical derision: nothing is required of the reader but what all readers are prepared to give. Since the publication of this work, the subject of popular tradition has been handled to triteness; *Volksmährchen* have been written and collected without stint or limit; and critics, in admitting that Musäus was the first to open this mine of entertainment, have lamented the incongruity between his subject and his style. But the faculty of laughing has been given to all men, and the feeling of imaginative beauty has been given only to a few: the lovers of primeval poetry, in its unadulterated state, may censure Musäus; but they join witn the public at large in reading him.

This book of *Volksmährchen* established the character of its author for wit and general talent, and forms the chief support of his reputation with posterity. A few years after, he again appeared before the public with a humorous performance, entitled, *Friend Hein's Apparitions, in the style of Holberg*, printed in 1785. *Friend Hein* is a name under which Musäus, for what reason his commentator Wieland seems unable to inform us, usually personifies Death: the essay itself, which I have never seen, may be less irreverent and offensive to pious feeling than its title indicates, and it is said to abound with "wit, humor, and knowledge of life," as much as any of his former works. He had also begun a second series of Tales, under the title of *Straussfedern* (Ostrich-feathers): but only the first volume had appeared, when death put a period to his labors. He had long been in weakly health: often afflicted with violent head-aches: his disorder was a polypus of the heart, which cut him off on the 28th of October 1787, in the fifty-second year of his age. The *Straussfedern* was completed by another hand; and a small volume of *Remains*, edited by Kotzebue in 1791, concludes the list of his writings. A simple but tasteful memorial, we are told, was erected over his grave by some unknown friend.

Musäus was a practical believer in the Horatian maxim, *Nil admirari:* of a jovial heart, and a penetrating, well-cultivated understanding, he saw things as they were, and had little disposition or aptitude to invest them with any colors but their own. Without much effort, therefore, he stood aloof from every species of cant; and *was* the man he thought himself, and wished others to think him. Had his temper been unsocial and melancholic, such a creed might have rendered him spiteful, narrow, and selfish: but nature had been kinder to him than education; he did not quarrel with the world, though he saw its barrenness, and knew not how to make it solemn any more than lovely; for his heart was gay and kind, and an imperturbable good-humor, more potent than a panoply of brass, defended him from the stings and arrows of outrageous Fortune to the end of his pilgrimage. Few laughers have walked so circumspectly, and acquired or merited so much affection. By profession a Momus, he looked upon the world as little else than a boundless Chase, where the wise were to recreate themselves with the hunting of Follies; and perhaps he is the only satirist on record of whom it can be said, that his jesting never cost him a friend. His humor is, indeed, untinctured with bitterness; sportful, ebullient, and guileless, as the frolics of a child. He could not reverence men; but with all their faults he loved them; for they were his brethren, and their faults were not clearer to him than his own. He inculcated or entertained no lofty principles of generosity; yet though never rich in purse, he was always ready to divide his pittance with a needier fellow-man. Of vanity, he showed little or none: in obscurity he was contented; and when his honors came, he wore them meekly, and was the last to see that they were merited. In society he was courteous and yielding; a universal favorite; in his chosen circle, the most fascinating of companions. From the slenderest trifle, he could spin a boundless web of drollery; and his brilliant mirth enlivened without wounding. With the foibles of others, he abstained from meddling; but among his friends, we are informed, he could for hours keep the table in a roar, when, with his dry inimitable vein, he started some banter on himself or his wife, and, in trustful abandonment, laid the reins on the neck of his fancy to pursue it. Without enthusiasm of character, or any pretension to high or even earnest qualities, he was a well-conditioned, laughter-loving, kindly man; led a gay, jestful life; conquering by contentment and mirth of heart, the long series of difficulties and distresses with which it assailed him; and died regretted by his nation, as a forwarder of harmless pleasure; and by those that knew him better, as a truthful, unassuming, affectionate, and, on the whole, very estimable person.

His intellectual character corresponds with his moral and social one; not high or glorious, but genuine so far as it goes. He does not approach the first rank of writers; he attempts not to deal with the deeper feelings of the heart; and for instructing the judgment, he ranks rather as a sound, well-informed, common-sense thinker, than as a man of high wisdom or originality. He advanced few new truths, but he dressed many old ones in sprightly apparel; and it ought to be remembered, that he kept himself unspotted from the errors of his time; a merit which posterity is apt to underrate; for nothing seems more stolid than a past delusion; and we forget that delusions, destined also to be past, are now present with ourselves, about us and within us, which were the task so easy, it is pity that we do not forthwith convict and cast away. Musäus had a quick vigorous intellect, a keen eye for the common forms of the beautiful, a fancy ever prompt with allusions, and an overflowing store of sprightly and benignant humor. These natural gifts he had not neglected to cultivate by study both of books and things; his reading distinguishes him even in Germany; nor does he bear it about him like an ostentatious burden, but in the shape of spiritual strength and plenty derived from it. As an author, his beauties and defects are numerous and easily discerned. His style sparkles with metaphors, sometimes just and beautiful, often new and surprising; but it is laborious, unnatural, and diffuse. Of his humor, his distinguishing gift, it may be remarked, that it seems copious rather than fine, and originates rather in the understanding than in the character: his heart is not delicate, or his affections tender; but he loves the ludicrous with true passion; and seeing keenly, if he feels obtusely, he can choose with sufficient skill the point of view from which his object shall appear distorted, as he requires it. This is the humor of a Swift or a Voltaire, but not of a Cervantes, or even of a Sterne in his best passages; it may produce a *Zadig* or a *Battle of the Books;* but not a *Don Quixote* or a *Corporal Trim.* Musäus is, in fact, no poet; he can see, and describe with rich graces what he sees; but he is nothing, or very little, of a maker. His imagination is not powerless: it is like a bird of feeble wing, which can fly from tree to tree; but never soars for a moment into the æther of Poetry, to bathe in its serene splendor, with the region of the Actual lying far below, and brightened into beauty by radiance not its own. He is a man of fine and varied talent, but scarcely of any genius.

These characteristics are apparent enough in his Popular Tales; they may be traced even in the few specimens of that work, by which he is now introduced to the English reader. As has been already stated, his *Volksmährchen* exhibit himself much better than his subject. He is not admitted by his critics to have seized the finest spirit of this species of fiction, or turned it to the account of which it is capable in other hands. Whatever was austere or earnest, still more, whatever bordered upon awe or horror, his riant fancy rejected with aversion: the rigorous moral sometimes hid in these traditions, the grim lines of primeval feeling and imagination to be traced in them, had no charms for him. These ruins of the remote time he has not attempted to complete into a perfect edifice, according to the first simple plan; he has rather pargetted them anew, and decorated them with the most modern ornaments and furniture; and he introduces his guests, with a roguish smile at the strange, antic contrast they are to perceive between the movables and the apartment. Sometimes he rises into a flight of simple eloquence, and for a sentence or two, seems really beautiful and affecting; but the knave is always laughing in his sleeve at our credulity, and returns with double relish to riot at will in his favorite domain.

Of the three Tales* here offered to the reader, nothing need be said in explanation; for their whole significance, with all their beauties and

---

* Only one is given in this volume.—Ed.

blemishes, lies very near the surface. I have selected them, as specimens at once of his manner and his materials, in the hope that, conveying some impression of a gifted and favorite writer, they may furnish a little entertainment both to the lovers of intellectual novelty, and of innocent amusement. To neither can I promise very much: Musäus is a man of sterling powers, but no literary monster; and his Tales, though smooth and glittering, are cold; they have beauty, yet it is the beauty not of living forms, but of well-proportioned statues. Meanwhile, I have given him as I found him, endeavoring to copy faithfully; changing nothing, whether I might think it good or bad, that my skill enabled me to keep unchanged. With all drawbacks, I anticipate some favor for him: but his case admits no pleading; being clear by its own light, it must stand or fall by a first judgment, and without the help of advocates.

DUMB LOVE.

THERE was once a wealthy merchant, Melchior of Bremen by name, who used to stroke his beard with a contemptuous grin, when he heard the Rich Man in the Gospel preached of, whom, in comparison, he reckoned little better than a petty shopkeeper. Melchior had money in such plenty, that he floored his dining-room all over with a coat of solid dollars. In those frugal times, as in our own, a certain luxury prevailed among the rich; only then it had a more substantial shape than now. But though this pomp of Melchior's was sharply censured by his fellow-citizens and consorts, it was, in truth, directed more to trading speculation than to mere vain-glory. The cunning Bremer easily observed, that those who grudged and blamed this seeming vanity, would but diffuse the reputation of his wealth, and so increase his credit. He gained his purpose to the full; the sleeping capital of old dollars, so judiciously set up for public inspection in the parlour, brought interest a hundred fold, by the silent surety which it offered for his bargains in every market; yet, at last, it became a rock on which the welfare of his family made shipwreck.

Melchior of Bremen died of a surfeit at a city-feast, without having time to set his house in order; and left all his goods and chattels to an only son, in the bloom of life, and just arrived at the years when the laws allowed him to take possession of his inheritance. Franz Melcherson was a brilliant youth, endued by nature with the best capacities. His exterior was gracefully formed, yet firm and sinewy withal; his temper was cheery and jovial, as if hung-beef and old French wine had joined to influence his formation. On his cheeks bloomed health; and from his brown eyes looked mirthfulness and love of joy. He was like a marrowy plant, which needs but water and the poorest ground to make it grow to strength; but which, in too fat a soil, will shoot into luxuriant overgrowth, without fruit or usefulness. The father's heritage, as often happens, proved the ruin of the son. Scarce had he felt the joy of being sole possessor and disposer of a large fortune, when he set about endeavouring to get rid of it as of a galling burden; began to play the Rich Man in the Gospel to the very letter; went clothed in fine apparel, and fared sumptuously every day. No feast at the bishop's court could be compared for pomp and superfluity with his; and never while the town of Bremen shall endure, will such another public dinner be consumed, as it yearly got from him; for to every burgher of the place he gave a Krusel-soup and a jug of Spanish wine. For this, all people cried: Long life to him! and Franz became the hero of the day.

In this unceasing whirl of joviality, no thought was cast upon the Balancing of Entries, which, in those days, was the merchant's vademecum, though in our times it is going out of fashion, and for want of it the tongue of the commercial beam too frequently declines with a magnetic virtue from the vertical position. Some years passed on without the joyful Franz's noticing a diminution in his incomes; for at his father's death every chest and coffer had been full. The voracious host of table-friends, the airy company of jesters, gamesters, parasites, and all who had their living by the prodigal son, took special care to keep reflection at a distance from him; they hurried him from one enjoyment to another; kept him constantly in play, lest in some sober moment Reason might awake, and snatch him from their plundering claws.

But at last their well of happiness went suddenly dry; old Melchior's casks of gold were now run off even to the lees. One day, Franz ordered payment of a large account; his cash-keeper was not in a state to execute the precept, and returned it with a protest. This counter-incident flashed keenly through the soul of Franz; yet he felt nothing else but anger and vexation at his servant, to whose unaccountable perversity, by no means to his own ill husbandry, he charged the present disorder in his finances. Nor did he give himself the trouble to investigate the real condition of the business; but after flying to the common Fool's-litany, and thundering out some scores of curses, he transmitted to his shoulder-shrugging steward the laconic order: Find means.

Bill-brokers, usurers, and money-changers now came into play. For high interest, fresh sums were poured into the empty coffers; the silver flooring of the dining-room was then more potent in the eyes of creditors, than in these times of ours the promissory obligation of the Congress of America, with the whole thirteen United States to back it. This palliative succeeded for a season; but, underhand, the rumour spread about the town, that the silver flooring had been privily removed, and a stone one substituted in its stead. The matter was immediately, by application of the lenders, legally inquired into, and discovered to be actually so. Now, it could not be denied, that a marble-floor, worked into nice Mosaic, looked much better in a parlour, than a sheet of dirty, tarnished dollars: the creditors, however, paid so little reverence to the proprietor's refinement of taste, that on the spot they, one and all, demanded payment of their several moneys; and as this was not complied with, they proceeded to procure an act of bankruptcy; and Melchior's house, with its appurtenances, offices, gardens, parks, and furniture, were sold by public auction, and their late owner, who in this extremity had screened himself from jail by some chicanery of law, judicially ejected.

It was now too late to moralize on his absurdities, since philosophical reflections could not alter what was done, and the most wholesome resolutions would not bring him back his money. According to the principles of this our cultivated century, the hero at this juncture ought to have retired with dignity from the stage, or in some way terminated his existence; to have entered on his travels into foreign parts, or opened his carotid artery; since in his native town he could live no longer as a man of honour. Franz neither did the one nor the other. The *qu'en-dira-t-on*, which French morality employs as bit and curb for thoughtlessness and folly, had never once occurred to the unbridled squanderer in the days of his profusion, and his sensibility was still too dull to feel so keenly the disgrace of his capricious wastefulness. He was like a toper, who has been in drink, and on awakening out of his carousal, cannot rightly understand how matters are or have been with him. He lived according to the manner of unprospering spendthrifts; repented not, lamented not. By good fortune, he had picked some relics from the wreck; a few small heir-looms of the family; and these secured him for a time from absolute starvation.

He engaged a lodging in a remote alley, into which the sun never shone throughout the year, except for a few days about the solstice, when it peeped for a short while over the high roofs. Here he found the little that his now much-contracted wants required. The frugal kitchen of his landlord screened him from hunger, the stove from cold, the roof from rain, the four walls from wind; only from the pains of tedium he could devise no refuge or resource. The light rabble of parasites had fled away with his prosperity; and of his former friends there was now no one that knew him. Reading had not yet become a necessary of life; people did not yet understand the art of killing time by means of those amusing shapes of fancy which are wont to lodge in empty heads. There were yet no sentimental, pedagogic, psychologic, popular, simple, comic, or moral tales; no novels of domestic life, no cloister-stories, no romances of the middle ages; and of the innumerable generation of our Henrys, and Adelaides, and Cliffords, and Emmas, no one had as yet lifted up its mantua-maker voice, to weary out the patience of a lazy and discerning public. In those days, knights were still diligently pricking round the tilt-yard; Dietrich of Bern, Hildebrand, Seyfried with the Horns, Rennewart the Strong, were following their snake and dragon hunt, and killing giants and dwarfs of twelve men's strength. The venerable epos, *Theuerdank*, was the loftiest ideal of German art and skill, the latest product of our native wit, but only for the cultivated minds, the poets and thinkers of the age. Franz belonged to none of those classes, and had therefore nothing to employ himself upon, except that he tuned his lute, and sometimes twanged a little on it; then, by way of variation, took to looking from the window, and instituted observations on the weather; out of which, indeed, there came no inference a whit more edifying than from all the labours of the most rheumatic meteorologist of this present age. Meanwhile, his turn for observation ere long found another sort of nourishment, by which the vacant space in his head and heart was at once filled.

In the narrow lane right opposite his window, dwelt an honest matron, who, in hope of better times, was earning a painful living by the long threads, which, assisted by a marvellously fair daughter, she winded daily from her spindle. Day after day the couple spun a length of yarn, with which the whole town of Bremen, with its walls and trenches, and all its suburbs, might have been begirt. These two spinners had not been born for the wheel; they were of good descent, and had lived of old in pleasant affluence. The fair Meta's father had once had a ship of his own on the sea, and, freighting it himself, had yearly sailed to Antwerp; but a heavy storm had sunk the vessel, "with man and mouse," and a rich cargo, into the abysses of the ocean, before Meta had passed the years of her childhood. The mother, a staid and reasonable woman, bore the loss of her husband and all her fortune with a wise composure; in her need she refused, out of noble pride, all help from the charitable sympathy of her relations and friends; considering it as shameful alms, so long as she believed, that in her own activity she might find a living by the labour of her hands. She gave up her large house, and all her costly furniture, to the rigorous creditors of her ill-fated husband, hired a little dwelling in the lane, and span from early morning till late night, though the trade went sore against her, and she often wetted the thread with her tears. Yet by this diligence she reached her object, of depending upon no one, and owing no mortal any obligation. By and by she trained her growing daughter to the same employment; and lived so thriftily, that she laid by a trifle of her gainings, and turned it to account by carrying on a little trade in flax.

She, however, nowise purposed to conclude her life in these poor circumstances; on the contrary, the honest dame kept up her heart with happy prospects into the future, and hoped that she should once more attain a prosperous situation, and in the autumn of her life enjoy her woman's-summer. Nor were these hopes grounded altogether upon empty dreams of fancy, but upon a rational and calculated expectation. She saw her daughter budding up like a spring rose, no less virtuous and modest than she was fair; and with such endowments of heart and spirit, that the mother felt delight and comfort in her, and spared the morsel from her own lips, that nothing might be wanting in an education suitable to her capacities. For she thought, that if a maiden could come up to the sketch which Solomon, the wise friend of woman, has left of the ideal of a perfect wife, it could not fail that a pearl of such price would be sought after, and bidden for, to ornament some good man's house; for beauty, combined with virtue, in the days of Mother Brigitta, were as important in the eyes of wooers, as, in our days, birth combined with fortune. Besides, the number of suitors was in those times greater; it was then believed that the wife was the most essential, not, as in our refined economical theory, the most superfluous item in the household. The fair Meta, it is true, bloomed only like a precious rare flower in the green-house, not under the gay, free sky; she lived in maternal oversight and keeping, sequestered and still; was seen in no walk, in no company; and scarcely once in the year passed through the gate of her native town; all which seemed utterly to contradict her mother's principle. The old Lady E—— of Memel understood it otherwise, in her time. She sent the itinerant Sophia, it is clear as day, from Memel into Saxony, simply on a marriage speculation, and attained her purpose fully. How many hearts did the wandering nymph set on fire, how many suitors courted her? Had she stayed at home, as a domestic modest maiden, she might have bloomed away in the remoteness of her virgin cell, without even making a conquest of Kubbuz the schoolmaster. Other times, other manners. Daughters with us are a sleeping capital, which must be put in circulation if it is to yield any interest; of old, they were kept like thrifty savings, under lock and key; yet the bankers still knew where the treasure lay concealed, and how it might be come at. Mother Brigitta steered towards some prosperous son-in-law, who might lead her back from the Babylonian captivity of the narrow lane into the land of superfluity, flowing with milk and honey; and trusted firmly, that in the urn of Fate, her daughter's lot would not be coupled with a blank.

One day, while neighbour Franz was looking from the window, making observations on the weather, he perceived the charming Meta coming with her mother from church, whither she went daily, to attend mass. In the times of his abundance, the unstable voluptuary had been blind to the fairer half of the species; the finer feelings were still slumbering in his breast; and all his senses had been overclouded by the ceaseless tumult of debauchery. But now the stormy waves of extravagance had subsided; and in this deep calm, the smallest breath of air sufficed to curl the mirror surface of his soul. He was enchanted by the aspect of this, the loveliest female figure that had ever flitted past him. He abandoned from that hour the barren study of the winds and clouds, and now instituted quite another set of Observations for the furtherance of Moral Science, and one which afforded to himself much finer occupation. He soon extracted from his landlord intelligence of this fair neighbour, and learned most part of what we know already.

Now rose on him the first repentant thought for his heedless squandering; there awoke a secret good-will in his heart to this new acquaintance; and for her sake he wished that his paternal inheritance were his own again, that the lovely Meta might be fitly dowered with it. His garret in the narrow lane was now so dear to him, that he would not have exchanged it with the Schudding itself.*

---

* One of the largest buildings in Bremen, where the meetings of the merchants are usually held.

Throughout the day he stirred not from the window, watching for an opportunity of glancing at the dear maiden; and when she chanced to show herself, he felt more rapture in his soul than did Horrox in his Liverpool Observatory, when he saw, for the first time, Venus passing over the disk of the Sun.

Unhappily the watchful mother instituted counter-observations, and ere long discovered what the lounger on the other side was driving at; and as Franz, in the capacity of spendthrift, already stood in very bad esteem with her, this daily gazing angered her so much, that she shrouded her lattice as with a cloud, and drew the curtains close together. Meta had the strictest orders not again to appear at the window; and when her mother went with her to mass, she drew a rain-cap over her face, disguised her like a favourite of the Grand Signior, and hurried till she turned the corner with her, and escaped the eyes of the lier-in-wait.

Of Franz, it was not held that penetration was his master faculty; but Love awakens all the talents of the mind. He observed, that by his imprudent spying, he had betrayed himself; and he thenceforth retired from the window, with the resolution not again to look out at it, though the *Venerabile* itself were carried by. On the other hand, he meditated some invention for proceeding with his observations in a private manner; and without great labour, his combining spirit mastered it.

He hired the largest looking-glass that he could find, and hung it up in his room, with such an elevation and direction, that he could distinctly see whatever passed in the dwelling of his neighbours. Here, as for several days the watcher did not come to light, the screens by degrees went asunder; and the broad mirror now and then could catch the form of the noble maid, and, to the great refreshment of the virtuoso, cast it truly back. The more deeply love took root in his heart,* the more widely did his wishes extend. It now struck him that he ought to lay his passion open to the fair Meta, and investigate the corresponding state of her opinions. The commonest and readiest way which lovers, under such a constellation of their wishes, strike into, was in his position inaccessible. In those modest ages, it was always difficult for Paladins in love to introduce themselves to daughters of the family; toilette calls were not in fashion; trustful interviews tête-a-tête were punished by the loss of reputation to the female sharer; promenades, esplanades, masquerades, pic-nics, goutés, soupés, and other inventions of modern wit for forwarding sweet courtship, had not then been hit upon; yet, notwithstanding, all things went their course, much as they do with us. Gossipings, weddings, lykewakes, were, especially in our Imperial Cities, privileged vehicles for carrying on soft secrets, and expediting marriage contracts: hence the old proverb, *One wedding makes a score*. But a poor runagate no man desired to number among his baptismal relatives; to no nuptial dinner, to no wake-supper, was he bidden. The by-way of negotiating, with the woman, with the young maid, or any other serviceable spirit of a go-between, was here locked up. Mother Brigitta had neither maid nor woman; the flax and yarn trade passed through no hands but her own; and she abode by her daughter as closely as her shadow.

In these circumstances, it was clearly impossible for neighbour Franz to disclose his heart to the fair Meta, either verbally or in writing. Ere long, however, he invented an idiom, which appeared expressly calculated for the utterance of the passions. It is true, the honour of the first invention is not his. Many ages ago, the sentimental Celadons of Italy and Spain had taught melting harmonies, in serenades beneath the balconies of their dames, to speak the language of the heart; and it is said that this melodious pathos had especial virtue in love matters; and, by the confession of the ladies, was more heart-affecting and subduing, than of yore the oratory of the reverend Chrysostom, or the pleadings of Demosthenes and Tully. But of all this the simple Bremer had not heard a syllable; and, consequently, the invention of expressing his emotions in symphonious notes, and trilling them to his beloved Meta, was entirely his own.

In an hour of sentiment, he took his lute: he did not now tune it merely to accompany his voice, but drew harmonious melodies from its strings; and Love, in less than a month, had changed the musical scraper to a new Amphion. His first efforts did not seem to have been noticed; but soon the population of the lane were all ear, every time the dilettante struck a note. Mothers hushed their children, fathers drove the noisy urchins from the doors, and the performer had the satisfaction to observe that Meta herself, with her alabaster hand, would sometimes open the window as he began to prelude. If he succeeded in enticing her to lend an ear, his voluntaries whirled along in gay *allegro*, or skipped away in mirthful jigs; but if the turning of the spindle, or her thrifty mother, kept her back, a heavy-laden *andante* rolled over the bridge of the sighing lute, and expressed, in languishing modulations, the feeling of sadness which love-pain poured over his soul.

Meta was no dull scholar; she soon learned to interpret this expressive speech. She made various experiments to try whether she had rightly understood it, and found that she could govern at her will the dilettante humours of the unseen lute-twanger; for your silent modest maidens, it is well known, have a much sharper eye than those giddy flighty girls, who hurry with the levity of butterflies from one object to another, and take proper heed of none. She felt her female vanity a little flattered; and it pleased her that she had it in her power, by a

---

* Ἀπὸ τοῦ ὁρᾷν ἔρχεται τὸ ἐρᾷν.

secret magic, to direct the neighbouring lute, and tune it now to the note of joy, now to the whimpering moan of grief. Mother Brigitta. on the other hand, had her head so constantly employed with her traffic on the small scale, that she minded none of these things; and the sly little daughter took especial care to keep her in the dark respecting the discovery; and, instigated either by some touch of kindness for her cooing neighbour, or perhaps by vanity, that she might show her hermeneutic penetration, meditated on the means of making some symbolical response to these harmonious apostrophes to her heart. She expressed a wish to have flower-pots on the outside of the window; and to grant her this innocent amusement was a light thing for the mother, who no longer feared the coney-catching neighbour, now that she no longer saw him with her eyes.

Henceforth Meta had a frequent call to tend her flowers, to water them, to bind them up, and guard them from approaching storms, and watch their growth and flourishing. With inexpressible delight the happy Franz explained this hieroglyphic altogether in his favour; and the speaking lute did not fail to modulate his glad emotions, through the alley, into the heedful ear of the fair friend of flowers. This, in her tender virgin heart, worked wonders. She began to be secretly vexed, when Mother Brigitta, in her wise table-talk, in which at times she spent an hour chatting with her daughter, brought their melodious neighbour to her bar, and called him a losel and a sluggard, or compared him with the Prodigal in the Gospel. She always took his part; threw the blame of his ruin on the sorrowful temptations he had met with; and accused him of nothing worse than not having fitly weighed the golden proverb, *A penny saved is a penny got*. Yet she defended him with cunning prudence; so that it rather seemed as if she wished to help the conversation, than took any interest in the thing itself.

While Mother Brigitta within her four walls was inveighing against the luckless spendthrift, he on his side entertained the kindest feelings towards her; and was considering diligently how he might, according to his means, improve her straitened circumstances, and divide with her the little that remained to him, and so that she might never notice that a portion of his property had passed over into hers. This pious outlay, in good truth, was specially intended not for the mother, but the daughter. Underhand he had come to know, that the fair Meta had a hankering for a new gown, which her mother had excused herself from buying, under pretext of hard times. Yet he judged quite accurately, that a present of a piece of stuff, from an unknown hand, would scarcely be received, or cut into a dress for Meta; and that he should spoil all, if he stept forth and avowed himself the author of the benefaction. Chance afforded him an opportunity to realize this purpose in the way he wished.

Mother Brigitta was complaining to a neighbour, that flax was very dull; that it cost her more to purchase than the buyers of it would repay; and that hence this branch of industry was nothing better, for the present, than a withered bough. Eaves-dropper Franz did not need a second telling; he ran directly to the goldsmith, sold his mother's ear-rings, bought some stones of flax, and, by means of a negotiatress, whom he gained, had it offered to the mother for a cheap price. The bargain was concluded; and it yielded so richly, that on All-Saints' day the fair Meta sparkled in a fine new gown. In this decoration she had such a splendour in her watchful neighbour's eyes, that he would have overlooked the Eleven Thousand Virgins, all and sundry, had it been permitted him to choose a heart's-mate from among them, and fixed upon the charming Meta.

But just as he was triumphing in the result of his innocent deceit, the secret was betrayed. Mother Brigitta had resolved to do the flax-retailer, who had brought her that rich gain, a kindness in her turn; and was treating her with a well-sugared rice-pap, and a quarter-stoop of Spanish sack. This dainty set in motion not only the toothless jaw, but also the garrulous tongue of the crone: she engaged to continue the flax-brokerage, should her consigner feel inclined, as from good grounds she guessed he would. One word produced another; Mother Eve's two daughters searched, with the curiosity peculiar to their sex, till at length the brittle seal of female secresy gave way. Meta grew pale with affright at the discovery, which would have charmed her, had her mother not partaken of it. But she knew her strict ideas of morals and decorum; and these gave her doubts about the preservation of her gown. The serious dame herself was no less struck at the tidings, and wished, on her side too, that she alone had got intelligence of the specific nature of her flax-trade; for she dreaded that this neighbourly munificence might make an impression on her daughter's heart, which would derange her whole calculations. She resolved, therefore, to root out the still tender germ of this weed, in the very act, from the maiden heart. The gown, in spite of all the tears and prayers of its lovely owner, was first hypothecated, and next day transmitted to the huckster's shop; the money raised from it, with the other profits of the flax speculation, accurately reckoned up, were packed together, and under the name of an old debt, returned to "Mr. Franz Melcherson, in Bremen," by help of the Hamburg post. The receiver, nothing doubting, took the little lot of money as an unexpected blessing; wished that all his father's debtors would clear off their old scores as conscientiously as this honest unknown person; and had not the smallest notion of the real position of affairs. The talking brokeress, of course, was far from giving him a true disclosure of her blabbing;

she merely told him, that Mother Brigitta had given up her flax-trade.

Meanwhile, the mirror taught him, that the aspects over the way had altered greatly in a single night. The flower-pots were entirely vanished; and the cloudy veil again obscured the friendly horizon of the opposite window. Meta was seldom visible; and if for a moment, like the silver moon from among her clouds in a stormy night, she did appear, her countenance was troubled, the fire of her eyes was extinguished, and it seemed to him, that, at times, with her finger, she pressed away a pearly tear. This seized him sharply by the heart; and his lute resounded melancholy sympathy in soft Lydian mood. He grieved, and meditated to discover why his love was sad; but all his thinking and imagining were vain. After some days were past, he noticed, to his consternation, that his dearest piece of furniture, the large mirror, had become entirely useless. He set himself one bright morning in his usual nook, and observed that the clouds over the way had, like natural fog, entirely dispersed; a sign which he at first imputed to a general washing; but ere long he saw that, in the chamber, all was waste and empty; his pleasing neighbours had in silence withdrawn the night before, and broken up their quarters.

He might now, once more, with the greatest leisure and convenience, enjoy the free prospect from his window, without fear of being troublesome to any; but for him, it was a dead loss to miss the kind countenance of his Platonic love. Mute and stupified, he stood, as of old his fellow-craftsman, the harmonious Orpheus, when the dear shadow of his Eurydice again vanished down to Orcus; and if the bedlam humour of those "noble minds," who raved among us through the by-gone lustre, but have now like drones disappeared with the earliest frost, had then been ripened to existence, this calm of his would certainly have passed into a sudden hurricane. The least he could have done, would have been to pull his hair, to trundle himself about upon the ground, or run his head against the wall, and break his stove and window. All this he omitted; from the very simple cause, that true love never makes men fools, but rather is the universal remedy for healing sick minds of their foolishness, for laying gentle fetters on extravagance, and guiding youthful giddiness from the broad way of ruin to the narrow path of reason; for the rake whom love will not recover, is lost irrecoverably.

When once his spirit had assembled its scattered powers, he set on foot a number of instructive meditations on the unexpected phenomenon, but too visible in the adjacent horizon. He readily conceived that he was the lever which had effected the removal of the wandering colony: his money-letter, the abrupt conclusion of the flax-trade, and the emigration which had followed thereupon, were like reciprocal exponents to each other, and explained the whole to him. He perceived that Mother Brigitta had got round his secrets, and saw from every circumstance that he was not her hero; a discovery which yielded him but little satisfaction. The symbolic responses of the fair Meta, with her flower-pots, to his musical proposals of love; her trouble, and the tear which he had noticed in her bright eyes shortly before her departure from the lane, again animated his hopes, and kept him in good heart. His first employment was to go in quest, and try to learn where Mother Brigitta had pitched her residence, in order to maintain, by some means or other, his secret understanding with the daughter. It cost him little toil to find her abode; yet he was too modest to shift his own lodging to her neighbourhood; but satisfied himself with spying out the church where she now attended mass, that he might treat himself once each day with a glance of his beloved. He never failed to meet her as she returned, now here, now there, in some shop or door which she was passing, and salute her kindly; an equivalent for a *billet-doux*, and productive of the same effect.

Had not Meta been brought up in a style too nun-like, and guarded by her rigid mother as a treasure, from the eyes of thieves, there is little doubt that neighbour Franz, with his secret wooing, would have made no great impression on her heart. But she was at the critical age, when Mother Nature and Mother Brigitta, with their wise nurture, were perpetually coming into collision. The former taught her, by a secret instinct, the existence of emotions, for which she had no name, and eulogized them as the panacea of life; the latter warned her to beware of the surprisals of a passion, which she would not designate by its true title, but which, as she maintained, was more pernicious and destructive to young maidens than the small-pox itself. The former, in the spring of life, as beseemed the season, enlivened her heart with a genial warmth; the latter wished that it should always be as cold and frosty as an ice-house. These conflicting pedagogic systems of the two good mothers, gave the tractable heart of the daughter the direction of a ship, which is steered against the wind, and follows neither the wind nor the helm, but a course between the two. She maintained the modesty and virtue which her education, from her youth upwards, had impressed upon her; but her heart continued open to all tender feelings. And as neighbour Franz was the first youth who had awakened these slumbering emotions, she took a certain pleasure in him, which she scarcely owned to herself, but which any less unexperienced maiden would have recognised as love. It was for this that her departure from the narrow lane had gone so near her heart; for this that the little tear had trickled from her beautiful eyes; for this that, when the watchful Franz saluted her as she came from church, she thanked him so kindly, and grew scarlet to the ears. The lovers had in truth never spoken any word to one another; but he understood her, and she him, so perfectly, that in the most secret interview they could not have explained themselves more clearly; and both contracting parties swore in their silent hearts, each for himself, under the seal of secresy, the oath of faithfulness to the other.

In the quarter, where Mother Brigitta had now settled, there were likewise neighbours, and among these likewise girl-spiers, whom the beauty of the charming Meta had not escaped. Right opposite their dwelling, lived a wealthy Brewer, whom the wags of the part, as he was strong in means, had named the Hop-King. He was a young, stout widower, whose mourning year was just concluding, so that now he was entitled, without offending the precepts of decorum, to look about him elsewhere for a new helpmate to his household. Shortly after the departure of his whilom wife, he had in secret entered into an engagement with his Patron Saint, St. Christopher, to offer him a wax-taper as long as a hop-pole, and as thick as a mashing-beam, if he would vouchsafe in this second choice to prosper the desire of his heart. Scarcely had he seen the dainty Meta, when he dreamed that St. Christopher looked in upon him, through the window of his bed-room in the second story,* and demanded payment of his debt. To the quick widower this seemed a heavenly call to cast out the net without delay. Early in the morning he sent for the brokers of the town, and commissioned them to buy bleached wax; then decked himself like a Syndic, and set forth to expedite his marriage speculation. He had no musical talents, and in the secret symbolic language of love he was no better than a blockhead; but he had a rich brewery, a solid mortgage on the city-revenues, a ship on the Weser, and a farm without the gates. With such recommendations, he might have reckoned on a prosperous issue to his courtship, independently of all assistance from St. Kit, especially as his bride was without dowry.

According to old use and wont, he went directly to the master hand, and disclosed to the mother, in a kind neighbourly way, his christian intentions towards her virtuous and honourable daughter. No angel's visit could have charmed the good lady more than these glad tidings. She now saw ripening before her the fruit of her prudent scheme, and the fulfilment of her hope again to emerge from her present poverty into her former abundance; she blessed the good thought of moving from the crooked alley, and in the first ebullition of her joy, as a thousand gay ideas were ranking themselves up within her soul, she also thought of neighbour Franz, who had given occasion to it. Though Franz was not exactly her bosom-youth, she silently resolved to gladden him, as the accidental instrument of her rising star, with some secret gift or other, and by this means likewise recompense his well-intended flax-dealing.

In the maternal heart the marriage-articles were as good as signed; but decorum did not permit these rash proceedings in a matter of such moment. She therefore let the motion lie *ad referendum*, to be considered by her daughter and herself; and appointed a term of eight days, after which "she hoped she should have it in her power to give the much-respected suitor a reply that would satisfy him;" all which, as the common manner of proceeding, he took in good part, and with his usual civilities withdrew. No sooner had he turned his back, than spinning-wheel and reel, swingling-stake and hatchel, without regard being paid to their faithful services, and without accusation being lodged against them, were consigned, like some luckless Parliament of Paris, to disgrace, and dismissed as useless implements into the lumber-room. On returning from mass, Meta was astonished at the sudden catastrophe which had occurred in the apartment; it was all decked out as on one of the three high Festivals of the year. She could not understand how her thrifty mother, on a work-day, had so neglectfully put her active hand in her bosom; but before she had time to question the kindly-smiling dame concerning this reform in household affairs, she was favoured by the latter with an explanation of the riddle. Persuasion rested on Brigitta's tongue; and there flowed from her lips a stream of female eloquence, depicting the offered happiness in the liveliest hues which her imagination could lay on. She expected from the chaste Meta the blush of soft virgin bashfulness, which announces the noviciate in love; and then a full resignation of herself to the maternal will. For of old, in proposals of marriage, daughters were situated as our princesses are still; they were not asked about their inclination, and had no voice in the selection of their legal helpmate, save the Yes before the altar.

But Mother Brigitta was in this point widely mistaken; the fair Meta did not at the unexpected announcement grow red as a rose, but pale as ashes. An hysterical giddiness swam over her brain, and she sank fainting in her mother's arms. When her senses were recalled by the sprinkling of cold water, and she had in some degree recovered strength, her eyes overflowed with tears, as if a heavy misfortune had befallen her. From all these symptoms, the sagacious mother easily perceived that the marriage-trade was not to her taste; at which she wondered not a little, sparing neither prayers nor admonitions to her daughter to secure her happiness by this good match, not flout it from her by caprice and contradiction. But Meta could not be persuaded that her happiness de-

---

* St. Christopher never appears to his favourites, like the other Saints, in a solitary room, encircled with a glory: there is no room high enough to admit him; thus the celestial Son of Anak is obliged to transact all business with his wards outside the window.

pended on a match to which her heart gave no assent. The debates between the mother and the daughter lasted several days, from early morning to late night: the term for decision was approaching; the sacred taper for St. Christopher, which Og King of Bashan need not have disdained had it been lit for him as a marriage torch at his espousals, stood in readiness, all beautifully painted with living flowers like a many-coloured light, though the Saint had all the while been so inactive in his client's cause, that the fair Meta's heart was still bolted and barred against him fast as ever.

Meanwhile she had bleared her eyes with weeping, and the maternal rhetoric had worked so powerfully, that, like a flower in the sultry heat, she was drooping together, and visibly fading away. Hidden grief was gnawing at her heart; she had prescribed herself a rigorous fast, and for three days no morsel had she eaten, and with no drop of water moistened her parched lips. By night sleep never visited her eyes; and with all this she grew sick to death, and began to talk about extreme unction. As the tender mother saw the pillar of her hope wavering, and bethought herself that she might lose both capital and interest at once, she found, on accurate consideration, that it would be more advisable to let the latter vanish, than to miss them both; and with kindly indulgence plied into the daughter's will. It cost her much constraint, indeed, and many hard battles, to turn away so advantageous an offer; yet at last, according to established order in household governments, she yielded unconditionally to the inclination of her child, and remonstrated no more with her beloved patient on the subject. As the stout widower announced himself on the appointed day, in the full trust that his heavenly deputy had arranged it all according to his wish, he received, quite unexpectedly, a negative answer, which, however, was sweetened with such a deal of blandishment, that he swallowed it like wine-of-wormwood mixed with sugar. For the rest, he easily accommodated himself to his destiny; and discomposed himself no more about it, than if some bargain for a ton of malt had chanced to come to nothing. Nor, on the whole, had he any cause to sorrow without hope. His native town has never wanted amiable daughters, who come up to the Solomonic sketch, and are ready to make perfect spouses; besides, notwithstanding this unprospered courtship, he depended with firm confidence upon his Patron Saint; who in fact did him such substantial service elsewhere, that ere a month elapsed, he had planted, with much pomp, his devoted taper at the friendly shrine.

Mother Brigitta was now fain to recall the exiled spinning-tackle from its lumber-room, and again set it in action. All once more went its usual course. Meta soon bloomed out anew, was active in business, and diligently went to mass; but the mother could not hide her secret grudging at the failure of her hopes, and the annihilation of her darling plan; she was splenetic, peevish, and dejected. Her ill-humour had especially the upper hand that day when neighbour Hop-King held his nuptials. As the wedding-company proceeded to the church, with the town-band bedrumming and becymballing them in the van, she whimpered and sobbed as in the evil hour when the Job's-news reached her, that the wild sea had devoured her husband, with ship and fortune. Meta looked at the bridal-pomp with great equanimity; even the royal ornaments, the jewels in the myrtle-crown, and the nine strings of true pearls about the neck of the bride, made no impression on her peace of mind; a circumstance in some degree surprising, since a new Paris cap, or any other meteor in the gallery of Mode, will so frequently derange the contentment and domestic peace of an entire parish. Nothing but the heart-consuming sorrow of her mother discomposed her, and overclouded the gay look of her eyes; she strove by a thousand caresses and little attentions to work herself into favour; and she so far succeeded that the good lady grew a little more communicative.

In the evening, when the wedding-dance began, she said, "Ah, child! this merry dance it might have been thy part to lead off. What a pleasure, hadst thou recompensed thy mother's care and toil with this joy! But thou hast mocked thy happiness, and now I shall never see the day when I am to attend thee to the altar."— "Dear mother," answered Meta, "I confide in Heaven; and if it is written above that I am to be led to the altar, you will surely deck my garland: for when the right wooer comes, my heart will soon say Yes."—"Child, for girls without dowry there is no press of wooers; they are heavy ware to trade with. Now-a-days the bachelors are mighty stingy; they court to be happy, not to make happy. Besides, thy planet bodes thee no good; thou wert born in April. Let us see how it is written in the Calendar; 'A damsel born in this month is comely of countenance, slender of shape, but of changeful humour, has a liking to men. Should have an eye upon her maiden garland, and so a laughing wooer come, not miss her therewith.' Alas, it answers to a hair! The wooer has been here, comes not again: thou hast missed him."—"Ah, mother, let the planet say its pleasure, never mind it; my heart says to me that I should love and honour the man who asks me to be his wife: and if I do not find that man, or he do not seek me, I will live in good courage by the labour of my hands, and stand by you, and nurse you in your old age, as beseems a good daughter. But if the man of my heart do come, then bless my choice, that it may be well with your daughter on the Earth; and ask not whether he is noble, rich, or famous, but whether he is good and honest, whether he loves and is loved."—"Ah, daughter! Love keeps a sorry kitchen, and feeds one poorly, along with bread and salt."—"But yet

Unity and Contentment delight to dwell with him, and these season bread and salt with the cheerful enjoyment of our days."

The pregnant subject of bread and salt continued to be sifted till the night was far spent, and the last fiddle in the wedding-dance was resting from its labours. The moderation of the prudent Meta, who, with youth and beauty on her side, pretended only to an altogether bounded happiness, after having turned away an advantageous offer, led the mother to conjecture that the plan of some such salt-trade might already have been sketched in the heart of the virgin. Nor did she fail to guess the trading-partner in the lane, of whom she never had believed that he would be the tree for rooting in the lovely Meta's heart. She had looked upon him only as a wild tendril, that stretches out towards every neighbouring twig, to clamber up by means of it. This discovery procured her little joy; but she gave no hint that she had made it. Only, in the spirit of her rigorous morality, she compared a maiden who lets love, before the priestly benediction, nestle in her heart, to a worm-eaten apple, which is good for the eye, but no longer for the palate, and is laid upon a shelf and no more heeded, for the pernicious worm is eating its internal marrow, and cannot be dislodged. She now despaired of ever holding up her head again in Bremen; submitted to her fate, and bore in silence what she thought was now not to be altered.

Meanwhile the rumour of the proud Meta's having given the rich Hop-King the basket, spread over the town, and sounded even into Franz's garret in the alley. Franz was transported with joy to hear this tale confirmed; and the secret anxiety lest some wealthy rival might expel him from the dear maiden's heart tormented him no more. He was now certain of his object; and the riddle, which for every one continued an insoluble problem, had no mystery for him. Love had already changed a spendthrift into a dilettante; but this for a brideseeker was the very smallest of recommendations, a gift which in those rude times was rewarded neither with loud praise nor with such pudding, as it is in our luxurious century. The fine arts were not then children of superfluity, but of want and necessity. No travelling professors were at that time known, save the Prague students, whose squeaking symphonies solicited a charitable coin at the doors of the rich. The beloved maiden's sacrifice was too great to be repaid by a serenade. And now the feeling of his youthful dissipation became a thorn in the soul of Franz. Many a touching monodrama did he begin with an O and an Ah, besighing his past madness: "Ah, Meta," said he to himself, "why did I not know thee sooner! Thou hadst been my guardian angel, thou hadst saved me from destruction. Could I live my lost years over again, and be what I was, the world were now Elysium for me, and for thee I would make it an Eden! Noble maiden, thou sacrificest thyself to a wretch, to a beggar, who has nothing in the world but a heart full of love, and despair that he can offer thee no happiness such as thou deservest." Innumerable times, in the paroxysms of these pathetic humours, he struck his brow in fury, with the repentant exclamation: "O fool! O madman! thou art wise too late."

Love, however, did not leave its working incomplete. It had already brought about a wholesome fermentation in his spirit, a desire to put in use his powers and activity, to try if he might struggle up from his present nothingness: it now incited him to the attempt of executing these good purposes. Among many speculations he had entertained for the recruiting of his wrecked finances, the most rational and promising was this: To run over his father's ledgers, and there note down any small escheats which had been marked as lost, with a view of going through the land, and gleaning, if so were that a lock of wheat might still be gathered from these neglected ears. With the produce of this enterprise, he would then commence some little traffic, which his fancy soon extended over all the quarters of the world. Already, in his mind's eye, he had vessels on the sea, which were freighted with his property. He proceeded rapidly to execute his purpose; changed the last golden fragment of his heritage, his father's hour-egg,* into money, and bought with it a riding nag, which was to bear him as a Bremen merchant out into the wide world.

Yet the parting with his fair Meta went sore against his heart. "What will she think," said he to himself, "of this sudden disappearance, when thou shalt no more meet her in the church-way? Will she not regard thee as faithless, and banish thee from her heart?" This thought afflicted him exceedingly; and for a great while he could think of no expedient for explaining to her his intention. But at last inventive Love suggested the idea of signifying to her from the pulpit itself his absence and its purpose. With this view, in the church, which had already favoured the secret understanding of the lovers, he bought a Prayer "for a young Traveller, and the happy arrangement of his affairs;" which was to last, till he should come again and pay his groschen, for the Thanksgiving.

At the last meeting, he had dressed himself as for the road; he passed quite near his sweetheart; saluted her expressively, and with less reserve than before; so that she blushed deeply; and Mother Brigitta found opportunity for various marginal notes, which indicated her displeasure at the boldness of this ill-bred fop, in attempting to get speech of her daughter, and with which she entertained the latter not in the most pleasant style the live-long day. From that morning Franz was no more seen in Bremen, and the finest pair of eyes within its cir-

---

* The oldest watches, from the shape they had, were named hour-eggs.

cuit sought for him in vain. Meta often heard the Prayer read, but she did not heed it, for her heart was troubled because her lover had become invisible. This disappearance was inexplicable to her; she knew not what to think of it. After the lapse of some months, when time had a little softened her secret care, and she was suffering his absence with a calmer mind, it happened once, as the last appearance of her love was hovering upon her fancy, that this same Prayer struck her as a strange matter. She coupled one thing with another, she guessed the true connection of the business, and the meaning of that notice. And although church litanies and special prayers have not the reputation of extreme potency, and for the worthy souls that lean on them, are but a supple staff, inasmuch as the fire of devotion in the Christian flock is wont to die out at the end of the sermon; yet in the pious Meta's case, the reading of the last Prayer was the very thing which fanned that fire into a flame; and she never neglected, with her whole heart, to recommend the young traveller to his guardian angel.

Under this invisible guidance, Franz was journeying towards Brabant, to call in some considerable sums that were due him at Antwerp. A journey from Bremen to Antwerp, in the time when road-blockades were still in fashion, and every landlord thought himself entitled to plunder any traveller who had purchased no safe-conduct, and to leave him pining in the ward-room of his tower, was an undertaking of more peril and difficulty, than in our days would attend a journey from Bremen to Kamtschatka: for the *Landfried* (or Act for suppressing Private Wars), which the Emperor Maximilian had proclaimed, was in force through the Empire, rather as a law than an observance. Nevertheless our solitary traveller succeeded in arriving at the goal of his pilgrimage, without encountering more than a single adventure.

Far in the wastes of Westphalia, he rode one sultry day till nightfall, without reaching any inn. Towards evening stormy clouds towered up at the horizon, and a heavy rain wetted him to the skin. To the fondling, who from his youth had been accustomed to all possible conveniences, this was a heavy matter, and he felt himself in great embarrassment how in this condition he should pass the night. To his comfort, when the tempest had moved away, he saw a light in the distance; and soon after, reached a mean peasant hovel, which afforded him but little consolation. The house was more like a cattle-stall, than a human habitation; and the unfriendly landlord refused him fire and water, as if he had been an outlaw. For the man was just about to stretch himself upon the straw among his steers, and, too tired to relight the fire on his hearth, for the sake of a stranger. Franz in his despondency uplifted a mournful *miserere*, and cursed the Westphalian steppes with strong maledictions: but the peasant took it all in good part; and blew out his light with great composure, troubling himself no farther about the stranger; for in the laws of hospitality he was altogether uninstructed. But as the wayfarer, standing at the door, would not cease to annoy him with his lamentations, he endeavoured in a civil way to get rid of him, consented to answer, and said : "Master, if you want good entertainment, and would treat yourself handsomely, you could not find what you are seeking here. But ride there to the left hand, through the bushes, a little way behind, lies the Castle of the valiant Eberhard Bronkhorst, a knight who lodges every traveller, as a Hospitaller does the pilgrims from the Holy Sepulchre. He has just one maggot in his head, which sometimes twitches and vexes him; he lets no traveller depart from him unbasted. If you do not lose your way, though he may dust your jacket, you will like your cheer prodigiously."

To buy a mess of pottage, and a stoop of wine, by surrendering one's ribs to the bastinado, is in truth no job for every man, though your spungers and plate-lickers let themselves be tweaked and snubbed, and from rich artists willingly endure all kinds of tar-and-feathering, so their palates be but tickled for the service. Franz considered for a while, and was undetermined what to do; at last he resolved on fronting the adventure. "What is it to me," said he, "whether my back be broken here on miserable straw, or by the Ritter Bronkhorst? The friction will expel the fever which is coming on, and shake me tightly if I cannot dry my clothes." He put spurs to his nag, and soon arrived before a castle-gate of old Gothic architecture; knocked pretty plainly on the iron door, and an equally distinct "Who's there?" resounded from within. To the freezing passenger, the long entrance ceremonial of this door-keeper precognition was as inconvenient, as are similar delays to travellers who, at barriers and gates of towns, bewail or execrate the despotism of guards and tollmen. Nevertheless he must submit to use and wont, and patiently wait to see whether the philanthropist in the Castle was disposed that night for cudgelling a guest, or would choose rather to assign him a couch under the open canopy.

The possessor of this ancient tower had served, in his youth, as a stout soldier in the Emperor's army, under the bold Georg von Fronsberg, and led a troop of foot against the Venetians; had afterwards retired to repose, and was now living on his property; where, to expiate the sins of his campaigns, he employed himself in doing good works; in feeding the hungry, giving drink to the thirsty, lodging pilgrims, and cudgelling his lodgers out of doors. For he was a rude wild son of war; and could not lay aside his martial tone, though he had lived for many years in silent peace. The traveller, who had now determined for good quarters to submit to the custom of the house, had not waited long till the bolts and locks began rattling within, and the creaking gate-leaves moved asunder, moaning in doleful notes, as if to warn or to deplore the entering stranger. Franz felt one cold shudder after the other running down his back, as he passed in: nevertheless he was handsomely received; some servants hastened to assist him in dismounting; speedily unbuckled his luggage, took his steed to the stable, and its rider to a large well-lighted chamber, where their master was in waiting.

The warlike aspect of this athletic gentleman,—who advanced to meet his guest, and shook him by the hand so heartily, that he was like to shout with pain, and bade him welcome with a Stentor's voice, as if the stranger had been deaf, and seemed withal to be a person still in the vigour of life, full of fire and strength,—put the timorous wanderer into such a terror, that he could not hide his apprehensions, and began to tremble over all his body.

"What ails you, my young master," asked the Ritter, with a voice of thunder, "that you quiver like an aspen leaf, and look as pale as if Death had you by the throat?"

Franz plucked up a spirit; and considering that his shoulders had at all events the score to pay, his poltroonery passed into a species of audacity.

"Sir," replied he, "you perceive that the rain has soaked me, as if I had swum across the Weser. Let me have my clothes dried or changed; and get me, by way of luncheon, a well-spiced aleberry, to drive away the ague-fit that is quaking through my nerves; then I shall come to heart, in some degree."

"Good!" replied the Knight; "demand what you want; you are at home here."

Franz made himself be served like a bashaw; and having nothing else but currying to expect, he determined to deserve it; he bantered and bullied, in his most imperious style, the servants that were waiting on him; it comes all to one, thought he, in the long run. "This waistcoat," said he, "would go round a tun; bring me one that fits a little better: this slipper burns like a coal against my corns; pitch it over the lists: this ruff is stiff as a plank, and throttles me like a halter; bring one that is easier, and is not plastered with starch."

At this Bremish frankness, the landlord, far from showing any anger, kept inciting his servants to go briskly through with their commands, and calling them a pack of blockheads, who were fit to serve no stranger. The table being furnished, the Ritter and his guest sat down to it, and both heartily enjoyed their aleberry. The Ritter asked: "Would you have aught farther, by way of supper?"

"Bring us what you have," said Franz, "that I may see how your kitchen is provided."

Immediately appeared the Cook, and placed upon the table a repast with which a duke might have been satisfied. Franz diligently fell to, without waiting to be pressed. When he had satisfied himself: "Your kitchen," said he, "is not ill-furnished, I perceive; if your cellar corresponds to it, I shall almost praise your house-keeping."

Bronkhorst nodded to his Butler, who directly filled the cup of welcome with common table wine, tasted, and presented it to his master, and the latter cleared it at a draught to the health of his guest. Franz pledged him honestly, and Bronkhorst asked: "Now, fair sir, what say you to the wine?"

"I say," answered Franz, "that it is bad, if it is the best sort in your catacombs; and good, if it is your meanest number."

"You are a judge," replied the Ritter: "Here, Butler, bring us of the mother-cask."

The Butler put a stoop upon the table, as a sample, and Franz having tasted it, said, "Ay, this is genuine last year's growth; we will stick by this."

The Ritter made a vast pitcher of it be brought in; soon drank himself into hilarity and glee beside his guest; began to talk of his campaigns, how he had been encamped against the Venetians, had broken through their barricado, and butchered the Italian squadrons, like a flock of sheep. In this narrative he rose into such a warlike enthusiasm, that he hewed down bottles and glasses, brandishing the carving-knife like a lance, and in the fire of action came so near his messmate with it, that the latter was in fright for his nose and ears.

It grew late, but no sleep came into the eyes of the Ritter; he seemed to be in his proper element, when he got to speak of his Venetian campaigns. The vivacity of his narration increased with every cup he emptied; and Franz was afraid that this would prove the prologue to the melodrama, in which he himself was to play the most interesting part. To learn whether it was meant that he should lodge within the Castle, or without, he demanded a bumper by way of good-night. Now, he thought, his host would first force him to drink more wine, and if he refused, would, under pretext of a drinking quarrel, send him forth, according to the custom of the house, with the usual *viaticum*. Contrary to his expectation, the request was granted without remonstrance; the Ritter instantly cut asunder the thread of his narrative, and said: "Time will wait on no one; more of it to-morrow!"

"Pardon me, Herr Ritter," answered Franz, "to-morrow by sunrise I must over hill and dale; I am travelling a far journey to Brabant, and must not linger here. So let me take leave of you to-night, that my departure may not disturb you in the morning."

"Do your pleasure," said the Ritter; "but depart from this you shall not, till I am out of the feathers, to refresh you with a bit of bread, and a toothful of Dantzig, then attend you to the door, and dismiss you according to the fashion of the house."

Franz needed no interpretation of these

words. Willingly as he would have excused his host this last civility, attendance to the door, the latter seemed determined to abate no whit of the established ritual. He ordered his servants to undress the stranger, and put him in the guest's-bed; where Franz, once settled on elastic swan's-down, felt himself extremely snug, and enjoyed delicious rest; so that ere he fell asleep, he owned to himself that, for such royal treatment, a moderate bastinado was not too dear a price. Soon pleasant dreams came hovering round his fancy. He found his charming Meta in a rosy grove, where she was walking with her mother, plucking flowers. Instantly he hid himself behind a thick-leaved hedge, that the rigorous duenna might not see him. Again his imagination placed him in the alley, and by his looking-glass he saw the snow-white hand of the maiden busied with her flowers; soon he was sitting with her on the grass, and longing to declare his heartfelt love to her, and the bashful shepherd found no words to do it in. Ah! he would have dreamed till broad mid-day, had he not been roused by the sonorous voice and clanking spurs of the Ritter, who, with the earliest dawn, was holding a review of kitchen and cellar, ordering a sufficient breakfast to be readied, and placing every servant at his post, to be at hand when the guest should awake, to dress him, and wait upon him.

It cost the happy dreamer no small struggling to forsake his safe and hospitable bed; he rolled to this side and to that; but the pealing voice of the worshipful Knight came heavy on his heart; and dally as he might, the sour apple must at last be bit. So he rose from his down; and immediately a dozen hands were busy dressing him. The Ritter led him into the parlour, where a small well-furnished table waited them; but now, when the hour of reckoning had arrived, the traveller's appetite was gone. The host endeavoured to encourage him. "Why do you not get to? Come, take somewhat for the raw foggy morning."

"Herr Ritter," answered Franz, "my stomach is still too full of your supper; but my pockets are empty; these I may fill for the hunger that is to come."

With this he began stoutly cramming, and stowed himself with the daintiest and best that was transportable, till all his pockets were bursting. Then observing that his horse, well curried and equipt, was led past, he took a dram of Dantzig, for good-b'ye, in the thought that this would be the watch-word for his host to catch him by the neck, and exercise his household privileges.

But, to his astonishment, the Ritter shook him kindly by the hand, as at his first entrance, wished him luck by the way, and the bolted door was thrown open. He loitered not in putting spurs to his nag; and, tip! tap! he was without the gate, and no hair of him harmed.

A heavy stone was lifted from his heart, as he found himself in safety, and saw that he had got away with a whole skin. He could not understand how the landlord had trusted him the shot, which, as he imagined, must have run pretty high on the chalk; and he embraced with warm love the hospitable man, whose club-law arm he had so much dreaded; and he felt a strong desire to search out, at the fountain-head, the reason or unreason of the ill report which had affrighted him. Accordingly, he turned his horse, and cantered back. The Knight was still standing in the gate, and descanting with his servants, for the forwarding of the science of horse-flesh, on the breed, shape, and character of the nag and his hard pace; he supposed the stranger must have missed something in his travelling gear, and he already looked askance at his servants for such negligence.

"What is it, young master," cried he, "that makes you turn again, when you were for proceeding?"

"Ah! yet a word, valiant Knight," cried the traveller. "An ill report has gone abroad, that injures your name and breeding. It is said that you treat every stranger that calls upon you with your best; and then, when he leaves you, let him feel the weight of your strong fists. This story I have credited, and spared nothing to deserve my due from you. I thought within myself, His worship will abate me nothing; I will abate him as little. But now you let me go, without strife or peril; and that is what surprises me. Pray, tell me, is there any shadow of foundation for the thing, or shall I call the foolish chatter lies next time I hear it?"

The Ritter answered: "Report has nowise told you lies; there is no saying, that circulates among the people, but contains in it some grain of truth. Let me tell you accurately how the matter stands. I lodge every stranger that comes beneath my roof, and divide my morsel with him, for the love of God. But I am a plain German man, of the old cut and fashion; speak as it lies about my heart, and require that my guest also should be hearty and confiding; should enjoy with me what I have, and tell frankly what he wants. Now, there is a sort of people that vex me with all manner of grimaces; that banter me with smirkings, and bows, and crouchings; put all their words to the torture; make a deal of talk without sense or salt; think they will cozen me with smooth speeches; behave at dinner as women at a christening. If I say, Help yourself! out of reverence, they pick you a fraction from the plate, which I would not offer to my dog; if I say, Your health! they scarcely wet their lips from the full cup, as if they set God's gifts at nought. Now, when the sorry rabble carry things too far with me, and I cannot, for the soul of me, know what they would be at, I get into a rage at last, and use my household privilege; catch the noodle by the spall, thrash him sufficiently, and pack him out of doors. This is the use and wont with me, and I do so with every guest that plagues me with these freaks. But a man of your stamp is always welcome : you told me plump out in plain German what you thought, as is the fashion with the Bremers. Call on me boldly again, if your road lead you hither. And so, God be with you."

Franz now moved on, with a joyful humour, towards Antwerp; and he wished that he might everywhere find such a reception as he had met with from the Ritter Eberhard Bronkhorst. On approaching the ancient Queen of the Flemish cities, the sail of his hope was swelled by a propitious breeze. Riches and superfluity met him in every street; and it seemed as if scarcity and want had been exiled from the busy town. In all probability, thought he, there must be many of my father's debtors who have risen again, and will gladly make me full payment whenever I substantiate my claims. After resting for a while from his fatigues, he set about obtaining, in the inn where he was quartered, some preliminary knowledge of the situation of his debtors.

"How stands it with Peter Martens?" inquired he one day, of his companions at table; "is he still living, and doing much business?"

"Peter Martens is a warm man," answered one of the party; "has a brisk commission trade, and draws good profit from it."

"Is Fabian van Plürs still in good circumstances?"

"O! there is no end to Fabian's wealth. He is a Councillor; his woollen manufactories are thriving incredibly."

"Has Jonathan Frischkier good custom in his trade?"

"Ah! Jonathan were now a brisk fellow, had not Kaiser Max let the French chouse him out of his Princess.* Jonathan had got the furnishing of the lace for the bride's dress, but the Kaiser has left poor Frischkier in the lurch, as the bride has left himself. If you have a fair one, whom you would remember with a bit of lace, he will give it you at half price."

"Is the firm Op de Bütekant still standing, or has it sunk?"

"There was a crack in the beams there some years ago; but the Spanish caravelles have put a new prop to it, and it now holds fast."

Franz inquired about several other merchants, who were on his list; found that most of them, though in his father's time they had "failed," were now standing firmly on their legs; and inferred from this, that a judicious bankruptcy had, as from of old, been the wine of future gains. This intelligence refreshed him mightily : he hastened to put his documents in order, and submit them to the proper parties. But with the Antwerpers, he fared as his itinerating countrymen do with shopkeepers in the German towns; they find everywhere a friendly welcome at their first appearance, but are looked upon with cheerfulness nowhere, when they come collecting debts. Some would have nothing to do with these former sins; and were of opinion, that by the tender of the legal five-per-cent composition, they had been entirely abolished: it was the creditor's fault if he had not accepted payment in time. Others could not recollect any Melchior of Bremen; opened their Infallible Books, found no debtor-entry marked for this unknown name. Others, again, brought out a strong counter-reckoning; and three days had not passed, till Franz was sitting in the Debtors' Ward, to answer for his father's credit, not to depart till he had paid the uttermost farthing.

These were not the best prospects for the young man, who had set his hope and trust upon the Antwerp patrons of his fortune, and now saw the fair soap-bubble vanish quite away. In his strait confinement, he felt himself in the condition of a soul in Purgatory, now that his skiff had run ashore and gone to pieces, in the middle of the haven where he thought to find security. Every thought of Meta was as a thorn in his heart; there was now no shadow of a possibility, that from the whirlpool which had sunk him, he could ever rise, and stretch out his hand to her; nor, suppose he should get his head above water, was it in poor Meta's power to pull him on dry land. He fell into a sullen desperation; had no wish but to die speedily, and give his woes the slip at once; and, in fact, he did attempt to kill himself by starvation. But this is a sort of death which is not at the beck of every one, so ready as the shrunk Pomponius Atticus found it, when his digestive apparatus had already struck work. A sound peptic stomach does not yield so tamely to the precepts of the head or heart. After the moribund debtor had abstained two days from food, a ravenous hunger suddenly usurped the government of his will, and performed, of its own authority, all the operations which, in other cases, are directed by the mind. It ordered his hand to seize the spoon, his mouth to receive the victual, his inferior maxillary jaw in motion, and itself accomplished the usual functions of digestion, unordered. Thus did this last resolve make shipwreck, on a hard bread-crust; for, in the seven-and-twentieth year of life, it has a heroism connected with it, which in the seven-and-seventieth is entirely gone.

At bottom, it was not the object of the barbarous Antwerpers to squeeze money from the pretended debtor, but only to pay him none, as his demands were not admitted to be liquid. Whether it were, then, that the public Prayer in Bremen had in truth a little virtue, or that the supposed creditors were not desirous of supporting a superfluous boarder for life, true it is, that after the lapse of three months, Franz was delivered from his imprisonment, under the condition of leaving the city within four-and-twenty hours, and never again setting foot

---

* Anne of Britanny.

on the soil and territory of Antwerp. At the same time, he received five crowns for travelling expenses from the faithful hands of Justice, which had taken charge of his horse and luggage, and conscientiously balanced the produce of the same against judicial and curatory expenses.

With heavy-laden heart, in the humblest mood, with his staff in his hand, he left the rich city, into which he had ridden some time before with high-soaring hopes. Broken down, and undetermined what to do, or rather altogether without thought, he plodded through the streets to the nearest gate, not minding whither the road into which chance conducted him might lead. He saluted no traveller, he asked for no inn, except when fatigue or hunger forced him to lift up his eyes, and look around for some church-spire, or sign of human habitation, when he needed human aid. Many days he had wandered on, as if unconsciously; and a secret instinct had still, by means of his uncrazed feet, led him right forward on the way to home; when, all at once, he awoke as from an oppressive dream, and perceived on what road he was travelling.

He halted instantly, to consider whether he should proceed or turn back. Shame and confusion took possession of his soul, when he thought of skulking about in his native town as a beggar, branded with the mark of contempt, and claiming the charitable help of his townsmen, whom of old he had eclipsed by his wealth and magnificence. And how in this form could he present himself before his fair Meta, without disgracing the choice of her heart? He did not leave his fancy time to finish this doleful picture; but wheeled about to take the other road, as hastily as if he had been standing even then at the gate of Bremen, and the ragged apprentices had been assembling to accompany him with jibes and mockery through the streets. His purpose was formed; he would make for the nearest seaport in the Netherlands; engage as a sailor in a Spanish ship, to work his passage to the new world; and not return to his country, till in the Peruvian land of gold he should have regained the wealth, which he had squandered so heedlessly, before he knew the worth of money. In the shaping of this new plan, it is true, the fair Meta fell so far into the back-ground, that even to the sharpest prophetic eye she could only hover as a faint shadow in the distance; yet the wandering projector pleased himself with thinking that she was again interwoven with the scheme of his life; and he took large steps, as if by this rapidity he meant to reach her so much the sooner.

Already he was on the Flemish soil once more; and found himself at sunset not far from Rheinberg, in a little hamlet, Rummelsburg by name, which has since, in the Thirty Years' War, been utterly destroyed. A caravan of carriers from Lyke had already filled the inn, so that Mine Host had no room left, and referred him to the next town; the rather that he did not draw too flattering a presage, from his present vagabond physiognomy, and held him to be a thieves' purveyor, who had views upon the Lyke carriers. He was forced, notwithstanding his excessive weariness, to gird himself for march, and again to take his bundle on his back.

As in retiring, he was muttering between his teeth some bitter complaints and curses of the Landlord's hardness of heart, the latter seemed to take some pity on the forlorn wayfarer, and called after him, from the door: "Stay, neighbour, let me speak to you: if you wish to rest here, I can accommodate you after all. In that Castle are empty rooms enow, if they be not too lonely; it is not inhabited, and I have got the keys." Franz accepted the proposal with joy, praised it as a deed of mercy, and requested only shelter and a supper, were it in a castle or a cottage. Mine Host, however, was privily a rogue, whom it had galled to hear the stranger drop some half-audible contumelies against him, and meant to be avenged on him, by a Hobgoblin that inhabited the old fortress, and had many long years before expelled the owners.

The Castle lay hard by the hamlet, on a steep rock, right opposite the inn, from which it was divided merely by the highway, and a little gurgling brook. The situation being so agreeable, the edifice was still kept in repair, and well provided with all sorts of house-gear; for it served the owner as a hunting-lodge, where he frequently caroused all day; and so soon as the stars began to twinkle in the sky, retired with his whole retinue, to escape the mischief of the Ghost, who rioted about in it the whole night over, but by day gave no disturbance. Unpleasant as the owner felt this spoiling of his mansion by a bugbear, the nocturnal sprite was not without advantages, for the great security it gave from thieves. The Count could have appointed no trustier or more watchful keeper over the Castle, than this same Spectre, for the rashest troop of robbers never ventured to approach its station. Accordingly he knew of no safer place for laying up his valuables, than this old tower, in the hamlet of Rummelsburg, near Rheinberg.

The sunshine had sunk, the dark night was coming heavily on, when Franz, with a lantern in his hand, proceeded to the castle-gate, under the guidance of Mine Host, who carried in his hand a basket of victuals, with a flask of wine, which he said should not be marked against him. He had also taken along with him a pair of candlesticks, and two wax-lights; for in the whole Castle there was neither lamp nor taper, as no one ever staid in it after twilight. In the way, Franz noticed the creaking, heavy-laden basket, and the wax-lights, which he thought he should not need, and yet must pay for. Therefore he said: "What is this superfluity and waste, as at a banquet? The light in the lantern is enough to see with, till I go to bed; and when I awake, the sun will be high enough, for I am tired completely, and shall sleep with both eyes."

"I will not hide from you," replied the landlord, "that a story runs of there being mischief in the Castle, and a Goblin that frequents it. You, however, need not let the thing disturb you; we are near enough, you see, for you to call us, should you meet with aught unnatural; I and my folks will be at your hand in a twinkling, to assist you. Down in the house there, we keep astir all night through, some one is always moving. I have lived here these thirty years; yet I cannot say that I have ever seen aught. If there be now and then a little hurly-burlying at nights, it is nothing but cats and martens rummaging about the granary. As a precaution, I have provided you with candles: the night is no friend of man; and the tapers are consecrated, so that sprites, if there be such in the Castle, will avoid their shine."

It was no lying in Mine Host to say that he had never seen anything of spectres in the Castle; for by night he had taken special care not once to set foot in it; and by day, the Goblin did not come to sight. In the present case, too, the traitor would not risk himself across the border. After opening the door, he handed Franz the basket, directed him what way to go, and wished him good-night. Franz entered the lobby without anxiety or fear; believing the ghost story to be empty tattle, or a distorted tradition of some real occurrence in the place, which idle fancy had shaped into an unnatural adventure. He remembered the stout Ritter Eberhard Bronkhorst, from whose heavy arm he had apprehended such maltreatment, and with whom, notwithstanding, he had found so hospitable a reception. On this ground he had laid it down as a rule deduced from his travelling experiences, when he heard any common rumour, to believe exactly the reverse, and left the grain of truth, which, in the opinion of the wise Knight, always lies in such reports, entirely out of sight.

Pursuant to Mine Host's direction, he ascended the winding stone stair; and reached a bolted door, which he opened with his key. A long dark gallery, where his footsteps resounded, led him into a large hall, and from this, a side-door, into a suite of apartments, richly provided with all furniture for decoration or convenience. Out of these he chose the room which had the friendliest aspect, where he found a well-pillowed bed; and from the window could look right down upon the inn, and catch every loud word that was spoken there. He lit his wax-tapers, furnished his table, and feasted with the commodiousness and relish of an Otaheitean noble. The big-bellied flask was an antidote to thirst. So long as his teeth were in full occupation, he had no time to think of the reported devilry in the Castle. If aught now and then made a stir in the distance, and Fear called to him, "Hark! hark! There comes the Goblin;" Courage answered: "Stuff! It is cats and martens bickering and caterwauling." But in the digestive half-hour after meat, when the sixth sense, that of hunger and thirst, no longer occupied the soul, she directed her attention from the other five exclusively upon the sense of hearing; and already Fear was whispering three timid thoughts into the listener's ear, before Courage had time to answer once.

As the first resource, he locked the door, and bolted it; made his retreat to the walled seat in the vault of the window. He opened this, and to dissipate his thoughts a little, looked out on the spangled sky, gazed at the corroded moon, and counted how often the stars snuffed themselves. On the road beneath him all was void; and in spite of the pretended nightly bustle in the inn, the doors were shut, the lights out, and everything as still as in a sepulchre. On the other hand, the watchman blew his horn, making his "List, gentlemen!" sound over all the hamlet; and for the composure of the timorous astronomer, who still kept feasting his eyes on the splendour of the stars, uplifted a rusty evening-hymn right under his window; so that Franz might easily have carried on a conversation with him, which, for the sake of company, he would willingly have done, had he in the least expected that the watchman would make answer to him.

In a populous city, in the middle of a numerous household, where there is a hubbub equal to that of a bee-hive, it may form a pleasant entertainment for the thinker to philosophize on Solitude, to decorate her as the loveliest playmate of the human spirit, to view her under all her advantageous aspects, and long for her enjoyment as for hidden treasure. But in scenes, where she is no exotic, in the isle of Juan Fernandez, where a solitary eremite, escaped from shipwreck, lives with her through long years; or in the dreary night-time, in a deep wood, or in an old uninhabited castle, where empty walls and vaults awaken horror, and nothing breathes of life, but the moping owl in the ruinous turret; there, in good sooth, she is not the most agreeable companion for the timid anchorite that has to pass his time in her abode, especially if he is every moment looking for the entrance of a spectre to augment the party. In such a case it may easily chance that a window conversation with the watchman shall afford a richer entertainment for the spirit and the heart, than a reading of the most attractive eulogy on solitude. If Ritter Zimmerman had been in Franz's place, in the castle of Rummelsburg, on the Westphalian marches, he would doubtless in this position have struck out the fundamental topics of as interesting a treatise on *Society*, as, inspired to all appearance by the irksomeness of some ceremonious assembly, he has poured out from the fulness of his heart in praise of *Solitude*.

Midnight is the hour at which the world of

spirits acquires activity and life, when hebetated animal nature lies entombed in deep slumber. Franz inclined getting through this critical hour in sleep rather than awake; so he closed his window, went the rounds of his room once more, spying every nook and crevice, to see whether all was safe and earthly; snuffed the lights to make them burn clearer; and without undressing or delaying, threw himself upon his bed, with which his wearied person felt unusual satisfaction. Yet he could not get asleep so fast as he wished. A slight palpitation at the heart, which he ascribed to a tumult in the blood, arising from the sultriness of the day, kept him waking for a while; and he failed not to employ this respite in offering up such a pithy evening prayer, as he had not prayed for many years. This produced the usual effect, that he softly fell asleep while saying it.

After about an hour, as he supposed, he started up with a sudden terror; a thing not at all surprising when there is tumult in the blood. He was broad awake: he listened whether all was quiet, and heard nothing but the clock strike twelve; a piece of news which the watchman forthwith communicated to the hamlet in doleful recitative. Franz listened for a while, turned on the other side, and was again about to sleep, when he caught, as it were, the sound of a door grating in the distance, and immediately it shut with a stifled bang. "Alack! Alack!" bawled Fright into his ear; "this is the Ghost in very deed!"—"'T is nothing but the wind," said Courage manfully. But quickly it came nearer, nearer, like the sound of heavy footsteps. Clink here, clink there, as if a criminal were rattling his irons, or as if the porter were walking about the Castle with his bunch of keys. Alas, here was no wind business! Courage held his peace; and quaking Fear drove all the blood to the heart, and made it thump like a smith's forehammer.

The thing was now beyond jesting. If Fear would still have let Courage get a word, the latter would have put the terror-struck watcher in mind of his subsidiary treaty with Mine Host, and incited him to claim the stipulated assistance loudly from the window; but for this there was a want of proper resolution. The quaking Franz had recourse to the bed-clothes, the last fortress of the timorous, and drew them close over his ears, as Bird Ostrich sticks his head in the grass, when he can no longer escape the huntsman. Outside it came along, door up, door to, with hideous uproar; and at last it reached the bed-room. It jerked sharply at the lock, tried several keys till it found the right one; yet the bar still held the door, till a bounce like a thunderclap made bolt and rivet start, and threw it wide open. Now stalked in a long lean man, with a black beard, in ancient garb, and with a gloomy countenance, his eyebrows hanging down in deep earnestness from his brow. Over his right shoulder he had a scarlet cloak; and on his head he wore a peaked hat. With a heavy step, he walked thrice in silence up and down the chamber; looked at the consecrated tapers, and snuffed them that they might burn brighter. Then he threw aside his cloak, girded on a scissor-pouch which he had under it, produced a set of shaving-tackle, and immediately began to whet a sharp razor on the broad strap which he wore at his girdle.

Franz perspired in mortal agony under his coverlet; recommended himself to the keeping of the Virgin; and anxiously speculated on the object of this manœuvre, not knowing whether it was meant for his throat or his beard. To his comfort, the Goblin poured some water from a silver flask into a basin of silver, and with his skinny hand lathered the soap into light foam; then set a chair, and beckoned with a solemn look to the quaking looker-on to come forth from his recess.

Against so pertinent a sign, remonstrance was as bootless as it is against the rigorous commands of the Grand Turk, when he transmits an exiled vizier to the Angel of Death, the Capichi Bashi with the Silken Cord, to take delivery of his head. The most rational procedure that can be adopted in this critical case, is to comply with necessity, put a good face on a bad business, and with stoical composure let one's throat be noosed. Franz honoured the Spectre's order; the coverlet began to move, he sprang sharply from his couch, and took the place pointed out to him on the seat. However strange this quick transition from the uttermost terror to the boldest resolution may appear, I doubt not but Moritz in his *Psychological Journal* could explain the matter till it seemed quite natural.

Immediately the Goblin Barber tied the towel about his shivering customer; seized the comb and scissors, and clipped off his hair and beard. Then he soaped him scientifically, first the beard, next the eye-brows, at last the temples and the hind-head; and shaved him from throat to nape, as smooth and bald as a Death's-head. This operation finished, he washed his head, dried it clean, made his bow, and buttoned up his scissor-pouch; wrapped himself in his scarlet mantle, and made for departing. The consecrated tapers had burnt with an exquisite brightness through the whole transaction; and Franz, by the light of them, perceived in the mirror that the shaver had changed him into a Chinese pagoda. In secret he heartily deplored the loss of his fair brown locks; yet now took fresh breath, as he observed that with this sacrifice the account was settled, and the Ghost had no more power over him.

So it was in fact; Redcloak went towards the door, silently as he had entered, without salutation or good-b'ye; and seemed entirely the contrast of his talkative guild-brethren. But scarcely was he gone three steps, when he paused, looked round with a mournful expression at his well-served customer, and stroked the flat of his hand over his black bushy beard.

He did the same a second time; and again, just as he was in the act of stepping out at the door. A thought struck Franz that the Spectre wanted something; and a rapid combination of ideas suggested, that perhaps he was expecting the very service he himself had just performed.

As the Ghost, notwithstanding his rueful look, seemed more disposed for banter than for seriousness, and had played his guest a scurvy trick, not done him any real injury, the panic of the latter had now almost subsided. So he ventured the experiment, and beckoned to the Ghost to take the seat from which he had himself just risen. The Goblin instantly obeyed, threw off his cloak, laid his barber tackle on the table, and placed himself in the chair, in the posture of a man that wishes to be shaved. Franz carefully observed the same procedure which the Spectre had observed to him, clipped his beard with the scissors, cropt away his hair, lathered his whole scalp, and the Ghost all the while sat steady as a wig-block. The awkward journeyman came ill at handling the razor; he had never had another in his hand; and he shore the beard right against the hair; whereat the Goblin made as strange grimaces as Erasmus's Ape, when imitating its master's shaving. Nor was the unpractised bungler himself well at ease, and he thought more than once of the sage aphorism, *What is not thy trade make not thy business;* yet he struggled through the task, the best way he could, and scraped the Ghost as bald as he himself was.

Hitherto the scene between the Spectre and the traveller had been played pantomimically; the action now became dramatic. "Stranger," said the Ghost, "accept my thanks for the service thou hast done me. By thee I am delivered from the long imprisonment, which has chained me for three hundred years within these walls; to which my departed soul was doomed, till a mortal hand should consent to retaliate on me what I practised on others in my lifetime.

"Know that of old a reckless scorner dwelt within this tower, who took his sport on priests as well as laics. Count Hardman, such his name, was no philanthropist, acknowledged no superior and no law, but practised vain caprice and waggery, regarding not the sacredness of hospitable rights: the wanderer who came beneath his roof, the needy man who asked a charitable alms of him, he never sent away unvisited by wicked joke. I was his Castle Barber, still a willing instrument, and did whatever pleased him. Many a pious pilgrim, journeying past us, I allured with friendly speeches to the hall; prepared the bath for him, and when he thought to take good comfort, shaved him smooth and bald, and packed him out of doors. Then would Count Hardman, looking from the window, see with pleasure how the foxes' whelps of children gathered from the hamlet to assail the outcast, and to cry as once their fellows to Elijah: 'Baldhead! Baldhead!' In this the scoffer took his pleasure, laughing with a devilish joy, till he would hold his pot-paunch, and his eyes ran down with water.

"Once came a saintly man, from foreign lands; he carried, like a penitent, a heavy cross upon his shoulder, and had stamped five nailmarks on his hands, and feet, and side; upon his head there was a ring of hair like to the Crown of Thorns. He called upon us here, requesting water for his feet, and a small crust of bread. Immediately I took him to the bath, to serve him in my common way; respected not the sacred ring, but shore it clean from off him. Then the pious pilgrim spoke a heavy malison upon me: 'Know, accursed man, that when thou diest, Heaven, and Hell, and Purgatory's iron gate, are shut against thy soul. As goblin it shall rage within these walls, till unrequired, unbid, a traveller come and exercise retaliation on thee.'

"That hour I sickened, and the marrow in my bones dried up; I faded like a shadow. My spirit left the wasted carcase, and was exiled to this Castle, as the saint had doomed it. In vain I struggled for deliverance from the torturing bonds that fettered me to Earth; for thou must know, that when the soul forsakes her clay, she panteth for her place of rest, and this sick longing spins her years to aeons, while in foreign elements she languishes for home. Now self-tormenting, I pursued the mournful occupation I had followed in my lifetime. Alas! my uproar soon made desolate this house! But seldom came a pilgrim here to lodge. And though I treated all like thee, no one would understand me, and perform, as thou, the service which has freed my soul from bondage. Henceforth shall no hobgoblin wander in this Castle; I return to my long-wished-for rest. And now, young stranger, once again my thanks, that thou hast loosed me! Were I keeper of deep-hidden treasures, they were thine; but wealth in life was not my lot, nor in this Castle lies there any cash entombed. Yet mark my counsel. Tarry here till beard and locks again shall cover chin and scalp; then turn thee homewards to thy native town; and on the Weser-bridge of Bremen, at the time when day and night in Autumn are alike, wait for a Friend, who there will meet thee, who will tell thee what to do, that it be well with thee on Earth. If from the golden horn of plenty, blessing and abundance flow to thee, then think of me; and ever as the day thou freedst me from the curse comes round, cause for my soul's repose three masses to be said. Now fare thee well. I go, no more returning."*

With these words the Ghost, having by his copiousness of talk satisfactorily attested his former existence as court-barber in the Castle of Rummelsburg, vanished into air, and left his deliverer full of wonder at the strange adven-

---

* I know not whether the reader has observed that our Author makes the Spectre speak in *iambics*, a whim which here and there comes over him in other tales also.—*Wieland.*

ture. He stood for a long while motionless; in doubt whether the whole matter had actually happened, or an unquiet dream had deluded his senses; but his bald head convinced him that here had been a real occurrence. He returned to bed, and slept, after the fright he had undergone, till the hour of noon. The treacherous Landlord had been watching since morning, when the traveller with the scalp was to come forth, that he might receive him with jibing speeches under pretext of astonishment at his nocturnal adventure. But as the stranger loitered too long, and mid-day was approaching, the affair became serious; and Mine Host began to dread that the Goblin might have treated his guest a little harshly, have beaten him to a jelly perhaps, or so frightened him that he had died of terror; and to carry his wanton revenge to such a length as this had not been his intention. He therefore rung his people together, hastened out with man and maid to the tower, and reached the door of the apartment where he had observed the light on the previous evening. He found an unknown key in the lock; but the door was barred within, for after the disappearance of the Goblin, Franz had again secured it. He knocked with a perturbed violence, till the Seven Sleepers themselves would have awoke at the din. Franz started up, and thought in his first confusion that the Ghost was again standing at the door, to favour him with another call. But hearing Mine Host's voice, who required nothing more but that his guest would give some sign of life, he gathered himself up and opened the room.

With seeming horror at the sight of him, Mine Host, striking his hands together, exclaimed: "By Heaven and all the saints! Redcloak" (by this name the Ghost was known among them) "*has* been here, and has shaved you bald as a block! Now, it is clear as day that the old story is no fable. But tell me how looked the Goblin: what did he say to you? what did he do?"

Franz, who had now seen through the questioner, made answer: "The Goblin looked like a man in a red cloak; what he did is not hidden from you, and what he said I well remember: 'Stranger,' said he, 'trust no innkeeper who is a Turk in grain. What would befall thee here he knew. Be wise and happy. I withdraw from this my ancient dwelling, for my time is run. Henceforth no goblin riots here; I now become a silent Incubus, to plague the Landlord; nip him, tweak him, harass him, unless the Turk do expiate his sin; do freely give thee prog and lodging till brown locks again shall cluster round thy head."*

The Landlord shuddered at these words, cut a large cross in the air before him, vowed by the Holy Virgin to give the traveller free board so long as he liked to continue, led him over to his house, and treated him with the best. By this adventure, Franz had well nigh got the reputation of a conjurer, as the spirit thenceforth never once showed face. He often passed the night in the tower; and a desperado of the village once kept him company, without having beard or scalp disturbed. The owner of the place, having learned that Redcloak no longer walked in Rummelsburg, was, of course, delighted at the news, and ordered that the stranger, who, as he supposed, had laid him, should be well taken care of.

By the time when the clusters were beginning to be coloured on the vine, and the advancing autumn reddened the apples, Franz's brown locks were again curling over his temples, and he girded up his knapsack; for all his thoughts and meditations were turned upon the Weser-bridge, to seek the Friend, who, at the behest of the Goblin Barber, was to direct him how to make his fortune. When about taking leave of Mine Host, that charitable person led from his stable a horse well saddled and equipt, which the owner of the Castle had presented to the stranger, for having made his house again habitable; nor had the Count forgot to send a sufficient purse along with it, to bear its travelling charges; and so Franz came riding back into his native city, brisk and light of heart, as he had ridden out of it twelve months ago. He sought out his old quarters in the alley, but kept himself quite still and retired; only inquiring underhand how matters stood with the fair Meta, whether she was still alive and unwedded. To this inquiry he received a satisfactory answer, and contented himself with it in the meanwhile; for, till his fate were decided, he would not risk appearing in her sight, or making known to her his arrival in Bremen.

With unspeakable longing, he waited the equinox; his impatience made every intervening day a year. At last the long-wished-for term appeared. The night before, he could not close an eye, for thinking of the wonders that were coming. The blood was whirling and beating in his arteries, as it had done at the Castle of Rummelsburg, when he lay in expectation of his spectre visitant. To be sure of not missing his expected Friend, he rose by day-break, and proceeded with the earliest dawn to the Weser-bridge, which as yet stood empty, and untrod by passengers. He walked along it several times in solitude, with that presentiment of coming gladness, which includes in it the real enjoyment of all terrestrial felicity; for it is not the attainment of our wishes, but the undoubted hope of attaining them, which offers to the human soul the full measure of highest and most heart-felt satisfaction. He formed many projects as to how he should present himself to his beloved Meta, when his looked-for happiness should have arrived; whether it would be better to appear before her in full splendour, or to mount from his former darkness with the first gleam of morning radiance, and discover to her by degrees the change in his condition.

---

* Here, too, on the spectre's score, Franz makes extempore *iambics.—Wieland.*

Curiosity, moreover, put a thousand questions to Reason in regard to the adventure. Who can the Friend be that is to meet me on the Weser-bridge? Will it be one of my old acquaintances, by whom, since my ruin, I have been entirely forgotten? How will he pave the way to me for happiness? And will this way be short or long, easy or toilsome? To the whole of which Reason, in spite of all her thinking and speculating, answered not a word.

In about an hour, the Bridge began to get awake; there was riding, driving, walking to and fro on it; and much commercial ware passing this way and that. The usual day-guard of beggars and importunate persons also by degrees took up this post, so favourable for their trade, to levy contributions on the public benevolence; for of poor-houses and work-houses, the wisdom of the legislature had as yet formed no scheme. The first of the tattered cohort that applied for alms to the jovial promenader, from whose eyes gay hope laughed forth, was a discharged soldier, provided with the military badge of a timber leg, which had been lent him, seeing he had fought so stoutly in former days for his native country, as the recompense of his valour, with the privilege of begging where he pleased; and who now, in the capacity of physiognomist, pursued the study of man upon the Weser-bridge, with such success, that he very seldom failed in his attempts for charity. Nor did his exploratory glance in anywise mislead him in the present instance; for Franz, in the joy of his heart, threw a white engelgroschen into the cripple's hat.

During the morning hours, when none but the laborious artisan is busy, and the more exalted townsman still lies in sluggish rest, he scarcely looked for his promised Friend; he expected him in the higher classes, and took little notice of the present passengers. About the council-hour, however, when the Proceres of Bremen were driving past to the hall, in their gorgeous robes of office, and about exchange-time, he was all eye and ear; he spied the passengers from afar; and when a right man came along the bridge, his blood began to flutter, and he thought here was the creator of his fortune. Meanwhile hour after hour passed on; the sun rose high; ere long the noontide brought a pause in business; the rushing crowd faded away; and still the expected Friend appeared not. Franz now walked up and down the Bridge quite alone; had no society in view but the beggars, who were serving out their cold collations, without moving from the place. He made no scruple to do the same; and, not being furnished with provisions, he purchased some fruit, and took his dinner *inter ambulandum*.

The whole club that was dining on the Weser-bridge had remarked the young man, watching here from early morning till noon, without addressing any one, or doing any sort of business. They held him to be a lounger; and though all of them had tasted his bounty, he did not escape their critical remarks. In jest, they had named him the Bridge-bailiff. The physiognomist with the timber-toe, however, noticed that his countenance was not now so gay as in the morning; he appeared to be reflecting earnestly on something; he had drawn his hat close over his face; his movement was slow and thoughtful; he had nibbled at an apple-rind for some time, without seeming to be conscious that he was doing so. From this appearance of affairs, the man-spier thought he might extract some profit; therefore he put his wooden and his living leg in motion, and stilted off to the other end of the Bridge, and lay in wait for the thinker, that he might assail him, under the appearance of a new arrival, for a fresh alms. This invention prospered to the full: the musing philosopher gave no heed to the mendicant, put his hand into his pocket mechanically, and threw a six-groat piece into the fellow's hat, to be rid of him.

In the afternoon, a thousand new faces once more came abroad. The watcher was now tired of his unknown Friend's delaying, yet hope still kept his attention on the stretch. He stept into the view of every passenger, hoped that one of them would clasp him in his arms; but all proceeded coldly on their way; the most did not observe him at all, and few returned his salute with a slight nod. The sun was already verging to decline, the shadows were becoming longer, the crowd upon the Bridge diminished; and the beggar-piquet by degrees drew back into their barracks in the Mattenburg. A deep sadness sank upon the hopeless Franz, when he saw his expectation mocked, and the lordly prospect which had lain before him in the morning, vanish from his eyes at evening. He fell into a sort of sulky desperation; was on the point of springing over the parapet, and dashing himself down from the Bridge into the river. But the thought of Meta kept him back, and induced him to postpone his purpose till he had seen her yet once more. He resolved to watch next day when she should go to church, for the last time to drink delight from her looks, and then forthwith to still his warm love for ever in the cold stream of the Weser.

While about to leave the Bridge, he was met by the invalided pikeman with the wooden leg, who, for pastime, had been making many speculations as to what could be the young man's object, that had made him watch upon the Bridge from dawn to darkness. He himself had lingered beyond his usual time, that he might wait him out; but as the matter hung too long upon the pegs, curiosity incited him to turn to the youth himself, and question him respecting it.

"No offence, young gentleman," said he: "allow me to ask you a question."

Franz, who was not in a very talking humour,

and was now meeting, from the mouth of a cripple, the address which he had looked for with such longing from a friend, answered rather testily: "Well, then, what is it? Speak, old graybeard!"

"We two," said the other, "were the first upon the Bridge to-day, and now, you see, we are the last. As to me and others of my kidney, it is our vocation brings us hither, our trade of alms-gathering; but for you, in sooth you are not of our guild; yet you have watched here the whole blessed day. Now I pray you, tell me, if it is not a secret, what it is that brings you hither; or what stone is lying on your heart, that you wished to roll away."

"What good were it to thee, old blade," said Franz, bitterly, "to know where the shoe pinches me, or what concern is lying on my heart? It will give thee small care."

"Sir, I have a kind wish towards you, because you opened your hand to me, and twice gave me alms, for which God reward you; but your countenance at night was not so cheerful as in the morning, and that grieves my heart."

The kindly sympathy of this old warrior pleased the misanthrope, so that he willingly pursued the conversation.

"Why, then," answered he, "if thou wouldst know what has made me battle here all day with tedium, thou must understand that I was waiting for a Friend, who appointed me hither, and now leaves me to expect in vain."

"Under favour," answered Timbertoe, "if I might speak my mind, this Friend of yours, be he who he like, is little better than a rogue, to lead you such a dance. If he treated *me* so, by my faith, his crown should get acquainted with my crutch next time we met. If he could not keep his word, he should have let you know, and not bamboozled you as if you were a child."

"Yet I cannot altogether blame this Friend," said Franz, "for being absent; he did not promise; it was but a dream that told me I should meet him here."

The goblin tale was too long for him to tell, so he veiled it under cover of a dream.

"Ah! that is another story," said the beggar; "if you build on dreams, it is little wonder that your hope deceives you. I myself have dreamed much foolish stuff in my time; but I was never such a madman as to heed it. Had I all the treasures that have been allotted to me in dreams, I might buy the city of Bremen, were it sold by auction. But I never credited a jot of them, or stirred hand or foot to prove their worth or worthlessness: I knew well it would be lost. Ha! I must really laugh in your face, to think that on the order of an empty dream, you have squandered a fair day of your life, which you might have spent better at a merry banquet."

"The issue shows that thou art right, old man, and that dreams many times deceive. But," continued Franz, defensively, "I dreamed so vividly and circumstantially, above three months ago, that on this very day, in this very place, I should meet a Friend, who would tell me things of the deepest importance, that it was well worth while to come and see if it would come to pass."

"O, as for vividness," said Timbertoe, "no man can dream more vividly than I. There is one dream I had, which I shall never in my life forget. I dreamed, who knows how many years ago, that my Guardian Angel stood before my bed in the figure of a youth, with golden hair, and two silver wings on his back, and said to me: 'Berthold, listen to the words of my mouth, that none of them be lost from thy heart. There is a treasure appointed thee, which thou shalt dig, to comfort thy heart withal for the remaining days of thy life. To-morrow, about evening, when the sun is going down, take spade and shovel on thy shoulder; go forth from the Mattenburg on the right, across the Tieber, by the Balkenbrücke, past the Cloister of St. John's, and on to the Great Roland.* Then take thy way over the Court of the Cathedral, through the Schüsselkorb, till thou arrive without the city at a garden, which has this mark, that a stair of three stone steps leads down from the highway to its gate. Wait by a side, in secret, till the sickle of the moon shall shine on thee, then push with the strength of a man against the weak-barred gate, which will resist thee little. Enter boldly into the garden, and turn thee to the vine trellices which overhang the covered-walk; behind this, on the left, a tall apple-tree overtops the lowly shrubs. Go to the trunk of this tree, thy face turned right against the moon: look three ells before thee on the ground, thou shalt see two cinnamon-rose bushes; there strike in, and dig three spans deep, till thou find a stone plate; under this lies the treasure, buried in an iron chest, full of money, and money's worth. Though the chest be heavy and clumsy, avoid not the labour of lifting it from its bed; it will reward thy trouble well, if thou seek the key which lies hid beneath it.' "

In astonishment at what he heard, Franz stared and gazed upon the dreamer, and could not have concealed his amazement, had not the dusk of night been on his side. By every mark in the description, he had recognized his own garden, left him by his father. It had been the good man's hobby in his life; but on this account had little pleased his son; according to the rule that son and father seldom sympathize in their favourite pursuit, unless indeed it be a vice, in which case, as the adage runs, the apple often falls at no great distance from the trunk. Father Melchior had himself laid out this gar-

---

* The rude figure of a man in armour, usually erected in the public square, or market-place of old German towns, is called the *Rolandsäule*, or *Rutlandsäule*, from its supposed reference to Roland the famous Peer of Charlemagne. The proper and ancient name, it seems, is *Rügelandsäule*, or Pillar of Judgment; and the stone indicated, of old, that the town possessed an independent jurisdiction.—*Ed.*

den, altogether to his own taste, in a style as wonderful and varied as that of his great-great-grandson, who has immortalized his paradise by an original description in *Hirschfeldts Garden-Calendar*. He had not, it is true, set up in it any painted menagerie for the deception of the eye; but he kept a very large one, notwithstanding, of springing-horses, winged-lions, eagles, griffins, unicorns, and other wondrous beasts, all stamped on pure gold, which he carefully concealed from every eye, and had hid in their iron case beneath the ground. This paternal Tempe the wasteful son, in the days of his extravagance, had sold for an old song.

To Franz, the pikeman had at once become extremely interesting, as he perceived that this was the very Friend, to whom the Goblin in the Castle of Rummelsburg had consigned him. Gladly could he have embraced the veteran, and in the first rapture called him friend and father: but he restrained himself, and found it more advisable to keep his thoughts about this piece of news to himself. So he said: "Well, this is what I call a circumstantial dream. But what didst thou do, old master, in the morning, on awakening? Didst thou not follow whither thy Guardian Angel beckoned thee?"

"Pooh," said the dreamer, "why should I toil, and have my labour for my pains? It was nothing, after all, but a mere dream. If my Guardian Angel had a fancy for appearing to me, I have had enow of sleepless nights in my time, when he might have found me waking. But he takes little charge of me, I think, else I should not, to his shame, be going hitching here on a wooden leg."

Franz took out the last piece of silver he had on him: "There," said he, "old father, take this other gift from me, to get thee a pint of wine for evening-cup; thy talk has scared away my ill humour. Neglect not diligently to frequent this Bridge; we shall see each other here, I hope, again."

The lame old man had not gathered so rich a stock of alms for many a day, as he was now possessed of; he blessed his benefactor for his kindness, hopped away into a drinking-shop, to do himself a good turn; while Franz, enlivened with new hope, hastened off to his lodging in the alley.

Next day he got in readiness everything that is required for treasure-digging. The unessential equipments, conjurations, magic-formulas, magic-girdles, hieroglyphic characters, and such like, were entirely wanting: but these are not indispensable, provided there be no failure in the three main requisites: shovel, spade, and before all—a treasure under ground. The necessary implements he carried to the place a little before sunset, and hid them for the meanwhile in a hedge; and as to the treasure itself, he had the firm conviction that the Goblin in the Castle, and the Friend on the Bridge, would prove no liars to him. With longing impatience he expected the rising of the moon; and no sooner did she stretch her silver horns over the bushes, than he briskly set, to work, observing exactly everything the Invalid had taught him; and happily accomplished the raising of the treasure, without meeting any adventure in the process, without any black dog having frightened him, or any bluish flame having lighted him to the spot.

Father Melchior, in providently burying this penny for a rainy day, had nowise meant that his son should be deprived of so considerable a part of his inheritance. The mistake lay in this, that Death had escorted the testator out of the world in another way than said testator had expected. He had been completely convinced, that he should take his journey, old and full of days, after regulating his temporal concerns with all the formalities of an ordinary sick-bed; for so it had been prophesied to him in his youth. In consequence he purposed, when, according to the usage of the Church, extreme unction should have been dispensed to him, to call his beloved son to his bed-side, having previously dismissed all bystanders; there to give him the paternal blessing, and by way of farewell memorial direct him to this treasure buried in the garden. All this, too, would have happened in just order, if the light of the good old man had departed, like that of a wick whose oil is done; but as Death had privily snuffed him out at a feast, he undesignedly took along with him his Mammon secret to the grave; and almost as many fortunate concurrences were required before the secreted patrimony could arrive at the proper heir, as if it had been forwarded to its address by the hand of Justice itself.

With immeasurable joy the treasure-digger took possession of the shapeless Spanish pieces, which, with a vast multitude of other finer coins, the iron chest had faithfully preserved. When the first intoxication of delight had in some degree evaporated, he bethought him how the treasure was to be transported, safe and unobserved, into the narrow alley. The burden was too heavy to be carried without help; thus, with the possession of riches, all the cares attendant on them were awakened. The new Crœsus found no better plan, than to entrust his capital to the hollow trunk of a tree that stood behind the garden, in a meadow: the empty chest he again buried under the rose-bush, and smoothed the place as well as possible. In the space of three days, the treasure had been faithfully transmitted by instalments from the hollow tree into the narrow alley; and now the owner of it thought he might with honour lay aside his strict incognito. He dressed himself with the finest; had his Prayer displaced from the church; and required, instead of it, "a Christian Thanksgiving for a Traveller, on returning to his native town, after happily arranging his affairs." He hid himself in a corner of the church, where he could observe the fair Meta, without himself being seen; he turned not his eye from the maiden, and drank from her looks the actual rapture, which in foretaste had restrained him from the break-neck somerset on the Bridge of the Weser. When the Thanksgiving came in hand, a glad sympathy shone forth from all her features, and the cheeks of the virgin glowed with joy. The customary greeting on the way homewards was so full of emphasis, that even to the third party who had noticed them, it would have been intelligible.

Franz now appeared once more on the Exchange; began a branch of trade, which in a few weeks extended to the great scale; and as his wealth became daily more apparent, Neighbour Grudge, the scandal-chewer, was obliged to conclude, that in the cashing of his old debts, he must have had more luck than sense. He hired a large house, fronting the Roland, in the Market-place; engaged clerks and warehousemen, and carried on his trade unweariedly. Now the sorrowful populace of parasites again diligently handled the knocker of his door; appeared in crowds, and suffocated him with assurances of friendship, and joy-wishings on his fresh prosperity; imagined they should once more catch him in their robber claws. But experience had taught him wisdom; he paid them in their own coin, feasted their false friendship on smooth words, and dismissed them with fasting stomachs; which sovereign means for scaring off the cumbersome brood of pickthanks and toad-eaters, produced the intended effect, that they betook themselves elsewhither.

In Bremen, the remounting Melcherson had become the story of the day; the fortune which in some inexplicable manner he had realized, as was supposed, in foreign parts, was the subject-matter of all conversations at formal dinners, in the Courts of Justice, and at the Exchange. But in proportion as the fame of his fortune and affluence increased, the contentedness and peace of mind of the fair Meta diminished. The friend *in petto* was now, in her opinion, well qualified to speak a plain word. Yet still his Love continued Dumb; and except the greeting on the way from church, he gave no tidings of himself. Even this sort of visit was becoming rarer; and such aspects were the sign not of warm, but of cold weather in the atmosphere of Love. Jealousy,* the baleful Harpy, fluttered round her little room by night, and when sleep was closing her blue eyes, croaked many a dolorous presage into the ear of the re-awakened Meta. "Forego the flattering hope of binding an inconstant heart, which, like a feather, is the sport of every wind. He loved thee, and was faithful to thee, while his lot was as thy own: like only draws to like. Now a propitious destiny exalts the Changeful far above thee. Ah! now he scorns the truest thoughts in mean apparel, now that pomp, and wealth, and splendour dazzle him once more;

---

* Jealousy, too, (at bottom a very sad spectre, but not here introduced as one), now *croaks* in iambics, as the Goblin Barber lately spoke in them.—*Wieland*.

and courts, who knows what haughty fair one that disdained him when he lay among the pots, and now with siren call allures him back to her. Perhaps her cozening voice has turned him from thee, speaking with false words: 'For thee, God's garden blossoms in thy native town: friend, thou hast now thy choice of all our maidens; choose with prudence, not by the eye alone. Of girls are many, and of fathers many, who in secret lie in wait for thee; none will withhold his darling daughter. Take happiness and honour with the fairest; likewise birth and fortune. The councillor dignity awaits thee, where vote of friends is potent in the city.'"

These suggestions of Jealousy disturbed and tormented her heart without ceasing: she reviewed her fair contemporaries in Bremen, estimated the ratio of so many splendid matches to herself and her circumstances; and the result was far from favourable. The first tidings of her lover's change of situation had in secret charmed her; not in the selfish view of becoming participatress in a large fortune; but for her mother's sake, who had abdicated all hopes of earthly happiness, ever since the marriage project with neighbour Hop-King had made shipwreck. But now poor Meta wished that Heaven had not heard the Prayer of the Church, or granted to the traveller any such abundance of success; but rather kept him by the bread and salt, which he would willingly have shared with her.

The fair half of the species are by no means calculated to conceal an inward care: Mother Brigitta soon observed the trouble of her daughter; and without the use of any great penetration, likewise guessed its cause. The talk about the re-ascending star of her former flax-negotiator, who was now celebrated as the pattern of an orderly, judicious, active tradesman, had not escaped her, any more than the feeling of the good Meta towards him; and it was her opinion, that if he loved in earnest, it was needless to hang off so long, without explaining what he meant. Yet out of tenderness to her daughter, she let no hint of this discovery escape her; till at length poor Meta's heart became so full, that of her own accord she made her mother the confident of her sorrow, and disclosed to her its true origin. The shrewd old lady learned little more by this disclosure than she knew already. But it afforded opportunity to mother and daughter for a full, fair, and free discussion of this delicate affair. Brigitta made her no reproaches on the subject; she believed that what was done could not be undone; and directed all her eloquence to strengthen and encourage the dejected Meta to bear the failure of her hopes with a steadfast mind.

With this view, she spelt out to her the extremely reasonable moral *a, b, ab;* discoursing thus: "My child, thou hast already said *a*, thou must now say *b* too; thou hast scorned thy fortune when it sought thee, now thou must sub mit when it will meet thee no longer. Experience has taught me, that the most confident Hope is the first to deceive us. Therefore, follow my example; abandon the fair cozener utterly, and thy peace of mind will no longer be disturbed by her. Count not on any improvement of thy fate; and thou wilt grow contented with thy present situation. Honour the spinning-wheel, which supports thee: what are fortune and riches to thee, when thou canst do without them?"

Close on this stout oration followed a loud humming symphony of snap-reel and spinning-wheel, to make up for the time lost in speaking. Mother Brigitta was in truth philosophising from the heart. After her scheme for the restoration of her former affluence had gone to ruin, she had so simplified the plan of her life, that Fate could not perplex it any more. But Meta was still far from this philosophical centre of indifference; and hence this doctrine, consolation, and encouragement, affected her quite otherwise than had been intended: the conscientious daughter now looked upon herself as the destroyer of her mother's fair hopes, and suffered from her own mind a thousand reproaches for this fault. Though she had never adopted the maternal scheme of marriage, and had reckoned only upon bread and salt in her future wedlock; yet, on hearing of her lover's riches and spreading commerce, her diet-project had directly mounted to six plates; and it delighted her to think, that by her choice she should still realize her good mother's wish, and see her once more planted in her previous abundance.

This fair dream now vanished by degrees, as Franz continued silent. To make matters worse, there spread a rumour over all the city, that he was furnishing his house in the most splendid fashion for his marriage with a rich Antwerp lady, who was already on her way to Bremen. This Job's-news drove the lovely maiden from her last defence: she passed on the apostate sentence of banishment from her heart: and vowed from that hour never more to think of him; and as she did so, wetted the twining thread with her tears.

In a heavy hour she was breaking this vow, and thinking, against her will, of the faithless lover: for she had just spun off a rock of flax; and there was an old rhyme which had been taught her by her mother for encouragement to diligence:

Spin, daughterkin, spin,
Thy sweetheart's within!

which she always recollected when her rock was done; and along with it the memory of the Deceitful necessarily occurred to her. In this heavy hour, a finger rapped with a most dainty patter at the door. Mother Brigitta looked forth: the sweetheart was without. And who could it be? Who else but neighbour Franz, from the alley? He had decked himself with a gallant wooing-suit; and his well-dressed, thick brown locks shook forth perfume. This stately decoration boded, at all events, something else than flax-dealing. Mother Brigitta started in alarm: she tried to speak, but words failed her. Meta rose in trepidation from her seat, blushed like a purple rose, and was silent. Franz, however, had the power of utterance; to the soft *adagio* which he had in former days trilled forth to her, he now appended a suitable text, and explained his dumb love in clear words. Thereupon he made solemn application for her to the mother; justifying his proposal by the statement, that the preparations in his house had been meant for the reception of a bride, and that this bride was the charming Meta.

The pointed old lady, having brought her feelings once more into equilibrium, was for protracting the affair to the customary term of eight days for deliberation; though joyful tears were running down her cheeks, presaging no impediment on her side, but rather answer of approval. Franz, however, was so pressing in his suit, that she fell upon a middle path between the wooer's ardour and maternal use and wont, and empowered the gentle Meta to decide in the affair according to her own good judgment. In the virgin heart there had occurred, since Franz's entrance, an important revolution. His presence here was the most speaking proof of his innocence; and as, in the course of conversation, it distinctly came to light, that his apparent coldness had been nothing else than zeal and diligence in putting his commercial affairs in order, and preparing what was necessary for the coming nuptials, it followed that the secret reconciliation would proceed forthwith without any stone of stumbling in its way. She acted with the outlaw, as Mother Brigitta with her disposted spinning gear, or the First-born Son of the Church with an exiled Parliament; recalled him with honour to her high-beating heart, and reinstated him in all his former rights and privileges there. The decisive three-lettered little word, that ratifies the happiness of love, came gliding with such unspeakable grace from her soft lips, that the answered lover could not help receiving it with a warm melting kiss.

The tender pair had now time and opportunity for deciphering all the hieroglyphics of their mysterious love; which afforded the most pleasant conversation that ever two lovers carried on. They found, what our commentators ought to pray for, that they had always understood and interpreted the text aright, without once missing the true sense of their reciprocal proceedings. It cost the delighted bridegroom almost as great an effort to part from his charming bride, as on the day when he set out on his crusade to Antwerp. However, he had an important walk to take; so at last it became time to withdraw.

This walk was directed to the Weser-bridge, to find Timbertoe, whom he had not forgotten, though he had long delayed to keep his word to him. Sharply as the physiognomist, ever since his interview with the open-handed Bridge-bailiff, had been on the outlook, he could never catch a glimpse of him among the passengers, although a second visit had been faithfully promised. Yet the figure of his benefactor had not vanished from his memory. The moment he perceived the fair-apparelled youth from a distance, he stilted towards him, and gave him kindly welcome. Franz answered his salutation, and said: "Friend, canst thou take a walk with me into the Neustadt, to transact a small affair? Thy trouble shall not be unpaid."

"Ah! why not?" replied the old blade; "though I have a wooden leg, I can step you with it as stoutly as the lame dwarf that crept round the city-common;* for the wooden leg, you must know, has this good property, it never tires. But excuse me a little while till Graycloak is come: he never misses to pass along the Bridge between day and night."

"What of Graycloak?" inquired Franz: "let me know about him."

"Graycloak brings me daily about nightfall a silver groschen, I know not from whom. It is of no use prying into things, so I never mind. Sometimes it occurs to me Graycloak must be the devil, and means to buy my soul with the money. But, devil or no devil, what care I? I did not strike him on the bargain, so it cannot hold."

"I should not wonder," answered Franz, with a smile, "if Graycloak were a piece of a knave. But do thou follow me: the silver groschen shall not fail thee."

Timbertoe set forth, hitched on briskly after his guide, who conducted him up one street and down another, to a distant quarter of the city, near the wall; then halted before a neat little new-built house, and knocked at the door. When it was opened: "Friend," said he, "thou madest one evening of my life cheerful; it is just that I should make the evening of thy life cheerful also. This house, with its appurtenances, and the garden where it stands, are thine; kitchen and cellar are full; an attendant is appointed to wait upon thee; and the silver groschen, over and above, thou wilt find every noon lying under thy plate. Nor will I hide from thee that Graycloak was my servant, whom I sent to give thee daily an honourable alms, till I had got this house made ready for thee. If thou like, thou mayest reckon me thy proper Guardian Angel, since the other has not acted to thy satisfaction."

He then led the old man into his dwelling, where the table was standing covered, and everything arranged for his convenience and comfortable living. The grayhead was so astonished at his fortune, that he could not understand or even believe it. That a rich man should take such pity on a poor one, was incomprehensible: he felt disposed to take the whole affair for magic or jugglery, till Franz removed his doubts. A stream of thankful tears flowed down the old man's cheeks; and his benefactor, satisfied with this, did not wait till he should recover from his amazement and thank him in words, but, after doing this angel-message, vanished from the old man's eyes, as angels are wont; and left him to piece together the affair as he best could.

Next morning, in the habitation of the lovely Meta, all was as a fair. Franz despatched to her a crowd of merchants, jewellers, milliners, lace-dealers, tailors, sutors, and semstresses, in part to offer her all sorts of wares, in part their own good services. She passed the whole day in choosing stuffs, laces, and other requisites for the condition of a bride, or being measured for her various new apparel. The dimensions of her dainty foot, her beautifully-formed arm, and her slim waist, were as often and as carefully meted, as if some skilful statuary had been taking from her the model for a Goddess of Love. Meanwhile, the bridegroom went to appoint the bans; and before three weeks were past, he led his bride to the altar, with a solemnity by which even the gorgeous wedding-pomp of the Hop-King was eclipsed. Mother Brigitta had the happiness of twisting the bridal-garland for her virtuous Meta; she completely attained her wish of spending her woman's-summer in propitious affluence; and deserved this satisfaction, as a recompense for one praiseworthy quality which she possessed: She was the most tolerable mother-in-law that has ever been discovered.

---

* There is an old tradition, that a neighbouring Countess promised in jest to give the Bremers as much land as a cripple, who was just asking her for alms, would creep round in a day. They took her at her word; and the cripple crawled so well, that the town obtained this large common by means of him.

MATTHIAS CLAUDIUS.

Born 1740. Died 1815.

THIS writer, better known in Germany by the assumed name of *Asmus*, is not usually numbered with the Classics of his country, but enjoyed a wider popularity than many who are so ranked. He is eminently a writer of and for the people, and would seem in some cases to affect a certain "Jack Downing" rudeness for the sake of rendering himself acceptable to uncultivated readers. But this sort of petulance, with him, never degenerates into gross vulgarity; and though we feel the want of refinement in all his productions, he never positively disgusts. The coarseness is in the manner, never in the thought. For the rest, he is thoroughly healthy, and acts with tonic effect on mind and heart. He is a humorist, never graceful, but always genial, hearty, downright. He resembles Jean Paul in childlike freshness of feeling and nobility of sentiment; and commends himself 'to every man's conscience' by the pure morality and moral purpose which pervade his writings; as also by his independent confession and defence of the popular religion, in a period of which Tieck says, that religion was then a contraband article in literature, and was pardoned in *Asmus* only on account of his genuine Germanism.

He was born at Reinfeld in Holstein, studied at Jena, and spent the greater part of his life as private citizen at Wandsbeck, where, under the name of *Asmus*, he wrote for the *Wandsbecker Bote*, (Wandsbeck Messenger). In 1776, he received the appointment of "Upper Land-Commissioner" at Darmstadt, where he was expected to edit a popular newspaper. But not liking the situation he resigned it the following year, and returned to Wandsbeck. In 1778, he was made first inspector of the Schleswig-Holstein bank at Altona, with the privilege of residing at Wandsbeck. He died, aged seventy-five, at the house of his son-in-law, the bookseller Friedrich Perthes: Hamburg, January 21st, 1815.

DEDICATION TO FRIEND HAIN.*

I HAVE the honour, Sir, to be acquainted with Mister, your brother; he is my good friend and patron. I have also, it may be, other introductions to you; but I think it best to come to you directly, in person. You are not in favour of introductions, and are not used to make many compliments.

I am told there are people — they are called men of strong minds — who never, in their life, have troubled themselves about *Hain*; and who, behind his back, even mock at him and his thin legs. I am not a man of strong mind. To tell the truth, my blood runs cold whenever I look at you, Sir. And yet I am willing to believe that you are a good man, when one is sufficiently acquainted with you; and yet I seem to have a kind of home-sickness and longing after thee, thou old porter, Ruprecht, — that thou mayest one day come and loose my girdle and lay me safely to rest in the place appointed, in expectation of better times.

* Death. Tr.

Here I've been writing a little book, and I bring it to you. It's poetry and prose. Don't know whether you are fond of poems. Should hardly think you were, since, as a general thing, you don't like jokes, and the times are past when poems were anything more than jokes. There are some things in the book which I hope will not be wholly displeasing to you. The greater part is mere setting, and trifling entertainment. Do what you please with it.

Your hand, dear *Hain!* And when you draw near at last, be not too hard upon me and my friends.

ADVERTISEMENT FOR SUBSCRIBERS.

I AM going to collect my works, like other folks, and publish them. No one has asked me to do so, it is true, as is sometimes the case; and I know better than any benevolent reader, how little would be lost if my works should remain as unknown as I am myself. But then subscribing and publishing is so nice, and such a pleasure and honour for me and my old aunt! Besides, it is every man's own choice whether he will subscribe or not. Therefore, I mean to publish them with the title, "*Asmus omnia sua secum portans,* or Complete works of the Wandsbeck Carrier." * * * *

I meant, at first, to have the portraits of all the subscribers engraved in the frontispiece. But they told me that would be inconvenient; so I gave it up. * * * * *

Finally, benevolent readers know, from the *Göttinger Musen-Almanach,* where I sometimes give myself another name, and particularly from the Wandsbeck Carrier, what they are to expect; and it is not my fault if any one subscribes and afterwards is dissatisfied.

Nov. 8th, 1774. ASMUS.

SPECULATIONS ON NEW-YEARS' DAY.

A HAPPY new year! A happy new year to my dear country, the land of old integrity and truth! A happy new year to friends and enemies, Christians and Turks, Hottentots and Cannibals! To all on whom God permits his sun to rise and his rain to fall! Also to the poor negro slaves who have to work all day in the hot sun. It's wholly a glorious day,—the new-years' day! At other times, I can bear that a man should be a little bit patriotic, and not make court to other nations. True, one must not speak evil of any nation. The wiser part are, everywhere, silent; and who would revile a whole nation for the sake of the loud ones? As I said, I can bear at other times, that a man should be a little patriotic; but on new-year's day my patriotism is dead as a mouse; and it seems to me on that day as if we were all brothers, and had one Father who is in heaven; as if all the goods of the world were water which God has created for all men, as I once heard it said, &c.

And so I am accustomed, every new-years' morning, to sit down on a stone by the wayside, to scratch with my staff in the sand before me, and to think of all of that. Not of my readers. I hold them in all honour; but on new-years' morning, on the stone by the way-side, I think not of them; but I sit there and think that during the past year I saw the sun rise so often, and the moon,—that I saw so many rainbows and flowers, and breathed the air so often, and drank from the brook,—and then I do not like to look up, and I take, with both hands, my cap from my head and look into that.

Then I think also of my acquaintance who have died during the year; and how they can talk now with Socrates and Numa, and other men of whom I have heard so much good, and with John Huss. And then it seems as if graves opened round about me, and shadows with bald crowns and long gray beards came out of them and shook the dust out of their beards. That must be the work of the "*Everlasting Huntsman,*" who has his doings about the twelfth. The old pious long-beards would fain sleep. But a glad new year to your memory and to the ashes in your graves!!

THE SORROWS OF YOUNG WERTHER.

FIRST AND SECOND PART. LEIPZIG. 1774.

DON'T know whether it's history or poetry. It is all very natural, and has a way of drawing the tears from one's head right movingly. Well, love is a strange thing! It will not be played with like a bird. I know it, how it goes through body and life, and beats and rages in every vein, and plays tricks with the head and reason.

Poor Werther! He had else such fine conceits and thoughts. Had he but taken a journey to Paris or to Pekin! But no! He would not leave the fire and the spit, and went round and round it till he went to pieces.

And there's the misery, that one can have such talents and gifts, and yet be so weak. Therefore they ought to make a turf-seat by his grave under the Linden-tree by the church-yard wall, that one might sit down upon it and lay his head in his hand, and weep over human weakness. But when thou hast finished weeping, good gentle youth! when thou hast finished weeping, lift up thy head with joy, and place thy hand against thy side! For there is such a thing as Virtue. That too goes through body and life, and beats and rages in every vein. She is said not to be attainable without much earnestness and conflict, and therefore not to be much known or loved. But he who has her has a rich reward in sunshine and frost and rain, and when Friend *Hain* comes with his scythe.

ON PRAYER.

EXTRACT FROM A LETTER "TO MY FRIEND ANDREW."

* * * * * * *

To distort one's eyes in prayer does not seem to me necessary; I hold it better to be natural. But then one must not blame a man on that account, provided he is no hypocrite. But that a man should make himself great and broad in prayer,—that, it seems to me, deserves reproach, and is not to be endured. One may have courage and confidence, but he must not be conceited and wise in his own conceit; for if one knows how to counsel and help himself, the shortest way is to do it. Folding the hands is a fine external decorum, and looks as if one surrendered himself without capitulation, and laid down his arms. But the inward, secret yearning, billow-heaving, and wishing of the heart,—that, in my opinion, is the chief thing in prayer; and therefore I cannot understand what people mean who will not have us pray. It is just as if they said one should not wish, or one should have no

beard and no ears. That must be a blockhead of a boy who should have nothing to ask of his father, and who should deliberate the whole day whether he will let it come to that extremity. When the wish within you concerns you nearly, Andrew, and is of a warm complexion, it will not question long; it will overpower you like a strong and armed man. It will just hurry on a few rags of words, and knock at the door of heaven. * * * * *
* * * * *

Whether the prayer of a moved soul can accomplish and effect anything, or whether the *Nexus Rerum* does not allow of that, as some learned gentlemen think — on that point I shall enter into no controversy. I have great respect for the *Nexus Rerum*, but I cannot help thinking of Samson who left the *Nexus* of the gate-leaves uninjured and carried the whole gate, as every one knows, to the top of the hill. And, in short, Andrew, I believe that the rain comes when it is dry, and that the heart does not cry in vain after fresh water, if we pray *aright* and are *rightly disposed.*

"Our Father" is once for all the best prayer, for you know who made it. But no man on God's earth can pray it after him, precisely as he meant it. We cripple it with a distant imitation; and each more miserably than the other. But that matters not, Andrew, if we only mean well; the dear God must do the best part at any rate, and he knows how it ought to be. Because you desire it, I will tell you sincerely how I manage with "Our Father." But it seems to me a very poor way, and I would gladly be taught a better.

Do you see, when I am going to pray, I think first of my late father, how he was so good and loved so well to give to me. And then I picture to myself the whole world as my Father's house, and all the people in Europe, Asia, Africa and America, are then, in my thoughts, my brothers and sisters; and God is sitting in heaven on a golden chair, and has his right hand stretched out over the sea to the end of the world, and his left full of blessing and good; and all around the mountain-tops smoke—and then I begin: —

Our Father who art in heaven.
Hallowed be thy name.

Here I am already at fault. The Jews are said to have known special mysteries respecting the name of God. But I let all that be, and only wish that the thought of God and every trace by which we can recognise him, may be great and holy above all things, to me and all men.

Thy kingdom come.

Here I think of myself, how it drives hither and thither within me, and now this governs and now that; and that all is sorrow of heart and I can light on no green branch. And then I think how good it would be for me, if God would put an end to all discord and govern me himself.

Thy will be done as in heaven so on earth.

Here I picture to myself heaven and the holy angels who do his will with joy, and no sorrow touches them, and they know not what to do for love and blessedness, and frolic night and day; and then I think: if it were only so here on the earth!

Give us this day our daily bread.

Everybody knows what daily bread means, and that one must eat as long as one is in the world, and also that it tastes good. I think of that. Perhaps too, my children occur to me, how they love to eat and are so lively and joyful at table. And then I pray that the dear God would only give us something to eat.

Forgive us our debt as we forgive our debtors.

It hurts when one receives an affront; and revenge is sweet to man. It seems so to me, too, and my inclination leads that way. But then the wicked servant in the gospel passes before my eyes and my heart fails, and I resolve that I will forgive my fellow-servant and not say a word to him about the *hundred pence.*

And lead us not into temptation.

Here I think of various instances where people, in such and such circumstances, have strayed from the good and have fallen; and that it would be no better with me.

But deliver us from evil.

Here I still think of temptations and that man is so easily seduced and may stray from the straight path. But at the same time I think of all the troubles of life, of consumption and old age, of the pains of child-birth, of gangrene and insanity and the thousand-fold misery and heart-sorrow that is in the world and that plagues and tortures poor mortals, and there is none to help. And you will find, Andrew! if tears have not come before, they will be sure to come here; and one can feel such a hearty yearning to be away and can be so sad and cast down in one's self, as if there were really no help at all. But then one must pluck up courage again, lay the hand upon the mouth and continue, as it were, in triumph:

For thine is the kingdom and the power and the glory forever. Amen.

A CORRESPONDENCE

BETWEEN ME AND MY COUSIN RESPECTING ORTHODOXY AND IMPROVEMENTS IN RELIGION.

Highly Larned,

Highly to be honoured Mr. Cousin,—

I have heard, for some time past, so much about the religion of reason and the religion of the bible, about orthodox and philosophical Theologians, that my head turns round, and I know no longer who is right and who is wrong.

To mend religion with reason,—that, to be sure, seems to me as if I should undertake to correct the sun by my old wooden house-clock. But, on the other hand, philosophy seems to me a good thing, too; and much that is objected to the orthodox strikes me as true. Mr. Cousin will do me a real favour, if he will expound this matter to me. Especially whether philosophy is a broom to sweep the filth out of the temple; and whether I must take my hat off with a more profound reverence to an orthodox or to a philosophical *Herr Pastor*.

I have the honour to remain with special esteem,
My highly larned,
Highly to be honoured Mr. Cousin's obedient servant and Cousin,
ASMUS.

Answer.

Dear Cousin,—

Philosophy is good and people are wrong who treat it with scorn. But revelation relates to philosophy, not as more and less but as heaven and earth, upper and under. I cannot explain it to you better than by the chart which you once made of the pond behind your late father's garden. You used to be fond of sailing on the pond, cousin, and so you had constructed, with your own hand, a chart of all the depths and shallows of the pond; and according to that you sailed about, and it answered very well. But if now a whirlwind, or the Queen of Otaheite, or a water-spout had taken you, with your boat and your chart, and had set you down in the midst of the ocean, Cousin, and you had attempted to sail there too by your chart, it would not have answered. The fault is not in the chart; it was a very good chart for the pond; but the pond is not the ocean, you see. Here you would have to make another chart; but that other chart would remain, for the most part, blank, because the sand-banks here lie very deep. And, Cousin, sail away there without fear; you may meet with sea-wonders, but you will not run ashore.

Hence, you may judge, yourself, how far philosophy is a broom to sweep the cobwebs from the temple. In a certain sense, it may be such a broom. Or you may call it a hare's foot to brush the dust from the sacred statues. But whoso should undertake therewith to carve and whittle at the statues himself,—look you! he expects more of the hare's foot than it is equal to. And that is highly ridiculous and a scandal to behold.

* * * * * *

That Christianity is to level all heights, that it is not merely, like virtue, to modify and regulate, but, like corruption, to carry away every peculiar form and beauty, in order that something new may be born out of it: that, indeed, will not appear to Reason. Nor need it, if only it be true. When Abraham was commanded to leave his country and his kindred and his father's house and to go out into a country which was afterward to be made known to him, do you not think that his natural feeling rebelled and that Reason had all sorts of well-grounded scruples and stately doubts to oppose to such a journey? But Abraham believed the word and went out. And there is and was no other way. For he could not see the promised land from Haran; and "Niebuhr's Travels" was not published then. If Abraham had debated the matter with his reason, he would certainly have remained in his country and with his kindred and would have taken his ease. The promised land would have lost nothing, in that case; but he would not have entered it. See, Cousin, so it is, and so it stands in the Bible.

Since then, the sacred statues cannot be restored by the help of Reason, it is patriotic, in a high sense of the word, to leave the ancient form uninjured and to let one's-self be slain for a tittle of the Law. And if that is what is meant by an orthodox *Herr Pastor*, you cannot bow too low to such an one. But they call other things orthodox, besides that.

Now farewell, dear Cousin, and wish for peace. But, for the rest, do not let the strife and the field-cry harm a hair of your head; and use religion more wisely than they. Touching that matter, I have Potiphar's wife before my eyes. You know the Potiphar? That sanguine and rheumatic person seized the mantle, and Joseph fled. Regarding the *point saillant*, the spirit of religion, it is idle to dispute; because, according to the Scripture, no one knows that but he who receives it; and then there is no time to doubt and to dispute.

To sum up all, Cousin, Truth is a giant who lies by the wayside and sleeps. They who pass by, see well his giant form, but him they see not, and in vain they lay the finger of their vanity on the nose of their reason. When he puts off the veil, then you will see his face. Until then, our consolation must be that he is under the veil. And do you go reverently and tremblingly by; and be not over wise, dear Cousin, &c.

ON KLOPSTOCK'S ODES.*

No, they're not verses; verses must rhyme together,—that's what Master Ahrens used to tell us at school. He would set me before him when he said so, and pull me by the ears, and say: Here an ear, and there an ear,—that rhymes, and so must verses.—And then, too, I can read a matter of two hundred verses an hour, and very often it affects me no more than wading through the water: the rhymes, too, play about one's head, as the waves do about one's heels; but *here* I can't stir from the spot, and it seems as if all the time shapes were putting themselves in my way, that I have seen before in dreams.

* Translated by Rev. C. T. Brooks.

To be sure, it's printed like verse, and there's a deal of melody and harmony in it, and yet it can't be verse, anyhow. Some time I'll ask cousin about it.——

Cousin says they are verses, too, and that almost every verse is a bold steed with free neck, that scents the warm-seated rider afar off and neighs inspiration. I had understood from Master Ahrens that verses were a sort of sounding, foamy substance, that must rhyme; but Herr Ahrens! Herr Ahrens! you have operated on my eye-teeth there. Cousin says it must not foam at all, but must be clear as a dew-drop, and penetrating as a sigh of love, and that in this dewy clearness and in warm-breathing tenderness lies the whole merit of modern poetry. He took the book out of my hand, and read (page 41) from the piece called "The Comforter."

* * * * * *

"Does that foam, cousin? How do you feel under it?"—How do I feel? It stirs up a Hallelujah in me, too, but I daren't express it, because I'm such a common churl; I could pluck the stars from heaven and strew them at the Comforter's feet, and then sink into the earth. That's how I feel! "Bravo! cousin! Those must be verses, that infect you with such an itching to pluck the stars. Read the book through; you'll relish it, and for the rest, don't be ashamed of the Hallelujah that stirs in you. Common! what's common? With odes there's no respect of persons; you or a king, one's as good as t'other! And, cousin, let me tell you, the fairest seraph, in the dreadful solemn pomp of his six wings, is only a poor vulgar churl in the sight of God! But, as I said, read the book through."—Have read it, and now I'll tell you how it went with me. When you read one of the pieces for the first time, you come out of the bright day into a glimmering chamber full of paintings; at first you see little or nothing, but when you have been there a while, by-and-bye the paintings begin to be visible and to take right hold of you, and then you shut-to the door and lock yourself in, and walk up and down, and find yourself mightily quickened with the pictures, and the rose-clouds, and fine rainbows, and light Graces with soft sensibility in their looks, and all that. Here and there I've hit upon passages, where I felt quite giddy, and it seemed just as if an eagle set out to fly right up to heaven, and now had got so high, that you could only see motion, but couldn't tell whether the eagle made it or whether it was only a *lusus aeris*, a play of the air. Then I like to put the book down, and take a whiff with Uncle Toby.

About the dove-tailing of the words, too, in these Odes, I've often had my own notions, and about the metre, and I'd be willing to bet, there's some special trick there, too, if one only understood it right. The metre isn't the same in all the Odes; not at all; in some it's like the roaring of a storm through a great forest, in others soft as the moon walking through the sky; and this don't seem to have come so accidentally either.

THE EARLY GRAVES.

"All hail to thee, silvery moon,
Lovely, lonely companion of night!
Dost thou flee? Haste thee not; linger, friend of thought!
Lo, she abides! 't was the cloud, only, swept by.

"Naught but the waking of May
Sweeter is than the summer night,
When the dew, pure as light, trickles from his locks,
And o'er the brow of the hill redly he climbs.

"Ye nobler ones, ah, even now
Sober moss on your grave-stones grows.
Oh how blest was I once, when with you I saw
Redden the dawn of the day, glimmer the night!"

There—I should like to have made that, or, at least, to be sleeping with the rest of 'em under a stone all overgrown with "sober moss," and hear, overhead, such a sigh from a good youth, whom in life I had held dear. My handful of dust would stir in the grave, and my shade would come up through the moss to the good youth, give him a hearty grip of the paw, and smack awhile at his neck in the moonshine.

And then the Titles over the pieces! yes, they are always so short and well given, and a good title over a piece is like a good face to a man. The Dedication, too, is brave—"To Bernstorf," and nothing more. And in fact what use of such a long talk about Mæcenas and grace and gracious? The great man don't relish it, and it eats up the little one's stomach.

On the whole this book has shed me a real light on Herr Ahrens and verse-making. I figure the poet to myself as a noble, tender-hearted youth, who at certain hours grows as plethorically desperate, as when one of us is ridden by the nightmare, and then comes on a fever which makes the fine, tender-hearted youth hot and sick, until the *materia peccans* secretes itself in the shape of an ode, elegy, or something of the sort; and whoever comes near him, catches the infection:

Braga comes down through the oak foliage to impregnate the soul of the patriot-poet, that it may bring to light in its time a ripe and vigorous fruit; but he who is wanton and flirts with foreigners, lays wind eggs.

The author is said to be one Klopstock;—should like right well to see him some day.

JOHANN CASPAR LAVATER.

Born 1741. Died 1801.

SWITZERLAND comes in for a share in the literary honors of Germany, whose language extends beyond the Rhine, and whose literature rejoices in the contributions of such men as Bodmer, Gessner, Lavater, von Zimmerman, von Salis, Pestalozzi.

Among these, the name of Lavater stands first in cosmopolitan significance, denoting one of the most remarkable men of his time; worshipped by one-half the world, and flouted by the other; a man in whom strength and weakness, depth and simplicity, liberality and narrowness were singularly blended. On the whole, an original mind and a true philosopher. His physiognomical essays, by which he is principally known at the present day, constitute but a small part of his literary labors. He wrote with acceptance on a great variety of subjects, and on none more effectively than on questions of theology. He was also a maker of poems. Among those who knew him best, he was distinguished more by his moral traits than by his intellectual gifts; by his purity of heart, his deep humility, his fervent piety, his Christian charity and zeal for mankind. A more thoroughly good man the annals of literature do not exhibit, nor a more devoted Christian.

Lavater* was born at Zurich, on the 14th November, 1741. His father, Henry Lavater, was Doctor of Medicine, and Member of the Government of Zurich; a man of universally acknowledged integrity, of unwearied application, and a sound understanding; an excellent economist. His mother, whose maiden name was Regula Escher, was a woman of marked character and extraordinary gifts. Whatever of genius he inherited, must have come from that side of the house.

His childhood promised poorly. He represents himself as excelling, at that period, in nothing but awkwardness and stupidity; "anything but apt to learn, very inattentive, changeful, impatient, pettish, thoughtless, and simple.

* The following sketch is taken principally from the Memoir, by Thomas Holcroft, prefixed to his translation of Lavater's Essays on Physiognomy. There is a biography of him, by his son-in-law, G. Gessner.

The slightest tendency to pleasantry or wit was never discovered in me. I recollect how much I suffered, at this early period of my life, from timidity and bashfulness. I observed and felt, but could never communicate my feelings and observations; or if I attempted such a communication, the manner in which I did it was so absurd and drew upon me so much ridicule, that I soon found myself incapable of uttering another word."

His imagination appears to have been, at this season, the most active of his mental powers. "My imagination was continually at work to conceive and plan what might appear uncommon and extraordinary. Every building appeared to me too small, every tower too low, every animal too diminutive." * * *

"My indefatigably inventive imagination was frequently occupied with two singular subjects, —with framing plans for impenetrable prisons, and with the idea of becoming the chief of a troop of banditti. In the latter case, however, it is to be understood that not the least tincture of cruelty or violence entered into my thoughts. I meant neither to murder nor distress; my timid and good heart shuddered at such an idea. But to steal with ingenious artifice and then bestow the stolen property with similar adroitness and privacy on another who might want it more; to do no serious injury, but to produce extraordinary changes and visible effects, while I myself remained invisible, was one of my favorite conceptions." Notwithstanding these mental vagaries, his religious feelings were early developed and very intense. He was, through life, a firm believer in the power of faith and the immediate, objective efficacy of prayer, of which he conceived himself to have had extraordinary personal experience. "It is scarcely possible to conceive the strength of my faith in these years, when I was in difficulty and trouble. If I could pray, it seemed to me that I had already obtained the object of my prayer. Once, when I had given in a Latin exercise on which much depended, I recollected, after it was in the hands of the master, that I had written *relata* instead of *revelata*. Can there be a stronger proof of the simplicity and strength of my childish faith than that I prayed to God that he would correct the word and write *ve* above it with black ink? The *ve* was written above in another hand with black ink, somewhat blacker than mine, and my exercise was adjudged faultless. I believe the correction was made by the master, from the partial kindness he entertained for me, and I think it was anxiety and presentiment on my part which assumed the form of prayer."

While at school in Zurich, he conceived the idea of being a minister of the gospel. It was suggested to him in the following manner: " Mr. Caspar Ulrich, minister at Fraumünster, and one of the superintendents of the gymnasium or college, came one day into the school and exclaimed among the scholars, " Which of you will be a minister?" Young Lavater, without ever having thought of such a thing before, cried out so hastily and loudly that all his companions burst out into a loud laugh, " I! I!" He answered thus without any consideration, or inclination. But scarcely had the word passed his lips when he began to feel a desire which soon became a wish, and that wish a firm resolution."

In 1755, Lavater left the grammar-school and entered the college in his native city, where he contracted an intimate friendship with Fuseli, afterwards so celebrated as a painter. In 1759 he was received into the theological class under Zimmerman, professor of divinity; and in 1762, was ordained a minister.

About this time, he distinguished himself, as a friend of the oppressed, by his efforts, in conjunction with his friends Fuseli and Pestalozzi, to bring to justice the bailiff of Grüningen, one of the bailiwicks of Zurich; Felix Grebel, a man "who grossly abused his authority as a magistrate and was notoriously guilty of acts of oppression and extortion, but whose victims being poor, dared not complain to the magistrates of Zurich, because the burgo-master was father-in-law of the delinquent."

In June, 1766, he married Miss Anna Schinz, the daughter of a respectable merchant, who held an office in the civil magistracy. The following year, he published his Swiss Songs which passed through a greater number of editions than any other of his numerous works.

In 1769 he was appointed deacon and preacher to the orphan-house at Zurich. In this situation he was unwearied in acts of benevolence. In the great dearth which occurred in Switzerland, in the years 1770 and 1771, a large portion of his own small income was given in charity, which, with his personal applications at the houses of the rich, caused him to be long remembered as the benefactor of the poor.

His first work on physiognomy was published in 1772; in 1775 the first volume of his celebrated Physiognomical Fragments for the Promotion of the Knowledge and Love of Mankind. In 1775 Lavater was made pastor or first preacher to the orphan-house, and, ten years after, pastor of the church of St. Peter, which office he held till his death.

When the French took possession of Switzerland in 1798, he protested against their ravages in a publication addressed to the Directory, entitled, " Words of a free Switzer to the Great Nation," which gained him the applause of Europe for its high-toned courage. The following year, he was seized and carried prisoner to Basel, on the charge of a conspiracy against the French, but was released, after a confinement of several weeks, for want of evidence.

In September, 1799, he received a gun-shot wound from a French soldier while standing before his door, which, though it healed for a while, proved ultimately fatal. The last year of his life was one of great bodily suffering occasioned by his wound which he bore with admirable patience, praying for the man who had wounded him, " that he might never suffer the pains he had caused him to endure." In the intervals of suffering his mental activity continued unabated, and several small works were published, during this period. On one occasion, he caused himself to be carried to church and addressed an affectionate farewell exhortation to his beloved flock.

About a fortnight before his death, he finished his last literary production, which was a poem (!) written with great spirit, and entitled " Zurich at the beginning of the Nineteenth Century." On the last of December he was so much exhausted that what he said could only be heard by applying the ear to his lips. Yet even in this condition he dictated some verses (German hexameters) for his colleague to read to his congregation on the morning of the new year's day.

He died Friday, January 2d, 1801.

As a physiognomist, the character to which he is principally indebted for his fame, Lavater has shown himself an original observer, and may even claim to be called, in some sense, a discoverer. He differed from all who had preceded him in this science, in directing his attention rather to the firm and stationary—"the defined and definable"—parts of the countenance than to those which are movable and accidental. He distinguished between what is superficial in the character,—the passions and accidental determinations of the individual,—and the original self. The former he supposed to be indicated by the movable and muscular parts of the countenance, the latter by the firm and bony. In order to form an opinion of the character from the face, he required to see the face at rest,—in sleep or in an unconscious state. "The greater part of the physiognomists," he says, "speak only of the passions, or rather of the exterior signs of the passions, and the expression of them in the muscles. But these exterior signs are only transient circumstances, which are easily discoverable. It has therefore always been my object to consider the general and fundamental character of the man, from which, according to the state of his exterior circumstances and relations, all his passions arise as from a root."*

The following anecdote is related by his son-in-law, G. Gessner, as an instance of his practical skill in this science. "A person to whom he was an entire stranger was once announced and introduced to him as a visitor. The first idea that rose in his mind, the moment he saw him, was: 'This man is a murderer.' He however immediately suppressed the thought as unjustifiably hasty and severe, and conversed with the person with his accustomed civility. The cultivated understanding, extensive information and ease of manner which he discovered in his visitor, inspired him with the highest respect for his intellectual endowments; and his esteem for these, added to his natural candor and benevolence, induced him to disregard the unfavorable impression he had received from his first appearance, with respect to his moral character. The next day he dined with him by invitation; but soon after it was known that this accomplished gentleman was one of the assassins of the late king of Sweden; and he found it advisable to leave the country as soon as possible."

The following extracts from Goethe's reminiscences of Lavater, contained in the "*Dichtung und Wahrheit*," give us the reflection of his personality in a mind of a very different order from his own.

"Not long after this, I came into connection with Lavater also. The 'Letter of a Pastor to his Colleagues'* had been very luminous to him, in passages; for there was much in it that fully coincided with his own sentiments. With his ceaseless driving, our correspondence soon became very brisk. He was just making earnest preparations for his larger *Physiognomik*. He called upon everybody to send him drawings, profiles, but especially pictures of Christ; and although what I could render in this way amounted to almost nothing, he insisted upon it, once for all, that he would have a Saviour drawn according to my conception of him. Such requisitions of the impossible gave rise to many jests, and I knew no other way of defending myself against his peculiarities but by turning out my own." * * * "He had commissioned a not unskilful painter in Frankfort to send him the profiles of several individuals whom he mentioned. The sender allowed himself the jest of sending Bahrdt's portrait at first, instead of mine; whereupon came back a pleasant indeed, but a thundering epistle, with all sorts of trumps and asseverations that this could not be my picture, and with whatever else Lavater, on such an occasion, might have to say in confirmation of his physiognomical doctrine." "The idea of humanity which had formed itself in him from his own humanity was so intimately connected with the conception of Christ, which he carried living within him, that it was inconceivable to him, how a man could live and breathe without being a Christian." "One must either be a Christian with him, a Christian after his sort, or one must draw him over to one's self, and convince him, too, of the truth of that in which one found repose. This requisition, so immediately opposed to the liberal, cosmopolitan feeling to which I gradually confessed myself, had not the best

---

* From a conversation with the Emperor Joseph II., quoted by Holcroft.

* One of Goethe's youthful productions.

effect with me. All attempts at conversion, when they are unsuccessful, render the intended proselyte obstinate and hardened; and this was my case; the rather when Lavater came forward at last with the hard dilemma; 'Either Christian or atheist.' I replied to this, that if he would not leave me my Christianity, as I had hitherto cherished it, I could perhaps make up my mind to atheism; especially, since I saw that no one knew exactly what was meant by either."

"Our first meeting was hearty; we embraced in the most friendly manner, and I immediately found him as he had been represented to me in so many pictures. An individual, unique, distinguished in a way which has not been seen and will not be seen again, I saw living and effective before me. He, on the contrary, betrayed in the first moment, by sundry singular exclamations, that he had expected me otherwise. Whereupon I told him, agreeably to my inborn and incultivated realism, that since God and Nature had once for all been pleased to make me so, we too would content ourselves with that. Now, the most important points upon which we had been least able to agree in our letters, came indeed into immediate discussion; but space was not allowed us for a thorough treatment of them, and I experienced what had never occurred to me before.

"We others, when we wished to discuss matters of the mind and heart, were accustomed to withdraw ourselves from the crowd, and even from society; because, with the manifold ways of thinking and different stages of culture, it is difficult to come to an understanding even with a few. But Lavater was of quite a different mind. He loved to extend his operations far and wide. He was never at home but in the congregation, for the instruction and entertainment of which he had a special talent, based on his great physiognomical gift. To him was given a correct discernment of persons and of spirits; so that he saw in each one quickly what was the probable state of his mind." "The profound meekness of his look, the determined loveliness of his lips, even his true-hearted Swiss dialect which sounded through his High German,—and how much else that distinguished him—imparted to every one with whom he conversed the most agreeable repose of mind. Even his somewhat forward bending position of the body—a consequence of his flat chest—contributed not a little to equalize the preponderance of his presence with the rest of the company.

"Toward assumption and conceit he knew how to bear himself very quietly and dexterously. For while he seemed to evade, he turned forth suddenly some great view, which the narrow-minded opponent could never have thought of, like a diamond shield; and yet knew then how to temper the light which flashed from it so agreeably, that men of this kind generally felt themselves instructed and convinced, at least in his presence. Perhaps the impression may have continued with many; for selfish men may be good too, at the same time. All that is required is that the hard shell which encloses the fruitful kernel should be dissolved by a gentle influence."

"For me the intercourse with Lavater was highly important and instructive." "Very remarkable and rich in results for me were the conversations of Lavater with the Fräulein von Klettenberg. Here now stood two decided Christians over against each other, and it was plain to see how the same confession changes its aspect with the sentiments of different individuals," — "how men and women need a different Savior. Fräulein von Klettenberg related to her's, as to a lover to whom one yields oneself unconditionally." "Lavater, on the other hand, treated his as a friend whom one emulates without envy, and full of love."

"Notwithstanding the religious and moral, but by no means anxious tendency of his mind, he was not insensible when the spirits were stimulated to cheerfulness and mirth by the events of life. He was sympathizing, ingenious and witty, and loved the same in others, provided it remained within the bounds which his delicate feelings prescribed to him. If one ventured beyond these, he used to pat him on the shoulder, and call the offender to order with a true-hearted "Behave now!"*

"One became virginal by his side, in order not to touch him with anything disgusting."

"Lavater's mind was altogether imposing. In his neighborhood one could not resist a decided influence."

"He who feels a synthesis right pregnant within himself, has properly the right to analyze; because, in external particulars, he proves and legitimates his inward whole. Of Lavater's manner of proceeding in this matter be one only

---

* "*Bisch guet,*" "be good." Swiss dialect.

example given. Sundays, after the sermon, he was required, as minister, to present the short-handled velvet bag to each one who came out, and to receive the alms with a blessing. Now he would impose it upon himself e. g. this Sunday, to look no one in the face, but only to watch the hands, and to interpret to himself their form. And not only the form of the fingers, but their expression in dropping the gift, did not escape his attention; and he had much to communicate to me about it afterward. How instructive and stimulating must such communications be to me who was also on the way to qualify myself for a painter of men!"

"Lavater's mind inclined strictly to realism. He knew nothing ideal, except under a moral form. If we hold fast this idea, we shall best understand a rare and singular man." "Scarcely ever was there one more passionately concerned to be rightly known than he; and it was this, especially, which qualified him for a teacher."

"The realization of the person of Christ was his favourite object."

"Every talent, which is founded in a decided natural tendency, appears to us to have something magical, because we cannot classify it or its effects, under an idea. And, really, Lavater's insight into individual men transcended all ideas. It was astounding to hear him, when he spoke confidentially of this or that person; nay, it was fearful to live in the vicinity of a man by whom every limit, with which Nature has been pleased to limit us individuals, was clearly perceived!"

ON THE NATURE OF MAN, WHICH IS THE FOUNDATION OF THE SCIENCE OF PHYSIOGNOMY.

Of all earthly creatures man is the most perfect, the most imbued with the principles of life.

Each particle of matter is an immensity; each leaf a world; each insect an inexplicable compendium. Who then shall enumerate the gradations between insect and man? In him all the powers of nature are united. He is the essence of creation. The son of earth, he is the earth's lord; the summary and central point of all existence, of all powers, and of all life, on that earth which he inhabits.

Of all organized beings with which we are acquainted, man alone excepted, there are none in which are so wonderfully united the three different kinds of life, the animal, the intellectual, and the moral. Each of these lives is the compendium of various faculties, most wonderfully compounded and harmonized.

To know, to desire, to act, or accurately to observe and meditate; to perceive and to wish; to possess the powers of motion and of resistance; these combined, constitute man an animal, intellectual, and moral being.

Man, endowed with these faculties, with this triple life, is in himself the most worthy subject of observation, as he likewise is himself the most worthy observer. Under whatever point of view he may be considered, what is more worthy of contemplation than himself? In him each species of life is conspicuous; yet never can his properties be wholly known, except by the aid of his external form, his body, his superficies. How spiritual, how incorporeal soever, his internal essence may be, still is he only visible and conceivable from the harmony of his constituent parts. From these he is inseparable.

He exists and moves in the body he inhabits, as in his element. This material man must become the subject of observation. All the knowledge we can obtain of man must be gained through the medium of our senses.

This threefold life, which man cannot be denied to possess, necessarily first becomes the subject of disquisition and research, as it presents itself in the form of body, and in such of his faculties as are apparent to sense.

There is no object in nature, the properties and powers of which can be manifest to us in any other manner than by such external appearances as affect the senses. By these all beings are characterized. They are the foundations of all human knowledge. Man must wander in the darkest ignorance, equally with respect to himself and the objects that surround him, did he not become acquainted with their properties and powers by the aid of their externals; and had not each object a character peculiar to its nature and essence, which acquaints us with what it is, and enables us to distinguish it from what it is not.

All bodies which we survey appear to sight under a certain form and superficies. We behold those outlines traced which are the result of their organization. I hope I shall be pardoned the repetition of such commonplace truths, since on these are built the science of physiognomy, or the proper study of man. However true these axioms, with respect to visible objects, and particularly to organized bodies, they are still more extensively true when applied to man, and his nature. The organization of man peculiarly distinguishes him from all other earthly beings; and his physiognomy, that is to say, the superficies and outlines of this organization, show him to be infinitely superior to all those visible beings by which he is surrounded.

We are unacquainted with any form equally

noble, equally majestic, with that of man, and in which so many kinds of life, so many powers, so many virtues of action and motion, unite, as in a central point. With firm step he advances over the earth's surface, and with erect body raises his head toward heaven. He looks forward to infinitude; he acts with facility, and swiftness inconceivable, and his motions are the most immediate and the most varied. By whom may their varieties be enumerated? He can at once both suffer and perform infinitely more than any other creature. He unites flexibility and fortitude, strength and dexterity, activity and rest. Of all creatures he can the soonest yield, and the longest resist. None resemble him in the variety and harmony of his powers. His faculties, like his form, are peculiar to himself.

How much nobler, more astonishing, and more attractive will this form become, when we discover that it is itself the interpreter of all the high powers it possesses, active and passive! Only in those parts in which animal strength and properties reside does it resemble animals. But how much is it exalted above the brute in those parts in which are the powers of superior origin, the powers of mind, of motion!

The form and proportion of man, his superior height, capable of so many changes, and such variety of motion, prove to the unprejudiced observer his supereminent strength, and astonishing facility of action. The high excellence and physiological unity of human nature are visible at the first glance. The head, especially the face, and the formation of the firm parts, compared to the firm parts of other animals, convince the accurate observer, who is capable of investigating truth, of the greatness and superiority of his intellectual qualities. The eye, the look, the cheeks, the mouth, the forehead, whether considered in a state of entire rest or during their innumerable varieties of motion, in fine, all that is understood by physiognomy, is the most expressive, the most convincing picture of interior sensation, desires, passions, will, and of all those properties which so much exalt moral above animal life.

Although the physiological, intellectual, and moral life of man, with all their subordinate powers and their constituent parts, so eminently unite in one being; although these three kinds of life do not, like three distinct families, reside in separate parts, or stories of the body; but coexist in one point, and by their combination form one whole; yet is it plain that each of these powers of life has its peculiar station, where it more especially unfolds itself, and acts.

It is beyond contradiction evident that, though physiological or animal life displays itself through all the body, and especially through all the animal parts, yet does it act most conspicuously in the arm, from the shoulder to the ends of the fingers.

It is equally clear that intellectual life, or the powers of the understanding and the mind, make themselves most apparent in the circumference and form of the solid parts of the head, especially the forehead; though they will discover themselves to an attentive and accurate eye in every part and point of the human body, by the congeniality and harmony of the various parts, as will be frequently noticed in the course of this work. Is there any occasion to prove that the power of thinking resides neither in the foot, in the hand, nor in the back; but in the head, and its internal parts?

The moral life of man, particularly, reveals itself in the lines, marks, and transitions of the countenance. His moral powers and desires, his irritability, sympathy, and antipathy; his facility of attracting or repelling the objects that surround him; these are all summed up in, and painted upon, his countenance when at rest. When any passion is called into action, such passion is depicted by the motion of the muscles, and these motions are accompanied by a strong palpitation of the heart. If the countenance be tranquil, it always denotes tranquillity in the region of the heart and breast.

This threefold life of man, so intimately interwoven through his frame, is still capable of being studied in its different appropriate parts; and did we live in a less depraved world we should find sufficient data for the science of physiognomy.

The animal life, the lowest and most earthly, would discover itself from the rim of the belly to the organs of generation, which would become its central or focal point. The middle or moral life would be seated in the breast, and the heart would be its central point. The intellectual life, which of the three is supreme, would reside in the head, and have the eye for its centre. If we take the countenance as the representative and epitome of the three divisions, then will the forehead, to the eyebrows, be the mirror, or image, of the understanding; the nose and cheeks the image of the moral and sensitive life; and the mouth and chin the image of the animal life; while the eye will be to the whole as its summary and centre. I may also add that the closed mouth at the moment of most perfect tranquillity is the central point of the radii of the countenance. It cannot however too often be repeated that these three lives, by their intimate connection with each other, are all, and each, expressed in every part of the body.

What we have hitherto said is so clear, so well known, so universal, that we should blush to insist upon such common-place truths, were they not, first, the foundation on which we must build all we have to propose; and, again, had not these truths (can it be believed by futurity?) in this our age been so many thousand times mistaken and contested, with the most inconceivable affectation.

The science of physiognomy, whether understood in the most enlarged or most confined sense, indubitably depends on these general and incontrovertible principles; yet, incontrovertible as they are, they have not been without their opponents. Men pretend to doubt of the most striking, the most convincing, the most self-evident truths; although, were these destroyed, neither truth nor knowledge would remain. They do not profess to doubt concerning the physiognomy of other natural objects, yet do they doubt the physiognomy of human nature; the first object, the most worthy of contemplation, and the most animated which the realms of nature contain.

OF THE TRUTH OF PHYSIOGNOMY.

All countenances, all forms, all created beings, are not only different from each other in their classes, races, and kinds, but are also individually distinct.

Each being differs from every other being of its species. However generally known, it is a truth the most important to our purpose, and necessary to repeat, that, "There is no rose perfectly similar to another rose, no egg to an egg, no eel to an eel, no lion to a lion, no eagle to an eagle, no man to a man."

Confining this proposition to man only, it is the first, the most profound, most secure, and unshaken foundation-stone of physiognomy that, however intimate the analogy and similarity of the innumerable forms of men, no two men can be found who, brought together, and accurately compared, will not appear to be very remarkably different.

Nor is it less incontrovertible that it is equally impossible to find two minds, as two countenances, which perfectly resemble each other.

This consideration alone will be sufficient to make it received as a truth, not requiring farther demonstration, that there must be a certain native analogy between the external varieties of the countenance and form, and the internal varieties of the mind. Shall it be denied that this acknowledged internal variety among all men is the cause of the external variety of their forms and countenances? Shall it be affirmed that the mind does not influence the body, or that the body does not influence the mind?

Anger renders the muscles protuberant; and shall not therefore an angry mind and protuberant muscles be considered as cause and effect?

After repeated observation that an active and vivid eye and an active and acute wit are frequently found in the same person, shall it be supposed that there is no relation between the active eye and the active mind? Is this the effect of accident? Of accident! Ought it not rather to be considered as sympathy, an interchangeable and instantaneous effect, when we perceive that, at the very moment the understanding is most acute and penetrating and the wit the most lively, the motion and fire of the eye undergo, at that moment, the most visible change?

Shall the open, friendly, and unsuspecting eye and the open, friendly, and unsuspecting heart be united in a thousand instances, and shall we say the one is not the cause, the other the effect?

Shall nature discover wisdom and order in all things; shall corresponding causes and effects be everywhere united; shall this be the most clear, the most indubitable of truths; and in the first, the most noble of the works of nature, shall she act arbitrarily, without design, without law? The human countenance, that mirror of the Divinity, that noblest of the works of the Creator,—shall not motive and action, shall not the correspondence between the interior and the exterior, the visible and the invisible, the cause and the effect, be there apparent?

Yet this is all denied by those who oppose the truth of the science of physiognomy.

Truth, according to them, is ever at variance with itself. Eternal order is degraded to a juggler, whose purpose it is to deceive.

Calm reason revolts at the supposition that Newton or Leibnitz ever could have the countenance and appearance of an idiot, incapable of a firm step, a meditating eye; of comprehending the least difficult of abstract propositions, or of expressing himself so as to be understood; that one of these in the brain of a Laplander conceived his Theodica; and that the other in the head of an Esquimaux, who wants the power to number farther than six, and affirms all beyond to be innumerable, had dissected the rays of light, and weighed worlds.

Calm reason revolts when it is asserted that the strong man may appear perfectly like the weak, the man in full health like another in the last stage of a consumption, or that the rash and irascible may resemble the cold and phlegmatic. It revolts to hear it affirmed that joy and grief, pleasure and pain, love and hatred, all exhibit themselves under the same traits; that is to say, under no traits whatever, on the exterior of man. Yet such are the assertions of those who maintain physiognomy to be a chimerical science. They overturn all that order and combination by which eternal wisdom so highly astonishes and delights the understanding. It cannot be too emphatically repeated, that blind chance and arbitrary disorder constitute the philosophy of fools; and that they are the bane of natural knowledge, philosophy and religion. Entirely to banish such a system is the duty of the true inquirer, the sage, and the divine.

All men, (this is indisputable), absolutely all men, estimate all things whatever by their physiognomy, their exterior, temporary superficies. By viewing these on every occasion, they draw their conclusions concerning their internal properties.

What merchant, if he be unacquainted with the person of whom he purchases, does not estimate his wares by the physiognomy or appearance of those wares? If he purchase of a distant correspondent, what other means does he use in judging whether they are or are not equal to his expectation? Is not his judgment determined by the colour, the fineness, the superficies, the exterior, the physiognomy? Does he not judge money by its physiognomy? Why does he take one guinea and reject another? Why weigh a third in his hand? Does he not determine according to its colour, or impression; its outside, its physiognomy? If a stranger enter his shop, as a buyer or seller, will he not observe him? Will he not draw conclusions from his countenance? Will he not, almost before he is out of hearing, pronounce some opinion upon him, and say: 'This man has an honest look,' 'That man has a pleasing, or forbidding, countenance?' What is it to the purpose whether his judgment be right or wrong? He judges. Though not wholly, he depends in part upon the exterior form, and thence draws inferences concerning the mind.

How does the farmer, walking through his grounds, regulate his future expectations by the colour, the size, the growth, the exterior; that is to say, by the physiognomy of the bloom, the stalk, or the ear, of his corn; the stem, and shoots of his vine-tree? 'This ear of corn is blighted,' 'That wood is full of sap; this will grow, that not,' affirms he, at the first or second glance. 'Though these vine-shoots look well, they will bear but few grapes.' And wherefore? He remarks, in their appearance, as the physiognomist in the countenances of shallow men, the want of native energy. Does not he judge by the exterior?

Does not the physician pay more attention to the physiognomy of the sick than to all the accounts that are brought him concerning his patient? Zimmermann, among the living, may be brought as a proof of the great perfection at which this kind of judgment has arrived; and among the dead, Kempf, whose son has written a treatise on Temperament.

The painter —— Yet of him I will say nothing; his art too evidently reproves the childish and arrogant prejudices of those who pretend to disbelieve physiognomy.

The traveller, the philanthropist, the misanthrope, the lover, (and who not?) all act according to their feelings and decisions, true or false, confused or clear, concerning physiognomy. These feelings, these decisions, excite compassion, disgust, joy, love, hatred, suspicion, confidence, reserve, or benevolence.

Do we not daily judge of the sky by its physiognomy? No food, not a glass of wine or beer, not a cup of coffee or tea, comes to table, which is not judged by its physiognomy, its exterior, and of which we do not thence deduce some conclusion respecting its interior, good or bad properties.

Is not all nature physiognomy, superficies and contents; body, and spirit; exterior effect and internal power; invisible beginning and visible ending?

What knowledge is there, of which man is capable, that is not founded on the exterior; the relation that exists between visible and invisible, the perceptible and the imperceptible?

Physiognomy, whether understood in its most extensive or confined signification, is the origin of all human decisions, efforts, actions, expectations, fears, and hopes; of all pleasing and unpleasing sensations, which are occasioned by external objects.

From the cradle to the grave, in all conditions and ages, throughout all nations, from Adam to the last existing man, from the worm we tread on to the most sublime of philosophers, (and why not to the angel, why not to the Mediator Christ?) physiognomy is the origin of all we do and suffer.

Each insect is acquainted with its friend and its foe; each child loves and fears, although it knows not why. Physiognomy is the cause; nor is there a man to be found on earth who is not daily influenced by physiognomy; not a man who cannot figure to himself a countenance which shall to him appear exceedingly lovely, or exceedingly hateful; not a man who does not more or less, the first time he is in company with a stranger, observe, estimate, compare, and judge him, according to appearances, although he might never have heard of the word or thing called physiognomy; not a man who does not judge of all things that pass through his hands, by their physiognomy; that is, of their internal worth by their external appearance.

The art of dissimulation itself, which is adduced as so insuperable an objection to the truth of physiognomy, is founded on physiognomy. Why does the hypocrite assume the appearance of an honest man, but because that he is convinced, though not perhaps from any systematic reflection, that all eyes are acquainted with the characteristic marks of honesty.

What judge, wise or unwise, whether he confess or deny the fact, does not sometimes in this sense decide from appearances? Who can, is, or ought to be, absolutely indifferent to the exterior of persons brought before him to be judged?* What king would choose a minister without examining his exterior, secretly at least, and to a certain extent? An officer will not enlist a soldier without thus examining his appearance, his height out of the question. What master or mistress of a family will choose a servant without considering the exterior; no matter whether their judgment be or be not just, or whether it be exercised unconsciously?

I am wearied of citing instances so numerous, and so continually before our eyes, to prove that men, tacitly and unanimously, confess the influence which physiognomy has over their sensations and actions. I feel disgust at being obliged to write thus, in order to convince the learned

---

* Franciscus Valesius says—Sed legibus etiam civilibus, in quibus iniquum sit censere esse aliquid futile aut varium, cautum est; ut si duo homines inciderent in criminis suspicionem, is primum torqueatur qui sit aspectu deformior.

of truths with which every child is or may be acquainted.

He that hath eyes to see, let him see; but should the light, by being brought too close to his eyes, produce phrenzy, he may burn himself by endeavouring to extinguish the torch of truth. I use such expressions unwillingly, but I dare do my duty, and my duty is boldly to declare that I believe myself certain of what I now and hereafter shall affirm; and that I think myself capable of convincing all real lovers of truth, by principles which are in themselves incontrovertible. It is also necessary to confute the pretensions of certain literary despots, and to compel them to be more cautious in their decisions. It is therefore proved, not because I say it, but because it is an eternal and manifest truth, and would have been equally truth, had it never been said, that, whether they are or are not sensible of it, all men are daily influenced by physiognomy; that, as Sultzer has affirmed, every man, consciously or unconsciously, understands something of physiognomy; nay, that there is not a living being that does not, at least after its manner, draw some inferences from the external to the internal; that does not judge concerning that which is not, by that which is, apparent to the senses.

This universal, though tacit confession, that the exterior, the visible, the superficies of objects, indicates their nature, their properties, and that every outward sign is the symbol of some inherent quality, I hold to be equally certain and important to the science of physiognomy.

I must once more repeat, when each apple, each apricot, has a physiognomy peculiar to itself, shall man, the lord of earth, have none? The most simple and inanimate object has its characteristic exterior, by which it is not only distinguished as a species, but individually; and shall the first, noblest, best harmonized, and most beauteous of beings be denied all characteristic.

But whatever may be objected against the truth and certainty of the science of physiognomy, by the most illiterate, or the most learned; how much soever he who openly professes faith in this science, may be subject to ridicule, to philosophic pity and contempt; it still cannot be contested that there is no object, thus considered, more important, more worthy of observation, more interesting than man, nor any occupation superior to that of disclosing the beauties and perfections of human nature.

Such were my opinions six or eight years ago. Will it in the next century be believed that it is still, at this time, necessary to repeat these things; or that numerous obscure witlings continue to treat with ridicule and contempt the general feelings of mankind, and observations which not only may be, but are demonstrated; and that they act thus without having refuted any one of the principles at which they laugh; yet that they are, notwithstanding, continually repeating the words, philosophy and enlightened age?

OF THE UNIVERSALITY OF PHYSIOGNOMONICAL SENSATION.

By physiognomonical sensation, I here understand "those feelings which are produced at beholding certain countenances, and the conjectures concerning the qualities of the mind, which are produced by the state of such countenances, or of their portraits drawn or painted."

This sensation is very universal; that is to say, as certainly as eyes are in any man or any animal, so certainly are they accompanied by physiognomonical sensations. Different sensations are produced in each by the different forms that present themselves.

Exactly similar sensations cannot be generated by forms that are in themselves different.

Various as the impressions may be which the same object makes on various spectators, and opposite as the judgments which may be pronounced on one and the same form, yet there are certain extremes, certain forms, physiognomies, figures, and lineaments, concerning which all, who are not idiots, will agree in their opinions. So will men be various in their decisions concerning certain portraits, yet will be unanimous concerning certain others; will say, "this is so like it absolutely breathes," or, "this is totally unlike." Of the numerous proofs which might be adduced of the universality of physiognomonical sensation, it is only necessary to select a few, to demonstrate the fact.

I shall not here repeat what I have already noticed, on the instantaneous judgment which all men give, when viewing exterior forms. I shall only observe that, let any person, but for two days, remark all that he hears or reads, among men, and he will everywhere hear and read, even from the very adversaries of physiognomy, physiognomonical judgments concerning men; will continually hear expressions like these: "You might have read it in his eyes," "The look of the man is enough," "He has an honest countenance," "His manner sets every person at his ease," "He has evil eyes," "You read honesty in his looks," "He has an unhealthy countenance," "I will trust him for his honest face," "Should he deceive me, I will never trust man more," "That man has an open countenance," "I suspect that insidious smile," "He cannot look any person in the face." The very judgments that should seem to militate against the science are but exceptions which confirm the universality of physiognomonical sensation. "His appearance is against him," "This is what I could not have read in his countenance," "He is better or worse than his countenance bespeaks."

If we observe mankind, from the most finished courtier, to the lowest of the vulgar, and listen to the remarks they make on each other, we shall be astonished to find how many of them are entirely physiognomical.

I have lately had such frequent occasion of observing this among people who do not know that I have published any such work as the present, people, who perhaps never heard the word physiognomy, that I am willing, at any time, to risk my veracity on the proof that all men, unconsciously, more or less, are guided by physiognomical sensation.

Another, no less convincing, though not sufficiently noticed, proof of the universality of physiognomical sensation, that is to say, of the confused feeling of the agreement between the internal character and the external form, is the number of physiognomonical terms to be found in all languages, and among all nations; or, in other words, the number of moral terms, which, in reality, are all physiognomonical; but this is a subject that deserves a separate treatise. How important would such a treatise be in extending the knowledge of languages, and determining the precise meaning of words! How new! How interesting!

Here I might adduce physiognomonical proverbs; but I have neither sufficient learning nor leisure to cite them from all languages, so as properly to elucidate the subject. To this might be added the numerous physiognomonical traits, characters, and descriptions, which are so frequent in the writings of the greatest poets, and which so much delight all readers of taste, sensibility, knowledge of human nature, and philanthropy.

Physiognomonical sensation is not only produced by the sight of man, but also by that of paintings, drawings, shades, and outlines. Scarcely is there a man in a thousand who, if such sketches were shown him, would not of himself form some judgment concerning them, or, at least, who would not readily attend to the judgment formed by others.

ON FREEDOM AND NECESSITY.

My opinion, on this profound and important question, is, that man is as free as the bird in the cage; he has a determinate space for action and sensation, beyond which he cannot pass. As each man has a particular circumference of body, so has he likewise a certain sphere of action. One of the unpardonable sins of Helvetius, against reason and experience, is, that he has assigned to education the sole power of forming, or deforming the mind. I doubt if any philosopher of the present century has imposed any doctrine upon the world so insulting to common sense. Can it be denied that certain minds, certain frames, are by nature capable, or incapable, of certain sensations, talents, and actions?

To force a man to think and feel like me, is equal to forcing him to have my exact forehead and nose; or to impart unto the eagle the slowness of the snail, and to the snail the swiftness of the eagle: yet this is the philosophy of our modern wits.

Each individual can but what he can, is but what he is. He may arrive at, but cannot exceed, a certain degree of perfection, which scourging, even to death itself, cannot make him surpass. Each man must give his own standard. We must determine what his powers are, and not imagine what the powers of another might effect in a similar situation.

When, oh! men and brethren, children of the common Father, when will you begin to judge each other justly? When will you cease to require, to force, from the man of sensibility the abstraction of the cold and phlegmatic; or from the cold and phlegmatic the enthusiasm of the man of sensibility? When cease to require nectarines from an apple-tree, or figs from the vine? Man is man, nor can wishes make him an angel; and each man is an individual self, with as little ability to become another self as to become an angel. So far as my own sphere extends, I am free; within that circle I can act. I, to whom one talent only has been intrusted, cannot act like him who has two. My talent, however, may be well or ill employed. A certain quantity of power is bestowed on me, which I may use, and by use increase, by want of use diminish, and by misuse totally lose. But I never can perform, with this quantity of power, what might be performed with a double portion, equally well applied. Industry may make near approaches to ingenuity, and ingenuity to genius, wanting exercise, or opportunity of unfolding itself, or rather may seem to make these approaches; but never can industry supply total absence of genius or ingenuity. Each must remain what he is, nor can he extend or enlarge himself beyond a certain size; each man is a sovereign prince, but, whether small or great, only in his own principality. This he may cultivate so as to produce fruits equal to one twice as large, that shall be left half uncultivated. But, though he cannot extend his principality, yet having cultivated it well, the lord of his neighbours may add that as a gift. Such being freedom and necessity, it ought to render each man humble yet ardent, modest yet active. Hitherto and no farther. Truth, physiognomy, and the voice of God, proclaim aloud to man, *Be what thou art, and become what thou canst.*

The character and countenance of every man may suffer astonishing changes; yet only to a certain extent. Each has room sufficient: the least has a large and good field, which he may cultivate, according to the soil; but he can only sow such seed as he has, nor can he cultivate any other field than that on which he is stationed. In the mansion of God, there are, to his glory, vessels of wood, of silver, and of gold. All are serviceable, all profitable, all capable of divine uses, all the instruments of God: but the wood continues wood, the silver, silver, the gold, gold. Though the golden should remain unused, still they are gold. The wooden may be made more serviceable than the golden, but they continue wood. No addition, no constraint, no effort of the mind, can give to man another nature. Let each be what he is, so will he be sufficiently good, for man himself, and God. The violin cannot have the sound of the flute, nor the trumpet of the drum. But the violin, differently strung, differently fingered, and differently bowed, may produce an infinite variety of sounds, though not the sound of the flute. Equally incapable is the drum to produce the sound of the trumpet, although the drum be capable of infinite variety.

I cannot write well with a bad pen, but with a good one I can write both well and ill. Being foolish I cannot speak wisely, but I may speak foolishly although wise. He who nothing possesses, can nothing give; but, having, he may give, or he may refrain. Though, with a thousand florins, I cannot buy all I wish, yet am I at liberty to choose, among numberless things, any whose value does not exceed that sum. In like manner am I free, and not free. The sum of my powers, the degree of my activity or inactivity, depend on my internal and external organization; on incidents, incitements, men, books, good or ill fortune, and the use I may make of the quantity of power I possess. "It is not of him that willeth, or of him that runneth, but of God that showeth mercy. Nor may the vessel say to the potter, Why hast thou made me thus? But the righteous lord reapeth not where he hath not sowed, nor gathereth where he hath not strewed. Yet, with justice, he demandeth five other talents from him who received five, two from him who received two, and one from him who received one."

OF THE UNIVERSAL EXCELLENCE OF THE FORM OF MAN.

The title of this fragment is expressive of the contents, or rather of the very soul, of the whole work; therefore, what I may here say, in a separate section, may be accounted as nothing; yet how vast a subject of meditation may it afford to man!

Each creature is indispensable in the immensity of the creations of God; but each creature does not know it is thus indispensable. Man alone, of all earth's creatures, rejoices in his indispensability.

No man can render any other man dispensable. The place of no man can be supplied by another.

This belief of the indispensability, and individuality, of all men, and in our own metaphysical indispensability and individuality, is, again, one of the unacknowledged, the noble fruits of physiognomy; a fruit pregnant with seeds most precious, whence shall spring lenity and love! Oh! may posterity behold them flourish; may future ages repose under their shade! The worst, the most deformed, the most corrupt of men, is still indispensable in this world of God, and is more or less capable of knowing his own individuality, and unsuppliable indispensability. The wickedest, the most deformed, of men, is still more noble than the most beauteous, most perfect animal.—Contemplate, oh man! what thy nature is, not what it might be, not what is wanting. Humanity, amid all its distortions, will ever remain wondrous humanity!

Incessantly might I repeat doctrines like this! —Art thou better, more beauteous, nobler, than many others of thy fellow-creatures? If so, rejoice, and ascribe it not to thyself, but to him who, from the same clay, formed one vessel for honour, another for dishonour; to him who, without thy advice, without thy prayer, without any desert of thine, caused thee to be what thou art.

Yea, to Him!—"For what hast thou, oh man, that thou didst not receive? Now if thou didst receive, why dost thou glory as if thou hadst not received?" "Can the eye say to the hand, I have no need of thee?" "He that oppresseth the poor, reproacheth his Maker." "God hath made of one blood all nations of men."

Who feels, more deeply, more internally, all these divine truths than the physiognomist? The true physiognomist, who is not merely a man of literature, a reader, an author, but—a man.

Yes, I own, the most humane physiognomist, he who so eagerly searches for whatever is good, beautiful, and noble in nature, who delights in the *Ideal*, who duly exercises, nourishes, refines his taste, with humanity more improved, more perfect, more holy, even he is in frequent danger, at least is frequently tempted to turn from the common herd of depraved men; from the deformed, the foolish, the apes, the hypocrites, the vulgar of mankind; in danger of forgetting that the misshapen forms, these apes, these hypocrites, also are men; and that, notwithstanding all his imagined or his real excellence, all his noble feelings, the purity of his views, (and who has cause to boast of these?) all the firmness, the soundness, of his reason, the feelings of his heart, the powers with which he is endowed, although he may appear to have approached the sublime ideal of Grecian art, still he is, very probably, from his own moral defects, in the eyes of superior beings, in the eyes of his much more righteous brother, as distorted as the most ridiculous, most depraved, moral or physical monster appears to be in his eyes.

Liable as we are to forget this, to be reminded thereof is necessary, both to the writer and the reader of this work. Forget not that even the wisest of men are men. Forget not how much positive good may be found, even in the worst; and that they are as necessary, as good in their place, as thou art. Are they not equally indispensable, equally unsuppliable? They possess not, either in mind or body, the smallest thing exactly as thou dost. Each is wholly and in every part as individual as thou art.

Consider each as if he were single in the universe. Then wilt thou discover powers and excellencies in him which, abstractedly of comparison, deserve all attention and admiration.

Compare him, afterward, with others; his similarity, his dissimilarity, to so many of his fellow-creatures. How must this awaken thy amazement! How wilt thou value the individuality, the indispensability of his being! How wilt thou wonder at the harmony of his parts, each contributing to form one whole, at their relation, the relation of his million-fold individuality, to such a multitude of other individuals! Yes! We wonder and adore the so simple yet so infinitely varied expression of almighty power inconceivable, so especially and so gloriously revealed in the nature of man.

No man ceases to be a man, how low soever he may sink beneath the dignity of human nature. Not being beast, he still is capable of amendment, of approaching perfection. The worst of faces still is a human face. Humanity ever continues the honour and ornament of man. It is as impossible for a brute animal to become man, although he may, in many actions, approach, or almost surpass him, as for man to become a brute, although many men indulge themselves in actions which we cannot view in brutes without abhorrence.

But the very capacity of voluntarily debasing himself in appearance, even below brutality, is the honour and privilege of man. This very capacity of imitating all things by an act of his will, and the power of his understanding,—this very capacity man only has, beasts have not. The countenances of beasts are not susceptible of any remarkable deterioration, nor are they capable of any remarkable amelioration, or beautifying. The worst of the countenances of men may be still more debased, but they may, also, to a certain degree, be improved and ennobled.

The degree of perfection or degradation, of which man is capable, cannot be described.

For this reason, the worst countenance has a well-founded claim to the notice, esteem, and hope of all good men.

Again; in every human countenance, however debased, humanity still is visible, that is, the image of the Deity.

I have seen the worst of men, in their worst of moments, yet could not all their vice, blasphemy, and oppression of guilt, extinguish the light of good that shone in their countenances; the spirit of humanity, the ineffaceable traits of internal, eternal perfectibility.—The sinner we would exterminate, the man we must embrace.

Oh physiognomy! What a pledge art thou of the everlasting clemency of God toward man!

Therefore, inquire into nature, inquire what actually is.—Therefore, O man, be man, in all thy researches; form not to thyself ideal beings, for thy standard of comparison.

Wherever power is, there is subject of admiration; and human, or, if so you would rather, divine power, is in all men. Man is a part of the family of men; thou art man, and every other man is a branch of the same tree, a member of the same body, is what thou art, and is more deserving regard than if he were perfectly similar, had exactly the same goodness, the same degree of worth thou hast; for he would then no longer be the single, indispensable, unsuppliable individual which he now is.—Oh man! Rejoice with whatever rejoices in its existence, and contemn no being whom God doth not contemn.

OF THE CONGENIALITY OF THE HUMAN FORM.

In organization nature continually acts from within outwards, from the centre to the circumference. The same vital powers that make the heart beat give the finger motion; that which roofs the scull arches the finger-nail. Art is at variance with itself; not so nature. Her creation is progressive. From the head to the back, from the shoulder to the arm, from the arm to the hand, from the hand to the finger, from the root to the stem, the stem to the branch, the branch to the twig, the twig to the blossom and fruit, each depends on the other, and all on the root; each is similar in nature and form. No apple of one branch can, with all its properties, be the apple of another; not to say another tree. There is a determinate effect of a determinate power. Through all nature each determinate power is productive only of such and such determinate effects. The finger of one body is not adapted to the hand of another body. Each part of an organized body is an image of the whole, has the character of the whole. The blood in the extremity of the finger has the character of the blood in the heart. The same congeniality is found in the nerves, in the bones. One spirit lives in all. Each member of the body is in proportion to that whole of which it is a part. As from the length of the smallest member, the smallest joint of the finger, the proportion of the whole, the length and breadth of the body may be found, so also may the form of the whole from the form of each single part. When the head is long, all is long, or round when the head is round, and square when it is square. One form, one mind, one root, appertain to all. Therefore is each organized body so much a whole that, without discord, destruction, or deformity, nothing can be added or diminished. Every thing in man is progressive, every thing congenial; form, stature, complexion, hair, skin, veins, nerves, bones, voice, walk, manner, style, passion, love, hatred. One and the same spirit is manifest in all. He has a determinate sphere in which his powers and sensations are allowed, within which they may be freely exercised, but beyond which he cannot pass. Each countenance is, indeed, subject to momentary change, though not perceptible, even in its solid parts; but these changes are all proportionate; each is measured, each proper and peculiar to the countenance in which it takes place. The capability of change is limited. Even that which is affected, assumed, imitated, heterogeneous, still has the properties of the individual, originating in the nature of the whole, and is so definite that it is only possible in this, but in no other, being.

I almost blush to repeat this in the present age. Posterity! what wilt thou think to see me obliged so often to demonstrate to pretended sages that nature makes no emendations? She labours from one to all. Hers is not disjointed organization; not mosaic work. The more of the mosaic there is in the works of artists, orators, or poets, the less are they natural; the less do they resemble the copious streams of the fountain, the stem extending itself to the remotest branch.

The more there is of progression, the more is there of truth, power, and nature; the more extensive, general, durable, and noble is the effect. The designs of nature are the designs of a moment. One form, one spirit, appears through the whole. Thus nature forms her least plant, and thus her most exalted man. I shall have effected nothing by my physiognomonical labours if I am not able to destroy the opinion, so tasteless, so unworthy of the age, so opposite to all sound philosophy, that nature patches up the features of various countenances, in order to make one perfect countenance; and I shall think them well rewarded if the congeniality, uniformity, and agreement of human organization be so demonstrated that he who shall deny it will be declared to deny the light of the sun at noon-day.

The human body is a plant; each part has the character of the stem. Suffer me to repeat this continually, since this most evident of all things is continually controverted, among all ranks of men, in words, deeds, books, and works of art.

Therefore it is that I find the greatest incongruities in the heads of the greatest masters. I know no painter of whom I can say he has thoroughly studied the harmony of the human outline, not even Poussin; no, not even Raphael himself. Let any one class the forms of their countenances, and compare them with the forms of nature; let him, for instance, draw the outlines of their foreheads, and endeavour to find similar outlines in nature, and he will find incongruities which could not have been expected in such great masters.

Excepting the too great length and extent, particularly of his human figures, Chodowiecki, perhaps, had the most exact feeling of congeniality, in caricature; that is to say, of the relative propriety of the deformed, the humorous, or other characteristical members and features; for as there is conformity and congeniality in the beautiful, so is there also in the deformed. Every cripple has the distortion peculiar to himself, the effects of which are extended to his whole body. In like manner the evil actions of the evil, and the good actions of the good, have a conformity of character, at least they are all tinged with this conformity of character.

Little as this seems to be remarked by poets and painters, still is it the foundation of their art, for wherever emendation is visible, there admiration is at an end. Why has no painter yet been pleased to place the blue eye beside the brown one? Yet, absurd as this would be, no less absurd are the incongruities continually encountered by the physiognomonical eye;—the nose of Venus on the head of a Madonna. I have been assured by a man of fashion, that at a masquerade he, with only the aid of an artificial nose, entirely concealed himself from the knowledge of all his acquaintance. So much does nature reject what does not appertain to herself.

To render this indisputable, let a number of shades be taken and classed according to the foreheads. We shall show, in its place, that all real and possible human foreheads may be classed under certain signs, and that their classes are not innumerable. Let him next class the noses, then the chins; then let him compare the signs of the noses and foreheads, and he will find certain noses are never found with certain foreheads; and, on the contrary, other certain foreheads are always accompanied by a certain kind of noses, and that the same observation is true with respect to every other feature of the face, unless the movable features should have something acquired which is not the work of the first formation and productive power of nature, but of art, of accident, of constraint. Experiment will render this indisputable. As a preliminary amusement for the inquiring reader, I will add what follows.

"Among a hundred profiles with circular foreheads, I have never yet met with one Roman nose. In a hundred other square foreheads I have scarcely found one in which there were not cavities and prominences. I never yet saw a perpendicular forehead, with strongly arched features, in the lower part of the countenance, the double chin excepted.

I meet no strong-bowed eyebrows combined with bony, perpendicular countenances.

Wherever the forehead is projecting, so, in general, are the under lips, children excepted.

I have never seen gently arched yet much retreating foreheads combined with a short snub nose, which in profile is sharp and sunken.

A visible nearness of the nose to the eye is always attended by a visible wideness between the nose and mouth.

A long covering of the teeth, or, in other words, a long space between the nose and mouth, always indicates small upper lips. Length of form and face is generally attended by well-drawn, fleshy lips. I have many further observations in reserve on this subject, which are withheld only till further confirmation and precision are obtained. I shall produce but one more example, which will convince all, who possess acute physiognomonical sensation, how great is the harmony of all nature's forms, and how much she hates the incongruous.

Take two, three, or four shades of men, remarkable for understanding, join the features so artificially that no defect shall appear, as far as relates to the act of joining; that is, take the forehead of one, add the nose of a second, the mouth of a third, the chin of a fourth, and the result of this combination of the signs of wisdom shall be folly. Folly is perhaps nothing more than the annexation of some heterogeneous addition.—'But let these four wise countenances be supposed congruous?'—Let them so be supposed, or as nearly so as possible, still their combination will produce the signs of folly.

Those, therefore, who maintain that conclusions cannot be drawn from a part, from a single section of the profile, to the whole, would be perfectly right if unarbitrary nature patched up countenances like arbitrary art; but so she does not. Indeed when a man, being born with understanding, becomes a fool, there an expression of heterogeneousness is the consequence. Either the lower part of the countenance extends itself, or the eyes acquire a direction not conformable to the forehead, the mouth cannot remain closed, or the features of the countenance in some other manner, lose their consistency. All becomes discord; and folly, in such a countenance, is very manifest. If the forehead be seen alone, it can only be said: "So much *can* or *could*, this countenance, by nature, unimpeded by accident." But if the whole be seen, the past and present general character may be determined.

Let him who would study physiognomy, study the relation of the constituent parts of the countenance; not having studied these he has studied nothing.

He, and he alone, is an accurate physiognomist, has the true spirit of physiognomy, who possesses sense, feeling, and sympathetic perception of the congeniality and harmony of nature; and who hath a similar sense and feeling for all emendations and additions of art and constraint. He is no physiognomist who doubts of the propriety, simplicity, and harmony of nature; or who has not this physiognomical essential; who supposes nature selects members to form a whole, as a compositor in a printing-house takes letters to make up a word; who can suppose the works of nature are the patchwork of a harlequin jacket. Not so is the most insignificant of insects compounded, much less the most perfect of organized beings, man. He breathes not the breath of wisdom who doubts of this progression, continuity, and simplicity of the structures of nature. He wants a general feeling for the works of nature, consequently of art, the imitator of nature. I shall be pardoned this warmth. It is necessary. The consequences are infinite, and extend to all things. He has the master-key of truth who has this sensation of the congeniality of nature, and by necessary induction of the human form.

All imperfection in works of art, productions of the mind, moral actions, errors in judgment; all scepticism, infidelity, and ridicule of religion, naturally originate in the want of this knowledge and perception. He soars above all doubt of the Divinity and Christ who hath them, and who is conscious of this congeniality. He also, who at first sight thoroughly perceives the congeniality of the human form, and feels that from the want of this congeniality arises the difference observed between the works of nature and of art, is superior to all doubt concerning the truth and divinity of the human countenance.

Those who have this sense, this feeling, call it what you please, will attribute that only, and nothing more, to each countenance which it is capable of receiving. They will consider each according to its kind, and will as little seek to add a heterogeneous character as a heterogeneous nose to the face. Such will only unfold what nature is desirous of unfolding, give what nature is capable of receiving, and take away that with which nature would only be encumbered. They will perceive any discordant trait of character, when it makes its appearance in the child, pupil, friend, or wife, and will endeavour to restore the original congeniality, the equilibrium of character and impulse, by acting upon the still remaining harmony, by co-operating with the yet unimpaired essential powers They will consider each sin, each vice, as destructive of this harmony; will feel how much each departure from truth in the human form, at least to eyes more penetrating than human eyes are, must distort, be manifest, and become displeasing to the Creator by rendering it unlike his image. Who, therefore, can judge better of the works and actions of man, who less offend, or be offended, who more clearly develope cause and effect, than the physiognomist, possessed of a full portion of this knowledge and perception?

RESEMBLANCE BETWEEN PARENTS AND CHILDREN.

The resemblance between parents and children is very commonly remarkable.

Family physiognomy is as undeniable as national. To doubt this is to doubt what is self-evident; to wish to interpret it is to wish to explore the inexplicable secret of existence. Striking and frequent as the resemblance between parents and children is, yet have the relations between the characters and countenances of families never been investigated. No one has, to my knowledge, made any regular observations on this subject. I must also confess that I have myself made but few, with that circumstantial attention which is necessary. All I have to remark is what follows.

When the father is somewhat stupid, and the mother strikingly the reverse, then will most of the children be endued with extraordinary understanding.

When the father is good, truly good, the children will in general be well disposed; at least most of them will be benevolent.

The son appears most to inherit moral goodness from the good father, and intelligence from the intelligent mother; the daughter to partake of the character of the mother.

If we wish to find the most certain marks of resemblance between parents and children, they should be observed within an hour or two after birth. We may then perceive whom the child most resembles in its formation. The most essential resemblance is usually afterwards lost, and does not, perhaps, appear for many years; or not till after death.

When children, as they increase in years, visibly increase in the resemblance of form and features to their parents, we cannot doubt that there is an increasing resemblance of character. Howmuchsoever the characters of children may appear unlike those of the parents they resemble, yet will this dissimilarity be found to originate in external circumstances, and the variety of these must be great indeed, if the difference of character be not, at length, overpowered by the resemblance of form.

From the strongly delineated father, I believe, the firmness and the kind (I do not say the form, but the kind) of bones and muscles is derived; and from the strongly delineated mother the kind of nerves and form of the countenance; if the imagination and love of the mother have not fixed themselves too deeply in the countenance of the man.

Certain forms of countenance in children appear for a time undecided whether they shall take the resemblance of the father or of the mother; in which case I will grant that external circumstances, preponderating love for the father or mother, or a greater degree of intercourse with either, may influence the form.

We sometimes see children who long retain a remarkable resemblance to the father, but, at length, change and become more like the mother.

I undertake not to expound the least of the difficulties that occur on this subject, but the most modest philosophy may be permitted to compare uncommon cases with those which are known, even though they too should be inexplicable; and this I believe is all that philosophy can and ought to do.

We know that all longing, or mother-marks, and whatever may be considered as of the same nature, which is much, do not proceed from the father, but from the imagination of the mother. We also know that children most resemble the father only when the mother has a very lively imagination, and love for, or fear of, the husband; therefore, as has been before observed, it appears that the matter and *quantum* of the power and of the life, proceed from the father; and from the imagination of the mother sensibility, the kind of nerves, the form, and the outward appearance.

If, therefore, in a certain decisive moment, the imagination of the mother should suddenly pass from the image of her husband to her own image, it might, perhaps, occasion a resemblance of the child, first to the father, and, afterward, to the mother.

There are certain forms and features of countenance which are long propagated, and others which as suddenly disappear. The beautiful and the deformed (I do not say forms of countenance, but what is generally supposed to be beauty and deformity) are not the most easily propagated; neither are the middling and insignificant; but the great and the minute are easily inherited, and of long duration.

Parents with small noses may have children with the largest and strongest defined; but the father or mother seldom, on the contrary, have a very strong, that is to say, large-boned nose, which is not communicated, at least to one of their children, and which does not remain in the family, especially when it is in the female line. It may seem to have been lost for many years, but, soon or late, will again make its appearance, and its resemblance to the original will be particularly visible a day or two after death.

If the eyes of the mother have any extraordinary vivacity, there is almost a certainty that these eyes will become hereditary; for the imagination of the mother is delighted with nothing so much as with the beauty of her own eyes. Physiognomonical sensation has been, hitherto, much more generally directed to the eyes than to the nose and form of the face; but, if women should once be induced to examine the nose, and form of the face, as assiduously as they have done their eyes, it is to be expected that the former will be no less strikingly hereditary than the latter.

Short and well-arched foreheads are easy of inheritance, but not of long duration; and here the proverb is applicable, *Quod cito fit, cito perit.* (Soon got, soon gone.)

It is equally certain and inexplicable, that some remarkable physiognomies, of the most fruitful persons, have been wholly lost to their posterity; and it is as certain and inexplicable that others are never lost.

Nor is it less remarkable that certain strong countenances, of the father or mother, disappear in the children and revive fully in the grandchildren.

As a proof of the power of the imagination of the mother, we sometimes see that a woman shall have children by her second husband that shall resemble the first, at least in the general appearance. The Italians, however, are manifestly too extravagant when they suppose children that strongly resemble their father are base born. They say that the imagination of the mother, during the commission of a crime so shameful, is wholly occupied with the possibility of surprise by, and of course with the image of, her husband. But, were this fear so to act, the form of the children must not only have the very image of the father, but also his appearance of rage and revenge; without which, the adulterous wife could not imagine the being surprised by, or image of, her husband. It is this appearance, this rage, that she fears, and not the man.

Natural children generally resemble one of their parents more than the legitimate.

The more there is of individual love, of pure, faithful, mild affection; the more this love is reciprocal, and unconstrained, between the father and mother, which reciprocal love and affection implies a certain degree of imagination, and the capacity of receiving impressions, the more will the countenances of the children appear to be composed of the features of the parents.

The sanguine of all the temperaments is the most easily inherited and with it, volatility; which, when once introduced, will require great exertion and suffering for its extermination.

The natural timidity of the mother may easily communicate the melancholy temperament of the father. Be it understood that this is easy, if, in the decisive moment, the mother be suddenly seized by some predominant fear; and that it is less communicable when the fear is less hasty, and more reflective. Thus we find those mothers, who, during the whole time of their pregnancy, are most in dread of producing monstrous, or marked children, because they remember to have seen objects that excited abhorrence, generally have the best formed, and freest from marks; for the fear, though real, was the fear of reflection, and not the sudden effect of an object exciting abhorrence, rising instantaneously to sight.

When both parents have given a deep root to the choleric temperament in a family, it may probably be some centuries before it be again moderated. Phlegm is not so easily inherited, even though both father and mother should be phlegmatic, for there are certain moments of life when the phlegmatic acts with its whole powers, although it acts thus but rarely, and these moments may, and must, have their effects; but nothing appears more easy of inheritance than activity and industry, when these have their origin in organization, and the necessity of producing alteration. It will be long before an industrious couple, to whom not only a livelihood, but business is, in itself, necessary, shall not have a single descendant with the like quality of industry, as such mothers are generally prolific.

OBSERVATIONS ON THE DYING AND THE DEAD.

I have seen one man of fifty, another of seventy years of age, who during life appeared not to have the least resemblance to their sons, and whose countenances seemed to be of a quite different class; yet, the second day after death, the profile of the one had a striking resemblance to the profile of his eldest, and that of the other, to the profile of his third son; stronger, indeed, and as a painter would say, harder. On the third day, a part of the resemblance disappeared.

Of the many dead persons I have seen, I have uniformly observed that sixteen, eighteen, or twenty-four hours, after death (according to the disease), they have had a more beautiful form, better defined, more proportionate, harmonized, homogeneous, more noble, more exalted, than they ever had during life.

May there not be, thought I, in all men an original physiognomy, subject to be disturbed by the ebb and flow of accident and passion, and is not this restored by the calm of death, as troubled waters, being again left at rest, become clear?

Among the dying, I have observed some who have been the reverse of noble or great during life, and who, some hours before their death, or perhaps some moments (one was in a delirium), have shown an inexpressible ennobling of the countenance. Everybody saw a new man; colouring, drawing, and grace, all was new, all bright, as the morning; heavenly; beyond expression, noble, and exalted; the most inattentive must see, the most insensible feel, the image of God. I saw it break forth and shine through the ruins of corruption, was obliged to turn aside in silence and adore. Yes, glorious God! still art thou there, in the weakest, most fallible men!

OF THE INFLUENCE OF COUNTENANCE ON COUNTENANCE.

As the gestures of our friends and intimates often become our own, so, in like manner, does their appearance. Whatever we love we would assimilate to ourselves; and whatever, in the circle of affection, does not change us into itself, that we change, as far as may be, into ourselves.

All things act upon us, and we act upon all things; but nothing has so much influence as what we love; and among all objects of affection, nothing acts so forcibly as the countenance of man. Its conformity to our countenance makes it most worthy our affection. How could it act upon, how attract our attention, had it not some marks, discoverable or undiscoverable, similar to, at least of the same kind with, the form and features of our own countenance?

Without, however, wishing farther to penetrate what is impenetrable, or to define what is inscrutable, the fact is indubitable that countenances attract countenances, and also that countenances repel countenances; that similarity of features between two sympathetic and affectionate men increases with the development, and mutual communication, of their peculiar, individual, sensations. The reflection, if I may so say, of the person beloved, remains upon the countenance of the affectionate.

The resemblance frequently exists only in a single point,— in the character of mind and countenance.

A resemblance in the system of the bones presupposes a resemblance of the nerves and muscles.

Dissimilar education may affect the latter so much that the point of attraction may be invisible to unphysiognomonical eyes.—Suffer the two resembling forms to approach, and they will reciprocally attract and repel each other; remove every intervening obstacle, and nature will soon prevail. They will recognize each other, and rejoice in the flesh of their flesh, and the bone of their bone; with hasty steps will proceed to assimilate. Countenances, also, which are very different from each other, may communicate, attract, and acquire resemblance: nay, their likeness may become more striking than that of the former, if they happen to be more flexible, more capable, and to have greater sensibility.

This resemblance of features, in consequence of mutual affection, is ever the result of internal nature and organization, therefore of the character of the persons. It ever has its foundation in a preceding, perhaps imperceptible resemblance, which might never have been animated, or suspected, had it not been set in motion by the presence of the sympathetic being.

It would be of infinite importance to give the characters of those countenances which most easily receive and communicate resemblance. It cannot but be known that there are countenances which attract all, others that repel all, and a third kind which are indifferent. The all-repelling render the ignoble countenances, over which they have continued influence, more ignoble. The indifferent allows no change. The all-attracting either receive, give, or reciprocally give and receive. The first change a little, the second more, the third most. "These are the souls," says Hemsterhuys the younger, "which happily, or unhappily, add the most exquisite discernment to that excessive internal elasticity which occasions them to wish and feel immoderately; that is to say, the souls which are so modified, or situated, that their attractive force meets the fewest obstacles in its progress."

It would be of the utmost importance to study this influence of countenance, this intercourse of mind. I have found the progress of resemblance most remarkable when two persons, the one richly communicative, the other apt to receive, have lived a considerable time together, without foreign intervention; when he who gave had given all, or he who received could receive no more, physiognomonical resemblance, if I so dare say, had attained its *punctum saturationis*. It was incapable of farther increase.

A word here to thee, youth, irritable and easy to be won. Oh! pause, consider, throw not thyself too hastily into the arms of a friend untried. A gleam of sympathy and resemblance may easily deceive thee. If the man who is thy second self have not yet appeared, be not rash; thou shalt find him at the appointed hour. Being found, he will attract thee to himself, will give and receive whatever is communicable. The ardour of his eyes will nurture thine, and the gentleness of his voice will temper thy too piercing tones. His love will shine in thy countenance, and his image will appear in thee. Thou wilt become what he is, and yet remain what thou art. Affection will make qualities in him visible to thee which never could be seen by an uninterested eye. This capability of remarking, of feeling what there is of divine in him, is a power which will make thy countenance assume his resemblance.

ON THE INFLUENCE OF THE IMAGINATION ON THE COUNTENANCE.

A word only, on a subject concerning which volumes might be written, for it is a subject I must not leave wholly in silence. The little, the nothing, I have to say upon it, can only act as an inducement to deeper meditation on a theme so profound.

Imagination acts upon our own countenance, rendering it in some measure resembling the beloved or hated image, which is living, present, and fleeting before us, and is within the circle of our immediate activity. If a man, deeply in love, and supposing himself alone, were ruminating on his beloved mistress, to whom his imagination might lend charms, which, if present, he would be unable to discover,—were such a man observed by a person of penetration, it is probable that traits of the mistress might be seen in the countenance of this meditating lover. So might, in the cruel features of revenge, the features of the enemy be read, whom imagination represents as present. And thus is the countenance a picture of the characteristic features of all persons exceedingly loved or hated. It is possible that an eye less penetrating than that of an angel may read the image of the Creator in the countenance of a truly pious person. He who languishes after Christ, the more lively, the more distinctly, the more sublimely, he represents to himself the very presence and image of Christ, the greater resemblance will his own countenance take of this image. The image of imagination often acts more effectually than the real presence; and whoever has seen him of whom we speak, the great HIM, though it were but an instantaneous glimpse, Oh! how incessantly will the imagination reproduce his image in the countenance!

Our imagination also acts upon other countenances. The imagination of the mother acts upon the child. Hence men have long attempted to influence the imagination for the production of beautiful children. In my opinion, however, it is not so much the beauty of surrounding forms as the interest taken concerning forms, in certain moments; and here, again, it is not so much the imagination that acts as the spirit, that being only the organ of the spirit. Thus it is true that *it is the spirit that quickeneth, the flesh* and the image of the flesh, merely considered as such, *profiteth nothing*. A look of love, from the sanctuary of the soul, has, certainly, greater forming powers than hours of deliberate contemplation of the most beautiful images. This forming look, if so I may call it, can as little be premeditatedly given as any other naturally beautiful form can be imparted by a studious contemplation in the looking-glass. All that creates and is profoundly active in the inner man, must be internal, and be communicated from above; as I believe it suffers itself not to be occasioned, at least not by forethought, circumspection, or wisdom in the agent to produce such effects. Beautiful forms, or abortions, are neither of them the work of art or study, but of intervening causes, of the quick-guiding providence, the predetermining God.

Instead of the senses, endeavour to act upon affection. If thou canst but incite love, it will of itself seek and find the powers of creation. But this very love must itself be innate before it can be awakened. Perhaps, however, the moment of this awakening is not in our power; and, therefore, to those who would, by plan and method, effect that which is in itself so extraordinary, and imagine they have had I know not what wise and physiological circumspection when they first awaken love, I might exclaim in the words of the enraptured singer : "I charge you, O ye daughters of Jerusalem, by the roes and the hinds of the field, that ye stir not up nor awake my love till he please."—Here, behold thy forming Genius.—" Behold he cometh, leaping upon the mountains, skipping upon the hills, like a young hart." (Song of Sol. chap. ii. 7, 8, 9.)

Moments unforeseen, rapid as the lightning, in my opinion, form and deform. Creation, of whatever kind, is momentaneous: the development, nutriment, change, improving, injuring, is the work of time, art, industry, and education. Creative power suffers not itself to be studied. Creation cannot be meditated. Masks may be moulded, but living essence, within and without resembling itself, the image of God, must be created, born, "*not of the will of the flesh, nor of the will of man, but of God.*"

MALE AND FEMALE.

In general (for I neither can nor will state anything but what is most known) how much more pure, tender, delicate, irritable, affectionate, flexible, and patient, is woman than man!

The primary matter of which she is constituted appears to be more flexible, irritable, and elastic than that of man.

Women are formed to maternal mildness, and affection; all their organs are tender, yielding, easily wounded, sensible, and receptible.

Among a thousand females there is scarcely one without the genuine feminine signs; the flexible, the round, and the irritable.

They are the counterpart of man, taken out of man, to be subject to man; to comfort him like angels, and to lighten his cares. " She shall be saved in child-bearing, if they continue in faith, and charity, and holiness, with sobriety." (1 Tim. ii. 15.)

This tenderness, this sensibility, this light texture of their fibres and organs, this volatility of feeling renders them so easy to guide and to tempt; so ready to submit to the enterprise and power of the man; but more powerful through the aid of their charms than man, with all his strength. The man was not first tempted, but the woman, afterward the man by the woman.

But, not only easily to be tempted, she is capable of being formed to the purest, noblest, most seraphic virtue; to everything which can deserve praise or affection.

Highly sensible of purity, beauty, and symmetry, she does not always take time to reflect on internal life, internal death, internal corruption. "The woman saw that the tree was good for food, and that it was pleasant to the eyes, and a tree to be desired to make one wise, and she took of the fruit thereof." (Gen. iii. 6.)

The female thinks not profoundly; profound thought is the power of the man.

Women feel more. Sensibility is the power of woman.

They often rule more effectually, more sovereignly, than man. They rule with tender looks, tears, and sighs; but not with passion and threats; for if, or when, they so rule, they are no longer women, but abortions.

They are capable of the sweetest sensibility, the most profound emotion, the utmost humility, and the excess of enthusiasm.

In their countenance are the signs of sanctity and inviolability, which every feeling man honours, and the effects of which are often miraculous.

Therefore, by the irritability of their nerves, their incapacity for deep inquiry and firm decision, they may easily, from their extreme sensibility, become the most irreclaimable, the most rapturous enthusiasts.

Their love, strong and rooted as it is, is very changeable; their hatred almost incurable, and only to be effaced by continued and artful flattery. Men are most profound; women are more sublime.

Men most embrace the whole; women remark individually, and take more delight in selecting the minutiæ which form the whole. Man hears the bursting thunder, views the destructive bolt with serene aspect, and stands erect amidst the fearful majesty of the streaming clouds.

Woman trembles at the lightning, and the voice of distant thunder; and shrinks into herself, or sinks into the arms of man.

Man receives a ray of light single, woman delights to view it through a prism, in all its dazzling colours. She contemplates the rainbow as the promise of peace; he extends his inquiring eye over the whole horizon.

Woman laughs, man smiles; woman weeps,

man remains silent. Woman is in anguish when man weeps, and in despair when man is in anguish; yet has she often more faith than man.

Man without religion is a diseased creature, who would persuade himself he is well and needs not a physician; but woman without religion is raging and monstrous.

A woman with a beard is not so disgusting as a woman who acts the free-thinker; her sex is formed for piety and religion; to women Christ first appeared; but he was obliged to prevent them from too ardently and too hastily embracing him.—*Touch me not.* They are prompt to receive and seize novelty, and become its enthusiasts.

The whole world is forgotten in the emotion caused by the presence and proximity of him they love.

They sink into the most incurable melancholy, as they also rise to the most enraptured heights.

The feelings of the man are more imagination; those of the female more heart.

When communicative, they are more communicative than man; when secret, more secret.

In general they are more patient, long-suffering, credulous, benevolent, and modest.

Woman is not a foundation on which to build. She is the gold, silver, precious stones, wood, hay, stubble (1 Cor. iii. 12); the materials for building on the male foundation. She is the leaven, or, more expressively, the oil to the vinegar of man; the second part of the book of man.

Man, singly, is but half man; at least but half human,—a king without a kingdom. Woman, who feels properly what she is, whether still or in motion, rests upon the man; nor is man what he may and ought to be but in conjunction with woman. Therefore, "It is not good that man should be alone, but that he should leave father and mother and cleave to his wife, and they two shall be one flesh."

A WORD ON THE PHYSIOGNOMICAL RELATION OF THE SEXES.

Man is the most firm—woman the most flexible.

Man is the straightest—woman the most bending.

Man stands steadfast—woman gently trips.

Man surveys and observes—woman glances and feels.

Man is serious—woman is gay.

Man is the tallest and broadest—woman less and taper.

Man is rough and hard—woman smooth and soft.

Man is brown—woman is fair.

Man is wrinkly—woman less so.

The hair of man is more strong and short—of woman longer and more pliant.

The eyebrows of man are compressed—of woman less frowning.

Man has most convex lines—woman most concave.

Man has most straight lines—woman most curved.

The countenance of man, taken in profile, is more seldom perpendicular than that of the woman.

Man is most angular—woman most round.

18

FRIEDRICH HEINRICH JACOBI.

Born 1743. Died 1819.

A DEVOUT soul, a penetrating intellect,—poet and philosopher in one. Jacobi has been called, by some, the "German Plato," in honour of the high religious tone which characterizes his writings.

Born at Düsseldorf, son of a merchant, he was early devoted to the same calling by his father, who sent him to Frankfort to be trained for the counting-room and the exchange. Here his pious spirit and studious habits drew upon him the ridicule of his companions, and foretold the future man. From Frankfort he went to Geneva, where he addicted himself to literary pursuits, and particularly to the French language and literature, while prosecuting the mercantile training which his father had marked out for him. After a residence of three years in this place, he returned to Düsseldorf and entered his father's establishment, whose business he conducted faithfully, though reluctantly, for several years. It was at this period that he married Betty von Clermont, a lady of Aix-la-Chapelle, who brought him wealth, together with great personal and mental attractions. A preponderating taste for letters, and an appointment under Government, which he received through his friend and patron Count von Goltstein, induced him to abandon his commercial engagements; and in 1779 he received a call, as Privy Councillor, to München. But his exposure of the abuses of the Bavarian system of customs was attended with consequences which rendered that post uncomfortable, and he retired to Pempelfort, an estate which he had purchased in the neighbourhood of Düsseldorf. He here applied himself with exclusive devotion to literature, and some of his best productions were written during this period. The death of his beautiful and accomplished wife, of whom Goethe speaks so enthusiastically in his memoirs, threw a gloom over this otherwise so happy interspace of private life. He still continued his establishment at Pempelfort, with the aid of the two maiden sisters so wittily celebrated by Frau von Arnim, until the progress of the French revolution, whose consequences began to be felt in that region, impelled him to move to the province of Holstein, the native country of his father. He resided for some time at Eutin, in this district, and in 1801 visited Paris. In 1804 he was invited to the newly-formed Academy of Sciences at Munich, of which he was afterwards made president. He was the rather induced to accept this invitation on account of the loss of a considerable part of his property by the misfortunes of his brother-in-law. At the age of seventy he resigned this office, the salary of which was continued to him during the remainder of his life. He died, March 10th, 1819.

Jacobi is ranked, and justly, among the philosophers of modern Germany, although his philosophy, far from shaping itself into a system, denies,—and that denial may be regarded as one of its leading characteristics,—on philosophical grounds, the possibility of a system, and maintains, that any system of philosophy carried to its legitimate results must lead to fanaticism. He vindicated the "*affective*" part of man's nature, which the Kantian exaltation of pure reason had seemed to disparage, at least to neglect, and gave to feeling* its due place and authority as a medium and interpreter of truth. Kant had shown the impossibility of absolute knowledge. Jacobi went farther, and maintained that the knowledge of the impossibility of absolute knowledge is also not absolute, as Kant had seemed to represent it;—that we have but an imperfect understanding of our own ignorance. He differed from contemporary philosophers, in being a devout believer in revelation,—in the Christian revelation. The gospel was to him the test and criterion of all truth. For the rest, he was an eclectic, and welcomed light from whatsoever quarter it came. In philosophical insight he is surpassed by none, and though his fixed idea of the impossibility of a systematic philosophy may have somewhat vitiated his view of existing philosophies, his criticisms on some of them are among the best that have been essayed.

---

* Closely connected with this merit, is the distinction between reason and the understanding, now so widely accepted, which Jacobi was the first to point out, or, at least, to make prominent.

As a writer of German, in the opinion of the author of this essay, he handles the language more skilfully than any of his contemporaries, Goethe only excepted. Many are more eloquent, but none (of the old school) possess his ease and grace. Some of the later writers, for example Heine, surpass him in this particular; but German rhetoric has undergone a great change for the better during the last thirty years. Of German philosophers, he is the least obscure, and the one whose writings, if translated, would prove most acceptable to the English mind.

His principal works are, "Woldemar" and "Alwill's Correspondence," two philosophical novels, "Letters on Spinoza," "Of Divine things and the revelation of them," "Letter to Fichte," "David Hume on faith, or Idealism and Realism."

On the whole, as Wieland has been denominated the Frenchman among German writers, so, and with greater justice, Jacobi may be termed English-German. In his strong practical tendency, and especially in his cautious, unscientific, but severely critical, not profound, but acute and ecclesiastical - mercantile way of judging philosophical questions, he manifests an affinity with the English mind which is not to be found, to the same extent, in any of his countrymen.

This is Mrs. Austin's view of him. "As a writer of fiction, he is distinguished for vigorous painting, admirable delineation of nature and the human heart, warmth and depth of feeling, and a lively, bold, yet correct, turn of expression. As a philosopher, he is admired for his rare depth of thought, (!) for the fervor of his religious feelings, and the originality and beauty of his style. At the same time, there are few authors concerning whom opinions vary more than concerning Jacobi. It seems as if his works of imagination injured him with the philosophers, and his philosophy with the poets.

"Jacobi's polemical merits were great. He pointed out the chasms, the unconnectedness, and the mischievous results of the prevalent opinions with critical acuteness, and with all the eloquence of a just aversion. With his peculiar modes of thinking, it was natural that he should not become the disciple of any other philosopher, and that he should come into conflict alternately with the dogmatic Mendelssohn, the critical Kant, the idealistical Fichte, and the pantheistical Schelling,* against the latter of whom, indeed, he expressed himself with too much bitterness. Jacobi's place among the pure searchers after truth must, however, remain for ever uncontested; and his character is rich in all that can attract the wise and good."†

Bouterwek, one of the most capable and judicious critics of Germany, characterizes Jacobi as follows:—

"This writer does not belong to the perfectly correct stylists, whose greatest merit, however, often consists merely in elegant phrases and turns of expression. But, like Herder and Johannes Müller, he towers above all other German prosaists of his age in the powerful and original manner in which he expresses his thoughts. His style is the true image of his mind. * * * * * *

"The supreme want of his heart was religion, but a religion which should consist with reason. By a severe criticism of the various metaphysical systems he had satisfied himself that no religious truth is susceptible of metaphysical demonstration; but also that *Reason*, by means of which man becomes capable of the idea of truth, is a higher principle in our mind than the mere *understanding* which forms general conceptions and combines them in judgments from which we draw conclusions. Reason, according to his view, included that same element of *feeling*, of which he could not divest himself in his search after pure truth. Nevertheless, there never perhaps was an understanding more clear and incorruptible than his. * * * *

"Jacobi's style is not laconic but pregnant. Every principal word has a deeply considered and sharply determined signification. Notwithstanding its easy and graceful turns, it exhibits no trace of flightiness. Not unfrequently it possesses a very agreeable rotundity. In his syntax he allows himself some liberties which are not common, but which have already been imitated by other writers, and which promote distinctness and force of expression. That Jacobi, ever intent on the most fitting expression, should have discovered in the German language some turns peculiar to it and hitherto little used, is the more remarkable, since, like Johannes Müller, he had received, in his youth, a part of his education in Geneva, and had

---

* See the "Conversations-Lexicon." Art. Jacobi. Ed.
† Mrs. Austin's "German Prose Writers."

become master of the French language as no philosophical writer in Germany, beside himself, is known to have been, since Leibnitz."*

What Goethe thought and hoped of Jacobi when both were young, may be seen from the following account which he gives of their meeting:

"Although the poetical mode of presentation occupied me chiefly and was properly congenial with my nature, yet reflections on subjects of every kind were not strange to me, and Jacobi's original and constitutional direction toward the inscrutable, was, in the highest degree, welcome and genial. Here, there was no controversy—neither a Christian one, as with Lavater, nor a didactic one, as with Basedow. The thoughts which Jacobi communicated to me sprung immediately from his feelings; and how peculiarly was I penetrated when, with unconditioned confidence, he hid not from me the deepest demands of his soul! From so wondrous a combination of want, passion and ideas, there could arise, for me also, only forefeelings of that which perhaps would be clearer to me at some future time. Happily I too had—if not cultivated—yet worked my nature on this side, and had received into myself the being and the way-of-thinking of an extraordinary man, imperfectly indeed, and as it were surreptitiously; but I was already experiencing therefrom the most important consequences. This mind which wrought so decidedly upon me, and which was to have so great an influence upon my whole way of thinking, was Spinoza. Namely, after I had looked about in all the world in vain for some means of forming my strange nature, I chanced at last on that man's "Ethics." Of what I may have read for myself out of that work, or of what I may have read into it, I can give no account. Enough, I found here a sedative for my passions; a large and free view of the sensual and moral world seemed to open itself before me. But what especially chained me to him, was the boundless disinterestedness which shone forth from every proposition. That wonderful word: "Whoso loveth God aright, must not demand that God should love him in return," with all the premises on which it rests, and all the consequences that flow from it, filled entirely my meditation. To be disinterested in all, and most disinterested in love and friendship, was my highest joy, my maxim, my exercise; so that that petulant later saying: "If I love thee, what's that to thee," is spoken from my very heart. For the rest, here also let it not be overlooked, that the most intimate connections spring from opposition. The all-composing quietism of Spinoza contrasted with my all-upstirring endeavor; his mathematical method was the antagonist to my poetical way of feeling and presenting; and precisely that ruled mode of treatment, which was thought not suitable to moral subjects, made me his passionate disciple, his most decided adorer. Mind and heart, understanding and sentiment, sought each other with necessary, elective affinity; and by this means a union of the most dissimilar natures was brought about.

"All this was still in the first stage of action and reaction, fermenting and seething. Fred. Jacobi, the first one whom I permitted to look into this chaos, he, whose nature was also laboring in the deepest, heartily accepted my confidence, returned it, and sought to guide me into his way of thinking. He too felt an unspeakable spiritual want; he too would not have it silenced by foreign aid, but satisfied by development and light from within. What he imparted to me of the state of his mind I could not comprehend, the rather because I could form no conception of my own. But he, who had advanced so far before me in philosophical thinking and even in the study of Spinoza, endeavored to guide and enlighten my dark striving. Such a pure, spiritual affinity, was new to me, and awakened a passionate longing for further communication. At night, after we had already parted and withdrawn into our sleeping-apartments, I would seek him again. The moonshine trembled on the broad Rhine; and we, standing at the window, revelled in the fulness of reciprocal giving and receiving which swells forth so richly in that glorious period of development.   *   *   *
*   *   *   *   *   *   *

"Then, when I returned to my friend Jacobi, I enjoyed the rapturous feeling of a union through the innermost mind. We were both animated by the liveliest hope of a common activity. I vehemently urged him to set forth vigorously, in some form or other, all that was moving and working within him. It was the means by which I had extricated myself from

---

* Bouterwek's "*Geschichte der Poesie und Beredsamkeit,*" quoted by Wolff.

so many perplexities, and I hoped that it would prove effectual with him also. He delayed not to seize it with spirit; and how much that is good, beautiful and heart-rejoicing has he not produced!

"And so we parted, at last, with the blessed feeling of eternal union, without any fore-feeling that our striving would take opposite directions, as, in the course of life, was but too manifest."*

* "*Aus meinem Leben.*" Part third. Book fourteenth.

FROM THE "FLYING LEAVES."

My aim is not to help the reader while away the time, but rather to aid those to whom, as to me, the time is already too fleeting.

I can live in harmony with every one who lives in harmony with himself.

What dost thou call a beautiful soul? Thou callest a beautiful soul one that is quick to perceive the good, that gives it due prominence and holds it immovably fast.

It is absurd for a man to say that he hates and despises men, but loves and honours Humanity. A general without a particular, a Humanity worthy of honour and love without men who are worthy of honour and love, is a fiction of the brain, a thing that has no existence.

It is the custom of virtue to note the failings of distinguished men not otherwise than with a certain timidity and shame. It is the custom of vice to cover impudence with the appellation of love of truth.

To lay aside all prejudices is to lay aside all principles. He who is destitute of principles is governed, theoretically and practically, by whims.

Man, according to Moses, was created last; all the varieties of irrational animals were created before him. This order is still repeated in each individual man. He follows first the animal, the coarser propensities,—coarse, animal pleasure; but he is created for immortality, and can find the way to immortality. But he can also become more beastly than a beast, and use the means of immortality in such a way as to become more mortal,—as to draw upon himself sufferings and diseases from which the brute is free. He can "with the armour of light extend the kingdom of darkness and of barbarism." Herder, in his "*Aelteste Urkunde,*" remarks that Adam, after the Fall, clothed himself in the life of animals. Man is guided by propensities, and all his propensities belong to his nature. But the propensity which makes him man, which distinguishes him, is the true life-propensity proper to his species,—the propensity to a higher life. Even in the mere faculty of perception, which may be regarded as opposed to the faculty of sensation, this propensity appears. For the faculty of perception, the power of projecting objects out of himself, of raising himself above them in order to contemplate them, is objective, and is the foundation of the regal dignity of man. It strikes the first spark of a love which differs so widely from what we call lust that it is capable of resisting and overcoming that lust. The earnest observer finds everywhere, from first to last, the same economy. But the innermost essence of the purely human propensity,—as the proper seat of liberty, as the mystery of substance,—is inscrutable for us.

There is no one thing in the world for which we can conceive an interest and a love that shall endure forever. Therefore *fidelity* is required of us, and a firm intent which the soul must be able to create for itself. He who learns this acquires freedom; acquires something of that great property, the property of having life in himself, which is the true philosopher's stone.

The secret of the moral sense and feeling is the secret of everlasting life, in contradistinction to our present existence, which is fleeting however we may strive against it, and leads to death. In moral feeling there is a presentiment of eternity. I know nothing sublimer and profounder than the saying of the New Testament, "Our life is hid in Christ (the God-man) with God." Unquestionably, our life, if there is any true life in us, is hidden deep within us. Nevertheless it commands, apodictically,* its own preservation; commands that we bring it forth to the light. Faith and experience, therefore, are the only way by which we can arrive at the knowledge of the truth. True, it is a mystic, and to brutalism altogether intolerable, way. We must be able to inflict pain upon ourselves if we would attain to virtue and honour. Courage, resolution, is, above all things, necessary to man.

What is it that we admire in a Bayard, a Montrose, a Ruyter, a Douglas, in the friends of Cimon, who offered themselves up at Tanagra? We admire this in them, that they did not doat on the body but lived exclusively the life of the

* *Apodiktisch*, equivalent to absolutely; from the Greek αποδεικνυμι, to demonstrate; also, to appoint, to require by law. Tr.

soul. They were not what accident would make of them, but what they themselves had resolved to be. He to whom the law, which he is to follow, does not stand forth as a God, has only a dead letter which cannot possibly quicken him.

Every aptitude to an end is a virtue. The inquiry after the highest virtue is an inquiry after the highest end. The rank of the virtues must therefore be determined according to the rank of the ends. To discover the system of ends it is necessary to ascertain what is the destination of man, his highest and ultimate aim.

The wise man is known by the choice of the ends which he proposes to himself; the prudent man is known by the choice of the means by which he attains his ends, whether they be wise or unwise. But how are the ends themselves to be known? Is the choice of the wisest to decide? Then we cannot say, as we have just said, that the wise man is known by his ends. *Semper idem velle atque idem nolle.* But what is this one, and the same which is to be always willed? It is the glory of God.

It is agreeable to the dignity of man to hold his passions in subjection, to govern them. But the feeling of dignity does not consist in the governing as such, but in that whereby we govern, in the consciousness of a higher destination. Man knows a higher good; this it is that overcomes, not his will.

Every activity proposes to itself a passivity, every labour enjoyment. But every enjoyment presupposes a want; when that is satisfied, the enjoyment ends. All pleasure is necessarily transient.

We enjoy ourself, however, only in our work, in our doing, and our best enjoyment is our best doing.

Man imputes to himself the ability to be constant by his own proper force, and places his honour in that ability. A man of his word, and a man of honor are synonymous terms. He who can embrace a purpose and persist in it, who can act from a resolve, unsupported by present inclination, nay, even in opposition to present inclination, emotion, or passion, of him we say, "he has character," "he is a man." We despise the man who is always only what things, accidents, circumstances, make of him; the fickle, the inconstant, the wavering. We honour him who can resist objects and the impressions which they make upon him, who knows how to maintain his self in the face of them, who lets himself be instructed but not changed by them.

To believe in humanity, to trust a friend unconditionally, we call great and noble. Want of faith, doubt, suspicion, have something little,

ignoble; they originate in fear. A noble and courageous mind then believes and confides. It believes and confides not because it is a good calculator; its faith, its confidence, is power of feeling, not a cold exercise of the understanding. On the contrary, this power is opposed to the understanding inasmuch as it raises itself above it.

When man abides in the creature, he sinks behind and before into nothing.

When feeling and sentiment vanish, words and ceremonies remain and make themselves important.

Where morals are, there reason reigns over sense. And, vice versa, where reason begins to obtain the ascendency over sense, there morals arise.

The first step in the corruption of morals is no longer to regard public opinion; the last step is the absence of public opinion. Every one does, then, what pleases him; to every one it seems right to follow his own lusts. Morals have ceased from the land.

Have not all virtues sprung up before they had either name or precept? The book of life must be written before an index can be affixed to it. Our moral philosophies are such indexes made after the book; and they are generally made by men who understand nothing of the book. Others, who also understand nothing of it, think that the index is the basis of the book, and the art of referring to it the true art of life. But they always refer to it for others, not for themselves.

Life is not a particular form of body, but the body is a particular form of life. The body relates to the soul as the word to the thought.

The essence of reason consists in self-perception. It returns into self. That which it perceives, so far as it is conditioned by sense, it calls nature. That which it perceives, so far as it is not conditioned by sense, it calls the Divine Being.

True enlightenment is that which teaches man that he is a law to himself. True culture is that which accustoms him to obey this law without regard to reward and punishment.

In an age in which the good and the true are considered as two different and often conflicting things, every thing must conflict.

All laws, considered in the origin of their power, are despotic. *Sic volo sic jubeo.* Laws of the will are not laws which the will receives, but laws which the will gives. There is nothing above the will; in it is original life. How should a law be able to produce a will? Where this seems to be the case, a law-giving will is already presupposed, which, in that particular instance, appears as executive power.

"Peace is the masterpiece of reason," says Johann Müller. This is true, not only in regard to civil polity, but in every regard.

It is not truth, justice, liberty, which men seek; they seek only themselves. And O! that they knew how to seek themselves aright!

What have not men tried and applied in order to guaranty to each other reciprocally, their identity,—the being and enduring of their *I*. All civil order has this for its first and last object, that the will of to-day may be valid also to-morrow. Hence, religion has been held so sacred among all nations. *They fixed by means of it the changeableness of their nature.*

He who cannot help himself seeks protection from others in return for service, subjection, all kinds of acknowledgment. Thus arose magistrates, judges, leaders. Right was sought first with the stronger; he helped to find it. The first natural potentates were fathers, afterwards patriarchs,—the patricians in Rome, later, freeholders. He who could help himself was more highly esteemed than he who was forced to seek help from others. Hence, it has come to pass that down to the present day, men boast more of strength than of justice, for justice makes equal.

So soon as man begins to believe in others no more than he believes in himself, all *Gouvernement de confiance* is at an end.

The aim of civil polities, so far as they are grounded in reason, is to give to pure, practical reason a body. Systems of ethics alone cannot do that. Reason must be expressed outwardly, embodied in external institutions, which serve, as far as possible, to supply the place of peculiar power,—its self-existence

Man esteems human feelings higher than the express laws by which it is intended to govern those feelings. He makes the love of parents, of children, the love of friends, fidelity, compassion, the basis of all duties; not only tolerating exceptions from the law on their account, but even reproving the strength of mind which exalts itself above every feeling by means of ideas.

As a countenance is made beautiful by the soul's shining through it, so the world is beautiful by the shining through it of a God.

As my own self is present to me in an incomprehensible manner, so God is present to me likewise, in an incomprehensible manner.

Instinct harmonizes the interior of animals, Religion the interior of man.

Through the dark of world-events there sometimes dart lightnings which tear asunder the clouds and discover heaven, the dwelling of God. In the heart of man, in his spirit, these lightnings are kindled and shoot upward.

Man as a finite being must everywhere make nature—finiteness—his foundation. He would not free himself from nature, but free his nature, or at least endue it with freedom.

Certain as it is that we live in time as our element, and cannot, for a moment, imagine ourselves out of time, without likewise imagining the cessation of our being; we can as little conceive ourselves as children of time and our existence as given in time alone. On the contrary, we have a most intense consciousness of something beyond time. In ourselves we call it self, out of ourselves, God; but that which is in time we call nature or the perishable. Every perishable is given in an imperishable, and presupposes it, or it could not be. We live thereby that we continually interrupt eternity and make a beginning and an end.

Nothing terrifies man so much, nothing brings such gloom over his spirit, as when, to his apprehension, God vanishes out of Nature, as when God hides his face from him, as when design, wisdom, goodness, do not appear to rule in Nature, but only blind necessity or senseless chance.

As man instinctively interprets the features, gestures, and accents of his fellow-men, and thus attains to language, even so he interprets Nature instinctively also. As men originally communicate, and understand one another by expressions of their interior which have been implanted by nature, not invented by themselves, so God communicates with the human race through his creation. Out of the natural language between man and man there arises an artificial one of arbitrary signs; and man can so abuse this art, as by means of it to deceive himself with regard to the original design. So it is with religion which degenerates, in his hands, into empty ceremonies, and at last into irreligion.

Without religion, whither will ye flee for safety, in a world full of death, full of pains, full of warring passions? Envy with its companions, slander and malice, assail you in every situation, so soon as ye begin to take comfort in it, so soon as ye begin, in any way, to distinguish yourselves in it. Wherever ye flee, injustice and wickedness are the stronger. Neither are ye true to yourselves; no inclination, no purpose, no living and strengthening thought can ye hold fast at will. Ye summon in vain all the powers and faculties of the understanding. The understanding can only elaborate, its deliberative will can only unite here and separate there what already is. What comfort, therefore, unless the spirit can lift itself up to something unchangeable, to something eternal? unless it can embrace a faith which shall overcome the world? Perfect blessedness is nowhere, and nowhere would there be consolation even, if religion were not. Everywhere man must help himself with something. One grasps at honour, another at pleasure, and destroys his inner life. Religion only can purify and deliver it.

Man is unceasingly employed in raising himself from the stuff to the form, from the actual to the possible, from the world to God.

It is impossible to be a hero in any thing unless one is first a hero in faith.

The characteristic sign of genius is to forget one's self by living in an idea. Life in an idea must entirely swallow up the proper, natural life.

As long as man forgets more slowly than he learns, he advances. He ceases to advance, and retrogrades, when he forgets sooner and more than he can learn.

With the approach of old age I experienced, as never before, that the living spirit in man is every thing, his knowledge nothing.

In love we exert ourselves to be all that we can be, in the presence of the beloved object. Through that we become acquainted with the feeling of shame for ourselves in the highest degree. In ordinary intimacies, the reverse is found; they help us to be less ashamed of ourselves; they put us at our ease; we relax in our intercourse with the friend, and precisely in his presence are the least that we can be.

Unwillingly I assail, unwillingly I refute, not only because I know from experience how little truth is benefited thereby, but because the nature of human knowledge itself convinces me of the same thing. Before I can expose an error, I must be able to demonstrate the truth which contradicts that error. Error in itself is always invisible; its nature is absence of light.

That which is written in the taste of the times needs no justification. Agreement supplies the place of proofs; whereas the most profound opposition awakens only anger.

Only those thoughts which the most profound earnestness has produced and perfected, take a cheerful form. They make a man joyful. This is the secret of the Socratic irony. And hence it is that the taste for genuine Socratic irony is so rare.

A man of taste is one who feels the beautiful immediately; who derives the feeling of the beautiful immediately from the beautiful. Any one who possesses a considerable degree of sagacity and understanding may judge very correctly, up to a certain point, in accordance with a received model; he may decide for others whether a given work of art is beautiful or not; he may determine the why and the degree of its beauty. But because he can do this, he is not therefore a man of taste, and not unfrequently he is guilty of gross error. The beautiful has this in common with all original (nature) that it is recognised without a mark. It is, and manifests itself; it may be indicated but not demonstrated.

We exhaust ourselves in the generation of our intellectual offspring. We weaken the power of representation in ourselves by representing for others; so that, in a strict sense, we give forth truth. What we communicate, (make common) of that we lose the proper possession. * * * * * We forget while teaching others, and, with our disciples, we become our own disciples by being obliged to stoop to them. It may come to pass, that one shall believe only that which one can succeed in imparting to others. All this, however, is true only of those labours in which truths are elicited from the innermost soul. In all other cases the "docendo discimus" holds good.

It happens to us with ideas* as with money. The general sign is metamorphosed, in our imagination, into the thing itself; we prefer it to that, the seemingly universal medium to each particular end.†
Avarice is a root of all evil.

We make ourselves giddy and sink down into the centre of nothing, i. e. of positive falsehood, when we undertake to restore from the understanding that which has perished as a feeling from the heart.

Our mundane system is said to be composed of the ruins of a sun. The dissecting, divelling understanding, when it attempts to create, devises only ruins. Man must annihilate a portion of every knowledge in order to grasp it, for he

---

* '*Begriffen.*' Conceptions, perhaps, is a more literal rendering; concipio, cum-capio, that which is *taken together* in one act of the mind. *Begreifen* is to grasp to take in, but *begriff*, as now used, lies between conception and idea: more objective than the former, more subjective than the latter, in its original acceptation. Tr.

† Coleridge says, somewhere, that our conceptions may be so adequate as to preclude the desire of realizing them. This I take to be the sense of the above; this is that intellectual avarice which contents itself with the means, the representative of values, without attempting to realize them in action. Tr.

can grasp only with his conception; he possesses the thing only so far as he knows how to bring it under a word.

Every mediate designation must have been preceded by an immediate, every artificial by a natural. The more mediated our designation becomes, the more artificial our language, the more confused and dim our conceptions of the truth.

All philosophising is only a more extended fathoming of the invention of language.

There is often such a silence in me, so profound a meditation, that I cannot express how distracted seem to me all men whom I see before me. No one listens.

In nature, and, in general, in the actual, the true, everything is positive. In the understanding and its possibility, everything is negative. For, in the understanding, everything *stands under* conceptions, and the most comprehensive are generally the most empty. At whatsoever the understanding aims, the *white* which it seeks to hit is nihility, or the All-*minus* diversity, individuality, personality.

Because man falls into self-contradiction, therefore he philosophises. In innumerable ways he loses the connection of his truths, i. e. they come into collision with each other, they mutually cancel each other. Here comes in the right of the stronger. Which is the more, the most positive? that is the controversy. To one man this seems most positive, to another that. Nay, in the same individual this may be most positive to-day, to-morrow that. When this happens frequently, the whole understanding of the man becomes confused; it finds nowhere a steady hold.

It is a strange pretence, that we seek truth disinterestedly. Man seeks it disinterestedly just as we may say of the brute that it seeks its food disinterestedly, solely in obedience to an instinct. Man seeks truth because untruth kills him, and because he seeks a foundation for his best feelings and wishes; he longs for the fountain of the good, the beautiful, of truth and life.

What do we mean when we say that truth should be sought for its own sake, and that we should sacrifice everything to that? Is it a command of instinct, or do I *see* something for which I strive! The aim of philosophy, it is said, is to understand ourselves. So it appears in reflection; but its origin is, that contradiction has arisen within us, that we see *double*, that a truth was taken from us which we are desirous of possessing again. We are looking round after the truth that has flown. There is, originally, no mere inconsiderate curiosity; but there is an original interest. We find ourselves in the truth, and only by degrees do we become aware that we did not possess it entire.

Of those who boast that they seek truth for its own sake, the greater part are seeking only a system, and when they have found one, no matter what one, they are satisfied.

Reason is the consciousness of the spirit. He who loses reason loses himself, his self-consciousness, his proper being and persistence, his person. Personality is inseparable from reason, reason from personality. * * * *
Reason also is necessarily connected with liberty, and *the consciousness of personality is the consciousness of liberty.*

He who philosophises for himself meets, at every step, with difficulties, of which he who philosophises for a school experiences nothing.

In my younger days it stood thus with me in regard to philosophy. I seemed to myself to be heir to immeasurable riches, and only some unimportant lawsuits and some unmeaning formalities seemed to hinder me from taking full possession of my inheritance. The suits, while pending, grew to be important. At last, it appeared that I had inherited nothing but lawsuits, and that the whole bequest was in insolvent hands.

Some men have, so to speak, only examples in their head, others have laws likewise. Vigorous reasoning is shown in finding laws for examples and examples for laws. The eye of the understanding contracts itself, as it were, in forming conceptions, and expands in applying them. The merely book-learned have, for the most part, very narrow minds, and so too have the merely mechanically practical.

Philosophy is an internal life. A philosophical life is a collected life. By means of *true* philosophy the soul becomes still, and, at last, devout.

Philosophising is striving to sail up the stream of being and of knowing, to its source.

In regard to the ultimate objects of human contemplation, the most common conceptions are the truest. After pondering till we are weary, we are forced to return to them at last, and to allow the truth of the saying, that to children and to men of simple understandings are revealed the things which are hidden from the wise.

I have been young and now I am old, and I bear my testimony that I have never found thorough, pervading, enduring morality with any but such as feared God,—not in the modern sense, but in the old child-like way. And only with such too, have I found a rejoicing in life,—

a hearty, victorious cheerfulness of so distinguished a kind, that no other is to be compared with it.

I too believe on account of miracles; namely, on account of the miracle of liberty, which is a continuous miracle, and has much analogy with the miracle on which Christendom is founded,—the reception of the Holy Spirit at Pentecost.

To be free and to be a spirit are one and the same. Where spirit is, there is invention, creative power, originality, self-existence.

Every great example takes hold of us with the authority of a miracle, and says to us: If ye had but faith, ye should also be able to do the things which I do.

Love, admiration, reverence, are the foundation of all morality. We feel ourselves as cause, as person, and so personify everything,—streams, winds, storms, trees,—whatever stirs and benefits or harms us. Whatever we know or judge of the internal powers of things, we know and judge by sympathy, by presentiment. Every man has his own individual universe. The more he is able to transport himself into other things, to live the life of those things, to unite his life with theirs, the greater his being becomes.

The best thing in being man, after all, is that the good which we have enjoyed does not perish from us,—that it establishes itself within and around us, propagates itself, multiplies; and that thus we acquire ever more power for greater enjoyment.

To embrace an object in such a way as to see nothing beyond it,—there is no other way to be a hero.

I have all reverence for principles which grow out of sentiments, but as to sentiments which grow out of principles, you shall scarcely build a house of cards thereon.

The first and necessary condition of morality—the power of acting in obedience to laws—is easily confounded with morality itself, which consists in a longing after something higher.

To perform noble and beautiful acts is natural to man; it is easy for him, he finds immediate impulses to such acts in himself. On the other hand, virtue, which, in the proper sense, is founded on self-denial, is everywhere difficult. To virtue he must accustom himself with great labour, and laboriously suffer the habit to be formed in him. Nevertheless Nature has implanted magnanimity in him, thereby indicating a power of self-control in his mind, which acts previous to all deliberation.

Most men can get accustomed to diligence and obedience; and the whole budget of ideas and sentiments by which it is proposed to control or regulate the animal propensities, amounts to nothing in comparison with acquired skill in work and the love of work which grows out of it.

It is never too late with us, so long as we are still aware of our faults and bear them impatiently,—so long as noble propensities, greedy of conquest, stir within us.

How happy you are, said I to L., in possessing so much freedom of will! While I said this, it struck me with new force that we place that which we call freedom of will, not so much in the power of choice, as in the power of executing our volitions.

The strongest passion in man is ambition. That which satisfies a true ambition promotes the love of God, and leads us nearer to the knowledge of Him.

It is sometimes necessary to let five be even.* I have all my life practised this doctrine, more than I ought, from natural facility of temper. But then I have never been able to prevail on myself, while letting five be even, to maintain solemnly that there is no such thing as even, or that five is the law of the even.

The Athenians, on the day after the assassination of Archias, sent to the Thebans, whom Pelopidas had set free, five thousand men, as auxiliaries against the Lacedæmonians. We often find this among the Greeks, that they regarded no danger in actions which honour and propriety demanded of them. Wisdom and prudence, with them, were very different things. With all the faults and vices of these people, there lived in them something of genuine freedom, which impelled them, strengthened them, and gave to their courage a sublime character, entirely wanting to the courage of the moderns. It stood very clear before their eyes that man has a better soul and that this better soul should hold the lower in subjection.

The greater a man's ability to act for distant ends, the stronger his mind.

Man cannot reform himself in detail, nor, in general, can he keep his promises to himself, for he himself is the sport of passions, and only the law *above him* is constant. That he can acknowledge this law, subject himself to its discipline, in fine, appropriate to himself the love of it and make it a part of his character,—therein consists his dignity. And the character of the righteous man is no other than this. It is folly to build upon a man who has only disposition (though it were the very best) without principles whereby to guide this disposition and to govern himself.

* * * * * *

---

* A proverbial expression signifying that one must not be too strict in a given case,—must let a thing pass. Tr.

We always live prospectively, never retrospectively, and there is no abiding moment. Therefore let us seek internal peace, before all things, and sacrifice everything to that. Every lot is tolerable; only dissatisfaction with ourselves is not tolerable; and there is a degree of remorse from which there is no deliverance.

We may surrender ourselves without danger to impressions made by Nature, also to impressions made by men. Call it enthusiasm, call it fanaticism, provided our feeling is only the result of an actual relation, there is no harm to be feared. But as soon as we attempt to perpetuate the feeling beyond its natural duration, as soon as we take pains to imitate it, and lastly, when we even go so far as to endeavour to awaken the feelings of others in ourselves, we are in the way of self-delusion and hypocrisy.

Mankind are forever employed in giving their unreason a different shape, and each time they persuade themselves that they have converted it into reason. They fall out of one superstition into another, and with every new start, they think they have gained in the knowledge of truth. It is error itself which continually drives them before it, while they think they are flying from it of their own accord. But it is contrary to the nature of error to drive men to the truth. The truth is altogether internal, and he who possesses it is in danger of losing it when he attempts to make it external, when he regards that which he has made external as the truth itself. For truth is not this or that opinion, but an insight which is elevated above every peculiar opinion.

Although man daily detects himself in mistaking the symptoms of an event for its cause, he continually commits the same error anew, and will rather help himself with the most absurd explanations, than be contented with a thorough account of the matter. For example, nothing lies more plain before his eyes than that no individual can originate from mere composition, and yet the materialist will rather suppose that this may take place in some incomprehensible way, than assume the incomprehensible directly and at once. His soul assures him with all its power and with a distinctness which exceeds all other distinctness, that the will is before the deed, life before food, but he reasons out the reverse.

When we call the system of the heavens a mechanism, we no longer wonder at that mechanism, but we wonder at a Newton, a Kepler, who with their intellect could explore it, and unfold it to us. But if we enter into the understanding of these great men, we no longer wonder even at that; the mechanism of its reflective action becomes intelligible to us, and that which we can thoroughly understand, that which follows from necessity, we cannot wonder at. At the utmost, we contemplate it with astonishment, as we contemplate a lofty mountain, or the boundless ocean. We can truly wonder, only at that which is a wonder (a miracle), or which seems to us such. The wonder-working from love is God; the wonder-working from malice is Satan. The brute can be astonished with terror or with joy, man alone can wonder.

The truly good can be preserved only by means of itself, and all efforts to preserve it by means of anything formal or external to itself, —with whatsoever kind of sugar or salt,—are vain.

Human reason is the symptom of the highest life that we know. But it has not its life in itself, it must receive it at every moment. Life is not in it, but it is in life. What life is,—its source and nature,—is for us the deepest mystery.

Man's light is in the impulse of elevation to something higher. Not because I raise myself *above* something, but because I raise myself *to* something, do I approve myself.

I know no deeper philosophy than that of Paul in the seventh chapter of his epistle to the Romans. In the merely natural man dwells sin. Regeneration is the basis of Christianity. He who banishes the doctrine of Grace from the bible, abolishes the whole bible.

"In the beginning was the Word;" means, the will was before the deed, the end before the means, the design before the act, the soul before the body, the form before the formless, life before death.

It is ever beneath the dignity of man to give laws, merely as the stronger, and to rejoice in the pressure which he exercises like a senseless block, by mere bulk, as if it were a living force.

The actual right of the stronger consists only in his being able to possess himself of the will of the less strong. It is with this just as it is with the ruling thoughts and sentiments in our soul.

True, the strongest is always king, not the strongest to subject the will of all to himself so that they shall do his will though contrary to their own, but the strongest to execute their will, to act in conformity with it.

Men will always act according to their passions. Therefore the best government is that which inspires the nobler passions and destroys the meaner.

The written, actual laws have grown out of

customs, which customs have no other origin than the natural inclinations and propensities of men who have united themselves in a certain body. Thus justice arose. If we were to take away from the law all that has grown up freely and naturally, there would be little good and much evil left. That which still holds society together and makes life tolerable is the work of liberty and Nature.

Despotism is easier than liberty, as vice is easier than virtue.

Justice is the freedom of those who are equal. Injustice is the freedom of those who are unequal.

It is impossible to diminish poverty by the multiplication of goods; for manage as we may, misery and suffering will always cleave to the border of superfluity.

Manage a mad-house as you will, you never can make a rational community of it. * * * It seems to me as if I should go mad myself when I hear those who only lust after the fruits of slavery raving about freedom.

As history is generally written, it is far from giving us a more accurate knowledge of man. On the contrary, it only makes him more unintelligible. And yet the true aim of the historian should be, so to represent the different modes of being which are natural to man, that we shall recognise them as natural.

The inventions and experiences of so many ages and nations have only, as it were, fastened themselves upon us. We have adopted them hastily, on account of certain prominent advantages, without investigating them in their origin and their consequences.

We cannot return to the old forms, and ought not to endeavour to do so, but we can return to the sentiments connected with those forms; and they lie very near us.

Nothing tends more to bring confusion and death into arts and morals, than when men blindly transfer the experience of one age to another.

It is a consequence of civilization, that man can produce without invention, know without insight. So far, civilization makes man mechanical. It is to be observed, however, that while it kills him *a parte post*, it may perhaps quicken him in the same degree, *a parte ante*.

"Mon ame active a besoin d'aliment." (Mem. d'Hipp. Clairon.) How ridiculous the requisition of those boastful philosophers, that man should despise all enjoyment! This being, so through and through necessitous, is to be blessed in himself alone, in his action, in his striving after nothing! Everything in us is to be contrary to nature, contempt of nature!

That which man seeks, which everywhere guides him,—yea! enlightens him even, is joy. Let him, it is said, seek joy in himself; that is constant, for his self can never desert him. False! The I of to-day is not the I of yesterday. The two are often so different that the one knows not how to find itself in the other. His empty form is pure nothing, and the permanent (that in him which is not form) is wholly unknown to him. He seeks himself everywhere in Nature, and finds himself not. That which he took for himself is only the reflection of something else. That something vanished; it was perishable, and he sank back into his own nothingness.

Man is a struggling creature. He feels in time, which never stands still, which has no proper moment. What is the present? An appearance compounded of the past and the future. And yet wise men have reproved man for forgetting the present, for dreaming away his life with hopes, and fondly sacrificing to them all actual enjoyment. Tell me, ye sages! whoso strives for show-good,—is he not deluded as well when he seizes it as when he only pursues it? Where is he among your disciples who has ever found peace and blessedness in what you call the present? A thing of the future is man, and strive he must without ceasing. But in the path of the true good, together with the joys of hope, he finds also the repose of enjoyment. Created for eternity, but created out of finite nature. Seize the Proteus which,—terrified by its changing forms,—thou hast so often let slip from thy hands; seize it and let it not go; for under every one of its forms lies the true, the prophetic, the divine.

Better make use of an asses' bridge than never be able to stir from the spot. Everything good has come to us in this way, and wo unto us should the bridge no longer hold!

In one thing men of all ages are alike; they have believed obstinately in themselves.

When we lose our faith in persons, we lose still more our faith in generalities.

The most universal rule that I know for the writer and also for the artist, is that his expression be always beneath the thing which he represents. I hold this to be the true secret of mind and of power.

True attention is the product of love.

Without repose of soul, nothing great is produced. When little passions are tugging at a man he can produce only little things, and that only at intervals. Even where strong passion brings great things to pass, there is a kind of repose in the soul. Everything is concentrated upon that one, and the soul reposes on that (central) point.

Nothing is more ruinous for a man than when he is mighty enough in any part, to right himself without right.

Is it supposed that liberty consists in the faculty of choosing opposite things? Only on that ground, and so far forth as we are able to do that, we are not free. Because the evening robs us of feelings, resolutions, views which we had in the morning; because we cannot hold fast our own wishes, our character, our person; because rain and sunshine, health and sickness, change us through and through; therefore we complain of bondage. If man were always of the same mind, his reason would keep its even course, and it would never occur to him that he was not free.

By every sensible impression we are divorced from ourselves, and never are we divorced from ourselves by free activity.

Where does Nature end? There where freedom begins. It is precisely this end that I seek. I follow after miracles as others follow after the science which abolishes miracles. He who makes an end of miracles is not my friend.

The true and the good resemble gold. Gold seldom appears obvious and solid, but it pervades invisibly the bodies that contain it.

The French rulers have too high an opinion of man's powers, and too low an opinion of his destination, which makes a strange, repulsive contrast.

No tradition assigns a beginning to justice, but only to injustice. Before the silver, the brazen, the iron age, there was a golden; man was at peace with himself. All governments are, to a certain extent, a treaty with the Devil.

We may have a perfect insight as to how it has come to pass, that in the same field where, a thousand years ago, justice was sown, nothing now springs from the same seed but tares, without being able, by means of this insight, to help the evil. What is to be done in this necessity? Burke's answer to this question is—" What necessity commands."

It is an indispensable condition of a morality that is to be efficient, to believe in a higher order of things, of which the common and visible is an heterogeneous part, that must assimilate itself to the higher. Both together must constitute but one kingdom, but one creation.

Are not understanding and reason organs of one and the same being? Assuredly. By means of the one the created,—Nature or the creature, —is unfolded to man; by means of the other, the Creator. In the consciousness of man that he is creature, but God's creature, understanding and reason are connected together in him. Humanity is destroyed by the separation of the one from the other. Without religion, man becomes a beast; without humanity, a visionary.

A want which can attain to its satisfaction, that is, to *a feeling of the good*, is no evil, but a stimulus which quickens. As the wants of a being, so is the being itself, and the worth of its life.

To philosophize is to recollect ourselves on all sides. We defend ourselves against the contradiction which threatens to destroy the unity of our consciousness, (our personality), which threatens to kill us. He who would recollect himself outside of sense, outside of all feeling, of all conception, by mere thinking as such, becomes mad.

Yesterday I despatched my answer to Kant, wherein I expressed my conviction that even the knowledge of our ignorance is patch-work. Three days I had plagued myself with this letter. I was tired, out of humour. My sisters came and begged me to read them something. They were not well, and I could not refuse their request. I asked, what? A portion of Stollberg's Sophocles? Without inward vocation or predilection I began to read the first piece in the second volume, the Ajax. And yet I scarce remember, in all my life, to have been so taken, so carried away by any reading, so wondrously filled with thoughts and feelings.

You know how strange and disagreeable the subject of this piece. Ajax sitting upon the slaughtered cattle presents a half-sickening, half-repellent spectacle. Minerva, who first appears, goddess of wisdom as she is, says many insipid things; and yet what an impression she immediately makes in her second dialogue with Ulysses, after Ajax has appeared in his madness! The insipid babbler becomes a celestial being the moment she says:

"Odysseus, seest thou now how great the power
Is of the Gods? Was e'er a wiser man
Than he? or furnished more for noble deeds?"

And Ulysses answers:

"More than at him, I look upon myself
And see that we, we mortals, all who live
Are visionary forms and shadows."

And then the Chorus and Tekmessa, and Ajax himself!

When, in connection with this sublime poem, we happen to think of the decent, probable, regular, dramas of the French, why are we seized with such disgust at those products of art which lay claim to faultlessness on the score of reason? Why does their art so fall to the ground before the art of the Greeks? It falls to the ground because the Greek is a true poet, because he is a Seer. "Thou art the mouth of Truth," we say to the Greek. "Thou givest to us again that which hath appeared to thyself." The other has only uncertain traditions, and gives us, out of them, only what seems to him probable.

Fulness of human sense! Yes! thou art exalted far above thine inflated substitute, abstraction! Alas for the pure cognition which is only skin and skeleton, without bowels, without soul! "Who knoweth the things of a man save the spirit of man which is in him?" Fountain of all certainty! thou art and I am! And I begin to doubt that I am, when I listen to you, ye lawgivers of reason! ye creators of a pure philosophy!

It belongs to the nature of man not to be able to imagine an end, that is, not to be able to imagine a genuine whole. Because he cannot imagine an end, he deludes himself with the notion that he can imagine the infinite, as something positive.

The respect for science, as such, is entirely the same with that which men have for property, and for that which secures to them its possession. Science incorporates the true, gives it a visible, serviceable body which eats and drinks, and renders services in return. Then, the living and philosophical in the sciences gradually dies out; the spirit which acquired them has vanished; the gatherer is followed by a spendthrift.

The natural striving of man to arrive at a perfect understanding of himself has much analogy with the wish to be as happy, according to the vulgar expression, "as a king;" that is, to be in possession of all the means of satisfying one's appetites and passions. The thoughtless dream of a condition in which there is nothing but joy and delight. But man can thrive only in want, in labour, and in dangers. And as to his mind, if that is to prosper, it must be conscious of a constant progress from one degree of clearness to another.

From the sensuous, however we may refine it, we cannot derive that which must be apprehended immediately by the spirit. When the process of abstraction from the sensuous is complete there remains = 0, and not the absolute, fair, and good, and true. Therefore we know nothing of an absolute fair and good and true, and nothing of God unless we possess a higher faculty for the perception of truth than the senses and the thinking power.

All my convictions rest on the single one of the liberty of man. This idea is peculiar to me, and distinguishes my philosophy (if men choose to honour a system of faith with that name,) from all that have preceded it.

It is much more dangerous, and a much greater evil to abrogate conscience with law and letter, than the reverse.

If we must be the victims either of feelings and inclinations, or of words and death, I would much sooner make up my mind to the former.

An elevation above sensual appetites and inclinations, without a whither, (a definite direction,) is an empty elevation; and a blind law is no better than a blind impulse. It is with morality as it is with the self-love of man; without given impulses, inclinations, and passions, they can neither of them become apparent, or have an application.

"Is there a progress of humanity in the good and in light?" If by good and light we understand what the sublimest philosophers of antiquity, Pythagoras and Plato, understood by these terms, then it is my decided opinion that there is no such progress of humanity. I even maintain that these men would not have deserved the name of divine, and that they must have had a very imperfect knowledge of their business, if they supposed that by means of civil institutions, of modes of education, by means of scholastic exercise and practice, they could establish a kind of learning by rote of the internal;* that they could gently and gradually, by means of deep-planned mechanism, make wisdom and virtue, and their daughter, liberty, the habit of a nation, nay, of the world; so that men should thenceforth not only be able to prefer, but should actually and universally prefer that happiness which is a property of the person, a quality of the mind, to that which depends on external things, and is a mere state of sensual enjoyment. Folly, vice, servitude, and, with the last, every evil, may be introduced; not virtue and liberty. Health is not contagious like the plague and the yellow fever. Neither can it be elaborated by art, still less created; for it is original and comes from the mother's womb, firmer or weaker, more perfect or less perfect.

If reason possessed power, says a profound writer, as she possesses authority, justice and peace would everywhere rule. But now, with her dwells only right; elsewhere, with sensual appetite, desire, passion, strength.

On account of this disproportion, mankind have divided themselves into two parties. The one—the earliest in its origin—cast about for means to bring force on the side of right. They invented wisely and also experimented successfully, but never with permanent results. All their undertakings proved failures, more or less, in the end, and dispersion ensued. But undestroyed and indestructible,—however frequently

* Auswendig lernen des inwendigen: literally, an external learning of the internal.

and strangely they have been scattered and may be again in time to come,—they steadfastly persevere and will persevere in their intent. No one, not even from their own midst, knows their present strength or weakness.

The other party, likewise dissatisfied with this twofold dominion in man, and desirous of putting an end to the schism,—after mature consideration of the hindrances which had caused the shipwreck of all the undertakings of the former,—hit upon the thought of an entirely opposite method. Instead of endeavouring to bring over force to the side of the right, they sought to bring over right to the side of force. They sought not to make the rational strong, but to make the strong rational. They accused the former system of hostility to Nature, of aiming at oppression and tyrannous despotism. On the other hand, they boasted that their own was in harmony with Nature, and, at the same time, did not conflict with Reason; that it only desired a good understanding between the two. Their plan was this. The whole gigantic progeny of sense, the lusts and passions should quietly come together, and consult among themselves what was best. The best was union. But, it was agreed, they would never be able to realize this union until they had put an end to the controversy with Reason, who dwelt together with them in their common country, the human mind. Experience had shown that she was never to be quite overpowered and entirely cast out. This, in fact, was no misfortune, since the senses could so easily make peace with Reason and then employ her to their own advantage, nay, make her entirely their own. The way to do this, was the establishment of a community, the plan of which might, without hesitation, be left to Reason to draw up. For, it was argued, Reason desires justice only for the sake of the common good, in other words, she desires only that each one should have his own; the individual she does not regard nor care for. Neither does she regard herself;—that is the property or vice only of that which is an individual, a person, a self. Reason has nothing of this sort, nor indeed, of genuine reality. Therefore, it was agreed, they could boldly rely on the impartiality of Reason, and not only confide to her, unconditionally, the organization of the commonweal to be established in connection with her, but even allot to her the dignity of the chief magistracy therein;—an office like the *royal one in Sparta*. An Ephorate* might be established in connection therewith, and committed to the jurisdiction of the understanding. The people had elected Reason and placed her over them, simply and solely that she should maintain order and harmony in their midst; she belonged to the commonweal, not the commonweal to her; the collective will was the true sovereign from whom Reason derived her royal title and the authority connected with it, merely as a fief. Should she ever forget this, assume independent powers, and attempt to exalt her nominal authority above the true, then the Ephorate must immediately come to the rescue and resist such attempt. They could place the utmost reliance on the watchfulness of the understanding, in this matter, because the understanding is thoroughly and altogether a *man of the people*.

The two systems which are here presented may be compared,—as formerly the systems of Idealism and Realism were compared,—with the two opposite astronomical systems of Ptolemy and Copernicus. Only the order of time, in this case, must be reversed; the latter must be considered as the elder, the former as the younger.

What history is not richer—does not contain far more than they by whom it is enacted, the present witnesses, see, experience and know? What mortal understandeth his way?

"Tous les goûts sont pour moi respectable," says Voltaire in a frivolous poem. I can adopt that saying of his, as a philosopher, and only require that every one should confess his taste clearly and distinctly. There are but two philosophies essentially distinct from each other. I will call them Platonism and Spinozism. Between these two spirits we may choose; that is, we may be taken with the one or the other, so that we shall attach ourselves to that alone, and be forced to regard that alone as the spirit of truth. It is the whole disposition of the man that must decide here. It is impossible to divide the heart between the two, still more impossible to unite them. Where there is the appearance of the latter, there language deceives, there is double-tonguedness.

Every man has some kind of religion; that is, a supreme truth by which he measures all his judgments,—a supreme will by which he measures all his endeavours;—these every one has who is at one with himself, who is everywhere decidedly the same. But the worth of such a religion, and the honour due to it, and to him who has become one with it, cannot be determined by its amount. Its quality alone decides and gives to one conviction, to one love or friendship, a higher value than to another.

At bottom every religion is anti-christian which makes the form the thing, the letter the substance. Such a materialistic religion, in order to be at all consistent, ought to maintain a material infallibility. * * * * *

There are but two religions, Christianity and paganism, the worship of God and idolatry. A third between these two is not possible. Where idolatry ends, there Christianity begins,

---

* The office of the Ephori. Εφοροι—a department of the Spartan Government. The word signifies properly, inspectors, from επι and οραω. Tr.

and where idolatry begins, there Christianity ends. Thus the apparent contradiction is done away between the two propositions;—"Whoso is not against me is for me;" and "whoso is not for me is against me."

As all men are, by nature, liars, so all men are also, by nature, idolaters,—drawn to the visible and averse from the invisible. Hamann called the body the first-born, because God first made a clod of earth, and then breathed into it a breath of life. The formation of the earth-clod and the spirit are both *of* God, but only the spirit is *from* God; and only on account of the spirit is man said to be made after the likeness of God.

Since man cannot do without the letter,— images and parables,—no more than he can dispense with time, which is incidental to the finite, although both shall cease, I honour the letter, so long as there is a breath of life in it, for that breath's sake.

LEARNED SOCIETIES—THEIR SPIRIT AND AIM.

A DISCOURSE PRONOUNCED AT THE PUBLIC RE-OPENING OF THE ROYAL ACADEMY OF SCIENCES AT MUENCHEN. 1807.

"E pur si move."—*Galilei.*

The most ancient of those academies which have become celebrated in Europe have grown out of voluntary associations of learned men, mutually attracted to each other by an equal desire for knowledge. The growth of science, the promotion of it by reciprocal aid, by collective diligence, by friendly emulation, was the design of their union.

So pure and vigorous a beginning could not but be attended with success. It surpassed every expectation; it became famous; it threw an astounding lustre far into the distance.

This lustre stimulated and awakened the desire of imitation. It was attempted to produce the like, to elaborate by artificial means what is least capable of being so elaborated, the spirit of inquiry, particularly of invention, without that holy flame which kindles the soul and causes it to strive with ardour, to struggle unceasingly for the knowledge of the truth, for virtue, for science and wisdom, as for ultimate and supreme ends which will not suffer themselves to be subordinated to any other. The love of imitation had other aims which were higher in its estimation, to which science and wisdom were to be subservient, and for whose sake alone they were to exist. This was to change wisdom into folly, to rob science of its proper life, to sever it from its own in order to make it produce from a foreign root such fruits as were desired.

The necessary consequence ensued. Nevertheless, imitation succeeded here and there in producing a sufficient illusion. Occasionally even, something praiseworthy was brought to pass; but no genuine tree of knowledge and of life. The results produced were plants resembling the chemical silver tree or tree of Diana; wonderful enough and often right pleasant to behold; only that interior life and the power of propagation were wanting.

The Bavarian Academy of Sciences, although one of the later born, in fact, the youngest of all, may boast an equality with those ancient ones as it regards the purity of its origin. It was founded in silence by two noble men, von Linbrun and Lori. These men conceived the purpose of establishing in München a learned society which should draw to itself the best heads, not only in Bavaria, but in all South Germany. They had been impelled to this enterprise by serious considerations of the disproportion in the state of the sciences, the arts and intellectual culture generally, between North and South Germany, and of the consequences flowing from the difference which was manifested here. They had observed how strikingly the progress of the one and the stationary character of the other were depicted in the whole social condition of the nations inhabiting the one and the other region; and how they were every day becoming more visible and more sensible. The nature of this difference may be found described with fidelity and truth by Loreng Westenrieder in the first part of the history of the Bavarian Academy of Sciences. pp. 3—9. * * * *

The abovementioned excellent men, Linbrun and Lori, confided the noble wish, which made their own breast too narrow for them, to a few friends who gave their assent and united themselves with them. The first meeting was held in the house of Herr von Linbrun, Oct. 12th, 1758.

The undertaking of these few men, banded together for the noblest purposes, was concealed at first with the greatest care. Nor did they venture to appear openly until, proceeding with the utmost caution, they had associated with themselves men of distinguished reputation or of great authority, in their own country and elsewhere. They knew what hindrances would even now interfere with the fulfilment of their wish to convert their enterprise into a public institution, and they overcame them by prudence. They carefully abstained from giving utterance to their higher aims, and only directed attention to those advantages of such an institution, by which even vulgar souls may be impressed and won. "They abstained"—it is verbally recorded in the history of the Bavarian Academy of Sciences—"from the mention of those things against which difficulties and objections might be raised, and spoke only of the use and the reputation of the thing."

Such a servile form has the best, the highest and the most venerable ever and everywhere been forced to assume, in order to gain admission and to pass for something in civil society. Ignorance, says Fontenelle, in his immortal history of the Parisian Academy of Sciences, affects to regard as useless that of which it has no knowledge. It revenges itself in this way. It says: 'Have we not our own moon to illumine our own nights? Of what use is it to know that the planet Jupiter has four? To what purpose so many observations, so many laborious calculations to determine their course with precision? We shall see none the clearer for them; and Nature, who placed these little stars so far from our eyes, appears not to have made them for us.'* And yet those four moons of Jupiter, invisible to the naked eye, have been of far greater use to us than our own moon which shines so brightly. Only since our acquaintance with them have Geography and Navigation been enabled to make important advances; incomparably better maps and charts have been produced; and, by means of the latter especially, the lives of innumerable seamen have been saved.

This example of the satellites of Jupiter is only one out of many which might be adduced, of the use of astronomical labours, and in justification of the great outlays of every kind which this science demands. But the mass of the high and low know nothing of the satellites of Jupiter; at the utmost, they have a dim and confused knowledge of them. Still less do they know of the connection of these satellites with Navigation. In fact, they have scarce heard the report of the perfection to which that science has arrived, within a short time.

Fontenelle then adds a great number of examples in illustration of the advantages which the diligence of a few men, devoted to the sciences, has conferred upon all classes of human society. Men enjoy these really countless advantages without considering their origin, without considering the way by which they have reached us. No one considers how much there was to be invented here; and few perhaps are competent even to imagine the powers of mind which must have been brought into action, in each one of these inventions, in order to originate or to complete them. But it ought to be remembered, that the innumerable processes which we now universally perform with unthinking facility, could not be performed in this way, unless thought,—unless the most strenuous efforts of reflection,—had preceded them. This antecedent living agency now manifests itself, embodied in serviceable manipulations, in mere acquired mechanical facilities, in lifeless instruments and machines. With these latter the spirit created for itself,—produced with free activity out of senseless matter,—unfeeling, dumb and deaf menials, the most perfect, because they are entirely destitute of volition, and never fail nor err. Thus, every workshop of mechanics and artificers announces to him that gives heed, a mind that has become invisible, which here wrought and bequeathed, and departed after it had fulfilled its task: announces it without words; silently represents that infinitely self-multiplying power of invention, which must throw every one, who is capable of apprehending what is admirable, into thoughtful astonishment.

Nevertheless, however exalted beyond contradiction the truth just propounded, however unquestionable the manifold use which the human race has derived for the ordinary purposes of life from the progress of science, it is equally certain and undeniable, on the other hand, that science in its origin and progress had, immediately in view, but solely and singly itself and its own extension. The impulse which seeks knowledge and insight has this in common with the impulse which seeks enjoyment, happiness, the sustenance of life: that it seeks its object simply for the object's sake, as ultimate end, not as means to other ends. It springs directly from the spirit of man; it is one of its peculiar powers and virtues, similar to that other sacred power of our spirit which produces those human qualities which we call virtuous qualities, and—in consideration of their immediate origin—virtues, such as courage, magnanimity, justice, general benevolence.

With respect to life and happiness, no one doubts that these are desired for their own sakes, and he who should propose the question, what are they good for, would only provoke our laughter. Of science, on the other hand, and of virtue, it is almost universally assumed, that they have a reason, a use, an end, beyond themselves, by which they first become desirable. They are supposed to have been arbitrarily invented to serve an arbitrary purpose. That virtue and knowledge belong to the being of man, that they unfold themselves necessarily out of that being, and with it, like language, without which men are not and never were; that where virtue, knowledge, and their beginning, the significant word, the intelligible speech, should be wanting, there all humanity would be also wanting, and the mere animal present itself instead; this the vulgar souls, who know only wants of the body, and none of the spirit, will never comprehend. These men, all earth, unconscious of any immediate instinct, except that which man has in common with the brute, the instinct of desire, of pleasure, of sensual enjoyment, have ever the objects of that instinct alone and unchangeably in view, as last and highest ends. Only that appears to them real, approved, and good, in respect to man, which is found substantiated in the *sounder* animal, and may be demonstrated from that, as the only revealer of unadulterated, pure truth. Whatsoever is more than that, is, to them, of evil. Still, they tolerate science, and even acknowledge that it deserves the support and encouragement of the State, provided it conforms itself to the State, and does not aspire beyond the state of

---

* More remarkable still, is another similar example. A Parisian lady of rank understood perfectly the use of the moon, "because it illumines our nights." But why the sun should appear in the heavens, in broad daylight, she could not comprehend.

bondage for which it was born. Any other science, that which would be an end unto itself, and assumes to be free-born, they will not acknowledge. They despise the fool, hate her, and persecute her for her pride's sake. No effort of the mind, no pursuit, shall be cherished, promoted, and rewarded, which cannot demonstrate its immediate utility in relation to ordinary life. Every science, and every fine art, must carry on, or at least assist in carrying on, some honest handicraft, and derive all its worth and all its dignity from its aptitude for this handicraft, or for some manual use. Each must declare what guild or what trade it belongs to, and be able also to demonstrate that belonging. They maintain that every science or art which cannot comply with this requisition ought to be banished from the country as a *breadless* art. Not to belong to the productive class, which is otherwise considered as a mark of nobility, is thought to render science ignoble, and to fix upon her the reproach of idleness.

These principles and demands of the common mind must appear ridiculous, and, in the highest degree, absurd to those who are at all acquainted with the history of human inventions, even supposing they were not otherwise disinclined to the common way of thinking on this subject. The history of inventions proves that the most important and the most useful of them have been a secondary and unexpected result of those efforts of mind from which this precise gain could nowise have been anticipated. "When, in the seventeenth century, the greatest geometricians employed themselves in investigating the nature of a new curve, which they called the cycloid, they had no other interest in that investigation than that of mere speculation and the ambition of discovering theorems, each more difficult than the former. None of these men had the most distant idea that they were exerting themselves for the general good. But afterward, when the nature of the cycloid had been thoroughly ascertained, it was found that, by means of this knowledge, the greatest possible perfection could be given to the pendulum, and the utmost precision introduced into the measurement of time."*

It would be superfluous to accumulate instances of this sort, since it lies in the nature of the thing, that the practical application must needs be subsequent to the scientific discovery. Every useful invention has compounded itself, as it were, out of several discoveries, observations, propositions, which had no probable relation to each other, which, in point of time, were often far distant from each other, and which belonged to men of the most different characters, views, and pursuits. "The confluence of several truths," remarks the sagacious Fontenelle, "even of the most abstract, almost always produces a useful application, which could not have been anticipated, because the combination was necessary to produce it. The ancients were acquainted with the magnet, but they had observed only its power of attracting iron. It needed but one experience more, and they would have discovered its polar tendencies, and the inestimable prize of the compass would have been theirs. Had they devoted a little more time and attention to a curiosity apparently useless and unprofitable, the hidden utility would have revealed itself to them. No human imagination was competent to presuppose the invention of the telescope and the microscope, with which a new eye was given to man for two worlds at once, the sublime world of the immeasurably great, and the still more wonderful one, it may be, of the immeasurably little. It was necessary that mathematics should enrich itself through a series of centuries with ever greater discoveries, before a Johannes Kepler could appear with his dioptrics, and bring the invention of the astronomical sight-instrument to light."

The result of all these considerations is, that governments, in the formal institution of learned societies, may indeed have respect to the benefits which such societies will confer on the common weal, and may make those benefits their aim, but never, on that account, should thus make utility a condition of science, and demand that this shall be its only object. A government which should do this would betray a want of insight into the nature of science, and would require the impossible. Still more incompatible with the nature of science would be the attempt to make it, any where, national or even provincial. There may be economical societies of this kind, which should, in each case, derive their names from the material want which led to their institution; fruit-growing, wood-saving, coal or turf-finding, bog-draining societies. But academies of sciences, which are merely national, or provincial, or economical, there cannot be.

It is by no means intended, however, in what has now been said, that scientific men, who feel a special impulse to employ themselves with objects of immediate utility, and to apply their scientific acquirements to those objects, like Duhamel du Monceau, Daubenton, and others, men who have rendered equal services to science and to their country, that such men should be excluded from an academy of sciences, or that, as members of such an academy, they should not hand in essays on national and provincial objects, and lay them before the society for examination. How many invaluable disquisitions of this kind are found in the annals of the French and other academies of sciences! But such productions should ever bear on their face the stamp of science; they should spring from the spirit of science, and be filled with it.

Even Colbert, when he founded the academy of sciences at Paris, more than a hundred years ago, planted himself on that higher stand-point, from which the immediate dignity of science is recognised in its whole extent, together with its

---

* Préf. de l'hist. de l'académie Royale de sciences.

indirect worth, I mean its utility, and it would be disreputable now to choose a lower one. "The penetrating mind of Colbert," says a judicious modern historian, "did not fail to perceive the close connection which exists between the sciences and the arts, and between the fine arts and the mechanical. He felt the necessity of perfecting the theories of mathematics, of astronomy, and of physics, in order to effect a manifold application of their principles. He had perceived that the progress of the mechanical arts presupposes the development of good taste, and that taste requires models and patterns for comparison. The academies of painting, of sculpture, of architecture, and of music, sprung up and yielded a flattering compensation to the masters of art, encouragement to the pupils, to all the citizens of the State instruction and examples. The beautiful had its temple, its service, its priests, as Truth had hers. Colbert's administration was wise. He had no occasion to fear the progress and diffusion of right views. Far from shunning men of learning and intellect, he attracted, he gathered them around him; he freed them from the cares of subsistence. Even foreigners experienced his favour, and many were first made known to their own country by the distinction so unexpectedly accorded to them by France."*

Although France, at the time when the academy exclusively devoted to mathematical and physical science was established, could exhibit a considerable number of important men who were qualified to come forward as members of this society and to give it authority, yet Colbert spared no expense in drawing to Paris learned men of other countries who might give to the new Institute still greater strength and splendour. Römer was summoned from Denmark, Cassini from Italy, Huyghens from Holland. Attracted by large emoluments they exchanged their native country for France. Other distinguished men in all parts of Europe were induced to take part in the new Institute, at least as foreign members. Others still, at home and abroad, who could not enter as fellow-labourers in any of the departments of the Academy of Sciences at Paris, but who otherwise possessed acknowledged merit and had made themselves a name as men of learning, received pensions, distinctions, gifts, without any requisition being made of them in return. Everywhere appeared the lofty ambition of the minister and of his king,—who in many respects was really and truly great-minded,—to manifest a wise disinterestedness and to make it prominent. They wished to encourage and reward, and in doing this, they attained also all those other ends, the pursuit of which, by any other method, will always be a vain undertaking.

A wise Government, and one of large views, establishes academies to effect what can only be effected by means of such institutions,—a collective force which shall accomplish and produce what disconnected individual powers, although of the greatest possible efficacy in themselves, would never be able to accomplish and produce. To this end it collects together a number of learned and judicious men thoroughly versed in their respective arts; unites them in an association, and provides this association with all the aids, stores, and instruments, which are necessary for their different pursuits. Through the union of the members of such a society in one place, the most rapid and manifold communication is rendered possible among them; and to make this communication more certain, regular meetings are appointed. Sciences, which thought themselves strangers to each other, now learn their near and nearer relations; onesidedness disappears; reciprocal action, mutual influence, and a scientific common-spirit arise.

Where the seat of a learned society of this description is at the same time the seat of government and the metropolis of the land, the advantages are still greater. Scientific intuition and the insight of experience impart themselves mutually, they interpenetrate each other; light gains new life, life new light; every sphere of vision is enlarged, every faculty is enhanced.

Even men of the world in the distinctive sense of that phrase, I mean those who claim to be exclusively such, who pride themselves thereon, as the highest boast,—even they are singly seized, changed and ennobled by instruction. They feel that they must relax something of the law of pure ignorance and solemn idleness, the strict and assiduous observance of which converts them into the most extraordinary kind of pedants; since the prerogative-maxim, "*the more worthless the more worthy*" dies of its own meaning, the moment it is distinctly pronounced. Be it that this maxim refuses to be so expressed and understood, let it seek palliation and pretexts, it only renders itself more hateful by its pains; it only accelerates its own downfall; in which downfall its whole aristocratic connection are inevitably involved.

To this connection belong especially the following assertions:

The assertion, that a living, far-reaching intuition, an intuition which affects the great, the universal, is incompatible with thorough knowledge and perfectly accurate conceptions,—altogether incompatible with true and genuine learning and science; on the contrary, that it is compatible only with very general and loose sketches of the understanding drawn from appearances alone;

The assertion, that you must guard against principles, because principles lead to systems, and all systems are false;

The assertion, that only the old method (routine) which arrogates to itself the honoured title of experience, guides in the right path, and that in order not to stray from that path, it is necessary to follow that guide in all cases.

---

* Tableau des révolutions du système politique de l'Europe depuis la fin du XV. Siècle par Frédéric Ancillon.—T. iv. p. 115, 204.

blindly, and that you must never use your own eyes for the sake of finding it;

The twin assertion, that you must distrust reason which only hatches mistaken theories, and always hold by the *positive;* by this positive we are to understand either a tradition which has become senseless and absurd by the change of times, or new and purely arbitrary arrangements;*

Finally, the assertion, which expresses the whole at once, that *theoretical shallowness is the condition of practical excellence.*

Not so did the truly great men of the world, of ancient, middle and modern times, contend. While earning the gratitude and admiration of posterity even more than of their contemporaries, they remembered well the source from which those powers that enabled them to become so mighty, so prominent, and so glorious, had flowed; and not only did they continue to draw from it, but they sought to render it more accessible, and especially more copious, so that, by channels and pipes, it might be conducted in all directions, for the use of the multitude. They all loved the sciences, sought the intercourse of the learned, and, with their counsel and aid, accomplished the most important and difficult undertakings. Several of these statesmen and men of the world were scientific men in the more proper and strict acceptation,—men of learning in the most comprehensive sense of the word.

History names to us, as belonging to this latter class, among the ancient Greeks, a Charaondas, Archytas, Zaleucus; a Dion, Epaminondas, Pericles and Xenophon; a Phocion and Demetrius of Phalera, together with many others. The Macedonian Alexander himself may be reckoned in this enumeration; after him, the first Ptolemies and their competitors, the kings of Pergamus.

Among the Romans—(I omit the first kings, a Numa, Servius Tullius, Tarquinius Priscus; as, in speaking of the Greeks, I omitted their eldest philosophers, who were all rulers, kings, princes and statesmen)—history names to us, as active friends and promoters of science, in the time of the Republic, a Scipio, Lælius, Lucullus, Asinius Pollio (founder of the first public library at Rome), Cato, Brutus, Cicero, *Julius Cæsar.*

The last in this catalogue, unquestionably the greatest statesman and military hero of them all, was also the most thorough scholar, the deepest and most comprehensive thinker of them all; although he himself gave Cicero the preference, in this respect, of whom he said that he had won for himself a crown of laurel which was more honourable than all triumphs; since it was greater glory to have extended the limits of Roman learning than to have extended the limits of the Roman territory. The emendation of the calendar, which he undertook with the Alexandrian astronomer, Sosigenes, his determination and division of the year, which, with some corrections since added, obtains to this day and continues to bear the name of its author,—these are sufficiently notorious. An ever-active military life, full of dangers and exploits, did not prevent him from writing philosophical, grammatical, and political works, besides his incomparable history of the Gallic war. It was because he could comprehend and penetrate with philosophic eye the connection of the ages, that he knew how to rule his own. He who wants the former,—the power of vision and the practice requisite for such insight,—will assuredly never succeed in the latter. His age will overcome him and make him a laughing-stock, with all his plans and labours. Not seeing what is, he will imagine himself to see with the greatest clearness what is not; everywhere he will see, as well in his fears as in his hopes and trusts. Such a one may have read all the books of history from the beginning of the world, and know them by heart; the great book of the world is still a closed book to him. He has never learned what occasioned the appearance of each particular crisis—the present among the rest—at that particular time when it appeared. This intuition which comprehends, at the same time, with a clear distinction, that which works by necessity and that which works with freedom, is the philosophic spirit itself, which, as something divine, alone possesses genuine power. That which exists merely as a consequence of the times, works on necessarily and blindly; its action is wholly earthly, and mere bondage. That which works with freedom interrupts the times, changes them for centuries to come, enlightens, ennobles, sets free.

Obviously to the dullest sense, the history of Rome under the emperors illustrates the close connection between the welfare of science and the welfare of the State. Along the whole series of the Cæsars, we find the one and the other always on the same level, now higher, now lower. Who does not know the history of the first four successors of Augustus? Exactly in proportion as any one of these rulers showed himself more unworthy of the throne, more inhuman, foolish, mad than another, were the sciences at Rome neglected, persecuted, banished the kingdom. Under the reign of Vespasian, beneficent as it was glorious, and under his successor Titus, art and science revived; they were promoted, rewarded. Quinctilian and the elder Pliny illustrated this period. Then followed the cruel Domitian. This man hoped to be able, together with the sciences and arts, to abolish from the foundation whatever ennobles and exalts the human soul. Not without reason, had he succeeded! Men of lofty purpose were no more to be; nothing venerable, says Tacitus, was permitted anywhere to spring up and show it-

---

* The warning of Tertullian, that *tradition nailed God himself to the cross,* has been elsewhere quoted by the author of this essay. This Father of the Church, on the same occasion, makes the important remark: Dominus noster, Jesus Christus *veritatem se non consuetudinem cognominavit.*

self. But in vain did he oppress and banish all the friends of the good and the true. His threats and his ravings were insufficient to prevent a multitude of noble youths from wandering to Bithynia to behold the example and to hear the wisdom of Epictetus. Exile and the sword had still spared many, out of the midst of whom, after the fall of the tyrant, a Nerva and a Trajan came forth to heal the wounds of Humanity once more.

After Domitian, five excellent rulers in turn ascended the throne. Then began, with Commodus, a new series of monsters, who trode in the steps of the Tiberii and the Neros, who purposely imitated, and in the variety of their vices and enormities, exceeded them; and still adopted the name of Antonine.—At length there appeared once more a man who was worthy to bear this great name; and he refused to assume it. This was the youth Alexander Severus. I should perish, said he, beneath the weight of a name which was borne by Pius and Marcus. Of the thirteen years' reign of this youth it has been justly said, that it might serve hoary heads for a model. With this great and good prince, the sun rose for the last time on the sciences and virtues and all good order. He died, and day returned not again to Rome. With the death of Philosophy (how could it be otherwise?) her daughter Jurisprudence also perished. Reason itself seemed to be extinguished. All was darkness and chaos. Barbarism triumphed in a twofold form, and, with blended savageness and degeneracy, produced a state of things never before experienced by man.

But that which works only destructively has its limit where its action must cease, and give place to a new and opposite principle,—a creative, a forming and reforming power. The destructive is not from the beginning, but the creative. This alone is eternal; its forces wax not old.

And so, in this case also, after a long night a new dawn began to break. He who introduced it was the same great individual with whom the German empire begins.

In his prosperous expedition against the Longobardi in Italy, Charlemagne became acquainted with the great spirit of antiquity, through its ruins; and his heart kindled for the revival of the sciences and arts throughout the whole extent of his dominions. He called Alcuin and other learned men and lovers of science, to his court. These established there a peculiar association, of which Charlemagne himself was a member, and gave it the name of Academy. Thus originated the first European learned Society. Alcuin appears, for a long time, to have been its head. Among its members were numbered, besides the emperor himself, and his famous chancellor, Eginhard,—the archbishop of Mayence, Riculph; farther, Theodulph, Angilbert and others. The numerous progeny of this institute shed their lustre over the whole of the ninth century.

That Charlemagne did not gather learned men around him merely because, with his fiery zeal for knowledge, their conversation must needs be dear to him; but that the education of the whole people, the ennobling of the national character, lay near his heart, is proved by the comprehensive provisions for public instruction which he made, and of which he is properly the *founder*. "With him," says Hegewisch very justly, " began the first transition of the Germans from merely sensuous activity to activity of mind."

If his plan were to succeed, it must begin with those who immediately surrounded the throne. On that account, Charlemagne founded the Academy at his court, and, by the powerful influence of his example, set in motion every mind that Nature had endowed with any degree of talent. No longer might the great look with contempt upon every species of intellectual employment, even to reading and writing; unless they were willing to see those whom they despised for their want of birth, exalted above them and enjoying exclusive favour. By this means, Charlemagne, in a few years, procured for himself able assistants and zealous participators in his lofty schemes.

He then went a step farther and ordered schools to be established in connection with every convent and every cathedral; and, what was most important, they were so arranged as to be useful not only in the education of those who devoted themselves to the clerical office, but also in the education of the laity, especially those of rank. For the benefit of the common people, and of those country-priests who were not sufficiently instructed, he caused passages to be collected from the Fathers, translated into the German, and read by the priests to the people on Sundays and public festivals of the Church.

From no one of the edicts of this truly great man, who wished not only to command but to rule, does his straight-forward and profound sense, his penetrating intellect, shine forth more conspicuously than from that just mentioned. He understood the direction which enlightenment must take, in order that it may be true and entirely sound.

Unfortunately, this great Reformer was, at the same time, a conqueror, and thought it necessary to convert obstinate pagans with the sword. Thus it came to pass, that he laboured against himself, and that what he planted did not attain sufficient strength. The schools which he established continued indeed; they even multiplied with the spread of Christendom and the wants of a more numerous clergy which that spread occasioned. But now, in the supply of these wants, everything else was forgotten. The schools educated only priests, and imparted to them only, in a very imperfect manner, what was absolutely essential to their calling. The most profound and pernicious ignorance prevailed. Hierarchy and feudal anarchy reached the summit of their power. State and Church ran wild; that epoch began which properly bears the name of the middle ages.

Towards the middle of this period, at the beginning of the thirteenth century, those four-limbed bodies for teaching and learning were formed, whose offspring to this day bear the barbarous name of Universities. With these,— with the unlimited power of scholasticism, which then culminated,— with the Dominicans and Franciscans,— the eclipse of Reason became central. Knowledge of the languages and ancient literature fell into utter contempt. They who occupied themselves with these in any degree were derided as dullards. Nevertheless, all this while, and through the whole medieval period, instruction, by way of preparation, in the seven liberal arts, as they were called, continued; and to this institution— to the preparatory schools— it is chiefly owing, that ancient literature did not pass into entire oblivion, and that the possibility remained of a return to the beautiful, the great and the true which had vanished with the fore-world.

It is very remarkable that though important progress was made in some departments of science during the middle ages—as in geometry and arithmetic with Gerbert, in natural science with Albertus Magnus and Roger Bacon;—and even though other branches of human knowledge unfolded themselves as new instincts, and introduced learned occupations even among the laity,— as jurisprudence and medicine which arose at the same time, toward the end of the eleventh century,— the former at Bologna, the latter at Salerno:— that notwithstanding these onward movements and the *mighty impulse given to the thinking faculty by scholastic studies*, the culture of reason, in its proper sense, did not arise or come to view. It arose first with the revival of ancient literature, and made mighty progress when, in Italy, through the instrumentality of Cosmo de Medicis, that *Platonic Academy*, celebrated not only in the annals of the learned, but in the history of the world, was formed, and, almost contemporary with it, a similar learned society in Germany, under the patronage of John of Dalburg, which called itself the Rhenish, and which proved even more fruitful than that of Florence.

Heeren remarks of the Florentine Institute, that "in an age when the institutions for the promotion of the sciences were all, as yet, under the control of the convents or of certain corporations, Cosmo, in his Platonic Academy, exhibited the first model of a free union for scientific culture, of which the many subsequent institutions of this kind were imitations, bearing the name (academies) without, for the most part, inheriting their spirit."*

Of the Rhenish Institute, Hegewisch says, after remarking that nothing of the kind had ever been seen in Germany before, except once at the court of Charlemagne: "so far as we are acquainted with this association, it was established precisely on that footing which seems most suitable for literary societies. The only bond which united the members, was mutual friendship originating in a common desire of being useful, and founded on reciprocal esteem. Among the members of this society were the Freiherr von Dalburg, afterward Bishop of Worms, the friend of Conrad Celtes, of Rudolph Agricola, of Johann Reuchlin, and of every man who, by virtue of distinguished talents, merited a place by the side of these; Wilibald Birkhaimer, who, as a statesman, a soldier, and an elegant writer, was an extraordinary phenomenon in Germany at that time; together with many others distinguished partly by their rank and station, and partly by their learning and talents."*

What made the preceding centuries so dark and ever darker is sufficiently notorious, after the labours of so many excellent men devoted to the illustration of this subject. Ignorance and barbarism grew in proportion as *hierarchy* and *feudalism* reared their summits over against each other, and wrought together, without concert, in the destruction of all true civil power.

This form of government could not reform itself, (as, in fact, no one has yet done; evil, in and of itself, can only grow worse continually;) it had to go down, and a new one to arise in its stead. This took place after a series of events, —crusades, and extended navigation, with all which they brought in their train,—had enlarged the sphere of vision of the nations, and given them the courage and the capacity to assert the feeling, common to all men, of self-property† against spiritual and personal tyranny. There arose a numerous class who, by virtue of their education, by their mode of living, their investigations and experiences, had attained to very different views of the world and man, and to quite other criteria of the know-worthy and the true, than those which the schools and the lecture-rooms of the time could furnish.‡ This class, or rather the taste for the good and the true, which had sprung from an understanding of the really useful, of that which benefits mankind in general, gained the ascendancy. The native oppressors and devastators of Ausonia disappeared, and citizen-princes arose in their place. The age of the Medicis began, and, at Florence, that Academy mentioned above, which numbered among its most active members and promoters, a Duke Frederic of Urbino, and the celebrated King Mathias Corvinus of Hungary. The inspiration of Italy passed over to Germany, but with this difference, that whereas there, citizen-scholars became princes, here, on the other hand, princes, and the companions of princes, became scholars, or, at least, friends,

---

* Gesch. des Studiums der classischen Lit. B. II. par. 20.

* Allgemeine Uebersicht der deutsch. Kulturgeschichte. S. 189. 191. 192.

† *Selbst angehörigkeit*—the belonging to one's self.

‡ Geschichte der Künste und Wissenschaften, v. Buhle. Abt. vi. B. 2. Absch. I.

lovers, and promoters of science. Who has not heard, in this connection, the names of Frederic the Wise of Saxony, of Philip of the Palatinate, of the Dukes Eberhard and Ulrich of Wittenberg, of Johannes von Dalburg, of Count Moritz von Spiegelberg, of Rudolph von Lange, and their pupils, Hermann von Nuenar and Hermann von dem Busche, above all, of Ulrich von Hutten?

Contemporary with these excellent men were the three patriarchs of German humanities,* Rudolph Agricola, Johann Reuchlin, and Conrad Celtes. The series of excellent writers who appeared in our country in the sixteenth century are to be regarded as the descendants of these. Yet they were not schoolmen, but only transient teachers, for a longer or shorter period, in universities, and belonged rather, especially the two former, to the great world and the life of affairs. To them chiefly it is to be ascribed, that classic literature, and with it philosophy and history, gained currency among the higher classes also, and were introduced at courts. On the other hand, they, for their part, received a kind of culture which is gained only by intercourse with the actual world, by participation in its affairs, and by intimate acquaintance with the principal conductors of those affairs; by mutual influence, action and reaction. Neither science nor government can thrive without some reciprocal action of this sort. For how can ignorance rule wisely, or even execute successfully its unwise plans? How can it preserve its *authority*, without which there is no true and enduring *power* in governments? And, on the other hand, how could science and wisdom make their dignity and their authority immediately felt? make it that which proves itself, universally, the stronger? Neither is compatible with the nature of man. Therefore let strength cleave to wisdom and wisdom to strength.

No one will question that the vast change which took place with the nations of Europe in the fifteenth and sixteenth centuries, and which has now been sketched with few strokes, was a change which ennobled humanity throughout this quarter of the globe, a real and general improvement of the human condition. It may be asked, however, with respect to the farther progress which has been making, for more than three centuries, in the same direction, or at least apparently in the same direction, whether this progress, the reality of which cannot be disputed, has been a progress toward a better and ever better? Consequently, whether humanity, in this age, may boast itself and rejoice to have drawn much nearer to the great end of the race, inward and outward peace, by universal and sure knowledge of the know-worthy, by universal and firm possession of the have-

---

* *Der deutschen humanisten*, i. e. of those who, in Germany, cultivated the "humanities," as they are called.

worthy, than our fathers were three hundred years ago?

This question, in order to be satisfactorily answered, must be put on higher grounds and in a form which concerns human nature in general. The problem would then read thus: Has the human race an attainable goal here on earth? And, if there is such a goal, is the whole race approaching it gradually, by different, and even apparently opposite paths? Or may single nations, at least, be moving toward it, by a continued approximation, until somewhere, at last, it is reached?

All the animal races have a goal which they may attain to. The tendency of each one is fulfilled, entirely satisfied; it completes its course, lives out its life. Not so man. He is a *yonder-sided* being. His senses and his understanding he has in common with the brute. Reason belongs to him alone. By means of that, he is made capable of a God and of virtue, of the beautiful, the good, the sublime. His instinct is religion.

The faculties which man possesses in common with the lower animals, he can use, cultivate, and apply in an infinitely greater variety of ways than they; and, with his more cunning understanding, which, as mere understanding, he owes, after all, only to a richer and more artificial organization, he may advance to such an extent that, compared with his speechless brothers, even on this stage, he shall be capable of seeming an essentially different being from them, living and free, endued with a creative spirit, a self-existing being.

But let us not forget to notice that the progress which man makes with the mere understanding, which necessarily relates to objects of sense alone, is, to say the least, *indifferent* in respect to reason, i. e. the cultivation of genuine humanity, of that which, exclusively and alone, makes man man. That is to say, the progress may be, and, in the beginning, always is, of such a nature as to prepare the way for the influence of true humanity, as to accompany and to promote it. But it may also acquire such a character, and has hitherto, in the most diverse ways, always acquired it, as to produce a strikingly opposite effect; as to destroy humanity, to suppress reason, and crowd everything divine out of the human breast.

The fact is but too evident, that a people may be admirably skilled in the arts, possess a many-sided culture, and even exhibit, outwardly, the most refined morals, and yet, at the same time, be inwardly, in the highest degree, corrupt, deeply immoral, God-forgetting, on the whole, destitute of all virtue.

Impressed with this truth, which the past and the present alike universally confirm, that a culture relating to the sensual life alone, far from aiding humanity by its progress, oppresses and corrupts it in its innermost being, and, in spite of all our refinement and affluence, makes us, in truth, only worse and more miserable *animals*,—deeply impressed with this truth, Rousseau wished, in order to get rid of our understanding which invents sciences, arts, and laws, to our undoing, that we might, renouncing our reason also, (in his zeal he forgot this part of our nature,) return to the forest, become four-footed and innocent once more, if this were only practicable now.

This fiery orator, and all who, since him, have handled the same subject, themselves saw by the light of the understanding only; and so the solution of this knot must needs be an impossibility for them. If reason, they maintained, is incapable of producing a 'heaven-on-earth,' she is deserving of no particular regard, at least, is not worth all the fuss which has hitherto been made about her. Others, who wished to preserve the authority of that which they denominated reason, contended that the heaven-on-earth would come, and that so soon as—no other should be talked of. The unphilosophical mocked at this, and, without waiting for that which reason might accomplish at some future period, they made their heaven-on-earth, as well as they could, on the spot. The philosophers, in silence, did the same.

The true word of this enigma, or its solution, is a yes and a no at the same time,—both equal in force, both equal in right, and of such a character, that the negation does not cancel the affirmation, nor the affirmation the negation, but both maintain themselves over against each other, and are mutually balanced.

When the faculty of desire has given the ends, the understanding assists to find the means necessary to the attainment of those ends. It distinguishes, combines, arranges, weighs, and considers. It calms the mind to prudence. But it is incapable of generating ends—original ends—out of itself. These all spring from sensual or supersensual, corporeal or spiritual wants. In and with *those*, works the understanding, in and with these, Reason.

It is a truth old as the human species, that sense and reason are in continual conflict with each other, that now one and now the other is in the ascendancy. Herein is manifested the discord of man with himself, caused by two propensities essentially different in their demands, and often diametrically opposite in their operation. One of these propensities produces the practical understanding, the other practical Reason.

There can be no dispute as to which of these propensities deserves, absolutely and always, the preference and the supremacy. No one denies that the highest authority belongs to Reason, and that unconditional obedience is due to her precepts.

Understanding may exist in the highest degree, even where the most profligate aims are manifest. It executes with equal assiduity the best and the worst. Of itself, it knows not what is good or bad, but only what is *more* or *less*. It can only mete according to a given measure; it can only deliberate, not subordinate;* it can only number, compute, calculate. To make out a first cause or an ultimate aim, lies entirely beyond its sphere.

"What is good," says the wise man of Stagira, "is so by the inherent power of the object; and life itself is a good, only because we learn what is good, by means of it." Reason alone makes known to us what is good in itself. Reason is the faculty of proposing to ourselves the highest. As such, it stood with the ancients, under the title of Wisdom, at the head of the virtues; it arranged them, it had invented them. Prudence is the virtue of the understanding. That faculty discovers and reveals what is before, unconcerned as to the worth of the end, whether good or bad.

"If Reason had the power as she has the authority," says a profound English thinker,† "Justice and Peace, the Good and the Beautiful would everywhere reign supreme." But now she has only right on her side; strength dwells elsewhere, with sensual desire, with the appetites and passions. This disproportion cannot be universally abolished, but the nobler or the ignobler may obtain more or less the ascendancy, and the times, accordingly, be better or worse.

Only that—according to the definition of one of our most acute and noble thinkers—deserves to be called a better age, in which human nature in a state of the most active self-development, although defective in some points, yet, on the whole, harmonious, has distinguished itself by nobleness of sentiment and energy of mind in entire nations; in which a noble and difficult aim was clearly discerned and boldly and steadfastly pursued. The value of an age, therefore, is not to be estimated by the bloom of the arts, or by the multitude of learned acquirements, by which particular classes of cultivated individuals may be distinguished; not by the powers and deeds of single, celebrated men, nor by the predominance of a so called enlightenment, in the best sense of the word; seeing that the faculty of moral self-determination is cultivated less by instruction than by living example, and, in an enervated century, all moral doctrines, although they may take root in the understanding, act but feebly on the character. Least of all, is the value of an age to be estimated by the standard of public self-content, which is generally considered a less fallible one; since man may easily sink so low that the manner of his well-being shall concern him but little, if only, on the whole, he is tolerably well. Let it first be ascertained what kind of well-being the people enjoy. Enjoyment is stimulating and honourable, only as a consequence of true self-development; and the real happiness of man,

---

* The epigrammatic force of the German is lost in this translation of the phrase, *nur ueber*: *nicht unterlegen*, i. e., only overlay, not underlay. But the rendering, it is believed, is otherwise exact. Tr.

† Joseph Butler.

which, at bottom, we all crave, is a noble happiness.*

Tried by these principles, the age in which we live, can hardly receive the testimony that it belongs to the better sort.

Means we have, as no generation ever had before us. But with this wealth of means what ends do we attain? What ends do we propose to ourselves? We are full of science, and are daily inventing new arts, but men, such as the ancient, and even the middle times — such as the fifteenth and sixteenth century produced, are proportionally rare among us. Our pride is to be able to dispense with such powers and virtues. So Pericles of old pronounced his Athenians happy, in that they had no need to be Spartans in virtue.† As, in the earliest times, men were at pains to subdue wild beasts, and to impart to the beasts which they subdued, habits contrary to their instincts; so, in later times, an entire, degenerate Humanity strives to subdue true humanity, wherever it is still active, to bring it beneath the power of a cultivated animalism which deems itself superior, to suppress or to pervert, on all sides, the higher instinct, so that, of all which has ever borne the name of virtue, there shall be nothing left but so called utilities, which may also be applied to vicious ends. To this class belong courage, industry, moderation, obedience, to which men may actually, to a certain extent, be merely *trained*, as we train animals. This is the true pedagogic of our time, the only one which the time esteems. It shows itself inexhaustible in devising new methods to attain the abovementioned end,—to separate what is merely useful in virtue from virtue itself, and to make it a matter of public opinion, that *naked* virtue, which would be estimated, not by what it fetches, but by what it costs, should be sent to the mad-house. And thus we become every day more intelligent,‡ more ingenious, and, in the same proportion, more irrational.§ Individually and in the mass,—nationally,—we have become more devoid of reason.

"Egoism and rage for enjoyment on principle," says the writer just quoted, "under the name of sound philosophy, destroy the fairest relations of life. The flattering happiness-doctrine, by which it was proposed at first to dam the stream of passion, has long since become a frail skiff, which follows the current. The more earnest and exalted morality which inspires man with a consciousness of his dignity, has become too strange and too high for the people. They cannot comprehend it. Man, in general, is conscientious, in the strictest sense, only then, when, in secret also, he feels the necessity of shame,

before another than himself. The belief in that other, has been, for centuries, by instruction and tradition, identified with attachment to a church. The inconsiderate cry of enlightenment has torn the people away from the Church, and Conscience is left without house or home. And now one party thirsts for sweet pleasure, to drain the cup of life to the dregs, and the other party crawls back to the cross in the literal sense of these words. Amid this disgusting (we may call it) opposition between a reviving priestcraft and a happiness-theory which knows not God, a generation is growing up whose destiny no philosophy can control. It would need no extraordinary occurrences to deliver up this generation to a new Mohammed. For it needs but few syllogisms now-a-days, to rob men of the principles of their 'human understanding,' as they call it. Popular enlightenment among us is unnaturally advanced. Its unnatural beginning and progress portend its natural termination. Posterity will not wonder if, in the desert of unbelief, men raise serpents and pray to golden calves once more; and if, in this serpent-and-calf-service, philosophers tend the altars."

Remarkable signs exhibit themselves. But twenty years ago, all shallow heads were agreed with Voltaire, Helvetius, Diderot, and their disciples, that philosophy and every method of cultivating and diffusing it, were good and wholesome. Now, all shallow heads are equally unanimous in the contrary opinion. All philosophising is affirmed to be useless and even pernicious. They became convinced, by an extraordinary event, that egoism cannot be made just, at least, not in the gross, in the way which their teachers had affirmed. They became convinced that a pure democracy of mere appetites and passions, however organized, can never become a kingdom of happiness and peace Hence they concluded (for the principle of egoism, as the only true principle, they once for all, could not let go) that it is better to renounce all hope of justice, to give up Humanity, and to abandon everything to Chance.

Far be it from us to concur with them. A loud appeal against them to the genius of Humanity, is the duty of every noble-minded man. We need heroes of humanity; and they will appear, as they have hitherto appeared in every case in which the highest necessity demanded them. As to the how and the when, let no one ask. Let each one perform, in his place, what the better, the *reliable* spirit within him enjoins.

This spirit, as it is its own highest end, so it is its own only means. Against the power thereof no other power may stand. It will pierce through and overcome.

It is impossible that a pure and clear understanding should be incompatible with an elevated reason. Rather, when used aright, they must mutually promote each other. There can be no bad use of the reason. And even of the understanding, there can only then be a bad

---

* See, Die goldenen Jahrhunderte, v. Fr. Bouterwek. Neues Museum der Phil. und Lit. Band I. Heft 2.
† Thucydides, ii. 34-39.
‡ *Verständig.*
§ *Unvernünftig.*—Observe all along the distinction, nowhere so prominent as with Jacobi, between the understanding and the reason. Tr.

use, when that faculty is already, in part, subjugated, and, in the same measure, eclipsed by the senses which it was ordained to rule. Only then will it prove itself hostile to reason,—place itself as a dark body before the sun of the spirit and intercept its rays. Its self-eclipses are not to be likened to the eclipses of the moon, in relation to which Thucydides says; "that the Greeks of his day had long since ceased to be afraid of eclipses of the sun, but that eclipses of the moon still excited their alarm." They did not comprehend how a body could stand in its own light.

It is plain, to him who reflects, in what way these general considerations connect themselves with what was said above, concerning learned societies of old and recent time, and what bearing they have on the new dedication of the Royal Bavarian Academy of Sciences. They came unsought. Dulness and narrowness cannot comprehend the design of these intellectual alliances. With bold assumption, they pronounce judgment upon them, or ask for results of immediate utility. These our Academy indeed, as the Keeper of the scientific (and what splendid!) treasures and collections of our illustrious monarch and of this kingdom, (a beautiful addition to its destination, which hitherto no other academy in the world has possessed, to this extent) can point to with serene brow; but they are not the only thing that gives value to this fair circle of the priests of humanity. The high ancestors of our Maximilian Joseph founded this Institute and made its conduct their care. The Genius of this kingdom would have mourned if our age had suffered it to become extinct. This was not to be apprehended. The lofty prince whom, with joy and triumph, we call *ours*,— whom, with full heart, we call the *king;* he who, in all ways, blesses his people, is willing also to increase their fame by helping to preserve to them so sacred an inheritance, by furnishing it anew, by enlarging its powers, by increasing its splendor.

Those who conclude, this day, the renewed alliance of truth and wisdom, are justly inspired with the hope of something better, and with courage to promote it. "*An institution of peace, and for the mediation of the antagonistic in time, by science,*"* has been founded. It is allowed us to speak freely of the advantages, but also of the defects of the time. Whatever it possesses that is costly and excellent in relation to science and art, is presented to us, in rich abundance, by royal liberality. To contribute something toward the promotion of the highest, and of whatsoever is wanting to the time, shall be the unalterable aim of our most zealous endeavours.

Blessings on the best of kings, who called this union into being, and who will foster and preserve it!

---

* Excellent words of Schelling.

HERDER.

JOHANN GOTTFRIED VON HERDER.

Born 1744. Died 1803.

This honored name, than which Germany has few more prized, represents a wide range of intellect, and covers a large space in the national literature. Herder is a literature in himself, including theology, philosophy, history, criticism, poetry; all the various departments of literary effort, and approved in all. He surpasses all his contemporaries in breadth, and most of them in depth. Such union of breadth and depth has seldom been seen. To him may be ascribed the epithet "myriad-minded." He towers above the ordinary level of humanity, not, like most great men, in a single peak, but with a many-headed elevation; a vast mountain-range whose highest summits mingle with the skies; whose sunny slopes are covered with luxurious vegetation; whose secret valleys are haunted by the Muse of Romance, and beneath whose surface are mines of gold.

Had Herder possessed the element of form in any degree proportioned to the sumless wealth of his intellect and his all-sided culture, he would have been the first poet, not of Germany only, but of his age, of any age. There lay his defect. He was no artist. Like king David, he collected materials from the ends of the earth, but it was not given to him to rear a temple therewith. With all his voluminousness he has left no perfect work. Even his "Ideas toward a philosophy of the history of Humanity" is fragmentary, as the name imports.

Herder was born at Mohrungen in East Prussia, where his father was *Cantor** of the church and usher in a female seminary. His early education was better adapted to make him a good man than a brilliant scholar, being confined to the reading of the bible and the hymn-book. Other books, which his thirst for knowledge constrained him to seek, he was obliged to read by stealth; and it is related that he used to climb a tree and lash himself with a leathern strap to one of the branches for this purpose.

He learned to write, and the beauty of his chirography procured him a patron in Trescho, a clergyman who employed him as amanuensis, and permitted him to share the instruction of his sons in the Latin and Greek languages. The intense application with which he devoted himself to the pursuit of knowledge brought on a disease of the eyes, from which he never entirely recovered. A Russian surgeon who had afforded him temporary relief, and who was then a visiter in the house of Trescho, persuaded him to study surgery in St. Petersburg, and offered not only to pay his expenses thither, but to give him gratuitous instruction. But at Königsberg, on their way, Herder was so overcome by the sight of a dissection which he witnessed, that he abandoned this project, and turned his attention to theology. He remained in Königsberg for this purpose, supporting himself, as a private instructor, while pursuing his studies at the university. He there formed an acquaintance with Hamann and with Kant.

In 1765, he was appointed teacher and preacher at the Cathedral school at Riga, where he kindled the enthusiastic devotion of his hearers and pupils by his word and his writings. For here commenced his career as an author. In 1768, he declined a call to St. Petersburg as inspector of the St. Peter's school in that city, and accepted the office of travelling chaplain to the prince of Holstein-Eutin. In this capacity he travelled through Germany as far as Strassburg, where he was induced to resign his office on account of his eyes, which began to trouble him again, and to undergo an operation which detained him for a long while in that city. Here he became acquainted with Goethe, who was then a student of Law at Strassburg. Goethe attributes great value to this acquaintance in his auto-biography, and makes much of Herder's influence on his mind and character at that forming period of his life. "I might count myself fortunate," he says, "that by an unexpected acquaintance, whatever of self-complacency, of self-mirroring, of vanity, pride, and highmindedness might slum-

---
* An office in the Lutheran Church, of which the principal duty is that of precentor—whence the name.

ber or work in me, was subjected to a very severe trial which was *unique* in its kind, by no means proportionate to the time, but so much the more penetrating and sensible.

"For the most significant occurrence and that which was to have the most important consequences for me, was an acquaintance and a consequent nearer connection with Herder. He had accompanied the prince of Holstein-Eutin, who was afflicted with melancholy, in his travels, and had come with him as far as Strassburg. Our society, as soon as they were aware of his presence, felt an earnest desire to approach him, and this gratification happened to me first in a quite unexpected and accidental manner. I had gone to the hotel '*Zum Geist*,' to visit I know not what distinguished stranger. At the foot of the stairs I met a man who was also on the point of ascending, and whom I might have taken for a clergyman. His powdered hair was rolled up into a round lock; a black dress likewise distinguished him, but still more a long black silk mantle, the end of which he had gathered together and thrust into his pocket. This somewhat striking, but, on the whole, gentlemanly and agreeable appearance, of which I had already heard speak, left me no doubt that he was the celebrated arrival, and my address must have convinced him at once that I knew who he was. He asked my name, which could be of no importance to him; but my frankness appeared to please him, for he responded to it with great kindness, and, as we ascended the stairs together, showed himself ready at once for a lively communication. It has escaped me whom we then visited. Enough, at parting, I begged permission to call upon him at his lodgings, which he accorded to me in a manner sufficiently friendly. I did not fail to avail myself repeatedly of this permission, and was more and more attracted by him. He had somewhat gentle in his carriage that was exceedingly fitting and graceful, without being exactly *adrett;* a round face, a significant brow, a somewhat blunt nose, a somewhat prominent but highly individual, agreeable, amiable mouth; under black eyebrows a pair of coal-black eyes which did not fail of their effect, although one of them was wont to be red and inflamed. By manifold questions he sought to make himself acquainted with me and my condition, and his power of attraction operated ever more strongly upon me. I was generally of a confiding nature, and for him, especially, I had no secret. But it was not long before the repellent pulse of his nature came in and occasioned me no little discomfort. * * * * * * * *

"Herder had now separated himself from the prince and removed to quarters of his own, resolved to submit himself to an operation by Lobstein. Here I found the benefit of those exercises by which I had endeavored to blunt my sensitiveness. I was able to assist at the operation, and, in various ways, to be helpful and serviceable to so worthy a man. I had every reason to admire his great fortitude and patience; for neither under the various wounds inflicted by the surgeon, nor under the oft-repeated, painful bandage, did he manifest the least vexation; and he appeared to be the one among us who suffered the least. But then, in the intervals, we had to bear in various ways the mutations of his humor. * * * * *

"Herder could be most sweetly engaging and genial; but he could as easily also turn forth a vexatious side. All men indeed have this attraction and repulsion according to their nature,—some more, some less,—some in slower, some in quicker pulses. Few can really overcome their peculiarity in this regard, although many appear to do so. In the case of Herder, the overweight of his contrary, bitter, biting humor was unquestionably owing to his malady and the sufferings which arose from it. This case often occurs in life, and we do not sufficiently consider the moral effects of diseased conditions, and therefore judge many characters very unjustly, because we regard all men as healthy, and require of them that they shall conduct themselves accordingly.

"During the whole time of this cure, I visited Herder morning and evening; I also remained with him sometimes the whole day, and accustomed myself in a short time to his chiding and fault-finding, the rather that I learned every day to estimate more highly his great and beautiful qualities, his extended knowledge, and his deep insight. The influence of this goodnatured grumbler was great and important. He was five years older than I, which makes a great difference in our younger days, and since I acknowledged him for what he was, since I knew how to value what he had already produced, he necessarily acquired a great superiority over me. But the relation was not an agreeable one. Older people with whom I had hitherto conversed had spared me while endeavoring to educate me; perhaps they had spoiled me by their yieldingness; but no approbation was ever to be had from Herder, whatever pains one might take to obtain it. While, therefore, on the one hand, my great attachment and reverence for him, and on the other, the discomfort which he awakened in me for ever contended together, there arose in me a contradiction, the first in its kind I had ever experienced. As his conversations were always significant, whether asking or answering, or in whatever way he imparted himself, it could not fail that I should be daily and hourly led on by him to new views. * * * * *

During so vexatious and painful a cure, our Herder lost nothing of his vivacity, but that vivacity grew ever less beneficent. He could not write a note containing a request, without spicing it with some kind of jeer. Thus, for example, he wrote to me once:

"If the epistles of Brutus thou hast in Cicero's Letters,
Thou whom, from well-polished shelves, the school-consolers—the classics
Comfort in splendid editions; but outwardly rather than inly;—
Thou who from Gods or from Goths, or, it may be, from mud* art descended,
Goethe send them to me."

To be sure, it was not handsome that he allowed himself this jest with my name; for the proper name of a man is not like a cloak which merely hangs round him, and at which one can pluck and twitch, but a close-fitting garment; nay, it is something which grows to him like the skin itself, and which cannot be scratched or wounded without injury to himself.

On the other hand, the preceding reproof was better founded. I had taken the authors which I had received in exchange from Langer, together with some beautiful editions out of my father's collection, with me to Strassburg, and arranged them in a neat book-case with the best intention to use them. But how should the time which was broken into fragments by a hundred different kinds of activity, suffice for this? Herder, who was a great observer of books, because he needed them every moment, noticed my beautiful collection on his first visit; but he noticed too, that I made no use of it; wherefore, as the greatest enemy of all seeming and ostentation, he used with every occasion to twit me on that point. * * *

Of such jests, more or less gay or abstruse, lively or bitter, I might mention many. They did not vex me, but they were unpleasant. But as I knew how to value whatever contributed to my education, and since I had sacrificed many of my earlier opinions and inclinations, I soon adjusted myself thereto, and only endeavoured, so far as it was possible for me from my then point of view, to separate just reproof from unjust invective. And so not a day passed that was not most fruitfully instructive for me. * * * * * * *
* * * * * * *

After the cure had been protracted beyond all reasonable bounds, and Lobstein began to waver and to repeat himself in his treatment, our whole relation was overcast. Herder became impatient and out of humor; he could not succeed in continuing his activity as heretofore, and he was obliged to restrain himself, the rather that the blame of the unsuccessful chirurgical undertaking was imputed to his too great intellectual activity, and his uninterrupted, lively and even merry intercourse with us. In short, after so much torture and suffering, the artificial lachrymal duct would not form, and the desired communication could not be brought about. It was found necessary to let the wound heal in order that the evil might not grow worse. If, during the operation, we were compelled to admire Herder's fortitude under such pains, his melancholy, nay, grim resignation to the idea of being obliged to bear such a blemish through life, had in it something sublime, whereby he secured to himself forever the veneration of those who saw him and loved him. This misfortune, which disfigured so significant a face, could not but be the more vexatious from the circumstance, that he had become acquainted with and had won the affections of a distinguished lady in Darmstadt. It was chiefly on this account that he had submitted to that cure, in order, on his return, to appear more free, more joyful, and with improved looks before his half-betrothed, and to connect himself more surely and inseparably with her."*

In 1770, Herder received a call to Bückeburg as superintendant, court-preacher, and member of the consistory. There he became the confidential friend of Count Wilhelm, of Schaumburg-Lippe and his wife, and added to

---

* "*Von Göttern von Gothen oder von Kothe;*" puns on Goethe's name.—*Ed.*

* Aus meinem Leben. Part 2d. Book 10th.

his literary fame by several important publications. In 1775, he was invited to a professorship of theology in Göttingen; but objections having been raised on the score of questionable orthodoxy, he accepted a call which came to him from Weimar to fill the offices of court-preacher, of general superintendent, and counsellor of the upper Consistory in that Electorate. Here he remained during the rest of his life, and by his fame as pulpit-orator, by his services as superintendent of the schools, and zealous promoter of all good works, by the establishment of a seminary for teachers, by the reforms which he introduced into the liturgy and the catechetical instruction, he endeared himself alike to prince and people. In 1789, he was made vice-president, in 1801, president of the upper Consistory. At the same time he received from the Elector of Bavaria the diploma of nobility.

He died, December 18th, 1803, in the sixtieth year of his age. His remains were deposited in the vault of the city-church, and, in 1819, a monument of cast-iron was erected over them, which expressed the characteristic aspirations of his soul with the brief inscription, *Licht, Liebe, Leben.*"*

The highest panegyric on Herder is that pronounced by his true friend and fervent admirer, Jean Paul, in his *Vorschule der Æsthetik*.

"That noble spirit was misunderstood by opposite times and parties, yet not entirely without fault of his own. For he had the fault, that he was no star of first or of any other magnitude, but a clump of stars out of which each one spells a constellation to please himself; one man a pair of scales, or the constellation of Autumn; another, a crab, or the constellation of Summer, and so on. Men, with powers of various kinds, are always misunderstood; those with powers of only one kind, seldom. The former come in contact with all, both like and unlike; the latter only with their like. * *

"Born, as it were, with a love-potion of fervid passion for nature, like a Brahmin, with the lofty Spinozism of the heart, he cherished and held fast to his heart every animalcule and every blossom. A travelling-carriage driven through greening life was his sun-chariot, and only under the free heaven, as also at the sound of music, would his heart, like a flower, with a right, wide-cheered expansion, unfold.

* * * * I can say but little about him, and insufficient at best. A man who could be resolved into words must be an every-day man. The star-heaven no star-map paints, although painting may represent a landscape. * * * * * *

"So this beloved spirit resembled the swans which, in the harsh season of the year, keep the waters open by their motion.
* * * * * * *

"I have not yet spoken the fullest word concerning him. If he was no poet, as he often, indeed, thought of himself, and also of other very celebrated people, standing, as he did, close by the Homeric and Shakspearian standard;—then he was merely something better, namely, a *poem*, an Indian-Greek *epos* made by some purest God. * * * *

"But how shall I analyze it? since in his beautiful soul, precisely as in a poem, everything coalesced, and the good, the true, the beautiful, constituted an inseparable triunity. Greece was to him the highest, and, however universal too his epic-cosmopolitan taste, praising and acknowledging—even the style of his Hamann —he still clung most intensely, like a much-wandered Odysseus after his return from all blossom lands, to his Greek home. He and Goethe only (each after his own fashion) are our restorers, or *Winkelmanns* of singing Greece, whose Philomel-tongue not all the prosers of foregone centuries had been able to loose.

Herder was, as it were, a Greek composition after the life. Poetry was not merely a horizon-appendix to his life,—as one often sees, in bad weather, a pile of rainbow-coloured clouds in the horizon,—but it rose shining, like a free, light rainbow, over the thick atmosphere of life, and spanned it as a heaven's-gate. Hence his Greek veneration for all the stages of life, his adjusting, epic manner in all his works, which, like a philosophical epos, brings all times, forms, people, spirits, as with the great hand of a god, impartially before the secular eye that measures years only by centuries, and so provides for them the widest arena. Hence his Greek disgust at every preponderance of the scale to one or the other side. Many storm-and-rack poems* could aggravate his mental torture into a bodily one. He wished to see the sacrifices of poesy as fair and undefiled as the thunder of heaven permits to scathed hu-

---

* "Light, Love, Life." See Wolff's Encyclopedia of German literature.

* His soul-words first reclaimed the author from the youthful confounding of force with beauty.

manity. Therefore, like a Grecian poem, he often drew, by mere dint of jest, around every fairest sentiment,—e. g. pathos,—an early boundary-line of beauty. Only men of shallow sentiments revel in them; those of more profound sensibility shun their despotism, and, therefore, have the appearance of coldness. A great poetical soul can more easily be anything else on the earth than happy, for man has something of the *Lavatere*-plant, which, for years, defies every winter, but grows tender and perishes as soon as it bears flowers. True, the poet is an eternal youth, and the dew of the morning lies upon him his whole life-day long; but without sun the drops are dim and cold.

"Few minds are learned after the same grand fashion as he. The greater part pursue only the rare, the least known in any science. He, on the contrary, received only the great streams, but those of all sciences, into his heaven-mirroring ocean, which, resolving, impressed upon them its own motion from west to east. Many are clasped by their learning as by a withering ivy, but he as by a grape-vine. Everywhere—organically poetizing—to appropriate to himself the opposite, was his character; and around the dry kernel-house of a Lambert he wove a sweet fruit-hull. Thus he combined the boldest freedom of philosophy, concerning Nature and God, with the most pious faith, a faith extending even to presentiments. Thus he exhibited the Greek humanity, to which he restored the name, in the most tender regard for all purely human relations, and in his Lutheran indignation against all whereby they were poisoned, however sanctioned by Church and State. He was a fort overgrown with flowers, a Northern oak whose branches were sensitive plants. How gloriously irreconcilable he burned against every creeping soul, against all looseness and self-contradiction, dishonesty, and poetical slime-softness; as also against German critical rudeness and all sceptres in paws; and how he exorcised the serpents of his time! But would you hear the softest of voices, it was his in love —whether for a child or a poem, or for music— or in mercy for the weak. He resembled his friend Hamann, who was at once a hero and a child; who, like an electrized person in the dark, stood harmless, with a glory encircling his head, until a touch drew the lightning from him.

"When he painted his Hamann as an angry prophet, as a demoniacal spirit, and even placed him above himself, (although Hamann was less Grecian and mobile, light-blooming and minutely organized,) and when we heard with grief that his true world and friendship's-island were merged in that writer's tomb, we became aware, from his longing, that, inwardly, he judged the age (according to his highest ideal) more severely than he outwardly appeared to do, with his toleration and his all-sidedness. Therefore there pervades his works a secret, now Socratic, now Horatian irony, which only those who knew him understand. Altogether, he was little weighed and little estimated; and only in particulars, not in the whole. That task remains for the diamond-scales of posterity, into which none of the flint-stones shall come, with which the rude prosaists, and ruder Kantians, and rude *poeticians*,* would half stone and half enlighten him.†

"The good spirit gave and suffered much. Two sayings of his, though unmeaning to others, remain to me always for contemplation. One was what he once said to me, with a melancholy feeling of the coldness and barrenness of the times, upon a Sunday amid the ringing of the near church-bells, whose tones flowed down to us as out of the old centuries: that he wished he had been born in the middle ages. The other, very different, was: that he wished to behold an apparition, and that he felt nothing and had no presentiment of the usual fear of ghosts. O, the pure soul, of spirit-kin! To him this was possible, poetical as he was, and although such natures usually shudder most at the long, silent veils which pass and rest behind death, — for he himself was a spiritual apparition to the earth, and never forgot his own kingdom. His life was a shining exception to ofttimes tainted geniality; he sacrificed, like the ancient priests, even at the altar of the Muses, only with white garments.

"He seems to me now,—much as Death usually lifts men up into a holy transfiguration,—in his present distance and elevation, no more shining than formerly, by my side, here below. I imagine him yonder, behind the stars, precisely in his right place, and but little changed, his griefs excepted. Well then! celebrate right festively yonder thy harvest-feast, thou pure, thou spirit-

---

* *Poetiker*. This word means neither poets nor poetasters, but men who theorize on the subject of poetry. Tr.
† In London transparent flints are ground into lenses.

friend! May thy coronal of heavy wheat-ears blossom on thy head into a light flower-chaplet! Thou sun-flower transplanted to thy sun at last!

"In his song to the night he says to his sleeping body:

> Slumber well, meanwhile, thou sluggish burden
> Of my earthly walk. Her mantle
> Over thee spreads the Night, and her lamps
> Burn above thee in the holy pavilion.

Otherwise now and colder stands the star-night above his mould. Alas! he who only read him has scarcely lost him; but he who knew and loved him is not to be consoled any more by *his* immortality, but only by the immortality of the human soul. If there were no such immortality, if our whole life here is only an evening twilight preceding the night, not a morning twilight; if the lofty mind is also let down after the body by coffin-ropes into the pit: O! then I know not why we should not, at the graves of great men, do from despair what the ancient savage nations did from hope, that is, throw ourselves after them into the pit, as those people did into the tombs of their princes, so that the foolish, violent heart that will obstinately beat for something divine and eternal, may be choked at once. * * * * * * O! I well know that he tolerated such griefs least of all. He would point now to the glittering stars of spring, above which he now dwells; he would beckon to us to listen to the nightingales which now sing to us and not to him; and he would be more moved than he seemed to be. * *
* * * * * * *
We will now love that great soul together, and if, at times, we are moved too painfully by his memory, we will read over again all whereby he made known to us the immortal and divine, and himself."

LOVE AND SELF.

AN APPENDIX TO THE LETTER OF HERR HEMSTERHUIS, ON DESIRE.

It is a beautiful legend of the most ancient poetry; that Love drew forth the world from chaos and bound the creatures reciprocally to each other with the bands of desire and longing; that, by these tender ties, she keeps all things in order and leads all to the One,— the great fountain of all light, as of all love. However various the names and garbs under which this poetical system has been presented, we recognise in all this general truth; that love unites and that hate divides; that all enjoyment of gods and of men consists in the love and union of homogeneous things; but, that longing and desire are, as it were, the bride-maids of Love,— the strong, yet tender arms, which induce and prepare all enjoyment, nay more, which confer in themselves the greatest enjoyment, by anticipation.

Soon, however, another side of this system became apparent, viz.: that this love has limits, and that a perfect union of beings in our universe is seldom or never known; that, therefore, the bands of this union, desire and longing, must often relax in the moment of the greatest strain, and yield, too often, alas! weariness and satiety instead of enjoyment. It was soon perceived, that, in this law, also, there was wisdom; since the Creator, by this means, has provided as carefully for the firm persistence of individual beings, as, by means of love and longing, he has provided for the union and kindly co-presence of many. It was seen that both these forces, which are, in the spiritual world, what attraction and repulsion are in the corporeal, are requisite to the preservation and firm tenure of the universe. And I believe it was Empedocles who first made Hatred and Love delineators of the outline of all beings.*
"By Hatred," he says, "things are separated, and each *individual* remains what it is; by Love they are united and connect themselves one with another." That is, as far as they can be united. For even Love, according to the Greeks, is ruled by Fate; and Necessity, the oldest of the gods, is mightier than Love. According to Plato's idea, the latter was born of Need and Superfluity, in the gardens of Jupiter. Accordingly, she partakes of the nature of both, and is always dependent on her parents.

I fancy it will not be unpleasant to follow this double walk; the rather, that Herr Hemsterhuis has led us very agreeably on one side, reserving to himself the other for another treatise; which, however, he has not yet written, or which I have not yet seen.

That love unites the different beings, and that all desire is only a striving after this union, as the only possible enjoyment of beings now separated,—this our author has proved with such exquisite examples, that too copious additions on this point would be a useless superfluity. Every craving for sensual and spiritual enjoyment, all desire of friendship and of love, thirsts after union with the object affected, because it forefeels, in that object, a new and delightful enjoyment of its own reality. The Godhead has wisely and kindly ordained that we shall be sensible of our existence, not in ourselves, but only by reaction, as it were, in some object without us; after which, accord-

---

* Εν δε κοτω διαμορφα και ανδιχα παντα πελονται
Συν δοιβη εν φιλοτητι και αλληλοισι ποθειται
Εκ των γαρ παντ' οσσ' ην οσσα τε εστι και εσται.

ingly, we strive, for which we live, in which we have a double and manifold existence. The multitude of attractive objects with which Nature has surrounded us, have, therefore, been placed by her at such various distances, and endowed with such various kinds and degrees of attraction, as to produce in us a rich and delicate concert of sensations, of various tones and modes; and to make our heart and life, as it were, a *Harmonica* of desire, the artistic image of an ever purer, insatiable, eternal longing.

Coarse, sensual enjoyment converts the object which we craved, into itself, and destroys it. It is vivid, therefore, for, in it there is a perfect union; but it is, likewise, coarse and transient. There are those who enjoy only with the tongue. Hence, in common life, the word *taste** is generally used in reference to this sense. Enjoyment, in this case, is a union.—that is, a solution of the finest juices. But it also ends with this, for the object is devoured, destroyed. In a certain sense, therefore, the finest enjoyment, here too, precedes the enjoyment. The craving for a beautiful fruit is pleasanter than the fruit itself. The eye excites the most agreeable sensation in the tongue. "Voluptatem præsagit multa cupido." Thus it is with the enjoyment of odors, and even of tones. We draw them into ourselves; we drink the stream of their delight with long draughts. And only then, do we say that we enjoy music, when it dissolves the heart and becomes one with the inward music of our sensations. The stream of melody, fine as it is, is nevertheless devoured. It continues to exist only in the harmonious effects,— the pleasant vibrations which it produced in us.

The more spiritual our enjoyment, the more permanent it is; the more permanent its object without us. But let us also add, the weaker it is; for the object is and remains without us; and only in its image, that is, — slightly or not all, — becomes one with us. The eye is never wearied with seeing: for how little does the heart receive with the sight! How little can the mere light-ray contribute to the most intense enjoyment!   *   *   *   *   *
*   *   *   *   *   *

Indeed, the *virtuosi* in regard to this organ — those who have cultivated their vision to a luxurious enjoyment — appear to be sensible of this. How do they seek to animate the object before them! They hunt after every impression of light and shade, of colour, form, gesture; in order to feel and grope out the spirit of the author, if they are artists, or the objects themselves, if they live in these, although it is a mere apparition which they have before them. Here again, the enjoyment consists in the conceit of a union. A feeble conceit, but a happy one! The eye does not destroy the essence of the beloved object, only because it cannot incorporate the same with itself. If this object seems to the deluded a fountain of inexhaustible charms, it is well for him, the blissfully deluded, who enjoys it. He draws forever, and never exhausts, because he can draw no perfect and intense draught. The beloved images flee before him and are still present to him. He lives in the sweet dream of a visible, intellectual phantom.

Imperceptibly, we have come upon that form of enjoyment, which, apparently, is the most enduring, but which, also, is the least satisfactory to our mortal nature,—the *ideal fruition* of corporeal beauty, — or, as it is called by enthusiasts, the enjoyment of Platonic love. The name of Plato is improperly applied to it; for he is speaking of intellectual Ideas, to be enjoyed by the intellect, and which cannot be enjoyed in any other way; and not of a mad spiritualizing of the corporeal, which often ends in a too coarse corporeity. That this is not a spiritual fruition, is evident from the fact that it destroys the body without satisfying the mind. It sins against the nervous fluid, as the passion of love, when of too coarse a character, sins against flesh and blood. It shows itself herein, not to be genuine enjoyment,—a happy contemplation of that kind, in which the beloved object becomes one with ourselves. How can that which is corporeal become one with pure spirit? Two things, that, properly speaking, have nothing in common, and could only be combined, in the beginning, as the Greeks fabled, by a kind of voluntary intoxication. The mind can enjoy spiritual qualities and objects. Its union with these is pure and so calm as that ancient Hymn makes God say : "*All is mine, for I have it in me!*" A possession and a fruition of which the soul is capable only in respect to the purest objects. Then it hovers and tastes like a beautiful butterfly which enjoys the flower without destroying it. Where it enjoys as a caterpillar, it devours, alas! leaf and flower.

We begin then to speak of the more genuine kinds of spiritual longing,—Friendship and Love. After what Hemsterhuis has told us of these, I shall add but a few traits.

The image of Friendship employed by the ancients,—two hands joined together,—appears to me the most fitting symbol of its union, its aim, and its enjoyment. More significant than the two according instruments. These express only companionship, which is far from being friendship. A companionable man is easy and well disposed. He adapts himself easily to every company, and every company adapts itself easily to him. He oppresses no one with his presence, he crowds no one; and therefore every one likes to be with him. In a certain degree, one is even intimate with him, because one feels that there is no mischief in the man. Characters of this sort are good for daily intercourse. But Friendship! what a different, sacred band is that! It unites hearts and hands in one common aim; and where that aim is obvious, where it is continuous, requiring exertion, where

---

* In German, *geniessen*, literally, to enjoy.

it lies among or behind dangers; there, the band of friendship is often so strict, so firm and hearty, that nothing but death has power to separate it. The phalanx of Greek friends in battle, who all conquered or died as one man,—those bright twin stars of friendship, which, in all nations, Hebrews and Greeks, Scythians and savages, shine forth from the night of ages, and are so grateful to the heart of man,—what made them friends? A common aim united them; danger drew the knot; tried faith, continuous, growing zeal, glorious labour, common enjoyment of that labour;—finally, necessity and death, made that knot indissoluble.

How truly said one, of his friend: "Thy love to me surpassed the love of women!" Creation knows nothing nobler than two voluntarily and indissolubly united hands,—two hearts and lives that have voluntarily become one. It matters not, whether these two hands are male or female, or of both sexes. It is a proud but irrational prejudice on the part of men, that only they are capable of friendship. Woman is often tenderer, truer, firmer, more golden-pure in that relation, than many a weak, unfeeling, impure, masculine soul. Where there is want of truth, where there is vanity, rivalry, heedlessness, there, friendship, in either sex, is impossible. Marriage, likewise, should be friendship; and wo! if it is not, if it is only love and desire. To a noble woman, it is sweet to suffer for her husband, as well as to rejoice with him, to feel that she is honoured, esteemed and happy in him and he in her. The common education of their children is the beautiful, leading aim of their friendship, which sweetly rewards them both, even in gray old age. They stand there, and will continue to stand like two trees with branches interlocked, begirt with a garland of youthful green,—saplings and twigs. In all cases, a life, in common, is the marrow of true friendship. Mutual unlocking and sharing of hearts, intense joy in each other, sympathy in each other's sufferings, counsel, consolation, effort, mutual aid,—these are its diagnostics, its delights, its interior recompense. What delicate secrets in friendship! Refinements of feeling, as if the soul of the one were directly conscious of the soul of the other, and, anticipating, discerned the thoughts of that soul as clearly as its own! And, assuredly, the soul has sometimes power thus to discern thoughts and to dwell immediately and intimately in the heart of another. There are moments of sympathy, even in thoughts, without the slightest external occasion, which indeed no psychology can explain, but which experience teaches and confirms. There are mutual, simultaneous recollections of one another—even at a distance—on the part of absent friends, which are often of the most wonderful, overpowering kind. And indeed, if ever the soul possesses the mysterious power to act directly, without organs, on another soul, where would such action be more natural than in the case of friends? This relation is purer, and therefore, assuredly, mightier also than love. For if love will lift itself up to the strength and duration of eternity, it must first purify itself from coarse sensuality, and become true and genuine friendship. How seldom does it arrive at this! It destroys itself or destroys its object with penetrating, devouring flames; and both the loving and the loved lie there, as it were, a heap of ashes. But the glow of friendship is pure, refreshing, human warmth. The two flames upon one altar play into each other, and frolicking, lift and bear one another aloft, and often, in the melancholy hour of separation, they soar rejoicing, and united, and victorious, upward to the land of the purest union, of truest, inseparable friendship.

May the reader pardon the explicitness with which I have handled this point! Since I look upon it as the true, singular, and most beautiful union of souls, and therefore also, as the noblest and sweetest enjoyment of which humanity is capable, to which even love itself is subservient;—since there are so many degrees of friendship, from easy companionship, to the most sublime, silent, enduring sacrifice, which, to be sure, has been the portion only of the most select souls, and only in very rare circumstances and combinations; but which is to be regarded in such instances as the highest privilege, the genuine antepast of a future, higher existence;—briefly, since, in friendship, there is union, almost without organs, pure, perfect and ever-growing;—therefore, as it seems to me, it is also the highest point of all desire, and, precisely, in seasons of the greatest strain and pressure, becomes the purest joy of earth. Here operates the genuine magnetism of human souls, and we know that the magnet attracts the more powerfully the more it is exercised. Unused, it is dead. Without confidence and truth severely tried, no friendship, no interchange of hearts is possible.

But Nature saw that this pure, heavenly flame is, for the most part, for us on the earth, too refined. Therefore she clothed it in earthly, sensible charms; and so Venus Urania appeared as—Aphrodite. Love was intended to invite us to friendship. Love is to become, itself, the most intense friendship.

I find its highest degree of rapture not there where, as Herr Hemsterhuis says, Nature deludes us with an instant of earthly union, (an instant which loses itself in mere surrounding want,) but in the first happy discovery,—in that moment, beyond all description sweet, when the beloved two become aware that they love, and tell each other so, with such certainty and sweet consent, however imperfect and involuntary the confession. Why must I use the word, 'tell.' How poor! What can the dead tongue,—what can pining language say, when even the soul-enkindled, fiery glance drops its wings and veils its glory? If there is a moment of heavenly rapture, and a pure union of embodied beings here on earth, it is this. So unlike that which pining enjoyment allows us! I know not what mythology of some Asiatic nation it is, which divides its periods of highest antiquity according to the manner in which men, while as yet they were paradisaical spirits, loved each other. At first, for many thousands of years, with looks; afterwards, with a kiss — a mere touch;—until, at last, in the course of long ages, they gradually degenerated into lower forms of enjoyment. That moment of spiritual recognition, that betraying of the soul by a look, transports us as it were into those primeval times, and, with them, into the joys of Paradise. Then we enjoy, with a retrospective sentiment, what we had so long sought and did not dare to confess to ourselves. Then too we enjoy prospectively the delights of the future,—not with presentiment merely, but with possession. Yes! if one may say so, with more than possession. The future can only unfold, seldom add. Often it detracts, and diminishes, with every enjoyment, the belief in enjoyment. That first moment, is when Psyche first beholds the god of love, whom, veiled, she had so long loved. Ah! why, unhappy one! didst thou let the spark fall, and thereby terminate, for so long a period, all thy joys?

Certain it is, that those souls which are created for the truest, purest, noblest love, fear this moment of betrayal as their worst foe, and defer it with the utmost shyness. The female sex which, in all matters of love, is more delicate than ours, feels how much its flame loses with every enjoyment, and how, contrary to the nature of all other flames, it goes out when it breaks forth, and with every manifestation, weakens its interior force and blessedness. Shy and holy, they seek, therefore, to preserve the secret in the heart of the lover himself, as soon as it is made certain. And nothing is more easily made certain than this. The secret is profaned, as it were, if it but touch the lips. It dies, in a measure, with the first kiss, with the first sigh. But since we are, once for all, bodies, Psyche, as the ancient fable teaches, must lose her celestial wings, with her first descent into matter. Is it strange that she should endeavor so long, and with so much pains, to delude herself with the belief, that she loves not the body, but only that which is connatural with herself, — the soul of the beloved? It is, as if she were ashamed of her degradation, and prophesied the brief duration of the pleasure which she seeks. How does she accordingly disguise that pleasure! In the kiss, she seeks only a union of souls, as sings the love-breathing poem below.*

Long passages in the fourth book of Lucretius describe this striving, this vain and ever unsatisfied striving after a union of beings, so emphatically, so philosophically and powerfully, as if Lucretius had written to illustrate the system of our author, or as if the latter had taken his system of love and enjoyment from the former.

It is fortunate that Nature coupled this deceptive phantom of intimate union, on the spiritual side, with friendship; and, on the side of the body, with an electric spark of her omnipotence, by which, from a union, incomprehensible to us, of two beings, a third is produced;—as it were a creation of love, of desire and unsatisfied longing. And so the fiery chain trails itself along. There is added to it, between need and excess, a new link, in which is propagated the kindling spark of desire. I remark in general, that the Creator has left no degree of union, among the creatures of his Nature, without fruit. The first degree of sensual enjoyment, which the very infant sucks in, yields us *life-sap*. It elaborates for us a nobler material out of a poorer. The finer the organ, the more *spiritual* the offspring of its conception. Odors strengthen and refresh the soul. Music comforts and soothes the heart with celestial drink. Pictures —" *Simulacra pabula amoris*" — bring thoughts to the mind, more delicate than their own material. And finally, Friendship and Love—the one the marriage of spirits, the other of bodies—offer us a cup of enjoyment, wreathed with the fairest fruits. Friendship awakens noble sentiments, aspirations, deeds. Love, like the divine spring-sun, quickens the tender, motherly vine with foliage and fruits. In it is laid the creative power of the first Cause.

It would seem also that Nature has taken care to replace and requite the brief and fleeting enjoyment of love, with a dower direct from her own bosom, by which it was designed that the humblest living creature should be honoured with a spark of the Godhead. That is, parental affection, the love of Father and Mother. This love is divine, for it is disinterested and often without return. It is heavenly, for it is capable of being shared among many, and still remains entire, undivided, and without envy. Finally, it is infinite and eternal, for it vanquishes love and death. Detestable is the mother who prefers her lover to her child. The very beasts shame her. They have often died joyfully for their young. * * * * *

Maternal tenderness is the pledge of love with which Nature, as it were out of her own heart, has requited the mother's pains. Nothing surpasses the anxiety with which the mother seeks

---

* *Dum semihulco suavio*
  Meum puellum suavior,
  Dulcemque florem spiritus
  Duco ex aperto tramite;
    Anima tunc, ægra et saucia,
    Cucurrit ad labias mihi,
    Orisque rictum pervium
    Et labra pueri mollia,
    Rimata itineri transitus,
    Ut transiliret nititur.

Tum, si moræ quid plusculæ
Fuisset in coitu osculi,
Amoris igne percita,
Transisset et me linqueret;
Et mira prorsum res foret,
Ut ad me fierem mortuus,
Ad puerum ut intus viverem.
    Aul: Gell: L. XIX. Cap. 11

a lost child, and nothing can equal the joy with which, after long seeking, after many years' separation, she finds it again, and embraces it as if new-born. The craving of a mother after children is the most beautiful form of longing which lay in the girdle of Love;—out of which that girdle seems to be wholly woven in pure female hearts. They are the priestesses at the sacred fire of Vesta; and wo to the despicable creature that glows with another flame instead of this! Only the point of his arrow has Cupid anointed with desire.* Alas! if the whole arrow glows with it.

From the tender, divine, eternal love of the parent, to whom can I ascend but to Thee? great universal Mother! Tender, highest Father! My language has no name for the feeling with which Thou hast established Thyself in every creature, in every nerve and corner of each beating heart, and hast given to each its own joys, immeasurable, inexplicable, insensible to every other. Thy whole creation is a weft which Power drew forth out of nothing, of which Wisdom laid the warp, and in which Love inwrought its thousandfold figures rich in significance and love. Who shall not love Thee, therefore, since every creature draws but to thee, points but to thee? And who can love Thee as he ought, seeing he is overwhelmed in the ocean of thy† thoughts and fore-reaching sensations; and even, regarding himself alone, sinks down into the deepest deep? Thou sharest the fate of all parents,—more loving than loved. But Thou art exalted above all others in this, that Thou thyself hast created in me the longing after Thee, and canst lead me ever nearer to Thyself by the bands of knowledge and of love. Thou wilt and must do this; my whole heart declares it. For the little spark of knowledge and of love that is in me is only an off-glance of thine infinite flame. Therefore must Thou know and name and seek and love me a thousand-fold more intensely than I can name and seek Thee. And this eternal drawing of thy heart to mine is, to me, an implanted voucher of my undying inclination to Thee, and of an ever-growing enjoyment of Thee.

But how is the Eternal enjoyed? By contemplation or by sensation? Our author has a hard remark about enthusiasts, which, if carefully examined, might prove alas! too true. It is a general experience that, in all cases of enthusiasm, women have been implicated. Often, the men have only caught the infection from the women, who, it was said, had borne them anew. The women were a kind of mediators of the Godhead to the men. And how they conceived of the Godhead, especially the human God, and with what feeling they embraced him, is known to the world, from many writings and letters. The fainting which the holy Theresa experienced before the altar, when the celestial Cupid touched her heart, considered in relation to the body alone, could hardly have differed from every other faintness caused by love. For love is the same in its action on the vital fluids of the body, whatever may be its object. In all sentiments of this kind, the greatest caution is necessary, even to the most innocent. Even upon the stream of divine love, the heart remains a human heart still. All mediatresses, even though it were the Mother of God, are dangerous. And so, to the female heart, all earthly mediators may become dangerous; and the heavenly mediator likewise, if too sensually felt. God requires to be loved with the whole soul and all its powers, but not with the effervescence of the nervous fluid, in a diseased, epileptic body.

We come naturally to the limits which have been set to love and longing, in every enjoyment here below. These are not merely, as Herr Hemsterhuis seems to think, our organs; but, as he himself discovers, at last, our *isolated individual existence*. He likens that property of the soul, which resists commixture with other beings, to the *vis inertiæ* in matter. And, assuredly, this power of inaction must be something different and more than the great mass of mechanical philosophers know or say about it. The words themselves,—Power and Inaction,—relate to each other like *Bewegung* (motion) and *Grund* (stationary ground) in the word *Bewegungsgründe* (motives). Moreover, Leibnitz and all the better class of thinkers have hazarded conjectures relative to the interior constitution of matter, to which I would fain hope for a pleasant addition in the promised observations of Herr Hemsterhuis. For the present, we will leave this resemblance where it is, and consider the limits which have been set to desire in the soul, by the nature of the soul itself. We are individual beings, and must continue so, unless, in the pursuit of enjoyment, we abandon the ground of all enjoyment—our own consciousness—and are willing to lose ourselves, in order to find ourselves again, in another being, that, after all, is not and never can be, our self. Even if I should lose myself in Deity, as mysticism requires, without any further feeling or consciousness of myself; it would no longer be I that enjoyed. The Godhead would have swallowed me up, and would enjoy in my stead. How well has Providence contrived, therefore, in awakening the music of our sensations gradually in various tones and modes; now exciting desire, now checking it, exercising it here actively, there passively, and ever, after the most honeyed enjoyment, throwing us back upon our poor self, as if saying to us, 'Thou art but a limited individual creation. Thou thirstest after perfection, but findest it not. Do not pine at the fountain of this one enjoyment, but gather thyself up and strive for something further.'

Let us look at this in some of the most striking proofs and examples.

All robber-like enjoyment, all enjoyment which

---

* Χρισας αφυκτον οισον ιμερῳ. *Euripides.*
† i. e. Inspired by thee. Tr.

destroys its object, is given us merely as a *want* by the hand of Necessity. It uses itself up and dies in itself. Man is a tyrant in the universe, but how soon is even this little tyrant satiated with plunder, if he keeps within the bounds of nature! Every sensual enjoyment is, strictly, but a modified necessity. Where mutual destruction ends, there, first, begins a freer, finer enjoyment,—a joyful consorting together of several beings who mutually seek and love each other. A tyrant who would be all in himself, who would devour all, as Saturn devours his children, is capable neither of friendship nor of love, not even of paternal affection. He oppresses and suppresses. Nothing can grow by his side, much less together with him, in a common crown.

Where several beings are in pleasant juxtaposition, and wish mutually to enjoy one another, it is evident that no one of them must aim at individual, peculiar, consequently, not at the *highest* enjoyment; otherwise he destroys all around him. He must give and take, suffer and act, attract toward himself and gently impart of himself. This, indeed, makes every enjoyment imperfect; nevertheless, it is the true tact and the very pulse of life;—the *modulation* and *economy* of desire, of love, and of all the sweets of longing. Here I direct attention to the beautiful wisdom of Nature, who, with sexes, moments, circumstances, ages, situations, has divided and, as it were, cradled all things in this systole and diastole of passive and active, giving and receiving. As yonder in the heavens two lights, so God has created here on the earth, two sexes which are designed to afford each other a mutual counterpoise, in the oscillation of feeling. One supplies to the other what is wanting of tenderness on the one side, and of strength on the other. And in the domain of love tenderness is mightier than strength. God has indemnified and veiled with attractions the weakness of woman. Where, in compliance with some necessity, he has departed from the law of beauty, there he has flung around her the girdle of love endowed with Desire, which, as said the Goddess, "vanquisheth all strength." In friendship also, one party is always the more active, the other, auxiliary and passive; one masculine, the other feminine; and often, in the inverse order of the sexes. In this marriage of souls, a monotone is neither agreeable nor profitable, nor possible. *Consonant* tones are required for the melody of life and enjoyment, not *unison*. Otherwise, friendship is soon lost in mere fellowship.

Hence it is evident, moreover, that the attractive power of an individual, human soul neither can nor ought to extend itself without limit. Nature has drawn narrow boundaries around each individual, and it is the most dangerous of all dreams to imagine one's self unlimited where one is limited, to believe one's self the Despot of the universe when one is living only on single alms. To embrace the whole creation with love sounds beautiful, but we must begin with the individual, with the nearest. And he who cannot love that, deeply, intensely, entirely, how should he be able to love that which is remote and which throws but feeble rays upon him from a foreign star? How should he be able to love it with any feeling which deserves the name of love? The greatest cosmopolites are generally the neediest beggars, and they who embrace the entire universe with love, for the most part, love nothing but their narrow self.

I come to the comparison which Herr H. makes between the States of Greece and our own; in which he seems to reproach the Christian religion with lessening the interest of its followers in the transient welfare of the secular State, through over-much care for the eternal well-being of the individual. The reproach would be well founded if the care for the eternal were *opposed* to the care for the temporal; and if a happy State could be anything else than a collection of happy individuals. It is only a misunderstood religion, a religion of priests, that will maintain the former. And with regard to the latter, the individual can only care for his own welfare and leave it to him who has contrived or who trains the machine, (as Herr Hemsterhuis himself calls the State,) to care for the welfare of the whole, according to his goodwill or power. That lawgivers have, almost uniformly, misused the Christian religion and mixed it up with their barbarous feudal and knightly institutions, is the crying evil in all Christian history. But, for this, we are not to blame the religion, but the coarse hands which have kneaded it with this heterogeneous political dough. Religion, as our author has justly defined it, is the free relation of the individual to the Supreme Being. Those who have sought to honour it with the name of a political machine, have, more than any others, deformed and degraded it.

But to our subject! Nature always begins with the individual, and not till she has adjusted and satisfied the propensities of the individual, in his own little circle, does she connect several together, and arrange their sentiments into a common weal. The welfare of the State consists of happy families, or else it is an imaginary quantity. When, in the individual man, sensual and spiritual joys, friendship and love, parental affection and personal virtue, are well-ordered and well-paired, then he is happy in himself and in others. He cannot, like ocean-slime, commingle with all; he cannot love, praise, and approve all in an *equal degree*, or change every mote into a sunbeam, in order to love it as a sunbeam. In attempting to do this, he injures the good as well as the bad, and, at last, loses entirely his judgment and his stand-point. Whoso should repel, neither can he attract. The two powers are but one pulsation of the soul.

Thus it is with us in this world; and how will it be, farther on, in our eternal pilgrimage? It can scarcely be otherwise. The existence of others, so far as they are connected with us, by love and longing, rests wholly on our own being and consciousness. If we could lose that, we could have no enjoyment from those. With each succeeding step, our existence must necessarily become more free and effective. Our enjoyments will become less corrupting and destructive. We shall learn evermore to find pleasure in giving and in doing, rather than in passive reception. Nevertheless, it should seem that the mutual relation which constitutes the sum of our whole happiness, can never entirely cease. In order to give, there must always be objects to receive. In order to act, there must always be those for whom to act. Friendship and love can never exist except between beings mutually free,—consonant, not unison, least of all identified. And finally, as to the enjoyment of the Highest, it must always be, as our author says, "*hyperbole and asymptote.*" The hyperbole forever approaches the asymptote, but never reaches it. It is our happiness that we can never lose the conception of our own being and attain to the infinite one,—that we are God. We shall always remain creatures, though we should become the creators of vast worlds. We shall approach perfection, but never become infinitely perfect. The greatest good which God could bestow on his creatures was, and will be, their individual existence. It is even through this that He exists for them; and, through this, he will be to them more and more, from stage to stage, ALL IN ALL.

TITHON AND AURORA.

ALTHOUGH, in general, no epitaph or panegyric uses to notice *how long a man has outlived himself,* yet is this one of the most remarkable and not infrequent phenomena in the history of human lives. The earlier the play of the faculties and passions begins, the more impetuously it is continued, and assailed in various ways by external accident, the oftener shall one discover cases of that early exhaustion of the soul,—of the warrior laid prostrate without death or wound,—of a manly, and, often even, of a youthful *extreme age.* A man may go about for a long while, with a living body, like the image of his own funeral monument; his spirit gone from him,—a shadow and a memory of his former name. Many causes may contribute to this early death: qualities of mind and heart, too great activity and too sluggish patience, relaxation as well as over-tension, too rapid prosperity and too protracted adversity. For it is a general truth, that health, cheerfulness, pleasure, and virtue, are ever the medium between two extremes. Either on the precipitous or the shallow shore of the stream, the vessel may be wrecked. In the middle, it is easy and pleasant sailing. Many a one has grown old because he wanted the true interior source of activity. He was a brook that contracts its waters into itself and soon dries up and shows its melancholy bed. This one endeavoured to make seeming supply the place of being. The darkness passed away, and the glow-worms in the hair glittered as sparkling diamonds no longer. That one would accomplish by toil and memory, what intelligence and genius alone can perform. The overloaded memory gave way, excessive labor tired, and the want of the essential was at last painfully apparent. Another, while a youth, overstrained his nobler powers; he piled up mountains of imagination to the skies, and soon, without the lightning of Jupiter, found under them his grave. Still another, whose learning and effort had no object but his own ease, abandoned learning and effort as soon as he had obtained that ease, and buried himself in a blessed decay. Here, one, without desert, has had his brain turned by an unexpected prosperity, a too rapidly acquired fame, an unlooked for success in action. He has no longer any thought beyond this success. His seductive goddess, Fortune, has crowned him at once with laurel, with poplar, and with poppy. He falls asleep or babbles nonsense in her enervating lap. There, one of great merit has suffered too long with undeserved misfortune, until his shoulders are bowed, his breast contracted, his arm paralysed, and he can no longer stand erect and recruit himself. A thunderbolt from heaven has stricken the oak even to its root and deprived it of the power of life. To this one—a man of manifold capacity—there was wanting a capacious breast to despise envy and to wait for better times. He suffered himself to be drawn into conflict with it, and the flying eagle was unworthily vanquished by the viper that held him in her folds. That one,—a man of honest industry,—was wanting in intelligence. His more cunning enemies soon made him powerless and wretched. And thus it befell ten other characters, in other situations. Hard by the theatre of civil life, there is generally a hospital, and in that the greater part of the actors gradually lose themselves.

Two things especially contribute to this result, and they, too, are extremes. In the first place, the arbitrariness of the ruling great; and, secondly, a too refined delicacy and carefulness. As to the former, it is a well-known and favorite saying, that nothing is so troublesome as gratitude, nothing so insupportable as continued respect and the daily spectacle of acknowledged merit. Accordingly, new favor purchases for itself new gratitude; and creatures whom the great purposely attract to themselves,—in whom they even pretend to find gifts and merits which the gods never gave them,—have, for them, a peculiar charm, as their own creation. The sap is withdrawn from the old trees that the young world may bloom and thrive. Whoso, in such cases, is not greater than he on whom he depends, dies inwardly with self-consuming vexation. The majestic voice of Philip the second,

"*Yo el Rey*" has slain many a one of this description. Opposed to this murder of human merits and powers, there is another, which may be termed the most refined species of self-murder. It is the more to be lamented because it occurs only in the case of the most elect of men; suddenly or gradually breaking in pieces their costly mechanism. Men of extreme delicacy of feeling have a 'Highest' after which they strive,—an idea to which they attach themselves with unspeakable longing,—an ideal perfection which they pursue with irresistible impulse. When deprived of this idea, when this fair image is destroyed before their eyes, the heart of their flower is broken, and feeble, withered leaves alone remain. Perhaps, more of the dead of this description go about in society, than one might at first suppose, because they, of all men, most carefully conceal their grief, and hide even from their friend the slow poison of their death,—that sad secret of the heart. Shakspeare, who depicted all conditions of the soul, has delineated, also, this epoch of the sinking or confusion of the faculties, in various situations and characters, with great truth and exactness. One,—perhaps the crown of lamentations over such a state,—may serve as an example of all.

> O! what a noble mind is here o'erthrown!
> The courtier's, soldier's, scholar's eye, tongue, sword,
> The expectancy and rose of the fair State,
> The glass of fashion and the mould of form,
> The observed of all observers! quite, quite down!
> ——Now see that noble and most sovereign reason,
> Like sweet bells jangled, out of tune and harsh;
> That unmatched form and stature of blown youth,
> Blasted with extasy.

Not only individual persons outlive themselves, but much oftener and longer, those politico-moral persons, so called,—*institutions, forms of polity, classes, corporations*. Often, their body remains, for centuries, as a show, when the soul of that body has long since fled; or they creep about as shadows among living forms. To be convinced of this, let any one enter a Jewish synagogue, or read Anquetil's Zend-Avesta, and the sacred books of the Brahmins. There is no doubt that all these religious institutions were once very useful, and that, in every one of these hulls, lay the germs of a great development. Time has developed each of them more or less, —one happily, so that we are disposed perhaps to look for more in it than was there; another imperfectly and feeble; as in the great course of Nature it will fall out. Nevertheless, everything has its goal, and the Rabbi, the Destur, the Mobed,—perhaps also the Brahmin,—has, in the great whole, outlived himself. In some regions of Mahommedanism, something similar is already reported of the Koran, although that is the youngest of bibles. And in Christendom, true as its pure fountain streams, with the water of eternal life, how many a vessel is already broken that was thought to have exhausted this fountain! How many a form which still stands there, had long ago outlived itself! Look at the Romish Mass! Listen to many of their litanies and prayers! Into what times do they take us back! What a strange savor of long-perished ages! As, in Religion, the priestly order, so in other institutions the orders connected with them follow each its living or its dead. Consider so many institutions and orders of the middle ages! Where they could not follow the Genius of opinion and renew their youth with him, they either remained stationary on the shore or else the stream bore them lifeless on, until they found somewhere their place of rest. Even in Cervantes' days the Duke of Bejar would not allow that Don Quixote should be dedicated to him, so long as he supposed it to be a serious book of knight-errantry; because the taste for such things had already begun to be ridiculous. He accepted the Dedication gladly when, as the book was read to him, he discovered its true character. Time has enacted novels of this kind with several institutions. The princes and heroes of Corneille are for the most part insupportable to us, and we wonder how other times could ever put together, believe and admire such nonsense. Shakspeare's court-scenes seem to us like Capital and State acts. The knights of our day are no longer of the ancient order; and that kingly word of Louis XIV.: "L'Etat? c'est moi!" will ever remain the appropriate epitaph of that great world-monarch.

"Whatsoever had a birth must die," says the Brahmin; and that, which seeks to defer its downfall by artificial methods, in resorting to such methods, has already outlived itself. In the early spring, the foliage and grass of the former year are often still visible; much of it has retained its place; but, in a short time, the whole is vanished, and a new raiment covers the trees and the bosom of the earth.

If there is anything in the circle of Humanity which ought not to outlive itself, it is Science and Art. The nature of these is eternal, and they are capable of the purest truth and of infinite extension. And indeed the real essence of Art and Science never dies, never changes. But their forms are all the more perishable, as they appear, above all things, to depend on their masters and discoverers,—to originate, to flourish, and to perish with them. So long as the discoverer lives, so long as the master teaches and directs, men draw living thoughts from his living fountain. In the second and third generation, one already wanders through schools that echo and ape him. The image of the master stands there dead. His science and his art has outlived itself, not in his own, but in his successors' works.

Travels give us a long catalogue of things which have thus outlived themselves. Travels in the history, as well as in the actual inspection of regions, countries, institutions, persons, classes. Who that enters an ancient castle, an old-fashioned knightly hall, an archive of old diplomas and treaties, of old arms and decorations;

old court-houses, churches,—convents, palaces and imperial cities, does not feel himself translated into a perished century? In a tour through Germany, one often finds, within a circle of a few miles, the ancient, the middle, the modern and *most* modern ages together. Here, we breathe still the air of the twelfth century; there, we hear the melodies of the sixteenth, the tenth, the fourth. All at once, you enter cabinets which have been instituted under the luxurious Ducal Government,—galleries collected under Louis XIV., and end with institutions which seem to have been devised for the twentieth century. Instructive as this chaos may be for the traveller, it would be very confusing and oppressive for the resident, did not human nature accustom itself to all things. "Lord, by this time he stinketh, for he hath been dead four days;" said the sorrowing sister; one might say, with regard to many institutions, four centuries, and still they are not offensive to their brothers and sisters. These are accustomed to the odor, and find it nourishing.

Italy seems to me the most instructive theatre of these life-epochs and world-ages. There, you can be with Egyptians, Greeks, Romans, Etruscans, nay, if you please, with Chineses, with Hindoos, and with the people of Madagascar! In Rome, alone, you may follow Paganism from Romulus to Diocletian, and Christianity from Constantine to Pius. There, and in the Italian provinces, you may live at pleasure in the fifteenth, the sixteenth, or the eighteenth century. And if you investigate the monuments of Nature, you will come upon self-survivals which will take you beyond the bounds of history. It requires a capacious mind to embrace, to distinguish, to classify all these scenes. But, to such a mind, they exhibit a compend of all history, which floods us, at last, with, I know not, what pleasing but dissolving melancholy.

> The cloud-capt towers, &c. &c.
> ————————We are such stuff
> As dreams are made of, and our little life
> Is rounded with a sleep.

Enough of sleep and of dying out! Let us now speak of waking and rejuvenescence! How is this brought about? By Revolution? I confess that, among the misused words of our modern, fashionable vocabulary, few are so displeasing to me as this; because it has entirely departed from its original, pure signification, and carries with it the most mischievous confusion of thought. In astronomy, we call revolution a movement of the great world-bodies which returns into itself,—determined by measure, number and forces; a movement, which is not only the most peaceful order in itself, but, in connection with other harmonious powers, establishes the kingdom of eternal order. Thus the earth revolves around itself and makes day and night, and by means of these, arranges and regulates the sleep and the waking of its creatures, their time for rest and the circle of their occupations. Thus the earth moves around the sun and makes the year, and by means of that, the seasons, and by means of them, the changes of labour and of mortal enjoyment. The revolution of the moon around our earth gives to the sea its ebb and flood, determines the periods of diseases, and perhaps, of the growth of plants. In this sense it is useful to notice revolutions; for, in them, we observe a course of affairs which returns into itself, and, in that course of things, the laws of a perpetual order. In such a course there is nothing abrupt, arbitrary, without reason. There is nothing of destruction in it, but a gently vibrating thread of conservation. Revolutions of this kind are the dance of the Hours around the throne of Jupiter. They are the chaplet of victory on the immortal head of the god, after the conquest of chaos.

Also, if we draw down this idea of Revolution from heaven to earth, it can be no other than the idea of a silent progress of things, of a re-appearance of certain phenomena, according to their peculiar nature, consequently, of the design of an ever-working Wisdom, Order and Goodness. In this sense, we speak of the revolutions of arts and sciences, that is, a periodical return of them, the causes of which, we endeavor to investigate in history, and, as it were, to calculate astronomically. Thus the Pythagoreans spoke of the revolutions of the human soul, that is, of its periodical return into other forms. Thus have men investigated the laws of the revolution of human thoughts; when they return from oblivion into remembrance; when visions and desires, when activities and passions which had gone to sleep, reappear once more. In all these things, it has been attempted to discover the laws of a hidden, silent order of Nature.

But the meaning of this word has undergone a detestable change, because, in the barbarous centuries, men knew of no other revolutions than conquests, overturns, oppressions, confusions without motive, aim or order. Then it was called revolution, when the nethermost was made uppermost,—when, by the so-called right of war, a nation lost more or less of its property, its laws, its goods; or when, by the right of monarchy, all those so-called rights were enforced, which St. Thomas, Machiavel and Naudè afterwards collected from actual events and brought together in one chapter. Then, finally, it was called a revolution, when the ministers did what the rulers themselves would not do; or when, here and there, the People undertook that which they could rarely execute so well as kings or ministers. Hence the numerous *Histoires des Revolutions*,—a kind of book whose title is all the more popular, that its contents are, for the most part, unintelligible or abominable. The notion of an aim or object was almost lost sight of. History became an exhibition of entanglements without a *denouement*. For, after the conclusion of each revolution, so called, the confusion, in the kingdoms where they occurred, was greater than before. Revolutions of this sort, whencesoever they may derive their origin, are signs of barbarism, of an insolent force, of a mad wilfulness. The more reason and moderation increase among men, the rarer they will become, until, at last, they entirely disappear. Then the word Revolution will revert to its pure and true meaning. Then it will mean, in history also as elsewhere, a course of things arranged according to laws,—a course of events which peacefully returns into itself. In this view alone is history worth the study; for, as to the revolutions of wild elephants, when they tear up trees and devastate villages,—from these there is not much to be learned.

Not to mislead, therefore, with this abused word, and not to make destructive violence a medicine for mortal ills, we will keep the path of healing Nature. Not Revolutions, but Evolutions are the silent process of the great mother, wherewith she awakens slumbering powers, brings germs to maturity, gives renewed youth to premature age, and new life to seeming death. Let us see what this remedy comprehends, and how it heals.

If we suppose Nature to have an aim on the earth, that aim can be no other than *the development of her powers in all forms, kinds and ways.* These evolutions proceed slowly, often imperceptibly; and, for the most part, they appear *periodically.* After a night of sleep, follows a morning of awakening. Under the shade of the former, Nature had re-collected her powers, in order to meet the latter with spirit. In the ages of man, childhood continues long; body and mind advance with a slow growth, until, with collected energies, the flower of youth breaks forth, and the fruit of later years comes gradually to maturity. Very improperly have these periods of development been called revolutions. There is nothing here that revolves, but faculties are evolved, developed. Ever, the more recondite and deeper-lying come forth to view, which, without many a preceding one, could not have been brought into action. Therefore Nature made periods. She gave the creature time to recover itself from one exertion gone through with, in order to begin, with joy, and to accomplish another and more difficult. For when the plant puts forth a flower, or when the fruit is forming in it, unquestionably more inward and finer forces are put in action than when the sap was entering the stem, and the lowest leaves were brought forth. In the ordinary course of things, Nature does not leave her work until all its physical powers have been brought into action; the innermost, as it were, turned outward, and the development, which, at every step, is assisted by a kindly *epigenesis,* has become as perfect as it could become, under the given conditions.

Men are accustomed to regard each individual object, and especially each living individual as an isolated whole; but a nearer view shows it to be connected with soil, climate, weather; with the periodical breath of all Nature; and that, according to these, it lasts for a longer or shorter time, grows early old or easily renews its youth. Man, a rational, moral and political creation, lives, by means of these capacities and powers, *in a peculiar and infinitely extended element.* His reason is connected with the reason of others, his moral culture with the conduct of others, his capacity to constitute himself a free being,—both in himself and in connection with others,—is so intimately connected with the way of thinking, the reasonableness, the active enterprise of many, that out of this element, he must needs be like a fish on dry land, or a bird in a space destitute of air. His best powers die out, his capacity remains a dead capability; and all effort, out of time and place, and without the co-operation of the elements, is like a flower in the midst of winter. It is Nature that makes seasons; it is she that furthers capacities. She furthers them also in human kind. Individual men, classes, corporations, whole societies and nations, can only advance with this stream, they have done all if they steer wisely upon it. Let no one think that, if all the regents of the earth from the proudest Negro King to the mightiest Khan of the Tartars should combine to make to-day yesterday and to hinder forever the progressive development of the human race, whether it lead to youth or to old age they could ever accomplish their aim. This can never be an aim with wise rulers, simply, because there is no sense in such fruitless endeavor.

A wise ruler then will always regard himself as the householder, not as the antagonist of Nature. He will improve every circumstance which she offers, to the best issues. Here leaves are falling, there a whole autumn of leaves lie already in their shrouds. He will not attempt to restore them again to their former places on limb and twig. Can he give them back their former freshness and sap which made them a living whole with the tree on which they hung? And if he cannot do this, how then? Will he crown himself with a withered wreath of dried leaves, because they were other once than they are now? What Nature could not keep, will the gardener keep it? and that too, not in conformity with the ends of Nature, but in direct opposition to them? Infinitely more beautiful the task to follow Nature, to mark her times, to awaken powers wherever they slumber, to promote thought, activity, invention, joy and love, in whatsoever field of useful employment. Necessity comes at last and compels with iron sceptre. He who obeys reason and measure will prevent necessity. Often, he will need only to beckon with the lily-staff of Oberon, and here new flowers will spring instead of the withered ones, and there, if the blossom-time is past, nourishing fruits will come to maturity. He will come to the aid of the young shoot and take it under his protection against oppressive weeds. The old wild tree he will not cut down, but graft more genial fruits upon it, and the rejuvenized tree will wonder, itself, at its nobler existence. A slight anticipation of this kind, by which one nation had got the start of another, has often secured to it, for centuries, unattainable advantages. England acquired the position which she now occupies, by a somewhat earlier adoption and application of certain points of constitutional finance and commerce, which had long before germinated in other countries, but which folly and passion had suppressed. After many violent revolutions which passed over her, like bloody thunder-showers, it was given to the most peaceful and silent revolution, to awaken a new activity, and thereby to establish, for centuries, the prosperity of a living constitution. If in the time of William the Third, she had attempted to renew the feudal, military and forest laws of William the Conqueror, where would she be now?

All orders and arrangements of society are the children of Time. This ancient mother produced, nourished, educated them; she adorned and fitted them out; and after a longer or shorter term of life, she buries them as she buries and renews herself. Whoever therefore confounds his own being with the duration of an order or institution, gives himself unnecessary torment. That which was before thee, will be behind thee too, if it is to be. For thine own part, act understandingly and wisely; time will proceed in its great course and accomplish its own. Be in thine own person more than thine order; and then, however that may grow old, thou wilt be, for thyself and for others, always young. Yea, the darker the night, the brighter shalt thou beam a star! He who does not raise himself above the breastwork of his order, is no hero within it. An order, as such, makes only puppets. Personality makes worth and merit. The more thou art idle, dead hull which conceals the best as well as the poorest kernel falls away, the more the fair and ripe fruit appears. Assuredly, therefore, it is no retrocession, but an evolution of the times, when the order ceases to be all, and men demand to see, in each order, persons, men, active beings. And since, without a new incursion of barbarism, and with the daily increasing necessities of Europe, this feeling must necessarily increase, there remains only one counsel which can secure each one against the senescence of his order. Be something in your order, and then you will be the first to perceive, to avoid and to amend its defects. Its old age will appear rejuvenized in you, precisely because there is something in you which would grace every form and live in all.

The excellent Paolo Sarpi wrote a treatise, the title of which attracted me exceedingly: "How opinions are born and die in us." I was very curious to become acquainted with its contents. And although I saw from Foscarini's extract in Griselini, that it was not likely to contain what I had supposed, this capital problem nevertheless was often in my thoughts.

Many are the ways in which, from earliest childhood, we arrive at opinions with which we clothe ourselves, body and soul. Many of them cleave to us with great tenacity, and the silliest we generally keep concealed behind our innermost, ninth skin, where, let no one presume to touch them! Unfortunately, however, Time will touch them, and often with very rude hands. And he who, in order to save his life, that is, his reason, peace and the self-consciousness of internal worth, cannot yield the skin and hair of his opinions to the meddling Satan, is in bad hands. For that which is mere opinion, or even false opinion, will assuredly perish in the fierce fire of purification. But is it not something better that shall arise in its place? Instead of opinions received on authority or even, as Franklin relates, from politeness, knowledge from conviction, reason approved by our own investigation, and a self-acquired felicity shall be our portion. The old man in us must die that a new youth may spring up.

"But how may this be! Can a man return into his mother's womb and be born again?" To this doubt of old Nicodemus, the only answer that can be given is: '*Palingenesia!*'—not Revolution, but a happy Evolution of the faculties which slumber in us, and by means of which we renew our youth. What we call outliving ourselves, — that is, a kind of death, — is, with souls of the better sort but sleep, which precedes a new waking, a relaxation of the bow which prepares it for new use. So rests the fallow-field, in order to produce the more plentifully hereafter. So dies the tree in winter, that it may put forth and blossom anew in the spring. Destiny never forsakes the good, as long as he does not forsake himself, and ignobly despair of himself. The Genius which seemed to have departed from him, returns to him again, at the right moment, bringing new activity, fortune and joy. Sometimes the Genius comes in the shape of a friend, sometimes in that of an unexpected change of times. Sacrifice to this Genius even though you see him not! Hope in back-looking, returning Fortune, even when you deem her far off! If the left side is sore, lay yourself on the right; if the storm has bent your sapling one way, bend it the other way, until it attains, once more, the perpendicular medium. You have wearied your memory? Then exercise your understanding. You have striven too diligently after seeming, and it has deceived you? Now seek being. That will not deceive. Unmerited fame has spoiled you? Thank Heaven that you are rid of it, and seek, in your own worth, a fame which cannot be taken away. Nothing is nobler and more venerable than a man, who, in spite of fate, perseveres in his duty, and who, if he is not happy outwardly, at least deserves to be so. He will certainly become so, at the right season. The Serpent of time often casts her slough, and brings to the man in his cave, if not the fabled jewel on her head and the rose in her mouth, at least medicinal herbs which procure him oblivion of the past, and restoration to new life.

Philosophy abounds in remedies designed to console us for misfortunes endured, but unquestionably, its best remedy is when it strengthens us to bear new misfortunes, and imparts to us a firm reliance on ourselves. The illusion which weakens the faculties of the soul, comes, for the most part, from without. But the objects which environ us are not ourselves. It is sad indeed, when the situation in which a man is placed, is so embittered and made so wretched, that he has no desire to touch one of its grapes or flowers, because they crumble to ashes in his hands, like those fruits of Sodom. Nevertheless, the situation is not himself; let him, like the tortoise, draw in his limbs and be what he can and ought. The more he disregards the consequences of his actions, the more repose he has in action. Thereby the soul grows stronger and revivifies itself, like an ever-springing fountain. The fountain does not stop to calculate through what regions of the earth its stream shall flow, what foreign matter it shall take in, and where it shall finally lose itself. It flows from its own fulness, with an irrepressible motion. That which others show us of ourselves is only appearance. It has always some foundation, and is never to be wholly despised; but it is only the reflection of our being in them, mirrored back to us from their own; often a broken and dim form, and not our being itself. Let the little insects creep over and around you, and be at the uttermost pains to make you appear dead; they work in their nature. Work you in yours, and live! In fact, our breast, our character, keeps us always more and longer upright, than all the acumen of the head, than all the cunning of the mind. In the heart we live, and not in the thoughts. The opinions of others may be a favorable or unfavorable wind in our sails. As the ocean its vessels, so circumstances at one time may hold us fast, at another may powerfully further us; but ship and sail, compass, helm and oar, are still our own. Never, then, like old Tithonus, grow gray in the conceit that your youth has passed away, Rather, with newly awakened activity, let a new Aurora daily spring from your arms.

I ought now to speak to the greater problem, so peculiarly adapted to our times: Whether nations, countries, states, must also decline with old age, or whether they too are capable of a new youth? And by what means that youth may be renewed? On this question there is great division of opinion, and, as each opinion knows how to fortify itself with examples from history, this very difference in the answers is itself a proof of the indefiniteness of the question. What is it that can grow old in a nation, a country, a state? What, in them, can or ought to be made young again? Is it the soul, the air, the sky? And how are these changed for the better or worse? Is it the farms, meadows, forests, salt-springs, mines, trees? Or is it the manner of working them, the profit and the application of their products? Is it these alone, or is it man himself, his race, his manners, his education and mode of living, his principles and opinions, his relations and conditions? And how shall these be changed? By speeches and writings, or by institutions and well-directed, consistent, continued action? And what object shall this change accomplish? Superfluity for the few, comfort and idleness for the many, or the happiness of all? And wherein consists the happiness of all? In arts and sciences? In seeming or in being? In loquacious enlightenment or in genuine culture? All these, and perhaps other questions, should be considered with careful reference to place, time and circumstances, and a comparison with more ancient examples and their consequences. And then, it would probably be found:

1. That land and people never grow old, or only at a very late period; but that States, as human institutions, as children of the times, or even, in many cases, as the mere growth of accident, have their age and their youth, and, consequently, an ever-progressive, imperceptible movement toward growth, toward blossoming, or toward dissolution.

2. That man, often individual men, may retard or promote these periods, nay, that they are mostly promoted by opposite measures.

3. That when forces are at work, either for bloom or for dissolution, their progress is rapid, and everything appears to assimilate itself with them, until trivial circumstances,—often again, individual men,—give the stream a different direction; which new direction, again, is the result of a living presence, although it sometimes appears to be the effect of chance.

4. That, finally, in order to forestall those fearful explosions which are called political revolutions, and which ought to be entirely foreign from the book of human affairs, the State has no other remedy, but to preserve or to restore the natural relation, the healthy action of all its parts, the brisk circulation of its juices, and must not contend against the nature of things. Sooner or later the strongest machine must succumb in that contest; but Nature never grows old. She only renews her youth periodically, in all her living forces.

The timid nature of man, always compassed about with hope and fear, often prophesies distant evils as near, and calls that death, which is only a wholesome slumber, a necessary, health-bringing relaxation. And so it generally deceives itself in its predictions concerning lands and kingdoms. Powers lie dormant which we do not perceive. Faculties and circumstances are developing themselves, on which we could not calculate. But even when our judgment is true, it usually leans too much to one side. "If this is to live," we say, "that must die." We do not consider, whether it may not be possible that both shall live and act favorably on each other?

The good Bishop Berkeley, who was no poet, was inspired, by his beneficent zeal for America, to write the following :   *   *   *

> Westward the star of empire takes its way;
> The four first acts already past,
> The fifth shall close the drama with the day,
> Time's noblest offspring is the last.*

So prophesied the good-natured Bishop, and if his spirit could now glance at yonder up-striving America, he would perhaps discover, with that same glance, that, in the arms of the old Tithon, Europe, also, a new Aurora was slumbering. Not four, scarcely three acts in the great drama of this, still youthful, quarter of the globe, are past; and who shall say how many times yet the old Tithon of the human race may and will renew his youth upon our earth!

METEMPSYCHOSIS,

IN THREE DIALOGUES.

DIALOGUE I.

CHARICLES AND THEAGES.

Char. You are just the person I wished to see, Theages. You will be surprised to find me in this laboratory of learning.

Theag. What books are these? Greek, Latin, English, even Hebrew! What are they all about?—*Metempsychosis.* Well! to be sure, that is a fertile subject to talk about and to write about.

Char. Let us talk about it then.

Theag. With all my heart; I have nothing else to do. An hypothesis so rich and concerning things so remote; for and against which so much may be said, certainly deserves a few words for and against. But we must first come to an understanding with ourselves as to the meaning of metempsychosis. There are three sorts, an *ascending*, a *descending*, and a *circular*. Do we understand each other?

Theag. Perfectly. The *ascending* is the refining of lower germs of life into higher; as if, for example, the soul of a plant should become an animal, the soul of an animal a man, &c. The descending is the Brahminical hypothesis; that good men are rewarded by being changed into cows, sheep, and white elephants, and the wicked punished by becoming tigers and swine. The third or *circular* is—circular. Which shall we discuss first?

Theag. Whichever you please. The first or ascending is very probable, and, if true, destroys the second and the third. If the upward course is the law of Nature with all living things, then nothing can move backward or in a perpetual circle. Then man too must forward. The chain cannot break with him—the highest link that we know. He is a being like all other beings, and if everything else advances, according to a universal law of Nature, then he too must advance.

Char. But we are supposing this law of Nature already proved.

Theag. We will not suppose it then. For the present, we will know nothing of the first sort of metempsychosis; whether, e. g., man was first a plant, then an animal, and has reached his present condition by a constant progress. We will speak only of the second and third journey,—*backwards* and *round about*. We will inquire whether there are *data in nature, experiences of the human species, fore-feelings in our soul, ideas in God,* as far as he is known to us, or in the general *course of the world*, which authorize such a supposition. Do you trust yourself to answer that question?

Char. Almost. And I will begin with the most intelligible — with the experiences of human kind. Do you not know great and rare men who cannot have become what they are, at once, in a single human existence? Who must have often existed before, in order to have attained that purity of feeling, that instinctive impulse for all that is true, beautiful and good; in short, that elevation and natural supremacy over all around them? Do you know none such?

Theag. I know none.

Char. Have you never read of such rare, great, eminent characters?

Theag. O friend, why amuse ourselves with ranging great men according to uniforms? I know great men in life and in history, but no one who must necessarily have been several times in a human mother's womb, in order to be the man he is. The greatest men, I have always found, were the most modest and sincere. They made no mystery of what they seemed to themselves, of what they once were, of what they became and how. They did not throw themselves into mount Ætna in order to become gods;† for the iron sandals will come to light in time. On the contrary, they confessed and gave their "Confessions" to the world and to posterity.

Char. And what did they confess? Do not you remember Pythagoras who had been Euphorbus? Do you not remember Apollonius of Tyana?

Theag. We will leave these fabulous shades, and come, if you please, to persons who stand in the light. Petrarch's, Cardanus's, Montaigne's, Luther's, Rousseau's Confessions,—do they breathe a syllable of those great, or at least rare men having been in the world before? of their feeling that they could not otherwise have become what they endeavored to be? On the contrary, do they not candidly confess how they had worked their way upward, how, with difficulty, they had raised themselves out of nothing, how they still felt all manner of faults and weaknesses within

---

* The original gives the entire poem of which the above is the concluding stanza, together with a German version of it.

† Deus immortalis haberi
Dum cupit Empedocles, ardentem frigidus Ætnam
Insiluit.—*Horat.*

themselves, and how, carried away thereby, they would undoubtedly have become bad men if they had given themselves the reins? You remember what Socrates said of the physiognomist? And Socrates was certainly very capable of Pythagorean dreams.

Char. Perhaps, of this Pythagorean dream, too. But altogether, we know too little about Socrates from his own mouth; he speaks only through the mouth of others. Therefore leave examples, and say: do you not think there have been very few truly great people in the world?

Theag. They would not be called great, were there not few of them.

Char. Do you suppose that these great men, rare as they have been in all centuries, became what they were and what, in all time, they will be, by mere industry, by pains-taking of which every mechanical mind is capable? or by Nature alone, by a kind of native sense, by an inspiration which they did not give to themselves, which never deserted them, which no one could imitate, and which every one who attempted to imitate, failed? They appeared like Genii, they vanished like Genii, and men could only say: "there he was, there he stood; he is no more; where is there another like him?" Is not that your opinion?

Theag. I need not opine, for all history confirms it. But what has this to do with metempsychosis?

Char. Hear me further. Do not these great characters appear, for the most part, all at once? Like a cloud of celestial spirits, they descended from on high;—like men risen from the dead, born again, who, after a long night of sleep, brought back the old time, and stood forth as youths in new and celestial beauty. Does it not seem as if the wheel of the times must revolve in order to produce the human race anew, to waken the understanding, to renovate virtue? What if these revolutions in the visible world are, what the name imports, revolutions also in the invisible,—the spirit-world,—a coming again of old, noble spirits and races of men?

Theag. That sounds fine. Let us see what the splendid vision amounts to. That great spirits are rare, I do not deny. I grant further, that what they were, they could be by nature alone, and not by an *improbus labor*. But this is no argument for Metempsychosis. Among brutes also, there are, in every species, large gradations and differences of faculty which only those observe, who live, as it were, on intimate terms with that species. Must the souls of these animals have therefore migrated? Must the more intelligent dog have been many times a dog, in order to become what he is? Or is it not rather evident, that everything depends on happier organization, a more sprightly genesis, a nobler lineage, on favorable local circumstances, on climate, birth, training and hundred-armed accident, which, with all its ramifications, it is so difficult to compute and to mould? Now compare brutes with man, a two-stringed fiddle with the organ! What an infinite diversity must there not be in the human species, even because the extent of man's powers is so great, his formation so delicate, his faculties so manifold, the climate in which he lives, the world of circumstances which acts upon him so wonderfully diverse, in short, the links of his chain so commensurable and so incommensurable, as you please to consider it! What may not man become? Who has ever determined the goal—so much and no more? What may not come to pass out of so great a multitude, in the stream of the ever-progressive development of the world and of human kind? Would it not be a far greater wonder, if all men were born blockheads, than that there should be, occasionally, a man of sense, as is now the case? Shall the electric spark, in no instance, shine forth pure and bright? Shall not the genuine human form show itself here and there in an army of *larvæ*? What need of goblins and *revenants?* since this nobler form is the true and peculiar form of humanity, from which we have only degenerated, by malformations too easily accounted for. You might as well maintain that angels embody themselves in these higher specimens of humanity, or,—if their genius works instinctively,—that certain animals endowed with certain artistic faculties are reproduced in them. I see not why we must needs disturb the dead and conjure up the prophet Samuel in his nightgown, merely that we may say; "I see gods arise out of the earth." View Humanity humanly, and it will appear human to you. View individual great men in their organization, their birth, their education, their place and position, and you will not need to cross the sea, in quest of shadows.

Char. But that these rare men should be, for the most part, cotemporary?—

Theag. Is that your proof, my good metempsychosist? As though a heap of shadows were blown along, as in Dante's hell, by a gust of wind; or as if a troop of giants, as in Bodmer's Noah, came sailing in a balloon, and were pleased to alight here! Consult history, you will always find that men are awakened by external causes, that circumstances, a demand, a want, a reward, called them forth; that emulation stimulated them; that a long series of errors had just run itself out; that a night of the ages had past away, and it was time, at last, that morning should dawn once more. Generally, there had been so much preparatory labor and discipline, that these more fortunate men needed only to profit by the failures and pains of their ancestors, to attain to honor. After many dissonances, they hit at last the consonant points of the cord.—That is all that our eye can discover from a comparison of periods and of men. As to groping farther into the invisible after the finger of the Godhead, and endeavoring to ascertain when and how he causes men to be born;—I hold that to be above our sphere. If we are going to *poetise*, I can as well derive them from the moon, under certain happy phases, as by a *palingenesia* from the fore-world, which does not change quite so regularly as the moon.

Char. The latter circumstance matters not. We are as yet far too young in history, we have experienced too few of those periodical revolutions, to be able to compute them as we do the changes of the moon.

Theag. Then also we are too young to cherish fictions which we cannot prove, for which all history furnishes no sure *data*. Young or old, the return of the human species must have become perceptible, the ebb and flood of spirits must have been observed, though only by way of conjecture. Nay, if with that return, the human understanding and moral refinement, the inward activity and elasticity of men be supposed to increase; heavens! what glorious men we should have, by this time, in those who have been here ten times before! And where are these? Where are they, my friend? The wisest, best and strongest men,—have they lived in modern times or in antiquity? And how often have the Homers, the Socrateses, the Pythagorases, the Epaminondases, the Scipios appeared in the world? to say nothing of their having grown from century to century. The human phœnixes have always been rare, and will always remain so. We need not expect that, suddenly, with the year 1800, gods will walk the earth instead of men, because the revolving wheel has dried the wet clay and brought the figures into shape. Let us therefore leave these divinations in their proper place, and content ourselves with being men, such as our forefathers were, once-baked men, and not sewed up, a second time, in Jupiter's thigh. Or if, my dear migrationist, you know any story out of your primeval world, which I also remember, bring it forwards.

Char. You shall have it; only I beg you to be candid, and not to deny the thoughts and reminiscences of your youth, especially of your early, unsophisticated childhood. Have you never had remembrances of a former state, which you could find no place for in this life? In that beautiful period, when the soul is yet a half-closed bud, have you not seen persons, been in places, of which you were ready to swear that you had seen those persons, or had been in those places before? And yet it could not have been in this life, as you can satisfy yourself on reflection. Whence then are those reminiscences? Whence can they be, but from some former state? Therefore are they so sweet, so elevating! The most blessed moments, the grandest thoughts, are from that source. In our more ordinary seasons, we look back with astonishment on ourselves, we do not comprehend ourselves. And such are *we ;* we who, from a hundred causes, have sunk so deep and are so wedded to matter, that but few reminiscences of so pure a character remain to us. The nobler class of men who, separated from wine and meat, lived in perfect simplicity, temperate, and according to the order of Nature, carried it further, no doubt, than others, as we learn from the example of Pythagoras of Iarchas, of Apollonius and others, who remembered distinctly what and how many times they had been in the world before. If we are blind, or can see but two steps beyond our noses, ought we therefore to deny that others may see a hundred or a thousand degrees farther, even to the bottom of time, into the deep, cool well of the fore-world, and there discern everything plain and bright and clear?

Theag. You are a true Pythagorean, my friend, and worthy to attain to the deepest well of the fore-time; yea! to the original fountain of truth itself, if men ever arrive there. I will freely confess to you, that those sweet dreams of memory are known to me also, among the experiences of my childhood and youth. I have been in places and circumstances of which I could have sworn that I had been in them before. I have seen persons with whom I seemed to have lived before; with whom I was, as it were, on the footing of an old acquaintance. But may there not be some other cause for such experiences?

Char. I know of none but the remembrance of a former state.

Theag. Certainly, of a former state; only not beyond this life, and in another body. Have you never watched yourself, and observed how the soul is always occupied in secret? how, especially, in childhood, it makes plans, combines thoughts, builds bridges, meditates romances, and repeats all this in dreams, with the magic colors of the dream-world? Look at that child playing and entertaining itself in silence. He talks with himself; he is in a dream of vivid images. These images and thoughts will some time return to him, at a time when he does not expect it, and no longer remembers whence they are. They will appear to him with all the decorations of the scene in which he first conceived them, or which, it may be, a youthful dream brought before his mind. The situation will create a pleasant delusion, as every retrospect which brings agreeable images before the mind deludes us. It will be taken for an inspiration because it actually comes like an inspiration from another world; that is, rich in images and without pains. A single trait of the *present* picture will recall it; a single sound which now touches the soul, awakens all the slumbering tones of former times. These are moments of the sweetest rapture, especially in beautiful, wild, romantic spots, in moments of pleasant intercourse with persons who, with an agreeable illusion, unexpectedly create in us, or we in them, the feeling, as it were, of an earlier acquaintance: reminiscences of paradise, but not of a previous human life; the paradise, rather, of youth, of childhood, or of pleasant dreams which we had either sleeping or waking, and which, in fact, are the true paradise. The *palingenesia* is therefore correct, only not so wonderful as you suppose, but, on the contrary, very natural.

Char. Your explanation is charming, but—

Theag. I think it will prove convincing, if we watch ourselves. Do you not think that man experiences the highest delight and even a kind of ecstasy, when he beholds a dream, which the soul had composed out of its dearest images, suddenly and unexpectedly, though only partially realized? Must not the soul welcome such a dream with rapture, and embrace it as Adam embraced Eve, when it sees in it the image of itself, the creation of its sweetest moments, the fruit of its secret love? Behold, my friend, hence come those surprises, those sudden and often so pleasing, so deeply prophetic and powerful sympathies; hence the divine and divining power of first impressions. The second impression can never give it. That only weakens the rapture of the first and decomposes the picture. As long as the soul realizes the first dream, it floats, as it were, in the Elysium of childhood. When the dream is dissolved, then, alas! the gods have become men, then we must till the ground and eat our bread in sorrow and in the sweat of our face. Observe particularly, that, with well-organized men, reminiscences of this kind are mostly beautiful, but wild, romantic, often exaggerated, precisely like the impressions and feelings of their youth. Sickly people retain ideas of pain, weak people feelings of difficulty and trouble— the reflections of their early impressions. These feelings return, at certain times, in moments of weakness, of sudden attack, when the soul is off its guard and gives itself up to involuntary combinations of thought; they return often; they become dominant feelings. I could mention striking examples of this, but they would lead us too far out of the way. Observe people in love, and insane people,— especially melancholy love and mild insanity,—you will see the power of first impressions, the entire youth of the soul in every trait of the pictures which filled their minds; you will hear them in all the complainings of their aberrations. Nay, observe your own soul in dreams. There, we all wander alike. After a certain age, we decorate all our dreams with scenes of our youth: the very persons who appear in them, if they were our nearest and most beloved, assume other, and, as it seems, more lovely and romantic forms. In all the fantasies of love the first impression is the dearest, the most indelible. In short, we spell together, where we can, an alphabet out of our youth whose traits are the most agreeable, the most impressive, the most familiar to us. Have I satisfied you with my solution?

Char. Not entirely. Some reminiscences are so wonderful, so foreign, and, to use your language, so incapable of being spelt with the impressions of the youth and childhood of this life, that—

Theag. That they necessarily require another world, a former life? Well, then, why are you not true to your own hypothesis? Why do you not actually assume another world, a foregone connection in the world of spirits and of souls, as Plato fabled, as the old Rabbins and many nations conceived? Methinks, if we must dream, we shall do well to dream the freest of dreams. Imagine, for example, how once, with your beloved in the land of spirits you

" Swarmed unseen, small as a ray of light;
Think how, upon an orange leaf,
You met for sport and jest;
In the luxurious lap of young auriculas,
Oft winged with converse sweet the laggard time."

Why must you make your scene so narrow and let the soul beg so often and laboriously, in our poor humanity, the spiritual alms which it may have far cheaper and all at once if you send it into the realm of spirits and divest it entirely of its corporeal nature. Have you never read letters from the dead to the living?

Char. Many.

Theag. Well, then, you know what freedom and absence of restraint there is in the kingdom of spirits. Therefore it is that children love dreams of this kind so much, because they blend them with their own dreams, which they seem to confirm therewith as with traditions from another world. For myself, though I tolerate these things in poetry, and once delighted in them, at my present time of life I am content to renounce the dream of pre-existence, and to study my soul in its present bonds, in its poor actuality.

Char. And what results do you draw from your studies in it?

Theag. Results? That's more than I know. But the study itself, it seems to me, is very profitable, and I wish that we might study our children for the same purpose.

Char. For what purpose?

Theag. To notice their first impressions, the manner in which their souls are affected by them, the secret ideas and images with which they entertain themselves, which they spin and spin, like a fine invisible web, according to their own will and pleasure. Have you never observed that children will sometimes, on a sudden, give utterance to ideas which make us wonder how they got possession of them, which presuppose a long series of other ideas and secret self-communings, which burst forth like a full stream, out of the earth, an infallible sign that the stream was not produced in a moment from a few rain-drops, but had long been flowing concealed beneath the ground, and, it may be, had broken through many a cave, had carried away many a rock, and contracted many defilements?

Char. And if we do observe this, who can resist Nature? Can we arrest the course of these streams or bring them to light? Can we change the constitution of the earth and of human souls according to our pleasure?

Theag. We can in one sense, and in another

sense we cannot. We can as far as we ought, and we ought as far as we can. If the souls of our children are dear to us, and we are as deeply convinced as I am, of the power of first impressions, ought we not imperceptibly to guide and to determine these first impressions, so far as they are in our power? I say, imperceptibly, for else it is all in vain. The soul, in its most secret operations, bears no restraint, no mechanical law; it works freely out of its own nature; and these first efforts contain the emblem of all its future workings through the whole course of its life. To watch it, therefore, and, when in pleasant wilds and agreeable labyrinths it wanders and loses its way, to guide it in the shape of a bright star, or like Minerva in Homer, in the form of a foreign traveller,—not teacher or overseer,—in short, as a certain philosopher desired for his daily portion, to supply to our children joyful morning-images and youthful pictures, that hereafter at evening and in old age, they may have glad reminiscences from the Platonic kingdom of spirits and may acquire no debasing and terrible ideas of metempsychosis;—that I think we can and ought to do; although, of course, subject to the power of fate.

Char. Yes! to be sure, subject to the power of fate.

Theag. For we are not masters of all our own ideas and impressions, much less of the impressions of our friends and our children. It is not we ourselves who have placed our souls here, much less have we armed their forces against the universe which streams to them from every side. There are actually persons who are destined to sorrows and misfortune, for whom early impressions and ideas, cares and disease have in a great measure diminished and destroyed the joy of life. The cup which they are to drink has been made bitter, or else turbid and distasteful; for there are evils which cannot be wholly done away with in this life. These persons, too, must content themselves, meanwhile, to bear with cheerfulness, at least with equanimity, the burden which is laid upon them, the inseparable burden of life, and to await in hope another, freer, better being.

Char. Do you see now how you arrive at my metempsychosis? Who knows what these people may have committed in their former state, that they are now made so miserable by the hand of fate and not by their own fault? But you are preparing to go.

Theag. It is late. Another time we will begin where we leave off, as is the law of metempsychosis. Sleep well, Charicles, and dream of the primeval realms of love, and not that you were once Sejanus or Ravaillac.

Char. In that case it were well that I am no longer so, and that my evil destiny lies already behind me. Sleep well!

DIALOGUE II.

Charicles. I hope, my friend, to hear you speak more reasonably to-day on the subject of our conversation. Yesterday you were somewhat warm.

Theages. That depends on what you mean by 'reasonable' and 'warm.' If equanimity is shown by investigating, then I had it yesterday; but if you desire that laxity and coldness to which everything is indifferent—

Char. Not exactly indifferent. To whom can it be a matter of indifference that poor, vexed man should find some indemnification for present, pressing evils, at least in the beautiful visions of hope? that he should receive some light concerning God, the world, the course of fate? Where Seneca's reasons cease, where even Religion does not explain, but only ties new knots, there—

Theag. Charicles, let us not bring religion into the play, especially in so disparaging manner. Religion, most surely, knows nothing of metempsychosis, but points in quite another direction, with all its promises, threats, commands, examples. The wheel of Ixion, the stone of Sisyphus, the drawing of the Danaides—such would be the eternal revolution of human destiny, not a comforting, heavenly recompense. In Dante's hell, the hypocrites walk with leaden mantles and averted, backward-looking-face, in a perpetual circle; they go forever and never move from the spot, and forever look behind them with their twisted necks.

Char. But, my friend, do you also look back calmly, a few moments. How many wretches are there behind you, who have not deserved to fall so low, who, therefore, must rise higher in this life in order to reconcile us, in some degree, with Divine justice and mercy.

Theag. To reconcile? You would then be an enemy of God, if there be no migration of souls in the circulations of Humanity? You must needs deny his justice and paternal goodness, if he did not permit you to return to this earth again and again? For myself, I confess I am heartily satisfied with having been once on the earth and lived my life, as man. For at best, says one of the eldest sages, it is "labor and sorrow:" and that is its everlasting circle. "Man who is born of woman is of few days and full of trouble. He cometh forth as a flower and is cut down; he fleeth also as a shadow and continueth not." That is his destiny.

Char. A sad destiny!

Theag. Sad or consoling,—enough, it is his destiny. When you look at human life in all its connections, does not everything within you seem to cry aloud: "God be praised! I am to be lived but once." The morning of our days, how soon past! The bud of our earthly being how soon withered! Now the day gets sultry, weariness of life succeeds; gradually the evening draws nigh, and the sun goes down. Man fades as he bloomed, he forgets his own thoughts, he distrusts his own powers, he dies before he dies, and rejoices to find his grave. This is the unchangeable circle of the days and seasons, of the life-period and human ages on our earth. And you would have the wretch tread this circle a thousand times when he rejoices to have trodden it but once! You would have Nature, like Penelope, forever weave her web and weave it anew, only to destroy it again. Unfortunate Humanity with all its talents, hopes and powers! Weak-minded Penelope! — for whose understanding at least I would not be a suitor.

Char. But, my friend, has not the tree, the flower, the day, the same destiny? and do they not return too? It appears to be the law of Nature; why should weak, proud man alone resist it?

Theag. Truly, he would be weak and proud, to resist it as a tree, as a flower, or as the day; but he is neither of the three; and furthermore these three do *not* return. The tree stands rooted in the earth, and if it has, as I doubt not, a life, it is only the first germ of an inferior kind of life. This, it is a great while in working out, and must remain long in its place. Every year is to it but one day; the spring its morning, the winter its sleep. It must endure, produce many leaves, blossoms and fruits which serve the air, animals, man, — the whole superior creation. Then it gradually grows old and dies. That which now shoots forth around it, is not itself but its offspring. What has become of its life-power and life-breath, in odors, blossoms, leaves, fruits, we know or do not know. Our glance cannot and must not penetrate the kingdom of productive powers. The tree, then, does not come within your *palingenesia;* it does not migrate, but lives out its life, as a world of changeable, unreturning leaves, blossoms and fruits. The same of the flower. And the simile of the day, which certainly never returns, was, undoubtedly, meant only as a simile. You are, therefore, entirely without example in the order of nature. And do you think that man, man alone, is to be this example of an Ixionic-Tantalistic-Danaidal destiny? an example without example, nay, almost without design?

Char. Not entirely without design. He would learn the science of life in the only way in which it can be learned; by the most many-sided view of it, and the most living experience. He would, therefore, always be tried, purified, refined, confirmed; the thread of his identity would continue and he would advance, however much he might seem to move in a circle.

Theag. A slow progress! in which Fate would treat us as Phrygians, who are always wise behindhand, and never know how the boy feels who receives the stripes, until they have received them themselves. And to receive these stripes forever!

Char. Fate will not inflict them without need; and since it is once for all established, that we really and truly know only that which we have ourselves tried and experienced—

Theag. It seems to me, my friend, that you abuse the truest of propositions, when you apply it in that way. I need not try everything in this world; else, wo to poor humanity! What wise man would wish to be inoculated with the plague in order to ascertain its true nature? What man would wish to be a patricide or a matricide, in order to learn how Nero or any other monster must have felt? And what kind of a destiny would that be, which should find pleasure in making me perform all sorts of detestable parts, in order to give me the feeling that I had performed them? You see what a system it is that can furnish occasion for all manner of enormities, making the lusts which the villain feels within himself, his present '*destination*,' and giving him, when he dies upon the gallows, the sweet consolation that "now he has expiated one of his debts; — it was his destination to tread that path at present; what he has not yet learned and experienced, he will have time to learn in other stations."

Char. We will not speak of these abuses. The best things may be abused, in the worst manner, by foolish and wicked men. I return to my question. How will you vindicate the goodness of God who has made the lot of man so unequal? Either, the ideas of evil and good, perfect or imperfect, happy or unhappy, must be very indifferent to him; or—

Theag. Or we ought not to measure him by our petty, narrow, pitiful standard. Who is happy? Who is unhappy? Is the civilized man more so than the savage? The slave in golden, more than the slave in iron chains? Where, on our earth, dwells perfection? Where has it built itself an house? Are we constituted its judges? We who live only on the dole of its grace and mercy? God created us not to judge the human species, but to live in it and to rejoice in our place, and to bless our kind wherever and as far as we can. He himself has done no more than, according to his wisdom, he *could ;*— than, according to his goodness, he *should.* He took counsel of both, and so he created the human race. Who can ask; "why no higher?" "why no lower?" Enough, it exists; and let each one rejoice that he too exists, enjoy his being, and trust in Him who brought him hither, that He will also lead him forth and lead him farther.

Char. So, the inequalities of the human condition, on our earth, find no explanation with you?

Theag. No other than this: "they lay in the plan of creation." Our planet, as it is once for all constituted, was intended to bear what it can, to produce what it can. Therefore it has been made a globe with all varieties of climate, of country, of vegetable, animal, human kinds. The ladder is erected in both hemispheres, its rounds are innumerable: where do they terminate? Through an hundred gates everything presses into the kingdom of God, and, through hundred thousand, forth again, in all gradations, upwards, forwards. Where God shall bless the poor, merchandised negro? whether in a paradise among the mountains,* or beneath a lazy bishop's mitre, because he has once ground himself weary,— let those decide who can. As diverse as this world is, so diverse will the future also be. Or if not,—if everything is to be united by simpler ends and more determinate magnitudes,—why, so much the better! Enough, I often find happiness here, where I sought it not; beauty beneath a covering which seemed most foreign to it; wisdom and virtue, for the most part, in rude, despised and undistinguishable forms. Precisely, where paint and prinking begin, there truth, justice, happiness cease; and shall we let our poor pilgrim migrate to these gilded pagodas, to lose the truth which they possess and to exchange inward worth and wealth for wretched outward tinsel? The more I learn to know Humanity by other tokens than the cut of the cloak, the more cause I find, even in this stage of being, to adore Providence with kneeling reverence. Where we expect the greatest misery, there dwells often the greatest happiness. Simplicity is not stupidity, and cunning is neither blessing nor wisdom. I therefore still hold with the poet;—

"Wisely doth Destiny its gifts allot;
To each, food, shelter, raiment and what not,
Strength to the poor and to the weak man, place."

Char. But, my dear friend, you surely know the law of economy which holds as well in regard to power as to space? It rules throughout all Nature. Is it not very probable that the Deity is guided by it in the propagation and progress of human souls? He who has not become ripe in one form of Humanity, is put into the oven again, and, some time or other, must be perfected.

Theag. But suppose he should be burned in the process? The mould of humanity is so narrow, the position—whether here or there, in rags or in purple — has so little to do with the result, that he who cannot be upright in one costume, will scarcely be so in another. At all events, there must be no necessity about it, else all the morality of free-agency is at an end, and man is thrown about like a stone, and shoved hither and thither like a clod of earth. Do you see where your hypothesis is leading you again? To a fatal necessity which enfeebles all striving and aspiration after happiness, beauty, virtue in every form, under every mask, and binds us in fetters of blind obedience to the car of Destiny. But we have been prating long enough in this narrow room; and that has made our conversation assume such a contracted, metaphysical character. Look at the beautiful, starry night! Yonder rises the moon. I propose, that we should betake ourselves, soul and body, out of this metaphysical atmosphere into free Nature.

---

* —"Simple Nature to his hope has given
Behind the cloud-topt hill an humbler heaven,
Some safer world in depth of woods embraced
Some happier island on the wat'ry waste."

They went forth and soon the tone of their conversation was changed. The holy silence which night spread around them, the bright celestial luminaries suspended like lamps above their heads, on the one side some lingering shimmer of the evening red, on the other the moon lifting herself softly from behind the shadows of the forest:—how does this magnificent temple exalt, expand, enlarge the soul! At such moments, one feels so perfectly the beauty and the nothingness of earth, and what refreshment God has provided for us on this star, on which sun and moon, the two fair lights of heaven, alternating, conduct us through life, and how low and small and vanishing is this speck of our earth, compared with the measureless splendor and glory of stars, suns and worlds.

What think you now, said Theages, of your *principium minimi,* according to which, you would be forever knocking about on the earth, chained to a grain of sand? Look at the heavens, God's star-writing, the primeval tradition of our immortality, the luminous chart of our far pilgrimage! Where does the universe end? And why do rays come down to us from yonder farthest star? Why have there been given to man the glance and the flaming flight of immortal hopes? Why, when we have been exhausted with the rays of the sun and bound fast to the dust all the day, does God unveil to us at night this sublime field of infinite eternal prospects? We stand lost amid the host of the worlds of God, lost in the abyss of his immensity round about us. And what should bind my spirit to this weary sand-grain, when my body, the hull, has sunk into the ground? All the laws which bind me here, evidently relate to my body only. That is formed of this earth and must return to this earth again. The laws of motion, the pressure of the atmosphere,—everything confines that, and only that, here below. The spirit once escaped, once rid of the delicate but strong bands of sense, impulse, propensity, duty and custom which bind it to this little sphere of visibility; what earthly power can hold it longer? What law of Nature has been discovered which should compel souls to revolve in this narrow race-course? The spirit is raised above the bounds of time, it despises space and the slow movements of earth. Once disembodied, it is immediately in its place, its sphere, in the new kingdom to which it belongs. Perhaps that kingdom is around us and we perceive it not; perhaps it is near us and we know not of it, except in occasional moments of happy fore-feeling, when the soul, as it were, attracts it to itself, or it the soul. Perhaps, too, there are appointed for us places of rest, regions of preparation, other worlds in which,—as on a golden heaven-ladder—ever lighter, more active and blest, we may climb upward to the fountain of all light, ever seeking, never reaching the centre of our pilgrimage,— the bosom of the Godhead. For we are and must ever be limited, imperfect, finite beings. But wherever I may be, through whatever worlds I may be led, I shall remain forever in the hands of the Father who hath brought me hither and who calls me further; forever in the infinite bosom of God.

I am sorry, said Charicles, to interrupt you in your contemplations which remove you so far from our earth; but do not leave me behind. Wherever you are free, wise and active, there is heaven; and why, then, do you shun and flee the earth? If you can live more freely, wisely, happily, in some other human form, and so ascend continually in your inward condition, what matters place and scene? Here or there, God's world is God's world; one theatre is as good as another. Our earth too is a star among stars.

Theag. Well, my friend; but how far is it possible to climb in our humanity? Is not its sphere as narrowly bounded, as dusty and as filthy as this star itself? The best of hearts is still but a human heart; body is body and earthly life is earthly life. The miserable details of business, the cares of life, so necessary and yet so unprofitable, still recur. The different life-periods, with their changing imperfections, recur. Even in regard to virtues, the human race is divided into its two sexes, which stand over against each other, on one root, mutually embrace and crown one another, but can never become one and the same perfection, in human life. What the one has, is wanting to the other. What one man has, another man wants. Birth, station, climate, education, office, mode of living forever limit and impede. Man grows for a few years only, and then stands still or declines and recedes. If he attempts, in old age, to appear a youth and to imitate others, he becomes ridiculous, he becomes childish. In short, it is a narrow sphere, this earthly life; and do what we will, as long as we are here, it is impossible to escape this narrowness without greater injury and the entire loss of ourselves. But hereafter, when death shall burst these bonds, when God shall transplant us like flowers into quite other fields and surround us with entirely different circumstances, then, — Have you never experienced, my friend, what new faculty a new situation gives to the soul? a faculty, which, in our old corner, in the stifling atmosphere of old circumstances and occupations, we had never imagined, had never supposed ourselves capable of?

Char. Who has not experienced that? From that very circumstance I drew the refreshing draught of the Lethe stream with which my *palingenesia* has already rejuvenized me, here on this earth. I feel, as you do, that, in spite of all our striving and effort, the sphere of humanity is insurmountable, and that our nature is circumscribed within fixed limits. Here, on this earth, no tree reaches to the heavens; certain stains, once contracted, all the rivers of the world cannot wash out; many weaknesses and imperfections, after a certain length of time, can scarcely be recognised, much less laid aside. Often, the coarser are exchanged for the more refined and more dangerous. All that is true. Moreover, I see very well, that, in the narrow, ever repeated circle of earthly life, nothing superlatively great is to be effected. There is so much useless trouble, and, from renewed effort, so little of fresh acquisition. The domain which *you* unfold is indeed more extensive, the field to which you invite is infinite,—the host of all the worlds that lie in my eternal path toward the Godhead. But, friend, who shall give me wings for such a flight? It seems, always, as if something hurled me back to my earth. It seems to me, as if I had not yet used up that, had not yet made myself sufficiently light to ascend higher; who shall give me wings?

Theag. If you will not receive them from the *sacred* hand which points thither, then receive at least some feathers from friendly—from your friend Newton's hands.

Char. From Newton's?

Theag. Even so. The system which he constructed out of stars and suns — let that be to you the fabric of your immortality, of an ever-during progress and upward flight. Are not all the planets of our solar system bound to each other and to their centre or focus, the sun, by the power of attraction?

Char. Unquestionably.

Theag. They constitute then a firm, an indestructible whole, in which, if anything should be changed or disturbed, the whole, with its great harmonies, must suffer and go to ruin.

Char. Precisely so. The planets all relate to the sun, and the sun, with its forces, its bulk, its light, its warmth and distance, relates to the planets.

Theag. And yet the planets are only the staging of the theatre, the dwelling-places of the creatures, who, on them, revolve around the infinitely more beautiful Sun of eternal goodness and truth, in various degrees of removal, with various eclipses, perihelia and aphelia. Is it possible that the scenes themselves should be so closely connected and not the contents of the scenes,—the play itself? Is it to be supposed, that the planets are so exactly arranged in relation to each other and to the Sun, and that the destiny of those who live in them, and for whose sake they have been prepared, is not as closely connected, and more closely, inasmuch as being is more than costume, matter more than place, life and subject more than theatre and stage? In nature everything is related,—morals and physics—like body and spirit. Morality is only a more beautiful *physique* of the spirit. Our future destination is a new link in the chain of our being, which connects itself with the present link most minutely and by the most subtile progression, as our earth is connected with the sun, and the moon with our earth.

Char. I surmise what you would say, my friend, but—

Theag. In these matters we can do nothing else but surmise and forebode. And beneath the silent gaze of the stars, in the face of the friendly moon, the surmises which we send into that immeasurable distance are so great, so elevating! Imagine, for a moment, that our star-fabric is as closely connected in regard to the moral condition of its inhabitants as it is in its physical circumstances,—that it is a choir of sisters praising the Creator in various tones and proportions, but with the harmony of a single power. Imagine that, from the farthest planet to the sun, there are gradations of being as of light, of distance, of masses, of forces, (and nothing is more probable); imagine the sun to be the *rendezvous* of all the beings of the system which he rules as he is the king of all light, of all warmth, of all beauty and truth which he communicates, in various gradations, to the creatures. Behold here the great ladder by which all ascend, and the long way which we have yet to tread, before we arrive at the centre and father-land of that which, in our star-system, we call Truth, Light, Love!

Char. So, then, the farther removed from our sun, the darker, the coarser? On the other hand, the nearer to that body, the brighter, the lighter, the warmer, the swifter? The beings in Mercury, which is always hidden in the rays of the sun, must indeed differ in their nature from the sluggish inhabitants of Saturn—those dark Patagonian giants who scarcely, in thirty years, get round the sun, and whose night, even with its five moons, is poorly lighted. Our earth then would occupy a middle station?

Theag. And perhaps that is the very reason why we are such middling creatures, standing half-way between the dark Saturnians and the bright sun-light, the fountain of all truth and beauty. Our reason is, in fact, but in its first dawn here; our freedom of will, too, and our moral energy is but so so. It is well, therefore, that we are not to tarry for ever on this earth-planet, where, it is most likely, we should never come to much.

Char. You think, then, that we are destined to travel through all the planets?

Theag. That I know not. Each planet may send its inhabitants, who are all, in various degrees, aspiring to one Sun, by the shortest route to that goal, and by such stages and gradations as the Creator shall judge to be necessary for them. How if our moon, for example,— and, if I remember right, Milton so describes her,* and several Oriental sects have so philosophized concerning her,—how if our moon should be the paradise of recreation, where weary pilgrims, escaped from the mists of this earth-valley, live in a purer atmosphere, in gardens of peace and social enjoyment, and prepare themselves for the contemplation of the higher light toward which the inhabitants of other planets are also travelling? It seems to me as if the moon promised us this with her calm consoling light,— as if she shone for no other purpose but to show us the glory of another world, and to inspire soft, dewy dreams of amaranthine bowers of peace, and an indissoluble, blessed friendship.

Char. You dream pleasantly, my friend, in the face of the moon, and I love to dream with you. It has often seemed to me too, when filled with sadness and gentle melancholy at the remembrance of departed, dearly loved friends, as if the moon-beams were their language, and I could almost hope to see their shining forms before me, or to feel, gliding down upon a ray, the kiss of their pure lips on my soul. But enough of this! We are both getting to be fantastic dreamers. Tell me further.

Theag. I have no inclination. I lack the blue, emerald gold-wings to carry you from star to star, to show you how our sun, too, speeds round a greater sun, how everything in creation rejoices in a harmony in which suns and earths are measured, numbered, weighed as notes, and doubtless, also, and how much more, the destiny, the life of their inhabitants. O! how great is the dwelling in which the Creator has placed me, and O, how fair! fair by night and by day, here and yonder, the view of sun, moon and star! My course is the path of the All of worlds; that uttermost star lights me on my way, and the harmony of all stars—the music of spiritual ideas and relations—accompanies me in it. But ah! my friend, all this is only twilight, conceit, surmise, compared with the infinitely purer and higher light of the religion of the spirit and the heart. On this earth everything is rounded with necessity, and we yearn, with 'the earnest expectation of the creature,' to be free. We have within us ideas of love, of friendship, of beauty, of truth which, here on earth, we know only in shadows and dream-images, so imperfect, so often disturbed, deceived, and always incomplete! We thirst for a river of purer joys; and it seems to me that the hope, the desire itself, is a sure prophecy of fruition. Take the purest relations of this world, the joys of a father, a mother, with what cares are they blended! with what pains and inconveniences are they interrupted; and how do they only minister, after all, to necessity, to a foreign, higher relation! "In that world," says the scripture, "they neither marry nor are given in marriage, but are as the angels of God." There love is freed from the coarser propensities, there friendship is pure and without the separations and burdens of this earth; there is more effective action with happy and beautiful concord, and a true, eternal aim; in fine, throughout, more of truth, of goodness, of beauty than this earth, even though we should return to it a hundred times, could afford.

"Him, O Parmeno!—him do I pronounce
The happiest, who when, from sorrow free,
His eyes have seen the things which we now see—
This sun, these stars, clouds, moon and fire—

---

* "Those argent fields, more likely, habitants,
Translated saints or middle spirits hold
Betwixt the angelical and human kind."

Again returneth thither whence he came.
For whether thou shalt live an hundred years
Or live but few, thou seest these, and aught
More beautiful than these hath no man seen.
Hold then this term of life, of which I speak,
But as a market or a caravan,
Where there is crowding, stealing, sport, and pains
Enow. The earlier thou departest hence,
The sooner shalt thou find the better hostelry,
If thou the pilgrim's penny—*Truth*
Provided hast, and hast no enemy.
Who long delays grows weary of the way
Him overtakes old age, and many wants
And plagues are his, and many foes.
He dies not happily who lives too long."*

How then would it be with him who should tarry here for ever, and again and again return to this 'market-place?'

Whether the silence of the night and the sublime harmony of the stars had reconciled the systems of the two friends, or whether Charicles had much to answer, they embraced and parted in silence. Theages seemed lost in the infinite blue of heaven and the shining star-ladder which so many nations, savages and sages, have denominated the *way of souls*. And truly a more sublime race that, and a richer, fairer *Palingenesia* than, even in its happiest forms, the needy narrow earth could afford.

"O Pater anne aliquas ad cœlum hinc ire putandum est
Sublimes animas? iterumque ad tarda reverti
Corpora? Quæ lucis miseris tam dira cupido?"

DIALOGUE III.

The next morning, as if by appointment, Theages and Charicles met in a walk of which both were fond, and where they were accustomed often to bathe their souls in the beams of the rising sun. Both were wrapped in the silence which twilight and waking bring with them, a holy silence from which the dawning day gently and gradually rouses us. They left each other undisturbed. With the blush of the morning before them and the joyous choir of all the newly awakened beings around them, they sat dumb for awhile, until, at last, when the sun had risen, and the scene became more animated, Charicles proposed that they should strike into the neighbouring wood through which, by a small circuit, they might take their way home. During the walk he imperceptibly directed the conversation to yesterday's topic.

Charicles. What did you dream of last night, Theages? Your visions must have been agreeable, for you seemed to be entirely lost last night among the stars and worlds.

Theages. When the sun is in the sky, one must not relate dreams, Charicles; then they lose the accompaniment of scene and decoration. There is a time for everything. See you not how the sun, with its glory, has veiled the entire host of those worlds of yesterday, and how sadly the moon looks in the heavens yonder—a pale cloudlet! Probably our conversation would be like it, if it should attempt to resume the prophecies of yesterday. Therefore, Charicles, put out the night-lamp and bring forward something of a more cheerful character, wherewith we may strengthen ourselves for the day.

Char. I think we may resume our yesterday's conversation and still attain that end. For, my friend, I feel now, very plainly, that the morning and not the evening is the time for discussions which take us back into the childhood of our race—the early morning of human ideas and images. Our studied night-wisdom has dazzled us. Where we should have conjectured, we asserted; where we should have thought humanly, we thought divinely.

Theag. Do you mean me?

Char. Perhaps a little. For you too, I am afraid, have been too much exalted by theology and philosophy, Newton and Christianity. You would soar to the stars; but our way at present is still on the earth; you are ashamed of your step-brothers, the brute animals, and would mount up into the society of beings whom you have never seen, and perhaps never will see—the inhabitants of Mercury, of the sun and of the moon.

Theag. No, I am not ashamed of my half-brothers, the brutes; on the contrary, as far as they are concerned, I am a great advocate of metempsychosis. I believe, for a certainty, that they will ascend to a higher grade of being, and am unable to comprehend how any one can object to this hypothesis which seems to have the analogy of the whole creation in its favor.

Char. Now you are in the right way.

Theag. It is the way I have always been in, as far as this point is concerned. Do not you remember that you yourself strayed from it yesterday? Do you like Æsop's fables, Charicles?

Char. Very much, but what have they to do with the matter?

Theag. I regard them as the compass which shows us our relation to the brutes. Severally and collectively the animals still play their fables. Æsop, the great philosopher and moralist, has only made their play intelligible to us; he has made their characters speak to our comprehension; for, to their own comprehension, they speak and act continually. And know you what is man's part in this progressive fable of the animals? He is the *general proposition*, the *moral of the fable*, the *tongue in the balance*. He uses the whole creation, and consequently the characters of animals. They act before him, they act for him, and he—thinks. His '*this fable teaches*,' he has to repeat every moment.

Char. And has this anything to do with the metempsychosis of animals?

Theag. Much, as it seems to me. To make the brute-fable a man-fable, there wants nothing but the conclusion, the general proposition, the doctrine. That brute-character, so determined, so sure, so rich in art and so instructive,—give it but a little spark of that light we call reason and you have the man. There he is, and he

* From a fragment of Menander.

gathers now instruction, doctrine, art from his former character as brute. He brings his former mode of life more or less into consciousness, and if he chooses, learns wisdom therefrom. He must learn, as man, to order wisely and well what, as brute. he can, and likes and wills. This, methinks, is the anthropogenesia and the palingenesia of brutes into men.

Char. The picture is fine: but the thing? Is it so certain, Theages, that every man has an animal character?

Theag. If you doubt it, look at the countenances of men under the influence of passion, of strong passion; observe in secret their mode of life and the sharply marked traits of their character; it shall go hard but you will discover in the formation, the air, the gesture, and still more in the progressive action of their life, the fox, the wolf, the cat, the tiger, the dog, the weasel, the vulture, the parrot, with the rest of the honorable company that came out of Noah's ark.

Char. You jest. I have hitherto considered the whole hypothesis as a joke, over the dessert, when we cover our mouths to the nose exclusive, with the napkin and ask: 'Who was I? What beast have I been?'

Theag. As things go, it is a joke and must remain so. Who knows himself to the bottom of his character? And how should another know us at a glance, as soon as we cover up the mouth with our napkin? What would come of it, if man should set the images of the animals with which he is daily conversant in his life's-almanac, and should converse with them in his own animal character in return? It was designed that we should be men, not animals. The tongue in the balance is to guide us, and not the dead weight of character and animal instincts laid in the scales. The animal-human countenance is human, enlightened. The features are separated, especially the most characteristic features. Forehead, nose, eyes and cheeks are infinitely dignified, ennobled, beautiful in man, as compared with the brute.

Char. Then the animal formation is only the basis of the human character, which is to be enlightened by the light of reason, and systematized, beautified, and elevated by the moral sentiments of the human heart? The ground of our capacities and traits, as beings of sense, — the remains of purely sensual faculties, propensities, and impulses—these are animal, and are afterward only polished and regulated by our reason?

Theag. Study men, and you will find abundant proofs of it. For when we separate the haughty moral element, we are all pretty much agreed in our judgment of traits and characters. In nature and in an Æsop's fable, we call a fox a fox, and not a lion. In human life our judgments are apt to be confused, as from hundred other causes, so also from this, that it is actually the aim of human culture and the destination of man to extinguish the animal character and the animal habits, to a certain extent, and to make men of us, or, if you will, angels in humanity. Every one would fain be thought to have reached this point himself; but envy and malice love to find in others the old, rude beast entire, with no trace of man or angel. Hence it is, that this hypothesis is so abused, and, at last, falls into contempt, either because it is misunderstood, or because it is feared. But, without it, I know not what is to become of the numerous host of creatures beneath us — our characteristic and sensitive half-brothers in field and forest.

Char. What is to become of them? Nothing different from what they are. They transmigrate into new forms of their own species; they become finer deer, finer birds.

Theag. Finer tigers, finer apes and wolves, and at the last day, I suppose, these will be raised too and accompany us? It is surely not your serious conviction, my friend, that the innermost creation — the ever-proceeding, new creation—must needs conform to the classifications of the late Baron Linné?

Char. Not mine exactly; but our friend Harmodius would suffer martyrdom for this opinion.

Theag. Well, he would die a very innocent death then. Our classifications are not so exhaustive as is usually supposed. They exist only for our senses, for our faculties; they are not the muster-rolls by which Nature arranges her creatures,—categories which she has prescribed to herself in order to keep each creature in its proper place. See how the different classes of creation run into each other! How the organizations ascend and struggle upward from all points, on all sides! And then again, what a close resemblance between them! Precisely as if, on all our earth, the form-abounding Mother had proposed to herself but one type, one *protoplasma* according to which and for which she formed them all. Know you what that form is? It is the identical one which man also wears.

Char. It is true; even in the most imperfect animal, some resemblance to this capital form of organization is not to be mistaken.

Theag. It is even more evident internally than it is externally. Even in insects, an analogon of the human anatomy has been discovered, though, compared with ours, enveloped and seemingly disproportionate. The different members, and consequently, also, the powers which work with them, are yet undeveloped, not organized to our fulness of life. It seems to me that throughout creation, this finger-mark of Nature is the Ariadne-thread that conducts us through the labyrinth of animal forms, ascending and descending.

But, my friend, we have walked and talked ourselves tired. Suppose we sit down beneath these pleasant trees and look at the swan that rows and glasses himself on yonder shining surface.

They seated themselves and rested awhile. The wash of the waves and the whispering trees agreeably damped their thoughts until, at last, Charicles resumed the thread of the conversation.

Char. * * * * * Tell me, beloved, something of your day-dreams on the subjects of which we have been speaking, as you told me yesterday of your night-dreams. The sight of this fair river, the sublime silence of this forest, methinks, are as favorable to such imaginings as the starred roof of heaven. Here, at least, we form, ourselves, a part of the chorus.

Theag. And did we not there, too? Or are we not here, also, in the midst of a river of heaven, a chorus of earthly stars! All the life of Nature, all the tribes and species of animated creation—what are they but sparks of the Godhead, a harvest of incarnate stars, among which, the two human sexes stand forth like sun and moon. We overshine, we dim the other figures, but, doubtless, we lead them onward in a chorus invisible to ourselves. O, friend, that an eye were given us to trace the shining course of this divine spark—to see how life flows to life, and ever refining, impelled through all the veins of creation, wells up into a purer, higher life! What a new city of God, what a creation within creation should we then behold! From the first atom, the most unfruitful dust scarce escaped from nonentity, through all the varieties of organization up to that little universe of multiform life — man, what a shining labyrinth! But the human understanding cannot detect it; it sees things only the outside, it sees only forms, not the transmigrating, up-striving souls. The interior mechanism of Nature, her living wheels and breathing forces, these, in their too exceeding glory, are to us a ἀδης, the *Kingdom of Night*, the hull and vein of unborn lives self-engendered in eternal progression.

* * * * "Alas our sight's so ill
That things which swiftest move, seem to stand still."

I need not veil myself before thee, great Pan! eternal fountain of life! Thou hast veiled me within myself. Do I know the world of lives which I call my body? Doubtless, my too feeble soul, could she see the countless host which ministers to her in all degrees and varieties of animation, would drop her imperial sceptre and sink from her throne. In my veins, in the minutest vascules allotted to me, these souls are pilgriming toward a higher life, as, already, through so manifold paths and preparations, they have travelled from all creation into me. I prepare them for their farther progress, as everything before has prepared them for me. No destruction, no death is there in creation, but dissolution, parturition, lustration. So the tree with its boughs and limbs elaborates the humors of the earth and the air, the fire of the soil and the heavens into its own nature—itself and its children into nobler sap. Its leaves imbibe and make fruitful. Every leaf is a tree, formed upon a green plain, in a slender fabric, because creation had not room to produce them all as perfect trees. From every bud, therefore, and every twig she thrusts forth tree-spirits. The all-bearing Mother clothes herself with green life; every flower which unfolds itself is a bride, every blossoming tree is a great family of lives. The kingdom of animals—our mute fellow-citizens—destroys thousand forms of inferior kind in order to animate its own higher forms; and finally, man, the chief artificer and destroyer in creation,—he gives life and takes it, he is, without knowing it, the goal of his inferior brethren, to which, perhaps, they are all imperceptibly conducted.

Beautiful, floating swan! In what a shining element thy creator has placed thee to love and admire thyself! With thy fair, bowed neck, in the pure, fresh whiteness of innocence, thou swimmest a queen, a soft splendor-form, on the clear surface of the waves. Thy world is a mirror, thy life a decoration and an art. What will be thine employment, when, hereafter, in a human form, thou projectest lines of beauty and studiest graces in thyself or in nature?

Char. Apropos! my friend, have you ever read Bishop Berkeley's* novel, "Gaudentio of Lucca?"

Theag. I am not acquainted with it.

Char. He has a very pretty idea of metempsychosis, which he ascribes to his Mezzoranians. He represents them as believing that the souls of animals covet the habitation of a human body, and seek, by every means, to steal into it. In this they succeed so soon as man lets fall the torch of his reason, and with it, the power of self-government. Then he becomes revengeful, cruel, lecherous, avaricious, according as this or that animal has pursued him, and usurped the place of his rational soul. Methinks, the allegory is fine.

Theag. As indeed, Berkeley was altogether a fine and rare man. That way of presenting it, clothes a truth so beautifully!

Char. And what think you of the metempsychosis of the Jews, which the Rabbins call *Ibbur?* They say that several souls, human souls, may adjoin themselves to an individual, and, at certain times,—when a friendly Spirit sees that he requires it and God permits,—help, strengthen, inspire him, dwelling with and in him. But they quit him again, when the business in which they were to aid him is accomplished, except in cases where God favors an individual with this sort of aid to the end of his days.

Theag. A very pretty fiction! It is founded in the perception that man acts very unequally at different times, and in old age, especially, often sinks far beneath himself. The foreign, auxiliary spirit has forsaken him, and he sits there naked with his own. Moreover, the fable is a beautiful commendation of extraordinary men; for what a compliment, to suppose that the soul of a sage is animated by the soul of an elder sage, or even by several at once! But surely you do not regard this beautiful, poetical invention, as physical historical truth!

Char. Who knows? The revolution of human souls has been universally believed by

---

* So, in the original. Tr.

many nations. You remember the question put to John: Art thou Elias? art thou that prophet? You know too, who even confirmed this idea, and said expressly, it is Elias.

Theag. And you have probably read the younger Helmont *de revolutione animarum?* He has adduced, in two hundred problems, all the sayings and all the arguments which can possibly be urged in favor of the return of souls into human bodies, according to Jewish ideas.

Char. I must say, I have always liked the Jewish doctrine of the revolution of souls. Are you well acquainted with it?

Theag. Pretty well. It asserts that the soul returns into life twice or thrice—in extraordinary cases oftener—and accomplishes what it had left unfinished. It supposes that God has divided the periods of the world's history according to these revolutions of souls; that he has determined the degrees of light and of twilight, of suffering and of joy; in fine, the destiny and the duration of beings in conformity with them. The first resurrection is a revolution of these perfected souls, returned into life.

Char. What have you to object to that?

Theag. Nothing, except that I can say nothing for it; because the whole is either a poetic fiction or rests in the counsels of God. At any rate, the passages which are quoted in favor of it prove nothing.

Char. And is there no weight in the arguments from reason which are adduced in its support? For example, that God, who is no respecter of persons, has shown so much respect for persons during one existence of souls in this world; that the Long-suffering and the Just gives every one space and time for repentance; that the fruition of life has been, to many, so embittered and so abridged, without any fault of their own? You slighted these reasons, my friend, because, if I may say so, you were prejudiced against the doctrine. But look at the thing humanly; consider the fate of the *misborn*, the deformed, the poor, the stupid, the crippled, the fearfully degraded and ill-treated; of young children who had scarce seen the light and were forced to depart. Take all this to heart, and you must either have weak conceptions of the progress of such people in the world to come, or they must first have wings made for them here, that they may learn to soar even at a distance after others, that they may be, in some measure, indemnified for their unhappy or unhappily abbreviated existence in this world. Promotion to a higher, human existence, is scarcely to be thought of in their case.

Theag. Why not? None can give as God gives, and no one can indemnify and compensate like God. To all beings he gave their existence, of his own free love. If some appear to have been more neglected than others, has he not places, contrivances, worlds enough, where, by a single transplantation, he can indemnify and compensate a thousand-fold? A child prematurely removed — a youth whose nature was too delicate, as it were, for the **rude** climate of this world—all nations have felt that such are loved by the gods,* and that they have transferred the treasured plant into a fairer garden. Or do you suppose that God has no other spot but this earth? Must he root up others in order to make room for these, and let the uptorn plant wait and wither in the store-chamber of unborn souls until he can find a place for it? How many are made happy in another world by having been unhappy here! My friend, do you know Kleist's fable of the maimed crane?

Char. I am not acquainted with it.

Theag. It is one of the finest that was ever made.

"When Autumn-winds had laid the forest bare
And scattered chrystal rime upon the plain,
There lighted on the strand a troop of cranes
Seeking a kinder earth beyond the sea.
Lamed by the fowler's shaft one luckless bird
Sat lone and sad and dumb, nor lent her voice
To swell the jubilee of the exulting host;
Mocked and contemned—the outcast of her tribe.
Not by mine own fault am I maimed, thought she,
Musing within herself. I served no less than ye
Our Commonwealth. Unjustly am I spurned.
But what shall be my fate whom pain
Hath reft of strength to endure the distant flight?
Ah, wretched me! the water soon must prove
My certain grave. Why left he life—
The cruel foe that robbed me of my powers?
Meanwhile the favoring wind blows fresh from shore;
The troop begin, in order due, their march,
And speed with sounding wings, and scream with joy.
Left far behind, that lone one lighted oft
Upon the lotus-leaves which strewed the sea,
And hopeless sighed with grief and bitter pain.
After long rest she saw the better land,
The kinder heaven which sudden healed her wound.
An unknown Providence had been her guide,
While many mockers found a watery grave.

* * * *

Ye whom the heavy hand of dire mischance
Bows to the earth, ye innocent who mourn,
Weary of life, despair not of the end,
But dare the necessary journey through.
There is a better land beyond the sea
And ye shall find your healing and reward."

Char. A beautiful fable for my side, too. Let us move, my friend, and on the way, you must allow me a few more questions. How comes it that the wisest nations of antiquity and those far removed from each other have believed so long in the doctrine of transmigration,—and that, too, of the worst kind,—in the return of human beings, in the doctrine which teaches that man becomes an animal once more?

Theag. You have already answered the question, Charicles; it was the childhood of the world and the world's wisdom respecting human destiny. With some nations, for example the Egyptians and Hindoos, and perhaps too with Pythagoras, it was designed as a moral fable, representing the doctrine of ecclesiastical penance in a sensuous and comprehensible form.

Char. A strange ecclesiastical penance, conveyed in a fiction!

Theag. To a certain extent, the two (the doctrine and the fiction) necessitated each other.

---

* ὃν οἱ θεοὶ φιλοῦσιν ἀποθνήσκει νέος.

You know that the wisdom of the most ancient nations was lodged with the priests. When they could give the rude people no right notions respecting the world to come or had none to give, was it not well that they should seek to deter them by a future of sensuous retribution? "You who are cruel, shall be changed into tigers, as even now you manifest a tiger-soul. You who are impure, shall be swine; you who are proud, shall be peacocks; and so you shall do penance for a long while, until you are found worthy to resume your desecrated humanity." These representations, addressed to the senses, and clothed with the authority of religion, would, undoubtedly, have a greater effect than metaphysical subtilties. Each one saw the nature of the threatened beast and its destiny before him. The vicious felt the beastly character in himself, and nothing was more natural than that he should fear a corresponding fate, that is, a real transition into that animal. This doctrine, once established, might deter from many vices and lead to many virtues. Who would not rather be a white elephant than a swine? especially one who viewed the nature and the fate of animals with the eyes of the Hindoos and the Egyptians,—with that quiet familiarity in which the childhood of the world lived with the brute creation. But you do not suppose, Charicles, that this doctrine is necessary or fitting for us?

Char. In many cases, a belief in it would be no evil. If the cruel man, who persecutes a poor stag to death, were seized, at that moment, with a lymphatic presentiment: "So will it fare with thee; thy soul shall pass into a stag and be tortured to death;" perhaps he might extinguish the joyless brutality in himself.

Theag. I doubt it, my friend, if the immediate contemplation of the pain is unable to extinguish it. For us, it seems to me, this whole doctrine of transmigration has lost its sting. If I am not good as man, am I likely to become so as tiger? since then, it is my nature to be that whereinto I am changed. If I am condemned to eat grass, like an irrational ox, how shall I begin, in that state, to use my reason better than I used it while a man. God himself has bound my eyes and taken from me the light of the understanding, and how then shall I learn to see more clearly? If my degradation is to be mere penance in the eyes of an arbitrary judge, why, be it so! but reformation — a rational, moral reformation in myself, it can never be; because, in my degradation, that which alone could reform me has been taken away. Is one not rather likely to be embittered against God, who deprives us of our eyes because we have not used them aright, and, because we have not disciplined our heart to right sentiments, hardens it in the shape of something vicious and wretched?

Char. There is much to be said in relation to that point; at any rate, the fiction had its use as parable for the people.

Theag. Even as parable for the people, the tale is not suited to our times. It seems to me that man should learn to look upon himself as occupying the highest grade, and use his present existence peremptorily. He must know of no retreat or by-way where he can bring up what he has neglected here. At least, the Deity has referred him to none. *Aut Cæsar aut nihil: aut nunc aut nunquam.* Even among the ancients, all active, noble nations that were not beguiled by fable-wisdom and the foolish penances of their priests, have proposed to themselves a nobler condition after death, as the goal of their endeavor. The being 'gathered to one's fathers' of the oriental nations, the Elysium of the Greeks, the Walhalla of the Norlanders, are certainly more beautiful views of death than that of the ox or the cow waiting for the dying man who holds the cow's tail in his hand; or the body of a strange mother into which he must slip, in order to whimper again as child.

Char. True, they are low ideas that gather about this hypothesis. But how then could the wise Pythagoras deem it worthy of being transplanted to Europe?

Theag. One brings all sorts of things from abroad, not only gold and jewels, but also monkeys and curiosities. Besides, it is not probable that Pythagoras made the same use of this doctrine that the later false Pythagoreans did. He too spoke of a Tartarus and an Elysium, like the other philosophers and poets of Greece. And, altogether, we know too little of that truly great man, to be able to judge of his parables and symbols; we know him only through the medium of fable.

And O! my friend, Pythagoras or no Pythagoras, what need of all this controversy and argument, with which we, too, have wasted our time? Ask your heart and the truth which dwells there. When you stand before the statue of a high-hearted Apollo, do you not feel what you lack of being that form? Can you ever attain to it here below, and can your heart ever rejoice in it, though you should return ten times? And yet, that was only the idea of an artist, the happy dream of a mortal,—a dream which our narrow breast also inclosed. How! has the almighty Father no nobler forms for us than those in which our heart now heaves and groans? Our language,—all communication of thought,— what bungling work it is! Hovering on the tip of our tongues, between lip and palate, in a few syllabled tones, our heart, our innermost soul would communicate itself to another, so that he shall comprehend us, shall feel the ground of our innermost being. Vain endeavor! Wretched pantomime with a few gestures and vibrations of air! The soul lies captive in its dungeon, bound as with a sevenfold chain, and only through a strong grating, and only through a pair of light and air-holes can it breathe and see. And always it sees the world on one side only, while there are a million other sides before us and in us, had we but more and other senses, and could we but exchange this narrow hut of our body for a freer prospect. And shall we be forever contented with this nook, this dungeon? What wretch, doomed to life-long misery in this life, confines his wishes to the throwing off of this world's burden, without the sense or the hope of requital for his present disappointment and degradation? When, even at the sweetest fountains of friendship and love, we so often pine, thirsty and sick, seeking union and finding it not, begging alms from every earthly object and always poor, always unsatisfied; and when we find, at last, that all the aims and plans of earth are vanity and vanity, and feel that daily,—what free and noble soul does not lift itself up and despise everlasting tabernacles and wanderings in the circle of earthly deserts.

"The soul longs from her prison-house to come,
And we would seal and sew up, if we could, the womb!
We seek to close and plaister up, by art,
The cracks and breaches of the extended shell,
And in that narrow cell
Would rudely force to dwell
The noble, vigorous bird already wing'd to part."

During these conversations, they had imperceptibly reached the end of the forest. At the last tree Charicles stood still. Before we leave this wood, Theages, said he, I must tell you the result of our conversations. In all the forms and conditions of humanity, the cultivation of our wit, our sagacity, or other branches of the human intellect, is of less consequence than the education of the heart; and that heart is in all men a human heart. And it may be educated, to a certain degree, in all the forms and situations of humanity. As to the extent to which it has been developed in this situation, and the way in which Providence may succor the unfortunate and the suffering, that I leave to Heaven, and venture not to make its secret ways the race-course or the beaten highway of an hypothesis by which man is to be scared, or in which the sluggish and the froward shall find their account. Sacred to me is the saying of the gospel: "Blessed are the poor in spirit, for theirs is the kingdom of heaven. Blessed are they that mourn, for they shall be comforted. Blessed are the pure in heart, for they shall see God." Purification of the heart, the ennobling of the soul, with all its propensities and cravings,— this, it seems, to me, is the true palingenesia of this life, after which, I doubt not, a happy, more exalted, but yet unknown metempsychosis awaits us. Herewith I am content, and I thank you that you have unfolded for me my thoughts.

They embraced each other, and parted.

JOHANN WOLFGANG VON GOETHE.

Born 1749.   Died 1832.

The biography of this extraordinary personage is yet to be written. His own memoirs, '*Aus meinem Leben*', &c.,—comprise but the first half of that full, rich life, of which the last half was the fullest, the richest. The materials for a farther and complete delineation are not wanting,* but the historian who shall collect, and arrange, and reproduce these in a 'Life of Goethe' worthy that name, has not yet been found. Shall we look to the author of the 'Life of Schiller' for this service? Or will Germany herself, out of the countless host of her literary artificers, furnish the historian of her own Genius?

Meanwhile, it is gratifying to learn that the autobiography is about to be given to the American Public, in a translation by one of our own countrymen,† which, if it fairly represents the original, can hardly fail to be a popular work. From this they will learn, if they have not already learned, that Johann Wolfgang v. Goethe was born at Frankfort on the Mayn, on the 28th of August, 1749, at midday, "as the clock struck twelve;" that his father was a wealthy and cultivated *Reichsbürger*, who lived much in his Italian reminiscences; that his maternal grandfather, Johann Wolfgang v. Textor, was a man of mark, the chief magistrate of the Imperial city; that the experiences and observations of his boyhood,—house-building, coronation, the seven years' war, the aspects of his native city, arts and trades, boyish love and shame and disappointment,—wrote imperishable records, materials for future creations, on the poet's heart; that, after a various and careful education at home, he was in due season matriculated at Leipzig, fell sick and returned to Frankfort, a confirmed invalid, much to his father's chagrin; that he recovered his health and studied law at Strassburg where he received the Doctor's degree, and where he diverged into an episode of love and romance of which the charming Friederike of Sesenheim was the heroine; that he began to practise his profession at Frankfort, but soon slid into literature, made an era therein, publishing *Werther's Leiden* and *Goetz von Berlichingen*, and so completed the first phase of his poetic life. Furthermore, if all the parts of these memoirs are given, we shall see the poet again in the character of declared and accepted lover,—the betrothed of the beautiful Lili;—since "it was the strange ordination of the High, above us ruling, that, in the progress of my wondrous life-course, I should also experience the feelings of a betrothed." We shall see him, next, this cold, impassive, self-sufficing Goethe,—as he has been depicted,—the man who lived only for self and Art,—we shall see him, on the summit of the Alps, turning his back upon Italy, the land of his youthful dreams, the pilgrim-goal of the artist, and hastening home, unable to resist any longer the passion which drew him back to his beloved:* and that,

---

* See the volumes of Goethe's correspondence with distinguished cotemporaries, published since his death, the '*Tag und Jahres Hefte,*" and the works of Eckermann, Falk, v. Müller, Döring and others.

† Parke Godwin, Esq. Since the above was written the work referred to has appeared. See No. LXXV. of Wiley and Putnam's Library of Choice Reading.

* Hear his own account of the matter. "It seems to me as if man, in such cases, had no power of decision in himself, but were rather governed and determined by earlier impressions. Lombardy and Italy lay as something wholly foreign before me, Germany as something known and love-worthy, full of friendly, domestic prospects. And—let me confess it—that which had so long compassed me about, which had borne up my existence, continued, at this moment also, to be the most indispensable element, out of whose limits I did not trust myself to pass. A small golden heart which I had received from her in the fairest hours, hung still, by the same riband by which she had fastened it, love-warmed upon my neck. I seized and kissed it. And here let me insert the poem occasioned by this circumstance.

"'Memorial thou of a joy whose sound has died away!
Which I yet wear about my neck,
Holdest thou, longer than the soul-band, us two?
Prolongest thou the brief days of love?
Do I flee, Lili, before thee? Must I, still led by thy hand,
Through distant vales and forests wander!
Ah Lili's heart could not so quickly
From my heart fall.
Like a bird who breaks his string
And returns to the forest;
He drags—captivity's dishonor,—
A bit of the string still after him.
It is the old, free-born bird no longer,
He has already been some one's property.'

"I rose quickly that I might get away from the steep spot, and that the friend storming toward me, with the knapsack-bearing guide, might not whirl me away with

after the resolution to separate himself from her, wrung from him by his sister, was already formed or forming within him. We shall see this connection sundered, for reasons which are not very obvious; but not till after long and dire struggles through "a cursed state which, in some respects, might be likened to Hades," and a "torture which, even in the remembrance, is well nigh insupportable."

Finally, we shall see him called to the court of Weimar by the hereditary prince, Karl August, afterward Grand Duke, there to become the client of a life-long patronage, as honorable to one party as it was beneficial to both.

Then, we have what may be regarded as the continuation of these memoirs, in the "*Italienische Reise*," the "*Zweiter römischer Aufenthalt*," and the "*Campagne in Frankreich*." And, be it remarked by the way, these are not the least impressive of Goethe's works. He maintains, as a writer of travels, the same rank which distinguishes him in every species of composition.

In 1779, Goethe was made Privy Counsellor; he received the title of nobility in 1782, travelled in Italy and Sicily, and sojourned in Rome during the two years from 1786 to 1788; made another visit in 1790; and, in 1792 accompanied the Grand Duke in the French campaign. In 1806, he married a Miss Vulpius, the mother of his only surviving child. In 1815, he was made Prime Minister; and although, during the last four years of his life, he withdrew himself from State affairs, he continued to labor in his vocation as a poet with unabated diligence, and apparently with unabated faculty, until the hour of his death, which overtook him, as it were with the pen in his hand, on the 22d March, 1832, in the eighty-third year of his age.

There is great satisfaction in contemplating so complete a life, a life in which the idea and the task have been so visibly and utterly fulfilled and accomplished.

At the age of eighty, Goethe often spoke of his death, and of how it might still be deferred.

"Yes!" said he, "we can make head against him for some time yet. As long as one creates there can be no room for dying. But yet the night, the great night will come in which no man can work." It was about this time that he lost his only son. "Here then," he writes to Zelter, "can the mighty conception of duty alone hold us erect. I have no other care but to keep myself in equipoise; the body *must*, the spirit *will;* and he who sees a necessary path prescribed to his will, has no need to ponder much." Was Goethe wanting in sensibility, because he did not give himself up to the lamentation of that loss? "Thus did he shut up the deepest grief within his breast, and hastily seized upon a long postponed labor, in order entirely to lose himself in it. In a fortnight he had nearly completed the fourth volume of his Life, when Nature avenged herself for the violence he had done her. The bursting of a blood-vessel brought him to the brink of the grave."*

He entirely recovered himself from this attack, and resumed his task. In the year preceding that of his death, he had still to finish the second part of Faust. God willing, he would not die till that was accomplished. "He laid it down as a law to himself, to complete it worthily; and on the day before his last birth-day he was enabled to announce that the highest task of his life was completed. He sealed it under a ten-fold seal, escaped from the congratulations of his friends, and hastened to revisit, after many years, the scenes of his earliest cares and endeavors, as well as of the richest and happiest hours of his life. He went to Ilmenau. The deep calm of the woods, the fresh breath of the hills, breathed new life into him. With refreshed and invigorated mind he returned home and felt himself inspired to undertake new observations of Nature. The Theory of Colors was revised, completed and confirmed, the nature of the rainbow more accurately examined, and unwearied thought bestowed on the spiral tendency of vegetation."*

And when, at last, the brief and painless sickness which terminated his earthly career had laid him prostrate, "faithful to his principles he continued to occupy himself that he might not give the thinking faculty time to grow dull and inactive. Even when he had

---

him into the steep abyss. I likewise greeted the pious *Pater*, and turned myself, without losing a word, toward the path by which we had come. A little lingering the friend followed, and, notwithstanding his love and attachment to me, he remained for awhile some distance behind, until, at last, the glorious waterfall brought us together again, kept us together, and that, which had once for all been determined, was also finally accepted as wholesome and good."—*Aus meinem Leben.*

* Chancellor von Müller, in Mrs. Austin's Characteristics.

lost the power of speaking, his hand preserved the character of his life. His voice was mute, but he traced characters in the air. And when his hand sank slowly on his knee, the radiant star had sunk beneath our horizon."*

The statesman-poet was inhumed with the pomp befitting his illustrious name. Agreeably to the wishes of the Grand Duke, who had preceded him by a few years, his remains were deposited by the side of that Prince and "the glorious Schiller." The royal vault of Weimar holds henceforth the honored frame in which that life was performed; to the living Weimar and to us and to all generations belongs "the absolute total of that life's vast sum."

The first thing that strikes us in the life of Goethe is the wonderful fortune of the man. No Genius was ever more favored from without. Sophocles alone, among the poets of all generations, may vie with him in this. We look in vain for another instance of so rich a nature coupled with so kind a destiny. It would seem as if all things had conspired for once to make a perfect lot; genius, organization, beauty of person, high culture, riches, rank, renown, length of days. Does the work performed correspond to the advantages enjoyed? Does the result justify the partiality of Fortune?—is a question which other ages must answer.

Goethe's genius is distinguished by its versatility. No other writer has shone with such various excellence. The two poles of the human intellect, poetry and science, define the range of his mind. His writings embrace both these extremes, and touch almost every topic of interest between the two. To speak only of more prominent and unquestioned excellences;—as a lyric poet, he has no equal. And this will be found, perhaps, in the final judgment, to constitute his chief merit. The union of perfect finish with perfect freedom; the uttermost abandonment of fancy, joined to the uttermost self-possession of artistic judgment; the wild freshness of poetic feeling—the very breath and aroma of Nature—accompanied by that profound philosophy which, rather felt than seen, pervades all his writings;—all this gives to Goethe's lyrics the highest relish of which that form of poetry is susceptible. The singular facility with which these pieces were produced, resembling improvisation or inspiration rather than composition, has contributed, in some cases, no doubt, to enhance their peculiar charm. "I had come," says he, "to regard the poetic talent dwelling in me, entirely as nature; the rather that I was directed to look upon external Nature as its proper subject. The exercise of this poetic gift might be stimulated and determined by occasion; but it flowed forth most joyfully, most richly, when it came involuntarily or even against my will.   *   *   *   *   *
I was so accustomed to say over a song to myself without being able to collect it again, that I sometimes rushed to the desk, and, without taking time to adjust a sheet that was lying crosswise, wrote the poem diagonally from beginning to end, without stirring from the spot. For the same reason, I preferred to use a pencil, which gives the characters more willingly. For it had sometimes happened that the scratching and sputtering of the pen would wake me from my somnambulistic poetizing, distract my attention, and stifle some small product in the birth. For such poetry I had a special reverence. My relation to it was something like that of a hen to the chickens, which, being fully hatched, she sees cheeping about her. My former desire to communicate these things only by reading them aloud, renewed itself again. To barter them for money seemed to me detestable."*

Goethe claims our admiration next, as a painter of character. Here too, the very highest rank, second to Shakspeare only, has been assigned to him. His characters have the Shakspearean merit of being, at the same time, universal and individual, impersonations of a general type, and veritable men and women, such as one might look to meet with, any day of the year, in their respective circles. And where he transcends the sphere of ordinary humanity, as in the case of Mignon, he gives us nothing inconceivable or inconsequent, but a nature that carries its constitutive law within itself, which all its movements obey, by which they are to be interpreted, and by which they must be judged. His success is greatest in female character, of which almost every variety is represented in his works. Running through the series of those works, we perceive a moral gradation of female character, from Gretchen the uncultivated, the unconscious, the betrayed but still pure, to Makaria, in whom female

---

* Notes to Mrs. Austin's Characteristics.

* Aus meinem Leben. IVth part.

virtue reaches its apotheosis, and whose only connection with this earth is to counsel and to bless. As we follow this ascending scale, we divine a moral purpose in the author, who, with each new character, has spread before us a distinct level of human culture, and by successive attractions has indicated the upward path of aspiration and self-conquest, by which Humanity must reach its destination.

Another characteristic excellence of Goethe is herewith suggested, viz: his veneration for women. This sentiment, with him, was not chivalry which, in assuming a protective attitude, assumes and emphasizes a weakness in the female nature, and thus degrades where it professes to honor; and whose very homage, fantastical and patronizing as it is, contains a latent irony the more bitter, perhaps, because unintentional. Goethe's respect for women was a philosophical appreciation of the real dignity and unacknowledged riches of the female character, coupled with the reverent homage of the heart for what the understanding so clearly discerned; a homage which two such living examples as the Grand Duchess and the Duchess Mother of Weimar could not fail to keep in active exercise. In the extent to which he carried this appreciation of female excellence he stands alone; far in the van of opinion as yet pronounced. No writer has estimated so highly, none so truly, the influence of woman on the social and moral destiny of man. The saving and benign power of the feminine element in human things is made prominent in all his creations. In some of them it is a cardinal point. It is the pivot in 'Wilhelm Meister' and the climax of 'Faust,' at the close of which it is announced with prophetic emphasis, as a fit conclusion "to the swelling theme:"—"*Das ewig weibliche zieht uns hinan.*"

A contemporary remarks in accordance with this view, that Goethe "always represents the highest principle in a feminine form." "As in Faust the purity of Gretchen resisting the demon always, even after all her faults, is announced to have saved her soul to heaven; and, in the second part, appears not only redeemed herself, but, by her innocence and forgiving tenderness, hallowed to redeem the being who had injured her; so, in the Meister, these women hover round the narrative, each embodying the spirit of the scene. The frail Philina, graceful though contemptible, represents the degradation incident to leading an exclusively poetic life. Mignon, gift divine as ever the Muse bestowed on the passionate heart of man, with her soft, mysterious inspiration, represents the high desire that leads to this mistake, as Aurelia the desire for excitement, Teresa practical wisdom, gentle tranquillity, which seem most desirable after the Aurelia glare. Of the "Beautiful Soul" and Natalia we have already spoken. The former embodies what was suggested to Goethe by the most spiritual person he knew in youth, Fräulein von Klettenberg, over whom, as he said, in her invalid loneliness, the Holy Ghost brooded like a dove. Entering on the Wanderjahre, Wilhelm becomes acquainted with another woman who seems the complement of all the former, and represents the idea which is to mould and to guide him in the realization of all the past experience. This person, long before we see her, is announced in various ways as a ruling power. She is the last hope in cases of difficulty, and, though an invalid, and living in absolute retirement, is consulted by her connections and acquaintance as an unerring judge in all their affairs. All things tend toward her as a centre; she knows all, governs all, but never goes forth from herself. Wilhelm at last visits her. He finds her infirm in body, but equal to all she has to do. Charity and counsel to men who need her, are her business; astronomy her pleasure." * *
* * * * "The apparition of the celestial Makaria seems to announce the ultimate destiny of the soul of man."[*]

As a writer of German prose, or, to use a coinage derived from that language,—as a *stylist,* Goethe's pre-eminence is undisputed and, even by his most determined opponents and detractors, emphatically affirmed. Menzel, whose work on German literature suggests the idea of having been written for the express purpose of abusing him and one or two others of like political sentiments, says: "He could make everything, even the smallest and meanest, delightful by the magic of his representation." "Goethe possesses in the highest degree the talent of making his reader an accomplice —of forcing from him a feeling of approbation. He carried in his hand the talisman which controls all hearts. No poet has so completely mastered the charm which language possesses. We cannot guard ourselves against the secret

---

[*] Dial. Vol. II. No. 1.

enchantment with which he captivates our inmost soul and seduces us to the very opposite of all that we had previously felt and believed."* And yet this author maintains that the writer who exercised this magic power was destitute of genius. The more pity for genius, if true!

Goethe's style is a puzzle. It excites our wonder how language can be so colorless, so free from mannerism, and, at the same time, so impressive, so suggestive, so individual. "It seems quite a simple style," says Carlyle, "remarkable chiefly for its calmness, its perspicuity, in short its commonness; and yet it is the most uncommon of all styles. We feel as if every one might imitate it, and yet it is inimitable."

His power, as a moral teacher, is not so generally understood and acknowledged as the other qualities which have been mentioned. Yet there are some by whom it is more strongly asserted and more deeply felt than all the other excellences which have been claimed for him. There are some who profess to have derived from him their strongest moral impressions, and who maintain that, as a teacher of moral truth, he has been more to them than any other, than all other writers. Nor will this seem strange, if we consider what constitutes an effective moralist, or what it is that gives force to the statement of moral truth. It is not enthusiasm, or fine sentiment, or declamation, but the clear intuition, the veritable experience, the unbiassed sincerity of a free and commanding mind. A character distinguished for moral worth is not necessary for this purpose, nor great activity of religious sentiment. The saint may instruct us better than all books by his life, but not necessarily — because he is a saint — by his writings. There may be great moral worth and a great deal of religious sentiment without that *intellectual sincerity* which brings us into immediate contact with the truth, and the want of which will vitiate the strongest statement. This sincerity of the intellect is something very different from conscientiousness. It is seemingly independent of any moral quality except the single one of courage. It is the rarest attribute in literature. It does not readily combine with natures in which sentiment predominates. It indicates rather a predominance of the intellectual. Only once in the tide of time, was the highest degree of it found united with the highest degree of moral purity and religious faith. It is the quality most essential in the communication of moral, as of all other truth.

We are apt to deceive ourselves as to the moral value of certain impressions derived from books. We mistake the transient excitation of the nobler sentiments produced by eloquent declamation or by the exhibition of romantic excellence in works of fiction, — by such characters, for instance, as the Marquis of Posa in Don Carlos, — for a genuine renewal of the moral man. We think we are burnt clean by the temporary glow into which we are thrown. The nature of such excitement differs but little from that produced by alcoholic stimulants, amid animated discussion and congenial friends. It is stimulus without nourishment, ebullition without growth. It has something maudlin. It acts chiefly on the nerves. Its final effect is rather to enervate than to educate the soul. He only instructs who gives me light, who effects a permanent lodgment, in the mind, of some essential truth. The effective moralist is not the enthusiast, but the impartial and clear-seeing witness; not he who declaims most eloquently about the truth, but he who makes me see it; who gives me a clear intuition of a moral fact.

Goethe was peculiarly fitted, by habit and endowment, to be a witness of the truth, so far as truth is a matter of intellectual discernment. Not over-scrupulous in his way of life, he practised the most scrupulous fidelity to himself, as a seeker of the truth. He gave no license to his mind. Where he could not or would not perform, he would know. He wanted not courage nor candor to see truly in morals and religion as in everything else. He loved sensual indulgence right well, but he loved truth more. A man of sincerest intellect, who suffered neither fear nor hope, nor prepossession of any kind, to come between him and the light; with whom to see was the first necessity of his nature; to state distinctly to himself and others what he saw, the next.

Unquestionably, he was no saint. His wildest admirers have sought no place for him in the Christian Calendar, though greater sinners than he may be found in it and among its most honored names. But neither was he a bad man in any allowable sense of the word, as every one must know who considers the moral conditions on which alone true poetry is possi-

---

* Menzel's German Literature translated by C. C. Felton.

ble. Wherein he transgressed the social law and the Christian standard, let judgment be pronounced without fear or favor. But for every count on which verdict is given, let irrefragable testimony be required. Let not the hero of his time, a hero of the true sort,—one who labored through life, with whatever judgment or success, to build up and not to destroy, to lead Humanity onward to the prize of beauty through the knowledge of the truth, — let not such a one be surrendered to the scourge of the tongue on grounds of hearsay and fallible inference. Let not a great and illustrious name be ruthlessly tossed to the dogs and to all the birds. If the good and evil of his life, the positive and the negative, were fairly weighed in the balance together, the result would probably indicate a higher grade of moral excellence than most of his accusers have attained to. It is not, however, on the moral character of the man that any safe judgment as to the moral character of his writings can be based. Grant him immoral; — still his testimony to moral truth, if sincere, (and no one versed in his writings can doubt his sincerity), may be all the more impressive on that account. It is the testimony of one who was biassed by no prepossessions in favor of that to which he testifies, who took nothing for granted, believed nothing because it was the general conviction, said nothing because it was expected, who would neither deceive himself nor be deceived by others. It is the testimony of one who had seen with his own eyes, and those eyes the keenest, the most unprejudiced, that ever sought to penetrate the relations of things;—who had experienced with his own heart, and that heart one to which all experiences were familiar, which gave itself up without reserve to all the discipline of life, which had proved all things and knew and confessed what was good.

In reading Goethe we do not feel, as when reading Dante or Milton, that we are conversing with a pure and lofty spirit; but we do feel that we are conversing with a competent witness, or better still, with an incorruptible judge. The verdict which he will give is a part of his life. It is a fact in Nature. The fault which most readers find with his writings is want of heat. He betrays no passionate interest in any subject, in any character, and seeks to excite none in his readers. To stir the blood is not his aim. Intense emotion he purposely avoids as incompatible with the higher purposes of art. There is no gush, no rush, no pouring forth of a full soul, excepting in his lyric poems. But what he wants in enthusiasm he makes up in sincerity and precision. If there is no declamation, there is also no cant, no straining, nothing said for effect. Therefore his words have weight. They drop like the oracles of destiny from his pen. When he states with characteristic calmness that "only with renunciation, can life, properly speaking, be said to begin;" that saying, though it does but repeat in substance what we had always been told, has all the freshness of an original discovery. This sincere word, wrung from the experience of such a mind, carries with it a deeper conviction than all the arguments and all the declamation that have ever been employed to enforce the duty of self-denial.

With strong propriety may Goethe be termed a moral teacher, and the highest rank assigned to him as such. He will be found, on a careful study, to have the moral law in view, and to aim at enforcing it; even there, where he has been charged with an immoral tendency;—and nowhere more emphatically, than in the "Elective Affinities." The imputation cast upon this work is a specimen of the hasty and superficial manner in which his writings have been judged. The aim of the "Elective Affinities" is to illustrate the ethics of married life, to expose the mischief of ill-considered and unequal matches, and the terrible consequences of even mental infidelity to the marriage vow. He who can read the book attentively and understandingly, and find in it any other meaning than this, might discover a plea for jealousy in Othello, or an apology for murderous ambition in Macbeth. A writer, already quoted, has better understood the worth and purport of this finished work. "The mental aberrations of the consorts from their plighted faith, though, in the one case never indulged, and though, in the other, no veil of sophistry is cast over the weakness of passion, but all that is felt, expressed with the openness of one who desires to legitimate what he feels,—are punished with terrible griefs and a fatal catastrophe. Ottilia, that being of exquisite purity, with intellect and character so harmonized in feminine beauty, as they never before were found in any portrait of woman painted by the hand of man, perishes on finding that she has been breathed upon by unhallowed passion, and led to err, even by her ignorant wishes, against what is held sacred. There is indeed a sadness, as of an irresistible fatality, brooding over the whole. It seems as if only a ray of angelic truth could have enabled these beings to walk in this twilight, at first so soft and alluring, then deepening into blind horror. But if no such ray came to prevent their earthly errors, it seems to point heavenward, in the saintly sweetness of Ottilia. Her nature, too fair for vice, too finely wrought even for error, comes lonely, intense and pale, like the evening star on the cold wintry night. It tells of other worlds, where the meaning of such passages as this must be read to those faithful and pure like her, victims perishing in the green garlands of youth, to atone for the unworthiness of others. An unspeakable pathos is felt from the minutest trait in this character, and deepens with every new study of it. Not even in Shakspeare, have I so felt the organizing power of Genius. I feel myself familiarized with all beings of her order. I see not only what she was, but what she might have been, and live with her in yet untrodden realms."*

Of Goethe's character, as a statesman and a citizen, no labored justification will be expected in a work like this. That he did not use his powers and influence for revolutionary purposes, seems to have been the chief cause of the disesteem into which he has fallen with certain revolutionary spirits of Germany, and of those aspersions which have acted on public opinion with us. True, he was decidedly conservative, so far as State institutions were concerned; for he saw little promise for man from measures, of which all that could with certainty be foreseen, was, that they were subversive of present order and peace. He believed that all which was wanted, or all which was really desirable, might be accomplished, with greater certainty, by the agency of existing institutions.

"*Narre wenn es brennt so lösche,*
Hat's gebrannt bau wieder auf.'

Heine refers this conduct of Goethe to his peculiar position. "The giant was minister in a German dwarf-state. He could never move naturally. They said of the sitting Jupiter of Phidias at Olympia, that, if he should suddenly stand up, he would burst the vaulted roof of the temple. This was precisely the position of Goethe at Weimar. If he had suddenly started up from his sitting rest, he would have broken through the ceiling of the State, or, what is more likely, he would have broken his own head against it. The German Jupiter quietly kept his seat." But in fact he needs no such apology. The question by which he must be tried, is not, whether he has adopted this or that particular method of advancing the interests of Humanity; but whether he has advanced the interests of Humanity at all, by any method whatsoever? Whether he labored, on the whole, to make men wiser, better, happier? The answer to this question must be sought in his works. We may demand of a man, that he should not be indifferent to certain ends; but the method we must leave to himself. "It cannot be too often repeated," says Mrs. Austin, "that Goethe was not a partisan. That he was indifferent to the progress of human improvement and the sum of human happiness, as some have maintained, seems to me incredible. Are we justified in accusing him of apathy and selfishness, because he had a dread of violent political convulsions? a distrust of the efficacy of abrupt changes in the mechanism of government? It was not surely indifference to the welfare of mankind, but that he thought it a pernicious illusion to look for healing there, from whence he was convinced no healing could ever come. His labors for the improvement of the human race were unwearied, calm and systematic."

With regard to his private character, it would be easy to accumulate testimony of the highest authority in favor of those qualities in which he has been supposed to be most deficient. But for those who have learned to believe in him for his works' sake, such testimony would be superfluous; and for those who are, once for all, determined against him, it would be unavailing. "Pity, that so few are acquainted with this excellent man in respect of his heart!" said the meek and pious Stilling, who could speak from personal experience of Goethe's worth. That he had faults it needs no testimony to prove. It may safely be taken for granted. That he had uncommon faults, or any which—as things go—might not naturally be expected from a man of the world: to prove this, requires more testimony than has yet been adduced. And so we will dismiss the subject with his own words: "Life to all of us is suf-

---

* S. M. Fuller. Dial. ubi supra.

fering; who save God alone shall call us to our reckoning? By the failings we recognise the species, by the excellences the individual. Defects we all have in common, virtues belong to each severally:" and with these of Wieland, which, though they refer rather to his official than his private action, are not out of place in this connection: "If I had cause to be ever so angry with Goethe, or to feel ever so much offended and aggrieved by his conduct; yet, when I recollect (what no one can know better than I) what incredible services he rendered to our Sovereign, during the early years of his reign, with what entire self-forgetfulness he devoted himself to his service; how much that was noble and great that yet slumbered in the princely youth he first called forth, I could fall on my knees before him, and praise and worship our Master Goethe more than for all the productions of his genius or his intellect."

It is time to conclude this essay, already drawn out beyond its legitimate bounds. The general misunderstanding which prevails among us respecting this hero of modern literature has caused it to assume a more apologetic character than its author could wish, than he feels to be consistent with his own respect for the man. In a few years, all external testimony as to his merits or demerits, will have perished from the earth; but his works will bear witness of him when there is no other. These have become a part of the world. Iphigenia and Tasso are indestructible possessions of the human mind, and Faust will endure while the Brocken stands or the Rhine flows. "In him," says Fichte, "the noblest blossom of Humanity, which Nature had put forth but once beneath the Grecian sky, by one of her miracles was repeated here in the North. To him it was given to measure two different epochs of human culture with all their gradations. And if our race are destined to ascend to higher degrees of excellence, it will not be without his co-operation."*

* *Fichte, ueber Geist und Buchstabe in der Philosophie. Philosophisches Journal*, vol. IX.

THE VICAR OF WAKEFIELD.

EXTRACT FROM GOETHE'S AUTOBIOGRAPHY.*

Now Herder came, and together with his great learning, he brought with him many other assistances, and the later publications besides. Among these he announced to us the *Vicar of Wakefield* as an excellent work, with the German translation of which he wished to make us acquainted by reading it aloud to us himself.

His method of reading was quite peculiar; one who has heard him preach will easily form an idea of it for himself. He delivered everything, and this romance as well as the rest, in a serious and simple style, perfectly removed from all imitative-dramatic representation, and avoiding even that variety which is not only permitted, but even required, in an epical delivery; I mean that slight change of voice which sets in relief what is spoken by the different characters, and by means of which the interlocutors are distinguished from the narrator. Without being monotonous, Herder let everything follow along in the same tone, just as if nothing of it was present before him, but all was only historical; as if the shadows of this poetic creation did not affect him in a life-like manner, but only glided gently by. Yet this manner of delivery had an infinite charm in his mouth: for, as he felt it all most deeply, and knew how to estimate the variety of such a work, so its whole merit appeared in perfect purity, and the more clearly, as you were not disturbed by passages sharply spoken out, nor interrupted in the feeling which the whole was meant to produce.

A Protestant country-clergyman is, perhaps, the most beautiful subject for a modern idyl; he appears, like Melchizedek, as Priest and King in one person. In the most innocent situation which can be imagined in the world, that of a husbandman, he is, for the most part, united to his people by similar occupations, as well as by similar family relationships; he is a father, a master of a family, an agriculturist, and thus a perfect member of the community. On this pure, beautiful, earthly foundation, reposes his higher calling; to him is it given to guide men through life, to take care for their spiritual education, to bless them at all the leading epochs of their existence, to instruct, to strengthen, to console them, and, if present consolation is not sufficient, he calls up before them the hope and firm assurance of a happier future. Imagine to yourself such a man, with feelings of pure humanity, strong enough not to deviate from them under any circumstances, and by this already elevated above the many, of whom one can expect neither purity nor firmness; give him the learning necessary for his office, as well as a cheerful, equable activity which is even passionate, for he neglects no moment for doing good,—and you will have him well endowed. But at the same time add the necessary limitedness, so that he must not only labor on in a small circle, but may also, perchance, pass over to a

* See No. LXXVI. of Wiley and Putnam's Library of Choice Reading.

smaller; grant him good-nature, placability, resolution, and everything else praiseworthy that springs from so decided a character, and over all this a serene condescension and a smiling forbearance towards his own failings and those of others: so will you have put together pretty well the image of our excellent Wakefield.

The delineation of this character on his course of life through joys and sorrows, and the ever increasing interest of the plot, by the combination of what is quite natural with the strange and the wonderful, make this romance one of the best which has ever been written; besides this, it has the great superiority of being quite moral, nay, in a pure sense, Christian, for it represents the reward of good intentions and perseverance in the right, it strengthens an unconditional confidence in God, and asserts the final triumph of good over evil, and all this without a trace of cant or pedantry. The author was preserved from both of these by an elevation of mind that shows itself throughout in the form of irony, by reason of which this little work must appear to us as wise as it is amiable. The author, Dr. Goldsmith, has without question great insight into the moral world, into its strength and its infirmities; but at the same time he may thankfully acknowledge that he is an Englishman,* and reckon highly the advantages which his country and his nation afforded him. The family, with whose delineation he has here busied himself, stands upon one of the lowest steps of citizen-comfort, and yet comes in contact with the highest; its narrow circle, which becomes still more contracted, extends its influence into the great world through the natural and common course of things; this little skiff floats full on the agitated waves of English life, and in weal or woe it has to expect injury or help from the vast fleet which sails around it.

I may suppose that my readers know this work and remember it; whoever hears it named for the first time here, as well as he who is induced to read it again, will thank me. For the former I would merely remark, *en passant*, that the Vicar's wife is of that busy, good sort, who allows herself and family to want for nothing, but who is also somewhat vain of herself and family. There are two daughters; Olivia, handsome and more devoted to the exterior, and Sophia, charming and more given to her inner self; nor will I omit mentioning an industrious son, Moses, who is somewhat astringent and emulous of his Father.

If Herder could be accused of any fault in his reading aloud, it was impatience; he did not wait until the hearer had heard and comprehended a certain part of the details, so as to be able to feel and think correctly about them; he would hurry on immediately to see their

------
* Goldsmith was an Irishman by birth, and received his education at Dublin, Edinburgh and Leyden, and spent six months at Padua, where he is supposed to have taken his degree.—*Trans.*

effect, and yet he was displeased with this too when it manifested itself in us. He blamed the excess of feeling which overflowed from me at every step in the story. I felt, like a man, like a young man; everything was living, true, and present before me. He, considering only the artistic keeping and form, saw clearly, indeed, that I was overpowered by the subject-matter, and this he was unwilling to allow. Peglow's reflections, besides, which were not of the most refined character, were still worse received; but he was especially angry at our want of keenness in not seeing beforehand the contrasts which the author often makes use of, and in suffering ourselves to be moved and carried away by them without remarking the oft-returning art. Nor would he pardon us for not having seen at once, or at least suspected from the first, where Burchell is on the point of discovering himself by passing over in his narration from the third to the first person, that he himself was the lord whom he was talking about; and when, finally, we rejoiced like children at the *dénouement*, and the transformation of the poor, needy wanderer, into a rich, powerful lord, he immediately recalled the passage, which, according to the author's plan, we had overlooked, and then he read us a powerful lecture on our stupidity. It will be seen from this that he regarded the work merely as a production of Art, and required the same of us who were yet wandering in that state where it is very allowable to let works of art affect us just as if they were productions of Nature.

I did not suffer myself to be at all confused by Herder's invectives; for young people have the happiness or unhappiness, that, when anything has produced an effect on them, this effect must be wrought out within themselves; from which much good, as well as much mischief arises. The above work had produced a great impression upon me, for which I could not account. Properly speaking, I felt myself in unison with that ironical tone of mind which elevates itself above every object, above fortune and misfortune, good and evil, death and life, and thus attains to the possession of a truly poetical world. In fact, though I could not become conscious of this until later, it was enough that it gave me much to do at the moment; but I could by no means have expected to see myself so soon transposed from this fictitious world into an actual one so similar.

My fellow-boarder, Weyland, who enlivened his quiet, laborious life, by visiting his friends and relations in the country, (for he was a native of Alsace,) did me many services on my little excursions, by introducing me to different localities and individuals, sometimes in person, sometimes by his recommendations. He had often spoken to me about a country clergyman who lived near Drusenheim, six leagues from Strasburg, in possession of a good benefice, with an intelligent wife and a pair of lovely daughters. The hospitality and agreeableness of this family were always highly extolled. It scarcely needed all this to draw thither a young rider who had already accustomed himself to spend all his leisure days and hours on horseback and in the open air. We decided upon this trip, too, on which my friend had to promise that, on introducing me, he would say neither good nor ill of me, but would treat me with general indifference, and would also allow me to make my appearance clad, if not meanly, yet somewhat poorly and slovenly. He consented to this, and promised himself some sport from it.

It is a pardonable whim in men of consequence to place their exterior advantages in concealment now and then, so as to give the fairer play to the intrinsic worth of their inner man. For this reason the incognito of princes, and the adventures resulting therefrom, are always highly pleasing; they appear like masked divinities, who can nobly reckon at double their value all the good offices shown to them as individuals, and are able either to make light of the disagreeable or to avoid it. That Jupiter should be well pleased in his incognito with Philemon and Baucis, and Henry the Fourth with his peasants after a hunting party, is quite conformable to Nature, and we like it well; but that a young man, of no importance or name, should take it into his head to derive any pleasure from an incognito, might be construed by many as an unpardonable arrogance. Yet since the question here is not whether such opinions and deeds are praiseworthy or blameable, but how they may have shown themselves and been put into execution, we will pardon the youngster his self-conceit for this time, for the sake of our own amusement; and the more so as I must here affirm, in my excuse, that from youth up, a love for masquerade had been excited in me even by my stern father himself.

This time too, partly with my own cast-off clothes, partly with some borrowed garments and by the manner of combing my hair, I had, if not disfigured myself, yet at least botched up my accoutrements so outlandishly that my friend could not help laughing along the way, especially since I knew how to take off to the life the bearing and gesture of the *Latin Riders* (as such-looking figures are called) when they sit on horseback. The fine road, the most splendid weather, and the neighborhood of the Rhine, put us in the best humor. We stopped a moment in Drusenheim, he to make himself spruce, and I to rehearse the part I was to play, for I was afraid of speaking now and then out of character. The country here has the characteristics of all the open, level parts of Alsace. We rode by a pleasant foot-path over the meadows, soon reached Sesenheim, left our horses at the tavern, and walked leisurely towards the parsonage. "Do not be put out," said Weyland, showing me the house from a distance, "that it looks like an old and miserable farm-house; it is so much the younger inside." We stepped into the court-yard; the whole pleased me well:

for it was just what is called picturesque, and what had so magically interested me in the Dutch school of art. The effect which time produces on all the works of man was strongly perceptible. House, barn and stable were just at that point of dilapidation where, in doubtful hesitation betwixt repairing and rebuilding, men often neglect the one without being able to accomplish the other.

As in the village, so in the court-yard of the Parsonage, everything was quiet and deserted. We found the father quite alone, a little man, wrapped up within himself, but friendly notwithstanding; the family were then in the field. He bade us welcome, and offered us some refreshment, which we declined. My friend hurried away to look after the ladies, and I remained alone with our host. "Perhaps," said he, "you are surprised to find me so miserably quartered in a wealthy village, and with a lucrative benefice; but," continued he, "it proceeds from irresolution. Long since it has been promised me by the parish, and even by those in higher places, that the house should be rebuilt; many plans have been already drawn, examined and altered, none of them altogether rejected, and none carried into execution. This has lasted so many years, that I scarcely know how to command my impatience." I answered him whatever I thought likely to cherish his hopes, and encourage him to take up the affair more vigorously. Thereupon he proceeded to describe familiarly the personages on whom such matters depend, and although he was no great hand at the delineation of character, yet I could easily comprehend how the whole business must have been delayed. The confidentialness of the man was something peculiar; he talked to me as if he had known me for ten years, though there was nothing in his look from which I could have suspected that he was directing any particular scrutiny to my character. At last my friend came in with the mother. She seemed to look at me with altogether different eyes. Her countenance was regular, and its expression intelligent; she must have been handsome in her youth. Her figure was tall and spare, but not more so than became her years, and when seen from behind she had yet quite a youthful and pleasing appearance. The elder daughter then came bouncing in briskly; she inquired after Frederica, just as both the others had also done. The father assured them that he had not seen her since all three had gone out together. The daughter again went out to the door to look for her sister; the mother brought us some refreshment, and Weyland continued the conversation with the old couple, which referred to nothing but known persons and circumstances; for it is usually the case, when acquaintances meet after some length of time, that they make inquiries about the members of a large circle, and mutually give each other information. I listened, and now learned how much I had to promise myself from this circle.

The elder daughter again came hastily back into the room, anxious at not having found her sister. They felt uneasy about her, and scolded at this or that bad habit; only the father said, very composedly: "Always let her alone; she is back again already!" At this instant, in fact, she entered the door; and then truly a most charming star arose in this terrestrial heaven. Both daughters still wore nothing but German, as they used to call it, and this almost obsolete national costume became Frederica particularly well. A short, white, full skirt, with a furbelow, not so long but it left the neatest little foot visible up to the ankle; a tight white bodice and a black taffeta apron,—there she stood, on the boundary between country beauty and city belle. Slender and airy, she tripped along as if she had nothing to carry, and her neck seemed almost too delicate for the luxuriant braids of flaxen hair on her elegant little head. A free, open glance beamed from her calm blue eyes, and her pretty little turned-up nose peered inquiringly into the air with as much unconcern as if there could be nothing like care in the world; her straw hat dangled on her arm, and thus, at the first glance, I had the delight of seeing her perfect grace, and acknowledging her perfect loveliness.

I now began to act my character subduedly, half ashamed to have played a joke on such good people, whom I had leisure enough to observe: for the girls continued the previous conversation, and that with feeling and humor. All the neighbors and connections were again brought upon the tapis, and to my imagination there seemed such a swarm of uncles and aunts, relations, cousins, comers and goers, gossips and guests, that I thought myself lodged in the liveliest world possible. All the members of the family had spoken some words with me, the mother looked at me every time she came in or went out, but Frederica first entered into conversation with me, and as I took up and glanced through the music that was lying around, she asked me if I played also? When I told her "Yes," she requested me to perform something; but the father would not allow this, for he maintained that it was becoming in her to serve her guest first, with some piece of music or other, or a song.

She played several things with some execution, in the style which one usually hears in the country, and on a harpsichord, too, that the schoolmaster should have tuned long since, if he had only had time. She was now to sing a song also, something of the tender-melancholy; but she could not succeed with it. She rose up and said, smiling, or rather with that touch of serene joy which ever reposed on her countenance: "If I sing poorly, I cannot lay the blame on the harpsichord or the schoolmaster; but let us go out of doors, then you shall hear my Alsatain and Swiss songs, they sound much better."

During tea, an idea which had already struck me before, occupied me to such a degree, that I became meditative and silent, although the liveliness of the elder sister, and the gracefulness of the younger, shook me often enough out of my contemplations. My astonishment at finding myself so actually in the Wakefield family was beyond all expression. The father, indeed, could not be compared with that excellent man; but where will you find his like? On the other hand, all the worth which is peculiar to the husband there, here appeared in the wife. You could not see her without at once reverencing and fearing her. In her we saw the fruits of a good education; her demeanor was quiet, easy, cheerful, and inviting.

If the elder daughter had not the celebrated beauty of Olivia, yet she possessed a fine figure, was lively, and rather impetuous; she everywhere showed herself active, and lent a helping hand to her mother in all things. It was not hard to put Frederica in the place of Primrose's Sophia: for of her there is little said, we take it for granted that she is lovely; and this girl was lovely indeed. Now as the same occupation and the same general situation, wherever they can occur, produce similar, if not the same effects, so here too many things were talked about and happened which had already taken place in the Wakefield family. But when a younger son, long spoken of and impatiently expected by the father, at last sprang into the room, and boldly sat himself down by us, taking but little notice of the guests, I could scarcely help exclaiming: "Moses, are you here too!"

The conversation at table extended my insight into this country and family circle, as they chatted about various pleasant incidents which had happened here and there. Frederica, who sat next to me, took occasion from that circumstance to describe to me different localities which it might be worth my while to visit. As one little story always calls out another, I was able to mingle in the conversation the better, and relate similar incidents, and, as, besides this, a good country wine was by no means spared, I stood in danger of slipping out of my character, for which reason my provident friend took advantage of the beautiful moonlight, and proposed a walk, which was immediately resolved on. He gave his arm to the elder, I to the younger, and thus we went through the wide plains, paying more attention to the heavens above than to the earth beneath, which lost itself in extension around us. There was nothing of moonshine about Frederica's conversation, however; by the clearness with which she spoke she turned night into day, and there was nothing in it which hinted at or would have excited feeling, only her expressions addressed themselves more than ever to me, while, as I walked by her side, she represented to me her own situation, as well as the neighborhood and her acquaintances, just as I wished to be made acquainted with them; then she added that she hoped I would make no exception, and would visit them again, as all strangers had willingly done who had once lodged at the Parsonage.

It was very pleasant to me to listen silently to the descriptions which she gave of the little world in which she moved, and of the persons whom she particularly valued. She thereby imparted to me a clear, and, at the same time, such an amiable idea of her situation, that it had a very strange effect on me: for I felt at once a deep regret that I had not lived with her sooner, and at the same time a right painful jealous feeling towards all who had hitherto had the good fortune to surround her. I also watched closely, as if I had had a right to do so, all her descriptions of men, whether they appeared under the names of neighbors, cousins, or familiar friends, and my conjectures inclined now to one, now to another; but how should I have discovered anything in my complete ignorance of all the circumstances? She at last became more and more talkative, and I constantly more and more silent. It was so good to listen to her, and as I heard only her voice, while the outlines of her countenance, like the rest of the world around, floated dimly in the twilight, it seemed to me as if I could see into her heart, and that I could not but find it very pure, since it unbosomed itself to me in such unembarrassed prattle.

When my companion and I retired to the guest-chamber which was prepared for us, he, with self-complacency, immediately broke out into pleasant jesting, and took great credit to himself for having surprised me so much with the likeness of the Primrose family. I chimed in with him, by showing myself thankful. "Truly," cried he, "the story is all here together. This family may well be compared to that, and the gentleman in disguise here, may assume the honor of passing for Mr. Burchell; moreover, since scoundrels are not so necessary in every-day life as in romances, I will for this time undertake the *rôle* of the Nephew, and will behave myself better than he did." However, I immediately changed this conversation, pleasant as it was to me, and first of all asked him, on his conscience, if he had not betrayed me? He answered me "No!" and I ventured to believe him. They had rather inquired, said he, after the jovial table-companion who boarded at the same house with him in Strassburg, and of whom they had heard all sorts of preposterous stuff. I now went to other questions: Had she ever been in love? Was she now in love? Was she engaged? He said "No" to them all. "In truth," replied I, "that such a serenity should come by nature is inconceivable to me. If she had loved and lost, and again recovered herself, or if she was betrothed, in both these cases I could account for it."

Thus we chatted together till deep in the night, and I was awake again at the dawn. My longing to see her once more seemed unconquerable; but while I was dressing I was horrified at the confounded wardrobe I had so capriciously selected. The further I advanced in putting on my clothes, the meaner I seemed in my own eyes: for everything was calculated for just that effect. I might perchance have set my hair to rights; but when at last I forced my arms into the borrowed, worn-out grey coat, the short sleeves of which gave me the most absurd appearance, I fell decidedly into despair, and the more so since I could see myself only piecemeal, in a little looking-glass, and then each part always looked more ridiculous than the rest.

During this toilette my friend awoke, and with the satisfaction of a good conscience, and in the feeling of pleasurable hopes for the day, he looked out at me from under the quilted silk coverlet. I had envied his fine clothes for a long time already, as they hung over the chair, and had he been of my size, I would have carried them off before his very eyes, dressed myself in them, and hurrying into the garden, left my cursed husks for him; he would have had good humor enough to deck himself out in my clothes, and our tale would have found a merry ending early in the morning. But that was not now to be thought of, as little as any other feasible accommodation. To appear again before Frederica in such a figure that my friend could give me out as a laborious and accomplished but poor student of Theology,—before Frederica, who yesterday evening had spoken so friendly to my disguised self,—that was altogether impossible. There I stood, vexed and thoughtful, and summoned up all my power of invention; alas! it deserted me! But now when he, comfortably stretched out in bed, after fixing his eyes upon me for a while, all at once burst out into a loud laugh, and exclaimed: "Yes! it is true, you do look most confoundedly!" I replied impetuously: "And I know what I will do. Good bye, and make my excuses!" "Are you crazy!" cried he, springing out of bed and trying to detain me. But I was already out of the door, down the stairs, out of the house and yard, to the tavern; in an instant my horse was saddled, and I hurried away in mad vexation, galloping towards Drusenheim, dashed through the place, and still onwards!

As I thought myself by this time in safety, I began to ride more leisurely, and now first felt how infinitely against my will I was going away. But I resigned myself to my fate, recalled to mind the promenade of yesterday evening with the greatest calmness, and cherished the secret hope of seeing her soon again. Yet this quiet feeling again changed itself into impatience, and I now determined to ride rapidly into the city, change my dress, take a good fresh horse, and then, as my passion made me believe, I could at all events return before dinner, or, as was more probable, to the dessert or towards evening, and beg my forgiveness.

I was just about to put spurs to my horse to execute this resolve, when another, and, as seemed to me, a happier thought came into my head. In the tavern at Drusenheim, the day before, I had noticed a son of the landlord very nicely dressed, who, up early to-day and busied about his rural arrangements, had saluted me from his court-yard as I rode by. He was of my size, and had slightly reminded me of myself. Thought, done! My horse was hardly turned around, when I found myself in Drusenheim; I brought him into the stable, and made the fellow my proposal in brief: that he should lend me his clothes, as I had something merry on foot at Sesenheim. I had no need to talk long; he agreed to the proposition with joy, and praised me for wishing to make some sport for the *Mamsells;* they were so gallant and good, especially Mamselle Rica, and the parents, too, liked to see everything go on merry and pleasant. He considered me attentively, and as from my appearance he might have taken me for a poor starveling, he said: "If you wish to insinuate yourself into their good graces, this is the right way." Meanwhile we had already made rapid advances in our toilette; he could not indeed trust me with his holiday clothes on the strength of mine; but he was honest-hearted, and had my horse in his stable. I soon stood there right trig, threw back my shoulders, and my friend seemed to contemplate his likeness with complacency. "Well, Mr. Brother!" said he, giving me his hand, which I grasped heartily, "don't come too near my gal, she might mistake you!"

My hair, which now had its full growth again, I could part at top pretty much like his, and as I looked at him repeatedly, I found it comical to imitate closely his thicker eyebrows, with a burnt cork, and bring mine nearer together in the middle, so as with my enigmatical intentions, to make myself an external riddle likewise. "Now have you not," said I, as he handed me his be-ribboned hat, "something or other to be done at the Parsonage, so that I may announce myself there in a natural manner?" "Good!" replied he, "but then you must wait two hours yet. There is a confinement at our house; I will offer to take the cake to the Parson's wife,* and you might carry it over there. Pride must be paid for, and so must a joke."—I concluded to wait, but these two hours were infinitely long, and I was dying of impatience when the third hour passed by before the cake came out of the oven. I got it at last, quite hot, and hastened away with my credentials in the most beautiful sunshine, accompanied for a space by my Ditto, who promised to come after me in the evening and bring me my clothes, which however, I briskly declined, and reserved to myself the privilege of returning him his own when I was done with them.

I had not skipped far with my present, which I carried neatly tied up in a napkin, when, in the distance, I saw my friend approaching with the two ladies. My heart was uneasy, although in fact it was unnecessary under this jacket. I stood still, took breath, and tried to think how I

* The general custom of the country villages in Protestant Germany on such interesting occasions.—*Trans.*

should begin; and now I first remarked that the nature of the ground was very much in my favor; for they were walking on the other side of the brook, which, together with the strips of meadow through which it ran, kept the two foot-paths pretty far apart. When they were just opposite to me, Frederica, who had already perceived me long before, cried: "George, what have you got there?" I was clever enough to cover my face with my hat, which I took off, at the same time holding up the loaded napkin high in the air. "A christening-cake!" cried she at that; "how does your sister do!" "Gooed," said I, for I tried to talk strange, if not exactly in the Alsatian dialect. "Carry it to the house!" said the elder, "and if you do not find mother, give it to the maid; but wait for us, we will be back soon, do you hear?" I hastened along my path in the joyous feeling of the best hope that, as the beginning was so lucky, all would go off well, and I soon reached the Parsonage. I found nobody either in the house or the kitchen; I did not wish to disturb the old gentleman, whom I might have supposed busy in the study; I therefore sat me down on the bench before the door, placed the cake beside me, and pressed my hat upon my face.

I cannot easily recall more delightful sensations. To sit here again on this threshold, over which, a short time before, I had blundered out in despair; to have seen her already, to have heard her dear voice again so soon after my chagrin had pictured to me a long separation, to be expecting every moment herself, and a discovery at which my heart throbbed fast, and yet, in this ambiguous case, it would be an exposure without shame; for from its very beginning it was a merrier prank than any of those they had laughed at so much yesterday. Love and Necessity are yet the best masters; they both worked together here, and their pupil was not unworthy of them.

But the maid came stepping out of the barn. "Now! did the cake turn out well!" cried she to me; "how does your sister do?" "All gooed," said I, and pointed to the cake without looking up. She took up the napkin and muttered: "Now what's the matter with you to-day again? Has little Barbara been looking at somebody else once more? Don't let us suffer for that! A happy couple you will make, if you carry on so!" As she spoke pretty loud, the Parson came to the window and asked: "What's the matter?" She showed him; I stood up and turned myself towards him, but yet kept the hat over my face. As he spoke rather kindly to me and had asked me to remain, I went towards the garden, and was just going in when the Parson's wife, who was entering the court-yard gate, called to me. As the sun shone right in my face, I once more took advantage of my hat, and saluted her with a ploughman's scrape; but she went into the house after she had bidden me not go away without eating something. I now walked up and down in the garden; everything had hitherto had the best success, yet I drew a deep breath when I reflected that the young people would soon return. But the mother unexpectedly stepped up to me, and was just going to ask me a question, when she looked me in the face so that I could not conceal myself any longer, and the question stuck in her mouth. "I was looking for George," said she, after a pause, "and whom do I find? Is it you, young sir? How many forms have you, then?" "In earnest only one," replied I; "in sport as many as you like." "Which sport I will not spoil," smiled she; "go out behind the garden and into the meadow until it strikes twelve, then come back, and I will already have contrived the joke." I did so; but when I was outside of the hedge that bounds the village gardens, and was going into the meadow, I saw some country people coming along the foot-path towards me, who embarrassed me. I therefore turned aside into a little grove which crowned an elevation near by, in order to conceal myself there till the appointed time. Yet how strangely was I surprised when I entered it! for it appeared to be a neatly trimmed place, with benches, from every one of which could be enjoyed a fine view of the country. Here was the village and the church tower, here Drusenheim, and behind it the woody islands of the Rhine, in the opposite direction was the Vosgian mountain-range, and at last the Minster of Strassburg. These different heaven-bright pictures were surrounded by frames of foliage, so that one could imagine nothing more joyous and more pleasing. I sat me down upon one of the benches, and noticed on the largest tree an oblong little board with the inscription: "Frederica's Repose." It never entered into my head that I could have come to disturb this repose: for a budding passion has this beauty about it, that, as it is unconscious of its origin, neither does it spend any thought upon its end, and as it feels itself glad and cheerful, it can have no presentiment that it may make mischief too.

Scarcely had I had time to look about me and lose myself in sweet reveries, when I heard somebody coming; it was Frederica herself. "George, what are you doing here?" she cried from a distance. "Not George!" cried I, running towards her, "but one who craves forgiveness of you a thousand times." She looked at me with astonishment, but soon collected herself and said, after drawing a deeper breath: "You abominable fellow, how you frighten me!" "The first disguise has led me into the second," exclaimed I; "the former would have been unpardonable if I had only known in any manner whom I was going to see, but this one you will certainly forgive, for it is the form of a man whom you meet in so friendly a manner." Her pale cheeks had colored up with the loveliest rosy-red. "You shall not be treated worse than George, at all events! But let us sit down! I confess that the fright has thrilled through all my limbs." I sat down beside her, exceedingly agitated. "We know everything already from your friend, up to this morning," said she, "now do you tell me the rest." I did not suffer her to ask twice, but described to her my horror at my yesterday's figure, and my rushing out of the house, so comically that she laughed heartily and delightedly; then I went on with what followed, with all modesty, indeed, yet passionately enough to have well passed for a declaration of love in historical form. At last I solemnized my pleasure at finding her again, by a kiss upon her hand, which she suffered to remain in mine. If she had taken upon herself the expense of the conversation during yesterday evening's moonlight walk, I now, on my part, richly repaid the debt. The pleasure of seeing her again, and being able to say to her everything that I had kept back yesterday, was so great, that, in my eloquence, I did not remark how meditative and silent she was becoming. Once more she drew a deep breath, and over and over again I begged her forgiveness for the fright which I had caused her. How long we may have sat there I know not; but all at once we heard some one call "Rica! Rica!" It was the voice of her sister. "That will be a pretty story to tell," said the dear girl, restored to her perfect serenity again; "she is coming hither from the side next to me," added she, bending over so as half to conceal me: "turn yourself away, so that she will not recognize you at once." The sister came up to the spot, but not alone; Weyland was with her, and both, as soon as they saw us, stood still as if petrified.

If we should all at once see a powerful flame burst out from a quiet roof, or should meet a monster whose deformity was at the same time revolting and fearful, we should not be struck with such massive astonishment as seizes us, when, unexpectedly, we see with our own eyes something we had believed morally impossible. "What is this?" cried the elder, with the rapidity of one who is frightened to death: "What is this? you with George! Hand-in-hand! How am I to understand this?"—"Dear sister," replied Frederica, very doubtfully, "the poor fellow is begging something of me; he has something to beg of you, too, you must forgive him beforehand." "I don't understand,—I don't comprehend—" said her sister, shaking her head and looking at Weyland, who, in his quiet way, stood by in perfect tranquillity, and contemplated the scene without any kind of expression. Frederica arose and drew me after her. "No hesitating!" cried she! "Pardon begged and granted!" "Now do!" said I, stepping pretty near the elder, "I have need of pardon!" She drew back, gave a loud shriek, and blushed over and over; then threw herself down on the grass, burst into a roar of laughter, and could not get enough of it. Weyland smiled as if pleased, and cried: "You are a rare youth!" Then he shook my hand in his. He was not usually liberal with his caresses, but his shake of the hand had something hearty and enlivening about it; yet he was sparing of this also.

After taking some time to recover and collect ourselves, we set out on our return to the village. On the way I learned how this singular rencounter had been occasioned. Frederica had at last parted from the promenaders to rest herself in her little nook for a moment before dinner, and when the other two came back to the house, the mother had sent them to call Frederica in the greatest haste, as dinner was ready.

The elder sister manifested the most extravagant delight, and when she learned that the mother had already discovered the secret, she exclaimed: "All that is left now is that father, brother, servant-man and maid, should be cheated likewise." When we were at the garden-hedge, Frederica insisted upon going beforehand into the house with my friend. The maid was busy in the kitchen-garden, and Olivia (for so I may be allowed to name the elder sister here), called out to her: "Here, I have something to tell you!" She left me standing by the hedge, and went towards the maid. I saw that she was speaking to her very earnestly. Olivia represented to her that George had quarrelled with Barbara, and seemed desirous of marrying her. The lass was not displeased at this; I was now called, and was to confirm what had been said. The handsome, stout girl cast down her eyes, and remained so till I stood quite near before her. But when, all at once, she looked into the strange face, she too gave a loud scream and ran away. Olivia bade me run after her and hold her fast, so that she should not get into the house and give the alarm; while she herself wished to go and see how it was with her father. On the way Olivia met the servant-boy, who was in love with the maid; I had in the mean time hurried after the maid, and held her fast. "Only think! what good luck!" cried Olivia: "it's all over with Barbara, and George marries Liese." "I have thought he would for a long while," said the good fellow, and stood there disconsolate.

I had given the maid to understand, that all we had yet to do was to cheat the father. We went up to the lad, who turned away and would have walked off; but Liese took him aside, and he, too, when he was undeceived, made the most extraordinary gestures. We went together to the house. The table was covered, and the father already in the room. Olivia, who kept me behind her, stepped to the threshold and said: "Father, you have no objections to George's dining with us to-day? but you must let him keep his hat on." "With all my heart!" said the old man, "but why such an unusual thing? Has he hurt himself?" She led me forward as I stood, with my hat on. "No!" said she, handing me into the room, "but he has a bird-cage under it, and the birds might fly out and make a deuce of a fuss; for there are nothing but loose wild birds there." The father was pleased with the joke, without precisely knowing what it meant. At this instant she took off my hat, made a ploughman's scrape, and required me to do the same. The old man looked at me, recognized me, but was not put out of his priestly self-possession. "Ay, ay, Mr. Candidate!" exclaimed he, raising a threatening finger at me: "You have changed saddles very quickly, and over-night I have lost an assistant, who yesterday promised me so faithfully that he would often mount my pulpit on week-days." Thereupon he laughed heartily, bade me welcome, and we sat down to table. Moses came in much later; for, as the youngest and spoiled child, he had accustomed himself not to hear the dinner-bell. Besides, he took very little notice of the company, scarce even when he contradicted them. In order to make surer of him, they had placed me, not between the sisters, but at the end of the table, where George often used to sit. As he came in at the door, which was behind me, he slapped me smartly on the shoulder, and said: "Good dinner to you, George!" "Many thanks, youngster!" replied I. The strange voice and the strange face startled him. "What say you?" cried Olivia: "does he not look very like his brother?" "Yes, from behind," replied Moses, who managed to recover his composure immediately, like other folk. He did not look at me again, and busied himself merely with zealously devouring the dishes, in order to make up for lost time. Then, too, he thought proper occasionally to find something for himself to do in the yard and the garden. At the dessert the genuine George came in, and made the scene still more lively. They rallied him for his jealousy, and would not praise him for having gotten himself a rival in me; but he was modest and clever enough, and, in a half-confused manner, he mixed up himself, his sweetheart, his ditto, and the *Mamsells* with each other to such a degree, that at last nobody could tell whom he was talking about, so that they were glad to give him a glass of wine and a piece of his own cake to eat, to keep him quiet.

At table there was some talk about going to walk; which however did not suit me very well in my peasant's clothes. But the ladies, early on that day already, when they learned who had run away in such a desperate hurry, had remembered that a hunting-coat of a cousin of theirs, in which he used to go sporting when he was here, was hanging in a clothes-press. Yet I declined, apparently with all sorts of jokes, but with a feeling of secret vanity, not wishing, as cousin, to disturb the good impression I had made in the character of peasant. The father had gone to take his afternoon nap; the mother, as always, was busy about her housewifery. But my friend proposed that I should tell them some story, to which I immediately agreed. We repaired to a spacious arbor, and I gave them a tale which I have since written out under the title of *The New Melusina,* (*post,* 324). It bears about the same relation to *The New Paris** as the Youth bears to the Boy, and I would insert it here, were I not afraid of injuring, by its outlandish play of Fancy, the rural reality and simplicity which agreeably surround us. Enough: I succeeded in that which rewards the inventors and narrators of such productions, I succeeded in awakening curiosity, in fixing the attention, in inciting them to give over-hasty solutions of impenetrable riddles, in deceiving their expectations, in confusing them by making that wonderful which was merely strange, in arousing sympathy and fear, in making them anxious, in moving them; and at last, by the inversion of what was apparently sober earnest into an ingenious and cheerful jest, this little tale satisfied the mind, leaving behind it materials for new images to the imagination, and to the understanding for further reflection.

Should any one hereafter read this tale in print, and doubt whether it could have and produce such an effect, let him remember that, properly speaking, man is only intended to have influence while present. Writing is an abuse of language, reading silently to one's self is a pitiful succedaneum of speech. The strongest influence in a man's power is made by his personal presence, youth is the most powerful upon youth, and hence too arise the purest influences. These are they which enliven the world, and can perish neither morally nor physically. I had inherited from my father a certain loquacious fondness for teaching; from my mother the faculty of representing, clearly and powerfully, everything that the imagination can produce or grasp, of giving a freshness to known stories, of inventing and relating others, and even making them up as I went along. By my paternal endowment I was for the most part rather a bore to the company: for who likes to listen to the opinions and sentiments of another, especially a youth, whose judgment, on account of his fragmentary experience, seems constantly insufficient? My mother, on the contrary, had thoroughly qualified me for social conversations. For to the imagination even the emptiest tale has an elevated charm, and even the smallest quantity of solid matter is thankfully received by the understanding.

By such recitals, which cost me nothing, I made myself beloved by children, I excited and delighted youth, and drew upon me the attention of older persons. But in society, such as it commonly is, I was soon obliged to stop these practices, and I have thereby lost but too much of the enjoyment of the world and of intellectual improvement; yet both these parental gifts accompanied me throughout my whole life, united with a third, namely, the necessity of expressing myself figuratively and by comparisons. In consideration of these peculiarities, Doctor Gall, a man of as much profundity as acuteness, discovering them by his Theory, assured me that I was properly speaking born for a popular orator. At this disclosure I was not a little confounded: for as I discovered, in my nation, no opportunity to harangue about anything, it would follow, if his assertion were well-grounded, that everything else I could undertake, would have been, alas, but a mistaken vocation!

FROM THE "ELECTIVE AFFINITIES."*

PART SECOND. CHAPTER THIRTEENTH.

OTTILIA this afternoon had taken a walk to the lake. She carried the child and read as she walked, according to her custom. In this manner she arrived at the oak by the ferry. The boy had fallen asleep: she seated herself, laid him down beside her, and continued her reading. The book was one of those that draw to them a tender soul and will not let it go. She forgot time and the hour, and did not consider that by land it was a long way back to the new building; but she sat absorbed in her book, in herself, so lovely to look upon that the trees and bushes around should have been animated and gifted with eyes to admire and delight in her. Just then a ruddy gleam of the sinking sun fell behind her, and gilded her cheeks and shoulders.

Edward, who had succeeded in making his way thus far unobserved, finding his park empty and the region solitary, ventured on still farther. At last he breaks through the thicket near the oak, sees Ottilia and she sees him; he flies to her and throws himself at her feet. After a long silent pause, in which both seek to collect themselves, he explains to her in a few words why and how he had come here; that he had sent the Major to Charlotte, that their common fate was at this moment deciding. That he had never doubted her love, she also certainly never his—that he now asks her consent.

* * * * * * *

Ottilia spoke thus in haste. She recalled at once to mind all that might occur. She was happy in Edward's presence, but felt that she must send him away. "I beg, I entreat you, dearest," she cried, "return and wait for the Major." "I obey your command," cried Edward, while he first gazed passionately on her and then seized her in his arms. She embraced him with hers, and pressed him most tenderly to her breast. Hope shot, like a star that falls from heaven, away over their heads. They imagined, they believed that they now belonged to each other; they exchanged, for the first time, decided, free kisses, and then, with a violent and painful effort, tore themselves apart.—The sun had set, it was growing dusk—and a damp vapor was rising from the lake. Ottilia stood perplexed and excited. She looked over toward the house on the hill, and thought she saw Char-

---

* See Part First, Book II.—*Trans.*

* Translated by Mr. G. P. Bradford.

lotte's white dress on the balcony. It was a long way round the lake, and she knew how impatiently Charlotte was waiting for the child. She sees the plane trees opposite her; only a piece of water separates her from the path that leads directly up to the building. In her thoughts, as with her eyes, she has already crossed. The risk of venturing on the water with the child vanishes in this extremity. She hastens to the boat, and does not feel that her heart beats violently, that her feet totter, and that her senses threaten to fail her. She springs into the boat, seizes the oar, and pushes off from the land. She is obliged to use force, and repeat the effort. The boat rocks and glides a little way out into the lake; with the child on her left arm, the book in her left hand, and the oar in her right, she staggers, loses her foothold, and falls into the boat. The oar escapes from her hand on one side, and, in her efforts to recover herself, child and book fall on the other into the water. She still grasps the child's clothes; but the helpless position in which she lies hinders her from rising herself. Her right hand, which remains free, is not sufficient to enable her to turn round and raise herself up. At last, however, she succeeds, draws the child out of the water, but its eyes are closed, it has ceased to breathe!

In an instant she recovers entirely her self-possession, but so much the greater is her pain. The boat has drifted nearly to the middle of the lake, the oar is floating far away, she sees no one on the shore, and indeed what would it have availed her to see any one? Separated from all, she floats on the faithless, inaccessible element.

In this emergency she has to look for aid within herself. Often has she heard of the resuscitation of the drowned. On her very birthday she had experienced this herself. She strips the child and dries it with her muslin dress. She tears open her bosom, and bares it for the first time to the free heaven; for the first time she presses a living being to her pure naked breast, alas! no longer a living being! The cold limbs of the unfortunate creature chilled her bosom to her inmost heart. Endless tears gush from her eyes, and impart a semblance of life and warmth to the surface of the stiffened corpse. * * * * * * * She does not give over her efforts, she wraps it in her shawl, and by rubbing, pressing, breathing on it, by kisses and tears, she thinks to supply the place of those remedies that are denied to her, cut off as she is from communication with others.

All in vain! Motionless the child lies in her arms, motionless stands the boat on the watery plain; but even here her beautiful spirit does not leave her helpless. She turns toward heaven. Kneeling she sinks down in the boat, and with both arms raises the stiffened child above her innocent breast, marble-like in whiteness, and alas! in coldness too. With moist eyes she looks upward and invokes help from thence where a tender heart hopes to find the greatest fulness when all else fails.

And not in vain does she turn to the stars, which already are beginning one by one to twinkle forth. A soft wind rises and drives the boat to the plane-trees.

CHAPTER FOURTEENTH.

She hastens to the new building, calls out the surgeon and gives him the child. The ever-ready man treats the delicate body with successive applications according to the customary manner. Ottilia assists him in all; she procures, she fetches, she assumes the care, moving, indeed, as in another world, for the height of misery like the highest happiness changes the face of all things; and only when, after all means have been tried, the worthy man shakes his head, first to her hopeful questions making no answer, then answering with a whispered No, she leaves Charlotte's chamber, where all this had taken place, and hardly has she entered the parlor, when, unable to reach the sofa, she falls on her face, exhausted on the floor.

At this moment they hear Charlotte's carriage drive up to the house. The surgeon earnestly beseeches the bystanders to remain behind. He will go to meet her and prepare her for what has happened; but already she has entered her apartment. She finds Ottilia on the floor, and one of the maids rushes toward her with cries and tears. The surgeon comes in and she learns all at once. But how can she, at once, give up all hope? The experienced, skilful and wise man begs her only not to see the child; and goes away to beguile her with new attempts. She has seated herself on her sofa; Ottilia still lies on the floor, but raised a little so that her head lies sunk on Charlotte's knees. The medical friend goes backward and forward. He appears to be busied about the child, while his care in reality is directed to the women. In this way midnight comes on, the death-stillness becoming always deeper. Charlotte no longer conceals from herself that the child can never be restored to life. She desires to see it. It has been wrapt in clean, warm, woollen cloths, and laid in a basket which they set by her on the sofa,—only the little face is uncovered. Calm and beautiful it lies there.

The news of the melancholy accident had excited a stir in the village and reached the inn. The Major had come up to the house by the well-known way: he went round the house, and meeting with one of the servants who had run out into the out-building to fetch something, he gained more exact information,—and sent for the surgeon to come out. The latter came, astonished at seeing his old patron, informed him of the present state of things, and undertook to prepare Charlotte to see him. He went in, and with this intention began a conversation by which he led her imagination from one object to another, until he at last brought before

Charlotte's mind her friend, intimated his certain sympathy, his nearness to her spirit in his modes of thinking, and at last his actual nearness in person. Enough, she learned that her friend was at the door, was apprized of all that had happened, and wished to be admitted.

The Major entered the room. Charlotte saluted him with a painful smile. He stood before her. * * * * Charlotte pointed to a seat, and thus they sat opposite to each other in silence, the night through. Ottilia still lay quietly on Charlotte's knees; she breathed softly as she slept or seemed to sleep.

The morning dawned, the light was extinguished, and both friends seemed to awake as from a gloomy dream. Charlotte looked at the Major, and said, "Explain to me, my friend, by what providence you came here to take part in this scene of sorrow?"

"This is neither the time nor place," said the Major, answering her as she had spoken in a low, subdued voice, as if they did not wish to waken Ottilia, "this is neither the time nor place for reserve, or delicate management in approaching the subject I would speak of. The situation in which I find you is so awful that the important matter itself, for which I came, loses its value by side of it." He then acknowledged to her very calmly and simply the object of his mission, so far as Edward had part in sending him, the design of his coming so far as his own free will, his own interest was concerned. He presented both with much tenderness and yet with sincerity. Charlotte listened calmly, and appeared to be neither surprised nor displeased at it.

When the Major had ended, Charlotte replied, and in so low a voice that he was obliged to move his seat nearer: "I have never before found myself in circumstances like these; but in similar cases, I have always said to myself, 'how will it be on the morrow?' I feel truly and deeply that the fate of several persons lies in my hands; and what I have to do is clear to me and soon explained. I consent to the separation. I ought to have resolved on it sooner. By my delay and opposition I have been the death of the child. There are certain things which Destiny obstinately determines shall be. In vain her Reason and Virtue, Duty and all that is holy throw themselves in the way. Something shall take place that is right to *it*, though it seems not right to us; and at last it carries its point let us demean ourselves as we may. Yet what do I say? Rather will Destiny again bring about my own wish, my own purpose, against which I inconsiderately acted. Have I not myself already thought of Ottilia and Edward together as a most suitable pair? Have I not even myself sought to bring them near to each other? Were not you yourself, my friend, knowing to this plan? And why could I not distinguish the caprice of a man from true love? Why did I accept his hand, when, as a friend, I might have made him and another wife happy? And consider, too, this unhappy slumberer! I tremble for the moment when she awakes from her half-death-sleep to consciousness. How shall she live, how shall she be consoled, if she cannot hope, by her love, to make good to Edward, what she, as the instrument of the strangest destiny, has robbed him of? And she can restore all to him, by the fondness, the passion with which she loves him. Love can bear all, it can do much more, it can restore all. As for myself, I must not be considered in the present posture of affairs.

"Retire quietly, my dear Major; say to Edward that I consent to the separation; that I give up the whole matter to him and you to manage in your own way. That I am unconcerned about my own future condition, and can be so in every sense. I will sign every paper which shall be brought to me. Only let it not be required of me to co-operate, to consider or advise."

The Major arose. She reached to him her hand over Ottilia. He pressed his lips on that dear hand. "And for myself, what may I hope?" he whispered gently.

"Allow me to remain still in your debt for the answer to that question," replied Charlotte: "we have not deserved to be unhappy; but neither have we deserved to be happy together."
* * * * * * *
Charlotte sat only a few minutes, absorbed in her reflections after the Major had left her; for hardly had he gone when Ottilia raised herself up with her eyes fixed intently on her friend. First she raised herself from her lap, then from the floor, and stood before Charlotte.

"For the second time," thus began the glorious child, with an invincible, graceful earnestness, "for the second time, I experience the same thing. You once said to me, 'It often happens that, at different times in our lives, we meet with like things, occurring in a similar way, and always in important moments.' I now find your remark to be true, and feel impelled to make a confession to you. Shortly after my mother's death, I, then a little child, had moved my stool to your side, you were sitting on a sofa as now, my head lay on your knees. I was neither asleep nor awake, but in a kind of slumber. I heard, very distinctly, everything that went on around me, especially everything that was said; and yet I could not move myself, nor speak, nor, even if I had wished it, so much as signify that I was conscious. At that time you spoke with a friend about me: you lamented my lot — in being left behind in the world, a poor orphan; you painted my dependent condition, and how unhappy it might be with me if a special star of good fortune did not rule over my destiny. I comprehended well and exactly, perhaps too strictly, all that you appeared to wish for me, and to demand of me. I made, hereupon, laws for myself, according to my limited views. By these I have lived for a long time; in conformity with these, what I did or forbore to do was regulated, at that time when you loved me and took care of me; when you received me into your house, and still for some time after.

But I have wandered away from my path, I have broken my laws, I have even lost the feeling of them; and now, after a terrible occurrence, you again give me light on my present situation which is more deplorable than the first. Resting on your lap, half-lifeless, as from a strange world, I hear once more your gentle voice over my ear. I learn the aspect of my condition; I shudder at myself; but, as at that time, so now also, in my half-lifeless sleep, I have marked out for myself my new path. I have resolved as I then did, and what that resolution is you must learn at once. Edward shall never be mine. In a fearful way has God opened my eyes to see in what a crime I am entangled. I will atone for it: and let no one think to turn me away from my purpose. Take then, dearest, your steps accordingly. Recall the Major; write to him that no steps be taken. How distressed was I that I could not move nor stir as he went away. I wished to start up, to cry out, that you might not allow him to go away with hopes so pernicious."

Charlotte saw Ottilia's state, she felt it, but hoped by time and her representations to make some change in her resolutions. Yet when she uttered some words that pointed to a future, to a mitigation of pain, to hope; "No!" cried Ottilia, with exaltation, "seek not to move me, to delude me: the moment I learn that you have consented to a separation, I expiate in that same lake my error, my crime."

CHAPTER FIFTEENTH.

While in a happy, peaceful daily intercourse, relations, friends, household companions, are wont to discuss what happens, or is to happen, more than is necessary or reasonable; while they repeatedly communicate to each other their purposes, undertakings, occupations, and without taking mutual counsel, yet always conduct their whole course of life as if by mutual advice; we find, on the other hand, that in moments of importance — the very occasions in which it would seem that the assistance and support of others are most needed — the individuals draw back into themselves, strive to transact everything for themselves, to conduct everything in their own way, and while they conceal from each other their own individual methods, only the result, the object, and what is attained, become common property once more.

After so many strange and unhappy events, a certain silent seriousness came over the two friends, which manifested itself in a lovely sparing of one another. Quite silently Charlotte had sent the child to the Chapel: there it rested as the first victim of a dark and fearful destiny.

Charlotte turned back as far as was possible toward life, and here she found that Ottilia had the first need of her aid. She occupied herself chiefly with her, without, however suffering it to be marked. She knew how much the heavenly child loved Edward; she had gradually inquired out the scenes that preceded the fatal accident, and learned every circumstance, partly from Ottilia herself, partly through the letters of the Major.

Ottilia, on her part, lightened, to a great extent, Charlotte's momentary life. She was open, talkative even, but never was the conversation of the present or of what had so lately happened. She had always noted, observed — she knew much — all this now turned to account. She entertained and diverted Charlotte, who still cherished in secret the hope of seeing so worthy a pair united. But it was otherwise with Ottilia. She had discovered to her friend the secret of her life-course; she was emancipated from her early narrowness, from servitude. By her repentance, by her resolution, she also felt herself freed from the burden of that guilt, that calamity. She had no longer need to do violence to herself. She had, in the depths of her heart, pardoned herself, but only on condition of complete renunciation, and this condition was unalterable for all the future.

Thus passed some time, and Charlotte felt how very much the house and park, water, rock and tree groups, only renewed, daily, painful feelings in them both. That the scene must be changed was but too clear; in what way to do this was not so easy to decide. Should the two women continue together? Edward's earlier wish seemed to enjoin this; his explanation, his threats to make it necessary. But how could it fail to be seen that both women, with all goodwill, with all reasonableness, found themselves in a painful relation to each other? Their conversation was evasive: often there were some things they chose but to half understand; but oftener an expression was misinterpreted, if not by the understanding, at least by the feelings. They feared to wound each other, and this very fear was the first thing to be wounded and the first to wound.

Did they wish to change the scene, and, at the same time, be separated, at least for a while, from each other, then the old question came up, where should Ottilia go? That rich and distinguished family beforementioned had made fruitless attempts to procure for a very promising daughter, the heiress of the house, female companions who should serve to amuse her and excite her emulation. Already on the last visit of the Baroness, and lately by letters, Charlotte had been urged to send Ottilia there, and she now proposed it again. But Ottilia decidedly refused to go, where she must find what is called the great world. "Suffer me, dear aunt," said she, "in order that I may not appear narrow-minded and wilful, to speak out that which, in any other case, it would be a duty not to speak of, but rather to conceal. A person distinguished by misfortune, even if without any fault, is marked in a fearful way. His presence excites in all who see and notice him a kind of horror. Every one thinks to see in him the dread thing which has been laid on him. Every one is curious and anxious at the same time. In like manner a house, a town in which something dreadful has happened, becomes fearful to every one who enters it. There the light of day shines not so clear, and the stars appear to lose their lustre. How great, and yet excusable perhaps, is the indiscretion of people towards such unhappy persons, their foolish obtrusiveness and awkward kindness! Pardon me that I say it; but I suffered incredibly with that poor maiden when Luciana dragged her out of the secret chambers of the house, kindly occupied herself with her, and, with the best intentions, wished to force her to play and dance. As the poor child, growing ever more frightened, fled and sunk away in a swoon, I caught her in my arms, the company were terrified and excited, and every one then first became really curious about the unhappy creature. I little thought then that a like fate was in reserve for me; but my sympathy, so true and vivid, still survives. I can now turn the compassion I felt for her upon myself, and guard myself from giving occasion to such scenes."

"But nowhere, dear child," replied Charlotte, "will you be able to withdraw yourself from the eyes of men; we have no cloisters, in which formerly an asylum for such feelings was to be found."

"It is not solitude that constitutes the asylum, dear aunt," answered Ottilia. "The refuge most to be prized is to be sought there where we can be active. All expiations, all renunciations are no way adapted to rescue us from a fatal, threatening destiny, if it is determined to pursue us. Only when I am forced, in an idle condition, to serve as a show to the world, does it disturb and pain me. But if I am found, cheerfully occupied with labor, unwearied in my duty, then can I endure the eyes of all, since I need not shrink from those of Heaven." "I am much mistaken," replied Charlotte, "if your inclination does not draw you again to the boarding-school."

"Yes," replied Ottilia, "I do not deny it. I _magine it to myself a happy destination to guide others in the common way, when the path in which we ourselves have been led has been most uncommon. Do we not in history see, that those who, on account of great moral calamities, have withdrawn into the deserts, have by no means remained concealed and buried as they hoped. They have been called back to the world in order to guide the wandering in the right way. And who could do it better than those already initiated in the error-paths of life? They have been called to aid the unhappy, and who are better fitted for this than those whom no earthly woes can any longer reach?"

"You choose a singular destination," answered Charlotte; "I will not oppose you; let it be so, though only, as I hope, for a short time."

"How very much I have to thank you," said Ottilia, "that you are willing to allow me to make this trial, this experience! If I do not flatter myself too much, it shall prove good for me. In that place, I shall be reminded how many trials I endured there, and how little, how utterly insignificant they were, in comparison with those I was afterwards doomed to experience. How serenely shall I look upon the troubles of the young folks, smile at their childish pains, and guide them with gentle hand through all their wanderings! The happy are not fitted to have charge of the happy; it lies in human nature always to require more of one's self and others, the more one has received. Only the self-recovered unhappy know how to cherish for themselves and others the feeling that even a moderate degree of happiness is to be enjoyed with rapture."

"Suffer me," said Charlotte, at last, after more consideration, "to bring forward one more objection which appears to me the most important. It relates not to yourself, but to a third person. The sentiments of the good, sensible, pious assistant are known to you. In the course you take, you will become every day more valuable and indispensable to him. As he already feels that he would not willingly live without you, so certainly, in future, when he has once become accustomed to your co-operation, he will no longer be able, without you, to carry on his affairs. You will thus aid him at first, only to prove an injury to him afterward."

"Destiny has not dealt gently with me," replied Ottilia, "and whoso loves me has, perhaps, nothing better to expect. As our friend is so good and intelligent, I hope, for this very reason, that the feeling of a pure relation to me will be developed in him. He will behold in me a consecrated person, who, in this way alone, perhaps, may hope to counterbalance a fearful evil to herself and others, by devoting herself to the Holy which, invisibly surrounding us, can alone protect us against those terrible powers that are ever pressing upon us."

CONFESSIONS OF A FAIR SAINT.*

TILL my eighth year, I was always a healthy child; but of that period I can recollect no more, than of the day when I was born. About the beginning of my eighth year, I was seized with a hemorrhage; and from that moment my soul became all feeling, all memory. The smallest circumstances of that accident are yet before my eyes, as if they had occurred but yesterday.

During the nine months, which I then spent patiently upon a sick bed, it appears to me, the ground-work of my whole turn of thought was laid; for the first means were then afforded to my spirit of developing itself in its own manner.

I suffered and I loved; this was the peculiar form of my heart. In the most violent fits of

* Wilhelm Meister. T. Carlyle's translation.

coughing, in the depressing pains of fever, I lay quiet, like a snail drawn back within its house: the moment I obtained a respite, I wanted to enjoy something pleasant; and as every other pleasure was denied me, I endeavored to amuse myself with the innocent delights of eye and ear. The people brought me dolls and picture books; and whoever chose to sit beside my bed, was forced to tell me something.

From my mother I rejoiced to hear the Bible histories: and my father entertained me with natural curiosities. He had a very pretty cabinet, from which he brought me first one drawer and then another, as occasion served; showing me the articles, and pointing out their properties. Dried plants and insects, with many kinds of anatomical preparations, such as human skin, bones, mummies and the like, were in succession laid upon the sick bed of the little one; the birds and animals he killed in hunting were shown to me before they passed into the kitchen: and that the Prince of the World might also have a voice in this assembly, my aunt related to me love adventures out of fairy tales. All was accepted, all took root. There were hours, in which I vividly conversed with the invisible Power: I can still repeat some verses, which I then dictated, and my mother wrote.

Frequently I told my father back again, what I had learned from him. I would scarce take any physic, without asking where the simples grew that it was made of, what look they had, what names they bore. Nor had the stories of my aunt alighted upon stony ground. I figured myself out in pretty clothes; and met the most delightful princes, who could find no peace or rest, till they discovered who the unknown Beauty was. One adventure of this kind with a charming little angel, dressed in white with golden wings, who warmly courted me, I dwelt upon so long, that my imagination painted out his form till it was almost visible.

After a year, I was pretty well restored to health; but nothing of the giddiness of childhood remained with me. I could not play with dolls; I longed for beings that were able to return my love. Dogs, cats and birds, of which my father kept a great variety, afforded me delight: but what would I have given for such a creature as my aunt once told me of! It was a lamb, which a peasant girl took up and nourished in a wood; but in the guise of this pretty beast, an enchanted prince was hid; who at length appeared in his native shape, a lovely youth, and recompensed his benefactress by his hand. Such a lamb as this I would have given the world for.

But none was to be had; and as everything about me went along quite naturally and commonly, I by degrees abandoned nearly all my hopes of such a precious treasure. Meanwhile I comforted myself by reading books, in which the strangest incidents were represented. Among them all, my favorite was the *Christian German Hercules;* that devout love history was altogether in my way. Whenever anything befel his dear Valiska, and cruel things befel her, he prayed before he hastened to her aid, and the prayers were standing there *verbatim.* My longing after the Invisible, which I had always dimly felt, was strengthened by such means: for, in short, it was ordained that God should also be my confidant.

As I grew older I continued reading, Heaven knows what, in a chaotic order. The *Roman Octavia* was the book I liked beyond all others. The persecutions of the first Christians, decorated with the charms of a romance, awoke the deepest interest in me.

But my mother now began to murmur at my constant reading; and to humor her, my father took away my books to-day, but gave them back to-morrow. She was wise enough to see that nothing could be done in this way; she next insisted merely that my Bible should be read with equal diligence. To this I was not disinclined: and I accordingly perused the sacred volume with a lively interest. Withal my mother was extremely careful that no books of a corruptive tendency should come into my hands: immodest writings I would, of my own accord, have cast away; for my princes and my princesses were all extremely virtuous.

To my mother, and my zeal for knowledge, it was owing that with all my love of books I also learned to cook; for much was to be seen in cookery. To cut up a hen, a pig, was quite a feast for me. I used to bring the entrails to my father, and he talked with me about them, as if I had been a student of anatomy. With suppressed joy, he would often call me his misfashioned son.

My twelfth year was now behind me. I learned French, dancing and drawing: I received the usual instructions in religion. In the latter many thoughts and feelings were awakened; but nothing properly relating to my own condition. I liked to hear the people speak of God; I was proud that I could speak on these points better than my equals. I zealously read many books, which put me in a case to talk about religion; but it never once occurred to me to think how matters stood with *me*, whether *my* soul was formed according to these holy precepts, whether it was like a glass from which the everlasting sun could be reflected in its glancing. From the first, I had presupposed all this.

My French I learned with eagerness. My teacher was a clever man. He was not a vain empiric, not a dry grammarian: he had learning, he had seen the world. Instructing me in language, he satisfied my zeal for knowledge in a thousand ways. I loved him so much, that I used to wait his coming with a palpitating heart. Drawing was not hard for me: I would have made a greater progress, had my teacher been possessed of head and science; he had only hands and practice.

Dancing was at first my smallest entertainment: my body was too sensitive for this, and I learned it only in the company of my sisters. But our dancing master took a thought of gathering all his scholars, male and female, and giving them a ball. This event gave dancing quite another charm for me.

Amid a throng of boys and girls, the most remarkable were two sons of the Marshal of the Court. The youngest was of my age, the other two years older; they were children of such beauty, that, according to the universal voice, no one had seen their equals. For my part, scarcely had I noticed them, when I lost sight of all the other crowd. From that moment I began to dance with care, and to wish that I could dance with grace. How came it, on the other hand, that these two boys distinguished me from all the rest? No matter; ere an hour had passed, we had become the warmest friends; and our little entertainment did not end, till we had fixed upon the time and place where we were next to meet. What a joy for me! And how charmed was I next morning, when both of them inquired about my health, each in a gallant note, accompanied with a nosegay! I have never since felt as I then did! Compliment was met by compliment; letter answered letter. The church and the public walks were grown a rendezvous; our young acquaintances, in all their little parties, now invited us together; while, at the same time, we were sly enough to veil the business from our parents, so that they could see no more of it than we thought good.

Thus had I at once got a pair of lovers. I had yet decided upon neither; they both pleased me, and we did extremely well together. All at once, the eldest of the two fell very sick. I myself had frequently been sick; and thus I was enabled, by despatching to him many little dainties and delicacies suited for a sick person, to afford some solace to the sufferer. His parents thankfully acknowledged my attention: in compliance with the prayer of their beloved son, they invited me, with all my sisters, to their house, so soon as he had risen from his sick bed. The tenderness, which he displayed on meeting me, was not the feeling of a child; from that day I gave the preference to him. He warned me to keep our secret from his brother; but the flame could no longer be concealed; and the jealousy of the younger completed our romance. He played us a thousand tricks; eager to annihilate our joys, he but increased the passion he was seeking to destroy.

At last, then, I had actually found the wished-for lamb; and this attachment acted on me like my sickness; it made me calm, and drew me back from noisy pleasures. I was solitary, I was moved; and thoughts of God again occurred to me. He was again my confidant, and I well remember with what tears I often prayed for this poor boy, who still continued sickly.

The more childishness there was in this adventure, the more did it contribute to the forming of my heart. Our French teacher had now turned us from translating, into daily writing him some letter of our own invention. I brought my little history to market, shrouded in the names of Phyllis and Damon. The old man soon saw through it; and to render me communicative, praised my labor very much. I still waxed bolder; came openly out with the affair, adhering even in the minute details to truth. I do not now remember what the passage was at which he took occasion to remark: "How pretty, how natural it is! But the good Phyllis had better have a care; the thing may soon grow serious."

It vexed me, that he did not look upon the matter as already serious; and I asked him, with an air of pique, what he meant by serious. He did not force me to repeat the question; he explained himself so clearly, that I scarce could hide my terror. Yet, as anger came along with it, as I took it ill that he should entertain such thoughts, I kept myself composed, I tried to justify my nymph; and said with glowing cheeks: "But, sir, Phyllis is an honorable girl."

He was rogue enough to banter me about my honorable heroine. While we were speaking French, he played upon the word *honnête*, and hunted the honorableness of Phyllis over all its meanings. I felt the ridicule of this, and was extremely puzzled. He, not to frighten me, broke off; but afterwards he often led the conversation to such topics. Plays and little histories, which I was reading and translating with him, gave him frequent opportunity to show how feeble a security our boasted virtue was against the rules of inclination. I no longer contradicted him; but I was in secret scandalized; and his remarks became a burden to me.

With my worthy Damon, too, I by degrees fell out of all connection. The chicanery of the younger boy destroyed our intercourse. Soon after, both these blooming creatures died. I lamented sore; however, in a short time I forgot.

But Phyllis rapidly increased in stature; was altogether healthy, and began to see the world. The hereditary Prince now married; and a short time after, on his father's death, began his rule. Court and town were in the liveliest movement: my curiosity had copious nourishment. There were plays and balls, with all their usual accompaniments; and though my parents kept retired as much as possible, they were obliged to show themselves at court, where I of course was introduced. Strangers were pouring in from every side; high company was in every house; even to us some cavaliers were recommended, others introduced; and at my uncle's, men of every nation might be met with.

My honest Mentor still continued, in a modest and yet striking way, to warn me; and I to take it ill of him in secret. With regard to his assertion, that women under every circumstance were weak, I did not feel at all convinced; and here perhaps I was in the right, and my Mentor in the wrong; but he spoke so earnestly, that once I grew afraid he might be right, and said to him.

with much vivacity: "Since the danger is so great, and the human heart so weak, I will pray to God that He may keep me."

This simple answer seemed to please him, for he praised my purpose; but on my side it was anything but seriously meant. It was in truth but an empty word; for my feelings towards the Invisible were almost totally extinguished. The hurry and the crowd with which I was surrounded dissipated my attention, and carried me along as in a powerful stream. These were the emptiest years of my life. All day long to speak of nothing, to have no solid thought; never to do anything but revel: such was my employment. On my beloved books I never once bestowed a thought. The people whom I lived among had not the slightest tinge of literature or science: they were German courtiers; a class of men at that time altogether destitute of mental culture.

Such society, it may be thought, must naturally have led me to the brink of ruin. I lived away in mere corporeal cheerfulness; I never took myself to task, I never prayed, I never thought about myself or God. Yet I look upon it as a providential guidance, that none of these many handsome, rich and well-dressed men could take my fancy. They were rakes, and did not hide it; this scared me back: their speech was frequently adorned with double meanings; this offended me, and made me act with coldness towards them. Many times their improprieties surpassed belief; and I did not prevent myself from being rude.

Besides, my ancient counsellor had once in confidence contrived to tell me, that, with the greater part of these lewd fellows, health as well as virtue was in danger. I now shuddered at the sight of them; I was afraid, if one of them in any way approached too near me. I would not touch their cups or glasses, even the chairs they had been sitting on. Thus morally and physically I remained apart from them; all the compliments they paid me I haughtily accepted of, as incense that was due.

Among the strangers then resident among us, there was one young man peculiarly distinguished, whom in sport we used to call Narciss. He had gained a reputation in the diplomatic line; and among the various changes now occurring at our court, he was in hopes of meeting with some advantageous place. He soon became acquainted with my father: his acquirements and manners opened for him the way to a select society of most accomplished men. My father often spoke in praise of him: his figure, which was very handsome, would have been more pleasing, had it not been for a certain air of self-complacency, which breathed from all his carriage. I had seen him; I thought well of him; but we had never spoken.

At a great ball, where we chanced to be in company, I danced a minuet along with him; but this too passed without results. The more violent dances, in compliance with my father's will, who felt anxieties about my health, I was accustomed to avoid: in the present case, when these came on, I retired to an adjoining room, and began to talk with certain of my friends, elderly ladies, who had set themselves to cards.

Narciss, who had jigged it for a while, at last came into the room in which I was; and having got the better of a bleeding at the nose, that had overtaken him in dancing, he began to speak with me about a multitude of things. In half an hour, the talk had grown so interesting, that neither of us could endure to think of dancing any more. We were rallied by our friends for this; but we did not let their bantering disturb us. Next evening, we recommenced our conversation, and were very careful not to hurt our health.

The acquaintance then was made. Narciss was often with my sisters and myself; and I now once more began to reckon over and consider what I knew, what I thought of, what I had felt, and what I could express myself about in conversation. My new friend had mingled in the best society; besides the department of history and politics, with every part of which he was familiar, he had gained extensive literary knowledge; there was nothing new that issued from the press, especially in France, that he was unacquainted with. He brought or sent me many a pleasant book; but this we kept as secret as forbidden love. Learned women had been made ridiculous, well-informed women were with difficulty tolerated; apparently, because it would have been uncourtly to put so many ill-informed gentlemen to shame. Even my father, much as he delighted in this new opportunity of cultivating my mind, expressly stipulated that our literary commerce should remain a secret.

Thus our intercourse continued almost for a year and a day; and still I could not say that in any wise Narciss had ever shown me aught of love or tenderness. He was always complaisant and kind; but manifested nothing like attachment: on the contrary, he even seemed to be in some degree affected by the charms of my youngest sister, who was then extremely beautiful. In sport, he gave her many little friendly names, out of foreign tongues; for he could speak two or three of these extremely well: and loved to mix their idiomatic phrases with his German. Such compliments she did not answer very liberally; she was entangled in a different noose; and being very sharp, while he was very sensitive, the two were often quarrelling about trifles. With my mother and my aunt, he kept himself on very pleasant terms; and thus by gradual advances, he was grown to be a member of the family.

Who knows how long we might have lived in this way, had a curious accident not altered our relations all at once. My sisters and I were invited to a certain house, to which we did not like to go. The company was too mixed; and persons of the stupidest if not the rudest stamp were often to be met with there. Narciss, on this occasion, was invited also; and on his account I felt inclined to go, for I was sure of finding one at least with whom I could converse as I desired. Even at table, we had many things to suffer; for several of the gentlemen had drunk too much: and after rising from it, they insisted on a game at forfeits. It went on with great vivacity and tumult. Narciss had lost a forfeit: they ordered him, by way of penalty, to whisper something pleasant in the ear of every member of the company. It seems, he staid too long beside my neighbor, the lady of a Captain. The latter on a sudden struck him such a box with his fist, that the powder flew about my eyes and blinded me. When I had cleared my sight, and in some degree recovered from my terror, I saw that both of them had drawn their swords. Narciss was bleeding; and the other, mad with wine and rage and jealousy, could scarcely be held back by all the company: I seized Narciss, led him by the arm up stairs; and as I did not think my friend even here in safety from his frantic enemy, I shut the door and bolted it.

Neither of us looked upon the wound as serious; for a slight cut across the hand was all we saw. Soon, however, I perceived a stream of blood running down his back, and a deep wound appeared upon his head. I now began to be afraid. I hastened to the lobby, to get help; but I could see no person; every one had staid below to calm the raving captain. At last a daughter of the family came skipping up; her mirth annoyed me; she was like to die with laughing at the bedlam spectacle. I conjured her for the sake of Heaven to get a surgeon; and she, in her wild way, sprang down the stair to fetch me one herself.

Returning to my wounded friend, I bound my handkerchief about his hand; and a neckkerchief, that was hanging on the door, about his head. He was still bleeding copiously: he now turned pale, and seemed as if he were about to faint. There was none at hand to aid me: I very freely put my arm around him; patted his cheek, and tried to cheer him up by little flatteries. It seemed to act upon him like a spiritual remedy; he kept his senses, but he sat as pale as death.

At last the active housewife entered: it is easy to conceive her terror when she saw my friend in this predicament, lying in my arms, and both of us bestreamed with blood. No one had supposed that he was wounded; all imagined I had carried him away in safety.

Now smelling-bottles, wine, and everything that could support and stimulate, were copiously produced. The surgeon also came; and I might easily have been dispensed with. Narciss, however, held me firmly by the hand; I would have staid without holding. During the dressing of his wounds, I continued wetting his lips with wine; I minded not though all the company were now about us. The surgeon having finished, his patient took a mute but tender leave of me, and was conducted home.

The mistress of the house now led me to her bed-room: she was forced to strip me altogether. * * * No portion of my clothes could be put on again; and as the people of the house were all either less or larger than myself, I was taken home in a strange disguise. My parents were, of course, astonished. They felt exceedingly indignant at my fright, at the wounds of their friend, at the captain's madness, at the whole occurrence. A very little would have made my father send a challenge to the captain, that he might avenge his friend without delay. He blamed the gentlemen that had been there, because they had not punished such a murderous attempt upon the spot: for it was but too clear, that the captain, instantly on striking, had pulled out his sword and wounded the other from behind. The cut across the hand had not been given, until Narciss himself was grasping at his sword. I felt unspeakably affected and altered: or, how shall I express it? The passion, which was sleeping at the deepest bottom of my heart, had at once broken loose, like a flame on getting air. And if joy and pleasure are well suited, for the first producing and the silent nourishing of love, yet this passion, bold by nature, is most easily impelled by terror to decide and to declare itself. My mother gave some physic to her little flurried daughter, and made her go to bed. With the earliest morrow, my father hastened to Narciss, whom he found lying very sick of a wound fever.

He told me little of what passed between them, but tried to quiet me about the probable results of this event. They were now considering whether an apology should be accepted of, whether the affair should go before a court of justice, and many other points of that description. I knew my father too well to doubt that he would be averse to see the matter end without a duel: but I held my peace; for I had learned from him before, that women should not meddle in such things. For the rest, it did not strike me as if anything had passed between the friends, in which my interests were specially concerned: but my father soon communicated to my mother the purport of their further conversation. Narciss, he said, appeared to be exceedingly affected at the help afforded by me; had embraced him, declared himself my debtor for ever, signified that he desired no happiness except what he could share with me, and concluded by entreating that he might presume to ask my hand. All this mamma repeated to me, but subjoined the safe reflection, that "as for what was said in the first agitation of mind in such a case, there was little trust to be placed in it." "Of course, none," I answered with affected coldness; though all the while I was feeling Heaven knows what and how.

Narciss continued sick for two months; owing to the wound in his right hand, he could not even write. Yet, in the meantime, he showed me his regard by the most obliging courtesies. All these unusual attentions I combined with what my mother had disclosed to me; and constantly my head was full of fancies. The whole city talked of the occurrence. With me they spoke of it in a peculiar tone; they drew inferences which, greatly as I struggled to avoid them, touched me very close. What had formerly been habitude and trifling, was now grown seriousness and inclination. The anxiety in which I lived was the more violent, the more carefully I studied to conceal it from every one. The idea of losing him affrighted me; the possibility of any closer union made me tremble. For a half-prudent girl, there is really something awful in the thought of marriage.

By such incessant agitations, I was once more led to recollect myself. The gaudy imagery of a thoughtless life, which used to hover day and night before my eyes, was at once blown away. My soul again began to wake: but the greatly interrupted intimacy with my Invisible Friend was not so easy to renew. We still continued at a frigid distance: it was again something; but little to the times of old.

A duel had been fought, and the captain been severely wounded, before I ever heard of it. The public feeling was in all senses strong on the side of my lover, who at length again appeared upon the scene. But first of all, he came with his head tied up and his arm in a sling, to visit us. How my heart beat while he was there! The whole family was present; general thanks and compliments were all that passed on either side; Narciss, however, found an opportunity to show some secret tokens of his love to me, by which means my inquietude was but increased. After his recovery, he visited us throughout the winter on the former footing; and in spite of all the soft private marks of tenderness, which he contrived to give me, the whole affair remained unsettled, undiscussed.

In this manner was I kept in constant practice. I could not trust my thoughts to mortal; and from God I was too far removed. Him I had quite forgot for four wild years: I now again began at times to think of him; but our acquaintance was grown cool; they were visits of mere ceremony, which I paid him; and as, besides, in paying them, I used to dress myself in fine apparel, to set before him self-complacently my virtue, honor and superiorities to others, he did not seem to notice me or know me in that finery.

A courtier would have been exceedingly distressed, if the prince who held his fortune in his hands had treated him in this way: but for me I did not sorrow at it. I had what I required, health and conveniences; if God should please to think of me, well; if not, I reckoned I had done my duty.

This, in truth, I did not think at that period: yet it was the true figure of my soul. But, to change and purify my feelings, preparations were already made.

The spring came on: Narciss once visited me, unannounced, and at a time when I happened to be quite alone. He now appeared in the character of lover; and asked me if I could bestow on him my heart, and when he should obtain some lucrative and honorable place, along with it my hand.

He had been received into our service: but at first they kept him back, and would not rapidly promote him, because they dreaded his ambition. Having some little fortune of his own, he was left with a slender salary.

Notwithstanding my regard for him, I knew that he was not a man to treat with altogether frankly. I drew up, therefore, and referred him to my father. About my father's mind he did not seem to doubt; but wanted previously to be at one with me, upon the spot. I at last said, yes; but stipulated as an indispensable condition that my parents should concur. He then spoke formally with both of them; they signified their satisfaction; mutual promises were given on the faith of his advancement, which it was expected would be speedy. Sisters and aunts were informed of this arrangement, and the strictest secrecy enjoined on them.

Thus from a lover I had got a bridegroom. The difference between the two soon showed itself to be considerable. If any one could change the lovers of all honorable maidens into bridegrooms, it would be a kindness to our sex, even though marriage should not follow the connection. The love between two persons does not lessen by the change, but it becomes more reasonable. Innumerable little follies, all coquetries and caprices, disappear. If the bridegroom tells us, that we please him better in a morning cap than in the finest head-dress, no discreet young woman will disturb herself about her hair-dressing; and nothing is more natural than that he too should think solidly, and rather wish to form a housewife for himself than a gaudy doll for others. And thus it is in every province of the business.

Should a young woman of this kind be fortunate enough to have a bridegroom who possesses understanding and acquirements, she learns from him more than universities and foreign lands can teach. She not only willingly receives instruction, when he offers it, but she endeavors to elicit more and more from him. Love makes much that was impossible possible. By degrees too that subjection, so necessary and so graceful for the female sex, begins: the bridegroom does not govern like the husband; he only asks; but his mistress seeks to notice what he wants, and to offer it before he asks it.

So did experience teach me what I would not for much have missed. I was happy; truly happy, as woman could be in the world; that is to say, for a while.

The *Serious* of my old French teacher now occurred to me; as well as the defence, which I had once suggested in regard to it.

With God I had again become a little more

acquainted. He had given me a bridegroom whom I loved; and for this I felt some thankfulness. Earthly love itself concentrated my soul, and put its powers in motion; nor did it contradict my intercourse with God. I naturally complained to him of what alarmed me: but I did not perceive that I myself was wishing and desiring it. In my own eyes, I was strong; I did not pray: "Lead us not into temptation!" My thoughts were far beyond temptation. In this flimsy tinsel-work of virtue I came to God: he did not drive me back. On the smallest movement towards him, he left a soft impression in my soul; and this impression caused me always to return.

Except Narciss, the world was altogether dead to me; excepting him, there was nothing in it that had any charm. Even my love for dress was but the wish to please him: if I knew that he was not to see me, I could spend no care upon it. I liked to dance; but if he was not beside me, it seemed as if I could not bear the motion. At a brilliant festival, if he was not invited, I could neither take the trouble of providing new things, nor of putting on the old according to the mode. To me they were alike agreeable, or rather I might say, alike burdensome. I used to reckon such an evening very fairly spent, when I could join myself to any ancient card-party, though formerly I was without the smallest taste for such things; and if some old acquaintance came and rallied me about it, I would smile, perhaps for the first time all that night. So likewise it was with promenades, and every social entertainment that can be imagined:

> Him had I chosen from all others,
> His would I be, and not another's;
> To me his love was all in all.

Thus I was often solitary in the midst of company; and real solitude was generally acceptable to me. But my busy soul could neither sleep nor dream; I felt and thought, and longed for the ability to speak about my feelings and my thoughts with God. From this were feelings of another sort unfolded; but they did not contradict the former: my affection to Narciss accorded with the universal scheme of nature; it nowhere hindered the performance of a duty. They did not contradict each other, yet they were immensely different. Narciss was the only living form which hovered in my mind, and to which my love was all directed; but the other feeling was not directed towards any form, and yet it was unspeakably agreeable. I no longer have it, I no longer can impart it.

My lover, whom I used to trust with all my secrets, did not know of this. I soon discovered that he thought far otherwise: he often gave me writings, which opposed with light and heavy weapons all that can be called connection with the Invisible. I used to read the books, because they came from him: but at the end, I knew no word of all that had been argued in them.

Nor in regard to sciences and knowledge was there any want of contradiction in our conduct. He did as all men do, he mocked at learned women; and yet he kept continually instructing me. He used to speak with me on all subjects, law excepted; and while constantly procuring books of every kind for me, he frequently repeated the uncertain precept, "That a lady ought to keep the knowledge she might have, more secret than the Calvinist his creed in Catholic countries." And while I, by natural consequence, endeavored not to show myself more wise or learned than formerly before the world, Narciss himself was commonly the first who yielded to the vanity of speaking about me and my superiorities.

A nobleman of high repute, and at that time valued for his influence, his talents and accomplishments, was living at our Court with great applause. He bestowed especial notice on Narciss, whom he kept continually about him. They had once an argument about the virtue of women. Narciss repeated to me what had passed between them; I was not wanting with my observations; and my friend required of me a written essay on the subject. I could write French fluently enough; I laid a good foundation with my teacher. My correspondence with Narciss was likewise carried on in French: except in French books, there was then no elegant instruction to be had. My essay pleased the Count; I was obliged to let him have some little songs, which I had lately been composing. In short, Narciss appeared to revel without stint in the renown of his beloved: and the story, to his great contentment, ended with a French epistle in heroic verse, which the Count transmitted to him on departing; in which their argument was mentioned, and my friend reminded of his happiness in being destined, after all his doubts and errors, to learn most certainly what virtue was, in the arms of a virtuous and charming wife.

He showed this poem first of all to me, and then to almost every one; each thinking on the matter what he pleased. Thus did he act in several cases; every stranger, whom he valued, must be made acquainted in our house.

A noble family was staying for a season in the place, to profit by the skill of our physician. In this house too, Narciss was looked on as a son: he introduced me there; we found among these worthy persons the most pleasant entertainment for the mind and heart. Even the common pastimes of society appeared less empty here than elsewhere. All knew how matters stood with us: they treated us as circumstances would allow, and left the main relation unalluded to. I mention this one family; because, in the after period of my life, it had a powerful influence upon me.

Almost a year of our connection had elapsed; and along with it, our spring was over. The summer came, and all grew drier and more earnest.

By several unexpected deaths, some offices were rendered vacant, which Narciss might make pretensions to. The instant was at hand, in which my whole destiny must be decided; and while Narciss and all our friends were making every effort to efface some impressions, which obstructed him at Court, and to obtain for him the wished-for situation, I turned with my request to my Invisible Friend. I was received so kindly, that I gladly came again. I confessed without disguise my wish that Narciss might obtain the place: but my prayer was not importunate; and I did not require that it should happen for the sake of my petition.

The place was obtained by a far inferior competitor. I was dreadfully troubled at this news; I hastened to my room, the door of which I locked behind me. The first fit of grief went off in a shower of tears; the next thought was, "Yet it was not by chance that it happened;" and instantly I formed the resolution to be well contented with it, seeing even this apparent evil would be for my true advantage. The softest emotions then pressed in upon me, and divided all the clouds of sorrow. I felt that, with help like this, there was nothing one might not endure. At dinner I appeared quite cheerful, to the great astonishment of all the house.

Narciss had less internal force than I, and I was called upon to comfort him. In his family, too, he had many crosses to encounter, some of which afflicted him considerably; and, such true confidence subsisting between us, he intrusted me with all. His negotiations for entering on foreign service were not more fortunate; the whole of this I deeply felt on his account and mine; the whole of it I ultimately carried to the place, where my petitions had already been so well received.

The softer these experiences were, the oftener did I endeavor to renew them; I hoped continually to meet with comfort, where I had so often met with it. Yet I did not always meet with it: I was as one that goes to warm him in the sunshine, while there is something standing in the way that makes a shadow. "What is this?" I asked myself. I traced the matter zealously, and soon perceived that it all depended on the situation of my soul: if this was not turned in the straightest direction towards God, I still continued cold; I did not feel his counter influence; I could obtain no answer. The second question was: "What hinders this direction?" Here I was in a wide field; I perplexed myself in an inquiry, which lasted nearly all the second year of my attachment to Narciss. I might have ended the investigation sooner; for it was not long till I had got upon the proper trace; but I would not confess it, and I sought a thousand outlets.

I very soon discovered that the straight direction of my soul was marred by foolish dissipations, and employment with unworthy things. The How and the Where were clear enough to me. Yet by what means could I help myself,

or extricate my mind from the calls of a world where everything was either cold indifference or hot insanity? Gladly would I have left things standing as they were, and lived from day to day, floating down with the stream, like other people whom I saw quite happy: but I durst not; my inmost feelings contradicted me too often. Yet if I determined to renounce society, and alter my relations to others, it was not in my power. I was hemmed in as by a ring drawn round me: certain connections I could not dissolve; and, in the matter, which lay nearest to my heart, fatalities accumulated and oppressed me more and more. I often went to bed with tears; and, after a sleepless night, arose again with tears: I required some strong support; and God would not vouchsafe it me, while I was running with the cap and bells.

I proceeded now to estimate my doings, all and each; dancing and play were first put upon their trial. Never was there anything spoken, thought, or written, for or against these practices, which I did not examine, talk of, read, weigh, reject, aggravate, and plague myself about. If I gave up these habits, I was certain that Narciss would be offended; for he was excessively afraid of the ridicule, which any look of straight-laced conscientiousness gives one in the eyes of the world. And doing what I now looked upon as folly, noxious folly, out of no taste of my own, but merely to gratify him, it all grew dreadfully irksome to me.

Without disagreeable prolixities and repetitions, it is not in my power to represent what pains I took, in trying so to counteract those occupations, which distracted my attention and disturbed my peace of mind, that my heart, in spite of them, might still be open to the influences of the Invisible Being. But at last with pain I was compelled to feel, that in this way the quarrel could not be composed. For no sooner had I clothed myself in the garment of folly, than it came to be something more than a mask; that foolishness pierced and penetrated me through and through.

May I here overstep the province of a mere historical detail, and offer one or two remarks on what was then taking place within me? What could it be, which so changed my tastes and feelings, that, in my twenty-second year, nay earlier, I lost all relish for the recreations with which people of that age are harmlessly delighted? Why were they not harmless for me? I may answer, Just because they were not harmless; because I was not, like others of my years, unacquainted with my soul. No! I knew from experiences, which had reached me unsought, that there are loftier emotions, which afford us a contentment such as it is vain to seek in the amusement of the world; and that in these higher joys there is also kept a secret treasure for strengthening the spirit in misfortune.

But the pleasures of society, the dissipations of youth, must needs have had a powerful charm for me, since it was not in my power to engage in them without participation, to act among them as if they were not there. How many things could I now do, if I liked, with entire coldness, which then dazzled and confounded me, nay threatened to obtain the mastery over me! Here there could no medium be observed; either those delicious amusements, or my nourishing and quickening internal emotions, must be given up.

But in my soul, the strife had, without my own consciousness, already been decided. Even if there still was anything within me that longed for earthly pleasures, I was now become unfitted for enjoying them. Much as a man might hanker after wine, all desire of drinking would forsake him, if he should be placed among full barrels in a cellar, where the foul air was like to suffocate him. Free air is more than wine: this I felt but too keenly; and from the first, it would have cost me little studying to prefer the good to the delightful, if the fear of losing the affection of Narciss had not restrained me. But at last, when after many thousand struggles, and thoughts continually renewed, I began to cast a steady eye upon the bond which held me to him, I discovered that it was but weak, that it might be torn asunder. I at once perceived it to be only as a glass bell, which shut me up in the exhausted airless space : One bold stroke to break the bell in pieces, and thou art delivered!

No sooner thought than tried. I drew off the mask, and on all occasions acted as my heart directed. Narciss I still cordially loved : but the thermometer, which formerly had stood in hot water, was now hanging in the natural air; it could rise no higher than the warmth of the atmosphere directed.

Unhappily it cooled very much. Narciss drew back, and began to assume a distant air: this was at his option; but my thermometer descended as he drew back. Our family observed this; questioned me, and seemed to be surprised. I explained to them with stout defiance, that heretofore I had made abundant sacrifices; that I was ready, still further and to the end of my life, to share all crosses that befell him; but that I required full freedom in my conduct, that my doings and avoidings must depend upon my own conviction; that indeed I would never bigotedly cleave to my own opinion, but on the other hand would willingly be reasoned with; yet, as it concerned my own happiness, the decision must proceed from myself, and be liable to no manner of constraint. The greatest physician could not move me by his reasonings to take an article of food, which perhaps was altogether wholesome and agreeable to many, so soon as my experience had shown that on all occasions it was noxious to me; as I might produce coffee for an instance; and just as little, nay still less, would I have any sort of conduct, which misled me, preached up and demonstrated upon me as morally profitable.

Having so long prepared myself in silence, these debates were rather pleasant than vexatious to me. I gave vent to my soul; I felt the whole worth of my determination. I yielded not a hair's breadth; and those to whom I owed no filial respect were sharply handled and despatched. In the family I soon prevailed. My mother from her youth had entertained these sentiments, though in her they had never reached maturity; for no necessity had pressed upon her, and exalted her courage to achieve her purpose. She rejoiced in beholding her silent wishes fulfilled through me. My younger sisters seemed to join themselves with me; the second was attentive and quiet. Our aunt had the most to object. The arguments, which she employed appeared to her irrefragable, and they were irrefragable, being altogether common-place. At last I was obliged to show her, that she had no voice in the affair in any sense; and after this, she seldom signified that she persisted in her views. She was indeed the only person who observed this passage close at hand, without in some degree experiencing its influence. I do not calumniate her, when I say that she had no character, and the most limited ideas.

My father acted altogether in his own way. He spoke not much, but often, with me on the matter: his arguments were rational; and being *his* arguments, they could not be impugned. It was only the deep feeling of my right that gave me strength to dispute against him. But the scenes soon changed; I was forced to make appeal to his heart. Straitened by his understanding, I came out with the most pathetic pleadings. I gave free course to my tongue and to my tears. I showed him how much I loved Narciss; how much constraint I had for two years been enduring; how certain I was of being in the right; that I was ready to testify that certainty by the loss of my beloved bridegroom and prospective happiness; nay, if it were necessary, by the loss of all that I possessed on earth; that I would rather leave my native country, my parents and my friends, and beg my bread in foreign lands, than act against these dictates of my conscience. He concealed his emotion; he said nothing on the subject for a while, and at last he openly declared in my favor.

During all this time Narciss forbore to visit us; and my father now gave up the weekly club, of which the former was a member. The business made a noise at court, and in the town. People talked about it, as is common in such cases, which the public takes a vehement interest in, because its sentence has usurped an influence on the resolutions of weak minds. I knew enough about the world to understand, that one's conduct is often censured by the very persons who would have advised it had one consulted them : and independently of this, with my internal composure, I should have looked on all such transitory speculations just as if they had not been.

On the other hand, I hindered not myself from yielding to my inclination for Narciss. To me he had become invisible, and to him my feelings had not altered. I loved him tenderly; as it were anew, and much more steadfastly than formerly. If he chose to leave my conscience undisturbed, then I was his: wanting this condition, I would have refused a kingdom with him. For several months, I bore these feelings and these thoughts about with me; and finding, at last, that I was calm and strong enough to go peacefully and firmly to work, I wrote him a polite but not a tender note, inquiring why he never came to see me.

As I knew his manner of avoiding to explain himself in little matters, but of silently doing what seemed good to him, I purposely urged him in the present instance. I got a long, and as it seemed to me a pitiful reply, in a vague style and unmeaning phrases, stating, that without a better place, he could not fix himself and offer me his hand; that I best knew how hardly it had fared with him hitherto; that as he was afraid lest a fruitless intercourse, so long continued, might prove hurtful to my reputation, I would give him leave to continue at his present distance; so soon as it was in his power to make me happy, he would look upon the word which he had given me as sacred.

I answered him upon the spot, that as our intercourse was known to all the world, it might perhaps be rather late to spare my reputation; for which, at any rate, my conscience and my innocence were the surest pledges: however, that I hereby freely gave him back his word, and hoped the change would prove a happy one for him. The same hour I received a short reply, which was, in all essential particulars, entirely synonymous with the first. He adhered to his former statement, that so soon as he obtained a situation, he would ask me if I pleased to share his fortune with him.

This I interpreted as meaning simply nothing. I signified to my relations and acquaintances, that the affair was altogether settled; and it was so actually. Having, nine months afterwards, obtained the much desired preferment, he offered me his hand; but under the condition, that as the wife of a man who must keep house like other people, I should alter my opinions. I returned him many thanks: and hastened with my heart and mind away from this transaction; as one hastens from the play-house when the curtain falls. And as he, a short time afterwards, found a rich and advantageous match, a thing now easy for him; and as I now knew him to be happy in the way he liked, my own tranquillity was quite complete.

I must not pass in silence the fact, that several times before he got a place, and after it, there were respectable proposals made to me; which, however, I declined without the smallest hesitation, much as my father and my mother could have wished for more compliance on my part.

At length, after a stormy March and April, the loveliest May weather seemed to be allotted me. With good health, I enjoyed an indescribable composure of mind: look around me as I pleased, my loss appeared a gain to me. Young and full of sensibility, I thought the universe a thousand times more beautiful than formerly, when I required to have society and play, that in the fair garden tedium might not overtake me. And now, as I did not conceal my piety, I likewise took heart to own my love for the sciences and arts. I drew, painted, read; and found enow of people to support me: instead of the great world which I had left, or rather which had left me, a smaller one was formed about me, which was infinitely richer and more entertaining. I had a turn for social life; and I do not deny that, on giving up my old acquaintances, I trembled at the thought of solitude. I now found myself abundantly, perhaps excessively, indemnified. My acquaintances ere long were very numerous; not at home only, but likewise among people at a distance. My story had been noised abroad; and many persons felt a curiosity to see the woman who had valued God above her bridegroom. There was a certain pious tone to be observed at that time generally over Germany. In the families of several counts and princes, a care for the welfare of the soul had been awakened. Nor were there wanting noblemen who showed a like attention; while in the inferior classes, sentiments of this kind were diffused on every side.

The noble family, whom I made mention of above, now drew me nearer to them. They had, in the meanwhile, gathered strength; several of their relations having settled in the town. These estimable persons courted my familiarity, as I did theirs. They had high connections; I became acquainted, in their house, with a great part of the princes, counts, and lords of the Empire. My sentiments were not concealed from any one; they might be honored or be tolerated; I obtained my object; none attacked me.

There was yet another way, by which I was again led back into the world. About this period, a step-brother of my father, who till now had never visited the house except in passing, staid with us for a considerable time. He had left the service of his court, where he enjoyed great influence and honor, simply because all matters were not managed quite according to his mind. His intellect was just, his character was rigid. In these points he was very like my father; only the latter had withal a certain touch of softness, which enabled him with greater ease to yield a little in affairs, and though not to do, yet to permit, some things against his own conviction; and then to evaporate his anger at them, either in silence by himself, or in confidence amid his family. My uncle was a great deal younger; and his independence of spirit had been favored by his outward circumstances. His mother had been very rich; and he still had large possessions to expect from her near and distant relatives: so he needed no foreign increase; whereas my father, with his moderate fortune, was bound to his place by the consideration of his salary.

My uncle had become still more unbending from domestic sufferings. He had early lost an amiable wife and a hopeful son; and from that time, he appeared to wish to push away from him everything that did not hang upon his individual will.

In our family, it was whispered now and then with some complacency, that probably he would not wed again, and so we children might anticipate inheriting his fortune. I paid small regard to this; but the demeanor of the rest was not a little modified by their hopes. In his own imperturbable firmness of character, my uncle had grown into the habit of never contradicting any one in conversation. On the other hand, he listened with a friendly air to every one's opinion; and would himself elucidate and strengthen it by instances and reasons of his own. All who did not know him fancied that he thought as they did: for he was possessed of a preponderating intellect; and could transport himself into the mental state of any man, and imitate his manner of conceiving. With me he did not prosper quite so well: for here the question was about emotions, of which he had not any glimpse; and with whatever tolerance, and sympathy, and rationality, he spoke about my sentiments, it was palpable to me that he had not the slightest notion of what formed the ground of all my conduct.

With all his secrecy, we by and by found out the aim of his unusual stay with us. He had, as we at length discovered, cast his eyes upon our youngest sister, with the view of giving her in marriage, and rendering her happy as he pleased; and certainly considering her personal and mental attractions, particularly when a handsome fortune was laid into the scale along with them, she might pretend to the first matches. His feelings towards me he likewise showed us pantomimically, by procuring me a post of Canoness, the income of which I very soon began to draw.

My sister was not so contented with his care as I. She now disclosed to me a tender secret, which hitherto she very wisely had kept back; fearing, as in truth it happened, that I would by all means counsel her against connection with a man who was not suited to her. I did my utmost, and succeeded. The purpose of my uncle was too serious and too distinct; the prospect for my sister, with her worldly views, was too delightful to be thwarted by a passion which her own understanding disapproved; she mustered force enough to give it up.

On her ceasing to resist the gentle guidance of my uncle, the foundation of his plan was quickly laid. She was appointed Maid of Honor at a neighboring court, where he could commit her to the oversight and the instructions of a lady, his friend, who presided there as Governess with great applause. I accompanied her to the place of her new abode. Both of us had reason to be satisfied with the reception which we met with; and frequently I could not help in secret smiling at the character, which now as Canoness, as young and pious Canoness, I was enacting in the world.

In earlier times, a situation such as this would have confused me dreadfully; perhaps have turned my head; but now, in midst of all the splendors that surrounded me, I felt extremely cool. With great quietness, I let them frizzle me, and deck me out for hours; and thought no more of it than that my place required me to wear that gala livery. In the thronged saloons, I spoke with all and each, though no shape or character among them made impression on me. On returning to my house, nearly all the feeling I brought back with me was that of tired limbs. Yet my understanding drew advantage from the multitude of persons whom I saw; and I grew acquainted with some ladies, patterns of every virtue, of a noble and good demeanor; particularly with the Governess, under whom my sister was to have the happiness of being formed.

At my return, hower, the consequences of this journey, in regard to health, were found to be less favorable. With the greatest temperance, the strictest diet, I had not been as I used to be, completely mistress of my time and strength. Food, motion, rising and going to sleep, dressing and visiting, had not depended, as at home, on my own conveniency and will. In the circle of social life, you cannot stop without a breach of courtesy: all that was needful I had willingly performed; because I looked upon it as my duty, because I knew that it would soon be over, and because I felt myself completely healthy. Yet this unusual restless life must have affected me more strongly than I was aware of. Scarcely had I reached our house, and cheered my parents with a comfortable narrative, when a hemorrhage attacked me, which, although it was not dangerous or lasting, yet left a weakness after it perceptible for many a day.

Here, then, I had another lesson to repeat. I did it joyfully. Nothing bound me to the world; and I was to be convinced that here the true good was never to be found: so I waited in the cheerfullest and meekest state; and after having abdicated life, I was retained in it.

A new trial was awaiting me: my mother took a painful and oppressive ailment, which she had to bear five years, before she paid the debt of nature. All this time we were sharply proved. Often when her terror grew too strong, she would make us all be summoned in the night before her bed, that so at least she might be busied if not bettered by our presence. The load grew heavier, nay scarcely to be borne, when my father too became unwell. From his youth, he frequently had violent headaches; which, however, at the longest, never used to last beyond six-and-thirty hours. But now they were continual; and when they mounted to a high degree of pain, his moanings tore my very heart. It was in these tempestuous seasons that I chiefly felt my bodily weakness; because it kept me from my holiest and dearest duties, or rendered the performance of them hard to an extreme degree.

It was now that I could try whether the path, which I had chosen, was the path of fantasy or truth; whether I had merely thought as others showed me, or the object of my trust had a reality. To my unspeakable support, I always found the latter. The straight direction of my heart to God, the fellowship of the "Beloved Ones"* I had sought and found; and this was what made all things light to me. As a traveller in the dark, my soul, when all was pressing on me from without, hastened to the place of refuge, and never did it return empty.

In later times, some champions of religion, who seem to be animated more by zeal than feeling for it, have required of their brethren to produce examples of prayers actually heard; apparently, because they wished for seal and writing, that they might proceed against their adversaries diplomatically and juridically. How unknown must the true feeling of the matter be to these persons! how few real experiences can they themselves have made!

I can say that I never returned empty, when in straits and oppression I called on God. This is saying infinitely much; more I must not and cannot say. Important as each experience was at the critical moment for myself, the recital of them would be flat, improbable and insignificant, were I to specify the separate cases. Happy was I, that a thousand little incidents in combination proved, as clearly as the drawing of my breath proved me to be living, that I was not without God in the world. He was near to me, I was before him. This is what, with a diligent avoidance of all theological systematic terms, I can with the greatest truth declare.

Much do I wish that in those times too I had been entirely without system. But which of us arrives early at the happiness of being conscious of his individual self in its own pure combination, without extraneous forms? I was in earnest with religion. I timidly trusted in the judgments of others; I entirely gave in to the Hallean system of conversion; but my nature would by no means tally with it.

According to this scheme of doctrine, the alteration of the heart must begin with a deep terror on account of sin; the heart in this agony must recognise in a less or greater degree the punishment which it has merited, must get a foretaste of Hell, and so embitter the delight of sin. At last it feels a very palpable assurance of grace; which, however, in its progress often fades away, and must again be sought with earnest prayer.

Of all this no jot occurred with me. When I sought God sincerely, he let himself be found of me, and did not reproach me about bygone things. On looking back, I saw well enough where I had been unworthy, where I still was so; but the confession of my faults was altogether without terror. Not for a moment did the fear of Hell occur to me: nay, the very notion of a wicked Spirit, and a place of punishment and torment after death, could nowise gain admission to the circle of my thoughts. I looked upon the men, who lived without God, whose hearts were shut against the trust in and the love of the Invisible, as already so unhappy that a hell and external pains appeared to promise rather an alleviation than an aggravation of their misery. I had but to turn my eyes upon the persons in this world, who in their breasts gave scope to hateful feelings; who hardened their hearts against the Good of whatever kind, and strove to force the Evil on themselves and others; who shut their eyes by day, that so they might deny the shining of the sun: How unutterably wretched did these persons seem to me! Who could have formed a Hell to make their situation worse?

This mood of mind continued in me, without change, for half a score of years. It maintained itself through many trials; even at the moving death-bed of my beloved mother. I was frank enough on this occasion not to hide my comfortable frame of mind from certain pious but rigorously orthodox people; and I had to suffer many a friendly admonition on that score. They reckoned they were just in season for explaining with what earnestness one ought to strive to lay a right foundation in the days of health and youth.

In earnestness I too determined not to fail. For the moment, I allowed myself to be convinced; and fain would I have grown for life, distressed and full of fears. But what was my surprise on finding absolutely that I could not! When I thought of God, I was cheerful and contented: even at the painful end of my dear mother, I did not shudder at the thought of death. Yet I learned many and far other things than my uncalled teachers thought of, in these solemn hours.

By degrees I grew to doubt the dictates of so many famous people, and retained my sentiments in silence. A certain lady of my friends, to whom I had at first disclosed too much, insisted still on interfering with my business. Of her too I was forced to rid myself; at last I firmly told her, that she might spare herself this labor, as I did not need her counsel; that I knew my God, and would have no guide but him. She felt exceedingly offended; I believe she never quite forgave me.

This determination to withdraw from the advices and the influence of my friends, in spiritual matters, produced the consequence, that also in my temporal affairs I gained sufficient courage to obey my own persuasions. But for the assistance of my faithful invisible Leader, I could

---

* So in the original.—*Ed.*

not have prospered here. I am still gratefully astonished at his wise and happy guidance. No one knew how matters stood with me; even I myself did not know.

The thing, the wicked and inexplicable thing, which separates us from the Being to whom we owe our life, and in whom all that deserves the name of life must find its nourishment; the thing, which we call Sin, I yet knew nothing of.

In my intercourse with my invisible Friend, I felt the sweetest enjoyment of all my powers. My desire of constantly enjoying this felicity was so predominant, that I abandoned without hesitation whatever marred our intercourse; and here experience was my surest teacher. But it was with me as with sick persons, who have no medicine, and try to help themselves by diet. Something is accomplished, but far from enough.

I could not always live in solitude; though in it I found the best preservative against the dissipation of my thoughts. On returning to the tumult, the impression it produced upon me was the deeper for my previous loneliness. My most peculiar advantage lay in this, that love for quiet was my ruling passion, and that in the end I still drew back to it. I perceived, as in a kind of twilight, my weakness and my misery; and tried to save myself by avoiding danger and exposure.

For seven years I had used my dietetic scheme. I held myself not wicked, and I thought my state desirable. But for some peculiar circumstances and occurrences, I had remained in this position: it was by a curious path that I got further. Contrary to the advice of all my friends, I entered on a new connection. Their objections made me pause at first. I turned to my invisible Leader, and, as he permitted me, I went forward without fear.

A man of spirit, heart and talents, had bought a property beside us. Among the strangers whom I grew acquainted with, were this person and his family. In our manners, domestic economy and habits, we accorded well; and thus we soon approximated to each other.

Philo, as I propose to call him, was already middle aged: in certain matters he was highly serviceable to my father, whose strength was now decaying. He soon became the friend of the family; and finding in me, as he was pleased to say, a person free alike from the extravagance and emptiness of the great world, and from the narrowness and aridness of the still world in the country, he courted intimacy with me, and ere long we were in one another's confidence. To me he was very pleasing and useful.

Though I did not feel the smallest inclination or capacity for mingling in public business, or seeking any influence on it, yet I liked to hear about such matters, liked to know whatever happened far and near. Of worldly things, I loved to get a clear though unconcerned perception: feeling, sympathy, affection, I reserved for God, for my people and my friends.

The latter were, if I may say so, jealous of Philo, in my new connection with him. In more than one sense, they were right in warning me about it. I suffered much in secret; for even I could not consider their remonstrances as altogether empty or selfish. I had been accustomed, from of old, to give a reason for my views and conduct; but in this case my conviction would not follow. I prayed to God, that here as elsewhere he would warn, restrain and guide me; and as my heart on this did not dissuade me, I went forward on my way with comfort.

Philo on the whole had a remote resemblance to Narciss; only a pious education had more enlivened and concentrated his feelings. He had less vanity, more character: and, in business, if Narciss was delicate, exact, persevering, indefatigable, the other was clear, sharp, quick and capable of working with incredible ease. By means of him, I learned the secret history of almost every noble personage with whose exterior I had grown acquainted in society. It was pleasant for me to behold the tumult, off my watch-tower, from afar. Philo could now hide nothing from me: he confided to me by degrees his own concerns both inward and outward. I was in fear because of him; for I foresaw certain circumstances and entanglements; and the mischief came more speedily than I had looked for. There were some confessions he had still kept back; and even at last he told me only what enabled me to guess the worst.

What an effect had this upon my heart! I attained experiences, which to me were altogether new. With infinite sorrow I beheld an Agathon, who, being educated in the groves of Delphi, yet owed his school fee, which he was now obliged to pay with its accumulated interest; and this Agathon was my especial friend. My sympathy was lively and complete; I suffered with him; both of us were in the strangest state.

After having long occupied myself with the temper of his mind, I at last turned round to contemplate my own. The thought: 'Thou art no better than he,' rose like a little cloud before me, and gradually expanded till it darkened all my soul.

I now not only thought myself no better than he; I felt this, and felt it as I should not wish to do again. Nor was it any transitory mood. For more than a year, I was constrained to feel that, if an unseen hand had not restrained me, I might have become a Girard, a Cartouche, a Damiens, or any wretch you can suppose. The tendencies to this I traced too clearly in my heart. Heavens! what a discovery!

If hitherto I never had been able, in the faintest degree, to recognise in myself the reality of sin by experience, its possibility was now become apparent to me by anticipation, in the most tremendous manner. And yet I knew not evil; I but feared it: I felt that I might be guilty, and could not accuse myself of being so.

Deeply as I was convinced that such a temperament of soul, as I now saw mine to be, could never be adapted for that union with the invisible Being, which I hoped for after death; I did not, in the smallest, fear that I should finally be separated from him. With all the wickedness, which I discovered in my heart, I still loved *Him;* I hated what I felt, nay, wished to hate it still more earnestly; my whole desire was to be delivered from this sickness, and this tendency to sickness; and I was persuaded that the great Physician would at length vouchsafe his help.

The sole question was: What medicine will cure this malady? The practice of virtue? This I could not for a moment think. For ten years, I had already practised more than mere virtue; and the horrors now first discovered had, all the while, lain hidden at the bottom of my soul. Might they not have broken out with me, as they did with David when he looked on Bathsheba? Yet was not he a friend of God; and was not I assured in my inmost heart that God was my friend?

Was it then an unavoidable infirmity of human nature? Must we just content ourselves in feeling and acknowledging the sovereignty of inclination? And, with the best will, is there nothing left for us but to abhor the fault we have committed, and on the like occasion to commit it again?

From systems of morality I could obtain no comfort. Neither their severity, by which they try to bend our inclinations, nor their attractiveness, by which they try to place our inclinations on the side of virtue, gave me any satisfaction. The fundamental notions, which I had imbibed from intercourse with my invisible Friend, were of far higher value to me.

Once, while I was studying the songs composed by David after that tremendous fall, it struck me very much that he traced his indwelling corruption even in the substance out of which he had been shaped; yet that he wished to be freed from sin, and that he earnestly entreated for a pure heart.

But how was this to be attained? The answer from the Scripture I was well aware of: 'That the blood of Jesus cleanseth us from all sin' was a Bible truth, which I had long known. But now for the first time, I observed that as yet I had never understood this oft-repeated saying. The questions: What does it mean? How is it to be? were day and night working out their answers in me. At last I thought I saw as by a gleam of light, that what I sought was to be found in the incarnation of the everlasting Word, by whom all things, even we ourselves, were made. That the Eternal descended as an inhabitant to the depths in which we dwell, which he surveys and comprehends; that he passed through our lot from stage to stage, from conception and birth to the grave; that by this marvellous circuit he again mounted to those shining Heights, whither we too must rise in order to be happy: all this was revealed to me, as in a dawning remoteness.

Oh! Why must we, in speaking of such things, make use of figures, which can only indicate external situations! Where is there in His eyes aught high or deep, aught dark or clear? It is we only that have an Under and Above, a night and day. And even for this did He become like us, since otherwise we could have had no part in him.

But how shall we obtain a share in this priceless benefit? 'By faith,' the Scripture says. And what is faith? To consider the account of an event as true—what help can this afford me? I must be enabled to appropriate its effects, its consequences. This appropriating faith must be a state of mind peculiar, and to the natural man, unknown.

'Now, gracious Father, grant me faith!' so prayed I once in the deepest heaviness of heart. I was leaning on a little table, where I sat; my tear-stained countenance was hidden in my hands. I was now in the condition, in which we seldom are, but in which we are required to be, if God is to regard our prayers.

O that I could but paint what I felt then! A sudden force drew my soul to the cross where Jesus once expired: it was a sudden force, a pull, I cannot name it otherwise, such as leads our soul to an absent loved one: an approximation, which perhaps is far more real and true than we imagine. So did my soul approach the Son of Man, who died upon the cross; and that instant did I know what faith was.

'This is faith!' said I; and started up as half affrighted. I now endeavored to get certain of my feeling, of my view; and shortly I became convinced that my spirit had acquired a power of soaring upwards, which was altogether new to it.

Words fail us in describing such emotions. I could most distinctly separate them from all fantasy: they were entirely without fantasy, without image; yet they gave us just the certainty of their referring to some object, which our imagination gives us when it paints for us the features of an absent lover.

When the first rapture was over, I observed that my present state of soul had formerly been known to me; only I had never felt it in such strength; I had never held it fast, never made it mine. I believe, indeed, that every human soul at intervals feels something of it. Doubtless it is this which teaches every mortal that there is a God.

With this power, which used to visit me from time to time, I had hitherto been well content: and had not, by a singular arrangement of events, that unexpected sorrow weighed upon me for a twelvemonth; had not my own ability and strength on this occasion altogether lost its credit with me; I perhaps might have been satisfied with this condition all my days.

But now, since that great moment, I had as it were got wings. I could mount aloft above what used to threaten me; as the bird can fly singing and with ease across the fiercest stream, while the little dog stands anxiously baying on the bank.

My joy was indescribable; and though I did not mention it to any one, my people soon observed an unaccustomed cheerfulness in me, and could not understand the reason of my joy. Had I but forever held my peace, and tried to nourish this serene temper in my soul! Had I not allowed myself to be misled by circumstances, so as to reveal my secret! Then might I again have saved myself a long and tedious circuit.

As in the previous ten years of my Christian course, this necessary force had not existed in my soul, I had just been in the case of other worthy people; had helped myself by keeping my fancy always full of images, which had some reference to God: a practice so far truly useful; for noxious images and their baneful consequences are by that means kept away. Often too our spirit seizes one or other of these spiritual images, and mounts with it a little way upwards; like a young bird fluttering from twig to twig.

Images and impressions pointing towards God are presented to us by the institutions of the Church, by organs, bells, singing, and particularly by the preaching of our pastors. Of these I used to be unspeakably desirous: no weather, no bodily weakness could keep me back from church; the sound of the Sunday bells was the only thing that rendered me impatient on a sick bed. Our head Court chaplain, a gifted man, I heard with great delight: his colleagues too I liked; and I could pick the golden apple of the word from the common fruit, with which on earthen platters it was mingled. With public ordinances, all sorts of private exercises were combined; and these too but nourished fancy and a finer kind of sense. I was so accustomed to this track, I reverenced it so much, that even now no higher one occurred to me. For my soul has only feelers, and not eyes; it gropes, but does not see: Ah! that it could get eyes and look!

On this occasion, therefore, I again went with a longing mind to sermon: but alas, what happened! I no longer found what I was wont to find. These preachers were blunting their teeth upon the shell, while I enjoyed the kernel. I soon grew weary of them; and I had already been so spoiled, that I could not be content with the little they afforded me. I required images, I wanted impressions from without; and reckoned it a pure spiritual desire that I felt.

Philo's parents had been in connection with the Herrnhuther community: in his library were many writings of Count Zinzendorf's. He had spoken with me very candidly and clearly on the subject more than once; inviting me to turn over one or two of these treatises, if it were but for the sake of studying a psychological phenomenon. I looked upon the Count, and those that followed him, as very heterodox: and so the Ebersdorf hymn-book, which my friend had pressed upon me, lay unread.

However, in my total destitution of external excitements for my soul, I opened up the hymn-book as it were by chance; and found in it, to my astonishment, some songs which actually, though under a fantastic form, appeared to shadow what I felt. The originality and the simplicity of their expression drew me on. It seemed to be peculiar emotions expressed in a peculiar way; no school technology suggested any notion of formality or common-place. I was persuaded that these people felt as I did: I was very happy to lay hold of here and there a stanza in their songs, to fix it in my memory, and carry it about with me for days.

Since the moment, when the truth had been revealed to me, some three months had in this way passed along. At last I came to the determination of disclosing everything to Philo, and asking him to let me have those writings, about which I was now become immoderately curious. Accordingly I did so, notwithstanding there was something in my heart, which earnestly dissuaded me.

I circumstantially related to him all the story; and, as he was a leading person in it, and my narrative conveyed the sharpest reprimand on him, he felt surprised and moved to an extreme degree. He melted into tears. I rejoiced at this; believing that in his mind also a full and fundamental change had taken place.

He provided me with all the writings that I could require; and now I had excess of nourishment for my imagination. I made rapid progress in the Zinzendorfic mode of thought and speech. And be it not supposed that I am yet incapable of prizing the peculiar turn and manner of the Count. I willingly do justice to him; he is no empty fantast; he speaks of mighty truths, and mostly in a bold figurative style; the people who despise him know not either how to value or discriminate his qualities.

At that time I became exceedingly attached to him. Had I been mistress of myself, I would certainly have left my friends and country, and gone to join him. We should infallibly have understood each other, and should hardly have agreed together long.

Thanks to my better genius that now kept me so confined by my domestic duties! I reckoned it a distant journey if I visited the garden. The charge of my aged weakly father afforded me employment enough, and in hours of recreation I had Fancy to procure me pastime. The only mortal whom I saw was Philo: he was highly valued by my father; but with me, his intimacy had been cooled a little by the late explanation. Its influence on him had not penetrated deep; and as some attempts to talk in my dialect had not succeeded with him, he avoided touching on this subject; and the more readily, as his extensive knowledge put it always in his power to introduce new topics in his conversation.

I was thus a Herrnhuth sister on my own footing. I had especially to hide this new turn of my temper and my inclinations from the head Court chaplain, whom, as my father confessor, I had much cause to honor; and whose high merits, his extreme aversion to the Herrnhuth community did not diminish in my eyes even then. Unhappily this worthy person had to suffer many troubles on account of me and others.

Several years before he had become acquainted with an upright pious gentleman, residing in a distant quarter; and had long continued in unbroken correspondence with him as with one who truly sought God. How painful was it to the spiritual leader, when this gentleman subsequently joined himself to the community of Herrnhuth, where he lived for a long while! How delightful, on the other hand, when at length he quarrelled with the brethren; determined to settle in our neighborhood; and seemed once more to yield himself completely to the guidance of his ancient friend!

The stranger was presented, as in triumph, by the upper Pastor to all the chosen lambs of his fold. To our house alone he was not introduced, because my father did not now see company. The gentleman obtained no little approbation: he combined the polish of the court with the winning manner of the Brethren; and having also many fine qualities by nature, he soon became the favorite saint with all who knew him; a result at which the chaplain was exceedingly contented. But, alas! it was merely in externals that the gentleman had split with the community; in his heart he was yet entirely a Herrnhuther. He was, in truth, concerned for the reality of the matter: but yet the gimcracks, which the Count had stuck around it, were at the same time quite adapted to his taste. Besides he had now become accustomed to this mode of speaking and conceiving; and if he had to hide it carefully from his ancient friend, it but became the more necessary for him, whenever he could get a knot of trusty persons round him, to come forth with his couplets, litanies, and little figures; in which, as might have been supposed, he met with great applause.

I knew nothing of the whole affair, and dawdled forward in my separate path. For a long time, we continued mutually unknown.

At a leisure hour, I happened once to visit a lady who was sick. I found several acquaintances along with her; and soon perceived that my appearance had cut short their conversation. I affected not to notice anything; but saw ere long, with great surprise, some Herrnhuth figures stuck upon the wall in elegant frames. Quickly comprehending what had passed before my entrance, I expressed my pleasure at the sight in a few suitable verses.

Conceive the wonder of my friends! We explained ourselves; instantly we were agreed, and in each other's confidence.

I henceforth often sought for opportunities of going out. Unhappily I found them only once in three or four weeks: yet I grew acquainted with our gentleman apostle, and by degrees with all the body. I visited their meetings, when I could: with my social disposition, it was quite delightful for me to communicate to others, and to hear from them, the feelings which till now I had conceived and harbored by myself.

But I was not so completely taken with my friends, as not to see that few of them could really feel the sense of those affecting words and emblems; and that from these they drew as little benefit, as formerly they did from the symbolic language of the Church. Yet, notwithstanding, I went on with them, not letting this disturb me. I thought I was not called to search and try the hearts of others; even although by long-continued guiltless exercisings, I had been prepared for something better. I had my share of profit from our meetings: in speaking, I insisted on attending to the sense and spirit, which, in things so delicate, is rather apt to be disguised by words than indicated by them; and for the rest I left with silent toleration each to act according to his own conviction.

These quiet times of secret social joy were shortly followed by storms of open bickering and contradiction; contentions which excited great commotion, I might almost say occasioned not a little scandal, in the Court and town. The period was now arrived when our Chaplain, that stout gainsayer of the Herrnhuth Brethren, must discover, to his deep, but I trust, sanctified humiliation, that his best and once most zealous hearers were now all leaning to the side of that Community. He was excessively provoked: in the first moments, he forgot all moderation: and could not, even if he had inclined it, afterwards retract. Violent debates took place; in which most happily I was not mentioned; both as I was but an accidental member of that hated body; and as our zealous preacher could not spare my father and my friend, in certain civic matters. With silent satisfaction, I continued neutral. It was irksome to me to converse about such feelings and objects, even with well affected people, if they could not penetrate the deepest sense, and lingered merely on the surface. But to strive with adversaries about things on which even friends could scarcely understand each other seemed to me unprofitable, nay pernicious. For I could soon perceive that many amiable noblemen, who on this occurrence could not shut their hearts to enmity and hatred, had very soon passed over to injustice; and, in order to defend an outward form, had almost sacrificed their most substantial duties.

Greatly as the worthy clergyman might, in the present case, be wrong; much as others tried to irritate me at him, I could never hesitate to give him my sincere respect. I knew him well: I could candidly transport myself into his way of looking at these matters. I have never seen a man without his weaknesses; only, in distinguished men they strike us more. We wish, and will at all rates have it, that persons privileged as they are should at the same time pay no tribute, no tax whatever. I honored him as a superior man: and hoped to use the influence of my calm neutrality to bring about, if not a peace, at least a truce. I know not what my efforts might have done; but God concluded the affair more briefly, and took the Chaplain to Himself. On his coffin, all wept who lately had been striving with him about words. His uprightness, his fear of God, no one ever had doubted.

I too was ere long forced to lay aside this Herrnhuth doll work, which, by means of these contentions, now appeared before me in a rather different light. Our uncle had in silence executed his intentions with my sister. He offered her a young man of rank and fortune as a bridegroom; and showed, by a rich dowry, what might be expected of himself. My father joyfully consented: my sister was free and forewarned, she did not hesitate to change her state. The bridal was appointed at my uncle's castle: family and friends were all invited; and we came in the highest spirits.

For the first time in my life, the aspect of a house excited admiration in me. I had often heard of my uncle's taste, of his Italian architect, of his collections and his library; but, comparing this with what I had already seen, I had formed a very vague and fluctuating picture of it in my thoughts. Great, accordingly, was my surprise at the earnest and harmonious impression which I felt on entering the house, and which every hall and chamber deepened. If elsewhere pomp and decoration had but dissipated my attention, I felt here concentrated and drawn back upon myself. In like manner, the preparatives for these solemnities and festivals produced a silent pleasure, by their air of dignity and splendor; and to me it seemed as inconceivable, that one man could have invented and arranged the whole of this as that more than one could have combined to labor in so high a spirit. Yet withal the landlord and his people were entirely natural; not a trace of stiffness or of empty form was to be seen.

The wedding itself was managed in a striking way: an exquisite strain of vocal music came upon us by surprise; and the clergyman went through the ceremony with a singular solemnity. I was standing by Philo at the time; and instead of a congratulation, he whispered in my ear: "When I saw your sister give away her hand, I felt as if a stream of boiling water had been poured upon me." "Why so?" I inquired. "It is always the way with me," said he, "when I behold two people joined." I laughed at him; but I have often since had cause to recollect his words.

The revel of the party, among whom were many young people, looked particularly glittering and airy, as everything around us was dignified and serious. The furniture, plate, table ware, and table ornaments, accorded with the general whole; and if in other houses, the furnisher and architect seemed to have proceeded from the same school, it here appeared that both furnisher and butler had taken lessons from the architect.

We staid together several days; and our intelligent and gifted landlord had variedly provided for the entertainment of his guests. I did not in the present case repeat the melancholy proof, which has so often in my life been forced upon me, how unhappily a large mixed company are situated, when, altogether left to themselves, they must select the most general and vapid pastimes, that the blockheads of the party may not want amusement, however it may fare with those that are not such.

My uncle had arranged it altogether differently. Two or three Marshals, if I may call them so, had been appointed by him: one of them had charge of providing entertainment for the young. Dances, excursions, little games, were of his invention, and under his direction; and as young people take delight in being out of doors, and do not fear the influences of the air, the garden and the garden hall had been assigned to them; while some additional pavilions and galleries had been erected and appended to the latter, formed of boards and canvas merely, but in such proportions, so elegant and noble, they reminded one of nothing else but stone and marble.

How rare is a festivity, in which the person who invites the guests feels also that it is his duty to provide for their conveniences and wants of every kind!

Hunting and card parties, short promenades, opportunities for trustful private conversations, were afforded to the elder persons: and whoever wished to go earliest to bed were certain to be lodged the most remote from noise.

By this happy order, the space in which we lived appeared to be a little world; and yet, considered narrowly, the castle was not large; without an accurate knowledge of it, and without the spirit of its owner, it would have been impossible to keep so many people in it, and to quarter each according to his humor.

As the aspect of a well-formed person pleases us, so also does a fair establishment, by means of which the presence of a rational intelligent mind is made apparent to us. We feel a joy in entering even a cleanly house, though it may be tasteless in its structure and its decorations; because it shows us the presence of a person cultivated in at least one sense. Doubly pleasing is it, therefore, when, from a human dwelling, the spirit of a higher though merely sensual culture speaks to us.

All this was vividly impressed upon my observation at my uncle's castle. I had heard and read much of art; Philo, too, was a lover of pictures, and had a fine collection; I myself had often practised drawing; but I had been too deeply occupied with my emotions for tasting aught that did not bear upon the one thing needful, which alone I was bent on carrying to perfection; and besides, such objects of art as I had seen appeared, like all other worldly objects, to distract my thoughts. But now for the first time, outward things had led me back upon myself: I now first perceived the difference between the natural charm of the nightingale's song, and that of a four-voice anthem pealed from the expressive organs of men.

I did not hide my joy at this discovery from my uncle; who, when all the rest were settled at their posts, was wont to come and talk with me in private. He spoke with great modesty of what he had produced and made his own; with great decision, of the views in which it had been gathered and arranged: and I could easily observe that he spoke with a forbearance towards me; seeming, in his usual way, to rate the excellence, of which he was himself possessed, below the excellence, which, in my opinion, was the best and properest.

"If we can conceive it possible," he once observed, "that the Creator of the world himself assumed the form of his creature, and lived in that manner for a time upon the earth, this creature must appear to us of infinite perfection, because susceptible of such a combination with its Maker. Hence, in our idea of man there can be no inconsistency with our idea of God: and if we often feel a certain disagreement with Him, and remoteness from Him, it is but the more on that account our duty, not like advocates of the wicked Spirit, to keep our eyes continually upon the nakedness and weakness of our nature; but rather to seek out every property and beauty, by which our pretension to a similarity with the Divinity may be made good."

I smiled and answered: "Do not make me blush, dear uncle, by your complaisance in talking in my language! What you have to say is of such importance to me, that I wish to hear it in your own most peculiar style; and then what parts of it I cannot quite appropriate, I will endeavor to translate."

"I may continue," he replied, "in my own most peculiar way, without any alteration of my tone. Man's highest merit always is as much as possible to rule external circumstances, and as little as possible to let himself be ruled by them. Life lies before us, as a huge quarry lies before the architect: he deserves not the name of architect, except when, out of this fortuitous mass, he can combine, with the greatest economy, suitableness and durability, some form, the pattern of which originated in his spirit. All things without us, nay, I may add, all things on us, are mere elements; but deep within us, lies the creative force, which out of these can produce what they were meant to be; and which leaves us neither sleep nor rest, till in one way or another, without us or on us, this has been produced. You, my dear niece, have, it may be, chosen the better part: you have striven to bring your moral being, your earnest lovely nature to accordance with itself and with the Highest; but neither ought we to be blamed, when we strive to get acquainted with the sentient man in all his comprehensiveness, and to bring about an active harmony among his powers."

By such discoursing, we in time grew more familiar; and I begged of him to speak with me as with himself, omitting every sort of condescension. "Do not think," replied my uncle, "that I flatter you, when I commend your mode of thinking and of acting. I reverence the individual who understands distinctly what he wishes; who unweariedly advances, who knows the means conducive to his object, and can seize and use them. How far his object may be great or little, may merit praise or censure, is the next consideration with me. Believe me, love, most part of all the misery and mischief, of all that is denominated evil, in the world, arises from the fact that men are too remiss to get a proper knowledge of their aims, and when they do know them to work intensely in attaining them. They seem to me like people who have taken up a notion, that they must and will erect a tower, and who yet expend on the foundation no more stones and labor than would be sufficient for a hut. If you, my friend, whose highest want it was to perfect and unfold your moral nature, had, instead of those bold and noble sacrifices, merely trimmed between your duties to yourself and to your family, your bridegroom, or perhaps your husband, you must have lived in constant contradiction with your feelings, and never could have had a peaceful moment."

"You employ the word sacrifice," I answered here; "and I have often thought that to a higher purpose, as to a divinity, we offer up, by way of sacrifice, a thing of smaller value; feeling, like persons who should willingly and gladly bring a favorite lamb to the altar, for the health of a beloved father."

"Whatever it may be," said he, "reason or feeling that commands us to give up the one thing for the other, to choose the one before the other, decision and perseverance are, in my opinion, the most noble qualities of man. You cannot have the ware and the money both at once: and he who always hankers for the ware without having heart enough to give the money for it, is no better off than he who repents him of the purchase when the ware is in his hands. But I am far from blaming men on this account: it is not they who are to blame: it is the difficult entangled situation they are in; they know not how to guide themselves in its perplexities. Thus, for instance, you will on the average find fewer bad economists in the country than in towns, and fewer again in small towns than in great; and why? Man is intended for a limited condition; objects that are simple, near, determinate, he comprehends, and he becomes accustomed to employ such means as are at hand; but on entering a wider field, he now knows neither what he would nor what he should; and it amounts to quite the same, whether his attention is distracted by the multitude of objects, or is overpowered by their magnitude and dignity. It is always a misfortune for him, when he is induced to struggle after anything, with which he cannot join himself by some regular exertion of his powers.

"Certainly," pursued he, "without earnestness there is nothing to be done in life: yet among the people whom we name cultivated men, but little earnestness is to be found: in labors and employments, in arts, nay, even in recreations, they proceed, if I may say so, with a sort of self-defence; they live, as they read a heap of newspapers, only to be done with it; they remind one of that young Englishman at Rome, who told, with a contented air, one evening in some company, that 'to-day he had despatched six churches and two galleries.' They wish to know and learn a multitude of things, and exactly those with which they have the least concern; and they never see that hunger is not stilled by snapping at the air. When I become acquainted with a man, my first inquiry is: With what does he employ himself, and how, and with what degree of perseverance? The answer regulates the interest which I shall take in him for life."

"My dear uncle," I replied, "you are perhaps too rigorous; you perhaps withdraw your helping hand from here and there a worthy man to whom you might be useful."

"Can it be imputed as a fault," said he, "to one who has so long and vainly labored on them and about them? How much we have to suffer in our youth from men, who think they are inviting us to a delightful pleasure party, when they undertake to introduce us to the Danaides or Sysiphus! Heaven be praised! I have rid myself of these people: if one of them unfortunately comes within my sphere, instantly, in the politest manner, I compliment him out again. It is from these people that you hear the bitterest complaints about the miserable course of things, the aridity of science, the levity of artists, the emptiness of poets, and much more of that sort. They do not recollect that they, and the many like them, are the very persons who would never read a book, which had been written just as they require it; that true poetry is alien to them; that even an excellent work of art can never gain their approbation save by means of prejudice. But let us now break off; for this is not the time to rail or to complain."

He directed my attention to the different pictures, which were fixed upon the wall: my eye dwelt on those whose look was beautiful or subject striking. This he permitted for a while; at last he said: "Bestow a little notice on the spirit, which is manifested in these other works. Good minds delight to trace the finger of the Deity in nature: why not likewise pay some small regard to the hand of his imitator?" He then led my observation to some unobtrusive figures; endeavoring to make me understand, that it was the history of art alone, which could give us an idea of the worth and dignity of any work of art; that we should know the weary steps of mere handicraft and mechanism, over which the man of talents has arisen in the course of centuries, before we can conceive how it is possible for the man of genius to move with airy freedom, on the pinnacle whose very aspect makes us giddy.

With this view, he had formed a beautiful series of works; and whilst he explained it, I could not help conceiving that I saw before me a similitude of moral culture. When I expressed my thoughts to him, he answered: "You are altogether in the right; and we see from this, that those do not act properly, who follow moral cultivation by itself exclusively. On the contrary, it will be found that he whose spirit strives for a development of this kind, has likewise every reason, at the same time, to improve his finer sentient powers, that so he may not run the risk of sinking from his moral height, by giving way to the enticements of a lawless fancy, and degrading his moral nature by allowing it to take delight in tasteless baubles, if not in something worse."

I did not in the least suspect him of levelling at me; but I felt myself struck, when I thought how many insipidities had been among the songs that used to edify me; and how little favor the figures, which had joined themselves to my religious ideas, would have found in the eyes of my uncle.

Philo, in the mean time, had frequently been busied in the library: he now took me along with him. We admired the selection as well as the multitude of books. They had been collected on my uncle's general principle; there were none among them to be found but such as either lead us to correct knowledge, or teach us right management; such as either give us fit materials, or further the concordance of our spirit.

In the course of my life, I had read very largely; in certain branches, there was scarce a work unknown to me: the more pleasant was it for me here, to speak about the general survey of the whole, and to observe deficiencies, where I had formerly seen nothing but a hampered confusion or a boundless expansion.

Here too we became acquainted with a very interesting, quiet man. He was a physician and a naturalist: he seemed rather one of the Penates than of the inmates. He showed us the museum, which like the library was fixed in glass cases to the walls of the chamber, adorning and ennobling the space which it did not crowd. On this occasion, I recalled with joy the days of youth, and showed my father many objects, which he formerly had laid upon the sick bed of his little child, that had yet scarcely looked into the world. At the same time, the Physician, in our present and following conversations, did not scruple to avow how nearly he approximated to me in respect of my religious sentiments: he warmly praised my uncle for his tolerance, and his esteem of all that testified or forwarded the worth and unity of human nature; admitting also, that he called for a similar return from others, and was wont to shun and to condemn nothing else so heartily as individual darkness and narrowness of mind. Since the nuptials of my sister, joy had sparkled in the eyes of our uncle: he often spoke with me of what he meant to do for her and for her children. He had several fine estates; he managed them himself, and hoped to leave them in the best condition to his nephews. Regarding the small estate, on which we were at present living, he appeared to entertain peculiar thoughts. "I will leave it to none," said he, "but to a person who can understand, and value and enjoy what it contains, and who feels how loudly every man of wealth and quality, especially in Germany, is called on to exhibit something like a model to others."

Most part of his guests were now gone; we too were making ready for departure, thinking we had seen the final scene of this solemnity; when his attention in affording us some dignified enjoyment produced a new surprise. We had mentioned to him the delight which the chorus of voices, that suddenly commenced without accompaniment of any instrument, had given us, at my sister's marriage. We hinted, at the same time, how pleasant it would be were such a thing repeated; but he seemed to pay no heed to us. The livelier, on this account, was our surprise, when he said one evening: "The music of the dance has died away; our transitory, youthful friends have left us; the happy pair themselves have a more serious look than they had some days ago: to part at such a time, when we perhaps shall never meet again, certainly never without changes, exalts us to a solemn mood, which I know not how to entertain more nobly than by the music that some of you were lately signifying a desire to have repeated."

The chorus, which had in the meanwhile gathered strength, and by secret practice more expertness, was accordingly made to sing us a series of four and of eight voiced melodies, which, if I may say so, gave a real foretaste of bliss. Till then, I had only known the pious mode of singing, as good souls practise it, frequently with hoarse pipes, imagining, like wild birds, that they are praising God, while they procure a pleasant feeling to themselves. Or perhaps I had hearkened to the vain music of concerts, in which one is at best invited to admire the talent of the singer, and very seldom even to a transient feeling of enjoyment. Now, however, I was listening to music, which, as it originated in the deepest principles of the most accomplished human beings, was by suitable and practised organs in harmonious unity made again to address the deepest and best principles of man, and to impress him at that moment with a lively sense of his likeness to the Deity. They were all devotional songs, in the Latin language: they sat like jewels in the golden ring of a polished intellectual conversation; and without pretending to edify, they elevated me and made me happy in the most spiritual manner.

At our departure, he presented all of us with handsome gifts. To me he gave the cross of my order, more beautifully and artfully worked and enamelled than I had seen it before. It was hung upon a large brilliant, by which it was likewise fastened to the chain, and to which it gave the aspect of the noblest stone in the cabinet of some collector.

My sister with her husband went to their estates; the rest of us to our abodes; appearing to ourselves, so far as outward circumstances were concerned, to have returned to quite an every-day existence. We had been, as it were, dropped from a palace of the fairies down upon the common earth; and were again obliged to help ourselves as best we could.

The singular experiences, which this new circle had afforded, left a fine impression on my mind. This, however, did not long continue in its first vivacity; although my uncle tried to nourish and renew it, by sending to me certain of his best and most pleasing works of art; changing them, from time to time, with others which I had not seen.

I had been so much accustomed to be busied with myself, in regulating the concerns of my heart and temper, and conversing on these matters with persons of a like mind, that I could not long study any work of art attentively without being turned by it back upon myself. I was used to look upon a picture or a copperplate merely as upon the letters of a book. Fine printing pleases well: but who would read a book for the beauty of its printing? In like manner, I required of each pictorial form that it should tell me something, should instruct, affect, improve me: and after all my uncle's letters to expound his works of art, say what he would, I continued in my former humor.

Yet not only my peculiar disposition, external incidents and changes in our family still further drew me back from contemplations of that nature, nay for some time even from myself. I had to suffer and to do, more than my slender strength seemed fit for.

My maiden sister had till now been as a right arm to me. Healthy, vigorous, unspeakably good-natured, she had managed all the housekeeping, I myself being busied with the personal nursing of our aged father. She was seized with a catarrh, which changed to a disorder in the lungs: in three weeks she was lying in her coffin. Her death inflicted wounds on me, the scars of which I am not yet willing to examine.

I was lying sick before they buried her: the old ailment in my breast appeared to be awakening; I coughed with violence, and was so hoarse I could not speak beyond a whisper.

My married sister, out of fright and grief, was brought to bed before her time. Our old father thought himself at once about to lose his children and the hope of their posterity: his natural tears increased my sorrow; I prayed to God that he would give me back a sufferable state of health. I asked him but to spare my life until my father should be dead. I recovered; I was what I reckoned well; being able to discharge my duties, though with pain.

My sister was again with child. Many cares, which in such cases are committed to the mother, in the present instance fell to me. She was not altogether happy with her husband; this was to be hidden from our father: I was frequently made judge of their disputes; in which I could decide with greater safety, as my brother trusted in me, and the two were really worthy persons, only each of them, instead of humoring, endeavored to convince the other; and out of eagerness to live in constant harmony, they never could agree. I now learned to mingle seriously in worldly matters, and to practise what of old I had but sung.

My sister bore a son: the feebleness of my father did not hinder him from travelling to her. The sight of the child exceedingly enlivened and cheered him; at the christening, contrary to his custom, he seemed as if inspired; nay, I might say like a Genius with two faces. With the one he looked joyfully forward to those regions which he soon hoped to enter; with the other, to the new, hopeful, earthly life, which had arisen in the boy that was descended from him. On our journey home, he never tired with talking to me of the child, its form, its health, and his wish that the endowments of this new denizen of earth might be cultivated rightly. His reflections on the subject lasted when we had arrived at home: it was not till some days afterwards, that I observed a kind of fever in him; which displayed itself, without shivering, in a sort of languid heat commencing after dinner. He did not yield, however; he went out as usual in the mornings, faithfully attending to the duties of his office, till at last continuous serious symptoms kept him in the house.

I never shall forget with what distinctness, clearness, and repose of mind, he settled in the greatest order the concerns of his house, the arrangements of his funeral, as if these had been the business of some other person.

With a cheerfulness, which he never used to show, and which now mounted to a lively joy, he said to me, "Where is the fear of death which once I felt? Shall I shrink at departing? I have a gracious God; the grave awakes no terror in me; I have an eternal life."

To recall the circumstances of his death, which shortly followed, forms one of the most pleasing entertainments of my solitude: the visible workings of a higher Power in that solemn time, no one shall argue from my memory and my belief.

The death of my beloved father altogether changed my mode of life. From the strictest obedience, the narrowest confinement, I passed at once into the greatest freedom; I enjoyed it like a sort of food from which one has long abstained. Formerly I very seldom spent two hours from home; now I very seldom lived a day there. My friends, whom I had been allowed to visit but by hurried snatches, wished to have my company uninterruptedly, as I did to have theirs. I was often asked to dinner: at walks and pleasure jaunts I never failed. But when once the circle had been fairly run, I saw that the invaluable happiness of liberty consisted, not in doing what one pleases and what circumstances may invite to, but in being able, without hindrance or restraint, to do in the direct way what one regards as right and proper: and in this case, I was old enough to reach a precious truth, without having smarted for my ignorance.

One pleasure I could not deny myself: it was, as soon as might be, to renew and strengthen my connection with the Herrnhuth Brethren. I made haste accordingly to visit one of their establishments at no great distance: but here I by no means found what I had been anticipating. I was frank enough to signify my disappointment, which they tried to soften by alleging that the present settlement was nothing to a full and fitly organized community. This I did not take upon me to deny; yet in my thought, the genuine spirit of the matter should have been displayed in a small body as well as in a great one.

One of their Bishops who was present, a personal disciple of the Count, took considerable pains with me. He spoke English perfectly, and as I too understood a little of it, he reckoned this a token that we both belonged to one class: I however reckoned nothing of the kind; his conversation did not in the smallest satisfy me. He had been a cutler; was a native of Moravia: his mode of thought still savored of the artisan. With Herr Von L——, who had been a Major in the French service, I got upon a better footing; yet I never could reduce myself to the submissiveness, which he displayed to his superiors; nay, I felt as if one had given me a box on the ear, when I saw the Major's wife, and other women more or less like ladies, take the Bishop's hand and kiss it. Meanwhile a journey into Holland was proposed; which, however, doubtless for my good, did not take place.

About this time, my sister was delivered of a daughter; and now it was the turn of us women to exult, and to consider how the little creature should be bred like one of us. The husband, on the other hand, was not so satisfied, when in the following year another daughter saw the light: with his large estates, he wanted to have boys about him, who in future might assist him in his management.

My health was feeble; I kept myself in peace; and observing a quiet mode of life, I enjoyed a tolerable equability. I was not afraid of death; nay, I wished to die; yet I secretly perceived that God was granting time for me to prove my soul, and to advance still nearer to himself. In my many sleepless nights especially, I have at times felt something, which I cannot undertake to describe.

It was as if my soul were thinking separately from the body; she looked upon the body as a foreign substance, as we look upon a garment. She pictured with extreme vivacity events and times long past, and felt by means of this, events that were to follow. Those times are all gone by; what follows likewise will go by; the body too will fall to pieces like a vesture; but I, the well-known I, I am.

The thought is great, exalted and consoling; yet an excellent friend, with whom I every day became more intimate, instructed me to dwell on it as little as I could. This was the Physician whom I met with in my uncle's house, and who since then had accurately informed himself about the temper of my body and my spirit. He showed me how much these feelings, when we cherish them within us independently of outward objects, tend as it were to excavate us, and to undermine the whole foundation of our being. "To be active," he would say, "is the primary vocation of man; all the intervals, in which he is obliged to rest, he should employ in gaining clearer knowledge of external things, for this will in its turn facilitate activity."

This friend was acquainted with my custom of looking on my body as an outward object; he knew also that I pretty well understood my constitution, my disorder, and the medicines of use for it; nay, that by continual sufferings of my own or other people, I had really grown a kind of half doctor; he now carried forward my attention from the human body, and the drugs which act upon it, to the kindred objects of creation: he led me up and down as in the Paradise of the first man; only, if I may continue my comparison, allowing me to trace in dim remoteness the Creator walking in the Garden in the cool of the evening.

How gladly did I now see God in nature, when I bore him with such certainty within my heart! How interesting to me was his handywork; how thankful did I feel that he had pleased to quicken me with the breath of his mouth!

We again had hopes that my sister would present us with a boy; her husband waited anxiously for that event, but did not live to see it. He died in consequence of an unlucky fall from horseback; and my sister followed him, soon after she had brought into the world a lovely boy. The four orphans they had left I could not look at but with sadness. So many healthy people had been called away before poor sickly me; might I not also have to witness blights among these fair and hopeful blossoms? I knew the world sufficiently to understand what dangers threaten the precarious breeding of a child, especially a child of rank; and it seemed to me that since the period of my youth these dangers had increased. I felt that weakly as I was, I could not be of much, perhaps of any service to the little ones; and I rejoiced the more on finding that my uncle, as indeed might have been looked for, had determined to devote his whole attention to the education of these amiable creatures. And this they doubtless merited in every sense: they were handsome; and with great diversities, all promised to be well conditioned, reasonable persons.

Since my worthy Doctor had suggested it, I loved to trace out family likenesses among our relatives and children. My father had carefully preserved the portraits of his ancestors, and got his own and those of his descendants drawn by tolerable masters; nor had my mother and her people been forgotten. We accurately knew the characters of all the family: and as we had frequently compared them with each other, we now endeavored to discover in the children the same peculiarities outward or inward. My sister's eldest son, we thought, resembled his paternal grandfather, of whom there was a fine youthful picture in my uncle's collection: he had been a brave soldier; and in this point too the boy took after him, liking arms above all other things, and busying himself with them whenever he had opportunity. In paying me a visit this was constantly remarkable: my father had possessed a very pretty armory; and the boy got neither peace nor rest till I had given him a pair of pistols and a fowling-piece out of it, and he had learned the proper way of using them. At the same time, in his conduct or his bearing, there was nothing which approached to rudeness: on the other hand, he was always meek and sensible.

The eldest daughter had attracted my especial love; of which perhaps the reason was that she resembled me, and of all the four held closest to me. But I may well admit that the more closely I observed her as she grew, the more she shamed me; I could not look on her without a sentiment of admiration; nay, I may almost say, of reverence. You would scarce have seen a nobler form, a more peaceful spirit, an activity so equable and universal. No moment of her life was she unoccupied; and every occupation in her hands grew dignified. All seemed indifferent to her, so that she could but accomplish what was proper in the place and time; and in the same manner, she could patiently continue unemployed, when there was nothing to be done. This activity without the need of occupation I have never elsewhere met with. In particular her conduct to the suffering and destitute was from her earliest youth inimitable. For my part, I freely confess that I never had the gift myself to make a business of beneficence: I was not niggardly to the poor; nay, I often gave too largely for my means; yet this was little more than buying myself off; and a person needed to be made for me, if I was to bestow attention on him. Directly the reverse was the conduct of my niece. I never saw her give a poor man money; whatever she obtained from me for this purpose, she failed not in the first place to change for some necessary article. Never did she seem more lovely in my eyes, than when rummaging my clothes-presses: she was always sure to light on something which I did not wear and did not need: and to sew these old cast articles together, and put them on some ragged child, she thought her highest happiness.

Her sister's turn of mind appeared already different: she had much of her mother; she promised to be soon very elegant and beautiful, and she now bids fair to keep her promise. She is greatly taken up with her exterior; from her earliest years, she could deck herself and bear herself in a way that struck you. I still remember with what ecstasy, when quite a little creature, she beheld her figure in a mirror, after I had been obliged to bind on her some precious pearls, once my mother's, which she had by chance discovered near me.

In reflecting on these diverse inclinations, it was pleasant for me to consider how my property would, after my decease, be shared among them, and again called into use by them. I saw the fowling-pieces of my father once more travelling round the fields upon my nephew's shoulder, and birds once more falling out from his hunting-pouch: I saw my whole wardrobe issuing from the church at the Easter Confirmation, on the persons of tidy little girls; while the best pieces of it were employed to decorate some virtuous burgher maiden on her marriage day. In furnishing such children and poor little girls, Natalia had a singular delight; although, as I must here remark, she did not show the smallest love, or if I may say it, smallest need of a dependence upon any visible or invisible Being, such as I had manifested in my youth so strongly.

When I further thought that her younger sister, on that very day, would wear my jewels and my pearls at court, I could view with peace my possessions like my body given back to the elements.

The children waxed apace: to my comfort, they are healthy, handsome, clever creatures. That my uncle keeps them from me I endure without repining: when staying in the neighborhood, or even in the town, they seldom see me.

A singular personage, regarded as a French clergyman, though no one rightly knows his history, has been intrusted with the oversight of all the children. He has them taught in various places; they are put to board now here now there.

At first I could perceive no plan whatever in this mode of education; till at last the Doctor told me that the Abbé had convinced my uncle, that in order to accomplish anything by education, we must first become acquainted with the pupil's tendencies and wishes: that when these are ascertained, he ought to be transported to a situation where he may, as speedily as possible, content the former and attain the latter; and so if we have been mistaken, may still in time perceive his error; and at last having found what suits him, may hold the faster by it, may the more diligently fashion himself according to it. I wish this strange experiment may prosper: with such excellent natures it perhaps is possible.

But there is one peculiarity in these instructers, which I never can approve of: they study to seclude the children from whatever might awaken them to an acquaintance with themselves and with the invisible, sole, faithful Friend. I often take it badly of my uncle that, on this account, he looks on me as dangerous for the little ones. Thus in practice there is no man tolerant! Many assure us that they willingly leave each to take his way; yet all of them endeavor to exclude from action every one that does not think as they do.

This removal of the children troubles me the more, the more I am convinced of the reality of my belief. How can it fail to have a heavenly origin, an actual object, when in practice it is so effectual? Is it not by practice only that we prove our own existence? Why then, by a like mode, may we not demonstrate to ourselves the influence of that Power who gives us all good things?

That I am still advancing, never retrograding; that my conduct is approximating more and more to the image I have formed of perfection; that I every day feel more facility in doing what I reckon proper, even while the weakness of my body hinders me so much: can all this be accounted for upon the principles of human nature, whose corruption I have seen so clearly? For me, at least, it cannot.

I scarce remember a command; to me there is nothing that assumes the aspect of a law; it is an impulse, which leads me, and guides me always rightly. I freely follow my emotions, and know as little of constraint as of repentance. God be praised that I know to whom I owe this happiness, and that I cannot think of these advantages without humility! Never shall I run the risk of growing proud of my own ability and power, having seen so clearly what a monster might be formed and nursed in every human bosom, did not higher influence restrain us.

INDENTURE.

FROM THE SAME.

Art is long, life short; judgment difficult, occasion transient. To act is easy, to think is hard; to act according to our thought is troublesome. Every beginning is cheerful; the threshold is the place of expectation. The boy stands astonished, his impressions guide him; he learns sportfully, seriousness comes on him by surprise. Imitation is born with us; what should be imitated is not easy to discover. The excellent is rarely found, more rarely valued. The height charms us, the steps to it do not; with the summit in our eye, we love to walk along the plain. It is but a part of art that can be taught; the artist needs it all. Who knows it half, speaks much and is always wrong; who knows it wholly, inclines to act and speaks seldom or late. The former have no secrets and no force; the instruction they can give is like baked bread, savory and satisfying for a single day; but flour cannot be sown, and seed corn ought not to be ground. Words are good, but they are not the best. The best is not to be explained by words. The spirit in which we act is the highest matter. Action can be understood and again represented by the spirit alone. No one knows what he is doing, while he acts rightly; but of what is wrong we are always conscious. Whoever works with symbols only is a pedant, a hypocrite, or a bungler. There are many such, and they like to be together. Their babbling detains the scholar; their obstinate mediocrity vexes even the best. The instruction, which the true artist gives us, opens up the mind; for where words fail him, deeds speak. The true scholar learns from the known to unfold the unknown, and approaches more and more to being a master.

THE EXEQUIES OF MIGNON.

FROM THE SAME.

The Abbé called them in the evening to attend the exequies of Mignon. The company proceeded to the Hall of the Past; they found it magnificently ornamented and illuminated. The walls were hung with azure tapestry almost from the ceiling to the floor, so that nothing but the cornices and friezes above and below were visible. On the four candilabras in the corners, large wax lights were burning; smaller lights were in the four smaller candilabras placed by the sarcophagus in the middle. Near this stood four Boys, dressed in azure with silver; they had broad fans of ostrich feathers, which they waved above a figure that was resting upon the sarcophagus. The company sat down: two invisible Choruses began in a soft musical recitative to ask: "Whom bring ye us to the still dwelling?" The four Boys replied with lovely voices: "'Tis a tired playmate whom we bring you; let her rest in your still dwelling, till the songs of her heavenly sisters once more awaken her."

CHORUS.

"Firstling of youth in our circle, we welcome thee! With sadness welcome thee! May no boy, no maiden follow! Let age only, willing and composed, approach the silent Hall, and in the solemn company, repose this one dear child!

BOYS.

Ah! reluctantly we brought her hither! Ah! and she is to remain here! Let us too remain; let us weep, let us weep upon her bier!

CHORUS.

Yet look at the strong wings; look at the light clear robe! how glitters the golden band upon her head! Look at the beautiful, the noble repose!

BOYS.

Ah! the wings do not raise her; in the frolic game, her robe flutters to and fro no more; when we bound her head with roses, her looks on us were kind and friendly.

CHORUS.

Cast forward the eyes of your spirits! Awake in your souls the imaginative power, which carries Life, the fairest, the highest of earthly endowments, away beyond the stars.

BOYS.

But ah! We find her not here; in the garden she wanders not; the flowers of the meadow she plucks no longer. Let us weep, we are leaving her here! Let us weep and remain with her!

CHORUS.

Children, turn back into life! Your tears let the fresh air dry which plays upon the rushing water. Fly from Night! Day and Pleasure and Continuance are the lot of the living.

BOYS.

Up! Turn back into life! Let the day give us labor and pleasure, till the evening brings us rest, and the nightly sleep refreshes us.

CHORUS.

Children! Hasten into life! In the pure garments of beauty, may Love meet you with heavenly looks and with the wreath of immortality!"

The Boys had retired; the Abbé rose from his seat, and went behind the bier. "It is the appointment," said he, "of the Man who prepared this silent abode, that each new tenant of it shall be introduced with a solemnity. After him, the builder of this mansion, the founder of this establishment, we have next brought a young stranger hither; and thus already does this little space contain two altogether different victims of the rigorous, arbitrary and inexorable goddess of Death. By appointed laws we enter into life; the days are numbered, which make us ripe to see the light; but for the duration of our life there is no law. The weakest thread will spin itself to unexpected length; and the strongest is cut suddenly asunder by the scissors of the Fates, delighting, as it seems, in contradictions. Of the child, whom we have here committed to her final rest, we can say but little. It is still uncertain whence she came; her parents we know not; the years of her life we can only conjecture. Her deep and closely shrouded soul allowed us scarce to guess at its interior movements; there was nothing clear in her, nothing open but her affection for the man, who had snatched her from the hands of a barbarian. This impassioned tenderness, this vivid gratitude, appeared to be the flame, which consumed the oil of her life: the skill of the physician could not save that fair life, the most anxious friendship could not lengthen it. But if art could not stay the departing spirit, it has done its utmost to preserve the body, and withdraw it from decay. A balsamic substance has been forced through all the veins, and now tinges, in the place of blood, these cheeks too early faded. Come near, my friends, and view this wonder of art and care!"

He raised the veil: the child was lying in her angel's dress, as if asleep, in the most soft and graceful posture. They approached it, and admired this show of life. Wilhelm alone continued sitting in his place; he was not able to compose himself: what he felt, he durst not think; and every thought seemed ready to destroy his feeling.

For the sake of the Marchese, the speech had been pronounced in French. That nobleman came forward with the rest, and viewed the figure with attention. The Abbé thus proceeded. "With a holy confidence, this kind heart, shut up to men, was continually turned to its God. Humility, nay an inclination to abase herself externally, seemed natural to her. She clave with zeal to the catholic religion, in which she had been born and educated. Often she expressed a still wish to sleep on consecrated ground: and according to the usage of the church we have therefore consecrated this marble coffin, and the little earth, which is hidden in the cushion that supports her head. With what ardor did she in her last moments kiss the image of the Crucified, which stood beautifully figured, on her tender arm, with many hundred points!" So saying, he stripped up her right sleeve; and a crucifix, with marks and letters round it, showed itself in blue upon the white skin.

The Marchese looked at this with eagerness, stooping down to view it more intensely. "O God!" cried he, as he stood upright, and raised his hands to Heaven; "Poor child! Unhappy niece! Do I meet thee here! What a painful joy to find thee, whom we had long lost hope of; to find this dear frame, which we had long believed the prey of fishes in the ocean, here preserved, though lifeless! I assist at thy funeral, splendid in its external circumstances, still more splendid from the noble persons who attend thee to thy place of rest. And to these," added he with a faltering voice, "so soon as I can speak, I will express my thanks."

Tears hindered him from saying more. By the pressure of a spring, the Abbé sank the body into the cavity of the marble. Four Youths, dressed as the Boys had been, came out from behind the tapestry; and lifting the heavy, beautifully ornamented lid upon the coffin, thus began their song.

THE YOUTHS.

"Well is the treasure now laid up; the fair image of the Past! Here sleeps it in the marble, undecaying; in your hearts too it lives, it works. Travel, travel back into life! Take along with you this holy Earnestness; for Earnestness alone makes life eternity."

The invisible Chorus joined in with the last words: but no one heard the strengthening sentiment; all were too much busied with themselves, and the emotions, which these wonderful disclosures had excited. The Abbé and Natalia conducted the Marchese out; Theresa and Lothario walked by Wilhelm. It was not till the music had altogether died away, that their sorrows, thoughts, meditations, curiosity again fell on them with all their force, and made them long to be transported back into that exalting scene.

EXTRACTS
FROM WILHELM MEISTER'S TRAVELS.*

By a short and pleasant road, Wilhelm had reached the town, to which his letter was directed. He found it gay and well built; but its new aspect showed too clearly that not long before it must have suffered by a conflagration. The address of his letter led him into the last small uninjured portion of the place, to a house of ancient, earnest architecture, yet well kept, and of a tidy look. Dim windows, strangely fashioned, indicated an exhilarating pomp of colours from within. Nor, in fact, did the interior fail to correspond with the exterior. In clean apartments, everywhere stood furniture which must have served several generations, intermixed with very little that was new. The master of the house received our traveller kindly, in a little chamber similarly fitted up. These clocks had already struck the hour of many a birth and many a death; everything which met the eye reminded one that the past might, as it were, be protracted into the present.

The stranger delivered his letter; but the landlord, without opening it, laid it aside, and endeavored, in a cheerful conversation, immediately to get acquainted with his guest. They soon grew confidential; and as Wilhelm, contrary to his usual habit, let his eye wander in-

---
* See Vol. IV. German Romance, by T. Carlyle.

quisitively over the room, the good old man said to him: "My domestic equipment excites your attention. You here see how long a thing may last; and one should make such observations now and then, by way of counterbalance to so much in the world that rapidly changes and passes away. This same tea-kettle served my parents, and was a witness of our evening family assemblages; this copper fire-screen still guards me from the fire, which these stout old tongs still help me to mend; and so it is with all throughout. I had it in my power to bestow my care and industry on many other things, as I did not occupy myself with changing these external necessaries, a task which consumes so many people's time and resources. An affectionate attention to what we possess makes us rich, for thereby we accumulate a treasure of remembrances connected with indifferent things. I knew a young man who got a common pin from his love, while taking leave of her; daily fastened his breast-frill with it, and brought back this guarded and not unemployed treasure from a long journeying of several years. In us little men, such little things are to be reckoned virtue."

"Many a one too," answered Wilhelm, "brings back, from such long and far travellings, a sharp pricker in his heart, which he would fain be quit of."

The old man seemed to know nothing of Lenardo's situation, though in the meanwhile he had opened the letter and read it; for he returned to his former topics.

"Tenacity of our possessions," continued he, "in many cases gives us the greatest energy. To this obstinacy in myself I owe the saving of my house. When the town was on fire, some people wished to snatch out their goods, and lodge them here. I forbade this; bolted my doors and windows; and turned out, with several neighbors, to oppose the flames. Our efforts succeeded in preserving this summit of the town. Next morning all was standing here as you now see it, and as it has stood for almost a hundred years."

"Yet you will confess," said Wilhelm; "that no man withstands the change which Time produces."

"That, in truth!" said the other: "but he who holds out longest has still done something.

"Yes! even beyond the limits of our being we are able to maintain and secure; we transmit discoveries, we hand down sentiments, as well as property: and as the latter was my chief province, I have for a long time exercised the strictest foresight, invented the most peculiar precautions; yet not till lately have I succeeded in seeing my wish fulfilled.

"Commonly the son disperses what the father has collected, collects something different, or in a different way. Yet if we can wait for the grandson, for the new generation, we find the same tendencies, the same tastes, again making their appearance. And so at last, by the care of our Pedagogic friends, I have found an active youth, who, if possible, pays more regard to old possession than even I, and has withal a vehement attachment to every sort of curiosities. My decided confidence he gained by the violent exertions with which he struggled to keep off the fire from our dwelling. Doubly and trebly has he merited the treasure which I mean to leave him: nay, it is already given into his hands; and ever since that time our store is increasing in a wonderful way.

"Not all, however, that you see here is ours. On the contrary, as in the hands of pawnbrokers you find many a foreign jewel, so with us I can show you precious articles, which people, under the most various circumstances, have deposited with us, for the sake of better keeping."

Wilhelm recollected the beautiful Box, which, at any rate, he did not like to carry with him in his wanderings; and showed it to his landlord. The old man viewed it with attention; gave the date when it was probably made; and showed some similar things. Wilhelm asked him if he thought it should be opened. The old man thought not. "I believe, indeed," said he, "it could be done without special harm to the casket; but as you found it in so singular a way, you must try your luck on it. For if you are born lucky, and this little box is of any consequence, the key will doubtless by and by be found, and in the very place where you are least expecting it."

"There have been such occurrences," said Wilhelm.

"I have myself experienced such," replied the old man; "and here you behold the strangest of them. Of this ivory crucifix I have had for thirty years, the body with the head and feet, in one place. For its own nature, as well as for the glorious art displayed in it, I kept the figure laid up in my most private drawer: nearly ten years ago I got the cross belonging to it, with the inscription; and was then induced to have the arms supplied by the best carver of our day. Far, indeed, was this expert artist from equalling his predecessor; yet I let his work pass, more for devout purposes, than for any admiration of its excellence.

"Now, conceive my delight! A little while ago the original, genuine arms, were sent me, as you see them here united in the loveliest harmony; and I, charmed at so happy a coincidence, cannot help recognising in this crucifix the fortunes of the Christian religion, which, often enough dismembered and scattered abroad, will ever in the end again gather itself together at the foot of the Cross."

Wilhelm admired the figure, and its strange combination. "I will follow your counsel," added he; "let the casket continue locked till the key of it be found, though it should lie till the end of my life."

"One who lives long," said the old man, "sees much collected and much cast asunder."

The young partner in the house now chanced

to enter, and Wilhelm signified his purpose of intrusting the Box to their keeping. A large book was thereupon produced, the deposit inscribed in it, with many ceremonies and stipulations; a receipt granted, which applied in words to any bearer, but was only to be honored on the giving of a certain token agreed upon with the owner.

So passed their hours in instructive and entertaining conversation, till at last Felix, mounted on a gay pony, arrived in safety. A groom had accompanied him, and was now for some time to attend and serve Wilhelm. A letter from Lenardo, delivered at the same time, complained that he could find no vestige of the Nut-brown Maid; and Wilhelm was anew conjured to do his utmost in searching her out. Wilhelm imparted the matter to his landlord. The latter smiled, and said: "We must certainly make every exertion, for our friend's sake; perhaps I may succeed in learning something of her. As I keep these old primitive household goods, so likewise have I kept some old primitive friends. You tell me that this maiden's father was distinguished by his piety. The pious have a more intimate connection with each other than the wicked; though externally it may not always prosper so well. By this means I hope to obtain some traces of what you are sent to seek. But, as a preparative, do you now pursue the resolution of placing your Felix among his equals, and turning him to some fixed department of activity. Hasten with him to the great Institution. I will point out the way you must follow in order to find the Chief, who resides now in one, now in another division of his Province. You shall have a letter, with my best advice and direction."

* * * * * * * *

The pilgrims pursuing the way pointed out to them, had, without difficulty, reached the limits of the Province, where they were to see so many singularities. At the very entrance, they found themselves in a district of extreme fertility; in its soft knolls, favorable to crops; in its higher hills, to sheep-husbandry; in its wide bottoms, to grazing. Harvest was near at hand, and all was in the richest luxuriance: yet what most surprised our travellers was, that they observed neither men nor women; but in all quarters, boys and youths engaged in preparing for a happy harvest, nay already making arrangements for a merry harvest-home. Our travellers saluted several of them, and inquired for the Chief, of whose abode, however, they could gain no intelligence. The address of their letter was: *To the Chief, or the Three.* Of this also the boys could make nothing; however, they referred the strangers to an Overseer, who was just about mounting his horse to ride off. Our friends disclosed their object to this man; the frank liveliness of Felix seemed to please him, and so they all rode along together.

Wilhelm had already noticed, that in the cut and color of the young people's clothes, a variety prevailed, which gave the whole tiny population a peculiar aspect: he was just about to question his attendant on this point, when a still stranger observation forced itself upon him; all the children, how employed soever, laid down their work, and turned with singular, yet diverse gestures, towards the party riding past them; or rather, as it was easy to infer, towards the Overseer, who was in it. The youngest laid their arms crosswise over their breasts, and looked cheerfully up to the sky; those of middle size held their hands on their backs, and looked smiling on the ground; the eldest stood with a frank and spirited air; their arms stretched down, they turned their heads to the right, and formed themselves into a line; whereas the others kept separate, each where he chanced to be.

The riders having stopped and dismounted here, as several children, in their various modes, were standing forth to be inspected by the Overseer, Wilhelm asked the meaning of these gestures; but Felix struck in, and cried gaily: "What posture am I to take, then?"

"Without doubt," said the Overseer, "as the first posture: The arms over the breast, the face earnest and cheerful towards the sky."

Felix obeyed, but soon cried: "This is not much to my taste; I see nothing up there: does it last long? But yes!" exclaimed he joyfully, "yonder are a pair of falcons flying from the west to the east: that is a good sign too?"

"As thou takest it, as thou behavest," said the other; "now mingle among them, as they mingle." He gave a signal, and the children left their postures, and again betook them to work, or sport, as before.

"Are you at liberty," said Wilhelm then, "to explain this sight which surprises me? I easily perceive that these positions, these gestures, are salutations directed to you."

"Just so," replied the Overseer; "salutations which at once indicate in what degree of culture each of these boys is standing."

"But, can you explain to me the meaning of this gradation?" inquired Wilhelm; "for that there is one, is clear enough."

"This belongs to a higher quarter," said the other: "so much, however, I may tell you, that these ceremonies are not mere grimaces; that on the contrary, the import of them, not the highest, but still a directing, intelligible import, is communicated to the children; while, at the same time, each is enjoined to retain and consider for himself whatever explanation it has been thought meet to give him; they are not allowed to talk of these things, either to strangers or among themselves; and thus their instruction is modified in many ways. Besides, secrecy itself has many advantages; for when you tell a man at once and straight forward, the purpose of any object, he fancies there is nothing in it. Certain secrets, even if known to every one, men find that they must still reverence by concealment and silence, for this works on modesty and good morals."

"I understand you," answered Wilhelm: "why should not the principle which is so necessary in material things, be applied to spiritual also? But perhaps, in another point, you can satisfy my curiosity. The great variety of shape and color in these children's clothes attracts my notice; and yet I do not see all sorts of colors, but a few in all their shades, from the lightest to the deepest. At the same time, I observe that by this no designation of degrees in age or merit can be intended; for the oldest and the youngest boys may be alike both in cut and color, while those of similar gestures are not similar in dress."

"On this matter also," said the other, "silence is prescribed to me: but I am much mistaken, or you will not leave us without receiving all the information you desire."

Our party continued following the trace of the Chief, which they believed themselves to be upon. But now the strangers could not fail to notice, with new surprise, that the farther they advanced into the district, a vocal melody more and more frequently sounded towards them from the fields. Whatever the boys might be engaged with, whatever labor they were carrying on, they accompanied it with singing; and it seemed as if the songs were specially adapted to their various sorts of occupation, and in similar cases, everywhere the same. If there chanced to be several children in company, they sang together in alternating parts. Towards evening, appeared dancers likewise, whose steps were enlivened and directed by choruses. Felix struck in with them, not altogether unsuccessfully, from horseback, as he passed; and Wilhelm felt gratified in this amusement, which gave new life to the scene.

"Apparently," he said to his companion, "you devote considerable care to this branch of instruction; the accomplishment, otherwise, could not be so widely diffused, and so completely practised."

"We do," replied the other: "on our plan, Song is the first step in education; all the rest are connected with it, and attained by means of it. The simplest enjoyment, as well as the simplest instruction, we enliven and impress by Song; nay, even what religious and moral principles we lay before our children, are communicated in the way of Song. Other advantages for the excitement of activity, spontaneously arise from this practice; for, in accustoming the children to write the tones they are to utter, in musical characters, and as occasion serves, again to seek these characters in the utterance of their own voice; and besides this, to subjoin the text below the notes, they are forced to practise hand, ear, and eye at once, whereby they acquire the art of penmanship sooner than you would expect; and as all this in the long run is to be effected by copying precise measurements and accurately settled numbers, they come to conceive the high value of Mensuration and Arithmetic much sooner than in any other way. Among all imaginable things, accordingly, we have selected music as the element of our teaching; for level roads run out from music towards every side."

Wilhelm endeavored to obtain still farther information, and expressed his surprise at hearing no instrumental music: "This is by no means neglected, here," said the other; "but practised in a peculiar district, one of the most pleasant valleys among the Mountains; and there again we have arranged it so that the different instruments shall be taught in separate places. The discords of beginners, in particular, are banished into certain solitudes, where they can drive no one to despair; for you will confess that in well-regulated civil society, there is scarcely a more melancholy suffering to be undergone, than what is forced on us by the neighbourhood of an incipient player on the flute or violin.

"Our learners, out of a laudable desire to be troublesome to no one, go forth of their accord, for a longer or a shorter time, into the wastes; and strive, in their seclusion, to attain the merit which shall again admit them into the inhabited world. Each of them, from time to time, is allowed to venture an attempt for admission, and the trial seldom fails of success; for bashfulness and modesty, in this, as in all other parts of our system, we strongly endeavor to maintain and cherish. That your son has a good voice, I am glad to observe: all the rest is managed with so much the greater ease."

They had now reached a place where Felix was to stop and make trial of its arrangements, till a formal reception should be granted him. From a distance, they had been saluted by a jocund sound of music; it was a game in which the boys were, for the present, amusing themselves in their hour of play. A general chorus mounted up; each individual of a wide circle striking in at his time, with a joyful, clear, firm tone, as the sign was given him by the Overseer. The latter more than once took the singers by surprise, when at a signal he suspended the choral song, and called on any single boy, touching him with his rod, to catch by himself the expiring tone, and adapt to it a suitable song, fitted also to the spirit of what had preceded. Most part showed great dexterity; a few, who failed in this feat, willingly gave in their pledges, without altogether being laughed at for their ill success. Felix was child enough to mix among them instantly; and in his new task he acquitted himself tolerably well. The First Salutation was then enjoined on him: he directly laid his hands on his breast, looked upwards, and truly with so roguish a countenance, that it was easy to observe no secret meaning had yet in his mind attached itself to this posture.

The delightful spot, his kind reception, the merry playmates, all pleased the boy so well, that he felt no very deep sorrow as his father moved away: the departure of the pony was perhaps a heavier matter; but he yielded here also, on learning that in this circle it could not possibly be kept; and the Overseer promised him, in compensation, that he should find another horse, as smart and well-broken, at a time when he was not expecting it.

As the Chief, it appeared, was not to be come at, the Overseer turned to Wilhelm and said: "I must now leave you, to pursue my occupations; but first I will bring you to the Three, who preside over our sacred things. Your letter is addressed to them likewise, and they together represent the Chief." Wilhelm could have wished to gain some previous knowledge of these sacred things, but his companion answered: "The Three will doubtless, in return for the confidence you show in leaving us your son, disclose to you in their wisdom and fairness what is most needful for you to learn. The visible objects of reverence, which I named sacred things, are collected in this separate circle; are mixed with nothing, interfered with by nothing: at certain seasons of the year only are our pupils admitted here, to be taught in their various degrees of culture, by historical and sensible means; and in these short intervals they carry off a deep enough impression to suffice them for a time, during the performance of their other duties."

Wilhelm had now reached the gate of a wooded vale, surrounded with high walls: on a certain sign the little door opened, and a man of earnest and imposing look received our traveller. The latter found himself in a large beautifully umbrageous space, decked with the richest foliage, shaded with trees and bushes of all sorts; while stately walls and magnificent buildings were discerned only in glimpses through this thick natural boscage. A friendly reception from the Three, who by and by appeared, at last turned into a general conversation, the substance of which we now present in an abbreviated shape.

"Since you intrust your son to us," said they, "it is fair that we admit you to a closer view of our procedure. Of what is external you have seen much, that does not bear its meaning on its front. What part of this do you chiefly wish to have explained?"

"Dignified, yet singular gestures of salutation I have noticed, the import of which I would gladly learn: with you, doubtless, the exterior has a reference to the interior, and inversely; let me know what this reference is."

"Well-formed, healthy children," replied the Three, "bring much into the world along with them: Nature has given to each whatever he requires for time and duration; to unfold this is our duty; often it unfolds itself better of its own accord. One thing there is, however, which no child brings into the world with him; and yet it is on this one thing that all depends for making man in every point a man. If you can discover it yourself, speak it out." Wilhelm thought a little while, then shook his head.

The Three, after a suitable pause, exclaimed: "*Reverence!*" Wilhelm seemed to hesitate. "Reverence!" cried they a second time. "All want it, perhaps you yourself.

"Three kinds of gestures you have seen; and we inculcate a threefold Reverence, which, when commingled and formed into one whole, attains its highest force and effect. The first is Reverence for what is above us. That posture, the arms crossed over the breast, the look turned joyfully towards Heaven; that is what we have enjoined on young children; requiring from them thereby a testimony that there is a God above, who images and reveals himself in parents, teachers, superiors. Then comes the second, Reverence for what is under us. Those hands folded over the back, and, as it were, tied together, that down-turned, smiling look, announce that we are to regard the Earth with attention and cheerfulness: from the bounty of the Earth we are nourished: the Earth affords unutterable joys; but disproportionate sorrows she also brings us. Should one of our children do himself external hurt, blameably or blamelessly; should others hurt him accidentally or purposely; should dead involuntary matter do him hurt; then let him well consider it; for such dangers will attend him all his days. But from this posture we delay not to free our pupil, the instant we become convinced that the instruction connected with it has produced sufficient influence on him. Then, on the contrary, we bid him gather courage, and turning to his comrades, range himself along with them. Now, at last, he stands forth, frank and bold; not selfishly isolated; only in combination with his equals does he front the world. Farther we have nothing to add."

"I see a glimpse of it!" said Wilhelm. "Are not the mass of men so marred and stinted, because they take pleasure only in the element of evil-wishing and evil-speaking? Whoever gives himself to this, soon comes to be indifferent towards God, contemptuous towards the world, spiteful towards his equals; and the true, genuine, indispensable sentiment of self-estimation corrupts into self-conceit and presumption. Allow me, however," continued he, "to state one difficulty. You say that reverence is not natural to man: now, has not the reverence or fear of rude people for violent convulsions of Nature, or other inexplicable, mysteriously-foreboding occurrences, been heretofore regarded as the germ out of which a higher feeling, a purer sentiment, was by degrees to be developed?"

"Nature is indeed adequate to fear," replied they; "but to reverence not adequate. Men fear a known or unknown powerful being; the strong seeks to conquer it, the weak to avoid it; both endeavor to get quit of it, and feel themselves happy when for a short season they have put it aside, and their nature has in some degree restored itself to freedom and independence.

The natural man repeats this operation millions of times in the course of his life; from fear he struggles to freedom; from freedom he is driven back to fear, and so makes no advancement. To fear is easy, but grievous; to reverence is difficult, but satisfactory. Man does not willingly submit himself to reverence; or rather he never so submits himself: it is a higher sense, which must be communicated to his nature; which only in some peculiarly favored individuals unfolds itself spontaneously, who on this account too have of old been looked upon as saints and gods. Here lies the worth, here lies the business of all true Religions; whereof there are likewise only three, according to the objects towards which they direct our devotion."

The men paused; Wilhelm reflected for a time in silence; but feeling in himself no pretension to unfold the meaning of these strange words, he requested the Sages to proceed with their exposition. They immediately complied. "No religion that grounds itself on fear," said they, "is regarded among us. With the reverence, to which a man should give dominion in his mind, he can, in paying honor, keep his own honor; he is not disunited with himself, as in the former case. The Religion which depends on reverence for what is above us, we denominate the Ethnic; it is the religion of the nations, and the first happy deliverance from a degrading fear: all Heathen religions, as we call them, are of this sort, whatsoever names they may bear. The Second Religion, which founds itself on reverence for what is around us, we denominate the Philosophical; for the philosopher stations himself in the middle, and must draw down to him all that is higher, and up to him all that is lower, and only in this medium condition does he merit the title of Wise. Here, as he surveys with clear sight his relation to his equals, and therefore to the whole human race; his relation likewise to all other earthly circumstances and arrangements necessary or accidental, he alone, in a cosmic sense, lives in Truth. But now we have to speak of the Third Religion, grounded on reverence for what is beneath us: this we name the Christian, as in the Christian religion such a temper is with most distinctness manifested: it is a last step to which mankind were fitted and destined to attain. But what a task was it, not only to be patient with the Earth, and let it lie beneath us, we appealing to a higher birth-place; but also to recognise humility and poverty, mockery and despite, disgrace and wretchedness, suffering and death, to recognise these things as divine; nay, even on sin and crime to look not as hindrances, but to honor and love them as furtherances, of what is holy. Of this, indeed, we find some traces in all ages: but the trace is not the goal; and this being now attained, the human species cannot retrograde; and we may say, that the Christian religion having once appeared cannot again vanish; having once assumed its divine shape, can be subject to no dissolution."

"To which of these religions do you specially adhere?" inquired Wilhelm.

"To all the three," replied they: "for in their union they produce what may properly be called the true religion. Out of those Three Reverences springs the highest reverence, reverence for one's self, and those again unfold themselves from this; so that man attains the highest elevation of which he is capable, that of being justified in reckoning himself the Best that God and Nature have produced; nay, of being able to continue on this lofty eminence, without being again by self-conceit and presumption drawn down from it into the vulgar level."

"Such a confession of faith, developed in this manner, does not repulse me," answered Wilhelm; "it agrees with much that one hears now and then in the course of life; only, you unite what others separate."

To this they replied: "Our confession has already been adopted, though unconsciously, by a great part of the world."

"How, then, and where?" said Wilhelm.

"In the Creed!" exclaimed they: "for the first Article is Ethnic, and belongs to all nations; the second, Christian, for those struggling with affliction and glorified in affliction; the third, in fine, teaches an inspired Communion of Saints, that is, of men in the highest degree good and wise. And should not therefore the Three Divine Persons, under the similitudes and names of which these threefold doctrines and commands are promulgated, justly be considered as in the highest sense One!"

"I thank you," said Wilhelm, "for having pleased to lay all this before me in such clearness and combination, as before a grown-up person, to whom your three modes of feeling are not altogether foreign. And now, when I reflect that you communicate this high doctrine to your children, in the first place as a sensible sign, then, with some symbolical accompaniment attached to it, and at last unfold to them its deepest meaning, I cannot but warmly approve of your method."

"Right," answered they: "but now we must show you more, and so convince you the better that your son is in no bad hands. This, however, may remain for the morrow: rest and refresh yourself, that you may attend us in the morning, as a man satisfied and unimpeded, into the interior of our Sanctuary."

* * * * * *

At the hand of the Eldest, our friend now proceeded through a stately portal, into a round, or rather octagonal hall, so richly decked with pictures, that it struck him with astonishment as he entered. All this, he easily conceived, must have a significant import, though at the moment he saw not so clearly what it was. While about to question his guide on this subject, the latter invited him to step forward into a gallery, open on the one side, and stretching round a spacious gay flowery garden. The wall, however, not the flowers, attracted the eyes of the stranger; it was covered with paintings, and Wilhelm could not walk far without observing that the Sacred Books of the Israelites had furnished the materials for these figures.

"It is here," said the Eldest, "that we teach our First Religion, the religion which, for the sake of brevity, I named the Ethnic. The spirit of it is to be sought for in the history of the world; its outward form, in the events of that history. Only in the return of similar destinies on whole nations, can it properly be apprehended."

"I observe," said Wilhelm, "you have done the Israelites the honor to select their history as the groundwork of this delineation, or rather, you have made it the leading object there."

"As you see," replied the Eldest; "for you will remark, that on the socles and friezes we have introduced another series of transactions and occurrences, not so much of a synchronistic, as of a symphonistic kind; since, among all nations, we discover records of a similar import, and grounded on the same facts. Thus you perceive here, while in the main field of the picture, Abraham receives a visit from his gods in the form of fair youths, Apollo, among the herdsmen of Admetus, is painted above on the frieze. From which we may learn, that the gods, when they appear to men, are commonly unrecognised of them."

The friends walked on. Wilhelm, for the most part, met with well-known objects, but they were here exhibited in a livelier and more expressive manner than he had been used to see them. On some few matters he requested explanation, and at last could not help returning to his former question: Why the Israelitish history had been chosen in preference to all others?

The Eldest answered: " Among all Heathen religions, for such also is the Israelitish, this has the most distinguished advantages; of which I shall mention only a few. At the Ethnic judgment-seat, at the judgment-seat of the God of Nations, it is not asked Whether this is the best, the most excellent nation, but whether it lasts, whether it has continued. The Israelitish people never was good for much, as its own leaders, judges, rulers, prophets, have a thousand times reproachfully declared; it possesses few virtues, and most of the faults of other nations: but in cohesion, steadfastness, valor, and when all this would not serve, in obstinate toughness, it has no match. It is the most perseverant nation in the world: it is, it was, and it will be; to glorify the name of Jehovah, through all ages. We have set it up, therefore, as the pattern figure; as the main figure, to which the others only serve as a frame."

"It becomes not me to dispute with you," said Wilhelm, "since you have instruction to impart. Open to me, therefore, the other advantages of this people, or rather of its history, of its religion."

"One chief advantage," said the other, is its excellent collection of Sacred Books. These stand so happily combined together, that even out of the most diverse elements, the feeling of a whole still rises before us. They are complete enough to satisfy; fragmentary enough to excite; barbarous enough to rouse; tender enough to appease: and for how many other contradicting merits might not these Books, might not this one Book, be praised!"

The series of main figures, as well as their relations to the smaller which above and below accompanied them, gave the guest so much to think of, that he scarcely heard the pertinent remarks of his guide; who, by what he said, seemed desirous rather to divert our friend's attention, than to fix it on the paintings. Once, however, the old man said, on some occasion: " Another advantage of the Israelitish religion, I must here mention; it has not embodied its god in any form; and so has left us at liberty to represent him in a worthy human shape, and likewise, by way of contrast, to designate Idolatry by forms of beasts and monsters."

Our friend had now, in his short wandering through this hall, again brought the spirit of universal history before his mind; in regard to the events, he had not failed to meet with something new. So likewise, by the simultaneous presentment of the pictures, by the reflections of his guide, many new views had risen on him; and he could not but rejoice in thinking that his Felix was, by so dignified a visible representation, to seize and appropriate for his whole life those great, significant, and exemplary events, as if they had actually been present, and transacted beside him. He came at length to regard the exhibition altogether with the eyes of the child, and in this point of view it perfectly contented him. Thus wandering on, they had now reached the gloomy and perplexed periods of the history, the destruction of the City and the Temple, the murder, exile, slavery of whole masses of this stiff-necked people. Its subsequent fortunes were delineated in a cunning allegorical way; a real historical delineation of them would have lain without the limits of true Art.

At this point, the gallery abruptly terminated in a closed door, and Wilhelm was surprised to see himself already at the end. " In your historical series," said he, "I find a chasm. You have destroyed the Temple of Jerusalem, and dispersed the people; yet you have not introduced the divine Man who taught there shortly before; to whom, shortly before, they would give no ear."

"To have done this, as you require it, would have been an error. The life of that divine Man, whom you allude to, stands in no connection with the general history of the world in his time. It was a private life; his teaching was a teaching for individuals. What has publicly befallen vast masses of people, and the minor parts which compose them, belongs to the general history of the world, to the general religion of the world; the religion we have named the First. What inwardly befalls individuals, belongs to the Second religion, the Philosophical: such a religion was it that Christ taught and practised, so long as he went about on Earth. For this reason, the external here closes, and I now open to you the internal."

A door went back, and they entered a similar gallery; where Wilhelm soon recognised a corresponding series of pictures from the New Testament. They seemed as if by another hand than the first: all was softer; forms, movements, accompaniments, light, and coloring.

"Here," said the guide, after they had looked over a few pictures, "you behold neither actions nor events, but Miracles and Similitudes. There is here a new world, a new exterior, different from the former; and an interior, which was altogether wanting there. By Miracles and Similitudes, a new world is opened up. Those make the common extraordinary, these the extraordinary common."

"You will have the goodness," said Wilhelm, "to explain these few words more minutely; for, by my own light, I cannot."

"They have a natural meaning," said the other, "though a deep one. Examples will bring it out most easily and soonest. There is nothing more common and customary than eating and drinking; but it is extraordinary to transform a drink into another of more noble sort; to multiply a portion of food that it suffice a multitude. Nothing is more common than sickness and corporeal diseases; but to remove, to mitigate these by spiritual, or spiritual-like means, is extraordinary; and even in this lies the wonder of the Miracle, that the common and the extraordinary, the possible and the impossible, become one. With the Similitude again, with the Parable, the converse is the case: here it is the sense, the view, the idea, that forms the high, the unattainable, the extraordinary. When this embodies itself in a common, customary, comprehensible figure, so that it meets us as if alive, present, actual; so that we can seize it, appropriate, retain it, live with it as with our equal: this is a second sort of miracle, and is justly placed beside the first sort; nay, perhaps preferred to it. Here a living doctrine is pronounced, a doctrine which can cause no argument: it is not an opinion about what is right and wrong; it is Right and Wrong themselves, and indisputably."

This part of the gallery was shorter; indeed it formed but the fourth part of the circuit enclosing the interior court. Yet if in the former part you merely walked along, you here liked to linger, you here walked to and fro. The objects were not so striking, not so varied: yet they invited you the more to penetrate their deep still meaning. Our two friends, accordingly, turned round at the end of the space, Wilhelm, at the same time, expressing some surprise that these delineations went no farther than the Supper, than the scene where the Master and his Disciples part. He inquired for the remaining portion of the history.

"In all sorts of instruction," said the Eldest, "in all sorts of communication, we are fond of separating whatever it is possible to separate; for by this means alone can the notion of importance and peculiar significance arise in the young mind. Actual experience of itself mingles and mixes all things together: here, accordingly, we have entirely disjoined that sublime Man's life from its termination. In life, he appears as a true Philosopher—let not the expression stagger you—as a wise man in the highest sense. He stands firm to his point; he goes on his way inflexibly; and while he exalts the lower to himself, while he makes the ignorant, the poor, the sick, partakers of his wisdom, of his riches, of his strength, he, on the other hand, in no wise conceals his divine origin; he dares to equal himself with God, nay, to declare that he himself is God. In this manner is he wont, from youth upwards, to astound his familiar friends; of these he gains a part to his own cause; irritates the rest against him; and shows to all men, who are aiming at a certain elevation in doctrine and life, what they have to look for from the world. And thus, for the noble portion of mankind, his walk and conversation are even more instructive and profitable than his death: for to those trials every one is called, to this trial but a few. Now, omitting all that results from this consideration, do but look at the touching scene of the Last Supper. Here the Wise Man, as it ever is, leaves those that are his own utterly orphaned behind him; and while he is careful for the Good, he feeds along with them a traitor by whom he and the Better are to be destroyed."

With these words the Eldest opened a door; and Wilhelm faltered in surprise, as he found himself again in the first hall at the entrance. They had, in the meanwhile, as he now saw, passed round the whole circuit of the court. "I hoped," said Wilhelm, "you were leading me to the conclusion, and you take me back to the beginning."

"For the present," said the Eldest, "I can show you nothing farther: more we do not lay before our pupils, more we do not explain to them, than what you have now gone through. All that is external, worldly, universal, we communicate to each from youth upwards; what is more particularly spiritual and conversant with the heart, to those only who grow up with some thoughtfulness of temper; and the rest, which is opened only once a-year, cannot be imparted save to those whom we are sending forth as finished. That last Religion which arises from the Reverence of what is beneath us; that veneration of the contradictory, the hated, the avoided, we give each of our pupils, in small portions by way of outfit, along with him into the world, merely that he may know where more is to be had, should such a want spring up within him.

I invite you to return hither at the end of a year, to visit our general festival, and see how far your son is advanced: then shall you be admitted into the Sanctuary of Sorrow."

"Permit me one question," said Wilhelm: "as you have set up the life of this divine Man for a pattern and example, have you likewise selected his sufferings, his death, as a model of exalted patience?"

"Undoubtedly we have," replied the Eldest. "Of this we make no secret; but we draw a veil over those sufferings, even because we reverence them so highly. We hold it a damnable audacity to bring forth that torturing Cross, and the Holy One who suffers on it, or to expose them to the light of the sun, which hid its face when a reckless world forced such a sight on it; to take these mysterious secrets, in which the divine depth of Sorrow lies hid, and play with them, fondle them, trick them out, and rest not till the most reverend of all solemnities appears vulgar and paltry. Let so much, for the present, suffice to put your mind at peace respecting your son; and to convince you, that on meeting him again, you will find him trained, more or less, in one department or another, but at least in a proper way; and, at all events, not wavering, perplexed, and unstable."

Wilhelm still lingered, looking at the pictures in this entrance-hall, and wishing to get explanation of their meaning. "This, too," said the Eldest, "we must still owe you for a twelvemonth. The instruction which, in the interim, we give the children, no stranger is allowed to witness: then, however, come to us; and you will hear what our best speakers think it serviceable to make public on these matters."

Shortly after this conversation, a knocking was heard at the little gate. The Overseer of last night announced himself: he had brought out Wilhelm's horse; and so our friend took leave of the Three; who, as he set out, consigned him to the Overseer with these words: "This man is now numbered among the Trusted, and thou understandest what thou hast to tell him in answer to his questions; for, doubtless, he still wishes to be informed on much that he has seen and heard while here: purpose and circumstance are known to thee."

Wilhelm had, in fact, some questions on his mind; and these he ere long put into words. As they rode along they were saluted by the children, as on the preceding evening; but to-day, though rarely, he now and then observed a boy who did not pause in his work to salute the Overseer, but let him pass unheeded. Wilhelm asked the cause of this, and what such an exception meant. His companion answered: "It is full of meaning; for it is the highest punishment which we inflict on our pupils; they are declared unworthy to show reverence, and obliged to exhibit themselves as rude and uncultivated natures: but they do their utmost to get free of this situation, and in general adapt themselves with great rapidity to any duty. Should a young creature, on the other hand, obdurately make no attempt at return and amendment, he is then sent back to his parents, with a brief but pointed statement of his case. Whoever cannot suit himself to the regulations, must leave the district where they are in force."

Another circumstance excited Wilhelm's curiosity to-day, as it had done yesterday: the variety of color and shape apparent in the dress of the pupils. Hereby no gradation could be indicated; for children who saluted differently, were sometimes clothed alike; and others agreeing in salutation, differed in apparel. Wilhelm inquired the reason of this seeming contradiction. "It will be explained," said the other, "when I tell you, that, by this means, we endeavor to find out the children's several characters. With all our general strictness and regularity, we allow in this point a certain latitude of choice. Within the limits of our own stores of cloths and garnitures, the pupils are permitted to select what color they please; and so likewise within moderate limits, in regard to shape and cut. Their procedure, in these matters, we accurately note; for by the color, we discover their turn of thinking; by the cut, their turn of acting. However, a decisive judgment in this is rendered difficult by one peculiar property of human nature, by the tendency to imitate, the inclination to unite with something. It is very seldom that a pupil fancies any dress that has not been already there; for most part, they select something known, something which they see before their eyes. Yet this also we find worth observing; by such external circumstances, they declare themselves of one party or another; they unite with this or that; and thus some general features of their characters are indicated; we perceive whither each tends, what example he follows.

"We have had cases where the dispositions of our children verged to generality; where one fashion threatened to extend over all; and any deviation from it to dwindle into the state of an exception. Such a turn of matters we endeavor softly to stop: we let our stores run out; this and that sort of stuff, this and that sort of decoration, is no longer to be had: we introduce something new and attractive; by bright colors and short smart shape, we allure the lively; by grave shadings, by commodious many-folded make, the thoughtful; and thus, by degrees, restore the equilibrium.

"For to uniform, we are altogether disinclined; it conceals the character, and, more than any other species of distortion, withdraws the peculiarities of children from the eye of their superiors."

Amid this and other conversation, Wilhelm reached the border of the Province; and this at the point, where, by the direction of his antiquarian friend, he was to leave it, to pursue his next special object.

At parting, it was now settled with the Overseer, that, after the space of a twelvemonth,

Wilhelm should return, when the grand Triennial Festival was to be celebrated; on which occasion all the parents were invited; and finished pupils were sent forth into the tasks of chanceful life. Then, too, so he was informed, he might visit at his pleasure all the other Districts; where, on peculiar principles, each branch of education was communicated and reduced to practice in complete isolation, and with every furtherance.

* * * * * * *

That a year must have passed since Wilhelm left the Pedagogic Province, is rendered certain, by the circumstance, that we now meet him at the Festival to which he had been invited: but as our wandering Renunciants sometimes unexpectedly dive down and vanish from our sight, and then again emerge into view at a place where they were not looked for, it cannot be determined with certainty what track they have followed in the interim.

Now, however, the Traveller advances from the side of the plain country into the Pedagogic Province: he comes over fields and pasturages; skirts, on the dry lea, many a little freshet; sees bushy rather than woody hills; a free prospect on all sides, over a surface but little undulated. On such tracks, he did not long doubt that he was in the horse-producing region; and accordingly, he failed not here and there to observe greater or smaller herds of mares and foals. But all at once the horizon darkens with a fierce cloud of dust, which, rapidly swelling nearer and nearer, covers all the breadth of the space; yet at last, rent asunder by a sharp side wind, is forced to disclose its interior tumult.

At full gallop, rushes forward a vast multitude of these noble animals, guided and held together by mounted keepers. The monstrous hurlyburly whirls past the wanderer; a fair boy among the keepers looks at him with surprise; pulls in, leaps down, and embraces his father.

Now commences a questioning and answering: the boy relates that an agricultural life had not agreed with him; the harvest-home he had indeed found delightful, but the subsequent arrangements, the ploughing and digging, by no means so. This the Superiors remark, and observe at the same time that he likes to employ himself with animals; they direct him to the useful and necessary domestic breeds; try him as a sequestered herdsman and keeper, and at last promote him to the more lively equestrian occupation; where accordingly he now, himself a young foal, has to watch over foals, and to forward their good nourishment and training, under the oversight of skilful comrades.

Father and son, following the herd, by various lone-lying spacious farm-yards, reached the town or hamlet, near which the great annual Market was held. Here rages an incredible confusion, in which it is hard to determine whether merchants or wares raise more dust. From all countries, purchasers assemble here to procure animals of noble blood and careful training; all the languages of the Earth, you would fancy, meet your ear. Amid all this hubbub, too, rises the lively sound of powerful wind-instruments: everything bespeaks motion, vigor, and life.

The wanderer meets his Overseer of last year, who presents him to the others: he is even introduced to one of the Three; and by him, though only in passing, paternally and expressively saluted.

Wilhelm, here again observing an example of exclusive culture and life-leading, expresses a desire to know in what else the pupils are practised, by way of counterpoise; that so in this wild, and, to a certain degree, savage occupation of feeding animals, the youth may not himself roughen into an animal. And, in answer, he is gratified to learn, that precisely with this violent and rugged-looking occupation the softest in the world is united; the learning and practising of languages.

"To this," it was said, "we have been induced by the circumstance, that there are youths from all quarters of the world assembled here: now to prevent them from uniting, as usually happens when abroad, into national knots, and forming exclusive parties, we endeavor by a free communication of speech to approximate them.

"Indeed, a general acquaintance with languages is here in some degree rendered necessary; since, in our yearly market-festivals, every foreigner wishes to converse in his own tones and idiom; and, in the course of cheapening and purchasing, to proceed with all possible convenience. That no Babylonish confusion of tongues, however, no corruption of speech, may arise from this practice, we employ a different language month by month, throughout the year: according to the maxim, that in learning anything, its first principles alone should be taught by constraint.

"We look upon our scholars," said the Overseer, "as so many swimmers, who, in the element which threatened to swallow them, feel with astonishment that they are lighter, that it bears and carries them forward: and so it is with everything that man undertakes.

"However, if any one of our young men show a special inclination for this or the other language, we neglect not, in the midst of this tumultuous-looking life, which nevertheless offers very many quiet, idly solitary, nay, tedious hours, to provide for his true and substantial instruction. Our riding grammarians, among whom there are even some pedagogues, you would be surprised to discover among these bearded and beardless Centaurs. Your Felix has turned himself to Italian; and in the monotonous solitude of his herdsman life, you shall hear him send forth many a dainty song with proper feeling and taste. Practical activity and expertness are far more compatible with sufficient intellectual culture, than is generally supposed."

Each of these districts was celebrating its peculiar festival; so the guest was now conducted to the Instrumental Music department. This tract, skirted by the level country, began from its very border to exhibit kind and beautifully changing valleys, little trim woods; soft brooks, by the side of which, among the sward, here. and there a mossy crag modestly stood forth. Scattered, bush-encircled dwellings you might see on the hill-sides; in soft hollows, the houses clustered nearer together. Those gracefully separated cottages lay so far apart, that neither tones nor mistones could be heard from one to the other.

They now approached a wide space, begirt with buildings and shady trees, where crowded, man on man, all seemed on the stretch of expectation and attention. Just as the stranger entered, there was sent forth from all the instruments a grand symphony, the full rich power and tenderness of which he could not but admire. Opposite the spacious main orchestra, was a smaller one, which failed not to attract his notice: here stood various younger and elder scholars; each held his instrument in readiness without playing; these were they who as yet could not, or durst not, join in with the whole. It was interesting to observe how they stood as it were on the start; and our friend was informed that such a festival seldom passed over, without some one or other of them suddenly developing his talent.

As among the instrumental music, singing was now introduced, no doubt could remain that this also was favored. To the question, What other sort of culture was here blended in kind union with the chief employment, our wanderer learned in reply, that it was Poetry, and of the lyrical kind. In this matter, it appeared, their main concern was, that both arts should be developed each for itself and from itself, but then also in contrast and combination with each other. The scholars were first instructed in each according to its own limitations; then taught how the two reciprocally limit, and again reciprocally free each other.

To poetical rhythm, the musical artist opposes measure of tone and movement of tone. But here the mastery of Music over Poesy soon shows itself; for if the latter, as is fit and necessary, keep her quantities never so steadily in view, still for the musician few syllables are decidedly short or long; at his pleasure he can overset the most conscientious procedure of the rhythmer, nay, change prose itself into song; from which, in truth, the richest possibilities present themselves; and the poet would soon feel himself annihilated, if he could not, on his own side, by lyrical tenderness and boldness, inspire the musician with reverence; and, now in the softest sequence, now by the most abrupt transitions, awaken new feelings in the mind.

The singers to be met with here are mostly poets themselves. Dancing also is taught in its fundamental principles; that so all these accomplishments may regularly spread themselves into every district.

The guest, on being led across the next boundary, at once perceived an altogether different mode of building. The houses were no longer scattered into separation, no longer in the shape of cottages: they stood regularly united, beautiful in their exterior, spacious, convenient, and elegant within; you here saw an unconfined, well-built, stately town, corresponding to the scene it stood in. Here the Plastic Arts, and the trades akin to them, have their home; and a peculiar silence reigns over these spaces.

The plastic artist, it is true, must still figure himself as standing in relation to all that lives and moves among men: but his occupation is solitary; and yet, by the strangest contradiction, there is perhaps no other that so decidedly requires a living accompaniment and society. Now here, in that circle, is each in silence forming shapes that are forever to engage the eyes of men; a holiday stillness reigns over the whole scene; and did you not here and there catch the picking of stone-hewers, and the measured stroke of carpenters, who are now busily employed in finishing a lordly edifice, the air were unmoved by any sound.

Our wanderer was struck, moreover, by the earnestness, the singular rigor with which beginners, as well as more advanced pupils, were treated; it seemed as if no one by his own power and judgment accomplished anything, but as if a secret spirit, striving towards one single great aim, pervaded and vivified them all. Nowhere did you observe a scheme or sketch; every stroke was drawn with forethought. As the wanderer inquired of his guide the reason of this peculiar procedure, he was told: That Imagination was in itself a vague, unstable power, which the whole merit of the plastic artist consisted in more and more determining, fixing, nay, at last, exalting to visible presence.

The necessity for sure principles in other arts was mentioned. "Would the musician," it was said, "permit his scholar to dash wildly over the strings, nay, to invent bars and intervals for himself at his own good pleasure? Here it is palpable that nothing can be left to the caprice of the learner: the element he is to work in is irrevocably given; the implement he is to wield is put into his hands; nay, the very way and manner of his using it, I mean the changing of the fingers, he finds prescribed to him; so ordered, that the one part of his hand shall give place to the other, and each prepare the proper path for its follower: by such determinate co-operation only can the impossible at last become possible.

"But what chiefly vindicates the practice of strict requisitions, of decided laws, is that genius, that native talent, is precisely the readiest to seize them, and yield them willing obedience. It is only the half-gifted that would wish to put his own contracted singularity in the place of the unconditioned whole, and justify his false attempts under cover of an unconstrainable originality and independence. To this we grant no currency: we guard our scholars from all such misconceptions, whereby a large portion of life, nay, often the whole of life, is apt to be perplexed and disjointed.

"With genius we love most to be concerned; for this is animated just by that good spirit of quickly recognising what is profitable for it. Genius understands that Art is called Art because it is *not* Nature. Genius bends itself to respect even towards what may be named conventional: for what is this but agreeing, as the most distinguished men have agreed, to regard the unalterable, the indispensable as the best? And does not such submission always turn to good account?

"Here, too, as in all our departments, to the great assistance of the teachers, our three Reverences and their signs, with some changes suitable to the nature of the main employment, have been introduced and inculcated."

The wanderer, in his farther survey, was surprised to observe that the Town seemed still extending; street unfolding itself from street, and so offering the most varied prospects. The exterior of the edifices corresponded to their destination; they were dignified and stately, not so much magnificent as beautiful. To the nobler and more earnest buildings in the centre of the Town, the more cheerful were harmoniously appended; till farther out, gay decorated suburbs, in graceful style, stretched forth into the country, and at last separated into garden-houses.

The stranger could not fail to remark, that the dwellings of the musicians in the preceding district were by no means to be compared, in beauty or size, with the present, which painters, statuaries, and architects inhabited. He was told that this arose from the nature of the thing. The musician, ever shrouded in himself, must cultivate his inmost being, that so he may turn it outwards. The sense of the eye he may not flatter. The eye easily corrupts the judgment of the ear, and allures the spirit from the inward to the outward. Inversely, again, the plastic artist has to live in the external world; and to manifest his inward being, as it were unconsciously, in and upon what is outward. Plastic artists should dwell like kings and gods: how else are they to build and decorate for kings and gods? They must at last so raise themselves above the common, that the whole mass of a people may feel itself ennobled in and by their works.

Our friend then begged an explanation of another paradox: Why at this time, so festive, so enlivening, so tumultuously excited, in the other regions, the greatest stillness prevailed here, and all labors were continued?

"A plastic artist," it was answered, "needs no festival; for him the whole year is a festival. When he has accomplished something excellent, it stands, as it has long done before his own eye, now at last before the eye of the world: in his task he needed no repetition, no new effort, no fresh success; whereas the musician constantly afflicts himself with all this; and to him, therefore, the most splendid festival, in the most numerous assemblage, should not be refused."

"Yet, at such a season," replied Wilhelm, "something like an exhibition might be desirable; in which it would be pleasant to inspect and judge the triennial progress of your best pupils."

"In other places," it was answered, "an exhibition may be necessary; with us it is not. Our whole being and nature is exhibition. Look round you at these buildings of every sort: all erected by our pupils; and this not without plans, a hundred times talked of and meditated; for the builder must not grope and experiment; what is to continue standing, must stand rightly, and satisfy, if not forever, yet at least for a long space of time. If we cannot help *committing* errors, we must *build* none.

"With statuaries we proceed more laxly, most so of all with painters; to both we give liberty to try this each in his own way. It stands in their power to select in the interior or exterior compartments of edifices in public places, some space which they may incline to decorate. They give forth their ideas, and if these are in some degree to be approved of, the completion of them is permitted, and this in two ways: either with liberty, sooner or later, to remove the work, should it come to displease the artist; or, with the condition that what is once set up shall remain unalterable in its place. Most part choose the first of these offers, retaining in their own hands this power of removal; and in the performance, they constantly avail themselves of the best advice. The second case occurs seldomer; and we then observe that the artist trusts less to himself, holds long conferences with companions and critics, and by this means produces works really estimable, and deserving to endure."

After all this, our Traveller neglected not to ask: What other species of instruction was combined with the main one here? and received for answer, that it was Poetry, and of the Epic sort.

This to our friend must have seemed a little singular, when he heard farther that the pupils were not allowed to read or hear any finished poems by ancient or modern poets. "We merely impart to them," it was said, "a series of mythuses, traditions, and legends, in the most laconic form. And now, from the pictorial or poetic execution of these subjects, we at once discover the peculiar productive gift of the genius devoted to the one or the other art. Both poet and painter thus labor at the same fountain; and each endeavors to draw off the water to his own advantage, and attain his own required objects with it; in which he succeeds much better, than if he attempted again to fashion something that has been fashioned already."

The Traveller himself had an opportunity of seeing how this was accomplished: several painters were busy in a room; a gay young friend was relating with great minuteness a very simple story; so that he employed almost as many words as the others did pencil-strokes, to complete the same exhibition and round it fully off.

He was told, that in working together the friends were wont to carry on much pleasant conversation; and that in this way several improvisatori had unfolded their gifts, and succeeded in exciting great enthusiasm for this twofold mode of representation.

Our friend now reverted his inquiries to the subject of plastic art. "You have no exhibition," said he; "and therefore, I suppose, give no prize either?"

"No," said the other, "we do not; but here, close by, we can show you something which we reckon more useful."

They entered a large hall, beautifully lighted from above; a wide circle of busy artists first attracted the eye; and from the midst of these, rose a colossal group of figures, elevated in the centre of the place. Male and female forms, of gigantic power, in violent postures, reminded one of that lordly fight between Heroic youths and Amazons, wherein hate and enmity at last issue in mutually regretful alliance. This strikingly intertwisted piece of art presented an equally favorable aspect from every point of its circuit. In a wide ring round it were many artists sitting and standing, each occupied in his own way; the painter at his easel, the drawer at his sketch-board; some were modelling it in full, others in bas-relief; there were even architects engaged in planning the pedestal, on which a similar group, when wrought in marble, was to be erected. Each individual was proceeding by his own method in this task : painters and drawers were bringing out the group to a plain surface; careful, however, not to destroy its figures, but to retain as much of it as possible. In the same manner were works in bas-relief going forward. One man only had repeated the whole group in a miniature scale; and in certain movements and arrangements of limbs, he really seemed to have surpassed his model.

And now it came out that this man was the maker of the model; who, before working it in marble, had here submitted his performance not to a critical, but to a practical trial; and by accurately observing whatever any of his fellow-artists in his special department and way of thought might notice, retain or alter in the group, was purposing, in subsequent consideration, to turn all this to his own profit; so that, when at length the grand work stood finished in marble, though undertaken, planned, and executed by one, it might seem to belong to all.

The greatest silence reigned throughout this apartment also; but the Superior raised his voice, and cried: "Is there any of you, then who in presence of this stationary work can, with gifted words, so awaken our imagination, that all we here see concreted, shall again become fluid, without losing its character; and so convince us, that what our artist has here laid hold of, was indeed the worthiest?"

Called forth on all sides by name, a fair youth laid down his work; and as he stept forward, began a quiet speech, seemingly intended merely to describe the present group of figures; but ere long he cast himself into the region of poetry, plunged into the middle of the action, and ruled this element like a master; by degrees, his representation so swelled and mounted by lordly words and gestures, that the rigid group seemed actually to move about its axis, and the number of its figures to be doubled and trebled. Wilhelm stood enraptured, and at last exclaimed: "Can we now forbear passing over into song itself, into rhythmic melody?"

"This I should wish to hinder," said the Overseer; "for if our excellent statuary will be candid, he will confess to us that our poet scarcely pleases him; and this because their arts lie in the most opposite regions: on the other hand, I durst bet, that here and there a painter has not failed to appropriate some living touches from the speech.

"A soft kindly song, however, I could wish our friend to hear: there is one, for instance, which you sing to an air so lovely and earnest; it turns on Art in general, and I myself never listen to it without pleasure."

After a pause, in which they beckoned to each other, and settled their arrangements by signs, the following heart and spirit stirring song resounded in stately melody from all sides:

When inventing, when selecting,
 Artist, by thyself continue long:
When some good thou art effecting,
 Haste and see it in the throng.
Here in others look, discover
 What thy own life's course has been;
And thy deeds of years past over
 In thy fellow man be seen.

The devising, the uniting,
 What and how the forms shall be;
One thing will the other lighten,
 And at last comes joy to thee!
Wise and true what thou impartest,
 Fairly shaped, and softly done:
Thus of old the cunning artist
 Artist-like his glory won.

As all Nature's thousand changes
 But one changeless God proclaim;
So in Art's wide kingdoms ranges
 One sole meaning still the same:
This is Truth, eternal Reason,
 Which from Beauty takes its dress,
And serene through time and season,
 Stands for aye in loveliness.

While the orator, the singer,
 Pour their hearts in rhyme and prose,
'Neath the painter's busy finger,
 Shall bloom forth Life's cheerful rose;
Girt with sisters: in the middle,
 And with Autumn's fruitage blent,
That of life's mysterious riddle
 Some short glimpses may be lent.

> Thousandfold, and graceful, show thou,
> Form from forms evolving fair;
> And of man's bright image know thou
> That a God once tarried there:
> And whate'er your tasks or prizes,
> Stand as brethren one and all,
> While, like song, sweet incense rises
> From the altar at your call.

All this Wilhelm could not but let pass, though it must have seemed paradoxical enough; and, had he not seen it with his eyes, might even have appeared impossible. But now, when it was explained and pointed out to him, openly and freely, and in fair sequence, he scarcely needed to put any farther question on the subject. However, he at last addressed his conductor as follows: "I see here a most prudent provision made for much that is desirable in life: but tell me farther, which of your regions exhibits a similar attention to Dramatic Poetry, and where could I instruct myself in that matter? I have looked round over all your edifices, and observed none that seemed destined for such an object."

"In reply to this question, we must not hide from you, that, in our whole Province, there is no such edifice to be seen. The drama presupposes the existence of an idle multitude, perhaps even of a populace; and no such class finds harbor with us; for birds of that feather, when they do not in spleen forsake us of their own accord, we soon take care to conduct over the marches. Doubt not, however, that in our Institution, so universal in its character, this point was carefully meditated: but no region could be found for the purpose, everywhere some important scruple came in the way. Indeed, who among our pupils could readily determine, with pretended mirth, or hypocritical sorrow, to excite in the rest a feeling untrue in itself, and alien to the moment, for the sake of calling forth an always dubious satisfaction? Such juggleries we reckoned in all cases dangerous, and could not reconcile with our earnest objects."

"It is said, however," answered Wilhelm, "that this far-stretching art promotes all the rest, of whatever sort."

"Nowise," answered the other: "it employs the rest, but spoils them. I do not blame a player for uniting himself with a painter; but the painter, in such society, is lost. Without any conscience, the player will lay hold of whatever art or life presents him, and use it for his fugitive objects, indeed with no small profit: the painter, again, who could wish in return to extract advantage from the theatre, will constantly find himself a loser by it; and so also in the like case will the musician. The combined Arts appear to me like a family of sisters, of whom the greater part were inclined to good economy, but one was light-headed, and desirous to appropriate and squander the whole goods and chattels of the household. The Theatre is this wasteful sister: it has an ambiguous origin, which in no case, whether as art or trade or amusement, it can wholly conceal."

Wilhelm cast his eyes on the ground with a deep sigh; for all that he had enjoyed or suffered on the Stage rose at once before his mind; and he blessed the good men who were wise enough to spare their pupils such pain, and, out of principle and conviction, to banish such errors from their sphere.

His attendant, however, did not leave him long in these meditations, but continued: "As it is our highest and holiest principle that no talent, no capacity be misdirected, we cannot hide from ourselves that among so large a number, here and there a mimical gift will sometimes decidedly come to light; exhibiting itself in an irresistible desire to ape the characters, forms, movements, speech of others. This we certainly do not encourage; but we observe our pupil strictly, and if he continue faithful to his nature, then we have already established an intercourse with the great theatres of all nations, and so thither we send any youth of tried capability, that, as the duck on the pond, so he on the boards, may be forthwith conducted, full speed, to the future quack-quacking, and gibble-gabbling of his life."

Wilhelm heard this with patience, but only with half-conviction, perhaps with some spleen: for so strangely is man tempered, that he may be persuaded of the worthlessness of any darling object, may turn away from it, nay, even execrate it, but yet will not see it treated in this way by others; and perhaps the Spirit of Contradiction which dwells in all men, never rouses itself more vehemently and stoutly than in such cases.

And the Editor of these sheets may himself confess, that he lets not this strange passage through his hands without some touch of anger. Has not he, too, in many senses, expended more life and faculty than was right on the Theatre? And would these men convince him that this has been an unpardonable error, a fruitless toil?

But we have no time for appending, in splenetic mood, such remembrances and after-feelings to the narrative: for our friend now finds himself agreeably surprised, as one of the Three, and this a particularly prepossessing one, again comes before his eyes. Kind, open meekness, announcing the purest peace of soul, came in its refreshing effluences along with him. Trustfully the Wanderer could approach, and feel his trust returned.

Here he now learned that the Chief was at present in the Sanctuary, instructing, teaching, blessing; while the Three had separated to visit all the Regions, and everywhere, after most thorough information obtained, and conferences with the subordinate Overseers, to forward what was in progress, to found what was newly planned, and thereby faithfully discharge their high duty.

This same excellent person now gave him a

more comprehensive view of their internal situation and external connections; explained to him the mutual influences of one Region on another; and also by what steps, after a longer or a shorter date, a pupil could be transferred from the one to the other. All this harmonized completely with what he already knew. At the same time, he was much gratified by the description given of his son; and their farther plan of education met with his entire approval.

He was now, by the Assistants and Overseer, invited to a Miners' Festival, which was forthwith to be celebrated. The ascent of the Mountains was difficult; and Wilhelm fancied he observed that his guide walked even slower towards evening, as if the darkness had not been likely to obstruct their path still more. But when deep night came round them, this enigma was solved: our Wanderer observed little flames come glimmering and wavering forth from many dells and chasms; gradually stretch themselves into lines, and roll over the summits of the mountains. Much kindlier than when a volcano opens, and its belching roar threatens whole countries with destruction, did this fair light appear; and yet, by degrees, it glowed with new brightness; grew stronger, broader, more continuous; glittered like a stream of stars, soft and lovely indeed, yet spreading boldly over all the scene.

After the attendant had a little while enjoyed the surprise of his guest, for they could clearly enough observe each other, their faces and forms as well as their path being illuminated by the light from the distance — he began: "You see here, in truth, a curious spectacle: these lights, which, day and night, the whole year over, gleam and work under ground, forwarding the acquisition of concealed and scarcely attainable treasures; these now mount and well forth from their abysses, and gladden the upper night. Scarcely could one anywhere enjoy so brave a review, as here, where this most useful occupation, which in its subterranean concealment is dispersed and hidden from the eye, rises before us in its full completeness, and bespeaks a great secret combination."

Amid such speeches and thoughts, they had reached the spot where these fire-brooks poured themselves into a sea of flame, surrounding a well-lighted insular space. The Wanderer placed himself in the dazzling circle, within which, glittering lights by thousands formed an imposing contrast with the miners, ranked round it like a dark wall. Forthwith arose the gayest music, accompanied by becoming songs. Hollow masses of rock came forward on machinery, and opened a resplendent interior to the eye of the delighted spectator. Mimetic exhibitions, and whatever else at such a moment can gratify the multitude, combined with all this at once to excite and to satisfy a cheerful attention.

But with what astonishment was Wilhelm filled, when, on being introduced to the Superiors, he observed Friend Jarno, in solemn stately robes, among the number! "Not in vain," cried Jarno, "have I changed my former name with the more expressive title of Montan: thou findest me here initiated in mountain and cave; and now, if questioned, I could disclose and explain to thee much that a year ago was still a riddle to myself."

* * * * * * *

As Wilhelm, in order to reach any point of the line marked out by the first Arrow, had to proceed obliquely through the country, he found himself necessitated to perform the journey on foot, leaving his luggage to be carried after him. For this walk of his, however, he was richly rewarded; meeting at every step, quite unexpectedly, with loveliest tracts of scenery. They were of that sort, which the last slope of a mountain region forms in its meeting with the plain country; bushy hills, their soft declivities employed in domestic use; all level spaces green; nowhere aught steep, unfruitful, or unploughed to be noticed. Ere long he reached the main valley, into which the side-waters flowed; and this too was carefully cultivated, graceful when you looked over it; with taper trees marking the bends of the river, and of the brooks which poured into it. On looking at his map, his indicator, he observed with surprise that the line drawn for him cut directly through this valley; so that, in the first place, he was at least on the right road.

An old castle, in good repair, and seemingly built at different periods, stood forth on a bushy hill; at the foot of which a gay hamlet stretched along, with its large inn rising prominent among the other houses. Hither he proceeded; and was received by the landlord kindly enough, yet with an excuse that he could not be admitted, unless by the permission of a party who had hired the whole establishment for a time; on which account he, the landlord, was under the necessity of sending all his guests to the older inn, which lay farther up the hamlet. After a short conference, the man seemed to bethink himself, and said: "Indeed there is no one of them at home even now; but this is Saturday, and the Bailiff will not fail to be here soon; he comes every week to settle the accounts of the last, and make arrangements for the next. Truly, there is a fair order reigns among these men, and a pleasure in having to do with them, though they are strict enough; for if they yield one no great profit, it is sure and constant." He then desired his new guest to amuse himself in the large upper hall, and await what farther might occur.

Here Wilhelm, on entering, found a large clean apartment; except for benches and tables, altogether empty. So much the more was he surprised to see a large tablet inserted above one of the doors, with these words marked on it in golden letters, *Ubi homines sunt modi sunt;* which in modern tongue may signify, that where men combine in society, the way and manner in which they like to be and to continue together is directly established. This motto made our Wanderer think; he took it as a good omen; finding here, expressed and confirmed, a principle which he had often, in the course of life, perceived for himself to be furthersome and reasonable. He had not waited long, when the Bailiff made his appearance; who being forewarned by the landlord, after a short conversation, and no very special scrutiny, admitted Wilhelm on the following terms: To continue three days; to participate quietly in whatever should occur; and happen what might, to ask no questions about the reason, and at taking leave, to ask none about the score. All this our traveller was obliged to comply with, the deputy not being allowed to yield in a single point.

The Bailiff was about retiring, when a sound of vocal music rolled up the stair: two pretty young men entered singing; and these the Bailiff, by a simple sign, gave to understand that their guest was accepted. Without interrupting their song, they kindly saluted the stranger, and continued their duet with the finest grace, showing clearly enough that they were well trained, and complete masters of their art. As Wilhelm testified the most attentive interest, they paused and inquired: If in his own pedestrian wanderings no song ever occurred to him, which he went along singing by himself? "A good voice," answered Wilhelm, "Nature has in truth denied me: yet I often feel as if a secret Genius were whispering some rhythmic words in my ear; so that, in walking, I move to musical measure; fancying, at the same time, that I hear low tones, accompanying some song, which, in one way or another, has pleasantly risen before me."

"If you recollect such a song, write it down for us," said they: "We shall see if we have skill to accompany your singing Demon." He took a leaf from his note-book, and handed them the following lines:

>From the mountains to the champaign,
By the glens and hills along,
Comes a rustling and a tramping,
Comes a motion as of song:
And this undetermined roving
Brings delight, and brings good heed;
And thy striving, be 't with Loving,
And thy living, be 't in Deed!

After brief study, there arose at once a gay marching melody, which, in its repetition and restriction still stepping forward, hurried on the hearer with it: he was in doubt whether this was his own tune, his former theme; or one now for the first time so fitted to the words, that no other movement was conceivable. The singers had for some time pleasantly proceeded in this manner, when two stout young fellows came in, whom, by their accoutrements, you directly recognised as masons; two others, who followed them, being as evidently carpenters. These four, softly laying down their tools, listened to the music, and soon struck in with sure and decided voices; so that to the mind it seemed as if a real wayfaring company were stepping along over hill and valley; and Wilhelm thought he had never heard anything so graceful, so enlivening to heart and mind. This enjoyment, however, was to be increased yet farther, and raised to the highest pitch, by the entrance of a gigantic figure, mounting the stair with a hard firm tread, which, with all his efforts, he could scarcely moderate. A heavy-laden dorsel he directly placed in the corner; himself he seated on a bench, which beginning to creak under his weight, the others laughed, yet without going wrong in their music. Wilhelm, however, was exceedingly surprised, when, with a huge bass voice, this Son of Anak joined in also. The hall quivered; and it was to be observed that in his part he altered the burden, and sang it thus:

>Life's no resting, but a moving,
Let thy life be deed on deed!

Farther, you could very soon perceive that he was drawing down the time to a slower step, and forcing the rest to follow him. Of this, when at last they were satisfied and had concluded, they accused him; declaring he had tried to set them wrong.

"Not at all!" cried he: "it is you who tried to set me wrong; to put me out of my own step, which must be measured and sure, if I am to walk with my loading up hill and down dale, and yet, in the end, arrive at my appointed hour, to satisfy your wants."

One after the other, these persons now passed into an adjoining room to the Bailiff; and Wilhelm easily observed that they were occupied in settling accounts; a point, however, as to which he was not allowed at present to inquire farther. Two fair lively boys in the meanwhile entered, and began covering a table in all speed, moderately furnishing it with meat and wine; and the Bailiff, coming out, invited them all to sit down along with him. The boys waited; yet forgot not their own concern, but enjoyed their share in a standing posture. Wilhelm recollected witnessing similar scenes during his abode among the players; yet the present company seemed to be of a much more serious cast; constituted not out of sport, for show, but with a view to important concerns of life.

The conversation of the craftsmen with the Bailiff added strength to this conviction. These four active young people, it appeared, were busy in the neighbourhood, where a violent conflagration had destroyed the fairest village in the country; nor did Wilhelm fail to learn that the worthy Bailiff was employed in getting timber and other building materials; all which looked the more enigmatical, as none of these persons seemed to be resident here, but in all other points announced themselves as transitory strangers. By way of conclusion to the meal, St. Christopher, such was the name they gave the giant, brought out, for good-night, a dainty glass of wine, which had before been set aside:

a gay choral song kept the party still some time together, after they were out of sight; and then Wilhelm was at last conducted to a chamber of the loveliest aspect and situation. The full moon, enlightening a rich plain, was already up; and in the bosom of our Wanderer it awoke remembrances of similar scenes. The spirits of all dear friends hovered past him: especially the image of Lenardo rose in him so vividly, that he might have fancied the man himself was standing before his eyes. All this had prepared him with its kind influences for nightly rest; when, on a sudden, there arose a tone of so strange a nature, that it almost frightened him. It sounded as from a distance, and yet seemed to be in the house itself; for the building quivered many times, and the floors reverberated when the sound rose to its highest pitch. Wilhelm, though his ear was usually delicate in discriminating tones, could make nothing of this: he compared it to the droning roar of a huge organ-pipe, which, for sheer compass, produces no determinate note. Whether this nocturnal terror passed away towards morning, or Wilhelm by degrees became accustomed to the sound, and no longer heeded it, is difficult to discover: at any rate, he fell asleep; and was in due time pleasantly awakened by the rising sun.

Scarcely had one of the boys who were in waiting brought him breakfast, when a figure entered, whom he had already noticed last night at supper, without clearly ascertaining his quality. A well-formed, broad-shouldered, yet nimble man; who now, by the implements which he spread out, announced himself as Barber, and forthwith prepared for performing his much-desired office on Wilhelm. For the rest, he was quite silent; and with a light hand he went through his task, without once having opened his lips. Wilhelm therefore began, and said: "Of your art you are completely master; and I know not that I have ever had a softer razor on my cheeks: at the same time, however, you appear to be a strict observer of the laws of the Society."

Roguishly smiling, laying his finger on his lips, the taciturn shaver glided through the door. "By my sooth!" cried Wilhelm after him, "I think you must be old Redcloak; if not himself, at least a descendant of his: it is lucky for you that you ask no counter service of me; your turn would have been but sorrily done."

No sooner had this curious personage retired, than the well-known Bailiff came in, inviting our friend to dinner for this day, in words which sounded pretty strange: the BOND, so said the speaker expressly, gave the stranger welcome; requested his company at dinner; and took pleasure in the hope of being more closely connected with him. Inquiries were then made as to the guest's health, and how he was contented with his entertainment; to all which he could only answer in terms of satisfaction. He would, in truth, have liked much to ask of this man, as previously of the silent Barber, some information touching the horrid sound, which throughout the night had, if not tormented, at least discomposed him: but, mindful of his engagement, he forbore all questions; hoping that, without importunity, from the good-will of the Society, or in some other accidental way, he might be informed according to his wishes.

Our friend, now when left alone, began to reflect on the strange person who had sent him this invitation, and knew not well what to make of the matter. To designate one or more superiors by a neuter noun, seemed to him a somewhat precarious mode of speech. For the rest, there was such a stillness all round, that he could not recollect of ever having passed a stiller Sunday. He went out of doors; and, hearing a sound of bells, walked towards the village. Mass was just over; and among the villagers and country-people crowding out of church, he observed three acquaintances of last night; a mason, a carpenter, and a boy. Farther on, he met among the Protestant worshippers the other corresponding three. How the rest managed their devotion was unknown to him: but so much he thought himself entitled to conclude, that in this Society a full religious toleration was practised.

About midday, at the castle-gate, he was met by the Bailiff; who then conducted him through various halls into a large antechamber, and there desired him to take a seat. Many persons passed through into an adjoining hall. Those already known were to be seen among them; St. Christopher himself went by: all saluted the Bailiff and the stranger. But what struck our friend most in this affair was, that the whole party seemed to consist of artisans; all dressed in the usual fashion, though extremely neat and clean: a few among the number you might at most perhaps have reckoned of the clerk species.

No more guests now making their appearance, the Bailiff led our friend through the stately door into a spacious hall. Here a table of immense length had been covered; past the lower end of which he was conducted, towards the head, where he saw three persons standing in a cross direction. But what was his astonishment when he approached, and Lenardo, scarcely yet recognised, fell upon his neck. From this surprise he had not recovered, when another person, with no less warmth and vivacity, likewise embraced him; announcing himself as our strange Friedrich, Natalia's brother. The rapture of these friends diffused itself over all present; an exclamation of joy and blessing sounded along the whole table. But in a moment, the company being seated, all again became silent; and the repast, served up with a certain solemnity, was enjoyed in like manner.

Towards the conclusion of the ceremony, Lenardo gave a sign: two singers rose; and Wilhelm was exceedingly surprised to hear in this place his yesternight's song; which we, for the sake of what follows, shall beg permission to insert once more.

> From the mountains to the champaign,
> By the glens and hills along,
> Comes a rustling and a tramping,
> Comes a motion as of song:
> And this undetermined roving
> Brings delight, and brings good heed;
> And thy striving, be't with Loving,
> And thy living, be't in Deed!

Scarcely had this duet, accompanied by a chorus of agreeable number, approached its conclusion, when two other singers, on the opposite side, started up impetuously; and, with earnest vehemence, inverted rather than continued the song; to Wilhelm's astonishment, proceeding thus:

> For the tie is snapt asunder,
> Trust and loving hope are fled;
> Can I tell, in fear and wonder,
> With what dangers now bested,
> I, cut off from friend and brother,
> Like the widow in her wo,
> With the one and not the other,
> On and on, my way must go!

The chorus, taking up this strophe, grew more and more numerous, more and more vociferous; and yet the voice of St. Christopher, from the bottom of the table, could still be distinctly recognised among them. The lamentation, in the end, rose almost to be frightful: a spirit of dispiritment, combining with the skilful execution of the singers, introduced something unnatural into the whole, so that it pained our friend, and almost made him shudder. In truth, they all seemed perfectly of one mind; and as if lamenting their own fate on the eve of a separation. The strange repetitions, the frequent resuscitation of a fatiguing song, at length became dangerous in the eyes of the Bond itself: Lenardo rose, and all instantly sat down, abruptly breaking off their hymn. The other, with friendly words, thus began:

"Indeed I cannot blame you for continually recalling to your minds the destiny which stands before us all, that so, at any hour, you may be ready for it. If aged and life-weary men have called to their neighbors: Think of dying! we younger and life-loving men may well keep encouraging and reminding one another with the cheerful words: Think of wandering! Yet, withal, of a thing which we either voluntarily undertake, or believe ourselves constrained to, it were well to speak with cheerfulness and moderation. You yourselves know best what, in our situation, is fixed, and what is movable: let us enjoy the former, too, in sprightly and gay tones; and to its success be this parting cup now drunk!" He emptied his glass, and sat down: the four singers instantly rose, and in flowing connected tones, thus began:

> Keep not standing fix'd and rooted,
> Briskly venture, briskly roam,
> Head and hand, where'er thou foot it,
> And stout heart, are still at home.

> In each land the sun does visit,
> We are gay, whate'er betide:
> To give room for wand'ring is it
> That the world was made so wide.

As the chorus struck in with its repetition of these lines, Lenardo rose, and with him all the rest. His nod set the whole company into singing movement; those at the lower end marched out, St. Christopher at their head, in pairs through the hall; and the uplifted wanderers' song grew clearer and freer, the farther they proceeded; producing at last a particularly good effect, when, from the terraces of the castle-garden, you looked down over the broad valley, in whose fulness and beauty you might well have liked to lose yourself. While the multitude were dispersing this way and that, according to their pleasure, Wilhelm was made acquainted with the third Superior. This was the Amtmann; by whose kind influence many favors had been done the Society; in particular, the Castle of his patron the Count, situated among several families of rank, had been given up to their use, so long as they might think fit to tarry here.

Towards evening, while the friends were in a far-seeing grove, there came a portly figure over the threshold, whom Wilhelm at once recognised as the Barber of this morning. To a low mute bow of the man, Lenardo answered: "You now come, as always, at the right season; and will not delay to entertain us with your talent. I may be allowed," continued he, turning towards Wilhelm, "to give you some knowledge of our Society, the Bond of which I may flatter myself that I am. No one enters our circle unless he have some talents to show, which may contribute to the use or enjoyment of society in general. This man is an excellent surgeon; of his skill as a beard-artist you yourself can testify: for these reasons, he is no less welcome than necessary to us. Now, as his employment usually brings with it a great and often burdensome garrulity, he has engaged, for the sake of his own culture, to comply with a certain condition; as, indeed, every one that means to live with us must agree to constrain himself in some particular point, if the greater freedom be left him in all other points. Accordingly, our Barber has renounced the use of his tongue, in so far as aught common or casual is to be expressed by it: but by this means, another gift of speech has been unfolded in him, which acts by forethought, cunningly and pleasurably; I mean the gift of narration.

"His life is rich in wonderful experiences, which he used to split in pieces, babbling of them at wrong times; but which he now, constrained by silence, repeats and arranges in his quiet thought. This also his power of imagination now forwards, lending life and movement to past occurrences. With no common art and skill, he can relate to us genuine Antique Tales, or modern stories of the same fabulous cast; thereby, at the right hour affording us a most pleasant entertainment, when I loose his tongue for him; which I now do; giving him, at the same time, this praise, that in the considerable period during which I have known him, he has never once been guilty of a repetition. I cannot but hope, that, in the present case, for love and respect to our dear guest, he will especially distinguish himself."

A sprightly cheerfulness spread over Redcloak's face; and without delay, he began speaking as follows.

THE NEW MELUSINA.

"Respected gentlemen! Being aware that preliminary speeches and introductions are not much to your taste, I shall without farther talk assure you, that in the present instance, I hope to fulfil your commission moderately well. From me has many a true history gone forth already, to the high and universal satisfaction of hearers: but, to-day I may assert, that I have one to tell, which far surpasses the former; and which, though it happened to me several years ago, still disquiets me in recollecting it, nay, still gives hope of some farther development.

"By way of introduction, let me confess, that I have not always so arranged my scheme of life as to be certain of the next period in it, or even of the next day. In my youth, I was no first-rate economist; and often found myself in manifold perplexity. At one time, I undertook a journey, thinking to derive good profit in the course of it: but the scale I went upon was too liberal; and after having commenced my travel with Extra-post, and then prosecuted it for a time in the Diligence, I at last found myself obliged to front the end of it on foot.

"Like a gay young blade, it had been from of old my custom, on entering any inn, to look round for the landlady, or even the cook, and wheedle myself into favor with her; whereby, for most part, my shot was somewhat reduced.

"One night at dusk, as I was entering the Post-house of a little town, and purposing to set about my customary operations, there came a fair double-seated coach with four horses, rattling up to the door behind me. I turned round; and observed in it a young lady, without maid, without servants. I hastened to open the carriage for her, and to ask if I could help her in anything. On stepping out, a fair form displayed itself; and her lovely countenance, if you looked at it narrowly, was adorned with a slight shade of sorrow. I again asked if there was aught I could do for her. 'O yes!' said she, 'if you will lift that little Box carefully, which you will find standing on the seat, and bring it in: but I beg very much of you to carry it with all steadiness, and not to move or shake it in the least.' I took out the Box with great care; she shut the coach-door; we walked up stairs together, and she told the servants that she was to stay here for the night.

"We were now alone in the chamber: she desired me to put the Box on the table, which was standing at the wall; and as, by several of her movements, I observed that she wished to be alone, I took my leave, reverently but warmly kissing her hand.

"'Order supper for us two,' said she then: and you may well conceive with what pleasure I executed the commission; scarcely deigning, in my pride of heart, to cast even a side-look on landlady and menials. With impatience I expected the moment that was to lead me back to her. Supper was served: we took our seats opposite each other; I refreshed my heart, for the first time during a considerable while, with a good meal; and no less with so desirable a sight beside me; nay, it seemed as if she were growing fairer and fairer every moment.

"Her conversation was pleasant; yet she carefully waived whatever had reference to affection and love. The cloth was removed: I still lingered, I tried all sorts of manœuvres to get near her; but in vain; she kept me at my distance, by a certain dignity which I could not withstand; nay, against my will, I had to part from her at a rather early hour.

"After a night passed in waking or unrestfully dreaming, I rose early; inquired whether she had ordered horses; and learning that she had not, I walked into the garden, saw her standing dressed at the window, and hastened up to her. Here, as she looked so fair, and fairer than ever, love, roguery, and audacity all at once started into motion within me: I rushed towards her, and clasped her in my arms. 'Angelic, irresistible being,' cried I, 'pardon! but it is impossible—!' With incredible dexterity she whisked herself out of my arms, and I had not even time to imprint a kiss on her cheek. 'Forbear such outbreakings of a sudden foolish passion,' said she, 'if you would not scare away a happiness which lies close beside you, but which cannot be laid hold of till after some trials.'

"'Ask of me what thou pleasest, angelic spirit!' cried I: 'but do not drive me to despair.' She answered with a smile: 'If you mean to devote yourself to my service, hear the terms. I am come hither to visit a lady of my friends, and with her I purpose to continue for a time: in the meanwhile, I could wish that my carriage and this Box were taken forward. Will you engage with it? You have nothing to do, but carefully to lift the Box into the carriage and out; to sit down beside it, and punctually take charge that it receive no harm. When you enter an inn, it is put upon a table, in a chamber by itself, in which you must neither sit nor sleep. You lock the chamber-door with this key, which will open and shut any lock, and has the peculiar property, that no lock shut by it can be opened in the interim.'

"I looked at her; I felt strangely enough at heart: I promised to do all, if I might hope to see her soon, and if she would seal this hope to me with a kiss. She did so; and from that moment, I had become entirely her bondman.

I was now to order horses, she said. We settled the way I was to take; the places where I was to wait, and expect her. She at last pressed a purse of gold into my hand, and I pressed my lips on the fair hand that gave it me. She seemed moved at parting; and for me, I no longer knew what I was doing or was to do.

"On my return from giving my orders, I found the room-door locked. I directly tried my master-key, and it performed its duty perfectly. The door flew up: I found the chamber empty; only the Box standing on the table where I had laid it.

"The carriage drove up: I carried the Box carefully down with me, and placed it by my side. The hostess asked: 'Where is the lady, then?' A child answered: 'She is gone into the town.' I nodded to the people; and rolled off in triumph from the door, which I had last night entered with dusty gaiters. That in my hours of leisure I diligently meditated on this adventure, counted my money, laid many schemes, and still now and then kept glancing at the Box, you will readily imagine. I posted right forward; passed several stages without alighting; and rested not till I had reached a considerable town, where my fair one had appointed me to wait. Her commands had been pointedly obeyed: the Box always carried to a separate room, and two wax candles lighted beside it, for such also had been her order. I would then lock the chamber; establish myself in my own, and take such comfort as the place afforded.

"For a while I was able to employ myself with thinking of her; but by degrees the time began to hang heavy on my hands. I was not used to live without companions: these I soon found, at tables-d'hôte, in coffee-houses, and public places, altogether to my wish. In such a mode of living my money began to melt away; and one night, it vanished entirely from my purse, in a fit of passionate gaming, which I had not had the prudence to abandon. Void of money; with the appearance of a rich man, expecting a heavy bill of charges; uncertain whether and when my fair one would again make her appearance, I felt myself in the deepest embarrassment. Doubly did I now long for her; and believe, that, without her and her gold, it was quite impossible for me to live.

"After supper, which I had relished very little, being forced for this time to consume it in solitude, I took to walking violently up and down my room: I spoke aloud to myself, cursed my folly with horrid execrations, threw myself on the floor, tore my hair, and indeed behaved in the most outrageous fashion. Suddenly, in the adjoining chamber where the Box was, I heard a slight movement, and then a soft knocking at the well-bolted door, which entered from my apartment. I gather myself, grope for my master-key, and the door-leaves fly up of themselves; and in the splendor of those burning wax-lights enters my Beauty. I cast myself at her feet, kiss her robe, her hands; she raises me; I venture not to clasp her, scarcely to look at her; but candidly and repentantly confess to her my fault. 'It is pardonable,' said she; 'only it postpones your happiness and mine. You must now make another tour into the world, before we can meet again. Here is more money,' continued she, 'sufficient if you husband it with any kind of reason. But as wine and play have brought you into this perplexity, be on your guard in future against wine and women, and let me hope for a glad meeting when the time comes.'

"She retired over the threshold; the door-leaves flew together: I knocked, I entreated; but nothing farther stirred. Next morning while presenting his bill, the waiter smiled, and said: 'So we have found out at last, then, why you lock your door in so artful and incomprehensible a way, that no master-key can open it. We supposed you must have much money and precious ware laid up by you; but now we have seen your treasure walking down stairs; and in good truth, it seemed worthy of being well kept.'

"To this I answered nothing; but paid my reckoning, and mounted with my Box into the carriage. I again rolled forth into the world, with the firmest resolution to be heedful in future of the warning given me by my fair and mysterious friend. Scarcely, however, had I once more reached a large town, when forthwith I got acquainted with certain interesting ladies, from whom I absolutely could not tear myself away. They seemed inclined to make me pay dear for their favor: for while they still kept me at a certain distance, they led me into one expense after the other; and I, being anxious only to promote their satisfaction, once more ceased to think of my purse, but paid and spent straight forward, as occasion needed. But how great was my astonishment and joy, when, after some weeks, I observed that the fulness of my store was not in the least diminished, that my purse was still as round and crammed as ever! Wishing to obtain more strict knowledge of this pretty quality, I set myself down to count; I accurately marked the sum; and again proceeded in my joyous life as before. We had no want of excursions by land, and excursions by water; of dancing, singing, and other recreations. But now it required small attention to observe that the purse was actually diminishing; as if by my cursed counting, I had robbed it of the property of being uncountable. However, this gay mode of existence had been once entered on; I could not draw back; and yet my ready money soon verged to a close. I execrated my situation; upbraided my fair friend, for having so led me into temptation; took it as an offence that she did not again show herself to me; renounced, in my spleen, all duties towards her; and resolved to break open the Box, and see if peradventure any help might be found there. I was just about proceeding with my purpose; but I put it off till night, that I might go through the business with full composure; and, in the mean time, I hastened off to a banquet, for which this was the appointed hour. Here again we got into a high key; the wine and trumpet-sounding had flushed me not a little, when by the most villanous luck it chanced, that during the dessert, a former friend of my dearest fair one, returning from a journey, entered unexpectedly, placed himself beside her, and, without much ceremony, set about asserting his old privileges. Hence, very soon arose ill-humor, quarrelling, and battle: we plucked out our spits; and I was carried home half-dead of several wounds.

"The surgeon had bandaged me and gone away: it was far in the night; my sick-nurse had fallen asleep; the door of the side-room went up; my fair mysterious friend came in, and sat down by me on the bed. She asked how I was: I answered not, for I was faint and sullen. She continued speaking with much sympathy: she rubbed my temples with a certain balsam, whereby I felt myself rapidly and decidedly strengthened, so strengthened that I could now get angry and upbraid her. In a violent speech I threw all the blame of my misfortune on her; on the passion she had inspired me with; on her appearing and vanishing, and the tedium, the longing which in such a case I could not but feel. I waxed more and more vehement, as if a fever had been coming on; and I swore to her at last, that if she would not be mine, would not now abide with me and wed me, I had no wish to live any longer; to all which I required a peremptory answer. As she lingered and held back with her explanation, I got altogether beside myself, and tore off my double and triple bandages, in the firmest resolution to bleed to death. But what was my amazement, when I found all my wounds healed, my skin smooth and entire, and this fair friend in my arms!

"Henceforth we were the happiest pair in the world. We both begged pardon of each other, without either of us rightly knowing why. She now promised to travel on along with me: and soon we were sitting side by side in the carriage; the little Box lying opposite us on the other seat. Of this I had never spoken to her, nor did I now think of speaking, though it lay there before our eyes; and both of us, by tacit agreement, took charge of it, as circumstances might require; I, however, still carrying it to and from the carriage, and busying myself, as formerly, with the locking of the doors.

"So long as aught remained in my purse, I had continued to pay; but when my cash went done, I signified the fact to her. 'That is easily helped,' said she, pointing to a couple of little pouches fixed at the top, to the side of the carriage. These I had often observed before, but never turned to use. She put her hand into the one, and pulled out some gold pieces, as from the other some coins of silver; thereby showing me the possibility of meeting any scale of expenditure, which we might choose to adopt. And thus we journeyed on from town to town, from land to land; contented with each other and with the world: and I fancied not that she would again leave me; the less so, that for some time she had evidently been as loving wives wish to be, a circumstance by which our happiness and mutual affection was increased still farther. But one morning, alas! she could not be found: and as my actual residence, without her company, became displeasing, I again took the road with my Box; tried the virtue of the two pouches, and found it still unimpaired.

"My journey proceeded without accident. But if I had hitherto paid little heed to the mysteries of my adventure, expecting a natural solution of the whole, there now occurred something which threw me into astonishment, into anxiety, nay, into fear. Being wont, in my impatience for change of place, to hurry forward day and night, it was often my hap to be travelling in the dark; and when the lamps, by any chance, went out, to be left in utter obscurity. Once in the dead of such a night, I had fallen asleep; and on awakening, I observed the glimmer of a light on the covering of my carriage. I examined this more strictly, and found that it was issuing from the Box; in which there seemed to be a chink, as if it had been chapped by the warm and dry weather of summer, which was now come on. My thoughts of jewels again came into my head; I supposed there must be some carbuncle lying in the Box, and this point I forthwith set about investigating. I postured myself as well as might be, so that my eye was in immediate contact with the chink. But how great was my surprise, when a fair apartment, well-lighted, and furnished with much taste and even costliness, met my inspection, just as if I had been looking down through the opening of a dome into a royal saloon! A fire was burning in the grate; and before it stood an arm-chair. I held my breath and continued to observe. And now there entered from the other side of the apartment a lady with a book in her hand, whom I at once recognised for my wife, though her figure was contracted into the extreme of diminution. She sat down in the chair by the fire to read; she trimmed the coals with the most dainty pair of tongs; and in the course of her movements, I could clearly perceive that this fairest little creature was also in the family way. But now I was obliged to shift my constrained posture a little; and the next moment, when I bent down to look in again, and convince myself that it was no dream, the light had vanished, and my eye rested on empty darkness.

"How amazed, nay, terrified I was, you may easily conceive. I started a thousand thoughts on this discovery, and in truth could think nothing. In the midst of this, I fell asleep; and on awakening, I fancied that it must have been a mere dream: yet I felt myself in some degree estranged from my fair one; and though I watched over the Box, but so much the more carefully, I knew not whether the event of her reappearance in human size was a thing which I should wish or dread.

"After some time she did in fact reappear: one evening, in a white robe, she came gliding in; and as it was just then growing dusky in my room, she seemed to me taller than when I had seen her last: and I remembered having heard that all beings of the mermaid and gnome species increased in stature very perceptibly at the fall of night. She flew, as usual, to my arms; but I could not with right gladness press her to my obstructed breast.

"'My dearest,' said she, 'I now feel by thy reception of me, what, alas, I already knew too well. Thou hast seen me in the interim: thou art acquainted with the state in which, at certain times, I find myself; thy happiness and mine is interrupted, nay, it stands on the brink of being annihilated altogether. I must leave thee; and I know not whether I shall ever see thee again.' Her presence, the grace with which she spoke, directly banished from my memory almost every trace of that vision, which indeed had already hovered before me as little more than a dream. I addressed her with kind vivacity, convinced her of my passion, assured her that I was innocent, that my discovery was accidental: in short, I so managed it that she appeared composed, and endeavored to compose me.

"'Try thyself strictly,' said she, 'whether this discovery has not hurt thy love, whether thou canst forget that I live in two forms beside thee, whether the diminution of my being will not also contract thy affection.'

"I looked at her: she was fairer than ever; and I thought within myself: Is it so great a misfortune, after all, to have a wife who from time to time becomes a dwarf, so that one can carry her about with him in a casket? Were it not much worse if she became a giantess, and put her husband in the box? My gaiety of heart had returned. I would not for the whole world have let her go. 'Best heart,' said I, 'let us be and continue ever as we have been. Could either of us wish to be better? Enjoy thy conveniency; and I promise thee to guard the Box with so much the more faithfulness. Why should the prettiest sight I have ever seen in my life make a bad impression on me? How happy would lovers be, could they but procure such miniature pictures! And after all it was but a picture, a little sleight-of-hand-deception. Thou art trying and teasing me: but thou shalt see how I will stand it.'

"'The matter is more serious than thou thinkest,' said the fair one: 'however, I am truly glad to see thee take it so lightly; for much good may still be awaiting us both. I will trust in thee; and for my own part do my utmost: only promise me that thou wilt never mention this discovery by way of reproach. Another prayer likewise I most earnestly make to thee: Be more than ever on thy guard against wine and anger.'

"I promised what she required; I could have gone on promising to all lengths; but she herself turned aside the conversation; and thenceforth all proceeded in its former routine. We had no inducement to alter our place of residence: the town was large, the society various; and the fine season gave rise to many an excursion, and garden-festival.

"In all such amusements the presence of my wife was welcome, nay, eagerly desired, by women as well as men. A kind insinuating manner, joined with a certain dignity of bearing secured to her on all hands praise and estimation. Besides, she could play beautifully on the lute, accompanying it with her voice; and no social night could be perfect, unless crowned by the graces of this talent.

"I will be free to confess that I have never got much good of music; on the contrary, it has always rather had a disagreeable effect on me. My fair one soon noticed this, and accordingly, when by ourselves, she never tried to entertain me by such means: in return, however, she appeared to indemnify herself while in society, where indeed she always found a crowd of admirers.

"And now, why should I deny it, our late dialogue, in spite of my best intentions, had by no means sufficed to abolish the matter within me: on the contrary, my temper of mind had by degrees got into the strangest tune, almost without my being conscious of it. One night, in a large company, this hidden grudge broke loose, and by its consequences produced to myself the greatest damage.

"When I look back on it now, I in fact loved my Beauty far less, after that unlucky discovery: I was also growing jealous of her; a whim that had never struck me before. This night at table, I found myself placed very much to my mind beside my two neighbours, a couple of ladies, who, for some time, had appeared to me very charming. Amid jesting and soft small talk, I was not sparing of my wine: while, on the other side, a pair of musical dilletanti had got hold of my wife, and at last contrived to lead the company into singing separately, and by way of chorus. This put me into ill-humor. The two amateurs appeared to me impertinent; the singing vexed me; and when, as my turn came, they even requested a solo-strophe from me, I grew truly indignant, I emptied my glass, and set it down again with no soft movement.

"The grace of my two fair neighbours soon pacified me, indeed; but there is an evil nature in wrath, when once it is set agoing. It went on fermenting within me, though all things were of a kind to induce joy and complaisance. On the contrary, I waxed more splenetic than ever when a lute was produced, and my fair one began fingering it and singing, to the admiration of all the rest. Unhappily, a general silence was requested. So then, I was not even to talk any more; and these tones were going through me like a toothach. Was it any wonder that, at last, the smallest spark should blow up the mine?

"The songstress had just ended a song amid the loudest applauses, when she looked over to me; and this truly with the most loving face in the world. Unluckily, its lovingness could not penetrate so far. She perceived that I had just gulped down a cup of wine, and was pouring out a fresh one. With her right forefinger, she beckoned to me in kind threatening. 'Consider that it is wine!' said she, not louder than for myself to hear it.—'Water is for mermaids!' cried I.—'My ladies,' said she to my neighbours, 'crown the cup with all your gracefulness, that it be not too often emptied.'—'You will not let yourself be tutored?' whispered one of them in my ear.—'What ails the Dwarf?' cried I, with a more violent gesture, in which I overset the glass.—'Ah, what you have spilt!' cried the paragon of women; at the same time, twanging her strings, as if to lead back the attention of the company from this disturbance to herself. Her attempt succeeded, the more completely as she rose to her feet, seemingly that she might play with greater convenience, and in this attitude continued preluding.

"At sight of the red wine running over the table-cloth, I returned to myself. I perceived the great fault I had been guilty of; and it cut me through the very heart. Never till now had music spoken to me: the first verse she sang was a friendly good-night to the company, here as they were, as they might still feel themselves together. With the next verse they became as if scattered asunder; each felt himself solitary, separated, no one could fancy that he was present any longer. But what shall I say of the last verse? It was directed to me alone; the voice of injured Love bidding farewell to Moroseness and Caprice.

"In silence I conducted her home; foreboding no good. Scarcely, however, had we reached our chamber, when she began to show herself exceedingly kind and graceful, nay, even roguish; she made me the happiest of all men.

"Next morning, in high spirits and full of love, I said to her: 'Thou hast so often sung, when asked in company; as, for example, thy touching farewell song last night. Come now, for my sake, and sing me a dainty gay welcome to this morning hour, that we may feel as we were meeting for the first time.'

"'That I may not do, my friend,' said she seriously. 'The song of last night referred to our parting, which must now forthwith take place: for I can only tell thee, the violation of thy promise and oath will have the worst consequences for us both; thou hast scoffed away a great felicity, and I too must renounce my dearest wishes.'

"As I now pressed and entreated her to explain herself more clearly, she answered:

'That, alas, I can well do; for, at all events, my continuance with thee is over. Hear, then, what I would rather have concealed to the latest times. The form, under which thou sawest me in the Box, is my natural and proper form: for I am of the race of King Eckwald, the dread Sovereign of the Dwarfs, concerning whom authentic History has recorded so much. Our people are still as of old laborious and busy, and therefore easy to govern. Thou must not fancy that the Dwarfs are behindhand in their manufacturing skill. Swords which followed the foe, when you cast them after him; invisible and mysteriously binding chains; impenetrable shields, and such like ware, in old times, formed their staple produce. But now they chiefly employ themselves with articles of convenience and ornament; in which truly they surpass all people of the Earth. I may well say, it would astonish thee to walk through our workshops and warehouses. All this would be right and good, were it not that with the whole nation in general, but more particularly with the royal family, there is one peculiar circumstance connected.'

She paused for a moment; and I again begged farther light on these wonderful secrets; which accordingly she forthwith proceeded to grant.

"'It is well known,' said she, 'that God, so soon as he had created the world, and the ground was dry, and the mountains were standing bright and glorious, that God, I say, thereupon, in the very first place, created the Dwarfs; to the end, that there might be reasonable beings also, who, in their passages and chasms, might contemplate and adore his wonders in the inward parts of the Earth. It is farther well known, that this little race by degrees became uplifted in heart, and attempted to acquire the dominion of the Earth; for which reason God then created the Dragons, in order to drive back the Dwarfs into their mountains. Now, as the Dragons themselves were wont to nestle in the large caverns and clefts, and dwell there; and many of them, too, were in the habit of spitting fire, and working much other mischief, the poor little Dwarfs were by this means thrown into exceeding straits and distress, so that not knowing what in the world to do, they humbly and fervently turned to God, and called to him in prayer, that he would vouchsafe to abolish this unclean Dragon generation. But though it consisted not with his wisdom to destroy his own creatures, yet the heavy sufferings of the poor Dwarfs so moved his compassion, that anon he created the Giants, ordaining them to fight these Dragons, and if not root them out, at least lessen their numbers.

"'Now, no sooner had the Giants got moderately well through with the Dragons, than their hearts also began to wax wanton; and, in their presumption, they practised much tyranny, especially on the good little Dwarfs, who then once more in their need turned to the Lord; and he, by the power of his hand, created the

Knights, who were to make war on the Giants and Dragons, and to live in concord with the Dwarfs. Hereby was the work of creation completed on this side: and it is plain, that henceforth Giants and Dragons, as well as Knights and Dwarfs, have always maintained themselves in being. From this, my friend, it will be clear to thee, that we are of the oldest race on the Earth; a circumstance which does us honor, but, at the same time, brings great disadvantage along with it.

"'For as there is nothing in the world that can endure forever, but all that has once been great, must become little and fade, it is our lot, also, that ever since the creation of the world, we have been waning and growing smaller; especially the royal family, on whom, by reason of their pure blood, this destiny presses with the heaviest force. To remedy this evil, our wise teachers have many years ago devised the expedient of sending forth a Princess of the royal house from time to time into the world, to wed some honorable Knight, that so the Dwarf progeny may be refected, and saved from entire decay.'

"Though my fair one related these things with an air of the utmost sincerity, I looked at her hesitatingly; for it seemed as if she meant to palm some fable on me. As to her own dainty lineage, I had not the smallest doubt: but that she should have laid hold of me in place of a Knight, occasioned some mistrust; seeing I knew myself too well to suppose that my ancestors had come into the world by an immediate act of creation.

"I concealed my wonder and scepticism, and asked her kindly: 'But tell me, my dear child, how hast thou attained this large and stately shape? For I know few women that in richness of form can compare with thee.'—'Thou shalt hear,' replied she. 'It is a settled maxim in the Council of the Dwarf Kings, that this extraordinary step be forborne as long as it possibly can; which, indeed, I cannot but say is quite natural and proper. Perhaps they might have lingered still longer, had not my brother, born after me, come into the world so exceedingly small, that the nurses actually lost him out of his swaddling-clothes, and no creature yet knows whither he is gone. On this occurrence, unexampled in the annals of Dwarfdom, the Sages were assembled; and without more ado, the resolution was taken, and I sent out in quest of a husband.'

"'The resolution!' exclaimed I: 'that is all extremely well. One can resolve, one can take his resolution: but to give a Dwarf this heavenly shape, how did your Sages manage that?'

"'It had been provided for already,' said she, 'by our ancestors. In the royal treasury, lay a monstrous gold ring. I speak of it as it then appeared to me, when I saw it in my childhood: for it was this same ring, which I have here on my finger. We now went to work as follows:

"'I was informed of all that awaited me; and instructed what I had to do and to forbear. A splendid palace, after the pattern of my father's favorite summer residence, was then got ready:' a main edifice, wings, and whatever else you could think of. It stood at the entrance of a large rock-cleft, which it decorated in the handsomest style. On the appointed day, our court moved thither, my parents also and myself. The army paraded; and four-and-twenty priests, not without difficulty, carried on a costly litter the mysterious ring. It was placed on the threshold of the building, just within the spot where you entered. Many ceremonies were observed; and after a pathetic farewell, I proceeded to my task. I stept forward to the ring; laid my finger on it; and that instant, began perceptibly to wax in stature. In a few moments I had reached my present size; and then I put the ring on my finger. But now, in the twinkling of an eye, the doors, windows, gates flapped to; the wings drew up into the body of the edifice; instead of a palace, stood a little Box beside me; which I forthwith lifted, and carried off with me; not without a pleasant feeling in being so tall and strong, still, indeed, a dwarf to trees and mountains, to streams and tracts of land; yet a giant to grass and herbs; and above all, to ants, from whom we Dwarfs, not being always on the best terms with them, often suffer considerable annoyance.

"'How it fared with me on my pilgrimage, I might tell thee at great length. Suffice it to say, I tried many; but no one save thou seemed worthy of being honored to renovate and perpetuate the line of the glorious Eckwald.'

"In the course of these narrations, my head had now and then kept wagging, without myself having absolutely shaken it. I put several questions; to which I received no very satisfactory answers; on the contrary, I learned, to my great affliction, that after what had happened, she must needs return to her parents. She had hopes still, she said, of getting back to me: but for the present, it was indispensably necessary to present herself at court; as otherwise, both for her and me, there was nothing but utter ruin. The purses would soon cease to pay; and who knew what all would be the consequences?

"On hearing that our money would run short, I inquired no farther into consequences: I shrugged my shoulders; I was silent, and she seemed to understand me.

"We now packed up, and got into our carriage; the Box standing opposite us; in which, however, I could still see no symptoms of a palace. In this way we proceeded several stages. Post-money and drink-money were readily and richly paid from the pouches to the right and left; till at last we reached a mountainous district; and no sooner had we alighted here, than my fair one walked forward, directing me to follow her with the Box. She led me by rather steep paths to a narrow plot of green ground, through which a clear brook now gushed in little falls, now ran in quiet windings. She pointed to a little knoll; bade me set the Box down there, then said: 'Farewell! Thou wilt easily find the way back; remember me; I hope to see thee again.'

"At this moment, I felt as if I could not leave her. She was just now in one of her fine days, or if you will, her fine hours. Alone with so fair a being, on the green sward, among grass and flowers, girt in by rocks, waters murmuring round you, what heart could have remained insensible! I came forward to seize her hand, to clasp her in my arms: but she motioned me back; threatening me, though still kindly enough, with great danger, if I did not instantly withdraw.

"'Is there no possibility, then,' exclaimed I, 'of my staying with thee, of thy keeping me beside thee?' These words I uttered with such rueful tones and gestures, that she seemed touched by them, and after some thought, confessed to me that a continuance of our union was not entirely impossible. Who happier than I! My importunity, which increased every moment, compelled her at last to come out with her scheme, and inform me that if I too could resolve on becoming as little as I had once seen her, I might still remain with her, be admitted to her house, her kingdom, her family. The proposal was not altogether to my mind; yet at this moment I positively could not tear myself away; so, having already for a good while been accustomed to the marvellous, and being at all times prone to bold enterprises, I closed with her offer, and said she might do with me as she pleased.

"I was thereupon directed to hold out the little finger of my right hand: she placed her own against it; then with her left hand, she quite softly pulled the ring from her finger, and let it run along mine. That instant, I felt a violent twinge on my finger: the ring shrunk together, and tortured me horribly. I gave a loud cry, and caught round me for my fair one, but she had disappeared. What state of mind I was in during this moment, I find no words to express; so I have nothing more to say, but that I very soon, in my miniature size, found myself beside my fair one in a wood of grass-stalks. The joy of meeting after this short yet most strange separation, or, if you will, of this re-union without separation, exceeds all conception. I fell on her neck; she replied to my caresses, and the little pair was as happy as the large one.

"With some difficulty, we now mounted a hill: I say difficulty, because the sward had become for us an almost impenetrable forest. Yet at length we reached a bare space; and how surprised was I at perceiving there a large bolted mass; which, ere long, I could not but recognise for the Box, in the same state as when I had set it down.

"'Go up to it, my friend,' said she, 'and do but knock with the ring: thou shalt see wonders.' I went up accordingly, and no sooner had I rapped, than I did, in fact, witness the greatest wonder. Two wings came jutting out; and at the same time there fell, like scales and chips, various pieces this way and that; while doors, windows, colonnades, and all that belongs to a complete palace at once came into view.

"If ever you have seen one of Röntchen's desks; how, at one pull, a multitude of springs and latches get in motion, and writing board and writing materials, letter and money compartments, all at once, or in quick succession, start forward, you will partly conceive how this palace unfolded itself, into which my sweet attendant now introduced me. In the large saloon, I directly recognised the fire-place which I had formerly seen from above, and the chair in which she had then been sitting. And on looking up, I actually fancied I could still see something of the chink in the dome, through which I had peeped in. I spare you the description of the rest: in a word, all was spacious, splendid, and tasteful. Scarcely had I recovered from my astonishment, when I heard afar off a sound of military music. My better half sprang up; and with rapture announced to me the approach of His Majesty her Father. We stept out to the threshold, and here beheld a magnificent procession moving towards us, from a considerable cleft in the rock. Soldiers, servants, officers of state, and glittering courtiers, followed in order. At last you observed a golden throng, and in the midst of it the King himself. So soon as the whole procession had drawn up before the palace, the King, with his nearest retinue, stept forward. His loving daughter hastened out to him, pulling me along with her. We threw ourselves at his feet; he raised me very graciously; and on coming to stand before him, I perceived, that in this little world I was still the most considerable figure. We proceeded together to the palace; where His Majesty, in presence of his whole court, was pleased to welcome me with a well-studied oration, in which he expressed his surprise at finding us here; acknowledged me as his son-in-law, and appointed the nuptial ceremony to take place on the morrow.

"A cold sweat went over me as I heard him speak of marriage: for I dreaded this event more than music, which otherwise appeared to me the most hateful thing on Earth. Your music-makers, I used to say, enjoy at least the conceit of being in unison with each other, and working in concord: for when they have tweaked and tuned long enough, grating our ears with all manner of screeches, they believe in their hearts that the matter is now adjusted, and one instrument accurately suited to the other. The band-master himself is in this happy delusion; and so they set forth joyfully, though still tearing our nerves to pieces. In the marriage-state, even this is not the case: for although it is but a duet, and you might think two voices, or even two instruments, might in some degree be attuned to each other, yet this happens very seldom: for while the man gives out one tone, the wife directly takes a higher one, and the man again a higher; and so it rises from the chamber to the choral pitch, and farther and farther, till at last wind-instruments themselves cannot reach it. And now, as harmonical music itself is an offence to me, it will not be surprising that disharmonical should be a thing which I cannot endure.

"Of the festivities in which the day was spent, I shall and can say nothing: for I paid small heed to any of them. The sumptuous victuals, the generous wine, the royal amusements, I could not relish. I kept thinking and considering what I was to do. Here, however, there was but little to be considered. I determined, once for all, to take myself away, and hide somewhere. Accordingly, I succeeded in reaching the chink of a stone, where I entrenched and concealed myself as well as might be. My first care after this was to get the unhappy ring off my finger; an enterprise, however, which would by no means prosper, for on the contrary, I felt that every pull I gave, the metal grew straiter and cramped me with violent pains, which again abated so soon as I desisted from my purpose.

"Early in the morning I awoke (for my little person had slept, and very soundly); and was just stepping out to look farther about me, when I felt a kind of rain coming on. Through the grass, flowers, and leaves, there fell as it were something like sand and grit in large quantities; but what was my horror when the whole of it became alive, and an innumerable host of Ants rushed down on me! No sooner did they observe me, than they made an attack on all sides; and though I defended myself stoutly and gallantly enough, they at last so hemmed me in, so nipped and pinched me, that I was glad to hear them calling to surrender. I surrendered instantly and wholly; whereupon an Ant of respectable stature approached me with courtesy, nay, with reverence, and even recommended itself to my good graces. I learned that the Ants had now become allies of my father-in-law, and by him been called out in the present emergency, and commissioned to fetch me back. Here then was little I in the hands of creatures still less. I had nothing for it but looking forward to the marriage; nay, I must now thank Heaven, if my father-in-law were not wroth, if my fair one had not taken the sullens.

"Let me skip over the whole train of ceremonies: in a word, we were wedded. Gaily and joyously as matters went, there were, nevertheless, solitary hours, in which you were led astray into reflection; and now there happened to me something which had never happened before: what, and how, you shall learn.

"Everything about me was completely adapted to my present form and wants; the bottles and glasses were in a fit ratio to a little toper, nay, if you will, better measure, in proportion, than with us. In my tiny palate, the dainty tidbits tasted excellently; a kiss from the little mouth of my spouse was still the most charming thing in nature; and I will not deny that novelty made all these circumstances highly agreeable. Unhappily, however, I had not forgotten my former situation. I felt within me a scale of bygone greatness; and it rendered me restless and cheerless. Now, for the first time, did I understand what the philosophers might mean by their Ideal, which they say so plagues the mind of man. I had an Ideal of myself; and often in dreams I appeared as a giant. In short, my wife, my ring, my dwarf figure, and so many other bonds and restrictions, made me utterly unhappy, so that I began to think seriously about obtaining my deliverance.

"Being persuaded that the whole magic lay in the ring, I resolved on filing this asunder. From the court-jeweller, accordingly, I borrowed some files. By good luck, I was left-handed, as, indeed, throughout my whole life, I had never done aught in the right-handed way. I stood tightly to the work: it was not small: for the golden hoop, so thin as it appeared, had grown proportionably thicker in contracting from its former length. All vacant hours I privately applied to this task; and at last, the metal being nearly through, I was provident enough to step out of doors. This was a wise measure: for all at once the golden hoop started sharply from my finger, and my frame shot aloft with such violence, that I actually fancied I should dash against the sky; and, at all events, I must have bolted through the dome of our palace; nay, perhaps, in my new awkwardness, have destroyed this summer-residence altogether.

"Here then was I standing again; in truth, so much the larger, but also, as it seemed to me, so much the more foolish and helpless. On recovering from my stupefaction, I observed the royal strong-box lying near me, which I found to be moderately heavy, as I lifted it, and carried it down the foot-path to the next stage; where I directly ordered horses, and set forth. By the road, I soon made trial of the two side-pouches. Instead of money, which appeared to be run out, I found a little key: it belonged to the strong-box, in which I got some moderate compensation. So long as this held out, I made use of the carriage: by and by I sold it, and proceeded by the Diligence. The strong-box, too, I at length cast from me, having no hope of its ever filling again. And thus in the end, though after a considerable circuit, I again returned to the kitchen-hearth, to the landlady and the cook, where you were first introduced to me."

WHERE IS THE TRAITOR?

"No! No!" exclaimed he, violently and hastily rushing into the chamber allotted him, and setting down his candle: "No! it is impossible! But whither shall I turn? For the first time I think otherwise than he; for the first time, I feel, I wish otherwise. O father! couldst thou but be present invisibly, couldst thou but look through and through me, thou wouldst see that I am still the same, still thy true, obedient, affectionate son. Yet to say No! To contradict my father's dearest, long-cherished wish! How shall I disclose it? How shall I express it? No, I cannot marry Julia! While I speak of it, I shudder. And how shall I appear before him, tell him this, him the good, kind father? He looks at me with astonishment, without speaking: the prudent, clear-sighted, gifted man, can find no words. Wo is me! Ah, I know well to whom I would confide this pain, this perplexity; who it is I would choose for my advocate! Before all others, thou, Lucinda! And I would first tell thee how I love thee, how I give myself to thee, and pressingly entreat thee to speak for me; and if thou canst love me again, if thou wilt be mine, to speak for us both."

To explain this short pithy monologue will require some details.

Professor N. of N. had an only boy of singular beauty, whom, till the child's eighth year, he had left entirely in charge of his wife. This excellent woman had directed the hours and days of her son, in living, learning, and all good behaviour. She died; and the father instantly felt, that to prosecute this parental tutelage was impossible. In their lifetime, all had been harmony between the parents: they had labored for a common aim, had determined in concert what was next to be done; and the mother had not wanted skill to execute wisely, by herself, what the two had planned together. Double and treble was now the widower's anxiety, seeing, as he could not but daily see, that for the sons of professors, even in universities, it was only by a sort of miracle that a happy education could be expected.

In this strait he applied to his friend the Oberamtmann of R., with whom he had already been treating of plans for a closer alliance between their families. The Oberamtmann gave him counsel and assistance: so the son was established in one of those Institutions, which still flourish in Germany, and where charge is taken of the whole man, and body, soul, and spirit are trained with all attention.

The son was thus provided for; the father, however, felt himself very lonely: robbed of his wife; shut out from the cheerful presence of the boy, whom he had seen, without effort of his, growing up in such desirable culture. But here again the friendship of the Oberamtmann served him in good stead: the distance of their abodes vanished before his affection, his desire for movement, for diversion of thought. In this hospitable home the widowed Man of Letters found, in a family circle motherless like his own, two beautiful little daughters growing up in diverse loveliness; a state of things which more and more confirmed the fathers in their purpose, in their hope, of one day seeing their families united in the most joyful bonds.

They lived under the sway of a mild good Prince: the meritorious Oberamtmann was certain of his post during life; and in the appointment of a successor, his recommendation was likely to go far. And now, according to the wise family arrangement, sanctioned also by the Minister, Lucidor was to train himself for the important office of his future father-in-law. This in consequence he did, from step to step. Nothing was neglected in communicating to him all sorts of knowledge, in developing in him all sorts of activity, which the State in any case requires: practice in rigorous judicial law; and also in the laxer sort, where prudence and address find their proper field; foresight for daily ways and means; not excluding higher and more comprehensive views, yet all tending towards practical life, and so as with effect and certainty to be employed in its concerns.

With such purposes had Lucidor spent his school-years: by his father and his patron, he was now warned to make ready for the university. In all departments he already showed the fairest talents; and to Nature he was farther indebted for the singular happiness of inclining, out of love for his father, out of respect for his friend, to turn his capabilities, first from obedience, then from conviction, on that very object to which he was directed. He was placed in a foreign university, and here, both by his own account in his letters, and by the testimony of his teachers and overseers, he continued walking in the path that led towards his appointed goal. It was only objected to him, that in certain cases he had been too impetuously brave. The father shook his head at this; the Oberamtmann nodded. Who would not have been proud of such a son?

Meanwhile, the two daughters, Julia and Lucinda, were waxing in stature and graces. Julia, the younger, waggish, lovely, unstable, highly entertaining; the other difficult to pourtray, for, in her sincerity and purity, she represented all that we prize most in woman. Visits were paid and repaid; and, in the Professor's house, Julia found the most inexhaustible amusement.

Geography, which he failed not to enliven by Topography, belonged to his province; and no sooner did Julia cast her eyes on any of the volumes, of which a whole series from Homann's warehouse were standing there, than the cities all and sundry had to be mustered, judged, preferred, or rejected: all havens especially obtained her favor; other towns, to acquire even a slight approval from her, must stand forth well supplied with steeples, domes, and minarets.

Julia's father often left her for weeks to the care of his tried friend. She was actually advancing in knowledge of her science; and already the inhabited world, in its main features, in its chief points and places, stood before her with some accuracy and distinctness. The garbs of foreign nations attracted her peculiar attention; and often when her foster-father asked her in jest; If among the many young handsome men who were passing to and fro before her window, there was not some one or other whom she liked? she would answer: "Yes, indeed, if he do but look odd enough." And as our young students are seldom behind-hand in this particular, she had often occasion to take notice of individuals among them: they brought to her mind the costume of foreign nations; however, she declared in the end, that if she was to bestow her undivided attention on any one, he must be at least a Greek, equipped in the complete fashion of his country; on which account, also, she longed to be at some Leipzig Fair where, as she understood, such persons were to be seen walking the streets.

After his dry and often irksome labors, our Teacher had now no happier moments, than those he spent in mirthfully instructing her; triumphing withal, in secret, that a being so attractive, ever entertaining, ever entertained, was in the end to be his own daughter. For the rest, the two fathers had mutually agreed, that no hint of their purpose should be communicated to the girls; from Lucidor, also, it was kept secret.

Thus had years passed away, as indeed they very lightly pass; Lucidor presented himself completed, having stood all trials to the joy even of the superior overseers, who wished nothing more heartily than being able, with a good conscience, to fulfil the hopes of old, worthy, favored, and deserving servants.

And so the business had at length by quiet regular steps come so far, that Lucidor, after having demeaned himself in subordinate stations to universal satisfaction, was now to be placed in a very advantageous post, suitable to his wishes and merits, and lying just midway between the University and the Oberamtmanship.

The father now spoke with his son about Julia, of whom he had hitherto only hinted, as about his bride and wife, without any doubt or condition; congratulating him on the happiness of having appropriated such a jewel to himself. The Professor saw in fancy his daughter-in-law again from time to time in his house; occupied with charts, plans, and views of cities: the son recalled to mind the gay and most lovely creature, who, in times of childhood, had, by her rogueries as by her kindliness, always delighted him. Lucidor was now to ride over to the Oberamtmann's, to take a closer view of the full-grown fair one; and, for a few weeks, to surrender himself to the habitudes and familiarity of her household. If the young people, as was to be hoped, should speedily agree, the Professor was forthwith to appear, that so a solemn betrothment might forever secure the anticipated happiness.

Lucidor arrives, is received with the friendliest welcome; a chamber is allotted him; he arranges himself there, and appears. And now he finds, besides the members of the family already known to us, a grown-up son; misbred certainly, yet shrewd and good-natured; so that if you liked to take him as the Jesting Counsellor of the party, he fitted not ill with the rest. There belonged, moreover, to the house, a very old, but healthy and gay-hearted man; quiet, wise, discreet; completing his life, as it were, and here and there requiring a little help. Directly after Lucidor, too, there had arrived another stranger; no longer young, of an impressive aspect, dignified, thoroughly well-bred, and, by his acquaintance with the most distant quarters of the world, extremely entertaining. He was called Antoni.

Julia received her announced bridegroom in fit order, yet with an excess rather than a defect of frankness: Lucinda, on the other hand, did the honors of the house, as her sister did those of herself. So passed the day; peculiarly agreeable to all, only to Lucidor not: he, at all times silent, had been forced, that he might avoid sinking dumb entirely, to employ himself in asking questions; and in this attitude, no one appears to advantage.

Throughout he had been absent-minded; for at the first glance he had felt, not aversion or repugnance, yet estrangement, towards Julia: Lucinda, on the contrary, attracted him, so that he trembled every time she looked at him with her full pure peaceful eyes.

Thus hard bested, he reached his chamber the first night, and gave vent to his heart in that soliloquy with which we began. But to explain this sufficiently, to show how the violence of such an emphatic speech agrees with what we know of him already, another little statement will be necessary.

Lucidor was of a deep character; and for most part had something else in his mind, than what the present scene required: hence talk and social conversation would never prosper rightly with him; he felt this, and was wont to continue silent, except when the topic happened to be particular on some department which he had completely studied, and of which, whatever he needed was at all times ready. Besides this, in his early years at school, and later at the university, he had been deceived in friends, and had wasted the effusions of his heart unhappily; hence every communication of his feelings seemed to him a doubtful step, and doubting destroys all such communication. With his father he was used to speak only in unison; therefore, his full heart poured itself out in monologues, so soon as he was by himself.

Next morning he had summoned up his resolution; and yet he almost lost heart and composure again, when Julia met him with still more friendliness, gaiety, and frankness, than ever. She had much to ask; about his journeys by land and journeys by water; how, when a student, with his knapsack on his back, he had roamed and climbed through Switzerland, nay, crossed the Alps themselves. And now of those fair islands on the great Southern Lake, she had much to say; and then backwards, the Rhine must be accompanied from his primary origin; at first, through most undelicious regions, and so downwards through many an alternation, till at length, between Maynz and Coblenz, you find it still worth while respectfully to dismiss the old River from his last confinement, into the wide world, into the sea.

Lucidor, in the course of this recital, felt himself much lightened in heart; he narrated willingly and well, so that Julia at last exclaimed in rapture: "It is thus that our other self should be!" At which phrase Lucidor again felt startled and frightened; thinking he saw in it an allusion to their future pilgrimage in common through life.

From his narrative duty, however, he was soon relieved: for the stranger, Antoni, very speedily overshadowed all mountain streams, and rocky banks, and rivers whether hemmed in or left at liberty. Under his guidance you now went forward to Genoa; Livorno lay at no great distance; whatever was most interesting in the country you took with you as fair spoil; Naples, too, was a place you should see before you died; and then, in truth, remained Constantinople, which also was by no means to be neglected. Antoni's descriptions of the wide world carried the imagination of every hearer along with him, though Antoni himself introduced little fire into the subject. Julia, quite enraptured, was still nowise satisfied: she longed for Alexandria, Cairo, and, above all, for the Pyramids: of which, by the lessons of her intended father-in-law, she had gained some moderate knowledge.

Lucidor, next night (he had scarcely shut his door; the candle he had not put down) exclaimed: "Now, bethink thee, then; it is growing serious! Thou hast studied and meditated many serious things: what avails thy law-learning, if thou canst not act like a man of law? View thyself as a delegate, forget thy own feelings, and do what it would behove thee to do for another. It thickens and closes round me horribly! The stranger is plainly come for the sake of Lucinda; she shows him the fairest, noblest social and hospitable attentions: that little fool would run through the world with any one for anything or nothing. Besides, she is a wag; her interest in cities and countries is a farce, by which she keeps us in silence. But why do I look at the affair so perplexedly, so narrowly? Is not the Oberamtmann himself the most judicious, the clearest, the kindest mediator? Thou wilt tell him how thou feelest and thinkest; and he will think with thee, if not likewise feel. With thy father he has all influence. And is not the one as well as the other his daughter? What would this Antoni the Traveller with Lucinda, who is born for home, to be happy and to make happy? Let the wavering quicksilver fasten itself to the Wandering Jew: that will be a right match."

Next morning Lucidor came down, with the firm purpose of speaking with the father; and waiting on him expressly to that end, at the hour when he knew him to be disengaged. How great was his vexation, his perplexity, on learning that the Oberamtmann had been called away on business, and was not expected till the day after the morrow! Julia, on this occasion, seemed to be expressly in her travelling fit; she kept by the world-wanderer, and, with some sportive hits at domestic economy, gave up Lucidor to Lucinda. If our friend, viewing this noble maiden from a certain distance, and under one general impression, had already, with his whole heart, loved her, he failed not now in this nearest nearness to discover with double and treble vividness in detail, all that had before as a whole attracted him.

The good old friend of the family now brought himself forward, in place of the absent father: he too had lived, had loved; and was now, after many hard buffetings and bruises of life, resting at last, refreshed and cheerful, beside the friend of his youth. He enlivened the conversation; and especially expatiated on perplexities in choice of wives; relating several remarkable examples of explanations, both in time and too late. Lucinda appeared in all her splendor. She admitted: That accident, in all departments of life, and so likewise in the business of marriage, often produced the best result; yet that it was finer and prouder when one could say he owed his happiness to himself, to the silent calm conviction of his heart, to a noble purpose and a quick determination. Tears stood in Lucidor's eyes as he applauded this sentiment: directly afterwards, the two ladies went out. The old president liked well to deal in illustrative histories; and so the conversation expanded itself into details of pleasant instances, which however, touched our hero so closely, that none but a youth of as delicate manners as his could have refrained from breaking out with his secret. He did break out, so soon as he was by himself.

"I have constrained myself!" exclaimed he: "with such perplexities I will not vex my good father: I have forborne to speak: for I see in this worthy old man the substitute of both fathers. To him will I speak; to him disclose the whole: he will surely bring it about; he has already almost spoken what I wish. Will he censure in the individual case what he praises in general? To-morrow I visit him: I must give vent to this oppression."

At breakfast, the old man was not present: last night he had spoken, it appeared, too much; had sat too long, and likewise drunk a drop or two of wine beyond his custom. Much was said in his praise; many anecdotes were related; and precisely of such sayings and doings as brought Lucidor to despair for not having forthwith applied to him. This unpleasant feeling was but aggravated, when he learned that in such attacks of disorder the good old man would often not make his re-appearance for a week.

For social converse, a country residence has many advantages; especially when the owners of it have, for a course of years, been induced, as thinking and feeling persons, to improve the natural capabilities of their environs. Such had been the good fortune of this spot. The Oberamtmann, at first unwedded, then in a long happy marriage, himself a man of fortune, and occupying a lucrative post, had, according to his own judgment and perception, according to the taste of his wife, nay, at last according to the wishes and whims of his children, laid out and forwarded many larger and smaller decorations; which by degrees being skilfully connected with plantations and paths, afforded to the promenader a very beautiful, continually varying, characteristic series of scenes. A pilgrimage through these, our young hosts now proposed to their guest; as in general we take pleasure in showing our improvements to a stranger, that so what has become habitual in our eyes, may appear with the charm of novelty in his, and leave with him, in permanent remembrance, its first favorable impression.

The nearest, as well as the most distant part of the grounds, was peculiarly appropriate for modest decorations, and altogether rural individualities. Fertile hills alternated with well-watered meadows; so that the whole was visible from time to time, without being flat; and if the land seemed chiefly devoted to purposes of utility, the graceful, the attractive, was by no means excluded.

To the dwelling and office-houses were united various gardens, orchards, and green spaces; out of which you imperceptibly passed into a little wood, with a broad, clear carriage-road winding up and down through the midst of it. Here, in a central spot, on the most considerable elevation, there had been a Hall erected, with side-chambers entering from it. On coming through the main-door, you saw in a large mirror the most favorable prospect which the country afforded; and were sure to turn round that instant, to recover yourself on the reality from the effect of this its unexpected image: for the approach was artfully enough contrived, and all that could excite surprise was carefully hid till the last moment. No one entered but felt himself pleasurably tempted to turn from the mirror to Nature, and from Nature to the mirror.

Once in motion in this fairest, brightest, longest day, our party made a spiritual campaign of it, over and through the whole. Here the daughters pointed out the evening seat of their good mother, where a stately box-tree had kept clear space all round it. A little farther on, Lucinda's place of morning-prayer was half-roguishly exhibited by Julia: close to a little brook, between poplars and alders, with meadows sloping down from it, and fields stretching upwards. It was indescribably pretty. You thought you had seen such a spot everywhere, but nowhere so impressive, and so perfect in its simplicity. In return for this, the young master, also half against Julia's will, pointed out the tiny groves, and child's gardens, which, close by a snug-lying mill, were now scarcely discernible : they dated from a time when Julia, perhaps in her tenth year, had taken it into her head to become a milleress; intending, after the decease of the two old occupants, to assume the management herself, and choose some brave millman for her husband.

"That was at a time," cried Julia, " when I knew nothing of towns lying on rivers, or even on the sea; nothing of Genoa, of Naples, and the like. Your worthy father, Lucidor, has converted me; of late I come seldom hither." She sat down with a roguish air, on a little bench, that was now scarcely large enough for her; under an elder-bough, which had bent deeply towards the ground: "Fie on this cowering !" cried she; then started up, and ran off with her gay brother.

The remaining pair kept up a rational conversation ; and in these cases, reason approaches close to the borders of feeling. Wandering over changeful, simple natural objects, to contemplate at leisure how cunning scheming man contrives to gain some profit from them; how his perception of what is laid before him, combining with the feeling of his wants, does wonders, first in rendering the world inhabitable, then in peopling it, and at last in overpeopling it: all this could here be talked of in detail. Lucinda gave account of everything; and, modest as she was, she could not hide that these pleasant and convenient combinations of distant parts by roads, had been her work, under the proposal, direction, or favor of her revered mother.

But as the longest day at last bends down to evening, our party were at last forced to think of returning; and while devising some pleasant circuit, the merry brother proposed that they should take the short road, though it commanded no fine prospects, and was even in some places more difficult to get over. "For," cried he, "you have preached all day about your decorations and reparations, and how you have improved and beautified the scene for pictorial eyes and feeling hearts: let me also have my turn."

Accordingly, they now set forth over ploughed grounds, by coarse paths, nay, sometimes picking their way by stepping-stones in boggy places; till at last they perceived, at some distance, a pile of machinery towering up in manifold combination. More closely examined, it turned out to be a large apparatus for sport and games, arranged not without judgment, and in a certain popular spirit. Here, fixed at suitable distances, stood a large swing-wheel, on which the ascending and the descending riders might still sit horizontally, and at their ease; other see-saws, swing-ropes, leaping-poles, bowling and nine-pins courses, and whatever can be fancied for variedly and equally employing and diverting a crowd of people gathered on a large common. "This," cried he, "is my invention, my decoration! And though my father found the money, and a shrewd fellow the brain necessary for it, yet without me, whom you often call a person of no judgment, money and brain would not have come together."

In this cheerful mood, the whole four reached home by sunset. Antoni also joined them; but the little Julia, not yet satisfied with this unresting travel, ordered her coach, and set forth on a visit to a lady of her friends, in utter despair at not having seen her for two days. The party left behind began to feel embarrassed before they were aware; it was even mentioned in words that the father's absence distressed them. The conversation was about to stagnate, when all at once the madcap sprang from his seat, and in a few moments returned with a book, proposing to read to the company. Lucinda forbore not to inquire how this notion had occurred to him, now for the first time in a twelvemonth. "Everything occurs to me," said he, "at the proper season: this is more than you can say for yourself." He read them a series of genuine Antique Tales; such as lead man away from himself, flattering his wishes, and making him forget all those restrictions, between which, even in the happiest moments, we are still hemmed in.

"What shall I do now!" cried Lucidor, when at last he saw himself alone. "The hour presses on: in Antoni I have no trust; he is an utter stranger, I know not who he is, how he comes to be here, nor what he wants; Lucinda seems to be his object; and if so, what can I expect of him? Nothing remains for me but applying to Lucinda herself: she must know of it, she before all others. This was my first feeling: why do we stray into sidepaths and subterfuges? My first thought shall be my last, and I hope to reach my aim."

On Saturday morning, Lucidor, dressed at an early hour, was walking to and fro in his chamber; thinking and conning over his projected address to Lucinda, when he heard a sort of jestful contention before his door, and the door itself directly afterwards went up. The mad younker was shoving in a boy before him, with coffee and baked ware for the guest; he himself carried cold meats and wine. "Go thou foremost," cried the younker: "for the guest must be first served;" I am used to serve myself. My friend, to-day I am entering somewhat early and tumultuously: but let us take our breakfast in peace; then we shall see what is to be done; for of our company there is nothing to be hoped. The little one is not yet back from her friend; they two have to pour out their hearts together every fortnight, otherwise the poor dear hearts would burst. On Saturdays, Lucinda is good for nothing; she balances her household accounts for my father; she would have had me taking share in the concern, but Heaven forbid! When I know the price of anything, no morsel of it can I relish. Guests are expected to-morrow; the old man has not yet got refitted; Antoni is gone to hunt, we will do the same."

Guns, pouches, and dogs were ready, as our pair stept down into the court; and now they set forth over field and hill, shooting at best some leveret or so, and perhaps here and there a poor indifferent undeserving bird. Meanwhile they kept talking of domestic affairs, of the household and company at present assembled in it. Antoni was mentioned, and Lucidor failed not to inquire more narrowly about him. The gay younker, with some self-complaisance, asserted, that strange as the man was, and much mystery as he made about himself, he, the gay younker, had already seen through him and through him. "Without doubt," continued he, "Antoni is the son of a rich mercantile family, whose large partnership concern fell to ruin at the very time when he, in the full vigor of youth, was preparing to take a cheerful and active hand in their great undertakings, and withal to share in their abundant profits. Dashed down from the summit of his hopes, he gathered himself together, and undertook to perform for strangers what he was no longer in a case to perform for his relatives. And so he travelled through the world; became thoroughly acquainted with it and its mutual traffickings; in the meanwhile, not forgetting his own advantage. Unwearied diligence and tried fidelity obtained and secured for him unbounded confidence from many. Thus in all places he acquired connections and friends; nay, it is easy to see that his fortune is as widely scattered abroad as his acquaintance; and accordingly his presence is from time to time required in all quarters of the world."

These things the merry younker told in a more circumstantial and simple style, introducing many farcical observations, as if he meant to spin out his story to full length.

"How long, for instance," cried he, "has this Antoni been connected with my father! They think I see nothing, because I trouble myself about nothing; but for this very reason, I see it better, as I take no interest in it. To my father he has intrusted large sums, who again has deposited them securely and to advantage. It was but last night that he gave our old dietetic friend a casket of jewels; a finer, simpler, costlier piece of ware, I never cast my eyes on, though I saw this only with a single glance, for they make a secret of it. Most probably it is to be consigned to the bride for her pleasure, satisfaction, and future security. Antoni has set his heart on Lucinda! Yet when I see them together, I cannot think it a well-assorted match. The hop-skip would have suited him better; I believe, too, she would take him sooner than the elder would. Many a time, I see her looking over to the old curmudgeon, so gay and sympathetic, as if she could find in her heart to spring into the coach with him, and fly off at full gallop." Lucidor collected himself: he knew not what to answer; all that he heard obtained his internal approbation. The younker proceeded: "All along the girl has had a perverted liking for old people: I believe, of a truth, she would have skipped away and wedded your father, as briskly as she would his son."

Lucidor followed his companion, over stock and stone, as it pleased the gay youth to lead him: both forgot the chase, which at any rate could not be productive. They called at a farm-house, where, being hospitably received, the one friend entertained himself with eating, drinking, and tattling: the other again plunged into meditations, and projects for turning this new discovery to his own profit.

From all these narrations and disclosures, Lucidor had acquired so much confidence in Antoni, that immediately on their return he asked for him, and hastened into the garden, where he was said to be. In vain! No soul was to be seen anywhere. At last he entered the door of the great Hall; and strange enough, the setting sun, reflected from the mirror, so dazzled him, that he could not recognise the two persons, who were sitting on the sofa; though he saw distinctly that it was a lady and a man, which latter was that instant warmly kissing the hand of his companion. How great, accordingly, was Lucidor's astonishment, when, on recovering his clearness of vision, he beheld Antoni sitting by Lucinda! He was like to sink through the ground: he stood, however, as if rooted to the spot; till Lucinda, in the kindest, most unembarrassed manner, shifted a little to a side, and invited him to take a seat on her right hand. Unconsciously he obeyed her, and while she addressed him, inquiring after his present day's history, asking pardon for her absence on domestic engagements, he could scarcely hear her voice. Antoni rose, and took his leave: Lucinda, resting herself from her toil, as the others were doing, invited Lucidor to a short stroll. Walking by her side, he was silent and embarrassed; she, too, seemed ill at ease: and had he been in the slightest degree self-collected, her deep-drawn breathing must have disclosed to him that she had heartfelt sighs to suppress. She at last took her leave, as they approached the house: he on the other hand turned round, at first slowly, then at a violent pace, to the open country. The park was too narrow for him; he hastened through the fields, listening only to the voice of his heart, and without eyes for the beauties of this loveliest evening. When he found himself alone, and his feelings were relieving their violence in a shower of tears, he exclaimed:

"Already in my life, but never with such fierceness, have I felt the agony which now makes me altogether wretched: to see the long-wished-for happiness at length reach me; hand-in-hand and arm-in-arm unite with me; and at the same moment announce its eternal departure! I was sitting by her, I was walking by her; her fluttering garment touched me, and I have lost her! Reckon it not over, torture not thy heart with it; be silent, and determine!"

He laid a prohibition on his lips; he held his peace, and planned and meditated, stepping over field and meadow and bush, not always by the smoothest paths. Late at night, on returning to his chamber, he gave voice to his thoughts for a moment, and cried: "To-morrow morning I am gone; another such day I will not front."

And so, without undressing, he threw himself on the bed. Happy, healthy season of youth! He was already asleep; the fatiguing motion of the day had earned for him the sweetest rest. Out of bright morning dreams, however, the earliest sun awoke him: this was the longest day in the year; and for him it threatened to be too long. If the grace of the peaceful evening star had passed over him unnoticed, he felt the awakening beauty of the morning only to despair. The world was lying here as glorious as ever; to his eyes it was still so; but his soul contradicted it; all this belonged to him no longer, he had lost Lucinda.

His travelling-bag was soon packed; this he was to leave behind him; he left no letter with it; a verbal message in excuse of absence from dinner, perhaps also from supper, might be left with the groom, whom at any rate he must awaken. The groom, however, was awake already: Lucidor found him in the yard, walking with large strides before the stable-door. "You do not mean to ride?" cried the usually good-natured man, with a tone of some spleen. "To you I may say it; but young master is growing worse and worse. There was he driving about far and near yesterday; you might have thought he would thank God for a Sunday to rest in. And see, if he does not come this morning before daybreak, rummages about in the stable, and while I am getting up, saddles and bridles your horse, flings himself on it, and cries: 'Do but consider the good work I am doing! This beast keeps jogging on at a staid juridical trot, I must see and rouse him into a smart life-gallop.' He said something just so, and other strange speeches besides."

Lucidor was doubly and trebly vexed: he liked the horse, as corresponding to his own character, his own mode of life: it grieved him to figure his good sensible beast in the hands of a madcap. His plan, too, was overturned; his purpose of flying to a college friend, with whom he had lived in cheerful cordial union, and in this crisis seeking refuge beside him. His old confidence had been awakened, the intervening miles were not counted; he had fancied himself already at the side of his true-hearted and judicious friend, finding counsel and assuagement from his words and looks. This prospect was now cut off: yet not entirely, if he could venture with the fresh pedestrian limbs, which still stood at his command, to set forth towards the goal.

First of all, accordingly, he struck through the park; making for the open country, and the road which was to lead him to his friend. Of his direction he was not quite certain, when looking to the left, his eye fell upon the Hermitage, which had hitherto been kept secret from him; a strange edifice, rising with grotesque joinery through bush and tree: and here, to his extreme astonishment, he observed the good old man, who for some days had been considered sick, standing in the gallery under the Chinese roof, and looking blithely through the soft morning. The friendliest salutation, the most pressing entreaties to come up, Lucidor resisted with excuses and gestures of haste. Nothing but sympathy with the good old man, who, hastening down with infirm step, seemed every moment in danger of falling to the bottom, could induce him to turn thither, and then suffer himself to be conducted up. With surprise he entered the pretty little hall: it had only three windows, turned towards the park; a most graceful prospect: the other sides were decorated, or rather covered, with hundreds of portraits, copperplate, or painted, which were fixed in a certain order to the wall, and separated by colored borders and interstices.

"I favor you, my friend, more than I do every one; this is the sanctuary in which I peacefully spend my last days. Here I recover myself from all the mistakes, which society tempts me to commit: here my dietetic errors are corrected, and my old being is again restored to equilibrium."

Lucidor looked over the place; and being well read in history, he easily observed that an historical taste had presided in its arrangement.

"Above, there, in the frieze," said the old virtuoso, "you will find the names of distinguished men in the primitive ages; then those of later antiquity; yet still only their names, for how they looked would now be difficult to discover. But here, in the main field, comes my own life into play: here are the men whose names I used to hear mentioned in my boyhood. For some fifty years or so, the name of a distinguished man continues in the remembrance of the people; then it vanishes, or becomes fabulous. Though of German parentage, I was born in Holland; and for me, William of Orange, Stadtholder, and King of England, is the patriarch of all common great men and heroes.

"Now, close by William, you observe Louis XIV. as the person who—" How gladly would Lucidor have cut short the good old man, had it but been permitted him, as it is to us the narrators: for the whole late and latest history of the world seemed impending; as from the portraits of Frederick the Great and his generals, towards which he was glancing, was but too clearly to be gathered.

And though the kindly young man could not but respect his old friend's lively sympathy in these things, or deny that some individual features and views in this exhibitory discourse might be interesting; yet at college he had heard the late and latest history of Europe already; and what a man has once heard, he fancies himself to know forever. Lucidor's thoughts were wandering far away; he heard not, he scarcely saw; and was just on the point, in spite of all politeness, of flinging himself out, and tumbling down the long fatal stair, when a loud clapping of hands was heard from below.

While Lucidor restrained his movement, the old man looked over through the window, and a well-known voice resounded from beneath: "Come down, for Heaven's sake, out of your historic picture gallery, old gentleman! Conclude your fasts and humiliations, and help me to appease our young friend, when he learns it. Lucidor's horse I have ridden somewhat hard; it has lost a shoe, and I was obliged to leave the beast behind me. What will he say? He is too absurd, when one behaves absurdly."

"Come up!" said the old man, and turned in to Lucidor: "Now, what say you?" Lucidor was silent, and the wild blade entered. The discussion of the business lasted long: at length it was determined to despatch the groom forthwith, that he might seek the horse and take charge of it.

Leaving the old man, the two younkers hastened to the house; Lucidor, not quite unwillingly, submitting to this arrangement. Come of it what might, within these walls the sole wish of his heart was included. In such desperate cases, we are, at any rate, cut off from the assistance of our free will; and we feel ourselves relieved for a moment, when, from any quarter, direction and constraint takes hold of us. Yet, on entering his chamber, he found himself in the strangest mood; like a man who, having just left an apartment of an inn, is forced to return to it, by the breaking of an axle.

The gay younker fell upon the travelling-bag, unpacking it all in due order; especially selecting every article of holiday apparel, which, though only on the travelling scale, was to be found there. He forced Lucidor to put on fresh shoes and stockings; he dressed for him his clustering brown locks, and decked him at all points with his best skill. Then stepping back, and surveying our friend and his own handiwork, from head to foot, he exclaimed: "Now, then, my good fellow, you do look like a man that has some pretensions to pretty damsels; and serious enough, moreover, to spy about you for a bride. Wait one moment! You shall see how I too can produce myself, when the hour strikes. This knack I learned from your military officers; the girls are always glancing at them; so I likewise have enrolled myself among a certain Soldiery; and now they look at me too, and look again, and no soul of them knows what to make of it. And so, from this looking and relooking, from this surprise and attention, a pretty enough result now and then arises; which, though it were not lasting, is worth enjoying for the moment.

"But, come along, my friend, and do the like service for me! When you have seen me case myself by piecemeal in my equipment, you will not say that wit and invention have been denied me." He now led his friend through several long spacious passages of the old castle. "I have quite nestled myself here," cried he. "Though I care not for hiding, I like to be alone; you can do no good with other people." They were passing by the office-rooms, just as a servant came out with a patriarchal writing-apparatus, black, massive, and complete; paper, too, was not forgotten.

"I know what is to be blotted here again," cried the younker: "go thy ways, and leave me the key. Take a look of the place, Lucidor; it will amuse you till I am dressed. To a friend of justice, such a spot is not odious, as to a tamer of horses." And with this, he pushed Lucidor into the hall of judgment.

Lucidor felt himself directly in a well-known and friendly element; he thought of the days when he, fixed down to business, had sat at such a table; and listening and writing, had trained himself to his art. Nor did he fail to observe, that in this case an old stately domestic Chapel had, under the change of religious ideas, been converted to the service of Themis. In the repositories, he found some titles and acts already familiar to him: in these very matters he had co-operated, while laboring in the Capital. Opening a bundle of papers, there came into his hands a rescript, which he himself had dictated; another, of which he had been the originator. Hand-writing and paper, signet and president's signature, everything recalled to him that season of juridical effort, of youthful hope. And here, when he looked round, and saw the Oberamtmann's chair, appointed and intended for himself; so fair a place, so dignified a circle of activity, which he was now like to cast away, and utterly lose, all this oppressed him doubly and trebly, as the form of Lucinda seemed to retire from him at the same time.

He turned to go out into the open air, but found himself a prisoner. His gay friend, heedlessly or roguishly, had left the door locked. Lucidor, however, did not long continue in this durance; for the other returned; apologised for his oversight, and really called forth good humor by his singular appearance. A certain audacity of color and cut in his clothes was softened by natural taste, as even to tattooed Indians we refuse not a certain approbation. "To-day," cried he, "the tedium of bygone days shall be made good to us. Worthy friends, merry friends are come; pretty girls, roguish and fond; and my father, to boot; and wonder on wonder! your father too. This will be a festival, truly; they are all assembled for breakfast in the parlor."

With Lucidor, at this piece of information, it was as if he were looking into deep fog; all the figures, known and unknown, which the words announced to him, assumed a spectral aspect: yet his resolution, and the consciousness of a pure heart, sustained him; and, in a few seconds, he felt himself prepared for everything. He followed his hastening friend with a steady step, firmly determined to await the issue, be it what it might, and explain his own purposes, come what come might.

And yet, at the very threshold of the hall, he was struck with some alarm. In a large half circle, ranged round by the windows, he immediately descried his father with the Oberamtmann, both splendidly attired. The two sisters, Antoni, and others known and unknown, he hurried over with a glance, which was threatening to grow dim. Half wavering, he approached his father; who bade him welcome with the utmost kindness, yet in a certain style of formality which scarcely invited any trustful application. Standing before so many persons, he looked round to find a place among them for the moment: he might have arranged himself beside Lucinda; but Julia, contrary to the rigor of etiquette, made room for him, so that he was forced to step to her side. Antoni continued by Lucinda.

At this important moment, Lucidor again felt as if he were a delegate; and, steeled by his whole juridical science, he called up in his own favor the fine maxim: That we should transact affairs delegated to us by a stranger, as if they were our own; why not our own, therefore, in the same spirit? Well practised in official orations, he speedily ran over what he had to say. But the company, ranged in a formal semicircle, seemed to outflank him. The purport of his speech he knew well; the beginning of it he could not find. At this crisis, he observed on a table, in the corner, the large ink-glass, and several clerks sitting round it: the Oberamtmann made a movement as if to solicit attention for a speech; Lucidor wished to anticipate him; and, at that very moment, Julia pressed his hand. This threw him out of all self-possession; convinced him that all was decided, all lost for him.

With the whole of these negotiations, these family alliances, with social conventions and rules of good manners, he had now nothing more to do: he snatched his hand from Julia's, and vanished so rapidly from the room, that the company lost him unawares, and he out of doors could not find himself again.

Shrinking from the light of day, which shone down upon him in its highest splendor; avoiding the eyes of men; dreading search and pursuit, he hurried forwards, and reached the large garden-hall. Here his knees were like to fail him; he rushed in, and threw himself, utterly comfortless, upon the sofa beneath the mirror.

Amid the polished arrangements of society, to be caught in such unspeakable perplexity! It dashed to and fro like waves about him and within him. His past existence was struggling with his present: it was a frightful moment.

And so he lay for a time, with his face hid in the cushion, on which last night Lucinda's arm had rested. Altogether sunk in his sorrow, he had heard no footsteps approach; feeling some one touch him, he started up, and perceived Lucinda standing by his side.

Fancying they had sent her to bring him back, had commissioned her to lead him with fit sisterly words into the assemblage to front his hated doom, he exclaimed: "You they should not have sent, Lucinda: for it was you that drove me away. I will not return. Give me, if you are capable of any pity, procure me convenience and means of flight. For, that you yourself may testify how impossible it was to bring me back, listen to the explanation of my conduct, which to you and all of them must seem insane. Hear now the oath which I have sworn in my soul, and which I incessantly repeat in words: with you only did I wish to live: with you to enjoy, to employ my days, from youth to old age, in true honorable union. And let this be as firm and sure as aught ever sworn before the altar; this which I now swear, now when I leave you, the most pitiable of all men."

He made a movement to glide past her, as she stood close before him; but she caught him softly in her arms. "What is this!" exclaimed he.

"Lucidor!" cried she, "not pitiable as you think: you are mine, I am yours; I hold you in my arms; delay not to throw your arms about me. Your father has agreed to all; Antoni marries my sister."

In astonishment he recoiled from her: "Can it be?" Lucinda smiled and nodded; he drew back from her arms. "Let me view once more, at a distance, what is to be mine so nearly, so inseparably." He grasped her hands: "Lucinda, are you mine?"

She answered: "Well, then, yes," the sweetest tears in the truest eyes; he clasped her to his breast, and threw his head behind hers; he hung like a shipwrecked mariner on the cliffs of the coast; the ground still shook under him. And now his enraptured eye, again opening, lighted on the mirror. He saw her there in his arms, himself clasped in hers; he looked down, and again to the image. Such emotions accompany man throughout his life. In the mirror, also, he beheld the landscape, which last night had appeared to him so baleful and ominous, now lying fairer and brighter than ever; and himself in such a posture, on such a background! Abundant recompense for all sorrows!

"We are not alone," said Lucinda; and scarcely had he recovered from his rapture, when, all decked and garlanded, a company of girls and boys came forward, carrying wreaths of flowers, and crowding the entrance of the Hall. "This is not the way," cried Lucinda: "how prettily it was arranged, and now it is all running into tumult!" A gay march sounded from a distance; and the company were seen coming on by the large road in stately procession. Lucidor hesitated to advance towards them; only on her arm did he seem certain of his steps. She stayed beside him, expecting from moment to moment the solemn scene of meeting, of thanks for pardon already given.

But by the capricious gods it was otherwise determined. The gay clanging sound of a postilion's horn, from the opposite side, seemed to throw the whole ceremony into rout. "Who can be coming?" cried Lucinda. The thought of a strange presence was frightful to Lucidor; and the carriage seemed entirely unknown to him. A double-seated, new, spick-and-span new travelling chaise! It rolled up to the Hall. A well-dressed, handsome boy sprang down; opened the door; but no one dismounted; the chaise was empty. The boy stept into it; with a dexterous touch or two he threw back the tilts; and there, in a twinkling, stood the daintiest vehicle in readiness for the gayest drive, before the eyes of the whole party, who were now advancing to the spot. Antoni, outhastening the rest, led Julia to the carriage. "Try if this machine," said he, "will please you; if you can sit in it, and over the smoothest roads, roll through the world beside me: I will lead you by no other but the smoothest; and when a strait comes, we shall know how to help ourselves. Over the mountains, sumpters shall carry us, and our coach also."

"You are a dear creature!" cried Julia. The boy came forward; and, with the quickness of a conjurer, exhibited all the conveniences, little advantages, comforts, and celerities of the whole light edifice.

"On Earth I have no thanks," cried Julia; "but from this little moving Heaven, from this cloud, into which you raise me, I will heartily thank you." She had already bounded in, throwing him kind looks and a kiss of the hand. "For the present you come not hither; but there is another whom I mean to take along with me in this proof excursion; he himself has still a proof to undergo." She called to Lucidor; who, just then occupied in mute conversation with his father and father-in-law, willingly took refuge in the light vehicle; feeling an irresistible necessity to dissipate his thoughts in some way or other, though it were but for a moment. He placed himself beside her; she directed the postilion where he was to drive. Instantly they darted off, enveloped in a cloud of dust; and vanished from the eyes of the amazed spectators.

Julia fixed herself in the corner, as firmly and commodiously as she could wish. "Now do you shift into that one too, good brother; so that we may look each other rightly in the face."

Lucidor. You feel my confusion, my embarrassment: I am still as if in a dream; help me out of it.

Julia. Look at these gay peasants, how kindly they salute us! You have never seen the Upper Hamlet yet, since you came hither. All good substantial people there, and all thoroughly devoted to me. No one of them so rich that you cannot, by a time, do a little kind service to him. This road, which we whirl along so smoothly, is my father's doing; another of his benefits to the community.

Lucidor. I believe it, and willingly admit it: but what have these external things to do with the perplexity of my internal feelings?

Julia. Patience a little! I will show you the riches of this world and the glory thereof. Here now we are at the top! Do but look how clear the level country lies all round us leaning against the mountains! All these villages are much, much indebted to my father; to mother and daughters too. The grounds of yon little hamlet are the border.

Lucidor. Surely you are in a very strange mood: you do not seem to be saying what you meant to say.

Julia. But now look down to the left; how beautifully all this unfolds itself! The Church, with its high lindens; the Amthaus, with its poplars, behind the village knoll! Here, too, are the garden and the park.

The postilion drove faster.

Julia. The Hall up yonder you know: it looks almost as well here, as this scene does from it. Here, at the tree, we shall stop a moment: now in this very spot our image is reflected in the large mirror; there they see us full well, but we cannot see ourselves. — Go along, postilion!—There, some little while ago, two people, I believe, were reflected at a shorter distance; and, if I am not exceedingly mistaken, to their great mutual satisfaction.

Lucidor, in ill humor, answered nothing: they went on for some time in silence, driving very hard. "Here," said Julia, "the bad road begins: a service left for you to do, some day. Before we go lower, look down once more. My mother's boxtree rises with its royal summit over all the rest. Thou wilt drive," continued she to the postilion, "down this rough road; we shall take the foot-path through the dale, and so be sooner at the other side than thou." In dismounting, she cried: "Well, now, you will confess, the Wandering Jew, this restless Antoni the Traveller, can arrange his pilgrimages prettily enough for himself and his companions: it is a very beautiful and commodious carriage."

And with this she tripped away down hill: Lucidor followed her, in deep thought; she was sitting on a pleasant seat; it was Lucinda's little spot. She invited him to sit by her.

Julia. So now we are sitting here, and one is nothing to the other. Thus it was destined to be. The little Quicksilver would not suit you. Love it you could not, it was hateful to you.

Lucidor's astonishment increased.

Julia. But Lucinda, indeed! She is the paragon of all perfections; and the pretty sister was once for all cast out. I see it, the question hovers on your lips: who has told us all so accurately?

Lucidor. There is treachery in it!

Julia. Yes, truly! There has been a Traitor at work in the matter.

Lucidor. Name him.

Julia. He is soon unmasked: You! You have the praiseworthy or blameworthy custom of talking to yourself: and now, in the name of all, I must confess that in turn we have overheard you.

Lucidor (starting up). A sorry piece of hospitality, to lay snares for a stranger in this way!

Julia. By no means! We thought not of watching you, more than any other. But, you know, your bed stands in the recess of the wall; on the opposite side is another alcove, commonly employed for laying up household articles. Hither, some days before, we had shifted our old man's bed; being anxious about him in his remote Hermitage: and here, the first night, you started some such passionate soliloquy, which he next morning took his opportunity of rehearsing.

Lucidor had not the heart to interrupt her. He withdrew.

Julia (rising and following him). What a service this discovery did us all! For I will confess, if you were not positively disagreeable, the situation which awaited me was not by any means to my mind. To be Frau Oberamtmannin, what a dreadful state! To have a brave gallant husband, who is to pass judgment on the people; and, for sheer judgment, cannot get to justice! Who can please neither high nor low; and, what is worst, not even himself! I know what my poor mother suffered from the incorruptibility, the inflexibility of my father. At last, indeed, but not till her death, a certain meekness took possession of him: he seemed to suit himself to the world, to make a truce with those evils which, till then, he had vainly striven to conquer.

Lucidor (stopping short; extremely discontented with the incident; vexed at this light mode of treating it). For the sport of an evening this might pass; but to practise such a disgracing mystification, day and night, against an unsuspicious stranger, is not pardonable.

Julia. We are all equally deep in the crime; we all hearkened you: yet I alone pay the penalty of eavesdropping.

Lucidor. All! So much the more unpardonable! And how could you look at me, throughout the day, without blushing, whom at night you were so contemptuously overreaching? But I see clearly with a glance, that your arrangements by day were planned to make mockery of me. A fine family! And where was your father's love of justice all this while! — And Lucinda!—

29*

Julia. And Lucinda! What a tone was that! You meant to say, did not you, How deeply it grieved your heart to think ill of Lucinda, to rank her in a class with the rest of us?

Lucidor. I cannot understand Lucinda.

Julia. In other words this pure noble soul, this peacefully composed nature, benevolence, goodness itself, this woman as she should be, unites with a light-minded company, with a freakish sister, a spoiled brother, and certain mysterious persons! That is incomprehensible!

Lucidor. Yes, indeed, it is incomprehensible.

Julia. Comprehend it then! Lucinda, like the rest of us, had her hands bound. Could you have seen her perplexity, how fain she would have told you all, how often she was on the very eve of doing it, you would now love her doubly and trebly, if indeed true love were not always tenfold and hundredfold of itself. I can assure you, moreover, that all of us at length thought the joke too long.

Lucidor. Why did you not end it then?

Julia. That, too, I must explain. No sooner had my father got intelligence of your first monologue, and seen, as was easy to do, that none of his children would object to such an exchange, than he determined on visiting your father. The importance of the business gave him much anxiety. A father alone can feel the respect which is due to a father. "He must be informed of it in the first place," said mine, "that he may not in the end, when we are all agreed, be reduced to give a forced and displeased consent. I know him well: I know how any thought, any wish, any purpose cleaves to him; and I have my own fears about the issue. Julia, his maps and pictures, he has long viewed as one thing; he has it in his eye to transport all this hither, when the young pair are once settled here, and his old pupil cannot change her abode so readily; on us he is to bestow his holidays; and who knows what other kind friendly things he has projected? He must forthwith be informed what a trick Nature has played us, while yet nothing is declared, nothing is determined." And with this, he exacted from us all the most solemn promise that we should observe you, and come what might, retain you here till his return. How this return has been protracted; what art, toil, and perseverance it has cost to gain your father's consent, he himself will inform you. In short, the business is adjusted; Lucinda is yours.

And thus had the two promenaders, sharply removing from their first resting-place, then pausing by the way, then speaking, and walking slowly through the green fields, at last reached the height, where another well-levelled road received them. The carriage came whirling up: Julia in the meanwhile turned her friend's attention to a strange sight. The whole machinery, of which her gay brother had bragged so much, was now alive and in motion; the wheels were already heaving up and down a multitude of people; the seesaws were flying; maypoles had their climbers; and many a bold artful swing and spring over the heads of an innumerable multitude you might see ventured. The younker had set all agoing, that so the guests, after dinner, might have a gay spectacle awaiting them. "Thou wilt drive through the Nether Hamlet," cried Julia; "the people wish me well, and they shall see how well I am off."

The Hamlet was empty: the young people had all run to the swings and seesaws; old men and women, roused by the driver's horn, appeared at doors and windows; every one gave salutations and blessings, exclaiming: "O what a lovely pair!"

Julia. There, do you hear? We should have suited well enough together after all; you may rue it yet.

Lucidor. But now, dear sister!——

Julia. Ha! Now dear, when you are rid of me?

Lucidor. One single word! On you rests a heavy accusation: what did you mean by that squeeze of the hand, when you knew and felt my dreadful situation? A thing so radically wicked I have never met with in my life before.

Julia. Thank Heaven, we are now quits; now all is pardoned. I had no mind for *you*, that is certain; but that you had utterly and absolutely no mind for me, this was a thing which no young woman could forgive; and the squeeze of the hand, observe you, was for the rogue. I do confess, it was almost too roguish; and I forgive myself, because I forgive you; and so let all be forgotten and forgiven! Here is my hand.

He took it; she cried: "Here we are again! In our park again; and so in a trice, we whirl through the wide world, and back too; we shall meet again."

They had reached the garden-hall; it seemed empty; the company, tired of waiting, had gone out to walk. Antoni, however, and Lucinda came forth. Julia stepping from the carriage flew to her friend; she thanked him in a cordial embrace, and restrained not the most joyful tears. The brave man's cheeks reddened, his features looked forth unfolded; his eye glanced moist; and a fair imposing youth shone through the veil.

And so both pairs moved off to join the company, with feelings which the finest dream could not have given them.

* * * * * *

"Thus, my friends," said Lenardo, after a short preamble, " if we survey the most populous provinces and kingdoms of the firm Earth, we observe on all sides that wherever an available soil appears, it is cultivated, planted, shaped, beautified; and in the same proportion, coveted, taken into possession, fortified and defended. Hereby we bring home to our conceptions the high worth of property in land; and are obliged to consider it as the first and best acquirement that can be allotted to man. And if on closer inspection we find parental and filial love, the union of countrymen and townsmen, and therefore the universal feeling of patriotism, founded immediately on this same interest in the soil, we cannot but regard that seizing and retaining of Space, in the great or the small scale, as a thing still more important and venerable. Yes, Nature herself has so ordered it! A man born on the glebe comes by habit to belong to it; the two grow together, and the fairest ties are spun from their union. Who is there then that would spitefully disturb this foundation-stone of all existence; that would blindly deny the worth and dignity of such precious and peculiar gifts of Heaven?

"And yet we may assert, that if what man possesses is of great worth, what he does and accomplishes must be of still greater. In a wide view of things, therefore, we must look on property in land as one small part of the possessions that have been given us. Of these the greatest and the most precious part consists especially in what is movable, and in what is gained by a moving life.

"Towards this quarter, we younger men are peculiarly constrained to turn; for though we had inherited from our fathers the desire of abiding and continuing, we find ourselves called by a thousand causes nowise to shut our eyes against a wider outlook and survey. Let us hasten, then, to the shore of the Ocean, and convince ourselves what boundless spaces are still lying open to activity; and confess that, by the bare thought of this, we are roused to new vigor.

"Yet not to lose ourselves in these vast expanses, let us direct our attention to the long and large surface of so many countries and kingdoms, combined together on the face of the Earth. Here we behold great tracts of land tenanted by Nomades; whose towns are movable, whose life-supporting household goods can be transferred from place to place. We see them in the middle of the deserts, on wide green pasturages, lying as it were at anchor in their desired haven. Such movement, such wandering, becomes a habit with them, a necessity; in the end they grow to regard the surface of the world as if it were not bulwarked by mountains, were not cut asunder by streams. Have we not seen the North-east flow towards the South-west, one people driving another before it, and lordship and property altogether changed?

"From over-populous countries, a similar calamity may again, in the great circle of vicissitudes, occur more than once. What we have to dread from foreigners, it may be difficult to say; but it is curious enough, that by our own over-population, we ourselves are thronging one another in our own domains, and without waiting to be driven, are driving one another forth, passing sentence of banishment each against his fellow.

"Here now is the place and season for giving scope in our bosoms, without spleen or anger, to a love of movement; for unfettering that impatient wish which excites us to change our abode. Yet, whatever we may purpose and intend, let it be accomplished not from passion, or from any other influence of force, but from a conviction corresponding to the wisest judgment and deliberation.

"It has been said, and over again said: Where I am well, is my country! But this consolatory saw were better worded: Where I am useful, is my country! At home, you may be useless, and the fact not instantly observed; abroad in the world, the useless man is speedily convicted. And now, if I say: Let each endeavor everywhere to be of use to himself and others, this is not a precept, or a counsel, but the utterance of life itself.

"Cast a glance over the terrestrial ball, and for the present leave the ocean out of sight; let not its hurrying fleets distract your thoughts: but fix your eye on the firm earth, and be amazed to see how it is overflowed with a swarming ant tribe, jostling and crossing, and running to and fro forever! So was it ordained of the Lord himself, when, obstructing the Tower of Babel, he scattered the human race abroad into all the world. Let us praise his name on this account, for the blessing has extended to all generations.

"Observe now, and cheerfully, how the young, on every side, instantly get into movement. As instruction is not offered them within doors, and knocks not at their gates, they hasten forthwith to those countries and cities whither the call of science and wisdom allures them. Here, no sooner have they gained a rapid and scanty training, than they feel themselves impelled to look round in the world, whether here and there some profitable experience, applicable to their objects, may not be met with and appropriated. Let these try their fortune! We turn from them to those completed and distinguished men, those noble inquirers into Nature, who wittingly encounter every difficulty, every peril, that to the world they may lay the world open, and, through the most Impassable, pave easy roads.

"But observe also, on beaten highways, how dust on dust, in long cloudy trains, mounts up, betokening the track of commodious top-laden carriages, in which the rich, the noble, and so many others, are whirled along; whose varying purposes and dispositions Yorick has most daintily explained to us.

"These the stout craftsman, on foot, may cheerily gaze after; for whom his country has made it a duty to appropriate foreign skill, and not till this has been accomplished, to revisit his paternal hearth. In still greater numbers, do traffickers and dealers meet us on our road: the little trader must not neglect, from time to time, to forsake his shop that he may visit fairs and markets, may approach the great merchant, and increase his own small profit, by example and participation of the boundless. But yet more restlessly do we descry cruizing on horseback, singly, on all high and bye ways, that multitude of persons whose business it is, in lawful wise, to make forcible pretension to our purses. Samples of all sorts, prize-catalogues, invitations to purchase, pursue us into town-houses and country-houses, and wherever we may seek refuge: diligently they assault us and surprise us; themselves offering the opportunity, which it would have entered no man's mind to seek. And what shall I say of that People which, before all others, arrogates to itself the blessing of perpetual wandering, and by its movable activity contrives to overreach the resting, and to overstep the walking? Of them we must say neither ill nor good; no good, because our League stands on its guard against them; no ill, because the wanderer, mindful of reciprocal advantage, is bound to treat with friendliness whomsoever he may meet.

"But now, above all, we must mention with peculiar affection, the whole race of artists; for they, too, are thoroughly involved in this universal movement. Does not the painter wander, with pallet and easel, from face to face; and are not his kindred laborers summoned, now this way, now that, because in all places there is something to be built and to be fashioned? More briskly, however, paces the musician on his way; for he peculiarly it is, that for a new ear has provided new surprise, for a fresh mind fresh astonishment. Players, too, though they now despise the cart of Thespis, still rove about in little choirs; and their moving world, wherever they appear, is speedily enough built up. So likewise, individually, renouncing serious profitable engagements, these men delight to change place with place, according as rising talents, combined with rising wants, furnish pretext and occasion. For this success they commonly prepare themselves, by leaving no important stage in their native land untrodden.

"Nor let us forget to cast a glance over the professorial class: these, too, you find in continual motion, occupying and forsaking one chair after the other, to scatter richly abroad on every side the seeds of a hasty culture. More assiduous, however, and of wider aim, are those pious souls who disperse themselves through all quarters of the world, to bring salvation to their brethren. Others, on the contrary, are pilgriming to seek salvation for themselves: they march in hosts to consecrated, wonder-working places, there to ask and receive what was denied their souls at home.

"And if all these sorts of men surprise us less by their wandering, as for most part, without wandering, the business of their life were impossible, of those again who dedicate their diligence to the soil, we should certainly expect that they, at least, were fixed. By no means! Even without possession, occupation is conceivable; and we behold the eager farmer forsaking the ground which for years has yielded him profit and enjoyment: impatiently he searches after similar or greater profit, be it far or near. Nay, the owner himself will abandon his new-grubbed clearage so soon as, by his cultivation, he has rendered it commodious for a less enterprising husbandman: once more he presses into the wilderness; again makes space for himself in the forests; in recompense of that first toiling, a double and treble space; on which also, it may be, he thinks not to continue.

"There we shall leave him, bickering with bears and other monsters; and turn back into the polished world, where we find the state of things no whit more stationary. Do but view any great and regulated kingdom: the ablest man is also the man who moves the oftenest; at the beck of his prince, at the order of his minister, the Serviceable is transferred from place to place. To him also our precept will apply: Everywhere endeavor to be useful, everywhere you are at home. Yet if we observe important statesmen leaving, though reluctantly, their high stations, we have reason to deplore their fate: for we can neither recognise them as emigrants nor as migrators: not as emigrants, because they forego a covetable situation without any prospect of a better even seeming to open; not as migrators, because to be useful in other places is a fortune seldom granted them.

"For the soldier, again, a life of peculiar wandering is appointed; even in peace, now this, now that post is intrusted to him; to fight, at hand or afar off for his native country, he must keep himself perpetually in motion or readiness to move; and not for immediate defence alone, but also to fulfil the remote purposes of nations and rulers, he turns his steps towards all quarters of the world; and to few of his craft is it given to find any resting-place. And as, in the soldier, courage is his first and highest quality, so this must always be considered as united with fidelity; and accordingly we find certain nations, famous for trustworthiness, called forth from their home, and serving spiritual or temporal regents as bodyguards.

"Another class of persons indispensable to governments, and also of extreme mobility, we see in those negotiators, who, despatched from court to court, beleaguer princes and ministers, and overnet the whole inhabited world with their invisible threads. Of these men also, no one is certain of his place for a moment. In peace, the ablest of them are sent from country to country; in war, they march behind the army when victorious, prepare the way for it when fugitive; and thus are they appointed still to be changing place for place; on which account, indeed, they at all times carry with them a stock of farewell cards.

"If hitherto at every step we have contrived to do ourselves some honor, declaring as we have done the most distinguished portion of active men to be our mates and fellows in destiny, there now remains for you, my beloved friends, by way of termination, a glory higher than all the rest, seeing you find yourselves united in brotherhood with princes, kings, and emperors. Think first, with blessings and reverence, of the imperial wanderer Hadrian, who on foot, at the head of his army, paced out the circle of the world which was subject to him, and thus in very deed took possession of it. Think then with horror of the Conqueror, that armed Wanderer, against whom no resistance availed, no wall or bulwark could shelter harmless nations. In fine, accompany with honest sympathy those hapless exiled princes, who, descending from the summit of the height, cannot even be received into the modest guild of active wanderers.

"And now while we call forth and illustrate all this to one another, no narrow despondency, no passionate perversion can rule over us. The time is past when people rushed forth at random into the wide world: by the labors of scientific travellers describing wisely and copying like artists, we have become sufficiently acquainted with the Earth, to know moderately well what is to be looked for everywhere.

"Yet for obtaining perfect information an individual will not suffice. Our Society is founded on the principle that each in his degree, for his purposes, be thoroughly informed. Has any one of us some country in his eye, towards which his wishes are tending, we endeavor to make clear to him, in special detail, what was hovering before his imagination as a whole: to afford each other a survey of the inhabited and inhabitable world, is a most pleasant and most profitable kind of conversation.

"Under this aspect, we can look upon ourselves as members of a Union belonging to the world. Simple and grand is the thought; easy is its execution by understanding and strength. Unity is all-powerful; no division, therefore, no contention among us! Let a man learn, we say, to figure himself as without permanent external relation; let him seek consistency and sequence not in circumstances but in himself; there will he find it; there let him cherish and nourish it. He who devotes himself to the most needful will in all cases advance to his purpose with greatest certainty: others again, aiming at the higher, the more delicate, require greater prudence even in the choice of their path. But let a man be attempting or treating what he will, he is not, as an individual, sufficient for himself; and to an honest mind, society remains the highest want. All serviceable persons ought to be related with each other, as the building proprietor looks out for an architect, and the architect for masons and carpenters.

"How and on what principle this Union of ours has been fixed and founded, is known to all. There is no man among us, who at any moment could not to proper purpose employ his faculty of action; who is not assured that in all places, whither chance, inclination, or even passion may conduct him, he will be received, employed, assisted; nay, in adverse accidents, as far as possible, refitted and indemnified.

"Two duties we have most rigorously undertaken: first, to honor every species of religious worship, for all of them are comprehended more or less directly in the Creed: secondly, in like manner to respect all forms of government; and since every one of them induces and promotes a calculated activity, to labor according to the wish and will of constituted authorities, in whatever place it may be our lot to sojourn, and for whatever time. Finally, we reckon it our duty, without pedantry or rigor, to practise and forward decorum of manners and morals, as required by that Reverence for ourselves, which arises from the Three Reverences; whereto we universally profess our adherence; having all had the joy and good fortune, some of us from youth upwards, to be initiated likewise in the higher general Wisdom taught in certain cases by those venerable men. All this, in the solemn hour of parting, we have thought good once more to recount, to unfold, to hear and acknowledge, as also to seal with a trustful Farewell.

> Keep not standing fix'd and rooted,
> Briskly venture, briskly roam!
> Head and hand, where'er thou foot it,
> And stout heart are still at home.
> In each land the sun does visit,
> We are gay whate'er betide;
> To give space for wand'ring is it
> That the world was made so wide."

NOVELLE.

FRASER'S MAGAZINE, 1832.*

The spacious courts of the Prince's Castle were still veiled in thick mists of an autumnal morning; through which veil, meanwhile, as it melted into clearness, you could more or less discern the whole Hunter-company, on horseback and on foot, all busily astir. The hasty occupations of the nearest were distinguishable: there was lengthening, shortening of stirrup-leathers; there was handing of rifles and shot-pouches, there was putting of game-bags to rights; while the hounds, impatient in their leashes, threatened to drag their keepers off with them. Here and there, too, a horse showed spirit more than enough; driven on by its fiery nature, or excited by the spur of its rider, who even now in the half-dusk could not repress a certain self-complacent wish to exhibit himself. All waited however on the Prince, who, taking leave of his young consort, was now delaying too long.

United a short while ago, they already felt the happiness of consentaneous dispositions; both were of active vivid character; each willingly participated in the tastes and endeavors of the other. The Prince's father had already, in his time, discerned and improved the season

---

* Translated by Thomas Carlyle.

when it became evident that all members of the commonwealth should pass their days in equal industry; should all, in equal working and producing, each in his kind, first earn and then enjoy.

How well this had prospered was visible in these very days, when the head-market was a holding, which you might well enough have named a fair. The Prince yester-even had led his Princess on horseback through the tumult of the heaped-up wares; and pointed out to her how on this spot the Mountain region met the Plain country in profitable barter: he could here, with the objects before him, awaken her attention to the various industry of his Land.

If the Prince at this time occupied himself and his servants almost exclusively with these pressing concerns, and in particular worked incessantly with his Finance-minister, yet would the Huntmaster too have his right; on whose pleading, the temptation could not be resisted to undertake, in this choice autumn weather, a Hunt that had already been postponed; and so for the household itself, and for the many stranger visitants, prepare a peculiar and singular festivity.

The Princess staid behind with reluctance: but it was proposed to push far into the Mountains, and stir up the peaceable inhabitants of the forests there with an unexpected invasion.

At parting, her lord failed not to propose a ride for her, with Friedrich, the Prince-Uncle, as escort: "I will leave thee," said he, "our Honorio too, as Equerry and Page, who will manage all." In pursuance of which words, he, in descending, gave to a handsome young man the needful injunctions; and soon thereafter disappeared with guests and train.

The Princess, who had waved her handkerchief to her husband while still down in the court, now retired to the back apartments, which commanded a free prospect towards the Mountains; and so much the lovelier, as the Castle itself stood on a sort of elevation, and thus, behind as well as before, afforded manifold magnificent views. She found the fine telescope still in the position where they had left it yester-even, when amusing themselves over bush and hill and forest-summit, with the lofty ruins of the primeval Stammburg, or Family Tower; which in the clearness of evening stood out noteworthy, as at that hour with its great light-and-shade masses, the best aspect of so venerable a memorial of old time was to be had. This morning too, with the approximating glasses, might be beautifully seen the autumnal tinge of the trees, many in kind and number, which had struggled up through the masonry unhindered and undisturbed during long years. The fair dame, however, directed the tube somewhat lower, to a waste stony flat, over which the Hunting-train was to pass: she waited the moment with patience, and was not disappointed: for with the clearness and magnifying power of the instrument her glancing eyes plainly distinguished the Prince and the Head-Equerry; nay, she forbore not again to wave her handkerchief, as some momentary pause and looking-back was fancied perhaps, rather than observed.

Prince-Uncle, Friedrich by name, now with announcement, entered, attended by his Painter, who carried a large portfolio under his arm. "Dear Cousin," said the hale old gentleman, "we here present you with the Views of the Stammburg, taken on various sides to show how the mighty Pile, warred on and warring, has from old times fronted the year and its weather; how here and there its wall had to yield, here and there rush down into waste ruins. However, we have now done much to make the wild mass accessible; for more there wants not to set every traveller, every visitor, into astonishment, into admiration."

As the Prince now exhibited the separate leaves, he continued: "Here where, advancing up the hollow-way, through the outer ring-walls, you reach the Fortress proper, rises against us a rock, the firmest of the whole mountain; on this there stands a tower built, yet when Nature leaves off, and Art and Handicraft begin, no one can distinguish. Farther you perceive sidewards walls abutting on it, and donjons terracewise stretching down. But I speak wrong, for to the eye it is but a wood that encircles that old summit; these hundred and fifty years no axe has sounded there, and the massiest stems have on all sides sprung up: wherever you press inwards to the walls, the smooth maple, the rough oak, the taper pine, with trunk and roots oppose you; round these we have to wind, and pick our footsteps with skill. Do but look how artfully our Master has brought the character of it on paper: how the roots and stems, the species of each distinguishable, twist themselves among the masonry, and the huge boughs come looping through the holes. It is a wilderness like no other; an accidentally unique locality, where ancient traces of long-vanished power of Man, and the ever-living, ever-working power of Nature show themselves in the most earnest conflict.'

Exhibiting another leaf, he went on: "What say you now to the Castle-court, which, become inaccessible by the falling in of the old gate-tower, had for immemorial time been trodden by no foot? We sought to get at it by a side; have pierced through walls, blasted vaults asunder, and so provided a convenient but secret way. Inside it needed no clearance; here stretches a flat rock-summit, smoothed by nature; but yet strong trees have in spots found luck and opportunity for rooting themselves there; they have softly but decidedly grown up, and now stretch out their boughs into the galleries where the knights once walked to and fro; nay, through the doors and windows into the vaulted halls; out of which we would not drive them: they have even got the mastery, and may keep it. Sweeping away deep strata of leaves, we have found the notablest place all smoothed, the like of which were perhaps not to be met with in the world.

"After all this, however, it is still to be remarked, and on the spot itself well worth examining, how on the steps that lead up to the main tower, a maple has struck root and fashioned itself to a stout tree, so that you can hardly with difficulty press by it, to mount the battlements and gaze over the unbounded prospect. Yet here, too, you linger pleased in the shade; for that tree is it which high over the whole wondrously lifts itself into the air.

"Let us thank the brave Artist, then, who so deservingly in various pictures teaches us the whole, even as if we saw it: he has spent the fairest hours of the day and of the season therein, and for weeks long kept moving about these scenes. Here in this corner has there for him, and the warder we gave him, been a little pleasant dwelling fitted up. You could not think, my Best, what a lovely outlook into the country, into court and walls, he has got there. But now when all is once in outline, so pure, so characteristic, he may finish it down here at his ease. With these pictures we will decorate our garden-hall; and no one shall recreate his eyes over our regular parterres, our groves and shady walks, without wishing himself up there, to follow, in actual sight of the old and of the new, of the stubborn, inflexible, indestructible, and of the fresh, pliant, irresistible, what reflections and comparisons would rise for him."

Honorio entered, with notice that the horses were brought out; then said the Princess, turning to the Uncle: "Let us ride up; and you will show me in reality what you have here set before me in image. Ever since I came among you, I have heard of this undertaking; and should now like of all things to see with my own eyes what in the narrative seemed impossible, and in the depicting remains improbable."
—"Not yet, my Love," answered the Prince: "what you here saw is what it can become and is becoming: for the present much in the enterprise stands still amid impediments; Art must first be complete, if Nature is not to shame it."
—"Then let us ride at least upwards, were it only to the foot: I have the greatest wish to-day to look about me far in the world."—"Altogether as you will it," replied the Prince.—"Let us ride through the Town, however," continued the Lady, "over the great market-place, where stands the innumerable crowd of booths, looking like a little city, like a camp. It is as if the wants and occupations of all the families in the land were turned outwards, assembled in this centre, and brought into the light of day: for the attentive observer can descry whatsoever it is that man performs and needs; you fancy, for the moment, there is no money necessary, that all business could here be managed by barter, and so at bottom it is. Since the Prince, last night, set me on these reflections, it is pleasant to consider how here, where Mountain and Plain meet together, both so clearly speak out what they require and wish. For as the Highlander can fashion the timber of his woods into a hundred shapes, and mould his iron for all manner of uses, so these others from below come to meet him with most manifold wares, in which often you can hardly discover the material or recognise the aim."

"I am aware," answered the Prince, "that my Nephew turns his utmost care to these things: for specially, on the present occasion, this main point comes to be considered, that one receive more than one give out: which is to manage is, in the long run, the sum of all Political Economy, as of the smallest private housekeeping. Pardon me, however, my Best: I never like to ride through markets; at every step you are hindered and kept back; and then flames up in my imagination the monstrous misery, which, as it were, burnt itself into my eyes, when I witnessed one such world of wares go off in fire. I had scarcely got to——"

"Let us not lose the bright hours," interrupted the Princess, for the worthy man had already more than once afflicted her with the minute description of that mischance: how he being on a long journey, resting in the best inn, on the market-place which was just then swarming with a fair, had gone to bed exceedingly fatigued; and in the night-time been, by shrieks, and flames rolling up against his lodging, hideously awakened.

The Princess hastened to mount her favorite horse: and led, not through the backgate upwards, but through the foregate downwards, her reluctant-willing attendant: for who but would gladly have ridden by her side, who but would gladly have followed after her. And so Honorio too had without regret staid back from the otherwise so wished-for Hunt, to be exclusively at her service.

As was to be anticipated, they could only ride through the market step by step; but the fair Lovely one enlivened every stoppage by some sprightly remark. "I repeat my lesson of yester-night," said she, "since Necessity is trying our patience." And in truth, the whole mass of men so crowded about the riders, that their progress was slow. The people gazed with joy at the young dame; and, on so many smiling countenances, might be read the pleasure they felt to see that the first woman in the land was also the fairest and gracefullest.

Promiscuously mingled stood, Mountaineers, who had built their still dwellings amid rocks, firs, and spruces; Lowlanders from hills, meadows, and leas; craftsmen of the little towns; and what else had all assembled there. After a quiet glance, the Princess remarked to her attendant, how all these, whencesoever they came, had taken more stuff than necessary for their clothes, more cloth and linen, more ribands for trimming. It is as if the women could not be bushy enough, the men not puffy enough, to please themselves.

"We will leave them that," answered the

uncle: "spend his superfluity on what he will, a man is happy in it; happiest when therewith decks and dizens himself." The fair dame nodded assent.

So had they by degrees got upon a clear space, which led out to the suburbs, when, at the end of many small booths and stands, a larger edifice of boards showed itself, which was scarcely glanced at till an ear-lacerating bellow sounded forth from it. The feeding-hour of the wild beasts there exhibited seemed to have come: the Lion let his forest and desert-voice be heard in all vigor; the horses shuddered, and all must remark how, in the peaceful ways and workings of the cultivated world, the King of the wilderness so fearfully announced himself. Coming nearer the booth, you could not overlook the variegated colossal pictures representing with violent colors and strong emblems those foreign beasts; to a sight of which the peaceful burgher was to be irresistibly enticed. The grim monstrous tiger was pouncing on a blackamoor, on the point of tearing him in shreds; a lion stood earnest and majestic, as if he saw no prey worthy of him; other wondrous party-colored creatures, beside these mighty ones, deserved less attention.

"As we come back," said the Princess, "we will alight and take a nearer view of these gentry."—"It is strange," observed the Prince, "that man always seeks excitement by Terror. Inside, there, the Tiger lies quite quiet in his cage; and here must he ferociously dart upon a black, that the people may fancy the like is to be seen within: of murder and sudden death, of burning and destruction, there is not enough; but ballad-singers must at every corner keep repeating it. Good man will have himself frightened a little; to feel the better, in secret, how beautiful and laudable it is to draw breath in freedom."

Whatever of apprehensiveness from such bugbear images might have remained was soon all and wholly effaced, as, issuing through the gate, our party entered on the cheerfullest of scenes. The road led first up the River, as yet but a small current, and bearing only light boats, but which by and by, as a renowned world-stream, would carry forth its name and waters, and enliven distant lands. They proceeded next through well-cultivated fruit-gardens and pleasure-grounds, softly ascending; and by degrees you could look about you in the now-disclosed much-peopled region, till first a thicket, then a little wood admitted our riders, and the gracefullest localities refreshed and limited their view. A meadow vale leading upwards, shortly before mown for the second time, velvet-like to look upon, watered by a brook rushing out lively copious at once from the uplands above, received them as with welcome; and so they approached a higher freer station, which, on issuing from the wood, after a stiff ascent, they gained; and could now descry, over new clumps of trees, the old Castle, the goal of their pilgrimage, rising in the distance, as pinnacle of the rock and forest. Backwards, again (for never did one mount hither without turning round), they caught, through accidental openings of the high trees, the Prince's Castle, on the left, lightened by the morning sun; the well-built higher quarter of the Town softened under light smoke-clouds; and so on, rightwards, the under Town, the River in several bendings with its meadows and mills; on the farther side, an extensive fertile region.

Having satisfied themselves with the prospect, or rather as usually happens when we look round from so high a station, become doubly eager for a wider, less limited view, they rode on, over a broad stony flat, where the mighty Ruin stood fronting them, as a green-crowned summit, a few old trees far down about its foot: they rode along; and so arrived there, just at the steepest most inaccessible side. Great rocks jutting out from of old, insensible of every change, firm, well-founded, stood clenched together there; and so it towered upwards: what had fallen at intervals lay in huge plates and fragments confusedly heaped, and seemed to forbid the boldest any attempt. But the steep, the precipitous is inviting to youth: to undertake it, to storm and conquer it, is for young limbs an enjoyment. The Princess testified desire for an attempt; Honorio was at her hand; the Prince-Uncle, if easier to satisfy, took it cheerfully, and would show that he too had strength; the horses were to wait below among the trees; our climbers make for a certain point, where a huge projecting rock affords a standing-room, and a prospect, which indeed is already passing over into the bird's-eye kind, yet folds itself together there picturesquely enough.

The sun, almost at its meridian, lent the clearest light; the Prince's Castle, with its compartments, main buildings, wings, domes, and towers, lay clear and stately; the upper Town in its whole extent; into the lower also you could conveniently look, nay, by the telescope distinguish the booths in the market-place. So furthersome an instrument Honorio would never leave behind: they looked at the River upwards and downwards, on this side the mountainous, terrace-like, interrupted expanse, on that the upswelling, fruitful land, alternating in level and low hill; places innumerable; for it was long customary to dispute how many of them were here to be seen.

Over the great expanse lay a cheerful stillness, as is common at noon; when, as the Ancients were wont to say, Pan is asleep, and all Nature holds her breath not to awaken him.

"It is not the first time," said the Princess, "that I, on some such high far-seeing spot, have reflected how Nature all clear looks so pure and peaceful, and gives you the impression as if there were nothing contradictory in the world; and yet when you return back into the habitation of man, be it lofty or low, wide or narrow, there is ever somewhat to contend with, to battle with, to smooth and put to rights."

Honorio who, meanwhile, was looking through the glass at the Town, exclaimed: "See! see! There is fire in the market!" They looked, and could observe some smoke, the flames were smothered in the daylight. "The fire spreads!" cried he, still looking through the glass; the mischief indeed now became noticeable to the good eyes of the Princess; from time to time you observed a red burst of flame, the smoke mounted aloft; and Prince-Uncle said: "Let us return; that is not good: I always feared I should see that misery a second time." They descended, got back to their horses. "Ride," said the Princess to the Uncle, "fast, but not without a groom; leave me Honorio, we will follow without delay." The Uncle felt the reasonableness, nay necessity of this; and started off down the waste stony slope, at the quickest pace the ground allowed.

As the Princess mounted, Honorio said: "Please your Excellency to ride slow! In the Town as in the Castle, the fire-apparatus is in perfect order; the people, in this unexpected accident, will not lose their presence of mind. Here, moreover, we have bad ground, little stones and short grass; quick riding is unsafe; in any case, before we arrive, the fire will be got under." The Princess did not think so; she observed the smoke spreading, she fancied that she saw a flame flash up, that she heard an explosion; and now in her imagination all the terrific things awoke, which the worthy Uncle's repeated narrative of his experiences in that market-conflagration had too deeply implanted there.

Frightful doubtless had that business been, alarming and impressive enough to leave behind it, painfully through life long, a boding and image of its recurrence, when, in the night-season, on the great booth-covered market-space, a sudden fire had seized booth after booth, before the sleepers in these light huts could be shaken out of deep dreams: the Prince himself, as a wearied stranger arriving only for rest, started from his sleep, sprang to the window, saw all fearfully illuminated; flame after flame, from the right, from the left, darting through each other, rolls quivering towards him. The houses of the market-place, reddened in the shine, seemed already glowing, threatened every moment to kindle, and burst forth in fire: below, the element raged without let; planks cracked, laths cracked, the canvass flew abroad, and its dusky fire-peaked tatters whirled themselves round and aloft, as if bad spirits, in their own element, with perpetual change of shape, were, in capricious dance, devouring one another; and there and yonder would dart up out from their penal fire. And then with wild howls each saved what was at hand: servants and masters labored to drag forth bales already seized by the flames, to snatch away yet somewhat from the burning shelves, and pack it into the chests, which too they must at last leave a prey to the hastening flame. How many a one could have prayed but for a moment's pause to the loud-advancing fire; as he looked round for the possibility of some device, and was with all his possession already seized: on the one side, burnt and glowed already, what on the other still stood in dark night. Obstinate characters, will-strong men grimly fronted the grim foe, and saved much, with loss of their eyebrows and hair. Alas, all this waste confusion now rose anew before the fair spirit of the Princess; the gay morning prospect was all overclouded, and her eyes darkened; wood and meadow had put on a look of strangeness, of danger.

Entering the peaceful vale, heeding little its refreshing coolness, they were but a few steps down from the copious fountain of the brook which flowed by them, when the Princess descried, quite down in the thickets, something singular, which she soon recognised for the tiger: springing on, as she a short while ago had seen him painted, he came towards her; and this image, added to the frightful ones she was already busy with, made the strangest impression. "Fly! your Grace," cried Honorio, "fly!" She turned her horse towards the steep hill they had just descended. The young man, rushing on towards the monster, drew his pistol and fired when he thought himself near enough; but, alas, without effect; the tiger sprang to a side, the horse faltered, the provoked wild beast followed its course, upwards straight after the Princess. She galloped, what her horse could, up the steep stony space; scarcely apprehending that so delicate a creature, unused to such exertion, could not hold out. It overdid itself, driven on by the necessitated Princess; it stumbled on the loose gravel of the steep, and again stumbled; and at last fell, after violent efforts, powerless to the ground. The fair dame, resolute and dextrous, failed not instantly to get upon her feet; the horse too rose, but the tiger was approaching; though not with vehement speed; the uneven ground, the sharp stones seemed to damp his impetuosity; and only Honorio flying after him, riding with checked speed along with him, appeared to stimulate and provoke his force anew. Both runners, at the same instant, reached the spot where the Princess was standing by her horse: the Knight bent himself, fired, and with this second pistol hit the monster through the head, so that it rushed down; and now, stretched out in full length, first clearly disclosed the might and terror whereof only the bodily hull was left lying. Honorio had sprung from his horse; was already kneeling on the beast, quenching its last movements, and held his drawn hanger in his right hand. The youth was beautiful; he had come dashing on as in sports of the lance and the ring the Princess had often seen him do. Even so in the riding-course would his bullet, as he darted by, hit the Turk's-head on the pole, right under the turban in the brow; even so would he, lightly prancing up, prick his naked sabre into the fallen mass, and lift it from the ground. In all such arts he was dextrous and felicitous; both now stood him in good stead.

"Give him the rest," said the Princess: "I fear he will hurt you with his claws."—"Pardon!" answered the youth: "he is already dead enough; and I would not hurt the skin, which next winter shall shine upon your sledge."—"Sport not," said the Princess: "whatsoever of pious feeling dwells in the depth of the heart unfolds itself in such a moment."—"I too," cried Honorio, "was never more pious than even now; and therefore do I think of what is joyfullest; I look at the tiger's fell only as it can attend you to do you pleasure."—"It would for ever remind me," said she, "of this fearful moment."—"Yet is it," replied the youth with glowing cheeks, "a more harmless spoil than when the weapons of slain enemies are carried for show before the victor."—"I shall bethink me, at sight of it, of your boldness and cleverness; and need not add that you may reckon on my thanks and the Prince's favor for your life long. But rise; the beast is clean dead, let us consider what is next: before all things rise!"—"As I am once on my knees," replied the youth, "once in a posture which in other circumstances would have been forbid, let me beg at this moment to receive assurance of the favor, of the grace which you vouchsafe me. I have already asked so often of your high consort for leave and promotion to go on my travels. He who has the happiness to sit at your table, whom you honor with the privilege to entertain your company, should have seen the world. Travellers stream in on us from all parts; and when a town, an important spot in any quarter of the world comes in course, the question is sure to be asked of us, were we ever there? Nobody allows one sense, till one has seen all that: it is as if you had to instruct yourself only for the sake of others."

"Rise!" repeated the Princess: "I were loth to wish or request aught that went against the will of my Husband; however, if I mistake not, the cause why he has restrained you hitherto will soon be at an end. His intention was to see you ripened into a complete self-guided nobleman, to do yourself and him credit in foreign parts, as hitherto at court; and I should think this deed of yours was as good a recommendatory passport as a young man could wish for to take abroad with him."

That, instead of a youthful joy, a certain mournfulness came over his face, the Princess had not time to observe, nor had he to indulge his emotion; for, in hot haste, up the steep, came a woman, with a boy at her hand, straight to the group so well known to us; and scarcely had Honorio, bethinking him, arisen, when they howling and shrieking cast themselves on the carcass; by which action, as well as by their cleanly decent, yet party-colored and unusual dress, might be gathered that it was the mistress of this slain creature, and the black-eyed black-locked boy, holding a flute in his hand, her son; weeping like his mother, less violent but deeply moved, kneeling beside her.

Now came strong outbreakings of passion from this woman; interrupted, indeed, and pulse-wise; a stream of words, leaping like a stream in gushes from rock to rock. A natural language, short and discontinuous, made itself impressive and pathetic: in vain should we attempt translating it into our dialects; the approximate purport of it we must not omit. "They have murdered thee, poor beast! murdered without need! Thou wert tame, and wouldst fain have laid down at rest and waited our coming; for thy foot-balls were sore, thy claws had no force left. The hot sun to ripen them was wanting. Thou wert the beautifullest of thy kind: who ever saw a kingly tiger so gloriously stretched out in sleep, as thou here liest, dead, never to rise more. When thou awokest in the early dawn of morning, and openedst thy throat, stretching out thy red tongue, thou wert as if smiling on us; and even when bellowing, thou tookest thy food from the hands of a woman, from the fingers of a child. How long have we gone with thee on thy journeys; how long has thy company been useful and fruitful to us! To us, to us of a very truth, meat came from the eater, and sweetness out of the strong. So will it be no more. Wo! wo!"

She had not done lamenting, when over the smoother part of the Castle Mountain, came riders rushing down; soon recognised as the Prince's Hunting-train, himself the foremost. Following their sport, in the backward hills, they had observed the fire-vapors; and fast through dale and ravine, as in fierce chase, taken the shortest path towards this mournful sign. Galloping along the stony vacancy, they stopped and stared at sight of the unexpected group, which in that empty expanse stood out so markworthy. After the first recognition there was silence; some pause of breathing-time; and then what the view itself did not impart, was with brief words explained. So stood the Prince, contemplating the strange unheard-of incident; a circle round him of riders, and followers that had run on foot. What to do was still undetermined; the Prince intent on ordering, executing, when a man pressed forward into the circle; large of stature, party-colored, wondrously-apparelled, like wife and child. And now the family in union testified their sorrow and astonishment. The man, however, soon restrained himself, bowed in reverent distance before the Prince, and said: "It is not the time for lamenting; alas, my lord and mighty hunter, the lion too is loose, hither towards the mountains is he gone: but spare him, have mercy that he perish not like this good beast."

"The Lion!" said the Prince: "Hast thou the

trace of him?"—"Yes, Lord! A peasant down there, who had heedlessly taken shelter on a tree, directed me farther up this way, to the left; but I saw the crowd of men and horses here; anxious for tidings of assistance, I hastened hither."—"So then," commanded the Prince, "draw to the left. Huntsmen; you will load your pieces, go softly to work, if you drive him into the deep woods, it is no matter: but in the end, good man, we shall be obliged to kill your animal; why were you improvident enough to let him loose?"—"The fire broke out," replied he, "we kept quiet and attentive; it spread fast, but at a distance from us, we had water enough for our defence; but a heap of powder blew up, and threw the brands on to us, and over our heads: we were too hasty, and are now ruined people."

The Prince was still busy directing; but for a moment all seemed to pause, as a man was observed hastily springing down from the heights of the old Castle; whom the troop soon recognised for the watchman that had been stationed there to keep the Painter's apartments, while he lodged there and took charge of the workmen. He came running, out of breath, yet in few words soon made known that the Lion had lain himself down, within the high ring-wall, in the sunshine, at the foot of a large beech, and was behaving quite quietly. With an air of vexation, however, the man concluded: "Why did I take my rifle to town yesternight, to have it cleaned; he had never risen again, the skin had been mine, and I might all my life have had the credit of the thing."

The Prince, whom his military experiences here also stood in stead, for he had before now been in situations where from various sides inevitable evil seemed to threaten, said hereupon: "What surety do you give me that if we spare your lion, he will not work destruction among us, among my people?"

"This woman and this child," answered the father hastily, "engage to tame him, to keep him peaceable, till I bring up the cage, and then we can carry him back unharmed and without harming any one."

The boy put his flute to his lips; an instrument of the kind once named soft, or sweet flutes; short-beaked like pipes: he, who understood the art, could bring out of it the gracefullest tones. Meanwhile the Prince had inquired of the watchman how the lion came up. "By the hollow-way," answered he, "which is walled in on both sides, and was formerly the only entrance, and is to be the only one still: two footpaths, which led in elsewhere, we have so blocked up and destroyed that no human being, except by that first narrow passage, can reach the Magic Castle which Prince Friedrich's talent and taste is making of it."

After a little thought, during which the Prince looked round at the boy, who still continued as if softly preluding, he turned to Honorio, and said: "Thou hast done much to-day, complete thy task. Secure that narrow path; keep your rifles in readiness, but do not shoot till the creature can no otherwise be driven back: in any case, kindle a fire, which will frighten him if he move downwards. The man and woman take charge of the rest." Honorio rapidly bestirred himself to execute these orders.

The child continued his tune, which was no tune; a series of notes without law, and perhaps even on that account so heart-touching: the bystanders seemed as if enchanted by the movement of a song-like melody, when the father with dignified enthusiasm began to speak in this sort:

"God has given the Prince wisdom, and also knowledge to discern that all God's works are wise, each after its kind. Behold the rock, how he stands fast and stirs not, defies the weather and the sunshine; primeval trees adorn his head, and so crowned he looks abroad; neither if a mass rush away, will this continue what it was, but falls broken into many pieces and covers the side of the descent. But there too they will not tarry, capriciously they leap far down, the brook receives them, to the river he bears them. Not resisting, not contradictory, angular; no, smooth and rounded they travel now quicker on their way, arrive, from river to river, finally at the ocean, whither march the giants in hosts, and in the depths whereof dwarfs are busy.

"But who shall exalt the glory of the Lord, whom the stars praise from Eternity to Eternity! Why look ye far into the distance? Consider here the bee: late at the end of harvest she still busily gathers, builds her a house, tight of corner, straight of wall, herself the architect and mason. Behold the ant: she knows her way, and loses it not; she piles her a dwelling of grass-halms, earth-crumbs, and needles of the fir; she piles it aloft and arches it in; but she has labored in vain, for the horse stamps, and scrapes it all in pieces: lo! he has trodden down her beams, and scattered her planks; impatiently he snorts and cannot rest; for the Lord has made the horse comrade of the wind and companion of the storm, to carry man whither he wills, and woman whither she desires. But in the Wood of Palms arose he, the Lion, with earnest step traversed the wilderness; there rules he over all creatures, his might who shall withstand? Yet man can tame him; and the fiercest of living things has reverence for the image of God, in which too the angels are made, who serve the Lord and his servants. For in the den of Lions Daniel was not afraid: he remained fast and faithful, and the wild bellowing interrupted not his song of praise."

This speech, delivered with expression of a natural enthusiasm, the child accompanied here and there with graceful tones; but now, the father having ended, he, with clear melodious voice and skilful passaging, struck up his warble, whereupon the father took the flute, and gave note in unison, while the child sang:

> From the Dens, I, in a deeper,
> Prophet's song of praise can hear;
> Angel-host he hath for keeper,
> Needs the good man there to fear?
>
> Lion, Lioness, agazing,
> Mildly pressing round him came;
> Yea, that humble, holy praising,
> It hath made them tame.

The father continued accompanying this strophe with his flute; the mother here and there touched in as second voice.

Impressive, however, in a quite peculiar degree, it was, when the child now began to shuffle the lines of the strophe into other arrangement; and thereby if not bring out a new sense, yet heighten the feeling by leading it into self-excitement:

> Angel-host around doth hover,
> Us in heavenly tones to cheer:
> In the dens our head doth cover:
> Needs the poor child there to fear?
>
> For that humble holy praising
> Will permit no evil nigh:
> Angels hover, keeping, gazing,
> Who so safe as I?

Hereupon with emphasis and elevation began all three:

> For th' Eternal rules above us,
> Lands and oceans rules his will;
> Lions even as lambs shall love us,
> And the proudest waves be still.
>
> Whetted sword to scabbard cleaving,
> Faith and Hope victorious see,
> Strong, who, loving and believing,
> Prays, O Lord, to thee.

All were silent, hearing, hearkening; and only when the tones ceased could you remark and distinguish the impression they had made. All was as if appeased; each affected in his way. The Prince, as if he now first saw the misery that a little while ago had threatened him, looked down on his spouse, who leaning on him forbore not to draw out the little embroidered handkerchief, and therewith covered her eyes. It was blessedness for her to feel her young bosom relieved from the pressure with which the preceding minutes had loaded it. A perfect silence reigned over the crowd; they seemed to have forgotten the dangers: the conflagration below; and above, the rising up of a dubiously-reposing Lion.

By a sign to bring the horses, the Prince first restored the group to motion; he turned to the woman, and said: "You think then that, once find the lion, you could, by your singing, by the singing of this child, with help of these flute-tones, appease him, and carry him back to his prison, unhurt and hurting no one?" They answered yes, assuring and affirming; the Castellan was given them as guide. And now the Prince started off in all speed with a few; the Princess followed slower with the rest of the train; mother and son, on their side, under conduct of the warder, who had got himself a musket, mounted up the steeper part of the height.

Before the entrance of the hollow-way which opened their access to the Castle, they found the hunters busy heaping up dry brushwood, to have, in any case, a large fire ready for kindling. "There is no need," said the woman: "it will all go well and peaceably, without that."

Farther on, sitting on a wall, his double-barrel resting in his lap, Honorio appeared; at his post, as if ready for every occurrence. However, he seemed hardly to notice our party; he sat as if sunk in deep thoughts, he looked round like one whose mind was not there. The woman addressed him with a prayer not to let the fire be lit; he appeared not to heed her words; she spoke on with vivacity, and cried: "Handsome young man, thou hast killed my tiger, I do not curse thee; spare my lion, good young man, I will bless thee."

Honorio was looking straight out before him, to where the sun on his course began to sink. "Thou lookest to the west," cried the woman; "thou dost well, there is much to do there; hasten, delay not, thou wilt conquer. But first conquer thyself." At this he appeared to give a smile; the woman stept on; could not, however, but look back once more at him: a ruddy sun was overshining his face; she thought she had never seen a handsomer youth.

"If your child," said the warder now, "with his fluting and singing, can, as you are persuaded, entice and pacify the lion, we shall soon get mastery of him after, for the creature has lain down quite close to the perforated vaults through which, as the main passage was blocked up with ruins, we had to bore ourselves an entrance into the Castle-Court. If the child entice him into this latter, I can close the opening with little difficulty; then the boy, if he like, can glide out by one of the little spiral stairs he will find in the corner. We must conceal ourselves; but I shall so take my place that a rifle-ball can, at any moment, help the poor child in case of extremity."

"All these precautions are unnecessary; God and skill, piety and a blessing, must do the work."—"May be," replied the warder; "however, I know my duties. First, I must lead you, by a difficult path, to the top of the wall, right opposite the vaults and opening I have mentioned: the child may then go down, as into the arena of the show, and lead away the animal, if it will follow him." This was done: warder and mother looked down in concealment, as the child descending the screw-stairs, showed himself in the open space of the Court, and disappeared opposite them in the gloomy opening; but forthwith gave his flute voice, which by and by grew weaker, and at last sank dumb. The pause was bodeful enough; the old Hunter, familiar with danger, felt heart-sick at the singular conjuncture; the mother, however, with cheerful face, bending over to listen, showed not the smallest discomposure.

At last the flute was again heard; the child stept forth from the cavern with glittering satisfied eyes, the lion after him, but slowly, and as it seemed with difficulty. He showed here and there desire to lie down; yet the boy led him in a half-circle through the few disleaved many-tinted trees, till at length, in the last rays of the sun which poured in through a hole in the ruins, he set him down, as if transfigured in the bright red light; and again commenced his pacifying song, the repetition of which we also cannot forbear:

> From the Dens, I, in a deeper,
> Prophet's song of praise can hear;
> Angel-host he hath for keeper,
> Needs the good man there to fear?
> Lion, Lioness, agazing,
> Mildly pressing round him came;
> Yea, that humble, holy praising,
> It hath made them tame.

Meanwhile the lion had laid itself down quite close to the child, and lifted its heavy right fore-paw into his bosom; the boy as he sung gracefully stroked it; but was not long in observing that a sharp thorn had stuck itself between the balls. He carefully pulled it out; with a smile, took the party-colored silk-handkerchief from his neck, and bound up the frightful paw of the monster; so that his mother for joy bent herself back with outstretched arms; and perhaps, according to custom, would have shouted and clapped applause, had not a hard hand gripe of the warder reminded her that the danger was not yet over.

Triumphantly the child sang on, having with a few tones preluded:

> For th' Eternal rules above us,
> Lands and oceans rules his will;
> Lions even as lambs shall love us,
> And the proudest waves be still.
> Whetted sword to scabbard cleaving,
> Faith and Hope victorious see,
> Strong, who, loving and believing,
> Prays, O Lord, to thee.

Were it possible to fancy that in the countenance of so grim a creature, the tyrant of the woods, the despot of the animal kingdom, an expression of friendliness, of thankful contentment could be traced, then here was such traceable; and truly the child in his illustrated look had the air as that of a mighty triumphant victor; the other figure, indeed, not that of one vanquished, for his strength lay concealed in him; but yet of one tamed, of one given up to his own peaceful will. The child fluted and sang on, changing the lines according to his way, and adding new:

> And so to good children bringeth
> Blessed Angel help in need;
> Fetters o'er the cruel flingeth,
> Worthy art with wings doth speed.
> So have tamed, and firmly iron'd
> To a poor child's feeble knee,
> Him the forest's lordly tyrant,
> Song and Piety.

THE TALE.*

In his little Hut, by the great River, which a heavy rain had swoln to overflowing, lay the ancient Ferryman, asleep, wearied by the toil of the day. In the middle of the night, loud voices awoke him; he heard that it was travellers wishing to be carried over.

Stepping out, he saw two large Will-o'-wisps, hovering to and fro on his boat, which lay moored: they said, they were in violent haste, and should have been already on the other side. The old Ferryman made no loitering; pushed off, and steered with his usual skill obliquely through the stream; while the two strangers whiffled and hissed together, in an unknown very rapid tongue, and every now and then broke out in loud laughter, hopping about, at one time on the gunwale and the seats, at another on the bottom of the boat.

"The boat is heeling!" cried the old man; "if you don't be quiet, it will overset; be seated, gentlemen of the wisp!"

At this advice they burst into a fit of laughter, mocked the old man, and were more unquiet than ever. He bore their mischief with patience, and soon reached the farther shore.

"Here is for your labor!" cried the travellers, and as they shook themselves, a heap of glittering gold-pieces jingled down into the wet boat. "For Heaven's sake, what are you about?" cried the old man; "you will ruin me forever! Had a single piece of gold got into the water, the stream, which cannot suffer gold, would have risen in horrid waves, and swallowed both my skiff and me; and who knows how it might have fared with you in that case: here, take back your gold."

"We can take nothing back, which we have once shaken from us," said the Lights.

"Then you give me the trouble," said the old man, stooping down, and gathering the pieces into his cap, "of raking them together, and carrying them ashore, and burying them."

The Lights had leaped from the boat, but the old man cried: "Stay; where is my fare?"

"If you take no gold, you may work for nothing," cried the Will-o'-wisps. — "You must know that I am only to be paid with fruits of the earth."—"Fruits of the earth? we despise them, and have never tasted them."—"And yet I cannot let you go, till you have promised that you will deliver me three Cabbages, three Artichokes, and three large Onions."

The Lights were making off with jests; but they felt themselves, in some inexplicable manner, fastened to the ground: it was the unpleasantest feeling they had ever had. They engaged to pay him his demand as soon as possible: he let them go, and pushed away. He was gone a good distance, when they called to him: "Old man! Holla, old man! the main point is forgotten!" He was off, however, and did not hear them. He had fallen quietly down that side of the River, where, in a rocky spot, which the water never reached, he meant to

---

* Translated by Carlyle. The editor has preferred to publish this "Tale" without the translator's comments. Whoever is curious to see these, and to have a key to this wondrous production, is referred to "Carlyle's Miscellanies." Boston: James Munroe & Co. Vol. IV Appendix.

bury the pernicious gold. Here, between two high crags, he found a monstrous chasm; shook the metal into it, and steered back to his cottage.

Now, in this chasm, lay the fair green Snake, who was roused from her sleep by the gold coming chinking down. No sooner did she fix her eye on the glittering coins, than she ate them all up, with the greatest relish, on the spot; and carefully picked out such pieces as were scattered in the chinks of the rock.

Scarcely had she swallowed them, when, with extreme delight, she began to feel the metal melting in her inwards, and spreading all over her body; and soon, to her lively joy, she observed that she was grown transparent and luminous. Long ago she had been told that this was possible; but now being doubtful whether such a light could last, her curiosity and the desire to be secure against the future, drove her from her cell, that she might see who it was that had shaken in this precious metal. She found no one. The more delightful was it to admire her own appearance, and her graceful brightness, as she crawled along through roots and bushes, and spread out her light among the grass. Every leaf seemed of emerald, every flower was dyed with new glory. It was in vain that she crossed the solitary thickets; but her hopes rose high, when, on reaching the open country, she perceived from afar a brilliancy resembling her own. "Shall I find my like at last, then?" cried she, and hastened to the spot. The toil of crawling through bog and reeds gave her little thought; for though she liked best to live in dry grassy spots of the mountains, among the clefts of rocks, and for most part fed on spicy herbs, and slaked her thirst with mild dew and fresh spring water, yet for the sake of this dear gold, and in the hope of this glorious light, she would have undertaken anything you could propose to her.

At last, with much fatigue, she reached a wet rushy spot in the swamp, where our two Will-o'-wisps were frisking to and fro. She shoved herself along to them; saluted them, was happy to meet such pleasant gentlemen related to her family. The Lights glided towards her, skipped up over her, and laughed in their fashion. "Lady Cousin," said they, "you are of the horizontal line, yet what of that? It is true we are related only by the look; for observe you," here both the Flames, compressing their whole breadth, made themselves as high and peaked as possible, "how prettily this taper length beseems us gentlemen of the vertical line! Take it not amiss of us, good Lady; what family can boast of such a thing? Since there ever was a Jack-o'-lanthorn in the world, no one of them has either sat or lain."

The Snake felt exceedingly uncomfortable in the company of these relations; for let her hold her head as high as possible, she found that she must bend it to the earth again, would she stir from the spot; and if in the dark thicket she had been extremely satisfied with her appearance, her splendor in the presence of these cousins seemed to lessen every moment, nay she was afraid that at last it would go out entirely.

In this embarrassment she hastily asked: if the gentlemen could not inform her, whence the glittering gold came, that had fallen a short while ago into the cleft of the rock; her own opinion was, that it had been a golden shower, and had trickled down direct from the sky. The Will-o'-wisps laughed, and shook themselves, and a multitude of gold-pieces came clinking down about them. The Snake pushed nimbly forwards to eat the coin. "Much good may it do you, Mistress," said the dapper gentlemen: "we can help you to a little more." They shook themselves again several times with great quickness, so that the Snake could scarcely gulp the precious victuals fast enough. Her splendor visibly began increasing; she was really shining beautifully, while the Lights had in the meantime grown rather lean and short of stature, without however in the smallest losing their good-humor.

"I am obliged to you for ever," said the Snake, having got her wind again after the repast, "ask of me what you will; all that I can I will do."

"Very good!" cried the Lights. "Then tell us where the fair Lily dwells? Lead us to the fair Lily's palace and garden; and do not lose a moment, we are dying of impatience to fall down at her feet."

"This service," said the Snake with a deep sigh, "I cannot now do for you. The fair Lily dwells, alas, on the other side of the water."—"Other side of the water? And we have come across it, this stormy night! How cruel is the River to divide us! Would it not be possible to call the old man back?"

"It would be useless," said the Snake; "for if you found him ready on the bank, he would not take you in; he can carry any one to this side, none to yonder."

"Here is a pretty kettle of fish!" cried the Lights: "are there no other means of getting through the water?"—"There are other means, but not at this moment. I myself could take you over, gentlemen, but not till noon."—"That is an hour we do not like to travel in."—"Then you may go across in the evening, on the great Giant's shadow."—"How is that?"—"The great Giant lives not far from this; with his body he has no power; his hands cannot lift a straw, his shoulders could not bear a faggot of twigs; but with his shadow he has power over much, nay all. At sunrise and sunset therefore he is strongest; so at evening you merely put yourself upon the back of his shadow, the Giant walks softly to the bank, and the shadow carries you across the water. But if you please, about the hour of noon, to be in waiting at that corner of the wood, where the bushes overhang the bank, I myself will take you over and present you to the fair Lily: or on the other hand, if you dislike the noontide, you have just to go at nightfall to that bend of the rocks, and pay a visit to the Giant; he will certainly receive you like a gentleman."

With a slight bow, the Flames went off; and the Snake at bottom was not discontented to get rid of them; partly that she might enjoy the brightness of her own light, partly satisfy a curiosity with which, for a long time, she had been agitated in a singular way.

In the chasm, where she often crawled hither and thither, she had made a strange discovery. For although in creeping up and down this abyss, she had never had a ray of light, she could well enough discriminate the objects in it, by her sense of touch. Generally she met with nothing but irregular productions of nature; at one time she would wind between the teeth of large crystals, at another she would feel the barbs and hairs of native silver, and now and then carry out with her to the light some straggling jewels. But to her no small wonder, in a rock which was closed on every side, she had come on certain objects which betrayed the shaping hand of man. Smooth walls on which she could not climb, sharp regular corners, well-formed pillars; and what seemed strangest of all, human figures which she had entwined more than once, and which appeared to her to be of brass, or of the finest polished marble. All these experiences she now wished to combine by the sense of sight, thereby to confirm what as yet she only guessed. She believed she could illuminate the whole of the subterranean vault by her own light; and hoped to get acquainted with these curious things at once. She hastened back; and soon found, by the usual way, the cleft by which she used to penetrate the Sanctuary.

On reaching the place, she gazed around with eager curiosity; and though her shining could not enlighten every object in the rotundo, yet those nearest her were plain enough. With astonishment and reverence she looked up into a glancing niche, where the image of an august King stood formed of pure Gold. In size the figure was beyond the stature of man, but by its shape it seemed the likeness of a little rather than a tall person. His handsome body was encircled with an unadorned mantle; and a garland of oak bound his hair together.

No sooner had the Snake beheld this reverend figure, than the King began to speak, and asked: "Whence comest thou?"—"From the chasms where the gold dwells," said the Snake.—"What is grander than gold?" inquired the King.—"Light," replied the Snake. "What is more refreshing than light?" said he.—"Speech," answered she.

During this conversation, she had squinted to a side, and in the nearest niche perceived another glorious image. It was a Silver King in a sitting posture; his shape was long and rather languid; he was covered with a decorated robe; crown, girdle, and sceptre were adorned with precious stones: the cheerfulness of pride was in his countenance; he seemed about to speak, when a vein which ran dimly-colored over the marble wall, on a sudden became bright, and diffused a cheerful light throughout the whole Temple. By this brilliancy the Snake perceived a third King, made of Brass, and sitting mighty in shape, leaning on his club, adorned with a laurel garland, and more like a rock than a man. She was looking for the fourth, which was standing at the greatest distance from her; but the wall opened, while the glittering vein started and split, as lightning does, and disappeared.

A Man of middle stature, entering through the cleft, attracted the attention of the Snake. He was dressed like a peasant, and carried in his hand a little Lamp, on whose still flame you liked to look, and which in a strange manner, without casting any shadow, enlightened the whole dome.

"Why comest thou, since we have light?" said the golden King.—"You know that I may not enlighten what is dark."—"Will my Kingdom end?" said the silver King.—"Late or never," said the old Man.

With a stronger voice the brazen King began to ask: "When shall I arise?"—"Soon," replied the Man.—"With whom shall I combine?" said the King.—"With thy elder brothers," said the Man.—"What will the youngest do?" inquired the King.—"He will sit down," replied the Man.

"I am not tired," cried the fourth King, with a rough faltering voice.

While this speech was going on, the Snake had glided softly round the temple, viewing everything; she was now looking at the fourth King close by him. He stood leaning on a pillar; his considerable form was heavy rather than beautiful. But what metal it was made of could not be determined. Closely inspected, it seemed a mixture of the three metals which its brothers had been formed of. But in the founding, these materials did not seem to have combined together fully; gold and silver veins ran irregularly through a brazen mass, and gave the figure an unpleasant aspect.

Meanwhile the gold King was asking of the Man, "How many secrets knowest thou?"—"Three," replied the Man.—"Which is the most important?" said the silver King.—"The open one," replied the other.—"Wilt thou open it to us also?" said the brass King.—"When I know the fourth," replied the Man.—"What care I?" grumbled the composite King, in an under tone.

"I know the fourth," said the Snake; approached the old Man, and hissed somewhat in his ear. "The time is at hand!" cried the old Man, with a strong voice. The temple re-echoed, the metal statues sounded; and that instant the old Man sank away to the westward, and the Snake to the eastward; and both of them passed through the clefts of the rock, with the greatest speed.

All the passages, through which the old Man travelled, filled themselves, immediately behind him, with gold: for his Lamp had the strange property of changing stone into gold, wood into silver, dead animals into precious stones, and of annihilating all metals. But to display this power, it must shine alone. If another light were beside it, the Lamp only cast from it a pure clear brightness, and all living things were refreshed by it.

The old Man entered his cottage, which was built on the slope of the hill. He found his Wife in extreme distress. She was sitting at the fire weeping, and refusing to be consoled. "How unhappy am I!" cried she: "Did not I entreat thee not to go away to-night?"—"What is the matter, then?" inquired the husband, quite composed.

"Scarcely wert thou gone," said she, sobbing, "when there came two noisy Travellers to the door: unthinkingly I let them in; they seemed to be a couple of genteel, very honorable people; they were dressed in flames, you would have taken them for Will-o'-wisps. But no sooner were they in the house, than they began, like impudent varlets, to compliment me, and grew so forward that I feel ashamed to think of it."

"No doubt," said the husband with a smile, "the gentlemen were jesting: considering thy age, they might have held by general politeness."

"Age! what age?" cried the Wife: "wilt thou always be talking of my age? How old am I then?—General politeness! But I know what I know. Look round there what a face the walls have; look at the old stones, which I have not seen these hundred years; every film of gold have they licked away, thou couldst not think how fast; and still they kept assuring me that it tasted far beyond common gold. Once they had swept the walls, the fellows seemed to be in high spirits, and truly in that little while they had grown much broader and brighter. They now began to be impertinent again, they patted me, and called me their queen, they shook themselves, and a shower of gold pieces sprang from them; see how they are shining there under the bench! But, ah! what misery! Poor Mops ate a coin or two; and look, he is lying in the chimney, dead. Poor Pug! O well-a-day! I did not see it till they were gone; else I had never promised to pay the Ferryman the debt they owe him."—"What do they owe him?" said the Man.—"Three Cabbages," replied the Wife, "three Artichokes, and three Onions: I engaged to go when it was day, and take them to the River."

"Thou mayest do them that civility," said the old Man; "they may chance to be of use to us again."

"Whether they will be of use to us I know not; but they promised and vowed that they would."

Meantime the fire on the hearth had burnt low; the old Man covered up the embers with a heap of ashes, and put the glittering gold pieces aside; so that his little Lamp now gleamed alone, in the fairest brightness. The walls again coated themselves with gold, and Mops changed into the prettiest onyx that could be imagined. The alternation of the brown and black in this precious stone made it the most curious piece of workmanship.

"Take thy basket," said the Man, "and put the onyx into it; then take the three Cabbages, the three Artichokes, and the three Onions; place them round little Mops, and carry them to the River. At noon the Snake will take thee over; visit the fair Lily, give her the onyx, she will make it alive by her touch, as by her touch she kills whatever is alive already. She will have a true companion in the little dog. Tell her not to mourn; her deliverance is near; the greatest misfortune she may look upon as the greatest happiness: for the time is at hand."

The old Woman filled her basket, and set out as soon as it was day. The rising sun shone clear from the other side of the River, which was glittering in the distance; the old woman walked with slow steps, for the basket pressed upon her head, and it was not the onyx that so burdened her. Whatever lifeless thing she might be carrying, she did not feel the weight of it; on the other hand, in those cases the basket rose aloft, and hovered along above her head. But to carry any fresh herbage, or any little living animal, she found exceedingly laborious. She had travelled on for some time, in a sullen humor, when she halted suddenly in fright, for she had almost trod upon the Giant's shadow, which was stretching towards her across the plain. And now, lifting up her eyes, she saw the monster of a Giant himself, who had been bathing in the River, and was just come out, and she knew not how she should avoid him. The moment he perceived her, he began saluting her in sport, and the hands of his shadow soon caught hold of the basket. With dexterous ease they picked away from it a Cabbage, an Artichoke, and an Onion, and brought them to the Giant's mouth, who then went his way up the River, and let the Woman go in peace.

She considered whether it would not be better to return, and supply from her garden the pieces she had lost; and amid these doubts, she still kept walking on, so that in a little while she was at the bank of the River. She sat long waiting for the Ferryman, whom she perceived at last, steering over with a very singular traveller. A young, noble-looking, handsome man, whom she could not gaze upon enough, stept out of the boat.

"What is it you bring?" cried the old man. "The greens which those two Will-o'-wisps owe you," said the Woman, pointing to her ware. As the Ferryman found only two of each sort, he grew angry, and declared he would have none of them. The Woman earnestly entreated him to take them; told him that she could not now go home, and that her burden for the way which still remained was very heavy. He stood by his refusal, and assured her that it did not rest with him. "What belongs to me," said he, "I must leave lying nine hours in a heap, touching none of it, till I have given the River its third." After much higgling, the old man at last replied: "There is still another way. If you like to pledge yourself to the River, and declare yourself its debtor, I will take the six pieces; but there is some risk in it."—"If I keep my word, I shall run no risk?" — "Not the smallest. Put your hand into the stream," continued he, "and promise that within four-and-twenty hours you will pay the debt."

The old Woman did so; but what was her affright, when on drawing out her hand, she found it black as coal! She loudly scolded the old Ferryman; declared that her hands had always been the fairest part of her; that in spite of her hard work, she had all along contrived to keep these noble members white and dainty. She looked at the hand with indignation, and exclaimed in a despairing tone: "Worse and worse! Look, it is vanishing entirely: it is grown far smaller than the other."

"For the present it but seems so," said the old man; "if you do not keep your word, however, it may prove so in earnest. The hand will gradually diminish, and at length disappear altogether, though you have the use of it as formerly. Every thing as usual you will be able to perform with it, only nobody will see it."—"I had rather that I could not use it, and no one could observe the want," cried she; "but what of that, I will keep my word, and rid myself of this black skin, and all anxieties about it." Thereupon she hastily took up her basket, which mounted of itself over her head, and hovered free above her in the air, as she hurried after the Youth, who was walking softly and thoughtfully down the bank. His noble form and strange dress had made a deep impression on her.

His breast was covered with a glittering coat of mail; in whose wavings might be traced every motion of his fair body. From his shoulders hung a purple cloak; around his uncovered head flowed abundant brown hair in beautiful locks: his graceful face, and his well-formed feet were exposed to the scorching of the sun. With bare soles, he walked composedly over the hot sand; and a deep inward sorrow seemed to blunt him against all external things.

The garrulous old Woman tried to lead him into conversation; but with his short answers he gave her small encouragement or information; so that in the end, notwithstanding the beauty of his eyes, she grew tired of speaking with him to no purpose, and took leave of him with these words: "You walk too slow for me, worthy sir; I must not lose a moment, for I have to pass the River on the green Snake, and carry this fine present from my husband to the fair Lily." So saying she stept faster forward; but the fair Youth pushed on with equal speed, and hastened to keep up with her. "You are going to the fair Lily!" cried he; "then our roads are the same. But what present is this you are bringing her?"

"Sir," said the Woman, "it is hardly fair, after so briefly dismissing the questions I put you, to inquire with such vivacity about my secrets. But if you like to barter, and tell me your adventures, I will not conceal from you how it stands with me and my presents." They soon made a bargain; the dame disclosed her circumstances to him; told the history of the Pug, and let him see the singular gift.

He lifted his natural curiosity from the basket, and took Mops, who seemed as if sleeping softly, into his arms. "Happy beast!" cried he; "thou wilt be touched by her hands, thou wilt be made alive by her; while the living are obliged to fly from her presence to escape a mournful doom. Yet why say I mournful! Is it not far sadder and more frightful to be injured by her look, than it would be to die by her hand? Behold me," said he to the Woman; "at my years, what a miserable fate have I to undergo. This mail which I have honorably borne in war, this purple which I sought to merit by a wise reign, Destiny has left me; the one as a useless burden, the other as an empty ornament. Crown, and sceptre, and sword are gone; and I am as bare and needy as any other son of earth; for so unblessed are her bright eyes, that they take from every living creature they look on all its force, and those whom the touch of her hand does not kill are changed to the state of shadows wandering alive."

Thus did he continue to bewail, nowise contenting the old Woman's curiosity, who wished for information not so much of his internal as of his external situation. She learned neither the name of his father, nor of his kingdom. He stroked the hard Mops, whom the sunbeams and the bosom of the youth had warmed as if he had been living. He inquired narrowly about the man with the Lamp, about the influences of the sacred light, appearing to expect much good from it in his melancholy case.

Amid such conversation, they descried from afar the majestic arch of the Bridge, which extended from the one bank to the other, glittering with the strangest colors in the splendors of the sun. Both were astonished; for until now they had never seen this edifice so grand. "How!" cried the Prince! "was it not beautiful enough, as it stood before our eyes, piled out of jasper and agate? Shall we not fear to tread it, now that it appears combined, in graceful complexity, of emerald and chrysopras and chrysolite?" Neither of them knew the alteration that had taken place upon the Snake: for it was indeed the Snake, who every day at noon curved herself over the River, and stood forth in the form of a bold-swelling bridge. The travellers stept upon it with a reverential feeling, and passed over it in silence.

No sooner had they reached the other shore, than the bridge began to heave and stir; in a little while, it touched the surface of the water, and the green Snake in her proper form came gliding after the wanderers. They had scarcely thanked her for the privilege of crossing on her back, when they found that, besides them three, there must be other persons in the company, whom their eyes could not discern. They heard a hissing, which the Snake also answered with a hissing; they listened, and at length caught what follows: "We shall first look about us in the fair Lily's Park," said a pair of alternating voices; "and then request you at nightfall, so soon as we are anywise presentable, to introduce us to this paragon of beauty. At the shore of the great Lake, you will find us."—"Be it so," replied the Snake; and a hissing sound died away in the air.

Our three travellers now consulted in what order they should introduce themselves to the fair Lady; for however many people might be in her company, they were obliged to enter and depart singly, under pain of suffering very hard severities.

The Woman with the metamorphosed Pug in the basket first approached the garden, looking round for her Patroness; who was not difficult to find, being just engaged in singing to her harp. The finest tones proceeded from her, first like circles on the surface of the still lake, then like a light breath they set the grass and the bushes in motion. In a green enclosure, under the shadow of a stately group of many diverse trees, was she seated; and again did she enchant the eyes, the ear, and the heart of the woman, who approached with rapture, and swore within herself that since she saw her last, the fair one had grown fairer than ever. With eager gladness from a distance she expressed her reverence and admiration for the lovely maiden. "What a happiness to see you, what a Heaven does your presence spread around you! How charmingly the harp is leaning on your bosom, how softly your arms surround it, how it seems as if longing to be near you, and how it sounds so meekly under the touch of your slim fingers! Thrice happy youth, to whom it were permitted to be there!"

So speaking she approached; the fair Lily raised her eyes; let her hands drop from the harp, and answered: "Trouble me not with untimely praise; I feel my misery but the more deeply. Look here, at my feet lies the poor Canary-bird, which used so beautifully to accompany my singing; it would sit upon my harp, and was trained not to touch me; but today, while I, refreshed by sleep, was raising a peaceful morning hymn, and my little singer was pouring forth his harmonious tones more gaily than ever, a Hawk darts over my head; the poor little creature, in affright, takes refuge in my bosom, and I feel the last palpitations of its departing life. The plundering Hawk indeed was caught by my look, and fluttered fainting down into the water; but what can his punishment avail me? my darling is dead, and his grave will but increase the mournful bushes of my garden."

"Take courage, fairest Lily!" cried the Woman, wiping off a tear, which the story of the hapless maiden had called into her eyes; "compose yourself; my old man bids me tell you to moderate your lamenting, to look upon the greatest misfortune as a forerunner of the greatest happiness, for the time is at hand; and truly," continued she, "the world is going strangely on of late. Do but look at my hand, how black it is! As I live and breathe, it is grown far smaller: I must hasten, before it vanish altogether! Why did I engage to do the Will-o'-wisps a service, why did I meet the Giant's shadow, and dip my hand in the River? Could you not afford me a single cabbage, an artichoke, and an onion? I would give them to the River, and my hand were white as ever, so that I could almost show it with one of yours.

"Cabbages and onions thou mayest still find; but artichokes thou wilt search for in vain. No plant in my garden bears either flowers or fruit; but every twig that I break, and plant upon the grave of a favorite, grows green straightway, and shoots up in fair boughs. All these groups, these bushes, these groves my hard destiny has so raised around me. These pines stretching out like parasols, these obelisks of cypresses, these colossal oaks and beeches, were all little twigs planted by my hand, as mournful memorials in a soil that otherwise is barren."

To this speech the old Woman had paid little heed; she was looking at her hand, which, in presence of the fair Lily, seemed every moment growing blacker and smaller. She was about to snatch her basket and hasten off, when she noticed that the best part of her errand had been forgotten. She lifted out the onyx Pug, and set him down, not far from the fair one, in the grass. "My husband," said she, "sends you this memorial; you know that you can make a jewel live by touching it. This pretty faithful dog will certainly afford you much enjoyment; and my grief at losing him is brightened only by the thought that he will be in your possession."

The fair Lily viewed the dainty creature with a pleased, and as it seemed, with an astonished look. "Many signs combine," said she, "that breathe some hope into me: but ah! is it not a natural deception which makes us fancy, when misfortunes crowd upon us, that a better day is near?

'What can these many signs avail me
 My Singer's Death, thy coal-black Hand!
 This Dog of Onyx, that can never fail me!
 And coming at the Lamp's command!

'From human joys removed forever,
  With sorrows compassed round I sit:
Is there a Temple at the River?
Is there a Bridge? Alas, not yet!'"

The good old dame had listened with impatience to this singing, which the fair Lily accompanied with her harp, in a way that would have charmed any other. She was on the point of taking leave, when the arrival of the green Snake again detained her. The Snake had caught the last lines of the song, and on this matter forthwith began to speak comfort to the fair Lily.

"The Prophecy of the Bridge is fulfilled!" cried the Snake: "you may ask this worthy dame how royally the arch looks now. What formerly was untransparent jasper, or agate, allowing but a gleam of light to pass about its edges, is now become transparent precious stone. No beryl is so clear, no emerald so beautiful of hue."

"I wish you joy of it," said Lily; "but you will pardon me if I regard the prophecy as yet unaccomplished. The lofty arch of your bridge can still but admit foot-passengers; and it is promised us that horses and carriages and travellers of every sort shall, at the same moment, cross this bridge in both directions. Is there not something said, too, about pillars, which are to arise of themselves from the waters of the River?"

The old Woman still kept her eyes fixed on her hand; she here interrupted their dialogue, and was taking leave. "Wait a moment," said the fair Lily, "and carry my little bird with you. Bid the Lamp change it into topaz; I will enliven it by my touch; with your good Mops it shall form my dearest pastime: but hasten, hasten; for, at sunset, intolerable putrefaction will fasten on the hapless bird, and tear asunder the fair combination of its form forever."

The old Woman laid the little corpse, wrapped in soft leaves, into her basket, and hastened away.

"However it may be," said the Snake, recommencing their interrupted dialogue, "the Temple is built."

"But it is not at the River," said the fair one.

"It is yet resting in the depths of the Earth," said the Snake; "I have seen the Kings and conversed with them."

"But when will they arise?" inquired Lily.

The Snake replied: "I heard resounding in the Temple these deep words, *The time is at hand.*"

A pleasing cheerfulness spread over the fair Lily's face: "'T is the second time," said she, "that I have heard these happy words to-day: when will the day come for me to hear them thrice?"

She rose, and immediately there came a lovely maiden from the grove, and took away her harp. Another followed her, and folded up the fine-carved ivory stool, on which the fair one had been sitting, and put the silvery cushion under her arm. A third then made her appearance, with a large parasol worked with pearls; and looked whether Lily would require her in walking. These three maidens were beyond expression beautiful; and yet their beauty but exalted that of Lily, for it was plain to every one that they could never be compared to her.

Meanwhile the fair one had been looking, with a satisfied aspect, at the strange onyx Mops. She bent down, and touched him, and that instant he started up. Gaily he looked around, ran hither and thither, and at last, in his kindest manner, hastened to salute his benefactress. She took him in her arms, and pressed him to her. "Cold as thou art," cried she, "and though but a half-life works in thee, thou art welcome to me; tenderly will I love thee, prettily will I play with thee, softly caress thee, and firmly press thee to my bosom." She then let him go, chased him from her, called him back, and played so daintily with him, and ran about so gaily and so innocently with him on the grass, that with new rapture you viewed and participated in her joy, as a little while ago her sorrow had attuned every heart to sympathy.

This cheerfulness, these graceful sports were interrupted by the entrance of the woful Youth. He stepped forward, in his former guise and aspect; save that the heat of the day appeared to have fatigued him still more, and in the presence of his mistress he grew paler every moment. He bore upon his hand a Hawk, which was sitting quiet as a dove, with its body shrunk and its wings drooping.

"It is not kind in thee," cried Lily to him, "to bring that hateful thing before my eyes, the monster, which to-day has killed my little singer."

"Blame not the unhappy bird!" replied the Youth; "rather blame thyself and thy destiny; and leave me to keep beside me the companion of my wo."

Meanwhile Mops ceased not teasing the fair Lily; and she replied to her transparent favorite, with friendly gestures. She clapped her hands to scare him off; then ran, to entice him after her. She tried to get him when he fled, and she chased him away when he attempted to press near her. The Youth looked on in silence, with increasing anger; but at last, when she took the odious beast, which seemed to him unutterably ugly, on her arm, pressed it to her white bosom, and kissed its black snout with her heavenly lips, his patience altogether failed him, and full of desperation he exclaimed: "Must I, who by a baleful fate exist beside thee, perhaps to the end, in an absent presence, who by thee have lost my all, my very self, must I see before my eyes, that so unnatural a monster can charm thee into gladness, can awaken thy attachment, and enjoy thy embrace? Shall I any longer keep wandering to and fro, measuring my dreary course to that side of the River and to this? No, there is still a spark of the old heroic spirit sleeping in my bosom; let it start this instant into its expiring flame! If stones may rest in thy bosom, let me be changed to stone; if thy touch kills, I will die by thy hands."

So saying he made a violent movement; the Hawk flew from his finger, but he himself rushed towards the fair one; she held out her hands to keep him off, and touched him only the sooner. Consciousness forsook him; and she felt with horror the beloved burden lying on her bosom. With a shriek she started back, and the gentle youth sank lifeless from her arms upon the ground.

The misery had happened! The sweet Lily stood motionless, gazing on the corpse. Her heart seemed to pause in her bosom; and her eyes were without tears. In vain did Mops try to gain from her any kindly gesture; with her friend, the world for her was all dead as the grave. Her silent despair did not look round for help; she knew not of any help.

On the other hand, the Snake bestirred herself the more actively; she seemed to meditate deliverance; and in fact her strange movements served at last to keep away, for a little, the immediate consequences of the mischief. With her limber body, she formed a wide circle round the corpse, and seizing the end of her tail between her teeth, she lay quite still.

Ere long one of Lily's fair waiting-maids appeared; brought the ivory folding-stool, and with friendly beckoning constrained her mistress to sit down on it. Soon afterwards there came a second; she had in her hand a fire-colored veil, with which she rather decorated than concealed the fair Lily's head. The third handed her the harp, and scarcely had she drawn the gorgeous instrument towards her, and struck some tones from its strings, when the first maid returned with a clear round mirror; took her station opposite the fair one; caught her looks in the glass, and threw back to her the loveliest image that was to be found in nature. Sorrow heightened her beauty, the veil her charms, the harp her grace; and deeply as you wished to see her mournful situation altered, not less deeply did you wish to keep her image, as she now looked, forever present with you.

With a still look at the mirror, she touched the harp; now melting tones proceeded from the strings, now her pain seemed to mount, and the music in strong notes responded to her wo; sometimes she opened her lips to sing, but her voice failed her; and ere long her sorrow melted into tears, two maidens caught her helpfully in their arms, the harp sank from her bosom, scarcely could the quick servant snatch the instrument and carry it aside.

"Who gets us the Man with the Lamp, before the sun set?" hissed the Snake, faintly, but audibly: the maids looked at one another, and Lily's tears fell faster. At this moment came the Woman with the Basket, panting and altogether breathless. "I am lost, and maimed for life!" cried she; "see how my hand is almost vanished; neither Ferryman nor Giant would take me over, because I am the River's debtor; in vain did I promise hundreds of Cabbages and hundreds of Onions; they will take no more than three; and no Artichoke is now to be found in all this quarter."

"Forget your own care," said the Snake, "and try to bring help here; perhaps it may come to yourself also. Haste with your utmost speed to seek the Will-o'-wisps; it is too light for you to see them, but perhaps you will hear them laughing and hopping to and fro. If they be speedy, they may cross upon the Giant's shadow, and seek the Man with the Lamp and send him to us."

The Woman hurried off at her quickest pace, and the Snake seemed expecting as impatiently as Lily the return of the Flames. Alas! the beam of the sinking Sun was already gilding only the highest summits of the trees, in the thicket, and long shadows were stretching over lake and meadow; the Snake hitched up and down impatiently, and Lily dissolved in tears.

In this extreme need, the Snake kept looking round on all sides; for she was afraid every moment that the Sun would set, and corruption penetrate the magic circle, and the fair youth immediately moulder away. At last she noticed sailing high in the air, with purple-red feathers, the Prince's Hawk, whose breast was catching the last beams of the Sun. She shook herself for joy at this good omen; nor was she deceived; for shortly afterwards the Man with the Lamp was seen gliding towards them across the Lake, fast and smoothly, as if he had been travelling on skates.

The Snake did not change her posture; but Lily rose and called to him: "What good spirit sends thee, at the moment when we were desiring thee, and needing thee, so much?"

"The spirit of my Lamp," replied the Man, "has impelled me, and the Hawk has conducted me. My Lamp sparkles when I am needed, and I just look about me in the sky for a signal; some bird or meteor points to the quarter towards which I am to turn. Be calm, fairest Maiden! whether I can help I know not; an individual helps not, but he who combines himself with many at the proper hour. We will postpone the evil, and keep hoping. Hold thy circle fast," continued he, turning to the Snake; then set himself upon a hillock beside her, and illuminated the dead body. "Bring the little Bird hither too, and lay it in the circle!" The maidens took the little corpse from the basket, which the old Woman had left standing, and did as he directed.

Meanwhile the Sun had set, and as the darkness increased, not only the Snake and the old Man's Lamp began shining in their fashion, but also Lily's veil gave out a soft light, which gracefully tinged, as with a meek dawning red, her pale cheeks, and her white robe. The party looked at one another, silently reflecting;

care and sorrow were mitigated by a sure hope.

It was no unpleasing entrance, therefore, that the woman made, attended by the two gay Flames, which in truth appeared to have been very lavish in the interim, for they had again become extremely meager; yet they only bore themselves the more prettily for that, towards Lily and the other ladies. With great tact, and expressiveness, they said a multitude of rather common things to these fair persons; and declared themselves particularly ravished by the charm which the gleaming veil spread over Lily and her attendant. The ladies modestly cast down their eyes, and the praise of their beauty made them really beautiful. All were peaceful and calm, except the old Woman. In spite of the assurance of her husband, that her hand could diminish no farther, while the Lamp shone on it, she asserted more than once, that if things went on thus, before midnight this noble member would have utterly vanished.

The Man with the Lamp had listened attentively to the conversation of the Lights; and was gratified that Lily had been cheered, in some measure, and amused by it. And, in truth, midnight had arrived they knew not how. The old Man looked to the stars, and then began speaking: " We are assembled at the propitious hour; let each perform his task, let each do his duty; and a universal happiness will swallow up our individual sorrows, as a universal grief consumes individual joys."

At these words arose a wondrous hubbub; for all the persons in the party spoke aloud, each for himself, declaring what they had to do; only the three maids were silent; one of them had fallen asleep beside the harp, another near the parasol, the third by the stool; and you could not blame them much, for it was late. The Fiery youths, after some passing compliments which they devoted to the waiting-maids, had turned their sole attention to the Princess, as alone worthy of exclusive homage.

"Take the mirror," said the Man to the Hawk; "and with the first sunbeam illuminate the three sleepers, and awake them, with light reflected from above."

The Snake now began to move; she loosened her circle, and rolled slowly, in large rings, forward to the River. The two Will-o'-wisps followed with a solemn air; you would have taken them for the most serious Flames in nature. The old Woman and her husband seized the Basket, whose mild light they had scarcely observed till now; they lifted it at both sides, and it grew still larger and more luminous; they lifted the body of the Youth into it, laying the Canary-bird upon his breast; the Basket rose into the air and hovered above the old Woman's head, and she followed the Will-o'-wisps on foot. The fair Lily took Mops on her arm, and followed the Woman; the Man with the Lamp concluded the procession, and the scene was curiously illuminated by these many lights.

But it was with no small wonder that the party saw, when they approached the River, a glorious arch mount over it, by which the helpful Snake was affording them a glittering path. If by day they had admired the beautiful transparent precious stones, of which the Bridge seemed formed; by night they were astonished at its gleaming brilliancy. On the upper side the clear circle marked itself sharp against the dark sky, but below, vivid beams were darting to the centre, and exhibiting the airy firmness of the edifice. The procession slowly moved across it; and the Ferryman who saw it from his hut afar off, considered with astonishment the gleaming circle, and the strange lights which were passing over it.

No sooner had they reached the other shore, than the arch began, in its usual way, to swag up and down, and with a wavy motion to approach the water. The Snake then came on land, the Basket placed itself upon the ground, and the Snake again drew her circle round it. The old Man stooped towards her, and said: " What hast thou resolved on?"

"To sacrifice myself rather than be sacrificed," replied the Snake; "promise me that thou wilt leave no stone on shore."

The old Man promised; then addressing Lily: "Touch the Snake," said he, " with thy left hand, and thy lover with thy right." Lily knelt, and touched the Snake, and the Prince's body. The latter in the instant seemed to come to life; he moved in the basket, nay, he raised himself into a sitting posture; Lily was about to clasp him; but the old Man held her back, and himself assisted the youth to rise, and led him forth from the Basket and the circle.

The Prince was standing; the Canary-bird was fluttering on his shoulder; there was life again in both of them, but the spirit had not yet returned; the fair youth's eyes were open, yet he did not see, at least he seemed to look on all without participation. Scarcely had their admiration of this incident a little calmed, when they observed how strangely it had fared in the meanwhile with the Snake. Her fair taper body had crumbled into thousands and thousands of shining jewels; the old Woman reaching at her Basket had chanced to come against the circle; and of the shape or structure of the Snake there was now nothing to be seen, only a bright ring of luminous jewels was lying in the grass.

The old Man forthwith set himself to gather the stones into the basket; a task in which his wife assisted him. They next carried the Basket to an elevated point on the bank; and here the man threw its whole lading, not without contradiction from the fair one and his wife, who would gladly have retained some part of it, down into the River. Like gleaming twinkling stars the stones floated down with the waves; and you could not say .whether they lost themselves in the distance, or sank to the bottom.

"Gentlemen," said he with the Lamp, in a respectful tone to the Lights, "I will now show you the way, and open you the passage; but you will do us an essential service, if you please to unbolt the door, by which the Sanctuary must be entered at present, and which none but you can unfasten."

The Lights made a stately bow of assent, and kept their place. The old Man of the Lamp went foremost into the rock, which opened at his presence; the Youth followed him, as if mechanically; silent and uncertain, Lily kept at some distance from him; the old Woman would not be left, and stretched out her hand that the light of her husband's Lamp might still fall upon it. The rear was closed by the two Will-o'-wisps, who bent the peaks of their flames towards one another, and appeared to be engaged in conversation.

They had not gone far till the procession halted in front of a large brazen door, the leaves of which were bolted with a golden lock. The Man now called upon the Lights to advance; who required small entreaty, and with their pointed flames soon ate both bar and lock.

The brass gave a loud clang, as the doors sprang suddenly asunder; and the stately figures of the Kings appeared within the Sanctuary, illuminated by the entering Lights. All bowed before these dread sovereigns, especially the Flames made a profusion of the daintiest reverences.

After a pause, the gold King asked: "Whence come ye?"—"From the world," said the old Man.—"Whither go ye?" said the silver King. —"Into the world;" replied the Man.—"What would ye with us?" cried the brazen King.— "Accompany you," replied the Man.

The composite King was about to speak, when the gold one addressed the Lights, who had got too near him: "Take yourselves away from me, my metal was not made for you." Thereupon they turned to the silver King, and clasped themselves about him; and his robe glittered beautifully in their yellow brightness. "You are welcome," said he, "but I cannot feed you; satisfy yourselves elsewhere, and bring me your light." They removed; and gliding past the brazen King who did not seem to notice them, they fixed on the compounded King. "Who will govern the world?" cried he with a broken voice.—"He who stands upon his feet," replied the old Man.—"I am he," said the mixed King.—"We shall see," replied the Man: "for the time is at hand."

The fair Lily fell upon the old Man's neck, and kissed him cordially. "Holy Sage!" cried she, "a thousand times I thank thee: for I hear that fateful word the third time." She had scarcely spoken, when she clasped the old Man still faster: for the ground began to move beneath them; the Youth and the old Woman also held by one another; the Lights alone did not regard it.

You could feel plainly that the whole Temple was in motion; as a ship that softly glides away from the harbor, when her anchors are lifted; the depths of the Earth seemed to open for the Building as it went along. It struck on nothing; no rock came in its way.

For a few instants, a small rain seemed to drizzle from the opening of the dome; the old Man held the fair Lily fast, and said to her: "We are now beneath the River; we shall soon be at the mark." Ere long they thought the Temple made a halt; but they were in an error: it was mounting upwards.

And now a strange uproar rose above their heads. Planks and beams in disordered combination now came pressing and crashing in, at the opening of the dome. Lily and the Woman started to a side; the Man with the Lamp laid hold of the Youth, and kept standing still. The little cottage of the Ferryman, for it was this which the Temple in ascending had severed from the ground and carried up with it, sank gradually down, and covered the old Man and the Youth.

The women screamed aloud, and the Temple shook, like a ship running unexpectedly aground. In sorrowful perplexity, the Princess and her old attendant wandered round the cottage in the dawn; the door was bolted, and to their knocking, no one answered. They knocked more loudly, and were not a little struck, when at length the wood began to ring. By virtue of the Lamp locked up in it, the hut had been converted from the inside to the outside into solid silver. Ere long too its form changed: for the noble metal shook aside the accidental shapes of planks, posts, and beams, and stretched itself out into a noble case of beaten ornamented workmanship. Thus a fair little temple stood erected in the middle of the large one; or if you will, an Altar worthy of the Temple.

By a stair which ascended from within, the noble Youth now mounted aloft, lighted by the old man with the Lamp; and, as it seemed, supported by another, who advanced in a white short robe, with a silver rudder in his hand; and was soon recognised as the Ferryman, the former possessor of the cottage.

The fair Lily mounted the outer steps, which led from the floor of the Temple to the Altar; but she was still obliged to keep herself apart from her Lover. The old Woman, whose hand in the absence of the Lamp had grown still smaller, cried: "Am I then to be unhappy after all? Among so many miracles, can there be nothing done to save my hand?" Her husband pointed to the open door, and said to her: "See, the day is breaking; haste, bathe thyself in the River."—"What an advice!" cried she: "it will make me all black: it will make me vanish altogether: for my debt is not yet paid." "Go," said the man, "and do as I advise thee; all debts are now paid."

The old Woman hastened away; and at that moment appeared the rising sun, upon the rim of the dome. The old Man stept between the Virgin and the Youth, and cried with a loud voice: "There are three which have rule on Earth; Wisdom, Appearance, and Strength." At the first word, the gold King rose; at the second, the silver one; and at the third, the brass King slowly rose; while the mixed King on a sudden very awkwardly plumped down.

Whoever noticed him could scarcely keep from laughing, solemn as the moment was: for he was not sitting, he was not lying, he was not leaning, but shapelessly sunk together.

The Lights, who till now had been employed upon him, drew to a side; they appeared, although pale in the morning radiance, yet once more well-fed, and in good burning condition; with their peaked tongues, they had dexterously licked out the gold veins of the colossal figure to its very heart. The irregular vacuities which this occasioned had continued empty for a time, and the figure had maintained its standing posture. But when at last the very tenderest filaments were eaten out, the image crashed suddenly together; and that, alas, in the very parts which continue unaltered when one sits down; whereas the limbs, which should have bent, sprawled themselves out unbowed and stiff. Whoever *could* not laugh was obliged to turn away his eyes; this miserable shape and no-shape was offensive to behold.

The Man with the Lamp now led the handsome Youth, who still kept gazing vacantly before him, down from the altar, and straight to the brazen King. At the feet of this mighty Potentate, lay a sword in a brazen sheath. The young man girt it round him. "The sword on the left, the right free!" cried the brazen voice. They next proceeded to the silver King; he bent his sceptre to the youth; the latter seized it with his left hand, and the King in a pleasing voice, said: "Feed the sheep!" On turning to the golden King, he stooped with gestures of paternal blessing, and pressing his oaken garland on the young man's head, said: "Understand what is highest!"

During this progress, the old Man had carefully observed the Prince. After girding on the sword, his breast swelled, his arms waved, and his feet trod firmer; when he took the sceptre in his hand, his strength appeared to soften, and by an unspeakable charm to become still more subduing; but as the oaken garland came to deck his hair, his features kindled, his eyes gleamed with inexpressible spirit, and the first word of his mouth was "Lily!"

"Dearest Lily!" cried he, hastening up the silver stairs to her, for she had viewed his progress from the pinnacle of the altar; "Dearest Lily! what more precious can a man, equipt with all, desire for himself than innocence and the still affection which thy bosom brings me? O my friend!" continued he, turning to the old Man, and looking at the three statues; "glorious and secure is the kingdom of our fathers; but thou hast forgotten the fourth power, which rules the world, earlier, more universally, more certainly, the power of Love." With these words, he fell upon the lovely maiden's neck; she had cast away her veil, and her cheeks were tinged with the fairest, most imperishable red.

Here the old Man said, with a smile: "Love does not rule; but it trains, and that is more."

Amid this solemnity, this happiness and rapture, no one had observed that it was now broad day; and all at once, on looking through the open portal, a crowd of altogether unexpected objects met the eye. A large space surrounded with pillars formed the fore-court, at the end of which was seen a broad and stately Bridge stretching with many arches across the River. It was furnished, on both sides, with commodious and magnificent colonnades for foot-travellers, many thousands of whom were already there, busily passing this way or that. The broad pavement in the centre was thronged with herds and mules, with horsemen and carriages, flowing like two streams, on their several sides, and neither interrupting the other. All admired the splendor and convenience of the structure; and the new King and his Spouse were delighted with the motion and activity of this great people, as they were already happy in their own mutual love.

"Remember the Snake in honor," said the man with the Lamp; "thou owest her thy life, thy people owe her the Bridge, by which these neighboring banks are now animated and combined into one land. Those swimming and shining jewels, the remains of her sacrificed body, are the piers of this royal bridge; upon these she has built and will maintain herself."

The party were about to ask some explanation of this strange mystery, when there entered four lovely maidens at the portal of the Temple. By the Harp, the Parasol, and the folding Stool, it was not difficult to recognise the waiting-maids of Lily; but the fourth, more beautiful than any of the rest, was an unknown fair one, and in sisterly sportfulness she hastened with them through the Temple, and mounted the steps of the Altar.

"Wilt thou have better trust in me another time, good wife?" said the man with the Lamp to the fair one: "Well for thee, and every living thing that bathes this morning in the River!"

The renewed and beautified old Woman, of whose former shape no trace remained, embraced with young eager arms the man with the Lamp, who kindly received her caresses. "If I am too old for thee," said he, smiling, "thou mayest choose another husband to-day; from this hour no marriage is of force, which is not contracted anew."

"Dost thou not know, then," answered she, "that thou too art grown younger?"—"It delights me if to thy young eyes I seem a handsome youth: I take thy hand anew, and am well content to live with thee another thousand years."

The Queen welcomed her new friend, and went down with her into the interior of the altar, while the King stood between his two men, looking towards the bridge, and attentively contemplating the busy tumult of the people.

But his satisfaction did not last; for ere long he saw an object which excited his displeasure. The great Giant, who appeared not yet to have awoke completely from his morning sleep, came stumbling along the Bridge, producing great confusion all around him. As usual, he had risen stupified with sleep, and had meant to bathe in the well-known bay of the River: instead of which he found firm land, and plunged upon the broad pavement of the Bridge. Yet although he reeled into the midst of men and cattle in the clumsiest way, his presence, wondered at by all, was felt by none; but as the sunshine came into his eyes, and he raised his hands to rub them, the shadows of his monstrous fists moved to and fro behind him with such force and awkwardness, that men and beasts were heaped together in great masses, were hurt by such rude contact, and in danger of being pitched into the River.

The King, as he saw this mischief, grasped with an involuntary movement at his sword; but he bethought himself, and looked calmly at his sceptre, then at the Lamp and the Rudder of his attendants. "I guess thy thoughts," said the man with the Lamp; "but we and our gifts are powerless against this powerless monster. Be calm! He is doing hurt for the last time, and happily his shadow is not turned to us."

Meanwhile the Giant was approaching nearer; in astonishment at what he saw with open eyes, he had dropt his hands; he was now doing no injury, and came staring and agape into the forecourt.

He was walking straight to the door of the Temple, when all at once in the middle of the court, he halted, and was fixed to the ground. He stood there like a strong colossal statue, of reddish glittering stone, and his shadow pointed out the hours, which were marked in a circle on the floor around him, not in numbers, but in noble and expressive emblems.

Much delighted was the King to see the monster's shadow turned to some useful purpose; much astonished was the Queen; who, on mounting from within the Altar, decked in royal pomp with her virgins, first noticed the huge figure, which almost closed the prospect from the Temple to the Bridge.

Meanwhile the people had crowded after the Giant, as he ceased to move; they were walking round him, wondering at his metamorphosis. From him they turned to the Temple, which they now first appeared to notice, and pressed towards the door.

At this instant the Hawk with the mirror soared aloft above the dome; caught the light of the sun, and reflected it upon the group, which was standing on the altar. The King, the Queen, and their attendants, in the dusky concave of the Temple, seemed illuminated by a heavenly splendor, and the people fell upon their faces. When the crowd had recovered and risen, the King with his followers had descended into the Altar, to proceed by secret passages into his palace; and the multitude dispersed about the Temple to content their curiosity. The three Kings that were standing erect they viewed with astonishment and reverence; but the more eager were they to discover what mass it could be that was hid behind the hangings, in the fourth niche; for by some hand or another, charitable decency had spread over the resting-place of the Fallen King a gorgeous curtain, which no eye can penetrate, and no hand may dare to draw aside.

The people would have found no end to their gazing and their admiration, and the crowding multitude would have even suffocated one another in the Temple, had not their attention been again attracted to the open space.

Unexpectedly some gold-pieces, as if falling from the air, came tinkling down upon the marble flags; the nearest passers-by rushed thither to pick them up; the wonder was repeated several times, now here, now there. It is easy to conceive that the shower proceeded from our two retiring Flames, who wished to have a little sport here once more, and were thus gaily spending, ere they went away, the gold which they had licked from the members of the sunken King. The people still ran eagerly about, pressing and pulling one another, even when the gold had ceased to fall. At length they gradually dispersed, and went their way; and to the present hour the Bridge is swarming with travellers, and the Temple is the most frequented on the whole Earth.

SCHILLER.

JOHANN CHRISTOPH FRIEDRICH VON SCHILLER.

Born 1759. Died 1805.

The life and character of this most popular of German writers have been made familiar to the English and American Public by Mr. Carlyle's excellent biography, republished in this country several years since, and still the best, if not the only one, in the English language. It has the credit of having been translated into German at the solicitation of his late Excellency, von Goethe. To this everywhere accessible and everywhere satisfactory work the reader is referred for a fuller account of Schiller than is compatible with the scope of the present publication. For readers of German, there is Döring's well-known work, and later and better, *Schiller's Leben*, &c., by *Frau von Wolzogen*, sister-in-law of the poet.

A very brief notice must suffice for these pages. Schiller was a native of Marburg, in the duchy of Würtemberg. His father, Johann Caspar Schiller, a military officer in the service of the Duke, was piously solicitous to procure for his son the best education which his circumstances would allow. For this purpose he was first placed under the tuition of a private instructer, a clergyman by the name of Möser, and afterward sent to the Latin school at Ludwigsburg. It was the wish of his parents — and his own choice, as he ripened toward manhood, coincided with theirs — that he should become a divine; but the offer of the Duke and the preference shown to the sons of military officers at the new seminary established by him at Stuttgard, induced them to place him at that institution, where his studies assumed a different direction, and where, after devoting himself awhile to law, he finally settled upon medicine.

The six years spent at this institution are represented as the most wretched of his life. "The Stuttgart system of education," says his biographer, "seems to have been formed on the principle, not of cherishing and correcting nature, but of rooting it out and supplying its place with something better. The process of teaching and living was conducted with the stiff formality of military drilling. Everything went on by statute and ordinance; there was no scope for the exercise of freewill, no allowance for the varieties of original structure. A scholar might possess what instincts or capacities he pleased, the 'regulations of the school' took no account of this; he must fit himself into the common mould which, like the old giant's bed, stood there appointed by superior authority to be filled alike by the great and the little. The same strict and narrow course of reading and composition was marked out for each beforehand, and it was by stealth if he read or wrote anything beside." * * * * "The pupils were kept apart from the conversation or sight of any person but their teachers; none ever got beyond the precincts of despotism to snatch even a fearful joy. Their very amusements proceeded by word of command."

This sort of discipline was ill adapted to educate a poet. Some natures would have been utterly perverted or crushed by it. In Schiller it produced an intense inwardness. His soul was thrust back within itself, and found refuge in the world of ideas from the hard formalities of his scholastic life. This effect was both a benefit and an evil. It is impossible to say whether, on the whole, he gained or lost by it. On the one hand, it stimulated his productiveness and was probably the chief and immediate cause of his literary efforts; and on the other hand, it gave his poetry that subjective character, the excess of which is its great defect. Perhaps, a more genial nurture would have corrected this error by awakening an interest in actual life; and perhaps too, such a nurture might have given his faculties a different direction and left the poet undeveloped. It is doubtful if any training could have supplied that intimate communication with external nature, that eye for forms, that love of things, that sunny realism which constitutes so essential a qualification of the true poet, and which seems to be a natural endowment, unattainable and inimitable.

In 1780 Schiller, having completed his medical studies, was appointed surgeon to the regiment *Augé*, in the Würtemberg army. In 1781 he published his "Robbers," composed, it is said, some years before, at the age of nineteen, but concealed, for fear of offence, until he had completed his studies. This juvenile effort is, in every point of view, a wonderful production. Considered as a specimen of precocious genius, it is one of the most remarkable extant. Moreover, it stands decidedly at the head of that class of writings to which it belongs, — a class characterized by stormy force and passionate extravagance of sentiment and diction, "a savageness of unreclaimed blood." The "Satanic school" it is denominated by Mr. Carlyle. Most of Byron's works rank in this rubric. Even the "Sorrows of Werter," though with some latitude of interpretation, has been thus classed. Schiller's drama stands pre-eminent among works of this description, surpassing everything of the sort in that peculiar power of fervid declamation which constitutes one of its distinguishing features. The "Corsair" and "Giaour" are milk-and-water idyls compared with it. The "Robbers" forms an era in literature. It was soon translated into most of the languages of Europe, and everywhere welcomed as the word which all men were waiting to hear. Not only did the pent volcano in the author's own breast find vent in those "power-words," but he appeared as the spokesman of his time, — the voice of that muttered uneasiness and impatience of existing institutions which marked the epoch immediately preceding the French revolution. In strong and terrible accents it spoke the hoarded wrath of long centuries of misrule and oppression. It was an angry scream which pierced every soul from the Rhine to the Baltic, and startled the eagles of dominion on their ancient sceptres,— a prophecy of that tempest which soon after burst upon the world and changed the face of empires. Popular as it was with the young, and on the stage, it is doubtful if the real merits of the "Robbers," to this day, have been duly appreciated by the critics. Its extravagances and puerilities, unhappily but too prominent, have thrown a shade over its great excellences and biassed the judgment of mature and less inflammable readers. It is not, as sometimes represented, a mere farrago of power-words and rodomontade. It is far more than that. It is a genuine work of genius, a work unsurpassed, with the exception of Faust, by anything since Shakspeare, in imaginative power, in the vivid delineation of vice and passion, and in tragic interest. Schiller has produced many things far superior to the "Robbers," as works of art, but nothing that equals it in vigor and effect. The promise implied in this first effort, which the author himself has stigmatised as a "monster born of the unnatural union of Genius with Thraldom," was never quite realized in his subsequent productions.

Meanwhile the publication of this tragedy was attended with some disagreeable consequences to the author. He drew down upon himself the wrath of the people of the Grisons by an offensive allusion, aspersing the reputation of that district; he incurred the suspicion of the Grand Duke by becoming an author, as well as by the specific character of his drama; and finally subjected himself to repeated arrests for going to Manheim "without leave" to witness its performance at the theatre in that city. The result was that Schiller made his escape from surgery and persecution at Stuttgart and fled to Manheim, where he found a temporary support by writing for the stage. After a short residence in this city he went to Mayence, then to Dresden, then to Leipzig. He also resided for a while at the estate of the Frau von Wolzogen. In 1784 he was made Counsellor by the Duke of Weimar, and in 1787 took up his residence in that city. Here, after some hesitation and coyness, and overcoming of prejudice on both sides, he became acquainted and finally intimate with Goethe, whose nature, in most respects the antipodes of his own, acted with decisive effect on Schiller's genius and destiny. Indeed, his acquaintance with Goethe seems to have been the most powerful influence to which his riper years were subjected. Goethe has given an account of the formation of this acquaintance, from which it appears how difficult it was for these two spirits, the idealist and the realist, — each so determined in his way, — to amalgamate or even to converse. The unbroken friendship subsisting between them for nearly twenty years, is a rare and beautiful passage in literary history, and highly creditable to both parties. In Goethe it required a severe struggle with fixed views and purposes, and some magnanimity, to make the first advances to the young poet whom, on his return from Italy, he found in full possession of the popular ear and heart, and threatening to re-induce a style and tendency which he, for his part, had laid aside with the crudities of his youth, and was every way endeavoring to counteract and supplant. Schiller himself thought they should never come together, and writes thus of their first interview: "Though it did not at all diminish the idea, great as it was, which I had previously formed of Goethe, I doubt if we shall ever come into close communication with each other. Much that still interests me has already had its epoch with him; his whole nature is from its very origin otherwise constructed than mine; his world is not my world, our modes of conceiving things appear to be essentially different." Goethe, on the other hand, relates that Schiller during this interview, in which the conversation turned on the metamorphosis of plants, said many things which pained him excessively, but that he determined to take no notice of them, and to discover, if possible, something which was common to both, and which might serve as the basis of an harmonious relation. Long after Schiller's death he remarks of their intimacy: "There was something providential in my connection with Schiller; it might have happened earlier or later without so much significance; but that it should occur just at this time, when I had my Italian journey behind me, and Schiller began to be weary of his philosophical speculations, led to very important consequences for both." Mr. Carlyle remarks: "If we regard the relative situation of the parties, and their conduct in this matter, we must recognise in both of them no little social virtue, at all events, a deep disinterested love of worth. In the case of Goethe, more especially, who, as the elder and every way greater of the two, has little to expect in comparison with what he gives, this friendly union, had we space to explain its nature and progress, would give new proof that, as poor Jung Stilling also experienced, 'the man's heart which few know, is as true and noble as his genius which all know.'"

In 1789 Schiller was made, through the mediation of Goethe, Professor extraordinary of philosophy at Jena, and, the year following, was married to Fräulein von Lengefeld. In 1791 he was attacked with a violent disease of the chest, which, for a long while, incapacitated him for literary and professional labor. During this interval, he received from the hereditary Prince of Denmark and Count von Schimmelman, a pension of one thousand rix dollars for three years. After his recovery he applied himself with renewed and suicidal devotion to his former pursuits, compelling himself to labor oftentimes, when nature was unequal to the effort, and seconding nature with stimulants. "His intolerance of interruption," says his biographer, "first put him on the plan of studying by night; an alluring but pernicious practice which began at Dresden and was never afterwards given up." * * * "During summer, his place of study was in a garden, which he at length purchased, in the suburbs of Jena." * * * In this garden "Schiller built himself a small house with a single chamber. It was his favorite abode during the hours of composition; a great part of the works he then wrote were written here." * * * "On sitting down to his desk at night he was wont to keep some strong coffee or wine-chocolate, but more frequently a flask of old Rhenish or Champagne standing by him, that he might repair the exhaustion of nature." * * * "In winter he was to be found at his desk till four or even five o'clock in the morning, in summer till towards three. He then went to bed, from which he seldom rose till nine or ten." As might be expected, this insane and ruinous mode of life soon used up the feeble remains of a constitution originally slender, and long impaired by disease. The only wonder is, that nature endured the outrage so long. Goethe says: "This habit not only injured his health but also his productions: the faults which some wise heads find in his works, proceed, I think, from this source. All the passages which they blame may be styled pathological passages; for they were written on those days when he had not strength to do his best."

In 1801, by the advice of his physician, he removed from Jena to Weimar, where he resided until his death. The Grand Duke allowed him a pension of a thousand dollars yearly, and offered to give him twice as much, in case he should be hindered by sickness. Schiller declined this last offer and never availed himself of it. "I have talents," said he, "and must help myself." His chief income was derived from his works, and he compelled himself to write two dramas yearly, to meet the growing expenses of his family. In 1802 he was ennobled by the emperor of Germany. He had previously received the rights of citizenship from the French Republic, at the commencement of the Revolution.

After attending a representation of his own "Tell" at Berlin, where he was received with great honor, he died at Weimar, May 19th, 1805, in his forty-seventh year; having, in the language of Goethe, "sacrificed life to the delineation of life."*

The forty years which have elapsed since his death have not diminished the estimation in which Schiller is held by his countrymen. He is still the most popular of German writers. Goethe, indeed, is preferred by men of the highest culture; Goethe is the prophet of the philosophical and profound; but Schiller is the poet of the people, and, in all probability, will long continue to hold the supreme rank in the popular estimation. In a great measure, this popularity is owing to intrinsic merit. Schiller's excellences are perfectly intelligible; they commend themselves at first sight; they lie on the surface. Not that he lacks profoundness; but he does not, like so many of his countrymen, court obscurity; he does not hide a second meaning behind the first; there is nothing esoteric in his writings; he never enigmatizes. Goethe maintained that a perfect work of art must leave something to conjecture. This was not Schiller's theory of art. At least, it was not his practice. Though eminently reflective, he is perfectly transparent. In part, however, the popularity of Schiller may be ascribed to the zeal with which, in early life, he advocated the cause of liberty; and another reason still, is the dramatic form which his genius assumed at the outset, and the wide circulation and commanding emphasis given to his writings by theatrical exhibition. The dramatic poet possesses a great advantage, in this respect, over other authors. "In the first place, it is evident," says Jean Paul, "how far one of the latter class, with his scattered recluse-readers, honored but little, and that only by cultivated men, read perhaps twice in succession, but not heard forty times in succession; —it is evident, I say, how far such an Irus in fame, such a John Lackland falls below the stage-poet, who not only wears these laurel-gleanings upon his head, but adds to them the rich harvest, that prince and chimney-sweep, and every generation and every age get his thoughts into their heads and his name into their mouths; that often the most miserable market-towns, whenever a more miserable strolling actor's company moves into them, harness themselves to the triumphal car in which such a writer is borne." * * * "There are a hundred other advantages which, by the figure of permission (*figura præteritionis*), I might mention, but which I prefer to omit; this, e. g., that a dramatic author (and oftentimes he is present and hears it all) employs, as it were, a whole corporation of hands in his service; * * * furthermore, that he is learned by heart, not only by the actors, but, after many repetitions, by the hearers also, and is continually praised anew in all the standing though tedious theatrical notices of the daily and monthly journals." * * * "Hence we may explain the fact, that our cold Germany has exerted itself so much and so well for Schiller and so little for Herder."*—— No writer of any nation, at present, fills so large a place in the mind of his country, or exercises such fascination over it, as Schiller. Scarcely less read than Scott, he is far more deeply loved, — loved with the passionate interest which attaches to a great unfinished life; with that yearning which follows a beautiful spirit too soon withdrawn from the earth. To him belongs the peculiar charm which made Byron, for a while, the idol of the young; but without the moral abatements so lamentable in his case,—the charm of intensity. Add to this the feminine delicacy of Racine, the masculine sincerity, if not the austere sanctity, of Milton, the soaring mind of Tasso, the studied elegance of Virgil, the tragic seriousness of Euripides: all these combine to render Schiller not only the favorite of his own nation, but the delight of the world. Frederic Schlegel characterizes him as "the true founder of the German drama," the man who gave it "its proper sphere and its most happy form."† The most elaborate eulogy of Schiller is that of Menzel, in his survey of German literature, in which the poet is not inaptly compared to Raphael. Mr. Longfellow has cited this full-mouthed panegyric in the notice of Schiller contained in "The Poets and Poetry of Europe." For this reason, it was thought best to omit it here and to substitute

---

*"He had," says Goethe, "an awful progressiveness. When I had been a week without seeing him, I was amazed and knew not where to take hold of him, and found him already advanced again. And so he went ever forward for forty-six years. Then, indeed, he had gone far enough."

* From "*Katzenberger's Badereise.*"
† Lectures on the History of Literature, vol. ii.

instead the more discriminating, if less laudatory criticism of Mr. Carlyle.*

"From many indications, we can perceive that to Schiller the task of the Poet appeared of far weightier import to mankind in these times than that of any other man whatever. It seemed to him that he was "casting his bread upon the waters, and would find it after many days;" that when the noise of all conjurors, and demagogues, and political reformers had quite died away, some tone of heavenly wisdom that had dwelt even in him might still linger among men, and be acknowledged as heavenly and priceless, whether as his or not; whereby, though dead, he would yet speak, and his spirit would live throughout all generations, when the syllables that once formed his name had passed into forgetfulness forever. We are told, "he was in the highest degree philanthropic and humane; and often said that he had no deeper wish than to know all men happy." What was still more, he strove, in his public and private capacity, to do his utmost for that end. Honest, merciful, disinterested, he is at all times found: and for the great duty laid on him no man was ever more unweariedly ardent. It was 'his evening song and his morning prayer.' He lived for it; and he died for it; 'sacrificing,' in the words of Goethe, 'his Life itself to this delineating of Life.' In collision with his fellow-men,—for with him as with others this also was a part of his relation to society,—we find him no less noble than in friendly union with them. He mingles in none of the controversies of the time; or only like a god in the battles of men. In his conduct towards inferiors, even ill-intentioned and mean inferiors, there is everywhere a true, dignified, patrician spirit. Ever witnessing, and inwardly lamenting, the baseness of vulgar Literature in his day, he makes no clamorous attacks on it; alludes to it only from afar: as in Milton's writings, so in his, few of his contemporaries are named, or hinted at; it was not with men, but with things that he had a warfare. In a word, we can say of Schiller, what can be said only of few in any country or time: He was a high ministering servant at Truth's altar; and bore him worthily of the office he held. Let this, and that it was even in our age, be forever remembered to his praise.

"Schiller's intellectual character has, as indeed is always the case, an accurate conformity with his moral one. Here too he is simple in his excellence; lofty rather than expansive or varied; pure, divinely ardent rather than great. A noble sensibility, the truest sympathy with Nature, in all forms, animates him; yet scarcely any creative gift altogether commensurate with this. If to his mind's eye all forms of Nature have a meaning and beauty, it is only under a few forms, chiefly of the severe or pathetic kind, that he can body forth this meaning, can represent as a Poet what as a Thinker he discerns and loves. We might say, his music is true spheral music; yet only with few tones, in simple modulation; no full choral harmony is to be heard in it. That Schiller, at least in his later years, attained a genuine poetic style, and dwelt, more or less, in the perennial regions of his Art, no one will deny: yet still his poetry shows rather like a partial than a universal gift; the labored product of certain faculties rather than the spontaneous product of his whole nature. At the summit of the pyre, there is indeed white flame; but the materials are not all in flame, perhaps not all ignited. Nay, often it seems to us, as if poetry were, on the whole, not his essential gift; as if his genius were reflective in a still higher degree than creative; philosophical and oratorical rather than poetic. To the last, there is a stiffness in him, a certain infusibility. His genius is not an Æolian harp, for the common wind to play with, and make wild, free melody; but a scientific harmonica, that being artfully touched will yield rich notes, though in limited measure. It may be, indeed, or rather it is highly probable, that of the gifts which lay in him only a small portion was unfolded: for we are to recollect that nothing came to him without a strenuous effort; and that he was called away at middle age. At all events, here as we find him we should say, that of all his endowments the most perfect is understanding. Accurate, thorough insight is a quality we miss in none of his productions, whatever else may be wanting. He has an intellectual vision, clear, wide, piercing, methodical,—a truly philosophic eye. Yet in regard to this also it is to be remarked, that the same simplicity, the same want of universality again displays itself. He looks aloft rather than around. It is in high, far-seeing philosophic views that he delights; in speculations on Art,—on the dignity and destiny of Man, rather than on the common doings and

---

* From "Carlyle's Miscellanies." Boston, James Munroe and Co., vol. ii.

interests of Men. Nevertheless these latter, mean as they seem, are boundless in significance; for every the poorest aspect of Nature, especially of living Nature, is a type and manifestation of the invisible spirit that works in Nature. There is properly no object trivial or insignificant: but every finite thing, could we look well, is as a window, through which solemn vistas are opened into Infinitude itself. But neither as a Poet nor as a Thinker, neither in delineation nor in exposition and discussion, does Schiller more than glance at such objects. For the most part, the Common is to him still the Common, or is idealized, rather as it were by mechanical art than by inspiration: not by deeper poetic or philosophic inspection, disclosing new beauty in its every-day features, but rather by deducting these, by casting them aside, and dwelling on what brighter features may remain in it. Herein Schiller, as, indeed, himself was modestly aware, differs essentially from most great poets; and from none more than from his great contemporary, Goethe. Such intellectual preëminence as this, valuable though it be, is the easiest and the least valuable; a preëminence that indeed captivates the general eye, but may, after all, have little intrinsic grandeur. Less in rising into lofty abstractions lies the difficulty, than in seeing well and lovingly the complexities of what is at hand. He is wise who can instruct us and assist us in the business of daily virtuous living; he who trains us to see old truth under Academic formularies may be wise or not as it chances; but we love to see Wisdom in unpretending forms, to recognise her royal features under week-day vesture.—There may be more true spiritual force in a Proverb than in a philosophical system. A King in the midst of his body-guards, with all his trumpets, war-horses, and gilt standard-bearers, will look great though he be little; but only some Roman Carus can give audience to satrap-ambassadors, while seated on the ground, with a woollen cap, and supping on boiled peas, like a common soldier.

"In all Schiller's earlier writings, nay, more or less, in the whole of his writings, this aristocratic fastidiousness, this comparatively barren elevation, appears as a leading characteristic. In speculation he is either altogether abstract and systematic, or he dwells on old, conventionally-noble themes; never looking abroad, over the many-colored stream of life, to elucidate and ennoble it; or only looking on it, so to speak, from a college window. The philosophy even of his Histories, for example, founds itself mainly on the perfectibility of man, the effect of constitutions, of religions, and other such high, purely scientific objects. In his Poetry we have a similar manifestation. The interest turns on prescribed, old-established matters, common love mania, passionate greatness, enthusiasm for liberty, and the like. This, even in Don Karlos, a work of what may be called his transition-period, the turning-point between his earlier and his later period, where we still find Posa, the favorite hero, 'towering aloft, far-shining, clear and cold, as a sea beacon.' In after years, Schiller himself saw well that the greatest lay not here. With unwearied effort he strove to lower and to widen his sphere, and not without success, as many of his Poems testify; for example, the *Lied der Glocke* (Song of the Bell), every way a noble composition; and, in a still higher degree, the tragedy of Wilhelm Tell, the last, and, so far as spirit and style are concerned, the best of all his dramas.

"Closely connected with this imperfection, both as cause and as consequence, is Schiller's singular want of Humor. Humor is properly the exponent of low things; that which first renders them poetical to the mind. The man of Humor sees common life, even mean life, under the new light of sportfulness and love; whatever has existence has a charm for him. Humor has justly been regarded as the finest perfection of poetic genius. He who wants it, be his other gifts what they may, has only half a mind; an eye for what is above him, not for what is about him or below him. Now, among all writers of any real poetic genius, we cannot recollect one who, in this respect, exhibits such total deficiency as Schiller. In his whole writings there is scarcely any vestige of it, scarcely any attempt that way. His nature was without Humor; and he had too true a feeling to adopt any counterfeit in its stead. Thus no drollery or caricature, still less any barren mockery, which, in the hundred cases, are all that we find passing current as Humor, discover themselves in Schiller. His works are full of labored earnestness; he is the gravest of all writers. Some of his critical discussions, especially in the *Aesthetische Briefe*, where he designates the ultimate height of man's culture by the title of *Spieltrieb* (literally, sport-impulse), prove that he knew what Humor was, and how essential; as indeed, to his intellect, all forms of excellence, even the most alien to his own, were painted with a wonderful fidelity. Nevertheless, he himself attains not that height which he saw so clearly; to the last the *Spieltrieb* could be little more than a theory with him. With the single exception of *Wallenstein's Lager*, where, too, the Humor, if it be such, is not deep, his other attempts at mirth, fortunately very few, are of the heaviest. A rigid intensity, a serious enthusiastic ardor, majesty rather than grace, still more than lightness or sportfulness, characterizes him. Wit he had, such wit as keen intellectual insight can give; yet even of this no large endowment. Perhaps he was too honest, too sincere, for the exercise of wit; too intent on the deeper relations of things to note their more transient collisions. Besides, he dealt in Affirmation, and not in Negation; in which last, it has been said, the material of wit chiefly lies.

"These observations are to point out for us the special department and limits of Schiller's excellence; nowise to call in question its reality. Of his noble sense for Truth, both in speculation and in action; of his deep, genial insight into nature; and the living harmony in which he renders back what is highest and grandest in Nature, no reader of his works need be reminded. In whatever belongs to the pathetic, the heroic, the tragically elevating, Schiller is at home, a master; nay perhaps the greatest of all late poets. To the assiduous student, moreover, much that lay in Schiller, but was never worked into shape, will become partially visible: deep, inexhaustible mines of thought and feeling: a whole world of gifts, the finest produce of which was but beginning to be realized. To his high-minded, unwearied efforts, what was impossible, had length of years been granted him! There is a tone in some of his later pieces, which here and there breathes of the very highest region of Art. Nor are the natural or accidental defects we have noticed in his genius, even as it stands, such as to exclude him from the rank of great Poets. Poets whom the whole world reckons great, have, more than once, exhibited the like. Milton, for example, shares most of them with him: like Schiller he dwells, with full power, only in the high and earnest; in all other provinces exhibiting a certain inaptitude, a certain elephantine unpliancy: he too has little Humor; his coarse invective has in it contemptuous emphasis enough, yet scarcely any graceful sport. Indeed, on the positive side also, these two worthies are not without a resemblance. Under far other circumstances, with less massiveness, and vehement strength of soul, there is in Schiller the same intensity; the same concentration, and towards similar objects, towards whatever is sublime in Nature and in Art, which sublimities they both, each in his several way, worship with undivided heart. There is not in Schiller's nature the same rich complexity of rhythm, as in Milton's, with its depths of linked sweetness; yet in Schiller too there is something of the same pure, swelling force, some tone which, like Milton's, is deep, majestic, solemn.

"It was as a Dramatic Author that Schiller distinguished himself to the world: yet often we feel as if chance rather than a natural tendency had led him into this province; as if his talent were essentially, in a certain style, lyrical, perhaps even epic, rather than dramatic. He dwelt within himself, and could not without effort, and then only within a certain range, body forth other forms of being. Nay, much of what is called his poetry seems to us, as hinted above, oratorical rather than poetical; his first bias might have led him to be a speaker, rather than a singer. Nevertheless, a pure fire dwelt deep in his soul; and only in Poetry, of one or the other kind, could this find utterance. The rest of his nature, at the same time, has a certain prosaic rigor: so that not without strenuous and complex endeavors, long persisted in, could its poetic quality evolve itself. Quite pure, and as the all-sovereign element, it perhaps never did evolve itself; and among such complex endeavors, a small accident might influence large portions in its course. —— Of Schiller's Philosophic talent, still more of the results he had arrived at in philosophy, there were much to be said and thought, which we must not enter upon here. As hinted above, his primary endowment seems to us fully as much philosophical as poetical; his intellect, at all events, is peculiarly of that character; strong, penetrating, yet systematic and scholastic, rather than intuitive; and manifesting this tendency both in the objects it treats, and in its mode of treating them. The transcendental Philosophy, which arose in Schiller's busiest era, could not remain without influence on him: he had carefully studied Kant's system, and appears to have not only admitted but zealously appropriated its fundamental doctrines; remoulding them, however, into his own peculiar forms, so that they seem no longer borrowed, but permanently acquired; not less Schiller's than Kant's. Some, perhaps little aware of his natural wants and tendencies, are of opinion that these speculations did not profit him.

"Among younger students of German Literature, the question often arises, and is warmly mooted: whether Schiller or Goethe is the greater Poet? Of this question we must be allowed to say that it seems rather a slender one, and for two reasons. First, because Schiller and Goethe are of totally dissimilar endowments and endeavors, in regard to all matters intellectual, and cannot well be compared together as Poets. Secondly, because if the question mean to ask, which Poet is on the whole the rarer and more excellent, as probably it does, it must be considered as long ago abundantly answered. To the clear-sighted and modest Schiller, above all, such a question would have appeared surprising: No one knew better than himself, that as Goethe was a born Poet, so he was in a great part a made Poet; that as the one spirit was intuitive, all-embracing, instinct with melody, so the other was scholastic, divisive, only partially and as it were artificially melodious. Besides, Goethe has lived to perfect his natural gift, which the less happy Schiller was not permitted to do. The former accordingly is the national Poet; the latter is not and never could have been. We once heard a German remark, that readers to their twenty-fifth year usually preferred Schiller; after their twenty-fifth year, Goethe. This probably was no unfair illustration of the question. Schiller can seem higher than Goethe only because he is narrower. Thus to unpractised eyes, a Peak of Teneriffe, nay, a Strassburg Minster, when we stand on it, may seem higher than a Chimborazo; because the former rise abruptly, without abutment or environment; the latter rises gradually, carrying half a world aloft with it; and only the deeper azure of the heavens, the widened horizon, the 'eternal sunshine' disclose to the geographer that the 'Region of Change' lies far below him.

"However, let us not divide these two Friends, who in life were so benignantly united. Without asserting for Schiller any claim that even enemies can dispute, enough will remain for him. We may say that, as a Poet and Thinker, he attains to a perennial Truth, and ranks among the noblest productions of his century and nation. Goethe may continue *the* German Poet, but neither through long generations can Schiller be forgotten."

As, of all German writers, Schiller is perhaps the best known, or least misunderstood, among us; as he has rank as poet rather than prose-writer, the following essay must suffice for the present collection.

UPON NAIVE AND SENTIMENTAL POETRY.*

THERE are moments in our life when we feel a kind of love and tender respect for Nature in plants, minerals, animals, landscapes, and in human nature in children, in the manners of rustics and of the primitive times: not on account of its sensuous interest, nor because it satisfies our intellect or taste, for the opposite may often occur with both, but solely because it is Nature. Every cultivated man, not entirely deficient in feeling, is sensible of this, when he walks in the open air, or is living in the country, or lingers near the monuments of past time: in short, when he is overtaken, in the midst of artificial relations and situations, by the simplicity of nature. It is this interest, often amounting to a want, which underlies many of our passions for flowers and creatures, for simple gardens, for walks, for the country and its inhabitants, for many products of distant antiquity, and the like. But this presupposes that neither affectation nor an otherwise accidental interest comes into play. Then this kind of interest in nature occurs only under two conditions. In the first place it is absolutely necessary, that the object which excites it should be Nature, or taken for such by us: secondly, that, in the widest signification of the term, it should be *naive*, that is, that nature should stand in contrast with art, and rebuke it. Nature becomes naive as soon as these two conditions are combined.

From this point of view nature becomes for us nothing more nor less than independent Being, the persistence of things by themselves, existence according to peculiar and immutable laws.

---

* Translated by Rev. J. Weiss.

This conception is absolutely prerequisite, if we would take interest in like phenomena. Could one, with the completest deception, give a natural look to an artificial flower, or carry the imitation of naive manners to the highest point of illusion, the discovery that it was all imitation would entirely destroy the feeling of which we speak.* Whence it is clear that this kind of pleasure in nature is moral and not aesthetic: for it is mediated by an idea, and is not created by direct contemplation. Besides which, it is by no means directed towards beauty of form. For instance: what attraction would a colorless flower, a fountain, a mossy stone, the twitter of birds, the humming of bees, have for us in themselves? What could give them a claim to our love? We do not love the objects themselves, but the ideas they represent. We love in each of them the still, creative life, the tranquil production out of itself, existence according to its own laws, eternal unity with itself.

They are what we were; they are what we again should be. Like them, we were Nature; and our culture ought to lead us back to Nature, by the path of reason and freedom. Then they are at the same time the representation of our lost childhood, which forever remains the dearest to us: hence, they fill us with a certain sadness; and at the same time the representation of our loftiest completion in the ideal: hence, they give us a sublime emotion.

But their completeness is not their merit, since it is not the work of their own choice. They secure for us, then, this entirely peculiar pleasure, that without making us ashamed, they are our model. They surround us, as a continual divine manifestation, but more refreshing than dazzling. What makes their character complete is exactly that in which our own is deficient: what distinguishes us from them is exactly that of divinity in which they fail. We are free, and they are necessary: we alter, they remain one. But the divine or the ideal obtains, only when the differences are blended, when the will follows freely the law of necessity, and the reason maintains its sway through every change of fancy. Then we forever perceive in them that which we lack, but for which we are invited to strive, and to which, even though we never attain it, we may yet hope to approximate in an infinite progression. We perceive in ourselves a superiority, which they lack, but which they can either never share, like the senseless creation, or only as they proceed in our path, like the state of childhood. Hence, as idea, they create for us the sweetest enjoyment of our manhood, although they must of necessity humiliate us with respect to *each determinate condition* of our manhood.

As this interest for nature is based upon an idea, it can be shown only in dispositions susceptible of ideas, that is, in moral ones. By far the majority of men only affect it; and the universality of this sentimental taste in our times, which displays itself, especially since the appearance of certain writings, in affected travels, gardens of like sort, walks and other fondnesses of the kind, is no proof at all for the universality of the true sentiment. Yet Nature will always exert something of this influence upon the most insensible, since for that the common bias of all men to the moral is adequate; and all of us without distinction, however great a disproportion there may be between our acts and the simplicity and truth of Nature, are compelled to that in idea. This sentiment for Nature and incitement from objects standing in a close relation with us, — as for example, children and childlike people,—and bringing nearer to us both self-retrospection and our own *unnature*, is especially strong and universal. It is erroneous to suppose, that it is only the appearance of helplessness which makes us, at certain times, linger with so much emotion near children. Perhaps that may be the case with some, who are wont to feel, in the presence of weakness, nothing but their own superiority. But the feeling of which I speak occurring only in entirely moral dispositions, and not to be confounded with that excited by the playful activity of children, is rather humiliating than gratifying to self-love; and indeed if any superiority is noticeable at all, it is by no means on our side. We experience emotion, not while we look down upon the child from the height of our power and perfection, but while we look up, out of the limitation of our condition which is inseparable from the definite mode to which we have attained, at the child's boundless determinableness and its perfect innocence. And, at such a moment, our feeling is too plainly mingled with a certain sadness, to allow us to mistake its source. The child represents the bias and determination, we represent the fulfilment, which forever remains infinitely far behind the former. Hence the child is an actualization of the ideal, not indeed of one fulfilled, but of one proposed; and so it is by no means the appearance of its neediness and limits which moves us, but, on the contrary, the appearance of its free and pure power, its integrity, its infinity. For this reason, a child will be a holy object to the man of morality and feeling, that is, an object which, by the magnitude of an idea, abolishes every actual magnitude, and which wins again in rich measure from the estimation of the reason all that

---

* Kant, the first to my knowledge who directed reflection expressly towards this phenomenon, remarks, that if we heard a man imitate with complete success the note of a nightingale, and yielded to the impression with profound emotion, all our pleasure would vanish with the dissipation of this illusion. See the chapter in the *Critique of Aesthetic Judgment*, upon Intellectual interest in the beautiful. Whoever has learned to admire the author only as a great thinker, will here be delighted to meet with a trace of his heart; and to be convinced, by the discovery, of his fitness for this lofty vocation, which unquestionably demands the union of both those qualities.

it may lose in the estimation of the understanding.

Out of this very contradiction between the judgment of the reason and of the understanding, proceeds the entirely peculiar phenomenon of mixed feeling, which a naive disposition excites in us. It unites childlike with childish simplicity. By the latter, it gives the understanding an idea of weakness, and produces that laughter by which we make known our (theoretic) superiority. But as soon as we have reason to believe that childish simplicity is at the same time childlike, and that consequently its source is not folly, or imbecility, but a loftier (*practical*) strength, a heart full of innocence and truth, which makes ashamed, by its internal greatness, the mediation of art,—then that triumph of the understanding is over, and a jest at simpleness passes over into admiration of simplicity. We feel ourselves compelled to respect the object at which we previously laughed, and, while casting a look into ourselves, to lament that we are not like it. Thus arises the entirely peculiar appearance of a feeling, in which are blended gay derision, reverence and sadness.*

* Kant, in a note to the Analysis of the Sublime (Critique of Aesth. Judg., p. 225, 1st Ed.), in like manner distinguishes this three-fold composition in the perception of the Naive, but he gives another explanation of it. "Something of both (the animal feeling of pleasure, and the spiritual feeling of respect) united, is found in naivete, which is the outbreak of the originally natural uprightness of humanity against the art of dissimulation become a second nature. We laugh at the simplicity which does not yet understand how to dissimulate, and still we enjoy that *natural* simplicity which disappoints such arts. If we expected the every-day style of an affected expression that is prudently established upon aesthetic show, behold, it is unsophisticated, blameless nature, which we were not at all prepared to meet, and which, it would seem, was not meant to be exposed. And because the aesthetic, but false, show, which commonly counts for much in our judgment, here suddenly vanishes, and because, so to speak, our waggery is exposed, this brings out in two opposite directions, a mental agitation, which at the same time gives the body a salutary shaking. But because something, which is infinitely better than all assumed style, that is, mental sincerity (at least the tendency thereto), is not yet entirely extinguished in human nature,—this it is which mingles seriousness and regard in this play of the judgment. But since the phenomenon lasts only for a little while, and the veil of dissimulation is soon again drawn before it, a regret, which is an emotion of tenderness, mingles also with our feeling; and it does not refuse to unite as play with a hearty laugh, at the same time relieving the embarrassment of the person who is the object of it, because he has not yet learned the way of the world." I must confess the explanation does not entirely satisfy me, and particularly for this reason, that it asserts something of the Naive in general, which is chiefly true of one species, the Naive of surprise, of which I shall afterwards speak. It certainly excites laughter, when anybody exposes himself by naivete; and in many cases this laughter may result from a previous expectation which is resolved into nothing. But also naivete of the noblest kind, the Naive of disposition, always excites a smile, which can hardly have for its cause an expectation resolved into nothing;

The Naive demands, that Nature should bear away the victory over Art,* whether it happen without the knowledge and will of the person, or with his full consciousness. In the first case it is the Naive of Surprise, and delights: in the other case it is the Naive of Disposition, and moves.

In the Naive of surprise, the person must be morally able to deny nature; in the Naive of disposition he need not be so, and yet, if it would affect us as naivete, we need not imagine him as physically unable to do so. Hence the talk and actions of children give us the pure impression of naivete, only so long as we do not remember their incapacity for art, but merely regard the contrast of their naturalness with the art in us. A childishness, where it is no longer expected, is Naive, and therefore that cannot be ascribed, in strictness of meaning, to actual childhood.

But in the cases, both of Naivete of Surprise and that of Disposition, nature must be right, but art be wrong.

The conception of the Naive is only completed by this final definition. Feeling is also nature, and the rule of propriety is something artificial; but yet the victory of feeling over propriety is nothing less than naive. If, on the other hand, the same feeling overcomes artifice, false propriety, dissimulation, we do not hesitate to call that naive.† It is necessary, then, that nature should triumph over art, not as a dynamic magnitude, by its blind force, but as a moral magnitude, by its form. The impropriety, and not the insufficing of art, must have afforded the victory to nature; for nothing which results but it is generally to be explained only by the contrast of a certain demeanor with the once assumed and expected forms. I also doubt, whether the pity, which is blended in our feeling at the Naive of the latter kind, relates to the naive person, and not rather to ourselves, or rather to mankind in general, of whose deterioration we are reminded by such a circumstance. It is too plainly a moral sadness, which must have a nobler object than the physical weakness with which sincerity is threatened in the customary routine of life; and this object cannot well be other than the decay of truth and simplicity in humanity.

* Perhaps I should briefly say; *truth over Dissimulation*. But the idea of the Naive appears to me to include still something more, while the simplicity which prevails over artifice, and the natural freedom which conquers stiffness and constraint, excite in us a similar perception.

† A child is ill bred, if it resists the precepts of a good education from desire, caprice or passion : but it is naive, if it releases itself by virtue of a free and healthy nature, from the mannerism of an unwise education, from the stiff postures of the dancing-master, and the like. The same also occurs with that loosely defined naivete which results from the transmission of humanity to the irrational. If the weeds got the upper hand in a badly kept garden, no one would find the appearance naive; but there is something positively naive when the *free* growth of outspreading branches destroys the laborious work of the shears in a French garden. And so it is not at all naive when a trained horse repeats his lesson badly out of natural fatness, but there is something naive when he forgets it out of natural freedom.

from deficiency can command respect. It is true, that in the Naive of Surprise, it is always the overplus of feeling and a deficiency of restraint which causes nature to be recognized: but this deficiency and that overplus by no means create the Naive, for they only afford an opportunity for nature to follow unimpeded its moral capacity, that is, the law of harmony.

The Naive of Surprise can only appertain to man, and to man alone, in so far as at that moment he is no longer pure and innocent nature. It presupposes a will which does not harmonize with that which nature does spontaneously. Such a person, if rendered conscious of it, will be frightened at himself: on the contrary, he who is naive by Disposition, will be surprised at men and at their astonishment. Then, as the truth does not here recognize the personal and moral character, but only the natural character released by feeling, so we attribute no merit to the man for his uprightness, and our laughter, which is restrained by no personal veneration for him, is merited sport. But as here also it is the uprightness of nature which breaks through the veil of falseness, a satisfaction of a higher kind unites with the mischievous pleasure at having surprised a man. For nature, in opposition to artifice, and truth, in opposition to deception, must always excite respect. We feel, then, in the naive of surprise also, an actual moral pleasure, though not from a moral character.*

It is true, we always respect nature in the naive of surprise, since we must respect the truth. On the contrary, we respect the person in the naive of disposition, and then we enjoy not only a moral pleasure, but also at a moral object. In the one as in the other case nature is right, so that she speaks the truth: but in the latter case nature is not only right, but the person is also worthy of respect. In the first case the uprightness of nature always redounds to the shame of the person, because it is involuntary; in the second it always redounds to his merit, even supposing that he incurs odium by what it expresses.

We ascribe a naive disposition to a man, if, in his judgments of things, he overlooks their artificial and forced relations, and adheres only to simple nature. We demand from him all the judgments that can be made within the limits of healthy nature; and we completely discharge him only from that which presupposes a separation from, at least a knowledge of, nature, whether in feeling or in thought.

If a father tells his child, that this or that man is pining in poverty, and the child hastens to carry to the man his father's purse of gold, the action is naive, for healthy nature acts out of the child: and it would be perfectly right so to proceed in a world where healthy nature rules. He only regards the need and the nearest method of satisfying it: such an extension of the right of property, whereby a part of humanity are left to perish, is not founded in simple nature. The action of the child, then, is a rebuke of the actual world, and our heart also confesses it by the satisfaction which the action causes it to feel.

If a man without knowledge of the world, but otherwise of good capacity, confesses his secrets to another, who betrays him,—but who knows how to artfully dissimulate,— and by this very candor lends him the means of doing him an injury, we find it naive. We laugh at him, but yet we cannot resist for that reason highly prizing him. For his confidence in the other results from the honesty of his own intentions: at least he is naive only so far as that is the case.

Hence the naive of reflection can never be a property of corrupted men, but can only belong to children and men with childlike dispositions. The latter often act and think naively in the most artificial relations of the great world. Out of their own fine humanity they forget that they have to do with a corrupted world, and they demean themselves at the courts of kings with an ingenuous innocence only to be found among a race of shepherds.

Now it is not so easy always correctly to distinguish childish from childlike innocence, since there are actions which waver between the extreme limits of both, and which actually leave us in doubt, whether we ought to laugh at simpleness or reverence a noble simplicity. A very remarkable instance of this kind is found in the political history of Pope Adrian VI., which Schröekh has described for us with the thoroughness and pragmatic truth peculiar to himself. This Pope, a Netherlander by birth, administered the pontificate at a critical moment for the hierarchy, when an embittered party exposed without mercy the weak points in the Roman church, and the adverse party was deeply interested to conceal them. What the truly naive character, if such a one ever strayed into the holy chair of Peter, would have to do in this case, is not the question: but rather, how far such a naivete of disposition might be compatible with the function of a Pope. This, by the way, was something which by no means embarrassed the predecessors and followers of Adrian. With perfect uniformity they adhered to the Romish system once for all accepted, nowhere to concede anything. But Adrian really had the simple character of his nation and the

---

* As the naive depends only upon the form in which something is said or done, this property disappears, as soon as the thing itself, either through its causes or through its effects, makes a preponderating or indeed contradictory impression. By naivete of this kind even a crime can be detected, but then we have neither the quiet nor the leisure to direct our attention to the form of the detection: and aversion for the personal character absorbs all our satisfaction at the nature. And as a revolted feeling steals the moral pleasure at the uprightness of nature, as soon as naivete gives knowledge of a crime, just so does an excited compassion destroy our mischievous pleasure, as soon as we see anybody placed in peril by his naivete.

innocence of his former rank. He was elevated from the narrow sphere of the student to his exalted post, and had never been false to the simplicity of that character on the eminence of his new dignity. The abuses in the church disturbed him, and he was much too honest openly to dissimulate his private convictions. In conformity to such a mood he suffered himself, in the instruction with which he furnished his legate to Germany, to fall into confessions, before unheard of from any pope, and to flatly impugn the principles of this court. Among other things it says: "We know well that for many years past much that is odious has been perpetrated in this holy chair: no wonder if the sickness has been transmitted from the head to the members, from the Pope to the prelates. We have all fallen away, and for a long time past there has not been one of us who has done a good thing, no, not one." Again, elsewhere, he enjoins the legate to declare in his name, "that he, Adrian, cannot be blamed on account of that which happened through former popes, and that such excesses had always displeased him, even when he filled an inferior station," &c. We can easily imagine what reception the Roman clerisy gave to such naivete on the part of the Pope. The least which they imputed to him was that he had betrayed the church to the heretics. Now this highly impolitic measure of the Pope would compel our whole respect and admiration, if we could only be convinced that he was actually naive, that is, that he had been forced to it only through the natural truth of his character, without any regard to the possible consequences, and that he would have done it none the less if he had anticipated the whole extent of its unseemliness. But we have some grounds for believing, that he did not deem this step so very impolitic, and in his innocence went so far as to hope, that he might gain a very important advantage for the church by his condescension toward the opposition. He not only presumed that as an honest man he ought to take this step, but to be able also as Pope to justify it: and while he forgot, that the most artificial of all structures could actually be sustained by a systematic denial of the truth, he committed the unpardonable error of using precepts in a position completely the reverse of those natural relations in which they might have been valid. This certainly modifies our judgment seriously: and although we cannot withhold our respect from the honesty of heart, out of which that action flowed, it is not a little weakened by the reflection, that nature had in art, and the heart in the head, a feeble rival.

That is not a true genius which is not naive. Nothing but its naivete makes it genius; and what it is in taste and intellect, it cannot contradict in its morality. Unacquainted with rules, the crutches of weakness and the taskmasters of perversity, guided only by nature or by instinct, its guardian angel, it passes tranquilly and safely through all the snares of a vicious taste, in which the pseudo-genius is inevitably caught, unless it is acute enough to anticipate them from afar. It is only granted to genius to be always at home beyond the limits of the familiar, and to extend, without transgressing, nature. It is true the greatest genius now and then commits the latter fault, but only because it also has its moments of fantasy, when protecting nature leaves it: only because the force of example wins it, or the corrupt taste of its age seduces it.

Genius must solve the most complicated problems with unpretending simplicity and skill. The egg of Columbus is a sample of every method of true spirit. It legitimates itself as genius only by triumphing through simplicity over the most factitious art. It proceeds not according to familiar principles, but by impulses and feelings. But its impulses are suggestions of a god, — all which healthy nature does, is divine,—and its feelings are laws for all ages and for every race of men.

The childlike character which genius stamps upon its works, it also manifests in its manners and its private life. It is chaste, because nature is always so: but it is not decent, because decency is only native to depravity. It is intelligent, for nature can never be the opposite; but it is not cunning, for only art can be so. It is true to its character and its inclinations, but not so much because it has principles, as because nature always returns through every vacillation to its first position, always restores the old necessity. It is modest, even bashful, because genius itself is always a mystery, but it is not anxious, because it does not know the perils of the road on which it travels. We know little of the private life of the greatest geniuses, but even that little which has been preserved, for example, concerning Sophocles, Archimedes, Hippocrates, among the ancients, and Ariosto, Dante and Tasso, Raphael, Albert Dürer, Cervantes, Shakspeare, Fielding, Sterne, and others of modern times, confirms this assertion.

And even, a fact which seems to present far greater difficulty, the great statesman and general will exhibit a naive character, as soon as their genius makes them great. Among the ancients, I will only here allude to Epaminondas and Julius Cæsar, and to Henry IV. of France, Gustavus Adolphus of Sweden, and Peter the Great, among the moderns. The Duke of Marlborough, Turenne, Vendome, all display this character. And in the other sex, nature has indicated her highest perfection of naivete. Feminine coquetry strives for nothing so much as for the appearance of naivete: proof enough, if we had no other, that the chief power of the sex rests upon this quality. But since the prevalent principles of female education are in lasting opposition to this character, it is as hard for the woman morally, as for the man intellectually, to maintain that noble gift of nature with the advantages bestowed by generous culture. The woman who unites this naiveté of manners with a demeanor appropriate to the world, merits our reverence as much as the scholar who combines a genial freedom of thought with all the severity of the schools.

A naive expression necessarily flows out of naive reflection, both in words and gestures: and it is the most important element of grace. Genius expresses thus naively its sublimest and deepest thoughts: they are oracles from the mouth of a child. While common sense, always afraid of error, nails its words and conceptions upon the cross of logic and grammar, while it is hard and stiff in order to be definite, multiplies words lest it say too much, and prefers to extract all the force and keenness from its thought, from dread of being inconsiderate, Genius, with a single happy dash of the pencil, gives to its thought a firm, forever definite and yet flowing outline. If, on the one hand, the symbol and the thing symbolized remain forever foreign and heterogeneous, on the other, the speech issues from the thought as by an inward necessity, and is so entirely one with it, that the spirit seems exposed even under its material veil. In composition, it is expression of this kind, where the symbol entirely vanishes in the thing symbolized, and where the language still leaves the thought which it expressed naked, while another never can present without at the same time concealing it, that we style by eminence spirited and genial.

Innocence of heart expresses itself freely and naturally in daily life, like genius in its works of thought. It is notorious that in social life a man eschews simplicity and severe integrity of expression in the same proportion as he lacks purity of intention: and where offence is so readily incurred, and the imagination so easily corrupted, a constrained demeanor is a necessity. Without being false, we often say what we do not think: we invent circumlocutions in order to say things which can offend only a sickly vanity, or injure only a corrupt imagination. An ignorance of these conventional laws, united with natural uprightness, which despises every labyrinth and show of falsehood (and not rudeness, which only rejects those laws because they incommode it), creates a naiveté of expression in intercourse, which consists in calling things, which we either may not designate at all or only artfully, by their right names and in the curtest way. The customary expressions of children are of this kind. They create laughter from their contrast with our customs; and yet in our hearts we confess that the child is right.

It is true that, strictly speaking, a naive disposition can be attributed to man only as a being not positively subject to nature, though still only so far as pure nature really acts in him. And yet, by an effect of the poetising imagination, it is often transferred from the rational to the irrational. Thus we often attribute a naive character to an animal, a landscape, a building, and to nature generally, in opposition to the caprice and fantasy of man. But this always demands that we should subjectively lend a will to that which has none, and have regard to its strict direction according to necessary laws. Dissatisfaction at our own ill exercised moral freedom, and at the lack of moral harmony in our actions, easily induces that kind of mood in which we address an irrational thing as a person, and imagine its eternal uniformity a merit, and envy its tranquil tenor, as if it really had to struggle with a temptation to be otherwise. At such a moment it jumps with our humor to consider our prerogative of reason an evil and a curse, and to deny justice to our capacity and destiny, from a vivid sense of the meagreness of our actual execution.

Then we see in irrational nature only a more fortunate sister, who remained in the maternal house, from which we stormed forth into the distance, in the exuberance of our freedom. With sorrowful longing we yearn to be back again, as soon as we begin to feel the oppressiveness of culture, and to hear in the foreign remoteness of art the winning voice of the mother. While we were only nature's children we were happy and perfect; we became free, and ceased to be both. Hence results a twofold and very dissimilar longing for nature, longing for her happiness, longing for her perfection. The loss of the former is lamented only by the sensuous man; but the moral man alone can mourn over the loss of the latter.

Ask yourself strictly then, sympathizing friend of nature, does your indolence pine for her repose? does your offended moral sense desire her harmony? Ask yourself candidly, does art disgust you, and do you take refuge in the solitude of inanimate nature from the abuses of society? do you abhor its privations, its burdens, its difficulties, or its moral anarchy, its disorders, its caprice? You must meet the former with joy and courage, and your compensation must be the very freedom out of which they flow. You may well propose the tranquil joy of nature for your distant goal, but only such as is the prize of your own worthiness. Then complain no longer of the hardship of life, of the inequality of conditions, of the stress of circumstances, of the insecurity of property, of ingratitude, oppression, persecution. You must submit to all the evils of culture with free resignation, you must respect them as the natural conditions of the only Good: you must lament only over its wickedness, but not with unmanly tears. Much rather care to act purely amid those contaminations, freely under that slavery, firmly through that fickle mutability, loyally through that anarchy. Do not fear external, but internal confusion: strive for unity, but seek it not in uniformity: strive for repose, but through the equipoise, not through the cessation, of your activity. That nature, which you begrudge to the irrational, deserves neither longing nor respect. It lies behind you: it must forever lie behind you.

When you no longer feel the ladder which upheld you, there remains for you no choice but to grasp the law with free consciousness and volition, or else to fall beyond deliverance into a fathomless abyss.

But if you become consoled for the loss of nature's happiness, then let her perfection be your heart's ideal. If you step forth unto her from your sphere of art, and see her before you in her great tranquillity, in her naive beauty, in her childlike innocence and simplicity, linger before the picture, cherish that feeling: it is worthy of your noblest manhood. Do not longer indulge the wish or fancy to exchange with her, but receive her into yourself, and strive to wed her infinite superiority to your own infinite prerogative, and create from that union the divine. Let her encompass you like a tender Idyll, in which you may always find yourself again out of the distractions of art, from which you may gather new courage and confidence for the race, and kindle afresh in your heart the flame of the Ideal, which flickers and sinks so soon in the storms of life.

If we call to mind the beautiful nature which surrounded the ancient Greeks, if we recollect how confidently that people could live under their fortunate heaven with free nature, how much nearer their conception, their sentiment, their manners lay to simple nature, and what a true reflection of her their works of fancy are, it must seem strange to observe that we find so few traces among them of that sentimental interest with which we moderns can cling to natural scenes and characters. It is true, the Greek is in the highest degree strict, true, circumstantial, in his description of nature, but yet not a whit more and with no heartier sympathy, than he is also in the description of an array, a shield, a suit of armor, a domestic utensil, or of any product of mechanics. He seems to make no distinction in his love for the object, between that which is in itself, and that which is through art and human will. Nature seems to interest his intellect and curiosity more than his moral sense: he does not cling to her, as we do, with heartiness, with sensibility, with a sweet sadness. And even when he personifies and deifies her single manifestations, and represents their effects as actions of a free being, he abolishes in her that tranquil necessity, by which precisely she is so attractive to us. His impatient fancy bears him away over her to the drama of human life. Nothing satisfies him but the free and living, nothing but characters, actions, fates and manners. And while we, in certain moral moods of mind, could wish to give up the superiority of our free volition, which causes us so much strife with ourselves, so much unrest and confusion, for the choiceless but tranquil necessity of the irrational, the Greek fancy, precisely the reverse, is busy making human nature inchoate even within the inanimate world, and giving influence to Will in the province of blind necessity.

Whence indeed this diversity of spirit? How comes it that we who are so far surpassed by the ancients in everything that is nature, can precisely here honor nature in a higher sense, cling to her with heartfulness, and embrace even the inanimate world with warmest sensibility? It is because with us nature has vanished out of humanity, and we meet her again in her truth only beyond the latter, in the world of matter. It is not our greater conformity with nature, but, quite the contrary, the incongruity of our relations, conditions and manners, which impels us to procure in the physical world that which is hopeless in the moral world, namely, satisfaction for the growing impulse for truth and simplicity, which lies incorruptible and ineffaceable in all human hearts, like the moral disposition whence it flows. It is for this reason that the feeling with which we cling to nature is so nearly akin to the feeling which laments the vanished age of childhood and of childlike innocence. Our childhood is the only unmutilated nature which we still find in cultivated manhood: then it is no wonder if every vestige of external nature conducts us back to our childhood.

It was very different with the ancient Greeks.* Their culture had not so far degenerated that nature was abandoned. The whole structure of their social life was based upon feelings, and not upon a composition of art: their mythology itself was the suggestion of a naive sentiment, the creation of a joyous fancy, and not of a refining reason, like the religion of later nations. Then as the Greek had not lost the nature in humanity, he could not be surprised by her beyond the limits of the latter: and so he could have no pressing necessity for objects in which he might recover her. In unison with himself, and happy in the feeling of his humanity, he fain held silently to that as his maximum, and approached all else with difficulty: while we, not in unison with ourselves, and unhappy in our experiences of humanity, have no pressing interest except to escape from it, and to thrust from our vision a form so unsuccessful.

The feeling to which we here allude, is not then, that which the ancients had: it is rather identical with that which we have for the an-

---

* But with the Greeks only: for just such a lively animation and such a rich fulness of human life as surrounded the Greek, was requisite, in order to transfer life into the lifeless also, and to pursue with that zeal the image of humanity. Ossian's human world, for example, was needy and monotonous: the inanimate around him was great, colossal, mighty. Thus it was imperative, and maintained its rights over man himself: and hence inanimate nature (in opposition to man) appears in the songs of this poet much more as an object of sentiment. But Ossian too laments a falling away of humanity; and however small was the circle of his people's culture and their corruptions, its experience was still lively and impressive enough, to repel the singer, with his tenderness and purity, back toward the inanimate, and to pour over his songs that elegiac tone which we find so moving and attractive.

cients. They perceived naturally: we perceive the natural. Without doubt, the feeling which filled Homer's soul when he let his celestial swineherd entertain Ulysses, was quite different from that which moved the soul of the young Werter, when he read the passage after a tedious company. Our sentiment for nature is like the feeling of the invalid for health.

In the same degree that Nature vanished out of human life as Experience and as the (active and perceptive) Subject, we see her appearing in the poetic world as Idea and as Object. That nation which has proceeded farthest both in unnature and in reflection upon it, must have been the first to be most strongly moved by the phenomenon of naivete, and to give to it a name. This nation, so far as I know, was the French. But perception of, and interest in, the naive, is naturally much earlier, and dates from the very commencement of moral and aesthetic depravation. This change in the perceptive mode is extremely striking even so early as Euripides; for example, when we compare him with his predecessors and with Æschylus especially, and yet that poet was the favorite of his age. The same revolution is apparent also among the old historians. Horace, the poet of a cultivated and corrupted age, extols tranquil happiness in his Tibur; and we may designate him as the true founder of this sentimental school of poetry, while as a model he has not yet been surpassed. We also find traces of this perception in Propertius, Virgil, and others, but few in Ovid, who lacked heartfulness, and who mourns, in his Exile at Tomi, the loss of that happiness which Horace so readily dispenses with in his Tibur.

Poets are universally, by their very conception, the guardians of nature. Where they can no longer be so, and already feel in themselves the destructive influence of capricious and artificial forms, or at least have had to struggle with it, they will then appear as the witnesses and as the avengers of nature. They will either be, or they will seek, a lost nature. Thus two very different schools of poetry arise, which cover and exhaust the whole province of that art. All who are really poets, will belong either to the naive or to the sentimental school, according to the constitution of the age in which they flourish, or as contingent circumstances affect their general culture and predominating neutral tone.

The early poet of a naive and spiritual world, and he, in an age of artificial culture, who is nearest to him, is austere and coy, like the virgin Diana in her forests. With no familiar manners, he eludes the heart that seeks him, and the longing that would embrace him. The homely truthfulness with which he handles an object often seems like insensibility. The object possesses him entirely: his heart does not lie, like a base metal, just beneath the surface, but will be sought after in the depths, like gold. He stands behind his work like the Infinite behind the structure of the world. He is the work and the work is him. We must first be unworthy of the work, or unequal to it, or weary, only to ask for him.

So appears, for example, Homer among the ancients and Shakspeare among the moderns: two very different natures, separated by the immeasurable lapse of ages, but in this particular characteristic completely one. When I first became acquainted with the latter poet, at a very early age, I was troubled at the coldness, the insensibility, which permitted him to jest in the deepest pathos, to disturb with a clown the heart-rending scenes in Hamlet, King Lear, Macbeth, and others, which now held him fast where my feelings hurried on, and now coldly hastened forward where the heart would so willingly have rested. Led by acquaintance with the later writers, to seek for the poet in the work, to meet his heart, to reflect familiarly with him concerning his object, in short, to contemplate the object in the subject,—it was intolerable to me that the poet would nowhere suffer contact, and never deign to talk with me. And for many years he had all my reverence and my study too, before I learned to win his personality. I was yet incapable of understanding nature at first hand. I could only tolerate her image reflected through the intellect and adjusted by the rules; and the sentimental poets both of the French and Germans, from 1750 to 1780, were just the proper subjects for that end. But I am not ashamed of this puerile judgment, since the mature critic passed a similar one, and was naive enough to publish it to the world.

The same thing happened to me with respect to Homer, also, whom I knew at a still later period. I remember now the remarkable place in the sixth book of the Iliad, where Glaucus and Diomed attack each other, and after one recognises the other as his guest, exchange presents. This affecting picture of the piety with which the laws of hospitality were observed in war itself, can be matched with a description of knightly magnanimity in Ariosto, where two knights and rivals, Ferran and Rinaldo, the one a Saracen, the other a Christian, make peace after being covered with wounds in a violent conflict, and mount the same horse in order to seek and bring back the flying Angelica. Different as both examples are, they still coincide in the effect upon our hearts, since both depict the beautiful triumph of manners over passion, and affect us with their naivete of disposition. But how differently do the poets undertake the description of this same action. Ariosto, the citizen of a later age, whose manners had deteriorated in simplicity, cannot conceal his own admiration and emotion at the relation of this event. The feeling of the remoteness of these manners from those which characterise his age, overpowers him. He abandons at once the delineation of the object and appears in his own person. The beautiful stanzas are well known, and have always excited special admiration:

> "O noble minds, by knights of old possess'd!
> Two faiths they knew, one love their hearts profess'd:
> And still their limbs the smarting anguish feel
> Of strokes inflicted by the hostile steel.
> Through winding paths and lonely woods they go,
> Yet no suspicion their brave bosoms know.
> At length the horse, with double spurring, drew
> To where diverging ways appeared in view."
> *(Hoole.)*

And now old Homer! Hardly does Diomed learn from the relation of Glaucus, his rival, that the latter is a guest of his family from the father's times downward, when he buries his spear in the ground, talks cordially with him, and they agree in future to avoid each other during battle. But hear Homer himself:

> "Henceforth let our spears
> Avoid each other in tumultuous war;
> For many Trojans and renown'd allies
> Have I to slay, whom to this arm some god
> May bring, or else my speed may overtake;
> And many Greeks there are for thee to slay,
> Whome'er thou canst; but let us arms exchange,
> That all who see our conference may know
> We boast to be hereditary guests.
> This said, both heroes leaping from their cars,
> With mutual kindness joined their hands and pledged
> The faith of friendship!"

A *modern* poet (at least one who is so in the moral sense of that word) would have hardly waited until now, in order to testify his pleasure at the action. And we should the easier pardon him for it, since our heart also makes a pause in the reading, and withdraws from the object, in order to contemplate itself. But no trace of all this in Homer: he proceeds in his barren truthfulness, as if he had announced an every-day affair, nay, as if he bore no heart in his bosom:

> "Then Saturnian love
> Exalted Glaucus' liberal mind, who gave
> His golden for Tydides' brazen arms,
> Although a hundred oxen his were worth,
> And those of Diomed no more than nine."
> *(Munfords' Translation.)*

Poets of this naive kind are properly no longer in their place in an artificial age. In fact they are hardly possible there, at least only if they run wild, and are saved from the crippling influence of their times by a fortunate destiny. They can never proceed out of society itself; but they sometimes appear beyond its limits, yet rather as strangers who astonish us, and as untamed children of nature who scandalise us. Beneficial as such phenomena are for the artist who studies them, and for the genuine connoisseur who knows how to estimate them, they prosper little on the whole with their period. The seal of ruler rests upon their brow; but we prefer to be rocked and carried by the muses. The Critics, who are the special hedge-trimmers of taste, hate them as bound-breakers, and would fain suppress them. For Homer himself need thank only the power of more than a Millenium of evidence, for the toleration of these aesthetic judges: it would harass them not a little to maintain their rules against his example, and his reputation against their rules.

I said that the poet either is nature, or he will seek her. If the former, he is naive; if the latter, he is sentimental.

The poetic spirit is immortal and inalienable in humanity: it cannot fail except simultaneously with that and with the poetic inclination. For when the man removes himself, by the freedom of his fancy and his understanding, from the simplicity, truth, and necessity of nature, not only the road to her remains forever open to him, but a mightier and more indestructible instinct, the moral, also impels him constantly back to her; and the poetic capacity stands in the closest relationship with this very instinct. That, then, is not also lost together with natural simplicity, but only operates in another channel.

Nature is still the only flame which nourishes the poetic spirit; it creates its whole energy out of her alone, and speaks to her even in the artificial man comprised within his culture. Every other mode of operation is foreign to the poetic spirit; hence, by the way, all so called works of humor are improperly styled poetic, although, guided by the reputation of French literature, we have for a long time confounded the two qualities. It is still nature, I say, that even in the artificial conditions of culture, gives energy to the poetic spirit; only she stands in a relation to it entirely new.

It is evident that, while man continues to be pure and not rude nature, he acts as an undivided sensuous unity and as a harmonizing whole. Sense and reason, the receptive and the creative faculty, are not yet separate in their operations, much less do they stand in opposition. The perceptions of the one are not the formless sport of chance, the ideas of the other are not the barren play of fancy; the former result from the law of necessity, the latter from reality. When man has passed into the state of culture, and art has lain her hand upon him, that sensuous harmony within him is removed, and he can only express himself as a moral unity, that is, as striving after unity. The agreement between his perception and reflection, which took place in the first condition actually, now exists only ideally. It is no longer in him, but out of him; as a thought which has yet to be realized, and no longer as a fact of his life. If now we apply the conception of poetry, which is none other than to give humanity its completest possible expression, to both the above conditions, the result is, that in the condition of natural simplicity, where the man still acts with all his powers at once as a harmonious unity, and where therefore the totality of his nature fully expresses itself in reality, the completest possible imitation of the actual must make the poet; that on the contrary, in the condition of culture, where that harmonious co-operation of his whole nature is only an idea, the elevation of reality to the ideal, or what amounts to the same thing, the representation of the ideal must make the poet. And these are also the two only possible modes in which the poetic genius can find expression. They are, as we see, entirely distinct; but there is a higher conception which comprehends them both, and we need not be surprised to find this conception coinciding with the idea of humanity.

This is not the place to pursue farther this thought, which only a special discussion can place in its full light. But whoever knows how to institute a comparison between the ancient and modern poets*, not only according to accidental forms, but according to the spirit, can easily be satisfied of its truth. The former affect us through their nature, through sensuous truth, through living presence: the latter affect us through ideas.

Moreover, this path which the modern poets travel, is the same which man must commonly pursue, as well in the part as in the whole. Nature makes him one with himself, Art separates and divides him, the Ideal restores his unity. But since the ideal is an infinity which man never reaches, the cultivated man can never become perfect in his mode, as the natural man is able to become in his. Then he must be infinitely inferior to the latter in perfection, if regard is had only to the relation in which both stand to their mode and their maximum. On the contrary, if we compare together the modes themselves, it is evident that the goal for which the man strives through culture, is infinitely superior to that which he attains through nature. The one then acquires his value through positive attainment of a finite, the other desires it through approximation to an infinite magnitude. But since the latter has only degree and progress, the relative worth of the cultivated man, taken as a whole, is never determinable, although when partially regarded he is found in necessary inferiority to him in whom nature acts in her whole perfection. But in so far as the final goal of humanity can only be reached through that progress, and the natural man can only proceed according as he cultivates himself, and consequently passes over into the other condition,—there is no question to which of the two the preference is to be awarded, with respect to that final goal.

What has here been said of the two distinct forms of humanity, may also be applied to both those poetic forms corresponding to them.

For this reason we ought not to compare together ancient and modern — naive and sentimental — poets, or, if we do, only beneath a higher conception common to both: for such an one there really is. For certainly, if we have once partially abstracted the generic conception of poetry from the old poets, nothing is easier, but nothing also is more trivial, than to undervalue the moderns in comparison. If we only call that poetry, which has uniformly affected simple nature in all times, the only result will be to render dubious the name of poet as applied to moderns exactly in their highest and most peculiar beauty, because it is precisely here that they speak only to the disciple of art, and have nothing to say to simple nature.* The richest contents will be empty show, and the highest flight of poetry will be exaggeration to him whose mind is not already prepared to pass out of reality into the province of ideas. The wish can never occur to a reasonable man, to set a modern side by side with that in which Homer is great; and it sounds laughable enough to hear a Milton or a Klopstock styled the modern Homer. And just as little would any ancient poet, least of all Homer, be able to maintain a comparison with the modern poet in *his* characteristics. The former, if I may so express it, is powerful through the art of limitation; the latter through the art of illimitation.

And from the fact that the strength of the ancient artist (for what has here been said of the poet, can also be applied in general to the liberal artist, under the restrictions which naturally occur) consisted in limitation, we may explain the high superiority which the plastic art of antiquity asserts over that of modern times; and, in general, the unequal relation of value in which modern poetry and modern plastic art stand to both species of art in antiquity. A work for the eye finds its perfection only in limitation: a work for the imagination can also attain it through the unlimited. Hence a modern's preponderance in ideas helps him little in plastic works; he is compelled here to *define in space* most rigidly the image of his fancy, and consequently to measure himself with the ancient artist precisely in that quality, in which the latter holds the indisputable palm. It is otherwise in poetic works; and though the ancient poets conquer here also in the simplicity of their means, and in that which is sensuously

---

* Perhaps it is not superfluous to mention, that if the modern poets are here set opposite to the ancient, we are to understand not so much the difference in time as the difference in manner. We have also in modern and even in the latest times, naive poems in all classes, though no longer of a style entirely pure; and there is no want of the sentimental among the old Latin, and even Grecian poets. We frequently find both kinds united, not only in the same poet, but even in the same work, as for example in the Sorrows of Werter. Productions of this kind will always have a superior effect.

* It became Moliere at any rate, as a naive poet, to leave to the decision of his maid-servant, what should stand in his comedies and what should be subtracted. It were to be wished that the masters of the French cothurn had also tried that test upon their tragedies. But I do not mean to propose that a similar test should be applied to the Odes of Klopstock, to the finest passages in the Messiah, in Paradise Lost, in Nathan the Wise, and many other pieces. But what do I say? This test is actually applied, and Moliere's maid reasons at full sweep, in our critical libraries, philosophical and literary annals and travels, upon poetry, art, and the like; only, as is reasonable, a little more insipidly on German than on French soil, and in keeping with the style in the servants'-hall of German literature.

presentable and corporeal,—the moderns in their turn leave them behind in profusion of material, in that which is irrepresentable and ineffable, and in short, in that which we call *spirit* in a work of art.

As the naive poet follows only simple nature and perception, and confines himself only to imitation of reality, he can only hold a single relation to his subject, and in this respect, he has no choice in his mode of handling. The different impression of naive poems depends (presupposing that we abstract all therein which pertains to the contents, and regard that impression only as the pure effect of the poetic handling), only, I remark, upon the different degree of one and the same perceptive method. Even the difference in the external forms can make no alteration in the quality of that aesthetic impression. Let the form be lyric or epic, dramatic or descriptive, we may indeed experience emotions more or less powerful, but never of different kinds, supposing the contents abstracted. Our feeling is altogether the same, composed entirely of one element, so that we can distinguish in it nothing else. Even the difference of tongues and times makes no alteration in this respect; for this pure unity of their origin and their effect is precisely one characteristic of naive poetry.

The case is entirely different with the sentimental poet. He reflects upon the impression which the objects make upon him, and the emotion into which he throws us and is thrown himself, is only based upon that reflection. Here the object is related to an idea, and its poetic power only rests upon that relation. Hence the sentimental poet is always involved with two conflicting representations and perceptions, with reality as a limit and with his idea as the unlimited: and the mingled feeling which he excites will always betray this two-fold source.* Since, then, a plurality of principles here occurs, it depends upon which of the two *predominates* in the poet's perception and in his representation, and a difference in the handling is consequently possible. For now the question arises, whether he will be more occupied with the real, or more with the ideal, whether he will treat the former as an object of aversion, or the latter as an object of inclination. Then his representation will either be *satirical*, or it will be *elegiac* (in a wider signification of this word, hereafter to be explained). Every sentimental poet will conform to one of these two methods of perception.

---

* Whoever notices the impression which naive poems make upon himself, and is able to disconnect therefrom the sympathy created by the contents, will find this impression, even in very pathetic subjects, always cheerful, always pure, always tranquil: while that of sentimental poems is always somewhat grave and intensive. The reason is, that while in the case of naive representations, be the action what it will. we always rejoice at the truth, at the living presence of the object in our imagination, and seek nothing more than this,—in the sentimental, on the contrary, we have to unite the presentation of the imagination with an idea of the reason, which always leaves us irresolute between two different conditions.

JOHANN GOTTLIEB FICHTE.

Born 1762. Died 1814.

This brave and devoted spirit claims our interest as the impersonation of transcendental ethics. Among the illustrious four* whose names are most intimately associated with the recent movement in German philosophy, his function is that of moralist; a preacher of righteousness. As a character, he is incomparably the most interesting of them all; as a writer, incomparably the most able and impressive. The eloquence of transcendentalism found in him its highest development.

Fichte recalls more than any modern the heroes of the Stoa. The stern Promethean vigor of that ancient school flowers anew in his word and in his character, which was no less emphatic than his word. Goethe, with customary aptness of characterisation, calls him "one of the most vigorous personalities"† that ever was seen. Few philosophers have so honored their theory with personal illustrations. He carried his philosophy into life and his life into philosophy, acting as he spoke, from an eminence above the level of the world. He created for himself, out of the fruitful bosom of his own ideality, a world of his own,—a world of great thoughts and lofty aims, in which he had his being and lived apart from his contemporaries, even while he mingled with them in the thickest tumult of life, and threw himself with all his presence into the sore conflict of his time.

In speculation, Fichte was closely and genetically related to Kant. The *Wissenschaftslehre* would never have been conceived, it is probable, had not the *Kritik der reinen Vernunft* preceded. But he differed from his predecessor in the practical tendency of his nature; and this it is which gives so decided a moral tone and direction to his philosophy. Kant was satisfied with the bare contemplation of abstract truth. Fichte would fain realise the truth in action; he would bring it to bear on the civil and social existence of man, or at least, on his own. He would make the word flesh in his life. The one resembled a mountain-lake embosomed in deep solitude, which, he who would know it, must make a special pilgrimage to visit. The other was like a river, which, springing from that lake, precipitates itself with passionate force on the plain below, and then, more calmly, gathers up its channelled waters and hastens with its full heart to make glad the region through which it flows. Fichte took a lively interest in the social and political questions of the day, and, as far as his function permitted, an active part in the great movements by which those questions were tried. He was an apostle of liberty to his countrymen, and by his "*Reden an die Deutschen*" did much to awaken that resistance to Napoleon which finally resulted in their emancipation from his dominion.

Notwithstanding this strong practical bias, Fichte was a thorough idealist in philosophy. A more radical and consistent system of idealism than the *Wissenschaftslehre* was never offered to the world. What Kant had indicated critically and negatively, Fichte endeavored to establish constructively; *i. e.* the subjectiveness of all our cognitions and experience. He reascends the path by which Kant had descended in his analysis, and taking his stand in the conscious I, endeavors thence to construct a world. Nothing exists but the I; and all our experience, and the external world, as the object of that experience, is a creation of the I, but a necessary creation. Fichte endeavors to develop the laws by which this creation proceeds. The idea of duty in this system is a creative principle. Beings exist for us only as we have duties toward them. The fact of moral obligation is the central fact which determines all things for moral agents.

The system was never popular, as, indeed, no idealistic system ever was or can be. It was made the subject of numberless satires, of which the most remarkable is the *Clavis Fichtiana* of Jean Paul. But Fichte's influence is independent of his system; the great thoughts which he put forth still heave the heart of Germany, and his word is one of the powers which now mould the world.

---

* Kant, Fichte. Schelling, Hegel.
† *Eine der tüchtigsten* (doughtiest) *Persönlichkeiten.*

FICHTE.

Fichte was the son of a ribbon-manufacturer at Rammenau, near Bischoffswerda, in Upper Lusatia. The distinguished promise of his childhood procured him a patron in a certain Herr von Miltitz, and, through him, the means of education which his father's poverty would not allow. He was placed at the High School, *Schulpforte*, then a Saxon Seminary. He studied theology successively at Jena, Leipzig, and Wittenberg. In 1788, he accepted the office of private tutor to a family in Zurich. Here he became acquainted with his future wife and was betrothed. In 1790, he returned to Leipzig, and devoted himself to study, particularly the study of the Kantian philosophy. In 1791, he went to Warsaw in compliance with an invitation to become a teacher in that city. But the situation did not please him, and he soon abandoned it. On his return, he tarried some time in Königsberg, where he became acquainted with Kant, and where, with the hope of making himself better known to that great philosopher, he published his "*Kritik aller Offenbarung*" (criticism of all revelation). The work was anonymous, and was universally believed to be Kant's, until he himself pointed out the true author. Then Fichte's name blossomed at once into a wide and brilliant reputation, as the second great philosopher of Germany; and in 1794, he was called to succeed Reinhold in the Professorial chair of Philosophy at Jena. His influence on the students was great and beneficent, but misunderstandings between him and his colleagues, the charge of atheism with which it was attempted to prejudice the Government against him, together with numerous other vexations, induced him to resign his office; and in 1799, he went to Berlin, where he lived for awhile in literary retirement. He was afterwards made Professor of Philosophy in Erlangen; but the war-troubles of that stormy period drove him to Königsberg, and later to Copenhagen. In 1807, he returned to Berlin once more, and with his "Addresses to the German Nation," and his lectures, labored intrepidly and indefatigably for the cause of freedom and German independence. In 1809, he was made Professor of Philosophy at the new University of Berlin, to which he rendered incalculable service, both as lecturer and as counsellor in its affairs. During the "war of liberation," as it is called, he distinguished himself anew by his courage and his patriotism, and died January 27th, 1814, of a fever contracted by assiduous watching at the sick-bed of his wife, who had contracted the same by her own ministrations to the sick and wounded, in a time of general distress.

In the first church-yard from the Oranienburg gate, of Berlin, stands a tall obelisk with this inscription:—

THE TEACHERS SHALL SHINE
AS THE BRIGHTNESS OF THE FIRMAMENT;
AND THEY THAT TURN MANY TO RIGHTEOUSNESS
AS THE STARS FOREVER AND EVER.

It marks the grave of FICHTE. The faithful partner of his life sleeps at his feet.

THE DESTINATION OF MAN.

INTRODUCTORY REMARK.

[THIS work is intended to present, in a popular form, certain results of the Transcendental Philosophy, or rather of the last Fichtean modification of that Philosophy. "Whatever of the new philosophy is available out of the School," says the author in his preface, "is to constitute the subject of this work; presented in that order in which it would naturally unfold itself to artless reflection."—"The book is not designed for philosophers by profession, and they will find nothing in it which has not already been set forth in the author's previous writings. It was meant to be intelligible to all readers who are capable of understanding a book at all. Undoubtedly, it will be thought unintelligible by those who seek for nothing but a repetition, in a somewhat different order, of phrases which they have already learned by heart, and who mistake this act of memory for an act of the understanding."

The plan of the work is this. The author supposes a mind,—as yet unversed in metaphysical inquiries, but otherwise cultivated,—just beginning to speculate on its own nature and destiny, and the grounds of all being and knowing. He follows what he supposes to be the natural course of such a mind, through three successive stages, which constitute the three divisions of the work. The first book is headed, "Doubt." It leaves the inquirer in a state of painful conflict between the instinctive belief of the soul and the fatalistic conclusions to which his reasonings have brought him. The second book, entitled "Knowledge," overthrows the whole fabric of sensible experience, and demonstrates that we properly *know* nothing beyond our momentary consciousness, and that consciousness, the mere reflection of a reflection, "the dream of a dream." I cannot say: *I feel, perceive, think*; but only: "there appears a thought" of somewhat, that I call me, feeling, perceiving, thinking. In short, this stage lands us in absolute Pyrrhonism. At the same time, the author refers us, for our satisfaction, to another "organ" than that of Knowledge. That other organ, "Faith," furnishes the title and constitutes the subject of the third book. Faith rebuilds, on moral grounds, the fabric which speculation had destroyed. Not speculation, but action, is the end of being. The call to act is instinctive; it is divine. If we accept that call in faith and obey it, we resolve ourselves of our doubts, so far as our act extends. We assure ourselves, at least, of the topics of action. Duty restores to us a God, an external world, our own identity and continuity of being; and unfolds to us, as individuals and as a race, a destination worthy all our powers and all our love.

Thus the inquiry ends by legitimating the innate convictions of the mind. It reconciles us to all that is or shall be, as divinely appointed process and end; and yields an impregnable peace, as its practical result. Tr.]

FROM THE FIRST BOOK.
DOUBT.

Now then, at length, I believe myself acquainted with a good part of the world which surrounds me! And indeed I have bestowed sufficient pains and care in becoming so. I have credited only the consenting testimony of my senses, and uniform experience. What I saw I have touched, what I touched I have analysed. I have repeated my observations and repeated them again. I have compared different appearances with each other; and not till I had comprehended their precise connection,—not till I could explain and derive the one from the other, could calculate beforehand the result that was to follow, and the observation of the result corresponded to my calculation,—have I allowed myself to be satisfied. Wherefore I am now as sure of the correctness of this portion of my knowledge, as of my own existence. I tread with firm step the familiar sphere of my world, and am ready at any moment to stake my being and well-being on the infallibility of my convictions.

But,—what am I myself, and what is my destination?

Superfluous question! It is long ago since my instruction on this point was brought to a close. It would require time to repeat to myself all that I have heard in detail and learned and believed respecting it.

And in what way did I arrive at this knowledge which I dimly remember to possess? Did I, impelled by a burning thirst for knowledge, work my way through uncertainty, through doubt and contradiction? Did I, when anything credible offered itself, suspend my judgment, prove what was probable, and prove it again, illustrate and compare; until an inward voice, unmistakeable and irresistible, called to me: It is so, and only so! as surely as thou livest and hast thy being? No! I remember no such state. Instruction on those subjects was offered me before I desired it. I was answered before I had put the question. I listened because I could not avoid it. There remained fixed in my memory so much as it pleased Chance to preserve. Without examination, and without interest, I let everything be as it was given.

How then can I persuade myself that I possess, in fact, any knowledge on this subject? If I can know and be convinced of that alone which I myself have discovered,—if I am actually acquainted with that only which I myself have experienced,—then I cannot say, in truth, that I possess the least knowledge respecting my own destination. I know only what others profess to know concerning it; and all that I can really affirm is this, that I have heard such and such things in relation to it.

So then, while I have investigated for myself with accurate care the less important, I have hitherto relied on the care and fidelity of strangers in regard to the most important. I have imputed to others an interest in the highest concerns of Humanity, an earnestness, a precision which I had by no means discovered in myself. I have estimated them unspeakably higher than myself.

Whatever truth they know, from whence can they know it except from their own reflection? And why may not I discover the same truth by the same reflection, since I avail as much as they? How have I hitherto undervalued and despised myself!

I will that it be so no longer. With this moment I will enter upon my rights and take possession of the dignity which belongs to me. Renounced be everything foreign! I will investigate for myself. Be it that secret wishes as to how the investigation may terminate,—be it that a fore-loving inclination to certain tenets stirs within me. I forget and deny it. I will allow it no influence on the direction of my thoughts. With severe accuracy I will go to work. With candor I will confess to myself the whole. Whatever I find to be truth, however it may sound, shall be welcome to me. I will KNOW. With the same certainty with which I reckon that this ground will bear me when I tread upon it, that this fire will burn me when I come in contact with it, I will be able to compute what I am and what I shall be. And if this shall be found impossible, I will at least know that it is impossible. And even to this issue of my investigation I will submit myself, if it shall discover itself to me as the Truth.—I hasten to solve the problem which I have proposed to myself.

I seize on-speeding Nature in her flight, arrest her for an instant, fix firmly in my eye the present moment, and reflect upon it!—upon this Nature by which my power of thought has hitherto been unfolded, and formed for those conclusions which are valid in her domain.

I am surrounded by objects which I am constrained to regard as wholes, existing for themselves, and mutually distinguished from each other. I see plants, trees, animals. I ascribe, to each individual, qualities and characteristics by which I distinguish them from each other; to this plant such a form, to another a different one; to this tree leaves of such a figure, to another tree leaves of a different figure.

Each object has its determinate number of qualities, none over and none under. To every question whether it be this or that? one who knows it thoroughly can always answer with a decisive yes or no, which puts an end to all vacillation between being and not being. Everything which exists is this something or it is not this something. It is colored or it is not colored; has this hue or has it not, is pleasant to the taste or unpleasant, is palpable or impalpable, and so on, indefinitely.

Each object possesses each of these qualities in a determinate degree. If there is a scale for a certain quality, and if I can apply that scale, I shall find a certain measure of that quality which it does not in the least degree exceed or fall below. If I measure the height of this tree, it is determined; it is not one line higher or lower than it is. If I consider the green of its leaves, it is a determined green, not, in the least degree, darker or brighter, fresher or more faded than it is; though I may have neither scale nor words to define it. If I cast my eye upon this plant, it stands at a certain stage between its germination and its maturity; not, in the least degree, nearer to or farther from either than it is. Everything that is, is thoroughly determined; it is what it is, and absolutely nothing else.

But Nature hurries on with her constant changes; and while I speak of the moment on which I have seized, it is flown, and everything has changed. And before I had seized it, it was likewise altogether different. As it was when I seized it, it had not always been. It became such.

Why now and from what cause did it become precisely such as it became? Why, among the infinitely various determinations which Nature is capable of assuming, did she assume, in this moment, precisely these which she did assume, and no other?

For this reason: Because they were preceded by precisely those which did precede them, and could not have been preceded by any other; and because they followed precisely those, and could not possibly have followed any other. If, in the preceding moment, anything had been, in the least degree, other than it was, then, in the present, also, something would have been other than it is. And why, in the preceding moment, was everything such as it was? For this reason: Because that which preceded it, was such as it was. And that again depended on the one which went before it, and that again on its predecessor, and so on, indefinitely upward. Even so, in the next following moment, Nature will be determined as she will be, because, in the present, she is determined as she is. And in this next following moment something would necessarily be otherwise than it will be, if, in the present, the least thing were other than it is. And, in the moment which shall follow that, everything will be such as it will be, because, in this next following, everything was as it will be. And so, the successor of that will depend upon that, as itself will have depended on its antecedent, and so on, indefinitely downward.

Nature travels through the infinite series of her possible determinations without pause; and the changes in these determinations are not lawless, but strictly lawful. Whatever exists in Nature is necessarily what it is, and it is absolutely impossible that it should be otherwise. I enter into a complete chain of phenomena, in which every link is determined by its predecessor, and determines its successor; a fixed connection of things, in which, from any given moment, I might discover by mere reflection, all possible states of the universe, ascending (a parte ante), if I should explain the given moment, descending (a parte post), if I should infer from it: if ascending, I should seek the causes by which alone it could be what it is: if descending, I should seek the consequences which must necessarily flow from it. In every part I receive the whole, because, it is only by means of the whole, that each part is what it is, and by means of that, it is necessarily what it is. * * * * *

In every moment of her duration, Nature is a connected whole. In every moment *each individual part* of her must be what it is, because, *all the other parts* are as they are; and you could not move a grain of sand from its place, without producing a change, invisible perhaps to your eyes, through all parts of the immeasurable whole. Every moment of this duration is determined by all the past moments and determines all the coming moments; and you cannot, in the moment that now is, suppose the position of a grain of sand to be different, without being obliged to suppose the whole past, indefinitely ascending, and the whole future, indefinitely descending, to be different. Make the experiment, if you will, with this grain of sea-sand, which you behold. Imagine it lying some paces farther toward the interior. Then, the storm-wind which drove it hither from the sea, must have been stronger than it actually was. But then, too, the preceding weather by which this storm-wind and the degree of its strength were determined, must have been other than it was; and the weather by which that, in like manner, was preceded and determined. And so you have, in an unlimited and indefinitely ascending series, an entirely different temperature of the air, than that which actually existed, and an entirely different character of the bodies which influence that temperature and are influenced by it. This temperature has unquestionably a very decided influence on the fruitfulness or unfruitfulness of countries, and by means of these, and even immediately, on the duration of human life. How can you know,— for, since it is not permitted us to penetrate into the interior of Nature, it is sufficient, here, to indicate possibilities,—how can you know but that, with such a quality of weather as would have been required to cast this grain of sand farther inward, one of your forefathers might have perished with hunger, or cold, or heat, before he begat the son from whom you have descended, accordingly, that you could not be, and that all which you think to effect, in the present and for the future, could not be, because a grain of sand lies in a different place?

I myself, with all that I call mine, am a link in this chain of Nature's strict necessity. There was a time — so others who lived in that time inform me, and I myself am necessitated, by reasoning, to suppose such a time, of which I am not directly conscious,—there was a time in which as yet I was not, and a moment in which I began to be. I existed only for others, not yet for myself. Since then, my self-consciousness has gradually unfolded itself, and I have discovered in myself certain faculties and dispositions, necessities and natural cravings. I am a determinate existence, which at some time or other began to be.

I did not originate of myself. It would be the greatest contradiction to suppose that I was before I was, in order to bring myself into being. I became actual, by means of another power, exterior to myself. And by what other power but the universal power of Nature, since I am a part of Nature? The time of my origin, and the qualities with which I originated, were determined by this universal power of Nature; and all the forms, under which these inborn ground-qualities have since manifested themselves, and will manifest themselves, so long as I shall continue to be, are determined by the same power of Nature. It was impossible that another than me should have originated in my place. It is impossible that the being which has so originated, can, in any moment of his existence, be other than he is and shall be.

* * * * * * *

It is true I am conscious of myself, in my innermost being, as self-subsisting and free in various particulars of my life. But this consciousness may be easily explained by the principles which have been established, and be made to appear perfectly consistent with the conclusions which have just been drawn. My immediate consciousness,—the real apperception,—does not extend beyond myself and my conditions. I know nothing immediately, except my own states. Whatever I am enabled to know, beyond these, I know only by inference, in the same way in which I have just now inferred original forces in Nature, which, by no means, come within the circle of my perceptions. But I—that which I call me,—my person—am not the man-making power of Nature itself, but only one of its manifestations. And only of this manifestation am I conscious, as of myself; not of that power. That is only an inference to which I am led by the necessity of accounting for my existence. This manifestation, however, in its proper essence, is indeed the product of an original and self-subsisting power; and must be found such in consciousness. Hence I appear to myself altogether as a *self-subsisting* being. For the same reason, I appear to myself free, in particular passages of my life, when these passages are manifestations of that self-subsisting power which has fallen to my share as an individual. On the other hand, I appear to myself restrained and limited, when, owing to a concatenation of external circumstances, originating in time,—not, however, lying in the original determination of my individuality,— I cannot do that which I might do, so far as my individual capacity is concerned. I appear to myself to be coerced when this individual capacity is compelled, by a superior power opposed to it, to manifest itself contrary to its own law.

Give a tree consciousness, and let it grow unobstructed, spread forth its boughs and produce leaves, buds, blossoms, fruits, according to its kind. It certainly will not feel itself restrained, because it happens to be a tree, and one of this particular species, and this particular individual of that species. It will feel itself free, because, in all those manifestations, it does nothing but what its nature requires. It will not choose to do anything else, because it can only choose what that nature requires. But let its growth be restrained by unfavorable weather, by want of nourishment, or other causes: it will feel itself limited and thwarted, because an impulse, which actually resides in its nature, is not satisfied. Bind its freely on all sides striving limbs to a trellis; force strange shoots upon it by grafting; and it will feel itself coerced in its action. Its limbs indeed continue to grow, but not in that direction which its forces would have taken, if left to themselves. It produces fruits, indeed, but not those which its original nature required. In my *immediate consciousness* I appear to myself free. When I reflect on the whole of Nature, I find that freedom is absolutely impossible. The former must be subordinated to the latter, for only by means of the latter can it be explained.

What high satisfaction does this system give to my understanding! What order, what firm connection, what an easy oversight does it introduce into all my knowledge. Consciousness, according to this system, is not that stranger in Nature, whose connection with being is so incomprehensible. It is at home there, and even constitutes one of Nature's necessary conditions. Nature rises gradually in the fixed gradation of her productions. In rude matter she is simple being. In organization she returns into herself in order to act upon herself internally;—in the plant to shape herself, in the animal to move herself, and in man, as her highest masterpiece, she returns into herself to behold and contemplate herself. She redoubles herself, as it were, in him, and from simple being, becomes being and consciousness in one.

It is easy to explain, in this connexion, how I should know of my own being and its conditions. My being and knowing have one common ground,—my nature in general. There is in me no being which does not know of itself, for the very reason that it is *my* being.

* * * * * * *

In each individual, Nature beholds herself from a different point of view. I call myself *I*, and you *you*. You call *yourself* I, and *me* you. I am external to you, as you are external to me. Of that which is external to me, I comprehend first my nearest limits. You comprehend your nearest limits. Starting from this point we proceed, each through the next succeeding links, and pass on. We describe very different series, which here and there perhaps intersect each other, but nowhere run side by side, in the same direction. All possible individuals, and, accordingly, all possible view-points of consciousness, become actual. This consciousness of all individuals combined, constitutes the perfected self-consciousness of the universe. And there is no other; for only in the individual, is there perfect determinateness and actuality.

The testimony of each individual consciousness is infallible, provided only, it is actually the consciousness hitherto described. For this consciousness unfolds itself out of the entire course of Nature, proceeding according to fixed laws; and Nature cannot contradict herself. Wherever there is a mental representation, there must be also a being corresponding thereto. For the representations in the mind are generated only contemporaneously with the being which corresponds to them. In each individual his particular consciousness is throughout determined, for it is a product of his own nature. No one has other cognitions, or has them in any other degree of vividness than he actually has. The *contents* of his cognitions are determined by the standpoint which he occupies in the universe. Their clearness and vividness are determined by the more or less of energy, with which the power of Humanity can manifest itself in his person. Give Nature a single condition of a single person, be it never so insignificant, the course of a single muscle, the flexure of a hair, and she would tell you—if she possessed general consciousness, and could answer —all the thoughts which this person will think during the whole period of his conscious existence.

Equally intelligible, according to this system, is that well-known phenomenon in our consciousness which we call the **will**. A volition is the immediate consciousness of the activity of our internal powers of Nature. The immediate consciousness of a striving of these powers, which is not yet effective, because hampered by opposing powers, is conscious inclination or desire. The struggle of conflicting powers is irresolution; the victory gained by one of them, a resolve of the will. If the endeavoring power is merely one which is common to us with the plant or the brute, there has already ensued, in our inner being, a division and a degradation. The craving is not consistent with our rank in the order of things, but beneath it; and may, with propriety, be called, according to a certain custom of speech, a low one. If that which endeavors, is the whole undivided power of our Humanity, then the craving is in harmony with our nature, and may be called a higher. The endeavor of this latter power, considered generally, may properly be termed a moral law. Its effective action is a virtuous will, and the act which flows from it, virtue. The triumph of the former, without harmony with the latter, is want of virtue. Its victory over the latter, and against the opposition of the latter, is vice.

The power which overcomes, in each case, overcomes necessarily. Its overweight is determined by the connection of the universe. Accordingly, the virtue, the want of virtue, the vice, of each individual, is also irrevocably determined by the same connection. Give Nature again, the course of a muscle, the flexure of a hair, in a certain individual, and if she could think in the whole, and could answer your inquiry, she would disclose to you all the good actions and all the evil actions of his life, from the beginning to the end. But virtue does not therefore cease to be virtue, and vice vice. The virtuous is a noble, the vicious, an ignoble and abominable nature; but one which necessarily flows from the connection of the universe.

There is remorse. It is the consciousness of the still continuing struggle of Humanity in me, even after it has been vanquished; combined with the unpleasant feeling, that it has been vanquished. A disquieting, but still a precious pledge of our nobler nature. From this consciousness of our radical impulse, springs *conscience* also, and its greater or less acuteness and sensitiveness,—down to the absolute want of it, —in different individuals. The less noble are incapable of remorse, because Humanity, in them, has not even power enough to contend against the lower appetites. Reward and punishment are the natural consequences of virtue and vice, which tend to produce new virtue and new vice. By often and important victories, namely, our individual power is extended and confirmed. From want of effectiveness and from frequent defeats it becomes weaker and weaker.

Only the ideas of blame and imputation have no meaning, except in relation to external justice. He has incurred blame, and to him his transgression is imputed, who forces Society to use external, artificial forces, in order to hinder the activity of those impulses which are prejudicial to the general safety.

My examination is concluded, and my desire for knowledge satisfied. I know what I am in general, and wherein consists the essence of my kind. I am a manifestation, conditioned by the entire universe, of a self-determining power of Nature. My particular, personal conditions it is impossible to discover *by means of their causes,* for I cannot penetrate into the interior of Nature. But I become directly conscious of them in myself. I know very well what I am at the present moment. I can remember pretty well what I was formerly, and I shall certainly experience what I am to be when I am it.

It cannot occur to me to make any use of this discovery, in action. For it is not I that act, but Nature acts in me. I cannot think of undertaking to make myself aught else than I am destined by Nature to be. For it is not I that make myself, but Nature that makes me, and all that I shall be. I may repent and be glad and make good resolutions, (although strictly speaking *I* cannot even do this, since everything must come to me of itself, if it is destined to come at all :) but I may be sure that all my repentance and all my resolutions cannot effect the least alteration in that which I am, once for all, destined to be. I am subject to the inexorable power of strict Necessity. If that determines me to be a fool or vicious, without doubt, I shall be a fool and vicious. If that determines me to be wise and good, without doubt, I shall be wise and good. It is not Necessity's fault or merit, nor mine. Necessity is subject to its own laws, and I to its. Since I am aware of this, it will be best for my peace of mind that I should subordinate my wishes also to this power, to which my being is, once for all, entirely subject.

O, these opposing wishes! For why should I longer conceal the sorrow, the abhorrence, the terror which has seized my inner man, from the moment that I perceived how the inquiry must terminate. I had made a sacred covenant with myself, that inclination should have no influence on the direction of my thought; and indeed I have, consciously, allowed it none. But shall I not therefore, at the conclusion, confess to myself, that this result contradicts my deepest, innermost presentiments, wishes, demands? And how can I, notwithstanding the correctness and the trenchant sharpness of the proofs which appear to me in this deliberation, believe in an interpretation of my existence which so decidedly conflicts with the most intimate root of that existence, and with the ends for whose sake alone I wish to be, and without which, I count my existence a curse?

Wherefore must my heart sorrow and be rent for that which so completely satisfies my understanding? While nothing in Nature contradicts itself, is man alone a contradictory being?—or, perhaps, not man, but only I and those who resemble me. Ought I perhaps to have gone on in the pleasant conceit which environed me, to have kept within the circle of my being's immediate consciousness, and never to have raised the question concerning the grounds of that being, the answer to which has now rendered me miserable? But if my answer is correct, I could but raise that question. It was not I that raised it, but thinking Nature in me. I was doomed to misery, and I mourn in vain the lost innocence of my mind, which can never return.

But courage! Let everything else forsake me, if only this forsake me not. For the sake of a mere preference, however deep in my interior that preference may lie, and however sacred it may seem to me, I cannot indeed relinquish what follows from incontrovertible reasons. But perhaps I have erred in my investigation. Perhaps I have but half considered the sources from which I was compelled to draw in conducting it, and have looked at them only from one side. I ought to repeat the investigation from the opposite end, that I may have a point from which to begin it. What is it then that so mightily repels and offends me in that decision? What is it that I wished to find instead of it? Let me, before all things, make clear to myself that preference to which I appeal.

That I should be destined to be wise or good, a fool or vicious, that I should be unable to effect any change in that destination, that I should be without merit in the former case, and without blame in the latter,—this it was that filled me with loathing and horror. That ground of my being and of the conditions of my being external to myself, whose manifestation, in turn, is determined by other grounds external to itself,—that it was that so violently repelled me. That freedom which is not my own, but belongs to a foreign power without me, and which, even in that power, is only a conditioned, only a half-freedom,—that it was that failed to satisfy me. *I myself,* that of which I am conscious as of a self, as of my own person, and which, in that system, appears only as the manifestation of a higher power, I myself would be self-subsisting, I would be something, not in another and by means of another, but for myself. I would be, in myself, as such, the ultimate ground of my conditions. The rank, which, in that system, is occupied by an original power of Nature, I would occupy, myself; but with this difference, that the mode in which I manifest myself, shall not be determined by foreign powers. I would possess an inward power peculiar to myself, of manifesting myself in an infinite variety of ways, like those powers of Nature; a power which should manifest itself exactly as it does, for no other reason than *because* it manifests itself thus; and not, like those powers of Nature, because it is subject to such or such external conditions.

Where now, according to this my wish, should be the proper seat and centre of that peculiar power of the *I?* Evidently, not in my body, which I am quite willing should pass—at least so far as its being is concerned, if not in its ulterior conditions—for a manifestation of the powers of Nature; neither in my sensual appetites, which I regard as a referring of those powers to my consciousness: consequently, in my thinking and willing. I would will with freedom, according to a freely proposed aim. And this will, as absolute, ultimate ground, determined by no possible higher than itself, should move and shape, first my body, and then, by means of that, the world which surrounds me. My active, natural power should be subject only to my will, and not be put in motion by anything else but that. So should it be. There should be a supreme good, according to spiritual laws. I would be able to seek this with freedom until I find it, to acknowledge it as such when I have found it; and it should be my fault if I found it not. This supreme good I would be able to will, simply because I will it; and if I willed anything else in its stead, it should be my fault.

* * * * *

Freedom, such as that which has been demanded above, is conceivable only in Intelligences; but without doubt, it is conceivable in them. On this supposition, also, man as well as Nature is perfectly intelligible. My body and my power of operating in the world of the senses, in this as in the other system, are a manifestation of limited natural powers; and my natural inclinations are the relations of this manifestation to my consciousness. The mere cognition of that which exists without my action, originates in the same way, on the supposition of freedom, as in the opposite system; and up to this point they both agree. But according to that,—and here begins the conflict of the two systems—according to that, my capacity of sensuous action continues subject to Nature, and is still put in motion by the same power which produced it; and thought has nothing to do in the matter but to look on. According to this, on the contrary, this capacity, when once it exists, is under the dominion of a power exalted above all Nature, and entirely independent of Nature's laws, the power of conceived purposes and of the will. Thought in this case is not a mere spectator, but itself the original of the action. There, it is external powers, invisible to me, which put an end to my irresolution and limit my activity, as well as the immediate consciousness of that activity, my will, to a single point; just as the activity of a plant, undetermined in itself, is limited. Here, it is *I* myself, independent and free from the influence of all external forces, who put an end to my irresolution and determine myself by a recognition, freely produced in myself, of the supreme good.

Which of these two opinions shall I embrace? Am I free and self-subsisting, or am I nothing in myself, and merely the apparition of a foreign power?

* * * * * *

The system of liberty satisfies; the opposite deadens and annihilates my heart. To stand there cold and dead, a mere spectator of changing events, an idle mirror of fleeting forms,— such an existence is intolerable to me. I scorn and curse it. I would love, I would lose myself in sympathy; I would rejoice and be sad. * * * I would do everything for the best; would rejoice in myself when I have done right, and would sorrow for myself when I have done wrong. And even this sorrow should be sweet to me, for it is interest in myself, and pledge of future amendment. Only in love there is life; without it is death and annihilation.

But cold and impertinent the opposite system steps in and mocks at this love. I am not and I act not, when I listen to that. The object of my intensest desire is a phantom of the brain, a palpably demonstrable, coarse illusion. Instead of me there is and acts a foreign, to me quite unknown power; and it becomes a matter of perfect indifference to me how that power may unfold itself. Ashamed I stand there, with my heartfelt affection and my good will, and blush at that which I know to be the best in me, and for whose sake alone I wish to be, as it were a laughable folly. My holiest is delivered up to mockery. * * * *

* * * The same system, dry and heartless, but inexhaustible in explaining, explains even this, my interest in liberty, my abhorrence for the opposite opinion. It explains everything which I bring forward against it out of my consciousness; and as often as I say it is so and so, it answers me in the same dry and imperturbable manner: "That is precisely what I say too; and I tell thee, moreover, the reasons why it must necessarily be so." * * * "Thou admittest, without controversy, that notwithstanding there is, in the plant, an instinct peculiar to itself to grow and shape itself, yet the determinate activity of this instinct depends on forces external to itself. Give this plant consciousness for a moment, and it will feel in itself this instinct to grow, with interest and love. Convince it by arguments drawn from reason, that this instinct cannot effect the least thing for itself, but that the measure of its manifestation is always determined by something external to itself, and perhaps it will talk exactly as thou hast just been talking. It will behave in a manner which may be pardoned in a plant, but which is altogether unbecoming in thee, as a higher product of Nature, capable of embracing the whole of Nature in thy thought."

What can I object to such representations? * * * Undecided I cannot remain. All my peace and all my dignity depends on the answer to this question. Just as impossible is it for me to come to a decision. I have absolutely no ground for deciding, one way or the other.

Intolerable state of uncertainty and irresolution, into which I have been forced by the best and most courageous resolve of my life! What power can deliver me from thee? What power can deliver me from myself?

FROM THE THIRD BOOK.
FAITH.

* * * "Not merely to know, but to act according to thy knowledge, is thy destination." So says the voice which cries to me aloud from my innermost soul, so soon as I collect and give heed to myself, for a moment. "Not idly to inspect and contemplate thyself, nor to brood over devout sensations;—no! thou existest to act. Thine act, and only thine act, determines thy worth." * * * * * *

* * * Shall I refuse obedience to that inward voice? I will not do it. I will give myself voluntarily the determination which that impulse imputes to me. And I will embrace, together with this resolution, the thought of its reality and truth, and of the reality of all that it presupposes. I will hold to the stand-point of natural thinking, which this impulse assigns to me, and renounce all those morbid speculations and refinements of the understanding which alone could make me doubt its truth. I understand thee now, sublime Spirit!* I have found the organ with which I embrace this reality, and with it, probably, all other reality. Knowledge is not that organ. No knowledge can ground and demonstrate itself. Every knowledge presupposes a higher as its ground, and this upward process has no end. It is Faith, that voluntary reposing in the view which naturally presents itself, because it is the only one by which we can fulfil our destination,—this it is that first gives assent to knowledge, and exalts to certainty and conviction what would otherwise be mere illusion. It is not knowledge, but a determination of the will to let knowledge pass for valid. I hold fast, then, forever to this expression. It is not a mere difference of terms, but a real deep-grounded distinction, exercising a very important influence on my whole mental disposition. All my conviction is only faith, and is derived from a disposition of the mind, not from the understanding. * * *

* * * There is only one point to which I have to direct incessantly all my thoughts: What I must do, and how I shall most effectu-

---
* This refers to the second Book, which takes the form of a dialogue between the inquirer and a Spirit.

---

ally accomplish what is required of me. All my thinking must have reference to my doing, —must be considered as means, however remote, to this end. Otherwise, it is an empty, aimless sport, a waste of time and power, and perversion of a noble faculty which was given me for a very different purpose.

I may hope, I may promise myself with certainty, that when I think after this manner, my thinking shall be attended with practical results. Nature, in which I am to act, is not a foreign being, created without regard to me. It is fashioned by the laws of my own thought, and must surely coincide with them. It must be everywhere transparent, cognisable, permeable to me, in its innermost recesses. Everywhere it expresses nothing but relations and references of myself to myself; and as certainly as I may hope to know myself, so certainly I may promise myself that I shall be able to explore that. Let me but seek what I have to seek, and I shall find. Let me but inquire whereof I have to inquire, and I shall receive answer.

I.

That voice in my interior, which I believe, and for the sake of which I believe all else that I believe, commands me not merely to act in general. That is impossible. All these general propositions are formed only by my voluntary attention and reflection directed to various facts; but they do not express a single fact of themselves. This voice of my conscience prescribes to me with certainty, in each particular situation of my existence, what I must do and what I must avoid in that situation. It accompanies me, if I will but listen to it with attention, through all the events of my life, and never refuses its reward where I am called to act. It establishes immediate conviction, and irresistibly compels my assent. It is impossible for me to contend against it.

To hearken to that voice, honestly and undisturbedly, without fear and without useless speculation, to obey it,—this is my sole destination, this the whole aim of my existence. My life ceases to be an empty sport, without truth or meaning. There is something to be done, simply because it must be done. That that which conscience demands of me in particular,—of me who have come into this situation,—may be fulfilled,—for this purpose alone do I exist. To perceive it, I have understanding; to do it, power.

Through these commandments of conscience alone come truth and reality into my conceptions. I cannot refuse attention and obedience to them, without renouncing my destination.

I cannot, therefore, withhold my belief in the reality which they bring before me, without, at the same time, denying my destination. It is absolutely true, without farther examination and demonstration,—it is the first true, and the ground of all other truth and certainty,—that I must obey that voice. Consequently, according to this way of thinking, everything becomes true and real for me, which the possibility of such obedience presupposes.

There hover before me appearances in space, to which I transfer the idea of my own being. I represent them to myself as beings of my own kind. Speculation, carried out, has taught me or will teach me that these supposed rational beings, without me, are only products of my own conception; that I am necessitated, once for all, by laws of thought which can be shown to exist, to represent the idea of myself out of myself, and that, according to the same laws, this representation can be transferred only to certain determinate intuitions. But the voice of my conscience cries to me: "Whatever these beings may be in and for themselves, thou shalt treat them as subsisting for themselves, as free, self-existent beings, entirely independent of thyself. Take it for granted that they are capable of proposing to themselves aims independently of thee, by themselves alone. Never disturb the execution of these, their designs, but further them rather, with all thy might. Respect their liberty. Embrace with love their objects as thine own." So must I act. And to such action shall, will, and must all my thinking be directed, if I have but formed the purpose to obey the voice of my conscience. Accordingly, I shall ever consider those beings, as beings subsisting for themselves, and forming and accomplishing aims independently of me. From this stand-point, I cannot consider them in any other light; and the above-mentioned speculation will vanish like an empty dream before my eyes. "I *think* of them as beings of my own species:" said I just now; but strictly, it is not a thought by which they are first represented to me as such. It is the voice of conscience; the command: "here restrain thy liberty, here suppose and respect foreign aims;" this it is which is first translated into the thought: "here is surely and truly, subsisting for itself, a being like me." To consider them otherwise, I must first deny the voice of my conscience in life, and forget it in speculation.

There hover before me other appearances, which I do not consider as beings like myself, but as irrational objects. Speculation finds it easy to show how the conception of such objects develops itself purely from my power of conception, and its necessary modes of action. But I embrace these same things also with necessity and craving and fruition. It is not the conception, no, it is hunger and thirst and the satisfaction of these that makes anything food and drink to me. Of course, I am constrained to believe in the reality of that which threatens my sensuous existence, or which alone can preserve it. Conscience comes in, at once hallowing and limiting this impulse of Nature. "Thou shalt preserve, exercise and strengthen thyself, and thy sensuous power: for this sensuous power forms a part of the calculation, in the plan of reason. But thou canst preserve it only by a suitable use, agreeable to the peculiar interior laws of such matters. And beside thyself, there are also others like thee, whose powers are calculated upon like thine own, and who can be preserved only in the same way. Allow to them the same use of their portion which it is commanded thee to make of thine own portion. Respect what comes to them, as their property. Use what comes to thee in a suitable manner, as thy property." So must I act, and I must think conformably to such action. Accordingly, I am necessitated to regard these things as standing under their own natural laws, independent of me, but which I am capable of knowing; that is, to ascribe to them an existence independent of myself. I am constrained to believe in such laws, and it becomes my business to ascertain them; and empty speculation vanishes like mist when the warming sun appears.

In short, there is for me, in general, no pure, naked existence, with which I have no concern, and which I contemplate solely for the sake of contemplation. Whatever exists for me, exists only by virtue of its relation to me. But there is everywhere but one relation to me possible, and all the rest are but varieties of this; that is my destination as a moral agent. My world is the object and sphere of my duties, and absolutely nothing else. There is no other world, no other attributes of my world, for me. My collective capacity, and all finite capacity is insufficient to comprehend any other. Everything which exists for me forces its existence and its reality upon me, solely by means of this relation; and only by means of this relation, do I grasp it. There is utterly wanting in me an organ for any other existence.

To the question, whether then in fact such a world exists as I represent to myself? I can answer nothing certain, nothing which is raised above all doubt, but this: I have assuredly and truly these definite duties, which represent themselves to me as duties toward such and such persons, concerning such and such objects. These definite duties I cannot represent to myself otherwise, nor can I execute them otherwise, than as lying within the sphere of such a world as I conceive. Even he who has never thought of his moral destination, if any such there could be, or who, if he has thought about it generally, has never entertained the slightest purpose of ever, in the indefinite future, fulfilling it; even he derives his world of the senses and his belief in the reality of such a world, no otherwise than from his idea of a moral world. If he does not embrace it with the idea of his duties, he certainly does so with the requisition of his rights. What he does not require of himself, he yet requires of others, in relation to himself; that they treat him with care and consideration, agreeably to his nature, not as an irrational thing, but as a free and self-subsisting being. And so he is constrained, in order that they may comply with this demand, to think of them also, as rational, free, and self-subsisting, and independent of the mere force of Nature. And even though he should never propose to himself any other aim in the use and fruition of the objects which surround him, than that of enjoying them, he still demands this enjoyment as a right, of which others must leave him in undisturbed possession. Accordingly, he embraces even the irrational world of the senses with a moral idea. No one who lives a conscious life can renounce these claims to be respected as rational and self-subsisting. And with these claims at least there connects itself in his soul, a seriousness, an abandonment of doubt, a belief in reality; if not with the acknowledgment of a moral law in his interior. Do but assail him who denies his own moral destination and your existence and the existence of a corporeal world, except in the way of experiment, to try what speculation can do,—assail him actively, carry his principles into life, and act as if he either did not exist, or as if he were a piece of rude matter, and he will soon forget the joke; he will become seriously angry with you, he will seriously reprove you for treating him so, and maintain that you ought not and must not do so to him; and, in this way, he will practically admit, that you possess indeed the power of acting upon him, that he exists, that you exist, and that there exists *a medium through which you act upon him;* and that you have at least duties toward him.

Hence it is not the action of supposed objects without us, which exist for us only, and for which we exist only, so far as we already know of them, just as little is it an empty fashioning, by means of our imagination and our thinking,—whose products would appear to us as such, as empty pictures;—it is not these, but the necessary faith in our liberty and our power, in our veritable action and in certain laws of human action, which serves as the foundation of all consciousness of a reality without us, a consciousness which is itself but a belief, since it rests on a belief, but one which follows necessarily from that belief. We are compelled to assume that we act in general, and that we ought to act in a certain way; we are compelled to assume a certain sphere of such action: this sphere is the truly and actually existing world as we find it. And *vice versa,* this world is absolutely nothing but that sphere, and by no means extends beyond it. The consciousness of the actual world proceeds from the necessity of action, and not the reverse,—i. e. the necessity of action from the consciousness of such a world. The necessity is first not the consciousness; that is derived. We do not act because we agnize, but we agnize because we are destined to act. Practical reason is the root of all reason. The laws of action for rational beings are *immediately* certain; their world is certain, *only because they are certain.* Were we to renounce the former, the world, and, with it, we ourselves, should sink into absolute nothing. We raise ourselves out of *this nothing,* and sustain ourselves above this nothing, solely by means of our morality.

II.

* * * * * * * *

When I contemplate the world as it is, independently of any injunction, there manifests itself in my interior the wish, the longing, no! not a longing merely,—the absolute demand for a better world. I cast a glance at the relations of men to each other and to Nature, at the weakness of their powers, at the strength of their appetites and passions. It cries to me irresistibly from my innermost soul: " thus it cannot possibly be destined always to remain. It must, O! it must all become other and better !"

I can in nowise imagine to myself the present condition of man as that which is designed to endure. I cannot imagine it to be his whole and final destination. If so, then would everything be dream and delusion, and it would not be worth the trouble to have lived and to have taken part in this ever-recurring, unproductive and unmeaning game. Only so far as I can regard this condition as the means of something better, as a point of transition to a higher and more perfect, does it acquire any value for me. Not on its own account, but on account of something better for which it prepares the way, can I bear it, honor it, and joyfully fulfil my part in it. My mind can find no place, nor rest a moment, in the present; it is irresistibly repelled by it. My whole life streams irrepressibly on toward the future and better.

Am I only to eat and to drink that I may hunger and thirst again, and again eat and drink, until the grave, yawning beneath my feet, swallows me up, and I myself spring up as food from the ground ? Am I to beget beings like myself, that they also may eat and drink and die, and leave behind them beings like themselves, who shall do the same that I have done ? To what purpose this circle which perpetually returns into itself; this game for ever re-commencing, after the same manner, in which everything is born but to perish, and perishes but to be born again as it was ? This monster which forever devours itself, that it may produce itself again, and which produces itself that it may again devour itself?

Never can this be the destination of my being and of all being. There must be something which exists because it has been brought forth, and which now remains and can never be brought forth again, after it has been brought forth once. And this, that is permanent, must beget itself amid the mutations of the perishing, and continue amid those mutations, and be borne along unhurt upon the waves of time.

As yet our race wrings with difficulty its sustenance and its continuance from opposing Nature. As yet the larger portion of mankind are bowed down their whole life long by hard labor, to procure sustenance for themselves and the few who think for them. Immortal spirits are compelled to fix all their thinking and scheming, and all their efforts, on the soil which bears them nourishment. It often comes to pass as yet, that when the laborer has ended, and promises himself, for his pains, the continuance of his own existence and of those pains; that then hostile elements destroy in a moment what he had been slowly and carefully preparing for years, and delivers up the industrious pains-taking man, without any fault of his own, to hunger and misery. It often comes to pass as yet, that inundations, storm-winds, volcanoes, desolate whole countries, and mingle works which bear the impress of a rational mind, as well as their authors, with the wild chaos of death and destruction. Diseases still hurry men into a premature grave, men in the bloom of their powers, and children whose existence passes away without fruit or result. The pestilence still stalks through blooming states, and leaves the few who escape it, bereaved and alone, deprived of the accustomed aid of their companions; and does all in its power to give back to the wilderness the land which the industry of man had already conquered for its own.

So it is, but so it cannot surely have been intended always to remain. No work which bears the impress of reason, and which was undertaken for the purpose of extending the dominion of reason, can be utterly lost in the progress of the times. The sacrifices which the irregular violence of Nature draws from reason, must at least weary, satisfy and reconcile that violence. The force which has caused injury by acting without rule, cannot be intended to do so more in that way, it cannot be destined to renew itself; it must be used up, from this time forth and forever, by that one outbreak. All those outbreaks of rude force, before which human power vanishes into nothing,—those desolating hurricanes, earthquakes, volcanoes, can be nothing else but the final struggle of the wild mass against the lawfully progressive, life-giving, systematic course to which it is compelled, contrary to its own impulse. They can be nothing but the last concussive strokes in the formation of our globe, now about to perfect itself. That opposition must gradually become weaker, and at last exhausted, since, in the lawful course of things, there can be nothing that should renew its power. That formation must at last be perfected, and our destined abode complete. Nature must gradually come into a condition in which we can count with certainty upon her equal step, and in which her power shall keep unaltered a determinate relation with that power which is destined to govern it, that is, the human. So far as this relation already exists, and the systematic cultivation of Nature has gained firm footing; the workmanship of man, by its mere existence and its effects, independent of any design on the part of the author, is destined to react upon Nature, and to represent in her a new and life-giving principle. Cultivated lands are to quicken and mitigate the sluggish, hostile atmosphere of the eternal forests, wildernesses, and morasses. Well-ordered and diversified culture is to diffuse through the air a new principle of life and fructification; and the sun to send forth its most animating beams into that atmosphere which is breathed by a healthy, industrious, and ingenious people. Science, awakened, at first, by the pressure of necessity, shall hereafter penetrate deliberately and calmly into the unchangeable laws of Nature, overlook her whole power, and learn to calculate her possible developments;—shall form for itself a new Nature in idea, attach itself closely to the living and active, and follow hard upon her footsteps. And all knowledge which reason has wrung from Nature, shall be preserved in the course of the times, and become the foundation of further knowledge, for the common understanding of our race. Thus shall Nature become ever more transparent and penetrable to human perception, even to its innermost secrets. And human power, enlightened and fortified with its inventions, shall rule her with ease, and peacefully maintain the conquest once effected. By degrees, there shall be needed no greater outlay of mechanical labor than the human body requires for its development, cultivation and health. And this labor shall cease to be a burden; for the rational being is not destined to be a bearer of burdens.

But it is not Nature, it is liberty itself, that occasions the most numerous and the most fearful disorders among our kind. The direst enemy of man is man.

* * * * * *

It is the destination of our race to unite in one body, thoroughly acquainted with itself in all its parts, and uniformly cultivated in all. Nature, and even the passions and vices of mankind, have, from the beginning, drifted towards this goal. A large part of the road which leads to it is already put behind us, and we may count with certainty that this goal, which is the condition of further, united progress, will be reached in due season. Do not ask History whether mankind, on the whole, have grown more purely moral! They have grown to extended, comprehensive, forceful acts of arbitrary will; but it was almost a necessity of their condition that they should direct that will exclusively to evil.

Neither ask History whether the aesthetic education and the culture of the understanding, of the fore-world, concentrated upon a few single points, may not have far exceeded, in degree, that of modern times. It might be that the answer would put us to shame, and that the human race would appear, in this regard, not to have advanced, but to have lost ground.

But ask History in what period the existing culture was most widely diffused and distributed among the greatest number of individuals? Undoubtedly, it will be found, that from the beginning of history down to our own day, the few light-points of culture have extended their rays farther and farther from their centres, have seized one individual after another, and one people after another; and that this diffusion of culture is still going on before our eyes.

And this was the first goal of Humanity, on its infinite path. Until this is attained, until the existing culture of an age is diffused over the whole habitable globe, and our race is made capable of the most unlimited communication with itself, one nation, one quarter of the globe must await the other, on their common path, and each must bring its centuries of apparent stationariness or retrogradation, as a sacrifice to the common bond, for the sake of which, alone, they themselves exist.

When this first goal shall be attained, when everything useful that has been discovered at one end of the earth, shall immediately be made known and imparted to all, then Humanity, without interruption, without cessation, and without retrocession, with united force, and with one step, shall raise itself up to a degree of culture which we want power to conceive.

* * * * * *

* * * By the institution of this one true State, and the firm establishment of this internal peace, external war also, at least with true States, will, at the same time, be rendered impossible. Even for the sake of its own advantage,—in order that no thought of injustice, plunder and violence may spring up in its own subjects, and no possible opportunity be afforded them for any gain, except by labor and industry, in the sphere assigned by law;—every State must forbid as strictly, must hinder as carefully, must compensate as exactly, and punish as severely, an injury done to the citizen of a neighbor State, as if it were inflicted upon a fellow-citizen. This law respecting the security of its neighbors is necessary to every State which is not a community of robbers. And herewith the possibility of every just complaint, of one State against another, and every case of necessary defence is done away.

There are no necessary, continuous, immediate relations of States, as such, to each other, that could engender warfare. As a general rule, it is only through the relations of single citizens of one State with the citizens of another,—it is only in the person of one of its members, that a State can be injured. But this injury will be instantly redressed, and the offended State satisfied. * * * * * *

* * * That a whole nation should determine, for the sake of plunder, to attack a neighboring country with war, is impossible. Since, in a State, in which all are equal, the plunder would not become the booty of a few, but must be divided equally among all, and so divided, the portion of each individual would never repay him for the trouble of a war. Only, then, when the advantage to be gained falls to the lot of a few oppressors, but the disadvantages, the trouble, the cost fall upon a countless army of slaves,—only then is a war of plunder possible or conceivable. Accordingly, these States have no war to fear from States like themselves, but only from savages or barbarians, tempted to prey by want of skill to enrich themselves by industry; or from nations of slaves, who are driven by their masters to plunder, of which they are to enjoy no part themselves. As to the first, each single State is undoubtedly superior to them in strength, by virtue of the arts of culture. As to the last, the common advantage of all the States will lead them to strengthen themselves by union with each other. No free State can reasonably tolerate, in its immediate vicinity, Polities whose rulers find their advantage in subjecting neighbor nations, and which, therefore, by their mere existence, perpetually threaten their neighbors' peace. Care for their own security will oblige all free States to convert all around them into free States like themselves, and thus, for the sake of their own well-being, to extend the dominion of culture to the savages, and that of liberty to the slave nations round about them. And so, when once a few free States have been formed, the empire of culture, of liberty, and, with that, of universal peace, will gradually embrace the globe. * * *

* * * In this only true State, all temptation to evil in general, and even the possibility of deliberately determining upon an evil act, will be cut off, and man be persuaded as powerfully as he can be to direct his will to the good. There is no man who loves evil because it is evil. He loves in it only the advantages and enjoyments which it promises, and which, in the present state of Humanity, it, for the most part, actually affords. As long as this state continues, as long as a price is set upon vice, a thorough reformation of mankind, in the whole, is scarcely to be hoped for. But in a civil Polity such as it should be, such as reason demands, and such as the thinker easily describes, although as yet he nowhere finds it, and such as will necessarily shape itself with the first nation that is truly disenthralled;—in such a Polity evil will offer no advantages, but, on the contrary, the most certain disadvantages; and the aberration of self love into acts of injustice, will be suppressed by self-love itself. According to infallible regulations, in such a State, all taking advantage and oppressing of others, every act of self-aggrandizement at another's expense, is not only sure to be in vain,—labor lost,—but it reacts upon the author, and he himself inevitably incurs the evil which he would inflict upon others. Within his own State and without it, on the whole face of the earth, he finds no one whom he can injure with impunity. It is not, however, to be expected that any one will resolve upon evil merely for evil's sake, notwithstanding he cannot accomplish it, and nothing but his own injury can result from the attempt. The use of liberty for evil ends is done away. Man must either resolve to renounce his liberty entirely,—to become, with patience, a passive wheel in the great machine of the whole,—or he must apply his liberty to that which is good.

And thus, then, in a soil so prepared, the good will easily flourish. When selfish aims no longer divide mankind, and their powers can no longer be exercised in destroying one another in battle, nothing will remain to them but to turn their united force against the common and only adversary which yet remains, resisting, uncultivated Nature. No longer separated by private ends, they will necessarily unite in one common end, and there will grow up a body everywhere animated by one spirit and one love. Every disadvantage of the individual, since it can no longer be a benefit to any one, becomes an injury to the whole, and to each particular member of the same; and is felt in each member with equal pain, and with equal activity redressed. Every advance which one man makes, human nature, in its entireness, makes with him.

Here, where the petty, narrow self of the person is already annihilated by the Polity, every one loves every other one truly, as himself, as a component part of that great *Self* which alone remains to his love, and of which he is nothing *but* a component part, that only through the Whole can gain or lose. Here the conflict of evil with good is done away, for no evil can any longer spring up. The contest of the good with each other, even concerning the good, vanishes, now that it has become easy to them to love the good for its own sake, and not for their sakes, as the authors of it;—now that the only interest they can have is that it come to pass, that truth be discovered, that the good deed be executed; not by whom it is accomplished. Here every one is prepared to join his power to that of his neighbor, and to subordinate it to that of his neighbor. Whoever, in the judgment of all, shall accomplish the best, in the best way, him all will support, and partake with equal joy in his success.

This is the aim of earthly existence which Reason sets before us, and for the sure attainment of which, Reason vouches. It is not a goal for which we are to strive merely that our faculties may be exercised on given objects, but which we must relinquish all hope of realizing. It shall and must be realized. At some time or other, this goal must be attained; as surely as there is a world of the senses, and a race of reasonable beings in time, for whom no serious and rational object can be imagined but this, and whose existence is made intelligible by this alone. Unless the whole life of man is to be considered as the sport of an evil Spirit, who implanted this ineradicable striving after the imperishable in the breasts of poor wretches, merely that he might enjoy their ceaseless struggle after that which unceasingly flees from them, their still repeated grasping after that which still eludes their grasp, their restless driving about in an ever-returning circle;—and laugh at their earnestness in this senseless sport:—unless the wise man, who must soon see through this game, and be tired of his own part in it, is to throw away his life, and the moment of awakening reason is to be the moment of earthly death;—that goal must be attained. O! it is attainable in life and by means of life; for Reason commands me to live. It is attainable, for I am.

III.

But how, when it is attained? when Humanity shall stand at the goal? What then? There is no higher condition on earth than that. The generation which first attains to it can do nothing farther than to persist in it, and maintain it with all their powers; die and leave descendants who shall do the same that they have done, and who, in their turn, shall leave descendants that shall do the same. Humanity would then stand still in its course. Therefore, its earthly goal cannot be its highest goal. This earthly goal is intelligible, and attainable, and finite. Though we consider the preceding generations as means of developing the last and perfected, still we cannot escape the inquiry of earnest Reason: "Wherefore then these last?" Given a human race on the earth, its existence must indeed be in accordance with Reason, and not contrary to it. It must become all that it can become on earth. But why should it exist at all, this human race? Why might it not as well have remained in the bosom of Nothing? Reason is not for the sake of existence, but existence for the sake of Reason. An existence which does not, in itself, satisfy Reason, and solve all her questions, cannot possibly be the true one.

Then, too, are the actions commanded by the voice of Conscience, whose dictates I must not speculate about, but obey in silence,—are they actually the means, and the only means, of accomplishing the earthly aim of mankind? That I cannot refer them to any other object but this, that I can have no other intent with them, is unquestionable. But is this my intent fulfilled in every case? Is nothing more needed but to will the best, in order that it may be accomplished? Alas! most of our good purposes are, for this world, entirely lost. And some of them seem even to have an entirely opposite effect to that which was proposed. On the other hand, the most despicable passions of men, their vices and their misdeeds, seem often to bring about the good more surely than the labors of the just man, who never consents to do evil that good may come. It would seem that the highest good of the world grows and thrives quite independently of all human virtues or vices, according to laws of its own, by some invisible and unknown power; just as the heavenly bodies run through their appointed course, independently of all human effort; and that this power absorbs into its own higher plan all human designs, whether good or ill; and, by its superior strength, appropriates what was intended for other purposes to its own ends.

If, therefore, the attainment of that earthly goal could be the design of our existence, and if no farther question concerning it remained to Reason, that aim, at least, would not be ours, but the aim of that unknown Power. We know not at any moment what may promote it. Nothing would be left us but to supply to that Power, by our actions, so much material, no matter what, to work up in its own way, for its own ends. Our highest wisdom would be, not to trouble ourselves about things in which we have no concern; to live, in each case, as the fancy takes us, and quietly leave the consequences to that Power. The moral law within us would be idle and superfluous, and wholly unsuited to a being that had no higher capacity and no higher destination. In order to be at one with ourselves, we should refuse obedience to the voice of that law, and suppress it as a perverse and mad enthusiasm.

* * * * * * *

If the whole design of our existence were to bring about an earthly condition of our race, all that would be required would be some infallible mechanism to direct our action; and we need be nothing more than wheels well fitted to the whole machine. Freedom would then not only be useless, but a contradictory power; and good will would be quite superfluous. The world, in that case, would be very clumsily contrived—would proceed to its goal with loss of power, and by circuitous paths. Rather, mighty World-Spirit, hadst thou taken from us this freedom, which, only with difficulty and by a different arrangement, thou canst fit to thy plans; and compelled us at once to act as those plans require. Thou wouldst then arrive at thy goal by the shortest road, as the meanest of the inhabitants of thy worlds can tell thee.

But I am free, and therefore such a concatenation of cause and effect, in which freedom is absolutely superfluous and useless, cannot exhaust my whole destination. I must be free; for not the mechanical act, but the free determination of free-will, for the sake of the command alone, and absolutely, for no other reason, so says the inward voice of conscience,—this alone determines our true worth. The band with which the law binds me is a band for living spirits. It scorns to rule over dead mechanism, and applies itself alone to the living and self-acting. Such obedience it demands. This obedience cannot be superfluous.

And herewith, the eternal world rises more brightly before me, and the ground-law of its order stands clear before the eye of my mind. In that world the *will*, purely and only, as it lies, locked up from all eyes, in the secret dark of my soul, is the first link in a chain of consequences which runs through the whole invisible world of spirits; as in the earthly world the *deed*, a certain movement of matter, becomes the first link in a material chain which extends through the whole material system. The will is the working and living principle in the world of Reason, as motion is the working and living principle in the world of sense. I stand in the centre of two opposite worlds, a visible in which the deed, and an invisible, altogether incomprehensible, in which the will decides. I am one of the original forces for both these worlds. My will is that which embraces both. This will is in and of itself a constituent portion of the supersensual world. When I put it in motion by a resolution, I move and change something in that world, and my activity flows on over the whole, and produces something new and ever-during, which then exists and needs not to be made anew. This will breaks forth into a material act, and this act belongs to the world of the senses, and effects, in that, what it can.

Not, when I am divorced from the connection of the earthly world, do I first gain admission into that which is above the earth. I am and live in it already, far more truly than in the earthly. Even now it is my only firm standpoint; and the eternal life, which I have long since taken possession of, is the only reason why I am willing still to prolong the earthly. That which they denominate Heaven, lies not beyond the grave. It is already here, diffused around our Nature, and its light arises in every pure heart. My will is mine, and it is the only thing that is entirely mine, and which depends entirely upon myself. By it I am already a citizen of the kingdom of liberty and of self-active Reason. My conscience, the tie by which that world holds me unceasingly and binds me to itself, tells me at every moment what determination of my will (the only thing by which, here in the dust, I can lay hold of that kingdom) is most consonant with its order; and it depends entirely upon myself to give myself the determination enjoined upon me. I cultivate myself then for this world, and, accordingly, work in it and for it, while elaborating one of its members. I pursue in it, and in it alone, without vacillation or doubt, according to fixed rules, my aim;—sure of success, since there no foreign power opposes my intent.

* * * * * * *

That our good-will, in and for and through itself, must have consequences, we know, even in this life; for Reason cannot require anything without a purpose. But what these consequences are,—nay, how it is possible that a mere will can effect anything,—is a question to which we cannot even imagine a solution, so long as we are entangled with this material world; and it is the part of wisdom not to undertake an inquiry concerning which, we know beforehand, that it must be unsuccessful. * *

* * * This then is my whole sublime destination, my true essence. I am member of two systems; a purely spiritual one, in which I rule by pure will alone; and a sensuous one, in which I work by my deed. * * *

* * * These two systems, the purely spiritual and the sensuous,—which last may consist of an immeasurable series of particular lives,—exist in me from the moment in which my active reason is developed, and pursue their parallel course. The latter system is only an appearance, for me and for those who share with me the same life. The former alone gives to the latter meaning, and purpose, and value. I *am* immortal, imperishable, eternal, so soon as I form the resolution to obey the law of Reason; and am not first to *become* so. The supersensuous world is not a future world, it is present. It never can be more present, at any one point of finite existence, than at any other point. After an existence of myriad lives, it cannot be more present, than at this moment. Other conditions of my sensuous existence are to come; but these are no more the true life, than the present condition. By means of that resolution, I lay hold on eternity, and strip off this life in the dust, and all other sensuous lives that may await me, and raise myself far above them. I become to myself the sole fountain of all my being and of all my phenomena; and have henceforth, unconditioned by aught without me, life in myself. My will, which I myself, and no stranger, fit to the order of that world, is this fountain of true life and of eternity.

But only my will is this fountain; and only when I acknowledge this will to be the true seat of moral excellence, and actually elevate it to this excellence, do I attain to the certainty and the possession of that supersensuous world.
* * * * *

The sense by which we lay hold on eternal life we acquire only by renouncing and offering up sense, and the aims of sense, to the law which claims our will alone, and not our acts;—by renouncing it with the conviction that to do so is reasonable and alone reasonable. With this renunciation of the earthly, the belief in the eternal first enters our soul, and stands isolated there, as the only stay by which we can still sustain ourselves, when we have relinquished everything else, as the only animating principle that still heaves our bosom and still inspires our life. Well was it said, in the metaphors of a sacred doctrine, that man must first die to the world and be born again, in order to enter into the kingdom of God.

I see, O! I see now, clear before mine eyes, the cause of my former heedlessness and blindness concerning spiritual things. Filled with earthly aims, and lost in them with all my scheming and striving; put in motion and impelled only by the idea of a result, which is to be actualized without us, by the desire of such a result and pleasure in it;—insensible and dead to the pure impulse of that Reason which gives the law to itself, which sets before us a purely spiritual aim, the immortal Psyche remains chained to the earth; her wings are bound. Our philosophy becomes the history of our own heart and life. As we find ourselves, so we imagine man in general and his destination. Never impelled by any other motive than the desire of that which can be realized in this world, there is no true liberty for us, no liberty which has the ground of its determination absolutely and entirely in itself. Our liberty, at the utmost, is that of the self-forming plant; no higher in its essence, only more curious in its result; not producing a form of matter with roots, leaves and blossoms, but a form of mind with impulses, thoughts, actions. Of the true liberty we are positively unable to comprehend anything, because we are not in possession of it. Whenever we hear it spoken of, we draw the words down to our own meaning, or briefly dismiss it with a sneer, as nonsense. With the knowledge of liberty, the sense of another world is also lost to us. Everything of this sort floats by like words which are not addressed to us; like an ash-grey shadow without color or meaning, which we cannot by any end take hold of and retain. Without the least interest, we let everything go as it is stated. Or if ever a robuster zeal impels us to consider it seriously, we see clearly and can demonstrate that all those ideas are untenable, hollow visions, which a man of sense casts from him. And, according to the premises from which we set out, and which are taken from our own innermost experience, we are quite right; and are alike unanswerable and unteachable, so long as we remain what we are. The excellent doctrines which are current among the people, fortified with special authority, concerning freedom, duty and eternal life, change themselves for us into grotesque fables, like those of Tartarus and the Elysian fields; although we do not disclose the true opinion of our hearts, because we think it more advisable to keep the people in outward decency by means of these images. Or if we are less reflective, and ourselves fettered by the bands of authority, then we sink, ourselves, to the true plebeian level. We believe that which, so understood, is foolish fable; and find, in those purely spiritual indications, nothing but the promise of a continuance, to all eternity, of the same miserable existence which we lead here below.

To say all in a word: Only through a radical reformation of my will does a new light arise upon my being and destination. Without this, however much I may reflect, and however distinguished my mental endowments, there is nothing but darkness in me and around me. The reformation of the heart alone conducts to true wisdom. So then, let my whole life stream incontinently toward this one end!

IV.

My lawful will, simply as such, in and through itself, must have consequences, certain and without exception. Every dutiful determination of my will, although no act should flow from it, must operate in another, to me incomprehensible, world; and, except this dutiful determination of the will, nothing can take effect in that world. What do I suppose when I suppose this? What do I take for granted?

Evidently, a law, a rule absolutely and without exception valid, according to which the dutiful will must have consequences. Just as in the earthly world which environs me, I assume a law according to which this ball, when impelled by my hand with this given force, in this given direction, must necessarily move in such a direction, with a determinate measure of rapidity; perhaps impel another ball with this given degree of force; which other ball then moves on with a determinate rapidity; and so on indefinitely. As in this case, with the mere direction and movement of my hand, I know and comprehend all the directions and movements which shall follow it, as certainly as if they were already present and perceived by me;—even so I comprehend, in my dutiful will, a series of necessary and infallible consequences in the spiritual world, as if they were already present;—only that I cannot, as in the material world, determine them; i. e., I merely know that they shall be, not how they shall be. I suppose a law of the spiritual world, in which my mere will is one of the moving forces, just as my hand is one of the moving forces in the material world. My firm confidence in the results of my volition and the thought of a law of the spiritual world are one and the same thing;—not two thoughts of which one is the consequence of the other, but precisely the same thought. Just as the certainty with which I count upon a certain motion, and the thought of a mechanical law of Nature, are the same. The idea of *Law* expresses generally nothing else but the fixed, immovable reliance of Reason on a proposition, and the impossibility of supposing the contrary.

I assume such a law of a spiritual world, which my own will did not enact, nor the will of any finite being, nor the will of all finite beings together; but to which my will and the will of all finite beings is subject.

* * * * * * *

Agreeably to what has now been advanced, the law of the supersensuous world should be a *Will*.

A Will which acts purely and simply as will, by its own agency, entirely without any instrument or sensuous medium of its efficacy; which is absolutely, in itself, at once action and result; which wills and it is done, which commands and it stands fast; in which, accordingly, the demand of reason, to be absolutely free and self-active, is represented. A Will which is law in itself; which determines itself, not according to humor and caprice, not after previous deliberation, vacillation and doubt, but which is forever and unchangeably determined, and upon which one may reckon with infallible security; as the mortal reckons securely on the laws of his world. A Will in which the lawful will of finite beings has inevitable consequences, but only their will, which is immovable to everything else, and for which everything else is as though it were not.

That sublime Will, therefore, does not pursue its course for itself, apart from the rest of Reason's world. There is between Him and all finite, rational beings, a spiritual band, and himself is this spiritual band of Reason's world. I will purely and decidedly my duty, and He then wills that I shall succeed, at least in the world of spirits. Every lawful resolve of the finite will enters into him, and moves and determines him—to speak after our fashion—not in consequence of a momentary good pleasure, but in consequence of the eternal law of his being.

With astounding clearness it now stands before my soul, the thought which hitherto had been wrapped in darkness, the thought, that my will, merely as such, and of itself, has consequences. It has consequences because it is infallibly and immediately taken knowledge of by another, related will, which is itself an act, and the only life-principle of the spiritual world.

In that Will it has its first consequence, and only through that, in the rest of the spiritual world which, in all its parts, is but the product of that infinite Will.

Thus I flow,—the mortal must speak according to his dialect,—thus I flow in upon that Will; and the voice of conscience in my interior, which, in every situation of my life, instructs me what I have to do in that situation, is that by means of which He, in turn, flows in upon me. That voice is the oracle from the eternal world, made sensible by my environment, and translated, by my reception of it, into my language; which announces to me how I must fit myself to my part in the order of the spiritual world, or to the infinite Will, which itself is the order of that spiritual world. I cannot oversee or see through this spiritual order; nor need I. I am only a link in its chain, and can no more judge of the whole, than a single tone in a song can judge of the harmony of the whole. But what I myself should be, in the harmony of Spirits, I must know; for only I myself can make myself that. And it is immediately revealed to me by a voice which sounds over to me from that world. Thus I stand in connection with the only being that *exists*, and partake of its being. There is nothing truly real, permanent, imperishable in me, but these two;—the voice of my conscience and my free obedience. By means of the first, the spiritual world bows down to me and embraces me, as one of its members. By means of the second, I raise myself into this world, lay hold of it, and work in it. But that infinite Will is the mediator between it and me; for, of it and me, himself is the primal fountain. This is the only true and imperishable, toward which my soul moves from its inmost depth. All else is only phenomenon, and vanishes and returns again, with new seeming.

This Will connects me with itself. The same connects me with all finite beings of my species, and is the universal mediator between us all. That is the great mystery of the invisible world, and its ground-law, so far as it is a world, or system of several individual wills: *Union and direct reciprocal action of several self-subsisting and independent wills among each other.* A mystery which, even in the present life, lies clear before all eyes, without any one's noticing it or thinking it worthy his admiration. The voice of Conscience, which enjoins upon each one his proper duty, is the ray by which we proceed from the Infinite, and are set forth as individual particular beings. It defines the boundaries of our personality; it is, therefore, our true original constituent, the ground and the stuff of all the life which we live.

* * * * * * *

That eternal Will, then, is indeed world-creator, as he alone can be,—in the finite reason. (The only creation which is needed.) They who suppose him to build a world out of an eternal sluggish matter, which world, in that case, could be nothing else but inert and lifeless, like implements fashioned by human hands, and not an eternal process of self-development; or who think they can imagine the going forth of a material something out of nothing, know neither the world nor him. If matter only is something, then there is nowhere anything, and nowhere, in all eternity, can anything be. Only Reason is, the infinite, in itself, the finite in that and by that. Only in our minds does he create the world; or, at least, that from which we unfold it, and that whereby we unfold it;—the call to duty, and the feelings, perceptions and laws of thought, agreeing therewith. It is *his* light whereby we see light, and all that appears to us in that light. In our minds he is continually fashioning this world, and interposing it by interposing in our minds with the call of duty, whenever another free agent effects a change therein. In our minds he maintains this world, and therewith, our finite existence, of which alone we are capable, in that he causes to arise out of our states new states continually. After he has proved us sufficiently for our next destination, according to his higher aim, and when we shall have cultivated ourselves for the same, he will annihilate this world for us by what we call death, and introduce us into a new one, the product of our dutiful action in this. All our life is his life. We are in his hand, and remain in it, and no one can pluck us out of it. We are eternal because He is eternal.

Sublime, living Will! whom no name can name, and whom no conception can grasp! well may I raise my mind to thee, for thou and I are not divided. Thy voice sounds in me, and mine sounds back, in thee; and all my thoughts, if only they are true and good, are thought in thee. In thee, the incomprehensible, I become comprehensible to myself, and entirely comprehend the world. All the riddles of my existence are solved, and the most perfect harmony arises in my mind.

Thou art best apprehended by childlike Simplicity, devoted to thee. To her thou art the heart-searcher who lookest through her innermost; the all-present, faithful witness of her sentiments, who alone knowest that she meaneth well, and who alone understandest her, when misunderstood by all the world. Thou art to her a Father, whose purposes toward her are ever kind, and who will order everything for her best good. She submitteth herself wholly, with body and soul, to thy beneficent decrees. Do with me as thou wilt, she saith, I know that it shall be good, so surely as it is thou that dost it. The speculative understanding, which has only heard of thee, but has never seen thee, would teach us to know thy being in itself, and sets before us an inconsistent monster, which it gives out for thine image, ridiculous to the merely knowing, hateful and detestable to the wise and good.

I veil my face before thee and lay my hand upon my mouth. How thou art in thyself, and how thou appearest to thyself, I can never know, as surely as I can never be thou. After thousand times thousand spirit-lives lived through, I shall no more be able to comprehend thee than now, in this hut of earth. That which I comprehend becomes, by my comprehension of it, finite; and this can never, by an endless process of magnifying and exalting, be changed into infinite. Thou differest from the finite, not only in degree but in kind. By that magnifying process they only make thee a greater and still greater man, but never God, the Infinite, incapable of measure. * * * *

* * * I will not attempt that which is denied to me by my finite nature, and which could avail me nothing. I desire not to know how thou art in thyself. But thy relations and connections with me, the finite, and with all finite beings, lie open to mine eye, when I become what I should be. They encompass me with a more luminous clearness than the consciousness of my own being. Thou workest in me the knowledge of my duty, of my destination in the series of rational beings. How? I know not, and need not to know. Thou knowest and perceivest what I think and will. How thou canst know it,—by what act thou bringest this consciousness to pass,—on that point I comprehend nothing. Yea! I know very well that the idea of an act, of a special act of consciousness, applies only to me but not to thee, the Infinite. Thou willest, because thou willest, that my free obedience shall have consequences in all eternity. The act of thy will I cannot comprehend. I only know that it is not like to mine. Thou *doest,* and thy will itself is deed. But thy method of action is directly contrary to that of which, alone, I can form a conception. Thou *livest* and *art,* for thou knowest, and willest, and workest, all present to finite Reason. But thou art not such as through all eternity I shall alone be able to conceive of Being.

In the contemplation of these thy relations to me, the finite, I will be calm and blessed. I know immediately, only what I must do. This will I perform undisturbed and joyful, and without philosophising. For it is thy voice which commands me, it is the ordination of the spiritual world-plan concerning me. And the power by which I perform it is thy power. Whatsoever is commanded me by that voice, whatsoever is accomplished by this power, is surely and truly good in relation to that plan. I am calm in all the events of this world, for they occur in thy world. Nothing can deceive, or surprise, or make me afraid, so surely as thou livest, and I behold thy life. For in thee and through thee, O infinite One! I behold even my present world in another light. Nature and natural consequences in the destinies and actions of free beings, in view of thee, are empty, unmeaning words. There is no Nature more. Thou, thou alone art.

It no longer appears to me the aim of the present world, that the above-mentioned state of universal peace among men, and of their unconditioned empire over the mechanism of Nature, should be brought about,—merely that it may exist; but that it should be brought about by man himself. And, since it is calculated for all, that it should be brought about by all, as one great, free, moral community. Nothing new and better for the individual, except through his dutiful will, nothing new and better for the community, except through their united, dutiful will, is the ground-law of the great moral kingdom, of which the present life is a part.

The reason why the good-will of the individual is so often lost for this world, is that it is only the will of the individual, and that the will of the majority does not coincide with it. Therefore, it has no consequences but those which belong to a future world. Hence, even the passions and vices of men appear to co-operate in the promotion of a better state, *not in and for themselves ;*—in this sense good can never come out of evil,—but by furnishing a counterpoise to opposite vices, and finally annihilating those vices and themselves, by their preponderance. Oppression could never have gained the upper hand, unless cowardice, and baseness, and mutual distrust had prepared the way for it. It will continue to increase, until it eradicates cowardice and the slavish mind; and despair re-awakens the courage that was lost. Then the two antagonist vices will have destroyed each other, and the noblest in all human relations, permanent freedom, will have come forth from them.

The actions of free beings have, strictly speaking, no other consequences than those which affect other free beings. For only in such, and for such, does the world exist; and that, wherein all agree, is the world. But they have consequences in free agents only by means of the infinite Will, by which all individuals exist. A call, a revelation of that Will to us, is always a requirement to perform some particular duty. Hence, even that which we call evil in the world, the consequence of the abuse of freedom, exists only through Him; and it exists for all, for whom it exists, only so far forth as it imposes duties upon them. Did it not fall within the eternal plan of our moral education and the education of our whole race, that precisely these duties should be laid upon us, they would not have been imposed; and that whereby they are imposed, and which we call evil, would never have been. In this view, everything which takes place is good, and absolutely accordant with the best ends. There is but one world possible,—a thoroughly good one. Everything that occurs in this world, conduces to the reformation and education of man, and, by means of that, to the furtherance of his earthly destination.

It is this higher world-plan that we call Nature, when we say Nature leads men through want to industry, through the evils of general disorder to a righteous polity, through the miseries of their perpetual wars to final, ever-during peace. Thy will, O Infinite! thy providence alone is this higher Nature. This too is best understood by artless simplicity, which regards this life as a place of discipline and education, as a school for eternity; which, in all the fortunes it experiences, the most trivial as well as the most momentous, beholds thy ordinations designed for good; and which firmly believes that all things will work together for good to those who love their duty and know thee.

O! truly have I spent the former days of my life in darkness. Truly have I heaped errors upon errors, and thought myself wise. Now first I fully understand the doctrine which seemed so strange to me, out of thy mouth, wondrous Spirit!* although my understanding had nothing to oppose to it. For now first I overlook it, in its whole extent, in its deepest ground, and in all its consequences.

Man is not a product of the world of sense; and the end of his existence can never be attained in that world. His destination lies beyond time and space and all that pertains to sense. He must know what he is and what he is to make himself. As his destination is sublime, so his thought must be able to lift itself up above all the bounds of sense. This

---

* An allusion to the second book.

must be his calling. Where his being is domesticated, there his thought must be domesticated also; and the most truly human view, that which alone befits him, that in which his whole power of thought is represented, is the view by which he lifts himself above those limits, by which all that is of the senses is changed for him into pure nothing, a mere reflection of the alone enduring, supersensual, in mortal eyes.

Many have been elevated to this view without scientific thought, simply by their great heart and their pure moral instinct; because they lived especially with the heart, and in the sentiments. They denied, by their conduct, the efficacy and reality of the world of sense; and in the shaping of their purposes and measures, they esteemed as nothing that, concerning which, they had not yet learned by thinking, that it *is* nothing, even to thought. They who could say, "our citizenship is in heaven; we have here no continuing place, but seek one to come;"—they whose first principle was, to die to the world and to be born anew, and even here, to enter into another life,—they, truly, placed not the slightest value upon all the objects of sense, and were, to use the language of the School, practical transcendental Idealists.

Others who, in addition to the sensual activity which is native to us all, have, by their thought, confirmed themselves in sense, become implicated, and, as it were, grown together with it;—they can raise themselves permanently and perfectly above sense only by continuing and carrying out their thought. Otherwise, with the purest moral intentions, they will still be drawn down again by their understanding; and their whole being will remain a continued and insoluble contradiction. For such, that philosophy, which I now first entirely understood, is the power by which Psyche first strips off her caterpillar-hull, and unfolds the wings on which she then hovers above herself, and casts one glance on the slough she has dropped, thenceforth to live and work in higher spheres.

Blessed be the hour in which I resolved to meditate on myself and my destination! All my questions are solved. I know what I can know, and I am without anxiety concerning that which I cannot know. I am satisfied. There is perfect harmony and clearness in my spirit, and a new and more glorious existence for that spirit begins.

My whole, complete destination, I do not comprehend. What I am called to be and shall be, surpasses all my thought. A part of this destination is yet hidden within myself, visible only to him, the Father of Spirits, to whom it is committed. I know only that it is secured to me, and that it is eternal and glorious as himself. But that portion of it which is committed to me, I know. I know it entirely, and it is the root of all my other knowledge. I know, in every moment of my life, with certainty, what I am to do in that moment. And this is my whole destination, so far as it depends upon me. From this, since my knowledge goes no farther, I must not depart. I must not desire to know anything beyond it. I must stand fast in this one centre, and take root in it. All my scheming and striving, and all my faculty, must be directed to that. My whole existence must inweave itself with it. * * * *
* * * I raise myself to this stand-point, and am a new creature. My whole relation to the existing world is changed. The ties by which my mind was heretofore bound to this world, and by whose secret attraction it followed all the movements of this world, are forever divided, and I stand free; myself, my own world, peaceful and unmoved. No longer with the heart, with the eye alone, I seize the objects about me, and, through the eye alone, am connected with them. And this eye itself, made clearer by freedom, looks through error and deformity to the true and the beautiful; as, on the unmoved surface of the water, forms mirror themselves pure, and with a softened light.

My mind is forever closed against embarrassment and confusion, against doubt and anxiety; my heart is forever closed against sorrow, and remorse, and desire. There is but one thing that I care to know: What I must do? And this I know, infallibly, always. Concerning all beside I know nothing, and I know that I know nothing; and I root myself fast in this my ignorance, and forbear to conjecture, to opine, to quarrel with myself concerning that of which I know nothing. No event in this world can move me to joy, and none to sorrow. Cold and unmoved I look down upon them all; for I know that I cannot interpret one of them, nor discern its connection with that which is my only concern. Everything which takes place belongs to the plan of the eternal world, and is good in relation to that plan; so much I know. But what, in that plan, is pure gain, and what is only meant to remove existing evil, accordingly, what I should most or least rejoice in I know not. In *His* world everything succeeds. This suffices me, and in this faith I stand firm as a rock. But what in His world is only germ, what blossom, what the fruit itself, I know not.

The only thing which can interest me is the progress of reason and virtue in the kingdom of rational beings; and that purely for its own sake, for the sake of the progress. Whether *I* am the instrument of this progress or another, whether it is my act which succeeds or is thwarted, or whether it is the act of another, is altogether indifferent to me. I regard myself in every case but as one of the instruments of a rational design, and I honor and love myself, and am interested in myself, only as such; and wish the success of my act, only so far as it goes to accomplish that end. Therefore I regard all the events of this world in the same manner;

only with exclusive reference to this one end; whether they proceed from me or from another, whether they relate to me immediately, or to others. My breast is closed against all vexation on account of personal mortifications and affronts; against all exaltation on account of personal merits; for my entire personality has long since vanished, and been swallowed up in the contemplation of the end.

* * * * * * *

Bodily sufferings, pain and sickness, should such befall me, I cannot avoid to feel, for they are events of my nature, and I am and remain nature here below. But they shall not trouble me. They affect only the Nature, with which I am, in some strange way, connected; not myself, the being which is elevated above all Nature. The sure end of all pain, and of all susceptibility of pain, is death; and of all which the natural man is accustomed to regard as evil, this is the least so to me. Indeed, I shall not die for myself, but only for others, for those that remain behind, from whose connexion I am severed. For myself, the hour of death is the hour of birth to a new and more glorious life.

Since my heart is thus closed to all desire for the earthly, since, in fact, I have no longer any heart for the perishable, the universe appears to my eye in a transfigured form. The dead, inert mass which but choked up space has vanished; and instead thereof flows, and waves, and rushes the eternal stream of life, and power, and deed;—of the original life, of thy life, O Infinite! For all life is thy life, and only the religious eye pierces to the kingdom of veritable beauty.

I am related to Thee, and all that I behold around me is related to me. All is quick, all is soul, and gazes upon me with bright spirit-eyes, and speaks in spirit-tones to my heart. Most diversely sundered and severed, I behold, in all the forms without me, myself again, and beam upon myself from them, as the morning sun, in thousand dew-drops diversely refracted, glances toward itself.

Thy life, as the finite can apprehend it, is a willing which shapes and represents itself by means of itself alone. This life, made sensible in various ways to mortal eyes, flows through me and from me downward, through the immeasurable whole of Nature. Here it streams, as self-creating, self-fashioning matter, through my veins and muscles, and deposites its fulness out of me, in the tree, in the plant, in the grass. One connected stream, drop by drop, the forming life flows in all shapes and on all sides, wherever my eye can follow it, and looks upon me, from every point of the universe, with a different aspect, as the same force which fashions my own body in darkness and in secret. Yonder it waves free, and leaps and dances as self-forming motion in the brute; and, in every new body, represents itself as another separate, self-subsisting world;—the same power which,

invisible to me, stirs and moves in my own members. All that lives follows this universal attraction, this one principle of all movement, which conducts the harmonious shock from one end of the universe to the other. The brute follows it without freedom. I, from whom, in the visible world, the movement proceeds, (without, therefore, originating in me,) follow it freely.

But pure and holy, and near to thine own essence as aught, to mortal apprehension, can be; this thy life flows forth as a band which binds spirits with spirits in one; as air and ether of the one world of Reason, inconceivable and incomprehensible, and yet lying plainly revealed to the spiritual eye. Conducted by this lightstream, thought floats unrestrained and the same from soul to soul, and returns purer and transfigured from the kindred breast. Through this mystery the individual finds, and understands, and loves himself only in another; and every spirit detaches itself only from other spirits; and there is no man, but only a Humanity;—no isolated thinking, and loving, and hating, but only a thinking, and loving, and hating in and through one another. Through this mystery the affinity of Spirits, in the invisible world, streams forth into their corporeal nature, and represents itself in two sexes, which, though every spiritual band could be severed, are still constrained, as natural beings, to love each other. It flows forth into the affection of parents and children, of brothers and sisters; as if the souls were sprung from one blood as well as the bodies;—as if the minds were branches and blossoms of the same stem. And from thence it embraces, in narrower or wider circles, the whole sentient world. Even the hatred of spirits is grounded in thirst for love; and no enmity springs up, except from friendship denied.

Mine eye discerns this eternal life and motion, in all the veins of sensible and spiritual Nature, through what seems to others a dead mass. And it sees this life forever ascend and grow, and transfigure itself into a more spiritual expression of its own nature. The universe is no longer, to me, that circle which returns into itself, that game which repeats itself without ceasing, that monster which devours itself in order to reproduce itself, as it was before. It is spiritualized to my contemplation, and bears the peculiar impress of the Spirit: continual progress toward perfection, in a straight line which stretches into infinity.

The sun rises and sets, the stars vanish and return again, and all the spheres hold their cycle-dance. But they never return precisely such as they disappeared; and in the shining fountains of life there is also life and progress. Every hour which they bring, every morning and every evening sinks down with new blessings on the world. New life and new love drop from the spheres, as dew-drops from the cloud, and embrace Nature, as the cool night embraces the earth.

All death in Nature is birth; and precisely in dying, the sublimation of life appears most conspicuous. There is no death-bringing principle in Nature, for Nature is only life, throughout. Not death kills, but the more living life, which, hidden behind the old, begins and unfolds itself. Death and birth are only the struggle of life with itself to manifest itself in ever more transfigured form, more like itself.

And *my* death,—can that be anything different from this? I, who am not a mere representation and copy of life, but who bear within myself the original, the alone true, and essential life? It is not a possible thought that Nature should annihilate a life which did not spring from her; Nature, which exists only for my sake, not I for hers.

But even my natural life, even this mere representation of an inward invisible life to mortal eyes, Nature cannot annihilate; otherwise she must be able to annihilate herself.— She who exists only for me and for my sake, and who ceases to exist, if I am not. Even because she puts me to death she must quicken me anew. It can only be my higher life, unfolding itself in her, before which my present life disappears; and that which mortals call death is the visible appearing of a second vivification. Did no rational being, who has once beheld its light, perish from the earth, there would be no reason to expect a new heaven and a new earth. The only possible aim of Nature, that of representing and maintaining Reason, would have been already fulfilled here below, and her circle would be complete. But the act by which she puts to death a free, self-subsisting being, is her solemn,—to all Reason apparent,—transcending of that act, and of the entire sphere which she thereby closes. The apparition of death is the conductor by which my spiritual eye passes over to the new life of myself, and of Nature, for me.

Every one of my kind who passes from earthly connexions, and who cannot, to my spirit, seem annihilated, because he is one of my kind, draws my thought over with him. He still *is*, and to him belongs a place.

While we, here below, sorrow for him with such sorrow as would be felt, if possible, in the dull kingdom of unconsciousness, when a human being withdraws himself from thence to the light of earth's sun;—while we so mourn, on yonder side there is joy, because a man is born into their world; as we citizens of earth receive with joy our own. When I, sometime, shall follow them, there will be joy for me; for sorrow remains behind, in the sphere which I quit.

It vanishes and sinks before my gaze, the world which I so lately admired. With all the fulness of life, of order, of increase, which I behold in it, it is but the curtain by which an infinitely more perfect world is concealed from me. It is but the germ out of which that infinitely more perfect shall unfold itself. My faith enters behind this curtain, and warms and quickens this germ. It sees nothing definite, but expects more than it can grasp here below, than it will ever be able to grasp in time.

So I live and so I am; and so I am unchangeable, firm and complete for all eternity. For this being is not one which I have received from without; it is my own only true being and essence.

PAINTED BY FORSTER.   ENGRAVED BY J. SARTAIN.

RICHTER.

JOHANN PAUL FRIEDRICH RICHTER.

Born 1763. Died 1825.

NEXT to Schiller there is no writer whom Germany cherishes with more enthusiastic attachment than *Jean Paul*,—so he called himself, while living, and is still called since his death. Confined to a narrower circle than Schiller, he is even more intensely loved within that circle than the great dramatist himself; for he is a writer to be loved, if tolerated. There is that in him which allows of no indifference. He must either attach or repel. Where he does not create an irreconcilable aversion, he binds with indissoluble friendship. Those who read him much, come into personal relations with him, and sympathize with him as with no other. Indeed, there is no other like him in the history of literature. He is incommensurable, and refuses to be classed; combining the most contradictory characters and gifts; the humorist and the prophet; the wildest fun with the steepest elevation of thought and an infinite pathos; the sharpest satire with an all-embracing love; a feeling for all littleness and little ones, with the loftiest sentiments and aspirations; a prevailing subjectiveness, with clear and original intuitions of men and things.

The humorist predominates; and such humor! It is not the humor of Cervantes, though sunny and wholesome as his. It is not the humor of Rabelais, having nothing of the satyr or the swine; and yet Rabelais himself is not more wildly fantastic. It is not the humor of Swift, though it lacks nothing of his irony; nor is it the humor of Sterne, though not less kind and contemplative, and stuffed with conceits. It is a humor quite his own, "compounded of many simples and extracted from many objects." In this, as in other things, he resembles no one else in the world but just Jean Paul. He is Jean Paul, "the only."

He was sumptuously, marvellously endowed, and if he wanted many essential qualifications of a great poet, or even of a good writer, there are others which he possessed in unrivalled perfection. He has but *one* rival, and that is Shakspeare, in exuberance of fancy. The incontinent, the inconceivable, the overwhelming affluence of images and illustrations, is what first strikes us in his writings. The paragraph labors and staggers with meanings and double meanings, and after-thoughts and side-thoughts, conceits appended to every third word, and ornaments stuck in, some sufficiently *bizarre*, and others of supernal beauty, making altogether "a piece of joinery so crossly indented and whimsically dovetailed, a cabinet so variously inlaid, such a piece of diversified Mosaic," as no other writing can parallel. He has absolutely no rival in what may be called the inborn poetry of the heart, that sympathy and identification of himself with all forms and ways of being, that secret understanding with Nature, that profound humanity which, in an inferior degree, so happily distinguishes Wordsworth among English poets. Some of his pieces, for example, Fibel and Quintus Fixlein, constitute a new and higher order of idyl; combining the subjective piquancy of modern thought with the classic outwardness of the ancient model.

In power of imagination, also, he takes rank among the first. Many of his characters are wholly new creations, and have an individuality and a self-subsistence which only true genius can impart. It is in his visions, however, with which his works abound, that Richter's imagination is most active, producing an apocalypse of the most extravagant and unheard-of portents, a swarming phantasmagory of beautiful and terrible apparitions, which make the application more appropriate to him than to any other, of those lines which describe one of his contemporaries:

"Within that mind's abyss profound,
As in some limbo vast,
More shapes and monsters did abound
To set the wondering world aghast,
Than wave-worn Noah fed or starry Tuscan found."

His faults as a writer are sufficiently prominent, but, for the most part, so blended and complicated with his peculiar merits, that we cannot imagine them removed without destroying some characteristic excellence. An utter want of grace and form, an habitual lugging in of irrelevant learning, an excessive delight in verbal quibbles and other conceits, obscurity, constant iteration of one or two types of character, exaggeration of one or two features of society, want of action in his narratives, a superfluity of tears and ecstasies not sufficiently motived, a passion for extremes — these are faults which have often been pointed out, and which his warmest admirers will hardly deny. On the other hand, the charge of affectation is unjust. A mannerist he certainly is, but it is the mannerism of idiosyncrasy, a bias in the nature of the man, a kink in his genius, a maggot in his brain, without which he would not be Jean Paul.

It is the moral qualities of Richter, far more than his intellectual, which endear him to his countrymen. To that true and loyal soul the deep heart of Germany responds with all its music. So loving, and believing, and hoping, and aspiring, so innocent of all guile, and free from all wrath, and bitterness, and evil speaking, so full of all fine sentiments and generous views, so abounding in compassion for all the suffering, willing to clasp them all to his great heart, which throbbed evermore with unebbing and unspeakable affection for all his kind; so devout, and pure, and good; he commends himself not only to his own people, but to humanity everywhere; to all that is best in the nature of man. It is good to converse with him. His word is sound and sanative, "pure as the heart of the waters," and "pure as the marrow of the earth."

The life's history of Jean Paul is gathered partly from his autobiography, commenced not many years before his death, and extending to his thirteenth year; partly from an appendix to that beginning by Herr Otto, a friend of the deceased; and partly from his correspondence with friends and contemporaries. A "Life of Jean Paul," in 2 vols. 12mo., embodying a translation of the autobiographical fragment, and continuing the narrative from the other sources above mentioned, was published in Boston,* a few years since, by a lady who seems to have spared no pains to make herself acquainted with her subject. To these two volumes the editor of this work refers with pleasure, as the best biography of Richter known to him.

Richter was born at Wunsiedel, in that part of Germany called the *Fichtelgebirge*, or Pine-mountain. His father, then organist and under-teacher at the gymnasium in that town, was soon after appointed pastor (Lutheran) of a church, in the small village of Joditz, and, some years later, promoted to the larger living of Schwarzenbach, on the Saale. From his father Richter received his first instruction in the languages. At sixteen, he was placed at the gymnasium in Hof, a neighboring small city. At eighteen, he entered the university of Leipzig, where he began the study of theology, but soon gave himself up to general culture, and began his career as author, with the publication of the "Greenland Lawsuits." His father had died meanwhile, and he was thrown entirely upon himself. His first attempts at authorship were not successful, his situation was perplexing, and the future looked grimly on the penniless youth. "Fortune seemed to have let loose her bandogs, and hungry Ruin had him in the wind."* His mother had removed to Hof, her birth-place, and there Jean Paul joined her, in a house which had but one apartment, pursuing his studies amid "the jingle of household operations;" writing books which would not sell, and tasting all the bitterness of extreme penury. "The prisoner's allowance," he says, "is bread and water, but I had only the latter."—"Nevertheless, I cannot help saying to Poverty: Welcome! so thou come not at quite too late a time! Wealth bears heavier on talent than Poverty. Under gold-mountains and thrones who knows how many a spiritual giant may lie crushed down and buried! When among the flames of youth, and above all, of hotter powers, the oil of Riches is also poured in — little will remain of the phœnix but his ashes; and only a Goethe has force to keep, even at the sun of good fortune, his phœnix-wings unsinged."* For ten years and upwards he fought this fight, during which time his only support was the money earned by the occasional but rare admission of one of his contributions to the public journals. Nevertheless he refused the situation of a private tutor, determined to succeed as author, or starve in the attempt. And he triumphed, at last.

---

* Life of Jean Paul Frederic Richter, compiled from various sources, together with his autobiography, translated from the German. Boston: Charles C. Little & James Brown.

* Carlyle's Miscellanies, vol. II.

After repeated failures, the publication of the "Invisible Lodge," in 1793, brought money, fame, troops of friends, and, altogether, decided his future. After the death of his mother, he resided successively in several different places, and finally fixed upon Baireuth, in the neighbourhood of the Fichtelgebirge, as his home. In 1801 he married Caroline Mayer, daughter of a professor of medicine in Berlin. In 1801 he received from the Prince Primate, Von Dalberg, a small pension, which was afterward paid to him by the King of Bavaria until his death. In 1824 the failure of his eyesight impaired his activity, without arresting it entirely. He continued to labor with the help of his nephews, revising his works in order to a uniform edition, and making the most of his declining strength, until, for all literary purposes, it failed him utterly. He died November 14, 1825. He was buried by torch-light; the unfinished manuscript of his Selina (a work on immortality) was borne upon his coffin, and Klopstock's Ode, "Thou shalt arise, my soul," was sung by the students of the Gymnasium.

ROME.*

HALF an hour after the earthquake the heavens swathed themselves in seas, and dashed them down in masses and in torrents. The naked *Campagna* and heath were covered with the mantle of rain. Gaspard was silent—the heavens black—the great thought stood alone in Albano that he was hastening on toward the bloody scaffold and the throne-scaffolding of humanity, the heart of a cold, dead heathen-world, the eternal Rome; and when he heard, on the *Ponte Molle*, that he was now going across the Tiber, then was it to him as if the past had risen from the dead, as if the stream of time ran backward and bore him with it; under the streams of heaven he heard the seven old mountain-streams, rushing and roaring, which once came down from Rome's hills, and, with seven arms, uphove the world from its foundations. At length the constellation of the mountain city of God, that stood so broad before him, opened out into distant nights; cities, with scattered lights, lay up and down, and the bells (which to his ear were alarm-bells) sounded out the fourth hour;† when the carriage rolled through the triumphal gate of the city, the *Porta del Popolo;* then the moon rent her black heavens, and poured down out of the cleft clouds the splendor of a whole sky. There stood the Egyptian Obelisk of the gateway, high as the clouds, in the night, and three streets ran gleaming apart. "So," (said Albano to himself, as they passed through the long *Corso* to the tenth ward) "thou art veritably in the camp of the God of war; here, where he grasped the hilt of the monstrous war-sword, and with the point made the three wounds in three quarters of the world!"—Rain and splendor gushed through the vast, broad streets—occasionally he passed suddenly along by gardens, and into broad city-deserts and market-places of the past. The rolling of the chariot amidst the rush and roar of the rain, resembled the thunder, whose days were once holy to this heroic city, like the thundering heaven to the thundering earth; muffled-up forms, with little lights, stole through the dark streets; often there stood a long palace with colonnades in the light of the moon, often a solitary gray column, often a single high fir-tree, or a statue behind cypresses. Once, when there was neither rain nor moonshine, the carriage went round the corner of a large house, on whose roof a tall, blooming virgin, with an uplooking child on her arm, herself directed a little hand-light, now toward a white statue, now toward the child, and so, alternately, illuminated each. This friendly group made its way to the very centre of his soul, now so highly exalted, and brought with it, to him, many a recollection; particularly was a Roman child to him a wholly new and mighty idea.

They alighted at last at the Prince *di Lauria's*, Gaspard's father-in-law and old friend. * * * Albano, dissatisfied with all, kept his inspiration sacrificing to the unearthly gods of the past round about him, after the old fashion, namely, with silence. Well might he, and could he, have discoursed, but otherwise; in odes, with the whole man, with streams which mount and grow upwards. He looked ever more and more longingly out of the window at the moon in the pure rain-blue, and at single columns of the Forum; out of doors there gleamed for him the greatest world.—At last he rose up, indignant and impatient, and stole down into the glimmering glory, and stepped before the Forum; but the moonlit night, that decoration-painter, which works with irregular strokes, made almost the very stage of the scene irrecognisable to him.

What a dreary, broad plain, loftily encompassed with ruins, gardens and temples, covered with prostrate capitals of columns, and with single, upright pillars, and with trees and a dumb wilderness! The heaped-up ashes out of the emptied urn of Time—and the potsherds of a great world flung around! He passed by three temple columns,* which the earth had

---

* From an unpublished translation (complete) of "The Titan" of J. Paul Richter, by Rev. C. T. Brooks.
† Ten o'clock.

* Of Jupiter Tonans.

drawn down into itself even to the breast, and along through the broad triumphal arch of Septimus Severus; on the right, stood a chain of columns without their temple; on the left, attached to a Christian church, the colonnade of an ancient heathen temple, deep sunken into the sediment of time; at last the triumphal arch of Titus, and before it, in the middle of the woody wilderness, a fountain gushing into a granite basin.

He went up to this fountain, in order to survey the plain, out of which the thunder-mouths of the earth once arose; but he went along as over a burnt-out sun, hung round with dark, dead earths. "O Man, O the dreams of Man!" something within him unceasingly cried. He stood on the granite margin, turning toward the Coliseum, whose mountain ridges of wall stood high in the moonlight, with the deep gaps which had been hewn in them by the scythe of Time —sharply stood the rent and ragged arches of Nero's golden house close by, like murderous cutlasses. The Palatine Hill lay full of green gardens, and, in crumbling temple-roofs, the blooming death-garland of ivy was gnawing, and living ranunculi still glowed around sunken capitals.—The fountain murmured babblingly and forever, and the stars gazed steadfastly down, with transitory rays, upon the still battle-field, over which the winter of time had passed without bringing after it a spring—the fiery soul of the world had flown up, and the cold, crumbling giant lay around—torn asunder were the gigantic spokes of the main-wheel, which once the very stream of ages drove. And in addition to all this, the moon shed down her light 'like eating silver-water upon the naked columns, and would fain have dissolved the Coliseum and the temples and all into their own shadows!

Then Albano stretched out his arm into the air, as if he were giving an embrace and flowing away as in the arms of a stream, and exclaimed, "O ye mighty shades, ye, who once strove and lived here, ye are looking down from Heaven, but scornfully, not sadly, for your great fatherland has died and gone after you! Ah, had I, on the insignificant earth, full of cold eternity, which you have made great, only done one action worthy of you! Then were it sweet to me and allowed me, to open my heart by a wound, and to mix earthly blood with the hallowed soil, and, out of the world of graves, to hasten away to you, eternal and immortal ones! But I am not worthy of it!"

At this moment there came suddenly along up the *Via sacra,* a tall man, deeply enveloped in a mantle, who drew near the fountain, without looking round, threw down his hat, and held a coal-black, curly, almost perpendicular, hind-head under the stream of water. But hardly had he, turning upward, caught a glimpse of the profile of Albano, absorbed in his fancies, when he started up, all dripping,—stared at the count—fell into an amazement—threw his arms high into the air—and said, "*Amico?*"—Albano looked at him.—The stranger said, "Albano!" "My Dian!" cried Albano; they clasped each other passionately and wept for love.

Dian could not comprehend it at all; he said in Italian; "But it surely cannot be you, you look old." He thought he was speaking German all the time, till he heard Albano answer in Italian. Both gave and received only questions. Albano found the architect merely browner, but there was the lightning of the eyes and every faculty in its old glory. With three words he related to him the journey, and who the company were. "How does Rome strike you?" asked Dian, pleasantly. "As life does," replied Albano, very seriously, "it makes me too soft and too hard."—"I recognise here absolutely nothing at all," he continued: "do those columns belong to the magnificent temple of Peace?" "No," said Dian, "to the temple of Concord; of the other there stands yonder nothing but the vault." "Where is Saturn's temple?" asked Albano. "Buried in St. Adrian's church;" said Dian, and added hastily, "close by stand the ten columns of Antonine's temple;—over beyond there the baths of Titus —behind us the Palatine hill, and so on. Now tell me —!"

They walked up and down the Forum, between the arches of Titus and Sévérus. Albano —especially, near the teacher who, in the days of childhood, had so often conducted him hitherward,—was yet full of the stream which had swept over the world, and the all-covering water sunk but slowly. He went on and said, "to-day, when he beheld the Obelisk, the soft, tender brightness of the moon had seemed to him eminently unbecoming for the giant city; he would rather have seen a sun blazing on its broad banner; but now the moon was the proper funeral-torch beside the dead Alexander, who, at a touch, collapses into a handful of dust."—"The artist does not get far with feelings of this kind," said Dian, "he must look upon everlasting beauties on the right hand and on the left."—"Where," Albano went on asking, "is the old lake of Curtius— the Rostrum— the pila Horatia—the temple of Vesta—of Venus, and of all those solitary columns?"—"And where is the marble Forum itself?" said Dian; "it lies thirty span deep below our feet." — "Where is the great, free people, the senate of kings, the voice of the orators, the procession to the Capitol? Buried under the mountain of potsherds. O Dian, how can a man who loses a father, a beloved, in Rome shed a single tear or look round him with consternation, when he comes out here before this battle-field of time, and looks into the charnel-house of the nations? Dian, one would wish here an iron heart, for fate has an iron hand!"

Dian, who nowhere stayed more reluctantly than upon such tragic cliffs, hanging over as it were into the sea of eternity, almost leaped off from them with a joke; like the Greeks, he blended dances with tragedy; "Many a thing is preserved here, friend!" said he: "in Adrian's church yonder they will still show you the bones of the three men that walked in the fire." "That is just the frightful play of destiny," replied Albano, "to occupy the heights of the mighty ancients with monks shorn down into slaves."

"The stream of time drives new wheels," said Dian: "yonder lies Raphael twice buried."* * * * And so they climbed silently and speedily over rubbish and torsos of columns, and neither gave heed to the mighty emotion of the other.

Rome, like the Creation, is an entire wonder, which gradually dismembers itself into new wonders, the Coliseum, the Pantheon, St. Peter's church, Raphael, &c.

With the passage through the church of St. Peter, the knight began the noble course through Immortality. The Princess let herself, by the tie of Art, be bound to the circle of the men. As Albano was more smitten with edifices than with any other work of man; so did he see from afar, with holy heart, the long mountain-chain of Art, which again bore upon itself hills; so did he stop before the plain, around which the enormous colonnades run like Corsos, bearing a people of statues;—in the centre shoots up the obelisk, and on its right and left an eternal fountain, and from the lofty steps, the proud Church of the world, inwardly filled with churches, rearing upon itself a temple toward Heaven, looks down upon the earth.—But how wonderfully, as they drew near, had its columns and its rocky wall mounted up and flown away from the vision!

He entered the magic church, which gave the world blessings, curses, kings and popes, with the consciousness, that, like the world-edifice, it was continually enlarging and receding more and more the longer one remained in it. They went up to two children of white marble, who held an incense-muscle-shell of yellow marble; the children grew by nearness, till they were giants. At length they stood at the main altar and its hundred perpetual lamps. What a stillness! Above them the heaven's arch of the dome, resting on four inner towers; around them an over-arched city of four streets in which stood churches.—The temple became greatest by walking in it; and when they passed round one column, there stood a new one before them, and holy giants gazed earnestly down.

Here was the youth's large heart, after so long a time, filled. "In no art," said he to his father, "is the soul so mightily possessed with the sublime as in architecture; in every other the giant stands within and in the depths of the soul, but here he stands out of and close before it." Dian, to whom all images were more clear than abstract ideas, said he was perfectly right.

Fraischdörfer replied, "The sublime also here lies only in the brain, for the whole church stands after all in something greater, namely, in Rome, and under the heavens, in the presence of which latter, we certainly should not feel anything." He also complained that the place for the sublime in his head was very much narrowed by the innumerable volutes and monuments which the temple shut up therein at the same time with itself." Gaspard, taking everything in a large sense, remarked, "When the sublime once really appears, it then, by its very nature, absorbs and annihilates all little circumstantial ornaments." He adduced as evidence the tower of the Minster,* and Nature itself, which is not made smaller by its grasses and villages.

Among so many connoisseurs of art, the Princess enjoyed in silence.

The ascent of the dome, Gaspard recommended to defer to a dry and cloudless day, in order that they might behold the queen of the world, Rome, upon and from the proper throne; he therefore proposed, very zealously, the visiting of the Pantheon, because he was eager to let this follow immediately after the impression of St. Peter's church. They went thither. How simply and grandly the hall opens! Eight yellow columns sustain its brow, and majestically as the head of the Homeric Jupiter its temple arches itself. It is the Rotunda or Pantheon.— "O the pigmies," cried Albano, "who would fain give us new temples! Raise the old ones higher out of the rubbish, and then you have built enough!"† They stepped in;—there rose itself around them a holy, simple, free world-structure, with its heaven-arches soaring and striving upward, an Odeum of the tones of the Sphere-music, a world in the world! And overhead,‡ the eye-socket of the light and of the sky gleamed down, and the distant rack of clouds seemed to touch the lofty arch over which it shot along! And round about them stood nothing but the temple-bearers, the columns! The temple of *all* gods endured and concealed the diminutive altars of the later ones.

Gaspard questioned Albano about his impressions. He said he preferred the larger church of St. Peter. The knight approved, and said that youth, like nations, always more easily found and better appreciated the sublime than the beautiful, and that the spirit of the young man ripened from strong to beautiful, as the body of the same ripens from the beautiful into the strong;—however, he himself preferred the Pantheon. "How could the moderns," said the Counsellor of Arts, Fraischdörfer, "build anything, except some little Bernim's Towers?" "That is why," said the offended Provincial Architect, Dian, (who despised the Counsellor

---

* The body in the Pantheon, the head in St. Luke's church.

* Strassburg.

† The hall of the Pantheon seems too low, because a part of its steps is hidden by the rubbish.

‡ This opening in the roof is twenty-seven feet in diameter.

of Arts, because he never made a good figure, except in the aesthetic hall of judgment as critic, never in the exhibition-hall as painter), "we moderns are, without contradiction, stronger in criticism; though in practice we are, collectively and individually, blockheads." Bouverot remarked, the Corinthian columns might be higher. The Counsellor of Arts said, after all he knew nothing more like this fine hemisphere than a much smaller one, which he had found in Herculaneum moulded in ashes, of the bosom of a fair fugitive." The knight laughed, and Albano turned away in disgust and went to the Princess.

He asked her for her opinion about the two temples. "Sophocles here, Shakspeare there; but I comprehend and appreciate Sophocles more easily," she replied, and looked with new eyes into his new countenance. For the supernatural illumination through the zenith of Heaven, not through a hazy horizon, transfigured, in her eyes, the beautiful and excited countenance of the youth; and she took for granted that the saintly halo of the dome must also exalt her form—when he answered her, "Very good! But in Shakspeare, Sophocles also is contained, not, however, Shakspeare in Sophocles—and in Peter's Church stands Angelo's Rotunda!" Just then the lofty cloud, all at once, as by the blow of a hand out of the ether, broke in two, and the ravished Sun, like the eye of a Venus floating through her ancient heavens,—for she once stood even here,—looked mildly in from the upper deep; then a holy radiance filled the temple, and burned on the porphyry of the pavement, and Albano looked around him in an ecstasy of wonder and delight, and said with low voice: "How transfigured at this moment is everything in this sacred place! Raphael's spirit comes forth from his grave in this noontide hour, and everything which its reflection touches, brightens into godlike splendor!" The Princess looked upon him tenderly, and he lightly laid his hand upon hers, and said, as one vanquished, "Sophocles!"

On the next moonlit evening, Gaspard bespoke torches, in order that the Coliseum, with its giant-circle, might the first time stand in fire before them. The knight would fain have gone around alone with his son dimly through the dim work, like two spirits of the olden time, but the Princess forced herself upon him, from a too lively wish to share with the noble youth his great moments, and perhaps, in fact, her heart and his own. Women do not sufficiently comprehend that an idea, when it fills and elevates man's mind, shuts it, then, against love, and crowds out persons; whereas with woman all ideas easily become human beings.

They passed over the Forum, by the *Via sacra*, to the Coliseum, whose lofty, cloven forehead looked down pale under the moonlight. They stood before the gray rock-walls, which reared themselves on four colonnades one above another, and the torchlight shot up into the arches of the arcades, gilding the green shrubbery high overhead, and deep in the earth had the noble monster already buried his feet. They stepped in and ascended the mountain, full of fragments of rock, from one seat of the spectators to another. Gaspard did not venture to the sixth or highest, where the men used to stand, but Albano and the Princess did. Then the youth gazed down over the cliffs, upon the round, green crater of the burnt-out volcano, which once swallowed nine thousand beasts at once, and which quenched itself with human blood. The lurid glare of the torches penetrated into the clefts and caverns, and among the foliage of the ivy and laurel, and among the great shadows of the moon, which, like recluses, kept themselves in cells. Toward the South, where the streams of centuries and barbarians had stormed in, stood single columns and bare arcades. Temples and three palaces had the giant fed and lined with his limbs, and still, with all his wounds, he looked out livingly into the world.

"What a people!" said Albano. "Here curled the giant snake five times about Christianity. Like a smile of scorn lies the moonlight down below there upon the green arena, where once stood the Colossus of the Sun-god. The star of the north[*] glimmers low through the windows, and the Serpent and the Bear crouch. What a world has gone by!"—The Princess answered, "that twelve thousand prisoners built this theatre, and that a great many more had bled therein." "O! we too have building prisoners," said he, "but for fortifications; and blood, too, still flows, but with sweat! No, we have no present; the past, without it, must bring forth a future."

The Princess went to break a laurel-twig and pluck a blooming wall-flower. Albano sank away into musing: the autumnal wind of the past swept over the stubble. On this holy eminence he saw the constellations, Rome's green hills, the glimmering city, the Pyramid of Cestius,—but all became Past, and on the twelve hills dwelt, as upon graves, the lofty old spirits, and looked sternly into the age, as if they were still its kings and judges.

"This to remember the place and time!" said the approaching Princess, handing him the laurel and the flower.—"Thou mighty One! a Coliseum is thy flower-pot; to thee is nothing too great, and nothing too small!" said he, and threw the Princess into considerable confusion, till she observed that he meant not her, but nature. His whole being seemed newly and painfully moved, and, as it were, removed to a distance: he looked down after his father, and went to find him; he looked at him sharply, and spoke of nothing more this evening.

---

[*] The Pole-star, as well as other northern constellations, stands lower in the south.

LEIBGEBER TO SIEBENKÄS.*

BAIREUTH, 21st September, 1785.

"MY dear brother, and cousin, and uncle, and father, and son,—The two ears and chambers of your heart, are my whole genealogical tree; wherein you resemble Adam, who, when he went out walking, carried with him the whole future race of his relations, and his long line of successors (which even yet is not all drawn out and unwound), until he became a father, and his wife bore a child. Would to God I had been the first Adam! * * * Siebenkäs, I adjure you, let me follow up this thought as though I were crazed; and don't expect another word in this letter except such as may assist in painting my portrait as the first father of mankind.

"Those scholars misunderstood me greatly who may suppose that I was to be Adam, because, according to Puffendorf and many others, the whole earth would then belong to me of right,—like a European possession in the India of the universe,—as my *patrimonium Petri, Pauli, Judæ*, inasmuch as I, the only Adam and man, consequently as the first and last universal monarch (though as yet without subjects), could and might lay claim to the whole earth. The Pope, as holy father, though not as first father, may think of such things; or rather, he did not think about them centuries ago, when he appointed himself guardian and heir of all the lands incorporated into the earth; nay, and did not even blush to pile upon his earthly crown yet two others—a heavenly crown and a crown of hell.

"How little I desire! My sole motive for wishing to have been the old and oldest Adam, is, that on my marriage-evening I might have walked up and down with Eve outside the espalier of Paradise, in our green honeymoon aprons and skins, and have held a Hebrew wedding-oration to the mother of mankind.

"Before I begin my speech, I must preface with the remark, that before my fall the extraordinarily felicitous idea suggested itself to me of noting down the cream of my omniscience; for in my state of innocence, I possessed a knowledge of all the arts and sciences, universal as well as scholastic history, the several penal and other codes of law, and all the old dead languages, as well as the living: I was, as it were, a living Pindus and Pegasus, a movable lodge of sublime light, a royal literary society, a pocket-seat of the Muses, and a short golden *siècle de Louis XIV*. With the understanding I then possessed, it was therefore less to be wondered at, than to be considered as a piece of good luck, that in my leisure moments I consigned the best of my omniscience to paper; so that when I afterwards fell, and became silly, I had extracts, or a *resumé*, of my former knowledge at hand, to which I was enabled to refer.

"'Virgin,' thus, beyond the gates of Paradise, did I begin my discourse; 'Virgin, we are indeed the first parents, and have a mind to beget other parents; but you think of nothing, as long as you can only stick your spoon into a forbidden mess of sweetmeat.

"'I, as man and protoplast, reflect and ponder; and to-day, as I walk up and down, I will be the marriage-priest and preacher (I wish I had begotten another for this purpose) at our holy ceremony, and represent to you and myself, in a short wedding-discourse, the grounds of doubt and decision, the *rationes dubitandi* and *decidendi* of the protoplasts, or first married pair (*i.e.* myself and thee), in the act of reflecting and considering; and, moreover, *how* they consider, in the first Pars, the grounds and reasons *not* to fructify the earth, but this very day to emigrate, the one into the old, the other into the new world; and, in the second Pars, the reasons nevertheless to leave it alone, and to marry; whereupon a short clench, or *usus epanorthoticus*, shall appear and conclude the night.

PARS I.

"'Pious hearer! such as thou now beholdest me in my sheep-skin, full of earnest and deep thought, I am nevertheless full, not so much of follies as of fools, between whom a wise man is occasionally inserted by way of a parenthesis. It is true, I am small of stature,* and the ocean rose some way above my ankles, and wet my new wild-beast skin; but, by heaven! I walk up and down here, girded with a seed-bag, containing the seeds of all nations, and I carry the *repertorium* and treasury-chest of the whole human race, a little world, and an *orbis pictus*, before me, as pedlars carry their open warehouse on their stomach; for Bonnet, who lives within me, when he comes forth, will seat himself down at his writing-desk, and show that all things are comprised one within the other, one parenthesis or box within the other; that the son is contained in the father, both in the grandfather, and consequently in the great-grandfather both the grandfather and his insertions lie waiting; in the great-great-grandfather the great-grandfather with the insertion of the insertion, and with all his episodes, and so on. Are not all religious sects—for I cannot make myself too intelligible to thee, beloved bride—incorporated in thy bridegroom here present, and with the exception of the Preadamites, even the Adamites,†—all giants, the great Christopher himself,—the people of all nations, all the ship-loads of negroes destined for America, and the red-marked packages, among which is the An-

---

* From "Flower, Fruit, and Thorn Pieces." Translated by Edw. Henry Noel. Boston: James Munroe & Co. 1845.

* The French Academician Nicolas Henrion stretched out Adam to the length of 123 feet, 9 inches; Heram, 118 feet, 9 3-4 inches. The above is related by the Rabbis, viz., that Adam after the fall ran through the ocean: vide the 4th Bibl. Disc. of Saurin.

† The well-known sect which went naked to church.

spach and Baireuth soldiery, bespoken by the English? When you contemplate my interior, Eve, do I not stand before you as a living street of Jews, a *Louvre* of governors and kings, all of whom I can beget if I please, supposing I am not decided to the contrary by this first Pars? You must admire me, though at the same time you may laugh, if you look at me attentively, and placing your hand upon my shoulder, just consider: Here in this man and protoplast lie side by side, without quarrelling, all the faculties and the whole race of man,—all the schools of philosophy, sewing-schools, and spinning-schools; the best and most ancient princely houses, though not yet cleanly picked out from the common ships' companies; the whole free imperial order of knighthood, though still packed up with their vassals, cottiers, and tenants; convents of nuns, bound up with convents of monks; barracks, and county-deputies, not to mention the ecclesiastical chapters of provosts, deacons, priors, sub-priors, and canons! What a man and Anak! wilt thou say. Right, dear one, so I am indeed! I am, in fact, the nest-dollar of the whole human cabinet of coins; the tribunal of all the courts of justice, which are, moreover, all full without the absence of a single member; the living *corpus juris* of all civilians, canonists, feudalists, and publicists. Have I not Meusel's learned Germany, and Jöcher's learned school-lexicon, complete within me? and, more than that, Jöcher and Meusel in person, not to speak of supplementary volumes?

"'I should like to show you Cain. Supposing I am persuaded by the second Pars, he would be our first seedling and tendril, our prince of Wales, of Calabria, of Asturia, and of the Brazils. If he were transparent, as I believe, you would see how every thing fits in him one within the other, like beer-glasses; all ecumenic councils, and inquisitions, and propaganda, and the devil and his grandmother. But, lovely one, you did not note down any of your *scientia media* before your fall, as I did, and consequently you gaze into futurity as blind as a beetle; but I, who see through it quite clearly, perceive by my chrestomathy that if I really avail myself of my Blumenbach's *nisus formativus*, and cast to-day a few protoplastic glances into the *jus luxandiæ coxæ*, or *primæ noctis*,* I shall not beget ten fools, like another person, but whole billions of tens, and the units besides, when one thinks of all the arrant Bohemians, Parisians, inhabitants of Vienna, Leipzic, Baireuth, Hof, Dublin, Kuhschnappel (together with their wives and daughters), who will come into life through me; amongst whom there are always a million for every five hundred who neither listen to reason nor possess it. Duenna, as yet you know but little of mankind; you only know two, for the snake is not one; but I know what I am about, and that with my *limbus infantum*

* Literally the "first night," because, according to many scholars, Eve became the fruit-thief on the very morning of her creation.

I shall at the same time open a bedlam. By heaven! I tremble and groan when I take but a cursory glance between the leaves of the course of centuries, and see nothing there but stains of blood and patchwork *quodlibets* of fools; when I think of the trouble it will cost before an age learns to write a legible hand as good as that of an elephant's trunk or of a minister—before poor humanity has passed through preparatory schools, and hedge-schools, and private French governesses, and can enter with honor the Latin lyceum, royal and Jesuit schools—before it can attend the fencing school, the dancing floor, a drawing academy, and a *dogmaticum* and *clinicum*. The devil! It makes me hot only to think of it! It is true nobody will call you the brood-hen of the future flight of starlings, the cod-fish spawner, wherein Leuenhock counts nine million and a half of stockfish eggs; it will not be laid at your door, my little Eve; but your husband will bear all the blame. He ought to have been wiser, people will say, and rather not have begotten anything at all than such a rabble as the greater number of these robbers are; such, for instance, as the crowned emperors on the Roman throne, and also the vicegerents on the Roman chair; the former of whom will name themselves after Antoninus and Cæsar, the latter after Christ and Peter, and amongst whom may be found some whose throne is a Lüneburg-chair of torture for humanity, and a birth-chair of the scaffold, if it be not indeed a *Place de Grève* reversed, serving at one and the same time as a place of execution for the mass, and of pleasure for the individual.* I shall also have Borgia, Pizarro, St. Domenico, and Potemkin, brought up against me; and even granting that I could free myself from the reproach of these black exceptions, I must nevertheless concede (and anti-Adams will take hold of it *utiliter*) that my descendants and colonists cannot exist half an hour without either thinking or committing some folly; that in their giant war of passions they never establish a peace, seldom a truce; that the chief fault of man consists in his having so many *little* faults that his conscience scarcely serves him for anything else but to hate his neighbor, and to have a morbid sensitiveness for the faults of others; that he will never part with his evil habits until he is on his death-bed, alongside which is pushed a confessional, much as children are made to go to stool before they are put to bed; that he learns and loves the language

* It seems almost emblematic of the incorporation of the fierce earnest tiger and the playful ape, that the Place de Grève in Paris is at once the place of execution for criminals, and the pleasure-ground for the public festivals; that on one and the same spot a king's assassin is torn asunder by horses, and a king's fête is celebrated by the citizens; and that the fire-wheels of the victims broken on the wheel and the fire-wheels of the fire-works play together in close fellowship. Horrible contrasts! which we must not accumulate, lest we fall into the error of those who have given occasion for this rebuke.

of virtue, while he shows enmity to the virtuous — resembling in this the citizens of London, who hate the French, while they keep French masters to learn their language. Eve, Eve! we shall gain little honor by our marriage. According to the fundamental text, Adam signifies red earth; and verily my cheeks will be entirely composed thereof, and blush when I think of the inexpressible and uninterrupted vanity and self-conceit of our great-grandchildren,—a vanity growing with every century. No one will pull his own nose but he who shaves himself; the high nobility will burn the family-escutcheon at the door of their secret chambers, and interweave the cruppers of their horses into their initials; reviewers will set themselves above the authors, the latter above the former; the Heimlicher von Blaise will present his hand for the orphan's kiss; the ladies theirs to every one; and the highest will kiss the hem of the embroidered garment. Eve, I had barely finished writing down my prophetic extracts of the world's history up to the sixth millennary, when you bit into the apple under the tree; and I, like an ass, followed your example, and then everything escaped me. God knows what may be the semblance of the male and female fools of the other millennaries. Virgin! wilt thou now use the *sternocleidomastoideum*, as Sömmering calls the nod of the head, and therewith say thy yea, when I ask thee, Wilt thou have this marriage-preacher to thy wedded lord and husband?

"'You will answer, without doubt: We will at least listen to the second Pars, wherein the affair is considered in another point of view; and truly, pious reader, we had almost forgotten to proceed to

PARS II.

and altogether to weigh the grounds which induce protoplasts and first parents to be such, and to marry, serving Destiny in the capacity of sewing and spinning machines of linseed and hemp, of flax and tow, which she may wind in infinite coils and net-work round the earthly sphere. My chief motive, and I hope thine also, is my conception of the last day; for in case we two become the *entrepreneurs* of the human race, I shall behold all my descendants steaming up on the last day from the calcined earth into the nearest neighboring planet, and arranging themselves in order for the last review; and in this blessed harvest of children and grandchildren I shall meet some who are gifted with understanding, and with whom one can exchange a word or two—men whose whole life passed under a thunder-cloud, and who lost it in a storm, as, according to the belief of the Romans, the favorites of the gods were struck dead by lightning — men who, nevertheless, neither bound their eyes or their ears in the tempest. Furthermore, I behold there the four glorious heathen evangelists, Socrates, Cato, Epictetus, and Antoninus, who went about to every house applying their throats, like the pipes of fire-engines 200 feet in length, to every damnable conflagration of the passions, and extinguishing them with the best and purest alpine water. In short, we shall, if we so please, be —I the grandpapa, and you the grandmamma, of the most excellent people. I tell thee, Eve, it is noted down here in my tracts and *collectanea*, black upon white, that I shall be the forefather, the ancestor, the Bethlehem, and plastic nature of an Aristotle, a Plato, a Shakspeare, Newton, Rousseau, Goethe, Kant, and Leibnitz, besides others who are still cleverer than their protoplast himself. Eve! thou acting and important member of this present fruit-bearing society, or productive class in the state, consisting of you and the wedding-orator, I swear to you that I shall enjoy an hour of some blissful eternities when I stand upon the neighboring planet, and cast my eyes flightily over the circle of classic and new-born men, and then kneel down in rapture upon the satellite, and exclaim, "Good morning, my children!"'

"Ye Jews formerly had the habit of uttering an ejaculatory prayer when ye met a wise man; but what prayer can I utter long enough, when I behold at one glance all the wise men and members of faculties, all of them, moreover, my relations, who, in spite of the wolfish hunger of the passions, yet knew how to renounce the forbidden apple and pear and ananas, and who, in their thirst after truth, committed no garden-robbery from the tree of knowledge, like their first parents, who seized the forbidden fruit, though they felt no hunger, and attacked the tree of knowledge, although they already possessed all knowledge, excepting that of the snake's nature. Then I shall rise from the ground, and rush among the crowd of my descendants, and fall on the bosom of one chosen one, and throw my arms round him, and say, 'Thou true, good, contented, gentle son, if, in the second Pars of my wedding-discourse, I could have shown my Eve, the queen-mother of the present swarm of bees around us, none other but thee, sitting in thy breeding-cell, verily the woman would have taken it to heart, and listened to reason:' and the true good son art thou, Siebenkäs; and thou wilt ever lie on the rough hairy breast of

"THY FRIEND."

SECOND EXTRACT FROM "FLOWER, FRUIT AND THORN PIECES."

Man lies under the yoke of a twofold necessity; that of the day, which he bears without murmur, and that of the year, which, though more rare, he cannot endure without wrangling and complaint. The daily and ever-renewed necessity is, that no wheat grows in winter; that we are not gifted with wings, like so many of the animal tribe; that we cannot set our foot upon the ring-shaped mountains of the moon, and thence gaze on the descending sun gloriously illumining the mile-deep abysses. The yearly and more rare necessity is, that it rains when the corn is in blossom; that we cannot walk conveniently in many a marshy meadow of earth; and that occasionally, because of corns or our want of shoes, we cannot walk at all. But the yearly necessity is, in fact, as great as the daily one; and it is just as foolish to resist and murmur at a paralysis of the limbs, as at our want of wings. All the past, and this alone is the subject of our sorrow, is so much a matter of iron-necessity, that in the eyes of a superior being it is an equal folly, on the part of an apothecary, whether he complain of his shop having been burnt down, or of his inability to go botanizing in the moon, though in the phials there he would find many things which are wanting in his.

I will here insert a little extra leaf upon the consolations in our windy, cold, damp life. Let those who are exceedingly vexed, and almost inconsolable, at this short digression, seek consolation in the

EXTRA LEAF ON CONSOLATION.

A time will come, that is, must come, when we shall be commanded by morality not only to cease tormenting others, but also ourselves. A time must come when man, even on earth, shall wipe away most of his tears, were it only from pride.

Nature, indeed, draws tears out of the eyes, and sighs out of the breast, so quickly, that the wise man can never wholly lay aside the garb of mourning from his body; but let his soul wear none. For if it is over a merit to bear a small suffering with cheerfulness, so must the calm and patient endurance of the worst be a merit, and will only differ in being a greater one; as the same reason which is valid for the forgiveness of small injuries is equally valid for the forgiveness of the greatest.

The first thing that we have to contend against and despise, in sorrow as in anger, is its poisonous enervating sweetness, which we are so loath to exchange for the labor of consoling ourselves, and to drive away by the effort of reason.

We must not exact of philosophy, that with one stroke of the pen it shall reverse the transformation of Rubens, who, with one stroke of his brush, changed a laughing child into a weeping one. It is enough if it change the full-mourning of the soul into half-mourning; it is enough if I can say to myself,—I will be content to endure the sorrow that philosophy has left me; without it, it would be greater, and the gnat's bite would be a wasp's sting.

Even physical pain shoots its sparks upon us out of the electrical condenser of the imagination. We could endure the most acute pangs calmly if they only lasted the sixtieth part of a second; but, in fact, we never have to endure an hour of pain, but only a succession of the sixtieth parts of a second, the sixty beams of which are collected into the burning focus of a second, and directed upon our nerves by the imagination alone. The most painful part of our bodily pain is that which is bodiless, or immaterial, namely, our impatience, and the delusion that it will last forever.

There is many a loss over which we all know for certain that we shall no longer grieve in twenty—ten—two years. Why do we not say to ourselves: I will at once then, to-day, throw away an opinion which I shall abandon in twenty years? Why should I be able to abandon errors of twenty years' standing, and not of twenty hours?

When I awake from a dream which an Otaheite has painted for me on the dark ground of the night, and find the flowery land melted away, I scarcely sigh, thinking to myself, "It was only a dream." Why is it that if I had really possessed this island while awake, and it had been swallowed up by an earthquake, why is it that I do not then exclaim, "The island was only a dream?" Wherefore am I more inconsolable at the loss of a longer dream than at the loss of a shorter—for that is the difference; and why does man find a great loss less probable and less a matter of necessity, when it occurs, than a small one?

The reason is, that every sentiment and every emotion is mad, and exacts and builds its own world. A man can vex himself that it is already, or only, twelve o'clock. What folly! The mood not only exacts its own world, its own individual[*] consciousness, but its own time. I beg every one to let his passions, for once, speak out plainly within himself, and to probe and question them to the bottom, as to what they really desire. He will be terror-struck at the enormity of these hitherto only half-muttered wishes. Anger wishes that all mankind had only one neck; love, that it had only one heart; grief, two tear-glands; and pride, two bent knees.

When I read in Widman's "Court Chronicle" of the terrible bloody times of the Thirty Years' War, and as it were lived them over again; when I heard once more the cries of the tortured for help, as they struggled in the Danube-whirlpools of their age, and again beheld the clasping of hands, and the delirious wandering to and fro on the several pillars of the crumbling bridges, against which struck foaming billows and fiercely-driven fields of ice—and thus reflected, "All the waves have subsided, the ice has melted, the storm is mute, and the human beings also with their sighs," I was filled with a peculiar melancholy feeling of consolation for all times; and I asked, "Was and is, then, this fleeting misery beneath the churchyard-gate of life, which three steps into the nearest cavern could put an end to, worth all this cowardly lamentation?" Verily, if there be, as I believe there is, true constancy under

---

[*] "Sein eignes ich." Tr.

an *eternal sorrow*, then is patience under a fleeting one scarcely worthy of the name.

A great and unmerited national calamity should not humble us, as the theologians demand, but rather make us proud. When the long heavy sword of war falls upon humanity, and when a thousand pale hearts are riven and bleeding; or when, on a blue serene evening, the hot smoky cloud of a city, cast on the funereal pyre, hangs darkly on the sky,—as though it were the cloud of ashes of a thousand consumed hearts and joys,—then be thy spirit lifted up in pride, and let it contemn the tear and that for which it falls, saying, "Thou art much too insignificant, thou every-day life, for the inconsolableness of an immortal,—thou tattered, misshapen, wholesale existence! Upon this sphere, which is rounded with the ashes of thousands of years, amid the storms of earth, made up of vapors, it is a disgrace that the sigh should only be dissipated together with the bosom that gives it birth, and not sooner; and that the tear should not perish except with the eye whence it flows."

But then, moderate thy sublime indignation, and put this question to thyself: If the hidden Infinite One, who is encompassed by gleaming abysses without bounds, and who himself creates the bounds, were now to lay immensity open to thy view, and to reveal himself to thee in his distribution of the suns, the lofty spirits, the little human hearts, and our days and some tears therein,—wouldst thou rise up out of thy dust against him, and say, "Almighty! be other than Thou art!"

But be one sorrow alone forgiven thee, or made good to thee—the sorrow for thy dead ones; for this sweet sorrow for the lost is itself but another form of consolation. When the heart is full of longing for them, it is but another mode of continuing to love them; and we shed tears as well when we think of their departure, as when we picture to ourselves our joyful re-union—and the tears, methinks, differ not.

DREAM.*

THE object of this composition must serve as the excuse of its boldness.

Man denies the existence of God with as little feeling as most of us grant it. Even in our true systems, we only collect words, counters and medals, as the avaricious accumulate cabinets of coins; and it is not until long after, that we exchange the words for sentiments, our coins for enjoyments. A man may believe in the immortality of the soul for twenty years, but only in the twenty-first, in some great moment, is he astonished at the rich substance of this belief, at the warmth of this naphtha-spring.

Even so was I horror-struck at the poisonous vapor which meets the heart of one who enters for the first time into the atheistic seminary, as though it would suffocate it. It would cause me less pain to deny immortality than the existence of the Deity. In the former case, I lose nothing but a world concealed by a fog; in the latter case, I lose the present world, namely, its Sun. The whole spiritual universe is split and shattered by the hand of Atheism into countless quicksilver points of individual existences,* which twinkle, melt into one another, and wander about, meet and part, without unity and consistency. No one is so much alone in the universe as a denier of God. With an orphaned heart, which has lost the greatest of fathers, he stands mourning by the immeasurable corpse of nature, no longer moved or sustained by the Spirit of the universe, but growing in its grave; and he mourns, until he himself crumbles away from the dead body.

The whole world lies before him like the great Egyptian sphinx of stone, which is half-buried in the sand, and the universe is the cold iron mask of the shapeless eternity.

Another aim of my composition is, to frighten some of the reading or deep-read professors; for verily these people, since they have become day-laborers, after the manner of condemned criminals, in the waterworks and mining operations of the critical philosophy, weigh the existence of God as apathetically and as cold-heartedly as though it were a question of the existence of the kraken or the unicorn.

To others, who are not so far advanced as these deep-read professors, I may observe, that it is no inconsistency to unite a belief in immortality with a belief in Atheism; for the same necessity which, in this life, threw the bright dewdrop of my individual existence into a flower-cup, and beneath a sun, can repeat it in a second life; indeed, it is easier to embody me a second time than the first time.

When we are told in childhood, that at midnight, when our sleep reaches near unto the soul, and even darkens our dreams, the dead rise out of *their* sleep and mimic the religious service of the living in the churches, we shudder at death on account of the dead; and in the loneliness of night we turn away our gaze from the long narrow windows of the silent church, fearing to examine whether their glitter proceeds from the moonbeams, or not.

Childhood and especially its terrors and raptures once more assume wings and brightness in our dreams, and play like glow-worms in the little night of the soul. Crush not these little fluttering sparks! Leave us even our dark painful dreams, as relieving middle tints of reality! And what could compensate us for our dreams, which bear us away from beneath the roar of the waterfall into the mountain-heights of childhood, where the stream of life,

---

* From the same.

* German, "*ichs*."

yet silent in its little plain, and a mirror of heaven, flowed towards its precipices?

Once on a summer evening I lay upon a mountain in the sunshine, and fell asleep; and I dreamt that I awoke in the church-yard, having been roused by the rattling wheels of the tower-clock, which struck eleven. I looked for the sun in the void night-heaven; for I thought that it was eclipsed by the moon. All the graves were unclosed, and the iron doors of the charnel-house were opened and shut by invisible hands. Shadows cast by no one flitted along the walls, and other shadows stalked erect in the free air. No one slept any longer in the open coffins but the children. A grey, sultry fog hung suspended in heavy folds in the heavens, and a gigantic shadow drew it in like a net, ever nearer, and closer, and hotter. Above me I heard the distant fall of avalanches; beneath me, the earnest step of an immeasurable earthquake. The church was heaved up and down by two incessant discords, which struggled with one another, and in vain sought to unite in harmony. Sometimes a grey glimmer flared up on the windows, and, molten by the glimmer, the iron and lead ran down in streams. The net of fog and the reeling earth drove me into the temple, at the door of which brooded two basilisks with twinkling eyes in two poisonous nests. I passed through unknown shadows, on whom were impressed all the centuries of years. The shadows stood congregated round the altar; and in all, the breast throbbed and trembled in the place of a heart. One corpse alone, which had just been buried in the church, lay still upon its pillow, and its breast heaved not, while upon its smiling countenance lay a happy dream; but on the entrance of one of the living he awoke, and smiled no more. He opened his closed eyelids with a painful effort, but within there was no eye; and in the sleeping bosom, instead of a heart there was a wound. He lifted up his hands, and folded them in prayer; but the arms lengthened out and detached themselves from the body, and the folded hands fell down apart. Aloft, on the church-dome, stood the dial-plate of Eternity; but there was no figure visible upon it, and it was its own index; only a black figure pointed to it, and the dead wished to read the time upon it.

A lofty, noble form, having the expression of a never-ending sorrow, now sank down from above upon the altar, and all the dead exclaimed—"Christ! is there no God?" And he answered—"There is none!" The whole shadow of each dead one, and not the breast alone, now trembled, and one after another was severed by the trembling.

Christ continued:—"I traversed the worlds. I ascended into the suns, and flew with the milky ways through the wildernesses of the heavens; but there is no God! I descended as far as Being throws its shadow, and gazed down into the abyss, and cried aloud—'Father, where art thou?' but I heard nothing but the eternal storm which no one rules; and the beaming rainbow in the west hung, without a creating sun, above the abyss, and fell down in drops; and when I looked up to the immeasurable world for the Divine Eye, it glared upon me from an empty, bottomless socket, and Eternity lay brooding upon chaos, and gnawed it, and ruminated it. Cry on, ye discords! cleave the shadows with your cries; for he is not!"

The shadows grew pale and melted, as the white vapor formed by the frost melts and becomes a warm breath, and all was void. Then there arose and came into the temple—a terrible sight for the heart—the dead children who had awakened in the church-yard, and they cast themselves before the lofty form upon the altar, and said, "Jesus! have we no Father?" and he answered with streaming eyes, "We are all orphans, I and you; we are without a Father."

Thereupon the discords shrieked more harshly; the trembling walls of the temple split asunder, and the temple and the children sunk down, and the earth and the sun followed, and the whole immeasurable universe fell rushing past us; and aloft upon the summit of infinite Nature stood Christ, and gazed down into the universe, chequered with thousands of suns, as into a mine dug out of the Eternal Night, wherein the suns are the miners' lamps, and the milky ways the veins of silver.

And when Christ beheld the grinding concourse of worlds, the torch-dances of the heavenly *ignes fatui*, and the coral-banks of beating hearts; and when he beheld how one sphere after another poured out its gleaming souls into the sea of death, as a drop of water strews gleaming lights upon the waves, sublime, as the loftiest finite being, he lifted up his eyes to the Nothingness, and to the empty Immensity, and said: "Frozen, dumb Nothingness! cold, eternal Necessity! insane Chance! know ye what is beneath you? When will ye destroy the building and me? Chance! knowest thou thyself when with hurricanes thou wilt march through the snow-storm of stars and extinguish one sun after the other, and when the sparkling dew of the constellations shall cease to glisten as thou passest by? How lonely is every one in the wide charnel of the universe! I alone am in company with myself. O Father! O Father! where is thine infinite bosom, that I may be at rest? Alas! if every being is its own father and creator, why cannot it also be its own destroying angel? * * * Is that a man near me? Thou poor one! thy little life is the sigh of Nature, or only its echo. A concave mirror throws its beams upon the dust-clouds composed of the ashes of the dead upon your earth, and thus ye exist, cloudy, tottering images! Look down into the abyss over which clouds of ashes are floating by. Fogs full of worlds arise out of the sea of death. The future is a rising vapor, the present a falling one. Knowest thou thy earth?" Here Christ looked down, and his eyes filled with tears, and he said, "Alas! I too was once like you: then I was happy, for I had still my infinite Father, and still gazed joyfully from the mountains into the infinite expanse of heaven; and I pressed my wounded heart on his soothing image, and said, even in the bitterness of death: 'Father, take thy Son out of his bleeding shell, and lift him up to thy heart.' Ah, ye too, too happy dwellers of earth, ye still believe in him. Perhaps at this moment your sun is setting, and ye fall amid blossoms, radiance, and tears, upon your knees, and lift up your blessed hands, and call out to the open heaven, amid a thousand tears of joy, 'Thou knowest me too, thou infinite One, and all my wounds, and thou wilt welcome me after death, and wilt close them all.' Ye wretched ones! after death they will not be closed. . . . . When the man of sorrows stretches his sore wounded back upon the earth to slumber towards a lovelier morning, full of truth, full of virtue and of joy, behold, he awakes in the tempestuous chaos, in the everlasting midnight, and no morning cometh, and no healing hand, and no infinite Father! Mortal who art near me, if thou still livest, worship him, or thou hast lost him forever!"

And as I fell down and gazed into the gleaming fabric of worlds, I beheld the raised rings of the giant serpent of eternity, which had couched itself round the universe of worlds, and the rings fell, and she enfolded the universe doubly. Then she wound herself in a thousand folds round Nature, and crushed the worlds together, and, grinding them, she squeezed the infinite temple into one church-yard church—and all became narrow, dark, and fearful, and a bell-hammer stretched out to infinity was about to strike the last hour of Time, and split the universe asunder—when I awoke.

My soul wept for joy, that it could again worship God; and the joy, and the tears, and the belief in him, were the prayer. And when I arose, the sun gleamed deeply behind the full purple ears of corn, and peacefully threw the reflection of its evening blushes on the little moon, which was rising in the east without an aurora. And between the heaven and the earth a glad fleeting world stretched out its short wings, and lived like myself in the presence of the infinite Father, and from all nature around me flowed sweet peaceful tones, as from evening bells.

LETTER TO MY FRIENDS, INSTEAD OF PREFACE.*

Of ways for becoming happier (not happy) I could never inquire out more than three. The first, rather an elevated road, is this: To soar away so far above the clouds of life, that you see the whole external world, with its wolf-dens, charnel-houses, and thunder-rods, lying far down beneath you, shrunk into a little child's garden. The second is: Simply to sink down into this little garden; and there to nestle yourself so snugly, so homewise, in some furrow, that, in looking out from your warm lark-nest, you likewise can discern no wolf-dens, charnel-houses, or thunder-rods, but only blades and ears, every one of which, for the nest-bird, is a tree, and a sun-screen, and rain-screen. The third, finally, which I look upon as the hardest and cunningest, is that of alternating between the other two.

This I shall now satisfactorily expound to men at large.

The Hero, the Reformer, your Brutus, your Howard, your Republican, he whom civic storm, or genius poetic storm, impels; in short, every mortal with a great Purpose, or even a perennial Passion (were it but that of writing the largest folios), all these men fence themselves in by their internal world against the frosts and heats of the external, as the madman in a worse sense does: every *fixed* idea, such as rules every genius, every enthusiast, at least periodically, separates and elevates a man above the bed and board of this Earth, above its Dog's-grottoes, buckthorns and Devil's-walls; like the Bird of Paradise, he slumbers flying; and on his outspread pinions, oversleeps unconsciously the earthquakes and conflagrations of Life, in his long fair dream of his ideal Mother-land.—Alas! To few is this dream granted; and these few are so often awakened by Flying Dogs!*

This skyward track, however, is fit only for the winged portion of the human species, for the smallest. What can it profit poor quill-driving brethren, whose souls have not even wing-shells, to say nothing of wings? Or these tethered persons with the best back breast and neck fins, who float motionless in the wicker Fish-box of the State, and are not allowed to swim, because the Box or State, long ago tied to the shore, itself swims in the name of the Fishes? To the whole standing and writing host of heavy-laden State-domestics, Purveyors, Clerks of all departments, and all the lobsters packed together heels over head in the Lobster-basket of the Government office-rooms, and for refreshment, sprinkled over with a few nettles; to these persons, what way of becoming happy *here*, can I possibly point out?

My *second* merely; and that is as follows: To take a compound microscope, and with it to discover, and convince themselves, that their drop of Burgundy is properly a Red Sea, that butterfly-dust is peacock-feathers, mouldiness a flowery field, and sand a heap of jewels. These microscopic recreations are more lasting than all costly watering-place recreations.—But I

---

* Life of Quintus Fixlein. German Romance. T. Carlyle, Vol. iii. Edinburgh. 1827.

* So are the Vampyres called.

must explain these metaphors by new ones. The purpose, for which I have sent *Fixlein's Life* into the Messrs. Lübeks' Warehouse, is simply that in this same *Life*—therefore in this Preface it is less needful—I may show to the whole Earth that we ought to value little joys more than great ones, the night-gown more than the dress-coat; that Plutus' heaps are worth less than his handfuls, the plum than the penny for a rainy day; and that not great, but little good-haps can make us happy.—Can I accomplish this, I shall, through means of my Book, bring up for Posterity, a race of men finding refreshment in all things; in the warmth of their rooms and of their night-caps; in their pillows; in the three High Festivals; in mere Apostles' days; in the Evening Moral Tales of their wives, when these gentle persons have been forth as ambassadors visiting some Dowager Residence, whither the husband could not be persuaded; in the bloodletting-day of these their newsbringers; in the day of slaughtering, salting, potting against the rigor of grim winter; and in all such days. You perceive, my drift is that man must become a little Tailor-bird, which, not amid the crashing boughs of the storm-tost, roaring, immeasurable tree of Life, but on one of its leaves, sews itself a nest together, and there lies snug. The most essential sermon one could preach to our century, were a sermon on the duty of staying at home.

The *third* skyward road is the alternation between the other two. The foregoing *second* way is not good enough for man, who here on Earth should take into his hand not the Sickle only, but also the Plough. The *first* is too good for him. He has not always the force, like Rugendas, in the midst of the Battle to compose Battle-pieces; and, like Backhuisen in the Shipwreck, to clutch at no board but the drawing-board to paint it on. And then his *pains* are not less lasting than his *fatigues*. Still oftener is Strength denied its Arena: it is but the smallest portion of life that, to a working soul, offers Alps, Revolutions, Rhine-falls, Worms Diets, and Wars with Xerxes; and for the whole it is better so: the longer portion of life is a field beaten flat as a threshing-floor, without lofty Gothard Mountains; often it is a tedious ice-field, without a single glacier tinged with dawn.

But even by walking, a man rests and recovers himself from climbing; by little joys and duties, for great. The victorious Dictator must contrive to plough down his battle Mars-field into a flax and carrot field; to transform his theatre of war into a parlour theatre, on which his children may enact some good pieces from the *Children's Friend*. Can he accomplish this, can he turn so softly from the path of poetical happiness into that of household happiness,—then is he little different from myself, who even now, though modesty might forbid me to disclose it—who even now, I say, amid the creation of this Letter, have been enabled to reflect, that when it is done, so also will the Roses and Elder-berries of pastry be done, which a sure hand is seething in butter for the Author of this Work.

THE MARRIAGE.*

RISE, fair Ascension and Marriage day, and gladden readers also! Adorn thyself with the fairest jewel, with the bride, whose soul is as pure and glittering as its vesture; like pearl and pearl-muscle, the one as the other, lustrous and ornamental! And so over the espalier, whose fruit-hedge has hitherto divided our darling from his Eden, every reader now presses after him!—

On the 9th of May, 1793, about three in the morning, there came a sharp peal of trumpets, like a light-beam, through the dim-red May-dawn: two twisted horns, with a straight trumpet between them, like a note of admiration between interrogation-points, were clanging from a house in which only a parishioner (not the Parson) dwelt and blew: for this parishioner had last night been celebrating the same ceremony which the pastor had this day before him. The joyful tallyho raised our Parson from his broad bed (and the Shock from beneath it, who some weeks ago had been exiled from the white sleek coverlid), and this so early, that in the portraying tester, where on every former morning he had observed his ruddy visage, and his white bedclothes, all was at present dim and crayoned.

I confess, the new-painted room, and a gleam of dawn on the wall, made it so light, that he could see his knee-buckles glancing on the chair. He then softly awakened his mother (the other guests were to lie for hours in the sheets), and she had the city cook-maid to awaken, who, like several other articles of wedding-furniture, had been borrowed for a day or two from Flachsenfingen. At two doors he knocked in vain, and without answer; for all were already down at the hearth, cooking, blowing, and arranging.

How softly does the Spring day gradually fold back its nun-veil, and the Earth grow bright, as if it were the morning of a Resurrection!—The quicksilver-pillar of the barometer, the guiding Fire-pillar of the weather-prophet, rests firmly on Fixlein's Ark of the Covenant. The Sun raises himself, pure and cool, into the morning-blue, instead of into the morning-red. Swallows, instead of clouds, shoot skimming through the melodious air. . . . O, the good Genius of Fair Weather, who deserves many temples and festivals (because without him no festival could be held), lifted an ætherial azure Day, as it were, from the well-clear atmosphere of the Moon, and sent it down, on blue butterfly-wings—as if it were a *blue* Monday—glitter-

---

* From the same.

ing below the Sun, in the zigzag of joyful quivering descent, upon the narrow spot of Earth, which our heated fancies are now viewing. . . . And on this balmy, vernal spot, stand amid flowers, over which the trees are shaking blossoms instead of leaves, a bride and a bridegroom. . . . . Happy Fixlein! how shall I paint thee without deepening the sighs of longing in the fairest souls?—

But soft! we will not drink the magic cup of Fancy to the bottom, at six in the morning; but keep sober till towards night!

At the sound of the morning prayer-bell, the bridegroom—for the din of preparation was disturbing his quiet orison—went out into the church-yard, which (as in many other places) together with the church, lay round his mansion like a court. Here, on the moist green, over whose closed flowers the church-yard wall was still spreading broad shadows, did his spirit cool itself from the warm dreams of Earth: here, where the white flat grave-stone of his Teacher lay before him like the fallen-in door on the Janus'-temple of Life, or like the windward side of the narrow house, turned towards the tempests of the world: here, where the little shrunk metallic door on the grated cross of his father uttered to him the inscriptions of death, and the year when his parent departed, and all the admonitions and mementos, graven on the lead;—there, I say, his mood grew softer and more solemn; and he now lifted up by heart his morning prayer, which usually he read; and entreated God to bless him in his office, and to spare his mother's life, and to look with favor and acceptance on the purpose of to-day.—Then, over the graves, he walked into his fenceless little angular flower-garden; and here, composed and confident in the divine keeping, he pressed the stalks of his tulips deeper into the mellow earth.

But on returning to the house, he was met on all hands by the bell-ringing and the Janizary-music of wedding-gladness;—the marriage-guests had all thrown off their nightcaps, and were drinking diligently;—there was a clattering, a cooking, a frizzling;—tea-services, coffee-services, and warm beer-services, were advancing in succession; and plates full of bride-cakes were going round like potter's frames or cistern-wheels.—The Schoolmaster, with three young lads, was heard rehearsing from his own house an *Arioso*, with which, so soon as they were perfect, he purposed to surprise his clerical superior.—But now rushed all the arms of the foaming joy-streams into one, when the sky-queen besprinkled with blossoms, the bride, descended upon Earth in her timid joy, full of quivering, humble love;—when the bells began;—when the procession-column set forth with the whole village round and before it;—when the organ, the congregation, the officiating priest, and the sparrows on the trees of the church-window, struck louder and louder their rolling peals on the drum of the jubilee-festival. . . . The heart of the singing bridegroom was like to leap from its place for joy, "that on his bridal-day, it was all so respectable and grand."—Not till the marriage benediction could he pray a little.

Still worse and louder grew the business during dinner, when pastry-work and marchpane-devices were brought forward,—when glasses, and slain fishes (laid under the napkins to frighten the guests) went round;—and when the guests rose, and themselves went round, and at length danced round: for they had instrumental music from the city there.

One minute handed over to the other the sugar-bowl and bottle-case of joy: the guests heard and saw less and less, and the villagers began to see and hear more and more, and towards night they penetrated like a wedge into the open door,—nay, two youths ventured even in the middle of the parsonage-court, to mount a plank over a beam, and commence seesawing.—Out of doors, the gleaming vapor of the departed Sun was encircling the Earth, the evening-star was glittering over parsonage and church-yard; no one heeded it.

However, about nine o'clock,—when the marriage-guests had well nigh forgotten the marriage-pair, and were drinking or dancing along for their own behoof; when poor mortals, in this sunshine of Fate, like fishes in the sunshine of the sky, were leaping up from their wet cold element; and when the bridegroom under the star of happiness and love, casting like a comet its long train of radiance over all his heaven, had in secret pressed to his joy-filled breast his bride and his mother,—then did he lock a slice of wedding-bread privily into a press, in the old superstitious belief, that this residue secured continuance of bread for the whole marriage. As he returned, with greater love for the sole partner of his life, she herself met him with his mother, to deliver him in private the bridal-nightgown and bridal-shirt, as is the ancient usage. Many a countenance grows pale in violent emotions, even of joy: Thiennette's wax-face was bleaching still whiter under the sunbeams of Happiness. O, never fall, thou lily of Heaven, and may four springs instead of four seasons open and shut thy flower-bells to the sun!—All the arms of his soul as he floated on the sea of joy were quivering to clasp the soft warm heart of his beloved, to encircle it gently and fast, and draw it to his own.

He led her from the crowded dancing-room into the cool evening. Why does the evening, does the night put warmer love in our hearts? Is it the nightly pressure of helplessness? or is it the exalting separation from the turmoil of life; that veiling of the world, in which for the soul nothing more remains but souls?—is it therefore, that the letters in which the loved name stands written on our spirit appear, like phosphorus-writing, by night, *in fire*, while by day in their *cloudy* traces they but smoke?

He walked with his bride into the Castle-garden: she hastened quickly through the Castle, and past its servants'-hall, where the fair flowers of her young life had been crushed broad and dry, under a long dreary pressure; and her soul expanded, and breathed in the free open garden, on whose flowery soil destiny had cast forth the first seeds of the blossoms which to-day were gladdening her existence. Still Eden! Green flower-chequered *chiaroscuro!*—The moon is sleeping under ground like a dead one; but beyond the garden the sun's red evening-clouds have fallen down like rose-leaves; and the evening-star, the brideman of the sun, hovers, like a glancing butterfly, above the rosy red, and, modest as a bride, deprives no single starlet of its light.

The wandering pair arrived at the old gardener's hut; now standing locked and dumb, with dark windows in the light garden, like a fragment of the Past surviving in the Present. Bared twigs of trees were folding, with clammy half-formed leaves, over the thick intertwisted tangles of the bushes.—The Spring was standing, like a conqueror, with Winter at his feet.—In the blue pond, now bloodless, a dusky evening-sky lay hollowed out, and the gushing waters were moistening the flower-beds.—The silver sparks of stars were rising on the altar of the East, and falling down extinguished in the red sea of the West.

The wind whirred, like a night-bird, louder through the trees, and gave tones to the acacia-grove; and the tones called to the pair who had first become happy within it: "Enter, new mortal pair, and think of what is past, and of my withering and your own; and be holy as Eternity, and weep not only for joy, but for gratitude also!"—And the wet-eyed bridegroom led his wet-eyed bride under the blossoms, and laid his soul, like a flower, on her heart, and said: "Best Thiennette, I am unspeakably happy, and would say much, and cannot—Ah, thou Dearest, we will live like angels, like children together! Surely I will do all that is good to thee; two years ago I had nothing, no, nothing; ah, it is through thee, best love, that I am happy. I call thee Thou, now, thou dear good soul!" She drew him closer to her, and said, though without kissing him: "Call me Thou always, Dearest!"

And as they stept forth again from the sacred grove into the magic-dusky garden, he took off his hat; first, that he might internally thank God, and secondly, because he wished to look into this fairest evening sky.

They reached the blazing, rustling, marriage-house, but their softened hearts sought stillness; and a foreign touch, as in the blossoming vine, would have disturbed the flower-nuptials of their souls. They turned rather, and winded up into the church-yard to preserve their mood. Majestic on the groves and mountains stood the Night before man's heart, and made that also great. Over the *white* steeple-obelisk the sky rested *bluer*, and *darker;* and behind it, wavered the withered summit of the May-pole with faded flag. The son noticed his father's grave, on which the wind was opening and shutting, with harsh noise, the little door of the metal cross, to let the year of his death be read on the brass plate within. An overpowering sadness seized his heart with violent streams of tears, and drove him to the sunk hillock, and he led his bride to the grave, and said: "Here sleeps he, my good father; in his thirty-second year, he was carried hither to his long rest. O thou good, dear father, couldst thou to-day but see the happiness of thy son, like my mother! But thy eyes are empty, and thy breast is full of ashes, and thou seest us not."—He was silent. The bride wept aloud; she saw the mouldering coffins of her parents open, and the two dead arise and look round for their daughter, who had stayed so long behind them, forsaken on the Earth. She fell upon his heart, and faltered: "O beloved, I have neither father nor mother, do not forsake me!"

O thou who hast still a father and a mother, thank God for it, on the day when thy soul is full of joyful tears, and needs a bosom wherein to shed them. . . .

And with this embracing at a father's grave, let this day of joy be holily concluded.

THOUGHTS.*

THE inner man, like the negro, is born white, but is colored black by life. In advanced age the grandest moral examples pass by us, and our life-course is no more altered by them than the earth is by a flitting comet; but in childhood the first object that excites the sentiment of love or of injustice flings broad and deep its light or shadow over the coming years; and as, according to ancient theologians, it was only the first sin of Adam, not his subsequent ones, which descended to us by inheritance, so that since the One Fall we make the rest for ourselves, in like manner the first fall and the first ascent influence the whole life.

HOW CHILDREN LEARN TO WORSHIP.

Sublimity is the staircase to the temple of religion, as the stars are to immensity. When the vast is manifested in nature, as in a storm, thunder, the starry firmament, death, then utter the name of God before your child. Signal calamity, rare success, a great crime, a noble action, are the spots upon which to erect the child's tabernacle of worship.

Always exhibit before children, even upon the borders of the holy land of religion, solemn and devout emotions. These will extend to them, unveiling at length the object by which they are excited, though at the beginning they are awe-struck with you, not knowing where-

---

* From the Diadem. 1846. Carey & Hart, Philadelphia. Translated by Miss L. Osgood.

fore. Newton, who uncovered his head when the greatest Name was pronounced, thus became without words a teacher of religion to children.

Instead of carrying children frequently to public worship, I should prefer simply to conduct them upon great days in nature or in human life into the empty church, and there show them the holy place of adults. To this I might add twilight, night, the organ, the hymn, the priest, exhortation; and so by a mere walk through the building, a more serious impression might remain in their young hearts than after a whole year of common church routine. Let every hour in which their hearts are consecrated to religion, be to them as absorbing as that in which they partake for the first time of the Lord's Supper.

Let the Protestant child show reverence to the Catholic images of saints by the road-side— the same as to the ancient Druidical oak of his ancestors. Let him as lovingly accept different forms of religion among men, as different languages, wherein there is still but one human mind expressed. Every genius has most power in his own tongue, and every heart in its own religion.

SUSCEPTIBILITY OF THE SENSES IN CHILDREN.

Who has not felt with me, that frequently a rural nosegay, which was our delight when we were children in the village, through its old fragrance produces for us in cities, in the advanced years of manhood, an indescribably rapturous return to godlike childhood, and like a flowery divinity wafts us upward to the first encircling Aurora-cloud of our earliest obscure sensations. But could such a remembrance so forcibly surprise us, were not the child's perception of flowers most powerful and interior?

JOYOUSNESS OF CHILDREN.

How should it be otherwise? I can bear a melancholy man, but never a melancholy child. Into whatever quagmire the former sinks, he may raise his eyes either to the realm of reason or to that of hope; but the little child sinks and perishes in a single black poison-drop of the present time.—Only imagine a child conducted to the scaffold—Cupid in a German coffin—or fancy a butterfly crawling like a caterpillar with his four wings pulled off, and you will feel what I mean.

TOYS.

You need not surround your children, like those of the nobility, with a little world of turner's toys. Let their eggs be white, not figured and painted; they can dress them out of their own imaginations. On the contrary, the older man grows, the larger reality appears. The fields which glisten for the young with the morning dew of love's brightness, chill the gray, half-blind old man with heavy evening damps, and at last he requires an entire world, even the second, barely to live in.

LANGUAGES.

Do not torment your pupil with a thousand tongues. The mere learning of languages is like expending one's money in the purchase of fine purses, or learning the Paternoster in every tongue, but never praying with it.

HAPPY FATHERS.

Two classes of men are happy fathers. The first is a country gentleman, who enjoys such golden means of exemption from other occupations, that his rural mansion can be a benevolent asylum for his children; since not even cards, hares, or rents are dearer to him than his posterity. The other is a country minister—the six days leisure, the rural seclusion from the whirl of cities, the free air, the office itself, which is a higher school of education, and on every seventh day presents to the children their dear father upon a glorious elevation, as the pastor and the saint, thus impressing the seal of office upon the instructions of the week—all this opens to the clergyman an arena for education, into which he may introduce with advantage other children, as well as his own.

FEMALE DELICACY.

Boys may derive advantage from the evil example of drunken Helots; girls should witness only what is good. Even boys do not come forth from the Augean stable of world-discipline without some smell of the barn. But girls are tender, white, Paris-apple blossoms, parlor flowers, whose delicate freshness cannot bear to be handled, but may only be touched with the finest brush. Like the priestesses of antiquity, they should be brought up only in holy places; the harsh, the indecorous, the violent, they may not hear, far less behold.

SEWING.

Most of the finger-works, whereby the female quicksilver is made stationary, bring with them this mischief—the mind, remaining idle, either grows rusty with dullness, or is given over to the circling maze of fancy, where wave succeeds to wave. Sewing and knitting-needles, for instance, keep open the wounds of disappointed love longer than all the romances in the world; they are thorns which prick through the drooping roses. But give the young girl such an occupation as young men generally have, which shall require a new thought every minute, and the old one cannot be continually raying up and glaring before her. Especially, change of employment contributes to heal woman's heart; constant progress in some one thing, man's.

RELIGION.

Upon the mount of religion, man may indeed still have sorrows, but they are brief. The nights linger in valleys, but on the mountains they are shortened, and ever a small red streak points towards the rising day.

36

THE IDEAL.

Ye holy matrons of by-gone times! As little did ye know of the ideal heart, as of the circulation of the pure blood which warmed and colored you, when ye cried, "I do this for my husband, for my children," and appeared in prosaic subjection to your cares and pursuits. Yet that holy Ideal was passing through you, as heaven's fire descends to the earth through clouds.

MERRIMENT.

Is there anything in life so lovely and poetical as the laugh and merriment of a young girl, who still in harmony with all her powers sports with you in luxuriant freedom, and in her mirthfulness neither despises nor dislikes? Her gravity is seldom as innocent as her playfulness; still less that haughty discontent which converts the youthful Psyche into a dull, thick, buzzing, wing-drooping night-moth. Among a certain Indian tribe the youth selected at a feast that maiden for marriage who laughed in her sport; perhaps my opinion inclines the same way.

Laughing cheerfulness throws day-light upon all the paths of life; discontent blows her ill-omened vapors from afar; depression produces more confusion and distraction of thought than the above-named giddiness. If, indeed, the wife could stereotype this comedy by playing it in wedded life, and sometimes enliven the dull epic of the husband or hero, by her own comic-heroic poetry, she would enjoy the delight of winning and enchanting both husband and children. Never fear that feminine playfulness will exclude depth of character and sensibility. The still energy of the heart is ever growing and filling itself beneath the outward glee. How heavenly, when at length for the first time the laughing eye melts in love, and gushing tears mirror forth the whole tender soul!

Let then the laughter-loving creatures giggle on at one another, and especially at the first clumsy make-game wight who comes among them, even should he be the writer of this paragraph.

TRUTH.

Truthfulness is not so much a branch as a blossom of moral, manly strength. The weak, whether they will or not, must lie. As respects children, for the first five years they utter neither truth nor falsehood—they only speak. Their talk is thinking aloud; and as one half of their thought is often an affirmative, and the other a negative, and, unlike us, both escape from them, they seem to lie, while they are only talking with themselves. Besides, at first they love to sport with their new art of speech; and so talk nonsense merely to hear themselves. Often they do not understand your question, and give an erroneous, rather than a false reply.—We may ask, besides, whether, when children seem to imagine and falsify, they are not often relating their remembered dreams, which necessarily blend in them with actual experience.

Children everywhere fly on the warm, sunny-side of hope. They say, when the bird or the dog has escaped from them, without any reason for the expectation—"he will come back again soon." And since they are incapable of distinguishing hope, that is, imagination, from reflection or truth, their self-delusion consequently assumes the appearance of falsehood. For instance, a truthful little girl described to me various appearances of a Christ-child, telling what it had said and done. In all those cases in which we do not desire to mirror before the child the black image of a lie, it is sufficient to say, "Be sober, have done with play."

Finally, we must distinguish between untruths relating to the future and the past. We do not attribute to a grown man who breaks his word in reference to some future performance, that blackness of perjury which we charge on him who falsifies what has been already done; so with children, before whose brief vision time, like space, is immeasurable, and who are as unable to look through a day, as we through a year, we should widely separate untruthfulness of promise from untruthfulness of assertion. Truth is a divine blossom upon an earthly root; of course, it is in time not the earliest, but the latest virtue.

THE CLASSICS.

The bulwarks around the city of God have been laid by the ancients for every age, through the history of their own. Manhood at the present day would sink immeasurably low, did not our youth pass through the still temple of the great old times and men, as a vestibule to the crowded Fair of modern life. The names of Socrates, Cato, Epaminondas, &c., are pyramids of human energy. Rome, Athens, Sparta, are three coronation cities of the giant Geryon, which, like primeval mountains of humanity, grapple with youthful manhood, while modern ones only attract the eye.

REVERENCE FOR LIFE.

Only place all life before the child, as within the realm of humanity, and thus the greater reveals to him the less. Put life and soul into everything: describe to him even the lily, which he would pull up as an unorganized thing, as the daughter of a slender mother, standing in her garden-bed, from whom her little white offspring derives nutriment and moisture. And let not this be done to excite an empty enervated habit of pity, a sort of inoculation-hospital for foreign pains, but from the religious cultivation of reverence for life, the God all-moving in the tree-top and the human brain. The love of animals, like maternal affections, has this advantage, that it is disinterested and claims no return, and can also at every moment find an object and an opportunity for its exercise.

ENGRAVED BY J. SARTAIN.

A. W. SCHLEGEL.

AUGUST WILHELM VON SCHLEGEL.

Born 1767. Died 1845.

A. W. VON SCHLEGEL, the eldest of the two brothers whose several and joint labors have contributed so largely to the literary and aesthetic culture of their nation and age, occupies the front rank among the scholars and critics of this century, whether we regard the extent and variety of his learning or the acuteness of his analysis and his luminous judgment. As a translator he surpasses all who have ever labored in that line. The fidelity with which he has rendered Shakspeare, or rather the skill with which he has reproduced him, has naturalized that poet in all the states of Germany, and made him not less a German than he is an English classic,—perhaps even more popular in the translation than in the original:—a solitary instance of literary transplantation, unless the popular versions of the old Hebrew poets may be regarded as another. "Such," says Mrs. Austin, " is Herr von Schlegel's masterly handling of his own language, and the exquisite nicety of his ear, that he has, in many cases (for example, Hamlet's Soliloquy), caught the very cadence of the original. With no other living language, perhaps, than the German, would this be possible; and even in that it is a wonderful achievement." "Calderon presented still greater difficulties of a metrical kind; these Herr von Schlegel has triumphantly overcome; he has adhered to the original even in metre, rhyme, and assonance, and has combined this exact imitation of form with an equally faithful interpretation of the meaning. The translation of the two greatest dramatic poets of two nations, so unlike in genius, shows a talent for discriminating, and a power of handling all the forms and resources of language, which have never been surpassed."

A. W. von Schlegel has attained no mean reputation as an original poet, and would probably have figured more illustriously in that capacity had not his poetic labors been eclipsed by his critical. His chief excellence, as a poet, consists in the perfection which he has given to the forms of poetic composition, and his magic mastery of language.

He was born at Hanover, on the 5th of September, 1767. His father held the office of Counsellor of the Consistory in the Lutheran Church. He received his early education in the Lyceum of his native city, where, at the age of eighteen, he recited before the Public, on the occasion of the King's birth-day, a poem on the history of German poetry, which attracted a good deal of attention at the time. In 1786 he entered the university of Göttingen, where he became intimate with the poet Bürger, and where he obtained the prize for a Latin disquisition on the geography of Homer. After he had finished his philological studies at the university, he resided for some time in Amsterdam, in the capacity of private tutor. In 1796 he returned to Germany, and resided at Jena, where he became a diligent contributor to various literary journals. He was soon made Professor in the university in that place, and produced a great impression far and wide by his lectures on aesthetics. In connection with his brother Friedrich, with Tieck, Schelling, and others, he edited a periodical work, in which he labored to establish the Romantic School of Art. In 1802 he removed to Berlin, where he lectured on literature and art, and contributed to various periodicals. In 1804 he travelled with Madame de Stael, and resided with her successively in Italy, in France, in Vienna, and finally in Stockholm, where the Crown-prince of Sweden cultivated his acquaintance, and employed him as political writer, and afterwards conferred upon him the title of nobility. In 1808 he read, in Vienna, the Lectures on Dramatic Art, from which the following extracts are taken. In 1818 he received an appointment as Professor at the new university at Bonn, which he held until his death. He commenced, in 1820, a journal devoted to the study of the Oriental languages, called the "Indian Library." He also published the *Bhagavad-Gita*, a philosophical poem in the Sanscrit, and accompanied it with a Latin translation. He wrote in the French and in the Italian, as well as in his vernacular tongue. His "Comparison of the Phædra of Euripides with that of Racine," in the former of those languages, and his treatise on the bronze horses at Venice, in the latter, are among the most important of his essays. He was twice married and twice divorced. He died at Bonn, 1845.

LECTURES ON DRAMATIC LITERATURE.
THE GREEK DRAMA.
(From the translation of John Black.)

WHEN we hear the word theatre, we naturally think of what with us bears the same name; and yet nothing can be more different from our theatre than the Grecian, in every part of its construction. If in reading the Grecian pieces we associate our own stage with them, the light in which we shall view them must be false in every respect.

The accurate mathematical dimensions of the principal part of it are to be found in Vitruvius, who also distinctly points out the great difference between the Greek and Roman theatres. But these and similar passages of the ancient writers have been most perversely interpreted by architects unacquainted with the ancient dramatists;* and the philologists on the other hand, who were altogether ignorant of architecture, have also fallen into egregious errors. The ancient dramatists are still, therefore, altogether in want of that sort of illustration which relates to scenic regulation. In many tragedies I conceive that my ideas on this subject are sufficiently clear; but others again present difficulties which are not so easily solved. We find ourselves most at a loss in figuring to ourselves the representation of the pieces of Aristophanes; the ingenious poet must have brought his wonderful inventions before the eyes of his audience in a manner equally bold and astonishing. Even Barthelemy's description of the Grecian stage is not a little confused, and the subjoined plan extremely erroneous; in the place which he assigns for the representation of the pieces in Antigone and Ajax, for instance, he is altogether wrong. The following observations will not therefore appear the less superfluous.†

The theatres of the Greeks were quite open above, and their dramas were always acted in open day, and beneath the canopy of heaven.

---

* We have a remarkable instance of this in the pretended ancient theatre of Palladio, at Vicenza. Herculaneum, it is true, had not then been discovered, and the ruins of the ancient theatre are not easily understood, if we have never seen one in an entire state.

† I am partly indebted for them to the illustrations of a learned architect, M. Genelli, of Berlin, author of the ingenious Letters on Vitruvius. We have compared several Greek tragedies with our interpretation of this description of Vitruvius, and endeavored to figure to ourselves the manner in which they were represented; and I afterwards found my ideas confirmed, on examination of the theatre of Herculaneum, and the two very small theatres at Pompeii.

The Romans, at an after period, endeavored by a covering to shelter the audience from the rays of the sun; but this degree of luxury was hardly ever enjoyed by the Greeks. Such a state of things appears very inconvenient to us; but the Greeks had nothing of effeminacy about them, and we must not forget, too, the beauty of their climate. When they were overtaken by a storm or a shower, the play was of course interrupted; and they would much rather expose themselves to an accidental inconvenience, than, by shutting themselves up in a close and crowded house, entirely destroy the serenity of a religious solemnity, which their plays certainly were.* To have covered in the scene itself, and imprisoned gods and heroes in dark and gloomy apartments with difficulty lighted up, would have appeared still more ridiculous to them. An action which so nobly served to establish the belief of the relations with heaven could only be exhibited under an unobstructed heaven, and under the very eyes of the gods as it were, for whom, according to Seneca, the sight of a brave man struggling with adversity is a becoming spectacle. With respect to the supposed inconvenience, which, according to the assertion of many modern critics, was felt by the poets from the necessity of always laying the scene of their pieces before houses, a circumstance that often forced them to violate probability, this inconvenience was very little felt by tragedy and the older comedy. The Greeks, like so many southern nations of the present day, lived much more in the open air than we do, and transacted many things in public which usually take place with us in houses. For the theatre did not represent the street, but a place before the house belonging to it, where the altar stood on which sacrifices to the household gods were offered up. Here the women, who lived in so retired a manner among the Greeks, even those who were unmarried, might appear without impropriety. Neither was it impossible for them to give a view of the interior of the houses; and this was effected, as we shall immediately see, by means of the encyclema.

But the principal reason for this observance was that publicity, according to the republican notions of the Greeks, was essential to a grave and important transaction. This is clearly proved by the presence of the chorus, whose

---

* They carefully made choice of a beautiful situation. The theatre at Tauromenium, at present Taormina, in Sicily, of which the ruins are still visible, was, according to Munter's description, situated in such a manner that the audience had a view of Ætna over the back-ground of the theatre.

remaining on many occasions when secret transactions were going on, has been judged of according to rules of propriety inapplicable to that country, and most undeservedly censured.

The theatres of the ancients were, in comparison with the small scale of ours, of a colossal magnitude, partly for the sake of containing the whole of the people, with the concourse of strangers who flocked to the festivals, and partly to correspond with the majesty of the dramas represented in them, which required to be seen at a respectful distance. The seats of the spectators consisted of steps, which rose backwards round the semicircle of the orchestra (called by us the pit), so that they all could see with equal convenience. The effect of distance was remedied by an artificial heightening of the subject represented to the eye and ear, produced by means of masks, and contrivances for increasing the loudness of the voice, and the size of the figures. Vitruvius speaks also of vehicles of sound, distributed throughout the building; but the commentators are very much at variance with respect to them. We may without hesitation venture to assume, that the theatres of the ancients were constructed on excellent acoustical principles.

The lowest step of the amphitheatre was still raised considerably above the orchestra, and the stage was placed opposite to it, at an equal degree of elevation. The sunk semicircle of the orchestra contained no spectators, and was destined for another purpose. It was otherwise however with the Romans, but we are not at present considering the distribution of their theatres.

The stage consisted of a strip which stretched from one end of the building to the other, and of which the depth bore little proportion to this breadth. This was called the logeum, in the Latin, pulpitum, and the usual place for persons who spoke was in the middle of it. Behind this middle part, the scene went inward in a quadrangular form, with less depth, however, than breadth. The space here comprehended was called the proscenium. The remaining part of the logeum, to the right and left of the scene, had, both before, the brink which adjoined the orchestra, and behind, a wall possessing no scenical decorations, but entirely simple, or at most architecturally ornamented, which was elevated to an equal height with the uppermost steps for the audience.

The decoration was contrived in such a manner, that the principal object in front covered the back-ground, and the prospects of distance were given at two sides, the very reverse of the mode adopted by us. This had also its rules: on the left appeared the town to which the palace, temple, or whatever occupied the middle, belonged; on the right the open country, landscape, mountains, sea-shore, &c. The lateral decorations were composed of triangles, which turned on an axis fastened underneath; and in this manner the change of scene was effected.* In the hindmost decoration it is probable that many things were exhibited in a bodily form which are only painted with us. When a palace or temple was represented, there appeared in the proscenium an altar, which answered a number of purposes in the performance of the pieces.

The decoration was for the most part architectural, but it was also not unfrequently a painted landscape, as in Prometheus, where it represented Caucasus; or in Philoctetus, where the desert island of Lemnos, with its rocks and his cave, were exhibited. It is clear, from a passage of Plato, that the Greeks, in the deceptions of theatrical perspective, carried things much farther than we might have inferred from some wretched landscapes discovered in Herculaneum.

In the back wall of this scene there was a large main entrance, and two side entrances. It has been maintained, that from them it might be discovered whether an actor played a principal or under part, as in the first case he came in at the main entrance, and in the second, at the side doors. But this should be understood with the distinction, that it must have been regulated according to the nature of the piece. As the hindmost decoration was generally a palace, in which the principal characters of royal descent resided, they naturally came through the great door, while the servants resided in the wings. There were two other entrances; the one at the end of the logeum, from whence the inhabitants of the town came; the other underneath in the orchestra, which was the side for those who had to come from a distance: they ascended a staircase of the logeum opposite to the orchestra, which could be applied to all sorts of purposes, according to circumstances. The entrance, therefore, with respect to the lateral decorations, declared the place from whence the players were supposed to come; and it might naturally happen, that the principal characters were in a situation to avail themselves with propriety of the two last-mentioned entrances. The situation of these entrances serves to explain many passages in the ancient dramas, where the persons standing in the middle see some one advancing, long before he approaches them. Beneath the seats of the spectators a stair was somewhere constructed, which was called the Charonic, and through which the shadows of the departed, without being seen by the audience, ascended into the orchestra, and then, by the stair which we formerly mentioned, made their appearance on the stage. The nearest brink of the logeum some-

---

* According to an observation on Virgil, by Servius, the change of scene was produced partly by revolving, and partly by withdrawing. The former applies to the lateral decorations, and the latter to the middle or background. The partition in the middle opened, disappeared at both sides, and exhibited to view a new picture. But all the parts of the scene were not always changed at the same time.

times represented the sea-shore. The Greeks were well skilled in availing themselves even of what lay beyond the decoration, and making it subservient to scenical effect. I doubt not, therefore, that in the Eumenides the spectators were twice addressed as an assembled people; first, by Pythia, when she calls upon the Greeks to consult the oracle; and a second time, when Pallas, by a herald, commands silence throughout the place of judgment. The frequent addresses to heaven were undoubtedly directed to a real heaven; and when Electra, on her first appearance, exclaims: "O holy light, and thou air which fillest the expanse between earth and heaven!" she probably turned towards the rising sun. The whole of this procedure is highly deserving of praise; and though modern critics have censured the mixture of reality and imitation, as destructive of theatrical illusion, this only proves that they have misunderstood the essence of the illusion which can be produced by an artificial representation. If we are to be truly deceived by a picture, that is, if we are to believe in the reality of the object which we see, we must not perceive its limits, but look at it through an opening; the frame at once declares it for a picture. In scenical decorations we are now unavoidably compelled to make use of architectural contrivances, productive of the same effect as the frames of pictures. It is consequently much better to avoid this, and to renounce the modern illusion, though it may have its advantages, for the sake of extending the view beyond the mere decoration. It was, generally speaking, a principle of the Greeks, that everything imitated on the stage should, if possible, consist of actual representation; and only where this could not be done were they satisfied with a symbolical exhibition.

The machinery for the descent of the gods through the air, or the withdrawing of men from the earth, was placed aloft behind the walls of the two sides of the scene, and consequently removed from the sight of the spectators. Even in the time of Æschylus great use was made of it, as he not only brings Oceanus through the air on a griffin, but also introduces the whole choir of ocean nymphs, at least fifteen in number, in a winged chariot. There were hollow places beneath the stage, and contrivances for thunder and lightning, for the apparent fall or burning of a house, &c.

An upper story could be added to the farthermost wall of the scene, when they wished to represent a tower with a wide prospect, or anything similar. The encyclema could be thrust behind the great middle entrance, a machine of a semicircular form within, and covered above, which represented the objects contained in it as in a house. This was used for producing a great theatrical effect, as we may see from many pieces. The side door of the entrance would naturally be then open, or the curtain which covered it withdrawn.

A stage curtain, which, we clearly see from a description of Ovid, was not dropped, but drawn upwards, is mentioned both by Greek and Roman writers, and the Latin appellation, aulœum, is even borrowed from the Greeks. I suspect, however, that the curtain on the Attic stage was not in use at its commencement. In the pieces of Æschylus and Sophocles the scene is evidently empty at the opening as well as at the conclusion, and therefore it did not require any contrivance for preventing the view of the spectators. However, in many of the pieces of Euripides, perhaps also in the Œdipus Tyrannus, the stage is at once filled, and represents a standing group, who could not have been first assembled under the eyes of the spectators. It must be recollected, that it was only the comparatively small proscenium, and not the logeum, which was covered by the curtain; for, from its great breadth, to have attempted to screen the logeum would have been almost impracticable, without answering any good end.

The entrances of the chorus were beneath in the orchestra, in which it generally remained, and in which also it performed its solemn dance, going backwards and forwards during the choral songs. In the front of the orchestra, opposite to the middle of the scene, there was an elevation with steps, resembling an altar, as high as the stage, which was called thymele. This was the station of the chorus when it did not sing, but merely took an interest in the action. The leader of the chorus then took his station on the top of the thymele, to see what was passing on the stage, and to communicate with the characters. For though the choral song was common to the whole, yet when it entered into the dialogue one person spoke for the rest; and hence we are to account for the shifting from *thou* to *ye* in addressing them. The thymele was situated in the very centre of the building; all the measurements were calculated from it, and the semicircle of the amphitheatre was described round that point. It was, therefore, an excellent contrivance to place the chorus, who were the ideal representatives of the spectators, in the very situation where all the radii were concentrated.

The tragical imitation of the ancients was altogether ideal, and rhythmical; and in forming a judgment of it, we must always keep this in view. It was ideal, as its chief object was the highest dignity and sweetness; and rhythmical, as the gestures and inflections of voice were measured in a more solemn manner than in real life. As the plastic art of the Greeks was formed, if we may so express ourselves, with scientific strictness on the most general conception, and embodied into various general characters which were gradually invested with the charms of animation, so that individuality was the last thing to which they turned their attention; in like manner in the mimetic art, their first idea was to exhibit their personages with heroical grandeur, a dignity more than human, and an ideal beauty: their second was character; and the last of all passion, which in the collision was thus forced to give way. The fidelity of the representation was less their object than its beauty: with us it is exactly the reverse. The use of masks, which appears astonishing to us, was not only justifiable on this principle, but absolutely essential; and far from considering them in the light of a last recourse, the Greeks would with justice have considered as a last recourse the being obliged to allow a player with vulgar, ignoble, or strongly marked individual features, to represent an Apollo or a Hercules. To them this would have appeared downright profanation. How limited is the power of the most finished actor, in changing the character of his features! And yet this has the most unfavorable influence on the expression of the passion, as all passion is tinged by the character. Neither are we obliged to have recourse to the conjecture, that they changed the masks in the different scenes, for the purpose of assuming a greater degree of joy or sorrow.* This would by no means have been sufficient, as the passions are often changed in the same scene; and then modern critics would still be obliged to suppose, that the masks exhibited a different appearance on one side from what they did on the other, and that that side was turned towards the spectators which the circumstances of the moment required.† No; the countenance remained from beginning to end the very same, as we may see from the antique masks cut out in stone. For the expression of the passion, the motion of the arms and hands, the attitudes, and the tone of voice, remained to them. We complain of the want of the expression of the face, without reflecting, that at such a great distance its effect would have been lost.

* I call it conjecture, though Barthelemy, in his Anacharsis, considers it a settled point. He cites no authorities, and I do not recollect any.

† Voltaire, in his essay on the Tragedy of the Ancients and Moderns, prefixed to Semiramis, has actually gone so far. Amidst a multitude of supposed improprieties, which he crowds together to confound the admirers of ancient tragedy, the following is one: Aucune nation (that is to say, excepting the Greeks) ne fait paraitre ses acteurs sur des especes d'echasses, le visage couvert d'un masque qui exprime la douleur d'un coté et la joye de l'autre. In a conscientious inquiry into the evidence for an assertion so very improbable, and yet so boldly made, I can only find one passage in Quinctilian, lib. 11. cap. 3, and an allusion of Platonius still more vague. (Vide Aristoph. ed. Küster, prolegom. p. 10.) Both passages refer only to the new comedy, and only amount to this, that in some characters the eyebrows were dissimilar. As to the view with which this took place, I shall afterwards say a word or two in considering the new Greek comedy. Voltaire, however, is without excuse, as the mention of the cothurnus leaves no doubt that he alluded to tragic masks. But his error had probably no such learned origin. In most cases, it would be a fruitless task to trace the source of his ignorance. The whole description of the Greek tragedy, as well as that of the cothurnus in particular, is worthy of the man whose knowledge of antiquity was such, that in his Essay on Tragedy, prefixed to Brutus, he boasts of having introduced the Roman Senate on the stage in *red mantles.*

We are not now inquiring whether, without the use of masks, it may not be possible to attain a higher degree of separate excellence in the mimetic art. This we would very willingly allow. Cicero, it is true, speaks of the expression. the softness, and delicacy of the acting of Roscius, in the same terms that a modern critic would apply to Garrick or Schröder. But I will not lay any stress on the acting of this celebrated player, the excellence of which has become proverbial, because it appears from a passage in Cicero that he frequently played without a mask, and that this was preferred by his contemporaries. I doubt, however, whether this ever took among the Greeks. But the same writer relates, that actors in general, for the sake of acquiring the most perfect purity and flexibility of voice (and not merely the musical voice, otherwise the examples would not have been applicable to the orator), submitted to such a course of uninterrupted exercises as our modern players, even the French, who are the strictest in their discipline, would consider a most intolerable oppression. The ancients could show their dexterity in the mimetic art, considered by itself without the accompaniment of words, in their pantomimes, which they carried to a degree of perfection altogether unknown to the moderns. In tragedy, however, the great object in the art was strict subordination; the whole was to appear animated by one spirit, and hence, not merely the poetry, but the musical accompaniment, the scenical decoration and representation, were all the creation of the poet. The player was a mere tool, and his excellency consisted in the accuracy with which he filled up his part, and by no means in arbitrary bravura, or an ostentatious display of skill.

As from the quality of their writing materials they had not the convenience of many copies, the parts were studied from the repeated delivery of the poet, and the chorus exercised in the same manner. This was called teaching a piece. As the poet was also a musician, and for the most part a player likewise, this must have greatly contributed to the perfection of the representation.

We may safely allow that the task of the modern player, who must change his person without concealing it, is much more difficult; but this difficulty affords us no just criterion for deciding which of the two merits the preference as a representation of the noble and the beautiful.

As the features of the player acquired a more decided expression from the mask, as his voice was strengthened by a contrivance for that purpose, the cothurnus, which consisted of several considerable additions to his soles, as we may see in the ancient statues of Melpomene, raised in like manner his figure considerably above the middle standard. The female parts were also played by men, as the voice and other qualities of women would have conveyed an inadequate idea of the energy of tragic heroines.

The forms of the masks,* and the whole appearance of the tragic figures, we may easily suppose, were sufficiently beautiful and dignified. We should do well to have the ancient sculpture always present to our minds; and the most accurate conception, perhaps, that we can possibly have, is to imagine them so many statues in the grand style endowed with life and motion. But, as in sculpture, they were fond of dispensing as much as possible with dress, for the sake of exhibiting the more essential beauty of the figure; on the stage they would endeavour, from an opposite principle, to clothe as much as they could well do, both from a regard to decency, and because the actual forms of the body would not correspond sufficiently with the beauty of the countenance. They would also exhibit their divinities, which in sculpture we always observe either entirely naked, or only half covered, in a complete dress. They had recourse to a number of means for giving a suitable strength to the forms of the limbs, and thus restoring proportion to the increased height of the player.

The great breadth of the theatre in proportion to its depth must have given to the grouping of the figures the simple and distinct order of the bas-relief. We prefer on the stage, as well as everywhere else, groups of a picturesque description, more crowded, in part covered by themselves, and stretching out into distance; but the ancients were so little fond of foreshortening, that even in their painting they generally avoided it. The gestures accompanied the rhythmus of the declamation, and were intended to display the utmost beauty and sweetness. The poetical conception required a certain degree of repose in the action, and that the whole should be kept in masses, so as to exhibit a succession of plastic attitudes; and it is not improbable that the player remained for some time motionless in the same position. But we are not to suppose from this, that the Greeks were contented with a cold and spiritless representation of the passions. How could we reconcile such a supposition with the fact, that whole lines in their tragedies are frequently dedicated to inarticulate exclamations of pain, with which we have nothing to correspond in any of our modern languages?

It has been often conjectured that the delivery of their dialogue must have resembled the modern recitative. For this conjecture there is no other foundation than that the Greek, like almost all the southern languages, must have been pronounced with a greater musical inflection of the voice than our languages of the north. In other respects I conceive that their tragic declamation must have been altogether unlike recitative, much more measured, and far removed from its learned and artificial modulation.

We come now to the essence of the Greek tragedy itself. In stating that the conception was ideal, we are not to understand that the different characters were morally perfect. In this case what room could there be for such an opposition or conflict, as the plot of a drama requires? Weaknesses, errors, and even crimes, were portrayed in them, but the manners were always elevated above reality, and every person was invested with such a portion of dignity and grandeur as was compatible with the share which he possessed in the action. The ideality of the representation chiefly consisted in the elevation to a higher sphere. The tragical poetry wished wholly to separate the image of humanity which it exhibited to us, from the ground of nature to which man is in reality chained down, like a feudal slave. How was this to be accomplished? By exhibiting to us an image hovering in the air? But this would have been incompatible with the law of gravitation and with the earthly materials of which our bodies are framed. Frequently, what we praise in art as ideal is really nothing more. But the production of airy floating shadows can make no durable impression on the mind. The Greeks, however, succeeded in combining in the most perfect manner in their art ideality with reality; or, dropping school terms, an elevation more than human with all the truth of life, and all the energy of bodily qualities. They did not allow their figures to flutter without consistency in empty space, but they fixed the statue of humanity on the eternal and immovable basis of moral liberty; and that it might stand there unshaken, being formed of stone or brass, or some more solid mass than the living

---

* We have obtained a knowledge of them from the imitations in stone which have come down to us. They display both beauty and variety. That great variety must have taken place in the tragical department (in the comic, we can have no doubt about the matter), is evident from the rich store of technical expressions in the Greek language for every gradation of the age, and character of masks. See the Onomasticon of Jul. Pollux. In the marble masks, however, we can neither see the thinness of the mass from which the real masks were executed, the more delicate coloring, nor the exquisite mechanism of their joinings. The abundance of excellent workmen possessed by Athens, in everything which had reference to the plastic arts, will warrant the conjecture that they were in this respect inimitable. Those who have seen the masks of wax in the grand style, which in some degree contain the whole head, lately contrived at the Roman carnival, may form to themselves a pretty good idea of the theatrical masks of the ancients. They imitate life even to its movements in a most masterly manner, and at such a distance as that from which the ancient players were seen, the deception is most perfect. They always contain the apple of the eye, as we see in the ancient masks, and the person covered sees merely through the aperture left for the iris. The ancients must have gone still farther, and contrived also an iris for the masks, according to the anecdote of the singer Thamyris, who, in a piece which was probably of Sophocles, made his appearance with a blue and a black eye. Even accidental circumstances were imitated; for instance, the cheeks of Tyro, down which the blood had rolled from the cruel conduct of his stepmother. The head from the mask must no doubt have appeared somewhat large for the rest of the figure; but this disproportion, in tragedy at least, would not be perceived from the elevation of the cothurnus.

human bodies, it made an impression by its own weight, and from its very elevation and magnificence it was only the more decidedly subjected to the law of gravity.

Inward liberty and external necessity are the two poles of the tragic world. Each of these ideas can only appear in the most perfect manner by the contrast of the other. As the feeling of internal dignity elevates the man above the unlimited dominion of impulse and native instinct, and in a word absolves him from the guardianship of nature, so the necessity which he must also recognise ought to be no mere natural necessity, but to lie beyond the world of sense in the abyss of infinitude; and it must consequently be represented as the invincible power of fate. Hence it extends also to the world of gods; for the Grecian gods are mere powers of nature, and although immeasurably higher than mortal man, yet, compared with infinitude, they are on an equal footing with himself. In Homer and the tragedians the gods are introduced in a manner altogether different. In the former their appearance is arbitrary and accidental, and can communicate no higher interest to the epic poem than the charm of the wonderful. But in tragedy the gods either enter in obedience to fate, and to carry its decrees into execution, or they endeavor in a godlike manner to assert their liberty of action, and appear involved in the same struggles with destiny which man has to encounter.

This is the essence of the tragic in the sense of the ancients. We are accustomed to give to all terrible or sorrowful events the appellation of tragic, and it is certain that such events are selected in preference by tragedy, though a melancholy conclusion is by no means indispensably necessary; and several ancient tragedies, viz. the Eumenides, Philoctetes, and in some degree also the Œdipus Colonus, without mentioning many of the pieces of Euripides, have a happy and enlivening termination.

But why does tragedy select those objects which are so dreadfully repugnant to the wishes and the wants of our sensible nature? This question has often been asked, and seldom answered in a very satisfactory manner. Some have said that the pleasure of such representations arises from the comparison between the calmness and tranquillity of our own situation, and the storms and perplexities to which the victims of passion are exposed. But when we take a warm interest in a tragedy, we cease to think of ourselves; and when this is not the case, it is the best of all proofs that we take but a feeble interest, and that the tragedy has failed in its effects. Others again have had recourse to our feelings for moral improvement, which is gratified by the view of poetical justice in the rewards of the good and the punishment of the wicked. But he whom the aspect of such dreadful examples could in reality improve, would be conscious of a sentiment of depression and humiliation, very far removed from genuine morality and elevation of mind. Besides, poetical justice is by no means indispensable in a good tragedy; it may end with the suffering of the just and the triumph of the wicked, when the balance is once restored by the prospect of futurity. Small will be our improvement, if with Aristotle we say that the object of tragedy is to purify the passions by pity and terror. In the first place the commentators have never been able to agree as to the meaning of this proposition, and have had recourse to the most forced explanations. Look for instance into the *Dramaturgie* of Lessing. Lessing gives a new explanation, and conceives he has found in Aristotle a poetical Euclid. But mathematical demonstrations are subject to no misconception, and geometrical evidence is not applicable to the theory of the fine arts. Supposing however tragedy to operate this moral cure in us, it must do so by the painful feelings of terror and compassion; and it remains to be proved how we should take a pleasure in subjecting ourselves to such an operation.

Others have been pleased to say that we are attracted to theatrical representations from the want of some violent agitation to rouse us out of the torpor of every-day life. I have already acknowledged the existence of this want, when speaking of the attractions of the drama: and to it we are even to attribute the fights of wild beasts and gladiators among the Romans. But must we who are less indurated, and more inclined to tender feelings, be desirous of seeing demi-gods and heroes descend into the bloody lists of the tragic stage, like so many desperate gladiators, that our nerves may be shaken by the aspect of their sufferings? No: it is not the aspect of suffering which constitutes the charm of a tragedy, or the amusement of a circus or wild beast fight. In the latter we see a display of activity, strength, and courage, qualities related to the mental and moral powers of man. The satisfaction which we derive from the representation of the powerful situations and overwhelming passions in a good tragedy, must be ascribed either to the feeling of the dignity of human nature, excited by the great models exhibited to us, or to the trace of a higher order of things, impressed on the apparently irregular progress of events, and secretly revealed in them; or to both of these causes together.

The true cause, therefore, why in tragical representations we cannot exclude even that which appears harsh and cruel is, that a spiritual and invisible power can only be measured by the opposition which it encounters from some external force that can be taken in by the senses. The moral freedom of man can therefore only be displayed in a conflict with the impulse of the senses: so long as it is not called into action by a higher power, it is either actually dormant in him, or appears to slumber, as it can fill no part as a mere natural entity. The moral part of our nature can only be preserved amidst struggles and difficulties, and if we were therefore to ascribe a distinctive aim to tragedy, as instructive, it should be this : that all these sufferings must be experienced, and all these difficulties overcome, to establish the claims of the mind to a divine origin, and teach us to estimate the earthly existence as vain and insignificant.

With respect to everything connected with this point, I refer my hearers to the Section on the Sublime in Kant's Criticism of the Judgment (*Kritik der Urtheilskraft*), to the complete perfection of which nothing is wanting but a more definite idea of the tragedy of the ancients, with which he does not seem to have been very well acquainted.

I come now to another peculiarity which distinguishes the tragedy of the ancients from ours, I mean the chorus. We must consider it as the personification of opinion on the action which is going on; the incorporation into the representation itself of the sentiments of the poet as the interpreter for the whole human race. This is the general poetical character which we must here assign to it, and that character is by no means affected by the circumstance that the chorus had a local origin in the feasts of Bacchus, and that it always had a peculiar national signification with the Greeks. We have already said that, with their republican way of thinking, publicity was considered essential to every important transaction. As in their compositions they went back to the heroic ages, they gave a certain republican cast to the families of their heroes, by carrying on the action either in presence of the elders of the people, or those persons whose characters entitled them to respect. This publicity does not, it is true, correspond with Homer's picture of the manners of the heroic age; but both in the costume and the mythology, the dramatic poetry generally displayed a spirit of independence and conscious liberty.

The chorus was therefore introduced to give the whole that appearance of reality which was most consistent with the fable. Whatever it might be in particular pieces, it represented in general, first the national spirit, and then the general participation of mankind. In a word, the chorus is the ideal spectator. It mitigates the impression of a heart-rending or moving story, while it conveys to the actual spectator a lyrical and musical expression of his own emotions, and elevates him to the region of consideration.

The modern critics have never known what to make of the chorus; and this is the less to be wondered at, as Aristotle affords no satisfactory solution of the difficulty. The business of the chorus is better painted by Horace, who ascribes to it a general expression of moral participation, instruction and admonition. But the critics in question have either believed that its chief object was to prevent the stage from ever being altogether empty, although the proper place for the chorus was not upon the stage; or they have censured it as a superfluous and laughable accompaniment, and seemed astonished at the supposed impropriety of carrying on secret transactions in the presence of assembled multitudes. This they consider as the principal reason for the observance of the unity of place, as it could not be changed by the poet without the dismission of the chorus, an act which would have required at least some sort of pretext; they believe that the chorus owed its continuance from the first origin of tragedy merely to accident; and as it is easy to perceive that in Euripides, the last tragic poet which we have, the choral songs have frequently little or no connection with the fable, and form a mere episodical ornament, they therefore conclude that the Greeks had only to take one other step in dramatic art to explode the chorus altogether. To refute these superficial conjectures, it is only necessary to observe, that Sophocles wrote a Treatise on the chorus, in prose, in opposition to the principles of some other poets, and that far from following blindly the practice which he found established, like an intelligent artist he could assign reasons for the system which he adopted.

Modern poets of the very first rank, since the revival of the study of the ancients, have often attempted to introduce the chorus in their pieces, for the most part without a correct, and always without a vivid idea of its destination. But we have no suitable singing or dancing; neither have we, as our theatres are constructed, any place for it; and it will hardly ever succeed, therefore, in becoming naturalized with us.

The Greek tragedy, in its pure and unaltered state, will always for our theatre remain an exotic plant, which we can hardly hope to cultivate with any success, even in the hot-house of learned art and criticism. The Grecian mythology, which constitutes the materials of ancient tragedy, is as foreign to the minds and imaginations of most of the spectators, as its form and mode of representation. But to endeavor to constrain another subject, an historical one for example, to assume that form, must always be a most unprofitable and hopeless attempt.

I have called mythology the chief material of tragedy. We know, indeed, of two historical tragedies, by Grecian authors: the Capture of Miletus, of Phrynichus, and the Persians, of Æschylus, a piece which still exists; but these singular exceptions, both belonging to an epoch when the art had not attained its full maturity, among so many hundred examples of a different description, serve to establish more strongly the truth of the rule. The sentence passed by the Athenians on Phrynichus, whom they subjected to a pecuniary fine because, in the representation of contemporary calamities which with due caution he might have avoided, he had agitated them in too violent a manner, however hard and arbitrary it may appear in a judicial point of view, displays nevertheless a correct feeling with respect to the subject and the limits of art. The mind suffering under the near reality of the subject cannot preserve the necessary repose and self-possession which are necessary for the reception of pure tragical impressions. The heroic fables, on the other hand, appear always at a certain distance, and in the light of the wonderful. The wonderful possesses the advantage of being believed, and in some degree disbelieved, at the same time: believed in so far as it is founded on the connection with other opinions; disbelieved while we never take such an immediate interest in it as we do in what wears the hue of the every-day life of our own age. The Grecian mythology was a web of national and local traditions, held in equal honor as a part of religion and as an introduction to history; everywhere preserved in full life among the people by customs and monuments, and by the numberless works of epic and mythical poets. The tragedians had only therefore to engraft one species of poetry on another: they were always allowed their use of certain established fables, invaluable for their dignity, grandeur, and remoteness from all accessary ideas of petty description. Everything, down to the very errors and weaknesses of that departed race of heroes who claimed their descent from the gods, was consecrated in the eyes of the people. Those heroes were painted as beings endowed with more than human strength; but, so far from possessing unerring virtue and wisdom, they were also represented as under the dominion of furious and unbridled passions. It was a wild age of effervescence: the cultivation of social order had not as yet rendered the soil of morality arable, and it yielded at the same time the most beneficent and poisonous productions, with the fresh and luxuriant fulness of a creative nature. Here the monstrous and ferocious were not a necessary indication of that degradation and corruption with which they are necessarily associated under the development of law and order, and which fill us with sentiments of horror and aversion. The criminals of the fabulous ages are not, if we may be allowed the expression, amenable to the tribunals of men, but consigned over to a higher jurisdiction. Some are of opinion that the Greeks, in their republican zeal, took a particular pleasure in witnessing the representation of the outrages and consequent calamities of the different royal families, and are almost disposed to consider the ancient tragedy, in general, as a satire on monarchical government. This party view would, however, have deadened the interest of the audience, and consequently destroyed the effect which it was the aim of the tragedy to produce. But we must remark, that the royal families, whose crimes and misfortunes afforded the most abundant materials for tragical pictures of a horrible description, were the Pelopidæ of Mycenæ, and the Labdacidæ of Thebes, families which were foreign to the Athenians, for whom the pieces were composed. We do not see that the Attic poets endeavored to exhibit the ancient kings of their country in an odious light; on the contrary, they always hold up their national hero, Theseus, for public admiration, as a model of justice and moderation, the champion of the oppressed, the first lawgiver, and even the founder of their liberty; and it was one of their favorite modes of flattering the people, to persuade them that, even in the heroic ages, Athens was distinguished above all the other states of Greece, for obedience to the laws, humanity, and a knowledge of the rights of nations. The general revolution, by which the independent kingdoms of ancient Greece were converted into a community of free states, had separated the heroic age from the age of social cultivation, by a wide interval, beyond which the genealogy of a very few families only was attempted to be traced. This was extremely advantageous for the ideal elevation of the characters of their tragedy, as few human things will admit of a close inspection into them, without betraying their imperfections. But in the very different relations of the age in which those heroes lived, the standard of mere civil and domestic morality was not applicable, and the feeling must go back to the primary ingredients of humanity. Before the existence of constitutions,—before the proper development of law and right, the sovereigns and rulers were their own lawgivers in a world not yet subjected to order; and the fullest scope was thus given to the dominion of will for good and for bad purposes. Hereditary rule, therefore, exhibited more striking instances of sudden changes of fortune than the late times of political equality. In these respects the high rank of the principal characters was essential, or at least favorable to tragic representation, and not because, according to the idea of some moderns, those only who can occasion the happiness or misery of numbers are sufficiently important to interest us in their behalf, nor because internal elevation of sentiment must be clothed with external dignity, to claim our honor and admiration. The Greek tragedians paint the downfall of kingly houses without any reference to the condition of the people; they show us the man in the king, and, far from veiling their heroes from our sight in their purple mantles, they allow us to look through their vain splendor, into a bosom torn and harrowed up by passions. That the regal pomp was not so necessary as the heroic costume is evident, not only from the practice of the ancients, but from the tragedies of the moderns having a reference to the throne, produced under different circumstances, namely, the existence of monarchical government. They dare not draw from existing reality, for nothing is less suitable for tragedy than a court, and a court life. When they do not therefore paint an ideal kingdom with distant manners, they fall into stiffness and formality, which are much more destructive to freedom and boldness of character, and to deep pathos, than the narrow circle of private life.

A few mythological fables only seem originally marked out for tragedy: such, for example, as the long-continued alternation of aggressions, vengeance, and maledictions, which we witness in the house of Atreus. When we examine the names of the pieces which are lost, we have great difficulty in conceiving how the mythological fables on which they are founded, as they are known to us, could afford sufficient materials for the development of an entire tragedy. It is true, the poets, in the various relations of the same story, had a great amplitude of selection; and this very variety justified them in going still farther, and making considerable alterations in the circumstances of an event, so that the inventions added to one piece sometimes contradict the accounts given by the same poet in another. We are, however, principally to ascribe the productiveness of mythology, for the tragic art, to the principle which we observe so powerful throughout the whole historical range of Grecian cultivation; namely, that the power which preponderated for the time assimilated everything to itself. As the heroic fables, in all their deviations, were easily developed into the tranquil fulness and light variety of epic poetry, they were afterwards adapted to the object which the tragedians proposed to accomplish, by earnestness, energy, and compression; and what in this change of destination appeared inapplicable to tragedy still afforded materials for a sort of half sportive, though ideal representation, in the subordinate walk of the satirical drama.

I shall be forgiven, I hope, if I attempt to illustrate the above reflections on the essence of the ancient tragedy, by a comparison borrowed from the plastic arts, which will, I trust, be found somewhat more than a mere fanciful allusion.

The Homeric epic is, in poetry, what half-raised workmanship is in sculpture, and tragedy the distinctly separated group.

The poem of Homer, sprung from the soil of the traditionary tale, is not yet purified from it, as the figures of a bas-relief are borne by a back-ground which is foreign to them. These figures appear depressed, and in the epic poem all is painted as past and remote. In the bas-relief they are generally thrown into profile, and in the epic characterized in the most artless manner: they are, in the former, not properly grouped, but follow one another; and the Homeric heroes, in like manner, advance singly in succession before us. It has been remarked that the Iliad is not definitively closed, but that we are left to suppose something both to precede and to follow. The bas-relief is equally boundless, and may be continued *ad infinitum*, either from before or behind, on which account the ancients preferred the selection of those objects for it which admitted of an indefinite extension, as the trains at sacrifices, dances, and rows of combatants, &c. Hence they also exhibited bas-reliefs on round surfaces, such as vases, or the frieze of a rotunda, where the two ends are withdrawn from our sight by the curvature, and where, on our advancing, one object appears as another disappears. The reading of the Homeric poetry very much resembles such a circumgyration, as the present object alone arrests our attention, while that which precedes and follows is allowed to disappear.

But in the distinctly formed group, as in tragedy, sculpture and poetry bring before our eyes an independent and definite whole. To separate it from natural reality, the former places it on a base, as on an ideal ground. It also removes as much as possible all foreign and accidental accessaries, that the eye may wholly rest on the essential objects, the figures themselves. These figures are wrought into the most complete rounding, yet they refuse the illusion of colours, and announce by the purity and uniformity of the mass of which they are constructed, a creation not endowed with perishable life, but of a higher and more elevated character.

Beauty is the object of sculpture, and repose is most advantageous for the display of beauty. Repose alone, therefore, is suitable to the figure. But a number of figures can only be connected together and grouped by one action. The group represents beauty in motion, and the object of it is to combine both in the highest degree. This can only be effected when the artist finds means, in the most violent bodily or mental anguish, to moderate the expression by manly resistance, calm grandeur, or inherent sweetness, in such a manner that, with the most moving truth, the features of beauty shall yet in nowise be disfigured. The observation of Winkelmann on this subject is inimitable. He says that beauty with the ancients was the tongue on the balance of expression, and in this sense the groups of Niobe and Laocoön are masterpieces; the one in the sublime and serious, the other in the learned and ornamental style.

The comparison with ancient tragedy is the more apposite here as we know that both Æschylus and Sophocles produced a Niobe, and that Sophocles was also the author of Laocoön. In Laocoön the conflicting sufferings and anguish of the body, and the resistance of the soul, are balanced with the most wonderful equilibrium. The children calling for help, tender objects of our compassion, and not of our admiration, draw us back to the appearance of the father, who seems to turn his eyes in vain to the gods. The convolving serpents exhibit to us the inevitable destiny which unites together the characters in so dreadful a manner. And yet the beauty of proportion, the pleasing flow of the attitude, are not lost in this violent struggle; and a representation the most frightful to the senses is yet treated with a degree of moderation, while a mild breath of sweetness is diffused over the whole.

In the group of Niobe there is also the most perfect mixture of terror and pity. The upturned looks of the mother, and the mouth half open in supplication, seem to accuse the invisible wrath of Heaven. The daughter, clinging in the agonies of death to the bosom of her mother, in her infantine innocence can have no other fear than for herself: the innate impulse of self-preservation was never represented in a manner more tender and affecting. Can there on the other hand be exhibited to the senses a more beautiful image of self-devoting heroic magnanimity than Niobe, as she bends her body forwards, that if possible she alone may receive the destructive bolt? Pride and repugnance are melted down in the most ardent maternal love. The more than earthly dignity of the features is the less disfigured by pain, as from the quick repetition of the shocks she appears, as in the fable, to have become insensible and motionless. But before this figure, twice transformed into stone, and yet so inimitably animated,—before this line of demarcation of all human suffering, the most callous beholder is dissolved in tears.

In all the agitation produced by the sight of these groups, there is still somewhat in them which invites us to composed contemplation; and in the same manner, the tragedy of the ancients leads us, even in the course of the representation, to the most elevated reflections on our existence, and those mysteries in our destiny which can never be wholly explained.

ÆSCHYLUS.

Æschylus is to be considered as the creator of tragedy, which sprung from him completely armed, liked Pallas from the head of Jupiter. He clothed it in a state of suitable dignity, and gave it an appropriate place of exhibition; he was the inventor of scenic pomp, and not only instructed the chorus in singing and dancing, but appeared in the character of a player. He was the first who gave development to the dialogue, and limits to the lyrical part of the tragedy, which still however occupies too much space in his pieces. He draws his characters with a few bold and strongly marked features. The plans are simple in the extreme: he did not understand the art of enriching and varying an action, and dividing its development and catastrophe into parts, bearing a due proportion to each other. Hence his action often stands still, and this circumstance becomes still more apparent, from the undue extension of his choral songs. But all his poetry betrays a sublime and serious mind. Terror is his element, and not the softer affections; he holds up the head of Medusa to his astonished spectators. His manner of treating fate is austere in the extreme: he suspends it over the heads of mortals in its gloomy majesty. The cothurnus of Æschylus has as it were an iron weight: gigantic figures alone stalk before our eyes. It seems as if it required an effort in him to condescend to paint mere men to us: he abounds most in representation of gods, and seems to dwell with particular delight in exhibiting the Titans, those ancient gods who signify the dark powers of primitive nature, and who had long been driven into Tartarus beneath a better regulated world He endeavors to swell out his language to a gigantic sublimity, corresponding with the standard of his character. Hence he abounds in harsh combinations and overstrained epithets, and the lyrical parts of his pieces are often obscure in the extreme, from the involved nature of the construction. He resembles Dante and Shakspeare in the very singular cast of his images and expressions. These images are nowise deficient in the terrible graces, which almost all the writers of antiquity celebrate in Æschylus.

Æschylus flourished in the very first vigor of the Grecian freedom, after its successful struggle, and he seems to have been thoroughly imbued with a proud feeling of the superiority which this struggle reflected on the nation to which he belonged. He was an eye-witness of the greatest and most glorious event in the history of Greece, the overthrow and annihilation of the Persian hosts under Darius and Xerxes, and had fought in the memorable battles of Marathon and Salamis with distinguished bravery. In the Persians he has, in an indirect manner, sung the triumph which he contributed to obtain, while he paints the downfall of the Persian projects, and the ignominious return of the fugitive monarch to his royal residence. He describes in the most vivid and glowing colors the battle of Salamis. In this piece, and in the Seven before Thebes, a warlike vein gushes forth; the personal inclination of the poet for the life of a hero shines throughout with the most dazzling lustre. It was well remarked by Gorgias, the sophist, that Mars, instead of Bacchus, dictated this last drama; for Bacchus, and not Apollo, was the patron of tragic poets, which may appear somewhat singular on a first view of the matter, but then we must recollect that Bacchus was not merely the god of wine and joy, but also the god of the highest degree of inspiration.

Among the remaining pieces of Æschylus, we have what is highly deserving of our attention, a complete triology. The antiquarian account of triologies is this, that in the more early times the poet did not contend for the prize with a single piece, but with three, which however were not always connected together by their contents, and that a fourth satirical drama was also attached to them. All these were successively represented in one day. The idea which we must form of the triology in relation to the tragic art is this; a tragedy cannot be indefinitely lengthened and continued, like the Homeric epic poem for example, to which whole rhapsodies have been appended; for this is too independent and complete within itself. Notwithstanding this circumstance, however, several tragedies may be connected together by means of a common destiny running throughout all their actions in one great cycle. Hence the fixing on the number three admits of a satisfactory explanation. It is the thesis, the antithesis, and the connection. The advantage of this conjunction was that, in the consideration of the connected fables, a more ample degree of gratification was derived than could possibly be obtained from a single action. The objects of the three tragedies might be separated by a wide interval of time, or follow close upon one another.

The three pieces of the triology of Æschylus are Agamemnon, the Choephoræ or Electra, and the Eumenides or Furies. The object of the first is the murder of Agamemnon by Clytemnestra, on his return from Troy. In the second, Orestes avenges his father by killing his mother: *facto pius et sceleratus eodem.* This deed, although perpetrated from the most powerful motives, is repugnant however to natural and moral order. Orestes as a prince was, it is true, entitled to exercise justice even on the members of his own family; but he was under the necessity of stealing in disguise into the dwelling of the tyrannical usurper of his throne, and of going to work like an assassin. The memory of his father pleads his excuse; but although Clytemnestra has deserved death, the blood of his mother still rises up in judgment against him. This is represented in the Eumenides in the form of a contention among the gods, some of whom approve of the deed of Orestes, while others persecute him, till at last the divine wisdom, under the figure of Minerva, reconciles the opposite claims, establishes a peace, and puts an end to the long series of crimes and punishments which desolated the royal house of Atreus.

A considerable interval takes place between the period of the first and second pieces, during which Orestes grows up to manhood. The second and third are connected together immediately in the order of time. Orestes takes flight after the murder of his mother to Delphi, where we find him at the commencement of the Eumenides.

In each of the two first pieces, there is a visible reference to the one which follows. In Agamemnon, Cassandra and the chorus prophesy, at the close, to the arrogant Clytemnestra and her paramour Ægisthus, the punishment which awaits them at the hands of Orestes. In the Choephoræ, Orestes, immediately after the execution of the deed, finds no longer any repose; the furies of his mother begin to persecute him, and he announces his resolution of taking refuge in Delphi.

The connection is therefore evident throughout, and we may consider the three pieces, which were connected together even in the representation, as so many acts of one great and entire drama. I mention this as a preliminary justification of Shakspeare and other modern poets, in connecting together in one representation a larger circle of human destinies, as we can produce to the critics who object to this the supposed example of the ancients.

In Agamemnon it was the intention of Æschylus to exhibit to us a sudden fall from the highest pinnacle of prosperity and fame, into the abyss of ruin. The prince, the hero, the general of the whole of the Greeks, in the very moment when he has succeeded in concluding the most glorious action, the destruction of Troy, the fame of which is to be re-echoed from the mouths of the greatest poets of all ages, on entering the threshold of his house, after which he has long sighed, is strangled amidst the unsuspected preparations for a festival, according to the expression of Homer, "like an ox in the stall," strangled by his faithless wife; her unworthy seducer takes possession of his throne, and the children are consigned to banishment, or to hopeless servitude.

With the view of giving the greater effect to this dreadful alternation of fortune, the poet has previously thrown a splendor over the destruction of Troy. He has done this in the first half of the piece in a manner peculiar to himself, which, however singular, must be allowed to be impressive in the extreme, and to lay fast hold of the imagination. It is of importance to Clytemnestra not to be surprised by the arrival of her husband. She has therefore arranged an uninterrupted series of signal-fires from Troy to Mycenæ to announce to her the great event. The piece commences with the speech of a watchman, who supplicates the gods for a release from his toils, as for ten long years he had been exposed to the cold dews of night, has witnessed the various changes of the stars, and looked in vain for the expected signal; at the same time he sighs in secret for the internal ruin of the royal house. At this moment he sees the blaze of the long wished-for fires, and hastens to announce it to his mistress. A chorus of aged persons appears, and in their songs they trace back the Trojan war, throughout all its eventful changes of fortune from its first origin, and recount all the prophecies relating to it, and the sacrifice of Iphigenia, at the expense of which the voyage of the Greeks was purchased. Clytemnestra declares the joyful cause of the sacrifice which she orders, and the herald Talthybius immediately makes his appearance, who as an eye-witness announces the drama of the conquered and plundered city consigned as a prey to the flames, the joy of the victors, and the glory of their leader. He displays with reluctance, as if unwilling to shade the brilliancy of his picture, the subsequent misfortunes of the Greeks, their dispersion, and the shipwreck suffered by many of them, an immediate symptom of the wrath of the gods. We easily see how little the unity of place was observed by the poet, and that he rather avails himself of the prerogative of his mental dominion over the powers of nature, and adds wings to the circling hours in their course towards their dreadful goal. Agamemnon now comes, borne in a sort of triumphal procession; and seated in another car, laden with booty, follows Cassandra, his prisoner of war and mistress, according to the privilege of the heroes of those days. Clytemnestra greets him with hypocritical joy and veneration; she orders her slaves to cover the ground with the most costly embroideries of purple, that it might not be touched by the foot of the conqueror. Agamemnon, with sage moderation refuses to receive an honor due only to the gods; at last he yields to their invitations and enters the house. The chorus then begins to utter dark forebodings. Clytemnestra returns to allure Cassandra to her destruction by the art of soft persuasion. The latter remains dumb and motionless, but the queen is hardly gone, when, seized with a prophetic rage, she breaks out into the most perplexing lamentations, afterwards unveils her prophecies more distinctly to the chorus; she sees in her mind all the enormities which have been perpetrated in that house; the repast of Thyestes, which the sun refused to look on; the shadows of the dilacerated children appear to her on the battlements of the palace. She also sees the death prepared for her master, and although horror-struck at the atrocious spectacle, as if seized with an overpowering fury, she rushes into the house to meet her inevitable death; we then hear behind the scenes the sighs of the dying Agamemnon. The palace opens; Clytemnestra stands beside the body of her king and husband, an undaunted criminal, who not only confesses the deed, but boasts of it as a just requital for Agamemnon's ambitious sacrifice of Iphigenia. The jealousy towards Cassandra, and the criminal union with the unworthy Ægisthus, which is first disclosed after the completion of the murder towards the conclusion of the piece, are motives which she throws entirely into the back-ground, and hardly touches on; this was necessary to preserve the dignity of the object. But Clytemnestra would have been improperly portrayed as a weak woman seduced from her duty; she appeared with the features of that heroic age so rich in bloody catastrophes, in which all the passions were violent, and in which, both in good and evil, men exceeded the ordinary standard of later and more puny ages. What is so revolting, what affords such a deep proof of the degeneracy of human nature, as the spectacle of horrid crimes conceived in a pusillanimous bosom? When such crimes are to be portrayed by the poet, he must neither endeavor to embellish them, nor to mitigate our horror and aversion. The consequence which is thus given to the sacrifice of Iphigenia has this particular advantage, that it keeps within some bounds our discontent at the fall of Agamemnon. He cannot be pronounced wholly innocent; an earlier crime recoils on his own head; and besides, according to the religious idea of the ancients, an old curse hung over his house: Ægisthus, the contriver of his destruction, is a son of that very Thyestes on whom his father Atreus took such an unnatural revenge; and this fatal connection is conveyed to our minds in the most vivid manner by the chorus, and more especially by the prophecies of Cassandra.

The scene of the Choephoræ is before the royal palace; the grave of Agamemnon appears on the stage. Orestes is seen with his faithful Pylades, and opens the play (which is unfortunately somewhat mutilated at the commencement) at the sepulchre with a prayer to Mercury, and with an invocation to his father, in which he promises to avenge him, and to whom he consecrates a lock. He sees a female train in mourning weeds issue from the palace, who bring a libation to the grave; and, as he thinks he recognizes his sister among them, he retires with Pylades that he may first overhear them. The chorus, which consists of captive Trojan virgins, reveals with mournful gestures the occasion of its mission, namely, a dreadful dream of Clytemnestra; it adds obscure forebodings of the impending revenge for the bloody crime, and bewails its lot in being obliged to serve unworthy superiors. Electra asks the chorus if they mean to fulfil the commission of her hostile mother, or if they are to pour out their offering in silence; and in compliance with their advice, she also offers up a prayer to the subterranean Mercury and the soul of her father, in her own name and that of the absent Orestes, that he may appear and avenge him. In pouring out the offering she joins in the lamentations of the chorus for the departed. She then conjectures, from finding a lock of hair resembling her own in color, and seeing footsteps near the grave, that her brother has been there; and when she is almost frantic with joy at the thought, her brother steps forward and discovers himself. He soon overcomes her doubts by exhibiting to her a tissue woven by herself: they give themselves up to their joy; he addresses a prayer to Jupiter, and makes known that Apollo has called on him, under the most dreadful threats of persecution from the furies of his father, to destroy those who were guilty of his death in the same manner in which he was destroyed, namely, by guile and cunning. We have now hymns on the part of the chorus and Electra, which consist of prayers to her father's shade and the subterranean divinities, and a recapitulation of the motives for the deed, especially those derived from the death of Agamemnon. Orestes inquires into the vision which induced Clytemnestra to offer the libation, and hears that she dreamt that she gave her breast to a dragon in her son's cradle and suckled it with her blood. He now resolves to become the dragon, and announces more distinctly his intention of stealing into the house as a disguised stranger, and attacking both her and Ægisthus by surprise. With this view he withdraws along with Pylades. The subject of the next choral hymn is the boundless audacity of men in general, and especially of women in their illicit passions, confirmed by the most terrible mythical examples, and the avenging justice which always at last overtakes them. Orestes returns as a stranger, with Pylades, and desires admission into the palace. Clytemnestra comes out, and when she learns from him the death of Orestes, at which Electra assumes a feigned grief, she invites him to enter and partake of their hospitality. After a short prayer of the chorus, the nurse comes and mourns her foster child; the chorus inspires her with some hopes of his being still in life, and advises her to contrive to bring Ægisthus to Clytemnestra without his body-guard. On the approaching aspect of danger, the chorus proffers prayers to Jupiter and Mercury for the success of the deed. Ægisthus enters into conversation with the messenger, can hardly allow himself to be persuaded of the truth of the joyful news of the death of Orestes, and hastens into the house for the purpose of ascertaining it, from whence, after a short prayer of the chorus, we hear the cries of the murdered. A servant rushes out and gives the alarm at the door of the female dwelling, to warn Clytemnestra. She hears it, comes forward, and demands an axe to defend herself; but as Orestes rushes instantaneously on her with the bloody sword, her courage fails her, and she holds up to him the maternal breast in the most moving manner. Hesitating in his purpose, he asks the counsel of Pylades, who in a few lines exhorts him by the most cogent reasons to persist; after an alternation of accusation and defence, he pursues her into the house, that he may sacrifice her beside the body of Ægisthus. The chorus rejoices in a grave hymn at the completion of the retaliation. The great door of the palace opens, and exhibits in the inside the two dead bodies on one bed. Orestes orders the servants to unfold the capacious vestment in which his father was entangled when he was slain, that it may be seen by all the beholders; the chorus recognize the bloody spots in it, and mourn afresh the murder of Agamemnon. Orestes, while he feels that his mind is becoming confused, lays hold of an opportunity of justifying himself; he declares his intention of repairing to Delphi to purify himself from the bloody deed, and flies with terror from the furies of his mother, whom the chorus does not perceive, but conceives to be a mere phantom of his imagination, but who nevertheless will no longer allow him any repose. The chorus concludes with a reflection on the threefold scene of murder, in the royal palace, since the repast of Thyestes.

The fable of the Eumenides is, as I have already said, the justification and absolution of Orestes from his bloody crime; it is a trial, but a trial where the gods are accusers, and defenders, and judges; and the manner in which the subject is treated corresponds with its majesty and importance. The scene itself brought before the eyes of the Greeks the highest objects of veneration which were known to them.

It opens before the celebrated temple at Delphi, which occupies the back-ground; the aged Pythia enters in sacerdotal pomp, addresses her prayers to all the gods who presided, or still preside, over the oracle, harangues the assembled people (the actual), and goes into the temple to seat herself on a tripod. She returns full of consternation, and describes what she has seen in the temple: a man stained with blood, supplicating protection, surrounded by sleeping women with serpent hair; she then makes her exit by the same entrance. Apollo now appears with Orestes in his traveller's garb, and a sword and an olive branch in his hands. He promises him his farther protection, commands him to flee to Athens, and recommends him to the care of the present but invisible Mercury, to whom travellers, and especially those who were under the necessity of concealing their journey, were usually consigned.

Orestes goes off at the side allotted to strangers; Apollo re-enters the temple, which remains open, and the furies are seen in the interior sleeping on their seats. Clytemnestra now ascends by the charonic stairs through the orchestra, and appears on the stage. We are not to suppose her a haggard skeleton, but a figure with the appearance of life, though paler, still bearing her wounds in her breast, and shrouded in ethereal-colored vestments. She calls repeatedly to the Furies in the language of vehement reproach, and then disappears, probably through a trap-door. The Furies awake, and when they no longer find Orestes, they dance in wild commotion round the stage during the choral song. Apollo returns from the temple, and expels them from his sanctuary as profanatory beings. We may here suppose him appearing with the sublime displeasure of the Apollo of the Vatican, with bow and quiver, or clothed in his sacred tunic and chlamys.

The scene now changes; but as the Greeks on such occasions were fond of going the shortest way to work, the back-ground remained probably unchanged, and had now to represent the temple of Minerva, on the hill of Mars (Areopagus), and the lateral decorations would be converted into Athens and the surrounding landscape. Orestes comes as from another land, and embraces as a suppliant the statue of Pallas placed before the temple. The chorus (who, according to the directions of the poet, were clothed in black, with purple girdles, and serpents in their hair,—the masks with something of the terrible beauty of Medusa heads, and even the age marked on plastic principles,—) follow him on foot to this place, but remain throughout the remainder of the piece beneath in the orchestra. The Furies had at first exhibited the rage of beasts of prey at the escape of their booty, but they now sing with tranquil dignity their high and terrible office among mortals, claim the head of Orestes as forfeited to them, and consecrate it with mysterious charms to endless pain. Pallas, the warlike virgin, appears in a chariot and four at the intercession of the suppliant. She listens with calm dignity to the mutual complaints of Orestes and his adversaries, and finally undertakes, after due reflection, the office of umpire, at the solicitation of the two parties. The assembled judges take their seats on the steps of the temple, the herald commands silence among the people by sound of trumpets, as at an actual tribunal. Apollo advances to advocate the cause of the youth, the Furies in vain oppose his interference, and the arguments for and against the deed are gone through in short speeches. The judges throw their calculi into the urn, Pallas throws in a white one; all are wrought up to the highest pitch of expectation; Orestes calls out full of anguish to his protector:

O Phœbus Apollo, how is the cause decided?

The Furies, on the other hand:

O black night, mother of all things, dost thou behold this?

In the enumeration of the black and white pebbles, they are found equal in number, and the accused is therefore declared by Pallas acquitted of the charge. He breaks out into joyful expressions of thanks, while the Furies on the other hand declaim against the arrogance of the young gods, who take such liberties with the race of Titan. Pallas bears their rage with equanimity, addresses them in the language of kindness, and even of veneration; and these beings, so untractable in their general disposition, are unable to withstand the power of her mild and convincing eloquence. They promise to bless the land over which she has dominion, while Pallas assigns them a sanctuary in the Attic territory, where they are to be called the Eumenides, that is, the benevolent. The whole ends with a solemn procession round the theatre, with songs of invocation, while bands of children, women, and old men, in purple robes, and with torches in their hands, accompany the Furies in their exit.

Let us now take a retrospective view of the whole triology. In Agamemnon we observe in the deed which is planned and executed, the greatest display of arbitrary will and power: the principal character is a great criminal; and the piece ends with the revolting impressions produced by the sight of triumphant tyranny and crime. I have already alluded to the circumstance of a previous destiny.

The deed in the Choephoræ is partly recommended by Apollo as an appointment of fate, and partly originates in natural motives: the desire of avenging the father, and the fraternal love for the oppressed Electra. After the deed the struggle between the most sacred feelings first becomes manifest, and allows no repose to the distracted youth.

From the very commencement, the Eumenides stands on the very highest tragical elevation: all the past is concentrated as it were in one focus. Orestes has merely been the passive instrument of fate; and free agency is transferred to the more elevated sphere of the gods. Pallas is properly the principal character. The opposition between the most sacred relations, which frequently appears beyond the power of mortal solution, is represented as a contention in the world of the gods.

And this leads me to the deep import of the whole. The ancient mythology is in general symbolical, although not allegorical; for the two are quite distinct. Allegory is the personification of an idea, a fable solely undertaken with such a view; but that is symbolical which has been created by the imagination for other purposes, or which has a reality in itself independent of the idea, but which at the same time is easily susceptible of a symbolical explanation, and even of itself suggests it.

The Titans, in general, mean the dark primary powers of nature and of mind; the later gods, what enters more within the circle of consciousness. The former are more nearly related to the original chaos, the latter belong to a world already subjected to order. The Furies are the dreadful powers of conscience, in so far as it rests on obscure feelings and forebodings, and yields to no principles of reason. In vain Orestes dwells on the just motives for the deed— the voice of blood resounds in his ear. Apollo is the god of youth, of the noble ebullition of passionate discontent, of the bold daring action: hence this deed was commanded by him. Pallas is cool wisdom, justice, and moderation, which alone can allay the dispute.

Even the sleep of the Furies in the temple is symbolical; for only in the holy place, in the bosom of religion, can the fugitive find rest from the stings of his conscience. Scarcely however has he again ventured into the world, when the image of his murdered mother appears, and again awakens them. The very speech of Clytemnestra is symbolical, as well as the attributes of the Furies, the serpents, and the sucking of blood. The same may be said of the aversion of Apollo for them; in fact this symbolical application runs throughout the whole.— The equal cogency of the motives for and against the deed is denoted by the divided number of the judges. When at last a sanctuary is allotted to the softened Furies in the Athenian territory, this is as much as to say that reason shall not everywhere assert her power against the instinctive impulse, that there are certain boundaries in the human mind which are not to be passed, and which every person possessed of a sentiment of reverence will beware of touching, if he wishes to preserve inward peace.

So much for the deep philosophical import, which we are not to wonder at finding in this poet, who, according to the testimony of Cicero, was a Pythagorean. Æschylus had also his political views. The first of these was the rendering Athens illustrious. Delphi was the religious centre of Greece, and yet how is it thrown into the shade! It can only shelter Orestes from the first onset of persecution, but not afford him a complete freedom; this is reserved for the land where law and humanity flourish. His principal object however was the recommending as essential to the welfare of Athens the Areopagus,* an uncorruptible yet mild tribunal, in which the white pebble of Pallas in favor of the accused does honor to the humanity of the Athenians. The poet shows us the origin of an institution fraught with blessings to humanity, in an immense circle of crimes.

But it will be asked, are not aims of this description prejudicial to the pure poetical impression which the whole ought to produce? Most undoubtedly, in the manner in which other poets, and especially Euripides, have proceeded in such cases. But in Æschylus the aim is much more subservient to the poetry than the poetry to the aim. He does not lower himself to a circumscribed reality, but elevates it on the contrary to a higher sphere, and connects it with the most sublime conceptions.

In the Orestiad (for so the three connected pieces are called) we certainly possess one of the most sublime poems that ever was conceived by the human imagination, and probably the most mature and faultless of all the productions of his genius. The period of their composition confirms this supposition; for he was at least sixty years old when he brought these dramas on the stage, the last which he ever submitted in competition for the prize at Athens. Every one of his pieces however which have come down to us is remarkable either for the display of some peculiar property of the poet, or as indicative of the step in the art on which he stood at the time.

The Chained Prometheus is the representation of constancy under suffering, and that the never-ending suffering of a god. Exiled to a naked rock on the shore of the encircling ocean, this drama still embraces the world, the Olympus of the gods, and the earth of mortals, all scarcely yet reposing in a secure state above the dread abyss of the dark Titanian powers. The idea of a self-devoting divinity has been mysteriously inculcated in many religions, as a confused foreboding of the true; here however it appears in a most alarming contrast with the consolations of revelation. For Prometheus does not suffer on an understanding with the power by whom the world is governed, but he atones for his disobedience, and that disobedience consists in nothing but the attempt to give perfection to the human race. It is thus an image of human nature itself: endowed with a miserable foresight and bound down to a narrow existence, without an ally, and with nothing to oppose to the combined and inexorable powers of nature, but an unshaken will and the consciousness of elevated claims. The other poems of the Greek tragedians are single tragedies: but this may be called tragedy itself: its purest spirit is revealed with all the annihilating and overpowering influence of its first unmitigated austerity.

There is little external action in this piece: Prometheus merely suffers and resolves from the beginning to the end; and his sufferings and resolutions are always the same. But the poet has contrived in a masterly manner to introduce variety and progress into that which in itself was determinately filled, and given us a scale for the measurement of the matchless power of his sublime Titans in the objects by which he has surrounded them. We have the first silence of Prometheus while he is chained down under the harsh inspection of Strength and Force, whose threats serve only to excite a useless compassion in Vulcan, who carries them into execution; then his solitary complaints, the arrival of the tender ocean nymphs, whose kind but disheartening sympathy induces him to give vent to his feelings, to relate the causes of his fall, and to reveal the future, though with prudent reserve he reveals it only in part; the visit of the ancient Oceanus, a kindred god of the race of Titans, who, under the pretext of a zealous attachment to his cause, advises him to submission towards Jupiter, and who is on that account dismissed with proud contempt; the introduction of the raving Io, driven about from place to place, the victim of the same tyranny from which Prometheus himself suffers; his prophecy of the wanderings to which she is still doomed, and the fate which at last awaits her, connected in some degree with his own, as from her blood he is to receive a deliverer after the lapse of many ages; the appearance of Mercury as a messenger of the tyrant of the world, who with threats commands him to disclose the secret by which Jupiter may remain on his throne secure from all the malice of fate; and lastly, the yawning of the earth before Prometheus has well declared his refusal, amidst thunder and lightning, storms and earthquake, by which he himself and the rock to which he is chained are swallowed up in the abyss of the nether world. The triumph of subjection was never celebrated in more glorious strains, and we have difficulty in conceiving how the

---

* I do not find that this aim has ever been ascribed to Æschylus by the express testimony of any ancient writer. It is however, not to be mistaken, especially in the speech of Pallas, beginning with the 680th verse. This coincides with the account that in the very year when the piece was represented, Olymp. lxxx. 1, a certain Ephialtes excited the people against the Areopagus, which was the best guardian of the old and more austere constitution, and kept democratic extravagance in check. This Ephialtes was murdered one night by an unknown hand. Æschylus received the first prize in the theatrical games, but we know at the same time that he left Athens immediately afterwards, and passed his remaining years in Sicily. It is possible that, although the theatrical judges did him the justice to which he was entitled, he might be held in aversion by the multitude notwithstanding, and that this without any express sentence of banishment might have induced him to leave his native city. The story of the sight of the terrible chorus of Furies having thrown children into mortal convulsions, and caused women to miscarry, appears to me fabulous. A poet would hardly have been crowned, who had been the occasion of profaning the festival by such occurrences.

poet in the Freed Prometheus could sustain himself on such an elevation.

In the dramas of Æschylus we have one of many examples that, in every art as well as nature, gigantic productions precede those that evince regularity of proportion, which again in their turn decline gradually into littleness and insignificance, and that poetry in its original appearance approaches always the nearest to the reverence of religion, whatever form the latter may assume among the various races of men.

A saying of the poet, which has been preserved, affords us a proof that he endeavored to maintain himself on this elevation, and purposely avoided all artificial cultivation, which might have the effect of lowering the divinity of his character. His brethren stimulated him to write a new Pæan. He answered: "The old one of Tynachus is the best, and the same thing would happen here that was observable in a comparison between the ancient and modern statues; for the former with all their simplicity were considered as divine, and the modern, with all the care bestowed on their execution, were indeed admired, but bore much less the impression of a divinity." He carries his boldness in religious matters, as in everything else, to the utmost limits; and he was even accused of having in one of his pieces disclosed the Eleusinian mysteries, and only absolved on the intercession of his brother Amynias, who displayed the wounds which he had received in the battle of Salamis. He perhaps believed that in the poetic communication was contained the initiation into the mysteries, and that nothing was in this way revealed to any one who was not worthy of it.

The tragic style of Æschylus is still imperfect, and not unfrequently runs into the unmixed epic and lyric. It is often disjointed, irregular, and hard. To compose more regular and skilful tragedies than those of Æschylus was by no means difficult; but in the more than mortal grandeur which he displayed, it was impossible that he should ever be surpassed; and even Sophocles, his younger and more fortunate rival, did not in this respect equal him. The latter, in speaking of Æschylus, gave a proof that he was himself a reflecting artist: "Æschylus does what is right without knowing it." These few simple words exhaust the whole of what we understand by powerful genius unconscious of its powers.

SOPHOCLES.

The birth-year of Sophocles was nearly at an equal distance between that of his prædecessor and of Euripides, so that he was about half a life-time from each: in this all the accounts are found to coincide. He was however during the greater part of his life the contemporary of both. He frequently contended for the tragic garland with Æschylus, and he outlived Euripides, who himself attained a good age. If I may speak in the spirit of the ancient religion, it seems that a beneficent Providence wished to evince to the human race, in the instance of this individual, the dignity and felicity of their lot, as he was endowed with every divine gift, with all that can adorn and elevate the mind and heart, and crowned with every blessing imaginable in this life. Descended from rich and honored parents, and born a free citizen of the most cultivated state of Greece, such were the advantages with which he entered the world. Beauty of body and of soul, and the uninterrupted enjoyment of both in the utmost perfection, till the extreme limits of human existence; an education the most extensive, yet select, in gymnastics and music, the former so important in the development of the bodily powers, and the latter in the communication of harmony; the sweet blossom of youth, and the ripe fruit of age; the possession and continued enjoyment of poetry and art, and the exercise of serene wisdom; love and respect among his fellow citizens, fame in other countries, and the countenance and favor of the gods; these are the general features of the life of this pious and virtuous poet. It would seem as if the gods, in return for his dedicating himself at an early age to Bacchus, as the giver of all joy, and the author of the cultivation of the human race, by the representation of tragical dramas for his festivals, had wished to confer immortality on him, so long did they delay the hour of his death; but as this was impossible, they extinguished his life as gently as possible, that he might imperceptibly change one immortality for another, the long duration of his earthly existence for an imperishable name. When a youth of sixteen, he was selected, on account of his beauty, to play on the lyre, and to dance in the Greek manner before the chorus of youths who, after the battle of Salamis (in which Æschylus fought, and which he has so nobly described), executed the Pæan round the trophy erected on that occasion; so that the fairest development of his youthful beauty coincided with the moment when the Athenian people had attained the epoch of their highest glory. He held the rank of general along with Pericles and Thucydides, and, when arrived at a more advanced age, the priesthood of a native hero. In his twenty-fifth year he began to represent tragedies; twenty times he was victorious; he often gained the second place, and he never was ranked in the third. In this career he proceeded with increasing success till he reached his ninetieth year; and some of his greatest works were even the fruit of a still later period. There is a story of an accusation brought against him by one or more of his elder sons, of having become childish from age, because he was too fond of a grandchild by a second wife, and of being no longer in a condition to manage his own affairs. In his defence he merely read to his judges his Œdipus in Colonos, which he had then composed in honor of Colonos, his birth-place; and the astonished judges, without farther consultation, conducted him in triumph to his house. If it be true that the second Œdipus was written at so late an age, as from its mature serenity and total freedom from the impetuosity and violence of youth we have good reason to conclude that it actually was, it affords us at once a pleasing picture of the delight and reverence which attended his concluding years. Although the various accounts of his death appear fabulous, they all coincide in this, that he departed without a struggle, while employed in his art, or something connected with it, and that like an old swan of Apollo, he breathed out his life in song. I consider also the story of the Lacedemonian general who had fortified the burying-ground of his fathers, and who, twice exhorted by Bacchus in a vision to allow Sophocles to be there interred, despatched a herald to the Athenians on the subject, with a number of other circumstances, as the strongest possible proof of the established reverence in which his name was held. In calling him virtuous and pious, I spoke in the true sense of the words; for although his works breathe the real character of ancient grandeur, sweetness and simplicity, of all the Grecian poets he is also the individual whose feelings bear the strongest affinity to the spirit of our religion.

One gift alone was refused to him by nature: a voice attuned to song. He could only call forth and direct the harmonious effusions of other voices; he was therefore compelled to depart from the established practice of the poet acting a part in his own pieces, and only once (a very characteristic trait) made his appearance in the character of the blind singer Thamyris playing on the cithera.

As Æschylus, who raised tragic poetry from its rude beginnings to the dignity of the cothurnus, was his predecessor; the historical relations in which he stood to Sophocles enabled the latter to avail himself of the inventions of his original master, so that Æschylus appears as the rough designer, and Sophocles as the finished successor. The more artful construction of the dramas of the latter is easily perceived: the limitation of the chorus with respect to the dialogue, the polish of the rhythmus, and the pure Attic diction, the introduction of a greater number of characters, the increase of contrivance in the fable, the multiplication of incidents, a greater degree of development, the more tranquil continuance of all the moments of the action, and the greater degree of theatrical effect given to incidents of a decisive nature, the more perfect rounding of the whole, even considered in a mere external point of view. But he excelled Æschylus in somewhat still more essential, and proved himself deserving of the good fortune of having such a preceptor, and of entering into competition with him in the same subjects: I mean the harmonious perfection of his mind, by which he fulfilled from inclination every duty prescribed by the laws of beauty, and of which the impulse was in him accompanied by the most clear consciousness. It was impossible to exceed Æschylus in boldness of conception; I am inclined however to believe that Sophocles appears only less bold from his wisdom and moderation, as he always goes to work with the greatest energy, and perhaps with even a more determined severity, like a man who knows the extent of his powers, and is determined, when he does not exceed them, to stand up with the greater confidence for his rights. As Æschylus delights in transporting us to the convulsions of the primary world of the Titans, Sophocles on the other hand never avails himself of the gods but when their appearance is necessary; he formed men, according to the general confession of antiquity, better, that is, not more moral, or exempt from error, but more beautiful and noble than they appeared in real life; and while he took everything in the most human signification, he was at the same time aware of their superior destination. According to all appearance he was also more moderate than Æschylus in his scenic ornaments; he displayed perhaps more taste and selection in his objects, but did not attempt the same colossal pomp.

To characterize the native sweetness and affection so eminent in this poet, the ancients gave him the appellation of the Attic bee. Whoever is thoroughly imbued with the feeling of this property may flatter himself that a sense for ancient art has arisen within him; for the affected sentimentality of the present day, far from coinciding with him in this opinion, would both in the representation of bodily sufferings, and in the language and economy of the tragedies of Sophocles, find much of an unsupportable austerity.

FRIEDRICH DANIEL ERNST SCHLEIERMACHER.

Born 1768. Died 1834.

THE respected divine who bore this name, distinguished alike by his intellectual pre-eminence and his beautiful piety, somewhat resembles Fenelon in his relation to his time, and the kind of influence which went forth from him. With nothing of the mysticism of the French saint, he possessed the same practical depth of spirit and the same devout earnestness; strongly contrasted in this respect with the rationalistic theologians of his day. As a German and a theologian, he was learned, of course; but he was far more than that; he was also a profound philosopher, and, in philosophy, a Platonist. No modern has entered more fully into the meaning and spirit of the immortal Greek, whose works he translated in part. The great aim of his life was to reconcile philosophy with Christianity, and to revive the religious sentiment in an age when the atheistic philosophy of France had brought a temporary blight upon all the nobler products of the soul. The "Discourses on Religion," from which the following extract is taken, is a contribution to this end. His last and his most important work is the *Christliche Glaubenslehre* (Doctrine of Christianity).

Schleiermacher was born at Breslau, and educated as a Moravian at the Seminary of the United Brethren at Niesky. At the age of twenty he left the society of the Moravians, and studied theology at Halle. Having been ordained as a preacher, he was minister for six years at the hospital, *Charité*, in Berlin. During this time, he published his Monologues and the Discourses on Religion, and translated Blair's and Fawcett's sermons. In 1802, he was appointed professor "extraordinary" of theology at Halle, and preached to the University. During the troublous period of the French invasion in 1807, when Halle was taken from the Prussians, he returned to Berlin, and lectured and preached with patriotic boldness on the state of the times, unawed by Davoust, who then occupied the city. In 1809, he was appointed preacher to the Trinity church in Berlin, and was married the same year. In 1810, at the establishment of the University at Berlin, he was made Professor of theology in that institution. This post he retained until his death. In 1833, he visited England, and opened the German church at the Savoy.

In person, Schleiermacher was diminutive and deformed. As a preacher, he was unboundedly popular, although his discourses had none of those qualities which stir the blood, but consisted, for the most part, in plain practical appeals to the understanding and the conscience. He preached extempore, and, it is said, with no other preparation than that which he allowed himself on Sunday morning,—an hour before service. His conduct during his last hours, as related by his wife, was characteristic, and illustrated the Christian faith and piety which distinguished him through life. His last act, a few minutes before death, was to administer the service of the Eucharist to himself and his family. "In these words of the Holy Scriptures," he said, "I place my trust; they are the corner-stone of my faith:" then turning to his wife and children, "In this love and communion of souls, then, we are and shall be one and undivided." He died February 12, 1834.

DISCOURSE IV.

ON THE SOCIAL ELEMENT IN RELIGION; OR ON THE CHURCH AND PRIESTHOOD.

Translated by Mr. George Ripley.

THOSE among you who are accustomed to regard religion as a disease of the human mind, cherish also the habitual conviction, that it is an evil more easily borne, if it cannot be restrained, so long as it is only insulated individuals here and there who are infected with it; but that the common danger is raised to the highest degree, and everything put at stake, as soon as a too close connexion is permitted between many patients of this character. In the former case it is possible by a judicious treatment, as it were by an antiphlogistic regimen, and by a healthy, spiritual atmosphere, to ward off the violence of the paroxysms; and if not to entirely conquer the exciting cause of the disease, to attenuate it to such a degree that it shall be almost innocuous. But in the latter case, we must despair of every other means of cure, except that which may proceed from some internal beneficent operation of Nature. For the evil is attended with more alarming symptoms, and is more fatal in its effects, when the too great proximity of other infected persons feeds and aggravates it in every individual; the whole mass of vital air is then quickly poisoned by a few; the most vigorous frames are smitten with the contagion; all the channels in which the functions of life should go on are destroyed; all the juices of the system are decomposed; and, seized with a similar feverous delirium, the sound spiritual life and productions of whole ages and nations are involved in irremediable ruin. Hence your antipathy to the church, to every institution which is intended for the communication of religion, is always more prominent than that which you feel to religion itself: hence, also, priests, as the pillars and the most efficient members of such institutions, are, of all men, the objects of your greatest abomination.

Even those among you who hold a little more indulgent opinion with regard to religion, and deem it rather a singularity than a disorder of the mind, an insignificant rather than a dangerous phenomenon, cherish quite as unfavourable impressions of all social organization for its promotion. A slavish immolation of all that is free and peculiar, a system of lifeless mechanism and barren ceremonies,—these, they imagine, are the inseparable consequences of every such institution; and these, the ingenious and elaborate work of men, who, with almost incredible success, have made a great merit of things which are either nothing in themselves, or which any other person was quite as capable of accomplishing as they. I should pour out my heart but very imperfectly before you, on a subject to which I attach the utmost importance, if I did not undertake to give you the correct point of view with regard to it. I need not here repeat how many of the perverted endeavors and melancholy fortunes of humanity you charge upon religious associations; this is clear as light, in a thousand indications of your predominant individuals; nor will I stop to refute these accusations, one by one, in order to fix the evil upon other causes. Let us rather submit the whole conception of the church to a new examination, and from its central point, throughout its whole extent, erect it again upon a new basis, without regard to what it has actually been hitherto, or to what experience may suggest concerning it.

If religion exists at all, it must needs possess a social character; this is founded not only in the nature of man, but still more in the nature of religion. You will acknowledge that it indicates a state of disease, a signal perversion of nature, when an individual wishes to shut up within himself anything which he has produced and elaborated by his own efforts. It is the disposition of man to reveal and to communicate whatever is in him, in the indispensable relations and mutual dependence not only of practical life, but also of his spiritual being, by which he is connected with all others of his race; and the more powerfully he is wrought upon by anything, the more deeply it penetrates his inward nature, so much the stronger is this social impulse, even if we regard it only from the point of view of the universal endeavor to behold the emotions which we feel ourselves, as they are exhibited by others, so that we may obtain a proof from their example that our own experience is not beyond the sphere of humanity.

You perceive that I am not speaking here of the endeavor to make others similar to ourselves, nor of the conviction that what is exhibited in one is essential to all; it is merely my aim to ascertain the true relation between our individual life and the common nature of man, and clearly to set it forth. But the peculiar object of this desire for communication is unquestionably that in which man feels that he is originally passive, namely, his perceptions and emotions. He is here impelled by the eager wish to know whether the power which has produced them in him be not something foreign and unworthy. Hence we see man employed, from his very childhood, with making revelations, which, for the most part, are of this character; the conceptions of his understanding, concerning whose origin there can be no doubt, he allows to rest in his own mind, and still more easily he determines to refrain from the expression of his judgments; but whatever acts upon his senses, whatever awakens his feelings, of that he desires to obtain witnesses, with regard to that he longs for those who will sympathise with him. How should he keep to himself those very operations of the world upon his soul which are the most universal and comprehensive, which appear to him as of the most stupendous and resistless magnitude? How should he be willing to lock up within his own bosom those very emotions which impel him with the greatest power beyond himself, and in the indulgence of which, he becomes conscious that he can never understand his own nature from himself alone? It will rather be his first endeavor, whenever a religious view gains clearness in his eye, or a pious feeling penetrates his soul, to direct the attention of others to the same object, and, as far as possible, to communicate to their hearts the elevated impulses of his own.

If, then, the religious man is urged by his nature to speak, it is the same nature which secures to him the certainty of hearers. There is no element of his being with which, at the same time, there is implanted in man such a lively feeling of his total inability to exhaust it by himself alone, as with that of religion. A sense of religion has no sooner dawned upon him, than he feels the infinity of its nature and the limitation of his own; he is conscious of embracing but a small portion of it; and that which he cannot immediately reach, he wishes to perceive, as far as he can, from the representations of others who have experienced it themselves, and to enjoy it with them. Hence, he is anxious to observe every manifestation of it; and, seeking to supply his own deficiencies, he watches for every tone which he recognizes as proceeding from it. In this manner, mutual communications are instituted; in this manner, every one feels equally the need both of speaking and hearing.

But the imparting of religion is not to be sought in books, like that of intellectual conceptions and scientific knowledge. The pure impression of the original product is too far destroyed in this medium, which, in the same way that dark-colored objects absorb a great proportion of the rays of light, swallows up everything belonging to the pious emotions of the heart, which cannot be embraced in the insufficient symbols from which it is intended again to proceed. Nay, in the written communications of religious feeling, everything needs a double and triple representation; for that which originally represented, must be represented in its turn; and yet the effect on the whole man, in its complete unity, can only be imperfectly set forth by continued and varied reflections. It is only when religion is driven out from the society of the living, that it must conceal its manifold life under the dead letter.

Neither can this intercourse of heart with heart, on the deepest feelings of humanity, be carried on in common conversation. Many persons, who are filled with zeal for the interests of religion, have brought it as a reproach against the manners of our age, that while all other important subjects are so freely discussed in the intercourse of society, so little should be said concerning God and divine things. I would defend ourselves against this charge by maintaining that this circumstance, at least, does not indicate contempt or indifference towards religion, but a happy and very correct instinct. In the presence of joy and merriment, where earnestness itself must yield to raillery and wit, there can be no place for that which should be always surrounded with holy veneration and awe. Religious views, pious emotions, and serious considerations with regard to them,—these we cannot throw out to each other in such small crumbs as the topics of a light conversation; and when the discourse turns upon sacred subjects, it would rather be a crime than a virtue to have an answer ready for every question, and a rejoinder for every remark. Hence, the religious sentiment retires from such circles as are too wide for it, to the more confidential intercourse of friendship, and to the mutual communications of love, where the eye and the countenance are more expressive than words, and where even a holy silence is understood.

But it is impossible for divine things to be treated in the usual manner of society, where the conversation consists in striking flashes of thought, gaily and rapidly alternating with each other; a more elevated style is demanded for the communication of religion, and a different kind of society, which is devoted to this purpose, must hence be formed. It is becoming indeed to apply the whole richness and magnificence of human discourse to the loftiest subject which language can reach,—not as if there were any adornment, with which religion could not dispense, but because it would show a frivolous and unholy disposition in its heralds, if they did not bring together the most copious resources within their power, and consecrate them all to religion: so that they might thus perhaps exhibit it in its appropriate greatness and dignity. Hence, it is impossible without the aid of poetry, to give utterance to the religious sentiment, in any other than an oratorical manner, with all the skill and energy of language, and freely using, in addition, the service of all the arts, which can contribute to flowing and impassioned discourse. He, therefore, whose heart is overflowing with religion, can open his mouth only before an auditory, where that which is presented, with such a wealth of preparation, can produce the most extended and manifold effects.

Would that I could present before you an image of the rich and luxurious life in this city of God, when its inhabitants come together each in the fulness of his own inspiration, which is ready to stream forth without constraint, but at the same time, each filled with a holy desire to receive and to appropriate to himself everything which others wish to bring before him. If one comes forward before the rest, it is not because he is entitled to this distinction, in virtue of an office or of a previous agreement, nor because pride and conceitedness have given him presumption: it is rather a free impulse of the spirit, a sense of the most heart-felt unity of each with all, a consciousness of entire equality, a mutual renunciation of all First and Last, of all the arrangements of earthly order. He comes forward, in order to communicate to others, as an object of sympathizing contemplation, the deepest feelings of his soul while under the influence of God; to introduce them within the sphere of religion, in which he breathes his native air; and to infect them with the contagion of his own holy emotions. He speaks forth the Divine which stirs his bosom, and in holy silence the assembly follows the inspiration of his words. Whether he unveils a secret mystery, or with prophetic confidence connects the future with the present; whether he strengthens old impressions by new examples, or is led by the lofty visions of his burning imagination into other regions of the world and into another order of things; the practised sense of his audience everywhere accompanies his own; and when he returns into himself from his wanderings through the kingdom of God, his own heart and that of each of his hearers are the common dwelling-place of the same emotion.

If now the agreement of his sentiments with that which they feel be announced to him, whether loudly or low, then are holy mysteries —not merely significant emblems, but, justly regarded, natural indications of a peculiar consciousness, and peculiar feelings—invented and celebrated, a higher choir, as it were, which in its own lofty language answers to the appealing voice. But not only, as it were; for as such a discourse is music without tune or measure, so there is also a music among the Holy, which may be called discourse without words, the most distinct and expressive utterance of the inward man. The Muse of Harmony, whose intimate relation with religion, although it has been for a long time spoken of and described, is yet recognized only by few, has always presented upon her altars the most perfect and magnificent productions of her selectest scholars, in honor of religion. It is in sacred hymns and choirs, with which the words of the poet are connected only by slight and airy bands, that those feelings are breathed forth which precise language is unable to contain; and thus the tones of thought and emotion alternate with each other in mutual support, until all is satisfied and filled with the Holy and the Infinite. Of this character is the influence of religious men upon one another; such is their natural and eternal union. Do not take it ill of them, that this heavenly bond,—the most consummate product of the social nature of man, but to which it does not attain until it becomes conscious of its own high and peculiar significance,—that this should be deemed of more value in their sight, than the political union, which you esteem so far above everything else, but which will nowhere ripen to manly beauty, and which compared with the former, appears far more constrained than free, far more transitory than eternal.

But where now, in the description which I have given of the community of the pious, is that distinction between priests and laymen, which you are accustomed to designate as the source of so many evils? A false appearance has deceived you. This is not a distinction between persons, but only one of condition and employment. Every man is a priest, so far as he draws around him others, in the sphere which he has appropriated to himself, and in which he professes to be a master. Every one is a layman, so far as he is guided by the counsel and experience of another, within the sphere of religion, where he is comparatively a stranger. There is not here the tyrannic aristocracy, which you describe with such hatred; but this society is a priestly people, a perfect republic, where every one is alternately ruler and citizen, where every one follows the same power in another which he feels also in himself, and with which he too governs others.

How then could the spirit of discord and division,—which you regard as the inevitable consequence of all religious combinations,—find a congenial home within this sphere? I see nothing but that All is One, and that all the differences which actually exist in religion, by means of this very union of the pious, are gently blended with each other. I have directed your attention to the different degrees of religiousness, I have pointed out to you the different modes of insight, and the different directions in which the soul seeks for itself the supreme object of its pursuit. Do you imagine that this must needs give birth to sects, and thus destroy all free and reciprocal intercourse in religion? It is true indeed in contemplation, that everything which is separated into various parts, and embraced in different divisions, must be opposed and contradictory to itself; but consider, I pray you, how Life is manifested in a great variety of forms, how the most hostile elements seek out each other here, and for this very reason, what we separate in contemplation, all flows together in life. They, to be sure, who on one of these points bear the greatest resemblance to each other, will present the strongest mutual attraction: but they cannot, on that account, compose an independent whole; for the degrees of this affinity imperceptibly diminish and increase, and in the midst of so many transitions there is no absolute repulsion, no total separation, even between the most discordant elements. Take which you will of these masses, which have assumed an organic form according to their own inherent energy; if you do not forcibly divide them by a mechanical operation, no one will exhibit an absolutely distinct and homogeneous character, but the extreme points of each will be connected at the same time with those which display different properties and properly belong to another mass.

If the pious individuals, who stand on the same degree of a lower order, formed a closer union with each other, there are yet some always included in the combination who have a presentiment of higher things. These are better understood by all who belong to a higher social union, than they understand themselves; and there is a point of sympathy between the two which is concealed only from the latter. If those combine together, in whom one of the modes of insight, which I have described, is predominant, there will always be some among them who understand at least both of the modes, and since they in some degree belong to both, they form a connecting link between two spheres which would otherwise be separated. Thus the individual who is more inclined to cherish a religious connection between himself and nature, is yet by no means opposed, in the essentials of religion, to him who prefers to trace the footsteps of the Godhead in history: and there will never be wanting those who can pursue both paths with equal facility. Thus in whatever manner you divide the vast province of religion, you will always come back to the same point.

If unbounded universality of insight be the first and original condition of religion, and hence also, most naturally, its fairest and ripest fruit, you perceive that it cannot be otherwise than that, in proportion as an individual advances in religion, and the character of his piety becomes more pure, the whole religious world will more and more appear to him as an indivisible whole. The spirit of separation, in proportion as it insists upon a rigid division, is a proof of imperfection: the highest and most cultivated minds always perceive a universal connection, and for the very reason that they perceive it, they also establish it. Since every one comes in contact only with his immediate neighbor, but, at the same time, has an immediate neighbor on all sides and in every direction, he is, in fact, indissolubly linked in with the whole. Mystics and Naturalists in religion, they to whom the Godhead is a personal Being, and they to whom it is not, they who have arrived at a systematic view of the Universe, and they who behold it only in its elements or only in obscure chaos,—all, notwithstanding, should be only one: one band surrounds them all; and they can be totally separated only by a violent and arbitrary force; every specific combination is nothing but an integral part of the whole, its peculiar characteristics are almost evanescent, and are gradually lost in outlines that become more and more indistinct; and at least those who feel themselves thus united will always be the superior portion.

Whence, then, but through a total misunderstanding, have arisen that wild and disgraceful zeal for proselytism to a separate and peculiar form of religion, and that horrible expression —"no salvation except with us." As I have described to you the society of the pious, and as it must needs be according to its intrinsic nature, it aims merely at reciprocal communication, and subsists only between those who are already in possession of religion, of whatever character it may be; how then can it be its vocation to change the sentiments of those who now acknowledge a definite system, or to introduce and consecrate those who are totally destitute of one? The religion of this society, as such, consists only in the religion of all the pious taken together; as each one beholds it in the rest,—it is Infinite, no single individual can embrace it entirely, since so far as it is individual, it ceases to be one, and hence no man can attain such elevation and completeness, as to raise himself to its level. If any one then, has chosen a part in it for himself, whatever it may be, were it not an absurd procedure for the society to wish to deprive him of that which is adapted to his nature,—since it ought to comprise this also within its limits, and hence some one must needs possess it?

And to what end should it desire to cultivate those who are yet strangers to religion? Its own especial characteristic—the Infinite Whole —of course it cannot impart to them; and the communication of any specific element cannot be accomplished by the Whole, but only by individuals. But perhaps then, the Universal, the Indeterminate, which might be presented, when we seek that which is common to all the members? But you are aware, that as a general rule, nothing can be given or communicated, in the form of the Universal and Indeterminate: specific object and precise form are requisite for this purpose; otherwise, in fact, that which is presented would not be a reality but a nullity. Such a society, accordingly, can never find a measure or rule for this undertaking.

And how could it so far abandon its sphere as to engage in this enterprise? The want on which it is founded, the essential principle of religious society, points to no such purpose. Individuals unite with each other and compose a Whole: the Whole, accordingly, rests in itself, and needs not to strive for anything beyond. Hence, whatever is accomplished in this way for religion is the private affair of the individual for himself, and if I may say so, more in his relations out of the church than in it. Compelled to withdraw into the inferior scenes of life, from the circle of religious communion, where the mutual existence and life in God afford him the most elevated enjoyment, and where his spirit, penetrated with holy feelings, soars to the highest summit of consciousness, it is his consolation that he can connect everything with which he must there be employed, with that which always retains the deepest significance in his heart. As he descends from those lofty regions, among those whose whole endeavor and pursuit are limited to earth, he easily believes—and you must pardon him the feeling —that he has passed from intercourse with Gods and Muses, to a race of coarse barbarians. He feels like a steward of religion among the unbelieving, a herald of piety among the savages; he hopes, like an Orpheus or an Amphion, to charm the multitude with his heavenly tones; he presents himself among them, like a priestly form, clearly and brightly exhibiting the lofty, spiritual sense, which fills his soul, in all his actions and in the whole compass of his Being. If the contemplation of the Holy and the Godlike awakens a kindred emotion in them, how joyfully does he cherish the first presages of religion in a new heart, as a delightful pledge of its growth even in a harsh and foreign clime! With what triumph does he bear the neophyte with him to the exalted assembly! This activity for the promotion of religion is only the pious yearning of the stranger after his home, the endeavor to carry his fatherland with him in all his wanderings, and everywhere to find again its laws and customs as the highest and most beautiful elements of his life; but the father-land itself, happy in its own resources, perfectly sufficient for its own wants, knows no such endeavor.

GEORGE WILHELM FRIEDRICH HEGEL.*

Born 1770. Died 1831.

GEORGE WILHELM FRIEDRICH HEGEL, the last of the four great German philosophers, was born August 27th, 1770, at Stuttgart, in the kingdom of Würtemberg. "It is quite remarkable," says his biographer, "that one of his sponsors was a professor of philosophy." He was matriculated as a student of theology in the University of Tübingen, in the year 1788. After completing his University career, he pursued an extensive and severe course of study in comparative retirement, being meanwhile chiefly employed as a teacher in private families. In 1801 he became a public lecturer in the University of Jena, dedicating his first work to an examination of the difference between the systems of Fichte and Schelling. Here he continued to give courses of lectures, and to develope his system, until the taking of Jena by the French in 1806. For the next two years he edited a newspaper, then he was rector of a gymnasium in Nuremberg, where he perfected his most important work, in which he gave a new character to the whole system of Logic. While professor of philosophy in Heidelberg (1816–18) he published his Encyclopædia, in which his whole scheme of philosophy is contained. He was called to Berlin in the year 1818, and remained there until his death, on the fourteenth of November, 1831, when he fell a victim to the cholera.

His philosophy claims to be the absolute system, the result and culmination of all other systems. In it he resumes the whole progress of the human mind, and alleges that his system, and that alone, is able to explain the whole course of history, and the phenomena of nature, all the problems of speculation. There is one *Absolute Substance* pervading all things. That Substance is *Spirit*. This Spirit is endued with the power of development; it produces from itself the opposing powers and forces of the universe. All that we have to do is to stand by and see the process going on. The process is at first the evolution of antagonistic forces; then a mediation between them. All proceeds by triplicates; there is the positive, then the negative, then the mediation between them, which produces a higher unity. This again is but the starting point for a new series. And so the process goes on, from stage to stage, until the Absolute Spirit has passed through all the stadia of its evolutions, and is exhibited in its highest form in the Hegelian system of philosophy. The system comprises three departments: Logic, Natural Philosophy, and the Philosophy of Spirit. Logic is the science of the Absolute Idea, in its abstract character; in the Philosophy of Nature we have the same Absolute in another, an external form; in the Philosophy of Spirit we have its highest stage. Here it manifests itself as the Subjective Spirit, the Objective Spirit, and the Absolute Spirit. The Absolute Spirit, in fine, has three stages of development, which are Religion, Art, and Philosophy.

The collective works of this philosopher have been published in eighteen octavo volumes. They embrace, besides those already specified, extensive courses of lectures upon Ethics, Art, the Philosophy of History, the History of Philosophy, and the Philosophy of Religion. His system has produced a profound impression upon the German mind. The theological and philosophical controversies of the day rage around it. It is reputed to be the most comprehensive and analytic of pantheistic schemes. Its author and some of his disciples assert, that it is the same system in the form of philosophy, which Christianity gives us in the form of faith. But its present position is that of hostility to Christianity.

The style of Hegel is declared by one of his friends to be "strong, pithy, and sometimes knotty." His terminology is often obscure. These characteristics may be noted in the following translations, which are chiefly taken from his Philosophy of History. Though this work was published after his death, yet the first portion of it, from which our extracts are derived, was printed from a full manuscript of the author.

* For this account of Hegel, and the translations from his writings which follow, with the exception of the last, the editor is indebted to a friend.

INTRODUCTION TO THE PHILOSOPHY OF HISTORY.

The subject of this course of Lectures is the Philosophical History of the World. By this is not meant general reflections upon history, such as one might draw from it and illustrate by appropriate examples, but the History of the World itself. That its true nature may be clearly seen, it seems to be necessary first of all to go through with the other modes in which history is treated. There are three general classes into which historical works may be divided:
1. Primitive History.
2. Systematic History, or History accompanied by the reflections of the author.
3. Philosophical History.

1. PRIMITIVE HISTORY.

To give a definite image of what I mean by this kind of history, I need only cite the names of Herodotus, Thucydides, and other historians of this stamp, who describe chiefly the deeds, events, and conditions which they had directly before them, and in the spirit of which they themselves participated. That which was externally present, they transferred in their histories into the domain of mental conceptions. The external phenomenon is here presented again in the form of an internal conception. So, for example, the poet takes the materials which his experience and emotions give him, and elaborates them into distinct and finished pictures. These primitive historians have also at hand the reports and narratives of other men, (it is not possible for one man to see everything,) but only as the poet has an ingredient in the cultivated language to which he owes so much. What memory carelessly keeps, the historian compounds into one whole, places it in the temple of *Mnemosyne*, and thus gives it immortal duration. Sagas, popular songs and traditions are to be excluded from such primitive history, for these are confused and unsettled things, and hence are peculiar to people that have not yet obtained a definite historical character. The sphere of events actually seen, or that could be seen, gives a firmer basis than does the dim antiquity where these sagas and fables grow up, and they do not constitute a part of the history of nations which have attained a fixed individuality.

These primitive historians now fashion the events, deeds, and conditions which were actually before them, into a work that gives to others a distinct picture of their times. The contents of such histories cannot, of course, be of great outward compass, (see the works of Herodotus, Thucydides, and Guicciardini;) for they are essentially made up of what is present and living around the authors. The state of culture of the author is *identical* with that in which those events were transacted, which he fashions into a work; the spirit of the author and the spirit of the deeds he narrates are *one* and *the same*. He describes that of which he has been more or less a part, or in the midst of which he has lived. There are short periods of time, distinct images of men and events, individual traits not reflected upon, from which he gathers his picture, in order to bring the scene and persons as definitely to the conception of after-times, as they stood before his own mind, whether in actual vision or in graphic narratives. He has nothing to do with reflections upon what he describes, for he lives in the spirit of the times, and has not yet got out beyond it: if he belong, as did Cæsar, to the class of generals or statesmen, then his own ends and aims are the ones which come out as historical. When it is here said that such a historian does not reflect, but that the persons and people themselves come forward, this seems to be contradicted by the speeches which we read, for example, in Thucydides, and which, it is quite certain, were not delivered as they are reported. But speeches are acts among men, and essentially effective acts also. People do indeed often say, it was only a speech, and mean by this that it was a harmless affair. Such speeches are mere talk, and talk has the important advantage of being harmless. But speeches from one people to another, orations addressed to people and princes are integral parts of history. Even if Thucydides did compose the speeches he puts into the mouth of Pericles, the most highly cultivated, genuine, and noble of statesmen, yet are they not foreign to Pericles. In these speeches, these men speak out the maxims of their people, of their own selves, their consciousness of their political relations, as well as of their moral and spiritual natures, the principles which guided their aims and acts. What the historian lets them say is not a loaned consciousness, but expresses the very culture of the orators.

Of such writers of history, whom we must study into, and by whom we must linger, if we would live with the nations, and sink ourselves into their spirit—of such historians, in whom we seek not merely learning, but deep and genuine delight, there are not so many to be found as we might perchance suppose. Herodotus, the father, that is the originator of history, and Thucydides, have been already named. Xenophon's Return of the Ten Thousand is a book equally original; Cæsar's Commentaries are the simple master-piece of a great spirit. In ancient times, these historians were necessarily great captains and statesmen; in the middle ages, if we except the bishops who stood at the centre of state affairs, the monks as naïve chroniclers are to be reckoned here; but they were as isolated from the events they describe, as those men of antiquity were connected with them. In later times, all the relations of things have changed. Our culture is essentially comprehensive, and immediately transforms all events into reports which give a distinct picture of them. We have admirable, simple, definite narratives of this kind, especially of military transactions, which may well be placed by the side of Cæsar's, and are even more instructive than his, on account of the fulness of their contents, and the details of means and conditions. The French Memoirs also belong here. Many of these are written by men of talent and wit about matters of limited interest, and they frequently contain much of anecdote; but others are true historical master-pieces, as those of Cardinal de Retz, and bring to view a wider historical field. In Germany there are but few masters in this art; Frederic the Great (*histoire de mon temps*) is an honorable exception. Such works can fitly come only from men in high stations. Only he who stands above can rightly survey the field, and look at everything; not he who has looked from below upwards through a scanty opening.

2. SYSTEMATIC HISTORY.

The second kind of history we may call Systematic History, or history accompanied by the reflections, and composed in view of the general scheme of the author. It is history, in the exhibition of which we are led beyond mere present and passing events, not in reference to time, but in respect of the spirit or views with which it is composed. Under this second genus, there are wholly different species to be distinguished.

a. We wish for a general view of the whole history of a people or country, or of the world, in short, what we call General History. Here the chief thing is the working up of the historical materials, and to this labor the author comes with a spirit which is different from the spirit of the periods of which he treats. In doing this, the points of chief importance will be, on the one hand, the principles which the author applies in judging of the character and tendency of the acts and events he describes, and, on the other hand, those which guide him in the composition of the history. The reflections and judgments of us Germans upon these points have been very manifold; every writer of history has got his own special way in his own head. The English and French, as a general thing, know how history should be written: their stage of culture is more general and national; among us, each one thinks out some subtle peculiarity, and instead of writing history, we are always trying to find out the way in which history should be written. This first species of excogitated history is near akin to primitive history, when it has no farther aim than to exhibit the whole history of a country. Such compilations (here belong the histories of Livy, Diodorus, Siculus, von Müller's History of Switzerland) when well made are highly serviceable. It would be best, if the historians would approximate to those of the first genus, and describe things so graphically, that the reader might suppose he was hearing contemporaries and eye-witnesses relate the events. But the peculiar tone of mind which every individual must have, who belongs to a particular stage of national culture, frequently becomes modified by the periods through which such a history takes its course, and the spirit which speaks from the historian is another than the spirit of these times. Thus Livy lets the old kings of Rome, the consuls and generals hold speeches befitting only a skilful advocate of the times of Livy, and which besides are most strongly contrasted with the genuine tales preserved from those ancient times; for example, the fable of Menenius Agrippa. Thus, too, the same author gives us descriptions of battles, as though he had himself seen them, the outlines of which, however, might be used for the battles of all ages; and the definitiveness of whose details, again, is in strong contrast with the want of connection and inconsistency with which in other passages he often speaks of the most important matters. The difference between such a compiler and a primitive historian may be best seen by comparing the work of Polybius, so far as it has been preserved to us, with the mode in which Livy makes use of extracts from, and abridges it in the corresponding portions of his history. John von Müller, in the endeavor to be true in his descriptions to the times which he describes, has given to his history a formal, grandiloquent and pedantic air. One would much rather read such things in the old Swiss chronicler, Tschudy himself; everything is more simple and natural than in such a mere made-up and affected antiquatedness.

A history of this kind which surveys long periods, or the whole history of the world, must in truth give up the exhibition of individual facts, and abridge by abstractions, not merely by leaving out events and actions, but by making the author's thoughts the great means of epitomising. A battle, a great victory, a siege, are no longer themselves, but are condensed into the simplest statements. When Livy tells of the wars with the Volsci, he says sometimes, (short enough,) this year war was carried on with the Volsci.

b. A second kind of systematic history is the *pragmatical.* When we have to do with what is past, and busy ourselves about a remote world, the mind, by its own activity, creates for itself a present there, which is the reward of its toil. The events are different, but what is universal and internal in them, the connection, is *one*. This abolishes the past, and makes the event present. Pragmatical reflections, abstract as they may be, do thus make the narrative of past events into a matter of present interest, and vivify them as with present life. Whether such reflections are really interesting and enlivening, depends upon the spirit of the author. Here we have especially called upon to make mention of those moral reflections, and that moral instruction to be got from history, for the sake of which it has often been worked up. Although it may be said that examples of virtue elevate the soul, and are to be applied in the moral instruction of children, in order to impress them with a love of excellence; yet the destinies of nations and states, their complicated interests, conditions and conflicts are quite another field. Regents, statesmen, and nations are very emphatically referred to the experience of history for their instruction. But what experience and history teach is this, that nations and governments have never learned anything from history, nor acted according to the lessons which might have been drawn from it. Every period has such peculiar circumstances, has such an individual character, that in it we must and can judge in view of its own circumstances alone. In the pressure of the world's events, neither a general principle, nor the recollection of similar relations is of service; for these, like a dim remembrance, have no power against the living force and freedom of the present. Nothing, in this respect, is emptier than the oft-repeated appeal to Greek and Roman examples, so often made among the French in the time of their revolution. Nothing can be more diverse than the character of those people and of our own times. John von Müller had such moral ends in view in his Universal as well as in his Swiss history; he prepared such instructions for princes, governments and people, especially for the Swiss; (he made special collections of such maxims and reflections, and often in his correspondence gives the exact number of such reflections, which he had finished in a week:) but all this can hardly be reckoned among the best things he has accomplished. It is only a thorough, free and comprehensive view of the situations, and the deep significancy of the idea by which we judge of them, (as, for example, in Montesquieu's Spirit of the Laws,) which can give truth and interest to such reflections. Hence *one* such history supersedes *another;* the materials are open to every writer, every one can easily think himself able to arrange and elaborate them, and to make his own spirit pass for the spirit of the times he describes. From satiety with such histories, men have frequently gone back, and given a picture of some one important event, described from all points of view. Such works are certainly of some value, but they give, for the most part, only materials. The Germans are content with them; the French, on the contrary, give such a spirited description of the past, as makes it seem living and present; they bring the past into direct connection with present circumstances.

ç. The third kind of systematic history is the *critical.* This is rather history of history, criticism of narratives, and investigation of their truth and credibility. Whatever there is extraordinary in it, and intended to be so, does not consist in the subject-matter, but in the acuteness of the writer, whose object is to pare away something from the narratives. The difference between what was before held to be fact, and what is now to be so held, is the measure of the fame of such a critical investigator of history; and it is not often considered, on the other hand, how arbitrary are the notions and combinations to which he may have surrendered himself.

d. The last kind of systematic history is that which does not pretend to be more than the history of some one department, as Art, Law, or Religion. The special subject is here, indeed, taken by itself, but since its history is written from general points of view, it forms a transition to the Philosophical History of the World. In our times this kind of history has been more cultivated; the philosophical principles contained in these different branches have been made more prominent. Such branches have a connection with the whole of a people's history; the main thing is, whether this connection is truly exhibited, or is sought for only in external relations. If the latter, then these separate departments seem to be only accidental and individual peculiarities of the nations.

3. PHILOSOPHICAL HISTORY.

The third kind of history is the Philosophical. In respect to the two previous divisions, there was no need of clearing up their meaning; this was understood of itself; but it is otherwise with this last kind, which seems to demand some explanation or justification.

The philosophy of history, then, in the most general point of view, signifies nothing other than a thoughtful consideration of history. As rational beings, we can never leave off thinking; thus we are distinguished from the brutes. In our sensations, in our knowledge and apprehension, in our impulses and will, so far as they are human, there is thought. It may seem that this appeal to thought, in connection with history, is unsatisfactory, since in history our thoughts must be subordinate to what actually exists, to the data given us,—must be founded upon, and guided by, the facts; while, on the other hand, it is said philosophy has thoughts of its own, engendered by mere speculation, without regard to what actually exists. If it goes to work upon history with such speculative notions, then it only handles it as so much mere material; does not leave it as it is, but fashions it after the thought, constructs it *à priori*, as we say. And since the only office of history is to grasp what is and has been, events and acts, and as it is more true in proportion as it adheres to its data, it seems as though the business of philosophy were in contradiction with such a procedure. This apparent contradiction, and the objection to a speculative treatment of history which springs from it, we will here explain and refute, without, however, going into a rectification of the infinitely varied and right special awry notions which are current, or always invented anew, respecting the end, the interests and the treatment of history, and its relation to philosophy.

The only idea which philosophy brings along with it to the consideration of history, is the simple idea of reason, that reason rules the world. This conviction and insight is indeed *an assumption* in respect to history, as such; in philosophy, however, it is no assumption. In philosophy, by means of speculative knowledge, it is evinced that reason—and we may here be allowed to abide by this expression, without entering into an investigation of the relation in which reason stands to God—that reason is the substance of all things, as well as the infinite power by which they are moved; is itself the illimitable material of all natural and spiritual life, as well as the source of the infinite variety of forms in which this material is livingly manifested. It is the substance of all things, that is, it is that whereby and wherein all that really exists has its being and continuance; it is the infinite power,—for reason is not so impotent that it can produce only an ideal, a something which ever should be and never is, and which has its being outside of and beyond all that actually does exist, nobody knows where, some very special thing in the heads of some men; it is the illimitable material of all essentiality and truth,—for it is not subjected, as is finite action, to the conditions forced upon it by external materials, from which it must receive nourishment and objects for its activity; it feeds upon itself, it creates its materials, viz. the infinite variety of extant forms; for only in the shape which reason prescribes and justifies do phenomena come into being, and begin to live. That it reveals itself in the world, and that nothing in the world but this is revealed; that this honor and glory are there, this is what, as we said, is proved by philosophy, and is here assumed as proved.

Though we have said that we here assume that reason rules the world, yet it is, in fact, not so much an assumption, as it is the result of the investigation we have started upon. From the consideration of the history of the world itself, we shall come to the result, that there has been a rational process of things in it; that it has been the rational and necessary course of the spirit which moves in the world,—a spirit whose nature does indeed ever remain one and the same, but which, in the existence of the world, unfolds this its one nature. This must, as was said, be the product of history. The history itself, however, we have to take as it is; we are to go to work historically, empirically. It might be stated, as the first condition, that we should truly comprehend the historical materials; but in such general expressions as *truly* and *comprehend*, there is an ambiguity. The ordinary and moderate historian, who thinks and declares that he stands only as a recipient, and gives himself up to the data, is yet not passive with his thinking; he brings with him some categories, through which he looks at what is before him. In everything, especially, which is meant to be scientific, reason may not slumber, reflection must be applied. He who looks at the world rationally, him the world also looks at rationally; the two are reciprocal.

There are some considerations which may serve to illustrate the general conviction, that reason has ruled in the world, and in its history, also. These will give us an opportunity to touch upon some of the chief points of difficulty. One is the historical fact, that Anaxagoras, the Greek, is said to have been the first to maintain that the νοῦς, understanding in general or reason, rules the world,—not an intelligence, in the sense of self-conscious reason — not a spirit, as such — for the two are to be carefully distinguished from each other. The movements of the solar system follow unchangeable laws; these laws are the reason of this system; but neither the sun, nor the planets which describe their orbits around it, according to these laws, have any consciousness thereof. Such an idea as this, that there is reason in nature, that it is immutably governed by general laws, does not strike us as strange; we are used to the like, and do not make much out of them. One reason, therefore, why I mention this historical circumstance is, to make it apparent that history teaches us that such like notions, which may seem to us trivial, have not always been in the world; that such thoughts make epochs in the history of the human mind. Aristotle says of Anaxagoras, as the originator of this thought: That he appeared like a sober man in the midst of the drunken. Socrates received this thought from Anaxagoras, and, with the exception of the notion of Epicurus, who ascribed all events to chance, it first became the predominant one in philosophy. Plato represents Socrates as saying: I rejoiced therein, and hoped that I had found a teacher who would interpret nature for me in accordance with reason,—who would show me in the special its special end, and in the whole its general purpose; this hope I would not have given up for much. But how greatly was I deceived, when I now zealously took up the writings of Anaxagoras himself, and found that he only brought forward external causes, as air, ether, water and the like, instead of reason. We see that what Socrates found to be unsatisfactory in the principle of Anaxagoras was not the principle itself, but the failing to apply it to nature in the concrete; the latter was not understood, comprehended, by means of the principle; the principle was held in the mere abstract, nature was not grasped as a development of it, as an organization produced by reason. I would call your attention here, in the very beginning, to the point; the difference there is between holding a formula, a principle, a truth only in the abstract, and the carrying it on and out in definitive and exact application into the concrete development. This difference is of the widest application.

This idea, that reason governs the world, is also connected with another application of it, well known to us in the form of the religious truth, that the world is not given over to accident, or to external and accidental causes, but is under the government of a Providence. I might appeal to your belief in this principle in this religious form, if it were not the peculiarity of the science of philosophy, that it does not allow authority to any assumptions; or to speak from another point of view, if it were not that the science of which we here treat is itself to furnish the proof, though not of the truth, yet of the correctness of that principle. The truth, now, that a Providence, that the Divine Providence presides over the events of the world, corresponds with the above principle; for the Divine Providence is wisdom and infinite power, realizing its purposes,— that is, the absolute, the rational end and destiny of the world; reason is thought, determining itself with perfect freedom. But, when further considered, the difference, the opposition even, of this faith and of our principle shows itself in the same way as with the demand of Socrates in respect to the maxim of Anaxagoras. This faith is equally indefinite, is what is called faith in Providence in general, and does not go forward to what is definite,— to an application to the whole comprehensive course of the world's history. Explaining history, generally means only the unveiling of the passions of men, their genius, their active powers; and the definite ends of Providence are called its *plan*. But it is this plan which is said to be concealed from our eyes, which it is audacity even to wish to know. The ignorance of Anaxagoras as to the mode in which the understanding (νοῦς) reveals itself in actual existence, was an unprejudiced one; he had not become conscious, nor had any one then in Greece, of any further application of his views; he was not yet able to apply his general principle to the concrete, to understand the latter by the former; for Socrates took the first step in grasping the union of the concrete with the universal. Anaxagoras was, then, not hostile to such an application; but this common faith in Providence is polemical, at least against the application of its principle to any wide extent, or against the attempt to understand the general plan of Providence. For, in special cases, those who hold it are willing sometimes to allow pious minds to see, in some single occurrences, not what is casual, but the very appointments of God; when, for example, help unexpectedly comes to an individual in great distress and need; but such Providential ends are only of a limited kind, are only the special ends of this individual. In the history of the world, however, we have to do with individuals which are nations, with wholes which are states; we cannot then limit ourselves to such retailing of faith in Providence, nor yet to that merely abstract, undefined faith, which only goes so far as to say that there is a Providence in general, but will not advance to the statement of its more definite acts. We should rather earnestly endeavor to understand the ways of Providence, its means and manifestations in history, and to bring those into connexion with our general principle.

HISTORY AS THE MANIFESTATION OF SPIRIT.

The true sphere of the history of the world is spiritual. The world comprises in itself both the physical and the psychical nature; physical nature plays a large part in the history of the world. But spirit, with the course of its development, is the substance of it. Nature is not here to be considered, so far as it is in itself, as it were, a system of reason, exhibited in a special and peculiar element, but only as it stands related to spirit. Spirit, however, in the theatre of the world's history, exists in its most concrete form, comes to its most real manifestations. In order to understand its connexions with history, we must make some preliminary and abstract statements respecting the nature of spirit.

The nature of spirit may be easily understood by comparison with that which is the entire opposite of it,—that is, matter. The substance of matter is weight, which is only this, that it is heavy; the substance, the essence of spirit, on the contrary, is freedom. Every one finds it immediately credible that spirit, among other attributes, also possesses freedom; but philosophy teaches us that all the attributes of spirit exist only through freedom, that they all are only the means of which freedom makes use, that this alone is what they all seek for and produce. The speculative philosophy recognises this fact, that freedom is the only truth of spirit. Matter shows that it is weight, by its tendency to one centre of gravity; it is essentially made up of parts, which parts exist separate from, and external to, each other; and it is ever seeking their unity, and thus seeks to abolish itself,— seeks the opposite of what it really is; if it attained this unity, it were no longer matter, it were destroyed; it strives to realize an idea, for in unity it is merely ideal. Spirit, on the other hand, is just this, that it has its centre in itself; its unity is not outside of itself, but it has found it; it is in itself and with itself. Matter has its substance out of itself; spirit consists in *being with itself*. This is freedom; for when I am dependent, I refer myself to something else which is not myself; I cannot be without something external; but I am free when I am with myself. This is self-consciousness, the consciousness of one's self. Two things are here to be distinguished: first, *that* I know or am conscious; secondly, *what* I know or am conscious of. In self-consciousness, the two come together, for spirit knows itself; it judges of its own nature.

In this sense, we may say that the history of the world is the exhibition of the process by which spirit comes to the consciousness of that which it really is,— of the significancy of its own nature. And as the seed contains in itself the whole nature of the tree, even to the taste and form of the fruit, so do the first traces of spirit virtually contain the whole of history.

The Oriental world did not know that spirit, man as such, is of himself free; since they knew it not, they were not free; they only knew that *one* is free; but just on this account their freedom was only arbitrariness, wildness, obtuse passion; or, if not so, yet a mildness and tameness of the passions, which is nothing but an accident or caprice of nature. This *one* is, therefore, only a despot, not a free man. Among the Greeks, the consciousness of freedom first arose, and therefore they were free; but they, as the Romans also, only knew that *some* are free, not that man, as such, is free. Even Plato and Aristotle did not know this. Hence, the Greeks not only held slaves, and had their life and the continuance of their fair freedom bound thereby, but their freedom itself was partly only an accidental and perishable flower, and partly a hard servitude of the human and humane. The German nations, under the influence of Christianity, first came to the consciousness that man, as man, is free,—that freedom of soul constitutes his own proper nature. This consciousness came first into existence in religion,—in the deepest religion of the spirit. But to fashion the world after this principle, was a further problem; the solution and application of which, demanded a severe and long labor. With the reception of the Christian religion, for example, slavery did not at once come to an end, still less did freedom at once become predominant in the States; their governments and constitutions were not immediately organized in a rational manner, or even based upon the principle of freedom. This application of the principle to the world at large, this thorough penetration and reformation of the condition of the world by means of it, is the long process which the history of the nations brings before our eyes. I have already called attention to the difference between a principle, as such, and its application,—that is, the introduction of it into the actual operations of spirit and life, and carrying it through all of them; this is a fundamental position in our science, and it is essential that we hold it fast in our thoughts. Here we have brought it out distinctly, in respect to the Christian principle of self-consciousness, of freedom; but it is no less essential in respect to the principle of freedom in general. The history of the world is the progress in the consciousness of freedom,— a progress which we shall have to recognise in its necessity.

What we have now said, in general terms, upon the difference in the knowledge of freedom which we find in different ages of the world, gives us, also, the true division of the history of the world, and the mode in which we shall proceed to its discussion. The scheme is this: the Oriental world only knew that *one* is free; the Greek and Roman world knew that *some* are free; but we know that all men, in their true nature, are free,—that man, as man, is free.

THE RELATION OF INDIVIDUALS TO THE WORLD'S HISTORY.

In the history of the world something else is generally brought out by means of the actions of individual men than they themselves aim at or attain, than they directly know of or will; they achieve their own ends, but something farther is brought to pass in connection with their acts, which also lies therein, but which did not lie in their consciousness and purposes. As an analogous example we cite the case of a man, who, out of revenge, which may have been justly excited, that is, by an unjust injury, goes to work and sets fire to the house of another man. Even in doing this, there is a connection made between the direct act, and other, although themselves merely external circumstances, which do not belong to this act, taken wholly and directly by itself. This act, as such, is the holding perhaps of a small flame to a small spot of a wooden beam. What is not yet accomplished by this act goes on and is done of itself; the part of the beam that was set on fire is connected with other parts of the same beam, this too with the rafters and joists of the whole house, this house with other houses, and a widespread conflagration ensues, which destroys the property and goods of many other men besides the one against whom the revenge was directed, and even costs many men their lives. All this lay not in the general act, nor in the intention of him who began it all. But, still farther, this action has another general character and destination: in the purpose of the actor it was only revenge against an individual by means of the destruction of his property; but it is also a crime, and this involves, farther, a punishment. This may not have been included in the consciousness, and still less in the will of the doer, but still such is his act in itself, the general character, the very substance of it, that which is achieved by it. In this example all that we would hold fast is, that in the immediate action there can lie something more than what was in the will and consciousness of the actor. The substance of the action, and thereby the act itself, here turns round against the doer; it becomes a return-blow against him, which ruins him. We have not here to lay any emphasis upon the action considered as a crime; it is intended only as an analogous example, to show, that in the definite action there may be something more than the end directly willed.

One other case may be adduced which will come up later in its own place, and which, being itself historical, contains, in the special form which is essential to our purpose, the union of the general with the particular, of an end necessary in itself with an aim which might seem accidental. It is that of Cæsar, in danger of losing the position he had obtained, if not of superiority over, yet of equality with, the other man who stood at the head of the Roman state, and of submitting to those who were upon the point of becoming his enemies. These enemies, who at the same time had their own personal ends in view, had on their side the formal constitution of the State and the power of seeming legality. Cæsar fought to maintain his own position, honor, and safety, and the victory over his opponents was at the same time the conquest of the whole kingdom: and thus he became, leaving only the forms of the constitution of the State, the sole possessor of power. The carrying out of his own at first negative purpose got for him the supremacy in Rome; but this was also in its true nature a necessary element in the history of Rome and of the world, so that it was not his own private gain merely, but an instinct which consummated that which, considered by itself, lay in the times themselves. Such are the great men of history—those whose private purposes contain the substance of that which is the will of the spirit of the world. This substance constitutes their real power; it is contained in the general and unconscious instinct of men; they are inwardly impelled thereto, and have no ground on which they can stand in opposing the man who has undertaken the execution of such a purpose in his own interest. The people assemble around his banner; he shows to them, and carries out, that which is their own immanent destiny.

Should we, farther, cast a look at the fate of these world-historical individuals, we see that they have had the fortune to be the leaders to a consummation which marks a stage in the progress of the general mind. That reason makes use of these instruments we might call its craft; for it lets them carry out their own aims with all the rage of passion, and not only keeps itself unharmed, but makes itself dominant. The particular is for the most part too feeble against the universal; the individuals are sacrificed. Thus the world's history presents itself as the conflict of individuals, and in the field of their special interests all goes on very naturally. In the animal world the preservation of life is the aim and instinct of each individual, and yet reason or general laws prevail, and the individuals fall; thus is it also in the spiritual world. Passions destroy each other; reason alone watches, pursues its end, and makes itself authoritative.

THE STATE.

That which is substantial and true in man's will is what we call morality and law; and this is what is divine in the external objects of history. Antigone in Sophocles says: 'The divine commands are not of yesterday or to-day; no, they live without end, and no one knows whence and when they came.' Moral laws are not accidental, but are reason itself. When these moral laws or ethical principles, which compose the true substance of humanity, have authority in the actions and sentiments of men, when they are really carried out and maintained, then we have the *State*. Now-a-days there are manifold errors current upon this matter which pass for established truths, and have all prejudices in their favor; we will only notice a few of them, and such as have a special bearing upon the aim of our history.

The State, we say, is the realisation of freedom in conformity with ethical laws. An opinion directly opposed to this view is current, which asserts that man is free by nature, and that the society, the State, of which he is naturally a member, must restrict this natural freedom. That man is free by nature is wholly correct in the sense, that this is the true idea of man, but this idea is something that is to be realized; it expresses his destination, and not what he actually is at first; the nature of any object can mean the same as the true conception of it. But this is not the whole meaning of the phrase; there is also included in it the notion of the mode in which man existed in his natural and undeveloped condition. In this sense, a state of nature is generally assumed in which man is represented as being in the possession of his natural rights in the unrestricted exercise and enjoyment of his freedom. This assumption does not pass for something verified by history; and if it were earnestly attempted, it would be difficult to show that such a state of nature either now exists, or has in past times anywhere existed. States of savageness can indeed be pointed out, but these are always connected with rude passions and violence, and, even when most cultivated, we find, among such tribes, social regulations which restrict true freedom. This whole assumption is one of those misty figments which a theorising spirit generates; a notion necessarily flowing from such a spirit, for which it then feigns a real existence, without justifying itself in an historical way.

Such as we find this state of nature to be in fact, so is it in the notion thereof. Freedom, being the ideality of what is primitive and natural, is not found in the primitive and natural condition of man; it must first be wrought out and won, and that, too, by an unending mediation between the impulses of knowledge and of will. Hence the state of nature is a state of injustice, of force, of unrestrained natural impulses to inhuman deeds and feelings. Society and the State do indeed make restrictions, but the restrictions are put upon these crude emotions and rude impulses, upon fickleness and passion. These limitations are made by that constant process of mediation between opposing principles, which is the only way in which such freedom is produced, as is conformed to the true idea thereof, and to the laws of reason. Right and ethics belong to the very idea of freedom; these are, in their very nature, universal essences, objects, and ends; they are found only as we, by the activity of thought, distinguish ourselves from whatever is sensual, and develope our characters in contrast with what is merely natural; and they must, so to speak, be moulded into and embodied in the will which is at first only sensuous, even in opposition to this will. This is the everlasting misapprehension of freedom, to know it only in its formal and subjective aspects, abstracted from its essential objects and aims; thus is it that the limitation of those impulses, desires, and passions, which belong only to single individuals as such, to the sphere of caprice and mere liking, is taken to be a restriction of freedom. Such limitation is rather absolutely necessary to the emancipation of the will; and society and the State are the conditions under which freedom is realised.

Another conception should be mentioned which goes against the development of right into its legal forms. The patriarchal state, taken as a whole, or at least in some of its branches, is looked upon as the condition in which the moral and social elements of our nature are best satisfied, in connection with the demands of law, and it is said that justice itself can be truly exercised only in conjunction with these elements. The family relation lies at the basis of the patriarchal condition; and here we have a development only of the first ethical elements; the State must also be added in order to bring about a conscious development of the second or higher elements. The patriarchal relation is a state of transition, in which the family has grown to a tribe or people; it has already ceased to have love and trust for its only bonds; it has come to be a connection of mutual service. The unity of the mere family is one of natural sentiment; the State adds higher bonds, and brings the members of the family into a higher moral condition and connections.

Finally it is said, that right and the true notion of freedom lie in the *general will*. When we speak of the will as general, we mean, that all individuals are to be subject to it; and when freedom is said to consist in this, that the individuals give their assent, it is easily seen that we have here got only the subjective elements of the will. It comes out at last to a mere majority and minority, and Rousseau has already remarked, that then there is no more freedom, for the will of the minority is no longer regarded. In the Polish diet every individual must give his assent to a measure, or it could not pass; and for the sake of such freedom the State was ruined; for every faction of the people can give itself out to be the people. That which constitutes the State is found rather in its culture than in the people as a mass.

The State, as such, is neither a natural, nor in its highest form, a patriarchal condition, nor is it the general will: but it is an *ethical* whole; the State, embodied in the individuals, is the true *ethics*. The State, its laws, its institutions are the rights of the individuals belonging to it, are their external possession; and its soil, its mountains, air, and waters, are their land, their fatherland; their deeds make the history of this State; that which their forefathers have done belongs to them, and lives in their memory. All is their possession — even as the State also possesses them — for it constitutes their substance, their being. Their conceptions are thus fulfilled; and their will is the willing of these laws and of this fatherland. It is this spiritual community which makes one essence, which we call the spirit of a people. The individuals belong to it; every individual is the son of his people, and at the same time, so far as the state is progressing, he is the son of his times; no one remains behind them, nor can he overleap them; this spiritual essence is his own, he is its representative; he came forth from it, and stands in it. Among the Athenians, Athena had a double significancy; first, she designated their institutions as a whole; and she was also the goddess who represented the unity, the spirit of the people.

This spirit of a people is a definite spirit; its character is determined by the historical stage of their development. This spirit is the basis out of which proceed all the forms of national culture. It is an individuality, which in religion is represented, reverenced, and loved in its essential character; in art, it is exhibited in visible images and forms; in philosophy, it is known and apprehended as thought. The forms which these things take are in inseparable union with the spirit of the people; the substance of which they are formed and their objects are originally the same; hence, only with such a religion can we have such a state; in such a state only such a philosophy and art. This remark is especially important in respect to the folly of our times, in wishing to invent and carry out state-constitutions independently of religion. The Catholic confession, although standing in common with the Protestant, within the bounds of Christianity, does not allow that internal justice and morality of the state, which lies in the more spiritual Protestant principle, and which Protestantism ascribes to it. This sundering of public law and the constitution of the state from its true basis, is the necessary result of the peculiar principle of the Catholic faith, which does not acknowledge that law and morals have a real, substantive existence of their own; but when they are thus torn loose from their spiritual foundation, from the last sanctuary of the conscience, from the same place where religion has its seat, then the principles and institutions of public law have no fixed centre, but remain abstract and undefined.

Hence it is to be taken as a general principle, that these essential things belong and go together, and that what is foreign to their spirit can have no ingress into a world which has its own limits. Thus Grecian art is the product of the Greek religion and governments, and no one can introduce it among ourselves. It is just so with the Greek philosophy; though we may learn much from it, yet it cannot satisfy us. Spirit takes the form of universality; and if a state is to advance in culture, if this is just its office, this culture must be in conformity with the laws of Spirit. Law, considered as freedom determining itself, is the objectivity of spirit: hence that alone is true volition, the will in the truth of it, which obeys law, for it then obeys only itself; it is then with itself and free; this is the freedom in the State for which the citizen is active, and which fills his soul. In that the State, the fatherland constitutes a community of existence, in that the subjective will of man becomes subject to the laws, the opposition between freedom and necessity vanishes. The rational, that which we have recognised as law, is necessary; and we are free when we follow what is rational; the objective and subjective will are thus reconciled. The ethics of the State are not to be regarded as the same thing with mere morality, are not the mere result of reflection, are not dependent upon private convictions alone; this is the system of morals familiar to the modern world, while the true and ancient system was based in this, that each man stood to his duty. A citizen of Athens did as it were by instinct what belonged to him to do; but if I reflect upon the object of my actions, I must then have the consciousness that my own will is first to come in as an essential element. But the true ethics consists in duty, in conformity with right, with law which has a real, substantial existence; it has been justly called the second nature, for the first nature of man is his primitive, animal existence.

RELIGION, ART, PHILOSOPHY.

All spiritual action has for its aim and result the production of the consciousness of the union of the objective and the subjective; in this is freedom. This union appears to be produced by the thinking subject, and to go out from it. Religion stands at the head of the forms of this union. Here the existing spirit, the spirit belonging to this world, becomes conscious of the Absolute Spirit; and in this consciousness of a being existing in and for itself, the will of man renounces its particular for private interests: in *devotion*, he puts this aside, for here he can have nothing to do with what is merely personal to himself. If he is truly penetrated with devotion, he knows that his particular interests are subordinate. This concentration of soul shows itself as feeling, but it also passes over into reflection; the *cultus*, meaning by this all forms of outward worship, is a manifestation of such reflection; the only destination and significance of these externals is to produce that internal union,—to lead the spirit thereto. By sacrifices, man expresses his willingness to give up his own possessions, his own will, his own particular feelings. Thus Religion is the first form of the union of the objective and subjective. The second shape it takes is Art: this comes more directly into the world of sense than religion; in its worthiest bearing its object is to exhibit, not, indeed, God as spirit, but the different visible representations which the different religions give of God; and, then, what is divine and spiritual in general. Art is intended to make what is divine more clear; it presents it to the imagination and contemplation in visible shapes. Truth, finally, appears not only in the form of feeling and of mental images of things, as in religion; not only in visible shapes, as in art; but it is also elaborated by the thinking spirit. Thus we attain the third mode of the union of the objective and subjective, and that is philosophy. This is the highest, freest, and purest shape which it assumes.

THE UNINTELLIGIBILITY OF PHILOSOPHY.

The difficulty here lies partly in the want of ability, in itself only a want of habit, to think abstractly, that is, to hold unmixed thoughts fast, and to move freely in them. In our ordinary consciousness, thoughts are overlaid and united with current materials from the world of sense and of spirit; and in our after-thoughts, reflections and reasonings, we mix up feelings, and mental images of visible objects, with the thoughts themselves: in every sentence where we speak only of what belongs to the world of sense, *e. g.* this leaf is green, the categories of *being* and *singleness* are involved. It is another thing to make the unmixed thoughts themselves the object of speculation. The other part of the unintelligibility arises from the impatient desire of having what exists in the consciousness, as a thought or idea, also before the mind, in the shape of some distinct image. It is a common saying, we do not know what we are to *think about* an idea which has been apprehended; with an idea there is nothing to be thought but the idea itself. The sense, however, of that expression is, that there is a longing for some already known and current notion: when these notions are taken away, it is, to the consciousness, as though the very ground were removed, upon which there was once a firm and homelike standing-place. When one is transferred into the pure region of ideas, he knows not where in the world he is. Hence, those writers, preachers and authors are found most intelligible, who tell their readers or hearers things which they already know by heart, which are current with them, and understood of themselves. There is a pretension, the opposite of this. Philosophy lays claim to *thinking*, as the peculiar *form* in which it works; and every man is by nature a thinking being. This science is, now, often disdainfully treated by persons who have never troubled themselves with studying it, and who imagine that they understand, *ab ovo*, all about philosophy and its conjunctures, and are able to philosophize, and judge about philosophy, just as they walk and talk with their common education; and especially on the ground of their religious feelings. It is granted that one must have studied the other sciences, in order to understand them; and that one is justified in passing judgment upon them only when they are understood. It is granted that, in order to make a shoe perfectly, one must have learned and practised the art; although every man has the measure in his own foot, and has hands, and, with these, natural adaptedness to the whole business. Only in philosophizing, such like study, learning and pains are not requisite. This convenient opinion has got confirmation in the latest times, by means of the theory of immediate knowledge,—of knowledge by intuitive wisdom.

EMPIRICISM AND PHILOSOPHY.

The principle of Experience contains one infinitely important element, that in order to receive and hold anything to be true, man must himself *be with it*, have a knowledge of it as connected with himself; to speak more definitely, that he must find such an external object united, and in unison with, *the certainty of himself*. He must himself be there with it, either by means of his external senses or his internal spirit, his essential self-consciousness. This principle is the same as what now-a-days is called faith, direct knowledge, the revelation in the external world, and especially in one's own self. We call those sciences which have been named *philosophy, empirical* sciences, on account of the point of departure which they take. But the essential thing which they aim at and produce is a knowledge of laws, of *general principles*, a theory—the *thoughts* that are contained in what is present around us. Thus the system of Newton is called Natural Philosophy; while, again, Hugo Grotius, combining together the historical relations of different nations to one another, and reasoning after the common fashion upon these data, arrived at some general principles, a theory which may be called the Philosophy of the Law of Nations. The word *philosophy* still retains this meaning universally in England. Newton has the credit of being the greatest of philosophers; even down to the price-currents of the fabricators of instruments we find it; those instruments which are not brought under some special rubric (as magnetic and electric apparatus), the thermometers, barometers, and such like, are called *philosophical instruments;* although one would think that Thought alone, and not a composition of iron, wood, &c., was the instrument of philosophy.* So, too, the science of Political Economy, for which we are indebted to these latest times, is called by them philosophy; while we Germans name it *rational* Economy of the State. In the mouths of English statesmen the expression, *philosophical* principles, is frequently used with reference to the general principles of State policy, even in public addresses. In a session of Parliament on the 2d of February, 1825, Brougham, by occasion of an Address in reply to the Speech from the Throne, spoke of "those *philosophical* principles of free trade, worthy of a statesman—for without doubt they are philosophical—on the adoption of which His Majesty has this day congratulated Parliament." And not only this member of the opposition, but the Secretary of State, Canning, in reply to a toast given him at the annual dinner of the Company of Ship-owners, where Lord Liverpool, the Prime Minister, presided, also said: "A period has lately begun in which ministers have it in their power to apply the correct maxims of a *deep philosophy* to our national government." However different the English Philosophy may be from the German, when the very name is elsewhere a by-word and reproach, or used as some hateful thing, it is an occasion of rejoicing to see it honored in the mouths of English statesmen.

It is an old maxim, falsely ascribed to Aristotle in the sense that it expresses the standpoint of his philosophy: *nihil est in intellectu, quod non fuerit in sensu:*—there is nothing in thought which was not first in sense, in experience. It is only a misunderstanding when it is said, that the speculative philosophy will not grant this principle. But, on the other hand, it also maintains: *nihil est in sensu, quod non fuerit in intellectu,*—first, in the very general sense, that the mind (νοῦς) or, with deeper significance of definition, *the spirit,* is the cause of the world; and, secondly, in the more special sense, that our feelings in respect to justice, morals and religion, are feelings, and so experiences, in respect to matters which have their root and seat in thought.

WHO THINKS ABSTRACTLY?
FROM HEGEL'S MISCELLANEOUS WRITINGS.

THINKS? Abstractly?—"Sauve qui peut!" "Save himself who can!" I hear a traitor exclaim, who, bribed by the enemy, would decry this essay, as one that treats of Metaphysics. For 'metaphysics' and 'abstract,' and, I had almost said, 'to think,' are words from which—as from one infected with the plague—every man is more or less disposed to run away.

I do not however intend here anything so atrocious as an explanation of what is meant by 'thinking' and by 'abstract.' I am frightened enough myself when any one begins to explain; for, at a pinch, I understand everything myself. Besides, any explanation of the words, 'to think' and 'abstract,' would be quite superfluous. For it is even because the polite world

---

* The Journal published by Thomson has the title, "*Annals of Philosophy*, or Magazine for Chemistry, Mineralogy, Mechanics, Natural History, Agriculture, and the Arts." One can from this see for himself what the materials are which are here called *philosophical.* Among the advertisements of new books in an English paper, I lately found the following: " The Art of Preserving the Hair, on Philosophical Principles, neatly printed in post, 8vo., price 7s." By philosophical principles are here probably meant chemical, physiological, and such like.

knows so well what is meant by 'abstract,' that it shuns the abstract. As no one craves what he does not know, so no one can hate what he does not know. Neither is it intended, by cunning stratagem, to attempt to reconcile the polite world to the abstract, as if, e. g. under the cover of a light conversation, 'thinking' and 'the abstract' should be tricked out, until, at last, without being recognised, and without awakening any abhorrence, they had crept into good company, and even been imperceptibly drawn in by said company, or, as they say in Suabia, "*gezäunselt*" in,—and then the author of the plot should come forward and uncover this otherwise strange guest, 'the abstract,' whom the whole company had been acknowledging and treating as a good friend, under a different name. These scenes of recognition, by which it is designed to instruct the world against its will, have this unpardonable fault—they mortify while they instruct; and they discover in the machinist the wish to acquire a little reputation by his arts. That mortification and this vanity neutralize the intended effect, and dissipate again the instruction purchased at such a price.

Besides, the stratagem, in this instance, if any such had been designed, is already defeated; inasmuch as its successful execution requires that the word of the enigma should not be pronounced at the outset. But that has been done in the present case, in the caption. If my essay had contemplated a *ruse* like that which has been described, these words, 'think' and 'abstract,' ought not to have made their appearance in the commencement; but, like the minister of state in the play, they should wear an over-coat through the whole piece, and then in the last scene unbutton it, and let the *star** of wisdom beam forth. But the unbuttoning of the metaphysical over-coat would not have so good an effect as the unbuttoning of the ministerial. It would only reveal a couple of *words;* and the best of the joke was to consist in showing that the company had long been in possession of the *thing*. So they would gain, in the end, nothing but the name; whereas the ministerial star indicates something more real, to wit, a purse with money in it.

It is presumed in good company—and that is the kind of company we are now in—that every one present knows what 'thinking' is, what 'abstract' is. We have only to inquire who it is that thinks abstractly. The design is not, as I have already remarked, to reconcile the company to these things, to expect of them that they should employ themselves with anything difficult, to speak to their consciences for heedlessly neglecting what is so worthy and befitting a rational being. The object is rather to reconcile the polite world with itself, in case it should feel—not exactly conscientious scruples on account of said neglect—but yet inwardly, at least, a certain respect for abstract thinking, as for something exalted, and should turn from it not because it is too mean, but because it is too high, not because it is too common, but because it is too distinguished; or, contrariwise, because it seems to be an *espèce*, something out of the way, something whereby one is, not distinguished in general society as by new finery, but rather excluded from it, or made ridiculous in it, as by a poor dress, or by a rich one, where the setting of the diamonds is old-fashioned, or where the embroidery, though never so costly, has long since come to be "Chinese."

Who thinks abstractly? The uncultivated man, not the cultivated. People who belong to good society do not think abstractly, because it is too easy, because it is too low—low, not according to outward condition;—they abstain from it, not out of empty *hauteur*, which affects to look with contempt on what is above its capacity, but on account of the intrinsic littleness of the thing.

The prepossession and respect for abstract thinking is so great, that refined noses will begin to scent and anticipate satire or irony here. But as my readers are readers of the *Morgenblatt*, they know that a price is paid for satire; and they must suppose that I would rather earn that price, and concur to obtain it, than give forth my matters in this way, without remuneration.

I need but adduce, in defence of my proposition, certain examples, which, as every one will allow, imply it. We will suppose, then, a murderer is led to the place of execution. To the common people he is nothing more than a murderer. Ladies, perhaps, will remark that he is a powerful, handsome, interesting man. But the people before mentioned, think that remark shocking. "What! a murderer handsome? How can any one be so evil-minded as to think a murderer handsome? It is to be feared you are not much better than murderers yourselves." "This is the corruption of morals which reigns among the higher classes," adds, perhaps, a priest, who knows the reason of things and the hearts of men.

One who understands human nature, investigates the course which the education of this murderer has taken; he finds in his history, in his bringing-up, bad domestic relations between his father and his mother; finds a monstrous severity exercised towards him on the occasion of some light offence,—a severity which has embittered his feelings in relation to the civil order;—finds a first reaction against this order, which caused his expulsion from it, and made it impossible for him, thenceforward, to maintain himself otherwise than by crime. There may be some who, when they hear this account of the matter, will say: that man wishes to apologize for this murderer! I remember to have heard, in my youth, a burgomaster complain that writers of books were going too far, were endeavoring to extirpate Christianity and

---

* In allusion to the star worn on the breast by certain dignitaries.—*Trans.*

justice altogether; that some one had written a defence of suicide!—dreadful! too dreadful! On inquiry, it appeared that he had in his mind the "Sorrows of Werter."

This is thinking abstractly,—to see in a murderer nothing but the abstract fact that he is a murderer; and by means of this single quality to expunge all else, all that is human in him.

Quite otherwise did a refined, sentimental Leipzig world. They bestrewed and bewreathed the wheel, and the criminal who was bound upon it, with flower-garlands. But this, again, is an abstraction of an opposite kind. Christians may well practise rosicrucianism, or rather cruciroseism, and wreathe the cross with roses. The cross is a long-since hallowed gibbet and wheel. It has lost its one-sided signification as an instrument of degrading punishment, and gives, on the contrary, the idea of the highest sorrow and the uttermost rejection, combined with extreme rapture and divine honor. The Leipzig cross, on the other hand, wreathed with violets and roses, represents an atonement in the manner of Kotzebue, a kind of maudlin agreement between sentiment and vice.

It was after a very different fashion that I once heard a vulgar old crone—a spital woman—slay the abstraction of a murderer, and raise him again to honor. The severed head was placed upon the scaffold, and the sun was shining. "How beautifully," said she, "God's sun of grace illumines Binder's head!" People say to a wight against whom they are incensed, "You are not worthy that the sun should shine upon you!" That woman saw that the murderer's head was shone upon by the sun, and consequently was still worthy of the sun's light. She raised him from the punishment of the scaffold into the sun-grace of God. She did not bring about the atonement with violets and sentimental vanity; but she saw him received with grace into a higher sun.

"Old woman! your eggs are rotten!" says the female purchaser to the huckster-woman. "What!" replies the latter; "my eggs rotten! Belike, you are rotten yourself. Do you say that of my eggs? You? Didn't the lice eat up your father on the public road? Didn't your mother run off with the French? Didn't your grandmother die in the Spital? Go! get you a whole smock, to go with your gauze neckerchief! Everybody knows where that neckerchief, and where all your caps come from. If there were no officers, many a girl would not be so prinked up now-a-days. And if mistresses would look more to their housekeeping, there's many a one would sit in the stocks. Go! patch the holes in your stockings!" In short, she does not leave her a whole thread. She thinks abstractly, and concludes her, together with neckerchief, caps, smock, &c., with fingers and other parts, also with her father and all her relations, under the single crime of having charged her (the huckster) with rotten eggs. Everything about her is colored through and through with these rotten eggs; whereas, on the contrary, those officers, of whom the huckster-woman spoke,—if (what is very doubtful) there is anything in the story,—must have seen something very different.

To come from the maid to servants:—a servant fares nowhere so badly as with men of inferior rank and small income. The higher the rank of the master, the better the condition of the servant. Here, again, the common man thinks more abstractly. He is haughty towards his servant, relates to him as to a servant only. To this one predicate he holds fast. A servant fares best with Frenchmen. The man of rank is familiar with his servant. The Frenchman is "hail! fellow, well met!" with him. When they are alone, the servant leads the conversation. See Diderot's *Jacques et son maître*. The master does nothing but take snuff and look at his watch; and, for the rest, lets the servant have his way. The man of rank knows that the servant is not merely a servant, that he is acquainted with the news of the city, knows the girls, and has good projects in his head. He asks him about these things, and the servant may say what he knows on the subjects on which the master questions him. With a French master, the servant may not only do this, but may also bring his own matter on the *tapis*, and have and maintain his own opinion. And if the master wants anything, he is not to command, but he must first reason his own opinion into the servant, and then give him a good word, in order that his own opinion may retain the ascendancy.

In military life, the same distinction is found. In Austria, the soldier can be flogged; consequently, he is a vile fellow; for one who has a passive right to be flogged, is a vile fellow. And so the common soldier passes with the officer for this abstraction, a floggable subject, one with whom a gentleman who has a uniform and *Port d'épée* must have intercourse. And that is to give one's self to the Devil.

JOHANN HEINRICH DANIEL ZSCHOKKE.

Born 1771.

ZSCHOKKE has become known to the American Public, within a few years past, by translations of several of his tales. But Zschokke is something more than a mere story-teller. He is known in Germany as an historical writer, and all his works discover the moral philosopher, well versed in human nature and human affairs, and one who has pondered deeply the social and individual destination of man.

He was born, according to Wolff's Encyclopædia of German Literature, at Magdeburg, March 22d, 1771, received a classical education in his native city, and studied at Frankfort on the Oder, where he afterwards took up his residence, and in 1793 was made Professor of Philosophy. He soon resigned this office, and moved to Graubündten, (Grisons,) where he undertook the management of a seminary of education. At the time of the French invasion he acted as mediator, devoting himself exclusively to the good of the country which he had adopted as a second father-land. He was made Government's Commissary for several Cantons, and officiated for some time as Lieutenant Governor at Basel. He then retired to Castle Biberstein in Aargau, but was soon summoned anew into public life, and made Superintendent of the Mining and Forest departments. In 1815, he was made member of the general Council of the Cantons. In 1829, he resigned all his public offices, and since that time has devoted himself exclusively to literary pursuits, living and laboring, as author by profession, at Aarau.

Zschokke has tried his hand at almost every species of literary production, and has been successful in all. He excels as narrator, combining artistic judgment with exuberant fancy, great power of characterization, a lively manner, and a style admirably suited to his material; natural, but at the same time dignified and correct. But his influence has been greatest as historian and popular teacher, skilled to comprehend and penetrate the spirit of the time, and indefatigable in developing and diffusing sound views of men and things.

LEAVES FROM THE JOURNAL OF A POOR VICAR IN WILTSHIRE.*

Dec. 15, 1764. — RECEIVED to-day from Dr. Snarl, £10 sterling, being my half-year's salary. The receipt even of this hardly-earned sum was attended with many uncomfortable circumstances.

Not until I had waited an hour and a half in the cold ante-room was I admitted to the presence of his Reverence. He was seated in an easy-chair at his writing-desk. My money was lying by him, ready counted. My low bow he returned with a lofty side-nod, while he slightly pushed back his beautiful black silk cap, and immediately drew it on again. Really he is a man of much dignity. I can never approach him without awe. I do not believe I should enter the king's presence with less composure.

He did not urge me to be seated, although he well knew that I had this very morning walked eleven miles in the bad weather, and that the hour and a half's standing in the ante-room had not much helped to rest my wearied limbs. He pointed me to the money.

My heart beat violently when I attempted to introduce the subject which I had so long thought over, of a little increase of my salary. I shall never be able to conquer my timidity, even in the most righteous cause. Twice, with an agony as if I were about to commit a crime, I endeavored to break ground. Memory, words, and voice failed me. The sweat started in great drops on my forehead.

"What do you wish?" said the Doctor, very politely.

"I am—everything is so dear—scarcely able to get along in these hard times, with this small salary."

"Small salary, Mr. Vicar! How can you think so? I can at any time procure another vicar for £15 sterling a year."

---

* From "The Gift," 1844, Philadelphia, Carey & Hart. Translated by Rev. W. H. Furness. The translator ventures the conjecture that the original fragment from which Zschokke took the idea of this journal, and which appeared in the British Magazine (1766), was written by Goldsmith. It may be, as the German writer suggests, the germ of the "Vicar of Wakefield," which appeared first in 1772.

"For £15! Without a family, one might indeed get along with that sum."

"Your family, Mr. Vicar," said the doctor, inquiringly, "has not received any addition, I trust. You have only two daughters?"

"Only two, your Reverence; but they are growing up. My Jenny, the eldest, is now eighteen, and Polly, the younger, will soon be twelve."

"So much the better. Can't your girls work?"

I was about to reply, when he cut me short by rising and observing, while he went to the window and drummed with his fingers on the pane, that he had no time to talk with me to-day. "Think it over," he concluded, "whether you will retain your place at £15 a year, and let me know. If you relinquish it, I hope you will have a better situation for a New Year's present."

He bowed very politely, and again touched his cap. I swept up the money, and took my leave. I was thunderstruck. He had never received nor dismissed me so coldly before. Without doubt somebody has been speaking ill of me. He did not once invite me to dinner, as had always before been his custom. I had depended upon it, for I came from home without breaking my fast. I bought a loaf in the outskirts of the town at a baker's shop, which I had observed in passing, and took my way home.

How cast down was I as I trudged along! I cried like a child. The bread I was eating was wet with my tears.

But fy, Thomas! Shame upon thy faint heart! Lives not the gracious God still? What if thou hadst lost the place entirely? And it is only £5 less! It is indeed a quarter of my whole little yearly stipend, and it leaves barely 10d. a day to feed and clothe three of us. What is there left for us? Who clothes the lilies of the field! Who feeds the young ravens! We must deny ourselves some of our luxuries.

Dec. 16.—I do believe Jenny's an angel. Her soul is even more beautiful than her body. I am almost ashamed of being her father. She is so much better and more pious than I.

I had not the courage yesterday to tell my girls the bad news. When I mentioned it to-day, Jenny at first looked very serious, but suddenly she brightened up and said, "Thou art disquieted, father!"

"Should I not be so?"

"No, thou shouldst not."

"Dear child, we shall never be free from debt and trouble. I do not know how we can stand it. Our need is sore. £15 hardly suffice for the bare necessaries of life. Who will assist us?"

Instead of answering, Jenny gently passed one arm round my neck, and pointed upwards with the other.—"He, there!" said she.

Polly seated herself on my lap, patted my face, and said, "I want to tell thee something. I dreamed last night that it was New Year's day, and that the king came to C——. There was a splendid show. The king dismounted from his horse before our front door, and came in. We had nothing to set before him, and he commanded some of his own dainties to be brought in dishes of gold and silver. The kettle-drums and trumpets sounded outside; and only think, with the sound of the music, in came some people with a bishop's mitre upon a satin cushion, a New Year's present for thee! It looked very funny, like the pointed caps of the bishops in the old picture-book. But it became thee right grandly. Yet I laughed myself almost out of breath; and then Jenny waked me up, which made me quite angry. This dream has certainly something to do with a New Year's present. It is only fourteen days to New Year's."

I said to Polly, "Dreams are but Seems;" but she said, "Dreams come from God."

I believe no such thing. Still I write the dream down, to see whether it be not a comforting hint from Heaven. A New Year's present would be acceptable to all of us.

All day I have been at my accounts. I do not like accounts. Reckoning and money matters distract my head, and make my heart empty and heavy.

Dec. 17.—My debts, God be praised, are all now paid, but one. At five different places I paid off £7 11s. sterling. I have therefore left in ready money, £2 9s. This must last a half-year. God help us!

The black hose that I saw at tailor Cutbay's I must leave unpurchased, although I need them sorely. They are indeed pretty well worn, yet still in good condition, and the price is reasonable. But Jenny needs a cloak a great deal more. I pity the dear child when I see her shivering in that thin camlet. Polly must be satisfied with the cloak which her sister has made for her so nicely out of her old one.

I must give up my share of the newspaper which neighbor Westburn and I took together. It goes hard with me. Here in C——, without a newspaper one knows nothing of the course of affairs. At the horse-races at Newmarket, the Duke of Cumberland won £5000 of the Duke of Grafton. It is wonderful how literally the words of Scripture are always fulfilled, "To him who hath, shall be given," and those other words, too, "From him who hath not, shall be taken away." I must lose £5 of even my poor salary.

Fy, Thomas, already murmuring again! and wherefore? For a newspaper, which thou art no longer able to take? Shame on thee! Thou mayst easily learn from others whether General Paoli succeeds in maintaining the freedom of Corsica. The French have indeed promised assistance to the Genoese; but Paoli has 20,000 veterans.

Dec. 18.—Ah! how happy are we poor people still! Jenny has got a grand cloak at the slop-shop for a mere song, and now she is sitting there with Polly, ripping it to pieces, in order to make it up anew. Jenny understands how to trade and bargain better than I. But they let her have things at her own price, her voice is so gentle. We have now joy upon joy. Jenny wants to appear in the new cloak for the first time on New Year's Day. Polly has a hundred comments and predictions about it. I wager, the Dey of Algiers had not greater pleasure in the costly present which the Venetians made him, the two diamond rings, the two watches set with brilliants, the pistols inlaid with gold, the costly carpets, the rich housings, and the 20,000 sequins in cash.

Jenny says we must save the cloak in eatables. Until New Year's, we must buy no meat. This is as it should be.

Neighbor Westburn is a noble man. I told him yesterday I must discontinue my subscription for the newspaper, because I am not sure of my present salary, nor even of my place. He shook my hand and said, "Very well, then I will take the paper, and you shall still read it with me."

One must never despair. There are more good men in the world than one thinks, especially among the poor.

The same day. Eve.—The baker is a crabbed man. Although I owe him nothing, yet when Polly went to fetch a loaf, and found it very small and badly risen or half-burnt, he struck up a quarrel with her, so that people stopped in the street. He declared that he would not sell upon trust—that we must go elsewhere for our bread. I pitied Polly.

I wonder how the people here know everything. Every one in the village is telling how the doctor is going to put another curate in my place. It will be the death of me.

The butcher, even, must have got a hint of it. It certainly was not without design that he sent his wife to me with complaints about the bad times, and the impossibility of selling any longer for anything but cash. She was indeed very polite, and could not find words to express her love and respect for us. She advised us to go to Colswood, and buy the little meat we want of him, as he is a richer man, and is able to wait for his money. I cared not to tell the good woman how that usurer treated us a year ago, when he charged us a penny a pound more than others for his meat, and, when his oaths and curses could not help him out, and he could not deny it, how he declared roundly that he must receive a little interest when he was kept out of his money a whole year, and then showed us the door.

I still have in ready money £2 1s. 3d. What shall I do, if no one will trust me, so that I may pay my bills quarterly? And if Dr. Snarl appoints another curate, then must I and my poor children be turned upon the street!

Be it so; God is in the street also!

Dec. 19, *early. A. M.*—I awoke very early to-day, and pondered what I shall do in my difficult situation. I thought of Master Sitting, my rich cousin at Cambridge; only poor people have no cousins, only the rich. Were New Year's day to bring me a bishop's mitre, according to Polly's dream, then I should have half England for my relations.

I have written, and sent by the post, the following letter to the Rev. Dr. Snarl:

"I write with an anxious heart. It is said that your reverence intends to appoint another curate in my stead. I know not whether the report has any foundation, or whether it has arisen merely from my having mentioned to some persons the interview I had with you.

"The office with which you entrusted me I have discharged with zeal and fidelity; I have preached the word of God in all purity; I have heard no complaints. Even my inward monitor condemns me not. I humbly requested for a little increase of my small salary. Your reverence spoke of reducing the small stipend, which scarcely suffices to procure me and my family the bare necessaries of life. Let your humane heart decide.

"I have laboured sixteen years under your reverence's pious predecessors, and a year and a half under yourself. I am now fifty years old. My hair begins to grow gray. Without acquaintances, without patrons, without the prospect of another living, without the means of earning my bread in any other way, mine and my children's fate depends upon your compassion. If you fail us, there remains no support for us but the beggar's staff.

"My daughters, gradually grown up, occasion, with the closest economy, increased expense. My eldest daughter, Jenny, supplies the place of a mother to her sister, and conducts our domestic concerns. We keep no maid; my daughter is maid, cook, washerwoman, tailoress, and even shoemaker, while I am the carpenter, mason, chimney-sweeper, woodcutter, gardener, farmer, and wood-carrier of the household.

"God's mercy has attended us hitherto. We have had no sickness. We could not have paid for medicines. C—— is a little place.

"My daughters have in vain offered to do other work, such as washing, mending, and sewing. They very rarely get any. Here in the country every one does her own housework; none are rich.

"It will be a hard task to carry me and mine through the year upon £20; but it will be harder still if I am to attempt it upon £15. But I throw myself on your compassion and on God, and pray your reverence at least to relieve me of this anxiety."

After I had finished this letter, I threw myself upon my knees, (while Polly carried it to the post-office,) and prayed for a happy issue. I then became wonderfully clear and calm in my mind. Ah! a word to God is always a word from God—so cheerfully came I from my little chamber, which I had entered with a heavy heart.

Jenny sate at work at the window. She sate there with the repose and grace of an angel. Light seemed to stream from her looks. A slender sunbeam came through the window, and transfigured the whole place. I was in a heavenly state. I seated myself at the desk, and wrote my sermon, "On the joys of poverty."

I preach in the pulpit as much to myself as to my hearers; and I come from church edified, if no one else does. If others do not receive consolation from my words, I find it myself. It is with the clergyman as with the physician. He knows the power of his medicines, but not always their effect upon the constitution of every patient.

The same day. A. M.—This morning I received a note from a stranger who had tarried over night at the inn. He begs me, on account of urgent affairs, to come to him.

I have been to him. I found him a handsome young man of about six-and-twenty, with noble features and a graceful carriage. He had on an old well-worn surtout and boots, which still bore the marks of yesterday's travel. His round hat, although originally of a finer material than mine, was still far more defaced and shabby. The young man appeared, notwithstanding the derangement of his dress, to be of good family. He had on at least a clean shirt of the finest linen, which perhaps had just been given him by some charitable hand.

He led me into a private room, begged pardon a thousand times for having troubled me, and proceeded to inform me in a very humble manner, that he found himself in most painful circumstances, that he knew nobody in this place, where he had arrived last evening, and had therefore had recourse to me as a clergyman. He was, he added, by profession, an actor, but without employment, and intending to proceed to Manchester. He had expended nearly all his money, and had not enough to pay his fare at the inn—to say nothing of the expense of proceeding on his journey. Accordingly he turned in his despair to me. Twelve shillings would be a great assistance to him. He promised, if I would favor him with that advance, that he would honorably and thankfully repay it, so soon as he was again connected with any theatre. His name is John Fleetman.

There was no necessity of his painting his distress to me so at large. His features expressed more trouble than his words. He probably read something of the same kind in my face; for as he turned his eyes upon me, he seemed struck with alarm, and exclaimed, "Will you leave me then without help?"

I stated to him that my own situation was full of embarrassment, that he had asked of me nothing less than the fourth part of all the money I had in the world, and that I was in great uncertainty as to the further continuance of my office.

He immediately became cold in his manner, and, as it were, drew back into himself, while he remarked, "You comfort the unfortunate with the story of your own misfortunes. I ask nothing of you. Is there no one in C—— who has pity, if he has no wealth?"

I cast an embarrassed look at Mr. Fleetman, and was ashamed to have represented my distressed situation to him as a reason for my refusal to assist him. I instantly thought over all my townsmen, and could not trust myself to name one. I did not perhaps know their hearts well enough.

I approached him, and laid my hand upon his shoulder, and said, "Mr. Fleetman, you grieve me. Have a little patience. You see I am poor. I will help you if I can. I will give you an answer in an hour."

I went home. On the way I thought to myself, "How odd! the stranger always comes first to me, and an actor to a clergyman! There must be something in my nature that attracts the wretched and the needy, like a magnet. Whoever is in need comes to me, who have the least to give. When I sit at table with strangers, one of the company is sure to have a dog who looks steadily at what I am eating, and comes and lays his cold nose directly on my knee."

When at home, I told the children who the stranger was, and what he wanted. I wished for Jenny's advice. She said tenderly, "I know, father, what thou thinkest, and therefore I have nothing to advise."

"And what do I think?"

"Why, that thou wilt do unto this poor actor as thou hopest God and Dr. Snarl will do unto thee."

I had thought no such thing, but I wished I had. I got the twelve shillings, and gave them to Jenny to carry to the traveller. I did not care to listen to his thanks. It humbles me. Ingratitude stirs my spirit up. And, besides, I had my sermon to prepare.

The same day. Eve.—The actor is certainly a worthy man. When Jenny returned from the inn, she had much to tell about him, and also about the landlady. This woman had found out that her guest had an empty pocket, and Jenny could not deny that she had brought him some money. So Jenny had to listen to a long sermon upon the folly of giving, when one has nothing himself, and the danger of helping vagrants, when one has not the wherewithal to clothe his own children. "The shirt is nearer than the coat," "To feed one's own maketh fat," &c. &c.

I had just turned to my sermon again, when Mr. Fleetman entered. He could not, he said, leave C—— without thanking his benefactor, by whose means he had been delivered from the greatest embarrassment. Jenny was just setting the table. We had an omelet and some turnips. I invited the traveller to dine with us. He accepted the invitation. It was very timely, he intimated, for he had eaten a very scanty breakfast. Polly brought some beer. We had not for a long while fared so well.

Mr. Fleetman seemed to enjoy himself with us. He had quite lost that anxious look he had, yet there was the shy, reserved manner about him, which is peculiar to the unfortunate. He inferred that we were very happy, and of that we assured him. He supposed also that I was richer and better to do in the world than I desired to appear. There he was mistaken. Without doubt the order and cleanliness of our parlor dazzled the good man, the clearness of the windows, the neatness of the curtains, of the dinner-table, the floor, and the brightness of our tables and chairs. One usually finds a great lack of cleanliness in the dwellings of the poor, because they do not know how to save. But order and neatness, as I always preached to my sainted wife and to my daughters, are great save-alls. Jenny is a perfect mistress therein. She almost surpasses her mother, and she is bringing up her sister Polly in the same way. Her sharp eyes not a fly-mark can escape.

Our guest soon became quite familiar and intimate with us. He spoke more, however, of our situation than of his own. The poor man must have some trouble on his heart, I hope not upon his conscience. I remarked that he often broke off suddenly in conversation, and became depressed, then again he would exert himself to be cheerful. God comfort him!

As he was quitting us after dinner, I gave him much friendly counsel. Actors, I know, are rather a light-minded folk. He promised me sacredly, as soon as he should have money, to send back my loan. He must be sincere in that, for he looked very honest, and several times asked, how long I thought I should be able with the remainder of my ready money to meet the necessities of my household.

His last words were, "It is impossible it should go ill with you in the world. You have heaven in your breast, and two angels of God at your side." With these words, he pointed to Jenny and Polly.

Dec. 20. — The day has passed very quietly, but I cannot say very agreeably, for the grocer, Jones, sent me his bill for the year. Considering what we had had of him, it was larger than we had expected, although we had had nothing of which we did not ourselves keep an account. Only he had raised the price of all his articles. Otherwise, his account agreed honestly with ours.

The worst is the arrears of my last year's bill. He begged for the payment of the same, as he is in great need of money. The whole of what I owe him amounts to eighteen shillings.

I went to see Mr. Jones. He is a very polite and reasonable man. I hoped to satisfy him by paying him in part, and promising to pay the remainder by Easter. But he was not to be moved, and he regretted that he should be forced to proceed to extremities. If he could, he would gladly wait; but only within three days he would have to pay a note which had just been presented to him. With a merchant, credit is everything.

To all this there was nothing to be said in reply, after my repeated requests for delay had proved vain. Should I have let him go to law against me, as he threatened? I sent him the money, and paid off the whole debt. But now my whole property has melted down to eleven shillings. Heaven grant that the actor may soon return what I loaned him. Otherwise I know not what help there is for us.

Now go to, thou man of little faith, if thou knowest not, God knoweth. Why is thy heart cast down? What evil hast thou done? Poverty is no crime.

Dec. 24. — One may be right happy after all, even at the poorest. We have a thousand pleasures in Jenny's new cloak. She looks as beautiful in it as a bride. But she wishes to wear it the first time abroad at church on New Year's day.

Every evening she reckons up, and shows me with how little expense she has got through the day. We are all in bed by seven o'clock, to save oil and coals. That is no great hardship. The girls are so much the more industrious in the day, and they chat together in bed until midnight. We have a beautiful supply of turnips and vegetables. Jenny thinks we can get through six or eight weeks, without running in debt. That were a stroke of management without parallel. And until then, we all hope that Mr. Fleetman will keep his word like an honest man, and pay us back the loan. If I appear to distrust him, it awakens all Jenny's zeal. She will allow no evil of the comedian.

He is our constant topic. The girls especially make a great deal out of him. His appearance interrupted the uniformity of our life. He will supply us with conversation for a full half year. Pleasant is Jenny's anger, when the mischievous Polly exclaims, "But he is an actor!" Then Jenny tells of the celebrated actors in London who are invited to dine with the princes of the royal family; and she is ready to prove that Fleetman will become one of the first actors in the world, for he has fine talents, and a graceful address and well-chosen phrases. "Yes, indeed!" said the sly Polly to-day, very wittily, "beautiful phrases! he called thee an angel." "And thee too," cried Jenny, somewhat vexed. "But I was only thrown into the bargain," rejoined Polly, "he looked only at thee."

This chat and childish raillery of my children awakened my anxiety. Polly is growing up; Jenny is eighteen. What prospect have I of seeing these poor children provided for? Jenny is a well-bred, modest, handsome maiden; but all C—— knows our poverty. We are therefore little regarded, and it will be difficult to find a husband for Jenny. An angel without money is not thought half so much of now-a-days, as a devil with a bag full of guineas. Jenny's only wealth is her gentle face. That everybody looks kindly on. Even the grocer, Jones, when she carried him his money, gave her a pound of almonds and raisins for a present, and told her how he was grieved to take my money, and that, if I bought of him, he would give me credit till Easter. He has never once said so much to me.

When I die, who will take care of my desolate children? Who! the God of Heaven. They are at least qualified to go to service anywhere. I will not distress myself about the future.

Dec. 26.—Two hard days these have been. I have never had so laborious a Christmas. I preached my two sermons in two days five times in four different churches. The road was very bad, and the wind and weather fearful. Age is beginning to make itself felt. I have not the freshness and activity I once had. Indeed, cabbage and turnips, scantily buttered, with only a glass of fresh water, do not afford much nourishment.

I have dined both days with Farmer Hurst. The people in the country are more hospitable by far than here in the town, where nobody has thought of inviting me to dinner these six months. Ah! could I have only had my daughters with me at table! What profusion was there! Could they have only had for a Christmas feast what the farmer's dogs received of the fragments of our meal! They did have some cake, and they are feasting on it now while I write. It was lucky that I had courage, when the farmer and his wife pressed me to eat more, to say that, with their leave, I would carry a little slice of the cake home to my daughters. The good-hearted people packed me a little bag full, and, besides, as it rained pitifully, sent me home in their wagon.

Eating and drinking are indeed of little importance, if one has enough to satisfy his hunger and thirst. Yet it may not be denied that a comfortable provision for the body is an agreeable thing. One's thoughts are clearer. One feels with more vivacity.

I am very tired. My conversation with Farmer Hurst was noteworthy. I will write it off to-morrow.

Dec. 27.—We have lived to know what perfect joy is. But one must be moderate in his joys. The girls must learn self-restraint, and practise themselves therein. Therefore I lay aside the packet of money which Mr. Fleetman has sent. I will not break the seal until after dinner. My daughters are Eve's daughters. They are dying of curiosity to know what Mr. Fleetman writes. They are examining the address, and the packet is passing from one to the other three times in a minute.

Indeed, I am more disturbed than rejoiced. I lent Mr. Fleetman only twelve shillings, and he sends me back £5. God be praised! He must have been very successful.

How joy and sorrow interchange! I went early this morning to the alderman, Mr. Fieldson, for I was told yesterday that the wagoner Brook at Watton Basset had, on account of his embarrassments, destroyed himself. Some eleven or twelve years ago I went security for him to the amount of £100. He was distantly related to my sainted wife. The bond has never been cancelled. The man has latterly had much trouble, and given himself up to drinking.

The alderman comforted me not a little. He said he had heard the report, but that it was very doubtful whether Brook had destroyed himself. There had been no authentic intelligence. So I returned home comforted, and prayed by the way that God would be gracious to me.

I had hardly reached the house, when Polly ran to meet me, exclaiming, almost breathless, "A letter! a letter from Mr. Fleetman, father, with £5! But the packet has cost seven pence." Jenny, with blushing looks, handed it to me before I laid down my hat and staff. The children were half out of their wits with joy. So I pushed aside their scissors, and said, "Do you not see, children, that it is harder to bear a great joy with composure than a great evil? I have often admired your cheerfulness when we were in the greatest want, and knew not where we were to find food for the next day. But now the first smile of fortune puts you beside yourselves. To punish you, I shall not open the letter nor the packet of money until after dinner."

Jenny would have it that it was not the money, but Mr. Fleetman's honesty and gratitude that delighted her, and that she only wanted to know what he wrote and how he was; but I adhered to my determination. This little curiosity must learn to practise patience.

The same day. Eve.—Our joy is turned into sorrow. The letter with the money came not from Mr. Fleetman, but from the Rev. Dr. Snarl. He gives me notice that our engagement will terminate at Easter, and he informs me that until that time I may look about for another situation, and that he has accordingly not only paid me up my salary in advance, that I may bear any travelling expenses I may be at, but also directed the new vicar, my successor, to attend to the care of the parish.

Thus the talk of the people here in town was not wholly without foundation, and it may also be true, what is said, that the new vicar had received his appointment thus readily, because he has married a near relative of his Reverence, a lady of doubtful reputation. So I must lose my office and my bread for the sake of such a person, and be turned into the street with my poor children, because a man can be found to buy my place at the price of his own honor.

Jenny and Polly turned deadly pale, when they found that the letter came not from Mr. Fleetman, but from the Doctor, and that the money, instead of being the generous return of a grateful heart, was the last wretched payment for my long and laborious services. Polly threw herself sobbing into a chair, and Jenny left the room. My hand trembled as I held the letter containing my formal dismissal. But I went into my little chamber, locked myself in, and fell upon my knees and prayed, while Polly wept aloud.

I rose from my knees refreshed and comforted, and took my Bible; and the first words upon which my eyes fell were, "Fear not, for I have redeemed thee, I have called thee by thy name; thou art mine."

Then all fear vanished out of my heart. I looked up, and said, "Yea, Lord, I am thine."

As Polly appeared to have ceased weeping, I went back into the parlor; but when I saw her upon her knees praying, with her clasped hands resting on a chair, I drew back and shut the door very softly, that the dear soul might not be disturbed.

After some time I heard Jenny come in. I then returned to my daughters. They were sitting at the window. I saw by Jenny's eyes that she had been giving relief to her anguish in solitude. They both looked timidly at me. I believe they feared lest they should see despair depicted on my countenance. But when they saw that I was quite composed, and that I addressed them with cheerfulness, they were evidently relieved. I took the letter and the money, and humming a tune, threw them into my desk. They did not allude to what had happened the whole day. This silence in them was owing to a tender consideration for me; with me it was fear lest I should expose my weakness before my children.

Dec. 28.—It is good to let the first storm go by, without looking one's troubles too closely in the face. We have all had a good night's sleep. We talk freely now of Dr. Snarl's letter, and of my loss of office, as of old affairs. We propose all kinds of plans for the future. The bitterest thing is that we must be separated. We can think of nothing better than that Jenny and Polly should go to service in respectable families, while I betake myself to my travels to seek somewhere a place and bread for myself and children.

Polly has again recovered her usual cheerfulness. She brings out again her dream about the bishop's mitre, and gives us much amusement. She counts almost too superstitiously upon a New Year's present. I have sometimes thought much of dreams, but I do not believe in them.

As soon as the new vicar, my successor, shall have arrived, and is able to assume the office, I shall hand over to him the parish-books, and take my way in search of bread elsewhere. In the meantime I will write to a couple of old friends at Salisbury and Warminster, to request them to find good places for my daughters, as cooks, seamstresses, or chambermaids. Jenny would be an excellent governess for little children.

I will not leave my daughters here. The place is poor, the people are unsocial, proud, and have the narrow ways of a small town. They talk now of nothing but the new vicar. Some are sorry that I must leave, but I know not who takes it to heart.

Dec. 29.—I have written to-day to my Lord Bishop of Salisbury, and laid before him in lively terms the sad, helpless situation of my children, and my long and faithful services in the vineyard of the Lord. He must be a humane pious man. May God touch his heart! Among the three hundred and four parishes of the county of Wiltshire, there must certainly be found for me at least some little corner! I do not ask much.

Dec. 30.—The bishop's mitre that Polly dreamt of must soon make its appearance, otherwise I shall have to go to jail. I see now very plainly that the jail is inevitable.

I am very weak, and in vain do I exert myself to practise my old heroism. Even strength fails me for fervent prayer. My distress is too much for me.

Yes, the jail is unavoidable. I will say it to myself plainly, that I may become accustomed to the prospect.

The All-merciful have mercy on my dear children! I may not—I cannot tell them.

Perhaps a speedy death will save me from the disgrace. I feel as if my very bones would crumble away; fever-shivering in every limb, I cannot write for trembling.

Some hours after.—Already I feel more composed. I would have thrown myself into the arms of God and prayed. But I was not well. I lay down on my bed. I believe I have slept, perhaps also I fainted. Some three hours have passed. My daughters have covered my feet with pillows. I am weak in body, but my heart is again fresh. Everything which has happened, which I have heard, flits before me like a dream.

So the wagoner Brook has indeed made way with himself. Alderman Fieldson has called and given me the intelligence. He had the coroner's account, together with the notice of my bond. Brook's debts are very heavy. I must account to Withell, a woollen-draper of Trowbridge, for the hundred pounds sterling.

Mr. Fieldson had good cause to commiserate me heartily. Good God! a hundred pounds sterling! How shall I ever obtain it? All that I and my children have in the world would not bring a hundred shillings. Brook used to be esteemed an upright and wealthy man. I never thought that he would come to such an end. The property of my wife was consumed in her long sickness, and I had to sacrifice the few acres at Bradford which she inherited. Now I am a beggar. Ah! if I were only a free beggar! I must go to prison, if Mr. Withell is not merciful. It is impossible for me even to think of paying him.

Same day. Eve.—I am ashamed of my weakness. What! to faint! to despair! Fy! And yet believe in a Providence! And a priest of the Lord! Fy, Thomas!

I have recovered my composure, and done what I should. I have just carried to the post-office a letter to Mr. Withell, at Trowbridge, in which I have stated my utter inability to pay the bond, and confessed myself ready to go to jail. If he has any human feeling, he will have pity on me; if not, he may drag me away, whithersoever he will.

When I came from the office, I put the courage of my children to the proof. I wished to prepare them for the worst. Ah! the maidens were more of men than the man, more of Christians than the priest.

I told them of Brook's death, of my debt, and of the possible consequences. They listened earnestly and in great sorrow.

"To prison!" said Jenny, silently weeping, while she threw her arms around me. "Ah, thou good, poor father, thou hast done no wrong, and yet hast to bear so much! I will go to Trowbridge; I will throw myself at Withell's feet; I will not rise until he releases thee!"

"No," cried Polly, sobbing, "do not think of such a thing. Tradesmen are tradesmen. They will not for all thy tears give up a farthing of father's debt. I will go the woollen-draper, and bind myself to live upon bread and water, and be his slave, until I have paid him with my labor what father owes."

In forming such plans, they gradually grew more composed. But they saw also the vanity of their hopes. At last said Jenny, "Why all these useless plans? Let us wait for Mr. Withell's answer. If he will be cruel, let him be so. God is also in the jail. Father, go to jail. Perhaps thou wilt be better there than with us in our poverty. Go, for thou goest without guilt. There is no disgrace in it for thee. We will both go to service, and our wages will procure thee everything needful. I will not be ashamed even to beg. To go a-begging for a father has something honorable and holy in it. We will come and visit thee from time to time. Thou shalt be well taken care of. We will fear no more."

"Jenny, thou art right," said Polly; "whoever fears, does not believe in God. I am not afraid. I will be cheerful—as cheerful as I can be, separated from father and thee."

Such conversations cheered my heart. Fleetman was right when he said that I had two angels of the Lord at my side.

Dec. 31.—The year is ended. Thanks be to Heaven, it has been, with the exception of some storms, a right beautiful and happy year! It is true, we often had scarcely enough to eat—still we have had enough. My poor salary has often occasioned me bitter cares, still our cares have had their pleasures. And now I scarcely possess the means of supporting myself and my children half a-year longer. But how many have not even as much, and know not where to get another day's subsistence! My place have I lost. In my old age I am without office or bread. It is possible that I shall spend the next year in a jail, separated from my good daughters. Still Jenny is right; God is there also in the jail!

To a pure conscience there is no hell even in hell, and to a bad heart no heaven in heaven. I am very happy.

Whoever knows how to endure privation is 'rich. A good conscience is better than that which the world names honor. As soon as we are able to look with indifference upon what people call honor and shame, then do we become truly worthy of honor. He who can despise the world enjoys heaven. I understand the gospel better every day, since I have learned to read it by the light of experience. The scholars at Oxford and Cambridge study the letter, not the spirit. Nature is the best interpreter of the Scriptures.

With these reflections I conclude the year.

I am very glad that I have now for some time persevered in keeping this journal. Everybody should keep one. One may learn more from himself than from the wisest books. When, by daily setting down our thoughts and feelings, we in a manner portray ourselves, we can see at the end of the year how many different faces we have. Man is not always like himself. He who says he knows himself, can answer for the truth of what he says only at the moment. Few know what they were yesterday; still fewer what they will be to-morrow.

A day-book is useful also, because it helps us to grow in faith in God and Providence. The whole history of the world does not teach us so much about these things as the thoughts, judgments, and feelings of a single individual for a twelvemonth.

I have also had this year new confirmation of the truth of the old saying, "Misfortunes seldom come singly, but the darkest hour is just before morning." When things go hard with me, then am I most at my ease, always excepting the first shock, for then I please myself with the prospect of the relief which is sure to succeed, and I smile because nothing can disturb me. On the other hand, when everything goes according to my wishes, I am timid and anxious, and cannot give myself up freely to joy. I distrust the continuance of my peace. Those are the hardest misfortunes which we allow to take us by surprise. It is likewise true that trouble looks more terrible in the distance than when it is upon us. Clouds are never so black when near as they seem in the distance.

I have learnt from all my calamities to consider, with the quickness of lightning, what will be their worst effect upon me. So I prepare myself for the worst, and it seldom comes.

This also I find good—I sometimes play with my hopes, but I never let my hopes play with me. So I keep them in check. I have only to remember how rarely fortune has been favorable to me; then all air castles vanish as if they were ashamed to appear before me. Alas for him who is the sport of his hopes! He pursues will-o'-the-wisps into bogs and mire.

New Year's Day, 1765. *A. M.*—A wonderful and sad affair opens the year. Here follows its history.

Early, about six o'clock, as I lay in bed thinking over my sermon, I heard a knocking at the front door. Polly was up and in the kitchen. She ran to open the door and see who was there. Such early visits are not usual with us. A stranger presented himself with a large box, which he handed to Polly with these words: "Mr. ———" (Polly lost the name) "sends this box to the Rev. Vicar, and requests him to be very careful of the contents."

Polly took the box with joyful surprise. The man disappeared. Polly tapped lightly at my chamber door to see whether I was awake. I answered, and she came in, and wishing me "a happy new year," as well as "good morning," added laughing, "you will see now, dear father, whether Polly's dreams are not prophetic. The promised bishop's mitre is come!" And then she told me how a New Year's present had been given her for me. It vexed me, that she had not asked more particularly for the name of my unknown patron or benefactor.

While she went out to light a lamp and call Jenny, I dressed myself. I cannot deny that I was burning with curiosity. For hitherto the New Year's presents for the Vicar of C———e had been as insignificant as they were rare. I suspected that my patron, the farmer, whose good-will I appeared to have won, had meant to surprise me with a box of cake, and I admired his modesty in sending me the present before it was light.

When I entered the parlour, Polly and Jenny were standing at the table on which lay the box directed to me, carefully sealed, and of an unusual size. I had never seen exactly such a box before. I lifted it, and found it pretty heavy. In the top were two smoothly cut round holes.

With Jenny's help, I opened the box very cautiously, as I had been directed to handle the contents carefully. A fine white cloth was removed, and lo!——but no, our astonishment is indescribable. We all exclaimed with one voice, "Good God!"

There lay a little child asleep, some six or eight weeks old, dressed in the finest linen, with rose-colored ribands. Its little head rested upon a soft blue silk cushion, and it was well wrapt up in a blanket. The covering as well as the little cap, was trimmed with the costliest Brabant lace.

We stood some moments gazing at it with silent wonder. At last Polly broke out into a comical laugh, and cried, "What shall we do with it? This is no bishop's mitre!" Jenny timidly touched the cheek of the sleeping babe with the tip of her finger, and in a tone full of pity, said, "Poor, dear little creature! thou hast no mother, or might as well have no mother! Great God! to cast off such a lovely, helpless being! Only see, father, only see, Polly, how peacefully and trustfully it sleeps, unconscious of its fate, as if it knew that it is lying in God's hand. Sleep on, thou poor, forsaken one! Thy parents are perhaps too high in rank to care for thee, and too happy to permit thee to disturb their happiness. Sleep on, we will not cast thee out. They have brought thee to the right place. I will be thy mother."

As Jenny was speaking, two large tears fell from her eyes. I caught the pious, gentle-hearted creature to my breast and said, "Be a mother to this little one! The stepchildren of fortune come to her stepchildren. God tries our faith—no, he does not try it, He knows it. Therefore is this forsaken little creature brought to us. We do not indeed know how we shall subsist from one day to another, but He knows, who has appointed us to be parents to this orphan."

Thus the matter was soon settled. The child continued to sleep sweetly on. In the meanwhile, we exhausted ourselves in conjectures about its parents, who were undoubtedly known to us, as the box was directed to me. Polly, alas! could tell us nothing more of the person who brought it than that she had already told. Now, while the little thing sleeps, and I run over my New Year's sermon upon "the Power of the Eternal Providence," my daughters are holding a council about the nursing of the poor stranger. Polly exhibits all the delight of a child. Jenny appears to be much moved. With me, it is as if I entered upon the New Year in the midst of miracles, and—it may be superstition, or it may be not—as if this little child were sent to be our guardian angel in our need. I cannot express the feelings of peace, the still happiness which I have.

Same day. Eve.—I came home greatly exhausted and weary with the sacred labors of the day. I had a long and rugged walk. But I was inspirited by a happy return home, by the cheerfulness of my daughters, by our pleasant little parlor. The table was ready laid for me, and on it stood a flask of wine, a New Year's present from an unknown benevolent hand.

The looks of the lovely little child in Jenny's arms refreshed me above all things. Polly showed me the beautiful little bed of our nursling, the dozen fine napkins, the dear little caps and night-clothes, which were in the box, and then a sealed packet of money directed to me, which they had found at the feet of the child when it awoke, and they took it out.

Anxious to learn something of the parentage of our little unknown inmate, I opened the packet. It contained a roll of twenty guineas and a letter, as follows:

"Relying with entire confidence upon the piety and humanity of your Reverence, the unhappy parents of this dear child commend it to your care. Do not forsake it. We will testify our gratitude when we are at liberty to make ourselves known to you. Although at a distance, we shall keep a careful watch, and know everything that you do. The dear boy is named Alfred. He has been baptized. His board for the first quarter accompanies this. The same sum will be punctually remitted to you every three months. Take the child. We commend him to the tenderness of your daughter Jenny."

When I had read the letter, Polly leaped with joy, and cried, "There's the bishop's mitre!" Bountiful Heaven! how rich had we suddenly become! We read the letter a dozen times. We did not trust our eyes to look at the gold upon the table. What a New Year's present! From my heaviest cares for the future was I thus suddenly relieved. But in what a strange and mysterious way! In vain did I think over all the people I knew, in order to discover who it might be who had been forced by birth or rank to conceal the existence of their child, or who were able to make such a liberal compensation for a simple service of Christian charity. I tasked my recollection, but I could think of no one. And yet it was evident that these parents were well acquainted with me and mine. Wonderful are the ways of Providence!

Jan. 2.—Fortune is heaping her favors upon me. This morning I again received a packet of money, £12, by the post, with a letter from Mr. Fleetman. It is too much. For a shilling he returns me a pound. Things must have gone well with him. He says as much. I cannot, alas, thank him, for he has forgotten to mention his address. God forbid I should be puffed up with my present riches. I hope now in time to pay off honestly my bond to Mr. Withell.

When I told my daughters that I had received a letter from Mr. Fleetman, there was a new occasion for joy. I do not exactly understand what the girls have to do with Mr. Fleetman. Jenny grew very red, and Polly jumped up laughingly, and held up both her hands before Jenny's face, and Jenny behaved as if she was right vexed with the playful girl.

I read out Fleetman's letter. But I could scarcely do it, for the young man is an enthusiast. He writes many flattering things which I do not deserve. He exaggerates everything, even indeed when he speaks of the good Jenny. I pitied the poor girl while I read. I did not dare to look at her. The passage, however, which relates to her, is worthy of note. It runs thus:

"When, excellent sir, I went from your door, I felt as if I were quitting a father's roof for the bleak world. I shall never forget you, never forget how happy I was with you. I see you now before me, in your rich poverty, in your Christian humility, in your patriarchal simplicity. And the lovely, fascinating Polly; and the—ah! for your Jenny I have no words! In what words shall one describe the heavenly loveliness by which everything earthly is transfigured? For ever shall I remember the moment when she gave me the twelve shillings, and the gentle tone of consolation with which she spoke to me. Wonder not that I have the twelve shillings still. I would not part with them for a thousand guineas. I shall soon perhaps explain everything to you personally. Never in my life have I been so happy or so miserable as I am now. Commend me to your sweet daughters, if they still bear me in remembrance."

I conclude from these lines that he intends to come this way again. The prospect gives me pleasure. In his unbounded gratitude, the young man has perhaps sent me his all, because I once lent him half of my ready money. That grieves me. He seems to be a thoughtless youth, and yet he has an honest heart.

We have great delight in the little Alfred. The little thing laughed to-day upon Polly, as Jenny was holding him, like a young mother, in her arms. The girls are more handy with the little citizen of the world than I had anticipated. But it is a beautiful child. We have bought him a handsome cradle, and provided abundantly for all his little wants. The cradle stands at Jenny's bedside. She watches day and night, like a guardian spirit, over her tender charge.

Jan. 3.—To-day, Mr. Curate Thomson arrived with his young wife and sent for me. I went to him immediately at the inn. He is an agreeable man, and very polite. He informed me that he was appointed my successor in office, that he wished, if I had no objections, to enter immediately upon his duties, and that I might occupy the parsonage until Easter: he would in the meanwhile take up his abode in lodgings prepared for him at Alderman Fieldson's.

I replied that, if he pleased, I would resign my office to him immediately, as I should thus be more at liberty to look out for another situation. I desired only permission to preach a farewell sermon in the churches in which I had for so many years declared the word of the Lord.

He then said that he would come in the afternoon to examine the state of the parsonage.

—He has been here with his wife and Alderman

Fieldson. His lady was somewhat haughty, and appears to be of high birth, for there was nothing in the house that pleased her, and she hardly deigned to look at my daughters. When she saw the little Alfred in the cradle, she turned to Jenny, and asked whether she were already married. The good Jenny blushed up to her hair, and shook her little head by way of negative, and stammered out something. I had to come to the poor girl's assistance. My lady listened to my story with great curiosity, and drew up her mouth, and shrugged her shoulders. It was very disagreeable, but I said nothing. I invited them to take a cup of tea. But they declined. Mr. Curate appeared to be very obedient to the slightest hint of the lady.

We were very glad when the visit was over.

Jan. 6. — Mr. Withell is an excellent man, to judge from his letter. He sympathizes with me in regard to my unfortunate bond, and comforts me with the assurance that I must not disquiet myself if I am not able to pay it for ten years or ever. He appears to be well acquainted with my circumstances, for he alludes to them very cautiously. He considers me an honest man. That gratifies me most. He shall not find his confidence misplaced. I will go to Trowbridge as soon as I can, and pay Mr. Withell Fleetman's £12 sterling, as an instalment of my monstrous debt.

Although Jenny insists that she sleeps soundly, that little Alfred is very quiet o' nights, and only wakes once, when she gives him a drink out of his little bottle, yet I feel anxious about the maiden. She is not so lively by far, as formerly, although she seems to be much happier than when we were every day troubled about our daily bread. Sometimes she sits with her needle, lost in a reverie, dreaming with open eyes; or her hands, once so active, lie sunk upon her lap. When she is spoken to, she starts, and has to bethink herself what was said. All this evidently comes from the interruption of her proper rest. But she will not hear a word of it. We cannot even persuade her to take a little nap in the daytime. She declares that she feels perfectly well.

I had no idea that she had so much vanity. Fleetman's praises have not displeased her. She has asked me for his letter, to read once more. And she has not yet returned it to me, but keeps it in her work-basket!

I don't care, for my part! the vain thing!

Jan. 8. — My farewell sermon was accompanied with the tears of most of my hearers. I see now at last that my parishioners love me. They have expressed their obligations on all hands and loaded me with gifts. I never before had such an abundance of provisions in the house, so many dainties of all kinds, and so much wine. A hundredth part of my present plenty would have made me account myself over-fortunate in past days. We are really swimming in plenty. But a goodly portion has already been disposed of. I know some poor families in C——e, and Jenny knows even more than I. The dear people share in our pleasures.

I was moved to the inmost by my sermon. With tears had I written it. It was a sketch of my whole past course from my call and settlement. I am driven from the vineyard as an unprofitable servant, and yet I have not labored as a hireling. Many noble vines have I planted, many deadly weeds cut away. I am driven from the vineyard where I have watched, and taught, and warned, and comforted, and prayed. I have shrunk from no sick bed. I have strengthened the dying for the last conflict with holy hope. I have gone after sinners. I have not left the poor, desolate. I have called back the lost to the way of life. Ah! all these souls that were knit to my soul, are torn from me—why should not my heart bleed? But God's will be done!

Gladly would I now offer to take charge of the parish without salary, but my successor has the office. I have been used to poverty from my birth, and care has never forsaken me since I stepped out of my boy's-shoes. I have enough for myself and my daughters in little Alfred's board. We shall be able indeed to lay up something. I would never again complain of wind and weather beating against my grey hairs, could I only continue to break the bread of life to my flock.

Be it so! I will not murmur. The tear which drops upon this page, is no tear of discontent. I ask not for riches and good days, nor have I ever asked. But, Lord! Lord! drive not thy servant for ever from thy service, although his powers are small. Let me again enter thy vineyard, and with thy blessing win souls.

Jan. 13. — My journey to Trowbridge has turned out beyond all expectation. I arrived late with weary feet at the pleasant little old city, and could not rouse myself from sleep until late the next morning. After I had put on my clean clothes (I had not been so finely dressed since my wedding-day—the good Jenny shows a daughter's care for her father,) I left the inn and went to Mr. Withell's. He lives in a splendid, great house.

He received me somewhat coldly at first; but when I mentioned my name, he led me into his little office. Here I thanked him for his great goodness and consideration, told him how I had happened to give the bond, and what hard fortunes had hitherto been mine. I then laid my £12 upon the table.

Mr. Withell looked at me for a while in silence, with a smile, and with some emotion. He then extended his hand, and shook mine, and said, "I know all about you. I have informed myself particularly about your circumstances. You are an honest man. Take your £12 back. I cannot find it in my heart to rob you of your New Year's present. Rather let me add a pound to it, to remember me by."

He arose, brought a paper from another room, opened it and said, "You know this bond and your signature? I give it to you and your children." He tore the paper in two, and placed it in my hand.

I could find no words, I was so deeply moved. My eyes filled. He saw that I would thank him, but could not, and he said, "Hush! hush! not a syllable, I pray you. This is the only thanks I desire of you. I would gladly have forgiven poor Brook the debt, had he only dealt frankly with me."

I don't know a more noble-hearted man than Mr. Withell. He was too kind. He would have me relate to him much of my past history. He introduced me to his wife, and to the young gentleman his son. He had my little bundle, containing my old clothes, brought from the inn, and kept me at his house. The entertainment was princely. The chamber in which I slept, the carpet, the bed, were so splendid and costly that I hardly dared to make use of them.

The next day Mr. Withell sent me home in his own elegant carriage. I parted with my benefactor with a heart deeply moved. My children wept with me for joy, when I showed them the bond. "See," said I, "this light piece of paper was the heaviest burthen of my life, and now it is generously cancelled. Pray for the life and prosperity of our deliverer!"

Jan. 16.—Yesterday was the most remarkable day of my life. We were sitting together in the forenoon; I was rocking the cradle, Polly was reading aloud, and Jenny was seated at the window with her needle, when she suddenly jumped up, and then fell back again deadly pale into her chair. We were all alarmed, and cried, "What is the matter?" She forced a smile, and said, "He is coming!"

The door opened, and in came Mr. Fleetman in a beautiful travelling cloak. We greeted him right heartily, and were truly glad to see him so unexpectedly, and, as it appeared, in so much better circumstances than before. He embraced me, kissed Polly, and bowed to Jenny, who had not yet recovered from her agitation. Her pale looks did not escape him. He inquired anxiously about her health. Polly replied to his questions, and he then kissed Jenny's hand, as though he would beg her pardon for having occasioned her such an alarm. But there was nothing to be said about it, for the poor girl grew red again like a newly-blown rose.

I called for cake and wine, to treat my guest and benefactor better than on a former occasion; but he declined, as he could not tarry long, and he had company at the inn. Yet at Jenny's request, he sate down and took some wine with us.

As he had spoken of the company which had come with him, I supposed that it must be a company of comedians, and inquired whether they intended to stop and play in C——, observing that the place was too poor. He laughed out, and replied, "Yes, we shall play a comedy, but altogether gratis." Polly was beside herself with joy, for she had long wanted to see a play. She told Jenny, who had gone for the cake and wine. Polly inquired whether many actors had come with him. "A gentleman and lady," said he, "but excellent players."

Jenny appeared unusually serious. She cast a sad look at Fleetman, and asked, "And you—will you also appear?" This was said in that tone peculiarly soft, yet very penetrating, which I have seldom observed in her, and only upon rare occasions, and at the most serious moments.

Poor Fleetman himself trembled at her tone, so like the voice of the angel of doom. He looked up to her with an earnest gaze, and appeared to struggle with himself for an answer, and then advancing towards her a step, he said, "Miss, by my God and yours, you alone can decide that!"

Jenny dropped her eyes. He continued to speak. She answered. I could not comprehend what they were about. They spoke—Polly and I listened with the greatest attention, but we neither of us understood a word, or rather we heard words without any sense. And yet Fleetman and Jenny appeared not only to understand one another perfectly, but, what struck me as very strange, Fleetman was deeply moved by Jenny's answers, although they expressed the veriest trifles. At last Fleetman clasped his hands passionately to his breast, raised his eyes, streaming with tears, to heaven, and with an impressive appearance of emotion, exclaimed, "Then am I indeed unhappy!"

Polly could hold out no longer. With a comical vivacity, she looked from one to the other, and at last cried out, "I do believe that you two are beginning to play already!"

He pressed Polly's hand warmly, and said, "Ah! that it were so!"

I put an end to the confusion by pouring out the wine. We drank to the welfare of our friend. Fleetman turned to Jenny, and stammered out, "Miss, in earnest, my welfare?" She laid her hand upon her heart, cast down her eyes, and drank.

Fleetman immediately became more composed. He went to the cradle, looked at the child, and when Polly and I had told him its history, he said to Polly, with a smile, "Then you have not discovered that I sent you this New Year's present?"

We all exclaimed in utter amazement, "Who! you?" He then proceeded to relate what follows: "My name," said he, "is not Fleetman. I am Sir Cecil Fairford. My sister and myself have been kept out of our rightful property by my father's brother, who took advantage of certain ambiguous conditions in my father's will, and involved us in a long and embarrassing lawsuit. We have hitherto lived with difficulty upon the little property left us by our mother, who died early. My sister has suffered most from the tyranny of her uncle, who was her guardian, and who had destined her for the son of an intimate and powerful friend of his. But my sister, on the other hand, was secretly contracted to the young Lord Sandom, whose father, then living, was opposed to their marriage. Without the knowledge either of my uncle or the old lord, they were secretly married. The little Alfred is their son. My sister, under the pretence of benefiting her health and availing herself of sea-bathing, left the house of her guardian, and put herself under my protection. When the child was born, our great concern was to find a place for it where it would have the tenderest care. I accidentally heard a touching account of the poverty and humanity of the parish minister of C——, and I came hither to satisfy myself. The manner in which I was treated by you decided me.

"I have forgotten to mention that my sister never returned to her guardian. For about six months ago I won the suit against him, and entered into possession of my patrimony. My uncle instituted a new suit against me for withdrawing my sister from his charge; but the old Lord Sandom died suddenly a few days ago of apoplexy, and my brother-in-law has made his marriage public. So that the suit falls to the ground, and all cause for keeping the child's birth secret is removed. Its parents have now come with me to take the child away, and I have come to take away you and your family, if the proposal I make you shall be accepted.

"During the lawsuit in which I have been engaged, the living, which is in the gift of my family, has remained unoccupied. I have at my disposal this situation, which yields over £200 per annum. You, sir, have lost your place. I shall not be happy unless you come and reside near me, and accept this living."

God only knows how I was affected at these words. My eyes were blinded with tears of joy. I stretched out my hands to the man who came a messenger from heaven. I fell upon his breast. Polly threw her arms around him with a cry of delight. Jenny thankfully kissed the baronet's hand. But he snatched it from her with visible agitation, and left us.

My happy children were still holding me in their embraces, and we were still mingling our tears and congratulations, when the baronet returned, bringing his brother-in-law, Lord Sandom, with his wife. The latter was an uncommonly beautiful young lady. Without saluting us, she ran to the cradle of her child. She knelt down over the little Alfred, kissed his cheeks, and wept freely with mingled pain and delight. Her lord raised her up, and had much trouble in composing her.

When she had recovered her composure, and apologized to us all for her behaviour, she thanked first me and then Polly, in the most touching terms. Polly disowned all obligation, and pointed to Jenny, who had withdrawn to the window, and said, "My sister there has been its mother!"

Lady Sandom approached Jenny, gazed at her long in silence, and with evidently delighted surprise, and then glanced at her brother with a smile, and folded Jenny in her arms. The dear Jenny, in her modesty, scarcely dared to look up. "I am your debtor," said my lady, "but the service you have rendered to a mother's heart it is impossible for me to repay. Become a sister to me, lovely Jenny; sisters can have no obligations between them." As they embraced each other, the baronet approached. "There stands my poor brother," said my lady; "as you are now my sister, he may stand nearer to your heart, dear Jenny, may he not?"

Jenny blushed and said, "He is my father's benefactor."

"Will you not be," replied the lady, "the benefactress of my poor brother? Look kindly on him. If you only knew how he loves you!"

The baronet took Jenny's hand and kissed it, and said, as Jenny struggled to withdraw it, "Miss, will you be unkind to me? I am unhappy without this hand." Jenny, much disturbed, let her hand remain in his. The baronet then led my daughter to me, and begged me for my blessing.

"Jenny," said I, "it depends upon thee. Do we dream? Canst thou love him? Do thou decide."

She then turned to the baronet, who stood before her, deeply agitated, and cast upon him a full, penetrating look, and then took his hand in both hers, pressed it to her breast, looked up to heaven, and softly whispered, "God has decided."

I blessed my son and my daughter. They embraced. There was a solemn silence. All eyes were wet.

Suddenly Polly sprang up, laughing through her tears, and flung herself upon my neck, while she cried, "There! we have it! The New Year's present! Bishop's mitres upon bishop's mitres!"

Little Alfred awoke.

It is in vain—I cannot describe this day. My happy heart is full, and I am continually interrupted.

FRIEDRICH VON SCHLEGEL.

Born 1772. Died 1829.

FRIEDRICH, a younger brother of A. W. von Schlegel, was born at Hanover, five years later. Destined by his father to mercantile pursuits, he was placed for that purpose in a counting-room at Leipzig; but feeling a strong predilection for Letters, and discovering more than ordinary capacity, he was recalled and suffered to take his own course. He studied Philology in Göttingen and in Leipzig, during which time he read every author of note in the Latin and Greek languages. He then resided for awhile in Berlin and in Dresden, published his "Greeks and Romans," 1797, and the following year, his "Poetry of the Greeks and Romans," a continuation of the former. In 1800, he went as *Privatdocent* (private teacher) to Jena, where he labored in conjunction with his brother and others, of like views, and published several poems. In 1803, at Cologne, he went over to the Roman Catholic church,* together with his wife, a daughter of Mendelssohn. He next resided for several years in Paris, where he lectured on Philosophy, and where he published his "*Europa*." While here he devoted himself to the study of the southern languages, and particularly to that of India. He also published, 1804, a collection of romantic poems of the middle ages, from printed sources and manuscripts; and illustrations of the history of Joan of Arc, drawn from the *Notices et Extraits*. His *Sprache und Weisheit der Indier* belongs to this period.

In 1808 he returned to Germany, and was made secretary of the Austrian Government at Vienna, where he exerted a powerful influence by his proclamations against Napoleon. After the conclusion of the peace, he gave lectures in Vienna, on modern history and on the literature of all nations. In 1815, he was appointed by Prince Metternich, Austrian Counsellor of Legation at the Diet in Frankfort. In 1818 he returned to Vienna, where he lived as Secretary of the Court, and devoted himself to literary pursuits. During this period he published his "View of the present Political Relations." In 1820 he undertook a periodical called *Concordia*, the object of which was to reconcile the different opinions on Church and State. In 1827 he gave a course of lectures in Vienna, on the Philosophy of Life, which was published the following year. In December 1828, he began another course in Dresden, on the Philosophy of Language and of the *Word*. These lectures he did not live to complete, but died in the midst of the course, January 11th, 1829. It has been noted as emblematic of the man, that the last word which came from his pen was *aber* (*but*). This was written at eleven o'clock at night. At one, he breathed his last.

Friedrich von Schlegel is thought to have surpassed his brother in originality, to have equalled him in depth and extent of learning, but to fall far behind him in point of taste and clearness. "Like his brother he opened to Poetry and to Science in Germany, new and hitherto unknown regions. He was the first who specially directed attention to the great intellectual treasures of the Indians, and introduced among us the studies relating to these. Later, after his change of faith, he assailed, in the most decided manner, French democracy and frivolity; but then, in his capacity of philosophical historian, he became an opponent of religious and political liberty and enlightenment, and completely lost himself at last in misty speculations and politico-religious vagaries."* With regard to this "change of faith," and the criticisms and imputations to which it gave rise, Mr. Carlyle judges thus: "Of Schlegel himself and his character and spiritual history we can profess no thorough or final understanding; yet enough to make us view him with admiration and pity, nowise with harsh, contemptuous censure; and must say, with clearest persuasion, that the outcry of his being 'a renegade,' &c., is but like other such out-

---

* According to Wolff in the *Encyclopädie der Deutschen Nationallitteratur*. The *Conversationslexicon* refers this apostasy to a later date,—1808.

* Wolff's *Encyclopädie*.

(472)

cries, a judgment where there was neither jury, nor evidence, nor judge. The candid reader in this book itself,* to say nothing of all the rest, will find traces of a high, far-seeing, earnest spirit, to whom 'Austrian Pensions' and the Kaiser's crown and Austria altogether, were but a light matter to the finding and vitally appropriating of truth. Let us respect the sacred mystery of a Person; rush not irreverently into man's Holy of Holies!"

* Schlegel's last work; Lectures on the Philosophy of Language, &c.

LECTURES ON THE PHILOSOPHY OF HISTORY.
From the Translation of Robinson.

THE CHINESE EMPIRE.

THE Chinese empire is the largest of all the monarchies now existing on the earth, and on this account alone may well challenge the attention of the historical inquirer. It is not absolutely the greatest in territorial extent, though even in this respect it is scarcely inferior to the greatest; but in point of population it is, in all probability, the first. Spain, could we now include in the number of her possessions her American colonies, would exceed all other empires in extent. The same may be said of Russia, with her colonies and boundless provinces in the north of Asia. But, great as the population of Russia may be, considered in itself and relatively to the other European states, it can sustain no comparison with that of China. England, with the East Indies and her colonial possessions in the three divisions of the globe, Polynesia, Africa, and America, has indeed a very wide extent, and perhaps, including the hundred and ten millions that own her sway in India, comes the nearest, in point of population, to China. Of the amount of the Chinese population, which is not certainly known, that of India may furnish a criterion for a conjectural and probable estimate. However, as this vast region is everywhere intersected by navigable rivers and canals, everywhere studded with large and populous cities, and enjoys a climate as genial, or even still more genial, and certainly far more salubrious, than that of India; as, like the latter country, it everywhere presents to the eye the richest culture, and is in all appearance as much peopled, or over-peopled, we may take India, whose total population is by no means included in the hundred and ten millions under British rule, as furnishing a pretty accurate standard for the computation of the Chinese population. Now, when we consider that even China proper is larger than the whole western peninsula of India, and that the vast countries dependent on China, such as Thibet and Southern Tartary, are very populous, the conjectural calculation of the English writer whom I follow in these remarks on the Chinese population, and who reckons it at one hundred and fifty millions, may be regarded as very moderate, and might, with perfect safety, be considerably raised. Thus then the Chinese population is nearly as large as the whole population of Europe, and constitutes, if not a fourth, at least a fifth, of the total population of the globe.

Cursory comparisons of this kind are not without value. The history of civilization, forming the basis, and as it were the outward body, of the philosophy of history, which should be the inner and highest sense of the whole, is deeply interesting in all that refers to the general condition of humanity. And such an interest, which does not of itself lie in mere statistical calculations, but in the outward condition of mankind, as the symbol of its inward state, may very well belong to comparisons of this nature.

The interest, however, which the philosophic historian should take in all that relates to humanity in general, and to the various nations of the earth, ought not to be regulated by the false standard of an indiscriminate equality, considering all nations of equal importance, and paying equal attention to all, without distinction. This would imply insensibility to man's higher nature, or ignorance of it. But this interest should be measured not merely by the population of a state, or by geographical extent of territory, or by external power, but by population, territory and power combined—by moral worth and intellectual pre-eminence, by the scale of civilization to which the nation has attained. The Tongoosses, though a very widely-diffused race—the Calmucks, though they have much to claim our attention, compared with the other nations of central Asia, cannot certainly excite equal interest, or hold a place in the history of human civilization with the Greeks or the Egyptians; though the territory of Egypt itself is certainly not particularly large, nor, according to our customary standard of population, were its inhabitants, in all probability, ever very numerous. In the same way, the Empire of the Moguls, which embraced China itself, has not the same importance in our eyes as the Roman Empire, either in its rise or in its fall. Writers of universal history have not however always avoided this fault, and have been too much disposed to place all nations on the same historical footing,—on the false level of an indiscriminate equality; and to regard humanity in a mere physical point of view, and according to the natural classification of tribes and races. In these sketches of history, the high and the noble is often ranked with the low and the vulgar; and neither what is truly great, nor what is of lesser importance (for this, too, should not be overlooked), has its due place in these portraits of mankind.

A numerous, or even excessive population, is undoubtedly an essential element of political power in a state; but it is not the only, nor in any respect the principal indication of the civilization of a country. It is only in regard to civilization that the population of China deserves our consideration. Although in these latter times, when Europe, by her political ascendancy over the other parts of the world, has proved the pre-eminence of her arts and civilization, England and Russia have become the immediate neighbors of China towards the north and west, yet these territorial relations affect not the rest of Europe; and China, when we leave out of consideration its very important commerce, cannot certainly be accounted a political power in the general system. Even in ancient, as well as in modern times, China never figured in the history of Western Asia or Europe, and had no connection whatever with their inhabitants; but this great country has ever stood apart, like a world within itself, in the remote, unknown Eastern Asia. Hence, the earlier writers of universal history have taken little or no notice of this great empire, shut out as it was from the confined horizon of their views. And this was natural, when we consider that the conquests and expeditions of the Asiatic nations were considered by these writers as subjects of the first importance. No conquerors have ever marched from China into Western Asia, like Xerxes, for instance, who passed from the interior of Persia to Athens; or Alexander the Great, who extended his victorious march from his small paternal province of Macedon to beyond the Indus, and almost to the borders of the Ganges, though the latter river, in despite of all his efforts, he was unable to reach. But great victorious expeditions have proceeded not from China, but from Central Asia, and the nations of Tartary, who have invaded China itself; though in those invasions the manners, mind, and civilization of the Chinese have evinced their power, since their Tartar conquerors, in the earliest as in the latest times, have, after a few generations, invariably conformed to the manners and civilization of the conquered nation, and become more or less Chinese. Not only the great population and flourishing agriculture of this fruitful country, but the cultivation of silk, for which it has been celebrated from all antiquity, the culture of the tea-plant, which forms such an important article of European trade, as well as the knowledge of several most useful medicinal productions of nature, and unique, and, in their way, excellent products of industry and manufacture, prove the very high degree of civilization to which this people have attained. And why should not that people be entitled to a high place, or one of the highest among civilized nations, which had known, many centuries before Europe, the art of printing, gunpowder, and the magnet—those three so highly celebrated and valuable discoveries of European skill? Instead of the regular art of printing with transposable letters, which would not suit the Chinese system of writing, this people make use of a species of lithography, which, to all essential purposes, is the same, and attended with the same effects. Gunpowder serves in China, as it did in Europe in the infancy of the discovery, rather for amusement and fireworks, than for the more serious purposes of war and conquest; and though this people are acquainted with the magnetic needle, they have never made a like extended application of its powers, and never employ it, either in a confined river and coasting navigation, or on the wide ocean, on which they never venture.

The Chinese are remarkable, too, for the utmost polish and refinement of manners, and even for a precise civility and love of stately ceremonial. In many respects, indeed, their politeness and refinement almost equal those of European nations, or at least are far superior to what we usually designate by the term of oriental manners—a term which, in our sense, can apply only to the nearer Mahometan countries of the Levant. Of this assertion, we may find a sufficient proof in any single tale that portrays the present Chinese life and manners; in the novel, for instance, translated by M. Remusat. In their present manners and fashions, however, there are many things utterly at variance with European taste and feelings; I need only mention the custom of the dignitaries, functionaries, and literary men letting their nails grow to the length of birds' claws, and that other custom in women of rank, of compressing their feet to an extreme diminutiveness. Both customs, according to the recent account of a very intelligent Englishman, serve to mark and distinguish the upper class; for the former renders the men totally incapable of hard or manual labor, and the latter impedes the woman of rank in walking, or at least gives her a mincing gait, and a languid, delicate and interesting air. These minute traits of manners should not be overlooked in the general sketch of the nation, for they perfectly correspond to many other characteristic marks and indications of the unnatural stiffness, childish vanity, and exaggerated refinement, which we meet with in the more important province of its intellectual character. Even in the basis of all intellectual culture, the language, or rather the writing of the Chinese, this character of refinement, pushed beyond all bounds and all conception, is visible, while, on the other hand, it is coupled with great intellectual poverty and jejuneness. A language where there are not many more than three hundred, not near four hundred, and (according to the most recent critical investigation) only 272 monosyllabic primitive roots without any kind of grammar; where the not merely various, but utterly unconnected significations of one and the same word are marked, in the first place, by a varying modulation of the voice, according to a fourfold method of accentuation; in the next place and chiefly, by the written characters, which amount to the prodigious number of eighty thousand, while the Egyptian hieroglyphs do not exceed the number of eight hundred—such a language must needs be the most artificial in the whole world;—an inference, not invalidated by the fact that, out of that great number of all actual or possible written characters, but a fourth part perhaps is really in use, and a still less portion is necessary to be learned. As the meaning, especially of more complex notions and abstract ideas, can be fully fixed and accurately determined only by such artificial ciphers, the language is far more dependent on these written characters than on living sound; for one and the same sound may often be designated by 160 different characters, and have as many significations. It not rarely occurs that the Chinese, when they do not very well understand each other in conversation, have recourse to writing, and by copying down these ciphers are enabled to divine each other's meaning, and become mutually intelligible. Indeed, it furnishes labor sufficient to fill up the life of man, for even the European scholars who have engaged in this study find it a matter of no small difficulty, to devise a system whereby a dictionary, or rather a systematic catalogue of all these written characters may be composed, to serve as a fit guide on this ocean of Chinese signs. But we shall again have occasion to recur to this subject; and, indeed, it is only in connection with the peculiarities of the Chinese mind that this writing system can be properly explained and understood in its true meaning, or rather its meaningless construction and elaborateness.

Although the construction of canals, and all the regulations of water-carriage, could have attained only by degrees to their present state of perfection, still this alone would prove the very early attention which this people had given to the arts of civilized life. Mention is often made of them in the old Chinese histories and imperial annals; and the canals of China, like the Nile in Egypt, were ever the objects of most anxious solicitude to the government. These annals, whenever they have occasion to speak of those great inundations and destructive floods which are of such frequent occurrence in Chinese history, invariably represent the attention bestowed on water-courses and water-regulations as the most certain mark of a wise, benevolent and provident administration. On the other hand, the neglect of this most important of administrative concerns is ever regarded as the proof of a wicked, reckless and unfortunate reign; and in these histories some great calamity, or even violent catastrophe, is sure to follow, like a stroke of divine vengeance, on this unpardonable neglect of duty.

The long succession of the different native dynasties of China, Tchin, Han, Tung, and Sung, down to the Moguls, which fills the diffuse annals of the empire, furnishes few important data on the intellectual progress of the Chinese; and everything of importance to the object of our present inquiries, that can be gathered out of the mass of political history, may be reduced to a very few plain facts. The English writer, whom we have already cited, though otherwise inclined to a certain degree of scepticism in his views, fixes the commencement of the historical ages of authentic history in the ancient dynasty of Chow, eleven hundred years before the Christian era. The first fact of importance, as regards the moral and intellectual civilization of China, is, that this country, originally divided into many small principalities and under petty sovereigns, whose power was more limited, enjoyed a greater share of liberty. The great burning of the books, of which more particular mention will be presently made, as well as the erection of the great wall, are attributed to the first general emperor of all China, Chihoangti; in whose reign, too, Japan became a Chinese colony, or received from China a political establishment. At a still later period, as in the fifth century of our era, and again at the time of the Mogul conquest under Zingis Khan, China was divided into two kingdoms, a northern and a southern. But there is another fact already mentioned, that throws still stronger light on the high civilization of China—it is, that at every period when this empire has been conquered by the Moguls and Tartars, the conquerors, overcome in their turn by the ascendancy of Chinese civilization, have, within a short time, invariably adopted the manners, laws, and even the language of China, and thus its institutions have remained, on the whole, unaltered. But here is a circumstance in Chinese history particularly worthy of our attention. In no state in the world do we see such an entire, absolute, and rigid monarchical unity as in that of China, especially under its ancient form; although this government is more limited by laws and manners, and is by no means of that arbitrary and despotic character which we are wont to attribute to the more modern oriental states. In China, before the introduction of the Indian religion of Buddhu, there was not even a distinct sacerdotal class—there is no nobility, no hereditary class with hereditary rights—education, and employment in the service of the state, form the only marks of distinction; and the men of letters and government functionaries are blended together in the single class of Mandarins; but the state is all in all. However, this absolute monarchical system has not conduced to the peace, stability, and permanent prosperity of the state, for the whole history of China, from beginning to end, displays one continued series of seditions, usurpations, anarchy, changes of dynasty, and other violent revolutions and catastrophes. This is proved by the bare statement of facts, though the official language of the imperial annals ever concedes the final triumph to the monarchical principle.

The same violent revolutions occurred in the department of science and of public doctrines, as in the instance already cited of the general burning of the books by order of the first general emperor, when the men of letters, or at least a party of them, were persecuted, and four hundred and sixty followers of Confucius burnt. This act of tyranny undoubtedly supposes a very violent contest between factions — an important political struggle between hostile sects, and a mighty revolution in the intellectual world. At the same time too, a favorite of this tyrannical prince introduced a new system of writing, which has led to the greatest confusion, even in subsequent ages. Such an intellectual revolution is doubtless evident on the introduction of the Indian religion of Buddhu, or Fo, (according to the Chinese appellation,) which took place precisely three-and-thirty years after the foundation of Christianity. The conquest of China by the Moguls, under Zingis Khan, occurred at the same time that their expeditions towards the opposite quarter of Europe spread terror and desolation over Russia and Poland, as far as the confines of Silesia. This conquest produced a reaction, and a popular revolution, conducted by a common citizen of China, by name Chow, restored the empire; this citizen afterwards ascended the throne, and became the founder of a new Chinese dynasty. The emperors of the present dynasty of Mantchou Tartars, that has now governed China since the middle of the seventeenth century, are distinguished for their attachment to the old customs and institutions of China, and even to its language and science; and their elevation to the throne has given rise to many great scientific enterprises, and has been singularly favorable to the investigations of those European scholars, whose object it is to make us better acquainted with China. But at the moment I am speaking, a great rebellion has broken out in the northern part of the kingdom, and in the opposite extremity the Christians are exposed to a more than ordinary persecution.

These few leading incidents in Chinese history may suffice to make known the principal epochs in the intellectual progress and civilization of this people. As the constitution and development of the human mind are in each of those ancient nations closely connected with the nature of their language, and even sometimes (as in the case of the Chinese) with their system of writing, the language of the latter people being, on account of its amazing copiousness, less fit for conversation than for writing, I shall now make a few remarks on the very artificial mode of Chinese writing, which is perfectly unique in its kind: but I shall confine my observation to its general character, and shall forbear entering into the vast labyrinth of the eighty thousand cipher-signs of speech, and all the problems and difficulties which they involve. The Chinese writing was undoubtedly in its origin symbolical, though the rude marks of those primitive symbols can now scarcely be discerned in the enigmatical abbreviations, and in the complex combinations of the characters at present in use. It is no slight problem even for the learned of China to reduce, with any degree of certainty, the boundless quantity of their written characters to their simple elements and primitive roots: in this, however, they have succeeded, and have shown that all these elements are to be found in the two hundred and fourteen symbols, or keys of writing, as they call them. The Chinese characters of the primitive ages comprise only representations, indicated by a few rude strokes, of those first simple objects which surround man while living in the most simple state of society — such as the sun and moon, the most familiar animals, the common plants, the implements of human labor, weapons, and the different parts of human dwellings. This is the same rude symbolical writing which we find among other civilized nations, the Americans, for example, and among them, the Mexicans in particular.

The celebrated French orientalist, Abel Remusat, who in our times has infused a new life into the study of Chinese literature, and especially thrown on the whole subject a much greater degree of clearness than originally belonged to it, has, in his examination of this first very meagre outline of the infant civilization of China, wherein he discovers the then very contracted circle of Chinese ideas, made many intelligent observations, and many historical deductions. And if, as he conjectures, the discovery of Chinese writing must date its origin four thousand years back, this would bring it within three or four generations from the deluge, according to the vulgar era—an estimate which certainly is not exaggerated. If this European scholar, intimately conversant as he is with Chinese antiquities and science, is at a loss adequately to describe his astonishment at the extreme poverty of these first symbols of Chinese writing, so no one, doubtless, possesses in a higher degree than himself all the necessary attainments to enable him to appreciate the immeasurable distance between this first extreme jejuneness of ideas, and the boundless wealth displayed in the latter artificial and complex writing of the Chihese.

But when, among other things, he calls our attention to the fact that, in this primitive writing, even the sign or symbol of a priest is wanting—a symbol which together with the class itself must exist among the very rudest nations —I must concur in the truth of the remark: for he himself adduces, among other characters, one which must represent a magician. Now among the heathen nations of the primitive age, the one personage was certainly identical with the other, as even among the Cainites was very probably the case. Even the combination of several of those simple characters, which generally serve to denote the more abstract ideas, seem often, or at least originally, not to have been regulated by any profound principle of symbolism, but to have arisen merely out of the vulgar perceptions or impressions of every-day life. For instance, the character denoting happiness is composed of two signs, of which one represents an open mouth, and the other a handful of rice, or rice by itself. Here we see no allusion is made to any very lofty or chimerical idea of happiness, or to any mystic or spiritual conception of it; but, as this written character well evinces, the Chinese notion of happiness is simply represented by a mouth filled and saturated with good wine. Another example of nearly the same kind, given by Remusat with a sort of polite reluctance, is the character designating woman, which, when doubled, signifies strife and contention, and when tripled, immoral and disorderly conduct. How widely removed are all those coarse and trivial combinations of ideas from an exquisite sense—a deep symbolism of Nature—from those spiritual emblems in the Egyptian hieroglyphics, so far as they have been deciphered; although these emblems may have been, and were in fact, applied to the purpose of alphabetic usage. In the hieroglyphics there is, besides the bare literal meaning, a high symbolic inspiration, like a soul of life, the breathing of a high, indwelling spirit, a deeply felt significancy, a lofty and beautiful design apparent through the dead characters denoting any particular name or fact.

But independently of this boundless chaos of written characters, the Chinese undoubtedly possess a system of scientific symbols and symbolical signs, which constitute the substance of their most sacred book, the I-King, which signifies the book of unity, or, as others explain it, the book of changes; and either name will agree with the meaning of those symbols which, when rightly understood, and conceived in the spirit of early antiquity, will appear to be of a very remarkable and scientific nature. There are only two primary figures or lines, from which proceed originally the four symbols and the eight kona or combinations representing Nature, which form the basis of the high Chinese philosophy. These first two primary principles are a straight, unbroken line, and a line broken or divided into two. If these first simple elements are doubled, namely, two straight lines put under each other like our arithmetical sign of equation, and two broken or divided lines also put together, the different lines are formed. According as one broken line occupies the upper or the lower place, there are two possible variations—when put together, there are four possible variations; and these constitute the four symbols. But if three lines of these two kinds, the straight and the broken, are united or placed under each other, so, according to the number or the upper, middle or lower place of either species of line, there are eight possible combinations, and these are the eight kona, which, together with the four symbols, refer to the natural elements, and to the primary principles of all things, and serve as the symbolical expression, or scientific designation of these.

What is now the real sense and proper signification of those scientific primary lines among the Chinese, which exert an influence over the whole of their ancient literature, and upon which they themselves have written an incredible number of learned commentaries? Leibnitz supposed them to contain a reference to the modern algebraical discoveries, and especially to the binary calculation. Other writers, especially among the English, drawing their observations more from real life, remark on the other hand, that this ancient system of mystical lines serves at present the purpose of a sort of oracular play of questions, like the turning up of cards among Europeans, and is converted to many superstitious uses, especially for making pretended discoveries in alchemy, to which the Chinese are very much addicted. But this is only an abuse of modern times, which no longer understand this primitive system of symbolical signs and lines. The high antiquity of these lines and of the eight kona can be the less a matter of doubt, as even mythology has ascribed them to the primitive patriarch of the Chinese, Fohi, who is represented as having espied these lines on the back of a tortoise, and having thence deduced the written characters; which many of the learned Chinese wish to derive from these eight kona or combinations of the first symbolical lines. But the French scholar, whom I have more than once had occasion to name, and who is well able to form a competent opinion on the subject, is most decidedly opposed to this Chinese derivation of all the written characters from the eight kona; and it would appear, indeed, that the latter differ totally from the common system of Chinese writing, and must be looked upon as of a distinct scientific nature.

Perhaps we may find a natural explanation of the true, and not very hidden sense of these signs, by comparing the fundamental doctrines of the elder Greek philosophy and science of Nature. Thus, in the writings of Plato, mention is often made of the one and of the other, or of unity and duality, as the original elements of Nature and first principles of all existence. By this is meant the doctrine of the first opposition and of the many oppositions derived from the first; and also of the possible, and conceivable, or required adjustment and compromise between the two, and of the restoration of the first unity and eternal equality anterior to all opposition, and which terminates and absorbs in itself all discord. Thus these eight kona, and mathematical signs or symbolical lines of ancient China, would comprise nothing more than a dry outline of all dynamical speculation and science. And it is therefore quite consistent that the old sacred book which contains these principles of Chinese science should be termed either the book of unity or the book of changes; for doubtless this title refers to the doctrine of an absolute unity, as the fundamental principle of all things, and to the doctrine of differences, or oppositions or changes springing out of that first unity.

This doctrine of an opposition in all things—in thought as in nature—will become more apparent if we reflect on the new and brilliant discoveries in natural philosophy. For as in this science, the oxygen and hydrogen parts in the chemistry of metals, or the positive or negative end of electrical phenomena, in the attracting and repelling pole of magnetism, reveal such an opposition and dynamic play of living powers in nature; so in this philosophy of China, the abstract doctrine of this opposition and dynamical change of existence seems to be laid down with a sort of mathematical generality, as the basis of all future science. In our higher natural philosophy, indeed, all this has been proved from facts and experience; and, besides, this dynamic life forms but one element, and the one branch of the science to be acquired; and a philosophy founded entirely on this dynamical law of existence, without any regard to the other and higher principle of internal experience and moral life, intellectual intuition and divine revelation, would be at best a very partial system, and by no means of general application; or if a general application of such a system were made, it must lead to endless mistakes, errors and contradictions. That such a system of dynamical speculation and science, if extended to objects where it cannot be corroborated by facts, to all things divine and human, real, possible, or impossible, will undoubtedly lead to such a chaotic confusion of ideas, we have had a memorable experience in the German "Philosophy of Nature" of the last generation; a philosophy which consisted in a fanciful play of thought with *Polarities, and oppositions, and points of indifference between them,* but which has been long appreciated in its true worth and real nature, and consigned to its proper limits.

Thus this outline of the old Chinese symbols of thought, which have a purely metaphysical import, would lay before us the most recent error clothed in the most antique form—but the Chinese system is in itself very remarkable and important. The fundamental text of the old sacred book on this doctrine of unity and oppositions, and which may now be easily comprehended, runs thus, according to Remusat's literal translation: "The great first principle has engendered or produced two equations and differences, or primary rules of existence: but the two primary rules or two oppositions, namely, Yn and Yang, or repose and motion (the affirmative and negative as we might otherwise call them), have produced four signs or symbols; and the four symbols have produced the eight kona, or further combinations." These eight kona are kien, or ether, kui, or pure water, li, or pure fire, tchin, or thunder, siun, the wind, kan, common water, ken, a mountain, and kuen, the earth.

On this ancient basis of Chinese philosophy, proceeding from indifference to differences, was afterwards founded the rationalist system of Lao-tseu, whose name occurs somewhat earlier than that of Confucius. The Taosse, or disciples of Reason, as the followers of this philosopher entitle themselves, have very much degenerated, and have become a complete atheistical sect; though the blame of this must be attributed, not to the founder, but to his disciples only. It is however acknowledged that the atheistical principles of this dead science of reason, have been very widely diffused throughout the Chinese empire, and for a certain period were almost generally prevalent.

As it is necessary to keep in view a certain chronological order, in our investigations of the progressive development of Chinese intellect, I may here observe that, as far as European research has been able to ascertain, we may distinguish three principal and successive epochs in the history both of the religion and science of China. The first epoch is that of sacred tradition, and of the old constitution of the Chinese empire, and discloses those primitive views, and that primitive system of ethics, on which the empire was founded. The second, which we may fix about six centuries before our era, is the period of scientific philosophy, pursuing two opposite paths of inquiry. Confucius applied his attention entirely to the more practical study of ethics, with which, indeed, the old constitution, history, and sacred traditions of the Chinese were very intimately connected; and the pure morality of Confucius, which was the first branch of Chinese philosophy known in Europe, excited to a high degree the enthusiasm of many European scholars, who, by their too exclusive admiration, were prevented from forming a right estimate of the general character of Chinese philosophy.

Another system of philosophy, purely speculative and widely different from the practical and ethical doctrine of Confucius, was the system of Lao-tseu and his school, whence issued the above-mentioned rationalist sect of Taosse, that has at last fallen into atheism. As to the question whether Lao-tseu travelled into the remote West, or in case he came only as far as Western Asia, whether he derived his system from the Persian or Egyptian doctrines, or mediately from the Greek philosophy—this question I shall not here stop to discuss, for the matter is very doubtful in itself, and, were it even proved, still all the doctrines borrowed from the West were invested in a form purely Chinese, and clothed in quite a native garb. Those signs in the I-King, we have already spoken of, evidently comprise the germ of such an absolute, negative, and consequently atheistic rationalism—a mechanical play of idle abstractions. The third epoch in the progress of Chinese opinions is formed by the introduction of the Indian religion of Buddha or of Fo. The great revolution which had previously occurred in the old doctrines and manners of China; and the ruling spirit of that false and absolute rationalism, had already paved the way for the foreign religion of Buddha, which, of all the Pagan imitations of truth, occupies the lowest grade.

The old sacred traditions of the Chinese are not so overlaid, nor disfigured with fictions, as those of most other Asiatic nations; those of the Indians, for example, and of the early nations of Pagan Europe; but their traditions breathe the purer spirit of genuine history. Hence, the poetry of the Chinese is not mythological, like that of other nations, but is either lyrical, (as in the Shi-King, a book of sacred songs, composed or compiled by Confucius,) or is entirely confined to the representation of real life, and of the social relations—as in the modern tales and novels, several of which have been translated into the European languages.

The old traditions of the Chinese have many traits of a kindred character with, or at least of a strong resemblance to, the Mosaic revelation, and even to the sacred traditions of the nations of Western Asia, particularly the Persians; and in these traditions we find much that either corroborates the testimony of Holy Writ, or at least affords matter for further comparison. We have before mentioned the very peculiar manner in which the Chinese speak of the great Flood, and how their first progenitors struggled against the savage waters, and how this task was afterwards neglected by bad or improvident rulers, who, in consequence of this neglect, were brought to ruin.

I will cite but one instance, where the parallel is indeed remarkable. In the I-King, mention is made of the fallen dragon, or of the spirit of the dragon, that, for his presumption in wishing to ascend to heaven, was precipitated into the abyss; and the words in which this event is described are precisely the same, or at least very similar to those which our Scriptures apply to the rebel angel, and the Persian books to Ahriman. However, this dragon is whimsically, we might almost say, artlessly, made the sacred symbol of the Chinese Empire and the Emperor. The paternal power of the latter is understood in a much too absolute sense; not only is the Emperor styled the lord of heaven and earth, and even the sun of God, but his will is revered as the will of God, or rather completely identified with it; and even the most determined eulogists of the Chinese constitution and manners, cannot deny that the monarch is almost the object of a real worship. Christianity teaches that all power is from God; but it does not thereby declare that all power is one and the same with God. Even a dominion over nature and her powers is ascribed to the Emperor of China, as the illustrious lord of heaven and earth.

Moreover, no hereditary nobility, no classes separated by distinctions of birth, exist in this country, as in India. The Emperor, half identified with the Deity, had alone the privilege in ancient times of offering on the sacred heights of the great sacrifice to God. Some European writers have, from this circumstance, conceived the Chinese constitution to be theocratic; but if it be so, it is only in its outward form or original mould; for it would be difficult to show in it any trace of a true, vital theocracy. All that pomp of sacred ceremony and religious titles, so strangely absurd, forms a striking contrast with real history, and with that long succession of profligate and unfortunate reigns, and perpetual revolutions, which fill most of the pages of the Chinese annals. We should err greatly, were we to regard all these high imperial titles as the mere swell and exaggeration of Eastern phraseology. The Chinese speak of their celestial Empire of the Medium, as they call their country, in terms which no European writer would apply to a Christian state; and such, indeed, as the Scriptures and religious authors use in reference only to the kingdom of God. They cannot conceive it possible for the earth to contain two emperors at one and the same time, and own the sway of more than one such absolute lord and master. Hence, they look on every solemn foreign embassy as a debt of homage; nor is this sentiment the idle effect of vanity or fancy—it is a firm and settled belief, perfectly coinciding with the whole system of their religious and political doctrines.——

THE HINDOOS.

When Alexander the Great had attained the object of his most ardent desires, and, realizing the fabulous expedition of Bacchus and his train of followers, had at last reached India, the Greeks found this vast region, even on this side of the Ganges—(for that river, the peculiar object of Alexander's ambition, the conqueror, in despite of all his efforts, was unable to reach)—the Greeks found this country extensive, fertile, highly cultivated, populous, and filled with flourishing cities, as it was divided into a number of great and petty kingdoms. They found there an hereditary division of castes, such as still subsists; although they reckoned not four, but seven, a circumstance, however, which, as we shall see later, argues no essential difference in the division of Indian classes at that period. They remarked, also, that the country was divided into two religious parties or sects, the *Brachmans* and the *Samaneans*. By the first, the Greeks designated the followers of the religion of Brahma, as well as of Vishnoo and Siva, a religion which still subsists, and is more deeply rooted and more widely diffused and prevalent in India than any other religious system; distinguished as it is by its leading dogma of the transmigration of souls, which has exerted the mightiest influence on every department of thought, on the whole bearing of Indian philosophy, and on the whole arrangement of Indian life. But by the Greek denomination of *Samaneans* we must certainly understand the Buddhists, as, among the rude nations of central Asia, and in other countries, the priests of the religion of Fo bear at this day the name of *Schamans*. These priests indeed appear to be little better than mere sorcerers and jugglers, as are the priests of all idolatrous nations that are sunk to the lowest degree of barbarism and superstition. The word itself is pure Indian, and occurs frequently in the religious and metaphysical treatises of that people; for originally, and before it had received such a mean acceptation among those Buddhist nations, it had quite a philosophical sense, as it still has in the Sanscrit. This word denotes that equality of mind, or that deep internal equanimity, which, according to the Indian philosophy, must precede, and is indispensably requisite to the perfect union with the Godhead. In general, all the names by which Buddha, the priests of his religion, and its important and fundamental doctrines are known, whether in Thibet, or among the Mongul nations, in Siam, in Pegu, or in Japan—in general, we say, all those names are pure Indian words; for the tradition of all those nations, with unanimous accord, deduces the origin of this sect from India.

The name of Buddha, which the Chinese have changed or shortened into that of Fo, is rather an honorary appellation, and is expressive of the divine wisdom with which, in the opinion of his followers, he was endowed; or which rather, according to their belief, became visible in his person. The period of his existence is fixed by many at six hundred years, by others again at a thousand years, before the Christian era. His real and historical name was Gautama; and it is remarkable that the same name was borne by the author of one of the principal philosophical systems of the Hindoos, the Nyaya philosophy, the leading principles of which will be the subject of future consideration, when we come to speak of the Indian philosophy. Indeed, the dialectic spirit, which pervades the Nyaya philosophy, would seem to be of a kindred nature and like origin with the confused metaphysics of the Buddhists. But the names, notwithstanding their identity, denote two different persons; although even the founder of the dialectic system, like almost all other celebrated names in the ancient history, traditions and sciences of the Indians, figures in the character of a mythological personage. But we must first take a view of the state of manners, and the state of political civilization, in India, in order to be able to form a right judgment and estimate of the intellectual and scientific exertions of its inhabitants, and of the peculiar nature and tendency of the Indian opinions.

By the manner in which the Greek writers speak of the two religious parties into which Alexander found the country divided, it can scarcely be doubted that the Buddhists at that period were far more numerous, and more extensively diffused throughout India, than they are at the present day, and this inference is even corroborated by many historical vouchers of the Indians themselves. Although the Buddhists are now but an obscure sect of dissenters in the western peninsula, they are still tolerably numerous in several of its provinces; while, on the other hand, they have complete possession of the whole eastern and Indo-Chinese peninsula. Besides this sect, there are many other religious dissenters even in Hindostan; such, for instance, as the sect of *Jains*, who steer a middle course between the followers of the old and established religion of Brahma and the Buddhists; for, like the latter, they reject the Indian division and system of castes. * * * This singular phenomenon of Indian life has even some points of connection with a capital article of their creed, the doctrine of the transmigration of souls — a doctrine which will be later the subject of our inquiries, and which we shall endeavor to place in a nearer and clearer light. In showing the influence of the institution of castes on the state of manners in India, I may observe, in the first place, that in this division of the social ranks there is no distinct class of slaves, (as was indeed long ago remarked by the Greeks,) that is to say, no such class of bought slaves — no men, the property and merchandise of their fellow-men — as existed in ancient Greece and Rome, as exist even at this day among Mahometan nations; and, as in the case of the Negroes, are still to be found in the colonial possessions of the Christian and European states. The laboring class of the *Sudras* is undoubtedly not admitted to the high privileges of the first classes, and is in a state of great dependence upon these; but this very caste of Sudras has its hereditary and clearly defined rights. It is only by a crime, that a man in India can lose his caste, and the rights annexed to it. These rights are acquired by birth, except in the instance of the offspring of unlawful marriages between persons of different castes. The fate of these hapless wretches is indeed hard — harder, almost, than that of real slaves among other nations. Ejected, excommunicated as it were, loaded with malediction, they are regarded as the outcasts of society, yea, almost of humanity itself. This terrible exclusion, however, from the rights of citizenship, occurs only in certain clearly specified cases. There are even some cases of exception explicitly laid down, where a marriage with a person of different caste is permitted, or where at least the only consequence to the children of such marriage is a degradation to an inferior class of society. But the general rule is, that a lawful marriage can be contracted only with a woman of the same caste. Women participate in all the rights of their caste; in the high prerogatives of Brahmins, if they are of the sacerdotal race, although there are not and never were priestesses among the Indians, as among the other heathen nations of antiquity; or in the privileges of nobility, if they belong to the caste of the Cshatriyas. These privileges which belong and are secured to women, and this participation in the rights and advantages of their respective classes, must tend much, undoubtedly, to mitigate the injurious effects of polygamy. The latter custom has ever prevailed, and still prevails in India, though not to the same degree of licentiousness, nor with the same unlimited and despotic control as in Mahometan countries; but a plurality of wives is there permitted only under certain conditions, and with certain legal restrictions, consequently in that milder form under which it existed of old in the warm climes of Asia, and according to the patriarchal simplicity of the yet thinly peopled world. The much higher social rank, and better moral condition of the female sex in India, are apparent from those portraits of Indian life, which are drawn in their beautiful works of poetry, whether of a primitive or a later date, and from that deep feeling of tenderness, that affectionate regard and reverence, with which the character of woman and her domestic relations are invariably represented. These few examples suffice to show the moral effects of the Indian division of castes; and while they serve to defend this institution against a sweeping sentence of condemnation, or the indiscriminate censure of too partial prejudice, they place the subject in its true and proper light, and present alike the advantages and defects of the system.

* * * * * * *

When the Greeks, who accompanied or followed Alexander into India, numbered seven instead of four castes in that country, they did not judge inaccurately the outward condition of things, but they paid not sufficient attention to the Indian notion of castes; and their very enumeration of those castes proves they had some points of detail. In this enumeration, they assign the first rank to the *Brachmans*, or wise men; and by the artisans, they no doubt understood the trading and manufacturing class of the Vaisyas. The counsellors and intendants of kings and princes do not constitute a distinct caste, but are mere officers and functionaries, who, if they be lawyers, belong to, and must be taken from, the caste of Brahmins; though the other two upper castes are not always rigidly excluded from these functions. The class, again, that tends the breeding of cattle, and lives by the chase, forms not a distinct caste, but merely follows a peculiar kind of employment. And when the Greeks make two castes of the agriculturists and the warriors, they only mean to draw a distinction between the laborers and the masters, or the real proprietors of the soil. Even the name of Cshatriyas signifies landed proprietor; and as in the old Germanic constitution, the arriere-ban was composed of landed proprietors, and the very possession of the soil imposed on the nobility the obligation of military service; so, in the Indian constitution, the two ideas of property in land and military service, are indissolubly connected. Some modern inquirers have attached very great importance to the undoubtedly wide and remarkable separation of the fourth or menial caste of Sudras from the three upper castes. They have thought they perceived, also, a very great difference in the bodily structure and general physiognomy of this fourth caste from those of the others; and have thence concluded that the caste of Sudras is descended from a totally different race, some primitive and barbarous people whom a more civilized nation, to whom the three upper castes must have belonged, have conquered and subdued, and degraded to that menial condition, the lowest grade in the social scale—a grade to which the iron arm of law eternally binds them down. This hypothesis is, in itself, not very improbable; and it may be proved from history, that the like has really occurred in several Asiatic and even European countries. In the back-ground of old, mighty and civilized nations, we can almost always trace the primeval inhabitants of the country, who, dispossessed of their territory, have been either reduced to servitude by their conquerors, or have gradually been incorporated with them. These primitive inhabitants, when compared with their later and more civilized conquerors, appear indeed in general rude and barbarous, though we find among them a certain number of ancient customs and arts, which by no means tend to confirm the notion of an original and universal savage state of nature. It is possible that the same circumstances have occurred in India, though this is by no means a necessary inference, for humanity in its progress follows not one uniform course, but pursues various and widely different paths; and hitherto, at least, no adequate historical proof has, in my opinion, been adduced for the reality of such an occurrence in India. It has also been conjectured that the caste of warriors, or the princes and hereditary nobility, possessed originally greater power and influence; and that it is only by degrees the race of Brahmins has attained to that great preponderance which it displays in later times, and which it even still possesses. We find, indeed, in the old epic, mythological, and historical poems of the Indians, many passages which describe a contest between these two classes, and which represent the deified heroes of India victoriously defending the wise and pious Brahmins from the attacks of the fierce and presumptuous Cshatriyas. This account, however, is susceptible of another interpretation, and should not be taken exclusively in this political sense. That in the brilliant period of their ancient and national dynasties and governments, the princes and warlike nobility possessed greater weight and importance than at present, is quite in the nature of things, and appears indeed to have been undoubtedly the case. From many indications in the old Indian traditions and histories, it would appear that the caste of Cshatriyas was partially, at least, of foreign extraction; while those traditionary accounts constantly represent the caste of Brahmins as the highest class, and nobler part, nay, the corner-stone of the whole community.

The origin of an hereditary caste of warriors, when considered in itself, may be easily accounted for, and it is nowise contrary to the nature of things that, even in a state of society where legal rights are yet undefined, the son, especially the eldest, should govern and administer the territory or property which his deceased father possessed, and even in those cases where it was necessary, should take possession, administer, and defend this property by open force and the aid of his dependants.

But afterwards, when the social relations became more clearly fixed by law, and a union on a larger scale was formed by a general league, as the duties of military service were annexed to the soil, so the right to the soil was again determined by, and depended on, military service; now, in that primitive period of history, such a political union might have been formed by a common subordination to a higher power, or by a confederacy between several potentates; and this has really been the origin of an hereditary, landed nobility, in many countries.

The hereditary continuance or transmission of arts and trades, whereby the son pursues the occupation of the father, and learns and applies what the latter has discovered, has nothing singular in itself, and appears indeed to contain its own explanation. But it is not easy, or, at least, equally so, to account for the exclusive distribution and the exact and rigid separation of castes, particularly by any religious motives and principles, which are, however, indubitably connected with this institution. Still less can we understand the existence of a great, hereditary class of priests, eternally divided from the rest of the community, such as existed both in India and Egypt. To comprehend this strange phenomenon, we must endeavor to discover its origin, and trace it back, as far as is possible, to the primitive ages of the world. If, for the sake of brevity, I have used the expression, "a class of hereditary priests," I ought to add, in order to explain my meaning more clearly, that the word *priests* must not be taken in that literal sense which antiquity attached to it; that the Brahmins are not confined merely to the functions of prayer, but are strictly and eminently theologians, since they alone are permitted to read and interpret the Vedas, while the other castes can read only with their sanction such passages of those sacred writings as are adapted to their circumstances, and the fourth caste are entirely prohibited from hearing any portion of them. The Brahmins are also the lawyers and physicians of India, and hence the Greeks did not designate them erroneously, when they termed them *the caste of philosophers.* * *

* * * Among the Indians, the ruling principle of existence was the doctrine of the transmigration of souls, which appears indeed to be the most characteristic of all their opinions, and was, by its influence on real life, by far the most important. We must in the first place remember, and keep well in our minds, that, among those nations of primitive antiquity, the doctrine of the immortality of the soul was not a mere probable hypothesis, which, as with many moderns, needs laborious researches and diffuse argumentations, in order to produce conviction on the mind. Nay, we can hardly give the name of faith to this primitive conception; for it was a lively certainty, like the feeling of one's own being, and of what is actually present; and this firm belief in a mere future existence exerted its influence on all sublunary affairs, and was often the motive of mightier deeds and enterprises, than any more earthly interest could inspire. I said above, that the doctrine of the transmigration of souls was not unconnected with the Indian system of castes; for the most honorable appellation of a Brahmin is *Tvija*, that is to say, a second time born, or regenerated. On one hand, this appellation refers to that spiritual renovation and second birth of a life of purity consecrated to God, as in this consists the true calling of a Brahmin, and the special purpose of his caste. On the other hand, this term refers to the belief that the soul, after many transmigrations through various forms of animals, and various stages of natural existence, is permitted in certain cases, as a peculiar recompense, when it has gone through its prescribed cycle of migrations, to return to the world, and be born in the class of Brahmins. This doctrine of the transmigration of souls through various bodies of animals or other forms of existence, and even through more than one repetition of human life (whether such migrations were intended as the punishment of souls for their viciousness and impiety, or as trials for their further purification and amendment)—this doctrine which has always been, and is still so prevalent in India, was held likewise by the ancient Egyptians. This accordance in the faith of these two ancient nations, established beyond all doubt by historical testimony, is indeed remarkable; and even in the minutest particulars on the course of migration allotted to souls, and on the stated periods and cycles of that migration, the coincidence is often perfectly exact. In this doctrine there was a noble element of truth—the feeling that man, since he has gone astray and wandered so far from his God, must needs exert many efforts, and undergo a long and painful pilgrimage, before he can join the source of all perfection;—

the firm conviction and positive certainty that nothing defective, impure, or defiled with earthly stains, can enter the pure region of perfect spirits, or be eternally united to God; and that thus, before it can attain to this blissful end, the immortal soul must pass through long trials and many purifications. It may now well be conceived, and indeed the experience of this life would prove it, that suffering, which deeply pierces the soul, anguish, that convulses all the members of existence, may contribute, or may even be necessary to the deliverance of the soul from all alloy and pollution, as, to borrow a comparison from natural objects, the generous metal is melted down in fire and purged from its dross. It is certainly true that the greater the degeneracy and the degradation of man, the nearer his approximation to the brute; and when the transmigration of the immortal soul through the bodies of various animals is merely considered as the punishment of its former transgressions, we can very well understand the opinion which supposes that man, who, by his crimes and the abuse of his reason, had descended to the level of the brute, should at last be transformed into the brute itself. But what could have given rise to the opinion that the transmigration of souls through the bodies of beasts was the road or channel of amendment, was destined to draw the soul nearer to infinite perfection, and even to accomplish its total union with the Supreme Being, from whom, in all appearance, it seemed calculated to remove it further? And as regards a return to the present state and existence of man, what thinking person would ever wish to return to a life divided and fluctuating as it is, between desire and disgust, wasted in internal and external strife, and which, though brightened by a few scattered rays of truth, is still encompassed with the dense clouds of error;—even though this return to earthly existence should be accomplished in the Brahminical class so highly revered in India, or in the princely and royal race so highly favored by fortune? There is in all this a strange mixture and confusion of the ideas of this world with those of the next; and how the latter is separated from the former by an impassable gulf, they seem not to have been sufficiently aware. Both these ancient nations, the Egyptians as well as the Indians, regarded, with few exceptions, the Metempsychosis, not as an object of joyful hope, but rather as a calamity impending over the soul; and whether they considered it to be a punishment for earthly transgressions, or a state of probation—a severe but preparatory trial of purification—they still looked on it as a calamity, which to avert or to mitigate, they deemed that no attempt, no act, no exertion, no sacrifice, ought to be spared.

In the manner, however, in which these two nations conceived this doctrine, there was a striking and fundamental difference; and if the leading tenet was the same among both, the views which each connected with it were very dissimilar. Deprived, as we are, of the old books and original writings of the Egyptians, we are unable perfectly to comprehend and seize their peculiar ideas on this subject, and state them with the same assurance as we can those of the Indians, whose ancient writings we now possess in such abundance, and which in all main points perfectly agree with the accounts of the ancient classics. But we are left to infer the ideas of the Egyptians on the Metempsychosis only from their singular treatment of the dead and the bodies of the deceased; from that sepulchral art (if I may use the expression) which with them acquired a dignity and an importance, and was carried to a pitch of refinement, such as we find among no other people; from that careful and costly consecration of the corpse, which we still regard with wonder and astonishment in their mummies and other monuments. That all these solemn preparations, and the religious rites which accompanied them, that the inscriptions on the tombs and mummies had all a religious meaning and object, and were intimately connected with the doctrine of the transmigration of souls, can admit of no doubt, though it is a matter of greater difficulty to ascertain with precision the peculiar ideas they were meant to express. Did the Egyptians believe that the soul did not separate immediately from the body which it has ceased to animate, but only on the decay and putrefaction of the corpse? Or did they wish, by their art of embalmment, to preserve the body from decay, in order to deliver the soul from the dreaded transmigration? The Egyptian treatment of the dead would certainly seem to imply a belief that, for some time at least after death, there existed a certain connection between the soul and body. Yet we cannot adopt this supposition to an unqualified extent, as it would be in contradiction to those symbolical representations that so frequently occur in Egyptian art, and in which the soul, immediately after death, is represented as summoned before the judgment-seat of God, severely accused by the hostile demon, but defended by the friendly and guardian spirit, who employs every resource to procure the deliverance and acquittal of the soul. Or did the Egyptians think that by all these rites, as by so many magical expedients, they would keep off the malevolent fiend from the soul, and obtain for it the succour of good and friendly divinities? Now, that the gates of hieroglyphic science have been at last opened, we may trust that a further progress in the science will disclose to us more satisfactory information on all these topics.

The Indians, however, who always remained total strangers to the mode of burial and treatment of the dead practised in Egypt, adopted a very different course to procure the deliverance of the human soul from transmigration: they had recourse to philosophy, to the highest aspirings of thought towards God, to a total and lasting immersion of feeling in the unfathomable abyss of the divine essence. They have never doubted that by this means a perfect union with the Deity might be obtained even in this life, and that thus the soul, emancipated from all mutation and migration through the various forms of animated nature in this world of illusion, might remain forever united with its God. Such is the object to which all the different systems of Indian philosophy tend —such is the term of all their inquiries. This philosophy contains a multitude of the sublimest reflections on the separation from all earthly things, and on the union with the Godhead; and there is no high conception in this department of metaphysics, unknown to the Hindoos. But this absorption of all thought and all consciousness in God—this solitary enduring feeling of internal and eternal union with the Deity, they have carried to a pitch and extreme that may almost be called a moral and intellectual self-annihilation. This is the same philosophy, though in a different form, which, in the history of European intellect and science, has received the denomination of *mysticism*. The possible excesses, the perilous abyss in this philosophy has been in general acknowledged, and even pointed out in particular cases, where egotism or pride has been detected under a secret disguise, or where this total abstraction of thought and feeling has spurned all limit, measure, and law. In general, however, the European mind, by its more temperate and harmonious constitution, by the greater variety of its attainments, and, above all, by the purer and fuller light of revealed truth, has been preserved from those aberrations of mysticism which in India have been carried to such a fearful extent, not only in speculation, but in real life and practice; and which, transcending as they do all the limits of human nature, far exceed the bounds of possibility, or what men have in general considered as such. And the apparently incredible things which the Greeks related more than two thousand years ago, respecting the recluses of India, or *Gymnosophists*, as they called those Yogis, are found to exist even at the present day; and ocular experience has fully corroborated the truth of their narratives.

* * * * * *

Of the political history of India, little can be said, for the Indians scarcely possess any regular history — any works to which we should give the denomination of historical; for their history is interwoven and almost confounded with mythology, and is to be found only in the old mythological works, especially in their two great national and epic poems, the Ramayan and the Mahabarat, and in the eighteen Puranas (the most select and classical of the popular and mythological legends of India), and perhaps in the traditionary history of particular dynasties and provinces; and even the works we have mentioned are not merely of a mythohistorical, but in a great measure of a theological and philosophical purport. The more modern history of Hindostan, from the first Mahometan conquest at the commencement of the eleventh century of our era, can indeed be traced with pretty tolerable certainty; but as this portion of Indian history is unconnected with, and incapable of illustrating the true state and progress of the intellectual refinement of the Hindoos, it is of no importance to our immediate object. The more ancient history of that country, particularly in the earlier period, is mostly fabulous, or, to characterize it by a softer, and at the same time more correct name, a history purely mythic and traditionary.; and it would be no easy task to divest the real and authentic history of ancient India of the garb of mythology and poetical tradition; a task which at least has not yet been executed with adequate critical acumen.

Chronology, too, shares the same fate with the sister science of history, for in the early period it is fabulous, and in the more modern, it is often not sufficiently precise and accurate. The number of years assigned to the first three epochs of the world must be considered as possessing an astronomical import, rather than as furnishing any criterion for an historical use. It is only the fourth and last period of the world— the age of progressive misery and all-prevailing wo, which the Indians term Caliyug—that we can in any way consider an historical epoch; and this, the duration of which is computed at four thousand years, began about a thousand years before the Christian era. Of the progress and term of this period of the world, considered in reference to the history of mankind, the Indians entertain a very simple notion. They believe that the condition of mankind will become at first much worse, but will be afterwards ameliorated. The regular historical epoch, when the chronology of India begins to acquire greater certainty, and from which indeed it is ordinarily computed, is the age of King Vikramaditya, who reigned in the more civilized part of India, somewhat earlier than the Emperor Augustus, in the West, perhaps about sixty years before our era. It was at the court of this monarch, that nine of the most celebrated sages and poets of the second era of Indian literature flourished; and among these was Calidas, the author of the beautiful dramatic poem of Sacontala, so generally known by the English and German translations. It was in the age of Vikramaditya, that the later poetry and literature of India, of which Calidas was so bright an ornament, reached its full bloom. The elder Indian poetry, particularly the two great epic poems above mentioned, entirely belong to the early and more fabulous ages of the world; so far at least as the poets themselves are assigned to those ages, and figure in some degree, as fabulous personages. We may, however, observe that in the style of poetry, in art, and even in the language itself, there reigns a very great difference between these primitive heroic poems, and the works of Calidas and other contemporary poets—the difference is at least as great as that which exists between Homer and Theocritus, or the other Bucolic poets of Greece. The oldest of the two epic poems of the Indians, the Ramayana, by the poet Valimki, celebrates Rama, his love for a royal princess, the beautiful Sita, and his conquest of Lanka, or the modern Isle of Ceylon. Although in the old historical Sagas of the Indians, we find mention made of far-ruling monarchs and all-conquering heroes, still these traditions seem to show, as in the instance first cited, that in the oldest, as in the latest times, prior to foreign conquest, India was not united in one great monarchy, but was generally parcelled out into a variety of states; and this fact serves to prove that such has ever been in general the political condition of that country. The whole body of ancient Indian traditions and mythological history is to be found in the other great epic of the Indians, the Mahabarata, whose author, or at least compiler, was Vyasa, the founder of the Vedanta philosophy, the most esteemed and most prevalent of all the philosophical systems of the Hindoos.

* * * * * *

In the whole Indian philosophy, there are in fact only three different modes of thought, or three systems absolutely divergent, and we shall give a sufficiently clear idea of these systems, if we say that the first is founded on nature, the second on thought, or on the thinking self, and the third attaches itself exclusively to the revelation comprised in the Vedas. The first system, which seems to be one of the most ancient, bears the name of the Sanchyá philosophy—a name which signifies "the philosophy of Numbers." This is not to be understood in the Pythagorean sense, that numbers are the principle of all things, or according to the very similar principle laid down in the books of I-King, where we find the eight kona, or the symbolic, primary lines of all existence. But the Sanchyá system bears this name because it reckons successively the first principles of all things and of all being to the number of four or five-and-twenty. Among these first principles, it assigns the highest place to Nature, the second to understanding, and by this is meant not merely human understanding, but general and even Infinite Intelligence; so that we may consider this system as a very partial philosophy of Nature; and indeed it has been regarded by some Indian writers as atheistical—a censure in which the learned Englishman, Mr. Colebrooke (to whose extracts and notices we are indebted for our most precise information on this whole branch of Indian literature), seems almost inclined to concur. This system was, however, by no means a coarse materialism, or a denial of the Divinity and of everything sacred. The doubts expressed in the passages cited by Mr. Colebrooke, are directed far more against the Creation than against God; they regard the motive which could have induced the Supreme Being, the Spirit of infinite perfection, to create the external world, and the possibility of such a creation.

This Sanchyá Philosophy would be more properly designated in our modern philosophic phraseology as a system of complete Dualism, where two substances are represented as coexistent—on one hand, a self-existent energy of Nature, which emanated, or eternally emanates, from itself; and on the other hand, eternal truth, or the Supreme and Infinite Mind.

The Indian Philosophers in general were so inclined to regard the whole outward world of sense, as the product of illusion, as a vain and idle apparition, that we can well imagine they were unable to reconcile the creation of such a world (which appeared to them a world of darkness, or perhaps, on a somewhat higher scale, as an intermediate state of illusion,) with their mystical notion of the infinite perfection of the Supreme Being and Eternal Spirit. For even in Ethics they were wont to place the idea of Supreme Perfection in a state of absolute repose, but not (at least to an equal degree) in the state of active energy or exertion. Great as the error of such a system of dualism may be, there is yet a mighty difference between a philosophy which denies, or at least misconceives, the Creation, and one which denies the existence of the Deity; for such atheism never occurred to the minds of those philosophers. The doctrine of a primary self-existing energy in Nature, or of the eternity of the Universe, may, in a practical point of view, appear as gross an error, but in philosophy we must make accurate distinctions, and forbear to place this ancient dualism on the same level with that coarse materialism, that destructive and atheistic Atomical philosophy, or any other doctrines professed by the later sects of a dialectic Rationalism.

Valuable, undoubtedly, as are such extracts and communications from the originals in a branch of human science still so little known, yet they will not alone suffice, and, without a certain philosophic flexibility of talent in the inquirer, they will fail to afford him a proper insight into the true nature, the real spirit and tendency of those ancient systems of philosophy. That the Indian philosophy, even when it has started from the most opposite principles, and when its circuitous or devious course has branched more or less widely from the common path, is sure to wind round, and fall into the one general track—the uniform term of all Indian philosophy—is well exemplified by the second part of the Sanchyá system (called the Yoga philosophy), where we find a totally different principle proclaimed; and while it utterly abandons the primary doctrine of a self-existent principle in Nature laid down in the first part of the philosophy, it unfolds those maxims of Indian mysticism which recur in every department of Hindoo literature. That total absorption in the one thought of the Deity, that entire abstraction from all the impressions and notions of sense—that suspension of all outward, and in part even of inward life, effected by the energy of a will tenaciously fixed and entirely concentrated on a single point, and by which, according to the belief of the Indians, miraculous power and supernatural knowledge are attained—are held up in the second part of the Sanchyá system as the highest term of all mental exertion. The word, Yoga, signifies the complete union of all our thoughts and faculties with God, by which alone the soul can be freed, that is, delivered from the unhappy lot of transmigration; and this, and this only, forms the object of all Indian philosophy.

The Indian name of Yogi is derived from the same word, which designates this philosophy. The Indian Yogi is a hermit or penitent, who, absorbed in this mystic contemplation, remains often for years fixed immovably to a single spot. In order to give a lively representation of a phenomenon so strange to us, which appears totally incredible and almost impossible, although it has been repeatedly attested by eye-witnesses, and is a well-ascertained historical fact, I will extract from the drama of Sacontalá by the poet Calidas, a description of a Yogi, remarkable for its vivid accuracy, or, to use the expression of the German commentator, its fearful beauty. King Dushmanta inquires of Indra's charioteer the sacred abode of him whom he seeks; and to this the charioteer replies:* "A little beyond the grove, where you see a pious Yogi, motionless as a pollard, holding his thick bushy hair and fixing his eyes on the solar orb. Mark— his body is half covered with a white ant's edifice made of raised clay; the skin of a snake supplies the place of his sacerdotal thread, and part of it girds his loins; a number of knotty plants encircle and wound his neck; and surrounding birds' nests almost conceal his shoulders." We must not take this for the invention of fancy, or the exaggeration of a poet; the accuracy of this description is confirmed by the testimony of innumerable eye-witnesses, who recount the same fact, and in precisely similar colors. During that period of wonderful phenomena and supernatural powers—the first three centuries of the Christian church—we meet with only one Simon Stylites, or columnstander; and his conduct is by no means held up by Christian writers as a model of imitation, but is regarded, at best, as an extraordinary exception permitted on certain special grounds. In the Indian forests and deserts, and in the neighborhood of those holy places of pilgrimage mentioned above, there are many hundreds of these hermits—those strange human phenomena of the highest intellectual abstraction or delusion. Even the Greeks were acquainted with them, and, among so many other wonders, make mention of them, in their description of India, under the name of the Gymnosophists. Formerly such accounts would have been regarded as incredible, and as exceeding the bounds of possibility; but such conjectures can be of no avail against historical facts repeatedly attested and undeniably proved. Now that men are better acquainted with the wonderful flexibility of human organization, and with those marvellous powers which slumber concealed within it, they are less disposed to form light and hasty decisions on phenomena of this description. The whole is indeed a magical intellectual self-exaltation, accomplished by the energy of the will concentrated on a single point: and this concentration of the mind, when carried to this excess, may lead not merely to a figurative, but to a real intellectual self-annihilation, and to the disorder of all thought, even of the brain. While on the one hand we must remain amazed at the strength of a will so tenaciously and perseveringly fixed on an object purely spiritual, we must, on the other hand, be filled with profound regret at the sight of so much energy wasted for a purpose so erroneous, and in a manner so appalling.

The second species of Indian philosophy, totally different from the other two kinds, and which proceeds not from Nature, but from the principle of thought and from the thinking self, is comprised in the Nyayá system, whose founder was Gautama, a personage whom several of the earlier investigators of Indian literature, particularly Dr. Taylor, in his Translation of the "Prabodha Chandrodaya" (page 116), have confounded with the founder of the Buddhist sect, as both bear the same name. But a closer inquiry has proved them to be distinct persons; and Mr. Colebrooke himself finds greater points of coincidence or affinity between the Sanchyá philosophy and Buddhism, than between the latter and the Nyayá system. This Nyayá philosophy, proceeding from the act of thought, comprises in the doctrine of particulars, distinctions and subdivisions, the application of the thinking principle; and this part of the system embraces all which among the Greeks went under the name of logic or dialectic; and which with us is partly classed under the same head. Very many writings and commentaries have been devoted to the detailed treatment and exposition of these subjects, which the Indians seem to have discussed with almost the same diffuseness, or at least copiousness, as the Greeks. Like the Indians, the learned Englishman, who has first unlocked to our view this department of Indian literature, has paid comparatively most attention to this second part of the Nyayá philosophy. But all this logical philosophy, though it may furnish one more proof (if such be necessary) of the extreme richness, variety, and refinement of the intellectual culture of the Hindoos, yet possesses no immediate interest for the object we here propose to ourselves. Mr. Colebrooke remarks, however, that the funda-

---

* We have transcribed Sir William Jones' own words, as given in his translation of Sacontalá.

mental tenets of this philosophy comprise, as indeed is evident, not merely a logic in the ordinary acceptation of the word, but the metaphysics of all logical science. On this part of the subject, I could have wished that in the authentic extracts he has given us from the Sancrit originals, he had more distinctly educed the leading doctrines of the system, and thus furnished us with adequate data for forming a judgment on the general character of this philosophy, as well as on its points of coincidence with other systems, and with the philosophy of the Buddhists. For although it appears to be well ascertained that the religion of Buddha sprang from some perverted system of Hindoo philosophy, yet the points of transition to such a religious creed existing in the Indian systems of philosophy have not yet been clearly pointed out. The Vedanta philosophy must here evidently be excepted; for to this Buddhism is as much opposed as to the old Indian religion of the Vedas. Moreover that endless confusion and unintelligibleness of the Buddhist metaphysics, which we have before spoken of, may first be traced to the source of Idealism; though in the progress of that philosophy, many errors have been associated with it, errors which even, in its origin, were most widely removed from it; for every system of error asserts and even believes that it is perfectly consistent, though in none is such consistency found.

The basis and prevailing tendency of the Nyayá system (to judge from the extracts with which we have been furnished) is most decidedly ideal. On the whole we can very well conceive that a system of philosophy beginning with the highest act of thought, or proceeding from the thinking self, should run into a course of the most decided and absolute idealism, and that the general inclination of the Indian philosophers to regard the whole external world of sense as vain illusion, and to represent individual personality as absorbed in the Godhead by the most intimate union, should have given birth to a complete system of self-delusion—a diabolic self-idolatry, very congenial with the principles of that most ancient of all anti-christian sects—the Buddhists.

The Indian authorities cited by Colebrooke impute to the second part of the Nyayá philosophy a strong leaning to the atomical system. We must here recollect that, as the Indian mind pursued the most various and opposite paths of inquiry even in philosophy, there were besides the six most prevalent philosophic systems, recognized as generally conformable to religion, several others in direct opposition to the established doctrines on the Deity and on religion. Among these the Charvacâ philosophy, which, according to Mr. Colebrooke, comprises the metaphysics of the sect of Jains, deserves a passing notice. It is a system of complete materialism founded on the atomical doctrines, such as Epicurus taught, and which met with so much favor and adhesion in the declining ages of Greece and Rome; doctrines which several moderns have revived in latter times, but which the profound investigations of natural philosophy, now so far advanced, will scarcely ever permit to take root again.

The third species or branch of Indian philosophy, is that which is attached to the Vedas, and to the sacred revelation and traditions they contain. The first part of this philosophy—the Mimansá—is, according to Mr. Colebrooke, more immediately devoted to the interpretation of the Vedas, and most probably contains the fundamental rules of interpretation, or the leading principles, whereby independent reason is made to harmonize with the word of revelation conveyed by sacred tradition. The second or finished part of the system is called the Vedanta philosophy. The last word in this term, "Vedanta," which is compounded of two roots, is equivalent to the German word *ende* (end), or still more to the Latin, *finis*, and denotes the end or ultimate object of any effort; and so the entire term Vedanta will signify a philosophy which reveals the true sense, the internal spirit, and the proper object of the Vedas, and of the primitive revelation of Brahma comprised therein. This Vedanta philosophy is the one which now generally exerts the greatest influence on Indian literature and Indian life; and it is very possible that some of the six recognized, or at least tolerated, systems of philosophy, may have been purposely thrown into the back-ground, or, when they clashed too rudely with the principles of the prevailing system, have been softened down by their partisans, and have thus come to us in that state. A wide field is here opened to the future research and critical inquiries of Indian scholars.

This Vedanta philosophy is, in its general tendency, a complete system of Pantheism; but not the rigid, mathematical, abstract, negative Pantheism of some modern thinkers; for such a total denial of all personality in God, and of all freedom in man, is incompatible with the attachment which the Vedanta philosophy professes for sacred tradition and ancient mythology; and accordingly a modified, poetical, and half-mythological system of Pantheism, may here naturally be expected, and actually exists. Even in the doctrine of the immortality of the soul, and of the Metempsychosis, the personal existence of the human soul, inculcated by the ancient faith, is not wholly denied or rejected by this more modern system of philosophy; though on the whole it certainly is not exempt from the charge of Pantheism. But all the systems of Indian philosophy tend more or less to one practical aim—namely, the final deliverance and eternal emancipation of the soul from the old calamity—the dreaded fate—the frightful lot—of being compelled to wander through the dark regions of nature—through the various forms of the brute creation—and to change ever anew its terrestrial shape. The second point in which the different systems of Indian philosophy mostly agree is this, that the various sacrifices prescribed for this end in the Vedas, are not free from blame or vice, partly on account of the effusion of blood necessarily connected with animal sacrifice — and partly on account of the inadequacy of such sacrifices to the final deliverance of the soul, useful and salutary though they be in other respects.

The general and fundamental doctrine of the Metempsychosis has rendered the destruction of animals extremely repulsive to Indian feelings, from the strong apprehension that a case may occur where, unconsciously and innocently, one may violate or injure the soul of some former relative in its present integument. But even the Vedas themselves inculcate the necessity of that sublime science which rises above nature, for the attainment of the full and final deliverance of the soul; as is expressed in an old remarkable passage of the Vedas, thus literally translated by Mr. Colebrooke.* "Man must recognise the soul—man must separate it from nature—then it comes not again—then it comes not again." These last words signify, Then the soul is delivered from the danger of a return to earth — from the misfortune of transmigration, and it remains forever united to God; a union which can be obtained only by that pure separation from nature, which is that sublimest science, invoked in the first words of this passage.

Animal sacrifices for the souls of the departed, particularly for those of deceased parents, which were regarded as the most sacred duty of the son and of the posterity, were among those religious usages which occupied an important place in the patriarchal ages, and were most deeply interwoven with the whole arrangement of life in that primitive period, as is evident from all those Indian rites, and the system of doctrines akin to them. These sacrifices are certainly of very ancient origin, and may well have been derived from the mourning father of mankind, and the first pair of hostile brothers. To these may afterwards have been added all that multitude of religious rites and doctrines, or marvellous theories respecting the immortal soul and its ulterior destinies. Hence the indispensable obligation of marriage for the Brahmins, in order to insure the blessing of legitimate offspring, regarded as one of the highest objects of existence in the patriarchal ages, for the prayers of the son only could obtain the deliverance, and secure the repose, of a departed parent's soul; and this was one of his most sacred duties. The high reverence for women, among the Indians, rests on the same religious notion, as is expressed by the old poet in these lines:

"Woman is man's better half,
Woman is man's bosom friend,
Woman is redemption's source,
From Woman springs the liberator."

This last line signifies, what we mentioned above, that the son is the Liberator appointed by God, to deliver by prayer the soul of his deceased father. The poet then continues:— "Women are the friends of the solitary—they solace him with their sweet converse; like to a father, in discharge of duty, consoling as a mother in misfortune."

We should scarcely conceive it possible (and it certainly tends to prove the original power, copiousness and flexibility of the human mind) that, by the side of a false mysticism totally sunk and lost in the abyss of the eternally incomprehensible and unfathomable, like the Indian philosophy, a rich, various, beautiful and highly-wrought poetry should have existed. The Epic narrative of the old Indian poems bears a great resemblance to the Homeric poetry, in its inexhaustible copiousness, in the touching simplicity of its antique forms, in justness of feeling, and accuracy of delineation. Yet in its subjects, and in the prevailing tone of its Mythological fictions, this Indian Epic poetry is characterized by a style of fancy incomparably more gigantic, such as occasionally prevails in the mythology of Hesiod—in the accounts of the old Titanic wars—or in the fabulous world of Æschylus, and of the Doric Pindar. In the tenderness of amatory feeling, in the description of female beauty, of the character and domestic relations of woman, the Indian poetry may be compared to the purest and noblest effusions of Christian poesy; though, on the whole, from the thoroughly mythical nature of its subjects, and from the rhythmical forms of its speech, it bears a greater resemblance to that of the ancients. Among the latter poets, Calidas, who is the most renowned and esteemed in the dramatic poetry of the Indians, might be called, by way of comparison, an Idyllic and sentimental Sophocles.

---

* See Colebrooke's article on the Vedas, in the eighth volume of Asiatic Researches.

NOVALIS. (FRIEDRICH VON HARDENBERG).

Born 1772. Died 1801.

Novalis is known as the associate of Tieck and the Schlegels in establishing the Romantic School of Poetry which blossomed in Germany toward the close of the last century. But Novalis possesses a significance independent of any clique, and, amid this famed constellation, shines as a particular star, with proper and individual lustre. The literary firmament of Germany has many greater lights, but none fairer. His contributions to the national literature are insignificant in extent, and consist, for the most part, of fragments and rhapsodies; but the little he wrote is instinct with a rare and noble spirit, and the effect has been altogether disproportionate to the bulk.

A singular charm invests this youth. For youth he was at the time of his death. His premature decease enhances the interest created by his lofty aims and his deep-eyed enthusiasm, imparting a certain ideal and heroic beauty to the early lost, whose germ of golden promise was not permitted to unfold in this present. Purity of heart, religious fervor, deep poetic feeling, and mystic inwardness, combined with true philosophic genius and scientific attainments far above the standard of general scholarship, constitute his distinguishing characteristics.

Friedrich von Hardenberg was born in the county of Mansfeld, in Saxony. His father (Baron von Hardenberg) and his mother were members of the Moravian Communion, profoundly religious, without narrowness or bigotry. He was one of eleven children, all of whom are said to have been distinguished by remarkable endowments of mind and heart. As a child, he was weakly, and discovered but little intellect. But after a dangerous illness, which occurred in his ninth year, he seemed to wake as from a dream, and thenceforward showed himself a youth of rare promise. He studied successively at the universities of Jena, Leipzig and Wittemberg, but chose a practical calling for his pursuit, in preference to the learned professions, and held an office under his father, who was director of the government salt-works in Saxony.

The critical event of his life was the death of his betrothed, Sophie v. K., who is represented as a being of preternatural beauty of person and of soul. "The first glimpse," says Tieck,* "of this beautiful and wondrous lovely form determined his whole life; nay, we may say, that the sentiment which penetrated and animated him became the theme of his whole life." * * * "All who knew this wonderful beloved of our friend, are agreed that no description can express with what a grace and heavenly charm this unearthly being moved, what beauty shone around her, what pathos and majesty invested her. Novalis became a poet whenever he spoke of her." She died the day but one succeeding her fifteenth birth-day, the 19th March, 1797. "No one dared to communicate the tidings to Novalis. At length, his brother Carl undertook it. The mourner locked himself up for three days and nights, and then journeyed to Arnstadt, that, with faithful friends, he might be nearer the beloved spot which now concealed the remains of this most precious being." * * * "At this period, Novalis lived only in his grief; it became natural to him to regard the visible and the invisible world as one, and to distinguish between life and death only by his longing for the latter. At the same time, life became to him transfigured, and his whole being was dissolved as in a lucid, conscious dream of a higher existence."

Novalis died within four years from the date of this affliction. That term comprises nearly all his writings.

"Since he had so far outstripped his age, his country was authorized to expect extraordinary things of him, had not this early death overtaken him. The unfinished writings he has left behind him have already wrought much; many of his great thoughts will exert their inspiration in the future, and noble minds and deep thinkers will be enlightened and inflamed by the scintillations of his spirit."

---

* See the biographical sketch prefixed to Tieck and Fr. Schlegel's edition of Novalis' works, from which this account is taken.

"Novalis was tall, slender, and of noble proportions. He wore his light-brown hair in pendent locks; his hazel eye was clear and gleaming; and the complexion of his countenance, especially of the intellectual forehead, almost transparent." * * * "Profile and expression resembled very nearly the Evangelist John, as we see him in the glorious great picture of A. Dürer, preserved at Nürnberg and München."

"His conversation was lively and loud, his gesticulation noble. I have never seen him wearied; even when we continued the conversation far into the night, he put a stop to it only by an effort of the will, in order to rest, and still read before he slept. Ennui he knew not, even in oppressive company with mediocre heads, for he was sure to discover some person who could impart to him a new knowledge which might be of use to him, insignificant as it seemed. His kindliness, his open communication, made him everywhere beloved. His skill in the art of conversation was so great, that inferior heads never perceived how far he overlooked them. Though in conversation he loved best to uncover the depths of the soul, and spoke with enthusiasm of the regions of the invisible, he was yet frolicsome as a child, jested with unembarrassed cheerfulness, and gave himself to the jests of the company. Without vanity or pride of learning, a stranger to all affectation and hypocrisy, he was a genuine, true man, the purest and loveliest embodiment of a lofty, immortal mind."

"His true studies, for several years, had been philosophy and physics. In the latter, his observations, combinations, and surmises, often outstripped his time. In philosophy, he studied especially Spinoza and Fichte. * * * His knowledge of mathematics and the mechanic arts, especially mining, was remarkable. On the other hand, he was but little interested in the fine arts. Music he loved much, but had only a superficial knowledge of it; to sculpture and painting his mind was not much drawn, although he could express the most original ideas and the highest surmises respecting all these arts. Thus I remember, e.g. a controversy respecting landscape-painting, in which I could not comprehend his view; but the excellent landscape-painter, Friedrich, in Dresden, has since actualized it, in great part, out of his own rich, poetic mind. * * * Goethe had long been his study; he preferred before all other works Wilhelm Meister, as little as one would suppose it, from his severe criticism of this work in his Fragments." * * *

"It had become with him the most natural view to regard the commonest, nearest, as miraculous, and the strange, the supernatural, as something common. Thus, every-day life itself environed him like a wondrous tale, and that region which most men but surmise or doubt, as distant, incomprehensible, was to him a beloved home. Thus he invented, unbribed by examples, a new mode of representation; and in many-sidedness of reference, in his view of love, in his faith in it—as for him, at once, instructress, wisdom, religion; — in that a single great life-moment and one deep pain and loss became the substance of his poetry and his contemplation, he alone among moderns resembles the sublime Dante, and sings to us, like him, an unfathomable mystic song, very different from that of many imitators who think they can put on and put off mysticism like an ornament. Therefore is, also, his Romance* consciously and unconsciously but the representation of his own mind and destiny; as he himself makes his Heinrich say, in the fragment of the second part, that destiny and mind are names of one idea."

Novalis did not leave the Lutheran Church for the Church of Rome, as has been falsely asserted.†

---

* Heinrich von Ofterdingen.

† See Tieck's preface to the fifth edition of Novalis' works, in which he says: "I may affirm that to my friend Hardenberg this transition into another Christian Communion from the Lutheran, in which he was born, was *utterly impossible.*" This fifth edition excludes the essay entitled "Christianity or Europe," which it seems had been inserted in the fourth edition without Tieck's consent, by Fr. von Schlegel, as seeming to favor Romanism. This essay, when offered for publication in the Athenæum, in 1799, had been rejected by a committee of the friends of the author, consisting of Tieck, the two Schlegels, and Schelling, as "weak and unsatisfactory," and altogether unworthy of Novalis' genius.

FROM HEINRICH VON OFTERDINGEN.[*]

THE VISIT TO THE CAVE.

[HEINRICH is travelling, with his mother, to Augsburg, the residence of his grandfather. Several merchants, bound in the same direction, join their company. At an inn on the road they fall in with an aged miner, who entertains them with matters pertaining to his craft. At length, he proposes an expedition to some caves in the vicinity, in which he is joined by Heinrich, by the merchants, and by several villagers.]

The evening was cheerful and warm. The moon stood in mild glory above the hills, and caused wondrous dreams to arise in all creatures. Herself a dream of the sun, she lay above the introverted dream-world, and led Nature, divided with innumerable boundaries, back into that fabulous prime, when each germ still slumbered within itself, and, solitary and untouched, longed in vain to unfold the dark fulness of its measureless being. The wonder-story of the evening mirrored itself in Heinrich's mind. It seemed to him as if the world reposed uncovered within him, and exhibited to him, as to a guest, all its treasures and its hidden charms. The grand and simple appearance around him seemed to him so intelligible. He thought Nature incomprehensible to man, only because she piles up around him the nearest, the most intimate, with such lavishness of manifold expression. The words of the old man had opened a hidden tapestry-door within him. He saw that his little chamber was built contiguous to a lofty minster, out of whose floor of stone arose the grave fore-world, while from the dome, the clear, glad future, in the form of angel-children, hovered singing above it. Mighty voices trembled through the silvery song, and through the wide portals all creatures entered in, each expressing its inner nature in a simple petition, and a dialect peculiar to itself. How did he wonder that this luminous view, which was now already become indispensable to his existence, had so long been foreign to him! Now he overlooked at once all his relations with the wide world around him, and comprehended all the strange conceptions and suggestions which he had often experienced in the contemplation of it. The story told by the merchants, of the youth who studied nature so diligently, and who became the son-in-law of a king, came into his mind, and a thousand other reminiscences of his life associated themselves, of their own accord, by a magic thread.

While Heinrich gave himself up to his meditations, the company had approached the cave. The entrance was low; the old man took a torch, and clambering over some stones, entered first. A quite perceptible current of air streamed toward him, and the old man assured them that they might follow with safety. The most timid went last, and held their weapons in readiness. Heinrich and the merchants walked behind the miner, and the boy strode briskly by his side. The way, at first, was through a somewhat narrow passage, but soon terminated in a very extensive and lofty cave, which the glare of the torches was unable wholly to illumine. One saw, however, in the background, several openings, which lost themselves in the wall of rock. The floor was soft and tolerably even; likewise the walls and the ceiling were not rough or irregular. But what especially engaged the attention of all, was the countless multitude of bones and teeth which strewed the floor. Some of them were perfectly preserved, in others there were marks of corruption, and those which here and there protruded from the walls, seemed to have become petrified. Most of them were of unusual size and strength. The old miner rejoiced in these relics of a primeval age; only the peasants had misgivings about them, for they regarded them as manifest traces of beasts of prey at hand, although the old man pointed out to them most convincingly the evidences of an inconceivable antiquity, and asked them if they had ever noticed any signs of ravages among their herds, or of the plunder of human neighbors, and whether they could regard these bones as those of known animals or men? The old man wished now to penetrate farther into the mountain, but the peasants deemed it advisable for them to retreat, and to await his entrance before the cave. Heinrich, the merchants, and the boy, remained with the miner, and provided themselves with ropes and torches. They soon reached a second cave, and the old man did not forget to mark the passage through which they had entered, by a figure composed of bones, which he placed before it. This cave resembled the first, and was equally rich in animal remains.

Heinrich experienced a strange awe; it struck him as if he were wandering through the forecourts of the inner earth-palace. Heaven and earth were suddenly far removed from him; and these dark, wide halls appeared to belong to a wondrous subterranean kingdom. He thought within himself, were it not possible that a separate world stirs this monstrous life beneath our feet? that unheard-of births have their being and their doings in the fastnesses of the earth, which the interior fire of the dark womb works up into gigantic forms of spirit-power? Might not, some time, these awful strangers, driven forth by the in-pressing cold, appear among us, while perhaps, at the same time, heavenly guests—living, speaking Powers of the star-world—became visible above our heads? Are these bones the remains of emigrations toward the surface, or signs of a flight into the deeps?

Suddenly, the old man called to the rest, and

---

[*] An unfinished Romance, which the author designed, he says, to be "an apotheosis of Poetry." The first part contains the initiation of the poet; the second his transfiguration. The name of the hero is that of an actual German poet or *Minnesinger* of the 13th century.—TR.

showed them a human footstep quite fresh on the floor of the cave. No others appeared; so he thought they might follow this trace without fear of meeting with robbers. *   *   *

After some searching, they found in an angle of the side-wall, on the right, a sloping passage, into which the footsteps appeared to lead. Soon they thought they could perceive a brightness, which grew stronger the nearer they approached. A new vault, of greater extent than the former, opened itself before them, in the background of which they saw, sitting by a lamp, the figure of a man, who had a large book lying before him on a stone tablet, in which he seemed to be reading. He turned himself toward them, rose and came to meet them. He looked neither old nor young, no traces of time were perceptible in him, except his straight grey hairs, which were parted on the forehead. He had soles bound to his feet, and seemed to have no other clothing except a wide mantle which was folded about him, and made more prominent his large and noble form. It seemed as if he were receiving expected guests in his dwelling.

"It is kind in you to visit me," he said; "you are the first friends I have seen here, as long as I have lived in this place. It would seem that people are beginning to consider more attentively our large and wondrous house." The old man replied: "We did not expect to find here so friendly a host. We were told of wild beasts and goblins, and find ourselves very agreeably deceived. If we have disturbed you in your devotions and profound contemplations, pardon thus much to our curiosity." "Can any contemplation be more delightful," said the unknown, "than that of glad and congenial human faces? Do not think me a misanthrope, because you find me in this solitude. I have not fled the world, I have only sought a place of rest, where I might pursue my meditations undisturbed."

"Do you never repent your resolution? and are there not hours when you feel afraid, and when your heart longs for a human voice?"

"Not now. There was a time, in my youth, when ardent enthusiasm induced me to become a recluse. Dim presentiments occupied my youthful imagination. I hoped to find full nourishment for my heart in solitude. Inexhaustible seemed to me the fountain of my inner life. But I soon perceived that one must bring with him abundance of experiences, that a young heart cannot be alone, nay, that it is only by manifold converse with his kind, that man can acquire a certain self-subsistence. *   *   * The dangers and vicissitudes of war, the high poetic spirit which accompanies a war-host, tore me from my youthful solitude, and determined the fortunes of my life. It may be, that the long tumult, the numberless events which I witnessed, have expanded yet farther my taste for solitude. Innumerable reminiscences are entertaining company,—the more entertaining the more varied the glance with which we overlook them, and which now first discovers their true connection, the deep meaning of their sequence, and the import of their phenomena. The true understanding of human history does not unfold itself till late, and rather under the still influences of recollection, than under the more powerful impressions of the present time. The nearest events seem but loosely connected, but they sympathize all the more wonderfully with remote ones; and only then when one is in a condition to overlook a long series, and neither to take everything literally, nor, with wanton vagaries, to confound the true order, does one perceive the secret concatenation of the former and the future, and learn to compound history out of hope and memory. Only he, however, to whom the entire fore-time is present, can succeed in discovering the simple rule of history. We attain only to imperfect, cumbrous formulas, and may be glad if we can but find for ourselves an available prescript, which shall give us satisfactory solutions for our own short life. But I may venture to affirm that every careful contemplation of the fates of life affords a deep and inexhaustible enjoyment, and, of all thoughts, exalts us most above earthly ills. Youth reads history only from curiosity, like an entertaining wonder-tale; to riper age it becomes a heavenly, consoling and edifying friend, who by her wise discourses gently prepares us for a higher, more comprehensive career, and by means of intelligible images, makes us acquainted with the unknown world. The Church is the dwelling-house of History, and the still churchyard her emblematic flower-garden. Only aged, God-fearing men should write of History, whose own history is nearly at an end, and who have nothing more to hope for, but to be transplanted into the garden. Not gloomy and troubled will their account be;— rather, a ray from the cupola will exhibit everything in the most correct and beautiful light, and a holy Spirit will hover over those strangely moved waters."   *   *   *   "When I consider all these things aright, it seems to me as if the historian should be a poet also, for only poets understand the art of presenting events in their true connection. In their narratives and fables, I have observed with silent pleasure a delicate feeling for the mysterious spirit of life. There is more truth in their wonder-stories than in learned chronicles. Although the personages and their fortunes are fictitious, the sense in which they are invented is true and natural. It is to a certain extent indifferent, as it regards our entertainment and our instruction, whether the persons in whose destinies we trace our own, actually lived or not. What we want is an intuition of the great, simple soul of the phenomena of time. If this wish is satisfied, we do not trouble ourselves about the accidental existence of the external figures."   *   *   *

"Since I have inhabited this cave," continued the recluse, "I have learned to meditate more of the olden time. It is indescribable how this study attracts. I can imagine the love which a miner must have for his handicraft. When I look at these strange old bones which are gathered together here in such a mighty multitude, when I think of the wild time in which these foreign, monstrous animals, impelled, perhaps, by fear and alarm, crowded in dense masses into these caves, and here found their death; when, again, I ascend to the times in which these caverns grew together, and vast floods covered the land, I appear to myself like a dream of the future, like a child of the everlasting peace. How quiet and peaceful, how mild and clear is Nature at the present day, compared with those violent, gigantic times! The most fearful tempest, the most appalling earthquake in our days, is but a faint echo of those terrific birth-throes. It may be, that the vegetable and animal world, and even the human beings of that time, if any there were on single islands in this ocean, had a different structure, more firm and rude. At least, one ought not to charge the traditions, which tell of a race of giants, with fabrication."

"It is pleasant," said the old man, "to observe the gradual pacification of nature. There appears to have formed itself gradually, a more and more intimate agreement, a more peaceful communion, a mutual assistance and animation; and we can look forward to ever better times. Possibly, here and there the old leaven may still ferment, and some violent convulsions may ensue, but we can discern, notwithstanding these, an almighty striving after a freer, a more harmonious constitution; and, in this spirit, each convulsion will pass by and lead us nearer to the great goal. It may be, that Nature is no longer so fruitful as formerly, that no metals or precious stones are formed in these days, that no more rocks and mountains arise, that plants and animals no longer swell up to such astonishing size and strength. But the plastic, ennobling, social powers of Nature have increased all the more. Her disposition has become more receptive and delicate, her fantasy more manifold and emblematic, her touch lighter and more artistic. She approaches human kind; and if once she was a wild-teeming rock, she is now a still, germinating plant, a mere human artist."

* * * * * * *

Heinrich and the merchants had listened attentively to this conversation, and the former, especially, experienced new developments in his fore-feeling soul. Many words, many thoughts, fell like quickening fruit-seed into his bosom, and transported him quickly from the narrow sphere of his youth to the height of the world. The hours just past lay like long years behind him, and it seemed to him as if he had never thought or felt otherwise than now.

The recluse showed them his books; they were old histories and poems. Heinrich turned over the leaves of the large and beautifully-illuminated manuscripts. The short lines of the verses, the titles, single passages, and the neat pictures which appeared here and there, like embodied words, for the purpose of seconding the imagination of the reader, excited mightily his curiosity. The recluse remarked his inward joy, and explained to him the singular representations. The most manifold life-scenes were depicted there. Battles, funeral solemnities, wedding-festivals, shipwrecks, caves and palaces, kings, heroes, priests, old men and young, men in foreign costume, and strange animals, appeared in various alternations and connections. Heinrich could not see his fill, and would have desired nothing better than to stay with the recluse, who attracted him irresistibly, and to be instructed by him concerning these books. Meanwhile the old man asked if there were any more caves, and the recluse answered that there were several very spacious ones in the vicinity, and that he would accompany him thither. The old man was ready, and the recluse, who had noticed the pleasure which Heinrich had in his books, induced him to remain behind, and to entertain himself with these during their absence. Heinrich was glad to remain with the books, and thanked him heartily for the permission. He turned over the leaves with infinite joy. At length there fell into his hands a book written in a foreign language, which appeared to him to bear some resemblance to the Latin and to the Italian. He longed very much to know the language, for the book particularly pleased him, although he understood not a word of it. It had no title, but he found, in seeking, several pictures. They seemed to him strangely familiar, and as he gazed more attentively, he discovered his own form quite distinguishable among the figures. He started and thought he had been dreaming, but after repeated inspection, he could not doubt the perfect similitude. He could scarcely believe his senses when, presently, he discovered in one of the pictures, the cave, with the recluse and the old man by his side. By degrees, he found in other pictures the Eastern maid, his parents, the count and countess of Thüringen, his friend the court-chaplain, and many others of his acquaintance. But their garments were different, and they appeared to belong to another age. A great number of figures he knew not how to name, yet they seemed familiar to him. He saw his similitude in various situations. Toward the end of the book, he appeared larger and nobler. A guitar was lying on his arm, and the countess was handing him a garland. He saw himself at the Imperial court, on shipboard, in close embrace with a slender, lovely maiden, in battle with wild-looking men, in friendly converse with Saracens and Moors. A man of earnest aspect appeared frequently in his company. He conceived a profound reverence for this lofty figure, and was rejoiced to see himself arm in arm with him. The last pictures were dark and unintelligible; but some of the forms of his dream surprised him with intense delight. The conclusion appeared to be wanting. Heinrich was much troubled, and wished nothing more ardently than to be able to read the book and to possess it entire. He viewed the pictures again and again, and was confused when he heard the company returning: An unaccountable shame came over him. He did not dare to make known his discovery, and merely asked the recluse, as unconcernedly as possible, respecting the title and the language. He learned that it was written in the Provençal tongue. "It is a great while since I have read it," said the recluse; "I do not remember exactly the subject. All I know is, that it is a Romance of the wonderful fortunes of a poet, in which poetry is represented and lauded in manifold relations. The conclusion is wanting to this copy, which I brought with me from Jerusalem, where I found it among the effects of a deceased friend, and kept it as a memorial of him.

THE POET AND HIS DAUGHTER.

The journey was now ended. It was toward evening when our travellers arrived, safe and in good spirits, in the world-renowned city of Augsburg, and rode through the lofty streets to the house of old Schwaning. * * * They found the house illuminated, and a merry music reached their ears. "What will you wager," said the merchants, "that your grandfather is giving a merry entertainment? We come as if called. How surprised he will be at the uninvited guests! Little does he dream that the true festival is now to begin."
* * * * * * * *
Among the guests, Heinrich had noticed a man who appeared to be the person that he had seen often at his side, in that book. His noble aspect distinguished him before all the rest. A cheerful earnestness was the spirit of his countenance. An open, beautifully arched brow; great, black, piercing and firm eyes; a roguish trait about the merry mouth, and altogether clear and manly proportions made it significant and attractive. He was strongly built, his movements were easy and full of expression, and where he stood, it seemed as if he would stand forever. Heinrich asked his grandfather about him. "I am glad," said the old man, "that you have remarked him at once. It is my excellent friend Klingsohr, the poet. Of his acquaintance and friendship you may be prouder than of the emperor's. But how stands it with your heart? He has a beautiful daughter; perhaps she will supplant the father in your regards. I shall be surprised if you have not observed her." Heinrich blushed. "I was absent, dear grandfather. The company was numerous, and I noticed only your friend." "It is very easy to see," replied Schwaning, "that you are from the north. We will soon find means to thaw you, here. You shall soon learn to look out for pretty eyes."
The old Schwaning led Heinrich to Klingsohr, and told him how Heinrich had observed him at once, and felt a very lively desire to be acquainted with him. Heinrich was diffident.

Klingsohr spoke to him in a very friendly manner of his country and his journey. There was something so confidential in his voice, that Heinrich soon took heart and conversed with him freely. After some time Schwaning returned, and brought with him the beautiful Mathilde. "Have compassion on my shy grandson, and pardon him for seeing your father before he did you. Your gleaming eyes will awaken his slumbering youth. In his country the spring is late."

Heinrich and Mathilde colored. They looked at each other with wondering eyes. She asked him with gentle, scarce audible words: "did he like to dance?" Just as he was affirming this question a merry dancing-music struck up. Silently he offered her his hand, she gave hers, and they mingled in the ranks of the waltzing pairs. Schwaning and Klingsohr looked on. The mother and the merchants rejoiced in Heinrich's activity, and in his beautiful partner. * * * Heinrich wished the dance never to end. With intense satisfaction his eye rested on the roses of his partner. Her innocent eye shunned him not. She seemed the spirit of her father in the loveliest disguise. Out of her large, calm eyes, spoke eternal youth. On a light, heaven-blue ground reposed the mild glory of the dusky stars. Around them brow and nose sloped gracefully. A lily inclined toward the rising sun, was her face; and from the slender white neck, blue veins meandered in tempting curves around the delicate cheeks. Her voice was like a far-away echo, and the small brown curly head seemed to hover over the light form.

THE FEAST.

The music banished reserve and roused every inclination to cheerful sport. Baskets of flowers in full splendor breathed forth odors on the table, and the wine crept about among the dishes and the flowers, shook his golden wings, and wove curtains of bright tapestry between the guests and the world. Heinrich now, for the first time, understood what a feast was. A thousand gay spirits seemed to him to dance about the table, and in still sympathy with gay men, to live by their joys and to intoxicate themselves with their delights. The joy of life stood like a sounding tree full of golden fruits before him. Evil did not show itself, and it seemed to him impossible that ever human inclination should have turned from this tree to the dangerous fruit of knowledge, to the tree of conflict. He now understood wine and food. He found their savor surpassingly delicious. They were seasoned for him by a heavenly oil, and sparkled from the cup of the glory of earthly life.
* * * * * * * *
It was deep in the night when the company separated. The first and only feast of my life! said Heinrich to himself when he was alone.

He went to the window. The choir of the stars stood in the dark sky, and in the east a white sheen announced the coming day. With full transport Heinrich exclaimed: "You, ye everlasting stars, ye silent pilgrims, you I invoke as witnesses of my sacred oath! For Mathilde I will live, and eternal truth shall bind my heart to hers. For me too the morn of an everlasting day is breaking. The night is past. I kindle myself, a never-dying sacrifice to the rising sun!

THE DREAM.

Heinrich was heated, and it was late, toward morning, when he fell asleep. The thoughts of his soul ran together into wondrous dreams. A deep blue river shimmered from the green plain. On the smooth surface swam a boat. Mathilde sat and rowed. She was decked with garlands, sang a simple song, and looked toward him with a sweet sorrow. His bosom was oppressed, he knew not why. The sky was bright, and peaceful the flood. Her heavenly countenance mirrored itself in the waves. Suddenly the boat began to spin round. He called to her, alarmed. She smiled, and laid the oar in the boat, which continued incessantly to whirl. An overwhelming anxiety seized him. He plunged into the stream, but could make no progress, the water bore him. She beckoned, she appeared desirous to say something. Already the boat shipped water, but she smiled with an ineffable inwardness, and looked cheerfully into the whirlpool. All at once it drew her down. A gentle breath streaked across the waves, which flowed on as calm and as shining as before. The terrific agony deprived him of consciousness. His heart beat no more. He did not come to himself until he found himself on dry ground. He might have swam far, it was a strange country. He knew not what had befallen him; his mind was gone;—thoughtless he wandered farther into the land. He felt himself dreadfully exhausted. A little fountain trickled from a hill, it sounded like clear bells. With his hand he scooped a few drops, and wetted his parched lips. Like an anxious dream the terrible event lay behind him. He walked on and on; flowers and trees spoke to him. He felt himself so well, so at home. Then he heard again that simple song. He pursued the sound. Suddenly some one held him back by his garment. Dear Heinrich! called a well-known voice. He looked round, and Mathilde clasped him in her arms. "Why didst thou run from me, dear heart?" said she, drawing a long breath, "I could scarce overtake thee." Heinrich wept. He pressed her to his bosom.— "Where is the river?" he exclaimed with tears. "Seest thou not its blue waves above us?" He looked up, and the blue river was flowing gently above their heads. "Where are we, dear Mathilde?" "With our parents." "Shall we remain together?" "Forever," she replied, while she pressed her lips to his, and so clasped him that she could not be separated from him again. She whispered a strange mysterious word into his mouth, which vibrated through his whole being. He wished to repeat it, when his grandfather called and he awoke. He would have given his life to remember that word.

THE VEGETABLE WORLD.

Plants are, as it were, the most direct language of the earth. Every new leaf, every strange flower, is some secret that is pressing forth, and which, because it cannot move or speak for joy and love, becomes a mute, quiet plant. When we find such a flower in a solitary place, does it not seem as if everything around were transfigured, and as if the little feathered tones loved best to dwell in its vicinity? One could weep for joy, and, secluded from the world, thrust hands and feet into the ground and strike root, in order never to leave the happy neighborhood. Over the whole dry world is flung this green, mysterious carpet of love. With every spring it is made new, and its strange writing is legible only to the beloved, like the posies of the Orient. Forever will he read, and never read his fill; and daily become aware of new meanings, new, transporting revelations of loving Nature.

CLOUDS.

"There is certainly something mysterious in the clouds," said Sylvester, "and certain kinds have often a quite wonderful influence over us. They march, and would take us up with their cool shadows and bear us away; and while their forms are lovely and variegated, like a breathed-out wish of our inner man, their brightness, and the splendid light that then reigns on the earth, are like a prophecy of an unknown, ineffable glory. But there are also dim, and grave, and terrible forms of clouds, in which all the terrors of the ancient night appear to threaten us. The heaven seems as if it would never become clear again, the cheerful blue is expunged, and a lurid, copper-red, on a black-grey ground, awakens awe and terror in every breast. When, then, the destructive beams dart down, and with mocking laughter, the crashing thunder-blows follow in their rear, we are terrified to the very centre of our being; and if, then, there arises not in us the sublime feeling of our moral supremacy, we think we are delivered up to the terrors of hell, to the power of evil spirits. These are echoes of the old, inhuman Nature; but they are also rousing voices of the higher Nature—the heavenly conscience within us. Mortality groans in its ground-fastnesses; but the immortality begins to shine with increased brightness, and to know itself.

CONSCIENCE.

"When," asked Heinrich, "when will there no longer be any need of terrors, of pains, of distress, and of evil in the world?"

When there is but *one* power,— the power of conscience; when Nature has become chaste and moral. There is but one cause of evi' the universal weakness; and this weakness is nothing but imperfect moral receptivity and insensibility to the charm of Freedom.

Conscience is the inborn mediator in every man. It is God's vicegerent on the earth, and is therefore regarded by many as the highest and the last. * * * Conscience is man's most proper essence, completely transfigured;—the celestial, aboriginal man. It is not this or that, it commands not in general propositions, it consists not of single virtues. There is but one virtue—the pure, earnest will which, in the moment of decision, resolves and chooses immediately. In living and peculiar indivisibility, it inhabits and animates the delicate symbol of the human body, and avails to call the spiritual members into truest activity.

Nature subsists only through the spirit of virtue, and is destined to become ever more steadfast.

FROM THE FRAGMENTS.

Where no gods are, spectres rule.

The best thing that the French achieved by their Revolution, was a portion of Germanity.

Germanity is genuine popularity, and therefore an ideal.

Where children are, there is the golden age.

Spirit is now active here and there: when will Spirit be active in the whole? When will mankind, in the mass, begin to consider?

Nature is pure Past, foregone freedom; and therefore, throughout, the soil of history.

The antithesis of body and spirit is one of the most remarkable and dangerous of all antitheses. It has played an important part in history.

Only by comparing ourselves, as men, with other rational beings, could we know what we truly are, what position we occupy.

The history of Christ is as surely poetry as it is history. And, in general, only that history is history which might also be fable.

The Bible begins gloriously with Paradise, the symbol of youth, and ends with the everlasting kingdom, with the holy city. The history of every man should be a Bible.

Prayer is to religion what thinking is to philosophy. To pray is to make religion.

The more sinful man feels himself the more Christian he is.

Christianity is opposed to science, to art, to enjoyment in the proper sense.

It goes forth from the common man. It inspires the great majority of the limited on earth.

It is the germ of all democracy, the highest fact in the domain of the popular.

Light is the symbol of genuine self-possession. Therefore light, according to analogy, is the action of the self-contact of matter. Accordingly, day is the consciousness of the planet, and while the sun, like a god, in eternal self-action, inspires the centre, one planet after another closes one eye for a longer or shorter time, and with cool sleep refreshes itself for new life and contemplation. Accordingly, here, too, there is religion. For is the life of the planets aught else but sun-worship?

The Holy Ghost is more than the Bible. This should be our teacher of religion, not the dead, earthly, equivocal letter.

All faith is miraculous, and worketh miracles.

Sin is indeed the real evil in the world. All calamity proceeds from that. He who understands sin, understands virtue and Christianity, himself and the world.

The greatest of miracles is a virtuous act.

If a man could suddenly believe, in sincerity, that he was moral, he would be so.

We need not fear to admit that man has a preponderating tendency to evil. So much the better is he by nature, for only the unlike attracts.

Everything distinguished (peculiar) deserves ostracism. Well for it if it ostracises itself. Everything absolute must quit the world.

A time will come, and that soon, when all men will be convinced, that there can be no king without a republic, and no republic without a king; that both are as inseparable as body and soul. The true king will be a republic, the true republic a king.

In cheerful souls there is no wit. Wit shows a disturbance of the equipoise.

Most people know not how interesting they are, what interesting things they really utter. A true representation of themselves, a record and estimate of their sayings, would make them astonished at themselves, would help them to discover in themselves an entirely new world.

Man is the Messiah of Nature.

The soul is the most powerful of all poisons. It is the most penetrating and diffusible stimulus.

Every sickness is a musical problem; the cure is the musical solution.

Inoculation with death, also, will not be wanting in some future universal therapia.

The idea of a perfect health is interesting only in a scientific point of view. Sickness is necessary to individualization.

If God could be man, he can also be stone, plant, animal, element, and perhaps, in this way, there is a continuous redemption in Nature.

Life is a disease of the spirit, a passionate activity. Rest is the peculiar property of the spirit. From the spirit comes gravitation.

As nothing can be free, so, too, nothing can be forced, but spirit.

A space-filling individual is a body, a time-filling individual is a soul.

It should be inquired, whether Nature has not essentially changed with the progress of culture.

All activity ceases when knowledge comes. The state of knowing is *eudæmonism*, blest repose of contemplation, heavenly quietism.

Miracles, as contradictions of Nature, are *amathematical*. But there are no miracles in this sense. What we so term, is intelligible precisely by means of mathematics; for nothing is miraculous to mathematics.

In music, mathematics appears formally, as revelation, as creative idealism. All enjoyment is musical, consequently mathematical. The highest life is mathematics.

There may be mathematicians of the first magnitude who cannot cipher. One can be a great cipherer without a conception of mathematics.

Instinct is genius in Paradise, before the period of self-abstraction (self-recognition).

The fate which oppresses us is the sluggishness of our spirit. By enlargement and cultivation of our activity, we change ourselves into fate. Everything appears to stream in upon us, because we do not stream out. We are negative, because we choose to be so; the more positive we become, the more negative will the world around us be, until, at last, there is no more negative, and we are all in all. God wills gods.

All power appears only in transition. Permanent power is stuff.

Every act of introversion — every glance into our interior — is at the same time ascension, going up to heaven, a glance at the veritable outward.

Only so far as a man is happily married to himself, is he fit for married life and family life, generally.

One must never confess that one loves one's self. The secret of this confession is the life-principle of the only true and eternal love.

We conceive God as personal, just as we conceive ourselves personal. God is just as personal and as individual as we are; for what we call *I* is not our true *I*, but only its off glance.

LUDWIG TIECK.*

Born 1773.

LUDWIG TIECK, born at Berlin, on the 31st of May, 1773, is known to the world only as a Man of Letters, having never held any public station, or followed any profession, except that of authorship. Of his private history the critics and news-hunters of his own country complain that they have little information; a deficiency which may arise in part from the circumstance, that till of late years, though from the first admired by the Patricians of his native literature, he has stood in no high favor, and of course awakened no great curiosity, among the reading *Plebs*; and may indicate, at the same time, that in his walk and conversation, there is little wonderful to be discovered.

His literary life he began at Berlin, in his twenty-second year, by the publication of three novels, following each other in quick succession: *Abdallah*, *William Lovell*, and *Peter Leberrecht*. These works found small patronage at their first appearance, and are still regarded as immature products of his genius; the opening of a cloudy, as well as fervid dawn; betokening a day of strong heat, and perhaps at last, of serene brightness. A gloomy tragic spirit is said to reign throughout all of them; the image of a high passionate mind, scorning the base and the false, rather than accomplishing the good and the true; in rapt earnestness "interrogating Fate," and receiving no answer but the echo of its own questions reverberated from the dead walls of its vast and lone imprisonment.

In this stage of spiritual progress, where so many not otherwise ungifted minds at length painfully content themselves to take up their permanent abode, where our own noble and hapless Byron perished from among us at the instant when his deliverance seemed at hand, it was not Tieck's ill fortune to continue too long. His *Popular Tales*, published in 1797, as an appendage to his last novel, under the title of *Peter Leberrechts Volksmährchen*, already indicate that he had worked his way through these baleful shades into a calmer and sunnier elevation; from which, and happily without looking at the world through a painted glass of any sort, he had begun to see that there were things to be believed, as well as things to be denied; things to be loved and forwarded, as well as things to be hated and trodden under foot. The active and positive of Goodness was displacing the barren and tormenting negative; and worthy feelings were now to be translated into their only proper language, worthy actions. In Tieck's mind, all Goodness, all that was noble or excellent in Nature, seems to have combined itself under the image of Poetic Beauty; to the service and defence of which he has ever since unweariedly devoted his gifts and his days.

These *Volkmährchen* are of the most varied nature: sombre, pathetic, fantastic, satirical; but all pervaded by a warm, genial soul, which accommodates itself with equal aptitude to the gravest or the gayest form. A soft abundance, a simple and kindly but often solemn majesty is in them: wondrous shapes, full of meaning, move over the scene, true modern denizens of the old Fairyland; low tones of plaintiveness or awe flit round us; or a starry splendor twinkles down from the immeasurable depths of Night.

It is by this work, as revised and perfected long afterwards, that we now purpose introducing Tieck to the notice of the English reader: it was by this also that he was introduced to the notice of his countrymen. *Peter Leberrechts Volksmährchen* was reviewed by August Wilhelm Schlegel, in the *Jena Litteraturzeitung*; and its author, for the first time, brought under the eye of the world as a man of rich endowments, and in the fair way for turning them to proper account. To the body of the world, however, this piece of news was surprising rather than delightful; for Tieck's merits were not of a kind to split the ears of the groundlings, and his manner of producing them was ill calculated to conciliate a kind hearing. Schiller and Goethe were at this

---

* The following notice, as well as the translation from Tieck, is from Carlyle's "German Romance."

time silent, or occupied with History and Philosophy: Tieck belonged not to the existing poetic guild; and, far from soliciting admission, he had not scrupled, in the most pleasant fashion, to inform the craftsmen that their great Diana was a dumb idol, and their silver shrines an unprofitable thing. Among these *Volksmährchen*, one of the most prominent is *Der Gestiefelte Kater*, a dramatised version of *Puss in Boots;* under the grotesque mask of which, he had laughed with his whole heart, in a true Aristophanic vein, at the actual aspect of literature; and without mingling his satire with personalities, or any other false ingredient, had rained it like a quiet shower of volcanic ashes on the cant of Illumination, the cant of Sensibility, the cant of Criticism, and the many other cants of that shallow time, till the gum-flower products of the poetic garden hung draggled and black under their unkindly coating. In another country, at another day, the drama of *Puss in Boots* may justly be supposed to appear with enfeebled influences; yet even to a stranger there is not wanting a feast of broad joyous humor in this strange phantasmagoria, where pit and stage, and man and animal, and earth and air, are jumbled in confusion worse confounded, and the copious, kind, ruddy light of true mirth overshines and warms the whole.

This What-d'ye-call it of *Puss in Boots* was, as it were, the key-note which for several years determined the tone of Tieck's literary enterprises. The same spirit lives in his *Verkehrte Welt* (World Turned Topsy-turvy), a drama of similar structure, which accompanied the former; in his tale of *Zerbino, or the Tour in search of Taste*, which soon followed it; and in numerous parodies and lighter pieces which he gave to the world in his *Poetic Journal;* the second and last volume of which periodical contains his *Letters on Shakspeare*, inculcating the same doctrines, in a graver shape. About this time, after a short residence in Hamburgh, where he had married, he removed his abode to Jena; a change which confirmed him in his literary tendencies, and facilitated the attainment of their objects. It was here that he became acquainted with the two Schlegels; and, at the same time, with their friend Novalis, a young man of a pure, warm, and benignant genius, whose fine spirit died in its first blossoming, and whose posthumous works it was, ere long, the melancholy task of Tieck, and the younger Schlegel, to publish under their superintendence. With Wackenroder of Berlin, a person of kindred mind with Novalis, and kindred fortune also, having died very early, Tieck was already acquainted and united; for he had co-operated in the *Herzensergiessungen eines einsamen Klosterbruders*, an elegant and impressive work on pictorial art, and Wackenroder's chief performance.

These young men sympathised completely in their critical ideas with Tieck; and each was laboring in his own sphere to disseminate them, and reduce them to practice. Their endeavors, it would seem, have prospered; for, in colloquial literary history, this gifted cinquefoil, often it is only the trefoil of Tieck and the two Schlegels, have the credit, which was long the blame, of founding a New School of Poetry, by which the Old School, first fired upon in the *Gestiefelte Kater*, and ever afterwards assailed, without intermission, by eloquence and ridicule, argument and entreaty, was at length displaced and hunted out of being; or, like Partridge the Astrologer, reduced to a life which could be proved to be no life.

Of this New School, which has been the subject of much unwise talk, and of much not very wise writing, we cannot here attempt to offer any suitable description, far less any just estimate. One thing may be remarked, that the epithet *School* seems to describe the case with little propriety. That since the beginning of the present century, a great change has taken place in German literature, is plain enough, without commentators; but that it was effected by three young men, living in the little town of Jena, is not by any means so plain. The critical principles of Tieck and the Schlegels had already been set forth, in the form both of precept and prohibition, and with all the aids of philosophic depth and epigrammatic emphasis, by the united minds of Goethe and Schiller, in the *Horen* and *Xenien*. The development and practical application of the doctrine is all that pertains to these reputed founders of the sect. But neither can the change be said to have originated with Schiller and Goethe; for it is a change originating not in individuals, but in universal circumstances, and belongs not to Germany, but to Europe. Among ourselves, for instance, within the last thirty years, who has not lifted up his voice with double vigor in praise of Shakspeare and Nature, and vituperation of French taste and French philosophy? Who has not heard of the glories of old English literature; the wealth of Queen Elizabeth's age; the penury of Queen Anne's; and the inquiry whether Pope was a poet? A similar temper is breaking out in France itself, hermetically sealed as that country seemed to be against all foreign influences; and doubts are beginning to be entertained, and even expressed, about Corneille and the Three Unities. It seems to be substantially the same thing which has occurred in Germany, and been attributed to Tieck and his associates: only, that the revolution, which is here proceeding, and in France commencing, appears in Germany to be completed. Its results have there been embodied in elaborate laws, and profound systems have been promulgated and accepted: whereas with us, in past years, there has been as it were a Literary Anarchy; for the Pandects of Blair and Bossu are obsolete or abrogated, but no new code supplies their place; and, author and critic, each sings or says that which is right in his own eyes. For the principles of German Poetics, we can only refer the reader to the treatises of Kant, Schiller, Richter, the Schlegels, and their many copyists and expositors; with the promise that his labor will be hard, but not unrewarded by a plenteous harvest of results, which, whether they be doubted, denied, or believed, he will find no trivial or unprofitable subject for his contemplation.

These doctrines of taste, which Tieck embraced every opportunity of enforcing as a critic, he did not fail diligently to exemplify in practice; as a long and rapid series of poetical performances lies before the world to attest. Of these, his *Genoveva*, a play grounded on the legend of that Saint, appears to be regarded as his master-piece by the best judges; though *Franz Sternebalds Wanderungen*, the fictitious History of a Student of Painting, was more relished by others; and, as a critic tells us, "here and there a low voice might be even heard voting that this novel equalled *Wilhelm Meister;* the peaceful clearness of which it however nowise attained, but only, with visible effort, strove to imitate." In this last work he was assisted by Wackenroder. At an earlier period, he had come forth, as a translator, with a new version of *Don Quixote:* he now appeared also as a commentator, with a work entitled *Minnelieder aus dem Schwabischen Zeitalter* (Minstrelsy of the Swabian Era), published at Berlin in 1803; with an able Preface, explaining the relation of these poets to Petrarca and the Troubadours. In 1804, he sent out his *Kaiser Octavianus*, a story which, like the other works mentioned in this paragraph, I have never seen, but which I find praised by his countrymen in no very intelligible terms, as "a fair revival of the old *Mährchen* (Traditionary Tale); in which, however, the poet moves freely, and has completed the cycle of the romance." *Die Gemälde* (the Pictures), another of his fictions, has lately been translated into English.

Tieck's frequent change of place bespeaks less settledness in his domestic, than happily existed in his intellectual circumstances. From Jena he seems to have again removed to Berlin; then to a country residence near Frankfort on the Oder; which, in its turn, he quitted for a journey into Italy. In this classic country he found new facilities for two of his favorite pursuits: he employed himself, it is said, to good purpose, in the study of ancient and modern art; to which, while in Rome, he added the examining of many old German manuscripts preserved in the Vatican Library. From his labors in this latter department, and elsewhere, his countrymen have not long ago obtained, in addition to the *Minstrelsy*, an *Altdeutsches Theater* (Old-German Theatre), in two volumes, with the hope of more. A collection of Old-German Poetry is still expected.

In 1806, he returned to Germany; first to Munich, then to his former retreat near Frankfort; but for the next seven years, he was little heard of as an active member of the literary world; and the regret of his admirers was increased by intelligence that ill health was the cause of his inactivity. That this inactivity was more apparent than real, he has proved by his reappearance in new vigor, at a time when he finds a readier welcome and more willing audience. He has since published abundantly in various forms; as a translator, an editor, and a writer both of poetry and prose. In 1812, appeared his early *Volksmährchen*, retouched, and improved, and combined into a whole, by conversations, critical, disquisitionary, and descriptive, in two volumes, entitled *Phantasus;* from which our present specimens of him are taken. His *Altdeutsches Theater* was followed by an *Altenglisches*, including the disputed plays of Shakspeare; a work gladly received by his countrymen, no less devoted admirers of Shakspeare than ourselves. Since that time, he has paid us a personal visit. In 1818, he was in London, and is said to have been well satisfied with his reception; which we cannot but hope was as respectful and kind as a guest so accomplished, and so friendly to England, deserved at our hands. The fruit of his residence among us, it seems, has already appeared in his writings. He has very lately given to the world a novel on Shakspeare and his Times; in which he has not trembled to introduce, as acting characters, the great dramatist himself, with Marlowe, and various other poets of that age. Such is the report, which adds, that his work is admired in Germany; but that any copy of it has crossed the Channel, I have not heard.

Of Tieck's present residence, or special pursuits, or economical circumstances, I am sorry to confess my entire ignorance. One little fact may perhaps be worth adding; that Sophia Bernhardi, an esteemed authoress, is his sister.——

THE ELVES.

"Where is our little Mary?" said the father.

"She is playing out upon the green there, with our neighbor's boy," replied the mother.

"I wish they may not run away and lose themselves," said he; "they are so thoughtless."

The mother looked for the little ones, and brought them their evening luncheon. "It is warm," said the boy; "and Mary had a longing for the red cherries."

"Have a care, children," said the mother, "and do not run too far from home, or into the wood; father and I are going to the fields."

Little Andres answered: "Never fear, the wood frightens us; we shall sit here by the house, where there are people near us."

The mother went in, and soon came out again with her husband. They locked the door, and turned towards the fields to look after their laborers, and see their hay-harvest in the meadow. Their house lay upon a little green height, encircled by a pretty ring of paling, which likewise enclosed their fruit and flower-garden. The hamlet stretched somewhat deeper down, and on the other side lay the castle of the Count. Martin rented the large farm from this nobleman; and was living in contentment with his wife and only child; for he yearly saved some money, and had the prospect of becoming a man of substance by his industry, for the ground was productive, and the Count not illiberal.

As he walked with his wife to the fields, he gazed cheerfully round, and said: "What a different look this quarter has, Brigitta, from the place we lived in formerly! Here it is all so green; the whole village is bedecked with thick-spreading fruit-trees; the ground is full of beautiful herbs and flowers; all the houses are cheerful and cleanly, the inhabitants are at their ease: nay, I could almost fancy that the woods are greener here than elsewhere, and the sky bluer; and, so far as the eye can reach, you have pleasure and delight in beholding the bountiful Earth."

"And whenever you cross the stream," said Brigitta, "you are, as it were, in another world, all is so dreary and withered; but every traveller declares that our village is the fairest in the country, far and near."

"All but that fir-ground," said her husband; "do but look back to it, how dark and dismal that solitary spot is lying in the gay scene: the dingy fir-trees, with the smoky huts behind them, the ruined stalls, the brook flowing past with a sluggish melancholy."

"It is true," replied Brigitta; "if you but approach that spot, you grow disconsolate and sad, you know not why. What sort of people can they be that live there, and keep themselves so separate from the rest of us, as if they had an evil conscience?"

"A miserable crew," replied the young farmer: "gipsies, seemingly, that steal and cheat in other quarters, and have their hoard and hiding-place here. I wonder only that his lordship suffers them."

"Who knows," said the wife, with an accent of pity, "but perhaps they may be poor people, wishing, out of shame, to conceal their poverty; for, after all, no one can say aught ill of them; the only thing is, that they do not go to church, and none knows how they live; for the little garden, which indeed seems altogether waste, cannot possibly support them; and fields they have none."

"God knows," said Martin, as they went along, "what trade they follow; no mortal comes to them; for the place they live in is as if bewitched and excommunicated, so that even our wildest fellows will not venture into it."

Such conversation they pursued, while walking to the fields. That gloomy spot they spoke of lay aside from the hamlet. In a dell, begirt with firs, you might behold a hut, and various ruined office-houses; rarely was smoke seen to mount from it, still more rarely did men appear there; though at times curious people, venturing somewhat nearer, had perceived upon the bench before the hut, some hideous women, in ragged clothes, dandling in their arms some children equally dirty and ill-favored; black dogs were running up and down upon the boundary; and, of an evening, a man of monstrous size was seen to cross the foot-bridge of the brook, and disappear in the hut; and, in the darkness, various shapes were observed, moving like shadows round a fire in the open air. This piece of ground, the firs, and the ruined huts, formed in truth a strange contrast with the bright green landscape, the white houses of the hamlet, and the stately new-built castle.

The two little ones had now eaten their fruit; it came into their heads to run races; and the little nimble Mary always got the start of the less active Andres. "It is not fair," cried Andres at last: "let us try it for some length, then we shall see who wins."

"As thou wilt," said Mary; "only to the brook we must not run."

"No," said Andres; "but there, on the hill, stands the large pear-tree, a quarter of a mile from this. I shall run by the left, round past the fir-ground; thou canst try it by the right, over the fields; so we do not meet till we get up, and then we shall see which of us is the swifter."

"Done," cried Mary, and began to run; "for we shall not mar one another by the way, and my father says it is as far to the hill by that side of the gipsies' house as by this."

Andres had already started, and Mary, turning to the right, could no longer see him. "It is very silly," said she to herself: "I have only to take heart, and run along the bridge, past the hut, and through the yard, and I shall certainly be first." She was already standing by the brook and the clump of firs. "Shall I? No; it is too frightful," said she. A little white dog was standing on the farther side, and barking with might and main. In her terror, Mary thought the dog some monster, and sprang back. "Fy! fy!" said she: "the dolt is gone half way by this time, while I stand here considering." The little dog kept barking, and, as she looked at it more narrowly, it seemed no longer frightful, but, on the contrary, quite pretty: it had a red collar round its neck, with a glittering bell; and as it raised its head, and shook itself in barking, the little bell sounded with the finest tinkle. "Well, I must risk it!" cried she: "I will run for life; quick, quick, I am through; certainly to Heaven, they cannot eat me up alive in half a minute!" And with this, the gay, courageous, little Mary, sprang along the foot-bridge; passed the dog, which ceased its barking, and began to fawn on her; and in a moment she was standing on the other bank, and the black firs all round concealed from view her father's house, and the rest of the landscape.

But what was her astonishment when here! The loveliest, most variegated flower-garden lay round her; tulips, roses, and lilies, were glittering in the fairest colours; blue and gold-red butterflies were wavering in the blossoms; cages of shining wire were hung on the espaliers, with many-colored birds in them, singing beautiful songs; and children, in short white frocks, with flowing yellow hair and brilliant eyes, were frolicking about; some playing with lambkins, some feeding the birds, or gathering flowers, and giving them to one another; some, again, were eating cherries, grapes, and ruddy apricots. No hut was to be seen; but instead of it, a large fair house, with a brazen door and lofty statues, stood glancing in the middle of the space. Mary was confounded with surprise, and knew not what to think; but, not being bashful, she went right up to the first of the children, held out her hand, and wished the little creature good even.

"Art thou come to visit us, then?" said the glittering child; "I saw thee running, playing on the other side, but thou wert frightened for our little dog."

"So you are not gipsies and rogues," said Mary, "as Andres always told me? He is a stupid thing, and talks of much he does not understand."

"Stay with us," said the strange little girl; "thou wilt like it well."

"But we are running a race."

"Thou wilt find thy comrade soon enough. There, take and eat."

Mary ate, and found the fruit more sweet than any she had ever tasted in her life before; and Andres, and the race, and the prohibition of her parents, were entirely forgotten.

A stately woman, in a shining robe, came towards them, and asked about the stranger child. "Fairest lady," said Mary, "I came running hither by chance, and now they wish to keep me."

"Thou art aware, Zerina," said the lady, "that she can be here but for a little while; besides, thou should'st have asked my leave."

"I thought," said Zerina, "when I saw her admitted across the bridge, that I might do it; we have often seen her running in the fields, and thou thyself hast taken pleasure in her lively temper. She will have to leave us soon enough."

"No, I will stay here," said the little stranger; "for here it is so beautiful, and here I shall find the prettiest playthings, and store of berries and cherries to boot. On the other side it is not half so grand."

The gold-robed lady went away with a smile; and many of the children now came bounding round the happy Mary in their mirth, and twitched her, and incited her to dance; others brought her lambs, or curious playthings; others made music on instruments, and sang to it.

She kept, however, by the playmate who had first met her; for Zerina was the kindest and loveliest of them all. Little Mary cried and cried again: "I will stay with you forever; I will stay with you, and you shall be my sisters;" at which the children all laughed, and embraced her. "Now, we shall have a royal sport," said Zerina. She ran into the palace, and returned with a little golden box, in which lay a quantity of seeds, like glittering dust. She lifted of it with her little hand, and scattered some grains on the green earth. Instantly the grass began to move, as in waves; and, after a few moments, bright rose-bushes started from the ground, shot rapidly up, and budded all at once, while the sweetest perfume filled the place. Mary also took a little of the dust, and, having scattered it, she saw white lilies, and the most variegated pinks, pushing up. At a signal from Zerina, the flowers disappeared, and others rose in their room. "Now," said Zerina, "look for something greater." She laid two pine-seeds in the ground, and stamped them in sharply with her foot. Two green bushes stood before them. "Grasp me fast," said she; and Mary threw her arms about the slender form. She felt herself borne upwards; for the trees were springing under them with the greatest speed; the tall pines waved to and fro, and the two children held each other fast embraced, swinging this way and that in the red clouds of the twilight, and kissed each other; while the rest were climbing up and down the trunks with quick dexterity, pushing and teasing one another with loud laughter when they met; if any one fell down in the press, it flew through the air, and sank slowly and surely to the ground. At length Mary was beginning to be frightened; and the other little child sang a few loud tones, and the trees again sank down, and set them on the ground as gradually as they had lifted them before to the clouds.

They next went through the brazen door of the palace. Here many fair women, elderly and young, were sitting in the round hall, partaking of the fairest fruits, and listening to glorious invisible music. In the vaulting of the ceiling, palms, flowers, and groves stood painted, among which little figures of children were sporting and winding in every graceful posture; and with the tones of the music, the images altered and glowed with the most burning colours; now the blue and green were sparkling like radiant light, now these tints faded back in paleness, the purple flamed up, and the gold took fire; and then the naked children seemed to be alive among the flower-garlands, and to draw breath, and emit it through their ruby-colored lips; so that by fits you could see the glance of their little white teeth, and the lighting up of their azure eyes.

From the hall, a stair of brass led down to a subterranean chamber. Here lay much gold and silver, and precious stones of every hue shone out between them. Strange vessels stood along the walls, and all seemed filled with costly things. The gold was worked into many forms, and glittered with the friendliest red. Many little dwarfs were busied in sorting the pieces from the heap, and putting them in the vessels; others, hunch-backed and bandy-legged, with long red noses, were tottering slowly along, half-bent to the ground, under full sacks, which they bore as millers do their grain; and, with much panting, shaking out the gold-dust on the ground. Then they darted awkwardly to the right and left, and caught the rolling ball that were likely to run away; and it happened now and then that one in his eagerness overset the other, so that both fell heavily and clumsily to the ground. They made angry faces, and looked askance, as Mary laughed at their gestures and their ugliness. Behind them sat an old crumpled little man, whom Zerina reverently greeted; he thanked her with a grave inclination of his head. He held a sceptre in his hand, and wore a crown upon his brow, and all the other dwarfs appeared to regard him as their master, and obey his nod.

"What more wanted?" asked he, with a surly voice, as the children came a little nearer. Mary was afraid, and did not speak; but her companion answered, they were only come to look about them in the chamber. "Still your old child's tricks!" replied the dwarf: "Will there never be an end to idleness?" With this, he turned again to his employment, kept his people weighing and sorting the ingots; some he sent away on errands, some he chid with angry tones.

"Who is the gentleman?" said Mary.

"Our Metal-Prince," replied Zerina, as they walked along.

They seemed once more to reach the open air, for they were standing by a lake, yet no sun appeared, and they saw no sky above their heads. A little boat received them, and Zerina steered it diligently forwards. It shot rapidly along. On gaining the middle of the lake, the stranger saw that multitudes of pipes, channels, and brooks, were spreading from the little sea in every direction. "These waters to the right," said Zerina, "flow beneath yon garden, and this is why it blooms so freshly; by the other side we get down into the great stream." On a sudden, out of all the channels, and from every quarter of the lake, came a crowd of little children swimming up; some wore garlands of sedge and water-lily; some had red stems of coral, others were blowing on crooked shells; a tumultuous noise echoed merrily from the dark shores; among the children might be seen the fairest women sporting in the waters, and often several of the children sprang about some one of them, and with kisses hung upon her neck and shoulders. All saluted the strangers; and these steered onwards through the revelry out of the lake, into a little river, which grew narrower and narrower. At last the boat came aground. The strangers took their leave, and Zerina knocked against the cliff. This opened like a door, and a female form, all red, assisted them to mount. "Are you all brisk here?" inquired Zerina. "They are just at work," replied the other, "and happy as they could wish; indeed, the heat is very pleasant."

They went up a winding stair, and on a sudden Mary found herself in a most resplendent hall, so that as she entered, her eyes were dazzled by the radiance. Flame-colored tapestry covered the walls with a purple glow; and when her eye had grown a little used to it, the stranger saw, to her astonishment, that, in the tapestry, there were figures moving up and down in dancing joyfulness; in form so beautiful, and of so fair proportions, that nothing could be seen more graceful; their bodies were as of red crystal, so that it appeared as if the blood were visible within them, flowing and playing in its courses. They smiled on the stranger, and saluted her with various bows; but as Mary was about approaching nearer them, Zerina plucked her sharply back, crying: "Thou wilt burn thyself, my little Mary, for the whole of it is fire."

Mary felt the heat. "Why do the pretty creatures not come out," said she, "and play with us?"

"As thou livest in the Air," replied the other, "so are they obliged to stay continually in Fire, and would faint and languish if they left it. Look now, how glad they are, how they laugh and shout; those down below spread out the fire-floods everywhere beneath the earth, and thereby the flowers, and fruits, and wine, are made to flourish; these red streams again, are to run beside the brooks of water; and thus the fiery creatures are kept ever busy and glad. But for thee it is too hot here; let us return to the garden."

In the garden, the scene had changed since they left it. The moonshine was lying on every flower; the birds were silent, and the children were asleep in complicated groups, among the green groves. Mary and her friend, however, did not feel fatigue, but walked about in the warm summer night, in abundant talk, till morning.

When the day dawned, they refreshed themselves on fruit and milk, and Mary said: "Suppose we go, by way of change, to the firs, and see how things look there?"

"With all my heart," replied Zerina; "thou wilt see our watchmen, too, and they will surely please thee; they are standing up among the trees on the mound." The two proceeded through the flower-garden by pleasant groves, full of nightingales; then they ascended a vine-hill; and at last, after long following the windings of a clear brook, arrived at the firs, and the height which bounded the domain. "How does it come," said Mary, "that we have to walk so far here, when without, the circuit is so narrow?"

"I know not," said her friend; "but so it is."

They mounted to the dark firs, and a chill wind blew from without in their faces; a haze seemed lying far and wide over the landscape. On the top were many strange forms standing; with mealy, dusty faces; their mis-shapen heads not unlike those of white owls; they were clad in folded cloaks of shaggy wool; they held umbrellas of curious skins stretched out above them; and they waved and fanned themselves incessantly with large bat's wings, which flared out curiously beside the woollen roquelaures. "I could laugh, yet I am frightened," cried Mary.

"These are our good trusty watchmen," said her playmate; "they stand here and wave their fans, that cold anxiety and inexplicable fear may fall on every one that attempts to approach us. They are covered so, because without it is now cold and rainy, which they cannot bear. But snow, or wind, or cold air, never reaches down to us; here is an everlasting spring and summer: yet if these poor people on the top were not frequently relieved, they would certainly perish."

"But who are you, then?" said Mary, while again descending to the flowery fragrance; "or have you no name at all?"

"We are called the Elves," replied the friendly child; "people talk about us in the Earth, as I have heard."

They now perceived a mighty bustle on the green. "The fair Bird is come!" cried the children to them: all hastened to the hall. Here, as they approached, young and old were crowding over the threshold, all shouting for joy; and from within resounded a triumphant peal of music. Having entered, they perceived the vast circuit filled with the most varied forms, and all were looking upwards to a large Bird with glancing plumage, that was sweeping slowly round in the dome, and in its stately flight describing many a circle. The music sounded more gaily than before; the colors and lights alternated more rapidly. At last the music ceased; and the Bird, with a rustling noise, floated down upon a glittering crown that hung hovering in air under the high window, by which the hall was lighted from above. His plumage was purple and green, and shining golden streaks played through it; on his head there waved a diadem of feathers, so resplendent that they glanced like jewels. His bill was red, and his legs of a glancing blue. As he moved, the tints gleamed through each other, and the eye was charmed with their radiance. His size was as that of an eagle. But now he opened his glittering beak; and sweetest melodies came pouring from his moved breast, in finer tones than the lovesick nightingale gives forth; still stronger rose the song, and streamed like floods of Light, so that all, the very children themselves, were moved by it to tears of joy and rapture. When he ceased, all bowed before him; he again flew round the dome in circles, then darted through the door, and soared into the light heaven, where he shone far up like a red point, and then soon vanished from their eyes.

"Why are ye all so glad?" inquired Mary, bending to her fair playmate, who seemed smaller than yesterday.

"The King is coming!" said the little one; "many of us have never seen him, and whithersoever he turns his face, there is happiness and mirth; we have long looked for him, more anxiously than you look for spring when winter lingers with you; and now he has announced, by his fair herald, that he is at hand. This wise and glorious Bird, that has been sent to us by the King, is called Phœnix; he dwells far off in Arabia, on a tree, which there is no other that resembles on Earth, as in like manner there is no second Phœnix. When he feels himself grown old, he builds a pile of balm and incense, kindles it, and dies singing; and then from the fragrant ashes, soars up the renewed Phœnix with unlessened beauty. It is seldom he so wings his course that men behold him; and when once in centuries this does occur, they note it in their annals, and expect remarkable events. But now, my friend, thou and I must part; for the sight of the King is not permitted thee."

Then the lady with the golden robe came through the throng, and beckoning Mary to her, led her into a sequestered walk. "Thou must leave us, my dear child," said she; "the King is to hold his court here for twenty years, perhaps longer; and fruitfulness and blessings will spread far over the land, but chiefly here beside us; all the brooks and rivulets will become more bountiful, all the fields and gardens richer, the wine more generous, the meadows more fertile, and the woods more fresh and green; a milder air will blow, no hail shall hurt, no flood shall threaten. Take this ring, and think of us: but beware of telling any one of our existence; or we must fly this land, and thou and all around will lose the happiness and blessing of our neighborhood. Once more, kiss thy playmate, and farewell." They issued from the walk; Zerina wept, Mary stooped to embrace her, and they parted. Already she was on the narrow bridge; the cold air was blowing on her back from the firs, the little dog barked with all its might, and rang its little bell; she looked round, then hastened over, for the darkness of the firs, the bleakness of the ruined huts, the shadows of the twilight, were filling her with terror.

"What a night my parents must have had on my account!" said she within herself, as she stept on the green; "and I dare not tell them where I have been, or what wonders I have witnessed, nor indeed would they believe me." Two men passing by saluted her, and as they went along, she heard them say: "What a pretty girl! Where can she come from?" With quickened steps she approached the house: but the trees which were hanging last night loaded with fruit, were now standing dry and leafless; the house was differently painted, and a new barn had been built beside it. Mary was amazed, and thought she must be dreaming. In this perplexity she opened the door; and behind the table sat her father, between an unknown woman and a stranger youth. "Good God! Father," cried she, "where is my mother?"

"Thy mother!" said the woman, with a forecasting tone, and sprang towards her: "Ha, thou surely canst not—Yes, indeed, indeed thou art my lost, long-lost dear, only Mary!" She had recognised her by a little brown mole beneath the chin, as well as by her eyes and shape. All embraced her, all were moved with joy, and the parents wept. Mary was astonished that she almost reached to her father's stature; and she could not understand how her mother had become so changed and faded; she asked the name of the stranger youth. "It is our neighbour's Andres," said Martin. "How comest thou to us again, so unexpectedly, after seven long years? Where hast thou been? Why didst thou never send us tidings of thee?"

"Seven years!" said Mary, and could not order her ideas and recollections. "Seven whole years?"

"Yes, yes," said Andres, laughing, and shaking her trustfully by the hand; "I have won the race, good Mary; I was at the pear-tree and back again seven years ago, and thou, sluggish creature, art but just returned!"

They again asked, they pressed her; but remembering her instruction, she could answer nothing. It was they themselves chiefly that, by degrees, shaped a story for her: How, having lost her way, she had been taken up by a coach, and carried to a strange remote part, where she could not give the people any notion of her parents' residence; how she was conducted to a distant town, where certain worthy persons brought her up, and loved her; how they had lately died, and at length she had recollected her birth-place, and so returned. "No matter how it is!" exclaimed her mother; "enough that we have thee again, my little daughter, my own, my all!"

Andres waited supper, and Mary could not be at home in anything she saw. The house seemed small and dark; she felt astonished at her dress, which was clean and simple, but appeared quite foreign; she looked at the ring on her finger, and the gold of it glittered strangely, inclosing a stone of burning red. To her father's question, she replied that the ring also was a present from her benefactors.

She was glad when the hour of sleep arrived, and she hastened to her bed. Next morning she felt much more collected; she had now arranged her thoughts a little, and could better stand the questions of the people in the village, all of whom came in to bid her welcome. Andres was there too with the earliest, active, glad, and serviceable beyond all others. The blooming maiden of fifteen had made a deep impression on him; he had passed a sleepless night. The people of the castle likewise sent for Mary, and she had once more to tell her story to them, which was now grown quite familiar to her. The old Count and his Lady were surprised at her good breeding; she was modest, but not embarrassed; she made answer courteously in good phrases to all their questions; all fear of noble persons and their equipage had passed away from her; for when she measured these halls and forms by the wonders and the high beauty she had seen with the Elves in their hidden abode, this earthly splendor seemed but dim to her, the presence of men was almost mean. The young lords were charmed with her beauty.

It was now February. The trees were budding earlier than usual; the nightingale had never come so soon; the spring rose fairer in the land than the oldest men could recollect it. In every quarter, little brooks gushed out to irrigate the pastures and meadows; the hills seemed heaving, the vines rose higher and higher, the fruit-trees blossomed as they had never done; and a swelling fragrant blessedness hung suspended heavily in rosy clouds over the scene. All prospered beyond expectation: no rude day, no tempest injured the fruits; the wine flowed blushing in immense grapes; and the inhabitants of the place felt astonished, and were captivated as in a sweet dream. The next year was like its forerunner; but men had now become accustomed to the marvellous. In autumn, Mary yielded to the pressing entreaties of Andres and her parents; she was betrothed to him, and in winter they were married.

She often thought with inward longing of her residence behind the fir-trees; she continued serious and still. Beautiful as all that lay around her was, she knew of something yet more beautiful; and from the remembrance of this, a faint regret attuned her nature to soft melancholy. It smote her painfully when her father and mother talked about the gipsies and vagabonds, that dwelt in the dark spot of ground. Often she was on the point of speaking out in defence of those good beings, whom she knew to be the benefactors of the land; especially to Andres, who appeared to take delight in zealously abusing them: yet still she repressed the word that was struggling to escape her bosom. So passed this year; in the next, she was solaced by a little daughter, whom she named Elfrida, thinking of the designation of her friendly Elves.

The young people lived with Martin and Brigitta, the house being large enough for all; and helped their parents in conducting their now extended husbandry. The little Elfrida soon displayed peculiar faculties and gifts; for she could walk at a very early age, and could speak perfectly before she was a twelvemonth old; and after some few years, she had become so wise and clever, and of such wondrous beauty, that all people regarded her with astonishment; and her mother could not keep away the thought that her child resembled one of those shining little ones in the space behind the Firs. Elfrida cared not to be with other children; but seemed to avoid, with a sort of horror, their tumultuous amusements; and liked best to be alone. She would then retire into a corner of the garden, and read, or work diligently with her needle; often also you might see her sitting, as if deep sunk in thought; or violently walking up and down the alleys, speaking to herself.

Her parents readily allowed her to have her will in these things, for she was healthy, and waxed apace; only her strange sagacious answers and observations often made them anxious. "Such wise children do not grow to age," her grandmother, Brigitta, many times observed; "they are too good for this world; the child, besides, is beautiful beyond nature, and will never find its proper place on Earth."

The little girl had this peculiarity, that she was very loath to let herself be served by any one, but endeavored to do everything herself. She was almost the earliest riser in the house; she washed herself carefully, and dressed without assistance: at night she was equally careful; she took special heed to pack up her clothes and washes with her own hands, allowing no one, not even her mother, to meddle with her articles. The mother humored her in this caprice, not thinking it of any consequence. But what was her astonishment, when, happening one holiday to insist, regardless of Elfrida's tears and screams, on dressing her out for a visit to the castle, she found upon her breast, suspended by a string, a piece of gold of a strange form, which she directly recognised as one of that sort she had seen in such abundance in the subterranean vault! The little thing was greatly frightened; and at last confessed that she had found it in the garden, and as she liked it much, had kept it carefully: she at the same time prayed so earnestly and pressingly to have it back, that Mary fastened it again on its former place, and, full of thoughts, went out with her in silence to the castle.

Sidewards from the farm-house lay some offices for the storing of produce and implements; and behind these there was a little green, with an old grove, now visited by no one, as, from the new arrangement of the buildings, it lay too far from the garden. In this solitude, Elfrida delighted most; and it occurred to nobody to interrupt her here, so that frequently her parents did not see her for half a day. One afternoon her mother chanced to be in these buildings, seeking for some lost article among the lumber; and she noticed that a beam of light was coming in, through a chink in the wall. She took a thought of looking through this aperture, and seeing what her child was busied with; and it happened that a stone was lying loose, and could be pushed aside, so that she obtained a view right into the grove. Elfrida was sitting there on a little bench, and beside her the well-known Zerina; and the children were playing, and amusing one another, in the kindliest unity. The Elf embraced her beautiful companion, and said mournfully: "Ah! dear little creature, as I sport with thee, so have I sported with thy mother, when she was a child; but you mortals so soon grow tall and thoughtful! It is very hard: wert thou but to be a child as long as I!"

"Willingly would I do it," said Elfrida; "but they all say, I shall come to sense, and give over playing altogether; for I have great gifts, as they think, for growing wise. Ah! and then I shall see thee no more, thou dear Zerina! Yet it is with us as with the fruit-tree flowers: how glorious the blossoming apple-tree, with its red bursting buds! It looks so stately and broad; and every one, that passes under it, thinks surely something great will come of it; then the sun grows hot, and the buds come joyfully forth; but the wicked kernel is already there, which pushes off and casts away the fair flower's dress; and now, in pain and waxing, it can do nothing more, but must grow to fruit in harvest. An apple, to be sure, is pretty and refreshing; yet nothing to the blossom of spring. So is it also with us mortals: I am not glad in the least at growing to be a tall girl. Ah! could I but once visit you!"

"Since the King is with us," said Zerina, "it is quite impossible; but I will come to thee, my darling, often, often, and none shall see me either here or there. I will pass invisible through the air, or fly over to thee like a bird; Oh! we will be much, much together, while thou art so little. What can I do to please thee?"

"Thou must like me very dearly," said Elfrida, "as I like thee in my heart: but come, let us make another rose."

Zerina took a well-known box from her bosom, threw two grains from it on the ground; and instantly a green bush stood before them, with two deep-red roses, bending their heads, as if to kiss each other. The children plucked them smiling, and the bush disappeared. "O that it would not die so soon!" said Elfrida; "this red child, this wonder of the Earth!"

"Give it me here," said the little Elf; then breathed thrice upon the budding rose, and kissed it thrice. "Now," said she, giving back the rose, "it will continue fresh and blooming till winter."

"I will keep it," said Elfrida, "as an image of thee; I will guard it in my little room, and kiss it night and morning, as if it were thyself."

"The sun is setting," said the other, "I must home." They embraced again, and Zerina vanished.

In the evening, Mary clasped her child to her breast, with a feeling of alarm and veneration. She henceforth allowed the good little girl more liberty than formerly; and often calmed her husband, when he came to search for the child; which for some time he was wont to do, as her retiredness did not please him, and he feared that, in the end, it might make her silly, or even pervert her understanding. The mother often glided to the chink; and almost always found the bright Elf beside her child, employed in sport, or in earnest conversation.

"Wouldst thou like to fly?" inquired Zerina once.

"Oh, well! How well!" replied Elfrida; and the fairy clasped her mortal playmate in her arms, and mounted with her from the ground, till they hovered above the grove. The mother, in alarm, forgot herself, and pushed out her head in terror to look after them; when Zerina, from the air, held up her finger, and threatened yet smiled; then descended with the child, embraced her, and disappeared. After this, it happened more than once that Mary was observed by her; and every time, the shining little creature shook her head, or threatened, yet with friendly looks.

Often, in disputing with her husband, Mary had said in her zeal: "Thou dost injustice to the poor people in the hut!" But when Andres pressed her to explain why she differed in opinion from the whole village, nay, from his Lordship himself; and how she could understand it better than the whole of them, she still broke off embarrassed, and became silent. One day, after dinner, Andres grew more violent than ever; and maintained that, by one means or another, the crew must be packed away, as a nuisance to the country; when his wife, in anger, said to him: "Hush! for they are benefactors to thee and to every one of us."

"Benefactors!" cried the other, in astonishment: "These rogues and vagabonds?"

In her indignation, she was now at last tempted to relate to him, under promise of the strictest secrecy, the history of her youth: and as Andres at every word grew more incredulous, and shook his head in mockery, she took him by the hand, and led him to the chink; where, to his amazement, he beheld the glittering Elf sporting with his child, and caressing her in the grove. He knew not what to say; an exclamation of astonishment escaped him, and Zerina raised her eyes. On the instant she grew pale, and trembled violently; not with friendly, but with indignant looks, she made the sign of threatening, and then said to Elfrida: "Thou canst not help it, dearest heart; but they will never learn sense, wise as they believe themselves." She embraced the little one with stormy haste; and then, in the shape of a raven, flew with hoarse cries over the garden, towards the Firs.

In the evening, the little one was very still, she kissed her rose with tears; Mary felt depressed and frightened, Andres scarcely spoke. It grew dark. Suddenly there went a rustling through the trees; birds flew to and fro with wild screaming, thunder was heard to roll, the Earth shook, and tones of lamentation moaned in the air. Andres and his wife had not courage to rise; they shrouded themselves within the curtains, and with fear and trembling awaited the day. Towards morning, it grew calmer; and all was silent when the Sun, with his cheerful light, rose over the wood.

Andres dressed himself, and Mary now observed that the stone of the ring upon her finger had become quite pale. On opening the door, the sun shone clear on their faces, but the scene around them they could scarcely recognise. The freshness of the wood was gone; the hills were shrunk, the brooks were flowing languidly with scanty streams, the sky seemed grey; and when you turned to the Firs, they were standing there no darker or more dreary than the other trees. The huts behind were no longer frightful; and several inhabitants of the village came and told about the fearful night, and how they had been across the spot where the gipsies had lived; how these people must have left the place at last, for their huts were standing empty, and within had quite a common look, just like the dwellings of other poor people: some of their household gear was left behind.

Elfrida in secret said to her mother: "I could not sleep last night; and in my fright at the noise, I was praying from the bottom of my heart, when the door suddenly opened, and my playmate entered to take leave of me. She had a travelling-pouch slung round her, a hat on her head, and a large staff in her hand. She was very angry at thee; since on thy account she had now to suffer the severest and most painful punishments, as she had always been so fond of thee; for all of them, she said, were very loath to leave this quarter."

Mary forbade her to speak of this; and now the ferryman came across the river, and told them new wonders. As it was growing dark, a stranger man of large size had come to him, and hired his boat till sunrise; and with this condition, that the boatman should remain quiet in his house, at least should not cross the threshold of his door. "I was frightened," continued the old man, "and the strange bargain would not let me sleep. I slipped softly to the window, and looked towards the river. Great clouds were driving restlessly through the sky, and the distant woods were rustling fearfully; it was as if my cottage shook, and moans and lamentations glided round it. On a sudden, I perceived a white streaming light, that grew broader and broader, like many thousands of falling stars; sparkling and waving, it proceeded forward from the dark Fir-ground, moved over the fields, and spread itself along towards the river. Then I heard a trampling, a jingling, a bustling, and rushing, nearer and nearer; it went forwards to my boat, and all stept into it, men and women, as it seemed, and children; and the tall stranger ferried them over. In the river were by the boat swimming many thousands of glittering forms; in the air white clouds and lights were wavering; and all lamented and bewailed that they must travel forth so far, far away, and leave their beloved dwelling. The noise of the rudder and the water creaked and gurgled between whiles, and then suddenly there would be silence. Many a time the boat landed, and went back, and was again laden; many heavy casks, too, they took along with them, which multitudes of horrid-looking little fellows carried and rolled; whether they were devils or goblins, Heaven only knows. Then came, in waving brightness, a stately freight; it seemed an old man, mounted on a small white horse, and all were crowding round him. I saw nothing of the horse but its head; for the rest of it was covered with costly glittering cloths and trappings: on his brow the old man had a crown, so bright, that as he came across, I thought the sun was rising there, and the redness of the dawn glimmering in my eyes. Thus it went on all night; I at last fell asleep in the tumult, half in joy, half in terror. In the morning all was still; but the river is, as it were, run off, and I know not how I am to steer my boat in it now."

The same year there came a blight; the woods died away, the springs ran dry; and the scene, which had once been the joy of every traveller, was in autumn standing waste, naked, and bald; scarcely showing here and there, in the sea of sand, a spot or two where grass, with a dingy greenness, still grew up. The fruit-trees all withered, the vines faded away, and the aspect of the place became so melancholy, that the Count, with his people, next year left the castle, which in time decayed and fell to ruins.

Elfrida gazed on her rose day and night with deep longing, and thought of her kind playmate; and as it drooped and withered, so did she also hang her head; and before the spring, the little maiden had herself faded away. Mary often stood upon the spot before the hut, and wept for the happiness that had departed. She wasted herself away like her child, and in a few years she too was gone. Old Martin, with his son-in-law, returned to the quarter where he had lived before.

FREDERIC WILLIAM JOSEPH VON SCHELLING.

Born 1775.

SCHELLING, the third and the only surviving one of the great quaternion of German philosophers, was born at Leonberg, in Würtemberg, January 27th, 1775. He studied philosophy and theology at Tübingen, Leipzig and Jena. At the latter university he was a pupil of Fichte, and afterward (1798) succeeded him as professor of philosophy. In 1803, he went to Würzburg, as professor *ordinarius* of philosophy; in 1807, to Munich, where he was made general secretary of the Academy of the Plastic Arts, and where he was ennobled by the King of Bavaria. In 1820, he left that place in disgust, in consequence of a literary controversy with the president of the Academy of Sciences, and lectured on philosophy in Erlangen; but accepted an invitation to return, seven years after, as professor *ordinarius* of philosophy, with the title of Privy Aulic Counsellor. He remained in Munich until the beginning of the present decade, when he was invited to Berlin by the reigning monarch of Prussia, to lecture at the university in the capacity of member of the Berlin Academy; a situation which he holds, it is believed, to this day, having entered upon it in November, 1841.

If Fichte's is the most interesting character among the transcendental philosophers of Germany, Schelling's is the richest genius and the widest influence. Incalculable has been the influence of his profound intuitions on Philosophy, Letters, Science, Art; on all departments of human Thought. His word was the breath of spring to the intellectual world of his time. It brought verdure and a sudden efflorescence to every branch of knowledge. Probably no man of his age, certainly no one in the province of abstract speculation, has put forth so many new and life-giving thoughts. His philosophy is creative, as that of Kant is destructive. He combines—what is so rare in philosophy—intuitive perception and poetic imagination, with dialectic subtlety and philosophical analysis. He is the *poet* of the transcendental movement, as Fichte is its preacher.

Schelling has given to the world no complete system of philosophy. There is no one work, as in the case of Kant and Fichte, which can be referred to as containing a full and systematic exposition of his distinctive views. They are scattered through a long series of works, each one of which presents some particular result of his speculations, or some particular aspect of his philosophy. Moreover, his view varies in different statements. His philosophy has received new modifications at different periods of his long life. But these modifications have not changed its identity; and the general direction of his opinions remains the same. The following are the titles of some of his works: "On the Possibility of a Form of Philosophy;" "Idea of a Philosophy of Nature;" "Introduction to a System of Natural Philosophy;" "Concerning the *I*;" "The Soul of the World;" "On the Relation between the Ideal and the Real in Nature;" "Philosophy and Religion," &c. &c.

Schelling differs from Fichte in the objective or realistic direction of his thought. Both endeavored to construct a philosophy of the Absolute. Both set out with the principle that there is but one being, one substance. Fichte sought it in the conscious self; Schelling finds it in Nature. Fichte regarded Nature, or the world of appearances, as a modification of Thought; Schelling regards Thought as a function or blossom of Nature. Accordingly, he gave to his philosophy the title, "Natural Philosophy," or "Philosophy of Nature." It is also called the "Philosophy of Identity," because he holds that matter and spirit, the ideal and the real, subject and object, are identical. The Absolute, according to him, is neither real nor ideal, (neither matter nor spirit,) but the identity of both. There is but one Being; that Being may be considered at once or alternately, as either wholly ideal or wholly real. God is the absolute identity of Nature and Thought, of matter and spirit. And this absolute identity is not the cause of the universe, but the universe itself—a God-universe.

From this account, it will be seen that the

philosophy of Schelling bears a close resemblance to that of Spinoza. What Spinoza dissected in dry mathematical formulas, Schelling gave forth a living soul. But, though they agree in substance, they differ in spirit. With Schelling, the spirit predominates; with Spinoza, the substance. Spinoza saw God immanent in Nature; Schelling sees Nature dissolved in God.

"By far the most important result of Schelling's philosophy," says Menzel, "seems to be the impartial epical view of the world which it imparts. In the system of Schelling, every party finds its place opposite another; the separation is shown to be a natural one; their contradictions are referred to an original and necessary opposition. This system throughout tolerates nothing exclusive, no unconditional persecution of another. It endeavors to secure to every spiritual existence, be it an opinion, a character or an event, the same right in a natural philosophy of mind and history which every material existence has in common science. It considers the historical periods as seasons of the year, nationalities as zones, temperaments as the elements, characters as creatures, and their manifestations in thought and action as necessarily founded in Nature, and as diverse as the instincts. According to this system, there is a growth and a progress, a multiplicity and an order, in the intellectual world, as in the natural. In it alone the endless war of opinion is hushed, and every contradiction finds its simplest and most natural solution."*

* Menzel's "German Literature." Translated by C. C. Felton.

ON THE RELATION OF THE PLASTIC ARTS TO NATURE.

A SPEECH ON THE CELEBRATION OF THE 12TH OCTOBER, 1807, AS THE NAME-DAY OF HIS MAJESTY THE KING OF BAVARIA.

Delivered before the Public Assembly of the Royal Academy of Sciences at Munich, by F. W. J. Schelling.*

* * * PLASTIC ART, according to the most ancient expression, is silent Poetry. The inventor of this definition no doubt meant thereby that the former, like the latter, is to express spiritual thoughts—conceptions whose source is the soul; only not by speech, but like silent Nature by shape, by form, by corporeal, independent works.

Plastic Art, therefore, evidently stands as a uniting link between the soul and Nature, and can be apprehended only in the living centre of both. Indeed, since Plastic Art has its relation to the soul in common with every other art, and particularly with Poetry, that by which it is connected with Nature, and, like Nature, a productive force, remains as its sole peculiarity. So that to this alone can a theory relate which shall be satisfactory to the understanding, and helpful and profitable to Art itself.

We hope, therefore, in considering Plastic Art in relation to its true prototype and original source, Nature, to be able to contribute something new to its theory—to give some additional exactness or clearness to the conceptions of it; but, above all, to set forth the coherence of the whole structure of Art in the light of a higher necessity.

But has not Science always recognised this relation? Has not indeed every theory of modern times taken its departure from this very position, that Art should be the imitator of Nature? Such has indeed been the case. But what should this broad general proposition profit the artist, when the notion of Nature is of so various interpretation, and when there are almost as many differing views of it, as various modes of life? Thus, to one, Nature is nothing more than the lifeless aggregate of an indeterminable crowd of objects, or the space in which, as in a vessel, he imagines things placed;—to another, only the soil from which he draws his nourishment and support;—to the inspired seeker alone, the holy, ever-creative original energy of the world, which generates and busily evolves all things out of itself.

The proposition would indeed have a high significance, if it taught Art to emulate this creative force; but the sense in which it was meant can scarcely be doubtful to one acquainted with the universal condition of Science at the time when it was first brought forward. Singular enough that the very persons who denied all life to Nature, should set it up for imitation in Art! To them might be applied the words of a profound writer:* "Your lying philosophy has put Nature out of the way; and why do you call upon us to imitate her? Is it that you may renew the pleasure by perpetrating the same violence on the disciples of Nature?"

Nature was to them not merely a dumb, but an altogether lifeless image, in whose inmost being even no living word dwelt; a hollow scaffolding of forms, of which as hollow an image was to be transferred to the canvass, or hewn out in stone.

* Translated by J. Elliot Cabot, Esq.

* J. G. Hamann.

This was the proper doctrine of those more ancient and savage nations, who, as they saw in Nature nothing divine, fetched idols out of her; whilst, to the susceptive Greeks, who everywhere felt the presence of a vitally efficient principle, genuine gods arose out of Nature.

But is, then, the disciple of Nature to copy everything in Nature without distinction? and of everything, every part? Only beautiful objects should be represented; and, even in these, only the Beautiful and Perfect.

Thus is the proposition farther determined; but, at the same time, this asserted, that, in Nature, the perfect is mingled with the imperfect —the beautiful with the unbeautiful. Now, how should he who stands in no other relation to Nature than that of servile imitation, distinguish the one from the other? It is the way of imitators to appropriate the faults of their model sooner and easier than its excellences, since the former offer handles and tokens more easily grasped; and thus we see that imitators of Nature in this sense have imitated oftener, and even more affectionately, the ugly than the beautiful.

If we regard in things, not their principle, but the empty abstract form, neither will they say anything to our soul; our own heart, our own spirit we must put to it, that they answer us.

But what is the perfection of a thing? Nothing else than the creative life in it, its power to exist. Never, therefore, will he, who fancies that Nature is altogether dead, be successful in that profound process (analogous to the chemical) whence proceeds, purified as by fire, the pure gold of Beauty and Truth.

Nor was there any change in the main view of the relation of Art to Nature, even when the unsatisfactoriness of the principle began to be more generally felt; no change, even by the new views and new knowledge so nobly established by John Winkelmann. He indeed restored to the soul its full efficiency in Art, and raised it from its unworthy dependence into the realm of spiritual freedom. Powerfully moved by the beauty of form in the works of antiquity, he taught that the production of ideal Nature, of Nature elevated above the Actual, together with the expression of spiritual conceptions, is the highest aim of Art.

But if we examine in what sense this surpassing of the Actual by Art has been understood by the most, it turns out that, with this view also, the notion of Nature as mere product; of things as a lifeless result, still continued; and the idea of a living creative Nature was in no wise awakened by it. So that these ideal forms also could be animated by no positive insight into their nature; and if the forms of the Actual were dead for the dead beholder, these were not less so. Was no independent production of the Actual possible, neither was it of the Ideal. The object of the imitation was changed, the imitation remained. In the place of Nature were substituted the sublime works of Antiquity, whose outward forms the pupils busied themselves in taking down, but without the spirit that fills them. These, however, are as unapproachable, nay, more so, than the works of Nature; and leave us yet colder, if we bring not to them the spiritual eye to penetrate through the veil, and feel the stirring energy within.

On the other hand, artists, since that time, have indeed received a certain ideal bias, and notions of a beauty superior to matter; but these notions were like fair words, to which the deeds do not correspond. While the previous method in Art produced bodies without soul, this view taught only the secret of the soul, but not that of the body. The theory had, as usual, passed with one hasty stride to the opposite extreme; but the vital mean it had not yet found.

Who can say that Winkelmann had not an insight into the highest beauty? But with him it appeared in its dissevered elements: on one side as beauty in idea, and flowing out from the soul; on the other, as beauty of forms. But what is the efficient link that connects the two? or by what power is the soul created together with the body, at once and as if with one breath? If this lies not within the power of Art, as of Nature, then it can create nothing whatever. This vital connecting link, Winkelmann did not determine; he did not teach how, from the idea, forms can be produced. Thus Art went over to that method which we would call the retrograde, since it strives from the form to come at the essence. But not thus is the Unlimited reached; it is not attainable by mere enhancement of the Limited. Hence, such works as have had their beginning in form, with all elaborateness on that side, show, in token of their origin, an incurable want at the very point where we expect the consummate, the essential, the final. The miracle by which the Limited should be raised to the Unlimited, the human become divine, is wanting: the magic circle is drawn, but the spirit that it should enclose, appears not, disobedient to the call of him who thought a creation possible through mere form. * * * *

* * * * * *

Nature meets us everywhere, at first with reserve, and in form more or less severe. She is like that quiet and serious beauty, that excites not attention by noisy advertisement, nor attracts the vulgar gaze.

How can we, as it were, spiritually melt this apparently rigid form, so that the pure energy of things may flow together with the force of our spirit, and pour forth in one united gush? We must transcend Form, in order to gain it again as intelligible, living, and truly felt. Consider the most beautiful forms: what remains behind after you have abstracted from them the efficient principle within? Nothing but mere unessential qualities, such as extension and the relations of space. Does the fact that one portion of matter exists near another, and distinct from it, contribute anything to its inner essence? or does it not rather contribute nothing? Evidently the latter. It is not mere contiguous existence, but the manner of it, that makes form; and this can be determined only by a positive force, which is even opposed to separateness, and subordinates the manifoldness of the parts to the unity of one idea — from the force that works in the crystal, to that which, as a gentle magnetic current, gives to the particles of matter in the human form a position and arrangement among themselves, through which the idea, the essential unity and beauty, can become visible.

Not only, however, as active principle, but as spirit and effective science, must the essence appear to us in the form, in order that we may truly apprehend it. For all unity must be spiritual in nature and origin: and what is the aim of all investigation of Nature, but to find science therein? For that wherein there were no Understanding, could not be the object of Understanding: the Unknowing could not be known. The science by which Nature works is not, indeed, like human science, connected with reflection upon itself: in it, the conception is not separate from the act, nor the design from the execution. Thus, rude matter strives, as it were, blindly, after regular shape, and unknowingly assumes pure stereometric forms, which belong, nevertheless, to the realm of ideas, and are something spiritual in the material.

The sublimest arithmetic and geometry are innate in the stars, and unconsciously displayed by them in their motions. More distinctly, but still beyond their grasp, the living cognition appears in animals; and thus we see them, though wandering about without reflection, bring about innumerable results far more excellent than themselves:—the bird that, intoxicated with music, transcends itself in soul-like tones; the little artistic creature, that, without practice or instruction, accomplishes light works of architecture;—but all directed by an overpowering spirit, that lightens in them already with single flashes of knowledge, but as yet appears nowhere as the full sun, as in Man.

This formative science in Nature and Art is the link that connects idea and form, body and soul. Before everything stands an eternal idea, formed in the Infinite Understanding; but by what means does this idea pass into actuality and embodiment? Only through the creative science that is as necessarily connected with the Infinite Understanding, as in the artist the principle that seizes the idea of unsensuous Beauty, with that which sets it forth to the senses.

Is the artist to be called happy and praiseworthy before all, to whom the gods have granted this spirit; so the work of art will appear in that measure excellent in which it shows to us, as in outline, this unadulterated energy of creation and activity in Nature.

It was long ago perceived that, in Art, not everything is performed with consciousness; that, with the conscious activity, an unconscious action must combine; and that it is of the perfect unity and mutual interpenetration of the two that the highest in Art is born.

Works that want this seal of unconscious science, are recognised by the evident absence of life self-supported and independent of the producer: as, on the contrary, where this acts, Art imparts to its work, together with the utmost clearness to the understanding, that unfathomable reality wherein it resembles a work of Nature.

It has often been attempted to make clear the position of the artist in regard to Nature, by saying that Art, in order to be such, must first withdraw itself from Nature, and return to it only in the last completeness. The true sense of this saying, it seems to us, can be no other than this: That in all things in Nature, the living idea shows itself only blindly active: were it so also in the artist, he would be in nothing distinct from Nature. But, should he attempt consciously to subordinate himself altogether to the Actual, and give back with servile fidelity the already existing, he would produce *larvæ*, but no works of Art. He must therefore withdraw himself from the product, from the creature; but only in order to raise himself to the creative energy, and spiritually to seize this. Thus he ascends into the realm of pure ideas; he forsakes the creature, to regain it with thousand-fold interest, and in this sense certainly to return to Nature. This spirit of Nature working at the core of things, and speaking through form and shape as by symbols only, the artist must certainly follow with emulation; and only so far as he seizes this with genial imitation, has he himself produced anything genuine. For works produced by aggregation, even of forms beautiful in themselves, would still be destitute of all beauty, since that, through which the work on the whole is truly beautiful, cannot be form. It is above form — it is Essence; the Universal; the look and expression of the indwelling spirit of Nature.

Now it can scarcely be doubtful what is to be thought of the so-called idealising of Nature in Art, so universally demanded. This demand seems to arise from a way of thinking, according to which not Truth, Beauty, Goodness, but the contrary of all these is the Actual. Were the Actual indeed opposed to Truth and Beauty, it would be necessary for the artist, not to elevate or idealise it, but to get rid of and destroy it, in order to create anything true and beautiful. But how should it be possible for anything to be actual except the True; and what is Beauty, if not full complete Being?

What higher aim, therefore, could Art have, than to represent that which in Nature truly is? Or how should it undertake to excel so-called actual Nature, since it must always fall short of it?

For does Art impart to its works actual sensuous life? This statue breathes not, is stirred by no pulsation, warmed by no blood.

But both the pretended excelling and the apparent falling short show themselves as the consequences of one and the same principle, so soon as we place the aim of Art in the exhibiting of that which truly is.

Only on the surface have its works the appearance of life; in Nature, life seems to reach deeper, and to be wedded entirely with the material. But does not the continual mutation of matter and the universal lot of final dissolution teach us the unessential character of this union, and that it is no intimate combination? Art, accordingly, in the merely superficial animation of its works, represents the unessential as not existing.

How comes it that to every tolerably cultivated taste, imitations of the so-called Actual, even though carried to deception, appear in the last degree untrue; nay, produce the impression of spectres; whilst a work in which the idea is predominant strikes us with the full force of truth, and alone places us in the genuine actual world? Whence comes it, if not from the more or less obscure feeling which tells us that the idea alone is the living principle in things, but all else unessential and vain shadow?

On the same ground may be explained all the opposite cases, which are brought up as instances of the surpassing of Nature by Art. In arresting the rapid course of human years; in uniting the energy of developed manhood with the soft charm of early youth; or exhibiting a mother of grown-up sons and daughters in the full possession of vigorous beauty, what does Art, except to strike out what is unessential, Time?

If, according to the remark of a discerning critic, every growth in Nature has but an instant of truly complete beauty, we may also say that it has too only an instant of full existence. In this instant it is what it is in all eternity: beside this, it has only a coming into and a passing out of existence. Art, in representing the thing at that instant, removes it out of Time, and sets it forth in its pure Being, in the eternity of its life.

After everything positive and essential had once been abstracted from Form, it necessarily appeared limiting, and, as it were, hostile, to the Essence; and the same theory that had called up the false and powerless Ideal, necessarily tended to the formless in Art. Form would indeed be a limitation to the Essence if it existed independent of it. But if it exists with and by means of the Essence, how could this feel itself limited by that which it has itself created? Violence would indeed be done it by a form forced upon it, but never by one proceeding from itself. In this, on the contrary, it must rest contented, and feel its own existence to be self-sustained and complete in itself.

Determinateness of form is in Nature never a

negation, but ever an affirmation. Commonly, indeed, the shape of a body seems a confinement; but could we behold the creative energy, it would reveal itself as the measure that this energy imposes upon itself, and in which it shows itself a truly intelligent force; for in everything is the power of self-rule allowed to be an excellence, and one of the highest.

In like manner most persons consider the particular in a negative manner; viz. as that which is not the whole or all. But no particular exists by means of its limitation, but through the indwelling force with which it maintains itself as a particular Whole, in distinction from the Universe.

This force of particularity, and thus also of individuality, showing itself as vital character, the negative conception of it is necessarily followed by an unsatisfying and false view of the characteristic in Art. Lifeless and of intolerable hardness would be the Art that should aim to exhibit the empty shell or limitation of the Individual. Certainly we desire to see not merely the individual, but more than this, its vital Idea. But if the artist have seized the inward creative spirit and essence of the Idea, and sets this forth, he makes the individual a world in itself, a class, an eternal prototype: and he who has grasped the essential character needs not to fear hardness and severity, for these are the conditions of life. Nature, who in her completeness appears as the utmost benignity, we see in each particular aiming even primarily and principally at severity, seclusion and reserve. As the whole creation is the work of the utmost externisation and renunciation [*Entäusserung*], so the artist must first deny himself and descend into the Particular, without shunning isolation, nor the pain, the anguish of Form.

Nature, from her first works, is throughout characteristic; the energy of fire, the splendor of light she shuts up in hard stone: the tender soul of melody in severe metal:—even in the threshold of Life, and already meditating organic shape, she sinks back overpowered by the might of Form, into petrifaction.

The life of the plant consists in still receptivity, but in what exact and severe outline is this passive life enclosed! In the animal kingdom the strife between Life and Form seems first properly to begin: her first works Nature hides in hard shells, and where these are laid aside, the animated world attaches itself again through its constructive impulse to the realm of crystallization. Finally she comes forward more boldly and freely, and vital, important characteristics show themselves, and are the same through whole classes. Art, indeed, cannot begin so far down as Nature. Though Beauty is spread everywhere, yet there are various grades in the appearance and unfolding of the Essence, and thus of Beauty. But Art demands a certain fulness, and desires not to strike a single note or tone, nor even a detached accord, but at once the full symphony of Beauty.

Art, therefore, prefers to grasp immediately at the highest and most developed, the human form. For since it is not given it to embrace the immeasurable whole, and as in all other creatures only single fulgurations, in Man alone full entire Being appear without abatement, Art is not only permitted but required to see the sum of Nature in Man alone. But precisely on this account,—that she here assembles all in one point, Nature repeats her whole multiformity, and pursues again in a narrower compass the same course that she had gone through in her wide circuit.

Here, therefore, arises the demand upon the artist first to be true and faithful in detail, in order to come forth complete and beautiful in the whole. Here he must wrestle with the creative spirit of Nature ;—[which in the moral world also deals out character and stamp in endless variety,]—not in weak and effeminate, but stout and courageous conflict.

Persevering exercise in the study of that by virtue of which the characteristic in things is a positive principle, must preserve him from emptiness, weakness, inward inanity, before he can venture to aim by ever higher combination and final melting together of manifold forms, to reach the extremest beauty in works uniting the highest simplicity with infinite meaning.

Only through the perfection of form can Form be made to disappear; and this is certainly the final aim of Art in the Characteristic. But as the apparent harmony that is even more easily reached by the empty and frivolous than by others, is yet inwardly vain; so in Art the quickly attained harmony of the exterior without inward fulness. And if it is the part of theory and instruction to oppose the spiritless copying of beautiful forms, especially must they oppose the tendency toward an effeminate characterless Art, which gives itself indeed higher names, but therewith only seeks to hide its incapacity to fulfil the fundamental conditions.

That lofty Beauty in which the fulness of form causes Form itself to disappear, was adopted by the modern theory of Art after Winkelmann, not only as the highest, but as the only standard. But as the deep foundation upon which it rests was overlooked, it resulted that a negative conception was formed of that which is the sum of all affirmation.

Winkelmann compares Beauty with water drawn from the bosom of the spring, which the less taste it has, the wholesomer it is esteemed. It is true that the highest Beauty is characterless, but it is so as we say of the Universe that it has no determinate dimension, neither length, breadth nor depth, since it has all in equal infinity: or that the Art of creative Nature is formless, because she herself is subjected to no form.

In this and in no other sense can we say that Grecian art in its highest cultivation rises into the characterless. But it did not aim immediately at this. It was from the bonds of Nature that it struggled upwards to divine freedom. From no lightly scattered seed, but only from a deeply enfolded kernel, could this heroic growth spring up. Only mighty emotions, only a deep stirring of the fancy through the impression of all-enlivening, all-commanding energies of Nature, could stamp upon Art that invincible vigor with which from the rigid, secluded earnestness of earlier productions up to the period of works overflowing with sensuous grace, it ever remained faithful to truth, and produced the highest spiritual Reality which it is given to mortals to behold.

In like manner as their Tragedy commences with the grandest characteristicness in morals, so the beginning of their Plastic Art was the earnestness of Nature, and the stern goddess of Athens its first and only Muse.

This epoch is marked by that style which Winkelmann describes as the still harsh and severe, from which the next or lofty style was able to develop itself by the mere enhancement of the Characteristic into the Sublime and the Simple.

For in the statues of the most perfect or divine natures, not only all the complexity of form of which human nature is capable had to be united, but moreover the union must be such as may be conceived to exist in the system of the Universe itself: viz. the lower forms, or those relating to inferior attributes, being comprehended under higher, and all at last under one supreme form, in which they indeed extinguish each other as separately existing, but still continue in Essence and efficiency.

Thus, though we cannot call this high and self-sufficing Beauty characteristic, so far as herewith is connected the notion of limitation or conditionality in the manifestation, yet still the characteristic continues efficient, though indistinguishable, within: as in the crystal, although transparent, the texture nevertheless remains.

Each characteristic element has its weight, however slight, and helps to bring about the sublime equipoise of Beauty.

The outer side or basis of all Beauty is beauty of form. But as Form cannot exist without Essence, wherever Form is, there also is Character; whether in visible presence or only perceptible in its effects. Characteristic Beauty, therefore, is Beauty in the root, from which alone Beauty can arise as the fruit. Essence may, indeed, outgrow Form, but even then the Characteristic remains as the still efficient ground-work of the Beautiful.

A most excellent critic,* to whom the Gods have given sway over Nature as well as Art, compares the Characteristic in its relation to

---

* Goethe. *Werke* (1840) xxx. 352. Mr. Ward's translation of Goethe's " Essays on Art," p. 76.

Beauty, with the skeleton in its relation to the living form. Were we to interpret this striking simile in our sense, we should say that the skeleton, in Nature, is not as in our thought detached from the living whole: that the firm and the yielding, the determining and the determined, mutually presuppose each other, and can exist only together: thus that the vitally Characteristic is already the whole form, the result of the action and reaction of bone and flesh, of Active and Passive. And although Art, like Nature, in its higher developments, thrusts inward the previously visible skeleton, yet this latter can never be opposed to Shape and Beauty, since it has always a determining share in the production of the one as well as of the other.

But whether that high and independent Beauty should be the only standard in Art, as it is the highest, seems to depend on the degree of fulness and extent that belongs to the particular Art.

Nature, in her wide circumference, ever exhibits the higher with the lower: creating in Man the godlike, she elaborates in all her other productions only its material and foundation, which must exist in order that in contrast with it the Essence as such may appear. And even in the higher world of Man the great mass serves again as the basis upon which the godlike that is preserved pure in the few, manifests itself in legislation, government, and the establishment of Religion. So that wherever Art works with more of the complexity of Nature, it may and must display together with the highest measure of Beauty, also its groundwork and raw material as it were, in distinct appropriate forms.

Here first prominently unfolds itself the difference in Nature of the forms of Art.

Plastic Art, in the more exact sense of the term, disdains to give Space outwardly to the object, but bears it within itself. This, however, narrows its field; it is compelled, indeed, to display the beauty of the Universe almost in a single point. It must therefore aim immediately at the highest, and can attain complexity only separately and in the strictest exclusion of all conflicting elements. By isolating the purely animal in human nature it succeeds in forming inferior creations too, harmonious and even beautiful, as we are taught by the beauty of numerous Fauns preserved from Antiquity: it can, indeed, parodying itself like the merry spirit of Nature, reverse its own Ideal, and for instance, in the extravagance of the Silenic figures, by light and sportive treatment, appear freed again from the pressure of matter.

But in all cases it is compelled strictly to isolate the work, in order to make it self-consistent and a world in itself; since for this form of Art there is no higher unity, in which the dissonance of particulars should be melted into harmony.

Painting, on the contrary, in the very extent of its sphere, can better measure itself with the Universe, and create with epic profusion. In an Iliad there is room even for a Thersites, and what does not find a place in the great epic of Nature and History!

Here the Particular scarcely counts anything by itself; the Universe takes its place, and that, which by itself would not be beautiful, becomes so in the harmony of the whole. If in an extensive painting, uniting forms by the allotted space, by light, by shade, by reflection, the highest measure of Beauty were everywhere employed, the result would be the most unnatural monotony; for, as Winkelmann says, the highest idea of Beauty is everywhere one and the same, and scarce admits of variation. The detail would be preferred to the whole, where, as in every case in which the whole is formed by multiplicity, the detail must be subordinate to it.

In such a work, therefore, a gradation of Beauty must be observed, by which alone the full Beauty concentrated in the focus becomes visible; and from an exaggeration of particulars proceeds an equipoise of the whole. Here, then, the limited and characteristic finds its place; and theory at least should direct the painter, not so much to the narrow space in which the entire Beauty is concentrically collected, as to the characteristic complexity of Nature, through which alone he can impart to an extensive work the full measure of living significance.

Thus thought, among the founders of modern art, the noble Leonardo; thus Raphael, the master of high Beauty, who shunned not to exhibit it in smaller measure, rather than to appear monotonous, lifeless, and unreal — though he understood not only how to produce it, but also how to break up uniformity by variety of expression.

For, although Character can show itself also in rest and equilibrium of form, yet it is only in action that it becomes truly alive.

By Character we understand a unity of several forces, operating constantly to produce among them a certain equipoise and determinate proportion, to which, if undisturbed, a like equipoise in the symmetry of the forms corresponds. But if this vital Unity is to display itself in act and operation, this can only be when the forces, excited by some cause to rebellion, forsake their equilibrium. Every one sees that this is the case in the Passions.

But here we are met by the well-known maxim of the theorists, which demands that Passion should be moderated as far as possible, in its actual outburst, that beauty of Form may not be injured. But we think this maxim should rather be reversed, and read thus:—that Passion should be moderated by Beauty itself. For it is much to be feared that this desired moderation too may be taken in a negative sense— whereas, what is really requisite is, to oppose to Passion a positive force. For as Virtue consists, not in the absence of passions, but in the mastery of the spirit over them, so Beauty is preserved, not by their removal or abatement, but by the mastery of Beauty over them.

The forces of Passion must actually show themselves—it must be seen that they are prepared to rise in mutiny, but are kept down by the power of Character, and break against the forms of firmly-founded Beauty, as the waves of a stream that just fills, but cannot overflow its banks. Otherwise, this striving after moderation would resemble only those shallow moralists, who, the more readily to dispose of Man, prefer to mutilate his nature; and who have so entirely removed every positive element from actions, that the people gloat over the spectacle of great crimes, in order to refresh themselves at last with the view of something positive.

In Nature and Art the Essence strives first after actualization, or exhibition of itself in the Particular. Thus in each the utmost severity is manifested at the commencement; for without bound, the boundless could not appear; without severity, gentleness could not exist: and if unity is to be perceptible, it can only be through particularity, detachment, and opposition. In the beginning, therefore, the creative spirit shows itself entirely lost in its form, inaccessibly shut up, and even in its grandeur still harsh. But the more it succeeds in uniting its entire fullness in one product, the more it gradually relaxes from its severity; and where it has fully developed the form, so as to rest contented and self-collected in it, it seems to become cheerful, and begins to move in gentle lines. This is the period of its fairest maturity and blossom, in which the pure vessel has arrived at perfection; the spirit of Nature becomes free from its bonds, and feels its relationship to the soul. As by a gentle morning blush stealing over the whole form, the coming soul announces itself: it is not yet present, but everything prepares for its reception, by the delicate play of gentle movements; the rigid outlines melt and temper themselves into flexibility; a lovely essence, neither sensuous nor spiritual, but which cannot be grasped, diffuses itself over the form, and entwines itself with every outline, every vibration of the frame.

This essence, not to be seized, as we have already remarked, but yet perceptible to all, is what the language of the Greeks designated by the name *Charis*, ours as Grace.

Wherever, in a fully developed form, Grace appears, the work is complete on the side of Nature; nothing more is wanting; all demands are satisfied. Here, already, soul and body are in complete harmony; Body is Form, Grace is Soul, although not Soul in itself, but the Soul of Form, or the Soul of Nature.

Art may linger, and remain stationary at this point; for, already, on one side at least its whole task is finished. The pure image of Beauty arrested at this point is the Goddess of Love.

But the beauty of the Soul in itself, joined to sensuous Grace, is the highest apotheosis of Nature.

The spirit of Nature is only in appearance opposed to the Soul; essentially, it is the instrument of its revelation; it brings about indeed the antagonism that exists in all things, but only that the one essence may come forth, as the utmost benignity, and the reconciliation of all the forces.

All other creatures are driven by the mere force of Nature, and through it maintain their individuality; in Man alone, as the central point, arises the soul, without which the world would be like the natural universe without the sun.

The Soul in Man, therefore, is not the principle of individuality, but that whereby he raises himself above all egoism, whereby he becomes capable of self-sacrifice, and of disinterested love, and (which is the highest,) of the contemplation and knowledge of the Essence of things; and thus of Art.

In him it is no longer employed about Matter, nor has to do with it immediately, but only with the spirit, (as the life) of things. Even while appearing in the body, it is yet free from the body, the consciousness of which hovers in the soul in the most beauteous shapes only as a light, undisturbing dream. It is no quality, no faculty, nor anything special of the sort; it knows not, but is Science; it is not good, but Goodness; it is not beautiful, as body even may be, but Beauty itself.

Most readily, or most immediately, indeed, in a work of art, the soul of the artist is seen as invention, in the detail, and in the total result, as the unity that hovers over it in serene stillness. But the Soul must be visible in objective representation, as the primœval energy of thought, in portraitures of human beings, altogether filled by an idea, by a noble contemplation; or as indwelling essential Goodness.

Each of these finds its distinct expression even in the completest repose, but a more living one where the Soul can reveal itself in activity and antagonism; and since it is by the passions mainly that the force of life is interrupted, it is the generally received opinion, that the beauty of the Soul shows itself especially in its quiet supremacy amid the storm of the passions.

But here an important distinction is to be made. For the Soul must not be called upon to moderate those passions which are only an outbreak of the lower spirits of Nature, nor can it be displayed in antithesis with these; for where calm considerateness is still in contention with them, the Soul has not yet appeared: they must be moderated by unassisted Nature in Man, by the might of the Spirit. But there are cases of a higher sort, in which, not a single force alone, but the intelligent Spirit itself breaks down all barriers: cases, indeed, where the Soul is subjected by the bond that connects it with sensuous existence, to pain, which should be foreign to its divine nature: where Man feels himself invaded and attacked in the root of his existence, not by mere powers of Nature, but by moral forces: where innocent error hurries him into crime, and thus into misery: where deep-felt injustice excites to rebellion the holiest feelings of humanity.

This is the case in all situations, truly, and in a high sense, tragical, such as the Tragedy of the ancients brings before our eyes. Where blindly passionate forces are aroused, the collected Spirit is present as the guardian of Beauty; but if the Spirit itself be hurried away, as by an irresistible might, what power shall watch over and protect sacred Beauty? Or, if the soul participate in the struggle, how shall it save itself from pain and from desecration?

Arbitrarily to limit the power of pain, of excited feeling, would be to sin against the very meaning and aim of Art, and would betray a want of feeling and soul in the artist himself.

Already therein, that Beauty, based on grand and firmly-established forms has become Character, Art has provided the means of displaying without injury to symmetry the whole intensity of Feeling. For where Beauty rests on mighty forms, as upon immoveable pillars, a slight change in its relations, scarcely touching the form, causes us to infer the great force that was necessary in order to effect it. Still more does Grace sanctify pain. It is the essential nature of Grace that it does not know itself; but not being wilfully acquired, it also cannot be wilfully lost. When intolerable anguish, when even madness, sent by avenging Gods, takes away consciousness and reflection, Grace stands as a protecting dæmon by the suffering form, and prevents it from manifesting anything unseemly, anything discordant to Humanity; but if it fall, to fall at least a pure and unspotted victim.

Not yet the Soul itself, but the prophecy of it; Grace accomplishes by natural means, what the Soul does by a divine power, in transforming pain, torpor, even death itself, into Beauty.

Yet Grace thus preserved amid the extremest discordance would be dead, without a transfiguration by the soul. But what expression can belong to the soul in this situation? It delivers itself from pain, and comes forth conquering, not conquered, by relinquishing its connection with sensuous existence.

It is for the natural Spirit to exert its energies for the preservation of sensuous existence, the Soul enters not into this contest; but its presence moderates even the storms of painfully-struggling life. Outward force can take away only outward goods, but not reach the Soul: it can tear asunder a temporal bond, not dissolve the eternal one of a truly divine love. Not hard and unfeeling, nor wanting in love itself, the Soul on the contrary displays in pain this alone, as the sentiment that outlasts sensuous existence, and thus raises itself above the ruins of outward life or fortune in divine glory.

It is this expression of the Soul that the creator of the Niobe has shown us in this statue. All the means by which Art tempers even the Terrible, are here made use of. Mightiness of form, sensuous Grace, nay, even the nature of the subject-matter itself softens the expression, since pain, transcending all expression, annihilates itself, and Beauty, which it seemed impossible to preserve from destruction, is protected from injury by the commencing torpor.

But what would it all be without the Soul; and how shall this manifest itself?

We see on the countenance of the mother, not grief alone for the already prostrated flower of her children; not alone deadly anxiety for the preservation of those yet remaining, and of the youngest daughter, who has fled for safety to her bosom; nor resentment against the cruel deities; least of all, as is pretended, cool defiance: all these we see, indeed, but not these alone; for, through grief, anxiety, and resentment streams, like a divine light, eternal love, as that which alone remains: and in this is preserved the mother, as one who was not, but now is a mother, and who remains united with the beloved ones by an eternal bond.

Every one acknowledges that greatness, purity, and goodness of soul have also their sensuous expressions. But how is this conceivable, unless the principle that acts in Matter be itself cognate and similar to Soul?

For the representation of the Soul there are again gradations in Art, according as it is joined with the merely Characteristic, or in visible union with the Charming and Graceful.

Who perceives not, in the tragedies of Æschylus, that lofty morality already predominant, which is at home in the works of Sophocles? But in the former it is enveloped in a bitter rind, and passes less into the whole work, since the bond of sensuous Grace is yet wanting. But out of this severity, and the still terrible charms of earlier Art, could yet proceed the grace of Sophocles, and with it the complete fusion of the two elements, which leaves us doubtful whether it is more moral or sensuous Grace that enchants us in the works of this poet.

The same is true of the plastic productions of the early and severe style, in comparison with the gentleness of the later.

If Grace, besides being the transfiguration of the spirit of Nature, is also the medium of connection between moral Goodness and sensuous Appearance, it is evident how Art must tend from all points towards it as its centre. This Beauty, which results from the perfect interpenetration of moral Goodness and sensuous Grace, seizes and enchants us when we meet it, with the force of a miracle. For, whilst the spirit of Nature shows itself everywhere else independent of the Soul, and, indeed, in a measure opposed to it, here, it seems, as if by voluntary accord, and the inward fire of divine love, to melt into union with it: the remembrance of the fundamental unity of the essence of Nature and the essence of the Soul, comes over the beholder with sudden clearness: the conviction that all antagonism is only apparent; that Love is the bond of all things, and pure Goodness the foundation and substance of the whole Creation.

Here Art as it were transcends itself, and becomes means only. On this summit sensuous Grace becomes in turn only the husk and body of a higher life: what was before a whole is treated as a part, and the highest relation of Art and Nature is reached in this, that it makes Nature the medium of manifesting the soul which it contains.

But though in this blossoming of Art, as in the blossoming of the vegetable kingdom, all the previous stages are repeated, yet on the other hand we may see in what various directions Art can proceed from this centre. Especially the difference in nature of the two forms of plastic Art here shows itself most strongly. For Sculpture, representing its ideas by corporeal things, seem to reach its highest point in the complete equilibrium of Soul and Matter—if it give a preponderance to the latter, it sinks below its own idea—but it seems altogether impossible for it to elevate the soul at the expense of Matter, since it must thereby transcend itself. The perfect sculptor indeed, as Winkelmann remarks on occasion of the Belvidere Apollo, will use no more material than is needful to accomplish his spiritual purpose: but also on the other hand he will put into the soul no more energy than is at the same time expressed in the material: for precisely upon this, fully to embody the spiritual, depends his art. Sculpture, therefore, can reach its true summit only in the representation of those natures in whose constitution it is implied that they actually embody all that is contained in their Idea or soul; thus only in divine natures. So that Sculpture, even if no Mythology had preceded it, would of itself have come upon Gods, and have invented such if it found none.

Moreover as the Spirit, on this lower platform, has again the same relation to Matter that we have ascribed to the Soul, (being the principle of activity and motion, as Matter is that of rest and inaction,) the law that regulates Expression and Passion, must be a fundamental principle of its nature.

But this law must be applicable not only to the lower passions, but also equally to those higher and godlike passions, if it is permitted so to call them, by which the Soul is affected in rapture, in devotion, in adoration. Hence, since from these passions the Gods alone are exempt, Sculpture is inclined from this side also to the imaging of divine natures.

The nature of Painting however seems to differ entirely from that of Sculpture. For the former represents objects not like the latter, by corporeal things, but by light and color; through a medium therefore itself incorporeal, and in a measure spiritual. And Painting moreover gives out its productions nowise as the things themselves, but expressly as pictures. From its very nature therefore it does not lay as much stress on the material as Sculpture, and seems indeed from this reason, when it exalts the material above the spirit, to degrade itself more than Sculpture in a like case: and on the other hand to be yet more justified in giving a clear preponderance to the soul.

Where it aims at the highest it will indeed ennoble the passions by Character, or moderate them by Grace, or manifest in them the power of the Soul: but on the other hand it is precisely those higher passions, depending on the relationship of the soul with a Supreme Being, that are entirely suited to the nature of Painting. Indeed while Sculpture maintains an exact balance between the force whereby a thing exists outwardly and acts in Nature, and that by virtue of which it lives inwardly and as soul, and excludes mere passivity even from Matter; Painting on the contrary may soften in favor of the soul the characteristicness of the force and activity in Matter, and transform it into resignation and endurance, by which Man seems to become more generally susceptible to the inspirations of the soul, and to higher influences.

This diametrical difference explains of itself not only the necessary predominance of Sculpture in the ancient, and of Painting in the modern world, (since in the former the tone of mind was thoroughly plastic, whereas the latter makes even the soul the passive instrument of higher revelations): but this also is evident; that it is not enough to strive after the Plastic in form and manner of representation, but that it is requisite before all to think and to feel plastically, that is, antiquely.

And as the deviation of Sculpture into the picturesque is destructive to Art, so the narrowing down of Painting to the conditions and forms belonging to Sculpture, is an arbitrarily imposed limitation. For while Sculpture, like Gravitation, acts towards one point, it is permitted to Painting, as to Light, to fill all space with its creative energy.

This unlimited universality of Painting is demonstrated by History itself, and by the examples of the greatest masters, who, without injury to the essential character of their art, have developed to perfection each particular stage by itself: so that we can find also in the history of Art the same sequence that may be pointed out in its nature. Not indeed in exact order of time, but yet substantially. For thus is represented in Michael Angelo the oldest and mightiest epoch of liberated Art; that in which it displays its yet uncontrolled strength in gigantic progeny: as in the fables of the symbolic Fore-world, the Earth, after the embrace of Uranus, brought forth at first Titans and heaven-storming giants, before the mild reign of the serene Gods began.

Thus the painting of the Last Judgment, with which, as the sum of his art, that giant spirit filled the Sistine Chapel, seems to remind us more of the first ages of the Earth and its products, than of its last. Attracted towards the most hidden abysses of organic, particularly of the human form, he shuns not the Terrible; nay, he seeks it purposely, and startles it from its repose in the dark workshops of Nature. Want of delicacy, grace, pleasingness, he balances by the extremest energy; and if he excites horror by his representations, it is the terror that, according to fable, the ancient god Pan spreads around him when he suddenly appears in the assemblies of men.

It is the method of Nature to produce the extraordinary by isolation and the exclusion of opposed qualities. Thus, it was necessary that, in Michael Angelo, earnestness and the deep significant energy of Nature should prevail, rather than a sense for the grace and sensibility that belong to the Soul, in order to display the extreme of pure plastic force in the painting of modern times.

After the earlier violence and the vehement impulse of birth is assuaged, the spirit of Nature is transfigured into Soul, and Grace is born. This point Art reached, after Leonardo da Vinci, in Correggio, in whose works the sensuous Soul is the active principle of Beauty.

* * * * * *

As the modern fable of Psyche closes the circle of the old mythology; so Painting, by giving a preponderance to the Soul, attained a new, though not a higher step of Art.

This Guido Reni strove after, and became the proper painter of the soul. Such seems to us to be the necessary interpretation of his whole endeavor, often uncertain, and, in many of his works, losing itself in the vague.

This is shown, as, perhaps, in few of his other pictures, in the masterpiece that is offered to the admiration of all in the great collection of our king.

In the figure of the heavenwards ascending virgin, all harshness and sternness is effaced even to the last trace: and, indeed, does not Painting itself seem in it to soar upwards, transfigured on its own pinions, as the liberated Psyche delivered from the severity of Form?

Here nothing outward remains, with separate natural force; everything expresses receptivity and still endurance, even the perishable flesh, the character of which the Italian language designates by the term *morbidezza*, altogether unlike that with which Raphael invests the descending Queen of Heaven, as she appears to the adoring pope and a saint.

Though the remark be well-founded, that the original of Guido's female heads is the Niobe of antiquity, yet the ground of this similarity is surely no mere intentional imitation; perhaps a like aim led to like means.

As the Florentine Niobe is an extreme in Sculpture, and the representation in it of the Soul; so this well-known picture is an extreme in Painting, which here ventures to lay aside even the requisite of shade and the obscure, and to work almost with pure Light.

Even though it might be permitted to Painting, from its peculiar nature, to give a distinct preponderance to the Soul, yet theory and instruction will do best constantly to aim at that original Centre, whence alone Art may be produced ever anew; whereas, at the stage last mentioned, it must necessarily stand still, or degenerate into cramped mannerism. For even that higher passivity is opposed to the idea of fully energetic Being, whose image and reflex Art is called upon to display.

A right perception will ever enjoy seeing a thing worthily, and, as far as possible, independently developed, even on this side of its individuality: yea, the Deity would look down with pleasure on a creature that, gifted with a pure soul, should stoutly assert the dignity of its nature outwardly also, and by its energetic sensuous existence.

We have seen how the work of Art, springing up out of the depths of Nature, begins with determinateness and limitation, unfolds its inward plenitude and infinity, is finally transfigured in Grace, and at last attains to Soul. But we can conceive only in detail what, in the creative act of mature Art, is but one operation. No theory and no rules can give this spiritual creative power. It is the pure gift of Nature, which here, for the second time, makes a close; for, having fully actualized herself, she invests the creature with her creative energy. But as, in the grand progress of Art, these different stages appeared successively, until, at the highest, all joined in one; so also, in particulars, sound culture can spring up only where it has unfolded itself regularly from the germ and root to the blossom.

The requirement that Art, like everything living, should commence from the first rudiments, and, to renew its youth, constantly return to them, may seem a hard doctrine to an age that has so often been assured that it has only to take from works of Art already in existence the most consummate Beauty, and thus as at a step to reach the final goal. Have we not already the Excellent, the Perfect? How then should we return to the rudimentary and unformed?

Had the great founders of modern Art thought thus, we should never have seen their miracles. Before them also stood the creations of the ancients, round statues and works in relief, which they might have transferred immediately to their canvas. But such an appropriation of a Beauty not self-won, and therefore unintelligible, would not satisfy an artistic instinct that aimed throughout at the fundamental, and from which the Beautiful was again to create itself with free original energy. They were not afraid, therefore, to appear simple, artless, dry, beside those exalted ancients; nor to cherish Art for a long time in the undistinguished bud, until the period of Grace had arrived.

Whence comes it that we still look upon these works of the older masters, from Giotto to the teacher of Raphael, with a sort of reverence, indeed with a certain predilection, if not that the faithfulness of their endeavor, and the grand earnestness of their serene voluntary limitation, compels our respect and admiration.

The same relation that they held to the ancients, the present generation holds to them. Their time and ours are joined by no living transmission, no link of continuous organic growth; we must reproduce Art in the way they did, but with energy of our own, in order to be like them.

Even that Indian-summer of Art, at the end of the sixteenth and the beginning of the seventeenth centuries, could call forth only a few new blossoms on the old stem, but no productive germs, still less plant a new tree of Art. But to set aside the works of perfected Art, and to seek out its scanty and simple beginnings, as some have desired, would be a new and perhaps greater mistake; it would be no real return to the fundamental: simplicity would be affectation, and grow into hypocritical show.

But what prospect does the present time offer for an Art springing from a vigorous germ, and growing up from the root? For it is in a great measure dependant on the character of its time; and who would promise the approbation of the present time to such earnest beginnings, when Art, on the one hand, scarcely obtains equal consideration with other instruments of prodigal luxury; and, on the other, artists and amateurs, with entire want of ability to grasp Nature, praise and demand the Ideal?

Art springs only from that powerful striving of the inmost powers of the heart and the spirit, which we call Inspiration. Everything that from difficult or small beginnings has grown up to great power and height, owes its growth to Inspiration. Thus empires and states, thus arts and sciences. But it is not the power of the individual that accomplishes this, but the Spirit alone, that diffuses itself over all. For Art especially is dependant on the tone of the public mind, as the more delicate plants on atmosphere and weather: it needs a general enthusiasm for Sublimity and Beauty, like that which, in the time of the Medici, as a warm breath of spring, called forth at once and together all those great spirits. * * * * * *

It is only when the public life is actuated by the same forces through whose energy Art is elevated, that the latter can derive any advantage from it; for Art cannot, without giving up the nobility of its nature, aim at anything outward.

Art and Science can move only on their own axes; the artist, like every spiritual laborer, can follow only the law that God and Nature have written in his heart. None can help him—he must help himself; nor can he be outwardly rewarded, since anything that he should produce for the sake of aught out of itself, would thereby become a nullity. Hence, too, no one can direct him, nor prescribe the path he is to tread. Is he to be pitied if he have to contend against his time, he is deserving of contempt if he truckle to it. But how should it be even possible for him to do this? Without great general enthusiasm there are only sects, no public opinion: not an established taste, not the great ideas of a whole people, but the voices of a few arbitrarily appointed judges, determine as to merit; and Art, which in its elevation is self-sufficing, courts favor, and serves where it should rule.

To different ages are given different inspirations. Can we expect none for this age, since the new world now forming itself, as it exists in part already outwardly, in part inwardly and in the hearts of men, can no longer be measured by any standard of previous opinion; and since everything, on the contrary, loudly demands higher standards and an entire renovation?

Should not the sense to which Nature and History have more livingly unfolded themselves, restore to Art also its great arguments? The attempt to draw sparks from the ashes of the Past, and fan them again into a universal flame, is a vain endeavor. Only a revolution in the ideas themselves is able to raise Art from its exhaustion: only new Knowledge, new Faith can inspire it for the work, by which it can display, in a renewed life, a splendor like the past.

An Art in all respects the same as that of foregoing centuries, will never return; for Nature never repeats herself. Such a Raphael will never be again, but another, who shall have reached in an equally original manner the summit of Art. Only let the fundamental conditions be fulfilled, and renewed Art will show, like that which preceded it, in its first works, its aim and intent. In the production of the distinctly characteristic, if it proceed from a fresh original energy, Grace is already present, even though hidden, and in both the advent of the soul already determined. Works produced in this manner, even in their rudimentary imperfection, are necessary and eternal. * * *

ERNST THEODOR AMADEUS HOFFMANN.

Born 1776. Died 1822.

Hoffman is celebrated chiefly for his successful use of the magic and demonic element in fiction. In this particular he stands first among the story-tellers of his time, and has had many imitators both in Germany and in France. But Hoffman does not revel in horrors for their own sake; he is not to be confounded with such writers as Maturin, and Lewis, and Mrs. Radcliffe, among English novelists. He does not seek to make the flesh creep and the hair bristle, but aims rather at the diaphragm. He views all these *infernalia* on the humorous side, and if any one trait is particularly prominent in his writings it is irony. In him Hogarth and Hell-Breughel unite. Then, he was a great musician, and had speculated, perhaps as profoundly as any man, on the philosophy of music, with which speculations his compositions are often occupied and everywhere tinged.

Hoffman was a native of Königsberg, where he received his education, and devoted himself to the study of the Law. After completing his course, he received an appointment to an office connected with his vocation, at Grosslogau, and afterwards at Berlin. In 1800, he was made assessor in the government of Posen; in 1802, he removed to Plozk, where he held the office of counsellor; and in 1803, to Warsaw. At the invasion of this city by the French, in 1806, he was forced to lay down his office, and to have recourse to music for a support. In 1808, he was appointed director of music at the new theatre in Bamberg, and thence went to Leipzig, and afterward to Dresden, in the same capacity. In 1816, he was reinstated as counsellor in the court of judicature, at Berlin, where he died, July 24th, 1822.

Hoffman had much that was noble in his character, but likewise much that was morbid and vicious. With a recklessness not unfrequently found in connection with fine artistic, and especially musical talent, he gave himself up to sensual excess, and wasted body and soul with riotous living.

His principal works are *Fantasiestücke in Callot's manier*, and the *Serapiansbrüder*. Besides these he published several volumes of tales and works of fiction, some of which, as the *Meister Floh* and the *Lebensansichten des Kater Murr*, are satirical.

The following is Menzel's judgment concerning him:

" With Hoffman the sentimentality of Kleist and the humor of Chamisso* appear to be fused together. He became the head of the new demonic school, and the poetic Pluto who ruled the dark realm in its widest extent. Or rather, was he not himself ruled by it? It is the poetry of fear that gives all his works such a peculiar stamp. Hence the sense of hearing, which is so closely connected with the feeling of terror, was with him so highly developed. Therefore his ear detected everywhere the mysterious tones of nature as well as of art. * * * And yet we can accuse him of no exaggerated softness or effeminate unmanliness; for his principal works employ themselves with a pain, with a despair, with a daring and an agony of the thoughts, of which only man is capable, not woman. It is disease, extravagance, delirium, but still always manly.

" From the devil down to a wry-faced child's-doll, from the dissonance of life which rends the soul, down to a dissonance in music which only rends the ear, the immeasurable kingdom of the ugly, the repulsive, the annoying, was gathered around him, and his descriptions paint alternately these tormenting objects and the torments which they prepare for a beautiful soul, with inimitable vividness and truth. He himself is that mad musician Kreisler, who, with his delicate sense for the purest and holiest tones, is driven to despair by the dissonances which everywhere assail him maliciously, as from hell. But he retained this delicate sense not in music alone. In all the spheres of life he finds, corresponding with musical dissonances, those ugly, hostile grimaces and demonic Powers by which precisely the noblest souls are most painfully stretched upon the rack. * * * * * *

* Author of Peter Sclemihl.

"Hoffman's innermost being was music, and the prayer of St. Anthony is never wanting to his hellish caricatures, nor the Christmas bell to the witches' Sabbath, nor to the concert of devils the pure and piercing tone with which the virgin soul takes leave of a shattered and priceless instrument. It is true he paints to us the soul only in its shattered state; but the soul was ever noble, and carried heaven with its harmony.

"Hoffman shares with Jean Paul his delicate sensibility to painful impressions. * * * Posterity will say that the dissonance which pervades our time was seized by no poet so poetically as by Hoffman; and perhaps the poetic spell consists precisely in this, that he did not, like so many other poets, seek a political solution of the dissonance, and appeal to the future, but held fast the illusion of a black, overshadowed fantasy, of a dream without waking."

It is scarcely necessary to say, that the tale from which the following extracts are given, is intended to allegorize the conflict between the poetic and the prosaic in human life.

THE GOLDEN POT.

FIRST VIGIL.

The Mishaps of the Student Anselmus. Conrector Paulmann's Tobacco-box, and the Gold-green Snakes.

On Ascension-day, about three o'clock in the afternoon, there came a young man running through the Schwarzthor, or Black Gate, out of Dresden, and right into a basket of apples and cakes, which an old and very ugly woman was there exposing to sale. The crash was prodigious; all that escaped being squelched to pieces, was scattered away, and the street-urchins joyfully divided the booty which this quick gentleman had thrown them. At the murder-shriek which the crone set up, her gossips, leaving their cake and brandy-tables, encircled the young man, and with plebeian violence stormfully scolded him: so that, for shame and vexation, he uttered no word, but merely held out his small, and by no means particularly well-filled purse, which the crone eagerly clutched, and stuck into her pocket. The firm ring now opened; but as the young man started off, the crone called after him: "Ay, run, run thy ways, thou Devil's bird! To the Crystal run! to the Crystal!" The squealing, creaking voice of the woman had something unearthly in it: so that the promenaders paused in amazement, and the laugh, which at first had been universal, instantly died away. The Student Anselmus, for the young man was no other, felt himself, though he did not in the least understand these singular phrases, nevertheless seized with a certain involuntary horror; and he quickened his steps still more, to escape the curious looks of the multitude, which were all turned towards him. As he worked his way through the crowd of well-dressed people, he heard them murmuring on all sides: "Poor young fellow! Ha! what a cursed beldam it is!" The mysterious words of the crone had oddly enough given this ludicrous adventure a sort of tragic turn; and the youth, before unobserved, was now looked after with a certain sympathy. The ladies, for his fine shape and handsome face, which the glow of inward anger was rendering still more expressive, forgave him this awkward step, as well as the dress he wore, though it was utterly at variance with all mode. His pike-gray frock was shaped as if the tailor had known the modern form only by hearsay; and his well-kept black satin lower habiliments gave the whole a certain pedagogic air, to which the gait and gesture of the wearer did not at all correspond.

The Student had almost reached the end of the alley which leads out to the Linke Bath; but his breath could stand such a rate no longer. From running, he took to walking; but scarcely did he yet dare to lift an eye from the ground; for he still saw apples and cakes dancing round him; and every kind look from this or that fair damsel was to him but the reflex of the mocking laughter at the Schwarzthor. In this mood, he had got to the entrance of the Bath: one group of holiday people after the other were moving in. Music of wind-instruments resounded from the place, and the din of merry guests was growing louder and louder. The poor Student Anselmus was almost on the point of weeping; for he too had expected, Ascension-day having always been a family-festival with him, to participate in the felicities of the Linkean paradise; nay, he had purposed even to go the length of a half *portion* of coffee with rum, and a whole bottle of double beer; and that he might carouse at his ease, had put more money in his purse than was entirely convenient or advisable. And now, by this fatal step into the apple-basket, all that he had about him had been swept away. Of coffee, of double or single beer, of music, of looking at the bright damsels; in a word, of all his fancied enjoyments, there was now nothing more to be said. He glided slowly past; and at last turned down the Elbe road, which at that time happened to be quite solitary.

Beneath an elder-tree, which had grown out through the wall, he found a kind green resting-place: here he sat down, and filled a pipe from the Sanitätsknaster, or Health-tobacco-box, of which his friend the Conrector Paulmann had lately made him a present. Close before him, rolled and chafed the gold-dyed waves of the fair Elbe-stream: behind him rose lordly Dresden, stretching, bold and proud, its light towers into the airy sky; which again, farther off, bent itself down towards flowery meads and fresh springing woods; and in the dim distance, a range of azure peaks gave notice of remote Bohemia. But, heedless of this, the Student Anselmus, looking gloomily before him, blew forth his smoky clouds into the air. His chagrin at length became audible, and he said: "Of a truth, I am born to losses and crosses for my life long! That in boyhood, at Odds or Evens, I could never once guess the right way; that my bread and butter always fell on the buttered side; of all these sorrows I will not speak: but is it not a frightful destiny, that now, when, in spite of Satan, I have become a student, I must still be a jolthead as before? Do I ever put a new coat on, without the first day smearing it with tallow, or on some ill-fastened nail or other, tearing a cursed hole in it? Do I ever bow to any Councillor or any lady, without pitching the hat out of my hands, or even sliding away on the smooth pavement, and shamefully oversetting? Had I not, every market-day, while in Halle, a regular sum of from three to four groschen to pay for broken pottery, the Devil putting it into my head to walk straight forward, like a leming-rat? Have I ever once got to my college, or any place I was appointed to, at the right time? What availed it that I set out half an hour before, and planted myself at the door, with the knocker in my hand? Just as the clock is going to strike, souse! some Devil pours a wash-basin down on me, or I bolt against some fellow coming out, and get myself engaged in endless quarrels till the time is clean gone.

"Ah! well-a-day! whither are ye fled, ye blissful dreams of coming fortune, when I proudly thought that here I might even reach the height of Privy Secretary? And has not my evil star estranged from me my best patrons? I learn, for instance, that the Councillor, to whom I have a letter, cannot suffer cropt hair; with immensity of trouble, the barber fastens me a little cue to my hindhead; but at the first bow, his unblessed knot gives way, and a little shock, running snuffing about me, frisks off to the Privy Councillor with the cue in his mouth. I spring after it in terror; and stumble against the table, where he has been working while at breakfast; and cups, plates, ink-glass, sand-box, rush jingling to the floor, and a flood of chocolate and ink overflows the Relation he has just been writing. 'Is the Devil in the man?' bellows the furious Privy Councillor, and shoves me out of the room.

"What avails it that Conrector Paulmann gave me hopes of a writership: will my malignant fate allow it, which everywhere pursues me? To-day even! Do but think of it! I was purposing to hold my good old Ascension-day with right cheerfulness of soul: I would stretch a point for once; I might have gone, as well as any other guest, into Linke's Bath, and called out proudly: 'Marqueur! a bottle of double-beer; best sort, if you please!' I might have sat till far in the evening; and, moreover, close by this or that fine party of well-dressed ladies. I know it, I feel it! heart would have come into me, I should have been quite another man; nay, I might have carried it so far, that when one or other of them asked: 'What o'clock may it be?' or 'What is it they are playing?' I should have started up with light grace, and without overturning my glass, or stumbling over the bench, but in a curved posture, moving one step and a half forward, I should have answered: 'Give me leave, mademoiselle! it is the overture of the *Donauweibchen;*' or, 'It is just going to strike six.' Could any mortal in the world have taken it ill of me? No! I say; the girls would have looked over, smiling so roguishly; as they always do when I pluck up heart to show them that I too understand the light tone of society, and know how ladies should be spoken to. And now the Devil himself leads me into that cursed apple-basket, and now must I sit moping in solitude, with nothing but a poor pipe of ———"
Here the Student Anselmus was interrupted in his soliloquy by a strange rustling and whisking, which rose close by him in the grass, but soon glided up into the twigs and leaves of the eldertree that stretched out over his head. It was as if the evening wind were shaking the leaves; as if little birds were twittering among the branches, moving their little wings in capricious flutter to and fro. Then he heard a whispering and lisping; and it seemed as if the blossoms were sounding like little crystal bells. Anselmus listened and listened. Ere long, the whispering, and lisping, and tinkling, he himself knew not how, grew to faint and half-scattered words:

"'Twixt this way, 'twixt that; 'twixt branches, 'twixt blossoms, come shoot, come twist and twirl we! Sisterkin, sisterkin! up to the shine; up, down, through and through, quick! Sunrays yellow; evening-wind whispering; dewdrops pattering; blossoms all singing: sing we with branches and blossoms! Stars soon glitter; must down: 'twixt this way, 'twixt that, come shoot, come twist, come twirl we, sisterkin!"

And so it went along, in confused and confusing speech. The Student Anselmus thought: "Well, it is but the evening-wind, which to-night truly is whispering distinctly enough." But at that moment there sounded over his head, as it were, a triple harmony of clear crystal bells: he looked up, and perceived three little Snakes, glittering with green and gold, twisted round the branches, and stretching out their heads to the evening sun. Then, again, began a whispering and twittering in the same words as before, and the little Snakes went gliding and caressing up and down through the twigs; and while they moved so rapidly, it was as if the elder-bush were scattering a thousand glittering emeralds through the dark leaves.

"It is the evening sun which sports so in the elder-bush," thought the Student Anselmus; but the bells sounded again; and Anselmus observed that one Snake held out its little head to him. Through all his limbs there went a shock like electricity; he quivered in his inmost heart; he kept gazing up, and a pair of glorious dark-blue eyes were looking at him with unspeakable longing; and an unknown feeling of highest blessedness and deepest sorrow was like to rend his heart asunder. And as he looked, and still looked, full of warm desire, into these kind eyes, the crystal bells sounded louder in harmonious accord, and the glittering emeralds fell down and encircled him, flickering round him in thousand sparkles, and sporting in resplendent threads of gold. The Elder-bush moved and spoke: "Thou layest in my shadow; my perfume flowed round thee, but thou understoodst it not. The perfume is my speech, when Love kindles it." The Evening-Wind came gliding past, and said: "I played round thy temples, but thou understoodst me not. That breath is my speech, when Love kindles it." The Sunbeam broke through the clouds, and the sheen of it burnt, as in words: "I overflowed thee with glowing gold, but thou understoodst me not: That glow is my speech, when Love kindles it."

And, still deeper and deeper sunk in the view of these glorious eyes, his longing grew keener, his desire more warm. And all rose and moved around him, as if awakening to glad life. Flowers and blossoms shed their odors round him; and their odor was like the lordly singing of a thousand softest voices; and what they sung was borne, like an echo, on the golden evening clouds, as they flitted away, into far-off lands. But as the last sun-beam abruptly sank behind the hills, and the twilight threw its veil over the scene, there came a hoarse deep voice, as from a great distance:

"Hey! hey! what chattering and jingling is that up there? Hey! hey! who catches me the ray behind the hills? Sunned enough, sung enough. Hey! hey! through bush and grass, through grass and stream. Hey! hey! Come dow-w-n, dow-w-w-n!"

So faded the voice away, as in murmurs of a distant thunder; but the crystal bells broke off in sharp discords. All became mute; and the Student Anselmus observed how the three Snakes, glittering and sparkling, glided through the grass towards the river; rustling and hustling, they rushed into the Elbe; and over the waves where they vanished, there crackled up a green flame, which, gleaming forward obliquely, vanished in the direction of the city.

SECOND VIGIL.

How the Student Anselmus was looked upon as drunk and mad. The crossing of the Elbe. Bandmaster Graun's Bravura. Conradi's Stomachic Liqueur, and the bronzed Apple-woman.

"THE gentleman is ailing some way!" said a decent burgher's wife, who, returning from a walk with her family, had paused here, and, with crossed arms, was looking at the mad pranks of the Student Anselmus. Anselmus had clasped the trunk of the elder-tree, and was calling incessantly up to the branches and leaves: "O glitter and shine once more, ye dear gold Snakes; let me hear your little bell-voices once more! Look on me once more, ye kind eyes; O once, or I must die in pain and warm longing!" And with this, he was sighing and sobbing from the bottom of his heart most pitifully; and in his eagerness and impatience, shaking the elder-tree to and fro; which, however, instead of any reply, rustled quite stupidly and unintelligibly with its leaves; and so rather seemed, as it were, to make sport of the Student Anselmus and his sorrows.

"The gentleman is ailing some way!" said the burgher's wife; and Anselmus felt as if you had shaken him out of a deep dream, or poured ice-cold water on him, that he might awaken without loss of time. He now first saw clearly where he was; and recollected what a strange apparition had assaulted him, nay, so beguiled his senses, as to make him break forth into loud talk with himself. In astonishment, he gazed at the woman; and at last snatching up his hat, which had fallen to the ground in his transport, was for making off in all speed. The burgher himself had come forward in the meanwhile; and, setting down the child from his arm on the grass, had been leaning on his staff, and with amazement listening and looking at the Student. He now picked up the pipe and tobacco-box which the Student had let fall, and, holding them out to him, said: "Don't take on so dreadfully, my worthy sir, or alarm people in the dark, when nothing is the matter, after all, but a drop or two of christian liquor: go home, like a pretty man, and take a nap of sleep on it."

The Student Anselmus felt exceedingly ashamed; he uttered nothing but a most lamentable Ah!

"Pooh! Pooh!" said the burgher, "never mind it a jot; such a thing will happen to the best; on good old Ascension-day a man may readily enough forget himself in his joy, and gulp down a thought too much. A clergyman himself is no worse for it: I presume, my worthy sir, you are a *Candidatus*.—But, with your leave, sir, I shall fill my pipe with your tobacco; mine went done a little while ago."

This last sentence the burgher uttered while the Student Anselmus was about putting up his pipe and box; and now the burgher slowly and deliberately cleaned his pipe, and began as slowly to fill it. Several burgher girls had come up: these were speaking secretly with the woman and each other, and tittering as they looked at Anselmus. The Student felt as if he were standing on prickly thorns, and burning needles. No sooner had he got back his pipe and tobacco-box, than he darted off at the height of his speed.

All the strange things he had seen were clean gone from his memory: he simply recollected having babbled all manner of foolish stuff beneath the elder-tree. This was the more frightful to him, as he entertained from of old an inward horror against all soliloquists. It is Satan that chatters out of them, said his Rector; and Anselmus had honestly believed him. But to be regarded as a *Candidatus Theologiæ*, overtaken with drink on Ascension-day! The thought was intolerable.

Running on with these mad vexations, he was just about turning up the Poplar Alley, by the Kosel garden, when a voice behind him called out: "Herr Anselmus! Herr Anselmus! for the love of Heaven, whither are you running in such haste?" The Student paused, as if rooted to the ground; for he was convinced that now some new mischance would befall him. The voice rose again: "Herr Anselmus, come back, then: we are waiting for you here at the water!" And now the Student perceived that it was his friend Conrector Paulmann's voice: he went back to the Elbe; and found the Conrector, with his two daughters, as well as Registrator Heerbrand, all on the point of stepping into their gondola. Conrector Paulmann invited the Student to go with them across the Elbe, and then to pass the evening at his house in the Pirna suburb. The Student Anselmus very gladly accepted this proposal; thinking thereby to escape the malignant destiny, which had ruled over him all day.

Now, as they were crossing the river, it chanced that, on the farther bank, in the Anton garden, a firework was just going off. Sputtering and hissing, the rockets went aloft, and their blazing stars flew to pieces in the air, scattering a thousand vague shoots and flashes round them. The Student Anselmus was sitting by the steersman, sunk in deep thought; but when he noticed in the water the reflection of these darting and wavering sparks and flames, he felt as if it was the little golden Snakes that were sporting in the flood. All the wonders that he had seen at the elder-tree again started forth into his heart and thoughts; and again that unspeakable longing, that glowing desire, laid hold of him here, which had before agitated his bosom in painful spasms of rapture.

"Ah! is it you again, my little golden Snakes? Sing now, O sing! In your song let the kind, dear, dark-blue eyes, again appear to me—Ah? are ye under the waves, then?"

So cried the Student Anselmus, and at the same time made a violent movement, as if he were for plunging from the gondola into the river.

"Is the Devil in you, sir?" exclaimed the steersman, and clutched him by the coat-breast. The girls, who were sitting by him, shrieked in terror, and fled to the other side of the gondola. Registrator Heerbrand whispered something in Conrector Paulmann's ear, to which the latter answered at considerable length, but in so low a tone, that Anselmus could distinguish nothing but the words: "Such attacks more than once?—Never heard of it." Directly after this, Conrector Paulmann also rose; and then sat down, with a certain earnest, grave, official mien, beside the Student Anselmus, taking his hand, and saying: "How are you, Herr Anselmus?" The Student Anselmus was like to lose his wits, for in his mind there was a mad contradiction, which he strove in vain to reconcile. He now saw plainly that what he had taken for the gleaming of the golden Snakes was nothing but the image of the fireworks in Anton's garden: but a feeling unexperienced till now, he himself knew not whether it was rapture or pain, cramped his breast together; and when the steersman struck through the water with his helm, so that the waves, curling as in anger, gurgled and chafed, he heard in their din a soft whispering: "Anselmus! Anselmus! seest thou not how we still skim along before thee? Sisterkin looks at thee again: believe, believe, believe in us!" And he thought he saw in the reflected light three green-glowing streaks: but then, when he gazed, full of fond sadness, into the water, to see whether these gentle eyes would not again look up to him, he perceived too well that the shine proceeded only from the windows in the neighbouring houses. He was sitting mute in his place, and inwardly battling with himself, when Conrector Paulmann repeated, with still greater emphasis: "How are you, Herr Anselmus?"

With the most rueful tone, Anselmus replied: "Ah! Herr Conrector, if you knew what strange things I have been dreaming, quite awake, with open eyes, just now, under an elder-tree at the wall of Linke's garden, you would not take it amiss of me that I am a little absent, or so."

"Ey, ey, Herr Anselmus!" interrupted Conrector Paulmann, "I have always taken you for a solid young man: but to dream, to dream with your eyes wide open, and then, all at once, to start up for leaping into the water! This, begging your pardon, is what only fools or madmen could do."

The Student Anselmus was deeply affected at his friend's hard saying; then Veronica, Paulmann's eldest daughter, a most pretty blooming girl of sixteen, addressed her father: "But, dear father, something singular must have befallen Herr Auselmus; and perhaps he only thinks he was awake, while he may have really been asleep: and so all manner of wild stuff has come into his head, and is still lying in his thoughts."

"And, dearest Mademoiselle! Worthy Conrector!" cried Registrator Heerbrand, "may one not, even when awake, sometimes sink into a sort of dreaming state? I myself have had such fits. One afternoon, for instance, during coffee, in a sort of brown study like this, in the special season of corporeal and spiritual digestion, the place where a lost *Act* was lying occurred to me, as if by inspiration; and last night, no farther gone, there came a glorious large Latin paper tripping out before my open eyes, in the very same way."

"Ah! most honoured Registrator," answered Conrector Paulmann; "you have always had a tendency to the *Poetica;* and thus one falls into fantasies and romantic humors."

The Student Anselmus, however, was particularly gratified that in this most troublous situation, while in danger of being considered drunk or crazy, any one should take his part; and though it was already pretty dark, he thought he noticed, for the first time, that Veronica had really very fine dark-blue eyes, and this too without remembering the strange pair which he had looked at in the elder-bush. On the whole, the adventure under the elder-bush had once more entirely vanished from the thoughts of the Student Anselmus; he felt himself at ease and light of heart; nay, in the capriciousness of joy, he carried it so far, that he offered a helping hand to his fair advocate, Veronica, as she was stepping from the gondola; and without more ado, as she put her arm in his, escorted her home with so much dexterity and good luck, that he only missed his footing once, and this being the only wet spot in the whole road, only spattered Veronica's white gown a very little by the incident.

Conrector Paulmann failed not to observe this happy change in the Student Anselmus; he resumed his liking for him, and begged forgiveness for the hard words which he had let fall before. "Yes," added he, "we have many examples to show that certain phantasms may rise before a man, and pester and plague him not a little; but this is bodily disease, and leeches are good for it, if applied to the right part, as a cor tain learned physician, now deceased, has directed." The Student Anselmus knew not whether he had been drunk, crazy, or sick; but at all events the leeches seemed entirely superfluous, as these supposed phantasms had utterly vanished, and the Student himself was growing happier and happier, the more he prospered in serving the pretty Veronica with all sorts of dainty attentions.

As usual, after the frugal meal, came music; the Student Anselmus had to take his seat before the harpsichord, and Veronica accompanied his playing with her pure clear voice : " Dear Mademoiselle," said Registrator Heerbrand, "you have a voice like a crystal bell!"

"That she has not!" ejaculated the Student Anselmus, he scarcely knew how. "Crystal bells in elder-trees sound strangely! strangely!" continued the Student Anselmus, murmuring half aloud.

Veronica laid her hand on his shoulder, and asked: "What are you saying now, Herr Anselmus?"

Instantly Anselmus recovered his cheerfulness, and began playing. Conrector Paulmann gave a grim look at him; but Registrator Heerbrand laid a music-leaf on the frame, and sang with ravishing grace one of Bandmaster Graun's bravura airs. The Student Anselmus accompanied this, and much more; and a fantasy duet, which Veronica and he now fingered, and Conrector Paulmann had himself composed, again brought all into the gayest humor.

It was now pretty late, and Registrator Heerbrand was taking up his hat and stick, when Conrector Paulmann went up to him with a mysterious air, and said: "Hem!—Would not you, honored Registrator, mention to the good Herr Anselmus himself—Hem! what we were speaking of before?"

"With all the pleasure in nature," said Registrator Heerbrand, and having placed himself in the circle, began, without farther preamble, as follows:

"In this city is a strange remarkable man, people say he follows all manner of secret sciences; but as there are no such sciences, I rather take him for an antiquary, and along with this, for an experimental chemist. I mean no other than our Privy Archivarius Lindhorst. He lives, as you know, by himself, in his old sequestered house; and when disengaged from his office, he is to be found in his library, or in his chemical laboratory, to which, however, he admits no stranger. Besides many curious books, he possesses a number of manuscripts, partly Arabic, Coptic, and some of them in strange characters, which belong not to any known tongue. These he wishes to have copied properly; and for this purpose he requires a man who can draw with the pen, and so transfer these marks to parchment, in Indian ink, with the highest strictness and fidelity. The work is carried on in a separate chamber of his house, under his own oversight; and besides free board during the time of business, he pays his man a speziesthaler, or specie-dollar, daily, and promises a handsome present when the copying is rightly finished. The hours of work are from twelve to six. From three to four, you take rest and dinner.

"Herr Archivarius Lindhorst having in vain tried one or two young people for copying these manuscripts, has at last applied to me to find him an expert drawer; and so I have been thinking of you, dear Herr Anselmus, for I know that you both write very neatly, and likewise draw with the pen to great perfection. Now, if in these bad times, and till your future establishment, you could like to earn a speziesthaler in the day, and this present over and above, you can go to-morrow precisely at noon, and call upon the Archivarius, whose house no doubt you know. But be on your guard against any blot! If such a thing falls on your copy, you must begin it again; if it falls on the original, the Archivarius will think nothing to throw you over the window, for he is a hot-tempered gentleman."

The student Anselmus was filled with joy at Registrator Heerbrand's proposal; for not only could the Student write well and draw well with the pen, but this copying with laborious calligraphic pains was a thing he delighted in beyond aught else. So he thanked his patron in the most grateful terms, and promised not to fail at noon to-morrow.

All night the Student Anselmus saw nothing but clear speziesthalers, and heard nothing but their lovely clink. Who could blame the poor youth, cheated of so many hopes by capricious destiny, obliged to take counsel about every farthing, and to forego so many joys which a young heart requires! Early in the morning he brought out his black-lead pencils, his crow-quills, his Indian ink; for better materials, thought he, the Archivarius can find nowhere. Above all, he mustered and arranged his calligraphic masterpieces and his drawings, to show them to the Archivarius, in proof of his ability to do what he wished. All prospered with the Student; a peculiar happy star seemed to be presiding over him; his neckcloth sat right at the very first trial; no tack burst; no loop gave way in his black silk stockings; his hat did not once fall to the dust after he had trimmed it. In a word, precisely at half-past eleven, the Student Anselmus, in his pike-grey frock, and black satin lower habiliments, with a roll of calligraphies and pen-drawings in his pocket, was standing in the Schlossgasse, or Castlegate, in Conradi's shop, and drinking one—two glasses of the best stomachic liqueur; for here, thought he, slapping on the still empty pocket, for here speziesthalers will be chinking soon.

Notwithstanding the distance of the solitary street where the Archivarius Lindhorst's antique residence lay, the Student Anselmus was at the front-door before the stroke of twelve. He stood here, and was looking at the large fine bronze knocker; but now when, as the last stroke tingled through the air with loud clang from the steeple-clock of the Kreuzkirche, or Cross-church, he lifted his hand to grasp this same knocker, the metal visage twisted itself, with horrid rolling of its blue-gleaming eyes, into a grinning smile. Alas, it was the Apple-woman of the Schwarzthor! The pointed teeth gnashed together in the loose jaws, and in their chattering through the skinny lips, there was a growl of: "Thou fool, fool, fool!—Wait, wait! —Why didst run!—Fool!" Horror-struck, the Student Anselmus flew back; he clutched at the door-post, but his hand caught the bell-rope, and pulled it, and in piercing discords it rung stronger and stronger, and through the whole empty house the echo repeated, as in mockery: "To the crystal, fall!" An unearthly terror seized the Student Anselmus, and quivered through all his limbs. The bell-rope lengthened downwards, and became a white transparent gigantic serpent, which encircled and crushed him, and girded him straiter and straiter in its coils, till his brittle paralysed limbs went crashing in pieces, and the blood spouted from his veins, penetrating into the transparent body of the serpent, and dyeing it red. "Kill me! Kill me!" he would have cried, in his horrible agony; but the cry was only a stifled gurgle in his throat. The serpent lifted its head, and laid its long peaked tongue of glowing brass on the breast of Anselmus; then a fierce pang suddenly cut asunder the artery of life, and thought fled away from him. On returning to his senses, he was lying on his own poor truckle-bed; Conrector Paulmann was standing before him, and saying: "For Heaven's sake, what mad stuff is this, dear Herr Anselmus?"

SIXTH VIGIL.

Archivarius Lindhorst's Garden, with some Mock-birds. The Golden Pot. English current-hand. Pot-hooks. The Prince of the Spirits.

"It may be, after all," said the Student Anselmus to himself, "that the superfine strong stomachic liqueur, which I took somewhat freely in Monsieur Conradi's, might really be the cause of all these shocking phantasms, which so tortured me at Archivarius Lindhorst's door. Therefore, I will go quite sober to-day; and so bid defiance to whatever farther mischief may assail me." On this occasion, as before when equipping himself for his first call on Archivarius Lindhorst, the Student Anselmus put his pen-drawings, and calligraphic masterpieces, his bars of Indian ink, and his well-pointed crow-pens, into his pockets; and was just turning to go out, when his eye lighted on the vial with the yellow liquor, which he had received from Archivarius Lindhorst. All the strange adventures he had met with again rose on his mind in glowing colours; and a nameless emotion of rapture and pain thrilled through his breast. Involuntarily he exclaimed, with a most piteous voice: "Ah, am not I going to the Archivarius solely for a sight of thee, thou gentle lovely Serpentina!" At that moment, he felt as if Serpentina's love might be the prize of some laborious perilous task which he had to undertake; and as if this task were no other than the copying of the Lindhorst manuscripts. That at his very entrance into the house, or more properly, before his entrance, all manner of mysterious things might happen, as of late, was no more than he anticipated. He thought no more of Conradi's strong water; but hastily put the vial of liquor in his waistcoat-pocket, that he might act strictly by the Archivarius' directions, should the bronzed Apple-woman again take it upon her to make faces at him.

And did not the hawk-nose actually peak itself, did not the cat-eyes actually glare from the knocker, as he raised his hand to it, at the stroke of twelve? But now, without farther ceremony, he dribbled his liquor into the pestilent visage; and it folded and moulded itself, that instant, down to a glittering bowl-round knocker. The door went up: the bells sounded beautifully over all the house: "Klingling, youngling, in, in, spring, spring, klingling." In good heart he mounted the fine broad stair; and feasted on the odors of some strange perfumery, that was floating through the house. In doubt, he paused on the lobby; for he knew not at which of these many fine doors he was to knock. But Archivarius Lindhorst, in a white damask night-gown, stept forth to him, and said: "Well, it is a real pleasure to me, Herr Anselmus, that you have kept your word at last. Come this way, if you please; I must take you straight into the Laboratory." And with this he stept rapidly through the lobby, and opened a little side-door, which led into a long passage. Anselmus walked on in high spirits, behind the Archivarius; they passed from this corridor into a hall, or rather into a lordly green-house: for on both sides, up to the ceiling, stood all manner of rare wondrous flowers, nay, great trees with strangely-formed leaves and blossoms. A magic dazzling light shone over the whole, though you could not discover whence it came, for no window whatever was to be seen. As the Student Anselmus looked in through the bushes and trees, long avenues appeared to open in remote distance. In the deep shade of thick cypress groves, lay glittering marble fountains, out of which rose wondrous figures, spouting crystal jets that fell with pattering spray into the gleaming lily-cups; strange voices cooed and rustled through the wood of curious trees; and sweetest perfumes streamed up and down.

The Archivarius had vanished: and Anselmus saw nothing but a huge bush of glowing fire-lilies before him. Intoxicated with the sight and the fine odors of this fairy-garden, Anselmus stood fixed to the spot. Then began on all sides of him a giggling and laughing; and light little voices railed and mocked him: "Herr Studiosus! Herr Studiosus! how came you hither? Why have you dressed so bravely, Herr Anselmus? Will you chat with us for a minute, how grandmammy sat squelching down upon the egg, and young master got a stain on his Sunday waistcoat?—Can you play the new tune, now, which you learned from Daddy Cockadoodle, Herr Anselmus?—You look very fine in your glass periwig, and post-paper boots." So cried and chattered and sniggered the little voices, out of every corner, nay, close by the Student himself, who now observed that all sorts of party-colored birds were fluttering above him, and jeering him in hearty laughter. At that moment, the bush of fire-lilies advanced towards him; and he perceived that it was Archivarius Lindhorst, whose flowered night-gown, glittering in red and yellow, had so far deceived his eyes.

"I beg your pardon, worthy Herr Anselmus," said the Archivarius, "for leaving you alone: I wished, in passing, to take a peep at my fine cactus, which is to blossom to-night. But how like you my little house-garden?"

"Ah, Heaven! Immeasurably pretty it is, most valued Herr Archivarius," replied the Student; "but those party-colored birds have been bantering me a little."

"What chattering is this?" cried the Archivarius angrily into the bushes. Then a huge grey Parrot came fluttering out, and perched itself beside the Archivarius on a myrtle-bough; and looking at him with an uncommon earnestness and gravity through a pair of spectacles that stuck on his hooked bill, it creaked out: "Don't take it amiss, Herr Archivarius; my wild boys have been a little free or so; but the Herr Studiosus has himself to blame in the matter, for ———"

"Hush! hush!" interrupted Archivarius Lindhorst; "I know the varlets; but thou must keep them in better discipline, my friend!—Now, come along, Herr Anselmus."

And the Archivarius again stept forth, through many a strangely-decorated chamber; so that the Student Anselmus, in following him, could scarcely give a glance at all the glittering wondrous furniture, and other unknown things, with which the whole of them were filled. At last they entered a large apartment; where the Archivarius, casting his eyes aloft, stood still; and Anselmus got time to feast himself on the glorious sight, which the simple decoration of this hall afforded. Jutting from the azure-colored walls, rose gold-bronze trunks of high palm-trees, which wove their colossal leaves, glittering like bright emeralds, into a ceiling far up: in the middle of the chamber, and resting on three Egyptian lions, cast out of dark bronze, lay a porphyry plate; and on this stood a simple Golden Pot, from which, so soon as he beheld it, Anselmus could not turn away an eye. It was as if, in a thousand gleaming reflexes, all sorts of shapes were sporting on the bright polished gold: often he perceived his own form, with arms stretched out in longing—ah! beneath the elder-bush,— and Serpentina was winding and shooting up and down, and again looking at him with her kind eyes. Anselmus was beside himself with frantic rapture.

"Serpentina! Serpentina!" cried he aloud; and Archivarius Lindhorst whirled round abruptly, and said: "How now, worthy Herr Anselmus? If I mistake not, you were pleased to call for my daughter; she is quite in the other side of the house at present, and indeed just taking her lesson on the harpsichord. Let us go along."

Anselmus, scarcely knowing what he did, followed his conductor; he saw or heard nothing more, till Archivarius Lindhorst suddenly grasped his hand, and said: "Here is the place!" Anselmus awoke as from a dream, and now perceived that he was in a high room, all lined on every side with book-shelves, and nowise differing from a common library and study. In the middle stood a large writing-table, with a stuffed arm-chair before it. "This," said Archivarius Lindhorst, "is your work-room for the present: whether you may work, some other time, in the blue library, where you so suddenly called out my daughter's name, I yet know not. But now I could wish to convince myself of your ability to execute this task appointed you, in the way I wish it and need it."

The Student here gathered full courage; and not without internal self-complacence in the certainty of highly gratifying Archivarius Lindhorst, pulled out his drawings and specimens of penmanship from his pocket. But no sooner had the Archivarius cast his eye on the first leaf, a piece of writing in the finest English style, than he smiled very oddly, and shook his head. These motions he repeated at every following leaf, so that the Student Anselmus felt the blood mounting to his face; and at last, when the smile became quite sarcastic and contemptuous, he broke out in downright vexation: "The Herr Archivarius does not seem contented with my poor talents."

"Dear Herr Anselmus," said Archivarius Lindhorst, "you have indeed fine capacities for the art of calligraphy; but, in the meanwhile, it is clear enough, I must reckon more on your diligence and good-will, than on your attainments in the business."

The Student Anselmus spoke largely of his often-acknowledged perfection in this art, of his fine Chinese ink, and most select crow-quills. But Archivarius Lindhorst handed him the English sheet, and said: "Be judge yourself!" Anselmus felt as if struck by a thunderbolt, to see his hand-writing look so: it was miserable, beyond measure. There was no rounding in the turns, no hair-stroke where it should be; no proportion between the capital and single letters; nay, villainous school-boy pot-hooks often spoiled the best lines. "And then," continued Archivarius Lindhorst, "your ink will not stand." He dipt his finger in a glass of water, and as he just skimmed it over the lines, they vanished without vestige. The Student Anselmus felt as if some monster were throttling him: he could not utter a word. There stood he, with the unlucky sheet in his hand; but Archivarius Lindhorst laughed aloud, and said: "Never mind it, dearest Herr Anselmus; what you could not perfect before, will perhaps do better here. At any rate, you shall have better materials than you have been accustomed to. Begin, in Heaven's name!"

From a locked press, Archivarius Lindhorst now brought out a black fluid substance, which diffused a most peculiar odor; also pens, sharply pointed and of strange color, together with a sheet of especial whiteness and smoothness; then at last an Arabic manuscript: and as Anselmus sat down to work, the Archivarius left the room. The Student Anselmus had often copied Arabic manuscripts already; the first problem, therefore, seemed to him not so very difficult to solve. "How these pot-hooks came into my fine English current-hand, Heaven, and Archivarius Lindhorst, know best," said he; "but that they are not from *my* hand, I will testify to the death!" At every new word that stood fair and perfect on the parchment, his courage increased, and with it his adroitness. In truth, these pens wrote exquisitely well; and the mysterious ink flowed pliantly, and black as jet, on the bright white parchment. And as he worked along so diligently, and with such strained attention, he began to feel more and more at home in the solitary room; and already he had quite fitted himself into his task, which he now hoped to finish well, when at the stroke of three the Archivarius called him into the side-room to a savory dinner. At table, Archivarius Lindhorst was in special gaiety of heart: he inquired about the Student Anselmus' friends, Conrector Paulmann, and Registrator Heerbrand, and of the latter especially he had store of merry anecdotes to tell. The good old Rhenish was particularly grateful to the Student Anselmus, and made him more talkative than he was wont to be. At the stroke of four, he rose to resume his labor; and this punctuality appeared to please the Archivarius.

If the copying of these Arabic manuscripts had prospered in his hands, before dinner, the task now went forward much better; nay, he could not himself comprehend the rapidity and ease, with which he succeeded in transcribing the twisted strokes of this foreign character. But it was as if, in his inmost soul, a voice were whispering in audible words: "Ah! couldst thou accomplish it, wert thou not thinking of *her*, didst thou not believe in *her* and in her love?" Then there floated whispers, as in low, low, waving crystal tones, through the room: "I am near, near, near! I help thee: be bold, be steadfast, dear Anselmus! I toil with thee, that thou mayest be mine!" And as, in the fulness of secret rapture, he caught these sounds, the unknown characters grew clearer and clearer to him; he scarcely required to look on the original at all; nay, it was as if the letters were already standing in pale ink on the parchment, and he had nothing more to do but mark them black. So did he labor on, encompassed with dear inspiring tones as with soft sweet breath, till the clock struck six, and Archivarius Lindhorst entered the apartment. He came forward to the table, with a singular smile; Anselmus rose in silence: the Archivarius still looked at him, with that mocking smile: but no sooner had he glanced over the copy, than the smile passed into deep solemn earnestness, which every feature of his face adapted itself to express. He seemed no longer the same. His eyes, which usually gleamed with sparkling fire, now looked with unutterable mildness at Anselmus; a soft red tinted the pale cheeks; and instead of the irony which at other times compressed the mouth, the softly-curved graceful lips now seemed to be opening for wise and soul-persuading speech. The whole form was higher, statelier; the wide night-gown spread itself like a royal mantle in broad folds over his breast and shoulders; and through the white locks, which lay on his high open brow, there winded a thin band of gold.

"Young man," began the Archivarius in solemn tone, "before thou thoughtest of it, I knew thee, and all the secret relations which bind thee to the dearest and holiest of my interests! Serpentina loves thee; a singular destiny, whose fateful threads were spun by enemies, is fulfilled, should she be thine, and thou obtain, as an essential dowry, the Golden Pot, which of right belongs to her. But only from effort and contest can thy happiness in the higher life arise; hostile Principles assail thee; and only the interior force with which thou shalt withstand these contradictions can save thee from disgrace and ruin. Whilst laboring here, thou art passing the season of instruction: Belief and full knowledge will lead thee to the near goal, if thou but hold fast, what thou hast well begun. Bear *her* always and truly in thy thoughts, her who loves thee; then shalt thou see the marvels of the Golden Pot, and be happy for ever more. Fare thee well! Archivarius Lindhorst expects thee to-morrow at noon in his cabinet. Fare thee well!" With these words Archivarius Lindhorst softly pushed the Student Anselmus out of the door, which he then locked; and Anselmus found himself in the chamber where he had dined, the single door of which led out to the lobby.

Altogether stupified with these strange phenomena, the Student Anselmus stood lingering at the street-door; he heard a window open above him, and looked up: it was Archivarius Lindhorst, quite the old man again, in his light-grey gown, as he usually appeared. The Archivarius called to him: "Hey, worthy Herr Anselmus, what are you studying over there? Tush, the Arabic *is* still in your head. My compliments to Herr Conrector Paulmann, if you see him; and come to-morrow precisely at noon. The fee for this day is lying in your right waistcoat-pocket." The Student Anselmus actually found the clear speziesthaler in the pocket indicated; but he took no joy in it. "What is to come of all this," said he to himself, "I know not: but if it be some mad delusion and conjuring work that has laid hold of me, the dear Serpentina still lives and moves in my inward heart; and before I leave her, I will die altogether; for I know that the thought in me is eternal, and no hostile Principle can take it from me: and what else is this thought but Serpentina's love?"

EIGHTH VIGIL.

The Library of the Palm-trees. Fortunes of an unhappy Salamander. How the Black Quill caressed a Parsnip, and Registrator Heerbrand was much overtaken with Liquor.

THE Student Anselmus had now worked several days with Archivarius Lindhorst; these working hours were for him the happiest of his life; still encircled with lovely tones, with Serpentina's encouraging voice, he was filled and overflowed with a pure delight, which often rose to highest rapture. Every strait, every little care of his needy existence, had vanished from his thoughts; and in the new life, which had risen on him as in serene sunny splendor, he comprehended all the wonders of a higher world, which before had filled him with astonishment, nay, with dread. His copying proceeded rapidly and lightly; for he felt more and more as if he were writing characters long known to him; and he scarcely needed to cast his eye upon the manuscript, while copying it all with the greatest exactness.

Except at the hour of dinner, Archivarius Lindhorst seldom made his appearance; and this always precisely at the moment when Anselmus had finished the last letter of some manuscript: then the Archivarius would hand him another, and directly after, leave him, without uttering a word; having first stirred the ink with a little black rod, and changed the old pens with new sharp-pointed ones. One day, when Anselmus, at the stroke of twelve, had as usual mounted the stair, he found the door through which he commonly entered, standing locked; and Archivarius Lindhorst came forward from the other side, dressed in his strange flower-figured night-gown. He called aloud: "To-day come this way, good Herr Anselmus; for we must to the chamber where Bhogovotgita's masters are waiting for us."

He stept along the corridor, and led Anselmus through the same chambers and halls, as at the first visit. The Student Anselmus again felt astonished at the marvellous beauty of the garden: but he now perceived that many of the strange flowers, hanging on the dark bushes were in truth insects glancing with lordly colors, hovering up and down with their little wings, as they danced and whirled in clusters, caressing one another with their antennæ. On the other hand again, the rose and azure-colored birds were odoriferous flowers; and the perfume which they scattered, mounted from their cups in low lovely tones, which, with the gurgling of distant fountains, and the sighing of the high groves and trees, mingled themselves into mysterious accords of a deep unutterable longing. The mock-birds, which had so jeered and flouted him before, were again fluttering to and fro over his head, and crying incessantly with their sharp small voices: "Herr Studiosus, Herr Studiosus, don't be in such a hurry! Don't peep into the clouds so! They may fall about your ears—He! He! Herr Studiosus, put your powder-mantle on; cousin Screech-Owl will frizzle your toupee." And so it went along, in all manner of stupid chatter, till Anselmus left the garden.

Archivarius Lindhorst at last stept into the azure chamber: the porphyry, with the Golden Pot, was gone; instead of it, in the middle of the room, stood a table overhung with violet-colored satin, upon which lay the writing-ware already known to Anselmus; and a stuffed arm-chair, covered with the same sort of cloth, was placed beside it.

"Dear Herr Anselmus," said Archivarius Lindhorst, "you have now copied me a number of manuscripts, rapidly and correctly, to my no small contentment: you have gained my confidence; but the hardest is yet behind; and that is the transcribing or rather painting of certain works, written in a peculiar character; I keep them in this room, and they can only be copied on the spot. You will, therefore, in future, work here; but I must recommend to you the greatest foresight and attention; a false stroke, or, which may Heaven forefend, a blot let fall on the original, will plunge you into misfortune."

Anselmus observed that from the golden trunks of the palm-trees, little emerald leaves projected: one of these leaves the Archivarius took hold of; and Anselmus could not but perceive that the leaf was in truth a roll of parchment, which the Archivarius unfolded, and spread out before the Student on the table. Anselmus wondered not a little at these strangely intertwisted characters; and as he looked over the many points, strokes, dashes, and twirls in the manuscript, he almost lost hope of ever copying it. He fell into deep thoughts on the subject.

"Be of courage, young man!" cried the Archivarius; "if thou hast continuing Belief and true Love, Serpentina will help thee."

His voice sounded like ringing metal; and as Anselmus looked up in utter terror, Archivarius Lindhorst was standing before him in the kingly form, which, during the first visit, he had assumed in the library. Anselmus felt as if in his deep reverence he could not but sink on his knee; but the Archivarius stept up the trunk of a palm-tree, and vanished aloft among the emerald leaves. The Student Anselmus perceived that the Prince of the Spirits had been speaking with him, and was now gone up to his study; perhaps intending, by the beams which some of the Planets had dispatched to him as envoys, to send back word what was to become of Anselmus and Serpentina.

"It may be too," thought he farther, "that he is expecting news from the Springs of the Nile; or that some magician from Lapland is paying him a visit: me it behoves to set diligently about my task." And with this, he began studying the foreign characters in the roll of parchment.

The strange music of the garden sounded over to him, and encircled him with sweet lovely odors; the mock-birds too he still heard giggling and twittering, but could not distinguish their words, a thing which greatly pleased him. At times also it was as if the leaves of the palm-trees were rustling, and as if the clear crystal tones, which Anselmus on that fateful Ascension-day had heard under the elder-bush, were beaming and flitting through the room. Wonderfully strengthened by this shining and tinkling, the Student Anselmus directed his eyes and thoughts more and more intensely on the superscription of the parchment roll; and ere long he felt, as it were from his inmost soul, that the characters could denote nothing else than these words: *Of the marriage of the Salamander with the green Snake.* Then resounded a louder triphony of clear crystal bells: "Anselmus! dear Anselmus!" floated to him from the leaves; and, O wonder! on the trunk of the palm-tree the green Snake came winding down.

"Serpentina! Serpentina!" cried Anselmus, in the madness of highest rapture; for as he gazed more earnestly, it was in truth a lovely glorious maiden that, looking at him with those dark blue eyes, full of inexpressible longing, as they lived in his heart, was hovering down to meet him. The leaves seemed to jut out and expand; on every hand were prickles sprouting from the trunk; but Serpentina twisted and winded herself deftly through them; and so drew her fluttering robe, glancing as if in changeful colors, along with her, that, plying round the dainty form, it nowhere caught on the projecting points and prickles of the palm-tree. She sat down by Anselmus on the same chair, clasping him with her arm, and pressing him towards her, so that he felt the breath which came from her lips, and the electric warmth of her frame.

"Dear Anselmus!" began Serpentina, "thou shalt now soon be wholly mine; by thy Belief, by thy Love thou shalt obtain me, and I will bring thee the Golden Pot, which shall make us both happy forevermore."

"O thou kind lovely Serpentina!" said Anselmus, "if I have but thee, what care I for all else! if thou art but mine, I will joyfully give in to all the wondrous mysteries that have beset me ever since the moment when I first saw thee."

"I know," continued Serpentina, "that the strange and mysterious things, with which my father, often merely in his sport of his humor, has surrounded thee, have raised distrust and dread in thy mind; but now, I hope, it shall be so no more; for I come at this moment to tell thee, dear Anselmus, from the bottom of my heart and soul, all and sundry to a tittle that thou needest to know for understanding my father, and so for seeing clearly what thy relation to him and to me really is."

Anselmus felt as if he were so wholly clasped and encircled by the gentle lovely form, that only with her could he move and live, and as it were but the beating of her pulse that throbbed through his nerves and fibres; he listened to each one of her words till it sounded in his inmost heart, and, like a burning ray, kindled in him the rapture of Heaven. He had put his arm round that daintier than dainty waist; but the changeful glistering cloth of her robe was so smooth and slippery, that it seemed to him as if she could at any moment wind herself from his arms, and glide away. He trembled at the thought.

"Ah, do not leave me, gentlest Serpentina!" cried he; "thou art my life."

"Not now," said Serpentina, "till I have told thee all that in thy love of me thou canst comprehend:

"Know then, dearest, that my father is sprung

from the wondrous race of the Salamanders; and that I owe my existence to his love for the green Snake. In primeval times, in the Fairyland Atlantis, the potent Spirit-prince Phosphorus bore rule; and to him the Salamanders, and other Spirits of the Elements, were plighted. Once on a time, the Salamander, whom he loved before all others (it was my father), chanced to be walking in the stately garden, which Phosphorus' mother had decked in the lordliest fashion with her best gifts; and the Salamander heard a tall Lily singing in low tones: 'Press down thy little eyelids, till my Lover, the Morning-wind, awake thee.' He stept towards it: touched by his glowing breath, the Lily opened her leaves; and he saw the Lily's daughter, the green Snake, lying asleep in the hollow of the flower. Then was the Salamander inflamed with warm love for the fair Snake; and he carried her away from the Lily, whose perfumes in nameless lamentation vainly called for her beloved daughter throughout all the garden. For the Salamander had borne her into the palace of Phosphorus, and was there beseeching him: 'Wed me with my beloved, and she shall be mine for evermore.'— 'Madman, what askest thou!' said the Prince of the Spirits; 'Know that once the Lily was my mistress, and bore rule with me; but the Spark, which I cast into her, threatened to annihilate the fair Lily; and only my victory over the black Dragon, whom now the Spirits of the Earth hold in fetters, maintains her, that her leaves continue strong enough to enclose this Spark, and preserve it within them. But when thou claspest the green Snake, thy fire will consume her frame; and a new Being rapidly arising from her dust, will soar away and leave thee.'

"The Salamander heeded not the warning of the Spirit-prince: full of longing ardor he folded the green Snake in his arms; she crumbled into ashes; a winged Being, born from her dust, soared away through the sky. Then the madness of desperation caught the Salamander; and he ran through the garden, dashing forth fire and flames; and wasted it in his wild fury, till its fairest flowers and blossoms hung down, blackened and scathed; and their lamentation filled the air. The indignant Prince of the Spirits, in his wrath, laid hold of the Salamander, and said: 'Thy fire has burnt out, thy flames are extinguished, thy rays darkened: sink down to the Spirits of the Earth; let these mock and jeer thee, and keep thee captive, till the Fire-element shall again kindle, and beam up with thee as with a new being from the Earth.' The poor Salamander sank down extinguished: but now the testy old Earth-spirit, who was Phosphorus' gardener, came forth and said: 'Master! who has greater cause to complain of the Salamander than I? Had not all the fair flowers, which he has burnt, been decorated with my gayest metals; had I not stoutly nursed and tended them, and spent many a fair hue on their leaves? And yet I must pity the poor Salamander; for it was but love, in which thou, O Master, hast full often been entangled, that drove him to despair, and made him desolate the garden. Remit him the too harsh punishment!'—'His fire is for the present extinguished,' said the Prince of the Spirits; 'but in the hapless time, when the Speech of Nature shall no longer be intelligible to degenerate man; when the Spirits of the Elements, banished into their own regions, shall speak to him only from afar, in faint, spent echoes; when, displaced from the harmonious circle, an infinite longing alone shall give him tidings of the Land of Marvels, which he once might inhabit while Belief and Love still dwelt in his soul: in this hapless time, the fire of the Salamander shall again kindle; but only to manhood shall he be permitted to rise, and entering wholly into man's necessitous existence, he shall learn to endure its wants and oppressions. Yet not only shall the remembrance of his first state continue with him; but he shall again rise into the sacred harmony of all Nature; he shall understand its wonders, and the power of his fellow-spirits shall stand at his behest. Then, too, in a Lily-bush, shall he find the green Snake again: and the fruit of his marriage with her shall be three daughters, which, to men, shall appear in the form of their mother. In the spring season these shall disport them in the dark Elder-bush, and sound with their lovely crystal voices. And then if, in that needy and mean age of inward stuntedness, there shall be found a youth who understands their song; nay, if one of the little Snakes look at him with her kind eyes; if the look awaken in him forecastings of the distant wondrous Land, to which, having cast away the burden of the Common, he can courageously soar; if, with love to the Snake, there rise in him belief in the Wonders of Nature, nay, in his own existence amid these Wonders, then the Snake shall be his. But not till three youths of this sort have been found and wedded to the three daughters, may the Salamander cast away his heavy burden, and return to his brothers.'— 'Permit me, Master,' said the Earth-spirit, 'to make these three daughters a present, which may glorify their life with the husbands they shall find. Let each of them receive from me a Pot, of the fairest metal which I have; I will polish it with beams borrowed from the diamond; in its glitter shall our Kingdom of Wonders, as it now exists in the Harmony of universal Nature, be imaged back in glorious dazzling reflection; and from its interior, on the day of marriage, shall spring forth a Fire-lily, whose eternal blossoms shall encircle the youth that is found worthy, with sweet wafting odors. Soon too shall he learn its speech, and understand the wonders of our kingdom, and dwell with his beloved in Atlantis itself.'

"Thou perceivest well, dear Anselmus, that the Salamander of whom I speak is no other than my father. Spite of his higher nature, he was forced to subject himself to the paltriest contradictions of common life; and hence, indeed, often comes the wayward humor with which he vexes many. He has told me now and then, that, for the inward make of mind, which the Spirit-prince Phosphorus required as a condition of marriage with me and my sisters, men have a name at present, which, in truth, they frequently enough misapply: they call it a childlike poetic character. This character, he says, is often found in youths, who, by reason of their high simplicity of manners, and their total want of what is called knowledge of the world, are mocked by the populace. Ah, dear Anselmus! beneath the Elder-bush, thou understoodest my song, my look: thou lovest the green Snake, thou believest in me, and wilt be mine forevermore! The fair Lily will bloom forth from the Golden Pot; and we shall dwell, happy, and united, and blessed, in Atlantis together!

"Yet I must not hide from thee that in its deadly battle with the Salamanders and Spirits of the Earth, the black Dragon burst from their grasp, and hurried off through the air. Phosphorus, indeed, again holds him in fetters; but from the black Quills, which, in the struggle, rained down on the ground, there sprung up hostile Spirits, which on all hands set themselves against the Salamanders and Spirits of the Earth. That woman who so hates thee, dear Anselmus, and who, as my father knows full well, is striving for possession of the Golden Pot; that woman owes her existence to the love of such a Quill (plucked in battle from the Dragon's wing) for a certain Parsnip beside which it dropped. She knows her origin and her power; for, in the moans and convulsions of the captive Dragon, the secrets of many a mysterious constellation are revealed to her; and she uses every means and effort to work from the Outward into the Inward and unseen; while my father, with the beams which shoot forth from the spirit of the Salamander, withstands and subdues her. All the baneful principles which lurk in deadly herbs and poisonous beasts, she collects; and, mixing them under favorable constellations, raises therewith many a wicked spell, which overwhelms the soul of man with fear and trembling, and subjects him to the power of those Demons, produced from the Dragon when it yielded in battle. Beware of that old woman, dear Anselmus! She hates thee; because thy childlike pious character has annihilated many of her wicked charms. Keep true, true to me; soon art thou at the goal!"

"O my Serpentina! my own Serpentina!" cried the Student Anselmus, "how could I leave thee, how should I not love thee forever!" A kiss was burning on his lips; he awoke as from a deep dream: Serpentina had vanished; six o'clock was striking, and it fell heavy on his heart that to-day he had not copied a single stroke. Full of anxiety, and dreading reproaches from the Archivarius, he looked into the sheet; and, O wonder! the copy of the mysterious manuscript was fairly concluded; and he thought, on viewing the characters more narrowly, that the writing was nothing else but Serpentina's story of her father, the favorite of the Spirit-prince Phosphorus, in Atlantis, the Land of Marvels. And now entered Archivarius Lindhorst, in his light-grey surtout, with hat and staff: he looked into the parchment on which Anselmus had been writing; took a large pinch of snuff, and said with a smile: "Just as I thought!—Well, Herr Anselmus, here is your speziesthaler; we will now to the Linke Bath: do but follow me!" The Archivarius stept rapidly through the garden, in which there was such a din of singing, whistling, talking, that the Student Anselmus was quite deafened with it, and thanked Heaven when he found himself on the street.

Scarcely had they walked twenty paces, when they met Registrator Heerbrand, who companionably joined them. At the Gate, they filled their pipes, which they had about them: Registrator Heerbrand complained that he had left his tinder-box behind, and could not strike fire. "Fire!" cried Archivarius Lindhorst, scornfully; "here is fire enough, and to spare!" And with this he snapped his fingers, out of which came streams of sparks, and directly kindled the pipes.—"Do but observe the chemical knack of some men!" said Registrator Heerbrand; but the Student Anselmus thought, not without internal awe, of the Salamander and his history.

In the Linke Bath, Registrator Heerbrand drank so much strong double beer, that at last, though usually a good-natured quiet man, he began singing student songs in squeaking tenor; he asked every one sharply, Whether he was his friend or not? and at last had to be taken home by the Student Anselmus, long after Archivarius Lindhorst had gone his ways.

NINTH VIGIL.

How the Student Anselmus attained to some Sense. The Punch Party. How the Student Anselmus took Conrector Paulmann for a Screech-Owl, and the latter felt much hurt at it. The Ink-blot, and its Consequences.

The strange and mysterious things which day by day befell the Student Anselmus, had entirely withdrawn him from his customary life. He no longer visited any of his friends, and waited every morning with impatience, for the hour of noon, which was to unlock his paradise. And yet while his whole soul was turned to the gentle Serpentina, and the wonders of Archivarius Lindhorst's fairy kingdom, he could not help now and then thinking of Veronica; nay, often it seemed as if she came before him and confessed with blushes how heartily she loved him; how much she longed to rescue him from the phantoms, which were mocking and befooling him. At times he felt as if a foreign power, suddenly breaking in on his mind, were drawing him with resistless force to the forgotten Veronica; as if he must needs follow her whither she pleased to lead him, nay, as if he were bound to her by ties that would not break. That very night after Serpentina had first appeared to him in the form of a lovely maiden; after the wondrous secret of the Salamander's nuptials with the green Snake had been disclosed, Veronica came before him more vividly than ever. Nay, not till he awoke, was he clearly aware that he had but been dreaming; for he had felt persuaded that Veronica was actually beside him, complaining with an expression of keen sorrow, which pierced through his inmost soul, that he should sacrifice her deep true love to fantastic visions, which only the distemper of his mind called into being, and which, moreover, would at last prove his ruin. Veronica was lovelier than he had ever seen her; he could not drive her from his thoughts: and in this perplexed and contradictory mood he hastened out, hoping to get rid of it by a morning walk.

A secret magic influence led him on to the Pirna gate: he was just turning into a cross street, when Conrector Paulmann, coming after him, cried out: "Ey! Ey!—Dear Herr Anselmus!—*Amice! Amice!* Where, in Heaven's name, have you been buried so long? We never see you at all. Do you know, Veronica is longing very much to have another song with you. So come along; you were just on the road to me, at any rate."

The Student Anselmus, constrained by this friendly violence, went along with the Conrector. On entering the house, they were met by Veronica, attired with such neatness and attention, that Conrector Paulmann, full of amazement, asked her: "Why so decked, Mamsell? Were you expecting visitors? Well, here I bring you Herr Anselmus."

The Student Anselmus, in daintily and elegantly kissing Veronica's hand, felt a small soft pressure from it, which shot like a stream of fire over all his frame. Veronica was cheerfulness, was grace itself; and when Paulmann left them for his study, she contrived, by all manner of rogueries and waggeries, so to uplift the Student Anselmus, that he at last quite forgot his bashfulness, and jigged round the room with the light-headed maiden. But here again the Demon of Awkwardness got hold of him : he jolted on a table, and Veronica's pretty little work-box fell to the floor. Anselmus lifted it; the lid had started up; and a little round metallic mirror was glittering on him, into which he looked with peculiar delight. Veronica glided softly up to him; laid her hand on his arm, and pressing close to him, looked over his shoulder into the mirror also. And now Anselmus felt as if a battle were beginning in his soul: thoughts, images flashed out—Archivarius Lindhorst,—Serpentina,—the green Snake—at last the tumult abated, and all this chaos arranged and shaped itself into distinct consciousness. It was now clear to him that he had always thought of Veronica alone; nay, that the form which had yesterday appeared to him in the blue chamber, had been no other than Veronica; and that the wild legend of the Salamander's marriage with the green Snake, had merely been written down by him from the manuscript, but nowise related in his hearing. He wondered not a little at all these dreams; and ascribed them solely to the heated state of mind into which Veronica's love had brought him, as well as to his working with Archivarius Lindhorst, in whose rooms there were, besides, so many strangely intoxicating odors. He could not but laugh heartily at the mad whim of falling in love with a little green Snake; and taking a well-fed Privy Archivarius for a Salamander: "Yes, yes! It is Veronica!" cried he aloud; but on turning round his head, he looked right into Veronica's blue eyes, from which warmest love was beaming. A faint soft Ah! escaped her lips, which at that moment were burning on his.

"O happy I!" sighed the enraptured Student: "What I yesternight but dreamed, is in very deed mine to-day."

"But wilt thou really wed me, then, when thou art Hofrath?" said Veronica.

"That I will," replied the Student Anselmus; and just then the door creaked, and Conrector Paulmann entered with the words:

"Now, dear Herr Anselmus, I will not let you go to-day. You will put up with a bad dinner; then Veronica will make us delightful coffee, which we shall drink with Registrator Heerbrand, for he promised to come hither."

"Ah, best Herr Conrector!" answered the Student Anselmus, "are you not aware that I must go to Archivarius Lindhorst's and copy?"

"Look you, *Amice!*" said Conrector Paulmann, holding up his watch, which pointed to half past twelve.

The Student Anselmus saw clearly that he was much too late for Archivarius Lindhorst; and he complied with the Conrector's wishes the more readily, as he might now hope to look at Veronica the whole day long, to obtain many a stolen glance, and little squeeze of the hand, nay, even to succeed in conquering a kiss. So high had the Student Anselmus' desires now mounted; he felt more and more contented in soul, the more fully he convinced himself that he should be delivered from all the fantastic imaginations, which really might have made a sheer idiot of him.

Registrator Heerbrand came, as he had promised, after dinner; and coffee being over, and the dusk come on, the Registrator, puckering his face together, and gaily rubbing his hands, signified that he had something about him, which, if mingled and reduced to form, as it were, paged and titled, by Veronica's fair hands, might be pleasant to them all, on this October evening.

"Come out, then, with this mysterious substance which you carry with you, most valued Registrator," cried Conrector Paulmann. Then Registrator Heerbrand shoved his hand into his deep pocket, and at three journeys, brought out a bottle of arrack, two citrons, and a quantity of sugar. Before half an hour had passed, a savory bowl of punch was smoking on Paulmann's table. Veronica drank their health in a sip of the liquor; and ere long there was plenty of gay, good-natured chat among the friends. But the Student Anselmus, as the spirit of the drink mounted into his head, felt all the images of those wondrous things, which for some time he had experienced, again coming through his mind. He saw the Archivarius in his damask night-gown, which glittered like phosphorus; he saw the azure room, the golden palm-trees; nay, it now seemed to him as if he must still believe in Serpentina: there was a fermentation, a conflicting tumult in his soul. Veronica handed him a glass of punch; and in taking it, he gently touched her hand. "Serpentina! Veronica!" sighed he to himself. He sank into deep dreams; but Registrator Heerbrand cried quite aloud: "A strange old gentleman, whom nobody can fathom, he is and will be, this Archivarius Lindhorst. Well, long life to him! Your glass, Herr Anselmus!"

Then the Student Anselmus awoke from his dreams, and said, as he touched glasses with Registrator Heerbrand: "That proceeds, respected Herr Registrator, from the circumstance, that Archivarius Lindhorst is in reality a Salamander, who wasted in his fury the Spirit-prince Phosphorus' garden, because the green Snake had flown away from him."

"How? what?" inquired Conrector Paulmann.

"Yes," continued the Student Anselmus; "and for this reason he is now forced to be a Royal Archivarius; and to keep house here in Dresden with his three daughters, who, after all, are nothing more than little gold-green Snakes, that bask in elder-bushes, and traitorously sing, and seduce away young people, like as many syrens."

"Herr Anselmus! Herr Anselmus!" cried Conrector Paulmann, "is there a crack in your brain? In Heaven's name, what monstrous stuff is this you are babbling?"

"He is right," interrupted Registrator Heerbrand: "that fellow, that Archivarius, is a cursed Salamander, and strikes you fiery snips from his fingers, which burn holes in your surtout like red-hot tinder. Ay, ay, thou art in the right, brotherkin Anselmus; and whoever says No, is saying No to me!" And at these words Registrator Heerbrand struck the table with his fist, till the glasses rung again.

"Registrator! Are you frantic?" cried the wroth Conrector. "Herr Studiosus, Herr Studiosus! what is this you are about again?"

"Ah!" said the Student, "you too are nothing but a bird, a screech-owl, that frizzles toupees, Herr Conrector!"

"What!—I a bird?—A screech-owl, a frizzler?" cried the Conrector, full of indignation: "Sir, you are mad, horn mad!"

"But the crone will get a clutch of him," cried Registrator Heerbrand.

"Yes, the crone is potent," interrupted the Student Anselmus, "though she is but of mean descent; for her father was nothing but a ragged wing-feather, and her mother a dirty parsnip: but the most of her power she owes to all sorts of baneful creatures, poisonous vermin which she keeps about her."

"That is a horrid calumny," cried Veronica, with eyes all glowing in anger: "old Liese is a wise woman; and the black Cat is no baneful creature, but a polished young gentleman of elegant manners, and her cousin german."

"Can he eat Salamanders without singing his whiskers, and dying like a candle-snuff?" cried Registrator Heerbrand.

"No! no!" shouted the Student Anselmus, "that he never can in this world; and the green Snake loves me, and I have looked into Serpentina's eyes."

"The Cat will scratch them out," cried Veronica.

"Salamander, Salamander beats them all, all," hollowed Conrector Paulmann, in the highest fury: "But am I in a madhouse? Am I mad myself? What unwise stuff am I chattering? Yes, I am mad too! mad too!" And with this, Conrector Paulmann started up; tore the peruke from his head, and dashed it against the ceiling of the room; till the battered locks whizzed, and, tangled into utter disorder, rained down the powder far and wide. Then the Student Anselmus and Registrator Heerbrand seized the punch-bowl and the glasses; and, hallooing and huzzaing, pitched them against the ceiling also, and the sherds fell jingling and tingling about their ears.

"*Vivat* the Salamander!—*Pereat, pereat* the crone!—Break the metal mirror!—Dig the cat's eyes out!—Bird, little Bird, from the air—*Eheu—Eheu—Evoe—Evoe*, Salamander!" So shrieked, and shouted, and bellowed the three, like utter maniacs. With loud weeping, Fränzchen ran out; but Veronica lay whimpering for pain and sorrow on the sofa.

At this moment the door opened: all was instantly still; and a little man, in a small grey cloak, came stepping in. His countenance had a singular air of gravity; and especially the round hooked nose, on which was a huge pair of spectacles, distinguished itself from all the noses ever seen. He wore a strange peruke too; more like a feather-cap than a wig.

"Ey, many good evenings!" grated and cackled the little comical mannikin. "Is the Student Herr Anselmus among you, gentlemen? — Best compliments from Archivarius Lindhorst; he has waited to-day in vain for Herr Anselmus; but to-morrow he begs most respectfully to request that Herr Anselmus would not forget the hour."

And with this he went out again; and all of them now saw clearly that the grave little mannikin was in fact a grey Parrot. Conrector Paulmann and Registrator Heerbrand raised a horse-laugh, which reverberated through the room; and in the intervals, Veronica was moaning and whimpering, as if torn by nameless sorrow; but, as to the Student Anselmus, the madness of inward horror was darting through him; and unconsciously he ran through the door, along the streets. Instinctively he reached his house, his garret. Ere long Veronica came in to him, with a peaceful and friendly look, and asked him why, in the festivity, he had so vexed her; and desired him to be on his guard against imaginations, while working at Archivarius Lindhorst's. "Good night, good night, my beloved friend!" whispered Veronica, scarce audibly, and breathed a kiss on his lips. He stretched out his arms to clasp her, but the dreamy shape had vanished, and he awoke cheerful and refreshed. He could not but laugh heartily at the effects of the punch; but in thinking of Veronica, he felt pervaded by a most delightful feeling. "To her alone," said he within himself, "do I owe this return from my insane whims. In good sooth, I was little better than the man who believed himself to be of glass; or he who durst not leave his room for fear the hens should eat him, as he was a barleycorn. But so soon as I am Hofrath, I marry Mademoiselle Paulmann, and be happy, and there's an end of it."

At noon, as he walked through Archivarius Lindhorst's garden, he could not help wondering how all this had once appeared so strange and marvellous. He now saw nothing past common; earthen flowerpots, quantities of geraniums, myrtles, and the like. Instead of the glittering party-colored birds which used to flout him, there were nothing but a few sparrows, fluttering hither and thither, which raised an unpleasant unintelligible cry at sight of Anselmus. The azure room also had quite a different look; and he could not understand how that glaring blue, and those unnatural golden trunks of palm-trees, with their shapeless glistening leaves, should ever have pleased him for a moment. The Archivarius looked at him with a most peculiar ironical smile, and asked: "Well, how did you like the punch last night, good Anselmus?"

"Ah, doubtless you have heard from the grey Parrot how——" answered the Student Anselmus, quite ashamed; but he stopt short, bethinking him that this appearance of the Parrot was all a piece of jugglery.

"I was there myself," said Archivarius Lindhorst; "did you not see me? But, among the mad pranks you were playing, I had nigh got lamed: for I was sitting in the punch-bowl, at the very moment when Registrator Heerbrand laid hands on it, to dash it against the ceiling; and I had to make a quick retreat into the Conrector's pipe-head. Now, adieu, Herr Anselmus! Be diligent at your task; for the lost day also you shall have a speziesthaler, because you worked so well before."

"How can the Archivarius babble such mad stuff?" thought the Student Anselmus, sitting down at the table to begin the copying of the manuscript, which Archivarius Lindhorst had as usual spread out before him. But on the parchment roll, he perceived so many strange crabbed strokes and twirls all twisted together in inexplicable confusion, offering no resting-point for the eye, that it seemed to him well nigh impossible to copy all this exactly. Nay, in glancing over the whole, you might have thought the parchment was nothing but a piece of thickly veined marble, or a stone sprinkled over with lichens. Nevertheless he determined to do his utmost; and boldly dipt in his pen: but the ink would not run, do what he liked; impatiently he spirted the point of his pen against his nail, and—Heaven and Earth!—a huge blot fell on the outspread original! Hissing and foaming, rose a blue flash from the blot; and crackling and wavering, shot through the room to the ceiling. Then a thick vapor rolled from the walls; the leaves began to rustle, as if shaken by a tempest; and down out of them darted glaring basilisks in sparkling fire; these kindled the vapor, and the bickering masses of flame rolled round Anselmus. The golden trunks of the palm-trees became gigantic snakes, which knocked their frightful heads together with piercing metallic clang; and wound their scaly bodies round Anselmus.

"Madman! suffer now the punishment of what, in capricious irreverence, thou hast done!" So cried the frightful voice of the crowned Salamander, who appeared above the snakes like a glittering beam in the midst of the flame: and now the yawning jaws of the snakes poured forth cataracts of fire on Anselmus; and it was as if the fire-streams were congealing about his body, and changing into a firm ice-cold mass. But while Anselmus' limbs, more and more pressed together, and contracted, stiffened into powerlessness, his sense passed away. On returning to himself, he could not stir a joint: he was as if surrounded with a glistening brightness, on which he struck if he but tried to lift his hand.—Alas! He was sitting in a well-corked crystal bottle, on a shelf, in the library of Archivarius Lindhorst.

TENTH VIGIL.

Sorrows of the Student Anselmus in the Glass Bottle. Happy Life of the Cross Church Scholars and Law Clerks. The Battle in the Library of Archivarius Lindhorst. Victory of the Salamander, and Deliverance of the Student Anselmus.

JUSTLY may I doubt whether thou, favorable reader, wert ever sealed up in a glass bottle; or even that any vivid tormenting dream ever oppressed thee with such necromatic trouble. If so were the case, thou wilt keenly enough figure out the poor Student Anselmus' woe: but shouldst thou never have even dreamed such things, then will thy quick fancy, for Anselmus' sake and mine, be obliging enough still to enclose itself for a few moments in the crystal. Thou art drowned in dazzling splendor; all objects about thee appear illuminated and begirt with beaming rainbow hues: all quivers and wavers, and clangs and drones, in the sheen; thou art swimming, motionless and powerless as in a firmly congealed ether, which so presses thee together that the spirit in vain gives orders to the dead and stiffened body. Weightier and weightier the mountain burden lies on thee; more and more does every breath exhaust the little handful of air, that still played up and down in the narrow space; thy pulse throbs madly; and cut through with horrid anguish, every nerve is quivering and bleeding in this deadly agony. Have pity, favorable reader, on the Student Anselmus! Him this inexpressible torture laid hold of in his glass prison: but he felt too well that death could not relieve him; for did he not awake from the deep swoon into which the excess of pain had cast him, and open his eyes to new wretchedness, when the morning sun shone clear into the room? He could move no limb; but his thoughts struck against the glass, stupifying him with discordant clang; and instead of the words, which the spirit used to speak from within him, he now heard only the stifled din of madness. Then he exclaimed in his despair: "O Serpentina! Serpentina! save me from this agony of Hell!" And it was as if faint sighs breathed around him, which spread like green transparent elder-leaves over the glass; the clanging ceased; the dazzling perplexing glitter was gone, and he breathed more freely.

"Have not I myself solely to blame for my misery? Ah! Have not I sinned against thee, thou kind, beloved Serpentina? Have not I raised vile doubts of thee? Have not I lost my Belief; and with it, all, all that was to make me so blessed? Ah! Thou wilt now never, never be mine; for me the Golden Pot is lost, and I shall not behold its wonders any more. Ah! But once could I see thee; but once hear thy kind sweet voice, thou lovely Serpentina!"

So wailed the Student Anselmus, caught with deep piercing sorrow: then spoke a voice close by him: "What the devil ails you Herr Studiosus? What makes you lament so, out of all compass and measure?"

The Student Anselmus now perceived that on the same shelf with him were five other bottles, in which he perceived three Cross Church Scholars, and two Law Clerks.

"Ah, gentlemen, my fellows in misery," cried he, "how is it possible for you to be so calm, nay so happy, as I read in your cheerful looks? You are sitting here corked up in glass bottles, as well as I, and cannot move a finger; nay, not think a reasonable thought, but there rises such a murder-tumult of clanging and droning, and in your head itself a tumbling and rumbling enough to drive one mad. But doubtless you do not believe in the Salamander, or the green Snake."

"You are pleased to jest, Mein Herr Studiosus," replied a Cross Church Scholar; "we have never been better off than at present: for the speziesthalers which the mad Archivarius gave us for all manner of pot-hook copies, are chinking in our pockets; we have now no Italian choruses to learn by heart; we go every day to Joseph's or other houses of call, where the double-beer is sufficient, and we can look a pretty girl in the face; so we sing like real Students, *Gaudeamus igitur*, and are contented in spirit!"

"They of the Cross are quite right," added a Law Clerk; "I too am well furnished with speziesthalers, like my dearest colleague beside me here; and we now diligently walk about on the Weinberg, instead of scurvy Act-writing within four walls."

"But, my best, worthiest masters!" said the Student Anselmus, "do you not observe, then, that you are all and sundry corked up in glass bottles, and cannot for your hearts walk a hairsbreadth?"

Here the Cross Church Scholars and the Law Clerks set up a loud laugh, and cried: "The Student is mad; he fancies himself to be sitting in a glass bottle, and is standing on the Elbebridge and looking right down into the water. Let us go along!"

"Ah!" sighed the Student, "they have never seen the kind Serpentina; they know not what Freedom, and life in Love, and Belief, signifies; and so by reason of their folly and low-mindedness, they feel not the oppression of the imprisonment into which the Salamander has cast them. But I, unhappy I, must perish in want and woe, if she, whom I so inexpressibly love, do not deliver me!"

Then waving in faint tinkles, Serpentina's voice flitted through the room: "Anselmus! believe, love, hope!" And every tone beamed into Anselmus' prison; and the crystal yielded to his pressure, and expanded, till the breast of the captive could move and heave.

The torment of his situation became less and less, and he saw clearly that Serpentina still loved him; and that it was she alone, who had rendered his confinement tolerable. He disturbed himself no more about his insane companions in misfortune; but directed all his thoughts and meditations on the gentle Serpentina. Suddenly, however, there arose on the other side a dull croaking repulsive murmur. Ere long he could observe that it proceeded from an old coffee-pot, with half-broken lid, standing over against him on a little shelf. As he looked at it more narrowly, the ugly features of a wrinkled old woman by degrees unfolded themselves; and in a few moments, the Applewife of the Schwarzthor stood before him. She grinned and laughed at him, and cried with screeching voice: "Ey, Ey, my pretty boy, must thou lie in limbo now? To the crystal thou hast run: did I not tell thee long ago?"

"Mock and jeer me; do, thou cursed witch!" said the Student Anselmus, "thou art to blame for it all; but the Salamander will catch thee, thou vile Parsnip!"

3 s

"Ho, ho!" replied the crone, "not so proud, good readywriter! Thou hast squelched my little sons to pieces, thou hast burnt my nose; but I must still like thee, thou knave, for once thou wert a pretty fellow; and my little daughter likes thee too. Out of the crystal thou wilt never come unless I help thee: up thither I cannot clamber; but my cousin gossip the Rat, that lives close behind thee, will eat the shelf in two; thou shalt jingle down, and I catch thee in my apron, that thy nose be not broken, or thy fine sleek face at all injured: then I carry thee to Mamsell Veronica; and thou shalt marry her, when thou art Hofrath."

"Avaunt, thou devil's brood!" cried the Student Anselmus full of fury; "it was thou alone and thy hellish arts that brought me to the sin which I must now expiate. But I bear it all patiently: for only here can I be, where the kind Serpentina encircles me with love and consolation. Hear it, thou beldam, and despair! I bid defiance to thy power: I love Serpentina, and none but her for ever; I will not be Hofrath, will not look at Veronica, who by thy means entices me to evil. Can the green Snake not be mine, I will die in sorrow and longing. Take thyself away, thou filthy rook! Take thyself away!"

The crone laughed, till the chamber rung: "Sit and die then," cried she: "but now it is time to set to work; for I have other trade to follow here." She threw off her black cloak, and so stood in hideous nakedness; then she ran round in circles, and large folios came tumbling down to her; out of these she tore parchment leaves, and rapidly patching them together in artful combination, and fixing them on her body, in a few instants she was dressed as if in strange party-colored harness. Spitting fire, the black Cat darted out of the ink-glass, which was standing on the table, and ran mewing towards the crone, who shrieked in loud triumph, and along with him vanished through the door.

Anselmus observed that she went towards the azure chamber; and directly he heard a hissing and storming in the distance; the birds in the garden were crying; the Parrot creaked out: "Help! help! Thieves! thieves!" That moment the crone returned with a bound into the room, carrying the Golden Pot on her arm, and with hideous gestures, shrieking wildly through the air; "Joy! joy, little son!—Kill the green Snake! To her, son! To her!"

Anselmus thought he heard a deep moaning, heard Serpentina's voice. Then horror and despair took hold of him: he gathered all his force, he dashed violently, as if nerve and artery were bursting, against the crystal; a piercing clang went through the room, and the Archivarius in his bright damask nightgown was standing in the door.

"Hey, hey! vermin!—Mad spell!—Witchwork!—Hither, holla!" So shouted he: then the black hair of the crone started up in tufts; her red eyes glanced with infernal fire, and clenching together the peaked fangs of her abominable jaws, she hissed: "Hiss, at him! Hiss, at him! Hiss!" and laughed and neighed in scorn and mockery, and pressed the Golden Pot firmly towards her, and threw out of it handfuls of glittering earth on the Archivarius; but as it touched the nightgown, the earth changed into flowers, which rained down on the ground. Then the lilies of the nightgown flickered and flamed up; and the Archivarius caught these lilies blazing in sparky fire and dashed them on the witch; she howled for agony, but still as she leapt aloft and shook her harness of parchment the lilies went out, and fell away into ashes.

"To her, my lad!" creaked the crone: then the black Cat darted through the air, and soused over the Archivarius' head towards the door; but the grey Parrot fluttered out against him; caught him with his crooked bill by the nape, till red fiery blood burst down over his neck; and Serpentina's voice cried: "Saved! Saved!" Then the crone, foaming with rage and desperation, darted out upon the Archivarius: she threw the Golden Pot behind her, and holding up the long talons of her skinny fists, was for clutching the Archivarius by the throat: but he instantly doffed his nightgown, and hurled it against her. Then, hissing, and sputtering, and bursting, shot blue flames from the parchment leaves, and the crone rolled round in howling agony, and strove to get fresh earth from the Pot, fresh parchment leaves from the books, that she might stifle the blazing flames; and whenever any earth or leaves came down on her, the flames went out. But now, from the interior of the Archivarius issued fiery crackling beams, and darted on the crone.

"Hey, hey! To it again! Salamander! Victory!" clanged the Archivarius' voice through the chamber; and a hundred bolts whirled forth in fiery circles round the shrieking crone. Whizzing and buzzing flew Cat and Parrot in their furious battle; but at last the Parrot, with his strong wing, dashed the Cat to the ground; and with his talons transfixing and holding fast his adversary, which, in deadly agony, uttered horrid mews and howls, he, with his sharp bill, picked out his glowing eyes, and the burning froth spouted from them. Then thick vapor streamed up from the spot where the crone, hurled to the ground, was lying under the nightgown: her howling, her terrific, piercing cry of lamentation, died away in the remote distance. The smoke, which had spread abroad with irresistible smell, cleared off; the Archivarius picked up his nightgown; and under it lay an ugly Parsnip.

"Honored Herr Archivarius, here let me offer you the vanquished foe," said the Parrot, holding out a black hair in his beak to Archivarius Lindhorst.

"Very right, my worthy friend," replied the Archivarius: "here lies my vanquished foe too: be so good now as to manage what remains. This very day, as a small douceur, you shall have six cocoa-nuts, and a new pair of spectacles also, for I see the Cat has villainously broken the glasses of these old ones."

"Yours forever, most honored friend and patron!" answered the Parrot, much delighted; then took the Parsnip in his bill, and fluttered out with it by the window, which Archivarius Lindhorst had opened for him.

The Archivarius now lifted the Golden Pot, and cried, with a strong voice, "Serpentina! Serpentina!" But as the Student Anselmus, joying in the destruction of the vile beldam who had hurried him into misfortune, cast his eyes on the Archivarius, behold, here stood once more the high majestic form of the Spirit-prince, looking up to him with indescribable dignity and grace. "Anselmus," said the Spirit-prince, "not thou, but a hostile Principle, which strove destructively to penetrate into thy nature, and divide thee against thyself, was to blame for thy unbelief. Thou hast kept thy faithfulness: be free and happy." A bright flash quivered through the spirit of Anselmus: the royal triphony of the crystal bells sounded stronger and louder than he had ever heard it: his nerves and fibres thrilled; but, swelling higher and higher, the melodious tones rang through the room; the glass which enclosed Anselmus broke; and he rushed into the arms of his dear and gentle Serpentina.

ELEVENTH VIGIL.

Conrector Paulmann's anger at the Madness which had broken out in his Family. How Registrator Heerbrand became Hofrath; and, in the keenest Frost, walked about in Shoes and silk Stockings. Veronica's Confessions. Betrothment over the steaming Soup-plate.

"But tell me, best Registrator! how the cursed punch last night could so mount into our heads, and drive us to all manner of *allotria?*" So said Conrector Paulmann, as he next morning entered his room, which still lay full of broken sherds; with his hapless peruke, dissolved into its original elements, floating in punch among the ruin. For after the Student Anselmus ran out of doors, Conrector Paulmann and Registrator Heerbrand had still kept trotting and hobbling up and down the room, shouting like maniacs, and butting their heads together; till Fränzchen, with much labor, carried her vertiginous papa to bed; and Registrator Heerbrand in the deepest exhaustion, sunk on the sofa, which Veronica had left, taking refuge in her bed-room. Registrator Heerbrand had his blue handkerchief tied about his head; he looked quite pale and melancholic, and moaned out: "Ah, worthy Conrector, not the punch which Mamsell Veronica most admirably brewed, no! but simply that cursed Student is to blame for all the mischief. Do you not observe that he has long been *mente captus?* And are you not aware that madness is infectious? One fool makes twenty; pardon me, it is an old proverb: especially when you have drunk a glass or two, you fall into madness quite readily, and then involuntarily you manœuvre, and go through your exercise, just as the crack-brained fugleman makes the motion. Would you believe it, Conrector? I am still giddy when I think of that grey Parrot!"

"Grey fiddlestick!" interrupted the Conrector: " it was nothing but Archivarius Lindhorst's little old Famulus, who had thrown a grey cloak over him, and was seeking the Student Anselmus."

"It may be," answered Registrator Heerbrand; "but, I must confess, I am quite downcast in spirit; the whole night through there was such a piping and organing."

"That was I," said the Conrector, "for I snore loud."

"Well, may be," answered the Registrator: "but, Conrector, Conrector! Ah, not without cause did I wish to raise some cheerfulness among us last night—And that Anselmus has spoiled all! You know not—O Conrector, Conrector!" And with this, Registrator Heerbrand started up; plucked the cloth from his head, embraced the Conrector, warmly pressed his hand, and again cried, in quite heart-breaking tone: "O Conrector, Conrector!" and snatching his hat and staff, rushed out of doors.

"This Anselmus comes not over my threshold again," said Conrector Paulmann; "for I see very well, that, with this moping madness of his, he robs the best gentlemen of their senses. The Registrator is now over with it too: I have hitherto kept safe; but the Devil, who knocked hard last night in our carousal, may get in at last, and play his tricks with me. So *Apage, Satanas!* Off with thee, Anselmus!" Veronica had grown quite pensive; she spoke no word; only smiled now and then very oddly, and liked best to be alone. "She too has Anselmus in her head," said the Conrector, full of spleen: "but it is well that he does not show himself here; I know he fears me, this Anselmus, and so he never comes."

These concluding words Conrector Paulmann spoke aloud; then the tears rushed into Veronica's eyes, and she said, sobbing: "Ah! how can Anselmus come? He has long been corked up in the glass bottle."

"How? What?" cried Conrector Paulmann. "Ah Heaven! Ah Heaven! she is doting too, like the Registrator; the loud fit will soon come! Ah, thou cursed, abominable, thrice-cursed Anselmus!" He ran forth directly to Doctor Eckstein; who smiled, and again said: "Ey! Ey!" This time, however, he prescribed nothing; but added, to the little he had uttered, the following words, as he walked away: "Nerves! Come round of itself. Take the air; walks; amusements; theatre; playing *Soutagskind, Schwestern von Prag.* Come round of itself."

"So eloquent I have seldom seen the Doctor," thought Conrector Paulmann; "really talkative, I declare!"

Several days and weeks and months were

gone; Anselmus had vanished; but Registrator Heerbrand also did not make his appearance: not till the fourth of February, when the Registrator, in a new fashionable coat of the finest cloth, in shoes and silk stockings, notwithstanding the keen frost, and with a large nosegay of fresh flowers in his hand, did enter precisely at noon into the parlor of Conrector Paulmann, who wondered not a little to see his friend so dizened. With a solemn air, Registrator Heerbrand stept forward to Conrector Paulmann; embraced him with the finest elegance, and then said: "Now at last, on the Saint's-day of your beloved and most honored Mamsell Veronica, I will tell you out, straight forward, what I have long had lying at my heart. That evening, that unfortunate evening, when I put the ingredients of our noxious punch in my pocket, I purposed imparting to you a piece of good news, and celebrating the happy day in convivial joys. Already I had learned that I was to be made Hofrath; for which promotion I have now the patent, *cum nomine et sigillo Principis*, in my pocket."

"Ah! Herr Registr—Herr Hofrath Heerbrand, I meant to say," stammered the Conrector.

"But it is you, most honored Conrector," continued the new Hofrath; "it is you alone that can complete my happiness. For a long time, I have in secret loved your daughter, Mamsell Veronica; and I can boast of many a kind look which she has given me, evidently showing that she would not cast me away. In one word, honored Conrector! I, Hofrath Heerbrand, do now entreat of you the hand of your most amiable Mamsell Veronica, whom I, if you have nothing against it, purpose shortly to take home as my wife."

Conrector Paulmann, full of astonishment, clapped his hands repeatedly, and cried: "Ey, Ey, Ey! Herr Registr—Herr Hofrath, I meant to say—who would have thought it? Well, if Veronica does really love you, I for my share cannot object: nay, perhaps, her present melancholy is nothing but concealed love for you, most honored Hofrath! You know what freaks they have!"

At this moment Veronica entered, pale and agitated as she now commonly was. Then Hofrath Heerbrand stept towards her; mentioned in a neat speech her Saint's day and handed her the odorous nosegay, along with a little packet; out of which, when she opened it, a pair of glittering earrings beamed up to her. A rapid flying blush tinted her cheeks; her eyes sparkled in joy, and she cried: "O Heaven! These are the very earrings which I wore some weeks ago, and thought so much of."

"How can this be, dearest Mamsell," interrupted Hofrath Heerbrand, somewhat alarmed and hurt, "when I bought these jewels not an hour ago in the Schlossgasse, for current money?"

But Veronica heeded him not; she was standing before the mirror to witness the effect of the trinkets, which she had already suspended in her pretty little ears. Conrector Paulmann disclosed to her, with grave countenance and solemn tone, his friend Heerbrand's preferment and present proposal. Veronica looked at the Hofrath with a searching look, and said; "I have long known that you wished to marry me. Well, be it so! I promise you my heart and hand; but I must now unfold to you, to both of you, I mean, my father and my bridegroom, much that is lying heavy on my heart; yes, even now, though the soup should get cold, which I see Fränzchen is just putting on the table."

Without waiting for the Conrector's or the Hofrath's reply, though the words were visibly hovering on the lips of both, Veronica continued: "You may believe me, best father, I loved Anselmus from my heart, and when Registrator Heerbrand, who is now become Hofrath himself, assured us that Anselmus might probably enough get some such length, I resolved that he and no other should be my husband. But then it seemed as if alien hostile beings were for snatching him away from me: I had recourse to old Liese, who was once my nurse, but is now a wise woman, and a great enchantress. She promised to help me, and give Anselmus wholly into my hands. We went at midnight on the Equinox to the crossing of the roads: she conjured certain hellish spirits, and by aid of the black Cat, we manufactured a little metallic mirror, in which I, directing my thoughts on Anselmus, had but to look, in order to rule him wholly in heart and mind. But now I heartily repent having done all this; and here abjure all Satanic arts. The Salamander has conquered old Liese; I heard her shrieks; but there was no help to be given: so soon as the Parrot had eaten the Parsnip, my metallic mirror broke in two with a piercing clang." Veronica took out both the pieces of the mirror, and a lock of hair from her work-box, and handing them to Hofrath Heerbrand, she proceeded: "Here, take the fragments of the mirror, dear Hofrath: throw them down, to-night, at twelve o'clock, over the Elbe-bridge, from the place where the Cross stands; the stream is not frozen there: the lock, however, do you wear on your faithful breast. I here abjure all magic: and heartily wish Anselmus joy of his good fortune, seeing he is wedded with the green Snake, who is much prettier and richer than I. You, dear Hofrath, I will love and reverence as becomes a true honest wife."

"Alake! Alake!" cried Conrector Paulmann, full of sorrow; "she is cracked, she is cracked; she can never be Frau Hofräthinn; she is cracked!"

"Not in the smallest," interrupted Hofrath Heerbrand; "I know well that Mamsell Veronica has had some kindness for the loutish Anselmus; and it may be that in some fit of passion, she has had recourse to the wise woman, who, as I perceive, can be no other than the card-caster and coffee-pourer of the Seethor; in a word, old Rauerin. Nor can it be denied that there are secret arts, which exert their influence on men but too balefully; we read of such in the Ancients, and doubtless there are still such; but as to what Mamsell Veronica is pleased to say about the victory of the Salamander, and the marriage of Anselmus with the green Snake, this, in reality, I take for nothing but a poetic allegory; a sort of song, wherein she sings her entire farewell to the Student."

"Take it for what you will, best Hofrath!" cried Veronica; "perhaps for a very stupid dream."

"That I nowise do," replied Hofrath Heerbrand; "for I know well that Anselmus himself is possessed by secret powers, which vex him and drive him on to all imaginable mad freaks."

Conrector Paulmann could stand it no longer; he broke loose: "Hold! For the love of Heaven, hold! Are we again overtaken with the cursed punch, or has Anselmus' madness come over us too? Herr Hofrath, what stuff is this you are talking? I will suppose, however, that it is love which haunts your brain: this soon comes to rights in marriage; otherwise I should be apprehensive that you too had fallen into some shade of madness, most honored Herr Hofrath; then what would become of the future branches of the family, inheriting the *malum* of their parents? But now I give my paternal blessing to this happy union; and permit you as bride and bridegroom to take a kiss."

This happened forthwith; and thus before the presented soup had grown cold, was a formal betrothment concluded. In a few weeks, Frau Hofräthinn Heerbrand was actually, as she had been in vision, sitting in the balcony of a fine house in the Neumarkt, and looking down with a smile on the beaux, who passing by turned their glasses up to her, and said: "She is a heavenly woman, the Hofräthinn Heerbrand."

TWELFTH VIGIL.

Account of the Freehold Property to which Anselmus removed, as Son-in-law of Archivarius Lindhorst; and how he lives there with Serpentina. Conclusion.

How deeply did I feel, in the centre of my spirit, the blessedness of the Student Anselmus, who now, indissolubly united with his gentle Serpentina, has withdrawn to the mysterious Land of Wonders, recognised by him as the home towards which his bosom, filled with strange forecastings, had always longed. But in vain was all my striving to set before thee, favorable reader, those glories with which Anselmus is encompassed, or even in the faintest degree to shadow them forth to thee in words. Reluctantly I could not but acknowledge the feebleness of my every expression. I felt myself enthralled amid the paltriness of every-day life; I sickened in tormenting dissatisfaction; I glided about like a dreamer; in brief, I fell into that condition of the Student Anselmus, which, in the Fourth Vigil, I have endeavored to set before thee. It grieved me to the heart, when I glanced over the Eleven Vigils, now happily accomplished, and thought that to insert the Twelfth, the keystone of the whole, would never be vouchsafed me. For whensoever, in the night season, I set myself to complete the work, it was as if mischievous Spirits (they might be relations, perhaps cousins-german, of the slain witch) held a polished glittering piece of metal before me, in which I beheld my own mean Self, pale, overwatched, and melancholic, like Registrator Heerbrand after his bout of punch. Then I threw down my pen, and hastened to bed, that I might behold the happy Anselmus and the fair Serpentina at least in my dreams. This had lasted for several days and nights, when at length quite unexpectedly I received a note from Archivarius Lindhorst, in which he addressed me as follows:

"Respected Sir,—It is well known to me that you have written down, in Eleven Vigils, the singular fortunes of my good son-in-law Anselmus, whilom Student, now Poet; and are at present cudgelling your brains very sore, that in the Twelfth and Last Vigil you may tell somewhat of his happy life in Atlantis, where he now lives with my daughter, on the pleasant Freehold, which I possess in that country. Now, notwithstanding I much regret that hereby my own peculiar nature is unfolded to the reading world; seeing it may, in my office as Privy Archivarius, expose me to a thousand inconveniences; nay, in the Collegium even give rise to the question: How far a Salamander can justly, and with binding consequences, plight himself by oath, as a Servant of the State? and how far, on the whole, important affairs may be intrusted to him, since, according to Gabalis and Swedenborg, the Spirits of the Elements are not to be trusted at all?—notwithstanding, my best friends must now avoid my embrace; fearing lest, in some sudden anger, I dart out a flash or two, and singe their hair-curls, and Sunday frocks; notwithstanding all this, I say, it is still my purpose to assist you in the completion of the Work, since much good of me and of my dear married daughter (would the other two were off my hands also!) has therein been said. Would you write your Twelfth Vigil, therefore, then descend your cursed five pair of stairs, leave your garret, and come over to me. In the blue palm-tree-room, which you already know, you will find fit writing materials; and you can then, in few words, specify to your readers, what you have seen; a better plan for you than any long-winded description of a life, which you know only by hearsay.

"With esteem, your obedient servant,
"THE SALAMANDER LINDHORST,
"P. T. Royal Archivarius."

This truly somewhat rough, yet on the whole friendly note from Archivarius Lindhorst, gave me high pleasure. Clear enough it seemed, indeed, that the singular manner in which the fortunes of his son-in-law had been revealed to me, and which I, bound to silence, must conceal even from thee, favorable reader, was well known to this peculiar old gentleman; yet he had not taken it so ill as I might readily have apprehended. Nay, here was he offering me his helpful hand in the completion of my work; and from this I might justly conclude, that at bottom he was not averse to have his marvellous existence in the world of spirits thus divulged through the press.

"It may be," thought I, "that he himself expects from this measure, perhaps, to get his two other daughters the sooner married: for who knows but a spark may fall in this or that young man's breast, and kindle a longing for the green Snake; whom, on Ascension-day, under the elder-bush, he will forthwith seek and find? From the woe which befell Anselmus, when inclosed in the glass bottle, he will take warning to be doubly and trebly on his guard against all Doubt and Unbelief."

Precisely at eleven o'clock, I extinguished my study-lamp; and glided forth to Archivarius Lindhorst, who was already waiting for me in the lobby.

"Are you there, my worthy friend? Well, this is what I like, that you have not mistaken my good intentions: do but follow me!"

And with this he led the way through the garden, now filled with dazzling brightness, into the azure chamber, where I observed the same violet table, at which Anselmus had been writing.

Archivarius Lindhorst disappeared: but soon came back, carrying in his hand a fair golden goblet, out of which a high blue flame was sparkling up. "Here," said he, "I bring you the favorite drink of your friend the Bandmaster, Johannes Kreisler.* It is burning arrack, into which I have thrown a little sugar. Sip a touch or two of it: I will doff my night-gown, and to amuse myself and enjoy your worthy company while you sit looking and writing, I shall just bob up and down a little in the goblet."

"As you please, honored Herr Archivarius," answered I: "but if I am to ply the liquor, you will get none."

"Don't fear that, my good fellow," cried the Archivarius; then hastily threw off his night-gown, mounted, to my no small amazement,

---

* An imaginary musical enthusiast of whom Hoffmann has written much; under the fiery sensitive wayward character of this crazy Bandmaster, presenting, it would seem, a shadowy likeness of himself. The *Kreisleriana* occupy a large space among these *Fantasy-pieces;* and Johannes Kreisler is the main figure in *Kater Murr*, Hoffmann's favorite but unfinished work. In the third and last volume, Kreisler was to end, not in composure and illumination, as the critics would have required, but in utter madness: a sketch of a wild, flail-like scarecrow, dancing vehemently and blowing soap-bubbles, and which had been intended to front the last title-page, was found among Hoffmann's papers, and engraved and published in his *Life and Remains.*—ED.

---

into the goblet, and vanished in the blaze. Without fear, softly blowing back the flame, I partook of the drink: it was truly precious!

Stir not the emerald leaves of the palm-trees in soft sighing and rustling, as if kissed by the breath of the morning wind? Awakened from their sleep, they move, and mysteriously whisper of the wonders, which from the far distance approach like tones of melodious harps! The azure rolls from the walls, and floats like airy vapor to and fro; but dazzling beams shoot through it; and whirling and dancing, as in jubilee of childlike sport, it mounts and mounts to immeasurable height, and vaults itself over the palm-trees. But brighter and brighter shoots beam on beam, till in boundless expanse opens the grove where I behold Anselmus. Here glowing hyacinths, and tulips, and roses, lift their fair heads; and their perfumes, in loveliest sound, call to the happy youth: "Wander, wander among us, our beloved; for thou understandest us! Our perfume is the Longing of Love: we love thee, and are thine forevermore!" The golden rays burn in glowing tones: "We are Fire, kindled by love. Perfume is Longing; but Fire is Desire: and dwell we not in thy bosom? We are thy own!" The dark bushes, the high trees rustle and sound: "Come to us, thou loved, thou happy one! Fire is Desire; but Hope is our cool Shadow. Lovingly we rustle round thy head: for thou understandest us, because Love dwells in thy breast!" The brooks and fountains murmur and patter: "Loved one, walk not so quickly by: look into our crystal! Thy image dwells in us, which we preserve with Love, for thou hast understood us." In the triumphal choir, bright birds are singing: "Hear us! Hear us! We are Joy, we are Delight, the rapture of Love!" But anxiously Anselmus turns his eyes to the glorious Temple, which rises behind him in the distance. The fair pillars seem trees; and the capitals and friezes acanthus leaves, which in wondrous wreaths and figures form splendid decorations. Anselmus walks to the Temple: he views with inward delight the variegated marble, the steps with their strange veins of moss. "Ah, no!" cries he, as if in the excess of rapture, "she is not far from me now; she is near!" Then advances Serpentina, in the fulness of beauty and grace, from the Temple; she bears the Golden Pot, from which a bright Lily has sprung. The nameless rapture of infinite longing glows in her meek eyes; she looks at Anselmus, and says: "Ah! Dearest, the Lily has sent forth her bowl: what we longed for is fulfilled; is there a happiness to equal ours?" Anselmus clasps her with the tenderness of warmest ardor: the Lily burns in flaming beams over his head. And louder move the trees and bushes; clearer and gladder play the brooks; the birds, the shining insects dance in the waves of perfume: a gay, bright rejoicing tumult, in the air, in the water, in the earth, is holding the festival of

Love! Now rush sparkling streaks, gleaming over all the bushes; diamonds look from the ground like shining eyes: strange vapors are wafted hither on sounding wings: they are the Spirits of the Elements, who do homage to the Lily, and proclaim the happiness of Anselmus. Then Anselmus raises his head, as if encircled with a beamy glory. Is it looks? Is it words? Is it song? You hear the sound: "Serpentina! Belief in thee, Love of thee has unfolded to my soul the inmost spirit of Nature! Thou hast brought me the Lily, which sprung from Gold, from the primeval Force of the world, before Phosphorus had kindled the spark of Thought; this Lily is Knowledge of the sacred Harmony of all Beings; and in this do I live in highest blessedness forevermore. Yes, I, thrice happy, have perceived what was highest: I must indeed love thee forever, O Serpentina! Never shall the golden blossoms of the Lily grow pale; for, like Belief and Love this Knowledge is eternal."

For the vision, in which I had now beheld Anselmus bodily, in his Freehold of Atlantis, I stand indebted to the arts of the Salamander; and most fortunate was it that, when all had melted into air, I found a paper lying on the violet-table, with the foregoing statement of the matter, written fairly and distinctly by my own hand. But now I felt myself as if transpierced and torn in pieces by sharp sorrow. "Ah, happy Anselmus, who hast cast away the burden of week-day life, who in the love of thy kind Serpentina fliest with bold pinion, and now livest in rapture and joy on thy Freehold in Atlantis! while I—poor I!—must soon, nay, in few moments, leave even this fair hall, which itself is far from a Freehold in Atlantis; and again be transplanted to my garret, where, enthralled among the pettinesses of necessitous existence, my heart and my sight are so bedimmed with thousand mischiefs, as with thick fog, that the fair Lily will never, never be beheld by me."

Then Archivarius Lindhorst patted me gently on the shoulder, and said: "Soft, soft, my honored friend! Lament not so! Were you not even now in Atlantis; and have you not at least a pretty little copyhold Farm there, as the poetical possession of your inward sense? And is the blessedness of Anselmus aught else but a Living in Poesy? Can aught else but Poesy reveal itself as the sacred Harmony of all Beings, as the deepest secret of Nature?"

ADALBERT VON CHAMISSO.*

Born 1781. Died 1839.

WE would fain perform in some degree an act of tardy justice to the memory of a poet of no mean order, and a man of rare and sterling worth. Considering the early and extensive popularity which the story of Peter Schlemihl obtained in this country, it is surprising how rarely the author's name is mentioned amongst us. Few English readers, we believe, are aware that he ever wrote a line of poetry, or acquired any other title to celebrity than that which his far-famed romance conferred upon him. Yet neither as to the man nor his works is this neglect deserved. Both have long been regarded in Germany with fervent love and admiration, and both commend themselves to our sympathies by qualities peculiarly adapted to win the cordial esteem of Englishmen. But even were it not so, even though Chamisso claimed our attention on no higher grounds, curiosity at least might well be directed towards the productions of a Frenchman, whose German style has been accepted in the country of his adoption as a model of purity, force, and elegance. Such an example of eminent mastery achieved both in prose and verse over a language which was not the writer's mother tongue, is almost unique in the history of literature.

Louis Charles Adelaide, or, as he was afterwards called, Adalbert von Chamisso, was one of the younger sons of the count of that name, and was born in the Château de Boncourt, in Champagne, in January, 1781. His family, which was of Lorrainian origin, had been distinguished for its loyalty to its suzerains, its ample feudal honors and possessions, and its intermarriages with many reigning houses. Not less eminent than its prosperous fortunes were the disasters that afterwards befel it. Adalbert's parents were residing in the château where he was born when the Revolution broke out. Boncourt was assailed, ransacked, and destroyed.

Little is known of Chamisso's childhood, except that he was even then remarkable for the taciturn and thoughtful disposition that characterized his manhood, and already evinced a propensity to the pursuits of the naturalist and the reveries of the poet. "I used," he says, "to observe insects, search out new plants, and at an open window on stormy nights, stand contemplating and reflecting." When his more volatile companions teased and ridiculed him for his backwardness to join in their romps, his mother would come to the rescue, and cry out, "Let him alone; he will outstrip you all by and by as a man, as much as he surpasses you now in good conduct and information." He used to say of his own fourth son, a delicate boy, whose apparent weakness of intellect occasioned his mother much uneasiness, "Never fear, the lad will come right in time; he is exactly such as I was myself at his age."

Chamisso was nine years old when his impoverished family fled from France. At thirteen, he studied drawing and miniature painting, at Wurtzburg. At fifteen, after having been for some time a pupil in the painting department of the royal porcelain manufactory of Berlin, he became one of the Queen of Prussia's pages. At seventeen, he entered the Prussian army; three years afterwards (1801) he was a lieutenant, and his family returned to France. The first occupation of the young Prussian officer was to make himself thoroughly acquainted with the German tongue; for at twenty years of age he was not yet perfectly familiar with the language, in the literature of which he was afterwards to take so prominent a place.

In 1810, he was called to France, to fill a professorship in the new college of Napoleonville; his errand was again a fruitless one, but the journey made him acquainted with Madame de Staël and M. de Barante, the historian, then prefect of Vendée. With the latter he spent the winter of 1810-11, agreeably enough, instructing the future translator of Schiller in German literature, and filling up his leisure with the perusal of old fabliaux and romances of chivalry. He was also a welcome guest of

* Abridged from Foreign Quarterly Review, No. LXXII.

(544)

Madame de Staël's, at Chaumont and Blois; and after her banishment he followed her to Geneva and Coppet.

It was during his visit to Coppet that Chamisso began the study of Botany, which was afterwards the professional occupation of his life. In 1812, he made a pedestrian tour in Switzerland, hesitated on the frontiers of Italy, and then turned short round to the north, hungering for his beloved Germany. Hastening to Berlin, he entered the university as a medical pupil, and began to study anatomy and physiology with intense zeal.

In 1813, he composed his famous tale of "Peter Schlemihl," the man who was rendered miserable by the loss of his shadow. Ampère has an ingenious passage on this subject, which is worth quoting:

"Is there a latent moral in this whimsical story? Without doing like Schlemihl, and running after a shadow, it seems to me we may attribute to the author the intention of expressing this truth, that in society, as it is now constituted, virtue, merit, and even fortune, are not everything. It is not enough that one is rich, something more is wanting to give one mark and consequence in the world; there needs a slight shadowy something, designated by the vague, but not insignificant words, speciality, notability, position. To be other than a nobody in society in these days, when men are no longer classed according to rank, one must bear a known name, or have produced a book, or possess some striking accomplishment; one must have the supplementary aid of fashion, or enjoy a celebrity, a notoriety, a distinction, as they phrase it, of one kind or another. This is the indispensable shadow for which the devil sometimes tempts us to sell our souls, and without which we succeed in nothing. The author of 'Peter Schlemihl' is right in concluding, that when one has not a shadow, one ought not to go into the sunshine."

We accept this interpretation, although since it was written Hitzig has published Chamisso's positive declaration that he had no didactic purpose in view when he composed the tale. We hold that every well-constructed story, inasmuch as it purports to present a regular series of events and circumstances, bound together by known laws, must of necessity supply data from which may be deduced one moral or more. In other words, the details of any fable will suggest pointed analogies just in proportion as they are consistent with each other and coherent. It is generally conceded that although the poet's functions have a moral tendency, he is not required to be solicitous about teaching categorically; and perhaps it would not be too much to say that if he thinks about his moral at all, the less he does so the better. Chamisso appears to have been of this opinion:

"I have seldom," he says, "any ulterior aim in my poetry; if an anecdote or a word strikes me in a particular manner (*mich selbst in Leibe von der Seite der linken Pfote bewegt*) I suppose it must have the same effect on others, and I set to work, wrestling laboriously with the language, till the thing comes out distinctly.

"If by chance I have had a notion to evolve, I am always disappointed with the way in which the thing turns out. It looks flimsy; there is no life in it. . . . . You may call me for this a nightingale, or a cuckoo, or any other singing bird, rather than a reasoning man; with all my heart! I ask no better. . . . . Schlemihl, too, came forth in this way. I had lost on a journey my hat, portmanteau, gloves, pocket-handkerchief, and all my movable estate. Fouqué asked me whether I had not also lost my shadow; and we pictured to ourselves the effects of such a disaster. Another time, in turning over the leaves of a book by Lafontaine (I do not know the title), was found a passage in which a very obliging man was described as producing all sorts of things from his pocket in a party, as fast as they were called for; upon this I remarked that, only ask him civilly, the good fellow would, no doubt, lug out a coach and horses from his pocket.—Here was Schlemihl complete in conception, and as time hung heavy enough on my hands in the country, I began to write. In truth I had no need to have read the 'Baron de Feneste' (Daubigné's philosophical romance) to have picked up all sorts of practical knowledge, touching the φαινεσθαι and the ειναι. But it was not my object to embody this knowledge, but to amuse Hitzig's wife and children, whom I looked upon as my public, and so it has come to pass that you and others have laughed over my performance."

He employed the latter part of 1813, and the greater part of the following year, upon natural history, attending lectures on mineralogy, which surprised him with the discovery "that stones had so much sense in them," assisting in the arrangement of the Crustacea in the Zoological Museum of Berlin, and exercising himself in writing and speaking Latin, preparatory to taking his doctor's degree. The storm of war broke out again in 1815, and made him more than ever solicitous to withdraw for a while from the scene of strife. He endeavored to join the Prince de Neuwied, who was about to travel in Brazil, but was disappointed in this and many other similar attempts. At last the opportunity he so much longed for arrived. Taking up a newspaper one day at Hitzig's, he chanced to see the announcement of a voyage of discovery towards the North Pole and in the Pacific, which was about to be undertaken on board the Russian ship of war, commanded by Otto von Kotzebue, son of the German author of that name. Stamping with his foot, Chamisso exclaimed, "I wish I was with these Russians at the North Pole." "Are you in earnest?" said Hitzig. "Quite so." And, on the 15th of July, Chamisso left Berlin for a voyage of three years.

He published a very lively and entertaining account of this voyage. In 1829, he produced his grandest work, Salas y Gomez, which probably first germinated in his mind during this voyage.

Returning to Berlin in the autumn of 1818, he employed the remainder of that year in arranging the specimens of natural history he had brought home, and which he bestowed on the Berlin Museum. In 1819 he was married, and of his bride he speaks thus: " She is young, blooming and strong, handsome and good, pure and innocent, clear, cloudless and serene, calm, rational and cheerful, and so amiable!"

Whilst he was writing verses for his young wife, and arranging the Herbaria of the Museum of Berlin, Chamisso, it is probable, scarcely recollected his quality of French emigrant. He was agreeably reminded of this, in the autumn of 1825, by a call to Paris to receive 100,000 francs lodged to his credit by the Commissioners of the Indemnity Fund. He was welcomed with marked distinction by the learned world of Paris, and passed his time far more pleasantly than he had done when he visited the luxurious capital in his needy and obscure youth. The letters he wrote home were filled with accounts of the many remarkable things, literary and theatrical, social and political, which Paris presented to his view at that stirring period. But in the midst of all this excitement he did not lose sight of the least every-day detail of his beloved home. " Don't forget," he says, writing to his wife, "don't forget the roses; don't forget the children's letters; don't forget to strew food for the sparrows on my window. I shall return to you the same as I left you; let me find everything again just as it was."

After his return from Paris, in 1827, a second German edition of "Schlemihl" was published, with an appendix containing a small collection of his poems. Up to this time he had no serious belief in his own poetical powers, and in a letter to Varnhagen's sister (May 24, 1827), he says, "That I am no poet, nor ever was, is manifest, but that does not prevent me from having a feeling for poetry." But the new publication began to attract public attention towards him, and, in June, 1828, he ventured to write to De la Foye. "I almost begin to think I am one of the poets of Germany." The matter was put beyond all doubt by the reception given to his " Salas y Gomez" in the following year. Soon after this we find him mentioning, with honest pride, that next to Uhland's Poems, none were in such frequent demand for presents as his own. Bridegrooms especially selected them as gifts for their brides.

Chamisso's existence had now reached the culminating point from which began its continuous descent. In 1831, he was seized by that worst form of influenza, which we all remember to have been the precursor of the cholera. It broke down his iron constitution, and left behind it a chronic affection of the lungs, from which he never recovered. His declining years were still cheered by the increasing honors conferred on him, both as a poet and a naturalist, but they were visited by a calamity for which there was no balm on earth. His wife died on the 21st of May, 1837, in her thirty-sixth year. He bore this fatal blow with manly fortitude, thankful for the blessings he had enjoyed, and patiently awaiting his dismissal. It was not long delayed. He survived his wife exactly fifteen months, and expired on the 21st of August, 1839.

Most characteristic of the man, was the manner in which he passed this interval. Earnest and strenuous to the last, he increased rather than relaxed his mental activity. He found in occupation the best alleviation of his sorrows, and employed himself simultaneously on two works of very dissimilar character. He published a grammar of the Havai language, spoken in some of the islands of the South Sea, and entered upon an elaborate philological investigation of the kindred dialects; and he joined Baron Gaudy in translating, or rather, as he says, *Germanizing* a selection of ninety-eight songs of Béranger. He continued also, the troublesome task of editing the "Musen Almanach," and shortly before his death, he showed that the old ardor was not extinct within him, by undertaking a journey to Leipzig, in order to run over the first portion of the Dresden Railway. He was radiant with delight. Speaking as a poet, he called the locomotive "*Time's wings;*" and in the language of a naturalist, he defined it as *a warm-blooded animal without eyes.* He looked on the invention as the certain commencement of a new era, and deemed that every moneyed man was morally bound to contribute a portion of his means towards the promotion of a system from which such grand results were to accrue.

THE WONDERFUL HISTORY OF PETER SCHLEMIHL.

CHAPTER I.

AFTER a fortunate, but for me very troublesome voyage, we finally reached the port. The instant that I touched land in the boat, I loaded myself with my few effects, and passing through the swarming people, I entered the first, and least house, before which I saw a sign hang. I requested a room; the boots measured me with a look, and conducted me into the garret. I caused fresh water to be brought, and made him exactly describe to me where I should find Mr. Thomas John.

"Before the north-gate; the first country-house on the right hand; a large new house of red and white marble, with many columns."

"Good." It was still early in the day. I opened at once my bundle; took thence my new black cloth coat; clad myself cleanly in my best apparel; put my letter of introduction into my pocket, and set out on the way to the man who was to promote my modest expectations.

When I had ascended the long North Street, and reached the gate, I soon saw the pillars glimmer through the foliage. "Here it is then," thought I. I wiped the dust from my feet with my pocket-handkerchief; put my neckcloth in order, and in God's name rung the bell. The door flew open. In the hall I had an examination to undergo; the porter, however, permitted me to be announced, and I had the honor to be called into the park, where Mr. John was walking with a select party. I recognised the man at once by the lustre of his corpulent self-complacency. He received me very well—as a rich man receives a poor devil,—even turned towards me, without turning from the rest of the company, and took the offered letter from my hand. "So, so, from my brother. I have heard nothing from him for a long time. But he is well? There," continued he, addressing the company, without waiting for an answer, and pointing with the letter to a hill, "there I am going to erect the new building." He broke the seal without breaking off the conversation, which turned upon riches.

"He that is not master of a million, at least," he observed, "is—pardon me the word—a wretch!"

"O! how true!" I exclaimed with a rush of overflowing feeling.

That pleased him. He smiled at me, and said—"Stay here, my good friend; in a while I shall perhaps have time to tell you what I think about this." He pointed to the letter, which he then thrust into his pocket, and turned again to the company. He offered his arm to a young lady; the other gentlemen addressed themselves to other fair ones; each found what suited him; and all proceeded towards the rose-blossomed mount.

I slid into the rear, without troubling any one, for no one troubled himself any further about me. The company was excessively lively; there was dalliance and playfulness; trifles were sometimes discussed with an important tone, but oftener important matters with levity; and especially pleasantly flew the wit over absent friends and their circumstances. I was too strange to understand much of all this; too anxious and introverted to take an interest in such riddles.

We had reached the rosary. The lovely Fanny, the belle of the day, as it appeared, would, out of obstinacy, herself break off a blooming bough. She wounded herself on a thorn, and as if from the dark roses, flowed the purple on her tender hand. This circumstance put the whole party into a flutter. English plaister was sought for. A still, thin, lanky, longish, oldish man, who stood near, and whom I had not hitherto remarked, put his hand instantly into the close-lying breast-pocket of his old French grey taffetty coat; produced thence a little pocket-book; opened it; and presented to the lady, with a profound obeisance, the required article. She took it without noticing the giver, and without thanks; the wound was bound up; and we went forward over the hill, from whose back the company could enjoy the wide prospect over the green labyrinth of the park to the boundless ocean.

The view was in reality vast and splendid. A light point appeared on the horizon between the dark flood, and the blue of the heaven. "A telescope here!" cried John; and already before the servants who appeared at the call, were in motion, the grey man, modestly bowing, had thrust his hand into his coat-pocket, and drawn thence a beautiful Dollond, and handed it to Mr. John. Bringing it immediately to his eye, he informed the company that it was the ship which went out yesterday, and was detained in view of port by contrary winds. The telescope passed from hand to hand, but not again into that of its owner. I, however, gazed in wonder at the man, and could not conceive how the great machine had come out of the narrow pocket: but this seemed to have struck no one else, and nobody troubled himself any farther about the grey man than about myself.

Refreshments were handed round; the choicest fruits of every zone, in the costliest vessels. Mr. John did the honors with an easy grace, and a second time addressed a word to me. "Help yourself; you have not had the like at sea." I bowed, but he saw it not, he was already speaking with some one else.

The company would fain have reclined upon the sward on the slope of the hill, opposite to the outstretched landscape, had they not feared the dampness of the earth. "It were divine," observed one of the party, "had we but a Turkey carpet to spread here." The wish was scarcely expressed when the man in the grey coat had his hand in his pocket, and was busied in drawing thence, with a modest and even humble deportment, a rich Turkey carpet interwoven with gold. The servants received it as a matter of course, and opened it on the required spot. The company without ceremony, took their places upon it; for myself, I looked again in amazement on the man; at the carpet, which measured above twenty paces long and ten in breadth; and rubbed my eyes, not knowing what to think of it, especially as nobody saw anything extraordinary in it.

I would fain have had some explanation regarding the man, and have asked who he was, but I knew not to whom to address myself, for I was almost more afraid of the gentlemen's servants than of the served gentlemen. At length I took courage, and stepped up to a young man who appeared to me to be of less consideration than the rest, and who had often stood alone. I begged him softly to tell me who the agreeable man in the grey coat there was.

"He there, who looks like an end of thread that has escaped out of a tailor's needle?"

"Yes, he who stands alone."

"I don't know him," he replied, and as it seemed in order to avoid a longer conversation with me, he turned away, and spoke of indifferent matters to another.

The sun began now to shine more powerfully, and to inconvenience the ladies. The lovely Fanny addressed carelessly to the grey man, whom as far as I am aware, no one had yet spoken to, the trifling question, "Whether he had not, perchance, also a tent by him?"—He answered her by an obeisance most profound, as if an unmerited honor were done him, and had already his hand in his pocket, out of which I saw come canvass, poles, cordage, iron-work, in short, everything which belongs to the most splendid pleasure-tent. The young gentlemen helped to expand it, and it covered the whole extent of the carpet, and nobody found anything remarkable in it.

I was already become uneasy, nay horrified at heart, but how completely so, as, at the very next wish expressed, I saw him yet pull out of his pocket three roadsters—I tell thee three beautiful great black horses, with saddle and caparison. Bethink thee! for God's sake!—three saddled horses, still out of the same pocket out of which already a pocket-book, a telescope, an embroidered carpet, twenty paces long and ten broad, a pleasure-tent of equal dimensions, and all the requisite poles and irons, had come forth! If I did not protest to thee that I saw it myself with my own eyes, thou couldst not possibly believe it.

Embarrassed and obsequious as the man himself appeared to be, little was the attention which had been bestowed upon him, yet to me his grisly aspect, from which I could not turn my eyes, became so fearful, that I could bear it no longer.

I resolved to steal away from the company, which from the insignificant part I played in it seemed to me an easy affair. I proposed to myself to return to the city, to try my luck again on the morrow with Mr. John, and if I could muster the necessary courage, to question him about the singular grey man. Had I only had the good fortune to escape so well!

I had already actually succeeded in stealing through the rosary, and in descending the hill, found myself on a piece of lawn, when fearing to be encountered in crossing the grass out of the path, I cast an enquiring glance round me. What was my terror to behold the man in the grey coat behind me, and making towards me! In the next moment he took off his hat before me, and bowed so low as no one had ever yet done to me. There was no doubt but that he wished to address me, and without being rude, I could not prevent it. I also took off my hat; bowed also; and stood there in the sun with bare head as if rooted to the ground. I stared at him full of terror, and was like a bird which a serpent has fascinated. He himself appeared very much embarrassed. He raised not his eyes; again bowed repeatedly; drew nearer, and addressed me with a soft, tremulous voice, almost in a tone of supplication.

"May I hope, sir, that you will pardon my boldness in venturing in so unusual a manner to approach you, but I would ask a favor. Permit me most condescendingly—"

"But in God's name!" exclaimed I in my trepidation, "what can I do for a man who—" we both started, and, as I believe, reddened.

After a moment's silence, he again resumed: "During the short time that I had the happiness to find myself near you, I have, sir, many times,—allow me to say it to you—really contemplated with inexpressible admiration, the beautiful, beautiful, shadow which, as it were, with a certain noble disdain, and without yourself remarking it, you cast from you in the sunshine. The noble shadow at your feet there. Pardon me the bold supposition, but possibly you might not be indisposed to make this shadow over to me."

I was silent, and a mill-wheel seemed to whirl round in my head. What was I to make of this singular proposition to sell my own shadow? He must be mad, thought I, and with an altered tone which was more assimilated to that of his own humility, I answered thus:

"Ha! ha! good friend, have not you then enough of your own shadow? I take this for a business of a very singular sort—."

He hastily interrupted me;—"I have many things in my pocket which, sir, might not appear worthless to you, and for this inestimable shadow I hold the very highest price too small."

It struck cold through me again as I was reminded of the pocket. I knew not how I could have called him good friend. I resumed the conversation, and sought, if possible, to set all right again by excessive politeness.

"But, sir, pardon your most humble servant; I do not understand your meaning. How indeed could my shadow"—He interrupted me—

"I beg your permission only here on the spot to be allowed to take up this noble shadow and put it in my pocket; how I shall do that be my care. On the other hand, as a testimony of my grateful acknowledgment to you, I give you the choice of all the treasures which I carry in my pocket,—the genuine Spring-root,* the Mandrake-root, the Change-penny, the Rob-dollar, the napkin of Roland's Page, a mandrake-man, at your own price. But these, probably don't interest you,—rather Fortunatus's Wishing-cap newly and stoutly repaired, and a lucky-bag such as he had!"

"The Luck-purse of Fortunatus!" I exclaimed, interrupting him; and great as my anxiety was, with that one word he had taken my whole mind captive. A dizziness seized me, and double ducats seemed to glitter before my eyes.

"Honored Sir, will you do me the favor to view, and to make trial of this purse?" He thrust his hand into his pocket, and drew out a tolerably large, well-sewed purse of stout Corduan leather, with two strong strings, and handed it to me. I plunged my hand into it, and drew out ten gold pieces, and again ten, and again ten, and again ten. I extended him eagerly my hand—"Agreed! the business is done; for the purse you have my shadow!"

He closed with me; kneeled instantly down before me, and I beheld him, with an admirable dexterity, gently loosen my shadow from top to toe from the grass, lift it up, roll it together, fold it, and finally, pocket it. He arose, made me another obeisance, and retreated towards the rosary. I fancied that I heard him there softly laughing to himself; but I held the purse fast by the strings; all round me lay the clear sunshine, and within me was yet no power of reflection.

CHAPTER II.

At length I came to myself, and hastened to quit the place where I had nothing more to expect. In the first place I filled my pockets with gold; then I secured the strings of the purse fast round my neck, and concealed the purse itself in my bosom. I passed unobserved out of the park, reached the highway and took the road to the city. As, sunk in thought, I approached the gate, I heard a cry behind me.

"Young gentleman! eh! young gentleman! hear you!"

I looked round, an old woman called after me.

"Do take care, sir, you have lost your shadow!"

"Thank you, good mother!" I threw her a gold piece for her well-meant intelligence, and stopped under the trees.

At the city gate I was compelled to hear again from the sentinel—"Where has the gentleman left his shadow?" And immediately again from some women—"Jesus Maria! the poor fellow has no shadow!" That began to irritate me, and I became especially careful not to walk in the sun. This could not, however, be accomplished everywhere, for instance, over the broad street which I next must approach actually, as mischief would have it, at the very moment that the boys came out of school. A cursed hunchbacked rogue, I see him yet, spied out instantly that I had no shadow. He proclaimed the fact with a loud outcry to the whole assembled literary street youth of the suburb, who began forthwith to criticise me, and to pelt me with mud. "Decent people are accustomed to take their shadow with them, when they go into the sunshine." To defend myself from them I threw whole handfuls of gold amongst them and sprang into a hackney-coach, which some compassionate soul procured for me.

As soon as I found myself alone in the rolling carriage I began to weep bitterly. The presentiment must already have arisen in me, that far as gold on earth transcends in estimation, merit and virtue, so much higher than gold itself is the shadow valued; and as I had earlier sacrificed wealth to conscience, I had now

---

* These are references to facts in the popular tales of Germany: as for instance, the Spring-wurzel, or Spring-root, is found in the story of Ruberzahl; and the Galgenmannlein, or gallows-men, were little figures cut out of a root, said by the dealers in such things in the middle ages, to be actual mandrake-roots growing in that shape at the feet of gallowses, etc., etc.

thrown away the shadow for mere gold. What in the world could and would become of me!—

I was again greatly annoyed as the carriage stopped before my old inn. I was horrified at the bare idea of entering that wretched cock-loft. I ordered my things to be brought down; received my miserable bundle with contempt, threw down some gold pieces, and ordered the coachman to drive to the most fashionable hotel. The house faced the north, and I had not the sun to fear. I dismissed the driver with gold; caused the best front rooms to be assigned me, and shut myself up in them as quickly as I could!

What thinkest thou I now began? Oh, my dear Chamisso, to confess it even to thee makes me blush. I drew the unlucky purse from my bosom, and with a kind of desperation which, like a rushing conflagration, grew in me with self-increasing growth, I extracted gold, and gold, and gold, and ever more gold, and strewed it on the floor, and strode amongst it, and made it ring again, and feeding my poor heart on the splendor and the sound, flung continually more metal to metal, till in my weariness, I sank down on the rich heap, and rioting thereon, rolled and revelled amongst it. So passed the day, the evening. I opened not my door; night and day found me lying on my gold, and then sleep overcame me.

I dreamed of thee. I seemed to stand behind the glass-door of thy little room, and to see thee sitting then at thy work-table, between a skeleton and a bundle of dried plants. Before thee lay open Haller, Humboldt, and Linnæus; on thy sofa a volume of Goethe and "The Magic-Ring." I regarded thee long, and every thing in thy room, and then thee again. Thou didst not move, thou drewest no breath;—thou wert dead!

I awoke. It appeared still to be very early. My watch stood. I was sore all over; thirsty and hungry too; I had taken nothing since the evening before. I pushed from me with loathing and indignation the gold on which I had before sated my foolish heart. In my vexation I knew not what I should do with it. It must not lie there. I tried whether the purse would swallow it again,—but no! None of my windows opened upon the sea. I found myself compelled laboriously to drag it to a great cupboard which stood in a cabinet, and there to pile it. I left only some handfuls of it lying. When I had finished the work, I threw myself exhausted into an easy chair, and waited for the stirring of the people in the house. As soon as possible I ordered food to be brought, and the landlord to come to me.

I fixed in consultation with this man the future arrangements of my house. He recommended for the services about my person a certain Bendel, whose honest and intelligent physiognomy immediately captivated me. He it was whose attachment has since accompanied me consolingly through the wretchedness of life, and has helped me to support my gloomy lot. I spent the whole day in my room among masterless servants, shoemakers, tailors, and tradespeople. I fitted myself out, and purchased besides a great many jewels and valuables for the sake of getting rid of some of the vast heap of hoarded up gold; but it seemed to me as if it were impossible to diminish it.

In the mean time I brooded over my situation in the most agonising despair. I dared not venture a step out of my doors, and at evening I caused forty waxlights to be lit in my room before I issued from the shade. I thought with horror on the terrible scene with the schoolboys, yet I resolved, much courage as it demanded, once more to make a trial of public opinion. The nights were then moonlight. Late in the evening I threw on a wide cloak, pressed my hat over my eyes, and stole, trembling like a criminal, out of the house. I stepped first out of the shade in whose protection I had arrived there, in a remote square, into the full moonlight, determined to learn my fate out of the mouths of the passers by.

Spare me, dear friend, the painful repetition of all that I had to endure. The women often testified the deepest compassion with which I inspired them, declarations which no less transpierced me than the mockery of the youth and the proud contempt of the men, especially of those fat, well-fed fellows, who themselves cast a broad shadow. A lovely and sweet girl, who, as it seemed, accompanied her parents, while these suspiciously only looked before their feet, turned by chance her flashing eyes upon me. She was obviously terrified; she observed my want of a shadow, let fall her veil over her beautiful countenance, and dropping her head, passed in silence.

I could bear it no longer. Briny streams started from my eyes, and cut to the heart, I staggered back into the shade. I was obliged to support myself against the houses to steady my steps and wearily and late reached my dwelling.

I spent a sleepless night. The next morning it was my first care to have the man in the grey coat everywhere sought after. Possibly I might succeed in finding him again, and how joyful! if he repented of the foolish bargain as heartily as I did. I ordered Bendel to come to me, he appeared to possess address and tact; I described to him exactly the man in whose possession lay a treasure without which my life was only a misery. I told him the time, the place in which I had seen him; I described to him all who had been present, and added, moreover, this token: he should particularly inquire after a Dollond's telescope; after a gold interwoven Turkish carpet; after a splendid pleasure tent; and, finally, after the black chargers, whose story, we knew not how, was connected with that of the mysterious man, who seemed of no consideration amongst them, and whose appearance had destroyed the quiet and happiness of my life.

When I had done speaking I fetched out gold, such a load that I was scarcely able to carry it, and laid upon it precious stones and jewels of a far greater value. "Bendel," said I, "these level many ways, and make easy many things which appeared quite impossible; don't be stingy with it, as I am not, but go and rejoice thy master with the intelligence on which his only hope depends."

He went. He returned late and sorrowful. None of the people of Mr. John, none of his guests, and he had spoken with all, were able in the remotest degree, to recollect the man in the grey coat. The new telescope was there, and no one knew whence it had come; the carpet, the tent were still there spread and pitched on the self-same hill; the servants boasted of the affluence of their master, and no one knew whence these same valuables had come to him. He himself took his pleasure in them, and did not trouble himself because he did not know whence he had them. The young gentlemen had the horses, which they had ridden, in their stables, and they praised the liberality of Mr. John who on that day made them a present of them. Thus much was clear from the circumstantial relation of Bendel, whose active zeal and able proceeding, although with such fruitless result, received from me their merited commendation. I gloomily motioned him to leave me alone.

"I have," began he again, "given my master an account of the matter which was most important to him. I have yet a message to deliver which a person gave me whom I met at the door as I went out on the business in which I have been so unfortunate. The very words of the man were these : 'Tell Mr. Peter Schlemihl he will not see me here again as I am going over sea, and a favorable wind calls me at this moment to the harbor. But in a year and a day I will have the honor to seek him myself, and then to propose to him another and probably to him more agreeable transaction. Present my most humble compliments to him, and assure him of my thanks.' I asked him who he was, but he replied, your honor knew him already."

"What was the man's appearance?" cried I, filled with foreboding, and Bendel sketched me the man in the grey coat, trait by trait, word for word, as he had accurately described in his former relation the man after whom he had inquired.

"Unhappy one!" I exclaimed, wringing my hands,—"that was the very man!" and there fell, as it were, scales from his eyes.

"Yes! it was he, it was, positively!" cried he in horror, "and I, blind and imbecile wretch have not recognized him, have not recognized him, and have betrayed my master!"

He broke out into violent weeping; heaped the bitterest reproaches on himself, and the despair in which he was inspired even me with compassion. I spoke comfort to him, assured him repeatedly that I entertained not the slightest doubt of his fidelity, and sent him instantly to the port, if possible to follow the traces of this singular man. But in the morning a great number of ships which the contrary winds had detained in the harbor, had run out, bound to different climes and different shores, and the grey man had vanished as tracelessly as a dream.

CHAPTER III.

OF what avail are wings to him who is fast bound in iron fetters? He is compelled only the more fearfully to despair. I lay like Faffner by his treasure far from every consolation, suffering much in the midst of my gold. But my heart was not in it, on the contrary, I cursed it, because I saw myself through it cut off from all life. Brooding over my gloomy secret alone, I trembled before the meanest of my servants, whom at the same time I was forced to envy, for he had a shadow; he might show himself in the sun. I wore away days and nights in solitary sorrow in my chamber, and anguish gnawed at my heart.

There was another who pined away before my eyes; my faithful Bendel never ceased to torture himself with silent reproaches, that he had betrayed the trust reposed in him by his master, and had not recognized him after whom he was despatched, and with whom he must believe that my sorrowful fate was intimately interwoven. I could not lay the fault to his charge; I recognised in the event the mysterious nature of the Unknown.

That I might leave nothing untried, I one time sent Bendel with a valuable brilliant ring to the most celebrated painter of the city, and begged that he would pay me a visit. He came. I ordered my people to retire, closed the door, seated myself by the man, and after I had praised his art, I came with a heavy heart to the business, causing him before that to promise the strictest secrecy.

"Mr. Professor," said I, "could not you, think you, paint a false shadow for one, who by the most unlucky chance in the world, has become deprived of his own?"——

"You mean a personal shadow?"

"That is precisely my meaning".——

"But," continued he, "through what awkwardness, through what negligence could he then lose his proper shadow?"

"How it happened," replied I, "is now of very little consequence, but thus far I may say," added I, lying shamelessly to him, "in Russia, whither he made a journey last winter, in an extraordinary cold his shadow froze so fast to the ground that he could by no means loose it again."

"The false shadow that I could paint him," replied the professor, "would only be such a one as by the slightest agitation he might lose again, especially a person, who, as appears by your relation, has so little adhesion to his own native shadow. He who has no shadow, let him keep out of the sunshine, that is the safest and most sensible thing for him." He arose and withdrew, casting at me a transpiercing glance which mine could not support. I sunk back in my seat, and covered my face with my hands.

Thus Bendel found me, as he at length entered. He saw the grief of his master, and was desirous silently and reverently to withdraw. I looked up, I lay under the burden of my trouble; I must communicate it.

"Bendel!" cried I, "Bendel, thou only one who seest my affliction and respectest it, seekest not to pry into it, but appearest silently and kindly to sympathise, come to me, Bendel, and be the nearest to my heart; I have not locked from thee the treasure of my gold, neither will I lock from thee the treasure of my grief. Bendel, forsake me not. Bendel, thou beholdest me rich, liberal, kind. Thou imaginest that the world ought to honor me, and thou seest me fly the world, and hide myself from it. Bendel, the world has passed judgment, and cast me from it, and perhaps thou too wilt turn from me when thou knowest my fearful secret. Bendel, I am rich, liberal, kind, but,—O God! —I have no shadow!"

"No shadow!" cried the good youth with horror, and the bright tears gushed from his eyes. "Woe is me, that I was born to serve a shadowless master!" He was silent, and I held my face buried in my hands.

"Bendel," added I, at length, tremblingly— "now hast thou my confidence, and now canst thou betray it—go forth and testify against me." He appeared to be in a heavy conflict with himself; at length, he flung himself before me and seized my hand, which he bathed with his tears.

"No!" exclaimed he, "think the world as it will, I cannot, and will not, on account of a shadow abandon my kind master; I will act justly, and not with policy. I will continue with you, lend you my shadow, help you when I can, and when I cannot, weep with you." I fell on his neck, astonished at such unusual sentiment, for I was convinced that he did it not for gold.

From that time my fate and my mode of life were in some degree changed. It is indescribable how much Bendel continued to conceal my defect. He was everywhere before me and with me; foreseeing everything, hitting on contrivances, and where danger threatened, covering me quickly with his shadow, since he was taller and bulkier than I. Thus I ventured myself again among men, and began to play a part in the world. I was obliged, it is true, to assume many peculiarities and humors, but such became the rich, and so long as the truth continued to be concealed, I enjoyed all the honor and respect which were paid to my wealth. I looked calmly forward to the promised visit of the mysterious unknown, at the end of the year and the day.

I felt, indeed, that I must not remain longer in a place where I had once been seen without a shadow, and where I might easily be betrayed. Perhaps I yet thought too much of the manner in which I had introduced myself to Thomas John, and it was a mortifying recollection. I would therefore here merely make an experiment, to present myself with more ease and confidence elsewhere, but that now occurred which held me a long time riveted to my vanity, for there it is in the man that the anchor bites the firmest ground.

Even the lovely Fanny, whom I in this place again encountered, honored me with some notice without recollecting ever to have seen me before; for I now had wit and sense. As I spoke, people listened, and I could not, for the life of me, comprehend myself how I had arrived at the art of maintaining and engrossing so easily the conversation. The impression which I perceived that I had made on the fair one, made of me just what she desired—a fool, and I thenceforward followed her through shade and twilight wherever I could. I was only so far vain that I wished to make her vain of myself, and found it impossible, even with the very best intentions, to force the intoxication from my head to my heart.

But why relate to thee the whole long ordinary story? Thou thyself hast often related it to me of other honorable people. To the old, well known play in which I goodnaturedly undertook a wornout part, there came in truth to her and me, and everybody, unexpectedly a most peculiar and poetic catastrophe.

As, according to my wont, I had assembled on a beautiful evening a party in a garden, I wandered with the lady, arm in arm at some distance from the other guests, and exerted myself to strike out pretty speeches for her. She cast down modestly her eyes, and returned gently the pressure of my hand, when suddenly the moon broke through the clouds behind me, and—she saw only her own shadow thrown forward before her! She started and glanced wildly at me, then again on the earth, seeking my shadow with her eyes, and what passed within her, painted itself so singularly on her countenance, that I should have burst into a loud laugh if it had not itself ran ice-cold over my back.

I let her fall from my arms in a swoon, shot like an arrow through the terrified guests, reached the door, flung myself into the first chaise which I saw on the stand, and drove back to the city, where this time, to my cost, I had left the circumspect Bendel. He was terrified as he saw me;—one word revealed to him all. Post horses were immediately fetched. I took only one of my people with me, an arrant knave, called Rascal, who had contrived to make himself necessary to me by his cleverness; and who could suspect nothing of the present occurrence. That night I left upwards of a hundred miles behind me. Bendel remained behind me to discharge my establishment, to pay money, and to bring me what I most required. When he overtook me next day, I threw myself into his arms, and swore to him, never again to run into the like folly, but in future to be more cautious. We continued our journey without pause, over the frontiers and the mountains, and it was not till we began to descend and had placed those lofty bulwarks between us and our former unlucky abode, that I allowed myself to be persuaded to rest from the fatigues I had undergone, in a neighboring and little frequented Bathing-place.

CHAPTER IV.

I must pass in my relation hastily over a time in which, how gladly would I linger, could I but conjure up the living spirit of it with the recollection. But the color which vivified it, and can only vivify it again, is extinguished in me; and when I seek in my bosom what then so mightily animated it, the grief and the joy, the innocent illusion,—then do I vainly smite a rock in which no living spring now dwells, and the god is departed from me. How changed does this past time now appear to me. I would act in the watering place an heroic character, ill studied, and myself a novice on the boards, and my gaze was lured from my part by a pair of blue eyes. The parents, deluded by the play, offer everything only to make the business quickly secure; and the poor farce closes in mockery. And that is all, all! That presents itself now to me so absurd and commonplace, and yet is it terrible, that that can thus appear to me which then so richly, so luxuriantly, swelled my bosom. Mina! as I wept at losing thee, so weep I still to have lost thee also in myself. Am I then become so old? Oh, melancholy reason! Oh, but for one pulsation of that time! one moment of that illusion! But no! alone on the high waste sea of thy bitter flood! and long out of the last cup of champagne the elfin has vanished!

I had sent forward Bendel with some purses of gold to procure for me a dwelling adapted to my needs. He had there scattered about much money, and expressed himself somewhat indefinitely respecting the distinguished stranger whom he served, for I would not be named, and that filled the good people with extraordinary fancies. As soon as my house was ready Bendel returned to conduct me thither. We set out.

About three miles from the place, on a sunny plain, our progress was obstructed by a gay festal throng. The carriage stopped. Music, sound of bells, discharge of cannon, were heard; a loud vivat! rent the air; before the door of the carriage appeared, clad in white, a troop of damsels of extraordinary beauty, but who were eclipsed by one in particular, as the stars of night by the sun. She stepped forth from the midst of her sisters; the tall and delicate figure kneeled blushing before me, and presented to me on a silken cushion a garland woven of laurel, olive branches, and roses, while she uttered some words about majesty, veneration and love, which I did not understand, but whose bewitching silver tone intoxicated my ear and heart. It seemed as if the heavenly apparition had sometime already passed before me. The chorus struck in, and sung the praises of a good king and the happiness of his people.

And this scene, my dear friend, in the face of the sun! She kneeled still only two paces from me, and I without a shadow, could not spring over the gulph, could not also fall on the knee before the angel! Oh! what would I then have given for a shadow! I was compelled to hide my shame, my anguish, my despair, deep in the bottom of my carriage. At length Bendel recollected himself on my behalf. He leaped out of the carriage on the other side. I called him back, and gave him out of my jewel-case, which lay at hand, a splendid diamond crown, which had been made to adorn the brows of the lovely Fanny! He stepped forward, and spoke in the name of his master, who could not and would not receive such tokens of homage; there must be some mistake; and the good people of the city were thanked for their good will. As he said this, he took up the proffered wreath, and laid the brilliant coronet in its place. He then extended respectfully his hand to the lovely maiden, that she might arise, and dismissed, with a sign, clergy, magistrates, and all the deputations. No one else was allowed to approach. He ordered the throng to divide, and make way for the horses; sprang again into the carriage, and on we went at full gallop, through a festive archway of foliage and flowers towards the city. The discharges of cannon continued. The carriage stopped before my house. I sprang hastily in at the door, dividing the crowd which the desire to see me had collected. The mob hurrahed under my window, and I let double ducats rain out of it. In the evening the city was voluntarily illuminated.

And yet I did not at all know what all this could mean, and who I was supposed to be. I sent out Rascal to make enquiry. He brought word to this effect:—that the people had received certain intelligence that the good king of Prussia travelled through the country under the name of a Graf; that my adjutant had been recognised; and, finally, how great the joy was as they became certain that they really had me in the place. They now saw clearly that I evidently desired to maintain the strictest incognito, and how very wrong it had been to attempt so importunately to lift the veil. But I had resented it so graciously, so kindly,—I should certainly pardon their good heartedness.

The thing appeared so amusing to the rogue, that he did his best, by reproving words, the more to strengthen the good folk in their belief. He made a very comical recital of all this: and as he found that it diverted me, he made a joke to me of his own additional wickedness. Shall

I confess it? It flattered me, even by such means, to be taken for that honored head.

I commanded a feast to be prepared for the evening of the next day, beneath the trees which over-shadowed the open space before my house; and the whole city to be invited to it. The mysterious power of my purse; the exertions of Bendel and the active invention of Rascal, succeeded in triumphing over time itself. It is really astonishing how richly and beautifully everything was arranged in those few hours. The splendor and abundance which exhibited themselves, and the ingenious lighting up, so admirably contrived that I felt myself quite secure, left me nothing to desire. I could not but praise my servants.

The evening grew dark; the guests appeared, and were presented to me. Nothing more was said about Majesty; I was styled with deep reverence and obeisance, Herr Graf. What was to be done? I allowed the Herr Graf to please, and remained from that hour the Graf Peter. In the midst of festive multitudes my soul yearned alone after one. She entered late, —she was and wore the crown. She followed modestly her parents, and seemed not to know that she was the loveliest of all. They were presented to me as Mr. Forest-master, his lady and their daughter. I found many agreeable and obliging things to say to the old people; before the daughter I stood like a rebuked boy, and could not bring out one word. I begged her, at length, with a faltering tone, to honor this feast by assuming the office whose insignia she graced. She entreated with blushes and a moving look to be excused; but blushing still more than herself in her presence, I paid her as her first subject my homage, with a most profound respect, and the hint of the Graf became to all the guests a command which every one with emulous joy hastened to obey. Majesty, innocence and grace, presided in alliance with beauty over a rapturous feast. Mina's happy parents believed their child only thus exalted in honor of them. I myself was in an indescribable intoxication. I caused all the jewels which yet remained of those which I had formerly purchased, in order to get rid of burthensome gold, all the pearls, all the precious stones, to be laid in two covered dishes, and at the table, in the name of the queen, to be distributed round to her companions and to all the ladies. Gold, in the mean time, was incessantly strewed over the inclosing lists among the exulting people.

Bendel, the next morning, revealed to me in confidence that the suspicion which he had long entertained of Rascal's honesty, was now become certainty. That he had yesterday embezzled whole purses of gold. "Let us permit," replied I, "the poor scoundrel to enjoy the petty plunder. I spend willingly on everybody, why not on him? Yesterday he and all the fresh people you have brought me, served me honestly; they helped me joyfully to celebrate a joyful feast."

There was no farther mention of it. Rascal remained the first of my servants, but Bendel was my friend and my confidant. The latter was accustomed to regard my wealth as inexhaustible, and he pried not after its sources; entering into my humor, he assisted me rather to discover opportunities to exercise it, and to spend my gold. Of that unknown one, that pale sneak, he knew only this, that I could alone through him be absolved from the curse which weighed on me; and that I feared him, on whom my sole hope reposed. That, for the rest, I was convinced that he could discover me anywhere; I him nowhere; and that therefore awaiting the promised day, I abandoned every vain enquiry.

The magnificence of my feast, and my behavior at it, held at first the credulous inhabitants of the city firmly to their preconceived opinion. True, it was soon stated in the newspapers that the whole story of the journey of the king of Prussia had been a mere groundless rumor; but a king I now was, and must spite of everything a king remain, and truly one of the most rich and royal who had ever existed; only people did not rightly know what king. The world has never had reason to complain of the scarcity of monarchs, at least in our time. The good people who had never seen any of them, pitched with equal correctness first on one and then on another; Graf Peter still remained who he was.

At one time appeared amongst the guests at the Bath, a tradesman, who had made himself bankrupt in order to enrich himself; and who enjoyed universal esteem, and had a broad though somewhat pale shadow. The property which he had scraped together, he resolved to lay out in ostentation, and it even occurred to him to enter into rivalry with me. I had recourse to my purse, and soon brought the poor devil to such a pass, that in order to save his credit he was obliged to become bankrupt a second time, and hasten over the frontier. Thus I got rid of him. In this neighborhood I made many idlers and good-for-nothing fellows.

With all the royal splendor and expenditure by which I made all succumb to me, I still in my own house lived very simply and retired. I had established the strictest circumspection as a rule. No one except Bendel, under any pretence whatever, was allowed to enter the rooms which I inhabited. So long as the sun shone, I kept myself shut up there, and it was said the Graf is employed in his cabinet. With this employment numerous couriers stood in connexion, whom I, for every trifle, sent out and received. I received company alone under my trees, or in my hall arranged and lighted according to Bendel's plan. When I went out, on which occasions it was necessary that I should be constantly watched by the Argus eyes of Bendel, it was only to the Forester's Garden, for the sake of one alone; for my love was the innermost heart of my life.

Oh, my good Chamisso! I will hope that thou

hast not yet forgotten what love is! I leave much unmentioned here to thee. Mina was really an amiable, kind, good child. I had taken her whole imagination captive. She could not, in her humility, conceive how she could be worthy that I should alone have fixed my regard on her; and she returned love for love with all the youthful power of an innocent heart. She loved like a woman, offering herself wholly up; self-forgetting; living wholly and solely for him who was her life; regardless if she herself perished;—that is to say—she really loved.

But I—oh what terrible hours—terrible and yet worthy that I should wish them back again, —have I often wept on Bendel's bosom, when, after the first unconscious intoxication, I recollected myself; looked sharply into myself;—I, without a shadow, with knavish selfishness destroying this angel, this pure soul which I had deceived and stolen. Then did I resolve to reveal myself to her; then did I swear with a most passionate oath to tear myself from her, and to fly; then did I burst out into tears, and concert with Bendel how in the evening I should visit her in the Forester's garden.

At other times I flattered myself with great expectations from the rapidly approaching visit from the grey man, and wept again when I had in vain tried to believe in it. I had calculated the day on which I expected again to see the fearful one; for he had said in a year and a day; and I believed his word.

The parents, good honorable old people, who loved their only child extremely, were amazed at the connexion, as it already stood, and they knew not what to do in it. Earlier they could not have believed that the Graf Peter could think only of their child; but now he really loved her and was beloved again. The mother was probably vain enough to believe in the probability of an union, and to seek for it; the sound masculine understanding of the father did not give way to such overstretched imaginations. Both were persuaded of the purity of my love! they could do nothing more than pray for their child.

I have laid my hand on a letter from Mina of this date, which I still retain. Yes, this is her own writing. I transcribe it for thee.

"I am a weak silly maiden, and cannot believe that my beloved, because I love him dearly, dearly, will make the poor girl unhappy. Ah! thou art so kind, so inexpressibly kind, but do not misunderstand me. Thou shalt sacrifice nothing for me, desire to sacrifice nothing for me. Oh God! I should hate myself if thou didst! No—thou hast made me immeasurably happy; hast taught me to love thee. Away! I know my own fate. Graf Peter belongs not to me, he belongs to the world. I will be proud when I hear—'that was he, and that was he again,—and that has he accomplished; there they have worshipped him, and there they have deified him!' See, when I think of this, then am I angry with thee, that with a simple child thou canst forget thy high destiny. Away! or the thought will make me miserable! I—oh! who through thee am so happy, so blessed. Have I not woven, too, an olive branch and a rosebud into thy life, as into the wreath which I was allowed to present to thee? I have thee in my heart, my beloved, fear not to leave me. I will die oh! so happy, so ineffably happy through thee!"

Thou canst imagine how the words must cut through my heart. I explained to her that I was not what people believed me, that I was only a rich but infinitely miserable man. That a curse rested on me, which must be the only secret between us, since I was not yet without hope that it should be loosed. That this was the poison of my days; that I might drag her down with me into the gulph,—she who was the sole light, the sole happiness, the sole heart of my life. Then wept she again, because I was unhappy. Ah, she was so loving, so kind! To spare me but one tear, she, and with what transport, would have sacrificed herself without reserve.

In the mean time she was far from rightly comprehending my words; she conceived in me some prince on whom had fallen a heavy bann, some high and honored head, and her imagination amidst heroic pictures limned forth her lover gloriously.

Once I said to her—"Mina, the last day in the next month may change my fate and decide it,—if not I must die, for I will not make thee unhappy." Weeping she hid her head in my bosom. "If thy fortune changes, let me know that thou art happy. I have no claim on thee. Art thou wretched, bind me to thy wretchedness, that I may help thee to bear it."

"Maiden! maiden! take it back, that word, that foolish word which escaped thy lips. And knowest thou this wretchedness? Knowest thou this curse? Knowest who thy love,—what he? Seest thou not that I convulsively shrink together, and have a secret from thee?" She fell sobbing to my feet, and repeated with oaths her intreaty.

I announced to the Forest-master, who entered, that it was my intention on the first approaching of the month to solicit the hand of his daughter. I fixed precisely this time, because in the interim many things might occur which might influence my fortunes. That I was unchangeable in my love to his daughter.

The good man was quite startled as he heard such words out of the mouth of Graf Peter. He fell on my neck, and again became quite ashamed to have thus forgotten himself. Then he began to doubt, to weigh, and to enquire. He spoke of dowry, security, and the fortune for his beloved child. I thanked him for reminding me of these things. I told him that I desired to settle myself in this country where I seemed to be beloved, and to lead a care-free life. I begged him to purchase the finest estate that the country had to offer, in the name of his daughter, and to charge the cost to me. A father could, in such matter, best serve a lover. It gave him enough to do, for everywhere a stranger was before him, and he could only purchase for about a million.

My thus employing him was, at the bottom, an innocent scheme to remove him to a distance, and I had employed him similarly before. For I must confess that he was rather wearisome. The good mother was, on the contrary, somewhat deaf, and not like him jealous of the honor of entertaining the Graf.

The mother joined us. The happy people pressed me to stay longer with them that evening,—I dared not remain another minute. I saw already the rising moon glimmer on the horizon,—my time was up.

The next evening I went again to the Forester's garden. I had thrown my cloak over my shoulders and pulled my hat over my eyes. I advanced to Mina. As she looked up and beheld me, she gave an involuntary start, and there stood again clear before my soul the apparition of that terrible night when I showed myself in the moonlight without a shadow. It was actually she! But had she also recognised me again? She was silent and thoughtful; on my bosom lay a hundred-weight pressure. I arose from my seat. She threw herself silently weeping on my bosom. I went.

I now found her often in tears. It grew darker and darker in my soul; the parents meanwhile swam in supreme felicity; the eventful day passed on sad and sullen as a thunder cloud. The eve of the day was come. I could scarcely breathe. I had in precaution filled several chests with gold. I watched the midnight hour approach.—It struck.

I now sat, my eye fixed on the fingers of the clock, counting the minutes, the seconds, like dagger-strokes. At every noise which arose, I started up;—the day broke. The leaden hours crowded upon each other. It was noon—evening—night: as the clock fingers sped on, hope withered; it struck eleven and nothing appeared; the last minutes of the last hour fell, and nothing appeared. It struck the first stroke,—the last stroke of the twelfth hour, and I sank hopeless and in boundless tears upon my bed. On the morrow I should—forever shadowless, solicit the hand of my beloved. Towards morning an anxious sleep pressed down my eyelids.

CHAPTER V.

It was still early morning when voices, which were raised in my ante-chamber in violent dispute, awoke me. I listened. Bendel forbade entrance; Rascal swore high and hotly that he would receive no commands from his fellow, and insisted in forcing his way into my room. The good Bendel warned him that such words, came they to my ear, would turn him out of his most advantageous service. Rascal threatened to lay hands on him if he any longer obstructed his entrance.

I had half dressed myself. I flung the door wrathfully open, and advanced to Rascal—"What wantest thou, villain?" He stepped two strides backwards, and replied quite coolly: "To request you most humbly, Herr Graf, just to allow me to see your shadow;—the sun shines at this moment so beautifully in the court."

I was struck, as with thunder. It was sometime before I could recover my speech. "How can a servant towards his master"—He interrupted very calmly my speech—

"A servant may be a very honorable man, and not be willing to serve a shadowless master—I demand my discharge." It was necessary to try other chords. "But honest, dear Rascal, who has put the unlucky idea into your head? How canst thou believe—?"

He proceeded in the same tone—"People will assert that you have no shadow—and, in short, you show me your shadow, or give me my discharge."

Bendel, pale and trembling, but more discreet than I, gave me a sign. I sought refuge in the all-silencing gold; and that had lost its power. He threw it at my feet. "From a shadowless man I accept nothing!" He turned his back upon me, and went most deliberately out of the room with his hat upon his head and whistling a tune. I stood there with Bendel as one turned to stone, thoughtless, motionless, gazing after him.

Heavily sighing and with death in my heart, I prepared myself to redeem my promise, and like a criminal before his judge, to appear in the Forest-master's garden. I alighted in the dark arbor, which was named after me, and where they would be sure also at this time to await me. The mother met me, care-free and joyous. Mina sate there, pale and lovely as the first snow which often in the autumn kisses the last flowers, and then instantly dissolves into bitter water. The Forest-master went agitatedly to and fro, a written paper in his hand, and appeared to force down many things in himself which painted themselves with rapidly alternating flushes and paleness on his otherwise immovable countenance. He came up to me as I entered and with frequently choked words, begged to speak with me alone. The path in which he invited me to follow him, conducted towards an open, sunny part of the garden. I sunk speechless on a seat, and then followed a long silence, which even the good mother dared not interrupt.

The Forest-master raged continually with unequal steps to and fro in the arbor, and suddenly halting before me, glanced on the paper which he held, and demanded of me with a searching look—

"May not, Herr Graf, a certain Peter Schlemihl be not quite unknown to you?" I was silent. "A man of superior character and singular attainments—" He paused for an answer.

"And suppose I were the same man?"

"Who," added he vehemently—"has by some means, lost his shadow!"

"Oh, my foreboding, my foreboding!" exclaimed Mina, "Yes, I have long known it, he has no shadow," and she flung herself into the arms of her mother, who terrified, clasped her convulsively, and upbraided her that to her own hurt she had kept to herself such a secret. But she, like Arethusa, was changed into a fountain of tears, which at the sound of my voice flowed still more copiously, and at my approach burst forth in torrents.

"And you," again grimly began the Forest-master, "and you, with unparalleled impudence, have made no scruple to deceive these and myself, and you give out that you love her whom you have so deeply humbled. See, there, how she weeps and writhes! Oh, horrible! horrible!"

I had to such a degree lost all reflection, that talking like one crazed, I began—"And, after all, a shadow is nothing but a shadow; one can do very well without that, and it is not worth while to make such a riot about it." But I felt so sharply the baselessness of what I was saying, that I stopped of myself, without his deigning me an answer, and I then added,—"What one has lost at one time, may be found again at another!"

He rushed fiercely towards me—"Confess to me, sir! confess to me, how became you deprived of your shadow!"

I was compelled again to lie. "A rude fellow one day trod so heavily on my shadow that he rent a great hole in it. I have only sent it to be mended, for money can do much, and I was to have received it back yesterday."

"Good, sir, very good!" replied the Forest-master. "You solicit my daughter's hand; others do the same. I have, as her father, to care for her. I give you three days in which you may see after a shadow. If you appear before me within these three days with a good, well-fitting shadow, you shall be welcome to me; but on the fourth day—I tell you plainly,—my daughter is the wife of another."

I would yet attempt to speak a word to Mina, but she clung, sobbing violently, only closer to her mother's breast, who motioned me to be silent and to withdraw. I reeled away, and the world seemed to close itself behind me.

Escaped from Bendel's affectionate oversight, I traversed in erring course, woods and fields. The perspiration of my agony dropped from my brow, a hollow groaning convulsed my bosom, madness raged within me.

I know not how long this had continued, when on a sunny heath, I felt myself plucked by the sleeve. I stood still and looked round—it was the man in the grey coat, who seemed to have run himself quite out of breath in pursuit of me. He immediately began:

"I had announced myself for to-day, but you could not wait the time. There is nothing amiss, however, yet. You consider the matter, receive your shadow again in exchange, which is at your service, and turn immediately back. You shall be welcome in the Forest-master's garden; the whole has been only a joke. Rascal, who has betrayed you, and who seeks the hand of your bride, I will take charge of; the fellow is ripe."

I stood there as still asleep. "Announced for to-day?" I counted over again the time,—he was right. I had constantly miscalculated a day. I sought with the right hand in my bosom for my purse: he guessed my meaning, and stepped two paces backwards.

"No, Herr Graf, that is in too good hands, keep you that." I stared at him with eyes of enquiring wonder, and he proceeded: "I request only a trifle, as memento. You be so good as to set your name to this paper." On the parchment stood the words:

"By virtue of this my signature, I make over my soul to the holder of this, after its natural separation from the body."

I gazed with speechless amazement, alternately at the writing and the grey unknown. Meanwhile, with a new made pen he had taken up a drop of blood which flowed from a fresh thorn-scratch on my hand and presented it to me.

"Who are you then?" at length I asked him.
"What signifies it?" he replied. "And is not that plain enough to be seen in me? A poor devil, a sort of learned man and doctor, who in return for precious arts, receives from his friends poor thanks, and for himself, has no other amusement on earth but to make his little experiments.—But, however, sign. To the right there—P E T E R S C H L E M I H L."

I shook my head, and said, "Pardon me, sir, I do not sign that."

"Not?" replied he, in amaze, "and why not?"

"It seems to me to a certain degree serious to stake my soul on a shadow."

"So, so," repeated he, "serious!" and he laughed almost in my face. "And if I might venture to ask, what sort of a thing is that soul of yours? Have you ever seen it? And what do you think of doing with it when you are dead? Be glad that you have found an amateur who in your lifetime is willing to pay you for the bequest of this X, of this galvanic power, or polarised Activity, or whatever this silly thing may be, with something actual; that is to say, with your real shadow, through which you may arrive at the hand of your beloved, and at the accomplishment of all your desires. Will you rather push forth, and deliver up that poor young creature to that low bred scoundrel Rascal? No, you must witness that with your own eyes. Here, I lend you the Tarn-cap," (the cap of invisibility)—he drew it from his pocket—"and we will proceed unseen to the Forester's garden."

I must confess that I was excessively ashamed of being ridiculed by this man. I detested him from the bottom of my heart; and I believe that this personal antipathy withheld me, more than principle, or prejudice, from purchasing my shadow, essential as it was, by the required signature. The thought also was intolerable to me of making the excursion which he proposed, in his company. To see this abhorred sneak, this mocking cobold, step between me and my beloved, two torn and bleeding hearts, revolted my innermost feeling. I regarded what was past as predestined, and my wretchedness as unchangeable, and turning to the man, I said to him,

"Sir, I have sold you my shadow for this in itself most excellent purse, and I have sufficiently repented of it. Let the bargain be at an end, in God's name!" He shook his head, and made a very gloomy face. I continued, "I will then sell you nothing further of mine, even for this offered price of my shadow; and, therefore, I shall sign nothing. From this you may understand, that the cap-wearing to which you invite me, must be much more amusing for you than for me. Excuse me, therefore; and as it cannot now be otherwise, let us part."

"It grieves me, Monsieur Schlemihl, that you obstinately decline the business which I propose to you. Perhaps another time I may be more fortunate. Till our speedy meeting again!—Apropos: Permit me yet to show you, that the things which I purchase I by no means suffer to grow mouldy, but honorably preserve, and that they are well used by me."

With that he drew my shadow out of his pocket and with a dexterous throw unfolding it on the heath, spread it out on the sunny side of his feet, so that he walked between two attendant shadows, his own and mine, for mine must equally obey him, and accommodate itself to and follow all his movements.

When I once saw my poor shadow again, after so long an absence, and beheld it degraded to so vile a service, whilst I, on its account, was in such unspeakable trouble, my heart broke, and I began bitterly to weep. The detested wretch swaggered with the plunder snatched from me, and impudently renewed his proposal.

"You can yet have it. A stroke of the pen, and you snatch therewith the poor unhappy Mina from the claws of the villain into the arms of the most honored Herr Graf;—as observed, only a stroke of the pen."

My tears burst forth with fresh impetuosity, but I turned away and motioned to him to withdraw himself. Bendel, who filled with anxiety, had traced me to this spot, at this moment arrived. When the kind, good soul, found me weeping, and saw my shadow, which could not be mistaken, in the power of the mysterious grey man, he immediately resolved, was it even by force, to restore to me the possession of my property; and as he did not understand going much about with tender phrases, he immediately assaulted the man with words, and without much asking, ordered him bluntly to allow that which was my own, instantly to follow me. Instead of answer, he turned his back, and went. But Bendel up with his buckthorn cudgel which he carried, and following on his heels, without mercy, and with reiterated commands to give up the shadow, made him feel the full force of his vigorous arm. He, as accustomed to such handling, ducked his head, set up his shoulders, and with silent and deliberate steps pursued his way over the heath, at once going off with my shadow and my faithful servant. I long heard the heavy sounds roll over the waste, till they were finally lost in the distance. I was alone, as before, with my misery.

CHAPTER VI.

LEFT alone on the wild heath, I gave free current to my countless tears, relieving my heart from an ineffably weary weight. But I saw no bound, no outlet, no end to my intolerable misery, and I drank besides with savage thirst of the fresh poison which the unknown had poured into my wounds. When I called the image of Mina before my soul, and the dear, sweet form appeared pale and in tears, as I saw her last in my shame, then stepped the shadow of the impudent and mocking Rascal between her and me; I covered my face and fled through the wild. But the hideous apparition left me not, but pursued me in my flight, till I sank breathless on the ground, and moistened it with a fresh torrent of tears.

And all for a shadow. And this shadow a pen-stroke had obtained for me. I thought on the strange proposition and my refusal. All was chaos in me. I had no longer either judgment or mastership of thought.

The day went over. I stilled my hunger with wild fruits; my thirst in the nearest mountain stream. The night fell; I lay down beneath a tree. The damp morning awoke me out of a heavy sleep in which I heard myself rattle in the throat as in death. Bendel must have lost all trace of me, and it rejoiced me to think so. I would not return again amongst men before whom I fled in terror, like the timid game of the mountains. Thus I lived through three weary days.

On the fourth morning I found myself on a sandy plain bright with the sun, and sate on the fragment of a rock in its beams, for I loved now to enjoy its long-withheld countenance. I still fed my heart with its despair. A light rustle startled me. Ready for flight I threw round me a hurried glance; I saw no one, but in the sunny sand there glided past me a human shadow, not unlike my own, which wandering there alone, seemed to have got away from its possessor. There awoke in me a mighty yearning. "Shadow," said I, "dost thou seek thy master? I will be he," and I sprang forward to seize it. I thought that if I succeeded in treading on it so that its feet touched mine, it probably would remain hanging there, and in time accommodate itself to me.

The shadow, on my moving, fled before me, and I was compelled to begin a strenuous chase of the light fugitive, for which the thought of rescuing myself from my fearful condition could alone have endowed me with the requisite vigor. It flew towards a wood, at a great distance, in which I must of necessity, have lost it. I perceived this,—a horror convulsed my heart, inflamed my desire, added wings to my speed; I gained evidently on the shadow, I came continually nearer, I must certainly reach it. Suddenly it stopped, and turned towards me. Like a lion on its prey, I shot with a mighty spring forwards to make seizure of it,—and dashed unexpectedly against a hard and bodily object. Invisibly I received the most unprecedented blows on the ribs that mortal man probably ever received.

The effect of the terror in me was convulsively to close my arms, and firmly to enclose that which stood unseen before me. In the rapid transaction, I plunged forward to the ground, but backwards and under me was a man whom I had embraced and who now first became visible.

The whole occurrence became now very naturally explicable to me. The man must have carried the invisible bird's nest which renders him who holds it, but not his shadow, imperceptible, and had now cast it away. I glanced round, soon discovered the shadow of the invisible nest itself, leaped up and towards it, and did not miss the precious prize. Invisible and shadowless, I held the nest in my hand.

The man swiftly springing up, gazing round instantly after his fortunate conqueror, descried on the wide sunny plain neither him nor his shadow, for which he sought with especial avidity. For that I was myself entirely shadowless he had no leisure to remark, nor could he imagine such a thing. Having convinced himself that every trace had vanished, he turned his hand against himself, and tore his hair. To me, however, the acquired treasure had given the power and desire to mix again amongst men. I did not want for self-satisfying palliatives for my base robbery, or rather I had no need of them; and to escape from every thought of the kind, I hastened away, not even looking round at the unhappy one, whose deploring voice I long heard resounding behind me.— Thus, at least, appeared to me the circumstances at the time.

I was on fire to proceed to the Forester's garden, and there myself to discern the truth of what the Detested One had told me. I knew not, however, where I was. I climbed the next hill, in order to look round over the country, and perceived from its summit the near city, and the Forester's garden lying at my feet. My heart beat violently, and tears of another kind than what I had till now shed, rushed into my eyes. I should see her again! Anxious desire hastened my steps down the most direct path. I passed unseen some peasants who came out of the city. They were talking of me, of Rascal and the Forest-master; I would hear nothing,—I hurried past.

I entered the garden, all the tremor of expectation in my bosom. I seemed to hear laughter near me. I shuddered, threw a rapid glance round me, but could discover nobody. I advanced farther. I seemed to perceive a sound as of man's steps at hand, but there was nothing to be seen. I believed myself deceived by my ear. It was yet early, no one in Graf Peter's arbor, the garden still empty. I traversed the well-known paths. I penetrated to the very front of the dwelling. The same noise more distinctly followed me. I seated myself with an agonised heart on a bench which stood in the sunny space before the house-door. It seemed as if I had heard the unseen cobold, laughing in mockery, seat himself near me. The key turned in the door, it opened, and the Forest-master issued forth with papers in his hand. A mist seemed to envelope my head. I looked up, and—horror! the man in the grey coat sate by me, gazing on me with a satanic leer. He had drawn his Tarncap at once over his head and mine; at his feet lay his and my shadow peaceably by each other. He played negligently with the well-known paper which he held in his hand, and as the Forest-master, busied with his documents, went to and fro in the shadow of the arbor, he stooped familiarly to my ear, and whispered in it these words, "So then you have notwithstanding accepted my invitation, and here sit we for once two heads under one cap. All right! all right! But now give me my bird's nest again; you have no further occasion for it, and are too honorable a man to wish to withhold it from me; but there needs no thanks: I assure you that I have lent it you with the most hearty good will." He took it unceremoniously out of my hand, put it in his pocket, and laughed at me, and that so loud that the Forest-master himself looked round at the noise. I sate there as if changed to stone.

"But you must allow," continued he, "that such a cap is much more convenient. It covers not only your person but your shadow at the same time, and as many others as you have a mind to take with you. See you, to-day again, I conduct two of them"—he laughed again. "Mark this, Schlemihl, what we at first won't do with a good will, that will we in the end be compelled to. I still fancy you will buy that thing from me, take back the bride (for it is yet time), and we leave Rascal dangling on the gallows, an easy thing for us so long as rope is to be had. Hear you—I will give you also my cap into the bargain."

The mother came forth, and the conversation began. "How goes it with Mina?"

"She weeps."

"Silly child! it cannot be altered!"

"Certainly not; but to give her to another so soon. Oh, man! thou art cruel to thy own child."

"No, mother, that thou quite mistakest. When she, even before she has wept out her childish tears, finds herself the wife of a very rich and honorable man, she will awake comforted out of her trouble as out of a dream, and thank God and us, that wilt thou see!"

"God grant it!"

"She possesses now, indeed a very respectable property; but after the stir that this unlucky affair with the adventurer has made, canst thou believe that a partner so suitable as Mr. Rascal could be readily found for her? Dost thou know what a fortune Mr. Rascal possesses?" He has paid six millions for estates here in the country free from all debts. I have had the title deeds in my own hands! He it was who everywhere had the start of me; and besides this, has in his possession bills on Thomas John for about five and a half millions."

"He must have stolen enormously."

"What talk is that again! He has wisely saved what would otherwise have been lavished away."

"A man that has worn livery—"

"Stupid stuff! he has, however, an unblemished shadow."

"Thou art right, but—"

The man in the grey coat laughed and looked at me. The door opened and Mina came forth. She supported herself on the arm of a chambermaid, silent tears rolled down her lovely pale cheeks. She seated herself on a stool which was placed for her under the lime trees, and her father took a chair by her. He tenderly took her hand, and addressed her with tender words, while she began violently to weep.

"Thou art my good, dear child, and thou wilt be reasonable, wilt not wish to distress thy old father, who seeks only thy happiness. I can well conceive it, dear heart, that it has sadly shaken thee. Thou art wonderfully escaped from thy misfortunes! Before we discovered the scandalous imposition, thou hadst loved this unworthy one greatly; see, Mina, I know it, and upbraid thee not for it. I myself, dear child, also loved him so long as I looked upon him as a great gentleman. But now thou seest how different all has turned out. What! every poodle has his own shadow, and should my dear child have a husband—no! thou thinkst, indeed, no more about him. Listen, Mina. Now a man solicits thy hand, who does not shun the sunshine, an honorable man, who truly is no prince, but who possesses ten millions; ten times more than thou; a man who will make my dear child happy. Answer me not, make no opposition, be my good, dutiful daughter, let thy loving father care for thee, and dry thy tears. Promise me to give thy hand to Mr. Rascal. Say, wilt thou promise me this?"

She answered with a faint voice,—"I have no will, no wish further upon earth. Happen with me what my father will."

At this moment Mr. Rascal was announced, and stepped impudently into the circle. Mina lay in a swoon. My detested companion glanced archly at me, and whispered in hurried words—"And that can you endure? What then flows instead of blood in your veins?" He scratched with a hasty movement a slight wound in my hand, blood flowed, and he continued—"Actually red blood!—So sign then!". I had the parchment and the pen in my hand.

CHAPTER VII.

My wish, dear Chamisso, is merely to submit myself to thy judgment, not to endeavor to bias it. I have long passed the severest sentence on myself, for I have nourished the tormenting worm in my heart. It hovered during this solemn moment of my life, incessantly before my soul, and I could only lift my eyes to it with a despairing glance, with humility and contrition. Dear friend, he who in levity only sets his foot out of the right road, is unawares conducted into other paths, which draw him downwards, and ever downwards; he then sees in vain the guiding stars glitter in heaven; there remains to him no choice; he must descend unpausingly the declivity, and become a voluntary sacrifice to Nemesis. After the false step which had laid the curse upon me, I had, sinning through love, forced myself into the fortunes of another being, and what remained for me but that where I had sowed destruction, where speedy salvation was demanded of me, I should blindly rush forward to the rescue?—for the last hour struck! Think not so meanly of me, my Adelbert, as to imagine that I should have regarded any price that was demanded as too high, that I should have begrudged anything that was mine even more than my gold. No, Adelbert! but my soul was possessed with the most unconquerable hatred of this mysterious sneaker along crooked paths. I might do him injustice, but every degree of association with him maddened me. And here stepped forth, as so frequently in my life, and as especially often in the history of the world, an event instead of an action. Since then I have achieved reconciliation with myself. I have learned, in the first place, to reverence Necessity; and what is more than the action performed, the event accomplished—her property. Then I have learned to venerate this Necessity as a wise Providence, which lives through that great collective Machine in which we officiate simply as co-operating, impelling and impelled wheels. What shall be, must be; what should be, happened, and not without that Providence, which I ultimately learned to reverence in my own fate, and in the fate of her on whom mine thus impinged.

I know not whether I shall ascribe it to the excitement of my soul under the impulse of such mighty sensations; or to the exhaustion of my physical strength, which during the last days such unwonted privations had enfeebled; or whether, finally, to the desolating commotion which the presence of this grey fiend excited in my whole nature; be that as it may, as I was on the point of signing, I fell into a deep swoon, and lay a long time as in the arms of death.

Stamping of feet and curses were the first

sounds which struck my ear, as I returned to consciousness. I opened my eyes: it was dark; my detested attendant was busied scolding about me. "Is not that to behave like an old woman? Up with you, man! and complete off-hand what you have resolved on, if you have not taken another thought and had rather blubber." I raised myself with difficulty from the ground and gazed in silence around. It was late in the evening; festive music resounded from the brightly illuminated Forester's house, various groups of people wandered through the garden walks. One couple came near in conversation, and seated themselves on the bench which I had just quitted. They talked of the union this morning solemnized between Mr. Rascal and the daughter of the house. So, then, it had taken place!

I tore the Tarncap of the already vanished Unknown from my head, and hastened in brooding silence towards the garden gate, plunging myself into the deepest night of the thicket, and striking along the path past Graf Peter's arbor. But invisibly my tormenting spirit accompanied me, pursuing me with keenest reproaches. "These then are one's thanks for the pains which one has taken to support Monsieur, who has weak nerves, through the long precious day. And one shall act the fool in the play. Good, Mr. Wronghead, fly you from me if you please, but we are, nevertheless, inseparable. You have my gold and I your shadow, and this will allow us no repose. Did anybody ever hear of a shadow forsaking its master? Your's draws me after you till you take it again into favor, and I get rid of it. What you have hesitated to do out of fresh pleasure, will you, only too late, be compelled to seek through new weariness and disgust. One cannot escape one's fate." He continued speaking in the same tone. I fled in vain; he relaxed not, but ever present insultingly talked of gold and shadow. I could come to no single thought of my own.

I struck through unfrequented ways towards my house. When I stood before it, and gazed at it, I could scarcely recognise it. No light shone through the dashed-in windows. The doors were closed; no throng of servants was moving therein. There was a laugh near me. "Ha! ha! so goes it! But you'll probably find your Bendel at home, for he was the other day purposely sent back so weary, that he has most likely kept his bed since." He laughed again. "He will have a story to tell! Well then, for the present, good night! We meet speedily again!"

I had rung repeatedly; light appeared; Bendel demanded from within who rung. When the good man recognised my voice, he could scarcely restrain his joy. The door flew open, and we stood weeping in each other's arms. I found him greatly changed, weak and ill; but for me,—my hair was become quite grey!

He conducted me through the desolated rooms to an inner apartment which had been spared. He brought food and wine, and we seated ourselves, and he again began to weep. He related to me that he the other day had cudgelled the grey-clad man whom he had encountered with my shadow, so long and so far, that he had lost all trace of me, and had sunk to the earth in utter fatigue. That after this, as he could not find me, he returned home, whither presently the mob, at Rascal's instigation, came rushing in fury, dashed in the windows, and gave full play to their lust of demolition. Thus did they to their benefactor. The servants had fled various ways. The police had ordered me, as a suspicious person to quit the city, and had allowed only four-and-twenty hours in which to evacuate their jurisdiction. To that which I already knew of Rascal's affluence and marriage, he had yet much to add. This scoundrel, from whom all had proceeded that had been done against me, must, from the beginning, have been in possession of my secret. It appeared that attracted by gold, he had contrived to thrust himself upon me, and at the very first had procured a key to the gold cupboard, where he had laid the foundation of that fortune, whose augmentation he could now afford to despise.

All this Bendel narrated to me with abundant tears, and then wept for joy that he again beheld me, again had me; and that after he had long doubted whither this misfortune might have led me, he saw me bear it so calmly and collectedly; for such an aspect had despair now assumed in me. I beheld my misery unchangeably before me; I had wept out to it my last tear; not another cry could be extorted from my heart; I presented to it my bare head with chill indifference.

"Bendel," I said, "thou knowest my lot. Not without earlier blame has my heavy punishment befallen me. Thou, innocent man, shalt no longer bind thy destiny to mine. I do not desire it. I ride to-night still forward; saddle me a horse; I ride alone; thou remainest: it is my will. Here still must remain some chests of gold; that retain thou; but I will alone wander incessantly through the world: but if ever a happier hour should smile upon me, and fortune look on me with reconciled eyes, then will I remember thee, for I have wept upon thy firmly faithful bosom in heavy and agonising hours."

With a broken heart was this honest man compelled to obey this last command of his master, at which his soul shrunk with terror. I was deaf to his prayers, to his representations, blind to his tears. He brought me out my steed. Once more I pressed the weeping man to my bosom, sprung into the saddle, and under the shroud of night hastened from the grave of my existence, regardless which way my horse conducted me, since I had longer on the earth, no aim, no wish, no hope.

CHAPTER VIII.

A PEDESTRIAN soon joined me, who begged,

after he had walked for some time by the side of my horse, that as we went the same way, he might be allowed to lay a cloak which he carried, on the steed behind me. I permitted it in silence. He thanked me with easy politeness for the trifling service; praised my horse, and thence took occasion to extol the happiness and power of the rich, and let himself, I know not how, fall into a kind of monologue, in which he had me now merely for a listener.

He unfolded his views of life and of the world, and came very soon upon metaphysics, in which the ultimate pretension extended to the discovery of the word that should solve all mysteries. He stated his premises with great clearness and proceeded to the proofs.

Thou knowest, my friend, that I have clearly discovered, since I have run through the schools of the philosophers, that I have by no means a turn for philosophical speculations, and that I have totally renounced for myself this field. Since then I have left many things to themselves; abandoned the desire to know and to comprehend many things; and as thou thyself advised me, have, trusting to my common sense, followed as far as I was able the voice within me on the direct course. Now this rhetorician seemed to me to raise with great talent a firmly put-together fabric, which was at once self-based and self-supported, and stood as by an innate necessity. I missed, however, in it completely, what most of all I was desirous to find, and so it became for me merely a work of art, whose ornamental compactness and completeness served only to charm the eye; nevertheless I listened willingly to the eloquent man who drew my attention from my grief to him; and I would have gladly yielded myself wholly up to him, had he captivated my heart as much as my understanding.

Meanwhile the time had passed, and unobserved the dawn had already enlightened the heaven. I was horrified as I looked suddenly up, and saw the pomp of colors unfold itself in the east, which announced the approach of the sun; while at this hour in which the shadows ostentatiously display themselves in their greatest extent, there was no protection from it; no refuge in the open country to be descried. And I was not alone! I cast a glance at my companion, and was again terror-struck. It was no other than the man in the grey coat!

He smiled at my alarm, and went on without allowing me to get in a word. "Let, however, as is the way of the world, our mutual advantage for awhile unite us. It is all in good time for separating. The road here along the mountain-range, though you have not yet thought of it, is, nevertheless, the only one into which you could prudently have struck. Down into the valley you may not venture; and still less will you desire to return again over the heights, whence you are come; and this is also exactly my way. I see that you already turn pale before the rising sun. I will, for the time we keep company, lend you your shadow, and you, on that account, tolerate me in your society. You have no longer your Bendel with you, I will do you good service. You do not like me, and I am sorry for it; but, notwithstanding, you can make use of me. The devil is not so black as he is painted. Yesterday you vexed me, it is true; I will not upbraid you with it to-day; and I have already shortened the way hither for you; that you must allow. Only just take your shadow again awhile on trial."

The sun had ascended; people appeared on the road; I accepted, though with internal repugnance, the proposal. Smiling he let my shadow glide to the ground, which immediately took its place on that of the horse, and trotted gaily by my side. I was in the strangest state of mind. I rode past a group of country-people, who made way for a man of consequence, reverently, and with bared heads. I rode on, and gazed with greedy eyes and a palpitating heart on this my quondam shadow which I had now borrowed from a stranger, yes, from an enemy.

The man went carelessly near me, and even whistled a tune. He on foot, I on horseback; a dizziness seized me; the temptation was too great; I suddenly turned the reins; clapped spurs to the horse, and struck at full speed into a side-path. But I carried not off the shadow, which at the turning glided from the horse, and awaited its lawful possessor on the high road. I was compelled with shame to turn back. The man in the grey coat when he had calmly finished his tune, laughed at me, set the shadow right again for me; and informed me, that it would then only hang fast and remain with me when I was disposed to become the rightful proprietor. "I hold you," continued he, "fast by the shadow, and you cannot escape me. A rich man, like you, needs shadow, it cannot be otherwise, and you only are to blame that you did not perceive that sooner."

I continued my journey on the same road; the comforts and the splendor of life again surrounded me; I could move about free and conveniently, since I possessed a shadow, although only a borrowed one; and I everywhere inspired the respect which riches command. But I carried death in my heart. My strange companion, who gave himself out as the unworthy servant of the richest man in the world, possessed an extraordinary professional readiness, prompt and clever beyond comparison, the very model of a valet for a rich man, but he stirred not from my side, perpetually directing the conversation towards me, and continually blabbing out the most confidential matters; so that, at length, were it only to be rid of him, I resolved to settle the affair of the shadow. He was become as burthensome to me as he was hateful. I was even in fear of him. He had made me dependent on him. He held me, after he had conducted me back into the glory of the world, which I had fled from. I was obliged to tolerate his eloquence upon myself, and felt, in fact, that he was in the right. A rich man in the world must have a shadow, and so soon as I desired to command the rank which he had contrived again to make necessary to me, I saw but one issue. By this, however, I stood fast;—after having sacrificed my love, after my life had been blighted, I would never sign away my soul to this creature, for all the shadows in the world. I knew not how it would end.

We sate, one day, before a cave which the strangers who frequent these mountains, are accustomed to visit. We heard there the rush of subterranean streams roaring up from immeasurable depths, and the stone cast in seemed, in its resounding fall, to find no bottom. He painted to me, as he often did, with a vivid power of imagination and in the lustrous charms of the most brilliant colors, the most carefully finished pictures of what I might achieve in the world by virtue of my purse, if I had but once my shadow in my possession. With my elbows rested on my knees, I kept my face concealed in my hands, and listened to the false one, my heart divided between the seduction and my own strong will. In such an inward conflict I could no longer contain myself, and the deciding strife began.

"You appear, sir, to forget that I have indeed allowed you, upon certain conditions, to remain in my company, but that I have reserved my perfect freedom."

"If you command it, I pack up."

He was accustomed to menace. I was silent. He began immediately to roll up my shadow. I turned pale, but I let it proceed. There followed a long pause; he first broke it.

"You cannot bear me, sir. You hate me; I know it; yet why do you hate me? Is it because you attacked me on the highway, and sought to deprive me by violence of my bird's nest? Or is it because you have endeavored in a thievish manner, to cheat me out of my property, the shadow, which was entrusted to you entirely on your honor? I, for my part, do not, therefore, hate you. I find it quite natural that you should seek to avail yourself of all your advantages, cunning, and power. For the rest, that you have the very strictest principles; and that you think like honor itself, is a taste that you have, against which I have nothing to say. In fact, I think not so strictly as you; I merely act as you think. Or have I at any time pressed my finger on your throat in order to bring to me your most precious soul, for which I have a fancy? Have I, on account of my bartered purse, let a servant loose on you? Have I sought thus to swindle you out of it?" I had nothing to oppose to him, and he proceeded.—"Very good, sir! very good! you cannot endure me: I know that very well, and am by no means angry with you for it. We must part, that is clear, and in fact, you begin to be very wearisome to me. In order, then, to rid you of my further, shame-inspiring presence, I counsel you once more purchase this thing from me." I extended to him the purse: "At that price?"—"No!"

I sighed deeply, and added, "Be it so, then. I insist, sir, that we part, and that you, no longer, obstruct my path in a world which is to be hoped, has room enough in it for us both." He smiled, and replied, "I go, sir; but first let me instruct you how you may ring for me when you desire to see again, your most devoted servant. You have only to shake your purse, so that the eternal gold pieces therein jingle, and the sound will instantly attract me. Every one thinks of his own advantage in this world. You see that I at the same time am thoughtful of yours, since I reveal to you a new power. Oh! this purse!—had the moths already devoured your shadow, that would still constitute a strong bond between us. Enough, you have me in my gold. Should you have any commands, even when far off, for your servant, you know that I can show myself very active in the service of my friends, and the rich stand particularly well with me. You have seen it yourself. Only your shadow, sir,—allow me to tell you that—never again, except on one sole condition."

Forms of the past time swept before my soul. I demanded hastily—"Had you a signature from Mr. John?". He smiled. "With so good a friend it was by no means necessary." "Where is he? By God I will know it!" He plunged hesitatingly his hand into his pocket, and, dragged thence by the hair, appeared Thomas John's ghastly disfigured form, and the blue death-lips moved themselves with heavy words—"*Justo judicio Dei judicatus sum; justo judicio Dei condemnatus sum.*" I shuddered with horror, and dashing the ringing purse into the abyss, I spoke to him the last words. "I adjure thee, horrible one, in the name of God! take thyself hence, and never again show thyself in my sight!"

He arose gloomily, and instantly vanished behind the masses of rock which bounded this wild, overgrown spot.

CHAPTER IX.

I SATE there without shadow and without money, but a heavy weight was taken from my bosom. I was calm. Had I lost my love, or had I in that loss felt myself free from blame, I believe that I should have been happy; but I knew not, however, what I should do. I examined my pockets: I found yet several gold pieces there; I counted them and laughed. I had my horses below at the inn; I was ashamed of returning thither; I must, at least, wait till the sun was gone down; it stood yet high in the heaven. I laid myself down in the shade of the nearest trees, and fell calmly asleep.

Lovely shapes blended themselves before me in charming dance into a pleasing dream. Mina with a flower-wreath in her hair floated by me, and smiled kindly upon me. The noble Bendel also was crowned with flowers, and went past with a friendly greeting. I saw many besides, and I believe thee too, Chamisso, in the distant throng. A bright light appeared, but no one had a shadow, and what was stranger, it had by no means a bad effect. Flowers and songs, love and joy, under groves of palm. I could neither hold fast nor single out the moving, lightly floating, loveable forms: but I knew that I dreamed such a dream with joy, and was careful to avoid waking. I was already awake, but still kept my eyes closed in order to retain the fading apparition longer before my soul.

I finally opened my eyes; the sun stood still high in the heaven, but in the east; I had slept through the night. I took it for a sign that I should not return to the inn. I gave up readily as lost, what I yet possessed there, and determined to strike on foot into a neighboring path, which led along the wood-grown feet of the mountains, leaving it secretly to fate to fulfil what it had yet in store for me. I looked not behind me, and thought not even of applying to Bendel, whom I left rich behind me, and which I could readily have done. I considered the new character which I should support in the world. My dress was very modest. I had on an old black Polonaise, which I had already worn in Berlin, and which, I know not how, had first come again into my hands for this journey. I had also a travelling cap on my head, a pair of old boots on my feet. I arose, and cut me on the spot a knotty stick as a memorial, and advanced at once on my wandering.

I met in the wood an old peasant who friendly greeted me, and with whom I entered into conversation. I inquired, like an inquisitive traveller, first the way, then about the country, and its inhabitants, the productions of the mountains, and many such things. He answered my questions sensibly and loquaciously. We came to the bed of a mountain torrent, which had spread its devastations over a wide tract of the forest. I shuddered involuntarily at the sun-bright space, and allowed the countryman to go first; but in the midst of this dangerous spot, he stood still, and turned to relate to me the history of this desolation. He saw immediately my defect, and paused in the midst of his discourse.

"But how does that happen,—the gentleman has actually no shadow!"

"Alas! alas!" replied I, sighing, "during a long and severe illness, my hair, nails, and shadow fell off. See, father, at my age, my hair, which is renewed again, is quite white, the nails very short, and the shadow,—that will never grow again."

"Ay! ay!" responded the old man, shaking his head,—"no shadow, that is bad! That was a bad illness that the gentleman had." But he continued not his narrative, and at the next cross way which presented itself, he left me without saying a word. Bitter tears trembled anew upon my cheeks, and my cheerfulness was gone.

I pursued my way with a sorrowful heart, and sought no further the society of men. I kept myself in the darkest wood, and was many a time compelled, in order to pass over a space where the sun shone, to wait for whole hours, least some human eye should forbid me the transit. In the evening I sought for a small inn in the villages. I went particularly in quest of a mine in the mountains where I hoped to get work under the oath; since, besides that my present situation made it imperative that I should provide for my support, I had discovered that the most active labor alone could protect me from my own annihilating thoughts.

A few rainy days advanced me well on the way, but at the expense of my boots, whose soles had been calculated for the Graf Peter, and not for the pedestrian laborer. I was already barefoot: I must procure a pair of new boots. The next morning I transacted this business with much gravity in a village where was held a Wake, and where in a booth old and new boots stood for sale. I selected and bargained long. I was forced to deny myself a new pair, which I would gladly have had, but the extravagant demand frightened me. I therefore contented myself with an old pair, which were yet good and strong, and which the handsome, blond-haired boy who kept the stall, for present cash payment handed to me with a friendly smile, and wished me good luck on my journey. I put them on at once, and left the place by the northern gate.

I was sunk very deep in my thoughts and scarcely saw where I set my feet, for I was pondering on the mine which I hoped to reach by evening, and where I hardly knew how I should propose myself. I had not advanced two hundred strides when I observed that I had got out of the way. I therefore looked round me, and found myself in a wild and ancient forest, where the axe appeared never to have been wielded. I pressed forward still a few steps, and beheld myself in the midst of desert rocks which were overgrown only with moss and lichens, and between which lay fields of snow and ice. The air was intensely cold; I looked round,—the wood had vanished behind me. I took a few strides more,—and around me reigned the silence of death: boundlessly extended itself the ice whereon I stood, and on which rested a thick, heavy fog. The sun stood blood-red on the edge of the horizon. The cold was insupportable.

I knew not what had happened to me; the benumbing frost compelled me to hasten my steps; I heard alone the roar of distant waters; a step and I was on the ice margin of an ocean. Innumerable herds of seals plunged rushing before me in the flood. I pursued this shore; I saw naked rocks, land, birch and pine forests; I now advanced for a few minutes right onwards. It was stifling hot. I looked around,— I stood amongst beautifully cultivated rice-fields, and beneath mulberry-trees. I seated myself in their shade; I looked at my watch; I had left the market town only a quarter of an hour before. I fancied that I dreamed; I bit my tongue to awake myself. I closed my eyes in order to collect my thoughts. I heard before me singular accents pronounced through the nose. I looked up. Two Chinese, unmistakeable from their Asiatic form of countenance, if indeed I would have given no credit to their costume, addressed me in their speech with the accustomed salutations of their country. I arose and stepped two paces backward; I saw them no more. The landscape was totally changed, trees and forests instead of rice-fields. I contemplated these trees, and the plants which bloomed around me, which I recognised as the growth of south-eastern Asia. I wished to approach one of these trees,—one step, and again all was changed. I marched now like a recruit who is drilled, and strode slowly, and with measured steps. Wonderfully diversified lands, rivers, meadows, mountain chains, steppes, deserts of sand, unrolled themselves before my astonished eyes. There was no doubt of it,—I had seven-leagued boots on my feet.

CHAPTER X.

I FELL in speechless adoration on my knees and shed tears of thankfulness, for suddenly stood my fortune clear before my soul. For early offence thrust out from the society of men, I was cast, for compensation, upon Nature, which I ever loved; the earth was given me as a rich garden, study for the object and strength of my life, and science for its goal. It was no resolution which I adopted. I have since then, with severe, unremitted diligence, striven faithfully to represent what then stood clear and perfect before my eye, and my satisfaction has depended on the agreement of the demonstration with the original.

I prepared without hesitation, with a hasty survey, to take possession of the field which I should hereafter reap. I stood on the heights of Thibet, and the sun, which had risen upon me only a few hours before, now already stooped to the evening sky. I wandered over Asia from east to west, overtaking him in his course, and entered Africa. I gazed about me with eager curiosity, as I repeatedly traversed it in all directions. As I surveyed the ancient pyramids and temples in passing through Egypt, I descried in the desert not far from hundred-gated Thebes, the caves where the christian anchorites once dwelt. It was suddenly firm and clear in me— here is thy home! I selected one of the most concealed which was at the same time spacious, convenient and inaccessible to the jackalls, for my future abode, and again went forward.

I passed at the pillars of Hercules, over to Europe, and when I had reviewed the southern and northern provinces, I crossed from northern Asia over the polar glaciers to Greenland and America; traversed both parts of that continent, and the winter which already reigned in the south drove me speedily back northwards from Cape Horn.

I tarried awhile till it was day in eastern Asia, and after some repose, continued my wandering. I traced through both Americas the mountain chain which comprehends the highest known inequalities on our globe. I stalked slowly and cautiously from summit to summit, now over flaming volcanoes, now snow-crowned peaks, often breathing with difficulty; when reaching Mount Elias, I sprang across Behring's Straits to Asia. I followed the western shores, in their manifold windings, and examined with especial care which of the islands there located were accessible to me. From the peninsula of Malacca my boots carried me to Sumatra, Java, Bali and Lamboc. I attempted often with danger, and always in vain, a northwest passage over the lesser islets and rocks with which this sea is studded to Borneo and the other islands of this Archipelago. I was compelled to abandon the hope. At length I seated myself on the extremest part of Lamboc, and gazing towards the south and east, wept, as at the fast closed grating of my prison, that I had so soon discovered my limits. New-Holland so extraordinary, and so essentially necessary to the comprehension of the earth and its sun-woven garment, of the vegetable and the animal world, with the South-Sea and its Zoophyte islands, was interdicted to me, and thus, at the very outset, all that I should gather and build up was destined to remain a mere fragment! Oh, my Adelbert, what after all, are the endeavors of men!

Often did I in the severest winter of the southern hemisphere, endeavor, passing the polar glaciers westward, to leave behind me those two hundred strides out from Cape Horn, which sundered me probably from Van Dieman's Land and New Holland, regardless of my return, or whether this dismal region should close upon me as my coffin-lid, making desperate leaps from ice-drift to ice-drift, and bidding defiance to the cold and the sea. In vain—I never reached New-Holland, but every time, I came back to Lamboc, seated myself on its extremest peak, and wept again, with my face turned towards the south and east, as at the fast closed bars of my prison.

I tore myself at length from this spot, and returned with a sorrowful heart into inner Asia. I traversed that farther, pursuing the morning dawn westward, and came yet in the night to my proposed home in the Thebais, which I had touched upon in the afternoon of the day before.

As soon as I was somewhat rested, and when it was day again in Europe, I made it my first care to procure everything which I wanted. First of all, stop-shoes; for I had experienced how inconvenient it was when I wished to examine near objects, not to be able to slacken my stride, except by pulling off my boots. A pair of slippers drawn over them had completely the effect which I anticipated, and later I always carried two pairs, since I sometimes threw them from my feet, without having time to pick them up again, when lions, men, or hyænas startled me from my botanising. My very excellent watch was, for the short duration of my passage, a capital chronometer. Besides this I needed a sextant, and some scientific instruments and books.

To procure all this, I made several anxious journeys to London and Paris, which, auspiciously for me, a mist just then overshadowed. As the remains of my enchanted gold was now exhausted, I easily accomplished the payment by gathering African ivory, in which, however, I was obliged to select only the smallest tusks, as not too heavy for me. I was soon furnished and equipped with all these, and commenced immediately, as private philosopher, my new course of life.

I roamed about the earth, now determining the altitudes of mountains; now the temperature of its springs and the air; now contemplating the animal, now inquiring into the vegetable tribes. I hastened from the equator to the pole; from one world to the other, comparing facts with facts. The eggs of the African ostrich or the northern sea-fowl, and fruits, especially of the tropical palms and Bananas, were even my ordinary food. In lieu of happiness I had tobacco, and of human society and the ties of love, one faithful poodle, which guarded my cave in the Thebais, and when I returned home with fresh treasures, sprang joyfully towards me, and gave me still a human feeling, that I was not alone on the earth. An adventure was yet destined to conduct me back amongst mankind.

CHAPTER XI.

As I once scotched my boots on the shores of the north, and gathered lichens and sea-weed, an ice-bear came unawares upon me round the corner of a rock. Flinging off my slippers, I would step over to an opposite island, to which a naked crag which protruded midway from the waves offered me a passage. I stepped with one foot firmly on the rock, and plunged over on the other side into the sea, one of my slippers having unobserved remained fast on the foot.

The excessive cold seized on me; I with difficulty rescued my life from this danger; and the moment I reached land, I ran with the utmost speed to the Lybian deserts in order to dry myself in the sun, but as I was here exposed, it burned me so furiously on the head that I staggered back again very ill towards the north. I sought to relieve myself by rapid motion, and ran with swift, uncertain steps, from west to east, from east to west. I found myself now in the day, now in the night; now in summer now in the winter's cold.

I know not how long I thus reeled about on the earth. A burning fever glowed in my veins; with deepest distress I felt my senses forsaking me. As mischief would have it, in my incautious career, I now trod on some one's foot; I must have hurt him; I received a heavy blow, and fell to the ground.

When I again returned to consciousness, I lay comfortably in a good bed, which stood amongst many other beds in a handsome hall. Some one sate at my head; people went through the hall from one bed to another. They came to mine, and spake together about me. They styled me *Number Twelve;* and on the wall at my feet stood,—yes, certainly it was no delusion, I could distinctly read on a black tablet of marble in great golden letters, quite correctly written, my name—

PETER SCHLEMIHL.

On the tablet beneath my name were two other rows of letters, but I was too weak to put them together. I again closed my eyes.

I heard something of which the subject was Peter Schlemihl read aloud, and articulately, but I could not collect the sense. I saw a friendly man, and a very lovely woman in black dress appear at my bedside. The forms were not strange to me, and yet I could not recognise them.

Some time went over, and I recovered my strength. I was called *Number Twelve*, and *Number Twelve*, on account of his long beard, passed for a Jew, on which account, however, he was not at all the less carefully treated. That he had no shadow appeared to have been unobserved. My boots, as I was assured, were, with all that I had brought hither, in good keeping, in order to be restored to me on my recovery. The place in which I lay was called the SCHLE-MIHLIUM. What was daily read aloud concerning Peter Schlemihl, was an exhortation to pray for him as the Founder and Benefactor of this institution. The friendly man whom I had seen by my bed was Bendel; the lovely woman was Mina.

I recovered unrecognised in the Schlemihlium; and learned yet farther that I was in Bendel's native city, where, with the remains of my otherwise unblessed gold, he had in my name founded this Hospital, where the unhappy blessed me, and himself maintained its superintendence. Mina was a widow. An unhappy criminal process had cost Mr. Rascal his life, and her the greater part of her property. Her parents were no more. She lived here as a pious widow, and practised works of mercy.

Once she conversed with Mr. Bendel at the bedside of *Number Twelve*. "Why, noble lady, will you so often expose yourself to the bad atmosphere which prevails here? Does fate then deal so hardly with you that you wish to die?"

"No, Mr. Bendel, since I have dreamed out my long dream, and have awoke in myself, all is well with me; since then I crave not, and fear not death. Since then, I reflect calmly on the past and the future. Is it not also with a still and inward happiness that you now, in so devout a manner, serve your master and friend?"

"Thank God, yes, noble lady. But we have seen wonderful things; we have unwarily drunk much good, and bitter woes, out of the full cup. Now it is empty, and we may believe that the whole has been only a trial; and armed with wise discernment, await the real beginning. The real beginning is of another fashion; and we wish not back the first jugglery, and are on the whole glad, such as it was, to have lived through it. I feel also within me a confidence that it must now be better than formerly with our old friend."

"In me too," replied the lovely widow, and then passed on.

The conversation left a deep impression upon me, but I was undecided in myself, whether I should make myself known, or depart hence unrecognised. I took my resolve. I requested paper and pencil, and wrote these words:—"It is indeed better with your old friend now than formerly, and if he does penance it is the penance of reconciliation."

Hereupon I desired to dress myself, as I found myself stronger. The key of the small wardrobe which stood near my bed, was brought, and I found therein, all that belonged to me. I put on my clothes, suspended my botanical case, in which I rejoiced still to find my northern lichens, round my black Polonaise, drew on my boots, laid the written paper on my bed, and as the door opened, I was already far on the way to the Thebais.

As I took the way along the Syrian coast, on which I for the last time had wandered from home, I perceived my poor Figaro coming towards me. This excellent poodle, who had long expected his master at home, seemed to desire to trace him out. I stood still and called to him. He sprang barking towards me, with a thousand moving assurances of his inmost and most extravagant joy. I took him up under my arm, for in truth he could not follow me, and brought him with me home again.

I found all in its old order; and returned gradually as my strength was recruited, to my former employment and mode of life, except that I kept myself for a whole year out of the, to me, wholly insupportable polar cold. And thus, my dear Chamisso, I live to this day. My boots are no worse for the wear, as that very learned work of the celebrated Tieckius, De Rebus Gestis Polticelli, at first led me to fear. Their force remains unimpaired, my strength only decays; yet I have the comfort to have exerted it in a continuous and not fruitless pursuit of one object. I have, so far as my boots could carry me, become more fundamentally acquainted than any man before me with the earth, its shape, its elevations, its temperatures, the changes of its atmosphere, the exhibitions of its magnetic power, and the life upon it, especially in the vegetable world. The facts I have recorded with the greatest possible exactness, and in perspicuous order in several works, and stated my deductions and views briefly in several treaties. I have settled the geography of the interior of Africa, and of the northern polar regions; of the interior of Asia, and its eastern shores. My Historia Stirpium Plantarum Utriusque Orbis stands as a grand fragment of the Flora Universalis Terræ, and as a branch of my Systema Naturæ. I believe that I have therein not merely augmented, at a moderate calculation, the amount of known species, more than one third, but have done something for the Natural System, and for the Geography of Plants. I shall labor diligently at my Fauna. I shall take care that, before my death, my works shall be deposited in the Berlin University.

And thee, my dear Chamisso, have I selected as the preserver of my singular history, which, perhaps, when I have vanished from the earth, may afford valuable instruction to many of its inhabitants. But thou, my friend, if thou wilt live among men, learn before all things to reverence the shadow, and then the gold. Wishest thou to live only for thyself and for thy better self—oh, then!—thou needest no counsel.

THE END.